TRADE AND INDUSTRI
DEVELOPING CO

Also by David Greenaway

INTERNATIONAL TRADE POLICY

ECONOMIC DEVELOPMENT AND INTERNATIONAL TRADE (*editor*)

CURRENT ISSUES IN INTERNATIONAL TRADE (*editor*)

CURRENT ISSUES IN MACROECONOMICS (*editor*)

Also by Chris Milner

EXPORT PROMOTION STRATEGIES: Theory and Evidence from Developing Countries (*editor*)

POLICY ADJUSTMENT IN AFRICA (*co-editor*)

TRADE AND INDUSTRIAL POLICY IN DEVELOPING COUNTRIES

A Manual of Policy Analysis

David Greenaway

and

Chris Milner

First published 1993 by
THE MACMILLAN PRESS LTD
Houndmills, Basingstoke, Hampshire RG21 2XS
and London
Companies and representatives
throughout the world

ISBN 0-333-46919-4 hardcover
ISBN 0-333-46920-8 paperback

A catalogue record for this book is available
from the British Library.

Printed and bound in Great Britain by
Mackays of Chatham PLC, Chatham, Kent

To Susan and Ruth

Contents

List of Tables

List of Figures

List of Charts

Preface

Trade policies and the formulation of trade strategy in developing countries has been a focus of attention for trade and development economists for several decades. The 1980s witnessed intensified interest in the relationship between trade policy and trade performance, and between trade performance and overall economic performance. There are a number of reasons for this. In academic and policy circles there has been a reevaluation of the relative merits of intervention-led and market-led development strategies. This has resulted from both a paradigm shift and the contrast between the experiences of some developing countries which adopted the most dirigiste and inward-oriented development strategies in the 1950s and 1960s and those of a number of NICs which apparently followed more outward-oriented policies. At the operational level there were no doubt some internal pressures on policy makers in developing countries as a result of dissatisfaction with what existing policies had delivered. But external influences have probably played a greater role. There has been a strong demonstration effect; the success of the export-oriented, newly industrialising countries, in particular of the Asian NICs, has received envious attention from politicians and the administrations in many less successful countries. There has also been a considerable amount of external pressure from multilateral agencies to undertake policy reform. The provision of significant amounts of financial resources, both short- and long-term, has become subject to policy conditions. In particular trade policy reform has invariably been a key component of the World Bank's structural adjustment programmes in developing countries.

Technical support in the form of funding for commissioned studies of current and possible future policies and their effects has frequently been a feature of structural adjustment lending (SAL). Indeed both of the present authors have been involved in the fieldwork for and production of reports on trade policy reform in countries involved with World Bank SAL negotiations – in Cote d'Ivoire, Madagascar, Tanzania, Burundi, Barbados and Trinidad for example. The governments of such countries seek independent advice on the costs and benefits of existing and other possible policies, and studies offer some opportunity for some 'technology transfer' about the available tools for analysing trade and industrial policies. But one-off studies prepared during periods of negotiation with an external agency, such as the World Bank, are likely to be of restricted value in providing a permanent basis for the on-going evaluation of policy and the monitoring of the implementation and impact of reforms. Herein lies one of the primary aims of this book, namely to provide a manual that will be of value to policy makers and economists in developing countries when designing and monitoring trade and industrial policy reform. It seeks to explain how concepts and tools of analysis can be used to examine specific policy issues – for instance how the concept of effective protection might be used to comment on anti-export bias, or how computable general equilibrium models might be used to examine the impact of trade policy reform on the distribution of economic activity across sectors. It also aims to investigate the implementation of specific tools of analysis – to explain for example what information from official sources or surveys is required to measure the structure of incentives or protection, to identify the problems of measurement where data quality is likely to be constrained or to show how specific models can be tested for their sensitivity to particular assumptions or parameter values. By understanding the purpose and limitations of trade policy analysis, the aim is to provide the policy analyst with the tools for investigating the effects of both partial or piecemeal reform and general or wholesale reform. The latter issue of the optimal timing and sequencing of large-scale trade and related-policy reform is clearly complex, and something that will be a central focus of policy debate in developing countries for many years to come.

Of course these issues are of considerable interest to any 'student' of trade and development, as well as to policy makers in developing countries. The last decade has seen substantial growth in our knowledge of the nature and effects of trade policies in developing countries – the SAL programmes and the World Bank have been prime movers in raising the quality of applied trade and trade policy analysis in developing countries. Much of this work, however, is either difficult to access or is available only from diverse sources. It is hoped therefore that this book will also provide a useful source of summary information on this recent empirical work.

As explained above, a considerable amount of the background research for this book was conducted 'at the coal face', undertaking trade policy studies in a number of developing countries in Africa, the Indian Ocean and the Caribbean. Operational experience gained while acting as economic advisers to Maxwell Stamp plc (London), the World Bank, UNIDO and UNCTAD provided an excellent opportunity to gain experience in applying the principles of trade policy analysis. We are grateful for this experience. In addition both authors have, jointly and independently, worked on a number of analytical problems in the field of trade policy and development. As well as the analytical work and operational experience, the preparation of this book was enriched by a period at the World Bank headquarters in Washington. That stay was financed by the Wincott Foundation and Maxwell Stamp plc. We are very grateful to both for making the visit possible.

The World Bank has been the leading force in the move to reduce trade policy distortions in developing countries. It has considerable operational experience and knowledge of local conditions in each of its country departments, and has attracted very able economists, including major trade economists from the academic community, to structure and develop its own research programmes. Our study visit to the World Bank during Easter 1988 provided us therefore with an invaluable opportunity to access its documentary resources, to gather case study material and to have discussions with World Bank officials who specialise in trade, and country specialists. In particular, we would like to thank the Research Administrative Department and the Economic Development Institute for the accommodation and facilities they provided; special thanks for their support and friendly interest in our work goes to Dennis de Tray and Richard Snape.

Finally our thanks also go to some other individuals. The typescript was expertly prepared by Su Spencer at Loughborough and Sue Berry and Sharon Tippier at Nottingham. Stephen Rutt at Macmillan displayed considerable support and patience during the project's long gestation. Finally, we would like to thank both of our families for their support and for the admirable way in which they coped while we were away gaining experience 'at the coal face' – not that fieldwork in some interesting 'southern' location is necessarily arduous!

DAVID GREENAWAY
University of Nottingham

CHRIS MILNER
Loughborough University

CHAPTER 1

Introduction and Overview

1.1 Background and aims

In general developing countries are small open economies. In the absence of intervention the traded goods sector invariably accounts for a large share of total output or final expenditure. The exact composition of output would in turn be determined by factor endowments, technology and tastes and preferences. Economic theory tells us that the allocation of resources across sectors, and the efficiency with which resources are utilised in a given sector, can be influenced by intervention. Governments have at their disposal a range of instruments which can be, and in general are, used in an endeavour to direct resource utilisation in a particular way. These instruments are collectively referred to as trade policy, or more generally trade and industrial policy. The former applies to border measures, the latter non-border measures, although drawing the line between the two is becoming increasingly difficult.

The instruments of trade policy have been extensively deployed in many developing countries. This is partly because of a genuine belief held by many that industrialisation can be effectively promoted through a policy of import substitution, partly because trade policy instruments have substituted for other forms of intervention (for example tariffs for fiscal purposes), and partly because GATT provisions have condoned intervention on a scale which would not have been possible in industrialised countries (particularly through Article XVIII).

Much has been written on trade policy and economic development on, *inter alia*, the relative efficiency of alternative instruments of intervention, the role of import substitution and export promotion, the links between trade strategy and economic performance and so on. In the process the trade policies and trade strategies of many developing countries have come in for close scrutiny, and an impressive literature is now available to the serious student of trade policy and economic development. There are however two potential entry barriers: first the scale of that literature is now quite intimidating; second the menu of techniques available to the applied economists is such that the necessary background to penetrate a particular study may sometimes be lacking.

This book is designed to lower these entry barriers. We sub-title it 'A Manual of Policy Appraisal' to signal that it is techniques oriented. Anyone interested in, or working on, applied trade policy should be able to familiarise him or herself with the full range of tools available to the analyst. It is not a 'cookbook', however. As well as introducing the techniques we aim to demonstrate how they have been used in the context of policy appraisal and, where appropriate, survey the relevant literature. Thus it is not a book about the theory of trade policy and economic development. Both of these feature, but the core is directed at the way in which we evaluate the impact of trade policy.

1.2 Outline of the manual

We have organised the material in five parts. Part I sets the context. In Chapter 2 we review the instruments of trade (and industrial) policy to highlight the range of fiscal and quantitative instruments which are available to policy makers, and to remind ourselves of the principles which economists use when assessing the relative efficiency of different instruments of intervention. Chapter 3 broadens the focus somewhat. It looks at trade strategy and economic development. We show how structuralist ideas were important to making the case for import substituting industrialisation in the 1950s and 1960s, with its emphasis on infant industry protection, direct controls and planning. In the later 1970s and 1980s 'getting prices right' emerged as a major theme and was associated with widespread trade liberalisation.

Part II concentrates on partial equilibrium techniques for policy appraisal. Chapter 4 is concerned with the measurement of nominal protection – nominal tariffs and the tariff equivalents of quantitative restrictions in particular. Measures of both are widely used by analysts. The theory of effective protection pointed up sharply the deficiencies associated with relying solely on measures of nominal protection. Chapter 5 systematically develops the effective protection measure, paying particular attention to practical difficulties in computation. In turn, a limitation of effective protection is that it only takes account of the impact of distortions in tradables. In contrast the domestic resource cost (DRC) ratio also takes account of non-border distortions, and this is dealt with in Chapter 6. Here again we develop the measure from its theoretical foundations, but focus particularly on practical aspects of its usage. In all the chapters in Part II we motivate the discussion of measures and measurement problems with frequent reference to empirical evidence – both cross-section and case study.

Part III switches the focus to general equilibrium approaches. The technique addressed in Chapter 7 is incidence analysis. Recent research suggests that this is a useful methodology for gaining insights into the way in which intervention in one sector impacts upon others. The theory is outlined, and recent empirical evidence is reviewed. Another technique of fairly recent origin is computable general equilibrium (CGE) modelling. Modern computer hardware and software has facilitated the translation of Walrasian ideas into an empirical setting. The technique is not without its critics, but nevertheless has become widely used. Because of its importance, and its proliferation, we devote two chapters to it (Chapters 8 and 9). In the first we outline the principles upon which CGE models are constructed; in the second we look at their implementation.

Trade policy intervention may be motivated by a desire to promote exports rather than protect imports. Some analysts believe it is possible to identify activities of potential comparative advantage, and a number of measures of revealed comparative advantage are used. This is the subject of Part IV. Again there are two chapters devoted to measurement issues and empirical applications.

One of the reasons why so much attention has been paid to trade policy, and trade policy reform, in developing countries is because it has figured so prominently in the conditional lending programmes of the major multilateral lending agencies, especially the World Bank. For this reason we devote Part V to structural adjustment lending and policy appraisal. Chapter 13 is concerned with the motivation behind SALs and their implementation. It pays particular attention to the role of policy appraisal in the whole process. Chapter 14 then looks at issues of timing, sequencing and adjustment, again with a view to assessing how our techniques of policy appraisal can be used to gain insight into these issues.

The book is intended for advanced undergraduate and postgraduate students of international trade, as well as 'practitioners', that is those involved in policy appraisal. As such it can be used as a work of reference as well as an advanced text. Many of the chapters and parts are designed to stand alone, although throughout we have tried to emphasise the interconnections between techniques, and between theory and practise. We hope that both students and analysts find it useful.

PART I

TRADE AND DEVELOPMENT

CHAPTER 2

Instruments of Trade and Industrial Policy

2.1 Introduction

Like Chapter 3, this is a scene setting chapter. In Chapter 3 we provide an overview of the links between trade policy and economic development, paying particular attention to the influences that have shaped particular strategies. In this chapter we review in a functional manner the economic effects of a range of instruments of trade and industrial policy. It should be emphasised at the outset that the aim is not to provide a 'ready reckoner' of analyses of different instruments. In the context of the present volume that would be both over-ambitious and in fact unnecessary. There are many texts devoted entirely to the microeconomics of commercial policy. As we emphasised in the introduction, this is a book devoted to applied aspects of commercial policy analysis and a basic familiarity with the microeconomics of alternative forms of intervention will therefore be assumed. Our intention in this chapter is simply to offer a brief refresher on the material by way of background.

Commercial policy can be directed at protecting firms in import substitute activities or in export oriented activities. As we shall see later, governments often believe, quite erroneously, that they can pursue both simultaneously. The distinction between the two is a useful one analytically and forms the framework for organising the material which follows. Section 2.2 examines the economic effects of a range of instruments of import substitution, whilst Section 2.3 does the same for instruments of export promotion. Section 2.4 discusses how instruments are often bundled together into policy packages in support of chosen strategies. In this section we will emphasise the key feature of protection as a relative concept. Finally Section 2.5 closes the chapter with some concluding comments.

2.2 Economic effects of instruments of import substitution

Table 2.1 provides a list of instruments of import substitution currently in use, to a greater or lesser degree, in many developing countries. The list is fairly exhaustive. It divides interventions into tariff and non-tariff barriers. The former probably remain the most pervasive form of import protection, although non-tariff barriers of various forms are common, especially in countries following inward oriented policies.

Tariff measures

PREVALENCE

Import tariffs are simply indirect taxes which apply, on a discriminatory basis, to imports. They may be ad valorem or specific. The former have the

Table 2.1 Instruments of import protection

Barriers	*Instruments*
Tariff	Ad valorem import tariff
	Specific import tariff
	Seasonal tariff
	Tariff quota
Non-tariff	Special levies
	Variable levies
	Border tax adjustments
	Anti-dumping duties
	Countervailing duties
	Prohibitions
	Global quotas
	Bilateral quotas
	Seasonal quotas
	Non-automatic licensing
	Import authorisations
	Voluntary export restraints
	Import surveillance
	Advance payment requirements
	Regulations on terms of payments
	Minimum pricing
	Price surveillance
	Sole importing agency
	Special entry procedures
	Additional customs formalities
	Customs valuation procedures
	Standards and regulations
	Local content requirements

Source: Based on Laird and Yeats (1990) Appendix 4.

advantage of being index linked, whilst the latter have the desirable feature of reducing opportunities for underinvoicing and other illegal practices designed to minimise tax liability. Sometimes particular tariffs can be used as quasi non-tariff barriers, for example when they apply on a seasonal basis or when they are linked into a quota.

Table 2.2 gives an indication of the prevalence of tariffs in developing countries. For purposes of comparison some information is also included on developed countries. Several points are notable. First the range of tariffs is relatively wide: in Singapore average nominal tariffs were only 1.3 per cent whilst in Bangladesh they are 68.8 per cent. Second the unweighted average for the developed countries in the table is 6.3 per cent whilst that for developing countries is 28.2 per cent. Admittedly these are non-random samples. Nevertheless the point holds. Nominal tariffs are in general higher in developing countries than in developed countries. Tariff rates in the former group have declined dramatically over the post-war period as a consequence of seven rounds of GATT multilateral trade negotiations. These have not impacted on developing countries, which have not been obliged to reciprocate tariff cuts. Moreover the GATT Charter waives the reciprocity obligation under Article 18 and Part IV permits developing countries greater freedom in the use of tariffs than applies to developed countries. The other point about Table 2.2 that should be noted is that these data apply to *nominal* tariffs. As we shall see in Chapter 5, in general average *effective* tariffs tend to be higher. In Chapter 4 we shall explore further issues in the measurement of nominal protection. Enough has been said thus far to make the central point that tariff protection is pervasive in developing countries.

ARGUMENTS FOR TARIFFS

As we explained in the introduction, this is a book devoted to techniques of policy appraisal. As such it is not our intention to probe deeply into normative issues. Moreover these are issues which have been investigated exhaustively elsewhere (for example Corden 1974). Nevertheless for purposes of reference it is important to review briefly the principal arguments advanced for import tariffs, or protection in general.

In a classic article Johnson (1965) distinguished between *economic*, *non-economic* and *non-arguments* for protection. The last of these can be dispensed with fairly easily. It applies to cases where an obviously fallacious case is put forward. The so-called 'cheap labour argument' is a good case in point. Here protection is sometimes requested on the grounds that overseas producers benefit from cheap labour and that confers an unfair advantage. As anyone familiar with the Heckscher–Ohlin model is aware, cheapness is relative and is driven by relative factor endowments.

Non-economic arguments revolve around socio-political objectives. For

Table 2.2 Trade weighted average MFN and applied tariffs in selected developed and developing countries

Country/ Country Group[1]	Trade Weighted Tariff Average					
	Developing Country trade weights:		Developed Country trade weights:		World trade weights:	
	MFN	Applied	MFN	Applied	MFN	Applied
Developed Countries:						
Australia	8.3	4.8	14.0	9.4	12.4	8.2
Austria	5.5	5.6	10.5	1.5	9.9	2.0
Canada	6.1	4.6	6.6	4.5	6.5	4.5
European Community[2]	3.2	2.1	4.8	2.8	4.2	2.5
Finland	6.7	4.6	4.7	0.7	4.8	1.0
Japan	3.0	2.4	4.2	4.0	3.5	3.0
New Zealand	5.2	3.3	16.0	13.0	13.6	10.9
Norway	3.2	2.8	4.9	0.8	4.8	1.0
Sweden	3.1	2.5	3.6	0.7	3.5	0.8
Switzerland	2.7	2.5	3.0	0.9	3.0	1.0
United States	4.9	4.5	3.4	3.4	3.9	3.8
Developing Countries:						
Algeria (1982)	11.0	–	11.9	11.9	11.7	–
Bangladesh (1983)	69.3	–	68.3	68.3	68.8	–
CARICOM (1979)	7.7	–	18.7	18.7	17.0	–
CEUCA (1977)	12.5	–	18.3	18.3	17.2	–
Egypt (1981)	35.5	–	22.8	22.8	24.2	–
India (1984)	26.9	–	60.2	60.2	44.8	–
Indonesia (1980)	20.2	–	24.7	24.7	23.0	–
Cote d'Ivoire (1980)	37.3	–	33.6	33.6	34.9	–
Kenya (1982)	37.5	–	31.8	31.8	34.0	–
Korea, Rep. of	6.9	–	16.2	16.2	13.0	–
Malaysia (1981)	6.6	–	14.3	14.3	11.6	–
Mexico (1984)	19.3	–	20.2	20.2	20.0	–
Morocco (1982)	33.2	–	36.7	36.7	35.7	–
Nigeria (1982)	29.3	–	22.1	22.1	23.1	–
Pakistan (1982)	30.3	–	54.7	54.7	43.4	–
Philippines (1985)	17.5	–	21.5	21.5	19.9	–
Saudi Arabia (1980)	5.5	–	11.9	11.9	10.9	–
Singapore (1983)	0.4	–	2.1	2.1	1.3	–
Sri Lanka (1983)	19.7	–	23.8	23.8	21.8	–
Tanzania, United Rep. (1981)	12.5	–	15.9	15.9	15.1	–
Thailand (1981)	6.1	–	20.5	20.5	14.5	–
Tunisia	14.5	–	18.9	18.9	18.5	–
Yugoslavia (1980)	4.5	–	12.1	12.1	10.0	–

Source: Laird and Yeats (1990).

Notes:
1. The dates shown in parentheses show the year for which the tariff data were drawn. Since the UNCTAD data base did not contain information on developing country preferential arrangements applied tariff averages could not be computed.
2. The trade weighted rates are based on the external trade of the EEC.

example a government may wish to exclude imports on health or safety grounds, or may wish to support a particular sector to preserve a particular 'way of life'. These are not arguments which the economist is well equipped to handle, involving as they do judgements about the desirability of given non-economic objectives. The economist may nonetheless have a role to play in commenting upon the instruments used to realise chosen objectives. Invariably there will be more than one instrument available. In principle the choice of instrument should rest upon efficiency considerations.

Economic arguments are of greatest interest to the economic analyst. These rest upon the notion that distortions are present in a particular market and intervention can successfully correct the distortion(s) in question. Table 2.3 illustrates the point. Distortions can exist in product or factor markets. When present they prevent the market from gravitating automatically to an optimum. Thus market power results in price exceeding marginal cost, negative externalities result in social costs exceeding private costs and so on. Resource misallocation is the inevitable outcome. In general there will be some instrument of intervention which can correct the distortion in question. It can be argued that certain distortions should be dealt with by instruments of trade policy. For example it is often argued that infant industries need to be protected from foreign competition whilst they mature. Another frequently cited argument for tariffs is that they provide central government with much-needed revenue, revenue which, due to administrative constraints and high collection costs, could not otherwise be collected through income-based or commodity-based taxes. Later in this chapter, when we have reviewed non-tariff measures, we will comment further on arguments for protection. For now let us review the simple welfare analytics of tariff imposition.

ECONOMIC EFFECTS OF TARIFFS

As with arguments for tariffs, there is no need to spend a great deal of time on the effects of nominal tariffs. This topic is covered exhaustively in most undergraduate texts on international economics (see for instance Williamson and Milner 1991). A review of some basics as a reference point is, however, in order.

For purposes of analysis we invoke the simple 2 × 2 × 2 Heckscher–Ohlin–Samuelson model, with all its attendant assumptions (perfectly competitive and efficient markets, incomplete specialisation in accordance with relative factor endowments, international immobility of factors and an inability of the home country to influence the international terms of trade). Figure 2.1 describes the case of a small open economy in a partial equilibrium framework. D^H, S^H and S^F denote domestic demand, domestic supply and foreign supply, respectively, of the import substitute. At the world

Table 2.3 Forms of distortions which result in market failure

Distortion	*Effects*
Domestic product market:	
1. Consumption externality	Private consumption levels which exceed or fall short of socially optimal levels
2. Monopoly sellers	Price in excess of marginal cost leading to private production and consumption at levels which are socially sub-optimal
3. Production externality	Private production levels which exceed or fall short of socially optimal levels
Domestic factor markets:	
1. Monopoly suppliers of labour	Wages in excess of marginal revenue products leading to employment below the socially optimal level
2. Interest rates in excess of social discount rates	Investment levels below the socially optimal level
3. Surplus labour	Wages in some sectors above their social opportunity cost leading to underemployment in those sectors
International product markets:	
1. Market power	Unexploited gains from trade available to the large country

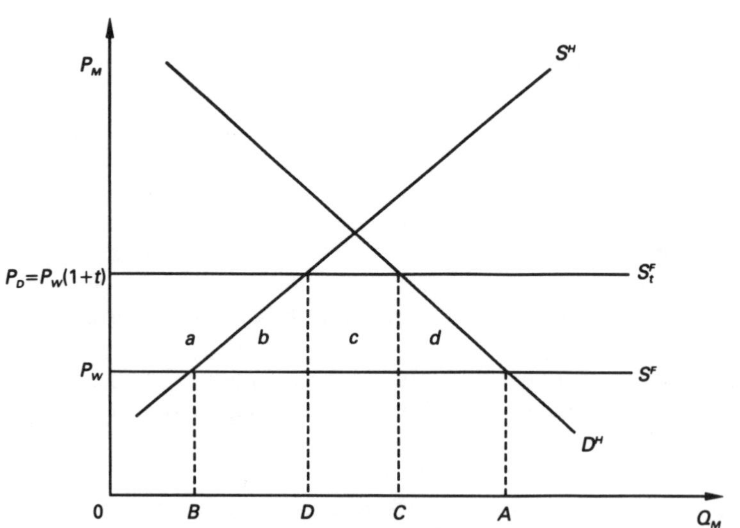

Figure 2.1 Economic effects of an import tariff: partial equilibrium, small open economy

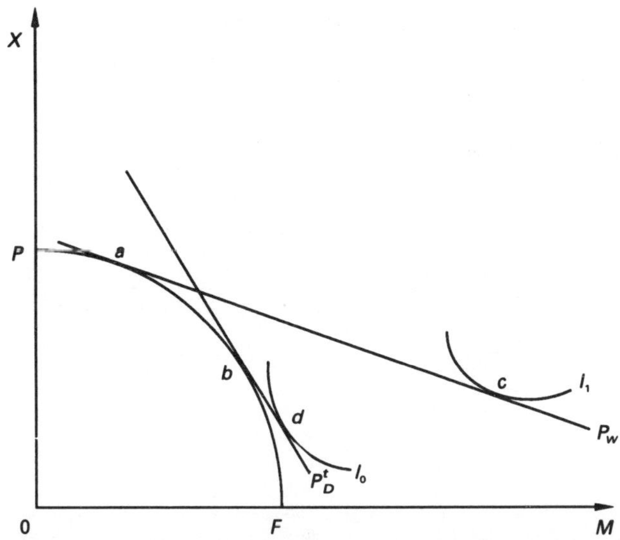

Figure 2.2 *Economic effects of an import tariff: general equilibrium, small open economy*

price of P_W, OA is consumed, of which OB is supplied domestically, the residual BA being imported. If an ad valorem tariff of t is levied the domestic price becomes:

$$P_D = P_W + P_W t$$

$$= P_W(1 + t) \quad (2.1)$$

At this price demand contracts to OC, domestic supply expands to OD and import penetration falls to DC/OC. The standard welfare effects follow. Consumer surplus declines by $a + b + c + d$. Part of this constitutes an internal redistribution. Producer surplus increases by a and government revenue increases by c. The residuals, b and d, are the well-known 'dead-weight losses' of tariff protection. d is incurred because at the margin some consumers are squeezed out, hence the term 'consumption loss'; b represents the excess cost of producing something domestically which could otherwise be imported, hence the term production, or efficiency, loss. *In the absence of distortions* these will be net losses to the domestic economy. As we shall see later, the gains to society from eliminating distortions could offset, in whole or in part, these losses.

Figure 2.2 presents the same analysis in a general equilibrium setting, with x as the exportable and m as the importable. Free trade production is located at a on the production frontier, consumption at c on indifference curve I_1. The tariff distorts the domestic relative price ratio from P_W to P_D^t, where:

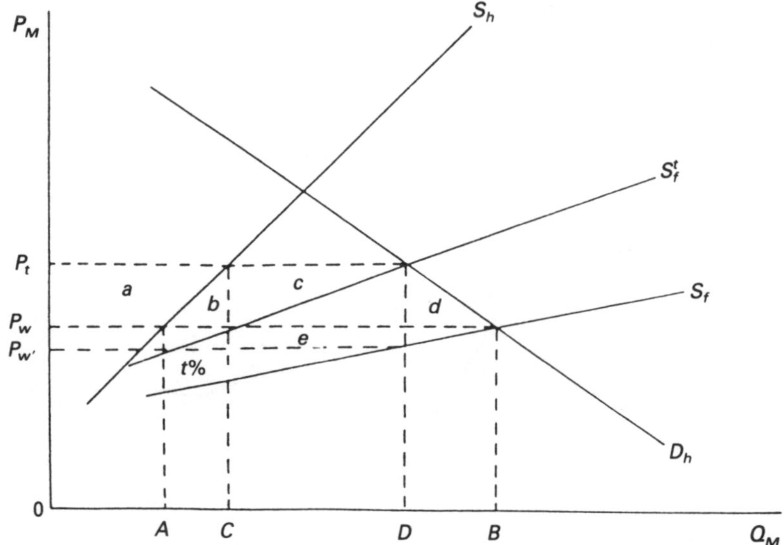

Figure 2.3 Economic effects of an import tariff: partial equilibrium, large open economy

$$P_D^t = \frac{P_m(1 + t)}{P_x} \tag{2.2}$$

At this price ratio production shifts from *a* to *b* as the export sector contracts to facilitate expansion of the import substitute sector. Consumption shifts from *c* to *d*, with the restriction of consumption possibilities taking the economy from I_1 to I_0. This is the analogue of the deadweight losses identified in Figure 2.1. Analytically, the key point which Figure 2.2 brings out is the fact that protection is a *relative* concept. In protecting one sector protection is removed from another. This is a feature of import protection that is often forgotten and to which we return in Chapter 7.

The large open economy case differs in one crucial respect. If a country is 'large' it can influence the prices at which it trades through changes in demand or supply. Thus when a tariff is levied it no longer leaves the post-tariff world price unchanged. Intuition suggests that the imposition of an import tariff by a large economy should drive down the world price, to the advantage, of course, of the importing country. The analytics are straightforward and are outlined in Figures 2.3 and 2.4. Figures 2.3 is the analogue of Figure 2.1. The key difference is the change in the world price from P_W to P'_W, which is driven by the tariff-induced restriction of demand. This actually has a beneficial impact on domestic welfare which is given by the area *e*. This area represents the tariff revenue which is in effect redistributed from foreign producers to the domestic government. If *e* exceeds *b* plus *d*, the country concerned is actually better off with the tariff.

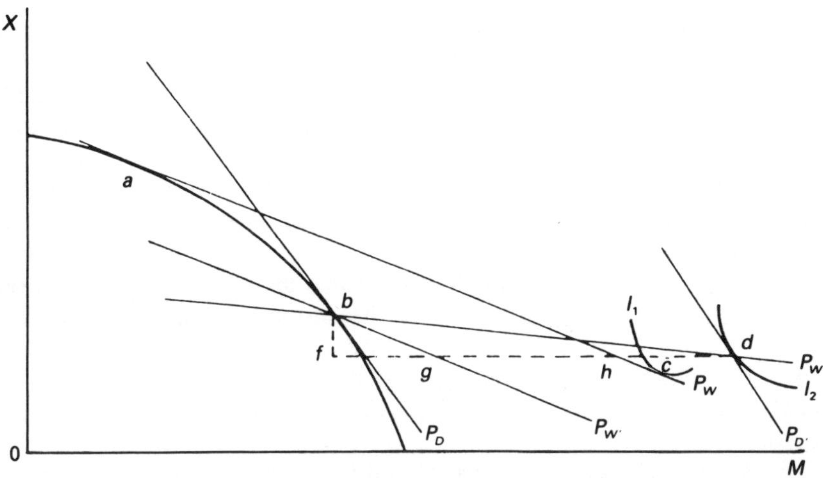

Figure 2.4 Economic effects of an import tariff: general equilibrium, large open economy

It could in fact levy an optimum tariff if the net gain is maximised. Figure 2.4 constructs the analysis in a general equilibrium setting. After the tariff has been imposed, the consumption point shifts to point *d* on indifference curve I_2, which lies above I_1. Note, of course, that the home country benefits by redistributing income from the rest of the world. Nonetheless the case is sometimes put forward as an argument for tariff protection.

In summary then, in the absence of distortions an import tariff results in net welfare losses in a small open economy. If however the country concerned is a large open economy, the tariff-imposing country can actually end up better off with the tariff.

Non-tariff measures

PREVALENCE

As can be seen from Table 2.1 above, the range of instruments that can be listed under the heading of non-tariff measures (NTMs) is large. It is also diverse, with some being fiscal, some quantitative, some involving monitoring and so on. Moreover, depending upon how one defines a NTM, the list could be longer still. Many measures are very carefully hidden.

From a documentary standpoint the diversity of NTMs is a major complication. One cannot easily 'add together' the restrictive impact of deliberately complicated customs valuations procedures with that of price surveillance, or an import quota. It is in part for this reason that summary statistics are hard to come by. However the situation is complicated further by the fact that many NTMs are quite deliberately opaque. From a political economy standpoint, opacity is a desirable characteristic. It means that policy makers can redistribute income from one group to another at low political cost. From the perspective of the economic analyst, the opacity has nothing to recommend it, leaving us struggling to pin down the existence of many measures, let alone their economic effects.

For these reasons it is just not possible to provide a summary of NTMs like that for tariffs reported in Table 2.2. As far as developing countries are concerned this kind of summary just does not exist. More information is available for developed countries where some analysts have recorded the frequency of NTMs by industry, or the proportion of trade which is covered by NTMs (see for instance Nogues, Olechowski and Winters, 1987). It might be noted in passing that this work shows that reliance on NTMs in developed countries has increased quite significantly over the last decade or so.

For developing countries one is forced to rely upon case study material which is either qualitative or which estimates the price-raising effects of particular NTMs. This kind of information must be used with great caution. Carefully interpreted, however, it can offer some guidance as to the pervasiveness or otherwise of NTMs. Table 2.4 reports the results of one of the few attempts to summarise information. This is taken from Greenaway (1986). For a (non-random) sample of developing countries, country-specific analyses were reviewed and the prevalence of direct controls qualitatively assessed according to whether they were pervasive, moderate, non-existent and so on. We should emphasise again that the information must be interpreted very carefully indeed. What it does appear to suggest is that NTMs in the form of direct controls are quite extensively deployed in many developing countries and especially those which have followed inward-oriented trade policies. This is consistent with the findings of a number of multi-country studies like those of Balassa (1982) and Krueger et al. (1981), as well as a multitude of case studies, some of which we will report on later. The impression that comes through strongly is that NTMs are widely used in many developing countries and their use is more pervasive than in developed countries. Having said that, it should be noted that there has been dismantling of some of the overt QRs in a large number of LDCs in the 1980s. As we shall see later, this is partly driven by adjustment lending programmes (see Thomas *et al.*, 1991 and Papageorgiou, Michaely and Choksi, 1991). It should also be noted, however, that in the process of trade reform some LDCs are utilising some of the features of the new protectionism, such as anti-dumping legislation.

ARGUMENTS FOR NTMs

Fundamentally the framework for putting forward arguments for NTMs is the same as that for tariffs. We can again distinguish between economic,

Table 2.4a Characteristics of trade and exchange rate regimes, 1965–73

Country	*Average EPR*[1]	*Range of EPRs*	*Use of direct controls*	*Export incentives*	*Bias in trade orientation*[2]	*Exchange rate alignment*	*Group*[3]
Korea, Rep. of	10 (1968)	−67→164 (1968)	Extensive until mid-1960s, limited thereafter	Extensive positive incentives	0.78 (1963) 0.91 (1966)	Realistic–low, undervalued	A1
Singapore	6 (1967)	−1→86 (1967)	Some instituted in 1963, removed in 1965	Extensive positive incentives	1.09 (1967)	Realistic	A1
Yugoslavia	28 (1970)	−3→66 (1970)	Moderate use of import controls	Extensive positive incentives	–	–	A2
Thailand	16 (1969) 27 (1973)	−38→68 (1969) −43→236 (1973)	Limited use of price controls and import controls	Moderate positive incentives	–	Realistic	A2
Colombia	−2 (1969)	−51→215 (1969)	Moderate use, increased reliance over period	Extensive positive incentives	1.23 (1969)	Low, overvalued	A2

continued on p. 18

Table 2.4a continued

Country	*Average EPR*	*Range of EPRs*	*Use of direct controls*	*Export incentives*	*Bias in trade Orientation*	*Exchange rate alignment*	*Group*
Malaysia	–8 (1963) 38 (1970) 39 (1973)	−42→212 (1963) 5→248 (1970) 0→307 (1973)	Limited use of import controls	Limited positive incentives and EPZ arrangements	–	Realistic	A2
Indonesia	33 (1971)	−19→5400 (1971)	Moderate use of import controls and industrial licensing	Limited positive incentives	–	–	A2
Ivory Coast	41 (1971)	−25→278 (1971)	Minimal use of direct controls pre-1974	Minimal positive incentives	–	Realistic	A2
Brazil	66 (1967)	25→362 (1967)	Extensive use of import controls until 1967	–	1.34 (1966)	Realistic to low overvalued	B1
Philippines	63 (1965)	−461→260 (1965)	Moderate use of direct controls and industrial licensing	–	1.36 (1962–4) 1.16 (1970)	Realistic	B1
Argentina	47 (1969)	−18→207 (1969)	–	–	1.94 (1969)	Significantly overvalued	B1

Mexico	49 (1970)	2→371 (1970)	Extensive use of import controls	–	–	Realistic	B1
Bolivia	54 (1970)	–	–	–	–	Realistic	B1
Israel	55 (1965) 62 (1968)	4→137 (1965) 0→188 (1968)	–	Moderate export incentives	1.5 (1968)	–	B1
Senegal	70 (1971)	–	Moderate use of import controls and industrial licensing	–	–	Low, overvalued	B1
Kenya	92 (1967)	−9→539 (1967)	Moderate use of import controls	–	–	Low, overvalued	B1
Nigeria	99 (1968)	−27→1063 (1968)	Extensive use of import controls and industrial licensing	Negligible	–	Overvalued	B2
Dominican Rep.	124 (1971)	−48→874 (1967)	–	–	–	Realistic	B2
Ghana	143 (1968–70) 105 (1972)	−10→1633 (1968–70)	Extensive use of import controls and industrial licensing	Negligible	–	Significantly overvalued	B2

continued on p. 20

Table 2.4a continued

Country	*Average EPR*	*Range of EPRs*	*Use of direct controls*	*Export incentives*	*Bias in trade orientation*	*Exchange rate alignment*	*Group*
India	125 (1968–9)	−21→3354 (1968–9)	Extensive use of import controls and industrial licensing	Negligible	–	–	B2
Sri Lanka	118 (1970)	2→382 (1970)	Extensive use of import controls and industrial licensing	Negligible	–	Significantly overvalued	B2
Tanzania	116 (1966)	−1→538 (1966)	Extensive use of import controls and industrial licensing	–	–	–	B2
Pakistan	356 (1963–4) 200 (1970–1)	−6→595 (1963–4) 36→595 (1970–1)	Extensive use of import controls and industrial licensing	Negligible	–	–	B2
Sudan	179 (1971)	32→783 (1971)	Extensive use of import controls	–	–	Low, overvalued	B2
Uruguay	384 (1965)	17→1014 (1965)	–	–	–	Significantly overvalued	B2

Ethiopia	125 (1970)	–	Extensive use of import controls	–	–	Realistic	B2
Tunisia	250 (1972)	1→737 (1972)	Extensive use of import controls	–	–	Low, overvalued	B2
Chile	175 (1967)	−23→1140 (1967)	Extensive use of import controls	–	1.79 (1967)	Significantly overvalued	B2
Peru	90 (1971)	–	Extensive use of import controls and licensing	–	–	Significantly overvalued	B2

Source: Greenaway (1986) Table 6.

Notes:
1. Effective rate of protection (see Chapter 5).
2. See section 2.4 for a definition of the bias index.
3. A1 – strongly outward oriented trade strategy; A2 – moderately outward oriented; B1 – moderately inward oriented; B2 – strongly inward oriented. See Greenaway and Nam (1988) for an explanation of the categories.

Table 2.4b Characteristics of trade and exchange rate regimes, 1973–84

Country	*Average EPR*	*Range of EPRs*	*Use of direct controls*	*Export incentives*	*Bias in trade orientation*	*Exchange rate alignment*	*Group*
Yugoslavia	9 (1974)	–	Extensive use of direct controls	Extensive positive incentives	–	–	A2
Malaysia	25 (1980)	−173→1175 (1980)	Limited use of import controls	Extensive positive incentives through EPZ	–	Undervalued	A2
Mexico	11 (1979) 3–10 (1980)	−32→249 (1979) −33→211 (1980)	Liberalisation of direct controls in late 1970s	Range of positive incentives available including EPZ incentives	–	Realistic	A2
Cameroon	31 (1975–6)	–	Some use of import controls	–	–	–	A2
Brazil	44 (1980–1)	−16→97 (1980–1)	Liberalisation of direct controls in 1970s	–	–	Low overvaluation	A2
Sri Lanka	38 (1979)	0→307 (1979)	Liberalisation of direct controls in 1977	Extensive positive incentives through EPZ	–	–	A2

Philippines	54 (1974) 44 (1978)	−41→18758 (1974)	Limited use of direct controls	Moderate positive incentives through EPZ	–	Realistic	B1
Indonesia	30 (1975)	−35→4314 (1975)	Extensive use of direct controls and industrial licensing	Limited	–	–	B1
Ivory Coast	76 (1978)	−8→118 (1978)	Moderate use of import controls post-1974	Limited	1.59 (1978)	Overvalued	B1
Colombia	44 (1979)	27→127 (1979)	Extensive use of import controls	Limited	–	Low, overvalued	B1
Thailand	54 (1978)	4→495 (1978)	Moderate use of import controls and industrial licensing	Moderate positive incentives through EPZ	–	Realistic	B1
Argentina	38 (1977)	−35→426 (1977)	Some liberalisation of direct controls in late 1970s	–	–	Significantly overvalued	B1
Pakistan	60 (1980)	−799→1543 (1980)	Moderate use of import controls and licensing	Limited	–	–	B1

continued on p. 24

Table 2.4b continued

Country	*Average EPR*	*Range of EPRs*	*Use of direct controls*	*Export incentives*	*Bias in trade orientation*	*Exchange rate alignment*	*Group*
Turkey	75 (1979)	−108→273 (1979)	Moderate use of import controls	–	1.33 (1979)	Overvalued	B1
Nigeria	82 (1979–80)	−62→1119 (1979–80)	Extensive use of import controls and industrial licensing	Negligible	–	Significantly overvalued	B2
Ghana	131 (1982)	−83→21632 (1982)	Extensive use of import controls and industrial licensing	Negligible	–	Overvalued	B2
Madagascar	164 (1982)	−23→4330	Extensive use of import controls and industrial licensing	–	–	Overvalued	B2
Burundi	91 (1984)	−4→7896	Extensive use of import controls and industrial licensing	–	–	Overvalued	B2
Bangladesh	144 (1976–7)	–	Extensive use of import controls	–	–	–	B2

Zambia	161 (1975)	−22→1251	Extensive use of import controls and industrial licensing	–	–	Realistic	B2
Bolivia	101 (1975–6)	−12→551	Extensive use of import controls and industrial licensing	Limited	–	Overvalued	B2
Peru	198 (1975) 122 (1978) 74 (1981)	27→121 (1981)	Extensive use of import controls Some liberalisation in early 1980	–	1.53 (1975)	Overvalued Realistic	B2

Source: Greenaway (1986) Table 7.

non-economic and non-arguments and nothing need be added here. It may, of course, be that certain NTMs are seen as being more effective in hitting particular targets and some will be less effective (for example the revenue motive will not apply unless quotas are auctioned). That, however, is a different matter and is something to which we will return later in this section.

ECONOMIC EFFECTS OF NTMs

As with tariff barriers, it is not necessary to dwell at length on the welfare analytics of NTMs, for at least some measures these are well known (see for example Anderson, 1988). Besides which the range of NTMs is so wide that one could write an entire text on this subject alone. For purposes of comparison with the tariff we will confine ourselves to a single but widely used measure, namely the quantitative restraint (QR). Extensive use is made of QRs in developing countries. Moreover a number of observations can be made about other instruments once we have evaluated the QR.

Figure 2.5 outlines the partial equilibrium effects of a QR. The upper limit on imports is $AF = CD$. This is represented by the effective supply curve becoming $P_WGS^H_Q$. In other words, beyond OF marginal supplies must come from domestic producers. For expository convenience we have set the quota to give us equivalent price effects with the tariff in Figure 2.1. Thus $P_Q = P_W(1 + t)$. The artificial scarcity created by the quota drives the domestic price above the world price, domestic supply expands and demand contracts. Because we have identical demand and supply conditions and have set the initial quantity effects as identical, there would appear to be complete equivalence between the welfare effects of the tariff and QR. In the sense that we end up with net welfare losses to the economy of $b + d$ (which should be interpreted in exactly the same way as the tariff case), this is so. However, the distributional consequences are somewhat different. Area a remains a redistribution from domestic consumers to domestic producers. Area c however is no longer a transfer to the domestic revenue authorities. In order to operate a QR, licences have to be issued to authorised importers. If the licences are distributed by some kind of administrative mechanism, the holders of these licences acquire rents which amount to the difference between P_W and P_Q. This arises because the world price remains at P_W whilst the domestic price is inflated to P_Q. The unit rent is the difference between the two, total rents amount to area c. If we ignore interpersonal utility comparisons the welfare effects of the two instruments are identical, although on equity grounds (the government should have the revenue rather than importers) or administrative grounds (developing country governments rely heavily on trade taxes for government revenue) one could make a case in favour of tariffs rather than

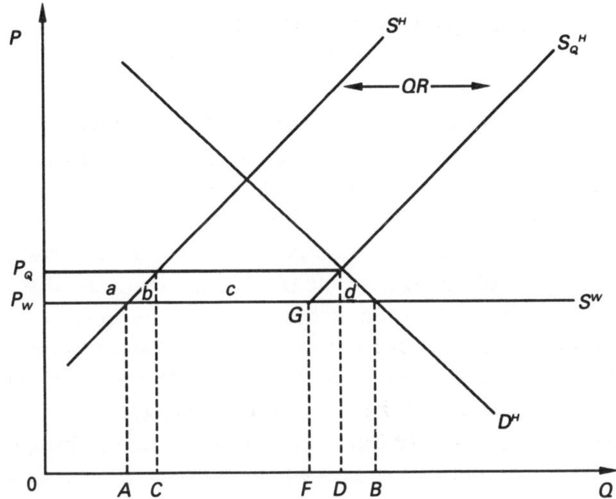

Figure 2.5 Economic effects of a QR: partial equilibrium, small open economy

quotas. However on efficiency grounds there would appear to be equivalence.

There are, however, important non-equivalences between tariffs and quotas which have been the subject of extensive analysis (Bhagwati, 1971; Anderson, 1988). Three in particular are worthy of mention. First, quotas can alter market structure and firm behaviour in a way that tariffs cannot. For instance, suppose the domestic market is dominated by a single firm or a cartel. If protection is provided via a tariff, this market power cannot be exploited. The market remains contestable at the margin. In contrast QRs eliminate competition at the margin and allow domestic firms to exploit their market power. As a consequence domestic price can rise beyond P_Q to the monopoly level. Second, if the market expands and D_H shifts out to the right, marginal supplies have to come from domestic producers rather than more efficient foreign producers. Thus, in an expanding market, the deadweight losses (*b* and *d*) grow. Third, the availability of rents results in rent-seeking behaviour. In other words agents compete by lobbying and other 'directly unproductive activities' (Bhagwati, 1971) to secure the rents. For these reasons, on efficiency grounds quotas are generally regarded as less efficient instruments of intervention than tariffs.

All of the above pertains to the small open economy, partial equilibrium case. We could replicate the analysis to large economy, general equilibrium cases. In fact there is no need to do so as equivalence holds for these cases also, subject to the points made above. The key result which comes out of this simple analysis is that the relative costs of securing a specific objective by alternative instruments might be quite different.

Optimal intervention analysis and NTMs

The last point of the previous section gives rise to the possibility that one can systematically compare instruments of intervention and rank them according to their relative costs or their by-product distortions (Corden, 1974). In fact this turns out to be a very powerful mechanism for policy analysis. The basic idea is very straightforward. First we identify a given argument for intervention, say to correct a particular distortion. Then we evaluate the impact of alternative means of correcting the distortion. The instrument which should be used is that which gets closest to the problem, that is that which minimises the by-product distortions of intervention. The ideas are traced out quite clearly in Meade (1955) and were subsequently formalised by Bhagwati (1958) and Johnson (1965a).

Table 2.5 illustrates the principle with a particular example. Here the distortion is taken to be a wage rate which exceeds the social opportunity cost of labour. This could be because of the influence of organised labour. The effect of the distortion is that employment is lower than it otherwise would be. The most efficient means of intervention would be to eliminate the distortion at source, that is break the power of organised labour. Of course this may be regarded as inadmissible because the presence of labour unions are regarded as important for socio-economic reasons. The next best instrument is a wage subsidy. This has a by-product distortion in that taxes have to be levied to finance the subsidy. It is however more efficient than a production subsidy which, by subsidising capital as well as labour, distorts the capital labour ratio in addition to introducing a distortion because the subsidy needs to be financed. A tariff is less efficient again because it also introduces a consumption distortion and so on as we go down the list.

From the standpoint of policy appraisal, the framework that optimal intervention analysis provides is potentially extremely useful to both policy maker and policy analyst. It provides a mechanism for encouraging investigation of alternative instruments for securing a given objective which emphasises efficiency criteria. This does not of course mean that the most efficient instrument of intervention will always be chosen. As we shall see later, greater reliance is often placed on relatively inefficient instruments. The reasons why this turns out to be the case are rather interesting and will be addressed later in this chapter.

2.3 Economic effects of instruments of export promotion

Table 2.6 gives details of the range of export incentives which have been used to some degree or other in some of the principal export-oriented developing countries. These are broken down according to whether they are input related, output related or externality related. The first two tend

Table 2.5 The hierarchy of policies

Instrument	*By-product distortions**
1. Remove distortions at source	None
2. Wage subsidy	Distortion from raising revenue (depending on tax used)
3. Production subsidy	(2) plus downward bias in labour intensity
4. Import tariff plus export subsidy	(3) minus distortion from raising revenue plus consumption distortion
5. Import tariff	(4) plus greater consumption distortion
6. Quantitative restriction	(5) plus potential loss of government revenue to license holders and greater administrative complexity and greater dynamic inefficiencies
7. Source specific quota/ voluntary export restraint	(6) plus export of rent to foreign licence-holders and trade diversion

* Distortion: private cost of labour exceeds the social opportunity cost.

to be firm or industry specific, the last tends to pertain to exports in general. The distinction between exports and imports relies upon an ability to trace the incentive specifically to a particular stage of the production process. As we can see, input-related incentives can be attached to intermediate or primary inputs, whilst output incentives can be direct (in the sense of being tied to volume of production) or indirect (in the form of systematic supports like infrastructure provision). Which instruments are used, and on what conditions, is fashioned by the arguments used to support intervention and the orientation of trade strategy (factors we will turn to later).

PREVALENCE

In Table 2.2 we were able to conveniently summarise the extent of tariff measures by reporting average tariffs for a range of developing countries. Unfortunately we are unable to do something similar for export incentives. This is the case for several reasons. Firstly, as we saw in Table 2.5, there is great diversity in the range of instruments used. As with NTMs and import substitution, there is no convenient way of 'adding' these up into a summary export incentive index. Second, and related to the above, many of the measures used are implicit. Governments have a strong incentive to provide support in this way on two counts: first, it ensures that the potential for demonstration effects on other sectors is minimised; second, it ensures that the scope for retaliatory action through GATT is minimised. Both are important, the latter especially so given the potential for use of

Table 2.6 Types of export incentives used in various LDCs[1]

A. 'Input-related' incentives[2]

1. *Intermediate input-related*:
   Tariff and tax exemptions/rebates on imported inputs for exporters and their domestic suppliers
   Import credits for exports
   Wastage allowance subsidies
   Reduced prices of public utility inputs
2. *Primary input-related*:
   Accelerated depreciation
   Reduced interest rates for exporters
   Investment loans (preferential access)

B. 'Output-related' incentives[2]

1. *Direct output-related*:
   Production loans for exporters (preferential access/interest rate subsidy)
   Domestic indirect and direct tax exemptions/rebates
   Import entitlement/licences linked to exports
   Export credits (preferential access/interest rate subsidy)
   Foreign exchange deposits held by central banks for use by individual exporters
   Foreign exchange loans (preferential access)
   Subsidised shipment insurance
   Direct export subsidies
2. *Indirect output-related*:
   Infrastructure provision
   Credits for, and government provision of, overseas marketing activities, R&D expenses, etc.

C. 'Externality-related' incentives

Export 'quality' inspection and incentives
Monopoly rights granted in new export markets

Source: Falvey and Gemmell (1990).

Notes:
1. These measures have operated at various dates in at least one of the following: Hong Kong, Indonesia, Korea, Malaysia, the Philippines, Singapore, Taiwan and Thailand.
2. The 'output-related', 'input-related' division is based on whether the amount of 'subsidy' received is determined primarily by levels of output or input use.

countervailing duties by trading partners alleging serious injury from subsidised exports. For these reasons assessments of the use of export incentives has tended to be qualitative rather than quantitative.

Table 2.7 reports some documentation for export incentives in four Asian countries that have provided extensive support – Malaysia, Philip-

Table 2.7 Export incentives in Malaysia, the Philippines, Thailand and Korea

Type of incentive	*Malaysia*	*Philippines*	*Thailand*	*Korea*
A. Tax Incentives for Priority Industries*				
Priority industries	*'Pioneer'* (exports; also socially desired goods not already produced on commercial terms)	*'Preferred'* (demand exists, not supply); *'pioneer'* (demand and supply must both be generated)	*'Promoted'* (development-oriented industries based on decisions by the Board of Investment)	*'Key'* (government determined)
Tax holidays	5–10 years based on investment, location, and employment: *cit, dit, dt* (2–8 years); indefinite loss carryover	All taxes, except *cit* are exempt on a diminishing basis up to 1981; loss carry forward to a maximum of 10 years	3–8 years plus 50 per cent reduction for 5 more years; includes *bt, cit*	All taxes: *cit, it* on unincorporated units; *dit, pt; pat*–for 5 years plus 50 per cent reduction for 3 additional years
Deductions	Does not apply due to exemptions	Organisational and pre-operating costs from taxable income	25 per cent of installation costs from net profits	Does not apply due to exemptions
Tax credit:				
1. Equipment	Post-exemption period: 25–40 per cent of capital expenses incurred during exemption period	100 per cent on domestic and imported equipment; penalty of twice the credit for unauthorised resales.	100 per cent exemption of *bt* on equipment	100 per cent on domestic and imported equipment; no penalty law

continued on p. 32

Table 2.7 continued

Type of incentive	*Malaysia*	*Philippines*	*Thailand*	*Korea*
2. Interest payments	Information unavailable	Conditionally, on foreign loan interest	Information unavailable	Full exemption from tax on interest on foreign loans
Accelerated depreciation	Conditionally available	Allowed to a maximum of twice the usual rate of 20 per cent	Conditionally available	Domestic equipment may receive up to four times usual rate
Tariffs on machinery and raw materials	*cd* exemption on raw materials and machinery not available locally	*cd* exemption on machinery not available locally; not so for materials	*cd* exemption on raw materials and machinery not available locally	*cd* exemption on 'capital goods' interpreted to include raw materials
B. Tax Incentives Specific to Export Industries*				
Priority exports	All export industries are included in the 'pioneer' category; the following incentives are additional	Export Incentives Act does not specify whether the following incentives are additive	All export areas are not 'promoted'. Following incentives related to exports (promoted as well as traditional exports)	All foreign exchange earning industries are defined within 'key' sectors; the following are additional incentives
Tax holidays	4–7 years holiday for capital investments (instead of usual 2-5 years for pioneer industries)	*et* exemption if revenues exceed US$5 million within 5 years from the registration	Exemption from *bt* and *et* on exportation of manufactures	*bt* exemption

Deductions	Expenses such as foreign advertising, export market research, transport costs deductible from tax base	*it* base reduced by a certain portion of export revenue, based also on domestic content	Not available	Not applicable due to total exemptions
Tax credit	Not available	Export producers: tax credit equivalent to the sales, compensating and specific taxes and raw material duties	7/8th of *cd* on raw materials	50 per cent for *it* and *cit*
Accelerated depreciation	Additional 40 per cent of the residual value of capital assets	Same as in priority industries	Same as in priority industries	Same as in priority industries

Source: Falvey and Gemmell (1990).

* Abbreviations used: *it* = income tax; *cit* = corporation income tax; *dit* = dividend income tax; *bt* = business tax; *dt* = development tax; *pt* = property tax; *pat* = property acquisition tax; *cd* = customs duty; and *et* = export tax.

pines, Thailand and Korea. The table is helpful in detailing the types of measures used, although it is not possible to provide summary measures, nor even to report the relative importance of each. Nevertheless it is useful in giving a flavour of the measures used, across industries and across countries.

There are a number of studies of trade policy which undertake this kind of exercise for different samples of countries (see for example Krueger *et al.*, 1981; Greenaway, 1986; Milner, 1990c). Summarising, the studies suggest the following. First, input measures tend to be more prevalent than output measures. This is partly to try to make them GATT-consistent, partly to tie them into protection of primary factors. Second, measures are much more widely applied to manufactures than primary products. Indeed the latter are very often explicitly taxed. Third, export incentives are more widely used by developing countries in Asia than in Latin America, the Middle East, or Sub-Saharan Africa. Fourth, to an increasing extent incentives operate through export processing zones (EPZs). These apply blanket incentives to any activity that produces exclusively for the export market. It is a phenomenon which has proliferated in recent years. Finally, typically the extent of export support provided falls short of that offered to import substitute activities.

ARGUMENTS FOR EXPORT INCENTIVES

In Section 2.2 we distinguished between economic, non-economic and non-arguments for intervention. The usefulness of this distinction is in forcing us to identify clearly circumstances where market failure of one form or another creates an a priori case for intervention. Later in that same section we saw that, having identified an a priori case, one could then use the optimal intervention framework to ensure that intervention was as efficient as possible, in the sense of minimising by-product distortions. The same approach can be applied to export incentives. One could for example make a case for supporting a particular export-oriented industry on infant industry grounds. Systematically working through the argument would help clarify whether the case was valid and, if so, determine the optimal intervention. The 'thought experiment' would be exactly analogous to the import protection case.

In addition to that class of argument there are two other lines of argument often used in connection with exportables, namely externalities which are peculiar to exports and compensatory export incentives. The first has been used to argue for export promotion in general. It stresses potential economy-wide benefits of exporting which derive from exposing indigenous producers to foreign competition. It is argued that this helps reduce X-inefficiency. In addition exposure to foreign competition facilitates technology transfer and accelerates technical process in the home economy. It has been argued by some that these kinds of considerations have been important in promoting growth in the South East Asian NICs.

Compensatory export incentives have a different kind of justification. The argument depends here on the pre-existence of import protection and an adverse impact of that import protection on the export sector. Suppose that in a simple three-sector economy the importable sector benefits from protection of some form. Protection is relative – to be effective it must protect one activity relative to another. If production of importables is supported, the sectors which find themselves without protection are the non-tradeable and exportable sectors. In Chapter 7 we outline a model which shows exactly how import protection can be shifted to the export sector. In crude terms it occurs through competition for resources. The point is, for present purposes, that a case can be made for intervention in order to neutralise the effects of the import protection. In other words some form of export incentive is provided to offset the import tariff. This is of course a second-best argument. The same result could be achieved more efficiently by removing the import protection (assuming an absence of distortions). If however the import protection cannot be removed, perhaps on political-economy grounds, a compensatory export incentive may be seen as appropriate.

Economic effects of export incentives

As with import protection, the basic welfare analytics of export incentives are well known and need not preoccupy us for too long. All that is required here are some background comments for reference. Having said that, we do face a difficulty of the sort we confronted in connection with NTMs, namely the range of export incentives upon which governments can call. To keep matters simple we will take as our reference point a straightforward export subsidy. This simplicity comes at a price in that we lose many of the subtleties associated with implicit measures, as well as ignoring the interactions with import measures. However we can evaluate implicit measures in a similar way if we are able to think of them in subsidy equivalent terms and we will be addressing interactions later in this chapter but more so in Chapter 7.

In Figure 2.6, D^H and S^H denote domestic demand and supply of the exportable, whilst P^W denotes the world price. At P^W, *OB* is produced, of which *AB* is exported. Suppose now an export subsidy of *s* is introduced. As this applies to only part of production it causes a movement along the existing supply curve, rather than a shift of the curve (as a production subsidy would). Exporting becomes more profitable at the margin and results in an expansion of total output from *OB* to *OD*. In addition, however, it also stimulates a reallocation of output. This follows because domestic consumers have to be willing to match the subsidy-inclusive price

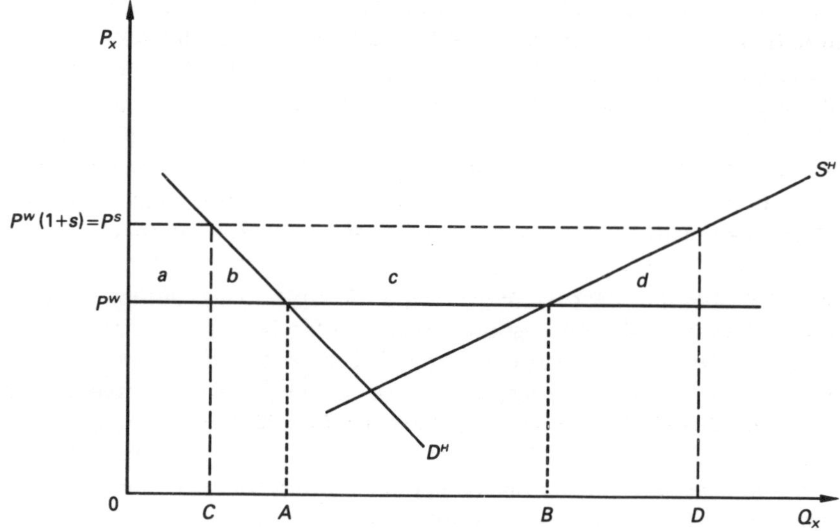

Figure 2.6 Economic effects of an export subsidy: partial equilibrium, small open economy

in order to prevent firms from exporting all of their output. Domestic price therefore increases from P^W to $P^S = P^W(1 + s)$, domestic demand contracts from *OA* to *OC* and the difference, *CA*, is exported. Total exports after the subsidy amount to *CD*.

The welfare effects are straightforward. Consumer surplus declines by $a + b$, and is a transfer to domestic producers. Government expenditure increases by $b + c + d$. Of this c is a transfer to domestic producers as producers' surplus increases by $a + b + c$. This leaves areas $b + d$, which is the net loss to the economy of the intervention. This is the waste of resources associated with reduced consumption and with producing *BD* relatively inefficiently, given a world price of P^W. In the absence of offsetting distortions, this is the net cost to the domestic economy of introducing the export subsidy. Clearly if some distortion were present the benefits of correcting it could outweigh areas $b + d$, making the policy justifiable on efficiency grounds.

This example could be easily extended into a general equilibrium setting by analogy with Figure 2.2. It is in fact a trivial extension and we leave it to the reader to carry it out. A more interesting extension is to the large economy, large producer case. In the case where we have a large producer facing competition from a number of small producers, and a perfectly elastic demand schedule, an export subsidy actually lowers the world price. The impact this has on area d depends on supply elasticities over the relevant range. One thing is clear however, the augmentation of total exports is less than in the small country. The large producer case has been extensively investigated in recent years, following the pioneering work of Brander and Spencer (1984a, 1984b). What this shows is that under certain circumstances providing an export subsidy to a domestic monopolist, who competes on the world market as an international duopolist, can be welfare improving. The way the subsidy works is to cause a reallocation of profits, or rents, from the foreign to the domestic firm, which more than outweighs the cost of the subsidy. This particular possibility has given rise to an interesting debate. For present purposes what we should note is that the circumstances under which this rent snatching occurs are really rather special and unlikely to be of relevance to most, if not all, developing countries (see Greenaway, 1991).

2.4 Instrument packages and policy strategies

So far we have treated instruments of import protection and export promotion as if they were alternatives and mutually exclusive. In fact the real situation, especially in developing countries, is rather more complicated. Not only do we often observe a wide range of instruments of import protection and a wide range of instruments of export promotion in use separately, as we have already indicated, in addition we frequently observe a range of instruments from each set in use simultaneously. From the standpoint of policy appraisal this creates complications. In a situation where both may be used, how do we summarise their impact?

This question has exercised the minds of many analysts and it is really rather an important one. If one of our aims is to evaluate how trade policy affects growth, in order to investigate this we need to be able to distinguish between different strategies. In simple theoretical models the distinction between inward orientation and outward orientation is generally a straightforward one to make, turning on the impact of policy intervention on relative prices. In practice however it tends to be rather complicated, for several reasons.

First, many governments support both import substitution and export promotion and the instruments used cannot always be reduced to comparable measurement units. Actually coming up with a summary statistic of some form or other is then quite a challenge. Second, relative reliance on alternative instruments can alter through time, further complicating assessment. For example Krueger (1978) defined a five-way classification scheme for policy orientation and identified one case which went through all five stages over the period 1950–72.

One response to the problem has been to develop single indicators of trade orientation (see Greenaway and Reed, 1990). These attempt to summarise relative price effects in a single measure. Krueger (1978) for example proposes a measure of bias in the trade regime as follows:

$$B = \frac{\sum_{i=1}^{m} w_i \left(\frac{P_{mi}}{Q_{mi}}\right)}{\sum_{j=1}^{n} w_j \left(\frac{P_{xj}}{Q_{xj}}\right)} \tag{2.3}$$

where P and Q refer to domestic and international prices respectively, m and x refer to importables and exportables respectively, w refers to weights, i and j are product groups, and the weights are defined as the share of these product groups in total imports or exports. Thus B measures the distortion of domestic prices relative to world prices in importables compared to that in exportables. A computed value of one represents neutrality. An index in excess of unity indicates inward orientation; an index of less than unity indicates outward orientation.

Use of the effective exchange rate facing exportables is in the same spirit as the bias index. This approach has been advocated by a number of analysts, including Balassa (1982) and Bhagwati (1986). The basic idea is simple: one calculates the effective exchange rate facing producers in the import substitute sector and compares this with the effective exchange rate facing producers in the export sector. If the former exceeds the latter, the country is said to be following an *IS* strategy; if the effective exchange rates are the other way around, the country is said to be following an *EP* strategy.

Inevitably there are measurement problems, for instance with the aggregation of individual subgroups within the tradeable goods sectors. Aggregation difficulties arise not only through problems in assigning weights to individual groups but also as a result of the fact that imports and exports may be recorded simultaneously in a given industry. Nevertheless both of the single indicators discussed have been used. For illustrative purposes estimates of both the bias index and effective exchange rate ratios are reported in Table 2.8.

Single indicators of this sort have the great virtue of simplicity – a single measure can summarise a complicated regime. However there are problems in interpreting these ratios, not the least of which is that a value of unity can mean more than one thing. Thus although we can correctly interpret an index of one as denoting 'neutrality' in the sense that incentives to producers of importables are exactly matched by those available to producers of exportables, this could arise from a free trade set of prices or a highly distorted set of prices. Put another way, it could arise from complete laissez-faire or from dirigisme. From the standpoint of making inferences about intervention and economic performance, this is really rather important. If one failed to probe behind the index, one could reach quite erroneous conclusions regarding the efficacy of intervention or non-intervention.

One response to this problem has been to try to use multiple criteria as a

Table 2.8a Estimates of bias in five developing countries

Country	*Year*	*Bias Index*
Brazil	1957	2.45
	1961	1.79
	1964	1.41
Chile	1956	3.69
	1959	1.94
	1965	1.95
Philippines	1960–2	2.01
	1970	1.37
South Korea	1961	0.67
	1964	0.78
Turkey	1958–9	6.31
	1970	3.01

Table 2.8b Ratio of import to export effective exchange rates in nine developing countries

Country	*Year*	*EERM/EERX*
Brazil	1957	1.28
	1961	1.64
	1964	1.00
Chile	1956	1.21
	1959	1.18
	1965	1.18
Egypt	1962	0.98
Ghana	1967	1.83
India	1966	1.29
Israel	1952	0.95
	1962	0.97
Philippines	1960–2	1.64
	1970	1.37
South Korea	1961	0.68
	1964	0.78
Turkey	1958–9	1.87
	1970	1.63

Source: Extracted from Krueger (1978), Tables 6.3 and 6.2.

basis for classifying trade orientation. This line of analysis endeavours to categorise trade strategy by reference to a number of different criteria. Sometimes this approach focuses on policy inputs. Thus, for instance, Greenaway and Nam (1988) used information on effective rates of protection, reliance on direct controls, export incentives and exchange rate misalignment to classify 41 LDCs into four categories, namely strongly outward-oriented, moderately outward-oriented, moderately inward-oriented and strongly inward-oriented. Donges (1975) also relied upon a number of quantitative and qualitative indicators in a similar type of cross-section study. Although Agarwala (1983) used a 'distortion index' in his analysis of growth patterns in LDCs, the index was constructed from information on a variety of qualitative and quantitative indicators. Thus, for instance, information on, *inter alia*, tariff levels, quantitative restrictions and exchange rate misalignment was used to distinguish between high, low and medium distortions in each. An overall inference on trade strategy could be made by reference to whether the overall degree of distortion was 'high', 'medium' or 'low'.

The advantage of this approach is that its information content is high. No one indicator is used. The principal disadvantage however is that an element of judgement is inevitably at work. This is not a problem if all the indicators point in the same direction (for example high import tariffs, pervasive direct controls, export taxes and an overvalued exchange rate). Where, however, they point in different directions (for example high import tariffs, no direct controls, no exchange rate misalignment and extensive export subsidies) it may be more problematic.

An alternative multiple indicator approach has been to use information on 'policy outputs' (that is relative prices, trade shares, and so on) to try to define a continuum of trade regimes from dirigisme on the import side, through laissez-faire, to dirigisme on the export side. This is the approach of Bradford and Branson and is summarised in Table 2.9. As can be seen, although this uses information such as estimates of relative effective exchange rates, it supplements this with other qualitative and quantitative information. The resulting spectrum is potentially rich and helpful. Again, however, it involves judgemental criteria, about trade ratios, critical degrees of discrimination and so on.

We have said enough to make the point that empirical identification of 'trade strategy' is far from easy in a world where intervention to protect both importables and exportables occurs. Our instinct as economists is to rely on relative prices. The problem with single indicators however is that their information content may be insufficiently high to convey an accurate picture of orientation. An appropriate response is to develop richer criteria and this is the direction research has recently taken. Further work in this direction will inevitably pay rich dividends.

2.5 Concluding comments

This has been intended as a 'scene setting' chapter. Before embarking on the main mission of this book we need to have some reference points. One such reference point is the range of policy instruments available to those charged with implementing commercial policy in developing countries. As we have seen, there is a great variety of potential instruments on both the import and export side. By way of background we reminded ourselves of

Table 2.9 Definition of trade regimes: the Bradford–Branson continuum

Trade regime	*Characteristics*
Autarky	No trade
	'Delinking'
	Self-reliance
Closed Economy	Exports and imports less than 5% as a share of GDP
Import Substitution	(a) Discriminates against all imports through controls: EERm > EERx
	(b) Selective discrimination
	(c) Mild and limited applications
Inward Orientation	Priority given to the domestic economy
Outward Orientation	Priority given to exports
Trade Economy	Exports 15% or more as a share of GDP
Open Economy	Internal liberalisation EERx = EERm
	(a) tradable goods
	(b) (a) + nontradable goods
	(c) (a) + (b) – macroeconomic variables
Export promotion	(a) Uniform subsidies for all exports: EERx > EERm
	(b) Selective subsidies:
	Industrial policy
	Import substitution

Note: EERx and EERm are the real effective exchange rates for exports and imports, respectively.

the economic effects of these instruments and alluded to their prevalence. Finally, we commented upon the difficulties of unambiguously identifying trade orientation in a situation where both the importable and exportable sectors benefit from protection.

Later in the volume we will look more carefully at economic effects. In the meantime the next stage in the analysis is to review thinking on trade policy and development to provide us with another reference point.

CHAPTER 3

Trade Policy and Development

3.1 Introduction

Economists of almost all persuasions acknowledge a role for government in the management of economic activity. Disagreement tends to revolve around the optimal degree of involvement. At one extreme good government intervention is equated with minimal government intervention. As far as possible agents should be permitted to make private contracts with each other in unfettered markets. Intervention should be confined to providing the appropriate legal infrastructure within which such contracts are enforceable. In such a world there are no areas of economic activity which require greater state involvement. Such a vision would be held by modern day Austrian economists. The antithesis of this view is that associated with neo-Marxists. Here a fundamental mistrust of the ability of markets to 'deliver' economically efficient outcomes combines with a belief that whatever the allocational outcome it will be distributionally inefficient, to identify a role for the state which is all-pervasive. The state is not simply seen as a vehicle for providing a framework of law within which free exchange can occur, but rather that body which plans economic activity at the macro level and, through publication of targets and guidelines, implements the plan through microeconomic policy. These are extreme views of the framework within which the fundamental allocative problem is to be solved. In between there are various shades of opinion which envisage, to a greater or lesser degree, some involvement in demand and supply management.

In a book of this type it is simply not possible to discuss the entire spectrum of views on trade and development – nor given its orientation is it desirable. However since policy appraisal is concerned with policy reform, and since policy reform presupposes a given set of policies, it is necessary to have some familiarity with the intellectual underpinnings of a given strategy and to see that strategy in an historical context. This chapter is directed to those ends. We begin in Section 3.2 with a brief historical overview of economic thought on development in general and the role of trade policy in particular. As we shall see in that section, the dominant 'schools of thought' over the postwar period have been structuralism and neo-classicism. Sections 3.3 and 3.4 address these respectively. Section 3.5 pulls together our analysis of policy instruments in Chapter 2 and the analysis of this chapter to evaluate policy orientation and trade policy. Finally, Section 3.6 offers some concluding comments.

3.2 Evolution of thought on trade and development

Many analysts have attributed to Adam Smith the accolade of the first development economist (which sits alongside his accolades as the first public finance economist, the first industrial economist and so on!) To the extent that Smith was concerned in *The Wealth of Nations* with problems of accumulation and allocation in an industrialising economy (the UK), this is an entirely reasonable suggestion. We will not however take such a long-term frame of reference. Interesting as the longer term is, this is simply not the place to address it. For two reasons our time frame will be restricted to the post-Second World War period: first it is really only over that period that a body of economic analysis dealing with the problems of developing countries has evolved; second the policy stances we are interested in appraising are essentially postwar.

One of the most influential postwar strands of thought on development is 'structuralism'. This is a body of analysis associated with the output of the United Nations Economic Commission for Latin America (ECLA) in the 1950s and 1960s, much of which is associated with the name of Raul Prebisch (who was in fact its first director). At the heart of the structuralist view of the world is a 'centre–periphery' dichotomy. At the 'centre' are the mature industrialised economies, specialised in manufactures and benefitting from scale economies. Moreover they produce commodities with an income-elastic demand. At the periphery are the developing countries. In the main they are specialised in producing low-productivity primary products. These fundamental structural differences ensure that the gains from trade are steered towards the centre, and ensure a dependency status on the part of the periphery. Moreover the periphery cannot rely upon international trade to break out of this situation. Industrialisation is the key ingredient in structural transformation:

> But this could not be expected to take place spontaneously, for it would be inhibited by the international division of labour which the centre would attempt to impose, and by a series of structural obstacles internal to the peripheral economies (Palma, 1989, p. 319).

This last point is elaborated by Little (1982) as follows:

> The structuralist sees the world as inflexible. Change is inhibited by obstacles, bottlenecks and constraints. People find it hard to move or adapt, and resources tend to be stuck. In economic terms, the supply of most things is inelastic. . . . Peasants were hardly economic men and were stuck in the mud; people were ruled by custom and authority; entrepreneurs were lacking; and communications were poor. There was little choice as to what to produce from the land. As a result of poverty, demands, too were inflexible, especially for food. If there was to be any development, the demand for imports would be highly inelastic, since capital goods must come from abroad. Demands also were inelastic, especially for food, for imports into developing countries, and for their exports (Little, 1982, p. 20).

In the next section we shall explore in detail the nature of these inelasticities and 'structural obstacles'. For the moment the important point to note is that they provided the justification for widespread intervention to regulate trade, finance, production and distribution.

Structuralist ideas have turned out to be a very influential input to policy formulation in developing countries. There can be no doubt that they provided the intellectual underpinnings to the inward orientation which is such a pervasive feature of many developing countries. Over the last fifteen years or so, however, very significant revisionism has occurred and as a result, what Toye (1987) refers to as neo-conservatist ideas have enjoyed a resurgence. This can be attributed to the interaction of several factors: first, a noticeable change in the intellectual climate in industrialised countries towards 'new conservatism'; second, the juxtaposition of the spectacular economic progress of outward-oriented developing countries with the poor performance of many of the most inward-oriented economies (Greenaway and Nam, 1988); third, growing evidence on and greater exposure being given to the costs of protection; fourth, growing evidence from fieldwork studies suggesting that agents in LDCs for the most part behaved as rational optimising agents (Stern, 1989); and finally the 'enforced' liberalisation associated with policy-conditioned lending in the 1980s.

There are at least two avenues along which this line of thinking has developed: an essentially neo-Austrian view associated in particular with the work of Bauer, and a more mainstream neo-classical view to be found in the work of, *inter alia*, Little (1982) and Lal (1983). The former takes an extreme view along the lines that dirigiste economic policies are fundamentally misconceived and misplaced, in part because problems of market failure are trivial and in part because dirigisme replaces market failure with government failure. The neo-classical position is less extreme. Most, though not all, neo-classical analysts acknowledge the existence of market imperfections and market failure. However they would distance themselves from structuralist commentators both with regard to the extent of the 'malady' and its remedy. Market failure would not be regarded as a general phenomenon, and where it is identified intervention should be carefully thought out and introduced. Where intervention is regarded as necessary it should be selective and chosen to minimise the 'by-product distortions' (Corden, 1974) associated with the intervention. Failure to assign appropriate instruments to given distortions not only raises the costs of intervention, but may also make the situation worse.

At the heart of this approach to policy, which emphasises microeconomic considerations, is social cost benefit analysis. As we shall see in Chapter 6, there are analytical problems with this technique, most notably second-best considerations, and implicit assumptions about income distribution. Nevertheless the 'new conservatism' generally, and neo-classical ideas in particular, have found willing sponsors in the form of the major multilateral lending agencies, especially the World Bank. Not only has the institution openly endorsed these ideas, it is clear from an inspection of the policy reform packages introduced by a wide range of developing countries as a condition for structural adjustment loans (SALs) that these ideas have influenced policy in a very profound way. Time will tell, but it may be that the counter-revolution will turn out to have just as profound an impact on policy formulation and implementation as structuralist ideas in the 1950s and 1960s. The SAL programme will be the subject of more detailed analysis in Chapters 12 and 13. In the meantime let us examine more thoroughly some aspects of structuralist and neo-classical thinking.

3.3 Trade as a source of impoverishment: structuralism

As we saw in the previous section, 'structuralism' is best thought of not as a school of thought, but rather as a touchstone for the belief that the structural characteristics one finds in developing countries ensure that unfettered markets cannot be relied upon to allow developing countries to gain from trade in the same way as industrialised countries can. At the heart of the structuralist case is a belief in market failure on a widespread scale. Thus market failure ensures that the vital signalling function performed by the market mechanism not only operates imperfectly, but may even emit signals that are quite misleading. Sources of market failure are manifold – capital market imperfections, production externalities, a complete absence of some markets. Moreover many of the imperfections are allegedly exogenous. Thus rather than giving the market a helping hand, policy should be directed at market replacement. Since most, if not all, developing countries were small open economies, this invariably meant that markets for traded goods were prime candidates for intervention. As indicated above, many market imperfections have been alleged but we will consider briefly the most influential (in the context of structuralism), namely terms of trade decline, export instability, pervasive infant industries and a maldistribution of the gains from trade. In terms of explaining the revealed preference of so many developing countries for inward orientation, these are the most important.

Terms of trade decline

The allegation that developing countries are faced with a secular tendency towards declining terms of trade can be traced back to the influential contributions of Singer (1950) and Prebisch (1950) – hence the nomenclature 'the Singer – Prebisch thesis'.

The argument is grounded in a simple 2 × 2 × 2 north–south model of the world economy. Southern developing countries are labour abundant, primary products are labour intensive, thus southern countries specialise in and export primary products. In contrast northern countries are relatively capital abundant, manufactures are relatively capital intensive, thus the north specialises in and exports manufactures. So far this is simply a description of the simple H-O-S model. In Figure 3.1 we would expect production to settle at a, consumption at b, and gains from trade to result. So what is the problem? The problem is that in a dynamic context this equilibrium shifts in a way that is disadvantageous from the standpoint of the south. T_1 shows a chronic tendency to drift towards T_2 with consequent welfare losses. The tendency for the terms of trade to deteriorate is explained by the structural characteristics of world markets for primary commodities and manufactures. It is claimed that demand for primary commodities is income inelastic. In the case of soft commodities this is simply an application of Engel's Law; in the case of hard commodities it follows from the emergence of fabricated substitutes for natural products. Thus as income grows in the north, the demand for primary products grows less than proportionately. This places downward pressure on prices which is exacerbated by the fact that world markets in these products are highly competitive. The presence of surplus labour ensures that productivity gains are passed forward in the form of lower prices. In contrast world markets in manufactures are dominated by multinational firms and uncompetitive markets. The fruits of any productivity gains are captured by cartelised groups and organised labour. Moreover demand for manufactures is income elastic. Thus income growth keeps upward pressure on their prices.

The initial support for this thesis was provided by Prebisch (1950). His examination of the British net barter terms of trade over the period 1870–1930 led him to a belief in the chronic tendency to secularly declining terms of trade. As we shall see, there are both theoretical and empirical question marks which can be placed against this alleged trend. For the moment however we shall take the argument as given, and return to the critique later.

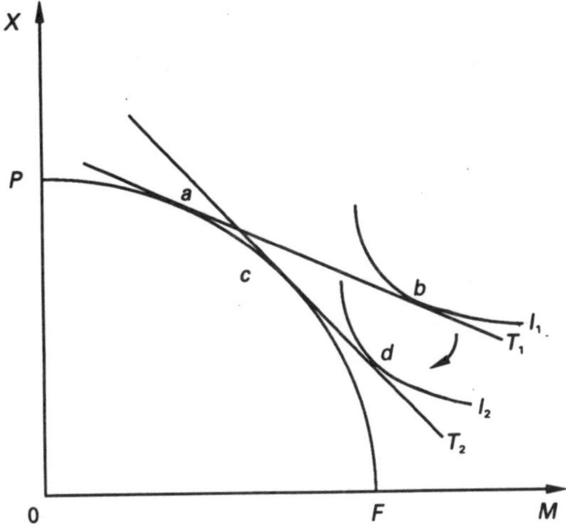

Figure 3.1 Terms of trade effects in a small open economy

Export instability

The potential problem of export instability is often confused with that of a decline in the terms of trade, although conceptually it is quite separate. It has the same starting point, namely dependence on primary commodity exports and the structural characteristics of primary markets. The structural characteristics emphasised are different here, namely price elasticities of supply and demand which are highly inelastic over the relevant range, and supply and demand schedules which are subject to random and unpredictable shocks. Thus (northern) demand for soft commodities is price inelastic (since we are dealing primarily with foodstuffs), and these products are particularly susceptible to supply side shocks (due for instance to pestilence, adverse weather conditions and so on). Demand for hard commodities is also price inelastic. In this case however the problem is demand side shocks driven largely by cyclical movements in output in the north.

As can be seen from Figure 3.2, when the appropriate schedules are inelastic over the relevant range small perturbations to supply and/or demand can result in relatively large perturbations to price. Moreover, if elasticities have the appropriate values, once the initial equilibrium is disturbed the adjustment path to a new equilibrium may be protracted and/or divergent. In some circumstances the classic 'cobweb adjustment' is possible. The essential point is that even if a cobweb does not result there may nevertheless be price instability which is then transmitted through to export earnings instability. One can certainly often find spectacular

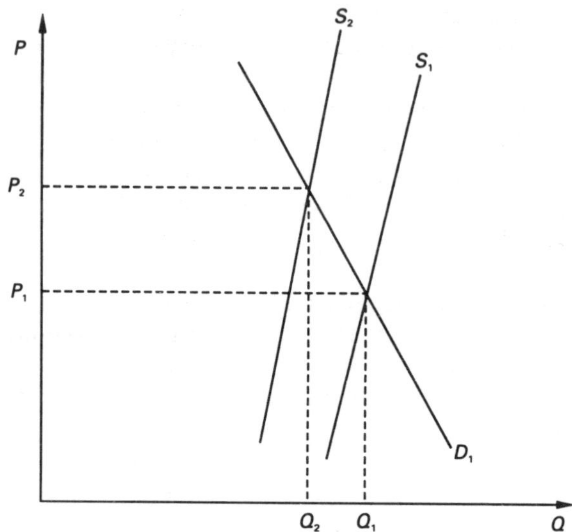

Figure 3.2 Supply shocks and export instability

examples of this phenomenon. For example the change in coffee prices in 1975 following the late frost in Brazil, the increase and decrease in hard commodity prices following the commodity price boom of the early 1970s, the aftermath of the oil shock of 1973–4 and so on. As with terms of trade decline one can question both the underlying theory and the empirical evidence. For now however we will again take the argument as given and note that it was influential in creating pressure for inward orientation. The argument is quite simple – to ameliorate the effects of export instability one must reduce dependence upon primary product exports. The most effective means of accomplishing this is via planned diversification. Although we shall consider some of the counter arguments later, one might be forgiven for asking at this point why the diversification does not come about 'naturally'. Why do producers need to be directed into the manufacturing sector? Why does the combination of secular decline in the terms of trade and export instability fail 'to stimulate manufacturing activity? The structuralist answer to this question is, as for many others, market failure. Many branches of manufacturing activity are infant industries. As such they require state support to nurture them.

Infant industry protection

Of all the arguments for inward orientation that have been advanced in developing countries, the infant industry argument has without question been the most pervasive, and probably the most influential. This is in part because it is an argument which is compatible with a range of market imperfections, and in part because it has a very obvious and very seductive appeal in a developing country context.

The crudest infant industry arguments are framed by reference to scale economies. The argument is quite simple. Established, mature producers benefit fully from scale economies. As a result they produce at minimum efficient scale and supply at minimum unit cost. So long as the scale curve is declining over the relevant range, developing countries are unable to compete. In Figure 3.3, established producers operate with unit costs of C_1, new entrants begin at C_2. They do not have the market share required to compete, nor are there any immediate prospects of acquiring that share. Thus temporary protection serves to raise the selling price of mature competitors. This allows the new entrant to expand capacity, gain market share and move down the scale curve. In time the infant matures and the protection can be removed. However, as Johnson (1970), Baldwin (1969) and others have argued, scale economies in themselves do not constitute a defensible argument for infant industry protection. After all scale economies are a pervasive feature of manufacturing activity in industrialised countries and the capital market has a mechanism for dealing with them: all 'infant' producers have to do is demonstrate that once scale economies are fully exploited, profits will be sufficient to offset initial losses and guarantee a rate of return at least equivalent to what could be earned elsewhere. However in a developing country the capital market may not exist! Even if it exists it may operate imperfectly. For example the inability to satisfactorily insure against possible inappropriate returns to investment in physical and/or human capital can result in first-mover disadvantages. Alternatively private discount rates may be significantly in excess of social discount rates. In such circumstances it is argued that infant industry protection is required. Since manufacturing activity is a key element in the industrial sector, and since the entire manufacturing sector may potentially be in its infancy, it follows that widespread protection of manufacturing is necessary. As with the other elements of structuralist thought we have discussed, there are counter arguments – again we will defer these until later.

3.4 Trade as a source of enrichment: neo-classicism

As we saw in Section 3.2, at a time when the influence of structuralist ideas was waning in the 1970s and 1980s the influence of neo-classical ideas was waxing. As we saw, this resurgence was partly associated with the perceived failure of structuralist policies and partly with a change in the intellectual climate. Fundamentally the revisionism is grounded on a belief that if markets are allowed to work in LDCs they will work. Even in the context of peasant economies, agents are claimed to be rational, optimising

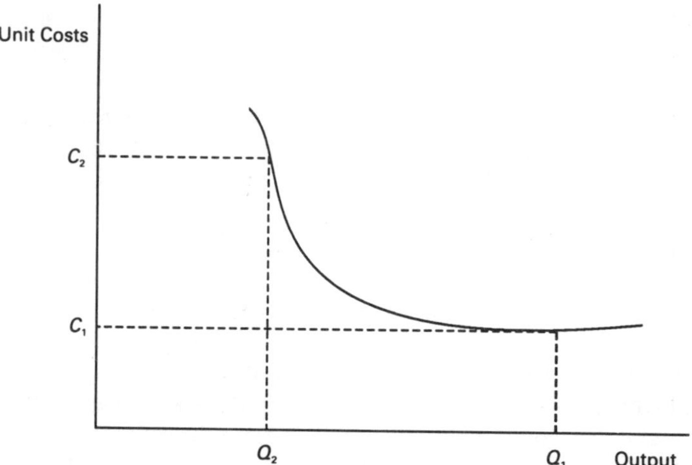

Figure 3.3 Unit costs and minimum efficient scale of production

subject to whatever constraints they face. In such circumstances international exchange, like intranational exchange, can be a source of enrichment rather than impoverishment. The sources of enrichment are argued to be static gains from interindustry exchange, dynamic gains from interindustry exchange and gains from intraindustry exchange. To underpin these sources of gain it is argued that the constraints alleged by structuralists are overstated. We shall deal with each of these in turn.

Static gains from interindustry exchange

The static gains from interindustry exchange are identified in Figure 3.4. In autarky the domestic price ratio is T_A, production and consumption taking place at *a*. The opportunity to trade at the price ratio T_T shifts the location of production from *a* to *b*, and consumption from *a* to *c*. The total gains from trade are represented by the shift from I_1 to I_3. Conceptually this gain can be broken down into two elements: a gain from specialisation and a gain from exchange. The latter can be isolated by bringing T_T back parallel to itself until it intersects the production frontier at *a*. In effect we are constraining production to the mix described by *a*, but allowing the country to exchange at the more favourable price ratio of T_T. This is a pure gain from exchange and can result without specialisation in production occurring. The benefit is represented by the move from indifference curve I_1 to I_2.

To benefit fully from trade, the economy's production mix has to be altered from *a* to *b*. When this occurs the net gain from specialisation results, that is the shift from I_2 to I_3. These gains from specialisation and

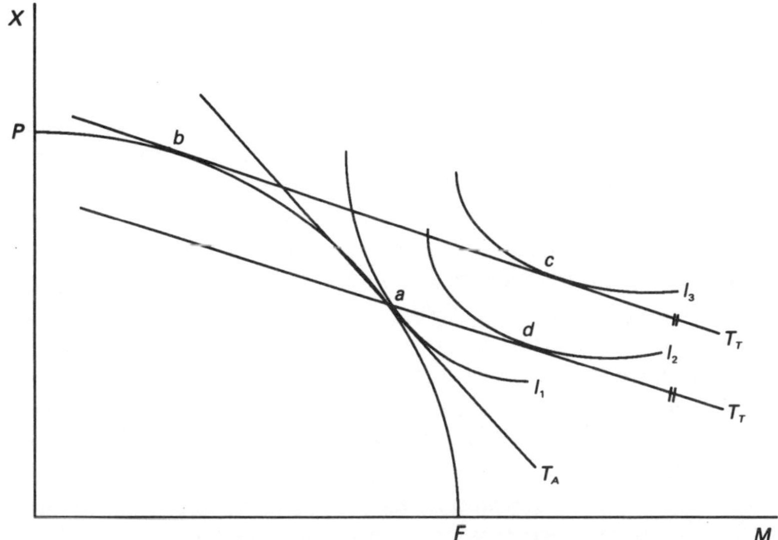

Figure 3.4 Static gains from trade

exchange are static gains in that they result from once and for all reallocations of resources. Placing orders of magnitude on these gains is rather difficult, if only because we rarely, if ever, have the opportunity to observe a discrete change from autarky to free trade. Analysts have however attempted to calibrate these gains via cost of protection analysis, in other words by calculating the static changes associated with tariff liberalisation. Typically these turn out to be of relatively small orders of magnitude (see Milner, 1985).

Dynamic gains from interindustry exchange

Most analysts argue that dynamic gains from interindustry exchange are quantitatively likely to be of greater magnitude than static gains. These can arise through various routes. If we stay within the confines of constant cost industries, the principal benefits arise from X-efficiency gains and a more rapid diffusion of technology. The former essentially refers to procompetitive effects of openness. If industries are sheltered they do not have an incentive to minimise costs. When exposed to international competition they have to eliminate management slack, overmanning and so on in order to meet that competition. The resulting gains are often labelled 'X-efficiency gains'.

Disentangling the contributory factors to economic growth is a notoriously difficult process. Most analysts argue however that technical change is the principal driving force behind the process. Growth-accounting exercises, which break down actual growth into that due to augmentation of the stocks of labour and capital and that due to improvements in the quality of capital and labour, consistently identify quality improvements as being overwhelmingly important. These quality improvements go under the generic heading of technical change. The forces responsible for technical change – education, investment in R&D, innovation and so on are not easily analysed, nor are the empirical relationships precise. One thing is clear however, developing countries tend not to enjoy a comparative advantage in promoting technical change – indeed relatively slow rates of technical change is one of the distinguishing characteristics of developing countries. One can legitimately argue that openness will tend to be associated with a more rapid rate of technical progress than autarky, especially where developing countries are concerned. Many technical improvements are 'embodied' in goods. Thus even armslength trade can stimulate new developments by promoting new ideas, prompting copying and so on. Of course many technical developments are 'disembodied' from goods but embodied in capital – access here can be gained, and is gained, via foreign direct investment (FDI). Capital flows from north to south to benefit from relatively cheap labour. Joint ventures, licencing agreements and direct production all offer the potential for direct access to new technology and human capital improvements through learning by doing.

Not all productive activities operate under conditions of constant costs. Indeed where manufacturing activity is concerned, decreasing costs are pervasive. For the vast majority of developing countries the domestic market is too small to facilitate efficient exploitation of economies of scale. This is so because the minimum efficient scale of production (MES) in many industries will exceed the 'average' market in a 'typical' developing country. Thus to produce a product efficiently the target market must be global rather than domestic. The pervasiveness of scale economies ensures that this is a major source of potential benefit from trade.

Estimates of dynamic benefits are not easily arrived at. Computationally it is difficult to calibrate technical change or X-efficiency gains with real precision. Benefits from scale economies are more tractable – even here however there are problems. Nonetheless many studies have attempted to gauge orders of magnitude, particularly with regard to scale economies and technical change, albeit largely in the context of industrialised countries. These studies suggest that greater competition and scale economics may bring benefits which exceed the deadweight gains by a factor of six or seven (Cline *et al.*, 1978; Cox and Harris, 1985). A recent study of the 1992 programme in the EC argued that the benefits of technical progress resulting from market integration might exceed the benefits from scale economies by a factor of seven or eight (Baldwin, 1989). Even if these estimates are on the optimistic side, it could be argued that the potential dynamic benefits from trade in developing countries are considerable.

Static and dynamic gains from intraindustry exchange

The foregoing refers to potential gains from trade in an interindustry exchange context. One of the most marked features of postwar trade has been the expansion of intraindustry exchange (see Greenaway and Milner, 1986a). This tends to be most prevalent in trade between industrialised countries. However there has been a significant growth of such trade among developing countries in general and NICs in particular (Havrylyshyn and Civan, 1985). Moreover it is probable that as these countries industrialise intraindustry trade will increase in importance. The welfare analytics of the gains from intraindustry trade are still being explored. Qualitatively there are both similarities with and differences from those arising from interindustry trade. On the production side there are deadweight production gains and scale economy benefits, on the consumption side the standard gains from exchange are augmented by benefits from greater product variety. Whether collectively these are likely to exceed or fall short of the gains from interindustry trade is an open question which would have to be explored on a case-by-case basis. What is clear however is that there are net benefits associated with such trade and it is argued that the benefits can only be realised through a policy of openness.

Rent seeking and directly unproductive activity

Public choice analysis applies the tools of optimising behaviour to the analysis of political action. In recent years neo-classical economists have deployed this framework in assessing interest group behaviour in developing countries (see for example Bhagwati, 1984). From this analysis it is argued that economies which rely heavily on direct controls (such as import licencing procedures, import quotas, planning licencing and so on) create an incentive structure which generates rents. Thus, as we saw in Chapter 2, when an import quota is binding, rents accrue to those licence holders fortunate enough to be in possession of an import licence. In turn the existence of rents gives rise to rent seeking. Agents compete for the attention and favours of bureaucrats and politicians in an endeavour to secure the rents. As a result much if not all of the rents are dissipated in the process of lobbying (through bribes and time spent). This activity is unproductive in that it does not add anything to national output. Indeed, insofar as the resources invested have an alternative use, it may even deplete output. Thus this kind of activity is growth inhibiting rather than growth enhancing. It is argued that if a policy of free trade is followed, the kind of incentive structure which engenders this kind of directly unproductive activity cannot arise. As a result energies are diverted into productive activity and the level and rate of growth of national output are higher than they otherwise would be.

Evidence against structural problems

A final element in the neo-classical case in favour of trade as a source of enrichment is an appeal to the evidence on alleged structural problems. As we saw above, potential terms of trade decline, export instability and infant industries have been powerful arguments in the structuralist case for intervention and import protection. The ground here has been fiercely contested, and the evidence is at best inconclusive. After an exhaustive review of the evidence, Spraos (1980) claimed there was no discernible evidence of a decline in the terms of trade of developing countries. Sapsford (1985) among others has contested this, arguing that if one acknowledges the existence of a structural break around the time of the Korean War, a long-term decline is evident. Bleaney and Greenaway (1993) confirm this, albeit with a smaller time trend (0.5 per cent per annum). However they and others have argued that even if a long-term decline is found, its welfare implications are far from clear for two reasons: first because broad indices of primary commodity and manufactures prices take no account of quality changes, which are likely to be more important in manufactures; second because not all primary producers are LDCs, nor are all LDCs primary producers.

The evidence on export instability is also conflicting (see MacBean and Nguyen, 1988). It is not clear that the prices of primary commodities are any more unstable than those of manufactures. If they are, the importance of this would derive from the impact of export instability on growth instability. The evidence here is again conflicting, however some analysts point to a positive association between export instability and unstable growth, others can find no such association (see Stein, 1978 and Krueger, 1984).

The evidence on infant industry protection is arguably more conclusive – most infants appear not to reach maturity (see Bell, Ross-Larson and Westphal, 1984). Protection provides the infant with access to rents in sheltered market, politically it then becomes a problem to remove the shelter. As a result inefficient production takes place behind productive barriers. Some of the evidence suggests that this may not be a feature of infant industry protection per se but rather of the form in which the support is given, namely a protected environment that relies heavily on direct controls.

This brings us to the final point to be made in this section – optimal intervention. The response of policy makers in many developing countries to alleged distortions such as unstable export prices, or infant industries, has been to provide protection from imports. As we saw in Chapter 2, there are alternative instruments for providing support. More importantly these instruments are not perfect substitutes for each other. For a given distortion it is possible to rank instruments of intervention according to the by-product distortions they create. To the neo-classical economist this is a crucially important point for the following reason: even if we find evidence of terms of trade decline and/or export instability and/or infant industries it does not follow that protection is the optimal form of intervention. Invariably some alternative instrument will be more efficient: in the case of terms of trade decline/export diversification via direct subsidies; in the case of export instability, price stabilisation through hedging or buffer stocks; in the case of infant industries, support through R&D or training subsidies. Appropriate instruments have a chance of efficiently correcting the distortion; inappropriate instruments may actually make the situation worse.

3.5 Policy orientation and trade policy

Before going on to the main theme of this book, namely techniques of policy appraisal, we will conclude Part I by clarifying how trade policy interlocks with the other levers of economic policy, and considering how the overall posture or orientation of policy can feed back onto trade policy.

Chart 3.1 schematically outlines the levers of economic policy. For purposes of exposition it is possible to distinguish between macroeconomic, microeconomic and social policy. Macroeconomic policy is directed at influencing the overall *level* of economic activity in the economy. Thus the classic targets of macropolicy are the rate of growth of national income, the level of unemployment, the rate of change of prices and aggregate payments balance. The instruments generally assigned to these targets are fiscal policy, monetary policy and exchange rate policy.

In contrast microeconomic policy is primarily concerned with influencing the *allocation* of resources across activities – the balance between industry and agriculture, between heavy industry and light industry and so on. To this end governments can make use of such instruments as competition policy, industrial policy and labour market policy. Thus anti-trust legislation could be used to expand output in monopolistically-controlled industries, or training subsidies could be offered to increase employment in manufacturing vis-à-vis non-manufacturing and so on.

Finally, social policy is essentially concerned with the *distribution* of resources between individuals and groups. Unfettered markets may generate distributional outcomes that are not regarded as socially optimal. A variety of instruments may be deployed to alter this distribution. For instance income transfers to low income groups, or income in kind via education and health which are free at the point of consumption.

All of the foregoing is in terms of the primary thrust of each of these types of policy. It is important to recognise that there will be secondary effects. Thus it is plausible, perhaps even inevitable, that microeconomic policy will impact upon the distribution of income, that social policy will influence the allocation of resources across activities and so on. Despite the fact that this may be so, the distinction being made is a useful one, and not

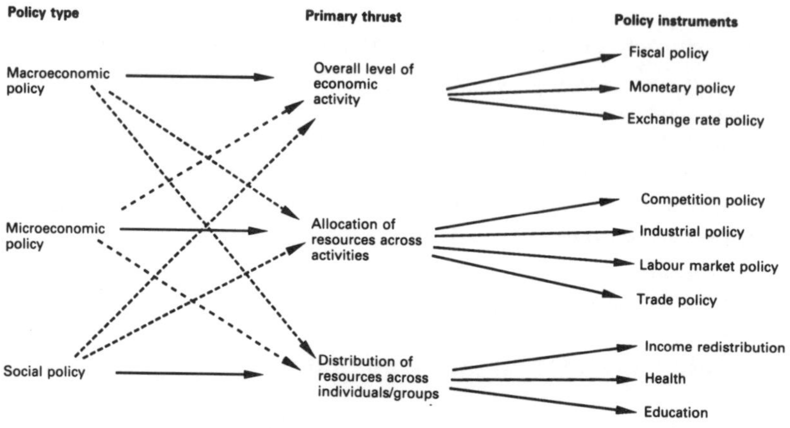

Chart 3.1 The levers of economic policy

simply for expositional convenience. In evaluating policy intervention one needs to assign policies appropriately. Thus, even if particular microeconomic policy instruments have macroeconomic effects, this is *not* an argument for using microinstruments to meet macroobjectives (or vice versa). This is an important principle which helps us in the appropriate classification of trade policy: trade policy is primarily an instrument (or to be more accurate, a collection of instruments) of microeconomic policy. As we saw in Chapter 2, protection is a relative concept. If one introduces an import tariff its purpose is to encourage production in the import substitute sector *relative to* the export sector (and vice versa with an export subsidy). We are therefore dealing with an instrument aimed at influencing the allocation of resources across activities. Trade policy can have macroeconomic consequences – even the GATT charter acknowledges this by sanctioning (under Article XII) temporary protection during balance of payments crises. Likewise it has consequences for the distribution of income – via the use of tariff revenue or the distribution of rent-yielding quota licences. This does not however mean that trade policy should be used to meet these objectives. As a general rule it should not. If trade policy has consequences for the level of macroeconomic activity or the distribution of income, then these should be countered by appropriate macroeconomic or social policies. This is not however always the case because the precise form which trade policy takes can be conditioned, at least in part, by a country's overall policy orientation.

Chart 3.2 outlines a scheme of alternative policy orientations. Of necessity this is simplistic and later in the volume we can consider possible extensions and embellishments. For the moment however it is an instructive basis for classifying further an important distinction already made – namely that between dirigisme and laissez-faire. Both are very general

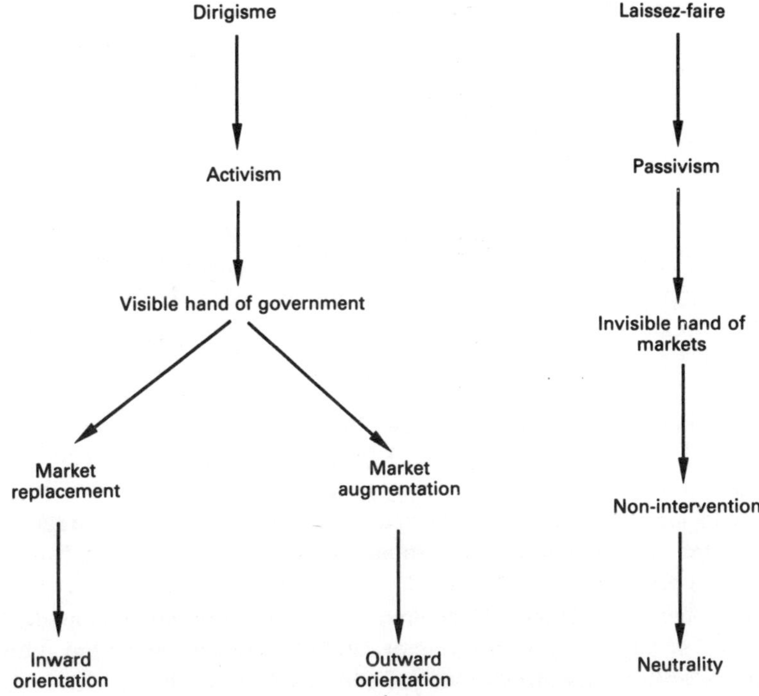

Chart 3.2 Alternative policy orientations

terms which describe the broad thrust of policy. It is important to note at the outset however that these terms cannot and should not be equated in any simple way with structuralism and neo-classicism.

Dirigisme describes a willingness on the part of the policy maker to become involved in all aspects of economic policy in a very active manner. Dirigiste policy is therefore activist policy guided by the visible hand of government. In its broadest sense dirigisme can be consistent with structuralist or neo-classical philosophy depending on what the precise role of government is seen to be. If this is in line with the structuralist vision of pervasive market failure then intervention will be pervasive, and very likely inward oriented. This is so by virtue of the extent of intervention perceived as necessary. Investment is controlled via planning licences; entry and therefore output is regulated; factor rewards may be constrained by minimum wage regulations; prices regulated by price controls and so on. If policy has this kind of thrust, trade policy is likely to emphasise import licencing, quantitative restrictions and the like. These are the kinds of instruments which provide the planner/regulator with most control. When trade policy analysts talk of dirigiste, inward-oriented regimes this is very much what they have in mind. As we shall see later, economies such as India, Nigeria and Tanzania have been held out as good examples of this form of regime.

Intervention however may also be a feature of a regime based on neo-classical principles, although its scale and form will differ from a structuralist scenario. As we saw earlier, neo-classical prescriptions on economic policy are guided by the principles of effective market classification and optimal intervention. Where market failure is found to exist, the policy maker should respond by appropriately assigning instruments to targets. This involves careful analysis of the relationships concerned and assigning policies in order to minimise by-product distortions. Fundamentally policy is directed at market augmentation rather than market replacement. The presumption is that with appropriate surgery, markets can continue to function well even where market failure precedes the surgery. This means there will be a tendency to rely upon market-based instruments such as subsidies and tariffs. Moreover, insofar as the intention is to reinforce market tendencies, it is likely to mean that the resultant policy orientation is outward. Thus although outward orientation is often associated with non-intervention, in fact it is a policy posture which generally results from interventionist policy, albeit interventionism aimed at market augmentation rather than market replacement. The strategy followed by South Korea is a good example of this.

Laissez-faire is qualitatively different. Whereas dirigisme is characterised by activism, laissez-faire is characterised by passivism. With the possible classic exceptions of defence, the judiciary and administration, everything is left to the invisible hand of markets. One does not need to worry about market imperfections because they are either trivial or transient. Thus so long as entry is free, monopoly cannot be a problem; externalities need not be a problem so long as agents can pursue claims on property rights to clean air, unpolluted rivers and so on through the courts. Non-intervention to this extent would be associated with the neo-conservatism of Bauer discussed earlier. From the standpoint of trade policy, the relevant outcome would be a posture of neutrality, that is classical free trade. There is no intervention whatsoever to support the import substitute sector or the export sector. Hong Kong is probably the sole example of this strategy in recent decades.

The terms we have used in this section are conceptually fairly precise. In practise however they are often difficult to apply. This is so for several reasons. First, countries often pursue mixed strategies, that is policy packages that combine elements of dirigisme and laissez-faire. Second, through time the emphasis of policy may change from dirigisme to laissez-faire, and vice versa. Third, there are no widely accepted, unambiguous indicators of policy orientation. From the practical standpoint, the last of these is particularly intractable. Some analysts have proposed alternative indicators. For example Agarwala (1983) reports a distortion index that is an unweighted average of seven different types of price distortion index (ranked as severe, less severe, and so on). Greenaway and Nam (1988) worked with a four-way classification which ranged from strongly outward to strongly inward oriented. Countries were classified using a wide range of information on, *inter alia*, effective protection, reliance on direct controls and exchange rate overvaluation. Krueger (1978) worked with a bias indicator calculated to reflect any distortions between domestic and world prices. All of these are useful, but not one is foolproof. For most dirigiste and most laissez-faire economies these indicators at least all point in the same direction. Inevitably it is in the intermediate cases that one faces most difficulties.

For the remainder of this book we shall use the terms in the senses discussed in this section. Thus neutrality in trade policy will denote free trade; inward orientation will denote active intervention to promote the import substitute sector; and outward orientation, active intervention to support the export sector.

3.6 Concluding comments

Like Chapter 2 this has been a scene-setting chapter. In Chapter 2 we were concerned with identifying the tools of trade policy. Here we have been concerned with the links between trade policy and development. We have seen that over the postwar period thinking on trade policy and development has evolved quite dramatically. In the early decades after the Second World War structuralism was in the ascendancy. This emphasised market failure as a pervasive feature of developing countries and stressed the role of active intervention. More recently neo-classical ideas have enjoyed something of a revival. Greater optimism with regard to the role markets can play in development is a recurring feature of these ideas. Both these schools of thought have exerted an impact on policy orientation in developing countries. Equipped with this background we are now in a position to proceed to Parts II and III and an evaluation of the tools of policy analysis.

PART II

TOOLS OF POLICY EVALUATION: PARTIAL ANALYSIS

CHAPTER 4

The Structure of Nominal Protection

4.1 Introduction

Part I of this volume was concerned with setting the scene for policy appraisal. There we reviewed arguments for inward and outward orientation and evaluated the impact of tariff and non-tariff measures in some simple models. These were essentially by way of revision. Now we turn our attention to estimating the impact of intervention. Some of the approaches we will evaluate are partial equilibrium, some are general equilibrium. Part II is devoted to partial equilibrium approaches.

In this chapter we begin by focusing on the initial impact of intervention. In order to estimate concepts such as effective protection, or to calibrate CGE models, we need the raw material of information on tariff and non-tariff measures. How do we acquire such information and/or estimate it? In the case of tariffs this may appear to be a non-question, after all does one not simply look at the tariff schedule? The answer to this question is 'yes and no'! 'Yes', one does begin with the schedule but 'no' it may not tell the whole story if there are exceptions, exemptions and so on. These and other aspects of estimating nominal tariffs are addressed in Section 4.2. As we have seen in Chapter 2, non-tariff measures are pervasive in developing countries and we need to be able to identify their extent and, if possible, estimate their tariff equivalence. This is the subject of Section 4.3. In Section 4.4 we report some evidence on both tariff and non-tariff measures. Finally in Section 4.5 we offer some concluding comments.

4.2 Measuring nominal tariffs

In terms of frequency, tariffs remain the most widely-used instrument of commercial policy in developing countries. Many of the measures we will discuss in subsequent chapters are concerned with evaluating the economic impact of tariffs in one way or another; by evaluating their restrictiveness, or their potential impact on resource reallocation, or their welfare effects. Before doing any of these things however we need to be able to clearly identify an import or export tariff, as well as being able to measure it. At one level this is quite straightforward: a tariff is an indirect tax, its rate is set by the fiscal authorities and, once set, is published in the tariff schedule as in Table 4.1 which, for illustrative purposes, reproduces a section from the tariff schedule of the Ivory Coast. The rates reported therein are the practical equivalent of the rate *t* in Figure 2.1. Thus, measuring nominal tariffs may be no more difficult than reading or even, given modern information technology, scanning a tariff schedule. The practicalities are however somewhat more complicated for four reasons: (1) the existence of secondary tariffs; (2) exceptions and exemptions to the scheduled tariff; (3) tariff redundancy; (4) aggregation problems. Let us consider each of these in turn.

Table 4.1 Extract from the tariff schedule of the Ivory Coast

Code	Chapter 15 Vegetable Oils *Product*	Tariff rate *(per cent)*
15–07–21	Soya oil – unrefined	6
15–07–24	Soya oil – refined	5
15–07–25	Cotton oil – unrefined	6
15–07–28	Cotton oil – refined	5
15–07–31	Groundnut oil – unrefined	6
15–07–34	Groundnut oil – refined	5
15–07–35	Olive oil – unrefined	6
15–07–36	Olive oil – refined	5
15–07–41	Sunflower oil – unrefined	6
15–07–44	Sunflower oil – refined	5
15–07–45	Mustard seed oil – unrefined	6
15–07–48	Mustard seed oil – refined	5
15–07–51	Linseed oil – unrefined	6
15–07–54	Linseed oil – refined	5
15–07–61	Palm oil – unrefined	4
15–07–64	Palm oil – refined	1.5
15–07–65	Coconut oil – unrefined	4
15–07–68	Coconut oil – refined	6
15–07–81	Sesame oil – unrefined	6
15–07–81	Sesame oil – refined	5
15–07–91	Other vegetable oils – unrefined	6
15–07–94	Other vegetable oils – refined	5

The existence of secondary tariffs

One of the reasons why liberal-minded economists favour tariffs over direct controls is their transparency: being indirect taxes they operate through the price mechanism and their price-raising effects are clearly visible. It is not unusual in developing countries to find, however, that the waters are a little bit muddied by the presence of other forms of interven-

Table 4.2 Nominal tariffs in Mauritius, 1980 (in per cent)

Activity	*Nominal tariff*	
	scheduled	*plus secondary tariffs*
Beverages	188	220
Tobacco	300	332
Textiles	13	45
Clothing	48	80
Leather products	75	107
Footwear	50	82
Wood products	25	57
Furniture	88	120
Paper products	40	72
Printing	16	48
Basic chemicals	5	37
Other chemicals	29	62
Rubber	53	85
Plastic	20	52
Glass	40	72
Base metals	2	34
Fabricated metals	32	64
Lime etc.	21	53
Non-electrical machinery	19	51
Electrical machinery	41	53
Transport equipment	70	102
Watches and lenses	37	69
Arithmetic mean	55.1	86.2
Standard deviation	65.8	66.0
Coefficient of variation	1.19	0.76
Range	2–300	34–332

Source: Greenaway and Milner (1989).

tion which do not go under the heading of 'tariffs" but which de facto are tariffs in that they apply discriminatorily to imported products. Such interventions might go under the heading of fiscal duty, or stamp duty, or import surcharge, or import surtax, or special levy, or even statistical tax! All of these are actual taxes which are in fact tariffs, and have been identified by the authors in case-study work. One might legitimately enquire why it is necessary for governments to have more than one import tariff, with some masquerading under different names. The most common reason is that they are introduced as part of a crisis package, often as alleged temporary measures. Developing countries are heavily dependent on trade taxes for government revenue. Faced with a need to raise taxes, it may be politically expedient to do so in the form of a new measure packaged as temporary. This increases the opacity of the action.

Whatever the justification for this proliferation it makes measurement more difficult. This would not be a great cause for concern if the measures in question were set at negligible rates. Often however these levels are well beyond nuisance values. Table 4.2 illustrates the impact of including hidden tariffs in the calculation of total nominal rates in Mauritius in 1980.

Then, as well as import tariffs and fiscal duty there was also an import surtax and stamp duty. These secondary tariffs added 32 per cent to the primary tariff, a non-marginal increment. In evaluating nominal protection it is important to seek out and incorporate these secondary tariffs.

Exceptions and exemptions to the scheduled tariff

The tariff rates reported in Table 4.1 for the Ivory Coast do not apply to all imports. Different rates apply to imports from different sources. Specifically, the Ivory Coast is a member of two different preferential trading arrangements (PTAs), ECOWAS and CEAO,[1] to which lower rates of tariff are applied. This is not at all uncommon. Of the 22 main preferential trading arrangements worldwide in 1990, 19 were agreements between developing countries involving over 90 different countries. So long as the preferential rates (which could of course be zero) apply to some share of imports, the implicit tariff will be less than the scheduled tariff. (These can also be referred to as ex-post and ex-ante rates respectively.)

The implicit, or ex-post, rate can be easily calculated as follows:

$$tp_i = \Sigma TR_i / \Sigma P_i Q_i \qquad (2.1)$$

where tp_i is the implicit tariff for product i, ΣTR_i is total customs collections for i and $\Sigma P_i Q_i$ is the total value of imports of i.

Thus the implicit tariff is that rate implied by actual customs collections. The method of calculation allows one to take account of duty-free and preferential-rate imports. Moreover it turns out that tp_i is a weighted average of all of the rates that apply, with the weights being the share of imports from each source. This can therefore be a very useful measure, although it is not problem free.[2] As we shall see below, it is sensitive to aggregation. Moreover it may also be sensitive to underinvoicing of import value if the tax is graduated (but not of course if the same rate applies to all imports) or corruption of the bill of origin. Notwithstanding these complications, this remains a useful and quite widely-used measure of nominal protection. Table 4.3 reports ex-ante and ex-post tariffs for Burundi for illustrative purposes. As one would expect, the ex-post rates are always less than the ex-ante rates, given the fact that some imports enter at less than the scheduled rates, partly due to Burundi's membership of several regional PTAs[3] and partly as a consequence of preferential rates applying to some 'priority imports' under the country's investment code.

Tariff redundancy

The concept of a redundant tariff is straightforward. It means exactly what its name implies, a tariff which has no impact on the level of imports. Why bother to introduce such a tariff in the first place? one may be tempted to

Table 4.3 'Ex-ante' and 'ex-post' nominal tariff rates for Burundi 1984

Product	*'Ex-ante' rate (%)*	*'Ex-post' rate (%)*
Coffee	154	148
Tea	154	114
Cigarettes	154	77
Concentrated milk (sugared)	31	0
Biscuits	104	57
Envelopes	46	39
Batteries	104	98
Cement	9	3
Sheets of corrugated iron	24	0
Paint (water)	64	2
Acetylene	19	0
Car tyres	36	33
Mineral water	104	75

Source: Greenaway and Milner (1990b).

ask. Perhaps the redundant tariff is a theoretical curiosm? In fact it is a relatively common phenomenon in developing countries. An obvious source of a redundant tariff is where an import prohibition applies to a given product but that same product has a scheduled tariff rate, possibly because the latter preceded the former. As we noted earlier, incrementalism is a common characteristic of the evolution of protectionist regimes. Another possibility is that the tariff rate is set above the prohibitive tariff. In such circumstances not all of the tariff is redundant, only that part beyond the prohibitive rate, a phenomenon sometimes referred to as 'water in the tariff'.

When measuring nominal protection, tariff redundancy can create problems, especially if we rely upon ex-ante/scheduled tariffs. In the event that there is some degree of redundancy, scheduled tariffs will overstate nominal protection. The phenomenon is less worrisome if we are using ex-post/implicit tariffs – clearly redundant tariffs do not yield revenue. This then is another reason why it might be preferable to rely on ex-post rather than ex-ante tariffs.

Aggregation problems

We measure tariffs because we are interested in their economic effects, in particular their impact on resource reallocation. For this purpose, as we shall see in subsequent chapters, we combine tariff line data with production data. Invariably however the former is much more disaggregated than the latter. Typically in developing countries, tariff lines run to thousands of items whilst production/input–output categories run to dozens of items. Thus, for instance when calculating nominal or effective protection for a given industry, one has to average data across a large number of tariff lines. A comparison of the components of Tables 4.1 and 4.2 gives an indication of the differences in detail with which we are dealing.

The process of averaging invariably creates problems. A simple average may not be terribly meaningful if it embraces a large number of lines covering different products and different sources of supply. Some kind of weighted average is invariably superior although the choice of weighting system is an issue: does one weight according to share of imports or share of domestic value added? The answer to this will be fashioned by the purpose to which the estimates are being put and, more importantly, data availability. The latter tends to be the key consideration. One often-used expedient is to calculate the ex-post tariff at the 'industry' level. As we saw earlier, this measure has the virtue of being a weighted average of sub-group tariffs, with the weights being the share of imports of different sub-groups in the total. If different origins of supply for a given product were the only source of differences in tariff rates this would be a reasonably satisfactory measure. Unfortunately however, when we work at relatively high levels of aggregation it is not. Different products from a given source that attract different rates become aggregated. This can make the resultant ex-post tariff more difficult to interpret. Moreover the measure is also known to be sensitive to changes in product composition through time. When working at relatively high levels of aggregation therefore, this measure must be used with some caution.

4.3 Measuring non-tariff barriers

Our discussion in Chapter 2 revealed that there are intrinsic problems associated with identifying non-tariff measures (NTMs). This is so because of grey areas between trade policy, industrial policy, investment policy and even fiscal policy. It is also hampered by the fact that there is a strong incentive on the part of governments not to disclose particular measures if at all possible. These problems clearly carry over to complicate measurement.

Assuming one can identify measures, there are two distinct approaches to quantifying NTMs – documentation and restrictiveness. The former essentially involves attempting to evaluate the extent of non-tariff protection and is sometimes referred to as the inventory approach; the latter attempts to go further in calculating the extent to which a given NTM influences prices and is sometimes known as tariff equivalence analysis.

Documentation of NTMs

A number of organisations, most notably UNCTAD and The World Bank, have amassed substantial inventories of NTMs, largely though not exclusively in industrialised countries. These data sets record the presence of NTMs at the tariff line and two different measures have been devised to summarise the information, namely the *frequency ratio* and the *coverage ratio*. The frequency ratio (*Fj*) is estimated as:

$$Fj = \sum D_i N_i / \sum N_t \qquad (2.2)$$

where D_i is the dummy variable, which takes a value of unity if one or more NTM applies to the product line *i*, and ΣNt is the total number of product lines in the import category.

Clearly the measure basically adds up the number of product lines subject to NTMs and expresses these as a proportion of all products, hence the term frequency ratio. The measure clearly has the virtue of simplicity, both in its computation and its interpretation. Thus a ratio of 0.6 tells us that 60 per cent of all imports in a given product line are subject to NTMs. Against this however the measure has a number of important limitations. First of all, and perhaps most obviously, NTMs are recorded as present or absent. Thus it does not matter if product *m* has four NTMs whilst product *n* only has one; both enter the ratio with equal weight. Second, and related to the previous point, it is implicitly assumed that all measures are equally restrictive. In other words a quota on product *r* is treated in the same way as one on product *w*, even if the former only applied to 10 per cent of the market, whilst the latter applies to 90 per cent. Thus although variations in the ratio through time can give some idea as to trends in the use of NTMs, they have to be interpreted cautiously.

The coverage ratio is calculated differently, as follows:

$$C_j = (\sum D_{i,t-m} V_{i,t-n}) / \sum V_{t,t-n} \qquad (2.3)$$

where D_i is as before, V_i is the value of imports affected by the NTM and V_t is the value of total imports.

Clearly what this ratio does is record the share of trade in a given product range subject to NTMs, hence the term coverage ratio. It is in fact analogous to the ex-post tariff. Because it incorporates import values it may appear to have a higher information content than the frequency ratio. However it shares its limitations in that non-tariff barriers are only recorded as present or absent, with no regard to their restrictiveness. In fact it may even be misleading regarding restrictiveness, depending upon the trade weights used. If the country's own trade weights are used then heavily restricted items enter with a low weight because the amount of trade taking place is restricted to a relatively low level. Clearly then the ratio is biased downwards. In practise analysts attempt to get around this problem by using global trade weights rather than own-country trade weights.

Tariff equivalence analysis

One can draw closer to proxying restrictiveness by calculating the tariff equivalent of a given NTM. What this involves is estimating the price-raising effect of the measure P_wP_Q in Figure 2.5. This does not of course give us full information on the economic impact of the measure, we would need information on demand and supply elasticities for that. What it does do is provide us with a measure of restrictiveness that is presented in the same terms as a tariff and can be readily compared with a tariff. Moreover it presents the information in a form which can then be used in investigating resource allocation effects using the techniques outlined in subsequent chapters.

What we want to get at with tariff equivalence analysis is the extent to which a particular measure raises the domestic price of the product concerned above the world price. For some of the measures listed in Table 2.1 this is well nigh impossible, for instance with 'import surveillance measures' or additional customs formalities. With some of the measures however there are procedures for estimating the price wedge.

For illustrative purposes, let us focus on an import quota. There are several ways in which the price-raising effect of a quota can, in principle, be estimated, namely *direct price comparisons*, *border price comparisons* and *border price–final price comparisons*. The first of these involves comparing the price prevailing in the quota-restricted situation with the price of an identical commodity in an unrestricted 'control'. In cases where this method has been used, Hong Kong has often been taken as the free-trade control. This approach has certain merits. It can be applied to identical products and one can rely upon the prices at which trade actually takes place. However one must be confident that supply conditions in the sample and control countries are similar. Moreover one is dealing with quotas that are not source specific. Where quotas are source specific, foreign exporters are generally in a position to capture the rent and the border price is inclusive of the quota rent. In those circumstances border-price comparisons might be the appropriate methodology. This involves comparing the border price of the restricted commodity in the restraining country with the border price in a country without restraints. The great advantage of this approach is that trade data for the computation of import unit values tends to be readily accessible. Against this however, one faces the difficulty of obtaining information on transportation costs in order to make the required adjustment to border prices.

The method of 'border price–final price' comparisons involves, as the name suggests, a comparison of border prices of a given commodity with retail prices of the same commodity. The former is taken as a proxy for the world price, the latter for the domestic distorted price. This methodology has certain features which commend it. First, one can make comparisons with an identical product. Second, the commodity concerned is entirely specific to the economy in question and there is no need to make cross-country comparisons. Third, the methodology is applicable to cases where there are general rather than source-specific quotas, which tends to be the typical situation in developing countries. Against this however, the major problem is one of 'stripping out' other influences on the border price–retail price wedge – import tariffs, retail margins and sales taxes for instance.

4.4 The extent of tariff and non-tariff protection

So much for techniques and problems of measurement; what of actual results? To some extent we need not spend a great deal of time on this as some of the specifics will be drawn out in later chapters and we have already commented briefly on these in Chapter 2. As we saw there, in Table 2.1, tariffs in developing countries are generally higher than those in industrialised countries. Developing countries have not been obliged to reciprocate in the GATT process of trade liberalisation and they have been allowed greater discretion in terms of introducing new tariffs under Article XVIII(b) of the GATT Charter (which covers action for balance of payments reasons). Developing countries also make more extensive use of tariffs for revenue purposes and to support infant industries. These are of course generalisations which have to be qualified in at least two important respects. First, as we have seen, some countries are more inward oriented than others and place greater reliance on tariffs than others. Second, considerable trade liberalisation has taken place recently in developing countries (see Whalley, 1991). Despite this the fact remains that for the most part tariff protection in developing countries exceeds that which we typically observe in industrialised countries.

As we emphasised at the outset, with so many countries in the set 'developing' there are dangers in generalising. Equally there are dangers in focusing on particular cases for illustrative purposes. Nevertheless it is helpful to take a few examples for discussion. Table 4.4 reports nominal tariffs for a number of East Asian countries, whilst Tables 4.5 to 4.8 report similar information for several African countries. Table 4.4 breaks down the information by tariff ranges, whilst Tables 4.5 to 4.8 categorise by product ranges. As one would expect, average nominal tariffs differ from one country to another. There is some tendency for tariffs to be lower in East Asia than in Africa, but one would anticipate this on a priori grounds from what is known about trade orientation in the two regions. The averages reported in these tables are certainly higher than those observed for industrialised countries and there are a greater number of 'tariff peaks'. Again, given what we know of the structure of protection, this much we would expect. One thing that does not show through especially clearly in these tables is tariff escalation, that is nominal tariffs which increase with the stage of production. The sample information is not rich enough to

Table 4.4 Nominal tariff structure and changes for East Asian countries (per cent share)

	Korea 1980	Korea 1985	Indonesia 1980	Indonesia 1984	Malaysia 1979	Malaysia 1982	Philippines 1979	Philippines 1984	Thailand 1981	Thailand 1985
Tariff range:										
0–10	22.5	24.4	32.7	52.8	—	—	23.5	33.4	34.2	17.3
11–30	57.2	59.1	33.3	37.1	—	—	29.8	40.9	39.4	34.8
31–60	19.0	15.5	25.9	9.5	—	—	15.8	20.3	13.8	43.4
>60	1.3	1.0	8.2	0.5	—	—	31.0	5.3	12.5	4.6
Average nominal tariff (unweighted)	25.0	21.9	28.0	23.0	11.6	13.6	43.0	29.0	31.0	34.0

Source: World Bank (1987).

Table 4.5 Comparison of protection from tariffs and quantitative controls for selected products; Ivory Coast, 1971 and 1978

	1971		1978	
Product	*Nominal protection: tariff*	*Nominal protection: quota*	*Nominal protection: tariff*	*Nominal protection: quota*
Canned and processed food:				
Instant coffee	37	106	37	97
Cocoa powder	35	–	25	–
Cocoa butter	40	–	40	–
Cocoa powder	35	–	40	–
Textiles:				
Cotton grey yarn	27	35	27	28
Cotton grey cloth	35	56	45	40
Fancy prints	40	72	50	68
Wax prints	45	120	50	123
Synthetic cloth	45	146	45	101
Blue denim	–	–	45	97
Blue jeans	–	–	50	68
Cotton blankets	35	–	45	50
Jute bags	30	103	40	249
Sisal bags	20	62	30	145
Chemicals:				
Matches	15	276	30	50
Oil paints	40	47	40	55
Insecticides	20	32	20	20
Ammonium sulphate	–	–	2	6
Superphosphates	–	–	5	6
Other mineral or chemical fertilisers	–	–	5	6
Other salts and peroxy-salts of inorganic acids	–	–	5	6
Sulphuric acid; oleum	25	41	10	6
Chemical fertiliser	0	0	–	–
Plastics:				
Pipes and tubes	–	–	25	30
Average (unweighted)	31	84	31	63

Source: Roger (1985).

Table 4.6 Comparison of protection from tariffs and quantitative controls for selected products, Mauritius, 1984

	Nominal protection: tariff	*Nominal protection: quota*
Foods:		
Jam/Marmalade	12	30
Biscuits	12	*
Sugar confectionery	48	64
Refined salt	12	48
Other consumer products:		
Autocycles	103	*
Bicycles	36	*
Dry cell batteries		
UM1	73	*
UM2	73	*
UM3	73	83
Electric bulbs	24	36
Matches	133	172
Socks	48	*
Brassieres	73	*
Agarbathis	73	83
Toilet paper	73	*
Toothbrushes	73	122
Toilet soap	73	*
Fridge/freezers	103	*
Television sets	103	*
Motorcycles	133	*
Industrial products:		
Poultry feed	12	*
Black steel tubes	24	34
Welding electrodes	48	72
Automotive lub. oil	14	*
Automotive filler	36	*
Paint brushes	73	133
Zip fasteners	73	109
Cotton sewing thread	48	55
Gumboots	73	*
Average (unweighted)	60	80

Source: Roger (1985).

* Tariff equivalent within 5 percentage points of actual tariff. Quota not binding.

Table 4.7 Comparison of protection from tariffs and quantitative controls for selected products, Zambia, 1981

	Nominal protection: tariff	*Nominal protection: import controls*
Consumer goods:		
Breakfast food	0	3
Wheat flour	0	–10
Cooking oil	43	94
Margarine	32	71
Soaps and detergents	43	87
Cotton cloth	49	67
Suiting material	49	67
Bicycles	0	47
Metal furniture	120	143
Intermediate goods:		
Polyethelene bags	43	81
Fertiliser	0	–4
Jute products	43	50
Plywood and block board	27	23
Portland cement	0	62
Capital goods:		
Structural metal products	43	104
Trailers	18	31
Average (unweighted)	32	57

Source: Roger (1985).

Table 4.8 Tariffs and tariff equivalents for a sample of products, Burundi, 1984

	Nominal tariff	*Unadjusted tariff equivalent*[1]		*Adjusted tariff equivalent*[2]	
	%	*%*	*M =10%*	*M =20%*	*M =30%*
Milk (sweet concentrate)	31	190	160	135	113
Butter (salted)	54	0	0	0	0
Cheese	106	209	169	136	108
Salt	19	667	594	533	482
Sugar	9	115	93	75	60
Milk (powdered)	31	399	349	308	273
Jams	111	339	287	243	206
Margarine	29	92	79	60	44
Biscuits	104	185	148	116	89
Vinegar	69	256	215	182	153
Roasted coffee	154	5	0	0	0
Wine	36	73	52	35	21
Vermouth	65	121	93	70	50
Spirit (methylalcohol)	87	0	0	0	0

Table 4.8 continued

	Nominal tariff	*Unadjusted tariff equivalent*[1]	*Adjusted tariff equivalent*[2]		
	%	*%*	*M =10%*	*M =20%*	*M =30%*
Shirt (male)	59	114	88	65	47
Shoes (male)	36	189	158	132	110
Shoes (female)	36	46	28	13	0
Shoes (children)	36	55	36	20	7
Polish	57	262	222	189	161
Soap powder	57	0	0	0	0
Soap (toilet)	57	98	73	53	35
Tooth brush	51	395	344	300	264
Typewriter	49	0	0	0	0
Calculator	49	0	0	0	0
Cement	9	8	0	0	0
Rolled metal	14	39	24	11	0
Corrugated iron	24	508	449	400	359
Car tyres	36	155	127	104	84
Trucks (over 5 tons)	19	149	123	102	84
Tobacco	154	297	262	232	207
Cigarettes	154	0	0	0	0
Tea	154	154	115	81	53
Flour (wheat)	9	66	49	35	23
Average (unweighted)	59	157	131	110	92

Source: Greenaway and Milner (1990b).

Notes:
1. No adjustment for profit.
2. Adjustment for alternative profit margins(M).

reveal this strongly, although some evidence is apparent (for example in The Ivory Coast and Burundi). We will comment on this further in the next chapter, when we focus on effective tariffs. Finally, note that these tables do not reveal evidence of tariff liberalisation. This does not contradict the earlier observation that in recent years there has been marked liberalisation in a number of developing countries, including some of those covered by the tables. Rather it reflects the time periods covered by the data reported. We will report evidence of this in Part V.

In Chapter 2, as well as earlier in this chapter, we referred to the difficulties of obtaining good information on NTMs: both on their presence and their restrictiveness. Tables 4.9 and 4.10 provide some illustrative details of NTMs in the five Asian countries for which we report tariff data in Table 4.4. Finally, Tables 4.5 to 4.8 report estimates of the tariff equivalence of QRs alongside the estimates of nominal tariffs discussed earlier. As with tariff data, this information is selective, being dictated by data availability. For the countries concerned it does seem as though NTMs are quite widely deployed. Moreover it also appears that they are generally a more restrictive form of protection than tariffs. This is not of course a sufficiently large sample upon which to base strong conclusions.

Table 4.9 Non-tariff trade barriers in East Asian countries

	Banned products	*Import quotas*	*Import licensing*	*Local content programmes*
Indonesia	27 products banned: vehicles, TVs, tyres, matches, etc.	Yes – linked to licensing system but fewer (300 items)	Yes – covers 17% import items	Yes – vehicles, generators, machine tools, tractors.
Korea	Few	Yes – quotas aimed unilaterally	12% of import items require import approval	Localisation for infant industries
Malaysia	Few	Yes – 32 products as of 1982	16 items in 1984	Yes – mainly motor vehicles
Philippines	On some agricultural products	Few formal quotas	Import approval on protective grounds required for 10% of import items	Mainly vehicles and electronics
Thailand	23 banned products: vehicles, sugar, ceramic products, etc.	No	22 products licensed – gold, tea, silk, used vehicles, etc.	Yes – vehicles, diesel engines, milks

Source: World Bank (1987).

Table 4.10 Trends in quantitative import restrictions in East Asian countries

Country	*Year*	*Proportion of import items subject to import restrictions (per cent)*
Indonesia	1985	28.0
	1986	21.9[1]
Malaysia	1984	less than 5
Korea[2]	1980	31.4
	1985	12.3
	1988	4.6
Philippines	1977	35.2
	1983	29.0
	1986	10.0
	1988	5.0
Thailand	1985	less than 5

Source: World Bank reports.

Notes:
1. An additional 4.2% of import licenses were substantially relaxed as part of October 1986 reforms.
2. Items not on 'automatic approval' list; about 40% of imports are still subject to exceptions and special laws.

The findings are not, however, inconsistent with work of a more qualitative nature (see for example the summary of evidence in Greenaway, 1988).

4.5 Concluding comments

This chapter has been essentially descriptive. It has briefly evaluated issues in measuring nominal protection and discussed some illustrative work on nominal protection. Much of what follows in this book is concerned with techniques used in evaluating the consequences of industrial and trade policies. A key data input to this process is information on nominal tariffs and the tariff equivalents of non-tariff measures.

As we have seen, even though the measurement of nominal protection may appear on the surface to be straightforward, in fact it can actually be quite complicated. This is especially true of non-tariff measures. It also applies to tariffs however. Having evaluated the various measurement complications we then went on to report some findings on both tariff and non-tariff measures. Notwithstanding the fact that these were from restricted samples, the data used does tend to suggest that tariff and non-tariff measures are typically deployed more widely in developing than industrialised countries and that NTMs are a more restrictive form of intervention than tariff barriers. We are now in a position to investigate further the impact of these various forms of intervention on resource allocation and economic welfare.

CHAPTER 5

Effective Protection Analysis

5.1 Introduction

Chapters 2 and 3 focused on the range of instruments of intervention available to the policy maker which go under the heading of 'trade and industrial policy'. In Chapter 4 we extended this analysis to the estimation of the nominal protection. Our interest there lay in the measurement of nominal tariffs and the estimation of the tariff equivalents of non-tariff barriers. As we argued in Chapter 4, the measurement of nominal protection can serve a very useful purpose. There are important respects however in which it can also be misleading. In particular it disregards the fact that the degree of protection conferred on an activity will depend not only on any interventions which affect the price of the final good produced, but also by any interventions which affect the price paid for inputs into the production process. This is a major shortcoming. Effective protection analysis offers a framework designed to overcome that shortcoming. This chapter is directed at outlining and explaining the effective protection method. Section 5.2 explains the concept formally. In Section 5.3 we explore a number of possible extensions to the basic model. Although, as we shall see, effective protection is in theoretical terms a very precise concept, there are a range of complications which arise when we attempt to estimate it empirically. These are discussed in Section 5.4. Section 5.5 continues by reviewing the evidence on effective protection in developing countries. As we shall see there is now an extensive literature on this subject. Section 5.6 explores the welfare and policy aspects of the measure and Section 5.7 offers some concluding comments.

5.2 The effective protection concept

Credit for the refinement of the effective protection concept is generally ascribed to Corden (1966) and Johnson (1960), although it is in fact explained fully in Meade (1951). Like many important concepts in economics, the basic idea is very simple and can be easily explained in intuitive terms.

As we saw in Chapter 2, trade policy affects consumers by raising the price of imports/importables relative to other commodities. Thus a 10 per cent tariff on imported personal computers (PCs) will raise the price of imported and locally produced PCs by 10 per cent. In the simple theory of nominal protection this encourages domestic suppliers of import substitutes to increase their output. Intuitively this seems obvious. However whether they increase their output, and the extent to which they do so, depends not only upon the tariff on PCs, but upon any protection given to inputs used in their manufacture. Thus, for example, if semiconductors are the sole input into the production of PCs, and if a tariff is levied on semiconductors at the same time as that levied on PCs, PC manufacturers may be no better off than they were before the tariffs. This follows because at the same time as they are given an implicit subsidy on their final good (the output tariff) they face a tax on their imported input (the input tariff). The latter in effect neutralises the former. The effective protection concept explicitly recognises that we should be concerned with the *net* protection conferred on a production *process*, rather than *gross* protection to an industry's *output*.

To elaborate the concept more formally, let us make the following assumptions:

- Initially we have a two stage production process. A single, homogenous, intermediate input (i) is used to produce a single, homogenous output (j).
- There are fixed physical input coefficients in the production of j.
- Both the inputs and output remain traded after any commercial policy changes.
- The home economy is a small open economy.
- Domestic markets are competitive and efficient.
- There is international immobility of factors of production.
- Initially the only instrument of intervention is a tariff (t).

Industry j therefore purchases inputs of i, combines these inputs with primary factors to add value and generate output of j. The effective protection provided to *value added* can therefore be defined as:

$$e_j = \frac{V_j^* - V_j}{V_j} = \frac{V_j^*}{V_j} - 1 \qquad (5.1)$$

where V_j is the value added to the final product j at free trade prices and V_j^* is the value added to the final product j at tariff distorted prices.

Given our assumptions we can define V_j and V_j^* as follows:

$$V_j \quad = P_j(1 - a_{ij}) \tag{5.2}$$

$$V_j^* \quad = P_j([1 + t_j] - a_{ij}\,[1 + t_i]) \tag{5.3}$$

where P_j is the world price of the final product j, t_j is the nominal tariff on j, t_i is the nominal tariff on i and a_{ij} is the share of final value of j accounted for by input i at world prices.

If (5.2) and (5.3) are substituted into (5.1) and rearranged we can write:

$$e_j = \frac{t_j - a_{ij}\, t_i}{1 - a_{ij}} \tag{5.4}$$

Differentiation of e_j with respect to t_j and t_i yields:

$$\frac{\delta e_j}{\delta t_j} = \frac{1}{1 - a_{ij}} > 0 \tag{5.5}$$

$$\frac{\delta e_j}{\delta t_i} = \frac{-\,a_{ij}}{1 - a_{ij}} < 0 \tag{5.6}$$

Thus from this analysis it should be obvious that when $a_{ij} < 1$,

$$e_j \gtreqless 0 \tag{5.7}$$

and

$$e_j \gtreqless t_j \gtreqless t_i \tag{5.8}$$

These are well-known results and are worth dwelling upon. They tell us that the effective protection rate is determined by three factors, t_j, t_i and a_{ij}. Other things being equal:

- Effective protection will be higher, the higher the nominal tariffs on output.
- Effective protection will be higher, the lower the nominal tariffs on inputs.
- Effective protection will be higher, the higher the value of a_{ij}.

The first of these two properties are intuitively obvious, the third less so. It follows because as a_{ij} rises, value added falls in absolute terms. As a result a given nominal tariff on output has a greater proportionate effect on value added. This point is worth noting – it is often what lies behind some spectacularly high rates of effective protection recorded in developing countries.

As Equation 5.8 indicates, effective protection will exceed nominal protection when the nominal tariff on the output exceeds that applied to the input. As we shall see later it is not unusual to find effective rates which are not only positive, but are in excess of nominal rates. As Equation 5.7 indicates however, it is also possible for effective protection to be negative. This arises when $t_j < a_{ij}t_i$. When $e_j < 0$ this indicates that value added in the industry concerned is actually *lower* than under free trade conditions. At first sight this may appear counter-intuitive. In fact it is quite a common phenomenon. For example it is frequently observed in export-oriented activities that typically enjoy zero tariff protection on their outputs, but find tariffs levied on their inputs.

As indicated above, all of the foregoing results depend upon the assumption that $a_{ij} < 1$. For the vast majority of cases this is an appropriate assumption. Occasionally however one finds circumstances where $a_{ij} > 1$. This arises when the value of inputs used in producing j exceeds the final value of j *at world prices*. Superficially this may appear to be a theoretical curiosus. What it is telling us is that value added at world prices is *negative*. Strange as it may seem this is not empirically irrelevant, because however agents observe distorted prices, the phenomenon does not readily manifest itself. Examples have been uncovered. In these circumstances the effective protection conferred on the activity in question is infinitely high. Where we do observe negative value added the value of resources used in producing a given product exceeds the value of the product itself, when both are valued at world prices.

Even from this account of the simplest possible concept of effective protection we can see that it is potentially a much richer measure than nominal protection. It forces us to direct our attention to the full range of interventions that may affect a given production process. As a result the information content of the measure is greater than in the case of nominal protection. We can see how, even with positive nominal tariffs, effective protection to an industry may be less than nominal protection. We can see how effective protection can be negative, such that the industry is actually penalised by intervention, and we can see how under certain circumstances it may be possible for an industry to be 'producing' negative value added, at world prices. Before we consider how, in practise, effective protection is measured, we should look at the ways in which the simple concept can be extended.

5.3 Extensions to the effective protection concept

The foregoing analysis is predicated on a number of simplifying assumptions, not all of which concur with reality. Thus it is rare to find a production process with a single intermediate input, some intermediate inputs are non-traded, tariffs are often not the sole form of protection, and tariff imposition itself may have induced exchange rate effects which influence the net protection conferred on a given activity. The simple effective protection concept elaborated in the previous section can be extended in various ways to incorporate these features of industrial market structure.

Take for example the case of many inputs. Most production processes employ a range of intermediate goods – the list can run to scores or even hundreds. Where many traded inputs are used Equation 5.4 should be revised to:

$$e'_j = \frac{t_j - \sum_{i=1}^{n} a_{ij} t_i}{1 - \sum_{i=1}^{n} a_{ij}} \tag{5.9}$$

where $\sum_{i=1}^{n} a_{ij}$ is the sum of the shares of intermediate inputs $(1, \ldots, n)$ in the final value of j and $\Sigma\, a_{ij} t_i$ is the weighted average of input tariffs on all intermediate inputs with weights applied according to input shares.

In principle this is a very straightforward amendment to make. Note that this does not mean it is straightforward in practise. There are for example possible measurement problems arising from tariff averaging. Nonetheless at the theoretical level it is very straightforward.

Less straightforward, even at the theoretical level, is the incorporation of non-traded inputs. Most production processes make some use of non-traded inputs like sewerage services, energy supplies, postal services and so on. Suppose we denote such inputs by b. We could then rewrite Equation 5.9 as:

$$e''_j = \frac{t_j - \sum_{i=1}^{n} a_{ij} t_i - \sum_{r=1}^{z} b_{rj} t_r}{1 - \sum_{i=1}^{n} a_{ij} - \sum_{r=1}^{z} b_{rj}} \tag{5.10}$$

where $\Sigma\, b_{rj} t_r$ is the sum of the shares of non-traded intermediate inputs $(r, \ldots, z)$ in the final value of j and t_r is the weighted average of implicit import tariffs on all importable inputs into non-tradeables.

There are at least two complications with Equation 5.10. First it assumes that non-traded inputs enter into the production function independently of tradeable inputs. In practise some non-tradeable inputs may be inputs into tradeable inputs. This is a measurement problem we shall return to later. The second problem relates to t_r. If inputs are non-traded, why should we incorporate an implicit tariff on such inputs? Analysts take different positions on this point. Balassa (1965c) argued that non-traded inputs could be treated as if they were traded inputs in infinitely elastic supply. In such circumstances their price would be insensitive to protection and t_r would equal zero. In contrast Corden (1966) argued that value added in non-traded inputs should be aggregated with all other value added. In effect then, non-traded inputs enjoy the same level of protection as primary factors. It can be argued that we can expect the price of non-traded inputs to increase with protection. This follows because of competition for resources and aggregate expenditure effects (of the type discussed in Chapter 7). The extent to which their price increases then depends upon elasticities of substitution between non-tradeables and tradeables, both in supply and demand. Quite how one measures this is another matter – it could be via the shift parameter discussed in Chapter 7, or via CGE modelling as in Chapter 8. However we arrive at the estimate, this is then proxied by t_r.

As we saw in Chapters 2 and 3, tariffs are not the most common nor, in the context of developing countries, necessarily the most important instrument of intervention. Other instruments such as subsidies and quotas are important. These can in principle be incorporated. For example if a subsidy were provided to a given production process, we would rewrite Equation 5.10 as:

$$e_j''' = \frac{t_j + s_j (1 + t_j) - \sum_{i=1}^{n} a_{ij}t_i - \sum_{r=1}^{z} b_{rj}t_r}{1 - \sum_{i=1}^{n} a_{ij} - \sum_{i=1}^{z} b_{rj}} \tag{5.11}$$

where s_j is the net subsidy available to producers of j.

So long as information is available on s_j the adjustment is straightforward. This also applies to quantitative restrictions. If a quota 'bites' it will have a price-raising effect. If this price-raising effect can be calibrated, Equation 5.11 should be revised to:

$$e_j^* = \frac{t_j^* + s_j (1 + t_j^*) - \sum_{i=1}^{n} a_{ij}t_i - \sum_{r=1}^{z} b_{rj}t_r}{1 - \sum_{i=1}^{n} a_{ij} - \sum_{t=1}^{z} b_{rj}} \tag{5.12}$$

where t_j^* is the nominal tariff on activity j, plus the tariff equivalent of any quantitative restraint.

If any QRs applied to traded inputs, t_i would be similarly adjusted. Note again that we are abstracting from measurement problems. Tariff equivalents are notoriously difficult to measure. Again this is something to which we shall return later. For the moment we should simply note that, so long as they can be measured, Equation 5.12 gives us a fully elaborated measure of effective protection, capable of incorporating all interventions that distort border prices.

There is one final point we should note, namely that protection may induce exchange rate changes. Thus if one group of industries are given protection (say import substitute activities), whilst some other group is not (say exporters), we might expect the trade balance to improve. Other things being equal this should result in exchange rate appreciation, thereby eroding some of the benefits of protection. Some analysts attempt to adjust for induced exchange rate changes. We shall return to this in the next section.

5.4 Measurement problems in effective protection analysis

Many of the measurement problems inherent in effective protection analysis have already been raised. This section will do two things. First it will briefly summarise the range of problems one could potentially confront. Many of these complications are 'study specific' however. Therefore this section will also develop a case study to illustrate some of these problems in a country-specific context.

Summary of measurement problems

As we saw in the previous section one can measure anything from an effective tariff through to total effective protection. What one does depends in large measure on data availability and measurement complications. Some combination of the following may turn out to be relevant.

(1) Choice of tariffs

In theory a tariff is a tariff! In practice however there are alternative means of defining a tariff. One could use the scheduled rate – what might be called the ex-ante rate. If there are no exemptions or preferential access agreements, this would be entirely appropriate. Where however such agreements exist, the scheduled tariff may be misleading. Thus if a country is a member of a customs union, and 90 per cent of its imports enter duty free, it may not be appropriate to use the ex-ante tariff, but to rely instead on the ex-post tariff, that is the tariff rate calculated from customs returns, sometimes called the implicit tariff). This has the advantage of being a weighted average of scheduled rates, with the weights being the shares of imports by source in total imports.

(2) Tariff averaging

Effective protection can be calculated from cost-based data or input–output returns. The latter is the more common. Either way, but particularly in the case of the latter, the number of production categories is invariably significantly smaller than the number of tariff lines. To take a specific example (from a non-LDC), the UK input–output tables comprise 101 sectors whilst the tariff classification runs to some 10 000 lines. Inevitably therefore tariff rates must be averaged in some way. The most common response here is to calculate weighted averages using trade shares. As Tumlir and Till (1971) demonstrate however, estimates of effective protection are in fact very sensitive to the averaging procedure used.

(3) INPUT–OUTPUT COEFFICIENTS

As we can see from Equation 5.4 , a fixed input–output coefficient (a_{ij}) is imposed in calculating effective protection. There are two issues here. First, when working with a published input–output table we are implicitly assuming that input–output relationships are identical across firms in a given sector/industry. By implication therefore all firms enjoy the same degree of effective protection from a given set of tariffs. Intraindustry differences will probably exist however, and there will almost certainly be differing output responses across firms. The second difficulty is that a_{ij} tends to be a post-protection input–output coefficient. If a_{ij} is unaffected by protection this does not matter. Clearly however, if there is scope for substitution between taxed inputs and primary factors, a_{ij} can be expected to alter. If substitution away from taxed inputs occurs, reliance on unadjusted a_{ij}s will lead to measured effective protection understating actual effective protection.

(4) CHOICE OF NON-TRADED INPUTS

What are non-traded inputs? Even at the conceptual level this is not a simple question to answer. One response is to define non-tradeables as those commodities which are not traded at *undistorted* international prices. There is a problem however in operationalising this definition. We do not observe undistorted international prices. A product which is not traded at distorted prices could be tradeable in the absence of distortions. Invariably one has to make a judgement here by reference to the data.

(5) IMPORT CONTENT OF NON-TRADEABLES

As we saw above, it is possible to incorporate non-tradeables into the effective protection measure in various ways depending upon how we think protection will affect the price of non-tradeable inputs. One way of attempting to estimate this price effect is by reference to the import content of non-tradeables. In principle this is a potentially worthwhile approach. The problem is however that the data requirements for so doing are very demanding. One may need to go 'behind' the input–output tables to uncover the detail of input–output relations in the input-supplying industries.

(6) NON-TARIFF BARRIERS

One of the advantages of tariffs over non-tariff barriers is that their price effects are generally more transparent. In contrast the price effects of non-tariff barriers in general, and quantitative restraints in particular, are opaque. If one wants an estimate of effective protection that includes non-tariff barriers, some means of estimating their tariff equivalent must be found. Different analysts have approached this problem in different ways. In a study of Burundi, Greenaway and Milner (1990a) begin from the price wedge between border prices and distorted prices and attempt to break down the wedge into its constituent components (sales taxes, import taxes, mark-up and quota rent). An alternative approach is to compare prices in distorted and undistorted markets. These and other approaches are both complicated and exacting in terms of data requirements. In the context of developing countries, this is not a trivial consideration.

(7) TREATMENT OF EXPORTABLE OUTPUT

In the simple trade models analysed in Chapter 2, industries conveniently fall under the headings of 'exportable' or 'importable'. Tariffs and other distortions in a given sector therefore only apply to importables or exportables. In practise industries may supply output to *both* the home and overseas market. In such circumstances, to what should the effective protection measure pertain – value added on total output, or value added on that share of total output produced for the home market only? One could make a case for either on theoretical grounds. A practical complication arises if one decides that it is desirable to separate output destined for the export market from output destined for the home market. Again there may be a data constraint. It should be noted however that this is potentially much more of a problem in the context of industrialised countries where intraindustry trade is more important than in developing countries.

(8) EXCHANGE RATE EFFECTS

We noted that protection can be expected to have induced exchange rate effects and one should take these into account in calculating net protection. Quite how this can be done is another matter however, as the exchange rate is itself a distorted price in many LDCs! In practise one approach here is to simply 'correct' the effective rates by some uniform adjustment factor designed to proxy the degree of induced exchange rate distortion. As output from different sectors is likely to vary in its sensitivity to exchange rate movements this is far from being a satisfactory procedure.

These then are the kinds of difficulties one can expect to confront in the measurement of effective protection. One can often gain a better 'feel' for the nature of the problems by reference to a specific example. Let us then focus upon the estimation of effective protection in the context of a developing country, drawing upon Greenaway and Milner, 1990b.

A case study of effective tariffs in Madagascar

As we can see from Equation 5.10, estimation of effective tariffs has two basic data requirements: input–output information on production techniques and information on the price-raising effects of tariffs. With regard to the former, two sources of information were used in this study. First, detailed cost data from a comprehensive survey of the Madagascan manufacturing industry grounded in 1983. This provided highly disaggregated data on ex-factory output values and detailed information on imported and locally-produced intermediate inputs. One major deficiency of the survey information however was the absence of information on the import content of non-tradeable inputs. This was estimated separately using an input–output table based on 1979. Using this it was then possible to impute a weighted-average import tariff applicable to each of the non-traded inputs.

In order to estimate the price-raising effects of protection, information on nominal tariffs is required. This may be gleaned from ex-ante or ex-post tariff information. As we saw earlier, arguments can be advanced for reliance on both measures. Ex-ante rates were relied upon due to the fact that customs collections were only available at a relatively high level of aggregation, raising the possibility of biased estimates as a result of product heterogeneity. The estimating equation used was:

$$e_j = \left[\frac{P_j^* - \sum a_{ij}' P_j^* - \sum b_{rj}' P_j^*}{\dfrac{P_j^*}{1 + t_j} - \dfrac{\sum a_{ij}' P_j^*}{1 + t_i} - \left(\sum\sum \dfrac{b_{rj}' P_j^* q_{ir}}{1 + t_i} + \sum\sum b_{rj}' P_j^* q_{vr} \right)} \right] - 1 \qquad (5.13)$$

where P_j^*, a_{ij}, t_j and t_i are as defined in Equation 5.2, b_{rj} is the share of non-traded input in the final value of product j, q_{ir} is the direct and indirect input–output coefficient for intermediate inputs used in producing non-traded goods in domestic prices, q_{vr} is the direct and indirect input–output coefficient for value added embodied in the production of non-traded goods in domestic prices and $q_{ir} + q_{vr} = 1$. (A $'$ denotes a coefficient at distorted prices.)

Thus the effective rate is estimated for each processing activity alone; it is assumed that non-traded inputs are supplied at constant cost, but this cost is influenced by tariff-induced changes if traded inputs enter into the production of non-traded goods. The effective rate for j is in effect an equivalent subsidy to value added in j which has the same impact as tariffs on j and its direct and indirect inputs.

The results of estimating Equation 5.13 are reported in Tables 5.1, 5.2 and 5.3. Table 5.1 provides details of effective tariffs on a product-by-product basis, 5.2 reports average effective tariffs by sector as well as the range and standard deviations of rates by sector and 5.3 reports the frequency distribution of rates. In reviewing these results particular attention will be paid to the interproduct variation in rates, the intersectoral variation and the intrasectoral variation. Interproduct variations are provided in Table 5.1. The maximum recorded effective tariff exceeded 4000 per cent. Strictly speaking however this does not represent the upper limit of the range of estimates since there were a number of instances of negative value added at world prices; in other words, cases where the level of effective protection was infinitely high. At the other end of the distribution, seven examples of negative effective protection were identified. These are activities where the tariff structure results in removal of protection. The largest concentration of rates is in the 50–99 per cent range, with some 30 per cent of activities falling into this category. The average for all products is 156 per cent. The intersectoral pattern is reported in Table 5.2. Three sectors have average effective tariffs in excess of 100 per cent, and five sectors are in the 50–100 per cent range.

As a result of the fact that most effective protection studies have to rely on fairly aggregate input–output data, it is rarely possible to comment on the intrasectoral pattern of protection. This study worked from highly disaggregated/establishment-based data and provides therefore a rare opportunity to comment on this pattern. As we can see from Table 5.2, the intrasectoral range of rates is very wide in some cases – from 20 per cent to infinitely high in chemicals and from 24 per cent to 310 per cent in construction materials. There are likely to be several sources of bias inherent in the above results. The fact that ex-ante rather than ex-post tariffs have been used may have imparted an upward bias. Since however the extent of preferential access of imports into Madagascar is limited this is probably not a serious problem. Another possible source of upward bias derives from the fact that the estimates calculate protection to all production. Where exports are important, reported effective tariffs will overstate actual effective tariffs. Manufactured exports are however of negligible importance in Madagascar. As a result any bias from this source is probably trivial. One other source of possible upward bias derives from the fact that the results are not adjusted for protection-induced exchange rate changes. The imposition of protective measures will generally permit

Table 5.1 Effective tariffs on manufactured products, Madagascar, 1983 (in per cent)

Food and Drink:	
Beer	81.9
Carbonated drinks	131.7
Processed meat	852.5
Concentrated milk	7.1
Sweets	131.1
Chocolate products	174.3
Boiled sweets	102.1
Sugar	24.4
Conserves	
Processed fish	87.5
Vegetable oil	0.6
Pharmaceuticals:	
Toilet soaps	61.9–65.0
Household soaps	40.8–49.3
Detergents	80.7
Tablets	26.4
Aspirins	256.8
Serums	–23.5
Syrups	10.6
Chemicals:	
Cellophane	–19.5
Plastic bags	139.5
Plastic	240.9
Paint	
Acetylene	–4.3
Mineral compounds	28.8
Industrial glues	154.3
Insecticides	58.1
Rubber products	69.5
Textiles:	
Elastic trimming	98.9
Fabric trimming	243.0
Elastic	47.7
Bags	
Lining	86.5
Leather and Footwear:	
Footwear components	78.2
Rubber footwear	102.3
Sandals	88.1
Leather footwear	79.7
Leather	55.8
Suitcases	14.8
Wood Products:	
Chipboard	5.9

continued on p. 90

Table 5.1 continued

Wooden doors	–10.6
Furniture	191.2
Metal Products:	
Metal cartons	23.5
Tin cans	84.2
Metal furniture	221.1
Aluminium bars	
Metal components	83.8–127.7
Cartons	10.3
Electrical Products:	
Batteries	73.1
Accumulators	81.9
Paper Products:	
Paper	–17.6
Cartons	–2.2
Stationery	13.5
Construction Materials:	
Bars	309.5
Nails	24.3
Miscellaneous:	
Pens	–93.2
Bottles	245.8
Glasses	157.7
Remoulded tyres	57.6

Source: Greenaway and Milner (1990b).

Table 5.2 Intersectoral pattern of effective tariffs, Madagascar, 1983

Industrial sector	*Average (%)*	*Standard deviation (%)*	*Range of effective tariff rates (%)*	*Number of activities with negative value added*
Food and drink	159.3	237.3	1–∞	2
Pharmaceuticals	40.0	27.7	24–81	0
Chemicals	83.4	83.0	20–∞	3
Textiles	961.4	1686.1	48–∞	1
Leather and footwear	70.9	26.3	15–102	0
Wood products	62.2	91.5	11–191	0
Metal products	90.0	65.3	24–222	0
Electrical goods	77.5	4.4	73–82	0
Paper products	–2.1	12.7	–18–14	0
Construction Materials	166.9	142.6	24–310	0
Miscellaneous	92.0	125.9	–93–245	0

Source: Greenaway and Milner (1990b).

Table 5.3 Distribution of effective tariffs, Madagascar, 1983

Range (%)	*Number of products in sample*
∞	6
>4000	1
1000–3999	0
500–999	1
250–499	1
200–249	4
150–199	4
100–149	6
50–99	21
0–49	17
>0	7

Source: Greenaway and Milner (1990b).

equilibrium in the trade balance to be reached at a lower exchange rate than under free trade. The elimination of protective measures in Madagascar would necessitate a devaluation. Net effective rates could therefore be estimated by downwardly adjusting the rates estimated at the prevailing exchange rate. The resulting estimates would indicate which activities were favoured (positive net rates) and which were disfavoured (negative net rates) compared to the free trade situation. But given the considerable scope for error in estimating the hypothetical free trade exchange rate and the uniform nature of the adjustment it was not undertaken.

A more important potential source of bias, insomuch as it may affect the rank order of the estimates, arises out of the fact that the results only take account of tariff barriers and ignore non-tariff barriers. There is a complete absence of information on the tariff equivalents of non-tariff barriers in Madagascar. Given the widespread use of quantitative restrictions, this is likely to be a non-trivial source of downward bias. It should be noted however that allowance for the price-raising effects of quantitative import restrictions (QRs) in effective protection studies is invariably for final output prices only. By ignoring the impact of QRs on input prices there is a tendency to upwardly bias the estimates, and therefore the consistent treatment of input and output protection may be viewed as a virtue.

5.5 Empirical evidence on effective protection

The preceeding section examined in detail the estimation of effective tariffs in Madagascar, paying particular attention to measurement aspects. In this section we review more generally the results of a wider set of studies. Table 5.4 reports details of a range of studies which encompass economies for various years between 1958 and 1985. For some economies (such as Brazil

Table 5.4 Evidence on effective protection in LDCs and NICs

Country	Year	Number of industries	Average EPR	Range of EPRs	Negative effective protection	Negative value added	Source
1. Brazil	1958	n.a.	108*	17–510	n.a.	n.a.	
2. Brazil	1963	n.a.	184*	60–687	n.a.	n.a.	
3. Brazil	1967	n.a.	63*	4–252	n.a.	n.a.	
4. Pakistan	1963–4	n.a.	356*	–6–595	n.a.	n.a.	
5. Pakistan	1970–1	n.a.	200*	36–595	n.a.	n.a.	
6. Korea	1968	n.a.	–1*	15–82	n.a.	n.a.	
7. Uruguay	1965	n.a.	384*	17–1014	n.a.	n.a.	Krueger et al., 1981
8. Colombia	1969	n.a.	19*	–8–140	n.a.	n.a.	
9. Chile	1967	n.a.	175*	–23–1140	n.a.	n.a.	
10. Indonesia	1971	n.a.	119*	–19–5400	n.a.	n.a.	
11. Thailand	1973	n.a.	27*	–48–236	n.a.	n.a.	
12. Tunisia	1972	n.a.	250*	1–737	n.a.	n.a.	
13. Ivory Coast	1973	n.a.	41*	–25–278	n.a.	n.a.	
14. Korea	1968	150	10	–67–164	(76)	n.a.	
15. Israel	1968	94	76	–943–750	(9)	n.a.	
16. Singapore	1967	69	6	–1–86	(29)	n.a.	Balassa et al., 1982
17. Taiwan	1969	61	46	–18,728–89	(26)	(6)	
18. Argentina	1969	82	94	–596–1308	(15)	(0)	
19. Colombia	1969	22	46	–51–215	(10)	(0)	
20. Brazil	1980–1	22	46	–16–97	(6)	n.a.	Tyler (1985)
21. Pakistan	1980–1	90	60	–799–1543	(22)	(13)	Naqvi et al., 1983
22. India	1968–9	69	n.a.	27–3354	n.a.	(4)	Bhagwati and Srinivasan 1975
23. Mauritius	1980	22	55	2–300	(0)	(0)	Greenaway and Milner, 1988
24. Madagascar	1983	58	156	–93–852	(7)	(5)	Greenaway and Milner, 1990a
25. Burundi	1985	46	–	–4–7896	(2)	(4)	Greenaway and Milner, 1990b

Notes:
* sample includes only manufacturing industries.
n.a. = not available.
Figures in parenthesis indicate number of activities falling into this category.

and Pakistan) several studies have been completed, which facilitates some intertemporal comparisons. In most cases however the studies pertain to a single year.

Before commenting on the detail of Table 5.4 it is important to make a number of caveats. As we saw in the previous section, complications in measurement exist relating to *inter alia*, the treatment of non-tradeable inputs and the treatment of exportable output. Conventions on the resolution of such complications vary from study to study. Having said this, many of the studies reported in Table 5.4 were prepared as part of larger projects. As a result some standardisation of methodology has taken place. For instance the first thirteen studies in Table 5.4 were prepared as part of a National Bureau of Economic Research (NBER) research programme and used a common methodology. This is also the case for studies 14–21, prepared as part of a World Bank study. One other difficulty is that the level of aggregation is not constant across studies. Finally, in addition to methodological differences and differences in the level of aggregation, most of the studies pertain to different years, and there is no guarantee that in all cases we have representative years. In summarising each of the studies we have provided information on the average rate of effective protection, the range of effective rates, details of whether or not evidence of negative effective protection was found, and details of whether or not evidence of negative value added was found.

Intercountry comparisons

Take first of all studies 1–13, since these use a common methodology. Here we observe a minimum *average* effective rate of −1 per cent (Korea in 1968) and a maximum average of 384 per cent (Uruguay in 1965). For the former the suggestion is that the protective structure is, on average, almost neutral with regard to effective rates. In Uruguay however, value added in the manufacturing industry would appear to have been some three and a half times the world value added. Of the thirteen studies, the average EPR exceeded 100 per cent in eight cases (Brazil in 1958 and 1963, Chile in 1967, Indonesia in 1971, Pakistan in 1963–4 and 1970–1, Tunisia in 1972), suggesting highly protective incentive structures. In four cases the average rates were moderately low, suggesting more neutral incentive structures (−1 per cent in Korea in 1968, 19 per cent in Columbia in 1969, 27 per cent in Thailand in 1973 and 41 per cent in the Ivory Coast in 1973).

Although studies 14–21 apply to roughly the same time period as studies 1–14 and there is some country overlap, the reported average EPRs are somewhat lower. The maximum for this group is recorded as 94 per cent (Argentina in 1969). Superficially the minimum here appears to be −300 per cent, for Taiwan in 1969. This however is a misleading estimate and is biased by the inclusion of activities which produce negative value added and whose EPR rates are estimated as negative. If one excludes the largest of these rates (−18 728) the average changes to a more realistic 46 per cent, which is the figure reported in the table. (The same remarks apply, *mutatis mutandis*, to Korea.) The most highly-protected economies in this group appear to be Argentina, Israel and Pakistan, with average EPRs of, respectively, 94, 75 and 60 per cent; the least protected appear to be Columbia, Singapore and Korea with averages of −2, 6 and 10 per cent respectively.

As we noted in our earlier discussion, *the range of EPRs* is of interest because it provides some guides as to the potential resource allocation effects of the protective structure. Referring first to studies 1–13, it would appear to be the case that the range of estimates is wider in the more highly protected economies. Thus in Burundi the range is −4–7896 per cent, in Indonesia the range is −19–5400 per cent, for Chile it is −23–1140 per cent and for Uruguay it is 17–1014 per cent. Those economies with relatively low average EPRs also appear to have somewhat narrower ranges. In the Ivory Coast it is reported as −25–278 per cent, in Colombia −8–140 per cent and in Korea −15–82 per cent. The potential for protection-induced resource misallocation would seem to be greater in the high-protection than in the low-protection economies. This inference can also be supported by studies 22 and 21 on India and Pakistan, two highly-protected economies, where the ranges are −27–3354 per cent and −799–1543 per cent respectively. The results from studies 14–21 are more ambiguous however. The ranges here are consistently wider than those for the NBER studies (1-13). This may be due to the fact that the data set for these studies is more disaggregated. Notwithstanding this, there is further support for more highly-protected economies having ranges which are wider than those recorded for the less highly-protected cases – compare, for instance, Argentina and Israel with Colombia and Taiwan. The association however is not as clear as with the NBER studies.

Table 5.4 also provides information on *negative effective protection* and *negative value added* for cases where these are reported. The former is not at all unusual. In Korea no less than seventy industries seem to have negative rates, almost half of the entire sample. There were over twenty instances in Taiwan, Singapore and Pakistan. It would seem then that cases where the protective structure works to the disadvantage of activities, that is leaves them without protection, are not at all unusual. Moreover, as we noted earlier, it will often be the case that these are (actual or potential) export activities that do not benefit from protection of their output but are subject to tariffs on their inputs.

It will be recalled that negative value added describes a sitution where domestic value added at world prices is negative. Such activities actually make a negative contribution to GNP. Some of the studies have discovered evidence of the phenomenon. In India in 1968–9 four instances were recorded, in Madagascar seven cases, while in Pakistan in 1980–1 thirteen cases were identified. What is particularly interesting in this context is the fact that the phenomenon is not confined to the most highly-protected economies. In both Taiwan in 1969 and Singapore in 1967 six cases of negative value added were reported. It is often assumed that the phenomenon only arises in the most highly-protected regimes. Clearly this would appear not to be the case.

It is not possible to say very much on *intertemporal comparisons*. As can be seen from Table 5.4, there are only two economies for which studies pertaining to several points in time exist, namely Brazil and Pakistan. Moreover even in these cases the same data set has not been consistently used, nor the same methodology, therefore any remarks must perforce be tentative. The evidence on Brazil seems to suggest that the economy became less protected between 1958 and 1980–1. The average EPR rose from 106 per cent to 184 per cent between 1958 and 1963, subsequently fell, and in 1980–1 was 46 per cent. This evidence that the economy was to some degree liberalised over that period is corroborated by other evidence (see for example Teitel and Thoumi, 1986). The evidence on Pakistan is more difficult to interpret. There are two average rates for the earliest years, 1963–4, which are significantly different – 200 per cent and 356 per cent. Comparing the 1980–1 figure with either does suggest a fall in the average EPR to 60 per cent. However the range for 1980–1 is wider than that reported in both of the 1963–4 studies. Clearly there must be some ambiguity in deciding whether or not the economy is more or less highly protected than in the earlier period.

Taking all these results together, it is clear that the structure of protection varies from one country to another, and in a given country from one period to another. Some economies are highly protected, others less so. In most economies there appears to be evidence of negative effective protection, suggesting that some activities are actually left without protection by commercial policy.

5.6 Policy appraisal issues

Having reviewed the theory of effective protection, and the evidence of the phenomenon for a range of developing countries, let us consider the usefulness or otherwise of the measure in the context of policy appraisal. In this regard one should begin by noting that the concept has been very widely used indeed, probably more widely used than any other single measure of the incentive structure in LDCs. This applies both to preappraisal and postappraisal analysis. Over the last twenty years or so a substantially larger amount of research effort has been expended in examining effective protection in developing countries than in industrialised countries. Why have so many policy appraisal studies relied upon the measure?

One factor which is undoubtedly relevant here is relative tractability. Notwithstanding the measurement and conceptual complications discussed above, effective protection remains a more tractable methodology than most alternatives, such as DRC or CGE modelling. The fundamental theory is well understood, and the data requirements less demanding than is the case of many alternatives. These of course are necessary but not sufficient conditions in explaining its popularity. After all it would be inadvisable to say the least to rely on a 'bad' or theoretically unsound indicator just because it was easy to measure! Some analysts have in fact argued that it is not theoretically sound. Thus Bhagwati and Srinivasan (1973) contend that the fundamental failing with effective protection analysis is that we are essentially using a partial equilibrium measure to make inferences about the general equilibrium effects of protection. They would argue that it is inappropriate to make statements about resource movements when we do not have information on supply elasticities across activities. Thus to argue that resources will be drawn from industry A into industry B because the former benefits from a 40 per cent rate of effective protection whilst the latter enjoys a 45 per cent rate is misleading and potentially quite wrong.

Strictly speaking this is quite correct. Does that mean we are misallocating resources in measuring effective protection? The answer to this question is 'no'. The measure most certainly does have some uses. Although it is potentially misleading to make inferences about resource allocation effects along the chain of effective rates, this does not invalidate the measure. Thus we can still make use of it in commenting upon the likely direction of resource pulls. This is why analysts devote attention to discussing the range of effective rates in a given set of estimates. For instance where the range is from 0 per cent to 4000 per cent one can state with some confidence that relative protection is having an impact on resource allocation, and in a particular direction. It may admittedly be more difficult where the range is from 40 per cent to 45 per cent; that however is another matter.

Average rates of effective protection are also of value in focusing attention upon the extent to which import substitute activities in general may be protected relative to other activities, such as exportables or non-tradeables. Since averages conceal useful information they should of course be used with caution. Sensibly used alongside information on the range of effective rates, the mean can be a useful indicator. Taken together the mean and variance can comprise valuable inputs into the process of appraising the impact of past policy intervention.

This also applies to negative effective protection and negative value added. Policy makers often introduce interventions on the assumption that they impact only on those sectors to which they are directed. This is a fallacy. The measurement of negative effective protection is one way of highlighting that fallacy, and a very useful way at that. Where negative effective protection is recorded, it signals quite clearly that the activity/industry in question is actually being penalised by the protective structure. In the context of policy appraisal this is useful in highlighting such possible cases.

Negative value added is, as we have seen, a quite different concept. From an empirical standpoint it is not an empty box. Where it does occur it illustrates just how costly an 'unplanned' protective regime can be. Incentives in this case draw resources into activities to produce commodities at a very high cost. If the objective of policy appraisal is to assist in the process of industry rationalisation, evidence of negative value added can contribute to this process in a very obvious way.

Overall then, effective protection analysis can be a potentially useful input into the process of policy appraisal, both in evaluating the possible impact of past policy and in assessing the possible effect of changes in policy regime. It is not a precise measure and can not be used for slide-rule type calculations. As we have seen there are conceptual and measurement complications which mean that the measure must be used with some caution. When sensibly used with appropriate 'health warnings' it has a useful and useable level of information content.

5.7 Concluding comments

This chapter has focused on a widely-used measure of protection, namely effective protection analysis. As we saw from the theoretical discussion, the measure is more complete than nominal protection and has a somewhat higher information content. The cost of this higher information content is inevitably greater complexity, both conceptually and empirically. As we saw however, procedures for dealing with many of the empirical complications have been developed and a substantial literature has evolved, providing us with a clearer perspective on the structure of protection in LDCs and a clearer notion of its potential resource-allocation effects. In Chapter 6 we examine more specifically the welfare effects of protection.

CHAPTER 6

Domestic Resource Cost Analysis

6.1 Introduction

As we saw in Chapter 5, a great merit of the effective protection concept is that it provides a summary measure of the impact of trade interventions. As a result both input tariffs and output tariffs are incorporated. If the only distortions to relative prices are those present in the market for traded goods, this makes it a complete measure. However tariffs and non-tariff measures are not the only source of distortion to relative prices in developing countries. There are a range of other direct controls and fiscal measures that can result in a divergence of market prices and shadow prices. Good examples are price controls, minimum wage legislation, repatriation limits on profits, state trading companies and so on. The domestic resource cost (DRC) ratio is in the same genre as the effective protection coefficient. It is however a broader measure. It attempts to take all distortions in a particular sector or production process into account when calculating the social opportunity cost of a given activity. The technique is more demanding in its data requirements than effective protection. Nevertheless it has been relatively widely used.

Our focus in this chapter is the DRC measure. The material is organized as follows. Section 6.2 outlines the basic idea behind the concept, explaining it intuitively and mathematically. Section 6.3 concentrates on the nature and problems of estimating DRC ratios and Section 6.4 looks specifically at applications of DRC methodology. Finally Section 6.5 offers concluding comments.

6.2 Domestic resource cost concepts

Basic principles

The idea behind DRC analysis is a very simple one: it attempts to provide an estimate of the value of domestic resources used in producing a particular product when all intermediate inputs are valued at world prices and all factor inputs are valued at their true opportunity cost prices. In other words, factor inputs are valued by reference to the rewards they could obtain when employed in some alternative activity – not any alternative activity, rather the activity they would most probably be engaged in if they were not employed in their current activity. A specific example can be used to explain the concept. Suppose a worker is engaged in the production of soap and his hourly wage is $1.80. Suppose also that were the worker not employed by the soap manufacturer he would be a farm labourer, earning $1.00. The higher rate of $1.80 may apply because there is minimum wage legislation in force which applies to the manufacturing sector. Alternatively labour may be organised and effective in the use of its bargaining power. Either way a distortion is present, such that wage rates do not reflect social opportunity costs. When estimating the DRC ratio for soap manufacture the worker's labour should be valued at $1.00 per hour and not the $1.80 per hour he is actually paid. This follows because $1.00 per hour is the *social opportunity cost* of the worker. In other words the cost *to the economy* of the worker being employed by the soap manufacturer is $1.00.

Analogous remarks apply to domestic capital. If the private rate of return differs from the social rate of return then some allowance should be made for this difference when estimating the DRC ratio. The social rate of return is the return the capital would earn in its best alternative use, for example investment in agriculture or even a bank deposit. The private rate of return may be higher than the social rate as a consequence of excessive protection being provided to a domestic firm enabling it to earn excess profits, or as a result of capital investments being subsidised. As with labour costs, whatever the reason for the divergence, where a divergence exists it must be allowed for so that capital can be valued at its true social cost. In both cases the intention is to estimate the shadow price of the factor, that is the price which would prevail if the market concerned were free of distortions.

Thus the domestic resource cost coefficient of a commodity compares the opportunity cost of the primary factors (land, labour and capital) used in the production of that commodity with value added in border prices. The coefficient shows the border priced value of the resources in their best alternative use per unit of border priced return from the resources in their existing use. If the estimated coefficient exceeds unity, it can be concluded that, in principle, the resources could be put to better use in an alternative activity, while if the estimated coefficient is less than one, resources are being used relatively efficiently. The DRC ratio can also be thought of as indicating the comparative advantages of competing activities. If a product is found to have a DRC of one then it takes a dollar's worth of resources to produce output that could be purchased internationally for one dollar. Consequently DRCs of less than one identify activities in which the country appears to have an international comparative advantage, whilst those in excess of one can be interpreted as indicating comparative disadvantage.[1]

The DRC ratio for a given activity can be estimated as:

$$DRC_j = (DC_j)/IVA_j \tag{6.1}$$

where: DC_j is the domestic cost of producing j with factors valued at their social opportunity costs and IVA_j is the value added to activity j at border prices.

The higher the DRC_j the more costly in terms of domestic resources it is to produce this product. Another infinitively more appealing, way of interpreting this ratio is to think of it as the cost to the economy of saving foreign exchange (through import substitution) or acquiring foreign exchange (through exporting). For example, if for a given activity the estimated DRC ratio comes out at two, this tells us that the value of domestic resources used up in producing a unit of the relevant product is twice what it would cost to import it. In contrast if the estimated DRC ratio were 0.5, then the domestic resources required to produce the commodity are 50 per cent of the foreign exchange required to import it. Other things being equal the DRC ratio can therefore be thought of as an (ex-post) index of comparative advantage. Ratios of less than one indicate activities of comparative advantage in the sense that they should be net foreign exchange earners; ratios in excess of one indicate comparative disadvantage in the sense that the value of domestic resources used up in producing the product exceeds the value of foreign exchange required to import it. The higher the ratio the greater the domestic resources needed to produce it.

More formally we can write Equation 6.1 as:

$$DRC_j = \frac{\sum_h v_{hj}\, s_h + \sum_n \sum_h d_{nj}\, v_{hn}\, s_h}{1 - \sum_i m_{ij} - \sum_f r_f\, v_{fj}} \tag{6.2}$$

where v_{hj} is the amount of the hth domestic factor of production used in the jth value-adding process (of traded goods), s_h is the shadow price of the hth factor, v_{hn} is the amount of the hth domestic factor of production used in the nth value-adding process (of non-traded goods), d_{nj} is the amount of non-traded good n used in the production of a unit of good j, r_f is the repatriated return per unit of the foreign-owned factor of production f, v_{fj} is the amount of the foreign-owned factor of production f used in the production of one unit of good j, m_{ij} is the amount of the traded input i

used in producing one unit of good *j* and all international prices are normalised at unity.

Relationship to other measures

Clearly the pivotal concepts in this measure are shadow prices, and in the next section we will evaluate this fully. Before we do however, let us consider how the DRC ratio relates to other indicators of intervention. Take first of all effective protection (e). To simplify, assume there are no distortions in factor markets, no expatriate labour or capital and an absence of non-traded goods. In these circumstances we could write.

$$DRC_j = \frac{DC_j}{IVA_j} = \frac{VA_j}{IVA_j} \tag{6.3}$$

It will be recalled from Chapter 5 that

$$e_j = \frac{VA_j - IVA_j}{IVA_j} = \frac{VA_j}{IVA_j} - 1 \tag{6.4}$$

Therefore:

$$DRC_j = e_j + 1 \tag{6.5}$$

Thus the DRC ratio is closely related to the e_j measure. It is even more closely related to the net social profitability (NSP) measure. This is equal to value added in world prices less domestic factors priced at their opportunity costs, viz,

$$NSP_j = \sum_i a_{ij}\, p_i - \sum_h f_{hj}\, s_h + E_j \tag{6.6}$$

where a_{ij} is the quantity of the ith commodity output produced by the jth activity (or the quantity of the ith material input used by j^{th} activity, in which case the term is negative, $i = 1, 2, 3, \ldots n$, p_i is the shadow price of the ith commodity output (or of the ith material input) (in domestic currency), f_{hj} is the quantity of the hth factor of production used by the jth activity, s_h is the shadow price of the hth factor of production (in domestic currency) $h = 1, 2, 3, \ldots$ m and E_j is a measure of the net external benefits or costs imported by the jth activity on the rest of the domestic economy.

Two adjustments to Equation 6.6 facilitate comparability of NSP with the DRC. First, all outputs are assumed to be tradeable. Second, all factor costs, incurred directly in the jth activity or indirectly in producing material inputs used by the jth activity, are divided into foreign and domestic costs.[2] With these two modifications, a second definition of NSP is:

$$NSP_j = (u_j - m_j - r_j)v_j - \sum_{s} f_{hj}\, s_h + E_j \tag{6.7}$$

where u_j is the total value at world prices (in foreign currency) of the output of the jth activity, m_j is the total (direct plus indirect) value (in foreign currency) of imported materials used by the jth activity, r_j is the total (direct plus indirect) value (in foreign currency) of repatriated earnings of foreign-owned factors of production employed by the jth activity (including repatriated portions of direct foreign factor costs, $f_{1j}\, V_1$, and of the indirect foreign factor costs), v_j is the shadow price of foreign exchange, expressed as a ratio of local currency to foreign currency and f_{hj} is the total (direct plus indirect) quantity of the hth domestic factor employed by the jth activity.

As Bruno (1967, p. 106; 1972, p. 20) noted, the DRC can be derived directly from the NSP. The DRC measure can be subtracted from the shadow price of foreign exchange and the difference multiplied by net foreign exchange earned or saved to find net social profitability. Note that if net foreign exchange earned or saved is negative, NSP must also be negative. When NSP is zero, the DRC measure is equal to the shadow price of foreign exchange. Similarly, when NSP is positive, DRC is less than v_j, when NSP is negative, DRC is greater than v_j.

Hence an activity is socially profitably if its DRC ratio, which measures its efficiency in transforming domestic resources into foreign exchange, is less than the shadow price of foreign exchange, which can be thought of as a weighted average of the efficiency of all tradeable activities in the economy in transforming domestic resources into foreign exchange.

6.3 Applications of the DRC methodology

The bulk of this section will concentrate on two case studies. Before we do that however, some comment on shadow pricing is appropriate. There is a vast literature on this subject (see Tower, 1991). In economies with long and extensive histories of government intervention, the need to have a set of prices which reflect as closely as possible the social gains and losses associated with actual policy and changes in that policy is apparent. Ideally one would attempt to calculate 'first best' shadow prices which assume that all government interventions will be dismantled. In this sense the shadow prices reflect true opportunity costs generated by a system completely free of distortions. In practice however one is frequently engaged in estimating 'second best' shadow prices, that is those which prevail on the assumption that preexisting non-optimal policies will remain in effect. The distinction matters, for as Findlay and Wellisz (1976) and Srinivasan and Bhagwati

(1978) have shown, shadow prices will vary according to whether first-best or second-best conditions hold.

As we shall see later, CGE modelling techniques offer a technology which can simulate the effect of removing a number of, or sub-set of, or all distortions in a given situation. Even here though the shadow prices one observes are driven by the model structure rather than the true structure of the economy. In the context of DRC analysis one is invariably estimating second-best shadow prices. Moreover the exercise tends, as with many of the other techniques we have discussed, to be constrained by data availability. The easiest way to illustrate this is to focus on a couple of case studies.

Domestic resource costs in Madagascar[3]

In a study of Madagascar grounded in 1984, Greenaway and Milner (1990) worked with the following estimating equation:

$$DRC_j = \frac{\sum v_{hj}\, s_h}{p_j\,(1 - m_{ij})} \tag{6.8}$$

where v_{hj} is the amount of primary factor h used in producing a unit of j, s_h is the social opportunity cost of primary factor i, p_j is the world price of commodity j and m_{ij} is the share of imported inputs in final value of j at world prices.

This differs from Equation 6.2 in two respects. First, the social opportunity cost of factors employed in the production of non-traded inputs into j are excluded; second, the income repatriated by foreign-owned factors of production is excluded. Both exclusions were necessitated by data constraints. Unfortunately the input–output table did not provide a breakdown of value added in non-tradeable activities (so as to obtain v_h separately for capital and labour). It was not therefore possible to include this component. The omitted component is likely to be of a fairly small order of magnitude for most activities (because it is in effect an input into an input). The extent of any error should be small and should not alter rank orders significantly. It should be obvious from a comparison of Equations 6.2 and 6.8 that the omission should result in a tendency for our DRC estimates to underestimate the true DRC ratios for manufacturing activity in Madagascar.

The omission of repatriated income may be even less of a problem. Madagascar does not have any foreign migrant labour and very few expatriate workers. Thus repatriation of wage income is likely to be negligible. Some companies are however either wholly or partly foreign owned. Therefore there exists at least a potential for repatriation of profit. It is however impossible to establish anything about the magnitude and pattern of any such transfers. Over the period 1972–82 repatriation provisions were suspended and in principle no profits could be transferred from a Madagascan subsidiary to a foreign parent. As a condition of an IMF credit these provisions have been relaxed somewhat. Since 1982 transfers have been permitted, up to a maximum of FMG 1 000 000 000 ($1.66 million). It is probable that some transfers occurred during the year to which our estimates apply (1983). In the absence of any detailed information however this had to be ignored. As with labour and capital inputs into non-tradeable goods this should, if anything result in the calculated DRC ratios being biased downwards.

In order to shadow price labour in manufacturing one must first ascertain what alternative employment labour would be engaged in, and secondly what the remuneration in this alternative activity is. The most probable alternative employment for manufacturing labour is either in the informal sector or in the agricultural sector. Information on the former is non-existent, therefore shadow prices were calculated using the wage differential between labour employed in the agricultural and manufacturing sectors. Various approaches to identifying the agriculture–manufacturing differential were explored. One possibility considered was to take the differential between the minimum wage in agriculture and the minimum wage for the lowest category of unskilled labour, which amounted to 13 per cent. This could have been used to adjust the firm's total wage bill.

Since wages for all categories of manufacturing labour, including the lowest category of unskilled labour, are in excess of minimum rates this is undoubtedly an understatement. A second possibility was to take the differential between the agricultural rate and the average wage *actually* paid in the lower category of unskilled labour, a differential which amounts to 47 per cent. In order to err on the side of caution and avoid possible upward bias in the DRC ratios, it was decided to regard this as the maximum differential and 13 per cent as the minimum differential. Taking the average of the two gives a differential of 30 per cent. Since the average wage actually paid for all categories of manufacturing labour was over 2.5 times the agricultural minimum wage rate, a figure of 30 per cent is very likely to be an underestimate of the differential. This was used to deflate actual wage bills.

Using the information contained in a survey of manufacturing firms it was possible to estimate the actual rate of return achieved by most companies in our sample. This was computed by expressing pre-tax profits as a proportion of total capital assets net of depreciation. Arriving at a shadow rate of return to capital proved problematic, primarily due to the paucity of alternative investment opportunities. One possibility was to estimate this by reference to the marginal cost of foreign borrowing. Since, however, most recent borrowing was on concessional terms this possibility was eschewed. With no detailed information available on the productivity of Madagascan capital an approximation to the shadow rate of return was

Table 6.1 Distribution of DRC ratios in Madagascar, 1983

Range	*Product DRC*
< 0.99	7
1.00–1.49	11
1.50–1.99	9
2.00–2.49	6
2.50–3.00	2
> 3.00	8
Number	42
Mean	3.70 2.18(n − 1)

Source: Greenaway and Milner (1990).

generated by assuming that funds not invested in manufacturing would be deposited with the banking system. This probably understates the real cost of capital to the Madagascan economy. Nevertheless it can be viewed as a feasible alternative and it had the merit of supplying an identifiable rate of return. Accordingly the nominal deposit rate of 14 per cent was taken as the shadow rate of return. To arrive at an estimate of shadow capital costs this 14 per cent return was applied to each firm's total assets net of depreciation. As we shall see below in some instances, frequently in cases where companies benefited from a relatively high effective tariff the shadow rate of return was less than that actual rate of return. In most instances however the shadow rate exceeded the actual rate.[4]

The sample size for the DRC estimates was dictated by data availability. It was seen as desirable to extract as much information as possible from a single data source. Labour and capital costs were available in the survey for some 29 firms producing 43 products. Table 6.1 provides details of the distribution of DRC ratios for the entire sample. The estimates range from a low of 0.60 for cartons to a high of 9.35 for processed meat. The (unweighted) mean DRC is 3.7, or 2.18 if the highest DRC is taken out. Even if we take the lower figure this implies that with an official exchange rate of around FMG 600 to $1, the average cost to the Madagascan economy of saving $1 through import substitution or earning $1 through exporting is FMG 1308 in terms of domestic resources. If one thinks of the DRC ratio as a cost–benefit ratio, the costs being domestic resources and the benefits being the potential foreign exchange contribution of the firm, then it would seem that this ratio is relatively disadvantageous.

Table 6.2 reports average DRCs by industry. Some caution must be exercised in interpreting these results given the fact that for some industries results for only one activity are available. Notwithstanding this some inferences can be drawn. The lowest average DRC appears to be in paper

Table 6.2 Pattern of DRC ratios by industry in Madagascar, 1983

Industry	*Number of firms*	*Average DRC*	*Industry range*
1. Food and drink	5	3.99	0.82–9.35
2. Pharmaceuticals	3	2.49	0.79–3.68
3. Chemicals	4	1.40	0.78–2.38
4. Textiles	1	1.71	–
5. Footwear and leather	2	1.65	1.39–1.91
6. Wood products	2	3.04	2.49–3.58
7. Metal products	5	2.15	1.33–3.02
8. Electrical products	1	1.40	–
9. Paper products	2	0.64	0.60–0.68
10. Construction goods	1	1.70	–
11. Miscellaneous	1	2.68	–

Source: Greenaway and Milner (1990).

products. Indeed this is the only industry for which an *average* DRC of less than one is found. (It is notable that this is also the only industry for which an *average* negative effective tariff was estimated.) At the other extreme food and drink has an average DRC of 3.49. It should be noted that in the case of food and drink there are two recorded instances of negative value added at world prices for which DRC ratios could not therefore be computed. The reported DRC average may therefore be an understatement. Moreover it is the industry with the third-highest average effective tariff. Of the remaining industries, six have below average DRCs (chemicals, textiles, footwear and leather, metal products, electrical products and construction goods) and three are estimated to have above average ratios, (pharmaceuticals, wood products and miscellaneous).

Since the simple average masks quite a wide range of estimates, in some cases it is instructive to consider interproduct variations in DRC ratios. As can be seen from Table 6.1 there are seven products with a DRC ratio of less than one, namely vegetable oils, serums, syrups, acetylene, paper and cartons.

Notwithstanding the caveats identified above a number of inferences can be drawn from this DRC analysis. First, the average DRC ratio in Madagascar is in excess of two. Thus on average the value of resources required to earn/save a unit of foreign exchange is more than twice that suggested by the official exchange rate. Secondly, the range of estimates is relatively wide, i.e. 0.60 to 9.35. This implies there may be considerable resource misallocation associated with commercial and industrial policy. It also suggests that greater allocative efficiency could be achieved by encouraging resources to shift from activities with relatively high DRCs to activities with relatively low DRCs.

Thirdly, the DRC analysis seems to reinforce the effective tariff analysis reported in Chapter 5 by suggesting that there are considerable potential gains to be reaped from policy reform. Fourth, with all analyses of this type there is inevitably a margin of error associated with the estimates, due in part to data deficiencies and in part to the nature of the assumptions which (of necessity) must be made. Where assumptions have had to be made they have consistently erred on the side of caution. Therefore if the results are systematically biased they are likely to be biased downwards. This point is reinforced by the fact that for those firms which enjoyed infinitely high protection, that is their value added was negative at world prices, a DRC could not be calculated (with the present methodology).[5]

Finally, in interpreting these results we have consistently used the official exchange rate. In practice many transactions may occur at a rate other than the official one. Indeed it would be surprising if the shadow rate was not less than the official. A black market exchange rate at some 30 per cent below the official rate is an imprecise estimate of the shadow rate. Using this rate would alter the detail of the results of course. However the use of any lower exchange rate would simply serve to raise, on average, the estimated value of Madagascan resources required in saving/acquiring foreign exchange without significantly altering the ranking and dispersion of DRC estimates.

Domestic resource cost ratios in Egyptian agriculture

Hassan, Greenaway and Reed (1992) have compiled a set of estimates for the Egyptian agricultural sector. Two sets of price data were collected. Domestic market prices were collected for all inputs and outputs. World prices were collected for all tradeable inputs and outputs. If the product is imported (exported), the world price is defined as the c.i.f (f.o.b) price (adjusted by the appropriate exchange rate). Shadow prices for domestic factors and the world price equivalent for non-traded inputs and outputs are calculated from the results of survey data (discussed below).

All traded inputs in the production process were treated as components of value added at world prices. If non-traded, however, the input was broken down into two categories. The first contains inputs that are defined as 'primary factors', for instance labour and land; the second category consists of inputs that are non-traded, for example manure, animal draft and sundries for irrigation. As Table 6.3 shows, primary factors are the most important component for the DRC. In general primary factors account for not less than 50 per cent of total domestic costs in Egypt.

For all commodities the market wage in Egyptian agriculture was considered to be the appropriate measure of the shadow price of labour. The rationale for taking the market wage was as follows. Labour is fully employed in the agricultural sector and acts as a reservoir for supplying demand in construction, services, expatriate production and so on. Thus a reserve army of unemployed labour does not exist. In shadow pricing for

Table 6.3 Relative importance of agricultural inputs in total production costs, Egypt 1980–7 (in per cent)

Crops	*Labour*	*Land*	*Machines*	*Seeds*	*Fertilizers*	*Insecticides*	*Animal draft*	*Manure*	*Sundries**
Wheat	34.4	23.3	16.5	4.6	8.1	0.0	4.8	3.7	4.5
Barley	30.5	22.8	18.7	4.8	7.8	0.0	5.0	5.6	4.8
Rice	43.1	12.9	16.6	7.5	5.6	0.6	6.2	3.1	4.4
Maize	42.8	14.7	12.9	2.3	9.7	0.0	3.8	8.8	5.0
Sorghum	50.2	16.3	15.6	1.6	8.7	0.0	2.2	1.2	4.2
Broadbeans	38.7	22.5	14.9	11.2	4.1	0.9	3.0	0.1	4.4
Soybeans	37.3	17.3	16.6	5.7	8.6	3.0	2.2	4.5	4.8
Groundnuts	45.6	20.3	9.6	7.2	4.4	0.8	4.0	4.3	3.9
Sesame	46.5	22.8	12.8	1.9	6.1	0.0	8.0	4.0	1.9
Cotton	53.6	17.3	8.5	0.7	5.0	3.1	1.9	6.2	3.7
Lentils	26.4	26.9	15.6	20.2	3.3	0.0	3.7	0.0	3.9
Onions	36.1	12.7	7.0	21.7	8.0	6.2	1.6	4.0	2.8
Flax	35.1	22.9	12.8	11.9	6.1	0.0	3.4	3.8	4.0
Sugarcane	47.4	13.8	12.4	5.3	11.2	0.5	4.9	0.4	4.1
Garlic	40.2	18.1	9.4	13.6	6.5	0.1	4.1	4.5	3.5
Potatoes	18.2	9.0	4.5	47.4	6.0	4.3	2.7	5.0	2.5
Tomatoes	41.7	15.5	7.3	6.3	8.2	7.5	2.5	8.2	2.7
Oranges	39.5	19.5	4.1	0.0	6.9	13.2	0.0	4.2	12.5

Source: Collected and computed from Egyptian Ministry of Agriculture data.
* Expenditure on water wheels, animal-powered irrigation, storage, haulage, interest and depreciation, and so forth.

non-agricultural activity, the agricultural wage is taken as the opportunity cost of labour. The labour market can be assumed to be fairly competitive and wages probably reflect fairly accurately the value of labour's marginal product, and therefore need only to be adjusted to take into account the impact that valuing tradeables at world prices would have on the value imputed to domestic resources. In the DRC calculations it has been assumed that the market wage of labour during the peak periods of May–June and October–November reflect the opportunity cost. In order to obtain its actual shadow cost for each crop, the market wage is multiplied by the crop's input–output coefficient for labour to obtain the labour shadow cost per feddan. To compute the labour shadow cost per unit (ton), it is divided by yield per feddan.[6]

Unlike labour, land is a basic depository of value and productive potential for agriculture. Its value is difficult to assess since it is not only a factor of production but also an asset, and related markets are often thin, unreliable and complex so that rental rates are not necessarily related either to the price of land or to its marginal product. The appropriate measure of the cost of land as an input is the producer's willingness to pay for the aggregate production benefits made possible by use of the land. In Egypt, with government intervention, rents are fixed by the land reform legislation to seven times the level of land tax. These taxes tend to remain constant at the same nominal level over long periods of time (about 10 years).

Table 6.4 shows the land tenure patterns in Egypt resulting from government intervention in the land market. It appears that about 60 per cent of the land is owner-operated and about 40 per cent is still cultivated by tenants. Tenancy tends on balance to consolidate land. Maximum rentals with protection of tenants against eviction were introduced in 1952 by the land reform legislation. The area rented decreased from about 42.6 per cent in 1972/73 to 35.1 per cent in 1981–82.

The cost of land is what it would have been worth in alternative uses. Thus the appropriate value for the opportunity cost of land in any crop is the return to land from the next best alternative use. In each sector, and for each district, the next best alternative crops were determined by comparison of (economic) returns to land. The opportunity cost of land in its existing use is then the result arrived at by taking the alternative crops with the highest return. Table 6.5 shows the crop alternatives assumed.

Although some farmers own tractors, they increasingly rely on tractor services provided by machinery renting stations to meet the needs of their production. These stations are under the supervision of the Ministry of Agriculture. Until recently, the charges for machinery services were controlled by the government, at £E 12 per hour for a farm tractor with driver and equipment. Even so, the farm tractor charge is subsidised, according to official data. The opportunity cost of tractor services are calculated using information on rentals in the British market. This involved computing costs

Table 6.4 Land tenure patterns in Egypt (1972–82)

Year	Owners (%)	Tenants (%)	Share croppers (%)	Total area (000 feddan)
1972/73	57.4	34.4	8.2	5642
1973/74	57.0	34.7	8.3	5625
1974/75	57.6	34.5	7.8	5661
1975/76	58.4	33.7	7.8	5675
1976/77	59.5	32.8	7.7	5667
1977/78	60.4	32.3	7.3	5655
1978/79	60.4	33.2	6.4	5648
1979/80	61.7	32.1	6.3	5635
1980/81	62.9	31.0	6.1	5610
1981/82	64.9	29.3	5.8	5645
Average	60.0	32.8	7.2	–

Source: Collected and computed using data from the Egyptian Ministry of Agriculture and the Agricultural Economics Research Institute, Cairo.

per hour after adjusting for the exchange rate (official and shadow exchange rates) for all crops.

Non-traded factors do not exceed 11.5 per cent on average of total production costs. Since their value to the economy cannot be measured in terms of border prices they should be assessed in relation to prices in the domestic market. To compute non-traded inputs, one could work with integrated industries in the 'sophisticated' Corden fashion. Alternatively, one could work with the disaggregated industries, but define the DRC in one of two different ways. The first would be to leave the numerator defined as the amounts of primary factors evaluated at shadow prices, while the denominator would be the value added at border prices. The second alternative would be to treat the non-traded inputs just like the primary factors of production and place them in the numerator instead of the denominator. This is the one used there.

On the basis of the above assumptions, DRC coefficients were derived for each agricultural product. These were computed twice, using official and shadow exchange rates. The main results are summarised in Tables 6.6 and 6.7. Table 6.6 presents DRC coefficients at the official exchange rates while Table 6.7 presents the coefficients at shadow exchange rates.

The results suggest a comparative advantage in all export commodities studied for 1980–7 (onions, tomatoes, oranges, groundnuts, garlic, potatoes, rice and cotton), either at the official exchange rate or the shadow exchange rate. They also show that DRC coefficients for all import and self-sufficient commodities are more than one, indicating that Egypt clearly does not have a comparative advantage in these crops. The estimates suggest a number of conclusions regarding comparative advantage within agriculture for the period 1980–7. In the import crops, for instance, sugar-

Table 6.5 Summary of next-best crop alternatives in Egypt

Crop	*Alternatives**
Wheat	Barley, lentils, onions, flax, garlic, tomatoes, broadbeans, *cotton*
Barley	Wheat, lentils, onions, flax, garlic, tomatoes, *broadbeans*
Rice	Groundnuts, soybeans, sesame, potatoes, maize, tomatoes, sorghum, *cotton*
Maize	Groundnuts, soybeans, sesame, potatoes, *rice*, tomatoes, sorghum, cotton
Sorghum	Groundnuts, soybeans, *sesame*, potatoes, rice, tomatoes, maize, cotton
Broadbeans	Wheat, barley, *lentils*, flax, onions, tomatoes, garlic
Soybean	Groundnuts, maize, rice, potatoes, sorghum, tomatoes, *sesame*, cotton
Groundnuts	Maize, rice, sorghum, potatoes, soybeans, tomatoes, *sesame*, cotton
Sesame	Maize, rice, sorghum, potatoes, soybeans, tomatoes, sesame, *cotton*
Cotton	Maize, rice, sorghum, potatoes, soybeans, tomatoes, sesame, *wheat*
Lentils	*Wheat*, barley, broadbeans, onions, flax, tomatoes, garlic
Onions	Wheat, barley, broadbeans, *lentils*, flax, tomatoes, garlic
Flax	Wheat, barley, broadbeans, *lentils*, onions, tomatoes, garlic
Sugarcane	*Cotton*
Garlic	Wheat, barley, broadbeans, lentils, *onions*, tomatoes, flax
Potatoes	Maize, *rice*, groundnuts, soybeans, sesame, tomatoes, sorghum, cotton
Tomatoes	Maize, rice, groundnuts, soybeans, *potatoes*, sesame, sorghum, cotton
Oranges	*Cotton*

* The italicised crops are the best alternative use.

Table 6.6 Egyptian agricultural crops, domestic resource costs (using official exchange rates), 1980–7

Crop	*1980*	*1981*	*1982*	*1983*	*1984*	*1985*	*1986*	*1987*	*1980–7*
Import-competing crops:									
Wheat	2.29	1.64	1.13	1.04	1.41	1.33	1.18	1.19	1.40
Maize	2.84	2.46	2.86	3.33	1.94	2.70	3.95	5.71	3.22
Soybean	1.06	1.01	0.77	1.28	1.12	1.21	2.43	2.74	1.46
Sesame	1.85	2.05	1.81	0.97	1.52	1.56	0.97	0.99	1.46
Lentils	0.97	1.14	1.24	1.21	1.02	0.92	0.94	0.99	1.05
Flax-seed	1.50	1.69	1.71	1.33	1.25	1.53	1.68	2.02	1.59
Sugarcane	0.72	0.56	0.65	1.54	1.89	2.27	1.42	3.11	1.52
Self-sufficient crops:									
Barley	0.74	0.74	1.12	1.46	1.15	1.23	1.41	1.66	1.19
Sorghum	1.48	1.34	1.30	1.48	1.71	1.88	2.31	2.21	1.71
Broadbeans	1.57	1.57	1.13	0.89	1.16	1.38	1.15	1.10	1.24
Export crops:									
Rice	0.98	0.79	0.52	0.59	1.04	0.99	0.74	0.82	0.81
Groundnuts	0.56	0.43	0.36	0.59	0.52	0.66	0.73	0.66	0.56
Cotton	0.52	0.68	0.95	1.00	0.82	0.85	1.02	1.00	0.86
Onions	0.25	0.23	0.21	0.29	0.35	0.35	0.40	0.22	0.29
Garlic	0.23	0.36	0.35	0.32	0.64	0.91	0.85	1.39	0.63
Potatoes	0.77	0.71	0.75	0.82	0.54	0.87	1.22	0.76	0.80
Tomatoes	0.29	0.40	0.40	0.35	0.60	0.51	0.33	0.28	0.40
Oranges	0.49	0.41	0.28	0.38	0.47	0.50	0.47	0.44	0.43

Source: Collected and computed from Egyptian Ministry of Agriculture data.

cane and lentils have a DRC coefficient which in some years turns out to be below one and in some years above one, depending on what was happening to world prices. The increased comparative advantage on lentils after 1984 is due to lower wheat prices.

6.4 DRC analysis and policy appraisal

These examples illustrate well the principles behind the technique, as well as some of the difficulties associated with its application. As we have seen, the key problem is the estimation of shadow prices. As with many other economic concepts, the contrast between theoretical precision and practical application is striking. The theorist enjoys the luxury of being able to disregard questions of data availability and policy evaluation in a second-best context. The analyst is not in such a luxurious position and invariably has to take a pragmatic perspective when it comes to estimation. Does this mean that the resultant estimates are of no value when it comes to policy appraisal? The answer to this question is 'no'. DRC analysis has been quite

Table 6.7 *Egyptian agricultural crops, domestic resource costs (using shadow exchange rates), 1980–7*

Crop	*1980*	*1981*	*1982*	*1983*	*1984*	*1985*	*1986*	*1987*	*1980–7*
Import-competing crops:									
Wheat	2.51	2.04	1.57	1.61	2.26	2.42	2.84	3.60	2.36
Maize	2.89	2.53	2.93	3.57	2.01	3.06	4.76	8.42	3.77
Soybean	1.04	0.99	0.76	1.29	1.14	1.24	2.67	3.37	1.56
Sesame	1.92	2.20	2.10	1.23	1.90	2.13	1.50	1.74	1.84
Lentils	0.95	1.09	1.19	1.29	0.95	0.77	0.95	0.98	1.02
Flax-seed	1.55	1.83	1.91	1.51	1.53	2.09	2.58	5.07	2.26
Sugarcane	0.70	0.53	0.60	1.39	1.74	2.07	1.19	2.38	1.33
Self-sufficient crops:									
Barley	0.75	0.78	1.23	1.65	1.29	1.57	2.12	3.04	1.55
Sorghum	1.47	1.36	1.29	1.46	1.65	1.79	2.37	2.29	1.71
Broadbeans	1.55	1.55	1.08	0.86	1.17	1.51	1.19	1.21	1.27
Export crops:									
Rice	0.99	0.82	0.56	0.68	1.19	1.14	0.91	1.07	0.92
Groundnuts	0.55	0.41	0.33	0.54	0.45	0.53	0.62	0.52	0.49
Cotton	0.47	0.55	0.73	0.74	0.56	0.53	0.47	0.43	0.56
Onions	0.22	0.19	0.16	0.20	0.24	0.23	0.23	0.12	0.20
Garlic	0.24	0.37	0.36	0.33	0.69	0.99	0.93	1.47	0.67
Potatoes	0.76	0.69	0.72	0.75	0.47	0.76	1.01	0.59	0.72
Tomatoes	0.29	0.40	0.39	0.34	0.58	0.47	0.30	0.27	0.38
Oranges	0.47	0.36	0.23	0.29	0.37	0.34	0.30	0.25	0.33

Source: Collected and computed from Egyptian Ministry of Agriculture data.

widely deployed in the process of policy appraisal by agencies like the World Bank, as well as by independent analysts. As it is more data demanding than effective protection it is not so widely used. Nevertheless, in the pre-appraisal stage of a structural adjustment programme, its use is not unusual.

The methodology has its attractions. As we saw earlier, it has a higher information content than the effective protection coefficient. In the context of developing countries this is a considerable virtue, given the pervasiveness of intervention. It is a measure with considerable intuitive appeal in that it can be interpreted as an indicator of comparative advantage. As such it can be used as an input into reflections on resource reallocation. Of course the measure also has its limitations, and one must interpret it with care. It would be unwise to rely on it to make judgements about the relative merits of investing in alternative activities with small differences in their DRCs. However one can use it in a similar way to the effective protection measure, using information on the mean DRC, its range and the ranking of activities in that range.

The mean can reveal something about the impact of intervention 'on average'. A mean of unity would suggest that, on average, activities are competitive internationally, a mean value of over two, as reported above in the Madagascan case, suggests quite the opposite. The distribution around the mean conveys information about potential damage in terms of resource misallocation associated with intervention, whilst the ranking within the distribution can convey information helpful to policy reform. Overall therefore the measure is a useful one. Used judiciously it is a valuable input to the policy appraisal process.

6.5 Concluding comments

DRC analysis belongs to the same family of policy-appraisal measures as effective protection and net social profitability in that it uses information on the relationship between domestic and world prices to describe the effects of intervention at a fairly disaggregated level. In this respect it has obvious similarities with the effective protection measure discussed in the last chapter. However it goes beyond effective protection in that it takes into account the impact of non-border distortions. Potentially therefore the measure has a high information content and can provide a neat summary of the relative efficiency of alternative activities. However, since it relies heavily on estimated shadow prices, it is a more complicated measure to work with. Moreover it is also inherently more difficult to estimate. Thus one has to use the measure judiciously. Notwithstanding this, it is a potentially useful tool in the analyst's toolbox.

PART III

TOOLS OF GENERAL EQUILIBRIUM ANALYSIS

CHAPTER 7

Shift Analysis and the Incidence of Protection

7.1 Introduction

The partial equilibrium tools of analysis outlined in Part II tend to focus on the impact of commercial policy interventions at the product or industry level. By design these tools are intended to comment on the impact of production and consumption effects and the resulting costs of discriminatory and protective measures. Analysts nonetheless are often drawn into using cross-sectional information on partial equilibrium estimates of the structure of protection to comment on resource allocation effects. As discussed in Chapter 5, information on average levels and the ranking and dispersion of effective protection can be used to make inferences about resource pulls between industries and sectors. But there are dangers in using partial equilibrium estimation techniques to comment upon general equilibrium effects. If the purpose of policy analysis is to comment upon *relative* incentives to invest and produce in particular sectors of the economy, then it would be preferable to set up a general equilibrium framework for the analysis of protection; one which focuses on the relative price effects of interventions across sectors of activity.

Incidence or shift analysis attempts to focus on these relative price effects, or true protection, as opposed to the nominal or net price effects. By examining the subsequent relative price adjustments to nominal interventions (tariffs, subsidies and so on) it is possible to comment on the ultimate incidence or burden of protective measures. In circumstances where countries simultaneously attempt to intervene or promote across the board, for example where LDCs try to both import-substitute and export-promote, it is also possible to use true protection measures to comment on policy conflicts and compatibility. In addition, as we shall see, this potentially powerful analytical tool is, in comparison with many of the other tools of analysis discussed in this book, relatively undemanding in terms of data requirements.

This chapter outlines the nature and uses of incidence analysis and illustrates its application in a number of developing countries. The rest of the chapter is organised as follows. Section 7.2 sets up the theoretical framework. Section 7.3 uses this framework to illustrate true protection and the incidence of protection under alternative conditions. Section 7.4 describes the estimation methodology required to operationalise the model and illustrates its application in a number of countries. Section 7.5 reviews the analytical value of the empirical work to policy appraisal. Finally section 7.6 offers some concluding comments.

7.2 The theoretical framework

The neoclassical model of international trade is usually based on two sectors, two factors of production and two goods. Such a model allows us to predict which *factor* loses from trade restriction and which gains. As Sjaastad (1980a) points out however, since it is generally assumed that both factors are used in both sectors it is not possible to examine the incidence of protection in *sectoral* terms. Import protection raises the price of importables relative to exportables but nothing can be inferred from this about the *incidence* of protection across the sectors. If a third sector is introduced, namely non-tradeables, a second relative price ratio, the price of non-tradeables relative to tradeables, is introduced. An examination of how an import tariff alters the price of importables relative to exportables *and* non-tradeables can provide an indication of the 'true' protection of importables and the extent to which the incidence of the tax is shifted onto exportables and non-tradeables. The incidence depends essentially on the degree of substitutability (in demand and production) between the products of the importables sector and the other unprotected sectors.

The model

Consider a simple general equilibrium model based on the following assumptions.[1]

- A small open economy with given factor endowments which produces and consumes importables (*M*), exportables (*X*) and non-tradeables or home goods (*H*).
- Initial (free-trade) internal relative prices of all goods which are unity. Moreover it will be assumed that the relative prices of both importables

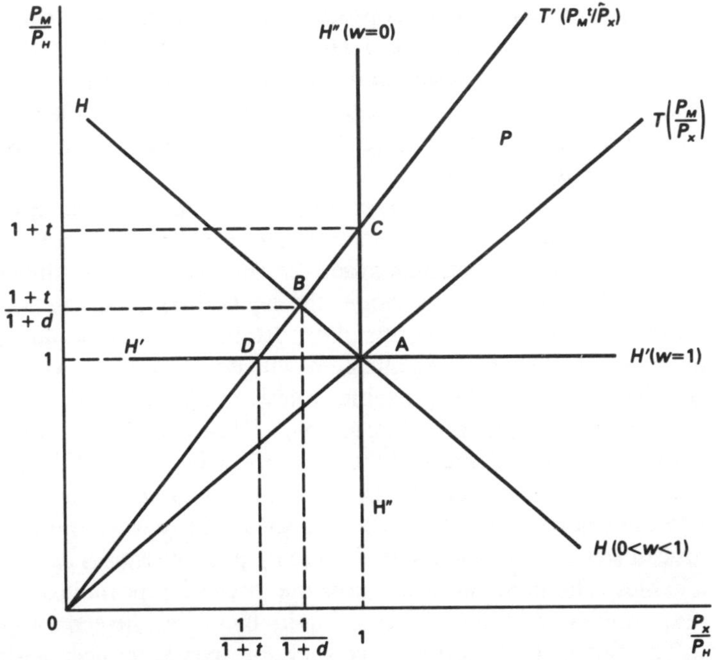

Figure 7.1 Relative prices and commercial policy interventions

and exportables in terms of home goods are flexible so as to allow market clearing.

- Commercial policy interventions which take the form of uniform tariffs on imports and/or uniform subsidies on exports.
- Factor intensities are such that $(K/L)_M \geqslant (K/L)_H \geqslant K/L)_X$, where K/L refers to the capital-labour ratio in each sector, and factor intensity reversals are ruled out.
- A fixed exchange rate and initial balanced trade.

As Dornbusch (1974) shows, equilibrium in the home goods market implies balanced trade. Therefore the equilibrium properties of the model can be examined in terms of equilibrium in either the market for non-tradeables or tradeables. Figure 7.1 illustrates a particular case. Here it is assumed that home goods are substitutable for exportables and/or importables in both production and consumption. Exportables and importables are not, however, substitutable.[2] The domestic price of importables relative to exportables (P_M/P_X) is determined by the given world terms of trade and any commercial policy intervention. This is represented by the ray OT. The schedule HH demonstrates alternative prices of importables and exportables (relative to home goods) that clear the home goods market. At points along HH, excess demand for home goods is zero. At points above and to the right, excess demand is positive, whilst at points below and to the left, excess demand is negative. *HH* is negatively sloped, reflecting the assumption that home goods substitute with *both* tradeables. A fall in P_M (relative to P_H) generates negative excess demand for non-tradeables and must be offset by an increase in P_X (relative to P_H). Free trade equilibrium is at *A* where *OT* intersects *HH*.

Using this framework one can examine the *relative* price effects of commercial policy interventions. Since initial relative prices are unity, a uniform tariff *t* on all importables raises the relative price of importables P_M/P_H to $1 + t$. In Figure 7.1 this rotates the ray *OT* to *OT′* as the domestic relative price of importables in terms of exportables rises by the amount of the nominal tariff. The new equilibrium will be at point *B* where *OT′* intersects *HH*. The price of exportables relative to home goods has fallen to $1/1 + d$, whilst the price of importables relative to home goods has increased to $1 + t/1 + d$. *d* refers to the proportional increase in the price of home goods ($\hat{P}_H$). This increase in the nominal price of home goods relative to the price of traded goods is necessary to remove the incipient tariff-induced trade surplus and corresponding positive excess demand for non-tradeables. The nominal tariff raises the price of importables in terms of both exportables and home goods as it initially moves the economy from *A* to *C*. The fall in the relative price of home goods induces a shift in demand towards home goods and a shift in production away from home goods, the extent of these shifts depending upon the substitutional relationships between *M* and *H*. The stronger the substitutional relationships the greater the proportional change in $\hat{P}_H$ $(=d)$. In Figure 7.1, $0 < d < t$ and full equilibrium is restored at *B*.

The role of substitutional relationships can be formally demonstrated as follows. The proportional increase in the price of home goods generated by an import tax is that required to restore equilibrium in the home goods market. Thus, following Sjaastad and Clements (1981),

$$\hat{S}_H = \hat{D}_H \qquad (7.1)$$

where $\hat{S}_H$ and $\hat{D}_H$ refer to the proportionate change in the supply of and demand for home goods respectively.

$$\hat{S}_H = h^S_X \hat{P}_X + h^S_M \hat{P}_M + h^S_H \hat{P}_H \qquad (7.2)$$

$$\hat{D}_H = h^D_X \hat{P}_X + h^D_M \hat{P}_M + h^D_H \hat{P}_H \qquad (7.3)$$

Since income effects are ignored, h^S and h^D are compensated supply and demand price elasticities for home goods with respect to the price of *X*, *M* and *H*, and ^ denotes a proportionate change.

These elasticities are subject to the homogeneity constraint:

$$\sum_{i=1}^{n} h_i^S = \sum_{i=1}^{n} h_i^D = 0 \tag{7.4}$$

From Equations 7.1, 7.2, 7.3 and 7.4 we obtain:

$$\hat{P}_H = w\hat{P}_M + (1 - w)\hat{P}_X \tag{7.5}$$

where

$$w = \frac{h_M^D - h_M^S}{h_H^S - h_H^D} \tag{7.6}$$

The effects of a tariff as shown by Equations 7.5 and 7.6 depend on the substitutional relationships between home goods and the two traded goods. In fact, the *shift parameter* (w) is an index of substitutability between home goods and importables in production and demand and will lie between zero and unity. Where importables and home goods are close substitutes, w will tend towards unity. In the limit where home goods and importables are perfect substitutes, $w = 1$. In this case the absolute price of both increases by the same extent, relative to the price of exportables, and the incidence of an import tax falls totally on exporters. Here the tariff, in fact, is fully equivalent to an implicit export tax. This is represented by point *D* in Figure 7.1, with *HH* being horizontal over the relevant range. In contrast, where exportables and home goods are close substitutes for each other the price of importables rises relative to both exportables and home goods and the incidence of the import tax is shared equally by those two sectors. In this case, $w = 0$ and we are at *C* in Figure 7.1 with *HH* being vertical over the relevant range.

Pre- and post-intervention equilibrium compared

Although both points *A* and *B* (for the case of an intermediate value for the shift parameter w or substitutability in production and demand) involve trade balance, there are some important differences in the characteristics of these equilibrium situations. First, the sectoral pattern of production, and consumption is different. Since the price of importables has risen relative to both non-tradeables and exportables, and the price of non-tradeables has risen relative to exportables, there has been a shift of resources away from the production of exportables and towards the production of importables, and a shift of domestic demand towards exportables and away from importables. The result is a larger importables sector, a smaller exportables sector and a reduced volume of both exports (the excess supply of exportables) and of imports (the excess demand for importables). Thus this discriminatory intervention alters the relative price and incentive structure, and has resource allocation effects. In this particular case import protection introduces a trade-regime and anti-export bias, although there has been no change in the nominal protection and therefore price of exportables. Protection and promotion are ultimately both relative, rather than nominal, concepts. (Measures of relative, or true protection, are set out in the next section.)

The second significant difference between the pre- and post-tariff equilibria concerns the real exchange rate. The initial effect of a tariff tended to move the economy from trade balance into trade surplus, as P_M/P_H rose to $1 + t$. The restoration of trade balance at *B* was achieved by an increase in the nominal price of non-tradeables (d), as P_M/P_H fell back to $1 + t/1 + d$. Although the nominal exchange rate is assumed to be fixed, this rise in P_H results in an implicit appreciation of the real exchange rate (a fall in the border price of tradeables relative to the price of non-tradeables). This same adjustment could have been achieved by a nominal currency appreciation, which would lower the nominal price of tradeables. Thus discriminatory commercial policy measures tend to cause exchange rate misalignment: import substitution measures for instance cause a country to maintain a given balance of trade position at a higher real (that is over-valued) exchange rate than would apply in the absence of intervention.

7.3 True protection and the incidence of protection

If we use the change in the price of importables or exportables relative to home goods as a measure of the 'true' effect of protecting or promoting a sector, we can define the true tariff ($\overset{*}{t}$) and true export subsidy ($\overset{*}{s}$) as:

$$\overset{*}{t} = \Delta\ (P_M/P_H) \qquad (7.7)$$

and

$$\overset{*}{s} = \Delta\ (P_X/P_H) \qquad (7.8)$$

In terms of Figure 7.1 the proportional change in P_H equals d and therefore Equations 7.7 and 7.8 can be rewritten as:

$$\overset{*}{t} = \left(\frac{1+t}{1+d}\right) - 1 = \frac{t-d}{1+d} \qquad (7.9)$$

and

$$\overset{*}{s} = \frac{s-d}{1+d} \qquad (7.10)$$

where s denotes the nominal export subsidy.

Thus the pattern of true protection depends upon the structure of protection (for example whether $t \geqslant s \geqslant 0$) and upon d.

Import protection only

In the case where import substitution measures ($t > 0$) are applied in the absence of any export promotion measures ($s = 0$) then:

$$d = wt \tag{7.11}$$

Therefore if we substitute Equation 7.11 into Equation 7.9 and 7.10:

$$\overset{*}{t} = \frac{t - wt}{1 + wt} \tag{7.12}$$

and

$$\overset{*}{s} = \frac{-wt}{1 + wt} \tag{7.13}$$

Thus $t \geqslant \overset{*}{t} \geqslant 0$ and $\overset{*}{s} \leqslant 0$ as $0 \leqslant w \leqslant 1$ (see Figure 7.2). If importables and home goods are perfect substitutes, that is $w = 1$, and $d = t$ the true tariff is zero. There is no net protection of importables relative to non-tradeables. But in this case the rise in P_H means that there is a negative true subsidy of exportables (if $s = 0$); $\overset{*}{s}$ equals $-t/(1 + t)$ where $w = 1$. Thus all the burden of import protection falls upon the exportables sector in this case.[3] It is somewhat ironic that this highest level of burden on exportables is associated with the lowest level of true protection for importables. It serves to illustrate however how the actual effects of policy intervention may differ substantially from the intended effects. It might be noted parenthetically that this may provide one explanation of the tendency for protection of importables in many less developed countries to increase through time. If true protection is low there is a motive to press for further nominal protection!

As w falls below unity (that is there is less than perfect substitutability between M and H and $d < t$), then the true tariff is positive (but less than the nominal tariff where $d > 0$) and the negative true subsidy becomes smaller in absolute terms. In this intermediate cause the burden of import protection falls on both exportables and non-tradeables (though more on exportables than non-tradeables). In the extreme, if exportables and home goods are perfect substitutes ($w = 0$) and import protection results in no change in P_H (that is $d = 0$), then $\overset{*}{s} = 0$ and the true tariff equals the

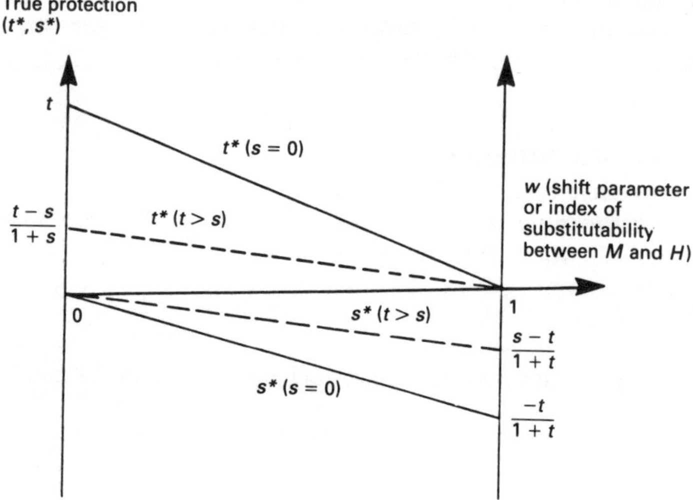

Figure 7.2 True protection and the structure of protection

nominal tariff. The cost of import protection falls equally on exportables and non-tradeables.[4] Thus the shift parameter w determines the pattern of true protection and the distribution of the incidence or burden of protection. The incidence on exports (y) in the import protection only case is as follows:

$$y = \tfrac{1}{2}(1 + w) \tag{7.14}$$

Thus the share of burden, which ranges between 50 per cent and 100 per cent as w ranges from 0 to unity, is endogenously determined by substitutability characteristics of the economy and not influenced by policy interventions.[5]

Mixed strategies

In many less developed countries the desire to industrialise has induced simultaneous attempts at import substitution and export promotion. In general the actual, net effects of simultaneously operating conflicting policies (in terms of their effects on internal relative prices) will be considerably different from the intended effects. Because protection alters *relative* prices, the protection of import-competing activities in isolation must 'disprotect' exporters, while the promotion of exports in isolation must 'disprotect' import-substitution activities. If import protection would, in isolation, result in a marked fall in the price of exportables relative to home goods, then the imposition of an export subsidy merely acts as a countervailing distortion. Similarly if the provision of an export subsidy raises the price of exportables relative to non-tradeables, an import tariff acts as a countervailing distortion.

The extent to which export subsidies offset the effects of import duties on relative prices depends on the relative magnitudes of the nominal rates of duty and subsidy and the nature of the substitutional relationships present in the economy. Traditional exports of primary products are invariably raw material or resource intensive. As such, one would anticipate somewhat limited substitution possibilities in demand and production between these and other sectors. In contrast, *non-traditional* exports (that is manufactures), tend to be relatively labour intensive and often have closer substitutional relationships with other sectors, in particular the home goods sector. As a result of this one might expect differences in the proportion of protection which is shifted, with a higher incidence on traditional exports.

Equations 7.9 and 7.10 show formally that what happens to the price of home goods has a critical influence on true rates of protection. The proportionate increase in the price of home goods ($\hat{P}_H$) following the imposition of an import tariff and export subsidy is composed of two elements: that part of the increase shifted on from the rise in the price of importables due to the tariff (wt) and that part shifted on from the domestic price of exportables due to the subsidy ($[1 - w]s$). That is, Equation 7.11 is amended so that:

$$d = wt + (1 - w)s \tag{7.15}$$

Consider first the uniform intervention case. If $t = s$, we have the result that $d = t = s$; the prices of all goods (tradeables and non-tradeables) have risen by the same proportion and no sector is protected because relative prices are unaltered. In other words, if import tariffs are used to protect the import substitute sector, whilst equivalent export subsidies are offered to the export sector, the overall pattern of relative prices will not differ from the preprotection level. This may seem self-evident. It is nonetheless an important point. To make a specific example, it implies that using resources to create an export processing zone, as many LDCs have done, may simply be a second-best means of achieving a 'free trade' pattern of relative prices!

The case where $t > s$ is probably of greater practical relevance. The division of true protection now depends critically on the value of w. The policy makers can set the extent to which actual or nominal t exceeds nominal s but the final relative price structure and therefore the true tariff and subsidy are determined by substitutional relationships in the economy which are dependent on preferences and technological characteristics. Consider Figure 7.2 again. True protection ($\overset{*}{t}$ or $\overset{*}{s}$) is absolutely smaller for any value of w. (The range of values for $\overset{*}{t}$ and $\overset{*}{s}$ given by the dotted lines in Figure 7.2 are obtained by substituting Equation 7.15 into Equation 7.9

Table 7.1 *True protection for alternative substitution possibilities and trade strategies*

	Degree of substitutability between M and H		
	Perfect $w = 1$	Intermediate $1 > w > 0$	Zero $w = 0$
Import protection only $(t > 0, s = 0)$	$\overset{*}{t} = 0$ $\overset{*}{s} < 0$	$0 < \overset{*}{t} < t$ $\overset{*}{s} < 0$	$\overset{*}{t} = t$ $\overset{*}{s} = 0$
Export promotion only $(t = 0, s > 0)$	$\overset{*}{t} = 0$ $\overset{*}{s} = s$	$\overset{*}{t} < 0$ $s > \overset{*}{s} > 0$	$\overset{*}{t} < 0$ $\overset{*}{s} = 0$
A mixed strategy $(t > s > 0)$	$\overset{*}{t} = 0$ $\overset{*}{s} < 0$	$0 < \overset{*}{t} < t$ $\overset{*}{s} < 0$	$\overset{*}{t} < t$ $\overset{*}{s} = 0$
Uniform intervention $(t = s)$	$\overset{*}{t} = 0$ $\overset{*}{s} = 0$	$\overset{*}{t} = 0$ $\overset{*}{s} = 0$	$\overset{*}{t} = 0$ $\overset{*}{s} = 0$

and 7.10 respectively.) But the critical feature of the diagram is that $\overset{*}{t} \geq 0$ and $\overset{*}{s} \leq 0$ as the value of w varies. The policy makers can raise $\overset{*}{t}(\overset{*}{s})$ for a given value of w except where $w = 1(0)$, but raising $\overset{*}{t}(\overset{*}{s})$ will lower $(\overset{*}{s})\overset{*}{t}$ and $\overset{*}{t}(\overset{*}{s})$ is always lower than $t(s)$. Policy conflict is inevitable if the aim is to simultaneously import protect and export promote on an across-the-board basis.

The range of possible true protection structures that can arise under alternative trade regimes and substitution arrangements is summarised in Table 7.1. We turn now to operationalising the model and reporting on a number of empirical studies that employed this framework.

7.4 Empirical application of the model

The extent to which nominal protection interventions confer true protection to particular sectors are shown by the model to depend upon substitutional relationships between the sectors. These substitutional relationships can in principle be measured directly or indirectly.

Direct estimation

Equation 7.6 defines the shift or incidence parameter in terms of demand and supply price elasticities for non-tradeables (H) with respect to the prices of each basket of goods (H, X and M). It is, in principle at least, possible to estimate these elasticities directly using time series data. Clements (1980) for instance has estimated a small-scale general equilibrium model with the three sectors H, X and M for the US. Using annual data for the postwar period, the estimated structural form price elasticities were; $\hat{h}^D_M = 0.044$, $\hat{h}^S_M = -0.532$, $\hat{h}^S_H = -0.598$ and $\hat{h}^D_H = -0.054$. Entering these values into Equation 7.6 gives an estimate of the shift parameter of 0.88.[6] The information requirements of this type of approach are however fairly high, in particular for developing countries. Although general equilibrium models have been applied to some developing countries, their purpose and form have not been suitable for testing the present three-sector model. Instead all existing work on applying shift analysis to developing countries has relied on indirect estimation methods, which are less demanding in terms of data requirements.

Indirect estimation

Equation 7.5 expresses a relationship between changes in the prices of importables, exportables and non-tradeables. Rearranging Equation 7.5 gives us:

$$\hat{P}_H - \hat{P}_X = w(\hat{P}_M - \hat{P}_X) \tag{7.16}$$

Since the shift model analyses proportional changes in the price of one group of commodities relative to another, a possible estimating procedure is to transform equation 7.16 to a double logarithmic specification, viz,

$$\log\left[\frac{P_H}{P_X}\right] = a + b\log\left[\frac{P_M}{P_X}\right] + u \tag{7.17}$$

where u is the random error term and the estimated coefficient $\hat{b}$ provides an estimate of the shift parameter ($\hat{w}$). Thus we can indirectly estimate w from times series data on prices (P_H, P_X and P_M) only, using regression techniques. A comparison of a number of estimates of w derived from this type of estimation procedure are set out in Table 7.2. These are discussed in greater detail below, but see also Greenaway, 1988a. Although this indirect estimation procedure only requires information on output prices, there are a number of methodological problems to confront.

(1) Time period identification

Since the aim of the analysis is to capture the shifting effects associated with import protection, then one should select a time period associated with sustained import substitution measures (and preferably increases in the level of protection) and without other significant influences on the structure of relative prices. Thus the nature and extent of the time period are of relevance; too long a period increases the possibility of extraneous influences[7] and too short a period reduces sample size and the probability of fully capturing relative price adjustments. The selection of the time period should therefore be undertaken with care, but the problem of observational equivalence does not disappear. Estimates of a shift parameter derived from this indirect methodology that are consistent with the model (that is lie in the 0–1 range) do not constitute a direct test of the model; the same set of results could be consistent with some alternative adjustment process and with some alternative source of change in the price of importables. What is offered is an empirical application, not a test, of the incidence model.

(2) Sector identification

In theory it is straightforward to distinguish between different sectors of economic activity. In practice it is very much more difficult. It is not always obvious what should comprise the components of a price index for importables or exportables. In principle the price indices P_H, P_M and P_X should exhaust all productive activities in the economy. In practice one has usually to work with a sub-set of information. In principle, also, it is domestic prices of tradeables and non-tradeables that are required. In practice prices may be available only for traded goods (that is imports and exports). Thus in the case of the study on Mauritius by Greenaway and Milner (1986b) a price series was constructed from official consumer price data for importables ($\hat{P}_M$) on furniture, furnishings, household appliances, alcoholic drinks and cotton yarns, and non-tradeables ($\hat{P}_H$) on household operations, shoe repairs, medical care, entertainment and education. The selection of these categories was partly constrained by the prevailing construction of the consumer price index, but was also undertaken after careful consideration of the import, export and production characteristics of the Mauritian economy. Two separate series were constructed for exportables: one for 'non-traditional' exportables (comprising finished clothing as identified also from consumer price data) and one for 'traditional' exportables (comprising sugar and tea but identified from unit value, export data). This configuration of information was influenced therefore by the selectivity of the researchers themselves, but it was also significantly fashioned by data availability.

(3) Price index construction

Having decided on the components of a particular index, it is necessary to decide on whether the aggregrate sector indices should be weighted or not, and for what frequency (monthly, quarterly or annually) they should be measured. Although frequency selection is invariably data constrained, some caution is required; with annual data an adequate sample size may extend the time period unsatisfactorily, while with monthly data adjustments of relative prices to policy changes may well be incomplete within one time period. The frequency of data is therefore likely to fashion the modelling of lag structures. This will invariably be determined by reference to the data and not to theory, which tells us little about the expected length or structure of lags.

Similarly the weighting issue has not been resolved in a common manner. Some studies use weighted composite indices, other unweighted indices. The weights that should be used are determined by relative substitution effects. In practice it is weights in production or consumption that are likely to be available.

Shift parameter estimates

Incidence analysis is of relatively recent vintage, and as a result the number of empirical studies that apply the model to developing countries is as yet relatively small. Studies on Latin American and African economies have been published; Sjaastad (1980b, 1980c) applied the technique to Uruguay and Argentina, Diaz (1980) to El Salvador, Fendt (1981) to Brazil, Garcia (1981) to Columbia, Sjaastad and Clements (1981) to Chile, Greenaway and Milner (1986b) to Mauritius, Greenaway (1989) to the Ivory Coast, Oyejide (1986) to Nigeria, and Milner (1990a, 1992) to Cameroon and Madagascar. Table 7.2 provides a comparison of some of these studies and their results, applying the type of model set out in Equation 7.17.[8]

As can be seen from the table, the studies cover a range of data periods and sets. Nonetheless, there is a degree of consistency between the results and with *a priori* expectations:

- All the estimates of w lie within the range zero and unity. The empirical evidence is to this extent consistent with the model.
- The value of w varies between countries and types of exportables. Substitutional relationships which determine w in the model can be expected to vary between countries and between traditional and non-traditional exportables.
- The estimated (long term) parameters fall within the range of 0.42 to 0.95, with all bar one exceeding 0.5. Thus the model predicts, given

Table 7.2 Shift parameter estimates for some developing countries

Country	*Shift parameter* ($\hat{w}$)	*Short-run shift parameter* ($\hat{w}'$)	*Type of exportable*[1]	*Data*[2]	*Period*	*Study*
Mauritius	0.71	0.22	NT	M	1976–82	Greenaway & Milner (1986b)
Mauritius	0.86	–	T	Q	1976–82	Greenaway & Milner (1986b)
Cameroon	0.81	0.62	NT	Q	1976–87	Milner (1990a)
Cameroon	0.73	0.95	T	Q	1976–87	Milner (1990a)
Ivory Coast	0.55	–	NT	A	1960–84	Greenaway (1989)
Ivory Coast	0.69	–	T	A	1960–84	Greenaway (1989)
Nigeria	0.83	–	AX	A	1960–82	Oyejide (1986)
Nigeria	0.82	–	T	A	1960–82	Oyejide (1986)
Madagascar	0.69	0.39–0.50	NT	M	1974–84	Milner (1992)
Chile	0.55	–	T	M	1959–71	Sjaastad & Clements (1981)
Uruguay	0.57	0.51	T	M	1966–79	Sjaastad (1980b)
Argentina	0.42	–	T	A	1935–79	Sjaastad (1980c)
Colombia	0.95	–	T	M	1970–8	Garcia (1981)

Notes:
1. All (AX), traditional (T) or non-traditional (NT).
2. Annual (A), quarterly (Q) or monthly (M).

Equation 7.14, that in most cases over 75 per cent of import protection is shifted to the export sector. In the case of Colombia (for traditional exportables) the estimated parameter comes close to unity (0.95), suggesting that protection is nearly shifted in its entirety to become an implicit export tax.

- In those cases (Mauritius, Cameroon and the Ivory Coast) where there is an estimate for both traditional and non-traditional exportables, the estimates for non-traditionals are significantly lower for traditionals. This suggests that there is greater substitutability between exportables and non-tradeables when the former are non-traditional. This accords with prior expectations, since there are less likely to be sector-specific factors in the production of non-traditional exportables than in traditional exportables.

For a few of the studies a short-run shift parameter is also reported on in Table 7.2. This distinction can be drawn where a lagged dependent variable is included in the estimating equation, such that:

$$\log \left[\frac{P_H}{P_X}\right] = a + b \log \left[\frac{P_M}{P_X}\right] + c \log \left[\frac{P_H}{P_X}\right]_{t-1} + u \qquad (7.18)$$

Its inclusion is a rather ad hoc attempt to allow for slowness in the adjustment of relative prices to changes in the relative price of importables. The coefficient b is now an estimate of the short-run shift parameter, and in the long-run as both (P_H/P_X and lagged P_H/P_X tend towards each other and in equilibrium, the long-run shift parameter will be given by:

$$w = \frac{\hat{b}}{1 - \hat{c}} \qquad (7.19)$$

where $\hat{b}$ and $\hat{c}$ are the estimated coefficients in Equation 7.18. (Milner, 1992, employs cointegration techniques to examine the dynamic adjustment path of relative prices more formally.)

As Milner (1992) shows, it is possible for the short-run shift parameter to be less or greater than its long-run value, depending on the magnitude of the short-run demand and supply elasticities (see Equation 7.5). Where the adjustment lags are such that the price of non-tradeables or home goods adjusts slowly (upwards) to a rise in the price of importables then the short-run parameter will be lower than the long-run rate. In four of the five cases reported on in Table 7.2 this result is obtained, the exception being the result for traditional exports for Cameroon. There is evidence therefore that if substitutability arrangements remain stable the burden on exportables tends to increase over some adjustment period.

True protection estimates

As explained in Section 3 of this chapter, estimates of the shift parameter can be combined with information on nominal tariffs and subsidies to estimate true tariffs and subsidies (substitute $\hat{w}$, $\hat{t}$ and $\hat{s}$ values into Equation 7.15 and then substitute $\hat{t}$, $\hat{s}$ and $\hat{d}$ into Equations 7.9 and 7.10). Few of the studies cited earlier have undertaken this type of work, largely because comprehensive information on nominal protection (including the effects of non-tariff interventions) and subsidisation is often not available. Greenaway and Milner (1986b) offer some hypothetical calculations for true tariffs and subsidies for Mauritius using the estimated shift parameter, actual data on nominal tariffs and assumed or guesstimated values for nominal subsidies. Greenaway (1989) provides similar estimates for the Ivory Coast, but this time using actual estimates of nominal export subsidies. These results are shown in Table 7.3.

According to these figures, the true tariff on importables ranges from 11.1 to 14.8 per cent depending on the value of the shift parameter and the value of any nominal duties on exportables. Other things being equal, t^* will increase as w falls, and will increase as s falls. Thus if we compare row 1 and row 2 of Table 7.3, we find that t^* falls from 14.1 to 11.1 per cent. The lower shift parameter (0.55 rather than 0.69) should mean a higher true tariff since importable prices rise to a greater extent vis-à-vis non tradeables. This however is more than offset by the change in s from an export tax of 28 per cent to an export subsidy of 2 per cent. Comparing rows 2 and 3, where s is held constant but the shift parameter falls, we observe an increase in the true tariff. Note that for all cases the estimated true tariff is substantially less than the nominal tariff.

In the case of exportables the true subsidy appears to range from −7.1 to −31.5 per cent. In other words, in all three scenarios interventions appear to operate as an implicit export tax. The case where the implicit tax is at a maximum is that which pertains to traditional exportables. This follows in part from the relatively high shift parameter and in part from the presence of explicit export taxes on these commodities. For non-traditional exportables the rates appear to be −7.1 per cent and −9.3 per cent depending on the value of the shift parameter. In other words, a positive export subsidy of 2 per cent is insufficient to offset the 'disprotection' from a 20 per cent import tariff and an *implicit* export tax still results.

7.5 Uses and implications of the analysis

Much of the analysis of industrial and commercial policy in developing countries until recent years has been founded predominantly on partial equilibrium analysis. Shift analysis should not be seen as a substitute for such partial analysis but rather as a complement to those techniques.

Table 7.3 Estimates of true tariffs and true subsidies for the Ivory Coast

	Nominal tariff on importables[1] *(%)*	*Nominal subsidy on exportables*[1] *(%)*	*Shift parameter*	t^* *(%)*	s^* *(%)*
1. Traditional exportables	20	–28	0.69	14.1	–31.5
2. Non-traditional exportables (annual data)	20	2	0.55	11.1	–9.3
3. Non-traditional exportables (monthly data)	20	2	0.34	14.8	–7.1

Source: Greenaway (1989).

Note:
1. Estimates taken from Monson (1981).

Although partial equilibrium analysis of effective protection, tariff equivalents and so on provides a great deal of detailed information relating to intervention in particular processes, product ranges and so on they are less robust as indicators of intersector allocation effects. In contrast shift analysis (which, as we have seen, is less data-intensive) permits one to focus explicitly on the relative price effects of interventions across broad sectors of economic activity. This ability of the technique to focus on ex-post general equilibrium effects has a number of important implications for policy evaluation and formulation:

- Protection or promotion are relative concepts. The technique permits one to make explicit the relative price effects of invisible as well as visible interventions. For example, as long as quantitative restrictions have relative price effects these will influence the value of the estimated shift parameter. Without having to undertake the very demanding (and resource-intensive) exercise of estimating individual tariff equivalents of quotas, one can gain some guidance as to their sectoral relative price effects (along with tariffs) through the shift coefficient.
- Through the medium of the true tariff and true subsidy concepts one can establish the true protection given to a particular sector. As long as separate incentives are given to different sectors, true protection will be less than apparent or (nominal) protection. The authorities can determine the structure of nominal protection, but the true effects are endogenously determined by the substitution arrangements specific to the economy.
- The technique allows one to make explicit the cancelling, or offsetting nature, of many interventions. Since most economies tend to pursue simultaneously policies of import protection and export promotion, this ability to identify policy conflict is an important feature of the methodology.
- Leading on from the above, the technique emphasises the need to design consistent policies in order to meet a given strategic objective – whether this be import protection or export promotion.
- By focusing on relative prices across sectors, one can infer something about relative investment incentives across sectors. Non-traditional exports may for instance fail to grow very rapidly, despite apparently generous incentives, because in relative terms there remains an anti-export bias.
- The analysis suggests that if the overall objective is export promotion, then one of the most direct routes to this goal may be simply to alter relative incentives through import liberalisation.

7.6 Concluding comments

This chapter has investigated the principles of incidence analysis and its implications for relative or true protection across sectors and within a general equilibrium framework. It has shown how the technique can be used to complement more traditional tools of commercial policy evaluation in developing countries. In part it can be used to comment upon the true intersectoral resource pulls induced by the (broad) nominal structure of protection or intervention. The approach clearly has considerable potential in highlighting conflict or inconsistencies between the actual and intended effects of policy. The principal output of the model is the shift parameter. This index is dependent upon the substitutional relationships in the economy – information which could only otherwise be obtained from more sophisticated computable general equilibrium models that are much more demanding in terms of data requirements than the incidence model. It is to a consideration of such alternative, general equilibrium models that we now turn.

CHAPTER 8

Computable General Equilibrium Modelling

8.1 Introduction

The rationale for general as opposed to partial equilibrium analytical techniques has been identified in the discussion in Chapter 7. The purpose of other general equilibrium models discussed there was rather specific and therefore restrictive assumptions allowed us to avoid much elaboration of the underlying structure of the economy. There is however a body of research, applied or computable general equilibrium analysis, that has the explicit aim of representing the (general equilibrium) structure of an economy. The aim is to convert Walrasian principles into realistic and operational models of actual economies by specifying production and demand parameters and using data that relates to the particular economy involved. Once operationalised these models can be used to identify the effects of existing policies and evaluate the medium- to long-term implications of policy reforms on an economy-wide basis.

The use of CGE models for policy analysis has become widespread in both developed and developing countries. In the case of developing countries however such models have been applied to a wider range of issues. This partly reflects the greater interest in wide-ranging policy or development strategy reform in developing countries. It can also be explained by the data-constraints on the use of macroeconometric models (which is dependent on reliable time series data for sufficient time periods) in the case of many developing countries. Our concern here is with the use of CGE modelling for trade and industrial policy analysis. We will focus specifically on illustrations of such applications in Chapter 9. It will be necessary first, however, to understand the principles that underpin the analysis and be aware of the process by which a model is constructed in practice. This chapter will seek to provide that groundwork. It is organised as follows. We begin in Section 8.2 with a brief outline of the origins and development of applied general equilibrium modelling. In Section 8.3 the principles of general equilibrium modelling are briefly developed. Section 8.4 then provides a systematic explanation of how to implement applied general equilibrium modelling, how to choose the model and specific functional forms, how to select parameter values and how to calibrate, solve and use the model. This is followed in Section 8.5 with a demonstration of the characteristics of a specific CGE model for a developing country. Finally, section 8.6 provides some conclusions.

8.2 Origins and development of CGE modelling

An individual market is in equilibrium when the quantity of the particular good demanded is equal to the quantity supplied. General equilibrium analysis deals explicitly with the interrelationships between different markets and different sectors of an economy. If there are c commodity markets and f factor markets there will be $c + f = n$ markets and $n - 1$ equilibrium prices to be determined if all markets are to be in equilibrium; when they are all in equilibrium the economy will be in a state of general equilibrium. Walras' Law states that for a given set of prices the sum of the excess demands over all markets must be equal to zero. In other words, if one market has positive excess demand, some others must have excess supply; and if all but one are in balance, so is that one. If all economic agents are satisfying their budget constraints and n − 1 markets are in equilibrium, then the nth market will also be cleared. These concepts about a Walrasian general equilibrium system were formalised and elaborated on in the 1950s by economists such as Arrow and Debreu (1954). In the Arrow–Debreu model[1] there is a specified number of consumers, each of which has an initial endowment of commodities and a given set of preferences. Thus there are market demand functions for each commodity, which are the sum of each individual's demand. These market demands for commodities are determined by all prices; the functions are well-behaved and satisfy Walras' Law, that is the total value of consumers' expenditures equals consumer incomes. On the production side constant returns to scale and profit-maximisation are assumed in order to generate the competitive solution. Given these model characteristics it is relative, not absolute, prices that are of significance. General equilibrium is characterised by a set of (relative) prices and pattern of production that clears the market for each commodity.

Two-sector general equilibrium models were popularised and applied to a range of analytical issues during the 1950s and 1960s. In international trade theory, work was pioneered for example by Meade and Johnson on the effect of policy distortions (for example tariffs) to trade. Most of the subsequent applied models are the numerical counterparts of those earlier theoretical models, though it must be recognised that the subsequent computational models also extend Leontief's work on Walrasian models based on fixed input–output coefficients. By including substitution possibilities in both production and consumption the later work was likely to be more useful in analysing medium- to long-term resource allocation issues. Examples of some of this early applied work are Johansen (1960), who formulated a multi-sector model to analyse resource allocation and policy issues in Norway, and Harberger (1962) who investigated tax policy issues with a two-sector general equilibrium model.

Numerical calculations of the effects of trade policy were rather limited while these early developments in general equilibrium trade theory and in applied general equilibrium modelling were taking place. A number of numerical studies of the effects of European integration were undertaken in the later 1950s (for example Scitovsky, 1958 and Johnson, 1958). But, despite calls for such work from trade theorists, these attempts at numerical trade modelling did not induce similar activity on a wider scale. It was not until the work by Scarf (1967) and Scarf and Hansen (1973) – which provided an ingenuous computation approach to the determination of equilibrium in a Walrasian system – that applied work of this nature on trade was widely undertaken. Miller and Spencer (1971 and subsequently published in 1977) for instance applied Scarf's computational methods to an assessment of the impact of UK entry into the EC. Subsequent CGE trade models have applied further algorithms for numerical solution and have developed the capacity to investigate a wide range of trade policy issues – from unilateral trade policy interventions (tariffs, quotas, and so on) to multilateral trade negotiations.

CGE models have been used extensively since the early 1980s to analyse a range of medium- to long-term policy issues in developing countries. Foreign exchange has considerable scarcity value in most developing countries, and as a result trade policy has occupied a central role in the majority of these applications. The extent to which the scarcity value of foreign exchange is influenced by policy change cannot be easily estimated with partial equilibrium tools of analysis. But even if the purpose of a developing country CGE model is not specifically to model trade policy impacts, the way that the foreign trade sector is modelled is likely to be important. The sensitivity of domestic resource allocation in highly open developing countries again means that general rather than partial equilibrium analysis is required to capture this interdependency.

8.3 General equilibrium models: some basic principles

Before turning to the examination of how general equilibrium models have been applied to the analysis of trade policy in general and to trade policy in developing countries in particular, we need to set out some of the basic principles involved.

The closed economy

Let us first consider a possible general equilibrium system for a simple, two-sector economy. The general equilibrium model must specify the demand and supply relations and the equilibrium condition for each market and must also specify the income or budget constraint on each agent in the economy. Here we assume two single-product (produced in quantities Q_A and Q_B) firms, each using only homogenous capital (K) and labour (L) of fixed or given endowments to the economy, the two products being owned by a single household. In this model therefore there are three economic agents: two firms and one consumer.

The consumer is assumed to maximise utility from the consumption of the two goods (C_A and C_B), subject to the constraint that total expenditure ($P_AC_A + P_BC_B$) equals the consumer's income (Y) (where P_i is the price of good i). If the utility function is well behaved, then the solution to the constrained optimisation problem produces the following demand or expenditure relationships:

$$C_A = C_A\,(P_A, P_B, Y) \tag{8.1}$$

$$C_B = C_B\,(P_A, P_B, Y) \tag{8.2}$$

The production side of the model is based on a two-stage optimisation procedure. Given a production function in general terms for each good or firm (i), that is $Q_i = Q_i(K_iL_i)$, the costs of production will be determined by the factor prices (r and w for capital and labour respectively). This is found by identifying the least-cost means of producing each (given) output level, subject to the technological or production function constraint. The firms' short-run supply functions are then determined by the second stage of the optimisation procedure, namely profit maximisation by each firm where the firm's revenue is a function of price (P_i) and costs are a function of factor prices (r and w). In general terms therefore:

$$Q_A = Q_A\,(P_A, w, r) \tag{8.3}$$

$$Q_B = Q_B\,(P_B, w, r) \tag{8.4}$$

For equilibrium in the product markets for A and B we must add the market clearing conditions:

$$C_A = Q_A \tag{8.5}$$

$$C_B = Q_B \tag{8.6}$$

Next we need to consider the factor markets. Given the profit-maximising levels of output, each firm will seek to employ the corresponding cost-minimising factor levels. Therefore the factor demand functions are:

$$K_A = K_A\,(Q_A, w, r) \tag{8.7}$$

$$K_B = K_B\,(Q_B, w, r) \tag{8.8}$$

$$L_A = L_A\,(Q_A, w, r) \tag{8.9}$$

$$L_B = L_B\,(Q_B, w, r) \tag{8.10}$$

For simplicity let us assume that factor supplies are exogenously given ($\bar{K}$, $\bar{L}$) rather than endogenously determined. Therefore the market clearing conditions for the factor markets are:

$$K_A + K_B = \bar{K} \tag{8.11}$$

$$L_A + L_B = \bar{L} \tag{8.12}$$

In order to complete the general equilibrium system we need to incorporate the household and firm income equations. For the firms their income or profits (π) is the difference between sales revenue and factor payments, that is:

$$\pi_A = P_A Q_A - wL_A - rK_A \tag{8.13}$$

$$\pi_B = P_B Q_B - wL_B - rK_B \tag{8.14}$$

Given that in this simple economy the single household supplies all factor services, then all income (Y) accrues to it, namely:

$$Y = w(L_A + L_B) + r(K_A + K_B) + \pi_A + \pi_B \tag{8.15}$$

The general equilibrium model for this simple closed economy is complete: there are 15 equations, 15 endogenous variables (Y, π_A, π_B, w, r, P_A, P_B, L_A, L_B, K_A, K_B, Q_A, Q_B, C_A, C_B) and two exogenous variables ($\bar{K}$, $\bar{L}$). Given appropriate functional forms for the (product and factor) demand and supply functions, it is possible to solve for all the equilibrium quantities produced and consumed in the product and factor markets and for relative product (P_A/P_B) and factor (w/r) prices. Similarly it can be solved for changes in the value of an exogenous variable. Herein lies the benefits of a general equilibrium methodology, since it allows the all-important interrelationships between markets to be traced through. If the labour endowment ($\bar{L}$) for example increases it directly alters the labour market equilibrium price ($\overset{*}{w}$). But a new value for $\overset{*}{w}$ will affect other relationships in the system: factor demands, output levels of the two goods, and consumer incomes and therefore expenditures on the two goods. Thus equilibrium relative prices will have to adjust to reflect the new patterns of demand and supply.

Note that we establish the structure of relative, not absolute, prices from a general equilibrium model, since real relationships in the model are affected by relative prices (that is if all prices increase in the same proportion relative prices arc unaltered, as are the structure of incentives to produce and consume particular commodities). Solving the model to identify the structure of equilibrium relative prices requires therefore that one price is arbitrarily set equal to unity; the commodity with a unitary price is the 'numeraire' of the system against which the prices of all other commodities are defined.

The open economy

The scope for international trade provides additional choices for consumers and producers: imports (M) are an alternative source of supply for the home consumer and exports (X) are an additional source of demand for the domestic producer. Compare Figure 8.1a with Figure 8.1b: the general equilibrium solution for a closed economy with that for an open economy. PP is the transformation curve, that is the alternative mixes of maximum levels of production of each good given the economy's factor endowments. In the absence of trade, consumption is constrained by these production possibilities. Maximisation of consumer's utility, represented by indifference curve (U_1) is at E_1, where the marginal rates of transformation and consumer substitution equal the domestic relative price ratio P_A/P_B (shown by the slope of the line dd). With the opening of trade the country has the option of purchasing and selling goods at world relative prices rather than (pre-trade) domestic prices. In Figure 8.1b we represent the (relative) world prices by the slope of (terms of trade) line TT. Since $dd \neq TT$ the domestic consumer has the ability to gain from trade; as P_A/P_B in this case rises then the consumer switches demand for good B from home towards foreign-produced goods, that is $M = C_B - Q_B$, and domestic resources are switched towards producing relatively more of good A (as the production equilibrium shifts from E_1 to F) and selling some of this production abroad, that is $X = Q_A - C_A$ (as the consumption equilibrium shifts from E_1 to a higher utility level [U_2] at E_2). The marginal rates of transformation and substitution, which previously reflected the domestic pre-trade price ratio, now reflect the world price ratio.

The above analysis implicitly incorporates the 'small country' assumption, namely that the country is a price-taker that does not effect world (w) prices through its trading activities. Thus we can treat world prices (Pw_A and Pw_B) as exogenous variables and (assuming no distortions) link world

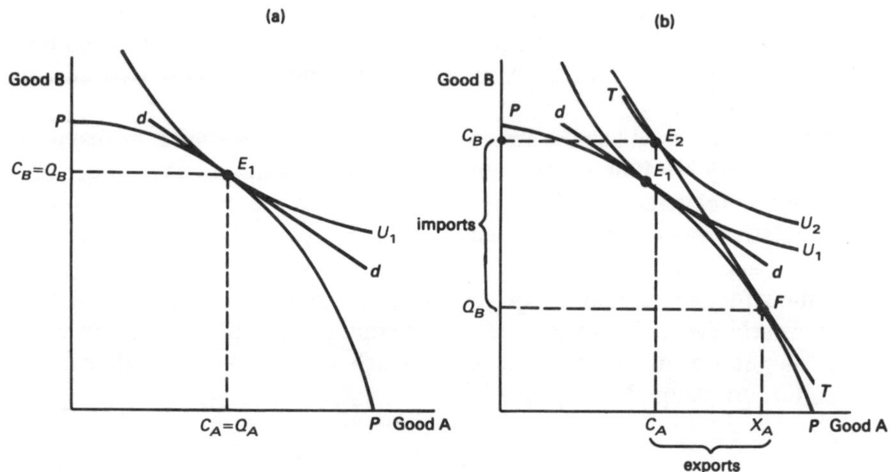

Figure 8.1 Two-sector general equilibrium with and without trade

and domestic prices directly through the exchange rate (e), for example $P_i = e\bar{P}_{wi}$. But e is an endogenous variable, that is the price of one unit of foreign purchasing power in terms of some numeraire, such as a good or factor price. Alternatively e can be normalised at unity and domestic prices are set at the price of traded goods. Besides the revised market-clearing conditions for the now-traded products and these revised price equations (which need to be incorporated with the type of closed economy relationships discussed above), it is also necessary to incorporate an overall balance of payments or foreign exchange constraint for the economy. If capital flows are excluded this requires that total expenditure on imports (Pw_BM) equals total export earnings (Pw_AX).

A two-sector open economy, general equilibrium model is illustrated in Table 8.1. Note that it embodies a constant returns to scale assumption. This means that the supply equations (Equations 8.3 and 8.4) have to be replaced by unit price equations (Equations 3 and 4 in the table, where k_i and l_i are the factor requirements per unit of output). Note also the assumptions of constant returns and given world prices ($\bar{P}w_i$) mean that this is a fixed- not flexi-price model. By normalising the exchange rate to unity, the domestic prices (P_A, P_B) are fixed by Equations 18 and 19. This in turn means that the factor prices are also fixed (Equations 3 and 4 in Table 8.1). Thus market clearing (product and factor) in this model will only come about through quantity, rather than price, adjustment. The general equilibrium needs to be numerically solved by identifying the conditions for factor market clearing. Fulfilment of these conditions will then determine the full employment output levels (Q_A, Q_B); general equilibrium being when these output levels are equal to total (domestic and foreign) demand for these final goods. Given the specific examples of

Table 8.1 A two-sector open economy, general equilibrium model

Description		*The model*	*Numerical example*
Commodity	(1)	$C_A = C_A(P_A, P_B, Y)$	$C_A = Y(2P_A)^{-1}$
Expenditures	(2)	$C_B = C_B(P_A, P_B, Y)$	$C_B = Y(2P_B)^{-1}$
Commodity	(3)	$P_A = rk_A + wl_A$	
Unit prices	(4)	$P_B = rk_B + wl_B$	
Product market	(5)	$X = Q_A - C_A$	
Clearing conditions	(6)	$M = C_B - Q_B$	
	(7)	$k_A = k_A(r, w)$	$k_A = (w/3r)^{3/4}$
	(8)	$K_A = k_A Q_A$	
	(9)	$k_B = k_B(r, w)$	$k_B = (w/r)^{1/2}$
Factor	(10)	$K_B = k_B Q_B$	
Demands	(11)	$l_A = l_A(r, w)$	$l_A = (3r/w)^{1/4}$
	(12)	$L_A = l_A Q_A$	
	(13)	$l_B = l(r, w)$	$l_B = (r/w)^{1/2}$
	(14)	$L_B = l_B Q_B$	
Factor market	(15)	$K_A + K_B = \bar{K}$	
Clearing conditions	(16)	$L_A + L_B = \bar{L}$	
Consumer's income	(17)	$Y = r\bar{K} + w\bar{L}$	
Price equations	(18)	$P_A = e\bar{P}w_A$	
	(19)	$P_B = e\bar{P}w_B$	
Foreign exchange	(20)	$P_{WA}X - P_{WB}M = 0$	

20 Endogenous variables are: $C_A, C_B, Q_A, Q_B, X, M, K_A, K_B, L_A, L_B, k_A, k_B, l_A, l_B, P_A, P_B, w, r, e, Y$

4 Exogenous variables are: $\bar{K}, \bar{L}, \bar{P}_{WA}, \bar{P}_{WB}$

Source: Dinwiddy and Teal (1988), Tables 5.1 and 5.2.

Cobb–Douglas functions (utility and production) represented in the demand or expenditure, and factor demand equations in the example in Table 8.1, it is possible to write a programme to solve the model (for particular values for world prices). (For details of the structure of the programme and an illustrative solution to the model in Table 8.1 see Dinwiddy and Teal, 1988, pp. 74–5.)

8.4 Applying general equilibrium analysis

A range of problems are encountered in designing and using CGE models. What type of model structure is required for the particular purpose? For that general structure, how are functional forms and parameter values to be chosen? How is the model to be solved? How is the calibrated model to be used to evaluate policy change? Let us consider these questions in turn.[2]

Model selection

The selection of a CGE model for trade policy analysis should be fashioned by the precise purpose of the model. The dimensions, that is the levels of aggregation and the degree of elaboration of particular market relationships and interrelationships, must inevitably involve judgement on the part of the modeller, since the model is an abstraction not an exact representation of reality. If the purpose is to examine current resource pulls between and within sectors associated with trade policies, then the model specification may well differ from one that is required to focus on the aggregate growth effects of trade policy change. Similarly model specification will vary according to the type of economy involved; for instance the degree of competition, the degree of input and factor substitutability, or the degree of substitutability in demand between imported and locally-produced goods will vary between economies as their production structures and development stages vary. The absence of a unique model form is of course a strength of CGE analysis: the ability to blend theory with actual market and policy conditions. However there is a danger, well recognised by most modellers, that model selection may to a large extent predetermine the (qualitative) conclusions of the analysis. But this is an inevitable danger resulting from the need for judgement. As with all good applied economic analysis, the robustness of the results/conclusions needs to be challenged by examining critically the assumptions underpinning the model.

We will return to some specific issues of model selection shortly. It is worth pointing out however that most of the models that have been developed so far have a similar form: static, two factors (capital and labour with sometimes some disaggregation of labour by skill) and a limited number of goods, with interindustry transactions incorporated through fixed (sometimes flexible) input–output matrices. There are a number of reasons for this similarity. Data availability is an important factor. For instance national accounts typically identify wages and profits (or operating surpluses). This encourages the use of a model with labour and capital inputs. Computational convenience is also a consideration. In the case of the choice of production technologies for instance, the specification could involve constant or increasing returns to scale. Some form of decreasing costs may seem appropriate for large ranges of industrial and manufacturing activity. But it has to be recognised that a constant returns assumption tends to make it easier to find an equilibrium concept upon which to base the analysis. Finally, it must also be recognised that many of the applied policy issues investigated quantitatively with CGE models are ones that have been examined qualitatively on previous occasions within a theoretical general equilibrium framework. Thus the legacy from trade theory of the two-sector–two-factor model is one that has had a strong influence on applied work.

An important issue in model specification is the treatment in the external sector. The traditional theoretical model of the dependent developing economy is one in which foreign prices are given, and as a result the terms of trade are treated as given, and domestically produced, tradeable goods are perfect substitutes for foreign goods. This assumption is applied in some CGE models for the external sector as a whole, or at least for primary products that are likely to be highly homogeneous. The implication of this specification is that changes in foreign prices, or changes in the domestic currency price of foreign goods induced by exchange rate or trade policy changes, are fully passed through to the prices of competing domestic goods. The realism of this assumption is increasingly questioned, and many CGE models now incorporate the alternative assumption that foreign and competing domestic goods are imperfect substitutes in use. This is consistent with empirical evidence at this disaggregated level that 'pass through' of exchange rate changes to domestic price is small.[3] It is consistent with the observed importance of simultaneous importing and exporting of similar goods by the same country; this being observed at the disaggregated commodity level and in the trade of developing countries. A common way of accommodating this specification of intercountry substitutability is to use the so-called Armington formulation, which treats similar products produced in different countries as different goods. Note that this specification can also be used on both the import and export side (with domestically produced goods for export sale being less than perfectly substitutable for domestically produced goods for sale on the domestic market) if heterogeneity is an appropriate assumption. Use of this formulation has the added advantage of allowing us to characterise sectors in terms of the degree of tradeability of the goods they produce. The elasticity (μ) of the prices of domestically produced goods with respect to change in the domestic currency price of imports (μ_m) and export (μ_x) will depend upon the model specification, as follows:

$$\mu = f(\theta, \Omega, \sigma, \varepsilon) \tag{8.16}$$

where θ is the share of traded goods in total production, Ω is the elasticity of transformation, ε is the elasticity of supply and σ is the elasticity of substitution.

When σ and Ω tend towards infinity then the domestic price system loses its independence from foreign prices and we have the traditional price-taker model (that is $\mu_m = \mu_x = 1$ and there is full 'pass-through'). Where $\mu < 1$ that is there is imperfect substitutability, then sectors can be classified in terms of tradeability as follows:

- Nontradeables have low import (θ_m) and export shares.
- Exportables have low import and high export shares.
- Importables have high import and low export shares, and are complementary where ($\sigma < \varepsilon$) and substitutes where ($\sigma > \varepsilon$).

Although the imperfect substitution assumption increases the parameter requirements, it does increase substantially the potential richness and realism of any policy simulations. Furthermore the approach is capable of dealing empirically with the theoretical conflicts that exist in the development literature between 'neo-classicists', who represent developing countries as having high elasticities, and 'structuralists', who maintain that they are characterised by low elasticities.

Some of the other issues in model selection that merit mention are the net savings–capital stock relationships and the treatment of investment. Investment is usually represented as reflecting household and corporate saving decisions, which are based on constant expenditure shares in static models or on intertemporal utility maximisation in genuine dynamic formulations. As a 'quasi-dynamic' approach, static equilibrium models are sometimes sequenced or linked through time to reflect changes in any economy's capital due to net savings (even if the constant expenditure share assumption is used to determine net savings at each point in time), that is a series of single period/static equilibria are linked through savings decisions that change the capital stock through time. Such a treatment of investment, like other aspects of the growth process (for example technical change which tends to be ignored or treated as an exogenous variable), is crude. This is unfortunate since a significant element of the effects of trade and trade policy may well be about how they affect investment and the pace of technical change. Here is an example of an area where computational difficulties are compounded by limited theoretical elaboration and consensus.

Choice of functional form

The choice of utility function (from which demand relationships derive) and of production functions in applied general equilibrium analysis is fashioned by the need to be theoretically consistent and analytically tractable. On the one hand the functions need to satisfy the restrictions required of a general equilibrium model, for example market clearing and zero abnormal profits in all markets. On the other hand the functions need to generate expenditure and production patterns that can be evaluated easily by any set of prices that are judged as a potential equilibrium set. Convenience, in particular in incorporating key parameters such as income and price elasticities, rather than appropriateness tends therefore to dominate the choice of functional form. 'Convenient' functional forms such as the Cobb–Douglas or constant elasticity of substitution (CES) tended to be used.

This dilemma facing the applied modeller can be illustrated for the demand side of a model. A Cobb–Douglas utility function (of the general form for the two-good case $U = C_1^{\alpha} C_2^{\beta}$) generates demand functions which impose the restrictions of zero cross-price elasticities and unit income and (uncompensated) own-price elasticities. The model is tractable but these restrictions are implausible. With the CES utility function (of the general form $U = [a_1C_1^{-\beta} + a_2C_2^{-\beta}]^{-1/\beta}$ where $\sigma = 1/[1 + \beta]$) unit own-price elasticities no longer apply, but all commodities now have the same (compensated) own-price elasticities (if the expenditure shares are small). Increasing the plausibility or acceptability of the model will be at the expense of greater complexity in the structure of the model.

CES functions tend also to be used on the production side. This allows for substitution between primary factors (usually capital and labour). The intermediate input relationships can be modelled with either fixed or flexible coefficients. One specification employed sometimes is to use fixed coefficients in terms of composite goods, but to allow substitution between the elements of the composite good. Thus a fixed cloth requirement per garment may be required for example, but a CES function can be used to allow substitution between imported and domestically produced cloth.

Benchmark data and construction of a SAM

The first step towards constructing a numerical model (see Chart 8.1) involves the construction of a benchmark data set from national income and other major data sources on the technological and trade characteristics of the economy. Typically data for a single and representative year is employed, but averaging over a period is a possibility. Frequently the information from different official sources is not consistent – for example household income from employment does not match the payments to labour by firms. The accuracy of some data is accepted and other data is adjusted in order to produce a consistent benchmark data set compatible with the equilibrium conditions the model is seeking to represent. This benchmark data set is often referred to as the (consistent) social accounting matrix (SAM). An illustration (one sector version) of a SAM for Turkey used in the CGE model constructed by Grais, de Melo and Urata (1986) is set out in Table 8.2. This SAM has 24 accounts; factors of production (accounts of rows 1–3), current accounts of institutions (4–9), capital account (10), rest of the world (11), production activities (12–13) and commodities (14–24). It indicates that the representative household receives payments from factors of production and from the rest of the world (in the form of workers' remittances), and it uses its income on consumption, savings and income taxes. Household consumption is split into committed and discretionary components. Note that government tax revenues (row 8) come from the taxation (that is tariffs) on imports (columns 18, 21 and 24) and on households (column 4) and production (column 13). (The SAM indicates the composition of imports in the base year, classifying imports by end use.) It should be evident to the reader that this SAM for

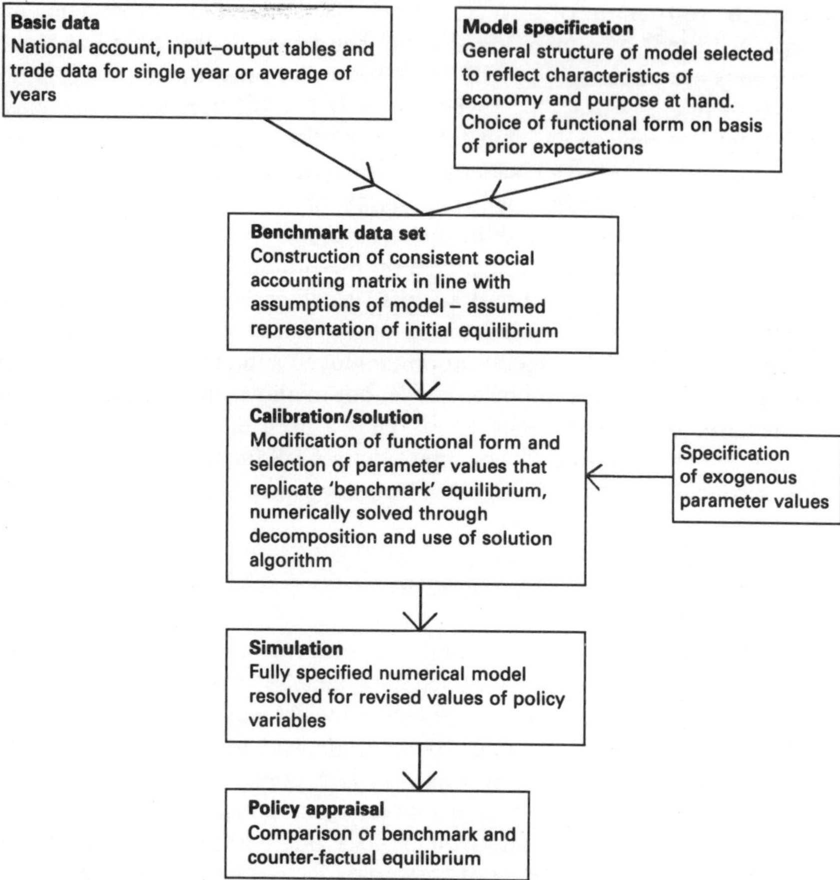

Chart 8.1 Calibration and simulation procedures with CGE models

Turkey, like all consistent ones, has the same number of rows and columns, respectively representing receipts and expenditures associated with each type of account. Row totals have to equal corresponding column totals in line with accounting requirements. But the construction of a SAM will also reflect the features, that is assumptions, of the model selected for the particular economy and circumstances. Thus in this particular example the SAM is also constructed according to the transactions value approach; only transactions with the same valuation appear in a given row. This allows the modeller(s) to incorporate his/her judgement about different assumptions regarding such considerations as factor mobility or the nature of policy influences. For example, in Table 8.2 labour is assumed to be perfectly mobile across all sectors. One uniform factor price applies therefore and one account only is needed in the SAM. If there were factor immobility resulting from sector specificity of that factor, then one needs as many accounts for that factor as there are separate or distinct factor prices.

Table 8.2 Social accounting matrix for Turkey (mm. th.), 1978

		1	2	3	4	5	6	7	8	9	10	11	12	13	14	15	16	17	18	19	20	21	22	23	24	25
Factors of production																										
Labour	1												597													597
Capital	2												590													590
Consolidated capital	3		590																							590
Household																										
Revenue	4	597		590								22						7								1216
Total income	5				999																					999
Total expenditure	6					845																				845
Discretionary expenditure	7						419																			419
Government																										
Revenue	8				217									47					8			24			8	304
Expenditure	9								169																	169
Capital account	10					154			135			24														313
Rest of the world	11																		25			71			25	121
Activities																										
Value added	12													1187												1187
Output	13														2053	75										2128
Domestic supply	14																805			733	66			449		2053
Exports	15											75														75
Commodities																										
Consumption																										
Domestic	16						443	362																		805
Rationed imports	17						−17	57																		40
Imports	18																	33								33
Intermediates																										
Domestic	19																						733			733
Rationed imports	20																						161			161
Imports	21																									95
Composite	22													894							95					894
Others																										
Domestic	23									165	284															449
Imports	24									4	29															33
Total	25	597	590	590	1216	999	845	419	304	169	313	121	1187	2128	2053	75	805	40	33	733	161	95	894	449	33	

Parameter values, calibration and solution

Parameter values for the selected functional forms are invariably crucial in determining the results of simulation exercises with CGE models. These parameter values are either generated 'exogenously' or through 'calibration' of the numerical model.

Calibration involves fitting the model to the benchmark data set. This may involve some modification of functional form, but since no statistical test of model specification is involved it more typically involves choosing and adjusting the parameters of the model 'endogenously' so that (or until) the model can reproduce what is to be taken to be the benchmark equilibrium. Herein lies the potential weakness of such a deterministic approach. The assumption of the equilibrium representation by the benchmark data may not be justified, and given that the stochastic elements of economic processes are excluded confidence in the robustness of policy simulations with the model are thereby reduced. Nevertheless there are strong practical grounds for adopting the 'calibration' approach. Given the dimensions of such models it would be difficult in practice to achieve the richness in specification that econometric estimation would offer. In order to estimate simultaneously all model parameters with time series statistical methods would require long runs of time series of observations for large numbers of variables. This is likely to be severely data-constrained in developing countries. Although partitioning models into blocks of relationships (for example into expenditure and production sub-models) is one way of reducing the number restrictions on identification and therefore on the number of data observations required for econometric estimation on a system basis, the coverage of time series data may still be inadequate and the partitioning is likely to conflict with some of the general equilibrium restrictions that can be satisfied via calibration.

Not all parameter values are necessarily 'endogenously' determined through calibration however. The benchmark data typically do not identify a unique set of parameter values. In any case with some functional forms it is necessary to prespecify certain key parameter values. With the widely employed CES functional form, for instance, exogenously or prespecified substitution elasticities are required; the curvature of indifference curves and isoquants cannot be inferred from the single observation on price and quantity recorded in the benchmark data. Other elasticities that are likely to need to be prespecified are the income elasticity for consumer goods, elasticity of substitution in production between factors and between (domestic and imported) intermediate inputs, and the elasticity of transformation between domestic and exported goods. Values for such elasticities are usually specified on the basis of other research. This could involve original work by the modellers themselves, but more typically they are taken from other models or earlier empirical studies not related to the study at hand. This places considerable reliance upon a careful survey of the existing literature and upon judgement about which study estimates (or guesstimates) should be 'borrowed' from. Careful judgement is required because elasticity values from different studies may be contradictory; this is not altogether surprising when they come from a range of countries, time periods and levels of aggregation. The transferability of 'exogenous' elasticity estimates, where information is not sparse, to the particular modelling exercise involved is therefore an important issue because it may well be crucial in fashioning the results of subsequent simulations. The modeller must consider carefully the comparability of the 'borrowed' source with the specific conditions being modelled.

Thus final solution of the model – a fully specified numerical model – is the outcome of an iterative procedure. The basic structure of the model (behavioural equations and functional specification) are combined with the information from the SAM. (Any partitioning of the model may be undertaken as necessary or convenient for solution purposes.) A solution algorithm is designed to solve for the particular model.[4] The increasing sophistication in computer software means that it is data availability rather than solution techniques that constrain this type of applied modelling. But judgement of the modeller is required to know whether the failure of the model to converge towards the benchmark equilibrium is a product of the solution method or of the functional forms and specific parameter values adopted. Where it is the latter some recalibration may be required in order to produce convergence towards a final numerical solution.

Policy simulation and appraisal

The numerical model can be used to examine a wide range of policy issues. By specifying new values for each policy instrument separately, or for a range of instruments simultaneously, it is possible to resolve the model to identify a new 'counter-factual equilibrium'. It is possible therefore to evaluate alternative reform packages or to compare specific reforms of alternative magnitudes by comparing the counter-factual and benchmark equilibrium. Comparison of alternative equilibrium outcomes means that the policy appraisal is medium to long term in nature. Although the model structure is not designed to capture the rich detail of dynamic adjustment paths, the fact that the model is solved in an iterative manner allows the nature of the convergence towards the new equilibrium to be plotted.

In the case of trade models of developing countries a CGE model can be used to comment on a wide range of issues of interest to the policy maker. For instance, changes in the use of factors of production across sectors, changes in the levels and composition of imports and exports, and changes in trade and other tax revenue (if unconstrained by the model) are likely to be important in policy evaluation. This type of positive information will be a direct 'output' of each, new numerical solution. Its richness (that is degree of disaggregation) will depend on the dimensions of the basic model structure.

In order to make normative assessments of policy, that is to comment on the desirability or ranking of alternative equilibria associated with alternative policy values, it is necessary to measure economic welfare. The most commonly-used measures are the Hicksian compensating (CV) or equivalent variations (EV); the former starts from the new equilibrium and asks how much income needs to be added or subtracted to return consumers to their original utility level; the latter starts from the original equilibrium and measures the change required to reach the new utility level. (For a welfare-raising change CV is negative and EV is positive.) Where the model provides detailed information on CVs or EVs (that is gainers and losers in utility terms), then the policy analyst may be interested in distributional effects, and it may not be necessary to aggregate individual welfare effects. Where net evaluations are required it is usual to aggregate CVs (or EVs) across households. There are obvious theoretical difficulties in interpreting the resulting net measure as an indicator of social welfare. Of course problems of distribution and aggregation are often abstracted from in applied trade models by assuming only one representative household or consumer. In this case aggregate efficiency and welfare effects of trade policy change are directly observable.

Having overviewed in general terms the nature of the process and problems involved in numerically applying general equilibrium analysis, let us now turn to an illustration of this in practice. We illustrate in the next section a CGE model that was developed to analyse foreign trade restrictions in a developing economy (Turkey for the year 1978).

8.5 A CGE model to analyse foreign trade restrictions illustrated

A tariff-quantitative restriction (TQR) model calibrated to 1978 Turkish data (see Table 8.2 discussed in Section 8.4 for the relevant social accounting matrix [SAM]) has been constructed by Grais, de Melo and Urata (1986). A brief overview of the model is provided in this section. (A full specification of the equations of the TQR model is contained in Appendix 8.1 of this chapter.)

The model

The broad features of the TQR model are summarised in Table 8.3. A number of the features of the model merit particular note.

First, distributional implications are minimised in a number of ways. The model assumes a single, representative consumer as the indicator of national welfare. Government expenditure is also fixed in real terms.

Second, given the emphasis on static (rather than dynamic) resource and welfare implications of trade restrictions, investment behaviour is modelled in a rudimentary manner; investment demand by sectors is in fixed proportions and capital inflows (in foreign currency) is fixed. However the adjustment to a new equilibrium (following policy adjustment) can be simulated where both capital specificity and capital mobility is assumed.

Third, the model allows for different demand behaviour by differing types of 'demanders'. For private consumption a demand system (a linear expenditure system) is specified; this allows for non-unitary income elasticities and cross-price substitution between imported and similar domestic goods. In contrast government and investment demand for different goods are assumed to be in fixed proportions (that is a Leontief-type assumption).

Fourth, the model retains the price-taker/small country assumption – infinite supply elasticities for unrestricted imports and infinite demand elasticities for exports – which is appropriate for a developing country. It does however allow for product differentiation, and does so for both imports and exports. In the case of the importables sector, imports and domestically produced goods are imperfect substitutes in end use. Domestic production is supplied for the domestic market and export sales according to a constant elasticity of transformation function (this is shown in the appendix by Equations 4(h) and 4(i) for the specification of composite prices and Equation 3a and 3b of the supply functions).

Fifth, a range of substitution possibilities in production are represented by Equations 1 and 2 of the appendix. There is no scope for substitution between primary and intermediate inputs in the aggregate production function. Value added is however a CES function of capital and labour. In the case of substitution between intermediate inputs there are mixed possibilities. There is a fixed intermediate input requirement across sectors, but from within a sector it is possible to substitute (via a CES function) between domestic and imported inputs.

Sixth, the representation of trade policy distortions is based on the simplifying assumption that imports can be clearly separated into those imports that are:

- Subject to tariffs only (assumed to be investment and government goods).
- Subject to tariffs and quantitative restrictions QRs, but not to rent-seeking activity (assumed to be consumer goods).
- Subject to tariffs, QRs and rent-seeking (assumed to be intermediate goods).

QRs are modelled (see Equation 6a in the appendix) by deriving the 'virtual prices' (*pv*) for a rationed import, that is the price that would induce an unconstrained consumer to behave in the same way as when faced with quantitative constraints. Thus the benefit to the consumer of a marginal relaxation of a quantitative import restriction is given by the difference between *pv* and the prevailing market price (*pm*). In turn the rents (*R*) associated with QRs are equal to (*pv* – *pm*) times the volume of rationed imports.

Seventh, given that producers in Turkey in 1978 (typically) directly received licenses to import specified commodities for intermediate uses, rent-seeking activity is introduced such that producers are induced to divert resources away from productive activities into acquiring import licenses for intermediates (that is directly unproductive activities – DUP) and the rents associated with them. The model assumes that the entire value of the rents is spent on the production of rent-seeking activity (assumed to be by the same technology as 'productive' activity). Thus the effect of rent seeking is to raise the price of intermediate inputs to the final user and to reduce the output of 'productive' activities, but not to generate utility since output from DUP activities is not an element in final demand.[5]

Calibration and solution

The construction of a consistent SAM was discussed in Section 8.4 and illustrated for one sector for this particular model of Turkey in Table 8.2. The exogenous parameters adopted by the modellers for the eight-sector disaggregation involved are set out in Table 8.4. Note that it is assumed that the income elasticities are lower for primary sector goods (agricultural and mining) than for non-primary sector goods and for domestically produced goods than for imported goods (compare rows 1 and 3). The higher income and (own) price elasticities for imported goods is consistent with the imperfect substitution assumption and with the view that import restrictions are likely to give rise to a pent-up demand for imports.

Numerical calibration of the model to the base year data set also required that rates of the premia associated with import QRs had to be estimated. Again the considerable data requirements of CGE modelling is demonstrated. Given crude estimates of the degree of quantitative restriction taken for earlier work it was only possible to approximate the premia using the following formula:

$$\frac{pv - pm}{pm} = \frac{1}{\eta} \frac{\Delta M}{(M_o + \Delta M)} \tag{8.17}$$

where *pv* is the 'virtual' price of imports, *pm* is the actual price of imports, M_o is the actual quantity of imports at *pm*, ΔM is the estimated level of

Table 8.3 Main features of the TQR model

1. Model dimensions	Eight sectors (one non-traded: construction); one consumer; two primary factors labour and capital with labour mobile and capital mobile or immobile across sectors.
2. Production	Cost-minimising producers using CES functions for value added; intermediate requirements involve fixed coefficients across intermediates in different sectors but allow for substitution between domestic and foreign intermediates within a sector.
3. Foreign trade	Imports and domestically produced goods are imperfect substitutes with different marginal rates of substitution by end use; capital inflows fixed in terms of foreign currency; the real exchange rate, defined as the relative price of foreign produced goods in terms of the numeraire, clears the market for domestically produced goods. Domestic production is supplied for domestic market and for export sales according to a CET transformation function. Small country assumption for import supplies and foreign export demand.
4. Final demand	Linear expenditure system for single household. Fixed coefficient investment demand by origin. Fixed coefficient demand by the government. Fixed real government consumption. Government savings determined residually.

Table 8.4 Parameter specifications for the TQR model

Parameter/Sector	*Agri-culture*	*Mining*	*Food Pro-cessing*	*Textiles*	*Inter-mediates*	*Machinery*	*Construc-tion*	*Services*
Domestic (D) final goods:								
1. Income elasticity	0.6	0.6	0.8	1.1	1.1	1.1	–	1.1
2. Own price elasticity	−0.2	−0.3	−0.4	−0.5	−0.5	−0.5	–	−0.3
Imported (M) final goods:								
3. Income elasticity	2.5	2.5	2.5	2.9	2.9	2.9	–	2.9
4. Own price elasticity	−1.2	−1.2	−1.2	−1.4	−1.4	−1.4	–	−1.4
Intermediate goods:								
5. Price elasticity (D)	–	−0.5	–	–	−0.1	−0.1	–	−0.1
6. Price elasticity (M)	–	−1.0	–	–	−0.3	−0.3	–	−0.8
Elasticity of substitution:								
7. Capital/labour	1.2	0.8	0.4	0.4	0.4	0.4	0.4	0.4
8. Domestic/imported goods	–	1.5	–	–	0.4	0.4	–	0.8
Elasticity of transformation:								
9. Domestic/exported goods	1.5	1.5	1.5	0.5	0.5	0.5	–	0.5
Import quota premia:								
10. Consumption goods	23.9%	32.0%	32.0%	13.7%	20.7%	21.0%	–	13.7%
11. Intermediate goods	–	40.0%	–	–	94.6%	101.4%	–	25.4%

Source: Grais, de Melo and Urata (1986), Tables 4, 5 and 6.

restricted imports and η is the assumed price elasticity of demand for imports.

The guesstimated premia rates by sector are reported in the last two rows of Table 8.4. Note the higher rates for intermediate than final consumption goods, which result not from higher rationing rates for intermediates but from lower demand elasticities (compare rows 4 and 6). (The estimated premia are used to compute the rents – R – accruing from rent-seeking activities.)

Simulation

More detailed consideration of the way in which a CGE model such as the TQR model can be used for policy appraisal purposes is provided in Chapter 9. At this stage we need to illustrate briefly the idea of simulation of policy experiments. Grais, de Melo and Urata (1986) report on the macroeconomic implications of a number of experiments (E). We consider only the following:

- E1: QRs on imports of intermediates eliminated *without* sectoral capital mobility.
- E2: QRs on imports of intermediates eliminated *with* sectoral capital mobility.
- E3: E1 plus removal of QRs on imported consumer goods.
- E4: E2 plus removal of QRs on imported consumer goods.

The impact of these simulated policy changes on imports, exports and GDP are reported in Table 8.5.

Clearly a wide range of other policy changes could be considered, as could the impact on other economic variables in the model (investment, consumption and so on). The context and focus of policy reform can vary. The danger is of course that the ease of experimentation could induce an unjustified confidence in the results, both qualitatively and quantitatively. It is easy to forget that the structure of the model embodies assumptions (which reflect beliefs or prejudices rather than reality) and that the data and the adopted elasticity values may be deficient. Nonetheless the importance of certain assumptions can themselves be tested through experimentation. In the case of the TQR model we can compare for example the implications of assuming intersectoral capital mobility rather than capital specificity – compare E1 with E2 and E3 with E4. In this case the magnitude of the results is not very sensitive to what is assumed about capital. Such a result is at odds, however, with the impact of capital specificity in models where perfect substitution between domestic and imported goods is assumed.[6] We need to consider clearly therefore what feature(s) of the model (in this case substitutability) produces a different result for the present model, and be assured that we are confident about the robustness of the relevant assumption.

Table 8.5 Results of some policy simulations with TQR model

	Import[1] volumes				Export volume	Real GDP
	Consumer	Inter-mediate	Other	Total		
Base values[2]	25.0	71.0	25.0	121.0	75.0	1281.0
Experiments[3]						
E1	25.0	70.6	27.1	122.7	76.8	1339.9
E2	25.0	73.5	27.5	126.0	79.9	1347.6
E3	31.8	69.5	27.1	128.4	81.5	1342.5
E4	31.7	72.3	27.4	131.4	84.5	1350.2

Source: Grais, de Melo and Urata (1986), adapted from Table 7.

Notes:
1. Exclusive of tariffs.
2. Millions of Turkish lira.
3. Defined in the text.

It is also possible to consider the sensitivity of the results to the composition of or level of simulated policy change. In the case of those simulations reported in Table 8.5 it is possible to compare the implications of QR liberalisation of intermediates only with that of consumer goods also included. In this case it turns out that the *incremental* effects of removing QRs on consumer goods are not very large. This reflects their lower share in imports and the lower rationing rate on this category of imports. Clearly considerable richness can be given to the appraisal of policy and the formulation of reforms by this type of sensitivity analysis. Even though complete QR liberalisation maximises the increase in real GDP (and presumably welfare), there are likely to be constraints (foreign exchange and political economy) on governments' abilities to reform completely and immediately. The information from policy experiments with GCE models can therefore be used to consider not only the nature of policy reform qualitatively and quantitatively, but also the timing and sequencing of reforms.

8.6 Concluding comments

This chapter has traced the development of general equilibrium analysis from its theoretical origins to the recent rapid growth of computable or numerical models supported by the computational convenience offered by modern computers and software. The structure and properties of the models typically developed in trade analysis have been investigated and illustrated, as has the process of model construction and of model use for policy simulation purposes. The advantages and limitations of CGE models should be clear to the reader from the discussion of their theoretical properties and of the calibration/solution methods. The additional insights of general equilibrium over partial equilibrium methodologies, the reduced data requirements relative to time-series econometric models and the ease of undertaking policy experiments are obvious strengths of the models. However it is also evident that there is room for improvement, in particular in the area of parameter estimation and of testing for model validity. This is true for all CGE models, be they single or multi-country ones applied to developed or developing countries. Given the special data problems likely to be experienced in developing countries, it does mean that CGE modelling should be viewed as a complementary technique and not one that replaces those discussed earlier in this volume. With these points in mind we turn to a more detailed consideration and illustration of the application of CGE models to trade policy issues in developing countries.

Appendix 8.1 The equations of the TQR model

This appendix presents the complete set of equations describing the model. Exogenous variables and parameters are denoted by Latin letters with an overbar or Greek letters; superscripts are used to distinguish commodities by end use and subscripts refer to sectors. The first list gives the sets of equations in the model, and the second list defines commodity prices in the model.

1. Factor markets

(a) $L_i^d = \alpha_i^{\sigma_i}(\mathrm{PN}_i/W)^{\sigma_i}\mathrm{X}_i$ — Labour (L) demand (σ is the elasticity of substitution between capital (K) and labour).

(b) $\sum_i L_i^d = \bar{L}$ — Equilibrium condition for the labour market.

(c) $K_i^d = (1 - \alpha_i)^{\sigma_i}(\mathrm{PN}_i/r)^{\sigma_i}\mathrm{X}_i$ — Demand for capital services.

(d) $\sum K_i^d = \bar{K}$ — Equilibrium condition for capital services (capital mobile across sectors). If capital is fixed, rental rates, r_i, are determined residually.

2. Demands for intermediate inputs (V)

(a) $V_i^c = \sum_j a_{ij}\, \mathrm{X}_j$ — Demands for composite intermediates, where X_j is total output.

(b) $V_j^d = \zeta_j^{n_j}(\mathrm{pc}_j^i/pd_j^i)^{n_j}V_j^c$ — Notional demands for domestic intermediates, $n_j > 0$, $0 < \zeta_j < 1$.

(c) $V_j^m = (1 - \zeta_j)^{n_j}\,(pc_j^i/pv_j^i)^{n_j}V_j^c$ — Notional demands for imported intermediates, $n_i > 0$, $0 < \zeta_j < 1$.

3. Supplies to domestic (S^d) and foreign (S^e) markets

(a) $S_j^d = \beta_j^{\theta_i} (PD_j/PD_j^d)^{\theta_j} X_j$ — Supplies to domestic markets, $\theta_j < 0$, where X_j is total output.

(b) $S_j^e = (1 - \beta_j)^{\theta_i} (PD_j/PD_j^e)^{\theta_j} X_j$ — Supplies to foreign markets, $\theta_j < 0$, where X_j is total output.

4. Relations between prices (variables starting with τ refer to corresponding ad valorem tax rates)

(a) $pd_j^c = (1 + \tau c_j^d)\, PD_j^d$ — Market prices (*pd*) of domestic consumer goods (*c*)

(b) $pd_j^i = (1 + \tau i_j^d)\, PD_j^d$ — Market prices of domestic intermediates.

(c) $pd_j^o = (1 + \tau o_j^d)\, PD_j^d$ — Market prices of other domestic goods.

(d) $pd_j^e = (1 + \tau e_j)\, PD_j^e$ — Export prices inclusive of taxes or subsidies with $pd_j^e = \overline{\pi e}_j$ ER.

(e) $pm_j^c = (1 + \tau c_j^m)\, \overline{\pi c}_j^m\, ER$ — Landed prices of consumer imports (pm).

(f) $pm_j^i = (1 + \tau i_j^m)\, \overline{\pi i}_j^m\, ER$ — Landed prices of intermediate goods.

(g) $pm_j^o = (1 + \tau o_j^m)\, \overline{\pi o}_j^m\, ER$ — Landed prices of other imports.

(h) $pc_j^i = (\zeta_j^{n_j} [pd_j^i]^{1-n_j} + [1 - \zeta_j]^{n_j} [pv_j^i]^{1-n_j})^{1/1-n_j}$ — Composite prices of intermediates (pc)

(i) $PD_j = (\beta_j^{\theta_j} [PD_j^d]^{1-\theta_j} + [1 - \beta_j]^{\theta_j} [PD_j^e]^{1-\theta})^{1/1-\theta_j}$ — Marginal revenues.

(j) $PD_j = \sum_i a_{ij} (pc_i^i) + a_{va,j} PN_j$ — Gross output prices, marginal costs of gross output.

(k) $PN_j = (\alpha_j^{\sigma_j} w^{1-\sigma_i} + [1 - \alpha_j]^{\sigma_i} r_j^{1-\sigma_j})^{1/1-\sigma_j}$ — Net prices/marginal costs of primary factors.

5. Market-clearing conditions

(a) $C_j^d + G_j^d + I_j^d + V_j^d = S_j^d$ — Domestic goods.

(b) $C_j^m = \bar{C}_j^m$ — Rationed consumer imports.

(c) $V_j^m = \bar{V}_j^m$ — Rationed intermediate imports.

(d) Perfectly elastic supplies — Other imports.

(e) Perfectly elastic demands — Exports.

(f) $\sum_j \overline{\pi c}_j^m + \sum_j \overline{\pi i}_j^m V_j^m + \sum_j \pi o_j^m (G_j^m + I_j^m) - \sum_j \overline{\pi e}_j S_j^e = \overline{FS}$ — Balance of payments.

6. Definition of rents

(a) $CR = \sum_j (pv_j^c - pm_j^c)\bar{C}_j^m$	Rents to consumers (CR).
(b) $PR = \sum_j (pv_j^i - pm_j^i)\bar{V}_j^m$	Rents to producers (PR).

7. Government revenues, expenditures, and savings

(a) $GREV = DTAX + NIT$	Government revenue (GREV).
(b) $GEXP = \overline{TG}$	Government expenditures (GEXP)
(c) $\left.\begin{array}{l} G_j^d = \delta_i^d\,\overline{TG} \\ G_i^m = \delta_i^m\,\overline{TG} \end{array}\right\} \sum (\delta_i^d + \delta_i^m) = 1$	Government demand (G) for domestic goods. Government demand for imported goods.
(d) $GSAV = GREV - GEXP$	Government savings (GSAV)
(e) $NIT = \sum_j[\tau c_j^d C_j^d + \tau i_j^d V_j^d + \tau o_j^d\,(G_j^d + I_j^d)]PD_j^d + (\sum_j \tau c_j^m\,\pi c_j^m\,C_j^m + \sum_j \tau i_j^m\,\pi i_j^m\,[V_j^m] + \sum_j \tau o_j^m\,\pi o_j^m\,[G_j^m + I_j^m])\,ER$	Net indirect taxes (NIT)

8. Savings and investment

(a) $SAV = HS + GSAV + ER \cdot \overline{FS}$	Total savings ($\overline{FS}$ is foreign capital inflow).
(b) $TINV = SAV$	Total investments.
(c) $I_i^d = \gamma_i^d(TINV/PI)$	Demands for domestic capital goods ($\sum (\gamma_i^d + \gamma_i^m) = 1$).
(d) $I_i^m = \gamma_i^m(TINV/PI)$	Demands for imported capital goods ($\sum (\gamma_i^d + \gamma_i^m) = 1$).

9. National income and Its allocation

(a) $Y = \sum_i wL_i^d + \sum_i r_i K_i^d + ER\,\overline{FS} + CR$	GNP at factor cost; CR is the total rent generated by the rationing of consumer imports.
(b) $HDI = (1 - t)\,Y$	Disposable income (HDI)
(c) $DTAX = tY$	Direct taxes (DTAX)
(d) $\overline{TC} = \mu HDI$	Private consumption (TC) ($0 < \mu < 1$).
(e) $HS = (1 - \mu)HDI$	Private savings (HS) ($0 < \mu < 1$).
(f) $C_i^d = \gamma_j^d + (b_i^d/pd_i^c)\,(\overline{TC} - \sum_j \gamma_j^d\,[pd_j^c] - \sum_j \gamma_j^m\,[pv_j^c])$	Notional private demands for domestic goods.

(g) $C_i^m = \gamma_i^m + (b_i^m/pv_i^c)(\overline{TC} - \sum_j \gamma_j^d [pd_j^c] - \sum \gamma_j^m [pv_j^c])$ — Notional private demands of import goods.

Prices in the TQR model:

$PN_j,\ j = 1, 2, \ldots, N$	Net prices.
$PD_j,\ j = 1, 2, \ldots, N$	Gross output prices, inclusive of production taxes.
$PD_j^d,\ j = 1, 2, \ldots, N$	Supply prices of domestic goods to domestic markets exclusive of commodity taxes or subsidies.
$PD_j^e,\ j = 1, 2, \ldots, N$	Supply prices of domestic goods to export markets exclusive of commodity taxes or subsidies.
$pd_j^k,\ j = 1, 2, \ldots, N$; $k = c, i, o, e$	Prices of domestic goods inclusive of commodity taxes or subsidies, where c, i, o, e refer to consumer, intermediate, other goods, and exports.
$pm_j^k,\ j = 1, 2, \ldots, N$; $k = c, i, o$	Tariff-inclusive landed prices of imports.
$pv_j^k,\ j = 1, 2, \ldots, N$; $k = c, i$	Virtual prices of consumer and intermediate imports.
$pc_j^i,\ j = 1, 2, \ldots, N$	Composite prices of intermediates.
$\overline{\pi c}_j$, $\overline{\pi i}_j^m$, $\overline{\pi o}_j^m$ $\}\ j = 1, 2, \ldots, N$	World prices of imports.
$\overline{\pi e}_j$	World prices of exports.
w	Wage rate.
$r_i,\ i = 1, 2, \ldots, N$	Sectoral rates of returns; $r_i = r_j$, where capital is mobile.
P	Consumer price index (numeraire).
PI	Investment price index.
PG	Government price index.
ER	Exchange rate.

CHAPTER 9

Applied CGE Analysis of Trade Policy

9.1 Introduction

In the previous chapter the focus of attention was with the principles and technique of CGE modelling. We turn now to illustrating the potential applications of CGE models in the case of medium- to long-term trade policy analysis in developing countries. There are of course policy applications beyond trade policy – taxation, income distribution, resource depletion, location, employment policies and so on – to which CGE analysis can and has been applied (see for example Devarajan, 1988). Our focus here is by necessity narrower, though it is the case that trade policy has been a central issue in the case of many applications to developing countries. Further, the way in which the foreign trade sector is modelled crucially influences policy simulations outside the foreign trade sector.

The aim of this chapter is to provide a focus on trade policy issues and to illustrate the modelling of them, rather than to provide a comprehensive review of what is now a very large literature. The remainder of the chapter is as follows. Section 9.2 considers the measurement of protection and resource pulls in a general equilibrium framework. In Section 9.3 the use of CGE modelling to analyse the welfare effects of protection and rent seeking is illustrated. The costs of trade interventions in the context of the non-competitive market structures that may often be a feature of small developing economies are investigated within a general equilibrium framework in Section 9.4. In Section 9.5 attention shifts to the issue of raising government revenue at minimum distortion through the use of trade taxes. The last application is the use of CGE simulation analysis of the growth implications of alternative trade strategies, and this is considered in Section 9.6. Finally some concluding comments are provided in Section 9.7.

9.2 Effective protection and resource pulls

The concept of effective protection was introduced in Chapter 5. There a partial equilibrium approach was adopted, and the problems of drawing inferences from this approach about general equilibrium adjustments (production effects and resource pulls) was that, although the lack of consideration of factor-price effects and input substitution possibilities introduces potential errors in the estimation of effective rates of protection in a partial equilibrium framework, the estimated effective rates may be used to provide a sensible indication of the effects of protective measures on resource allocation. This is supported by empirical work that has investigated the theoretical work (Bhagwati and Srinivasan, 1973) about how well effective rates of protection estimated in a partial framework will predict resource flows.

Taylor and Black (1974) have compared the output changes predicted by partial equilibrium effective rates with output changes estimated in a 35-sector general equilibrium model of the Chilean economy for 1962. They conclude that the specification of the way in which intermediate inputs enter into the production function is numerically important in determining output responses to, for example, tariff changes. But rank correlation between partial and general equilibrium estimates is not very sensitive to the specification, and is high. If intermediate input coefficients are assumed to be constant the rank correlation coefficient between the two sets of estimates is 0.885. If instead a unitary elasticity of substitution between primary and intermediate inputs is assumed, there are larger absolute differences between the estimates than in the first case but the rank correlation remains high (0.851).

Taylor and Black (1974) assume that capital is immobile between industries and that labour is the only mobile factor. This is clearly a restrictive assumption and one that is inconsistent with a long-run, general equilibrium theory of protection. De Melo (1978) investigates the sensitivity of the Taylor–Black results to this assumption. The model distinguishes between land, labour and capital (with substitutability between primary factors and fixed intermediate input coefficients) in a 15-sector general equilibrium model for Columbia. With capital mobile he found a rank correlation coefficient of 0.864 between partial equilibrium effective rates and resource pulls; lower but not substantially lower than the 0.955 rank correlation between comparable general equilibrium estimates and resource pulls. Similar results have been obtained by de Melo (1980) for a model which splits labour into skilled and unskilled groups. Interestingly, in the later study de Melo obtains a closer correspondence between partial equilibrium estimates and resource pulls for a more disaggregated model of the traded goods sector. We can therefore identify a possible complementarity between partial and general equilibrium analyses, since data is likely to constrain general equilibrium modelling to higher levels of aggregation than is possible for estimation of partial equilibrium effective rates.

The closer correspondence between resource pulls and partial equilibrium effective rate estimates may well be explained by the fact that the effects of protection on product prices are more important in determining resource pulls within sectors (with similar factor input requirements) than are the effects of protection on factor prices. As factor intensities vary between traded good sectors then the factor price effects of protection can be expected to have a greater influence on incentives to produce and therefore resource pulls. It should be noted that general equilibrium estimates of effective protection may not correlate perfectly with resource pulls, since a given protection-induced change in value added in a particular process can be brought about by alternative 'mixes' of product price and factor price changes (de Melo, 1978, finds an 0.95 rank correlation between resource pulls and general equilibrium effective rates). Indeed it is conceivable that a process with a lower effective rate of protection (or smaller policy-induced increase in value added) will receive a greater incentive to increase output than an activity with higher effective protection (or greater policy-induced increase in value added) if factor intensity differences are sufficient to cause factor price effects of protection to offset the product price effects of protection. Thus the essential purpose of CGE modelling is not to generate alternative, that is general equilibrium estimates of effective protection, but rather to comment upon the broad intersectoral resource pulls associated with policy interventions or policy reforms.

We can illustrate the long-run structural effects of trade policy from work by Chenery *et al.* (1986). They construct a dynamic CGE model in two parts. First there is a static CGE model which is solved for a one year equilibrium, based on data for South Korea for 1963. (Korea had completed a period of development based on import substitution up to 1963, and was poised for a shift towards a more outward-orientated strategy.) Table 9.1(a) summarises the main features of the static model and the dynamic features, that is the intertemporal linkage equations which update on exogenous variables and parameters that are influenced by policy decisions. (See Section 9.6 below for further discussion of the dynamic features of the model.) The authors use the model to simulate the effects of alternative trade strategies. We concentrate here on the effects of export promotion through the lowering of average tariffs (from 17 per cent to 9 per cent over a 20 year period) and the necessary devaluation of the real exchange rate to clear the foreign exchange market. This policy reform alters the structure of relative prices and factor allocation in turn responds

Table 9.1(a) Outline of the static and dynamic CGE model (Chenery et al, 1986)

Economic relations	Static model: Principal relations	Static model: Structural features	Dynamic model: cumulative processes
Factor markets:			
Labour	Labour demand equations	Segmented rural–urban labour markets	Labour force growth
Capital	Marginal product equations	Fixed sectoral capital stocks	Capital stock growth
Product markets:			
Production	Production functions	—	Productivity growth
Demand	Expenditure functions	—	Composition changes
Foreign trade:			
Exports	Export supply functions	Segmented domestic and export markets	World market trends
Imports	Trade aggregation functions	Imperfect substitutability	Induced import substitution
Trade balance	Exchange rate or premium rate	Foreign exchange rationing, exogenous inflow	Sequence of capital inflows
Macroeconomic balance:			
Savings–investment	Domestic savings rates	—	Trends in savings rates
External capital	Endogenous foreign capital inflows	Fixed exchange rate	—

Table 9.1(b) Simulated growth and structural changes of trade liberalisation/export promotion (Chenery et al. model)

			Percentage contribution			
Strategy and sector	*Output growth*	*Share of output change*	*Domestic demand*	*Exports*	*Import substitution*	*Change in input–output coefficients*
Agriculture	3.2	9.0	103.4	31.2	−4.6	−30.2
Food processing	7.3	9.1	79.4	23.4	−0.7	−2.1
Consumer goods	9.4	24.9	64.4	38.1	0.2	−2.6
Intermediate goods	12.4	23.0	51.0	30.9	1.7	16.4
Machinery	12.6	8.9	70.1	16.4	−1.5	14.9
Services	6.6	25.1	89.5	14.9	0.1	−4.5
Total	7.5	100.0	73.0	26.7	−0.2	0.4

Source: Chenery *et al.*, 1986, Tables 11.1 and 11.8.

to these changes in price incentives. Table 9.1(b) summarises the sectoral output growth effects over the whole period, the sectoral shares of output change and the decomposition of sectoral output growth. Note the significant contribution of export expansion (26.7 per cent) to the total growth of output as the incentive to produce for export rather than for domestic market increases. Note also the significant intersectoral differences in the contribution to the total change in output – ranging from 8.9 per cent in the case of machinery to 24.9 per cent from production of consumer goods. This confirms the possibility of trade reforms having long-term effects on the structure of the economy and on the allocation of resources.

The above model is not designed to explore the short-run resource reallocation effects associated with the transitional period of trade reforms or of change of development strategy. 'Structural adjustment' issues may be better addressed with an annual or 'static' model where the structure and detail of the model can be fashioned so as to concentrate on adjustment problems (see for example Robinson and Tyson, 1985). Some of the models examined in subsequent sections of this chapter could be used for this type of purpose. We focus however on other issues of interest to the policy analyst or policy maker.

9.3 Costs of protection and rent seeking

Developing countries have typically used quantitative restrictions on imports, as well as tariffs, to protect domestic producers and ration foreign exchange.

The (TQR) model of Grais, de Melo and Urata (1986) has been used to analyse the effects of quantitative imports restrictions (QRs) in Turkey in 1978. The characteristics of the model are outlined in Section 8.5. We consider here how that model can be used to estimate the welfare costs of this protection and of the extensive rent-seeking activity by industrialists that was induced by the use of QRs by Turkey.

The regulation of imports in the late 1970s in Turkey involved the classification of imports as follows: an unrestricted list of non-competing imports of raw materials and parts; a restricted list of competing intermediate and final goods imports for which an import license was required; and a quota list (with quotas for specific commodities) of allocations between producers and importers.[1] It is evident that the producers' response to this rationing of imports was to indulge in rent-seeking activity.

The modelling of a trade regime like this is of course extremely difficult. The restrictiveness of the regime, and therefore the effects of any liberalisation, will depend upon the extent to which the QRs alone or QRs and tariffs combined have a binding, pre-policy change effect on the volume of imports. It is difficult to estimate with precision what the effects of the lowering of either policy instruments will be on import volumes, in particu-

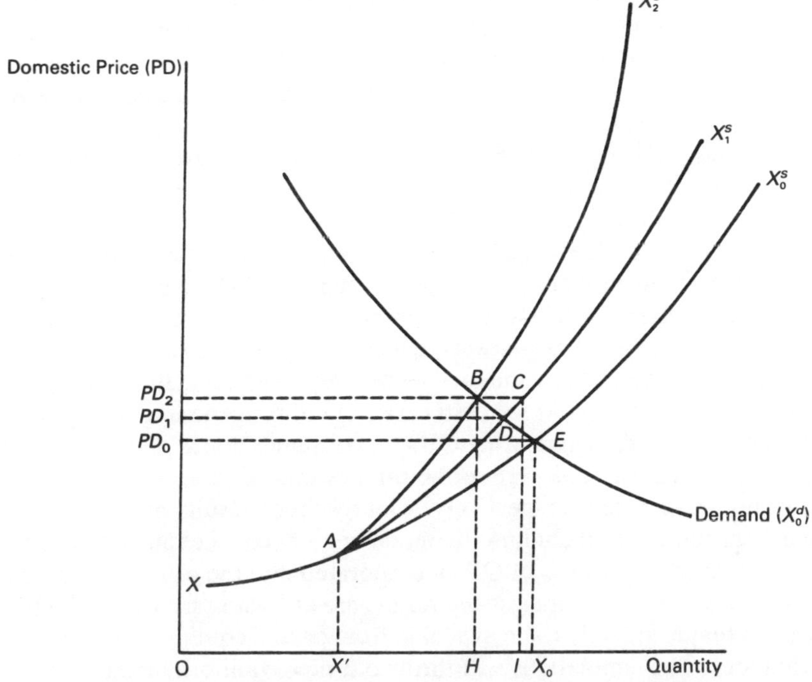

Figure 9.1 Welfare cost of rationing and rent seeking

lar of new products. This difficulty is compounded when, as might be expected, import restrictions induce smuggling and other illegal means of circumventing the controls. Thus, in order to simplify the model and the analysis, the model sharply divides imports into the three categories described on page 153. The authors estimate the welfare costs of quantity rationing and rent-seeking; rationing of consumers in their purchase of imports of final goods and rationing and rent-seeking by producers whose purchases of intermediate imports are restricted. (Again the modelling procedure to capture rent-seeking is described on page 154.)

The costs resulting from rationing and rent seeking can be illustrated by Figure 9.1 for a single sector. In the absence of rationing the domestic price is PD_0, which corresponds with the intersection of the initial domestic demand (X_0^d) and supply to the domestic market (X_0^s). Thus the 'traditional' output level (without rent-seeking activity) would be X_0. The rationing of intermediates causes the marginal costs of production to rise, and the supply schedule beyond X' (the level at which import rationing is binding) shifts to the left from X_0^s to X_1^s. At the resulting higher domestic price (PD_1) and reduced output of 'traditional' output associated with point *D*, there is a deadweight loss which can be represented by the area *ADE*. The effect of rent seeking is to push the supply curve further to the left, that is to X_2^s, as output is diverted from 'traditional' to rent-seeking activity.

Relative to the numeraire, this raises the domestic price to PD_2 and the deadweight loss by the area *ABD*. Thus the total deadweight loss associated with the restriction of output (*ABE*) can be broken down into a cost of rationing (*ADE*) and cost of rent seeking (*ABD*). At the final (distorted) domestic price (PD_2) producers would be willing to supply quantity *OI*, but only produce 0H quantity of 'traditional' output because of rent-seeking production. *HI* 'production' of rent-seeking activity at price PD_2 values these rents at a level represented by the area *HBCI*.

The welfare effects of trade liberalisation in Turkey in 1978 using the eight-sector TQR model are reported in summary in Table 9.2. The gains of liberalisation (or if the signs are reversed the costs of rationing and rent seeking) are expressed as percentage increases over the base values. Overall gains in real GDP are estimated to be over 5 per cent. Interestingly the bulk of the potential gains (or costs) arise out of the rationing of imports of intermediate goods; eliminating QRs on consumer goods and then lowering tariffs across the board raise the total estimated gains by only 0.2 per cent and 0.1 per cent respectively. Clearly these results are sensitive to model specification (including the modelling of rent-seeking activity) and to the price-raising effects of QRs incorporated into the calibrated solution for the base case. Nonetheless the results are at least indicative and offer a richness that is unlikely to be available from partial equilibrium estimation techniques. The simulations will throw out new equilibrium values for all the endogenous variables in the model. In this case, for example, we are also able to comment on the costs of QRs in terms of foresaken consumption and the reduced productive potential associated with lower investment levels.

9.4 Trade regimes and market structure

The analysis of the costs of protection (whether it be deadweight consumption or rent-seeking costs) is traditionally conducted in the context of competitive markets. In the case of many developing countries the size of the domestic market may well not support more than a few firms. This tendency to concentration may be reinforced by industrial policies (licensing procedures and investment incentives) that deter entry. As a result the costs of a restrictive trade regime (especially where quantitative import restrictions eliminate foreign competition at the margin) may induce greater costs in the presence of oligopolistic market structures than the standard welfare costs that we would identify in the face of competitive behaviour.

Pioneering work in the area of general equilibrium assessment of trade liberalisation in a developing country context in the presence of economies of scale and imperfect competition has been undertaken by Condon and de Melo (1986) and Rodrik (1987). It has extended work by Harris (1985) and

Table 9.2 Welfare gains from trade liberalisation[1] in Turkey (% increase relative to base values in 1978)

	Real GDP	*Real consumption*	*Real investment*
Removal of QRs on intermediate goods	+5.2	+3.8	+11.2
Removal of QRs on intermediate and consumer goods	+5.4	+4.2	+11.0
Removal of all QRs and a 50% cut in tariffs across the board	+5.5	+5.7	+7.1

Source: Grais, de Melo and Urata (1986), Table 7.

Note:
1. Assuming capital mobility across sectors.

empirical analysis for Canada by Cox and Harris (1985) to the structural characteristics of a typical semi-industrial economy.

The standard costs of import rationing need to be modified first to capture the effect of protection on the scale of production and therefore on per unit costs, and its effect on the price as a result of the departure from average cost pricing implied by non-competitive behaviour. We can show this formally, as in Rodrik (1987). If the expenditure (E) function for the single representative consumer is as follows,

$$E = E(p_1 \ldots p_n, W) \tag{9.1}$$

where p_i is the price of good i, W is the welfare index and sectoral production (X_i) takes place in n identical firms (that is $X_i = nx_i$) with unit cost (C_i) functions as follows,

$$C_i = C_i(f, X_i) \tag{9.2}$$

where f is the vector of factor prices, then the welfare effect for a given sector ($E_n dW$) of a change in trade policy can be expressed as:

$$E_n dW = \sum_i (p_i - p_i^w) dC_i + \sum_i (c_i - p_i^w) dX_i + n_i c_i (1 - 1/\pi_i) dX_i \tag{9.3}$$

where p_i^w is the world price of good i and Π_i is the ratio of average to marginal cost or scale elasticity.

The three terms on the right-hand side of Equation 9.3 relate to the consumption, competition and scale economy effects respectively. As domestic price (p_i) exceeds world price (p_i^w) following the application of an import restriction, then welfare falls for the normal good as consumption of good i contracts. The first term, therefore, is the traditional cost associ-

Table 9.3 Welfare costs of import rationing for alternative market structures and returns to scale

	Welfare costs[1] (% of base[2] national income)	
	20% import rationing[3]	50% import rationing
Policy Experiments:[4]		
E(1)	1.7	13.0
E(2)	6.1	16.0
E(3)	6.5	16.7
E(4)	6.5	17.1

Source: Condon and de Melo (1986) Table 5.

Notes:
1. Hicksian-compensated variation from indirect utility function in linear expenditure system.
2. The base was taken as the free trade situation.
3. Rationing of consumer and intermediate goods.
4. The nature of the policy experiments are described in the text.

ated with the policy-induced distortion. There are, in contrast to the traditional production cost of protection, two elements to the production distortion. The second term captures the effect of imperfect competition on production; the greater the degree of market concentration and the more that price exceeds unit cost ($p_i > c_i$) because of monopoly power, then the greater the degree of contraction of output and the more that unit cost will rise above the world price ($c_i > p_i^w$). Finally, the third term captures the effect of trade policy on the degree to which scale economies are exploited. Thus the greater the expansion of production and the greater the scale elasticity or fall in costs as output increases, the greater the increase in welfare.

Condon and de Melo (1986) investigate the trade-off between the scale and anticompetitive effects of import restrictions in the context of a stylised three-sector model. In their model the primary and non-traded goods sectors are characterised by constant returns and competitive conditions, while the manufacturing sector is represented as being subject to increasing returns and non-competitive behaviour. The results of their simulations of the effects of import rationing are summarised in Table 9.3. Four policy simulation experiments are reported on:

- E(1): constant returns to scale, no firm entry, and no collusive behaviour.
- E(2): increasing returns to scale, no firm entry, and no collusive behaviour.

– E(3): increasing returns to scale, firm entry and no collusive behaviour.
– E(4): increasing returns to scale, no firm entry and collusive behaviour.

Of course the results in Table 9.3 can only be viewed as indicative of the potential implications for trade policy analysis in the context of scale effects and non-competitive behaviour. The scale elasticities were based on evidence from the manufacturing sector in Canada, while the policy-induced changes in price–cost margin and firm numbers were set in line with the experience after trade liberalisation of the Chilean manufacturing sector. The results are for a hypothetical rather than an actual developing economy. Nonetheless they suggest that the costs of import restriction (or the gains of trade liberalisation) can be considerably greater in the imperfect competition/increasing returns context than in the traditional competition/constant returns framework. Compare the results of experiments E(1) and E(2), but note also the advantages of being able to simulate within a general equilibrium framework. One might have anticipated that the freedom of firm entry would have reduced the costs of import rationing by restricting the degree of production distortion resulting from monopoly or market concentration. But by incorporating the assumption that the number of firms in a sector is an increasing function of the rents available from rationing, then there is the possibility of excessive entry which increases the extent to which each firm underexploits available scale economies. (There is evidence from developing countries of 'excessive entry', that is too many firms behind protective barriers, where the restrictiveness on industrial licensing is not too great.)[2] Of course experiment E(4) shows that this is not the only danger in the case of imperfectly competitive markets. In this experiment the possibility of the 'excessive entry problem' is eliminated, but now rationing provides an opportunity for greater departures from average cost pricing in the domestic market as a result of collusive behaviour by firms. The welfare costs of policy experiment E(4) are no lower than for E(3) and increase above those of E(3) as the degree of import rationing and opportunity for collusion increases.

The potential complexity of the links between trade policy, scope for scale economies and industrial organisation or market structure has meant that the robustness of the postulates of trade policy in the context of the traditional (constant returns/perfect competition) framework has been challenged. The costs of import restriction are always positive for the small, undistorted economy in the traditional model. There is a possibility of welfare-raising interventions in the context of an increasing returns/imperfect competition world. But the discussion in this section has identified two important features of the recent work on trade policy. First, we have been able to show the value of using general equilibrium analysis when seeking to capture the complex interactions between trade policy and market structure. And second, although welfare-raising intervention is a possibility in this second-best world, the evidence from recent empirical works suggests that the costs of restricting trade (or gains from liberalising trade) in these circumstances can be considerably greater than they are in a traditional, neo-classical framework.

9.5 Trade taxation and government revenue

In the earlier sections of this chapter we have been able to demonstrate how CGE modelling can be used to focus on the allocation effects and misallocation costs of trade policy interventions. But trade taxes are not always used for protective purposes alone. In many developing countries there is a fairly high fiscal dependence on trade taxes. Greenaway and Milner (1991a) show that the average share of trade taxes in total government revenue is 17 per cent for a sample of non-oil developing countries. There is however a wide dispersion around this mean, and the trade tax share is considerably higher than this in many cases (62 per cent in the case of Gambia for example). Indeed for 31 countries in the sample fiscal dependence of over 20 per cent was identified. On efficiency and equity grounds trade taxes are not 'first best' means of raising revenue. If we ignore lump-sum taxes, then the optimal taxation literature (for example, Dixit, 1985; Stern, 1987) establishes that commodity consumption taxation should be used to raise revenue. However the choice of taxes may be severely constrained in low-income developing countries. Some subsistence sectors (rural agriculture) cannot be taxed, and in some sectors administrative costs and pervasive tax evasion (for example of income taxes) forces the authorities to rely on trade and producer taxes as major sources of revenue. Thus the willingness of developing countries to undertake trade policy reform will not only be fashioned by consideration of efficiency and growth gains or by adjustment and income redistribution considerations, it will also be influenced by the impact of border taxation changes on trade and non-trade tax revenue.[3] Herein lies the benefits of a general equilibrium framework since a CGE model can be used to simulate simultaneously the effects of trade policy change on the output and structure of an economy and the effects on tax revenue – directly from trade taxes and indirectly from non-trade taxes. (The ability of general, as opposed to partial, equilibrium analysis to capture indirect effects also should be noted.)

The CGE framework can be used as a positive tool, that is to identify actual revenue effects of non-optimal trade policy reforms. It can of course also be employed as a normative tool to identify how to raise a given amount of revenue at minimum distortionary cost, given the constraint that distortionary taxes (such as production and trade taxes) have to be used to raise the revenue. It is this latter type of work on 'optimal' tariff structure that has been tackled by Mitra (1986) and Dahl, Devarajan and van Wijnbergen (1986), the former for India and the latter for Cameroon.

Interesting results have come out of this type of analysis, and these contrast with the traditional public finance and trade analysis. The traditional and more pragmatic approach emphasises the benefits of more uniform taxation and protection. More uniform tariffs across final goods and between intermediate and final goods is seen as a means of simplifying the complexity of the system, reducing resource misallocation and the spread of effective protection rates and therefore resource misallocation and the opportunities for rent-seeking activity. Indeed this orthodoxy has fashioned the form of the trade policy reform components of most SAL programmes (see Chapters 12 and 13). It has been possible to design programmes that achieved greater uniformity and which could also be revenue-neutral or enhancing. The replacement of quantitative import restrictions by tariffs or the reduction of tariff exemptions on intermediate inputs are obvious sources of direct revenue-enhancement, which can be achieved with greater uniformity as well. These reforms have often been defended on *a priori* grounds, but CGE modelling has also been used to quantify and compare the revenue effects of alternative reform packages and alternative tariff rates.

But the orthodox approach tends to presume that related reforms of the tax system will take place, and with it the dependence on distortionary trade taxes will decline over time. If, in contrast, we adopt the position that the fiscal systems of the lowest income developing countries will remain inherently weak for some considerable time and that the present distortionary taxes are not removable, then the recent CGE analysis of 'optimal' tariffs shows that the recommendations for uniform (nominal and effective) tariffs may not be robust. The work has identified a number of rules analogous to those derived by the optimal tax analysis. Only if price elasticities of import demand are uniform across goods (ignoring cross-price effects) and if the substitutability of production between the domestic and export market is identical, would an 'optimal' tariff structure involve uniform tariff rates. *Ceteris paribus* the 'optimal' tariff should be higher the more inelastic the import demand and the lower the substitutability between import and export goods; the higher tariff induces a lower consumption and/or production distortion and a lower 'tax' on exports than would apply if the same tariff rate were applied when import demand is elastic and imports are closer substitutes for exports.

This has been illustrated by Dahl, Devarajan and van Wijnbergen (1986) in an eight-sector model of Cameroon that captured the above influences on the optimal tariff structure. The model was calibrated to data for Cameroon for the year 1979/80 and assumed the structure of indirect taxes and import tariffs that actually applied at that time. Very high export demand elasticities (uniformly −20, in line with Cameroon's minimal world market power) are also assumed. This implies that the optimal export tax will be positive in an undistorted economy. The model is used to simulate the structure of 'optimal' tariffs that generate the same level of

Table 9.4 'Optimal' revenue-constrained tariff rates

	Base rates		*Optimal revenue-constrained rates*		
			with zero export taxes		*with optimal export taxes*
	Ind. tax[1] rates	*Tariff rates*	*Existing ind. taxes*	*Ind. tax = 0*	*Ind. tax = 0*
Food crops	0.02	0.22	−0.06	0.09	0.15
Cash crops	0.19	0.23	−0.28	0.13	0.14
Forestry	0.06	0.28	9.31[2]	0.12	0.14
Food processing	0.04	0.35	0.27	0.11	0.15
Consumer goods	0.10	0.38	0.28	0.11	0.14
Intermediate goods	0.03	0.18	0.22	0.15	0.14
Services	0.00	0.00	0.04	0.19	0.14
Uniform rate			**0.16**	**0.15**	**0.14**

Source: Dahl, Devarajan and van Wijnbergen (1986) Table 2.

Notes:
1. Indirect production tax rates.
2. This very high 'optimal' rate is due to the fact that imports of this commodity are miniscule.

revenue as was collected in 1979; 'optimal' being those tariff rates that maximise the utility of the representative consumer. (Given that investment goods play no role in the consumer's single period utility function, then the tariff on investment goods was constrained to prevailing levels to avoid the shifting of the bulk of the tax burden to this sector.) 'Optimal' tariffs are identified for: the existing structure of domestic indirect taxes and with them eliminated; for export taxes at zero and with them set optimally; and when tariffs are constrained to be uniform – in all cases generating the same amount of revenue. Table 9.4 summarises the results of these alternative policy experiments.

The distinctive feature of these results is the sensitivity of the 'optimal' tariff structure to the degree of policy distortion assumed to remain. With optimal export taxes and indirect production taxes set at zero, the optimal structure is highly uniform (at 14 per cent or 15 per cent). (The variability of the 'optimal' rate is of course dependent in part on the degree of disaggregation possible in the model.) However as we move into a second-best world where distortions due to both non-optimal export and production taxes are present, then the 'optimal' tariff rates vary widely across sectors (from plus 28 per cent to minus 28 per cent if we ignore the exceptional figure for forestry). The negative rates in the area of food and cash crops is particularly interesting. Much of the output of these sectors was exported in 1979, so that production tax (which is sizeable in the case of cash crops) acts like an export tax. The negative optimal tariff therefore attempts to dampen the effects of this tax.

One message from this analysis is that uniform protection is not necessarily optimal (though it may be welfare-raising relative to existing non-optimal patterns of protection) if fiscal or other constraints are present. Whether or not one should recommend greater uniformity is not the purpose of the current discussion. Some authors would advocate greater uniformity of protection, irrespective of whether related reforms were going to reduce the other policy-induced constraints. They would recommend greater simplicity in anticipation of future reforms. A preference for 'long-term' optimisation does rule out the use of CGE modelling of the type we are examining here. The policy experiments allow us to identify the 'second-best' optimal tariff rates, and to identify the potential benefits of lowering other policy constraints through complementary policy reform. Therein lies the motivation for a general equilibrium approach to policy modelling, and for the avoidance of piecemeal reform based on partial analysis.

9.6 Growth and trade strategy simulation

The final application of CGE simulation we shall illustrate is that of examining the long-term growth implications of alternative foreign trade strategies. This is clearly of central interest to policy makers in developing countries who are considering trade policy reform: sufficient long-term growth advantages are likely to be necessary to encourage policy makers to initiate change which induces significant adjustment costs and income redistribution.

Modelling the growth process is of course problematic. There has been much controversy surrounding causality issues, the measurement of capital and about the form and role of technical progress. A modelling exercise of this form inevitably has to side-step many of these problems by taking the determinants or sources of growth as exogenous to the model. Even so the results are likely to be sensitive to the nature of the linkages of the model into the exogenous growth sources. We report here on work by Chenery, Lewis, de Melo and Robinson (1986) on the impact of alternative (representative) trade strategies on various macroeconomic variables, including growth. This model was introduced in Section 9.2 above and its broad features are summarised in Table 9.1(a). Disembodied technical progress and labour force growth are exogenously given, but the model also has to capture the response of trade (imports and exports) to relative price

Table 9.5 Trade strategies and macroeconomic performance

Components	*Import substitution (IS)*	*Balanced (B)*	*Export promotion (EP)*
Trade Policy/Trends:			
Sectoral trends (i.e. exogenous variation in trade shares)	Low/falling	Constant	Rising
Macroeconomic policy instruments	Tariffs/import rationing	Real exchange rate adjustment	Real exchange rate adjustment
Productivity growth	Low/intermediate	Intermediate	High
Macroeconomic Indicators:			
Incremental capital–output ratio, terminal year	3.26	3.02	2.95
Export growth rate	7.9	10.3	14.1
Import growth rate	4.5	6.4	9.3
GDP growth rate	5.7	6.2	6.5
Bias of the trade regime in terminal year	2.0	1.0	0.95
Relative price of capital goods in terminal year	1.2	1.05	0.95

Source: Chenery *et al.* (1986) Chapter 4.

changes induced by the selection of alternative trade strategies. Thus further exogenous trends were imposed on the parameters of the import demand and export supply functions. The authors revised the trade share parameters in these functions in line with shifts in relative prices.[4] The trends in trade shares for an import substitution (IS), balanced (B) and export promotion (EP) strategy are shown in Table 9.5.

In addition to differential trends in trade shares, trade strategy is modelled by assuming differential effects on productivity growth, different forms of macroeconomic adjustment and by affecting the cost of capital. The former is potentially controversial since there are differing schools of thought about the role of openness and competition on innovation and technical progress. There is however empirical evidence of a positive link between productivity growth and outward-orientation, which provides a reasonable initial working assumption that can be modified for sensitivity analysis purposes. The differences in macroeconomic adjustment between an IS and EP strategy are also summarised in Table 9.5. In the case of an IS strategy all the adjustment to any excess demand for imports is assumed to come on the import side through import rationing. In contrast any ex-ante excess demand for foreign exchange is eliminated by real exchange rate adjustment, depreciation of the real exchange rate relieving the constraint by squeezing imports and stimulating exports. Thus in the case of the IS strategy the premium on foreign exchange (that is induced by import rationing) means that the effective exchange rate (EER) for imports (M) is considerably higher than it is for exports (X). This results in a significant trade regime bias (B) against exports (that is $EER_M > EER_X$), which is avoided by other strategies. Table 9.5 shows that $EER_M/EER_X = 2$ in the terminal year in the case of the IS strategy, while the bias index remains around unity for the other strategies. The table also shows that an IS strategy tends to raise the relative price or cost of capital (by 20 per cent compared with a fall of 5 per cent in the case of an EP strategy).

The authors undertook extensive sensitivity analysis of the key parameters of the model, given the obvious elements of subjectivity embodied in the model. The significance of particular assumptions can thereby be brought to the attention of the policy maker, and the reasons why the choice of development/trade strategy may affect growth can be identified. The simulations reported in Table 9.5 provide a rough guide to the bounds of influence of trade strategy on growth. The growth rate differences do not appear to be particularly large: the GDP annual growth rate ranging from 5.7 per cent for the IS strategy to 6.5 per cent for the EP strategy. Growth depends on many factors besides trade policy, but an (approximate) one percentage point differential in the average growth rate over a 20-year period will result in a substantial GDP differential over the period as a whole – a differential which certainly suggests that governments should be concerned with the impact of the choice of trade strategy on growth and development.

9.7 Concluding comments

This chapter has reviewed[5] a number of the recent applications (from what is a burgeoning literature) of CGE modelling to the analysis of trade policy in developing countries. Space constrained any description of the detailed structure of the models, but the broad features (and their potential strengths and weaknesses) have been outlined. Some of the more detailed issues were considered in the previous chapter, but the reader interested in the detailed properties of a specific model will need to refer to the original study. The aim here was rather to illustrate the range of trade policy issues (cost, structural and growth effects) that could be investigated within a CGE modelling framework. Some of the numerical results of specific policy exercises have been provided in order to show the reader how simulation and sensitivity analysis can be used as a tool to guide policy makers and policy formulation.

It is evident from the results reported and the discussion of the model's characteristics that the absolute values of the numerical results often need to be viewed with some scepticism, especially in a developing country context where data deficiencies (rather than model limitations) may be particularly serious. But orders of magnitude and the qualitative content of the results are also often instructive. It is generally advisable to avoid excessive confidence in the precision of empirical economic analysis. This is particularly true of applied CGE analysis, but it is also true that this is an area of analysis that is undergoing rapid 'technical progress'. As software developments continue to reduce the computational task of model calibration and solution, so attention will no doubt increasingly shift to improving parameter estimation (and reduce dependence on the use of 'borrowed' values) and improving the formal methods of testing for model validity.

It must be recognised however that the advance of computing technology and the ability of modellers to build models that are more realistic (in the case of developing countries capturing 'structuralist' rigidities and macro-imbalances which imply a departure from the strict Walrasian/neo-classical framework) may lead to methodological problems and problems of interpretation.[6] There is a danger of ad hoc addition of model features that are not rooted in adequate theory. But ability to accommodate both neo-classical and structuralist perspectives is also a potential strength. Theoretical progress needs to keep pace with applied work.

PART IV

EVALUATING COMPARATIVE ADVANTAGE

CHAPTER 10

Revealed Comparative Advantage

10.1 Introduction

Most models of international trade explain the commodity composition and direction of trade in terms of the law of comparative advantage: countries tend to export those goods which have the lowest relative costs (and therefore prices) under autarky. Different models focus on particular commodity characteristics and/or country characteristics to determine the pattern of relative autarkic costs; for instance technological factors in the case of the Ricardian model and factor intensity/endowment differences in the case of the Heckscher–Ohlin model. Indeed the concept of comparative advantage can be regarded as one of the triumphs of economic thought. It is logically irrefutable and widely accepted. It is also however a concept that is difficult to quantify and test directly: relative prices under autarky are not observable for countries that have long engaged in international trade, and even if they were the law does not imply a simple, deterministic relationship between comparative advantage and the volume of trade.

Despite these difficulties and given the central nature of the concept of comparative advantage to both theoretical and policy discussions, economists have persisted in their attempts to apply it to real-world circumstances. These involve indirect methods which use information derived or revealed from post-trade situations and assumptions about the relationship between observable and unobservable variables. Such indirect approaches are often concerned with explaining trade patterns in terms of a particular model, that is of a particular set of trade determinants, rather than with the explicit assessment of comparative advantage. It is on the attempts to assess the latter, that is to 'measure' revealed comparative advantage in the context of developing countries, that we report in this chapter. The chapter is organised as follows. In Section 10.2 we consider the conceptual issues and problems involved in testing and measuring comparative advantage. This is followed by review of the principles and empirical evidence relating to the use of revealed trade performance (Section 10.3) and price-based measures of revealed comparative advantage (Section 10.4) as indicators of comparative advantage. Section 10.5 provides some conclusions.

10.2 Conceptual issues and problems

Most trade models are designed to answer the very specific question: what goods do countries trade and why? As argued in the previous section, most models provide an answer to this question in terms of comparative advantage; comparative advantage (or the structure of autarkic relative prices) being the proximate or immediate determinant of the commodity trade pattern. The empirical researcher does not have information however on autarkic prices because countries are already engaged in international trade. We therefore cannot construct direct estimates of comparative advantage. Clearly that may be a considerable frustration to the policy maker anxious to promote selectively activities of comparative advantage (or to protect selectively activities of comparative disadvantage). But can the economic analyst infer anything from information derived from the post-trade situation to assist the policy maker?

Certainly we can test the trade models themselves without a direct measure or test of comparative advantage. The models explain comparative advantage in terms of factors which are themselves observable. If the model is constructed such that the vector of an economy's relative autarky prices ($\tilde{p}$) is linearly related to product characteristics (captured by matrix X and relative country characteristics (contained in vector a):

$$\tilde{p} = X.a \tag{10.1}$$

then we can derive a relationship between trade and the characteristics of X and a, independent of the relationship between trade and $\tilde{p}$. Thus in the context of the Heckscher–Ohlin model autarkic prices will be relatively low for those goods whose production is (relatively) intensive in the country's (relatively) abundant factor; the country will tend to export these goods of comparative advantage. Testing the H–O theorem therefore requires data on trade, factor intensities and factor endowments but no direct measure of comparative advantage. Given that each trade model implies a (derivable) relationship between the observable determinants of trade and the resulting (and also observable) post-trade pattern of trade, production and consumption, is it also legitimate to use revealed patterns of trade and production (for example trade performance) to assess or measure comparative advantage?

The key difficulty is that there is not a simple/deterministic relationship between trade and autarkic relative prices ($\tilde{p}$) or comparative advantage. It would be convenient if it could be established that the volume of trade by commodity was linearly related to $\tilde{p}$. In the Ricardian model for example we can show that with *free and costless* trade the direction of trade in a particular commodity does depend upon autarkic prices, but the volume of trade does not; this depends on the foreign demand for and the domestic capacity to produce the good. The story is further complicated by the inclusion of trade barriers and transport costs, and by higher dimensionality issues (multi-product and multi-factor conditions) in the case of the Heckscher–Ohlin model. In the simplest H–O model – with only two countries, two products and two factors – it is easier to derive a deterministic relationship between comparative advantage and revealed trade performance. But the real world does not look like the textbook H–O model and a deterministic link no longer holds (Drabicki and Takayama, 1979). Such problems are often conveniently forgotten in empirical work on trade, where a continuous, rather than binary, dependent variable is used in regressions of the volume of trade against the hypothesised determinants of comparative advantage.[1]

Where does this leave us? Is it possible to identify comparative advantage and test the theory of comparative advantage? It is possible to be pessimistic, even nihilistic in the light of the preceding discussion. However there is a large body of evidence using regression analysis that is consistent with the existence of a fairly systematic relationship between trade and its proposed determinants, and this gives encouragement to explore the relationship further. In this regard we can draw some support from the theoretical work that has been done on weaker forms of the trade – comparative advantage relationship. Deardorff (1980) for example, using a fairly general model, has shown that autarkic prices and (net) exports (T) are negatively correlated, that is

$$\tilde{p}'\, T = a'\, X'\, T < 0 \tag{10.2}$$

Since relative country characteristics (a), relative product characteristics (X) and (net) exports (T) can all be observed, the above correlation (Equation 10.2) means that there are testable propositions that can be derived from any trade model that relies on the law of comparative advantage. The issue remains however about the extent to which the pattern of trade will diverge from a deterministic relationship between trade and its determinants. In Section 10.3 we presume that the deterministic relationship is sufficiently plausible to justify the cautious use of trade performance indices as a way of 'revealing' comparative advantage.[2] As an alternative to reliance on the deterministic specification and direct measurement of comparative advantage, we consider in Section 10.4 how price-based measures of revealed comparative advantage can be used to draw inferences about the pattern of comparative advantage.

10.3 Trade performance and 'revealed' comparative advantage

In this section we adopt a 'second-best' position; accepting the fundamental criticism[3] that the use of any revealed comparative advantage (RCA) statistic may not be a consistent measure of 'true' comparative advantage. We consider the issues of how an RCA statistic might be constructed, how cross-sectional information on RCA may be interpreted, and review some empirical results based on this type of methodology.

Alternative measures

The literature offers a variety of measures or proxies for RCA based upon:

- The use of production, consumption and trade statistics.
- The use of actual trade statistics only.
- Deviations between actual and expected production and consumption values.

The first class of measures does permit some 'normalisation' for country size. By relating exports to domestic production (*X*/*P*) for instance, it may be possible to improve the comparison between a 'large' and 'small' country. Table 10.1 illustrates this point for the case of the steel industries of Brazil and South Korea. The higher export or net trade to production ratios (rows 7 and 8) suggest that Korea has a greater comparative advantage in steel than Brazil. The table however also demonstrates the problem of using observed data for *X*, *M*, *P* and *C*. In terms of the share of imports in total consumption (*M*/*C* in row 9) Brazil is revealed to have a greater advantage than South Korea.

Before considering whether this ambiguity can be eliminated by concentrating on trade data only, it should be noted that any measure of RCA can be distorted by aggregation and policy effects. By choosing to measure RCA in Table 10.1 at the level of aggregation of all steel exports and imports, there is a risk that the selection of this particular level of aggregation is obscuring the true pattern of comparative advantage. A country may specialise for instance in the production of high-quality finished steel in which it has a comparative advantage, and import crude and semi-processed steel in order to meet the input requirements of the higher stage of processing. Measurement of an RCA index at the industry level may not capture this effect if total imports of steel are relatively high. Applied researchers must give careful thought to the level of aggregation at which RCA indices are constructed. There is a tendency in fact to calculate the indices for as narrowly-defined product lines as data and resources will permit. But that may aggravate the problems caused by policy distortions were tariffs, non-tariff barriers and subsidies are product-specific and non-

Table 10.1 Some alternative trade performance indicators: Brazilian and South Korean steel industries, 1979–80

	Brazil	*South Korea*
1. Production (*P*) ($US mill.)	7144	4403
2. Imports (*M*) ($US mill.)	551	1073
3. Exports (*X*) ($US mill.)	834	1473
4. Consumption (*C*) ($US mill.)	6861	4003
5. Net trade ($X - M$)	283	400
6. Gross trade ($X + M$)	1385	2546
7. Export/production ratio (X/P)	0.117	0.334
8. Net trade/production ratio $(X-M)/P$	0.040	0.091
9. Import/consumption ratio (M/C)	0.080	0.268
10. Net: gross trade ratio $\left(\frac{X-M}{X+M}\right)$	0.204	0.157

Source: Ballance (1988) Table 2.1.

uniform within industries. Products within a given industry may be revealed to have both a comparative advantage and disadvantage, not because the factor intensities vary significantly within the industry but because of policy distortions. At higher aggregation there may be less bias in the measured RCA because there are offsetting errors. Of course at any level of aggregation non-uniform or distortionary policy may remain. It is for this reason that some analysts (for example Balassa, 1977) have chosen to exclude imports from their calculations on the ground that import restrictions are more pervasive than export interventions. Of course exports will be affected by the import restrictions of other countries, but the more important criticism of the exclusion of information about imports is that it runs the risk of dismissing intraindustry or 'two-way' trade as aggregation bias rather than the outcome of *within-industry* specialisation forces that are compatible with broader *between-industry* specialisation influences. It is for this reason that many analysts prefer to construct RCA indices based on net trade flows.

The preceding discussion would suggest that there is a need to strike a careful balance in avoiding both excessive aggregation and disaggregation when calculating RCA indices. But the choice may be data-constrained. This is particularly the case where different classifications are employed for production and trade data, and the process of concordance forces the researcher into using the level of aggregation dictated by the least finely disaggregated classification. It is for this reason, and the potential ambiguity associated with composite indices such as the X/P, $(X - M)/P$ and M/C ratios, that RCA indices are derived often from trade data only.

There are several variants of the 'trade-only' measure. Let us illustrate two of these variants in order to capture the key issues involved in index construction:

$$\mathrm{RCA}_1 = \frac{X_{ij}}{X_{wj}} \div \frac{\sum_j X_{ij}}{\sum_j X_{wj}} \tag{10.3}$$

$$\mathrm{RCA}_2 = \frac{X_{ij} - M_{ij}}{X_{ij} + M_{ij}} \tag{10.4}$$

where i is the country, j is the commodity and w is the world.

RCA_1 is the original formulation used by Balassa (1965b) and retained in his subsequent work (Balassa, 1977, 1979a). If country i's share of 'world' exports of j (X_{ij}/X_{wj}) is greater than country's i's share of world exports (of all goods or all goods of a certain type for example manufactured goods, $\sum_j X_{ij}/\sum_j X_{wj}$) then $\mathrm{RCA}_1 > 1$ and a comparative advantage is revealed. As argued above, this index may be distorted by the omission of imports, and this omission may be particularly important where there is a country-size effect. In the case of many small developing countries the denominator of RCA_1 (Equation 10.3) is likely to be negligible. In contrast its exports may well be concentrated on a few traditional exports where its share of world trade is significant. Thus RCA_1 may reveal very high 'levels' of comparative advantage for a few traditional export commodities, and low levels (that is comparative disadvantage) for most other non-traditional goods. This calls for careful selection of the range of goods (j) over which we aggregate $\left(\sum_j\right)$ when formulating the denominator in Equation 10.3.

The alternative index (RCA_2) set out in Equation 10.4 makes reference to the 'own' country trade performance only, and recognises the possibility of simultaneous exporting and importing within a particular product category. The most recent work on measuring revealed comparative advantage appears to reflect the theoretical preference for a focus on some form of net export ratio. In the case of the simple ratio in Equation 10.4 the ratio ranges from -1 ($X_{ij} = 0$ and revealed comparative disadvantage) to $+1$ ($M_j = 0$ and revealed comparative advantage). Around zero values for RCA_2 there is ambiguity. Indeed the limitations of this particular index are evident when we consider that any specific value of the index is consistent with any volume of trade. It is for this reason that a number of studies (Donges and Riedel, 1977; and UNIDO, 1986) have sought to normalise for the relative importance of a particular (net) trade flow in world trade.

The final set of RCA measures adopts a probabilistic approach; RCA is expressed in terms of deviations between actual and expected levels of trade, production and consumption. This requires that a 'norm' is formulated to represent conditions under autarky. The principle underpinning this approach is of course appealing since it recognises that it is the interaction between production and consumption that fashions revealed comparative advantage. The approach gives rise to ambiguities since alternative forms of the pre-trade world can be hypothesised. If preferences are assumed, as in the standard H–O model, to be identical across countries pre-trade (Kunimoto, 1977) or identical and homothetic (Bowen, 1983), then the comparison of expected and actual trade flows may be very misleading if the assumptions about preferences do not approximately hold in reality.[4]

Given that there is a range of RCA indices that have been proposed and employed to measure comparative advantage then we may anticipate that there will be some inconsistency in the results obtained by each index. This sensitivity of results to proxy choice is empirically confirmed by Ballance, Forstner and Murray (1986). They show the inconsistency to be greatest when the indices are interpreted cardinally rather than in an ordinal or dichotomous fashion. The policy maker should be encouraged therefore to interpret RCA indices with caution, and as a means of discriminating between activities with a greater or lower probability of revealing a comparative advantage or disadvantage.

Some evidence for developing countries

UNIDO (1982) is one of the most comprehensive studies. It used several of the RCA indices discussed above and had a coverage of 47 countries and 129 industries. The results showed that in general developing countries' comparative advantage was limited to the production of manufactures involving simple processing, often linked to agriculture or other resource-intensive primary activities. In line with the ladder of development principle embodied in the stages approach to comparative advantage (see Balassa, 1979b and Section 11.2), more advanced developing countries were found to be less dependent on natural resource-based manufacturing activity; they revealed clear comparative advantage in labour-intensive goods or stages of processing involving standardised technologies. This can be seen from an examination of Table 10.2. All 'classes' of developing countries show a much greater tendency to reveal comparative advantage in labour-intensive/standardised than capital intensive/standardised goods (compare rows 1 and 2), and there is a much greater incidence throughout of comparative advantage in standardised than non-standardised products. This pattern of revealed trade performance is consistent with a factor endowments explanation of trade; relative to the industrialised countries the developing countries have large amounts of unskilled labour and little technological expertise. Note however that the results are consistent with the ladder of development view of comparative advantage; the NICs are less dependent on natural resource-based activities than other developing countries and the recently developed countries show greater evidence of breaking into capital-intensive and less standardised product ranges.

Depending on our confidence in our ability to measure comparative advantage and the factor intensity of goods, and in the H–O and stages

Table 10.2 Share of manufactured exports with a strongly revealed comparative advantage[1] in different types of developing countries (percentages)

Product type[2]	Recently[3] developed	Newly[4] industrialising (NIC)	Other LDCs
Standardised:			
Labour-intensive	22.3	34.6	20.3
Capital-intensive	3.1	0.7	1.5
Unstandardised:			
Labour-intensive	2.9	3.2	2.9
Capital-intensive	5.2	1.2	0.6

Source: Adapted from Ballance (1988) Table 2.3.

Notes:
1. RCA index exceeded a normalised level of 100 by at least 50 per cent.
2. Products were distinguished by the rate of product development, with standardisation involving low product development.
3. Countries such as Greece, Israel, Portugal, Spain and Yugoslavia.
4. Includes Argentina, Brazil, Hong Kong, Mexico, Singapore, South Korea and Turkey.

model, then we will place differing degrees of confidence in these results. Certainly the NICs and other newly exporting developing countries have been able to compete in world markets for mature manufactured goods, and it is tempting to interpret this revealed trade performance as evidence of where comparative advantage lies.

10.4 A price-based measure of revealed comparative advantage

Using revealed trade performance to indicate comparative advantage has one obvious drawback – actual trade flows are affected by policy-induced barriers to trade. Indeed trade barriers may affect both the volume and direction of trade. Consider Figure 10.1 below. If two varieties (u, v) of final good (j) can be produced (S^u_{Dj} and S^v_{Dj}) by country D using the same amount of a common intermediate input (i) available at world price (P_{wi}), then supply of each variety is a function of net price which may be influenced by import duties on final and intermediate goods. Without border interventions then there would be AB quantity of imports of variety u and BC amount of exports of variety v. Consider now the effect of an import tariff on the intermediate input; the effective supply schedule to domestic users shifts to S'_{wi}. At each gross price for the final goods involved domestic producers are willing to supply less; the supply schedules for the final good are now $S^{u'}_{Dj}$ and $S^{v'}_{Dj}$. In the absence of output 'subsidisation' from output tariffs (in domestic sales) or export subsidies, then the volume of imports of variety u increases from AB to EB while variety v ceases to be exported and is now imported (volume DB).

The use of the post-policy intervention trade volumes to comment on revealed comparative advantage in this example would be very misleading. Clearly this is a potentially serious problem when conducting single-country studies of revealed trade performance for developing countries where policy-induced trade barriers are extensive and substantial. In fact, as the discussion of effective protection analysis (Chapter 5) showed, low tariffs or duty-exemptions on intermediate goods means that effective rates of protection of exportables are typically (absolutely) small. Import protection of final goods means that the trade distortions are greater in the importables sector. Thus RCA indices based on gross exports (X) rather than net trade ($X - M$) are likely to be subject to less distortion. Nevertheless the possibility of eliminating the effects of protection should not be ignored.

In principle it is possible to calculate the percentage changes in (net) price, that is the rates of (effective) protection, and therefore use specific supply elasticities to calculate the domestic production distortion. The non-distorted trade flows would equal the revealed or actual trade flows less the production distortions. The protection effects are capable of estimation (see Chapter 5), but data is likely to constrain calculation on an across-the-board basis and with much disaggregation in the absence (as is likely to be the case) of an input–output table with large dimensions. Similarly (net) price supply elasticities are not likely to be available or calculable with broad coverage. Thus we could focus instead on the implicit (relative) prices that would define tradeability or determine trade patterns in the absence of trade policy distortions.

'Implicit' revealed comparative advantage (IRCA)

The basis of the IRCA measure is the calculation of a notional price for each commodity or activity, that is the price that would apply in the absence of policy distortions in intermediate and final goods markets. The total value of the (per unit) output of each activity can be adjusted (P_j') in order to:

- Remove the effect of net (direct) subsidies (s_j).
- Revalue tradeable inputs (1. . . n) at 'world prices'.
- Revalue non-tradeable inputs to the value that apply if all tradeable inputs used in the production of each non-tradeable (1. . . m) were set at 'world prices'.

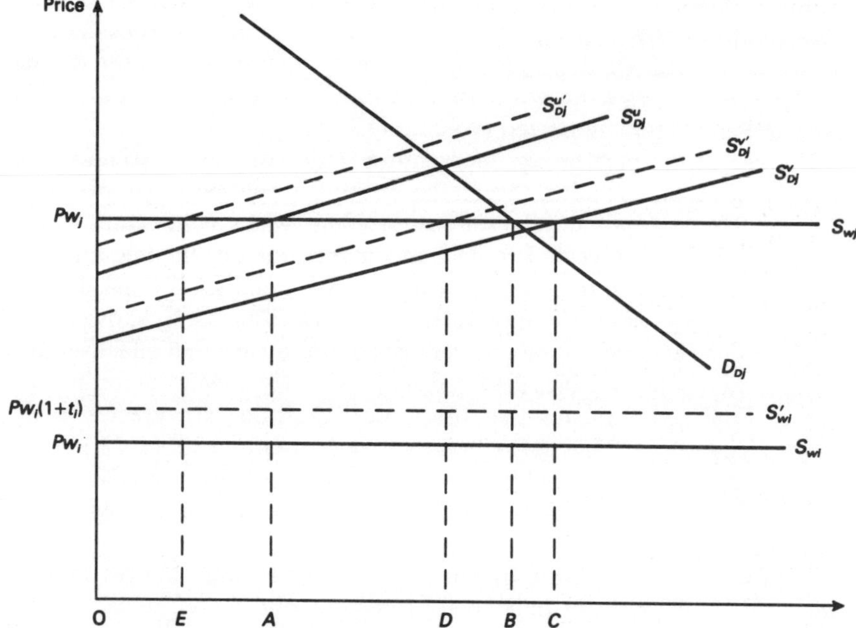

Figure 10.1 Policy-induced distortions of revealed trade

Thus the adjusted value (P') is given by:

$$P'_j = VA_j + s_j + \sum_{i=1}^{n} (a_{ij}p_{iw}) + \sum_{n=1}^{m} (a_{nj}p'_n) \tag{10.5}$$

where VA_j is the value-added at current factor prices, S_j net subsidies, a_{ij} is the amount of tradeable input i in producing one unit of j, a_{nj} is the amount of non-tradeable input n in producing one unit of j and p'_n is the notional price of non-traded input n calculated as in Equation (10.5)

The notional price can be constructed from input–output relationships and evidence on the price-changing effects of subsidies and border taxes, using the fixed technological assumptions and the type of information that is used in effective protection calculations (see Chapter 5). Note that the effect of factor market distortions on comparative advantage are not investigated by the IRCA measure. Further adjustments for such distortions are investigated in the context of domestic resource cost analysis (see Chapters 6 and 11).

The adjusted or notional price can be expressed as a notional domestic relative price by expressing it relative to a trade (export)-weighted average of the notional prices ($\bar{P}'$) of each commodity. This provides an estimate of, or hypothetical relative price of, commodity j that would apply in the absence of product market interventions. In order to construct a measure of implicit revealed comparative advantage (expressed in terms of deviations from unity) we can express the domestic relative price (P_j') relative to the world relative price of j (P_w):

$$\text{IRCA} = \left(\frac{P_W}{P_j'}\right) - 1 \tag{10.6}$$

where $P_w = P_j/\overline{P}$ and $P_j' = P_j'/\overline{P}'$ (with identical trade weights used to estimate $\overline{P}$ and $\overline{P}'$).

In theory this measure is positively correlated with the unobservable set of autarkic relative prices and with net exports under Deardorff's 'natural trade' concept (Deardorff, 1979). Thus a country is expected to have a comparative advantage for those commodities where the (adjusted) domestic (relative) price (P_j') is lower than the world (relative) price (P_w). In terms of the formula in Equation 10.6 this means that a comparative advantage is indicated where the IRCA measure is positive and a disadvantage where it is negative.

The information requirements of IRCA are very similar to those of effective protection analysis – information on the price effects of policy interventions and input–output relationships. The methodological and data issues are dealt with in detail in the chapters on nominal and effective protection. It should be evident however that the data requirements are considerably greater than the revealed trade peformance indicators of comparative advantage. Indeed there is only limited published information on input–output relationships for many developing countries. Input–output tables may not exist, or may exist only for a specific year which is now some time ago, or they may be constructed at a very high degree of aggregation. In such cases it will be necessary to conduct large-scale enterprise surveys in order to apply the technique. There is as a result little evidence to report on. Webster (1991) has calculated IRCA indices for the UK using 80 categories of tradeable goods from the 1979 published input–output table. Otherwise the technique has been applied in large-scale consultancy studies on specific countries where large-scale enterprise surveying has been funded by agencies such as the World Bank, for example Maxwell Stamp (1991) on Trinidad and Tobago.

Table 10.3 lists those industries that were identified by the IRCA analysis in the above studies as having a comparative advantage. In the case of the UK results it is interesting that the areas revealing strongest advantage were relatively technologically-sophisticated manufactures, chemicals and chemical-based activities and machinery and equipment. Although not reported in the table, the activities 'revealing' comparative disadvantage tended to involve relatively unsophisticated and traditional manufactures: food processing, leather goods, textiles, clothing and footwear. We would have expected this if trade- and price-based indicators of RCA produced reasonably consistent results, and it is again consistent with the picture that emerged from trade-based measures: direct links between the degree of

Table 10.3 Industries with (implicit) revealed comparative advantage: UK and Trinidad and Tobago compared

UK (1979)[1]	*Trinidad and Tobago (1990)*
Structural clay products	Rubber products
Cement, lime, plaster	Electrical appliances
Asbestos and abrasives	Transport equipment
Inorganic chemicals	Wood products
Organic chemicals	Printing and publishing
Synthetic resins, plastics	Textiles
Paints, dyes etc.	Pharmaceuticals
Industrial chemicals	Metal building materials
Pharmaceuticals	Petroleum
Soaps and toiletries	Beverages
Man-made fibres	Footwear
Metal castings, forgings etc.	
Other metal goods	
Engineer's small tools	
Process machinery	
Power transmission equipment	
Insulated wire and cable	
Industrial electrical equipment	
Telecommunications equipment	
Electric lighting equipment	
Other vehicles	
Grain milling	
Bread, biscuits etc.	
Alcoholic drink	

Source: Webster (1991) for the UK and Maxwell Stamp (1991) for Trinidad and Tobago.

Note:
1. Both revealed by trade performance indicators (RCA) and the price-based indicator (IRCA) of comparative advantage.

technological sophistication and the pattern of export performance. There is support for this link in the activities of comparative advantage listed for Trinidad in Table 10.3. Resource-based activities are evident (petroleum, pharmaceuticals and wood products) as are some of the labour-intensive activities that do not appear on the UK's list, such as textiles and footwear. Interestingly in the case of Trinidad there are some items on the list that would not be there if a trade-based measure of RCA is used. Apparel and chemicals for instance would look to have immediate potential on the basis of trade performance, but the IRCA analysis provides a cautionary note about the possible influence of policy on transitory trade performance. Chemicals, as indicated by the UK results, require a level of technological sophistication that has not yet been reached by Trinidad. Wages levels are also such that it is difficult to envisage sustained competition against clothing exports from low-wage economies in Asia and South-east Asia in particular. Therein lies the benefit of avoiding an excessively mechanistic approach to the interpretation of a single indicator of comparative advantage.

10.5 Concluding comments

Despite the obvious difficulties of bridging the gap between the theoretical concept of comparative advantage and an operational measure, it is evident that empirical estimates of revealed comparative advantage can, if used judicially and in an ordinal manner, add to our understanding of the international differences in sources of relative efficiency, competitiveness and international patterns of specialisation and trade. They also allow us to understand, in part at least, how these sources of trade change over time. The principle that relative rather than absolute costs largely determine trade patterns is a theoretically robust principle, and there is, as this chapter shows, a large amount of empirical evidence that is consistent with the orthodox view of the broad determinants of comparative advantage. Developing countries do reveal a comparative advantage in those products which are *apparently* relatively intensive in the factors with which they are *assumed* to be relatively well endowed. Policy makers in developing countries should not ignore the principle or the evidence. Indeed they should consider this when formulating the broad trade strategy and trade policy environment. They may also use evidence about revealed comparative advantage when seeking to lower policy or market distortions that restrict changes in relative factor endowments. However to assume that RCA indices can serve as a basis for specific policy decisions about which activities to promote, and which not to promote, would be wholly unjustifiable. Policy makers generally, and in developing countries in particular, already have a regrettable propensity for trying to 'pick winners' on the basis of subjectivity. They should not be encouraged to believe that there are objective indicators that they can use with confidence!

CHAPTER 11

Potential Comparative Advantage

11.1 Introduction

There is a considerable amount of evidence of developing countries either wishing or being encouraged to promote particular activities; promotion which increases exports of existing products and/or diversifies exports into non-traditional manufacturing activities. As we argued in Chapter 10, governments should be cautious about trying to select or identify specific activities for either the domestic or the export market. There are many examples of the failure of governments to identify appropriate activities. Indeed a primacy needs to be placed on demonstrating the responsibility of governments to create an environment conducive to facilitating efficient resource allocation. For example the encouragement of exports may require reductions of anti-export bias in incentive structures induced by existing policies (see for example Greenaway and Milner, 1986b, 1987a). The creation of more neutral incentive structures is likely to be a major element in export promotion.

There is nonetheless likely to be a legitimate interest by governments of developing countries to identify appropriate activities to promote or encourage. In the case of export promotion for example, measures of import protection are unlikely to be totally eliminated and some anti-export bias is likely to remain. If there is a budget constraint on the provision of compensatory fiscal and financial incentives for export promotion, then selective promotion may be necessary. Indeed where the government itself, directly or indirectly through quasi-official agencies, is involved in the allocation of investment funds, information on export potential may be of immediate value, especially if market signals are deficient. Even if the government and the public sector are not major actors in investment decisions, then the identification of export potential may still be of value in the making of decisions about the provision of infrastructure support.

Developing countries should be encouraged, of course, to employ appropriate investment appraisal techniques, once specific/individual investment proposals have been identified. But there are also economy-wide appraisal techniques, such as domestic resource cost analysis, that can be employed. But before the (specific) project appraisal stage is reached there may be a need to select or filter out a finite number of projects from a nearly infinite number of possibilities. Revealed comparative advantage, that is past performance, is of course a possible starting point. But in looking to the future we need to consider how an economy's resource endowments, and therefore its comparative advantage and competitiveness, may change.

The rest of this chapter is organised as follows. Section 11.2 examines how comparative advantage and the factor content of trade evolve over time with the process of development. Section 11.3 shows how information on the trade performance of similar economies might be used as a guide to export potential. Section 11.4 considers how information on domestic resource cost indices might be used as further information about how comparative advantage may change with policy reform. Finally Section 11.5 offers some summary conclusions.

11.2 Factor content and the stages approach

The empirical analysis of trade flows and revealed comparative advantage shows that trade is about much more than the processing of local raw materials into final goods for consumption. Some countries produce and export raw materials to others where they are processed into intermediate goods that are then exported for further processing. The complexity of this process depends upon the location of raw materials, the nature of the product and factor input requirements of each stage of processing. Consider the case of textiles and clothing. The developing countries tend to be net importers of textile fibres, to have a more competitive position in intermediate processing (yarns and fabrics), and to enjoy a clear comparative advantage in the final stage of labour-intensive production of clothing for the mass market. But this is only a generalisation. Countries such as Hong Kong and Mauritius are large net importers of yarns and textiles and exporters of finished clothing, while other NICs and industrialising countries are highly specialised in specific processing operations, importing cotton and man-made fibres from elsewhere. This is not a permanent pattern. There are dynamic aspects to comparative advantage which mean that the pattern of international specialisation shifts and relative resource endowments change as technologies and market needs change. Thus in the case of clothing there is now some tendency for the location of cutting, matching and finishing of clothing to shift back to the industrialised countries. Computer-controlled processes ensure reliability and quick response to market needs.

Such variations in competitiveness at different stages of production and changes in them over time are typical of many manufacturing activities. There are systematic links between the factor endowments of countries and the factor intensities or contents of production processes. There also appears to be systematic patterns of change in countries' factor endowments, and therefore their comparative advantage, that provide us with some guidance as to how we might anticipate comparative advantage to change.

Stages approach to comparative advantage

Balassa (1979b) argues that a country's comparative advantage will systematically change as a result of the accumulation of physical and human capital and increasing technological sophistication in production. Thus with the passage of time the competitive advantage of the more advanced developing countries will be lost in those processes that require a relative abundance of cheap, unskilled labour, and will shift instead to those processes and products which require more capital and skill input and are technologically more sophisticated. The developing countries can expect, in this model, to move along a ladder of comparative advantage as development proceeds. Certainly the post-war experience of Japan and other Asian NICs would appear to be in general accord with this interpretation of the dynamic aspects of comparative advantage.

There is also wider cross-country evidence (Leamer, 1984) on the sources of comparative advantage that show the industrialising countries losing their revealed comparative advantage first in labour- and then in capital-intensive activities as newly industrialising countries displaced them in these areas. But the support for a smooth, systematic transition appears to exist only for very broad aggregates of goods/activities. Using data for 79 industries in 28 countries during the mid-1960s and mid-1970s, Ballance, Ansari and Singer (1982) were unable to find support for a sequential evolution of comparative advantage. This is probably not surprising given the problems of measuring revealed comparative advantage and of testing the 'stages' hypothesis. It does indicate however that developing countries should be cautious about using this approach in a prescriptive manner. It does not provide a rationale for governments of countries that have had export successes in some labour-intensive products to believe that they should promote further export growth and diversification through the general promotion/subsidisation of capital- and technologically-intensive activities. It is in any case necessary to know first what the factor content of existing exports are. Armed with this information, it may be appropriate to implement policies that induce the socially-optimal rate of physical and human capital accumulation.

Factor content analysis

The effects of a country's existing factor endowments on its comparative advantage can be inferred from the factor content of its current trade, to the extent that the H–O–S model of trade applies. Factor content analysis seeks to convert trade in goods (and services) into the implied trade in services (direct and indirect) of factors of production embodied in that trade, on the assumption that:

$$F.T = E_k - E.w_k \qquad (11.1)$$

where F is the matrix of coefficients of direct or direct and indirect quantities of each factor per unit of gross output, T is the vector of net exports, E is the vector of world endowments of factors, E_k is country k's vector of factor endowments and w_k are the scales indicating country k's share of world factor endowments.

Calculation of $F.T$ is equivalent to measuring the net export of country k's endowment of factor services, if trade is balanced. If trade is imbalanced it is necessary to measure the factor content of net trade relative to that of domestic consumption. Thus factor j will be a source of comparative advantage for the country if its net exports require more j per unit than its consumption.

There are a number of practical difficulties in applying factor content analysis to developing countries. First, the F matrix (the technological coefficients or the Leontief-inverse matrix depending on whether direct only or gross inputs are measured) can only be identified if there is an input–output table available that is reasonably reliable, up-to-date and sufficiently disaggregated to match our definition of net exports by 'industries' in vector T. Second, even if an appropriate input–output table is available there may be difficulties in applying the table for the present purpose if the economy is small and/or highly distorted. If there is no domestic production of many imported goods, it will not be possible to measure the factor content of net exports. Alternatively if the technological relationships in the economy are severely distorted by import substitution policies we would be measuring the effect of policy rather than that of free trade on the use of factors. Estimating undistorted from distorted technological coefficients is difficult and requires a considerable amount of information on the nature and extent of the policy distortions. Third, measures of factor inputs or content may not be available or may not be sufficiently disaggregated or reliable.

For these reasons factor content analysis has tended to focus on the trade of developed economies, in particular the US. Even here much of the work has been involved with low dimension versions of the H–O–S model, and with the verification or otherwise of the 'Leontief paradox' (for a summary of this type of work see Deardorff, 1984). Certainly in order to comment on potential comparative advantage much higher dimensions are required, with a meaningful breakdown of each type of factor input (for example breakdown of labour inputs into skill types). More recently there has been some factor content analysis work which is of a much richer form than the investigations of the 2 × 2 × 2 H–O–S model, but it relates to developed countries. Work with relevance to the developing countries is much less sophisticated and partial in nature.[1] It often relates to developing countries' bilateral trade with a particular industrial country and for data limitation reasons looks at the factor content of their imports.[2]

Clearly there is a need for much more systematic factor-content work on the trade of developing countries, as production and input–output data becomes more comprehensive and reliable. In the meantime there is some scope for basing analysis on the assumption that technologies are internationally invariant. Thus detailed (and probably more comprehensive) input–output information from an industrialised country (such as the US or UK) where policy distortions are limited could be used to proxy 'world' production techniques. A developing country's net exports (for which information is more likely to be available) could then be applied to this technological information to measure the factor content of the developing country's trade, as if 'world' production techniques were operative. Empirical work of this kind on Trinidad and Tobago for example (Maxwell Stamp, 1991) has produced results that are consistent with the country's factor endowments, and the information content of which is valuable for policy purposes. Much more work of this kind is needed if we are to understand the complex interactions between the characteristics of economies and of products or processes that determine international competitiveness.

11.3 Export similarity and comparative trade performance

As was shown in Chapter 10 trade performance measures have in fact been widely employed to comment on comparative advantage on a cross-country basis. We saw in Section 11.2 how comparative advantage may systematically change with progress up the ladder of development. Thus we may be able to employ trade performance information from an appropriate comparator country to identify export potential.

There are three analytically separate but interrelated aspects of the process of identifying comparative advantage and export potential: the identification of similar or comparator economies, the identification of products with export potential and the identification of potential export markets. For each of the goods produced or producable by a developing country, we can ask the following question: may we expect this country to compete with similar goods from other countries in third market(s)?

Identification of similar economies

A central feature of this approach is the prior identification of comparator countries; countries which, due to their local resource endowments, stage of industrial development and/or revealed export performance, are likely to be guides to export possibilities. These countries may have, or once had, similar resource endowments and therefore compete for inward investment; they may export similar but not identical products. These dissimilarities can therefore become a source of information for the country concerned on export potential. They may export similar products but to different markets; the comparison again offers information on potential for market diversification. The possible method of identifying potential competing countries in export markets has two stages: initial selection of a number of countries based on qualitative judgements and subsequent discrimination between the selected countries based on export similarity indices.

Following the qualitative selection of potential comparator countries, it is possible to measure the revealed similarity between the home country's actual exports and those of the selected countries. An export similarity index (ES) is defined as a measure of the similarity of the exports of any two countries to the world market in general or to a specific third market:

$$ES = \sum \min\left(xj[ac], xj[bc]\right) . 100 \qquad (11.2)$$

where *a* is the home country, *b* is the selected comparator country, *c* is the world (or specific) market and *xj* is the share of industry *j*'s exports in the country's total exports.

If the industry distribution of country *a* and *b*'s exports to market *c* are identical (that is $xj(ac) = xj(bc)$ for all *j*), there is total (scaled) similarity and the index will take on a value of 100. If there is total dissimilarity in the product or industry pattern of *a* and *b*'s exports (that is $xj(ac)$ or $xj(bc)$ equal 0 for all *j*), the index will take on a value of 0. Note that the exports of each country are scaled relative to total exports and as a result the index compares only patterns of trade across product categories and not absolute levels. This is a useful characteristic which makes possible a comparison between countries of different size and stage of development. (An export similarity index was first articulated by Finger and Kreinin, 1979, and has been employed fairly widely in trade analysis.)[3]

Although the index utilises actual export data, it is capable of application in a way that may indicate potential competitors and as a consequence potential export products and markets. For instance, where there is a 'high' degree of measured (scaled) export similarity between two countries (with perceived similar resource endowments) at the industry level of aggregation, then:

- Differences in the absolute level of the competitor country's exports can be identified. Such information may be indicative of the scope for export growth through the displacement of existing suppliers.
- Differences in the detailed product breakdown of each industry's exports may indicate scope for product diversification of exports, that is for intraindustry diversification of exports.
- Differences in the geographical composition, that is direction of exports, may indicate the opportunities for export expansion through diversification.

Thus a range of issues may be judicially tackled with the aid of export similarity indices. The attractiveness of such an index is that it requires only international trade data. Indices can be calculated for total exports (to the world or specific markets) and for exports excluding significant primary products, at for example the third digit level or a more detailed product level.[4]

Product identification

In addition to the information on export similarity indices, which can indicate on disaggregation sources of unfulfilled export potential, complementary analysis entails the identification of revealed comparative advantage (RCA). The sources of revealed advantage can then be compared with those for competitor countries. Thus if other similar economies (in terms of prior expectations about resource endowments and in terms of recorded export similarity) have a comparative advantage in certain industries/product ranges that the country of focus has not so far revealed, again we have an indicator to potential product development for that country. This may identify potential for export diversification of an inter-, as opposed to intraindustry nature. (RCA indicators are defined and discussed in Chapter 10.)

Market identification

The final stage of the methodology is to identify potential markets for these products. There are two features of market identification which are relevant to the question of export promotion: one is the identification of new markets for the current or similar export product range; the other is the identification of market potential for new export products. It was mentioned earlier that export similarity and revealed comparative advantage indices could be used to identify competing exporters and how the geographical pattern of exports of similar economies might identify currently untapped markets for the home country's current exports.

An illustration of the methodology: Cameroon

(1) IDENTIFICATION OF COMPARATORS

The Cameroon is a small economy rich in natural resources. It is a 'price-taker' in world markets and relatively distant from the main high income/industrial markets. It is classified by the World Bank as a lower–middle income developing country. It has benefited significantly since 1979 from oil-producer status, and its natural resource endowments have facilitated near-self-sufficiency in food. It has a range of agricultural exportables (fruit, vegetables, coffee, cocoa, cotton) and there is obvious specialisation in forestry products (wood, rubber and palm oil). The more recent diversification into industrial production has been in the areas of agro-industries, construction materials (aluminium products and cement) and textiles.

We will take Nigeria, Kenya, the Ivory Coast, Indonesia, Malaysia, Ecuador and Venezuela as an illustrative group of potential comparator countries. Clearly the larger the number of countries in the initial selection the smaller the possibility of random errors and distortions undermining the robustness of the later analysis. Some prior criteria for selection of countries (for example relating to size, development and structural characteristics) could also be used. In this case there are countries at similar (Nigeria, the Ivory Coast) and higher (Malaysia and Venezuela) stages of income and industrial development. It includes other countries with relatively abundant (underdeveloped) natural resources (Ecuador and Indonesia). In terms of per capita incomes, Nigeria, the Ivory Coast and Ecuador are very similar to Cameroon. Venezuela, with its high level of dependence on fuel and mineral exports and its subsequent diversification of exports, may offer some guidelines for Cameroon. Alternatively Malaysia's industrial and export growth, despite its relative smallness in terms of population, may be informative.

The scaled exports for Cameroon at the 3rd digit of the SITC and for the six countries (where their exports matched those of Cameroon) for 1982 are set out in Table 11.1. These export shares can be applied to Equation 11.2 to calculate export similarity indices. The resulting indices are as follows:

	% degree of similarity	*% accounted for by crude oil*
Cameroon/Ecuador	59.4	46.8
Cameroon/Indonesia	54.2	46.8
Cameroon/Ivory Coast	46.1	2.4
Cameroon/Venezuela	49.3	46.8
Cameroon/Kenya	18.1	0.0
Cameroon/Malaysia	38.0	27.4

Table 11.1 Scaled exports of Cameroon and potential competitor countries, 1982 (in matched categories)

*SITC** *Digit 3* *R2 (R1)*	*Cameroon*	*Ecuador*	*Indonesia*	*Ivory Coast*	*Venezuela*	*Kenya*	*Malaysia*
030	.0015	.0768	.0104	.0209	–	–	.0097
057	.0025	.0938	–	.0274	–	.0126	–
061	.0022	–	–	.0099	–	.0076	–
071	.1558	.0684	.0154	.2218	.0002	.2544	–
072	.1416	.0384	–	.2667	.0012	–	.0087
073	.0005	.0136	–	.0047	–	–	–
112	.0047	–	–	–	–	.0009	–
121	.0029	–	–	–	–	–	–
232 (231)	.0069	–	.0272	.0094	–	–	.0945
247 (242)	.0440	–	.0147	.0928	–	–	.1203
248 (243)	.0154	.0044	.0099	.0278	–	–	.0414
263	.0359	–	–	.0242	–	.0000	–
292	.0047	–	.0042	.0029	–	.0278	–
333 (331)	.4683	.6425	.6648	.0243	.7875	–	.2737
424 (422)	.0058	–	.0161	.0185	–	–	.1094
553	.0044	–	–	–	–	–	–
554	.0070	–	–	.0025	–	.0097	–
634 (631)	.0165	.0101	.0142	.0094	–	–	.0129
652	.0180	–	–	.0176	–	–	.0033
684	.1630	–	.0010	–	.0233	–	–
690 (691)	.0036	–	–	.0061	–	.0067	.0042
890 (899)	.0044	–	–	–	–	.0085	.0057

* Standard International Trade Classification, Revision 2 (R2) (or Revision 1 (R1) in brackets).

In terms of total exports (including crude petroleum) therefore, the structure of Cameroon's exports appears to be closer to those of Ecuador, Indonesia and Venezuela. In all these cases, however, the similarity is substantially accounted for by the shared importance of crude oil exports – the export shares in 1982 for the four countries being Cameroon 46.8 per cent, Ecuador 64.3 per cent, Indonesia 66.5 per cent and Venezuela 78.8 per cent. In contrast the index for overall similarity with the Ivory Coast is 46.1 per cent, but only 2.4 per cent of the Ivory Coast's exports in 1982 were crude oil. For this reason Ecuador, Indonesia and the Ivory Coast were selected as the reference or comparator countries for the subsequent analysis of export potential.

(2) Product identification

For the three-digit categories identified in Table 11.1 as significant exports by Cameroon, revealed comparative advantage indices greater than unity (that is comparative advantage is revealed) are reported in Table 11.2. Thus comparative advantage is revealed for Cameroon in SITC (Revision 2) as:

057	(fruit and nuts)	262	(cotton)
071	(coffee)	333	(crude petroleum)
072	(cocoa)	553	(perfumery, cosmetics)
121	(tobacco)	554	(soap)
232	(natural rubber)	634	(veneer, plywood)
247	(wood: rough)	652	(cotton fabrics)
248	(wood shaped, supply worked)	684	(aluminium)

By implication all the other categories listed in Table 11.2 have indices below unity. These results are not at all unexpected given Cameroon's resource endowments. Natural resource-intensive products predominate in the exports of this relatively natural resource-abundant economy.

The comparative information on revealed comparative advantage (at the third digit) set out in Table 11.2 can be used to identify possibilities for both intra- and inter-industry export promotion. (For illustrative purposes the subsequent discussion will concentrate on manufactured goods, that is SITC sections 5–8.)

(3) INTRA-INDUSTRY EXPORT POTENTIAL

Cameroon reveals comparative advantage in manufacturing activities at the third-digit level in SITC (R2) categories 553 (perfumery, cosmetics), 554 (soap), 634 (veneers, plywoods) and 652 (cotton fabrics). In each case a detailed analysis of the product composition and market direction of exports by the comparator countries (in particular the regional comparator, the Ivory Coast) in each of the three-digit categories could be undertaken. To the extent that the competitor countries are exporting related but different products, or are exporting identical products to different markets, this is valuable information for existing export industries.

(4) INTERINDUSTRY EXPORT DIVERSIFICATION

The comparator countries are also shown in Table 11.2 as having revealed comparative advantage for three-digit categories for which the Cameroon does not have at present. Given the similarity achieved in other categories, it is possible that similarity may be achievable in these areas if resource endowments are indeed sufficiently similar (and any technological and policy constraints can be overcome). Thus we have a basis for investigating the scope for export diversification. The activities of revealed advantage in

Table 11.2 A comparison of revealed comparative advantage[1] for Cameroon and similar economies,[2] 1982

SITC (Revision 2)	*Cameroon*	*Ecuador*	*Indonesia*	*Ivory Coast*
030		9.93	1.18	
037		12.97		
057	3.83	22.11		8.59
058				4.27
061				3.94
071	63.69	24.23	5.46	78.47
072	154.87	42.01		291.46
073		11.89		4.12
074			4.36	
075			7.53	
081		2.53		
098				1.70
121	3.99			
122				3.65
232	1.77		5.37	1.85
247	12.64		5.95	37.53
248	1.49		1.66	4.64
263	11.05			7.93
265		21.61		
292			1.32	
333	11.03	53.54		
424			1.69	6.94
553	2.21			
554	2.61			1.33
634	4.25	3.34	4.67	3.09
652	2.85			4.06
661				2.62
684	8.16			
687			14.81	
775		1.05		
842				1.01

Notes:
1. Revealed comparative advantage indices greater than unity.
2. Ignoring refined petroleum products.

the similar countries which *might* for example achieve comparative advantage in Cameroon are 661 (lime, cement and building products), 775 (household equipment) and 842 (men's outerwear, not knitted).

To the extent that aggregate or overall 'similarity' between countries (possibly on different steps of the development ladder) is accounted for by the similarity of relative factor endowments, more detailed comparisons of the revealed trade performance of these similar economies may provide a useful initial guide to potential for export growth and diversification. Where comparator economies reveal mutual activities of comparative advantage at a specific level of aggregation or industry-proxy, evidence of dissimilarity in the composition and direction of exports at a higher level of disaggregation may indicate potential for product and market diversification. Similarly, revealed comparative advantage in competitor countries that is not matched in the reference country might indicate future scope for new export industries.

Of course there are dangers in using this approach. Revealed similarity does not ensure that there is actual similarity of resource endowment and market opportunities. The actual trade flows of 'similar' and 'dissimilar' economies are likely to be subject to the influence of distortions, in particular policy ones in both the exporting and importing countries. But it is not always obvious which distortions should be taken as given. In this case basing analysis on revealed evidence is not necessarily unsatisfactory – the methodology only seeks to identify possibilities for export potential. It offers a search methodology, and export potential can only be expected to turn into actual exports if appropriate resource allocation criteria are applied and if an appropriate policy environment is created. This 'health-warning' needs to be attached to any such procedure. The proposed approach – one which places an emphasis on resource and market constraints on export opportunities – is preferable to one in which non-economic and administrative influences predominate. International comparisons serve to focus attention on some of the critical issues: the nature of techniques of production and costs, and the nature of incentives to inward investment in comparator countries, for example.

The case study for Cameroon does in fact provide results that conform with prior expectations about the importance of relative resource endowments. The scope for expansion and diversification of manufactured exports appears to be constrained in the shorter term. Recognition of the constraints on industrial export growth in a country like Cameroon should not necessarily be viewed with pessimism however. Natural resource-intensive and traditional exports should not be discouraged for the sake of non-traditional exports if this is not consistent with prevailing relative resource endowments. Acceptance of the 'ladder of development' principle is not an argument for the continuation of the status quo, but rather a recognition of the need for specific steps or stages of development to be fulfilled.

11.4 Policy reform and cost competitiveness

A crucial aspect of export promotion and diversification is likely to be policy reform itself. We have seen in earlier chapters how import protection acts as a relative disincentive to produce for export markets. The direct manifestation of the cost of this anti-export bias is resource misallocation (higher resource costs associated with production distortions) and higher prices to consumers (consumption distortions). But the policy-induced distortions may well mean also that an economy's true factor endowments, and therefore its genuine comparative advantage, are not reflected in the revealed trade performance or the factor content of its trade. Thus use of information that is subject to policy distortions may provide a very misleading foundation upon which to base an analysis of potential comparative advantage. The analyst needs to be able to comment upon relative costs and competitiveness in the absence of policy distortions. By doing so he is able to comment also on how market-enhancing policy reform might be expected to alter the pattern of production and trade.

Domestic resource costs and comparative advantage

The domestic resource cost (DRC) concept and its measurement were discussed in detail in Chapter 6. Since the DRC ratio seeks to measure the true opportunity cost of domestic resources used in a particular activity, it was indicated there that the DRC ratio could be viewed in two ways: either as a measure of the actual (true) resource costs of existing policy distortions (that is as a cost of protection measure) or as an indicator of potential comparative advantage. It is this latter interpretation of the DRC ratio that is relevant to the present discussion. Since the ratio can be thought of as a measure of the true resource costs of saving foreign exchange (through import substitution) or acquiring foreign exchange (through exporting), then the lower the ratio for a particular activity, the lower the marginal cost of acquiring or saving foreign exchange.[5] Where the ratio is less than unity (see equation 6.1) there are potential 'cost' savings or net resource benefits associated with local production. In a static setting, activities with DRC ratios less than unity are ones of potential comparative advantage, towards which resources might be drawn if 'cost' savings can be sustained over a significant range of production increase. In a dynamic setting where efficiency gains from 'learning by doing' or increased scale might be reaped, then the rank order rather than absolute value of DRC ratios may be of more interest to the policy maker. Expansion of activities with relatively low DRC ratios, and the corresponding contraction of activities of DRC ratios well above unity, is indicated on efficiency grounds.

Note that in order to obtain measures of domestic resource cost we are identifying what the true resource cost of producing goods is in the absence of policy-induced distortions in both final product markets and all factor markets. In other words in the two-factor, capital (K) and labour (L) case:

$$\mathrm{DRC}_j = \frac{S_L + S_K}{V_j} = \frac{S_L + S_K}{V_j'\left(\dfrac{1}{1 \times e_j}\right)} \tag{11.3}$$

where S_L are the labour costs at shadow prices, S_K are the capital costs at shadow prices, V_j is the value added in j at world prices, V_j' is the value added in j at distorted output and intermediate input prices and e_j is the effective rate of protection of activity j.

Product market distortions are eliminated in the numerator of Equation 11.3 by estimating what value added would be without tariffs and non-tarriff barriers on competing imports of product j and without tariffs on importable intermediate inputs, while factor market distortions can be separately or jointly eliminated in the denominator.

The reader should of course be reminded that there are methodological and measurement problems associated with the estimation of DRC ratios as a form of policy analysis: it is demanding in information terms, and sampling and proxying problems are likely to result in measurement error and incomplete coverage in the case of most developing countries. These issues are discussed in some detail in Chapter 6 and the reader is advised to refer back to that discussion. Suffice it to say at this point that the value of DRC ratios in commenting on potential comparative advantage is information-constrained.

Table 11.3 reports upon some estimated DRC ratios for a sample of activities in Cameroon; domestic factor inputs are revalued at estimated shadow values and international value added is estimated from border prices. Individual DRC estimates for identical local activities may sometimes be available, but given that sample evidence only is likely to be available and that we may be concerned with the potential for activities

Table 11.3 Estimates of domestic resource cost ratios by sector, Cameroon, 1986

	Range of DRC ratios
Forestry	0.29–0.90
Agriculture and fisheries	0.66–0.71
Agro-industrial	0.36–1.50
Metal products	0.70–2.05
Wood and paper products	1.16–4.41
Leather and rubber products	1.28–3.47
Textiles	1.79–4.11
Chemicals and pharmaceuticals	1.75–160.60
Engineering	potentially ∞[1]
Construction goods	potentially ∞[1]

Source: Maxwell Stamp, 1987.

Note:

1. All activities in these sectors had estimated negative value added at world or border prices. DRC ratios cannot, strictly speaking, be identified but this can also be interpreted as evidence of potentially infinitely high domestic resource cost.

without currently-revealed comparative advantage then it is the DRC ratio (average or range of values) for the relevant sector (that is for activities with similar technological characteristics or factor intensities) that are likely to be of particular interest in this case.

The results shown are in fact consistent with traditional factor-endowment explanations of comparative advantage. Existing primary sector activities at this stage of Cameroon's development are shown to be 'resource' efficient; DRC ratios less than unity consistently apply in the case of forestry and agriculture and fisheries. The DRC ratios rise however as the relative importance of natural resources and local factor inputs decrease. Thus engineering and construction goods are shown to be highly resource-inefficient. The fact also that the intermediately ranked sectors tends to have ratios in excess of unity suggests that the scope for 'efficient' industrialisation is currently limited, and in turn therefore that there is limited potential for manufactured exports. But there are some instances even in manufacturing of DRC ratios below unity (agro-industrial and metal products) and of relatively low DRC ratios which may fall at higher scale and capacity utilisation (for example wood and paper products and leather and rubber products). Note that these activities tend to be higher-stage ones based on local/primary sector inputs.

11.5 Concluding comments

'Picking winners' is a dangerous exercise. There are good grounds for believing that the 'market' is in general likely to be more efficient than the policy maker in this regard. The policy maker's primary concern should be with identifying and remedying sources of market failure and with reducing policy-induced distortions or impediments to efficient resource allocation. But for both positive reasons (such as the need to provide appropriate institutional and infrastructure support) and negative reasons (such as avoiding inappropriate investments) policy makers are likely to continue to be interested in identifying where an economy's future comparative advantage lies. This chapter has illustrated how the factor content of trade, the revealed trade behaviour of comparator or 'similar' economies, and domestic resource cost analysis might be used to guide policy makers. Such filtering devices could be used judicially to identify activities that merit more detailed and formal project appraisal.

PART V

THE MODELLING AND REFORMULATION OF POLICY

CHAPTER 12

Structural Adjustment Lending: Rationale and Trade Policy Aspects

12.1 Introduction

In Part I of this volume the role of trade policy in the process of economic development was emphasised. Parts II and III focused on empirical aspects of trade policy – the techniques of policy appraisal and their potential use in policy evaluation. In this part we take the analysis a stage further and examine how the techniques of policy appraisal have been used in the process of policy reform in LDCs. In recent years a major new source of conditional finance has emerged from The World Bank. As we shall see this has opened a window for substantial resources which can quickly be disbursed to LDCs. The disbursements are however conditional upon policy reforms being agreed and implemented. Many of the required policy reforms revolve around changes in trade policy.

In this chapter we will focus upon the role of trade policy in the adjustment process, both from an ex-ante and an ex-post standpoint. Prior to any loan agreement a package of reforms has to be proposed. Often evaluations of the effects of trade policy, using the techniques discussed earlier, forms an input to this process. Even when agreement is reached on a reform package, actual outcomes may differ from intended outcomes due for instance, to exogenous shocks or problems with government commitment. The lessons to be learned from individual country experiences thus far will be appraised in Chapter 13.

Trade policy is just one element (albeit a very important one) in structural adjustment programmes; other areas of policy are also included. Thus we begin this chapter with an analysis of the characteristics of SALs. Section 12.3 narrows the focus by looking at trade policy in SALs, whilst Section 12.4 considers how policy appraisal can form an important input to the SAL process. Finally Section 12.5 offers some concluding comments.

12.2 Structural adjustment lending: origins and structure

The World Bank is the largest multilateral lending agency in the world, both in terms of the range of its lending operations and its country involvement. Traditionally World Bank lending activities have concentrated on specific investment loans, sector-specific loans, and to a lesser extent technical assistance loans. In 1980 a new programme of structural adjustment lending was initiated. Since that date SALs and SECALs (mini SALs which pertain to specific sectors) have grown in importance and now account for around 20 per cent of total World Bank lending, about $4.0 billion in 1990 (Figure 12.1). To put this in perspective, it is equivalent to about 20 per cent of official overseas development assistance to non-oil developing countries. It is therefore an extremely important source of finance. This growing importance of SALs is documented in Table 12.1. As can be seen, both the number of SALs and the funds disbursed therein grew dramatically in the 1980s.

According to a recent World Bank appraisal, the SAL programme was initiated in response to fundamental disequilibrium in developing countries – disequilibrium which resulted from the second oil shock and domestic policy weakness (World Bank, 1988). Whilst these were undoubtedly important factors, as Mosley and Toye (1988) argue, a third factor was also influential, namely the desire of officials at the World Bank to secure a seat at the 'high table' of policy making alongside the IMF, whose stabilisation loans are also subject to conditionality. In this respect the SAL programme can be thought of as a political track, as opposed to the administrative track in project lending. Conditions are negotiated and administered at an altogether higher level.

The Operational Manual of the World Bank defines SALs as:

> non-project lending to support programmes of policy and institutional change necessary to modify the structure of the economy so that it can maintain both its growth rate and the viability of its balance of payments in the medium term.

As can be seen from this definition there are several important characteristics which set them apart from IMF stabilisation loans. First, they are medium term rather than short term in outlook. Second, they involve programmes of policy reform. Third, in emphasising institutional change and the structure of the economy their thrust is oriented primarily to

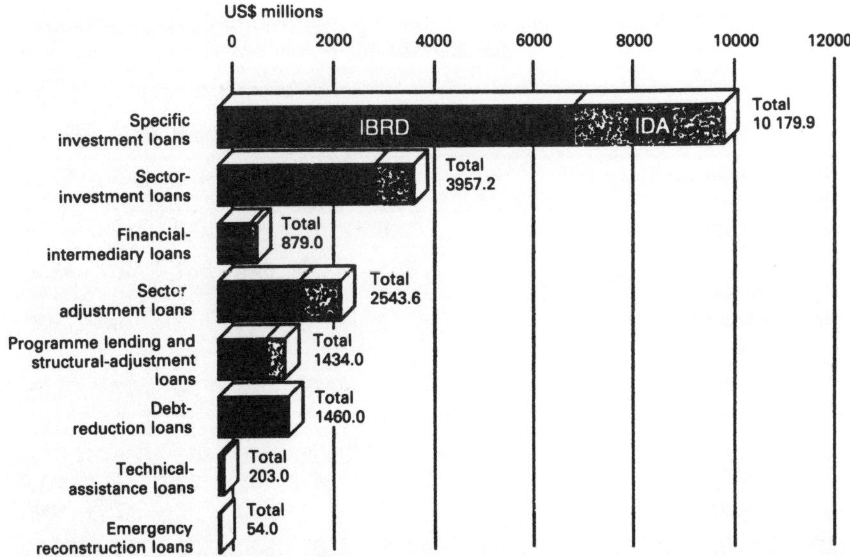

Figure 12.1 IBRD and IDA lending, by lending instrument, fiscal year 1990

supply-side reforms rather than the management of aggregate demand. In simple microeconomic terms, the objective of SAL programmes is to encourage an evolution of the economy from point a in Figure 12.2, through point b to point c. In other words, relative prices are adjusted in a way which facilitates a more efficient use of existing resources (a → b). In time the mobilisation and investment of new resources results in economic growth (b → c). To achieve these objectives the broad policy focus is directed at altering relative incentives in the economy and facilitating the more efficient mobilisation of resources. As we shall see, the former is directed at changing the price of tradeables relative to non-tradeables and/or agricultural relative to non-agricultural products, as well as exportables relative to importables. More effective mobilisation of domestic resources may be facilitated by budget deficit reduction, financial sector reforms, reforming public sector management structures and so on.

In the context of development finance the operation of SALs is quite unique. The process begins with policy appraisal. Past policies are evaluated and current problems diagnosed. On the basis of this appraisal the bank and host government enter into a dialogue about policy reform. Ultimately recommendations are made for reforms and disbursement of SAL funds is conditional upon the acceptance of these reform proposals. The process can be thought of as a stick and carrot mechanism. The carrot comes in several forms: quickly disbursed finance; often a great deal of latitude over the way in which the finance can be utilised; finance which is

Table 12.1 Adjustment loans and lending commitments by the World Bank, 1980–9[1]

	1980–2[3]	1983–5[3]	1986	1987	1988	1989	Total 1980–9[4]
Africa[2] ($ millions)	190	468	1497	754	1472	1235	6933
(% total AL)	24	21	35	17	31	20	24
(no. of loans)	3	8	16	11	13	14	85
Asia ($ millions)	200	383	0	840	600	1130	4320
(% total AL)	25	18	0	19	13	19	15
(no. of loans)	1	2	0	4	2	6	20
EMENA[5] ($ millions)	357	657	803	990	1150	1064	7047
(% total AL)	44	30	19	22	24	17	25
(no. of loans)	2	3	5	4	5	6	34
LAC[5] ($ millions)	62	675	2005	1840	1485	2665	10 206
(% total AL)	8	31	47	42	32	44	36
(no. of loans)	1	4	7	10	7	7	48
HICs[5] ($ millions)	171	1095	2607	1840	2135	3166	13 545
(% total AL)	21	50	61	42	45	52	48
(no. of loans)	2	6	8	10	8	6	55
Total ($ millions)	809	2183	4305	4424	4707	6094	28 506
(no. of loans)	7	17	28	29	27	33	187

Source: *Report on Adjustment Lending II: Policies for the Recovery of Growth*, World Bank, 1990.

Notes:
1. All figures are based on Calendar Year.
2. Africa includes Special Facility for Africa (for dollar amounts but not number of operations).
3. Per year, average of three years.
4. Total sum of CY 1980–9.
5. EMENA = Eastern Mediterranean and North Africa; LAC = Latin American countries; HICs = highly indebted countries.

often provided on concessional terms. The stick takes the form of a commitment to policy reform by the recipient government. Commitment to policy reform is a prerequisite to disbursement. Often loans are tranched, that is, disbursed in slices. This provides the opportunity for periodic appraisal of the extent to which loan conditions are being met. In the event of non-compliance the bank tightens the conditions associated with further disbursements – or it could even suspend the loan and has on occasions done so.

Tables 12.2 and 12.3 provide details of the policy areas where conditionality is most frequently applied in connection with SALs and SECALs. Table 12.2 shows the content of conditionality broken down by supply-side growth-oriented reforms, absorption reduction policies and

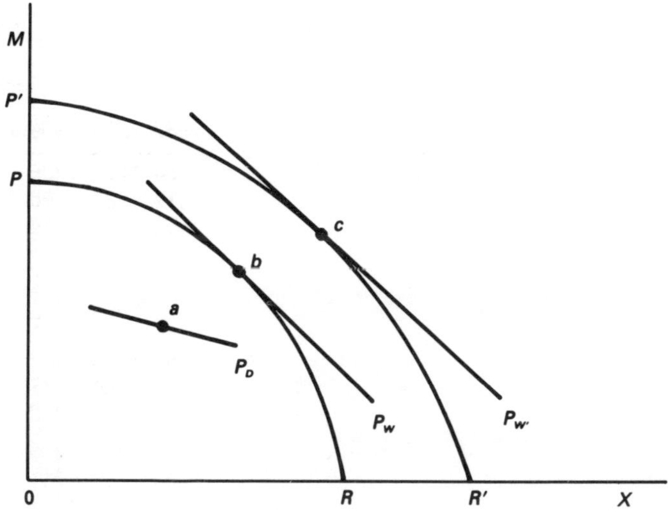

Figure 12.2 Structural adjustment loans and economic growth

switching policies. These are also cross-classified by country type. Table 12.3 then breaks down lending operations by loan agreement conditions in various policy areas. The most striking feature of Table 12.2 is the overwhelming importance of supply-side policies compared to absorption and switching policies – the proportion of conditions by policy areas being 84 per cent, 11 per cent and 5 per cent respectively. This reflects two factors: first the emphasis on medium-term policy reform to which we have already alluded; second the fact that demand-side conditionality, which focuses on absorption and switching policies, is much more the preserve of the IMF. Insofar as conditions apply in these areas in World Bank lending, they are generally subject to 'cross-conditionality' with the IMF.

Turning to the detail of policy reform, from Table 12.3 we can see that the area most frequently subject to conditionality is trade policy. Almost 80 per cent of all loans have trade policy reform conditions attached. This is by far the most important area of conditional lending. The specific details of these reform programmes will be examined in the next section. Other important areas of conditionality are public sector reform (fiscal policy, budgetary expenditures and public enterprises), agricultural policy and financial sector reform. A little less important are industrial policy and energy policy. The broad thrust of these conditions is directed at industrial restructuring (such as divestiture of assets in parastatals), more effective mobilisation of resources (such as reform of indirect taxes) and changing relative incentives through changing relative prices (for example reducing export taxes on agricultural products).

Table 12.2 Content of conditionality in World Bank lending

	Distribution of loan-agreement conditions by policy area and country type (per cent)											*Distribution of all actions in Presidents' Reports[3]*
	All countries	*HICs*	*SSA[4]*	*SAL*	*SECAL*	*Hybrid-loans[1]*	*EIAL countries[2]*			*Other AL countries*		
							79–85	*86–8*	*89*	*79–85*	*86–9*	*(per cent)*
1. *Supply-side, growth-oriented polices*:	85	89	82	77	91	90	88	88	88	87	80	84
Trade policies	16	22	14	15	17	4	26	17	11	10	13	16
Sectoral policies	28	23	26	18	35	62	36	21	44	53	23	28
Industry	4	4	4	3	4	5	6	4	7	4	2	5
Energy	6	3	2	3	7	31	5	4	24	2	4	5
Agricultural	17	16	19	12	20	19	25	13	12	47	14	17
Financial sector	10	12	7	10	9	1	3	14	18	9	7	10
Rationalisation of gov't finance & administration	7	7	6	11	4	0	8	6	5	3	8	9
Public enterprise reforms	16	18	19	15	17	7	14	21	6	6	18	14
Social policy reforms	4	5	5	2	5	14	0	8	0	2	5	3
Others	4	2	5	4	3	1	1	2	2	3	7	5
2. *Absorption reduction policies*:	12	9	13	18	8	8	11	10	9	9	15	11
Fiscal policy	9	7	12	16	6	7	9	9	7	8	11	8
Monetary policy [money supply targets]	2	2	2	2	2	0	1	1	3	2	4	3
3. *Switching policies*:	3	2	4	5	2	2	1	2	3	4	5	5
Exchange rate	2	2	2	2	1	0	1	2	2	2	2	3
Wage policy	2	0	3	3	1	2	0	1	1	3	3	2
Total	100	100	100	100	100	100	100	100	100	100	100	100

Source: World Bank (1990), based on an analysis of 183 SALs and SECALs to 61 developing countries. A total of 7723 actions were considered in all.

Notes:
1. Based on a subset of 10 hybrid SECALs.
2. EIAL – early intensive adjustment lending. Years refer to fiscal year of Board approval.
3. All actions in all countries, including conditions in loan agreements.
4. SSA – Sub-Sahara Africa.

Table 12.3 Content of lending operations of World Bank

	Share of loans with loan-agreement conditions in various policy areas (per cent)[1]											
							EIAL countries			Other AL countries		Share of loans with actions in various policy areas[2] (per cent)
	All countries (183)	SSA (84)	HICs (64)	SAL (73)	SECAL (110)	Hybrid (10)	79–85 (55)	86–8 (49)	89 (15)	79–85 (9)	86–9 (55)	
1. *Supply-side, growth-oriented polices*:												
Trade policies	58	58	67	64	55	30	60	69	33	56	55	79
Sectoral policies												
Industry	22	30	16	25	20	10	24	20	27	22	20	44
Energy	15	12	14	21	11	30	15	14	7	22	16	27
Agricultural	45	62	33	56	37	30	44	35	27	89	53	62
Financial sector	31	26	31	40	25	20	16	35	27	44	40	51
Rationalisation of gov't finance & administration	51	57	50	71	38	10	51	53	40	44	55	72
Public enterprise reforms	44	58	34	49	40	40	31	49	33	33	56	65
Social policy reforms	11	13	9	11	11	10	4	20	0	22	11	24
Other	28	42	17	33	25	10	7	27	20	33	51	49
2. *Absorption reduction polices*:												
Fiscal policy	51	69	41	78	34	30	47	51	53	33	58	67
Monetary policy [Money Supply Targets]	16	14	13	14	16	10	7	16	13	11	24	42
3. *Switching policies*:												
Exchange rate	16	18	20	22	13	0	9	18	20	11	22	45
Wage policy	13	23	5	25	6	20	4	8	7	11	29	22

Source: World Bank (1990), based on an analysis of 183 SALs and SECALs to 61 developing countries.

Notes:
1. Numbers in brackets are total number of loans.
2. All countries. All conditions called for in all loan agreements or other actions called for in all Presidents' Reports.

The range of policy instruments affected by SAL programmes makes them difficult to negotiate and agree for three reasons. First, there are problems of policy interdependence. Policy instruments interact. Thus, for example, tariff reduction may impact on government fiscal constraints, reducing agricultural taxes may also affect government budget constraints, introducing new taxes may distort relative prices and so on. When changes are taking place simultaneously across a range of areas it may be extremely difficult to predict *a priori* quite how these changes will ultimately affect economic activity. Second, the greater the number of policy areas involved in a particular reform package, the greater the number of government agencies involved in the negotiation of the package. As the number of interested parties increases, the potential trade-offs between agencies increases. This can make the process of negotiation very complicated indeed. The third reason is the resistance which host governments often have to liberalisation in a world where they feel they are facing increasing restrictions. One can of course argue about differences in initial levels. The fact remains however that the new protectionism has not helped here.

The potential for policy conflict and the manner in which it interacts with government commitment to a programme are important issues. This is not the place for a full and detailed appraisal of all aspects of the SAL programme and we will return to these issues later. The principal thrust of our analysis is on the trade policy-related aspects of SALs, to which we now turn.

12.3 Trade policy reform in SALs

Trade policy has been the area of policy reform where most SAL conditions have been assigned. As we saw in Tables 12.2 and 12.3, almost 80 per cent of all SALs have a trade policy condition, and some 16 per cent of all SAL conditions are trade policy related. Why has trade policy figured so prominently in the SAL programme? Five considerations are relevant here.

First, as we saw earlier, basic trade theory suggests that the optimal trade policy for a small open economy with no distortions is free trade. Of course if distortions exist, as they often do in developing countries, there may be an economic argument for intervention. However protection will rarely be a first best policy. Thus, there is a presumption in trade theory that reliance upon trade policy should be carefully circumscribed.

Second, a growing body of empirical evidence suggests that protectionist interventions are costly. Moreover a substantial literature indicates a positive association between exports and growth, and a possible association between outward orientation and economic performance (see Greenaway and Nam, 1988). In other words it appears that strongly inward-oriented economies may have performed less well as a consequence of their protective structures.

Third, trade policy performs a pivotal role. Arguably if trade policy is liberal in orientation the significance of other policy interventions declines. For example, if one has free trade one may not have to worry about domestic monopolies abusing their market power for the simple reason that exposure to international competition keeps the market contestable. Thus getting prices right in the traded goods sector is viewed as being of crucial importance.

Fourth, there is evidence to suggest that protectionist trade regimes, particularly those grounded in direct controls, encourage rent seeking and directly unproductive activity. Reforming trade policy can alter the structure of property rights in a more equitable direction.

Fifth, many of the instruments of trade policy are readily identifiable and compliance/non-compliance with particular conditions relatively easily monitored. For instance it is more straightforward to monitor a condition that all import tariffs be reduced by 25 per cent than one which states that the rate of growth of the money supply should be maintained in a band of 10–15 per cent.

These considerations have interacted in thrusting trade policy to the fore in the SAL process. As we shall see later, this emphasis on trade policy and the justification for it have not been universally accepted. For the time being we will take it as given and examine the reform packages involved.

The detail of reform varies from one programme to another depending upon, *inter alia*, initial protective structures, the prospects for sustainability and political considerations. Most reform packages tend to be guided by a combination of factors that can be readily adduced from the points made earlier – a desire on the part of the World Bank to reduce protection, reduce anti-export bias, simplify protective structures and increase the transparency of policy. Table 12.4 summarises the main components of trade policy reform for a sample of 40 countries subject to SALs. The table breaks down import policy into seven instruments, and export policy into three. Where possible, policy changes are designated as significant, less significant and negligible. These are essentially qualitative indicators (see Halevi, 1988, for definitions). Nevertheless they do provide us with an indication of the relative importance of alternative reform measures.

As can be seen, reforms in overall import policy were regarded as significant in almost half of all cases, and negligible in just a quarter. Recommendations relating to the overall level of protection were significant in one-third of cases. Conditions here pertained more to quantitative restrictions (QRs) than tariffs. Significant reforms on protective QRs and on QRs for non-protective imports were recorded in almost one-third of all cases. This reflects a view that is relatively widely held outside the World Bank, and even more strongly held within it, that quotas are a relatively

Table 12.4 Main components of trade policy reform in 40 AL countries[1]

	Number of countries where reforms were:						
Area of reform	*Significant*	*Less significant*	*Negligible*	*Total*	*Present*	*Not present*	*Total*
Overall import policy	19	10	11	40	–	–	–
QRs on non-competitive imports	12	16	12	40	–	–	–
Protective QRs	12	17	11	40	–	–	–
Tariff level	7	20	13	40	–	–	–
Tariff dispersion	8	22	10	40	–	–	–
Protection level	13	26	1	40	–	–	–
Schedule of future reduction	6	29	5	40	–	–	–
Protection studies	–	–	–	–	28	12	40
Overall export policy[2]	15	14	11	40	–	–	–
Exchange rate[3]	–	–	–	–	38	2	40
Export promotion[4]	–	–	–	–	33	7	40
Imports for exports	17	15	8	40	–	–	–

Source: World Bank (1988) Table 3.1.

Notes:
1. The assessments refer to proposals supported by the World Bank. They do not necessarily refer to policy implementation.
2. Judgment on the significance of the overall reform proposals.
3. Often these were not explicit conditions, but constituted understandings frequently made under the programme.
4. Includes such schemes as export credits, insurance, guarantees and institutional development.

inefficient form of protection and tend to have less acceptable distributional consequences than tariffs. Thus even where a QR is replaced with an equivalent tariff, this in itself would be regarded as an act of liberalisation on the grounds that the tariff is more transparent, maintains competition at the margin and has a desirable impact on government revenues.

Reform provision on tariff levels and tariff dispersion were significant in about 20 per cent of all cases. However they were of negligible significance in only one-third and one-quarter of cases respectively. Clearly tariff reductions ought to be liberalising on a *ceteris paribus* basis. Such changes are regarded as desirable in improving resource allocation. In addition however, tariff liberalisation is viewed as reducing anti-export bias. The rationale behind reducing tariff dispersion is that if one reduces the range of nominal tariffs, reductions in effective tariffs should follow, with potentially beneficial implications for resource allocation. Typically reduction schedules are specified in terms of nominal tariffs, although occasionally they may be specified by reference to effective tariffs (as in the case of the Ivory Coast for instance).

Reforms in overall export policy were significant or less significant in almost three-quarters of cases, negligible in the remaining quarter. A major objective of SALs has been to reduce anti-export bias in developing countries. Protection is a relative concept. As recent research has shown, if one protects the import-competing sector of an economy, one does so at the expense of other sectors – typically the export sector. Thus, as noted above, liberalisation of import policy may in itself have a beneficial impact on incentives to export. Arguably, complete import liberalisation would obviate the need for any positive export promotion policies, since complete liberalisation will, *ceteris paribus*, result in neutrality in the structure of relative prices.

However in SAL programmes complete liberalisation is not typical, either because reforms are gradually phased in or because a certain 'core' level of protection is conceded. Thus positive export policy is frequently recommended. This sometimes takes the form of understandings on the exchange rate with a view to reducing the extent of exchange rate overvaluation. An overvalued exchange rate distorts the price of tradeables relative to non-tradeables to the disadvantage of the former. Moreover since the costs of, and risks associated with, exporting tend to be greater than those of competing on the home market, it is often argued that an overvalued exchange rate disadvantages the export sector in particular. As we saw earlier however, recommendations on exchange rate policy tend to be in the bailiwick of the IMF rather than the World Bank.

The range of possible recommendations on export promotion is wide. They can include duty drawback schemes, export credit guarantee schemes, institutional reform designed to improve market reseach and market intelligence, and export subsidies. Reforms of export policy have been less pervasive and less marked than those of import policy, in the sense that less conditionality has been applied. This does not reflect a lack of concern with export policy, but rather results from a combination of technical and practical constraints. First, the (non-traditional) manufacturing sector is often relatively small – the emphasis therefore tends not to be in terms of encouraging existing firms in that sector, but in creating conditions which will encourage entry. In turns this relies, at least in part, on dismantling structures of import protection. Second, many areas of reform on the export side rely on institutional change. One does not have obvious 'indicators' here as with tariffs or QRs. Thus rather than explicit conditionality applying, often recommendations refer to feasibility studies and the like. Third, the provision of export subsidies can in the short run represent a drain on fiscal resources, which could discourage their use. Moreover explicit export subsidies can readily run afoul of countervailing duty action in industrialised countries.

Overall then, recommendations on trade policy reform are directed at reducing anti-export bias, increasing transparency in the protective structure and improving the efficiency with which relative price signals are transmitted. We will consider in Chapter 13 how these and other aspects of the SAL programme have operated, and what their impact on economic performance may have been. In the meantime let us consider the role of policy appraisal as an input to the SAL programme.

12.4 The role of policy appraisal in SALs

As can be seen from Table 12.4, in 28 of the 40 adjustment loans reviewed, studies of protection levels were included in the conditionality package. It is not unusual then to have policy reviews explicitly included as a loan condition. These figures however understate the role of explicit appraisal, since in most cases appraisal of some form will take place *prior* to the loan conditions being negotiated. Thus policy appraisal may be pre-loan or post-loan.

Pre-loan policy appraisal performs a number of important functions. Specifically one can identify an *informative function*, a *simulation function* and a *persuasive function*. Relatively little is known of the economic effects of trade and industrial policy in developing countries. We have at various points confronted the reasons for this situation – data is relatively scarce and frequently 'contaminated'; policy stacking makes it very difficult to disentangle the economic effects of different interventions; the incentive structure within the bureaucracy creates natural resistance to full information, and a tendency to obfuscation. Thus the information function of pre-loan policy appraisal is arguably a very important one. Generating information on effective protection rates, domestic resource cost ratios and cost of protection details is particularly useful in this regard. The information content of these measures is high. Of course, as we have seen, there are difficulties involved with their calculation and often problems with their interpretation. This is not however an argument against generating such information – some information is generally better than none at all. So long as the results of any such exercise are appropriately qualified and carefully interpreted they can be extremely useful. Thus, as we saw in the case of EP analysis, the precise details of given estimates of effective protection are less important than the ranking and range of rates in a given series. Even if we have concerns regarding the precision of particular point estimates, we may have more confidence regarding the probable direction of resource pulls induced by the protective structure. This type of information is clearly important as an input to the process of policy reform. As far as possible reform proposals should be grounded on evidence which supports the need for change.

This last point leads on to the persuasive function of pre-loan policy appraisal. A SAL is provided by a multilateral lending agency to a sovereign government. That sovereign government cannot be forced to adopt particular adjustment measures. Although the willingness of a government to follow a given set of measures will be directly related to the severity of the constraints it perceives itself to be facing, and the perceived strength of the lobbies it faces, the fact is that it still cannot be forcibly driven down a particular path. Effective and meaningful reform is more likely where government officials can be persuaded that a particular course of action is in their interests. Now whilst appeals to the principle of comparative advantage and the theory of tariffs could be helpful, in themselves they are unlikely to persuade policy makers of the need for reform. Argumentation grounded on 'theory' is likely to be dismissed as an act of faith. The ability to offer empirical evidence to illuminate the effects of current policy is therefore important. This does not mean of course that if one provides a given set of estimates of effective protection (EP) the case is won – far from it. Providing detailed data can create a different set of problems. Skilled negotiators wishing to resist change can deploy selective information very effectively as a delaying tactic. (This point does not incidentally only pertain to developing countries!) Nevertheless the fact remains that this kind of information can perform an important persuasive function. Given the nature of policy formulation, and incrementalism, policy makers and policy administrators rarely have any real feel for the economic effects of a given policy regime. Information on EP, domestic resource costs, cost of protection and incidence analysis all have a potentially valuable role to play, especially when used to enlighten the relative effects of protection. When incidence analysis was discussed we saw that although the information content was less than with EP and DRC, it had the virtue of being a simple, transparent measure which can be readily understood. With regard to the persuasive function, this makes it particularly useful.

The simulation function ties in with both the informative and persuasive functions of pre-loan policy appraisal. If a particular package of reforms is to be adopted and implemented, one ought to attempt to provide some indication of its likely impact, otherwise the reform package might launched on the basis of uncertain impact. Now forecasting is a dangerous business. Sceptics would no doubt describe it as a graveyard, and moreover a graveyard that is not short of tombstones. This is true for industrialised countries where data series are more complete and probably more reliable than in developing countries. Nevertheless forecasting and policy simulation in the context of policy appraisal are not directed at generating point estimates of output, employment, the current account and so on. Rather the process is directed at providing information of a qualitative nature or on *relative* orders of magnitude. This is where computable general equilibrium (CGE) modelling is useful. As we saw earlier, there are a great many pitfalls with CGE modelling in developing countries. In many cases the technology is just too sophisticated for the data base it relies upon. The technique must therefore be used with great caution. However when used with appropriate caution it can provide some enlightenment on alternative policy scenarios. In particular it can be helpful in comparing a base case, simulating the continuation of present policies, with projected outcomes of a range of reform possibilities. Although CGE modelling may exhaust its usefulness more quickly than other policy appraisal techniques it can perform a useful role.

Before proceeding further, one final point should be made. Although we have distinguished between the informative, persuasive and simulation functions we need to acknowledge that in practice they may be interdependent. A political scientist might argue that pre-loan appraisal is geared towards involving outside experts in the process. According to this view, simulation is then no more than a means of generating the types of information an expert political outsider must have in order to be persuasive. In the context of the bargaining that takes place between governments and the lending agencies, this view has some legitimacy. Notwithstanding this, it is still helpful to try to disentangle the three functions in order to highlight the role of economist cum technician, as opposed to the adviser cum persuader.

So much for pre-loan policy appraisal, what about post-loan appraisal? This process too can perform several functions. Again the *informative function* may be important. In addition the process performs a *monitoring function*. Finally we can identify a *bargaining function*. In the light of our comments above the information function is largely self-explanatory. Some time after the loan conditions have been agreed and implemented it is useful to recalculate EP or DRC rates. As well as providing basic information on changes in the protective structure this facilitates monitoring of actual effects. As we saw earlier a particular reform package may have certain expected effects. As a matter of good practise one should subsequently evaluate whether these particular effects materialised and if not, why not. This is arguably an important process with regard to any episode of policy reform. It is especially important in the context of SALs as this programme is still relatively young. As we shall see later, there is evidence to suggest that some early SALs were over-ambitious in terms of the conditionality they required. This clearly compromised their prospect of success. In order to improve the design and implementation of SALs it is important that learning take place. Post-loan appraisal has an obvious role to play in this regard.

From a political economy standpoint, post-loan appraisal has a third function, namely a bargaining role. SAL programmes generally encompass more than one single loan and/or tranching within a given loan programme. Thus in the countries covered by Tables 12.1–12.4, many received three or more loans. As Mosley (1987) has stressed, the bargaining process that occurs within and between loans has a vital bearing on actual conditionality. Both parties have an interest in underpinning their position with evidence on the economic effects of prior programmes. Where the World Bank is concerned this can be viewed as the analogue of the persuasive function discussed in connection with pre-loan appraisal. Information is required in order to reinforce the case for continuing with a particular programme, or to support the case for readopting a suspended programme.

Thus policy appraisal, using the techniques discussed earlier, has a very important role to play in the context of the SAL programme. This role is multi-faceted. The range of tools available allows the applied economist/ policy analyst the opportunity to provide the raw material to facilitate informed debate. Of course the information generated may ultimately do little to alter entrenched positions. That is however a problem for negotiators rather than economists, and it is not a convincing argument against using the techniques available to enlighten and inform. As with all techniques of applied economics they have to be used with caution and care – one wants to avoid at all costs being confronted with Turvey's famous dictum 'if you torture the data long enough, it will confess'!

12.5 Concluding comments

The SAL programme is an important one from the standpoint of developing countries: it provides substantial resources. These are quick to disburse and there is considerable flexibility in their usage. SALs are conditional lending programmes that emphasise supply-side reforms. A crucial element in the reform package is trade policy reform. SALs agreed thus far have resulted in changes in a number of instruments of trade policy. In deciding upon which instruments to change, as well as the general thrust of policy reform, policy appraisal using the techniques we have discussed has been an important input. Policy appraisal has figured in both pre-loan and post-loan bargaining about the detail of conditionality, and has probably made for more informed debate that would otherwise have been the case. This does not of course mean that the 'right' policies have always been adopted, nor that they have always been implemented in the 'right' order. That is another issue. It simply means that the tools of policy appraisal can have an important operational function to play in the context of trade policy reform. The issue of actual outcomes will be addressed in Chapter 13. Having evaluated the rationale behind SALs, and assessed the trade policy components, it is now time to consider in more detail actual adjustment experience and economic performance under SALs.

CHAPTER 13

Structural Adjustment Lending: Timing, Sequencing and Economic Effects

13.1 Introduction

As we saw in Chapter 12, SALs have rapidly become an important source of finance to developing countries. These quick to disburse loans now account for the equivalent of one-quarter of all official development assistance to non-oil developing countries. As we also saw, trade policy is the most important area of conditionality in these lending programmes. In turn policy appraisal forms an important element in the negotiation of conditionality.

Having examined the main thrust of SAL reforms, we come now to an assessment of the economic effects of those reforms. Of necessity this must focus primarily on the SAL programmes overall. Where possible however the economic effects of trade policy aspects will be highlighted. In the course of this assessment we will draw out the interaction of trade policy with other areas of policy reform. In turn this will permit us to emphasise the importance of timing and sequencing.

The remainder of this chapter is organised as follows. Section 13.2 looks at the detail of adjustment experience and economic performance and Section 13.3 concentrates on issues of timing, sequencing and other constraints to reform. Section 13.4 examines the factors affecting sustainability. Section 13.5 considers whether policy appraisal has any role to play with respect to timing and sequencing. Finally, Section 13.6 offers some concluding comments.

13.2 Adjustment experience and economic performance

How does one evaluate the SAL programme? This is an extremely important question. However it is also a difficult question to answer. In principle there are two quite separate approaches we could use. First, we could evaluate actual outcomes relative to SAL objectives. Second, we could attempt to compare economic performance under SALs with economic performance in their absence.

Compliance with conditionality

Assessing compliance with conditionality is a relatively simple exercise. We take the information on conditionality and assess the degree to which this conditionality was adhered to. Any such assessment would be necessarily qualitative. One would have to make judgements as to when a condition was 'fully implemented', and when 'substantial progress' towards implementation had been made. World Bank (1988) makes such an assessment. This is summarised in Table 13.1. As one can see, for the 40 countries studied 60 per cent of all conditions were assessed as fully implemented in the period concerned. When those conditions where 'substantial progress' was made are also included the proportion was 84 per cent. If one allows for a lag, these proportions increase to 67 per cent and 89 per cent respectively.

This kind of exercise can convey potentially useful information. It can tell us, for example, something about differences in implementation by policy instrument. Thus the percentage of trade policy conditions implemented was relatively low, whilst those for energy policy and the exchange rate were relatively high. This may have something to do with the nature of the reforms involved. Thus if those for energy just involve price changes whilst those for trade policy involve replacing QRs with equivalent tariffs, one can see how the greater complexity of the latter could make for greater difficulty of compliance. Another possibility is that greater political interests may be at stake with trade policy than with, say, energy policy. As we saw earlier substantial rents are often associated with direct controls. Agents acquire property rights to such rents and give them up with great reluctance. As a result conditionality may be more difficult to meet. We shall consider these issues in greater detail later when we evaluate the role of constraints, slippage and timing and sequencing. This is where this kind of information is potentially most useful. It is less useful however as a basis for evaluating the impact of SALs on recipient countries. This is so for several reasons.

First, it is possible that it is the least important conditions which are adhered to, and the most important which are resisted. World Bank (1988)

Table 13.1 Degree of implementation of World Bank conditionality

	Percentage of conditions:			
	During the loan period		*Current situation*	
Item	*Conditions fully implemented (1)*	*(1) plus 'substantial progress' (2)*	*Conditions fully implemented (3)*	*(3) plus 'substantial progress' (4)*
1. Exchange rate	70.0	90.0	62.5	87.5
2. Trade policies	54.9	84.2	63.4	89.3
Import QRs	62.8	93.0	69.0	90.4
Import duties	61.5	76.9	72.7	81.8
Import/export finance	20.0	80.0	42.9	85.7
Export incentives	60.6	81.8	62.5	91.7
Other trade policies	33.3	76.2	41.1	94.1
3. Fiscal policy	53.2	78.3	69.8	95.3
Tax policy	46.2	53.8	86.7	100.0
4. Budget/public expenditures	68.0	78.0	71.7	84.8
5. Public enterprise reforms (incl. restructuring)	61.3	86.7	70.0	90.0
6. Financial sector	71.4	85.7	73.5	89.8
7. Industrial policy (excl. restructuring)	53.3	93.3	42.9	85.7
8. Energy policy	79.2	83.3	83.3	88.9
Energy pricing	84.6	84.6	100.0	100.0
9. Agriculture policy	57.1	81.6	58.1	83.7
Agricultural pricing	64.3	85.7	61.5	80.8
All conditions, total	60.3	83.7	67.5	89.0
All conditions, SALs	68.3	84.1	73.5	92.4
All conditions, SECALs	59.9	83.2	60.0	84.9
All conditions, SSA countries	52.4	84.6	62.2	86.7
All conditions, HICs	66.9	88.6	73.2	91.4
All conditions, other developing countries	52.8	79.7	56.0	84.0

Source: World Bank (1988) Table 4.3.

did acknowledge this problem. It distinguished between 'key' conditions and other conditions. It concluded that, 'on balance, the performance on key conditions is better than the performance on all conditions' (p. 62).

Second, even if key conditions have been implemented more than other conditions, it could be that implementation has occurred in the most flexible countries with the best economic prospects. In this regard it is notable from Table 13.1 that the proportion of conditions implemented in Sub-Saharan Africa is less than the overall average, although it is also the case that for another problem group, the HICs, it is higher than average.

Third, it may be that misguided or inappropriate conditions have been applied! As we saw in Part I, there continues to be debate over the role of liberal trade policies in development. The SAL programme promotes the adoption of more liberal trade policies. Not all analysts would regard this as appropriate.

Fourth, the conditions we are focusing on are, after all, *inputs* into the policy reform process. Ultimately what we should focus on are the *outputs* of that process – that is to say the eventual impact of the programme on economic performance (however defined).

Thus although compliance with conditionality provides us with useful information for programme assessment, it is not a substitute for evaluating economic performance under adjustment programmes.

Performance under adjustment programmes

Assessing the experience of countries subject to SALs presents us with an entirely different set of analytical constraints. This is so for several reasons. First, as we have seen, many of the SAL reforms are supply side, directed at altering relative incentives in the medium to long run rather than in the short to medium run. It may therefore take some time for the reforms to have an impact on economic activity. Second, we do not have any clear *ante monde*. What would have happened in the absence of the SAL? It is tempting simply to assume that preexisting policies would have continued. Preexisting policies may however have been unsustainable. As a result taking these as a reference point could be misleading. Third, other policy shocks and lending programmes could overlap/interact with a SAL. For instance, it is not unusual to find that a country is simultaneously subject to a SAL and an IMF stabilisation loan – how does one disentangle the effects of the two programmes? Fourth, in any cross-section study one faces the difficulty that different countries start from different positions, they have different conditionality, the sequencing of programmes may be different, and so on. Finally, the conditions of a given SAL may not have been fully adhered to. How does one allow for this? For all these reasons, any evaluation must of necessity be to some extent partial, to some extent qualitative and to some extent incomplete. Notwithstanding these difficulties however, there have been several attempts to evaluate the impact of SALs on the recipient countries, some of which have been cross-section, some case study. The most comprehensive cross-section analyses are World Bank (1988, 1990) and Harrigan and Mosley (1991). A great deal of case study material has now been assembled, including Thomas *et al.* (1992) and Mosley, Harrigan and Toye (1991).

What are the measuring rods for SAL success or failure? On page 212 we set out the objectives for the programme. It will be recalled that medium-term growth and sustainability of the balance of payments are seen as the

Table 13.2 Details of SAL studies

Study	*Number of Countries*	*Time Period*
World Bank (1988)		All SALs 1980–7, evaluation of impact three years after disbursement
World Bank (1990)	78	1985–8 with 1970–90 1985–8 with 1981–4
Harrigan and Mosley (1991)	40	SALs 1980–7 with 1982–6

key objectives. In assessing the impact of SALs therefore, these are obvious indicators to refer to. Methodologically there are two approaches one can take: 'before and after', and 'with–without' performance. The former traces the path of, for example, GDP growth before the SAL, then compares it with post-SAL performance, the difference being attributed to the impact of the lending programme. There are two major shortcomings with this: first it presupposes the sustainability of preexisting policies. Typically SALs are negotiated in crisis conditions. In other words, against the backdrop of unsustainable policies. The other problem is that it is difficult to control for exogenous shocks such as commodity price changes. 'With–without' relies upon the experience of comparing performance in SAL countries (the 'with' group) against that of non-SAL countries (the 'without' group). Differences are then attributed to the impact of adjustment lending. The principal problem here is in the choice of 'control' and the impact of 'other factors' on the control. This however is the approach used by World Bank (1988, 1990) and Harrigan and Mosley (1991), although the World Bank studies do have a before–after element in them. Table 13.2 gives details of the samples. The number of countries varies from 40 to 78, whilst the data period is constrained by the limited time-frame within which SALs have operated – 1980–8 at the longest. All three studies attempt to evaluate the impact of SALs on the growth of real GDP, growth of real exports, investment as a proportion of GDP and current account balance as a proportion of GDP. World Bank (1988) and Harrigan and Mosley (1991) are close in terms of the time-frame they cover, as well as the country samples. We shall therefore take these as a pair, then refer to the results of World Bank (1990).

Table 13.3 reports the key results from these two studies. Before commenting on them, one methodological observation is in order, namely the SAL/non-SAL comparisons. The World Bank pooled the relevant data, that is all SAL countries were treated as one discrete sub-sample, all non-SAL countries as a separate sub-sample. Harrigan and Mosley regard

Table 13.3 Effectiveness of adjustment lending: comparison of results, (percentage of SAL countries which outperformed non-SAL countries)

Study	Growth of real GDP	Investment as % of GDP	Growth of real exports	Current account as % of GDP
World Bank (1988)	53	37	57	70
Mosley and Harrigan (1991)	50	38	65	79

this as flawed because the countries in each sub-sample may be unrepresentative. Instead they match with and without countries on a pairwise basis using information on, *inter alia*, economic structure, income per capita, growth of GDP and so on. In some cases the pairings work out rather well (for example Burundi and Rwanda or Kenya and Tanzania); in other cases the pairs do not look quite as well matched (for example Pakistan and Egypt, or Turkey and Greece). Nevertheless the approach offers an alternative to that of the World Bank (1988). Despite this difference, one cannot help being struck at the similarity of outcomes across the two studies. Harrigan and Mosley's study is more favourable on exports and the current account (despite excluding two of the most successful adjusting countries from their sample, namely Mauritius and Korea); slightly less favourable on GDP growth, and almost identical on investment. Overall both studies appear to suggest that adjustment lending might encourage real export growth and might contribute to improvements in the current account of the balance of payments. On the other hand, however, they imply that the impact on real GDP growth is neutral, whilst the effect on investment is negative.

The presentation of results in World Bank (1990) is somewhat different. These are reported in Table 13.4. They do not tell a markedly different story to Table 13.3. There is some evidence to suggest an improvement in real export growth, though it is noteable that this only shows up in nominal terms. When measured in real terms the change is still positive but not statistically significant. The impact on GDP growth appears to be positive, although the results are only statistically significant when we compare 1985–8 with 1981–4, a period of recession. Finally, there again appears to be a negative impact on investment and this *is* statistically significant when 1985–8 is compared with 1970–80.

Before appraising these findings, one final piece of evidence should be cited. As well as the with–without comparisons, Harrigan and Mosley also undertook some regression analysis. They correctly observe that the with–without results are likely to be influenced to an unknown extent by several non-SAL factors, in particular the conjunction of other finance with disbursements from the World Bank (notably from the IMF); a differential impact of exogenous shocks across countries; and the possible diversity of responses to adjustment lending across the sample due to different

Table 13.4 Effectiveness of adjustment lending: World Bank's assessment

Period/ dependent variable	*Change in rate[1] of growth of GDP (%)*	*Change in investment/ GDP (%)*	*Change in domestic saving/ GDP (%)*	*Change in export/ GDP (%)*
Current prices:				
1985–8 with 1970–80	1.3	−4.1[3]	4.0[4]	6.4[3]
1985–8 with 1981–4	2.0[4]	0.5	4.2[2]	5.0[4]
Constant prices:				
1985–8 with 1970–80	1.0	−5.6[3]	2.0	1.2
1985–8 with 1981–4	1.9[5]	−0.1	5.8[2]	2.3

Source: World Bank (1990).

Notes:
1. The rate of growth of GDP is measured at constant prices in both cases but the estimation procedure requires the use of lagged values of all the performance indicators and that is the reason for slightly different estimation of the effect of programs on rate of growth of GDP in the top and bottom of the table.
2. Statistically significant at the 2.5% level.
3. Statistically significant at the 5% level.
4. Statistically significant at the 7.5% level.
5. Statistically significant at the 10% level.

implementation and sequencing patterns. Thus they regress GDP growth, real export growth, investment growth and so on, on a set of independent variables for the period 1980–6. The results are reported in Table 13.5. It has to be acknowledged that there are some fairly fundamental problems with these estimates. What we have is a series of ad hoc equations designed to scan the characteristics of the data. Whilst this can be a useful starting point in empirical analysis, it makes it difficult to offer a convincing economic interpretation. For example it is not clear why we should truncate the lags on SALs at two periods; nor is it obvious why there are no lags on IMF stabilisation loans. Moreover there are very likely to be statistical problems with the results – collinearity between some of the independent variables (for example EPI and gEX), and, judging from the DW statistics, autocorrelation in at least some cases. One must therefore interpret the results with great caution. In terms of the signs of many of the coefficients,

Table 13.5 Effectiveness of adjustment lending: further evidence

Dependent variable (R squared in brackets)	*Regression coefficients on independent variables (student's T-statistics in brackets beneath coefficient)*													
	Constant	*IMF(t)*	*SAL(t)*	*SAL(t-1)*	*SAL(t-2)*	*CI(t)*	*CI(t-1)*	*CI(t-2)*	*W(t)*	*TOT(t)*	*DPI(t)*	*INV(t)*	*gEX(t)*	*DW Statistic*
GDP growth (0.40)	–24.65** (–5.65)	–0.11 (–0.46)	0.03 (0.50)	–1.85* (–2.54)	0.98 (1.30)	0.23 (0.53)	1.35** (2.87)	0.23 (0.52)	0.12** (4.54)	0.16** (4.07)	n/a	0.01 (0.16)	0.04* (2.57)	1.68
Export growth (0.17)	–0.51 (–0.02)	2.64 (1.83)	–10.03** (–3.08)	3.72 (0.84)	1.89 (0.41)	9.63** (3.96)	–6.04* (–2.15)	1.72 (0.64)	–0.15 (–0.97)	n/a	–0.20 (–0.94)	–0.25 (–0.71)	n/a	2.49
Import growth (0.13)	24.84 (0.93)	2.91* (1.99)	–6.13 (–1.86)	–2.07 (–0.46)	3.57 (0.77)	6.69** (2.71)	–4.58 (–1.61)	0.34 (0.13)	–0.18 (–1.13)	–0.15 (–0.63)	n/a	0.12 (0.34)	n/a	2.62
Investment as % of GDP (0.25)	–16.37 (–2.42)	0.00 (0.00)	–0.70 (–0.83)	0.53 (0.46)	–0.72 (–0.60)	–0.38 (–0.60)	0.49 (0.67)	–0.20 (–0.28)	0.10* (2.39)	0.32** (6.03)	n/a	n/a	n/a	0.66
Private Foreign Finance (0.18)	–1269.71* (–1.97)	–61.81 (–1.76)	–30.62 (0.39)	–16.16 (–0.15)	–108.64 (–0.97)	–25.46 (–0.43)	–2.04 (–0.03)	62.43 (0.96)	8.17* (2.15)	6.67 (1.17)	n/a	16.99* (2.01)	n/a	0.81

Source: Harrigan and Mosley (1991).

Note:
** denotes significance of a coefficient at the 1% level and * at the 5% level.

CI = Conditionality index
W = Weather index
DPI = Export price index
INV = Investment as a share of GDR
gEX = Growth rate of exports

the results do not appear to be inconsistent with the results of the with–without analysis. For the most part however the coefficient estimates fail to reach statistical significance. They should not therefore be taken as seriously as the other results reported earlier.

What can we make of all of this? The results suggest several conclusions. First it would seem that some current account improvement has been experienced in adjustment lending countries. The evidence on real export growth suggests that this is partly attributable to improved export performance. However more detailed analysis also suggests that it is in part due to import compression. Since many SAL countries also have IMF stabilisation loans in place, and since conditionality there tends to apply to demand-side restraint, this effect could be due to the impact of Fund lending rather than SALs. As yet no work has successfully disentangled the impact of structural adjustment and stabilisation lending.

Second, there may be a modest growth bonus from adjustment lending. The evidence here is somewhat more equivocal. Harrigan and Mosley suggest SALs are neutral in their impact on real growth, whilst the World Bank (1990) suggests that the bonus could be up to two percentage points (in nominal terms, less in real terms). This is a case where it may genuinely be too early to judge. At present we do not have a great many data points from which to work.

Third, it would appear that adjustment lending is associated with investment slumps. This is an alarming finding, particularly from the perspective of those who make a case for adjustment lending programmes. Since investment is directly related to growth, it may not augur well for the future.

There are several possible explanations for the finding. The World Bank (1990) argues that since an integral aim of adjustment lending is to curtail private and public sector investment whose efficiency is low, some reduction was to be expected. This may be so. In itself it is not a convincing explanation however, if only because proponents of adjustment lending would also argue that reduction of the public sector should have 'crowded in' private sector investment. A second possibility is that the greater fungibility of adjustment finance facilitates a switch from investment expenditure to consumption expenditure to alleviate repressed consumption. Thirdly, as public sector budgets are squeezed, one finds this impacting on capital expenditure to a greater degree than current expenditure. The latter is dominated by wage costs. As a result there is far greater resistance to cuts than with capital expenditure. For political economy reasons then, investment expenditures fall. Both of these explain why public-sector investment falls. What about the failure of private investment to increase? A convincing explanation here relates to the role of credibility. In the early stages of a SAL the private sector has doubts about its sustainability and holds off from making investments until it is clear whether or not the regime change is permanent. In view of the unstable policy environment in many developing countries this is an appealing explanation and is certainly consistent with the facts. Unfortunately however it means that the lags associated with an investment response could be 'long and variable' (to coin a phrase!)

As is often the case with empirical work, both sides could probably find some comfort in these findings. Those who emphasise the need for supply-side reforms, and who do not see them coming without the threat of conditional finance, would emphasise the findings on real export growth, the current account, and perhaps even GDP growth. In contrast those who see the entire philosophy as fundamentally flawed would emphasise the findings on investment and probably those on GDP growth. Whilst it is true that adjustment lending programmes have been associated with very rapid and impressive growth in some countries, for example in Mauritius (see Greenaway and Milner, 1991c), the aggregate results are disappointing, especially those pertaining to investment performance. There is a good case to be made that it is simply too early to judge – we need more evidence. Only time can resolve this one. One could also argue that, especially in the early years, insufficient attention has been paid to issues of sequencing and infrastructural support. In other words reform programmes have not addressed themselves to the order in which reforms were implemented, nor have they concerned themselves sufficiently with the resources required for effective implementation.

13.3 Timing, sequencing and adjustment

To an increasing extent, attention is being paid to the timing of liberalisation reforms, the sequencing of reforms across sectors/markets and adjustment of agents to the reform programme. As Chart 13.1 shows, these issues are interrelated and, as experience with adjustment programmes demonstrates, they have important implications for the sustainability of a given reform programme and its eventual success or failure. Although the issues of liberalisation mechanisms, timing and sequencing are interdependent, for expository purposes it is helpful to treat them separately.

In designing a liberalisation programme the first decision one faces, as Chart 13.1 shows, is whether the programme should be partial or complete. This actually has two dimensions: should reforms pertain to all sectors (capital controls, traded goods, non-traded goods, financial sector, labour market and so on), or to a specific sector (for example traded goods); second, should the reforms sweep away all interventions or modify existing policy. Thus for example, in the event that policy was aimed at liberalising trade policy, should the objective be free trade or reduction of existing tariffs? Economic theory offers some guidance, although for most practical purposes it may not be terribly helpful. One can show relatively easily that, if the economy is free of distortions, on efficiency grounds complete liberalisation is superior to partial liberalisation (see for instance

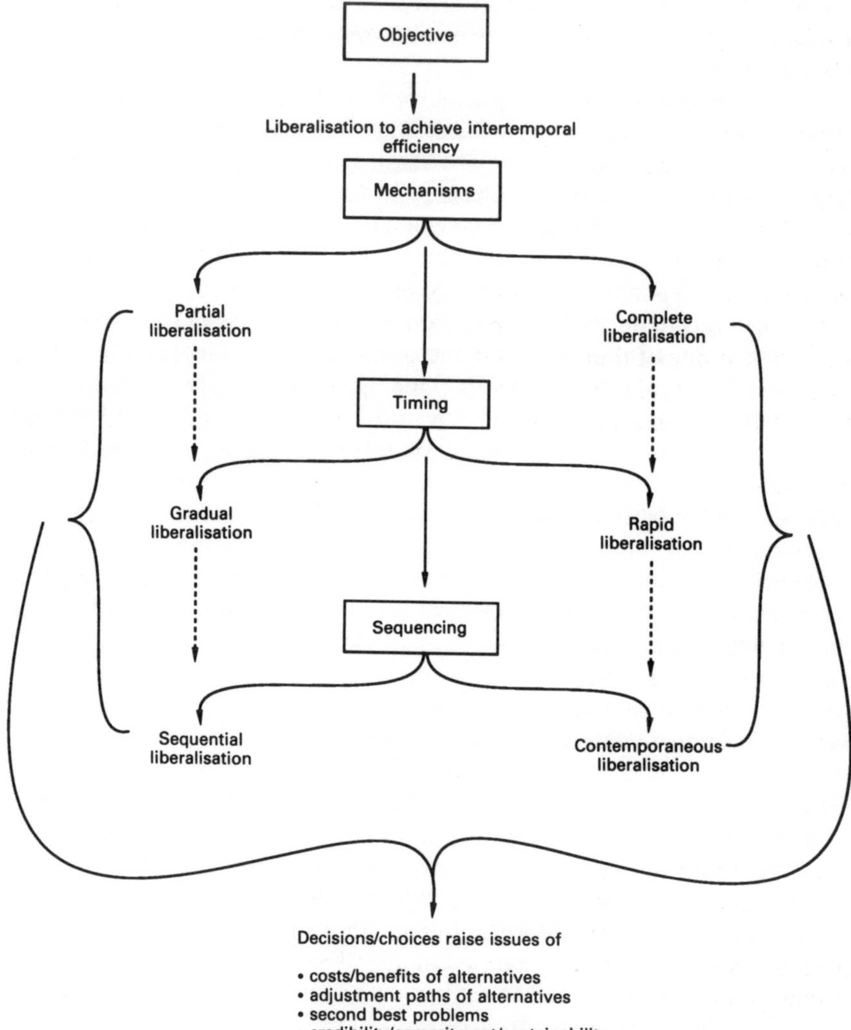

Chart 13.1 Timing and sequencing of liberalisations

Michaely, 1986). This in fact is a fairly standard result of welfare theory. Sadly however, as we have seen elsewhere in this volume, the economies of many developing countries are typically not free of distortions. In such circumstances the lead given by economic theory is less conclusive in that we face a classic second-best problem. In principle this applies to any partial liberalisation, whether this refers to liberalisation of one sector with others left untouched, or partial removal of restraints in a given sector.

The danger of using second-best theory as a touchstone in policy reform is that it becomes a recipe for inactivity. Being a purist also involves being a nihilist in this respect. In practice advice tends to be given on a *ceteris paribus* basis. Thus, notwithstanding the general theory of second-best, economic theory shows quite clearly that a tariff is generally superior to a quota as an instrument of protection. This can be used to defend the replacement of quotas with equivalent tariffs as an act of liberalisation. Moreover political economy considerations will often also be brought to bear. For example replacing quotas with tariffs can be defended on distributional grounds. Ultimately of course the issue of whether liberalisation is general or partial is a political one determined by bargaining between the World Bank and the government of the host country.

Having taken a decision to liberalise, whether partially or generally, the next issue is one of timing: should the programme be implemented rapidly or gradually? Again this is a tricky issue. Economic theory would suggest that, in the absence of distortions and with full factor mobility, liberalisation should be rapid – the 'big bang' approach. In such circumstances adjustment would be smooth. Theory also shows, however, that even without distortions adjustment might be sticky if some factors are sector specific (see for instance Mussa, 1986). Factor specificity results in some wage/price rigidities and quantity rationing. As a result sector-specific unemployment follows liberalisation. This can be used to make a case for gradualism on one of two counts, depending upon the specific factor: first it allows time for sector-specific labour to retrain; second, it permits sector-specific capital to be written off at some 'optimal' rate. Of course one could take the view that adjustment costs are the price we pay for change and are simply a short-run phenomenon. Since the discounted value of the benefits from liberalisation will typically exceed to a significant degree the discounted value of any adjustment costs, we should still go ahead and implement reforms quickly in order to realise the benefits quickly. At least two objections are often raised against this proposition. On the one hand it is sometimes argued that 'fairness' demands adjustment assistance in the form of time to adjust; on the other hand it is often argued that gradualism makes good sense on political economy grounds – with rapid adjustment you are likely to get maximum resistance to liberalisation. The former point is not wholly convincing. Although 'fairness' is (quite rightly) a powerful motive force, it is not clear why traded goods sectors should be singled out – as they often are. In other words, if this is to be used as an argument for gradualism it should apply to *all* economic policy where there are gainers and losers. The second argument is potentially more cogent. If the costs of adjustment are heavily concentrated in a specific factor, or on specific sectors, one might find that powerful lobbies opposed to the policy change are galvanised in their opposition by rapid adjustment. If so, this could then constitute a real threat to the sustainability of the entire programme.

This is certainly plausible. Equally however another perspective can be taken, *viz.*, gradualism allows lobbies opposed to liberalisation to organise, resist and ultimately undermine the programme. In practice this has been a problem in some countries – gradualist programmes have never reached full fruition. This is not, incidentally, a problem peculiar to developing countries. It arises because the benefits from liberalisation are widely dispersed whilst the losses are concentrated. Thus beneficiaries are poorly organised and ineffectually counter the lobbying efforts of losers from liberalisation. This problem has led Laird and Yeats (1990) to propose the establishment of permanent commissions which record the costs of protection/benefits of liberalisation and are charged with the responsibility of defending the gains realised from liberalisation programmes.

Tied in with timing is the question of sequencing – no matter whether we are dealing with partial or complete liberalisation, should all sectors be liberalised contemporaneously or should liberalisation in some precede that in others? This question has been scrutinised fairly closely by analysts, especially by reference to Latin American experience (see for instance Edwards, 1990). Again theory is not unequivocal in its recommendations, although practical experience does give us a few useful counters. Thus, for example, Latin American experience suggests that financial market liberalisation should precede the removal of capital controls. Removal of capital controls prior to reforming financial markets appears to be a recipe for capital flight. In turn capital flight creates pressures for a policy reversal and potentially erodes commitment.

McKinnon (1973, 1982) has argued that not only should abolition of capital controls follow financial market liberalisation, it should also follow trade liberalisation. His reasoning is as follows: if financial markets are reformed and capital controls are abolished prior to trade liberalisation, there will be capital inflows to the reforming economy. In turn these lead to real exchange rate appreciation which erodes the competitiveness of industries producing tradeables. This would then make trade liberalisation much more difficult. Clearly, if reform of policy in traded goods sectors precedes the abolition of capital controls, the problem simply does not arise. Frenkel (1983) has given a slightly different gloss on this by emphasising relative speed of adjustment across markets. Specifically, asset markets clear much more quickly than goods and labour markets. Consequently he argues that these markets need a shorter time to adjust. Appropriate sequencing then means liberalising the trade account some time ahead of the current account.

As we can see therefore, issues of timing and sequencing are complex and complicated. From a policy standpoint they are crucially important. If the wrong decisions are taken regarding the scale of liberalisation and/or speed of implementation and/or sequencing across sectors, government commitment to the programme and/or the credibility of government's commitment could be eroded. In these circumstances the programme would simply not be sustainable. It is to the issue of sustainability that we now turn.

13.4 Factors influencing sustainability

For the most part SALs tend to involve partial liberalisation, they tend to be implemented gradually and, to an increasing extent, reforms which apply to real sectors precede those which apply to financial markets. Some SALs are sustained, others show evidence of slippage at an early stage and *in extremis* complete collapse results. The sustainability of a given lending programme appears to be fashioned by a combination of programme design, government commitment, adequacy of funding and external environment.

Programme design clearly overlaps our discussion in Section 13.3, particularly regarding sequencing. In addition however, several other points are relevant. Experience has shown that consistency of policies within a package is important – ideally policy reforms should reinforce each other. In practice this is not always the case. For instance, incentives may be given to exporters to reduce anti-export bias. If at the same time protection to producers of intermediate goods is raised, then exporters are disadvantaged. As a result a potentially vocal lobby in support of reforms is alienated. Related to the above, where lending programmes from more than one agency are in place simultaneously it is crucially important to ensure that they are consistent. An interesting example of conflict here occurred in the Ivory Coast in the early 1980s. At the same time as the World Bank was recommending tariff liberalisation on allocative grounds, the IMF was pushing for tariff increases on fiscal grounds. In addition to compromising the credibility of the institutions, such conflicting advice must compromise sustainability. Fortunately greater attention is now being paid to cross-conditionality between the key multilateral agencies and the prospects of this occurring are, as a result, lower. A final aspect of programme design that should be acknowledged is feasibility – conditions should be capable of implementation. This is an obvious point. On occasions however, conditions have simply been too ambitious. To illustrate this point we can refer again to the experience of the Ivory Coast in the early 1980s, when tariff reforms were set by reference to effective rather than nominal tariffs. Quite apart from the advisability of the objective of a uniform effective tariff, setting the bureaucracy the task of calibrating and monitoring uniform effective tariffs was simply too ambitious. Clearly in such circumstances the policy reform is not sustainable.

Government commitment is central to sustainability. Here several influences are relevant, some of which overlap the points made in Section 13.3. We can identify two sources of pressure – internal and external. The former refers to the way in which responsibility for implementing different elements of the programme is devolved within the government machinery and the extent of any infrastructural support provided. As we saw in Chapter 12, SALs can be very complex packages involving policy reforms in a wide range of areas. Typically government bureaucracies are fragmented, with different agencies responsible for carefully delineated spheres of influence. Moreover it is not unusual to find that these spheres of influence are jealously guarded. This means that internal coordination may be difficult. It also means that officials some way down the chain of command can be readily identified as targets for lobbying activity. Both may help erode commitment. It has been argued by Halevi (1988) that this was an important factor in Ghana.

The other internal factor, infrastructural support, overlaps comments made in Section 13.3 above about feasibility of reforms and in Section 13.5 below regarding adequacy of funding. The point is a simple one: if the necessary administrative infrastructure is not in place, the ability of a government to see a particular programme through must be in question. A good example here was in Tanzania in the late 1980s when wholesale tariff reform was proposed in order to raise customs collections. At the time there were only 12 customs posts in the country and no formal mechanism for training new customs officers.

'Externally' the key influences on commitment are the speed of any positive supply response to an adjustment programme and the impact of the programme on protected sectors. If implementation of conditionality results in a rapid contraction of previously protected sectors but a sluggish response from export orientated industries, as may be the case due to credibility problems, the social costs of adjustment would appear to be relatively high. As occurred for instance in the Philippines, the government then comes under early and severe pressure to slow down, or even reverse, some of the changes and slippages take place. Typically producer lobbies are well organised and effective. Often they are 'pushing against an open door' in dealing with governments that have implemented policy reforms in which they may not have complete conviction and which have uncertain outcomes. As we noted earlier, this can be used as an argument for making adjustment assistance available to exposed sectors in order to enhance the prospects for sustainability.

Adequacy of funding is implicit in some of the points made above but should be mentioned in its own right. The point is that expectations on the part of the lender may be unrealistically high, given the level and distribution of funding. This was certainly the case with many of the early SALs for Sub-Saharan African countries – too much was being asked given the absence of funding earmarked for infrastructural support in the form of training and internal mechanisms for monitoring and evaluation. Inevitably, if the internal machinery for seeing reform through is not properly resourced, commitment will wane.

External environment. As we saw in Section 12.2, exogenous shocks can impact on countries whilst they are subject to a lending programme. Shocks may be beneficial or adverse. In the event of the latter they can easily erode commitment. A good example here is Zambia in 1987. In that year the Zambian government implemented a series of radical reforms, including auctioning foreign exchange and reducing quantitative restrictions. During the programme, however, the world price of copper fell significantly. As copper accounted for around 90 per cent of Zambian exports (by value), this not only reduced export revenues quite dramatically, it also reduced government revenue and as a result the reform programme was reversed. There is probably not a lot one can do within the context of an SAL to insure against such contingencies, beyond perhaps making available more compensatory finance.

Sustainability cannot be taken for granted therefore. It depends upon the characteristics of programme design, the nature and adequacy of funding, external shocks during the lending period and, above all, government commitment. Can policy appraisal help?

13.5 Policy appraisal, timing, sequencing and adjustment

The answer to the above question is, regretfully, probably not a lot. We saw in Chapter 12 how the techniques of policy appraisal can be helpful in pre-loan and post-loan evaluation. We can make use of many of the techniques discussed in Chapters 4 to 11 to inform and persuade. Many of these techniques are partial equilibrium and therefore incapable of being used to evaluate adjustment paths as a basis for evaluating timing and sequencing. Some were of course general equilibrium, most notably CGE modelling. However as we saw this particular methodology tends to be used against the backcloth of necessarily restrictive assumptions. Apart from the fact that some of the results are not always robust, the technique is still in its infancy and is not as yet a perfectly reliable basis for analysing adjustment paths. The comparison of endstates is one thing, tracking sectoral and intersectoral adjustment over time is quite another.

Referring back to our discussion in Chapter 12, what this means is that the 'persuasive' function is probably uppermost in this context. In the light of experience the economist qua adviser can allude to experience with sequencing in countries where a series of lending programmes have been implemented and use this as an input to policy design. The only role that measures such as effective protection, DRC and the like then play is in highlighting the consequences of past policy and emphasising the potential benefits of sustaining a particular reform programme.

13.6 Concluding comments

In Chapter 12 we evaluated the characteristics of SALs and the rationale behind the programme as a whole. In this chapter we have focused on the economic effects of adjustment lending. In particular we have been interested in how those countries subject to lending programmes appear to have fared, as well as the impact of different sequencing arrangements.

Evaluating SALs is not easy, partly because of the difficulty of disentangling the effects of adjustment lending from everything else that is going on; partly because it may just be too early to tell. The evidence adduced so far appears to suggest that the impact on export growth and the balance of payments may have been beneficial whilst that on output growth and investment has been disappointing. Various explanations for these findings were discussed, including programme design. We saw that the timing and sequencing of a particular programme is likely to have an impact on the effects of that programme and on its sustainability. There is evidence to suggest that the international agencies are learning from experience and greater thought is being given to issues of timing and sequencing with a view to enhancing the prospects of sustainability. One of the items for the research agenda of the mid to late 1990s should be an evaluation of the relative impact of SALs in the early to mid 1980s with those of the late 1980s to early 1990s to see whether this may have had an impact on performance.

Notes

4. The Structure of Nominal Protection

1. Economic Community of West African States and Communaute Economique de l'Afrique de l'Ouest
2. Weighting by import share downwardly biases the measure of protection with the import share and scheduled tariff positively related.
3. Burundi is a member of the Communaute Economique Pays de Grand Lacs (CEPGL), the Communaute Economique des Etats de l'Afrique Centrale (CEEAC), and of the Preferential Trading Arrangement for Eastern and Southern African States.

6. Domestic Resource Cost Analysis

1. Note that if competitive conditions prevail, with undistorted markets and free trade, there is no reason in principle why we should observe DRCs of less than unity.
2. This approach and notation are adapted from Bruno, 1972, pp. 18–22.
3. This section draws upon Greenaway and Milner, 1990b.
4. This is an opportunity cost valuation of factors which differs somewhat from the shadow prices concept using general equilibrium, cost–benefit analysis. In that case the shadow price of a factor is the social value of endowing the private sector with one more unit of the factor.
5. International value added in process j (IVA_j in for example Equation 6.4) was estimated by revaluing domestic Madagascan value added at border prices, and not identified in a non-Madagascan setting.
6. The most extensive data on labour utilisation in rural Egypt is provided by the labour-force surveys carried out by the Agricultural Development System Project (ARE Ministry of Agriculture–University of California), Egypt Agricultural Mechanisation Project (Egypt–USAID Project) and the Ministry of Agriculture's Economics Research Unit.

7. Shift Analysis and the Incidence of Protection

1. This analysis draws on the work of Dornbusch (1974), Sjaastad (1980a), Sjaastad and Clements (1981), Clements and Sjaastad (1985) and Greenaway and Milner (1987a).
2. The implications of relaxing this assumption are explored in Greenaway and Milner (1988a) and Milner (1989).

3. This theoretical extreme is rather perverse in that the relative price changes induce no substitution in domestic demand towards exportables nor in production away from exportables. There is no resource effect for the exportables sector, but real income in the sector is reduced by the implicit tax paid on the consumption of higher priced importables and home goods.
4. Incidence is equally shared insomuch as the implicit tax rate on the consumption of importables is the same for producers of both exportables and non-tradeables.
5. Singh (1988) argues that the limits for w are not necessarily zero and unity. But Greenaway and Milner (1988b) show it to be the case for the model as currently specified.
6. Clements (1980) also computes an alternative set of price elasticities derived from income elasticities by applying separability theory. The estimated shift parameter for these revised values is 0.65.
7. Smeets (1989) argues for instance that application of Equation 7.17 involves a misspecification, where price change is influenced by other variables such as the domestic money supply and international prices. Although there is a problem of observational equivalence, correct interpretation of Smeets' results shows that relative prices are not fundamentally affected in the way that Smeets argues.
8. OLS results for time series regressions are likely to suffer from autocorrelation. Many of the studies report results for both OLS and other estimations which have corrected for serially correlated error terms.

8. Computable General Equilibrium Modelling

1. The Arrow–Debreu model was further elaborated on in Arrow and Hahn (1971).
2. For other useful considerations of these issues see Shoven and Whalley (1984), Dervis, de Melo and Robinson (1982) and de Melo (1988).
3. See for example Isard (1977).
4. Early models used Scarf's algorithm (1967) or approximated an equilibrium using Johansen's (1960) procedure. Other possibly more rapid solution methods have been developed subsequently. These include other local linearisation techniques and a Newton-type algorithm. For a further discussion of this last type of solution procedure see Drud, Grais and Pyatt (1983).
5. It was convenient in this case that QRs were modelled as inducing rent-seeking activity in intermediate goods only. Rent-seeking activities in consumer goods would complicate the utility specification. For an alternative approach to rent seeking see Dervis, de Melo and Robinson (1982).
6. See for instance de Melo (1978).

9. Applied GCE Analysis of Trade Policy

1. In 1981 (the nearest year for which information is available) 70 per cent of imports (by value) were subject to licensing and 8 per cent were on the quota list. In addition durable and non-durable consumer goods such as cars, washing machines and televisions were not listed, with imports *de facto* prohibited in the absence of specific authorisation by the government.
2. This problem was first noted by Eastman and Stykolt (1960) for Canada.
3. Arguably it may be the transitional impact on revenue that is important if reform of non-trade taxation is possible. But if the administrative costs of other, potentially more efficient, forms of taxation are expected to remain high, then the longer term revenue impact of trade tax reform may also be a concern.

4. This is an ad hoc response to the inadequacies for long-run analysis of the standard foreign trade specifications in CGE models. Further elaboration of modelling technique is required in this area.
5. This has been a selective review in order to illustrate types of applications, rather than a comprehensive review. A similar approach can be found in de Melo (1988) and Dervis, de Melo and Robinson (1982). More comprehensive reviews can be found in Robinson (1988), DeCaluwe and Martens (1986), Devarajan, Lewis and Robinson (1986) and Bandara (1991).
6. See for example Bell and Srinivasan (1984).

10. Revealed Comparative Advantage

1. Baldwin (1971) is a pioneering example of this type of empirical analysis. For a review of this type of work see Deardorff (1984).
2. See for example Hillman (1980) and Bowen (1983).
3. Hillman (1980) and Forstner (1984) identify circumstances where cross-country comparisons of RCA indices for specific commodities may provide consistent results. Webster (1991), reviewing recent theoretical developments, concludes however that 'we should treat single good, many country comparisons of RCA with considerable caution. Comparison between a single country and the rest of the world across several industries are more capable of justification' p. 938.
4. Ballance, Forstner and Murray (1985, 1986) express these concerns about comparisons of actual and expected values derived from the hypothesised autarkic situation.

11. Potential Comparative Advantage

1. This evidence is surveyed in Greenaway and Milner (1987b).
2. There is some more comprehensive evidence for India for example (Bhagwati and Bharadwaj, 1967), but here again there is limited factor disaggregation.
3. The index has also been used by Pomfret (1981) to examine the similarity of manufactured exports to the EEC from Spain, Greece and Portugal.
4. It is possible that the rankings arising from the index may not be consistent over time and at different levels of statistical aggregation (see for example Kellman and Schroder, 1983). In the present context there is no attempt to use the index for formal testing purposes. There is, in any case, less likelihood of product heterogeneity in the case of developing countries. It would also be possible to calculate the index for a number of years if rapid structural change was evident.
5. The dangers of inferring total resource cost effects of non-marginal resource allocations from DRC ratios are discussed in Chapter 7.

References

Agarwala, R. (1983) 'Price distortions and growth in developing countries', *World Bank Staff Working Paper*, no. 575 (Washington, DC: World Bank).

Anderson, J. (1988) *The Relative Inefficiency of Quotas* (Cambridge: MIT Press).

Arrow, K.J. and G. Debreu (1954) 'Existence of an equilibrium for a competitive economy', *Econometrica*, vol. 22, pp. 265–90.

Arrow, K.J. and F.H. Hahn (1971) *General Equilibrium Analysis* (San Francisco: Holden-Day).

Balassa, B. (1965a) *Economic Development and Integration* (Mexico, DF: Centro de Estudios Monetarios Latinamericanos).

Balassa, B. (1965b) 'Trade liberalisation and "revealed" comparative advantage', *Manchester School*, vol. 33, pp. 99–123.

Balassa, B. (1965c) 'Tariff Protection in Industrial Countries: An Evaluation', *Journal of Political Economy*, vol. 73, pp. 579–94.

Balassa, B. (1977) '"Revealed" comparative advantage revisited: an analysis of relative export shares of industrial countries: 1953–71', *Manchester School*, vol. 45, pp. 327–44.

Balassa, B. (1979a) 'The changing pattern of comparative advantage in manufactured goods', *Review of Economics and Statistics*, vol. 61, pp. 259–66.

Balassa, B. (1979b) 'A "stages approach" to comparative advantage' in *Economic Growth and Resources*, vol. 4, (London: Macmillan).

Balassa, B. (ed.) (1982) *Development Strategies in Semi Industrialized Economies* (Baltimore: Johns Hopkins University Press).

Baldwin, R.E. (1969) 'The case against infant industry protection', *Journal of Political Economy*, vol. 77, pp. 295–305.

Baldwin, R.E. (1971) 'Determinants of the commodity structure of US trade', *American Economic Review*, vol. 61, pp. 126–46.

Baldwin, R. (1989) 'The Growth Effects of 1992', *Economic Policy*, no. 9, pp. 248–81.

Ballance, R.H. (1988) 'Trade performance as an indicator of comparative advantage', in D. Greenaway (ed.) (1988a).

Ballance, R.H., J. Ansari and H. Singer (1982) *The International Economy and Industrial Development*, (Totowa, NJ: Allanheld, Osmun).

Ballance, R.H., H. Forstner and T. Murray (1985) 'On measuring comparative advantage: a note on Bowen's indices', *Weltwirtschaftliches Archiv*, vol. 121, pp. 346–50.

Ballance, R.H., H. Forstner and T. Murray (1986) 'Consistency tests of alternative measures of comparative advantage', *Review of Economics and Statistics*, vol. 69, pp. 157–61.

Bandara, J.S. (1991) 'Computable general equilibrium models for development policy analysis in LDCs', *Journal of Economic Surveys*, vol. 5, pp. 3–70.

Bell, M., B. Ross-Larson and L. Westphal (1984) 'Assessing the performance of infant industries', *Journal of Development Economics*, vol. 16, pp. 101–28.

Bell, C.L.G. and T.N. Srinivasan (1984) 'On uses and abuses of economy-wide models in development policy analysis' in M. Syrquin, L. Taylor and L.E. Westphal (eds), *Economic Structure and Performance*, (New York: Academic).

Bertrand, T.J. (1979) 'Shadow pricing in distorted economies', *American Economic Review*, vol. 69, pp. 902–14.

Bhagwati, J.N. (1958) 'Immiserizing growth: a geometric note', *Review of Economic Studies*, vol. 25, pp. 201–5.

Bhagwati, J.N. (1964) 'The pure theory of international trade: a survey', *Economic Journal*, vol. 74, pp. 1–84.

Bhagwati, J.N. (1969) *Trade, Tariffs and Growth* (Cambridge, Mass.: MIT Press).

Bhagwati, J.N. (1971) 'The generalised theory of distortions and welfare', in J.N. Bhagwati, R.W. Jones, R.A. Mundell and J. Vanek (eds), *Trade, Balance of Payments and Growth* (Amsterdam: North-Holland).

Bhagwati, J.N. (1978a) *Anatomy and Consequences of Exchange Control Regimes* (Cambridge, Mass.: Ballinger, for NIER).

Bhagwati, J.N. (1978b) *Foreign Trade Regimes and Economic Development* (Cambridge, Mass.: Ballinger).

Bhagwati, J.N. (1984) 'DUP Activities and Economic Theory', in D. Colander (ed.), *Neoclassical Political Economy* (Cambridge: Ballinger).

Bhagwati, J.N. (1990) 'Export-Promoting Trade Strategy: Issues and Evidence', in Milner (1990c).

Bhagwati, J.N. and R. Bharadwaj (1967) 'Human capital and the pattern of foreign trade: the Indian case', *Indian Economic Review*, vol. 2, pp. 117–42.

Bhagwati, J.N. and T.N. Srinivasan (1973) 'The general equilibrium theory of effective protection and resource allocation', *Journal of International Economics* vol. 3, pp. 259–81.

Bhagwati, J.N. and T.N. Srinivasan (1975) *Foreign Trade Regimes and Economic Development: India* (New York: National Bureau of Economic Research).

Bhagwati, J.N. and H. Wan (1979) 'The "stationarity" of shadow prices of factors in project evaluation with and without distortions', *American Economic Review*, vol. 69, pp. 261–73.

Bleaney, M.F. and D. Greenaway (1993) 'Long Run Trends in the Relative Price of Primary Commodities and in the Terms of Trade of Developing Countries', *Oxford Economic Papers*.

Bowen, H. (1983) 'On the theoretical interpretation of indices of trade intensity and revealed comparative advantage', *Weltwirtschaftliches Archiv*, vol. 119, pp. 464–72.

Brander, J.A. and B.J. Spencer (1984a) 'Tariff protection and imperfect competition', in Kierzkowski (1984).

Brander, J.A. and B.J. Spencer (1984b), 'Trade warfare: tariffs and cartels', *Journal of International Economics*, vol. 16, pp. 227–42.

Bruno, M. (1967) 'The optimal selection of export-promoting and import-substituting projects', in *Planning the External Sector: Techniques, Problems and Policies* (New York, United Nations).

Bruno, M. (1972) 'Domestic resource cost and effective protection: clarification and synthesis', *Journal of Political Economy*, vol. 80, pp. 16–33.

Chenery, H., J. Lewis, J. de Melo and S. Robinson (1986) 'Alternative routes to development', in H. Chenery, S. Robinson and M. Syrquin (eds), *Industrializa-*

tion and Growth: A Comparative Study (New York: Oxford University Press and World Bank).

Chenery, H. and M. Syrquin (1975) *Patterns of Development* (Oxford University Press) 2nd edition.

Clements, K.W. (1980) 'A general equilibrium econometric model of the open economy', *International Economic Review*, vol. 21, pp. 469–88.

Clements, K.W. and L.A. Sjaastad (1985) *How Protection Taxes Exporters*, Thames Essay, 39 (London: Trade Policy Research Centre).

Cline, W.R., N. Kronso, T. Kawanabe and T. Williams (1978) *Trade Negotiations in the Tokyo Round: A Quantitative Assessment* (Washington: Brookings Institution).

Condon, T. and J. de Melo (1986) 'Industrial organisation implications of QR trade regimes: evidence and welfare costs' (Washington, DC: World Bank), processed.

Corden, W.M. (1966) 'The Structure of a Tariff System and the Effective Protective Rate', *Journal of Political Economy*, vol. 74, pp. 221–37.

Corden, W.M. (1971) *The Theory of Protection* (Oxford: Clarendon Press).

Corden, W.M. (1974) *Trade Policy and Economic Welfare* (Oxford: Clarendon Press).

Cox, D. and R. Harris (1985) 'Trade liberalisation and industrial organisation: some estimates for Canada', *Journal of Political Economy*, vol. 93, pp. 115–45.

Dahl, H., S. Devarajan and S. van Wijnbergen (1986) 'Revenue-neutral tariff reform: theory and an application to Cameroon', discussion paper no. 1986–25 (Washington: Country Policy Department, World Bank).

Deardorff, A.V. (1979) 'Weak links in the chain of comparative advantage', *Journal of International Economics*, vol. 9, pp. 197–209.

Deardorff, A.V. (1980) 'The general validity of the law of comparative advantage', *Journal of Political Economy*, vol. 86, pp. 941–57.

Deardorff, A.V. (1984) 'Testing trade theories and predicting trade flows', in R.W. Jones and P.B. Kenen (eds), *Handbook of International Economics*, vol. 1 (Amsterdam: North Holland).

DeCaluwe, B. and A. Martens (1986) *CGE Modelling and Developing Economies: A Concise Empirical Survey of 56 Applications to 24 Countries*, CRDE study no. 1686 (University of Montreal).

de Melo, J. (1978) 'Protection and resource allocation in a Walrasian trade model', *International Economic Review*, vol. 19, pp. 25–44.

de Melo, J. (1980) 'Tariffs and resource allocation in partial and general equilibrium', *Weltwirtschaftliches Archiv*, vol. 116, pp. 169–77.

de Melo, J. (1988) 'Computable general equilibrium models for trade policy analysis in developing countries: a survey', *Journal of Policy Modelling*, vol. 10, pp. 469–503.

Dervis, K., J. de Melo and S. Robinson (1982) *General Equilibrium Models for Development Policy* (New York: Cambridge University Press).

Devarajan, S. (1988) 'Natural resources and taxation in computable general equilibrium models of developing countries', *Journal of Policy Modelling*, vol. 10, pp. 505–28.

Devarajan, S., J. Lewis and S. Robinson (1986) 'A bibliography of computable general equilibrium (CGE) models for developing countries', working paper no. 400, Department of Agricultural and Resource Economics (Berkeley: University of California).

Diaz, C. (1980) 'The effects of commercial policy in El Salvador', unpublished thesis, Graduate Institute of International Studies, Geneva.

Dinwiddy, C.L. and F.J. Teal (1988) *The Two-Sector General Equilibrium Model: A New Approach* (Oxford: Philip Allan).

Dixit, A. (1985) 'Tax policies in open economies', in A. Auerbach and M. Feldstein (eds), *Handbook of Public Economics* (Amsterdam: North Holland).

Donges, J.B. (1975) 'A comparative survey of industrialization policies in fifteen semi-industrialized countries', *Weltwirtschaftliches Archiv*, vol. 112, pp. 626–59.

Donges, J.B. and J. Riedel (1977) 'The expansion of manufactured goods in developing countries: an empirical assessment of supply and demand issues', *Weltwirtschaftliches Archiv*, vol. 113, pp. 58–87.

Dornbusch, R. (1974) 'Tariffs and non-traded goods', *Journal of International Economics*, vol. 4, pp. 177–85.

Drabicki, J. and A. Takayama (1979) 'An antimony in the theory of comparative advantage', *Journal of International Economics*, vol. 9, pp. 211–23.

Drud, A., W. Grais and G. Pyatt (1983) 'The TV-approach: a systematic method of defining economy-wide models based on social accounting matrices', *Proceedings of 4th IFAC/IFORS/ILASA Conference on the Modelling and Control of National Economies*, pp. 231–38.

Eastman, H. and S. Stykolt (1960) 'A model for the study of protected oligopolies', *Economic Journal*, vol. 70, pp. 336–47.

Edwards, S. (1990) 'The sequencing of economic reform: analytical issues and lessons from Latin America', *The World Economy*, vol. 13, pp. 1–14.

Falvey, R. and N. Gemmell (1990) 'Trade taxes and welfare: the case of export incentives in South East Asian countries', *Australian Economic Review*, pp. 61–73.

Fendt, R. (1981) 'Brazilian trade liberalisation: a reassessment', in L.A. Sjaastad (ed.), *The Free Trade Movement in Latin America* London: Macmillan.

Findlay, R. and S. Wellisz (1976) 'Project evaluation, shadow prices, and trade policy', *Journal of Political Economy*, vol. 84, pp. 543–552.

Finger, J. and M. Kreinin (1979) 'A measure of "export similarity" and its possible uses', *Economic Journal*, vol. 89, pp. 905–13.

Forstner, H. (1984) 'The changing pattern of international trade in manufactures: a logit analysis', *Weltwirtschaftliches Archiv*, vol. 120, pp. 1–17.

Frenkel, J. (1983) 'Remarks on the Southern Case', *IMF Staff Papers*.

Garcia, R. (1981) *The Effects of Exchange Rates and Commercial Policy on Agriculture Incentives in Columbia, 1957–78* (Washington: International Food Policy Research Institute).

Grais, W., J. de Melo and S. Urata (1986) 'A general equilibrium estimation of the effects of reduction in tariffs and quantitative restrictions in Turkey in 1978', in T.N. Srinivasan and J. Whalley (eds), *General Equilibrium Trade Policy Modelling* (Cambridge, Mass.: MIT Press).

Greenaway, D. (1980) 'Trade taxes as a source of government revenue: an international comparison', *Scottish Journal of Political Economy*, vol. 27, pp. 175–82.

Greenaway, D. (1985) 'Models of trade in differentiated goods and commercial policy', in D. Greenaway (ed.), *Current Issues in International Trade* (London: Macmillan).

Greenaway, D. (1986) 'Characteristics of industrialisation and economic performance under alternative development strategies', background paper to *World Development Report 1987* (Washington DC: World Bank).

Greenaway, D. (ed.) (1988a) *Economic Development and International Trade* (London: Macmillan).

Greenaway, D. (1988b) 'Evaluating the structure of protection in less developed countries', in D. Greenaway (ed.), *Economic Development and International Trade* (London: Macmillan).

Greenaway, D. (1989) 'Commercial policy and policy conflict: an evaluation of the incidence of protection in a non-industrialised economy', *Manchester School*, vol. 57, pp. 125–41.

Greenaway, D. (1991) 'New Trade Theories and Developing Countries', in V.N. Balasubramanyam and S. Lall (eds), *Current Issues in Development Economics*, (London: Macmillan).

Greenaway, D., R.C. Hine, A. O'Brien and R. Thornton (eds) (1991) *Global Protectionism* (London: Macmillan).

Greenaway, D. and C.R. Milner (1986a) *The Economics of Intra-Industry Trade* (Oxford: Basil Blackwell).

Greenaway, D. and C.R. Milner (1986b) 'Estimating the shifting of protection across sectors: an application to Mauritius', *Industry and Development*, vol. 16, pp. 1–22.

Greenaway, D. and C.R. Milner (1987a) 'True protection concepts and their role in evaluating trade policies in LDCs', *Journal of Development Studies*, vol. 23, pp. 200–19.

Greenaway, D. and C.R. Milner (1987b) 'Trade theory and less-developed countries', in N. Gemmell (ed.), *Surveys in Development Economics* (London: Blackwells).

Greenaway, D. and C.R. Milner (1988a) 'Intra-industry trade and the shifting of protection across sectors', *European Economic Review*, vol. 32, pp. 823–42.

Greenaway, D. and C.R. Milner (1988b) 'Some features of "true protection": a reply', *Journal of Development Studies*, vol. 25, pp. 122–25.

Greenaway, D. and C.R. Milner (1989) 'Nominal and effective tariffs in a small industrialising economy: the case of Mauritius', *Applied Economics*, vol. 21, pp. 995–1010.

Greenaway, D. and C.R. Milner (1990a) 'The estimation of "true protection": a comment on the Smeets procedure', *Journal of Development Studies*, vol. 26, pp. 330–4.

Greenaway, D. and C.R. Milner (1990b) 'Industrial incentives, domestic resource costs and resource allocation in Madagascar', *Applied Economics*, vol. 22, pp. 805–22.

Greenaway, D. and C.R. Milner (1990c) 'Policy appraisal and the structure of protectionism in a low income LDC: the case of Burundi', *Journal of Development Studies*, vol. 27, pp. 22–42.

Greenaway, D. and C.R. Milner (1991a) 'Fiscal dependence on trade taxes and trade policy reform', *Journal of Development Studies*, vol. 27, pp. 95–132.

Greenaway, D. and C.R. Milner (1991b) 'Structural adjustment, trade policy reforms and fiscal constraints in development countries', report to the Trade Policy Division, World Bank, Washington.

Greenaway, D. and C.R. Milner (1991c) 'Did Mauritius really constitute a case study in Malthusian economics?', *Journal of International Development*, vol. 3, pp. 325–8.

Greenaway, D. and C. Nam (1988) 'Industrialisation and macroeconomic performance in developing countries under alternative trade strategies', *Kyklos*, vol. 41, pp. 419–36.

Greenaway, D. and G.V. Reed (1990) 'Empirical evidence on trade orientation and economic performance in developing countries', in Milner (ed.) (1990c).

Halevi, N. (1988) 'Trade liberalisation in adjustment lending', mimeo (World Bank).

Harberger, A.C. (1962) 'The incidence of the corporation income tax', *Journal of Political Economy*, vol. 70, pp. 215–40.

Harrigan, J. and P. Mosley (1991) 'Evaluating the impact of World Bank structural adjustment lending', *Journal of Development Studies*, vol. 27, pp. 63–94.

Harris, R. (1985) 'Applied general equilibrium analyses of small open economies with scale economies and imperfect competition', *American Economic Review*, vol. 74, pp. 1017–32.

Hassan, R., D. Greenaway and G.V. Reed (1992) 'Nominal and effective protection in the Egyptian agricultural sector: a multicommodity analysis', *Applied Economics*, vol. 24, pp. 473–82.

Havrylyshyn, O. and E. Civan (1985) 'Intra-industry trade among developing countries', *Journal of Development Economics*, vol. 18, pp. 253–72.

Hillman, A. (1980) 'Observations on the relation between "revealed comparative advantage" and comparative advantage as indicated by pre-trade relative prices', *Weltwirtschaftliches Archiv*, vol. 116, pp. 315–21.

Isard, P. (1977) 'How far can we push the law of one price', *American Economic Review*, vol. 67, pp. 942–8.

Johansen, L. (1960) *A Multi-sectoral Study of Economic Growth* (Amsterdam: North Holland).

Johnson, H.G. (1958) 'The gains from freer trade with Europe: an estimate', *Manchester School*, vol. 26, pp. 247–55.

Johnson, H.G. (1965a) 'Optimal trade intervention in the presence of domestic distortions', in R. Baldwin *et al.*, *Trade Growth and the Balance of Payments* (Chicago: Rand McNally).

Johnson, H.G. (1965b) 'The theory of tariff structure with special reference to world trade and development', in H.G. Johnson and P.B. Kenen (eds), *Trade and Development* (Geneva: Graduate Institute of International Studies).

Johnson, H.G. (1970) 'A new view of the infant industry argument', in I.A. McDougall and R.H. Snape (eds), Studies in International Economics (Amsterdam: North-Holland).

Kellman, M. and T. Schroder (1983) 'The export similarity index: some structural tests', *Economic Journal*, vol. 93, pp. 193–8.

Kierzkowski, H. (ed.) (1984) *Monopolistic Competition and International Trade* (Oxford University Press).

Kirkpatrick, C. (1982) 'Trade policy and industrialization in LDCs', in N. Gemmell (ed.), *Surveys in Development Economics* (Oxford: Blackwells).

Krueger, A.O. (1972) 'Evaluating restrictionist trade regimes: theory and measurement', *Journal of Political Economy*, vol. 80, pp. 48–62.

Krueger, A.O. (1978) *Liberalisation Attempts and Consequences* (New York: National Bureau of Economic Research).

Krueger, A.O. (1984) 'Trade policies in developing countries', in R.W. Jones and P.B. Kenen (eds), *Handbook of International Economics* (Amsterdam: North-Holland).

Krueger, A.O., H.B. Lary, T. Monson and N. Akransanee (1981) *Trade and Employment in Developing Countries* (University of Chicago Press).

Kunimoto, K. (1977) 'Typology of trade intensity indices', *Hitotsubashi Journal of Economics*, vol. 17, pp. 15–32.

Laird, S. and A. Yeats (1990) *Quantitative Methods for Trade Policy Analysis* (London: Macmillan).

Lal, D. (1983) *The Poverty of "Development Economics"*, Hobart Paperback no. 16 (London: Institute of Economic Affairs).

Lal, D. and S. Rajapatirana (1987) 'Foreign trade regimes and economic growth in developing countries', *The World Bank Research Observer*, vol. 2, pp. 189–218.

Leamer, E.E. (1984) *Sources of International Comparative Advantage: Theory and Evidence* (Cambridge, Mass.: MIT Press).

Little, I.M.D. (1982) *Economic Development: Theory, Policies and International Relations* (New York: Basic Books).

Little, I.M.D. and J.A. Mirrlees (1974) *Project Appraisal and Planning for Developing Countries* (New York: Basic Books).

Lucas, R.E.B. (1984) 'On the theory of DRC criteria', *Journal of Development Economics*, vol. 14, pp. 407–17.

MacBean, A.I. and T. Nguyerns (1988) 'Export instability and growth performance', in Greenaway (1988a).

Maxwell Stamp (1987) *Assistance in the Elaboration of an Industrial Masterplan in the Cameroon* (London: Maxwell Stamp PLC).

Maxwell Stamp (1991) Trinidad and Tobago Trade Policy Study (London: Maxwell Stamp PLC).

McKinnon, R. (1973) *Money and Capital in Economic Development* (Washington, DC: Brookings Institution).

McKinnon, R. (1982) 'The order of economic liberalisation: lessons from Chile and Argentina' in K. Brunner and A. Meltzer (eds) *Economic Policy in a World of Change* (Amsterdam: North-Holland).

Meade, J.E. (1955) *Trade and Welfare* (Oxford University Press).

Messerlin, P. and S. Laird (1990) 'Institutional reform for trade liberalisation', *The World Economy*, vol. 13, pp. 230–49.

Michaely, M. (1986) 'The timing and sequencing of a liberalisation policy', in A. Choksi and D. Papageorgiou (eds), *Economic Liberalisation in Developing Countries* (Oxford: Basil Blackwell).

Miller, M.H. and J.E. Spencer (1977) 'The static economic effects of the UK joining the EEC: a general equilibrium approach', *Review of Economic Studies*, vol. 44, pp. 71–93.

Milner, C.R. (1985) 'Empirical analyses of the costs of protection', in Greenaway (1985).

Milner, C.R. (1987) 'Trade strategies and economic development: theory and evidence', in D. Greenaway (ed.), *Economic Development and International Trade* (London: Macmillan).

Milner, C.R. (1989) 'True protection in "capital-rich" and "capital-poor" developing countries: some policy implications', *Journal of Economic Studies*, vol. 16.

Milner, C.R. (1990a) 'Identifying and quantifying anti-export bias: the case of Cameroon', *Weltwirtschaftliches Archiv*, vol. 126, pp. 142–55.

Milner, C.R. (1990b) 'Trade and industrial policies in developing countries: the use of domestic resource cost analysis', mimeo.

Milner, C.R. (ed.) (1990c) *Export Promotion Strategies: Theory and Evidence from Developing Countries* (London: Harvester Wheatsheaf).

Milner, C.R. (1992) 'Short and long run true protection: the case of Madagascar', *Applied Economics*, vol. 24, pp. 257–63.

Mitra, P. (1986) 'Revenue-raising tariffs: theory and application to India' (Washington: World Bank), processed.

Monson, T. (1981) 'Trade strategies and employment in the Ivory Coast, in Krueger *et al.* (1981).

Mosley, P. (1987) *Conditionality as Bargaining Process: Structural Adjustment Lending 1980–86*, Essays in International Finance No. 168 (Princeton, N.J.).

Mosley, P. and J. Toye (1988) 'The design of Structural Adjustment Programmes', *Development Policy Review*, vol. 6, pp. 395–413.

Mussa, M. (1986) 'The adjustment process and the timing of a trade liberalisation', in A. Choksi and D. Papageorgiou (eds) *Economic Liberalisation in Developing Countries* (Oxford: Basil Blackwell).

Naqvi, S., A. Kemal and A. Heston (1983) *The Structure of Protection in Pakistan 1980–81* (Islamabad: Pakistan Institute of Development Economics).

Nogues, J., A. Olechowski and L.A. Winters (1987) 'The extent of non-tariff barriers to industrial countries' imports', *World Bank Economic Review*, vol. 1, pp. 181–99.

Oyejide, T.A. (1986) *The Effects of Trade and Exchange Rate Policies on Agriculture in Nigeria*, (Washington: International Food Policy Research Institute).

Palma, J.G. (1989) 'Structuralism' in J. Eatwell, M. Milgate and P. Newman (eds) *The New Palgrave: Economic Development* (London: Macmillan).

Papageorgiou, A., M. Michaely and A. Choksi (eds) (1991) *Liberalising Foreign Trade* (7 vols) (Oxford: Basil Blackwell).

Pearson, S.R. (1976) 'Net social profitability, domestic resource costs and effective protection', *Journal of Development Studies*, vol. 12, pp. 320–33.

Pomfret, R. (1981) 'The impact of EEC enlargement on non-member Mediterranean countries' exports to the EEC', *Economic Journal*, vol. 19, pp. 726–30.

Prebisch, R. (1950) *The Economic Development of Latin America and its Principal Problems* (New York: United Nations).

Reidel, J.A. (1987) 'Trade as an engine of growth', in D. Greenaway (ed.) (1987b).

Robinson, S. (1988) 'Multisectoral models', in H. Chenery and T.N. Srinivasan, *Handbook of Development Economics*, vol. 2 (Amsterdam: North Holland).

Robinson, S. and L. Tyson (1985) 'Foreign trade, resource allocation and structural adjustment in Yugoslavia 1976–80', *Journal of Comparative Economics*, vol. 9, pp. 46–70.

Rodrik, D. (1987) 'Imperfect competition, scale economies and trade policy in developing countries', processed (Cambridge, Mass.: Harvard University Press).

Roger, N. (1985) 'Tariff and non-tariff protection in mauritius', mimeo (Washington: World Bank).

Sapsford, D. (1985) 'The statistical debate on the net barter terms of trade: a comment and some additional information', *Economic Journal*, vol. 95, pp. 781–8.

Scarf, H.E. and T. Hansen (1973) *The Computation of Economic Equilibria* (New Haven: Yale University Press).

Scarf, H.E. (1967) 'On the computation of equilibrium prices', in W.J. Fellner (ed) *Ten Economic Studies in the Tradition of Irving Fisher* (New York: Wiley).

Scitovsky, T. (1958) *Economic Theory and Western European Integration* (Stanford University Press).

Shoven, J.B. and J. Whalley (1984) 'Applied general-equilibrium models of taxation and international trade: an introduction and survey', *Journal of Economic Literature*, vol. 22, pp. 1007–51.

Singer, H.W. (1950) 'The distribution of gains between borrowing and investing countries', *American Economic Review*, vol. 40, pp. 473–85.

Singh, H.V. (1988) 'A comment on some features of "true protection"', *Journal of Development Studies*, vol. 25, pp. 118–21.

Sjaastad, L.A. (1980a) 'Commercial policy, true tariffs and relative prices', in J. Black and B.V. Hindley (eds) *Current Issues in Commercial Policy and Diplomacy* (London: Macmillan).

Sjaastad, L.A. (1980b) 'The incidence of a uniform tariff in Uruguay', mimeo (University of Chicago).

Sjaastad, L.A. (1980c) 'Commercial policy reform in Argentina: implications and consequences', mimeo, (University of Chicago).

Sjaastad, L.A. and K.W. Clements (1981) 'The incidence of protection: theory and measurement', in L.A. Sjaastad (ed.), *The Free Trade Movement in Latin America* (London: Macmillan).

Smeets, H.D. (1989) 'The "true protection" concept: a comment on Greenaway and Milner', *Journal of Development Studies*, vol. 25, pp. 401–7.

Spraos, J. (1980) 'The statistical debate on the net barter terms of trade', *Economic Journal*, vol. 90, pp. 107–28.

Srinivasan, T.N. and J.N. Bhagwati (1978) 'Shadow prices for project selection in the presence of distortions: effective rates of protection and domestic resource costs', *Journal of Political Economy*, vol. 86, pp. 97–116.

Stein, L. (1978) 'Export instability and development: a review of some recent findings', *Banca Nazionale del Lavoro Review*, vol. 30, pp. 279–90.

Stern, N.H. (1987) 'Aspects of the general theory of tax reform', in D.M.G. Newbery and N.H. Stern (eds), *The Theory of Taxation for Developing Countries* (new York: Oxford University and World Bank).

Stern, N. (1989) 'The economics of development: a survey', *Economic Journal*, vol. 99, pp. 597–685.

Taylor, L. and S.L. Black (1974) 'Practical general equilibrium estimates of resource pulls under trade liberalisation', *Journal of International Economics*, vol. 4, pp. 37–58.

Teitel, S. and F. Thoumi (1986) 'From import substitution to exports: the manufacturing exports experience of Argentina and Brazil', *Economic Development and Cultural Change*, vol. 34, pp. 455–90.

Thomas, V., A. Chibber, M. Dailami and J. de Melo (1991) *Restructuring Economies in Distress* (Oxford: Oxford University Press).

Tower, E. (1984) 'Effective protection, domestic resource costs, and shadow prices: a general equilibrium perspective', *World Bank Staff Working Paper*, no. 664, (Washington, DC).

Tower, E. (1991) 'Cost benefit analysis and project appraisal', in D. Greenaway, M. Bleaney and I. Stewart (eds), *Companion to Contemporary Economic Thought* (London: Routledge).

Toye, J. (1987) *Dilemmas of Development* (Oxford: Basil Blackwell).

Tumlir, J. and L. Till (1971) 'Tariff averaging in international comparisons', in H.G. Grubel and H.G. Johnson (eds), *Effective Tariff Protection* (Geneva: Graduate Institute of International Studies).

Tyler, W.G. (1985) 'Effective incentives for domestic market sales and exports: a view of anti-export biases and commercial policy in Brazil 1980–81', *Journal of Development Economics*, vol. 18, pp. 219–42.

UNIDO (1982) *Changing Patterns of Trade in World Industry* (New York: United Nations).

UNIDO (1986) *International Comparative Advantage in Manufacturing* (Vienna: UNIDO).

Webster, A. (1991) 'Some issues in the measurement of comparative advantage', *Applied Economics*, vol. 23, pp. 937–48.

Whalley, J. (1991) 'Recent trade liberalisation in the developing world: what is behind it and where is it headed?', in Greenaway *et al.* (1991).

Williamson, J. and C.R. Milner (1991) *The World Economy* (London: Harvester Wheatsheaf).

World Bank (1988) *Interim Report on Adjustment Lending*, report no. R88–179 (Washington DC: World Bank).

World Bank (1990) *Report on Adjustment Lending II: Policies for the Recovery of Growth*, report R90–49, (Washington DC: World Bank).

Name Index

Subject Index

MATCHBOX TOYS 1947 TO 2007

FIFTH EDITION

IDENTIFICATION & VALUE GUIDE

DANA JOHNSON

COLLECTOR BOOKS

A Division of Schroeder Publishing Co., Inc.

On the Cover:
Front cover:
Top Left: Lincoln Continental Mark V, 1979 #28, $6 – 7
Top Right: Dump Trunk, from 2005 5-pack, $1 – 2
Center Left: Trash Titan/Trash Truck (MB678), 2006 #36, $1 – 2
Center Right: 1961 Jaguar E-Type Coupe, 2007 #28, $1 – 2
Bottom Left: 1957 Licoln Premiere, 2004 Superfast #50, $3 – 4
Bottom Right: International 4700 Armored Car, 2000 Speedy Delivery #58, $1 – 2

Back cover:
Top Left: Double-Decker London Bus, 2006 #56, $1 – 2
Top Right: Rolls Royce Silver Cloud, 1985 #62, $1 – 2
Center Left: Refuse Truck, 2006 Superfast #22, $1 – 2
Center Right: Euclid Quarry Truck, 2⅝", 1964 #6, $10 – 15
Bottom Left: Rolls Royce Phantom V, 1964 #44, $15 – 20
Bottom Right: Hoveringham Tipper, 1963 #17, $60 – 80

Cover design by Beth Summers
Book design by Barry Buchanan

Collector Books
P.O. Box 3009
Paducah, KY 42002-3009

www.collectorbooks.com

CONTENTS

Preface

Since 1953, Matchbox toys have captured the hearts, minds, and imaginations of children all around the world. As these children have grown up, they have remembered the fun and fascination they had for their little toys. As adults, they have been transformed into Matchbox collectors.

From their humble beginnings in 1947 in a burned-out London pub, partners Leslie Smith and Rodney Smith built an everlasting legacy to their ingenuity and entrepreneurial spirit through their company, Lesney, and their Matchbox brand of diecast toys. Fifty years and several owners later, Matchbox toys remain some of the world's most popular toys and collectibles.

This book is the result of author Dana Johnson's 50-year fascination with these wonderful toys. His first book on Matchbox toys was published in 1994, to fill a void in the collector's reference library. He has since produced three more books on the subject, the latest of which is this one. The key difference between this latest effort and the rest is that this book is arranged alphabetically, for reasons which will be made clear later in this book. Suffice it to say that it's about time such a book was published, as it promises to be the most useful and user-friendly book on Matchbox toys ever produced...But you can decide that for yourself.

About the Author

Dana Johnson has enjoyed collecting and studying Matchbox toys since he was seven years old, in 1962. Originally from Skandia, Michigan, he lived in several other places in Michigan before moving to Bend, Oregon, in 1985. He has lived there ever since.

His interest in diecast toys has since expanded to many other brands besides Matchbox, including Majorette, Tomica, Siku, Hot Wheels®, Bburago, Maisto, Yatming, and hundreds of other brands.

He has discovered so many brands of automotive toys and models (over 1,000) that he has written a book on them entitled *Toy Car Collector's Guide*, available from Collector Books, your favorite bookstore, or from the author for $24.95 retail plus shipping and handling.

INTRODUCTION

HOW TO USE THIS BOOK

This book is arranged in two sections: the Introduction, and An Alphabetical Guide to Values.

The Introduction provides information on how to most effectively use this book and how to identify, date, and evaluate your collection, and offers a short history of Matchbox toys.

An Alphabetical Guide to Values is an illustrated guide to values and variations by model name and/or description.

MODEL NUMBER DESIGNATIONS

There is a good reason for making this book an alphabetical collector's guide rather than a numerical guide. Since 1953, each Matchbox toy has been issued with a corresponding model number, but the model number was originally only on the box, not on the model itself. The eventual assortment of 75 models in the primary Matchbox Series, also known as Matchbox Miniatures or the 1 – 75 Series, established the size of the series at 75 models for any given year.

In addition, model numbers 76, 77, 78, and 79 were applied to variations of Japanese cars offered to the Japanese market.

In 1996, an error in the planning department resulted in four models issued for the US being misnumbered as 76, 77, 78, and 79.

Also, a series of inexpensive versions with no interiors and less detail were at one time assigned Roman numerals from I to X (1 to 10).

To further complicate matters, Super GTs and Neon Racers were assigned two consecutive numbers per model, for a total of 24 numbers for 12 models.

The latest change to this system was in 1999, when the series was expanded to 100 models. The 100-model series continued through another year before being returned to 75 models in 2001. The 2008 line has again been increased to 100. (See page 215.)

The problem with listing models by model number is that they have to be in their original package to identify them by that method, since the earliest Matchbox models had no numbers imprinted on the bases, nor do models issued after 1982.

In the case of a model with many variations, the variations are arranged in order of color, starting with red and proceeding through the color spectrum to orange, yellow, green, blue, and purple, with black, gray, white, silver, and gold following.

GUIDE TO DETERMINING VALUES

Values indicated in this book generally represent the average value for a given model. Although collectors are often willing to pay top dollar, occasionally even higher than book value, for models in new, or mint, condition, especially when a model is in its original box or package, it is often possible to purchase models for considerably less. In the same spirit, you will often need to sell a model, and particularly an entire collection, at a much lower price than indicated by this or any book; this is particularly likely when you need to sell an entire collection, since buyers of entire collections usually wish to quickly sell individual models at a reasonable profit. It is also important to know that most dealers will not buy toys in less than near-mint condition.

For standardization, all values mentioned in this book are for models in new condition. Two values are provided. The first value is for the model in new condition but without its original container; the second value is for the model in its original container.

A numerical value from 0 to 10 is most commonly used to define an item's condition. The chart below is intended to assist in determining value for less-than-mint-condition toys. Note that "mint condition" denotes a model with no wear, no chips, and no flaws. Models in sealed blisterpacks, for instance, may sometimes suffer wear from rubbing on the insides of the plastic blisters and therefore be considered less-than-mint condition. So not everything still in the package should automatically be considered mint.

Rating	Percent of Book Value	Evaluation
10	100%	Mint condition with original container
9	90 – 95%	Mint condition without container
8	80 – 85%	Near mint condition, close inspection reveals minor wear
7	70 – 75%	Excellent condition, visible minor wear
6	25 – 35%	Very good condition, visible wear, all parts intact
5	7 – 10%	Good condition, excessive wear, paint chipped or heavily worn
4	4 – 5%	Fair condition, parts broken or missing
1 – 3	2 – 3%	Poor condition, paint worn off, parts broken or missing
0	0.5 – 1%	Salvage, for parts only

HISTORY OF MATCHBOX TOYS

BEGINNINGS

It was 1947, and two school chums, Leslie Smith and Rodney Smith, unrelated but sharing the same dream and last name, decided to start a diecasting firm in a vacant pub previously known as the Rifleman, which had been burned out during the German blitz of London in 1940. Leslie and Rodney Smith got together enough funds to purchase the building and start manufacturing diecast zinc alloy components for industry and the military.

It wasn't long before the Smiths started tinkering with the idea of producing a toy or two. Early toys included a walking Jumbo the Elephant tin windup and a marionette puppet named Muffin the Mule.

One of the earliest diecast toys ever produced by Lesney was a horse-drawn "rag and bone" cart, a rag and bone cart being the English equivalent of a junk wagon. This unusual toy featured a driver and assorted junk: a bicycle frame, a washtub, part of a bed frame, a bucket, a crate, and what appears to be a kitchen sink.

Other models included a soap-box racer, a road roller, a Caterpillar tractor and bulldozer, a Massey Harris Tractor, a Hand Cement Mixer, and a Prime Mover truck with low-loader trailer and bulldozer.

THE CORONATION COACH

The introduction of the Coronation Coach in 1953 secured Lesney's honored place in British industry. A large and small version were produced to commemorate Queen Elizabeth II's coronation. But producing the coach to commemorate her coronation was not the original intent.

In 1949, Lesney originally planned to produce a 15¾" long toy coach to commemorate the silver wedding celebrations of King George VI and Queen Elizabeth I (later referred to as the Queen Mother), which had revived interest in British royalty. At the same time, England was planning a celebration in 1951 known as the Festival of Britain. The miniature coach would have been perfect for both occasions. But by the time the toy was ready to market, a ban on the use of zinc was declared, as it was needed for the Korean War effort.

The molds remained unused for two years. Meanwhile, King George VI died, and the throne passed to the oldest daughter, Elizabeth. It was only then that the ban on zinc use was lifted and the coach went into production.

Two hundred or so large Coronation Coaches were produced with the king and queen inside, now intended to represent Queen Elizabeth II and her husband, Prince Philip. But as her June 2nd coronation neared, it was discovered that the queen would be riding alone in the coach.

So Lesney removed the male figure from the mold, and added "Made In England" to the casting to conform to new government regulations that required the name of the country of origin on all products. Roughly 32,800 were made with these modifications.

Most models issued were painted gold. But a few versions were released with the queen in either a gold-plated or silver-plated coach.

The smaller, 4½" version of the coach was also produced in 1953, either chrome-plated or painted gold and embossed with "A Moko Toy by Lesney, British Made."

Benbros of England made a similar version, but with "Made in England" on the upper side of the center bar and "E II R" (for *Elizabeth the Second Regina*) on the doors of the coach.

MATCHBOX IS BORN

Leslie and Rodney realized they had a good thing going, and in 1953 introduced the Matchbox series of toys, starting with three models, the Number 1 Diesel Road Roller, Number 2 Dumper, and Number 3 Cement Mixer, each based on early Lesney toys but smaller.

By 1960, the Matchbox Miniatures series settled at 75 models, but in 1981 numbers 76 through 79, miniatures of popular Japanese cars, were issued for the Japanese market. Another exception to the 1 – 75 series was a set of vehicles issued with Roman numerals I through X.

MATCHBOX MARKETING

The first Matchbox toys were marketed through the Moko firm, a century-old firm founded by Moses Kohnstam in 1875 and carried on by his sons until 1959.

Later, the Fred Bronner Corporation took over marketing. The relationship continued through the mid-1960s, when till Lesney took over its own marketing.

JACK ODELL PROVIDES DIECASTING EXPERTISE

Almost from the beginning, John W. (Jack) Odell provided the diecasting expertise. After leaving Lesney, returning, and leaving again in 1982, Jack Odell started his own toy company, Lledo, which is Odell spelled backwards. His toys remain as popular today as when he first started the company. Lledo is now a subsidiary of Zindart, which also now owns the Corgi brand of diecast toys.

COMPETITION CUTS INTO MATCHBOX MARKET

Until 1968, Matchbox toys had a solid corner on the market of diecast toys. But then Mattel introduced Hot Wheels cars. The popularity of these new toys forced Lesney to introduce Superfast. These revamped Matchbox toys sported thinner axles and new-style wheels, and were designed to compete with Hot Wheels cars on their own track.

One year later, Johnny Lightning cars were introduced by Topper Toys, representing yet another threat to the market for Matchbox toys. By their third year, Johnny Lightning cars were making a notable dent in both the Matchbox and Hot Wheels markets. If it weren't for indictments for business fraud, which forced the company out of business, Topper would have surely dominated the diecast toy market through the 1970s.

In 1994, Johnny Lightning cars made a comeback through a new company, Playing Mantis, founded by Tom Lowe, himself an aficionado of the original Topper versions. Playing Mantis and the Johnny Lightning brand were purchased by Action Performance in 2006.

MATCHBOX SELLS OUT — THREE TIMES

First Time — 1982 was the year that Lesney finally called it quits in the toy business and sold the Matchbox line to the Universal Holding Company of Hong Kong, headed by David Yeh, himself a toy enthusiast. While in possession of the brand, Universal also purchased the venerable Dinky brand of England in 1987 and incorporated it into the Matchbox product line. "Matchbox Toys Intl." and "Matchbox Toys Inc." replaced the Lesney name on the bases of all models. Model numbers no longer appeared on the bases of new models released after 1983, making identification more difficult. The reason for this change was that it enabled the company to assign different model numbers for different markets. At the same time, Universal purchased Kidco and inherited Burnin' Key Cars, which was briefly incorporated into the Matchbox lineup.

Second Time — The Matchbox name was sold again in October 1992, to Tyco Toys. With the purchase of Matchbox by Tyco, several of the lines — Dinky, Models of Yesteryear, Kingsize — were discontinued or absorbed into the newly formed Matchbox Collectibles division.

Third Time — Once again, the Matchbox name was purchased, along with Tyco Toys and the Dinky Collection, this time by Mattel. The purchase began in the fall of 1996 and was completed in May of 1997. New Mattel Matchbox toys started appearing on the market after the New York Toy Fair in February 1998.

MATCHBOX COLLECTIBLES, INC.

In 1994 Matchbox Collectibles were introduced, as a new outlet for marketing Models of Yesteryear and the Dinky Collection from Matchbox. Through they had previously been sold only through direct-marketing, an effort started in September 1998 to sell them through retail stores. They were first offered through high-end gift and specialty stores, including a few Hallmark shops, beginning at $20.00 each. Within two years the marketing strategy changed, and Matchbox Collectibles started showing up in retail chain stores such as Target, Wal-Mart, ShopKo, Fred Meyer, and many others, for about half the price.

WHITE ROSE AND NUTMEG COLLECTIBLES

As the collector market expanded, Universal (and later Tyco) established a symbiotic relationship, which it has maintained, with two independent companies that take stock Matchbox models and modify them especially for the collectibles market.

White Rose Collectibles has marketed limited-edition variations of Matchbox models under contract to Tyco, mostly racing transporters and customized race cars, but also produced a line of 24 versions of production models for 1994 with particularly nice color and detail. White Rose agreed to purchase and market a quantity of models produced by Matchbox to White Rose's specifications. In turn, Matchbox packaged them as White Rose Collectibles. The practice is not unlike, say, Sears contracting Whirlpool to produce appliances under the Kenmore brand.

Nutmeg Collectibles, meanwhile, focused on Sprint Racers and Modified Racers to produce a distinctive line of modified Matchbox models that have since been mimicked by Racing Champions, Road Champs, and others.

ASAP and COLOR COMP

ASAP and Color Comp are the two primary companies responsible for producing custom promotional models from Matchbox blank castings. Primarily, they take a plain model and apply a simple message, logo, or design, usually a corporate name or an event designation.

MATCHBOX LIVES

While sometimes experiencing great challenges in its 50-year history, Matchbox continues to offer a diversity of diecast toys, producing new models and updated versions of older models to replace existing models in the 1 – 75 series. Mattel has made a commitment to maintain the integrity of the Matchbox series by continuing to produce realistic models of cars and trucks under the Matchbox brand while maintaining the Hot Wheels series as a more sporty, hot, wild, and imaginative line of models.

ALPHABETICAL GUIDE TO VALUES AND VARIATIONS

EARLY LESNEY TOYS

Lesney Products Company started manufacturing toys in 1948, a year after the company was begun. As industrial orders declined, Leslie Smith and Rodney Smith, with the help of their friend Jack Odell, started experimenting with the manufacture of diecast and tin lithographed toys. Many of the early models created were later reproduced in smaller versions as the first of the Matchbox series.

Aveling Barford Diesel Road Roller, 4³/₈", 1948
1. green with driver, yellow flywheel, red wheels.................... $1,250 – 1,500
2. green with no driver, no flywheel, unpainted wheels .... $600 – 800
3. green with driver, no flywheel, unpainted wheels.......................... $600 – 800
4. green with no driver, no flywheel, red wheels.......................... $700 – 900
5. gray-brown with no driver, no flywheel, green wheels.............. $800 – 1,200
6. red with no driver, no flywheel, green wheels....................... $800 – 1,200

Bread Bait Press, 2", 1954
1. red with green wing nut, green inner mechanism, "Lesney Milbro"... $125 – 175
2. red with unpainted wing nut, green inner mechanism, "Lesney"....... $100 – 125
3. red with unpainted wing nut and inner mechanism, "Lesney"....... $100 – 125

Caterpillar Bulldozer, with blade, 4¹/₂", 1948
1. green...................... $1,000 – 1,250
2. yellow........................... $700 – 900
3. orange .... $700 – 900

Caterpillar Tractor, no blade, 3¹/₈", 1948
1. green........................ $900 – 1,200
2. yellow........................... $700 – 900
3. orange .... $700 – 900

Cement Mixer, 3⁹/₁₆", 1948
1. light green with red barrel and handle, red wheels.................... $400 – 600
2. dark green with red barrel and handle, red wheels.................... $400 – 600
3. dark green with red barrel and handle, yellow wheels................. $400 – 600
4. dark green with green barrel and handle, green wheels........... $400 – 600
5. dark green with green barrel and handle, red wheels .... $400 – 600
6. red with dark green barrel and handle, green wheels................. $400 – 600
7. red with dark green barrel and handle, yellow wheels................. $400 – 600

Conestoga Wagon, 4⁷/₈", 1955
1. no barrels on sides......... $175 – 225
2. red barrels on sides .... $175 – 225

Coronation Coach, large, 15³/₄", 1952
1. gold-painted coach with king and queen inside .... $1,200 – 1,600
2. gold-painted coach with queen only.............................. $500 – 700
3. gold plated, queen only..... $600 – 800
4. silver plated, queen only........................... $800 – 1,200

Coronation Coach, small, 4¹/₂", 1953
1. silver plated.................... $150 – 200
2. gold painted .... $250 – 350

Horse-drawn Milk Float, 5³/₈", 1949
1. orange .... $1,500 – 2,000
2. blue .... $2,500 – 4,000

Jumbo the Elephant, lithographed tin wind-up with key, 4", 1950.... $900 – 1,250

Massey Harris Tractor, red with beige wheels, black rubber tires, 7¹³/₁₆", 1954........................ $900 – 1,250

Muffin the Mule, cast-metal marionette, 5¹/₂", 1951... $500 – 700

Prime Mover with Trailer & Bulldozer, 18", 1950
1. orange with orange trailer, green bulldozer .... $2,000 – 2,500
2. orange with blue trailer, orange bulldozer...................... $1,500 – 2,000
3. orange with blue trailer, yellow bulldozer with red blade........... $1,000 – 1,500

Rag and Bone Cart, 5¹/₄", 1949
1. yellow...................... $3,000 – 4,000
2. green...................... $4,000 – 5,000

Ruston Bucyrus 10RB Power Shovel Excavator, 4",1949...$1,000 – 1,500

Soap Box Racer, gold painted, 3¹/₈", 1949
.... $2,500 – 3,000

MATCHBOX MINIATURES BASIC SERIES

From 1953 to the present, the mainstay of the Matchbox product line has been the 1-75 series, or basic series, also referred to as Matchbox Miniatures, a line of small transportation toys each generally 3" or less in length. This listing also incorporates variations that were issued as Matchbox Collectibles, World Class, Select Class, and promotional models.

In 1999 and 2000 the series was expanded to 100 models, and it was returned to 75 models in 2001. Below is an alphabetical listing of Matchbox Miniatures and variations, with current values. The section that follows this one lists the larger Matchbox models, including Major Pack, Kingsize, Models of Yesteryear, Sea Kings, Sky Busters, and others.

A

Abrams M1 A1 Tank, #54, 1995 – 1998; #84, 1999; #61, 1995, international

1. green with black and brown camouflage, multipack .... $1 – 2

2. **army green with white star and "T-7521-6," 1996................ $1 - 2**
3. army green with brown and black camouflage, 1996 5-pack .... $2 – 4
4. army green with black and tan camouflage, Premiere Collection .... $5 – 7
5. army green with gray and brown camouflage, play set .... $1 – 2

6. **light army green with yellow "476 BD98675," 1999 Military Patrol series .... $1 - 2**
7. dark army green with yellow "476 BD98675" .... $1 – 2
8. black with rose and white design, Australia issue .... $4 – 6

9. **black with green and brown camouflage, 5-pack .... $1 - 2**

10. **white with gray and army green camouflage, 1997 Tundra Defense Force 5-pack .... $1 - 2**
11. light brown with white star and "T-7521-6," multipack .... $3 – 4
12. khaki with brown and white camouflage, 1995 .... $1 – 2

13. **khaki with brown camouflage, 1997 Desert Assault Force 5-pack .. $1 - 2**
14. dark khaki with detailed graphics, 2003 Matchbox Heroes .... $3 – 4

15. **camouflage green with black gun, Battle Kings Jungle Recon set, 2006, K5530 .... $1 - 2**
16. beige with black painted tread, opening features, 2001 Feature Cars (designed to replace Premiere Collections) .... $9 – 12

Abrams Main Battle Tank (see Abrams M1 A1 Tank)

AEC Ergomatic Eight-Wheel Tipper, 3", #51, 1969

1. **red cab, silver dumper, white grille, "Douglas," black plastic wheels, 1969 .... $75 - 125**
2. orange cab, silver dumper, white grille, "Douglas," black plastic wheels, 1969 .... $160 – 240
3. orange cab, silver dumper, silver grille, "Douglas," black plastic wheels, 1969 .... $40 – 60
4. yellow cab, silver dumper, silver grille, "Douglas," black plastic wheels, 1969 .... $30 – 50

5. **yellow cab, silver dumper, silver grille, "Pointer," black plastic wheels, 1969 .... $15 - 20**
6. yellow cab, silver dumper, "Pointer," Superfast wheels, 1970 .... $30 – 50
7. yellow cab, silver dumper, no labels, Superfast wheels, 1970 .... $30 – 50

AEC Ergomatic Horse Box, with two horses, $2^3/_4$", #17, 1969

1. **red cab, green box, gray door, black plastic wheels, 1969 .... $6 - 9**
2. red cab, green box, gray door, Superfast wheels, 1970 .... $30 – 40
3. mustard yellow, green box, gray door, Superfast wheels, 1970 ..... $25 – 35
4. orange cab, light gray box, light brown door, Superfast wheels, 1970 .... $25 – 35

Aero Junior, #95, 1999; #70, 2000; #75, 1999, international; #50, 2000, international

1. **red and yellow with blue pilot, 1999 Mountain Cruisers .... $1 - 2**

2. metallic blue with red pilot, "NP-20035, 2000 Air Travel .... $1 – 2
3. metallic blue with red pilot, "NP-20035," "Matchbox 2000," 2000 Air Travel .... $3 – 4

Airboat, #63, 2001

1. white hull with red accents, light blue "Rescue 2" bordered in black, red deck, metallic gray fan cage, 2001 Scuba Dudes ....$4 – 5

2. green with black hull with camouflage graphics, brown cage, black seats, Battle Kings Jungle Recon set, 2006, K5530 ....$1 – 2

Air-Lift Helicopter, #68, 2000; #73, 2001; #34, 2002; #47, 2003; #48, 2000, international

1. dark red with yellow and black design, gray base, 2000 Air Travel ...... $1 – 2
2. dark red with yellow and black design, "Matchbox 2000," gray base, 2000 Air Travel .... $3 – 4

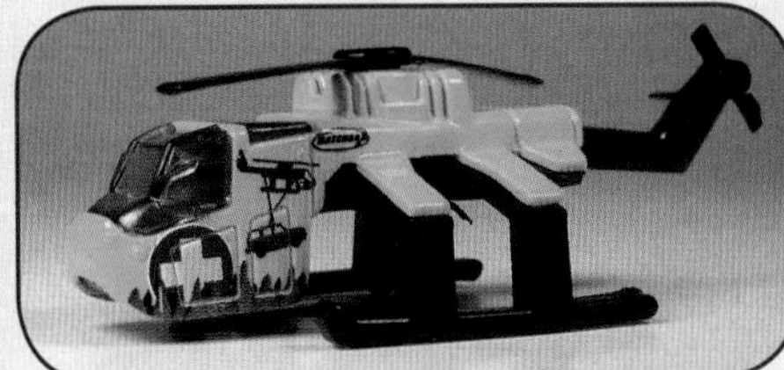

3. lime green with black, red, and white illustration, black base, 2002 Ultimate Rescue ....$1 – 2

4. black with green, yellow, and red graphics, blue base, 2003 Hero City 5-pack #3 ....$1 – 2

5. gold with green base, 2003 Forest Rescue .... $1 – 2
6. gold with green base, 2003 Hero City 10-pack #2 .... $1 – 2

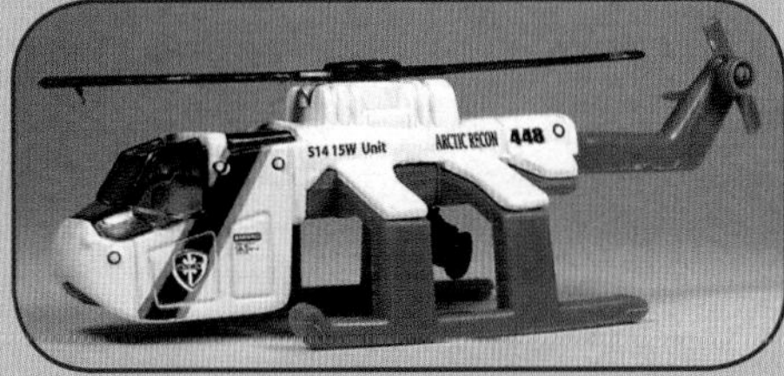

7. white with gray base, Battle Kings Polar Rescue set, 2007, K5537 .... $1 – 2

Airplane Transporter, 3", #72, 1985; #65, 1986; #10, 1999; #69, 2000; #49, 2000, international (similar casting: NASA Rocket Transporter)

1. yellow, "Rescue" and checkerboard pattern, China cast .... $7 – 9
2. yellow, "Rescue" and checkerboard pattern, Macau cast .... $7 – 9
3. army green with black and tan camouflage, China cast, Commando ...$45 – 55
4. black with yellow dashes and plane silhouette graphics, "Matchbox 2000," China cast, 2000 Air Travel ..... $3 – 4
5. black with yellow dashes and plane silhouette graphics, China cast, 2000 Air Travel .... $1 – 2

6. black with red, blue, and yellow graphics, 2003 Hero City 5-pack #3 ....$1 – 2

7. metallic gray with red dashes, plane silhouette, China cast, 1999 Air Traffic ....$1 – 2

8. white, "NASA," Macau cast ..... $4 – 5
9. white, "Rescue" and checkerboard pattern, Thailand cast .... $3 – 4

10. white with gray-green camouflage, Thailand cast, 1997 Tundra Defense Force 5-pack ....$4 – 5

Airport Coach, 3", #65, 1977

1. "Alitalia," white with white roof, amber windows, England cast .... $8 – 10
2. "Alitalia," white with white roof, amber windows, Macau cast .... $4 – 5
3. "Alitalia," white with green roof, amber windows, Thailand cast .... $6 – 8

4. "American Airlines," metallic blue with white roof, amber windows, England cast ....$5 – 6

5. "American Airlines," metallic blue with white roof, amber windows, no origin cast, Brazil issue .... $40 – 50
6. "American Airlines," metallic blue with white roof, clear windows, England cast .... $5 – 6
7. "Australian," metallic blue with white roof, amber windows, Macau cast, Australia issue .... $8 – 10

8. "British," metallic blue with white roof, amber windows, England cast ....$8 – 10

9. "British Airways," metallic blue with white roof, amber windows, England cast .... $5 – 6
10. "British Airways," metallic blue with white roof, no origin cast, Brazil issue .... $40 – 50

11. "British Airways," metallic blue with white roof, clear windows, England cast ....$5 – 6
12. "Girobank," metallic blue with white roof, blue windows, Macau cast, UK issue ....$8 – 10
13. "KLM," white with blue roof, amber windows, Thailand cast .... $6 – 8

14. "Lufthansa," metallic blue with white roof, amber windows, England cast .... $5 – 6
15. "Lufthansa," metallic blue with white roof, amber windows, no origin cast, Brazil issue .... $40 – 50
16. "Lufthansa," metallic blue with white roof, clear windows, England cast ....$5 – 6
17. "Lufthansa," orange with white roof, amber windows, Macau cast ... $4 – 5
18. "Lufthansa," white with white roof, amber windows, England cast ..$30 – 40
19. "Lufthansa," white with white roof, amber windows, Thailand cast ... $6 – 8
20. "Pan Am," white with white roof, amber windows, Macau cast .... $4 – 5
21. "Qantas," red with white roof, amber windows, England cast .... $9 – 12
22. "SAS," white with blue roof, amber windows, Thailand cast .... $6 – 8
23. "Schulbus," orange with white roof, amber windows, England cast, Germany issue .... $40 – 50
24. "Stork SB," white, amber windows, Macau cast, on-package premium, Australia issue .... $9 – 12

25. "TWA," red with white roof, amber windows, England cast .... $8 – 10
26. "TWA," green with white roof, amber windows, Manaus cast, Brazil issue .... $50 – 60
27. "TWA," red with white roof, amber windows, Manaus cast, Brazil issue .... $40 – 50
28. "Virgin Atlantic," red with white roof, amber windows, Macau cast ... $4 – 5
29. "Virgin Atlantic," red with white roof, amber windows, Thailand cast ....$4 – 5

Airport Fire Pumper/Runway Hero, with extending snorkel and translucent tank, 3"; #26, 2001; #71, 2002; #41, 2003

1. red with white, yellow and blue design, translucent blue tank, 2003 Airport .... $1 – 2
2. red with white, yellow and blue design, translucent blue tank, 2003 Hero City 10-pack #2 .... $1 – 2
3. yellow, "Birthday Party" .... $30 – 40

4. fluorescent yellow with orange and black, blue tank, 2001 Flame Eaters .... $1 – 2

5. metallic silver with blue tank, red snorkel, 2002 Kids' Cars Of The Year .... $1 – 2

6. gray with yellow boom, "De-Icer," 2007 5-pack K9613 .... $1 – 2

Airport Fire Tanker, #31 Fire Flooder, 2004; #45 Runway Patrol, 2006

1. metallic copper with blue water gun, black base, "Alarm" graphics, 2004 .... $1 – 2

2. metallic red, 2006 #45 Runway Patrol (K2620 on package) .. $1 – 2

3. orange with white and black graphics, 2007 5-pack K9407 ...... $1 – 2

Airport Fire Tender (see Airport Fire Truck, Airport Fire Pumper)

Airport Fire Truck, with short nozzle and ladder, 3", #8, 1992 – 1999; #24, 1992, international; #29, 2000; #41, 2002
1. red with white ladder, "5 Alarm" and yellow stripes .... $1 – 2

2. red with white ladder, "Matchbox Fire Dept." and white stripe, 1997 Fire 5-pack .... $1 – 2

3. red with white ladder, "Feuerwehr" ... $4 – 5

4. orange with red, white, and black, "Alarm," 2002 Airport Alarm .. $1 – 2

5. orange with red, white and black, "Alarm," 2003 Hero City 5-pack .... $1 – 2

6. fluorescent orange with white ladder, blue and white accents, "Airport Fire Service" .... $1 – 2

7. fluorescent orange with white ladder, blue and white accents, "Airport Fire Service," "IC," Intercom City ... $40 – 50

8. fluorescent yellow with metallic gray ladder, "Metro Alarm" and red stripes .... $1 – 2

9. yellow with silver ladder, "Matchbox Fire Dept." and red stripe, 2000 Fire 5-pack .... $1 – 2

10. yellow with red ladder, "Airways Fire & Rescue," 1999 Airport 5-pack .... $1 – 2

11. yellow with white ladder, "Newfield Airport Fire Rescue," rubber tires on chrome rims, Premiere Collection .... $4 – 5

12. fluorescent yellow with metallic gray ladder, "34" and dashed line, 1998 Emergency Rescue 5-pack .... $1 – 2

13. fluorescent yellow with metallic gray ladder, "Westford Airport Fire Rescue," rubber tires on chrome rims, Premiere Collection .... $4 – 5

14. fluorescent lime green with metallic gray ladder, "DIA 2," rubber tires on chrome rims, Premiere Fire Collection #3 .... $12 – 16

15. fluorescent lime green with metallic gray ladder, "Metro 24" and blue stripe, Germany issue .... $4 – 6

16. bright blue with metallic gray ladder, "Runway Rescue" and yellow stripe, 2000 Fire Fighters .... $1 – 2

17. white and red with metallic gray ladder, "Fire Dept.," gold crest and star, 5-pack .... $1 – 2

18. white with black ladder, "34" and hash marks, 2000 Fire Fighters ...... $1 – 2

19. white with black ladder, "34" and hash marks, "Matchbox 2000," 2000 Fire Fighters .... $3 – 4

20. yellow with red windows, "Matchbox FDMB" on shield with flame graphics, "14," 2001 Action Launcher Fire Truck set .... $3 – 4

21. red with yellow plastic grille and inserts, silver ladder and snorkel, yellow, red, black and white graphics, 2003 Hero City 5-pack #7 .... $3 – 4

Airport Foam Pumper, $3\frac{1}{4}$", #54, 1984, nozzle, sirens and lights on forward part of roof (similar castings: Command Vehicle, Mobile Home, NASA Tracking Vehicle)

1. red with "3" and Japanese lettering, Japan issue .... $9 – 12

2. red with red roof, "Fire Rescue," gold crest, white band, black and gold stripes .... $1 – 2

3. red with red roof, "Foam Unit 3," "Metro Airport," metal base ... $3 – 4

4. red with red roof, "Foam Unit 3," "Metro Airport," plastic base, Macau cast .... $3 – 4

5. red with red roof, "Foam Unit 3," "Metro Airport," plastic base, Thailand cast .... $1 – 2

6. red with white roof, "Foam Unit," black and white checkerboard pattern .... $40 – 50

7. fluorescent orange, "Foam Unit," "City Airport," "Emergency Rescue," Emergency multipack .... $1 – 2

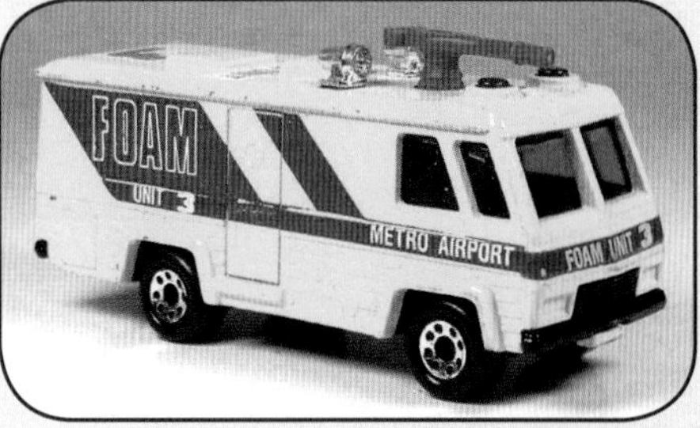

8. yellow with yellow roof, "Foam Unit 3," "Metro Airport," metal base, Macau cast .... $3 - 4
9. yellow with yellow roof, "Foam Unit 3," "Metro Airport," plastic base, Thailand cast .... $1 – 2
10. blue, "Police Command Center," white diagonal stripes, 1997 Police 5-pack .... $1 – 2
11. black with tan and green camouflage, tan nozzle and roof light, 5-pack .... $1 – 2

Airport Foamite Crash Tender, 2¼", #63, 1964
1. silver nozzle .... $5 – 10
2. gold nozzle .... $20 – 25

Airport Pumper (see Airport Fire Pumper, Airport Fire Truck)

Airport Tender (see Airport Fire Truck)

Albion Chieftain Flatbed Transporter, "Blue Circle Portland Cement," 2½", #51, 1958
1. metal wheels .... $30 – 40

2. gray plastic wheels .... $30 - 40
3. silver plastic wheels .... $60 – 80
4. black plastic wheels .... $80 – 100

Alfa 155 (see Alfa Romeo 155)

Alfa Carabo, 3", #75, 1971; BR 21 – 22, 1985
1. red with yellow base, accents .... $9 – 12
2. pink with yellow base, no accents .... $80 – 120
3. pink with yellow base, accents ..$20 – 30

4. metallic pink with no accents .... $12 - 18
5. yellow, England cast, Super GT, BR 21-22, 1985 .... $30 – 40
6. orange with blue and white, England cast, Super GT, BR 21-22, 1985 .... $4 – 6
7. orange, no markings, England cast, Super GT, BR 21-22, 1985 .....$12 – 15
8. orange with light and dark blue accents, England cast, Super GT, BR 21-22, 1985 .... $12 – 15
9. orange with green and light blue accents, England cast, Super GT, BR 21-22, 1985 .... $12 – 15
10. green, China cast, Super GT, BR 21-22, 1985 .... $3 – 5
11. green, England cast, Super GT, BR 21-22, 1985 .... $12 – 15
12. pale blue, China cast, Super GT, BR 21-22, 1985 .... $3 – 5
13. light purple with unpainted base .... $16 – 24
14. light purple with yellow base .. $16 – 24
15. silver, China cast, Super GT, BR 21-22, 1985 .... $8 – 10
16. silver, England cast, Super GT, BR 21-22, 1985 .... $12 – 15
17. silver with accents, England cast, Super GT, BR 21-22, 1985 .... $5 – 10
18. beige, England cast, Super GT, BR 21-22, 1985 .... $30 – 40

Alfa Romeo 155, #3, 1997; #62, 1998
1. red, "7," cross and snake, chrome hubs, rubber tires .... $5 – 7
2. unpainted, chrome hubs, rubber tires .... $5 – 7

3. red, "8," cross and snake, 5-spoke concave star wheels .... $1 - 2
4. red, "7," cross and snake, 5-spoke concave star wheels, China issue .... $35 – 40
5. white, "8" graphics, cross and snake, 5-spoke concave star wheels ... $1 – 2
6. metallic gold, 1997 75 Challenge .... $6 – 12
7. red, "Coca-Cola" and polar bears, Coca-Cola 5-pack .... $1 – 2

Alfa Romeo Giulia Sprint GTR, #32, 2007
red .... $1 – 2

Alfa Romeo SZ, 2⅞", #15, 1991, US; #6, 1991, international

1. red with black roof, no markings ..$2 - 4
2. red with red roof, no markings, Germany gift set .... $9 – 12
3. red with black roof, "Alfa Romeo" ..$2 – 4
4. red with red roof, "Alfa Romeo" ...$2 – 4
5. lime with lime roof, "Alfa Romeo" .... $9 – 12
6. blue, "Go Eagles! 1997," Australia issue ....$4 – 6

All-Terrain Fire Tanker, #64, 2002; #67, 2003; #37 Beach Patrol, 2004; #43 Critter Cruncher, 2006

1. metallic red with metallic gray interior and tank, black chassis, 2002 Rescue Rookies .... $1 - 2
2. black with metallic gray interior and tank, 2003 Pumper Squad ...... $1 – 2

3. metal flake burgundy with metallic gray interior and tank, bright lemon yellow chassis, 2004 Hero City pkg. .... $1 - 2

4. metallic silver with black interior and tank, Beach Patrol #37, 2004 .... $1 - 2

5. **white, "Termite Terminators" graphics, metallic gray interior and tank, black base, orange wheel hubs, 2006 Critter Cruncher #43 .... $1 – 2**

6. **red with white interior and tank, "Airport Emergency," 2006 5-pack J4678 .... $1 – 2**

7. **pale gray-green with white interior, "Sanitation Department Power Steamer," 2007 5-pack K9618 .... $1 – 2**

Alvis Stalwart "BP Exploration," $2^{5}/_{8}$", #61, 1966

1. yellow wheels .... $30 – 40

2. **green wheels .... $9 – 12**

Ambulance (also see Chevrolet Ambulance, Bedford Lomas Ambulance, Daimler Ambulance, Mercedes-Benz Ambulance, etc.)

Ambulance, #66, 2005; #37, 2006; Superfast #31, 2006 (MB679)

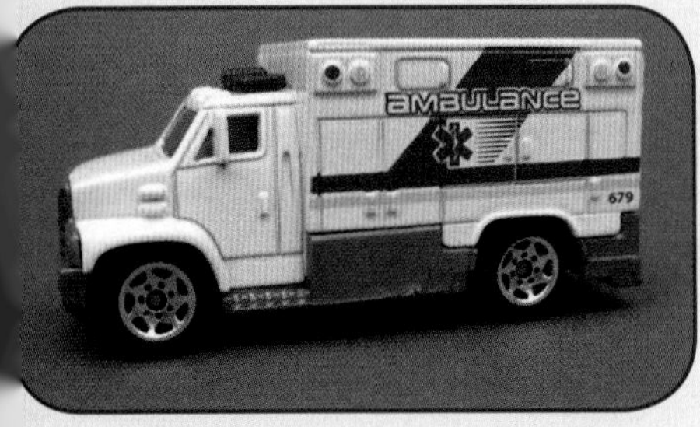

1. **white with red, yellow, and blue graphics, 2005 #66 .... $1 – 2**

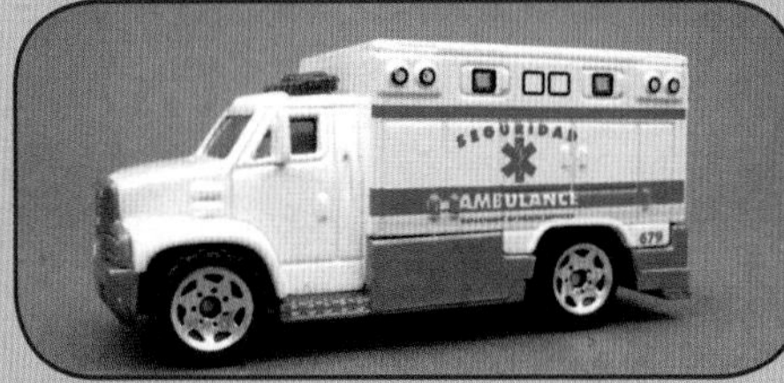

2. **white with yellow and blue graphics, "Seguridad," "Ambulance," 2006 #37 .... $1 – 2**

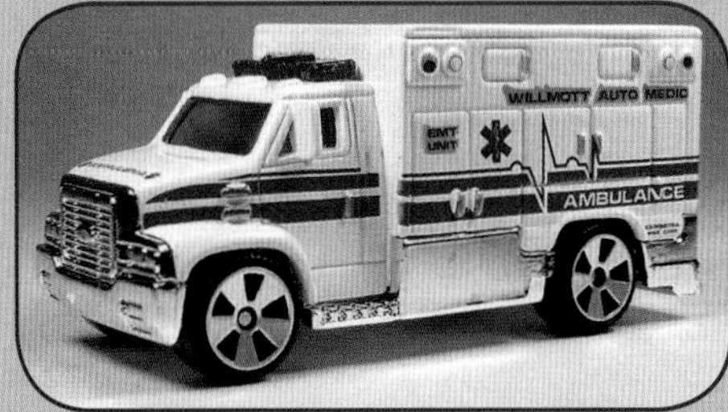

3. **white with red, blue, and silver graphics, 2006 Superfast #31 ...... $1 – 2**

Ambulance, #26, 2002; #12, 2003; #46, 2004

1. white with blue windows, green plastic grille, fenders and base, "Medis M3," 2001 Rescue Squad .... $1 – 2

2. **metallic gold with orange, brown, and white, "Ultra Med Alert," blue windows, metallic gray plastic grille, fenders and base, 2002 Red Hot Rescue, #26 .... $1 – 2**

3. **blue with orange and yellow, amber windows, metallic gray plastic grille, fenders and base, 2003 Hospital, #12 .... $1 – 2**

4. **white with red windows, blue plastic grille, fenders and base, labels, 2003 McDonald's Happy Meal premium .... $3 – 4**

Ambulance, #42, 2001

1. white with green base, checkerboard pattern along roof line, "Medic" graphics, 2001 #42 .... $3 – 4

2. **white with green base, brown roof, "Ice Age 2: The Meltdown," "Crash & Eddie" illustration, 2006 Ice Age 2 5-pack .... $2 – 3**

3. **metallic blue with silver base, white roof, "Elemental Hero Bubbleman" illustration, 2006 Yu-Gi-Oh GX 5-pack .... $2 – 3**
4. lime green with green roof, "Diego" illustration, 2006 Nickelodeon 5-pack H4108 .... $2 – 3

5. **red with white roof, "24/7 Ambulance" graphics, 2006 5-pack J4682 .... $1 – 2**

AMC Javelin AMX, 3", #9, 1972

1. lime with chrome hood scoop, bright yellow interior, doors open ... $12 – 16

2. lime with black hood scoop, bright yellow interior, doors open .... $6 – 9
3. lime with black hood scoop, orange interior, doors open .... $12 – 16
4. lime with black hood scoop, white interior, doors open .... $60 – 80
5. lime with black hood scoop, blue interior, doors open .... $120 – 160
6. lime with black hood scoop, yellow-orange interior, doors open ...... $6 – 9
7. metallic blue, black hood scoop, doors open .... $6 – 9
8. metallic blue, black hood scoop, doors don't open .... $6 – 9
9. metallic green, black hood scoop, doors open .... $6 – 9
10. red with black hood scoop, doors don't open .... $40 – 50

AMC Javelin AMX Pro Stocker, $2^{5}/_{8}$", #17, 1983

1. metallic gray with red and black stripes, "AMX" graphics, Macau cast .... $2 – 4
2. metallic gray with red and black stripes, "AMX" graphics, China cast ... $9 – 12
3. maroon with "Dr. Pepper" .... $6 – 9

AMG Mercedes-Benz 500 SEC (see Mercedes-Benz AMG 500 SEC)

Amphibious Personnel Carrier, #55, 2000
1. olive green with mud spatter, "Bravo Co. 17," 2000 Military .... $1 – 2
2. olive green with mud spatter, "Bravo Co. 17," "Matchbox 2000," 2000 Military .... $3 – 4
3. dark khaki with dark brown and yellow detailed graphics, 2003 Matchbox Heroes .... $3 – 4

4. flat black, Battle Kings Night Landing set, 2006, K5532 .... $1 – 2

AMX Javelin (see AMC Javelin AMX)

AMX Pro Stocker (see AMC Javelin AMX Pro Stocker)

Arctic Track Truck (see Snow Doctor)

Armored Police Truck (see Armored Response Vehicle)

Armored Response Vehicle, #47, 2001; #39, 2002; 69, 2004

1. red with black base, black canopy, 2003 Hero City 5-pack #3 ... $1 – 2

2. metallic burgundy with red base, phosphorescent canopy, 2002 Nite Glow .... $1 – 2

3. blue sides, red-brown front, metallic gray canopy, "Stratos" graphics, 2003 Matchbox Collectibles Masters of the Universe .... $4 – 6

4 dark gray with black base, gray canopy, "ARV 05," 2001 Pull Over .... $1 – 2
5. gray with pale green base, "Secret Force," detailed graphics, 2003 Matchbox Heroes .... $3 – 4
6. metallic gray, "Diego" illustration, 2006 Ice Age 2 5-pack J4720 .... $1 – 2

7. metallic green with "Scooby-Doo!" graphics, Scooby-Doo! 5-pack L1574, 2007 .... $4 – 5

Armored Truck, $2^{13}/_{16}$", #69, 1978
1. red, "Wells Fargo," "732-2031," clear windows, England cast .... $35 – 45

2. red, "Wells Fargo," "732-2031," blue windows, England cast .. $5 – 6
3. red, "Wells Fargo," "QZ-2031," blue windows, England cast .... $5 – 6
4. red, no markings, blue windows, England cast .... $30 – 40
5. green, "Dresdner Bank," blue windows, England cast, Germany issue .. $40 – 50
6. dark army green, "Dresdner Bank," blue windows, England cast, Germany issue .... $60 – 80

Army Halftrack (see Army M3 Halftrack Personnel Carrier)

Army Jeep (see Jeep, #38)

Army M3 Halftrack Personnel Carrier, 2½", #49, 1958
1. metal front wheels and rollers ....$40 – 50
2. gray plastic front wheels, metal rollers ....$45 – 60
3. gray plastic front wheels and rollers ....$90 – 100
4. gray plastic front wheels, silver plastic rollers ....$70 – 80
5. black plastic front wheels and rollers ....$30 – 40

Army M3 A2 Halftrack, 2001 Feature Cars, with opening features, designed to replace Premiere Collection
1. olive green with star and black treads ....$9 – 12

Army Saracen Personnel Carrier (see Saracen Personnel Carrier)

Artic Track Truck (see Snow Doctor)

Articulated Trailer, 3", #50, 1980 (goes with #50 Articulated Truck)
1. blue container, yellow trailer base, 2-pack ....$5 – 6
2. metallic gray container, red trailer base, 2-pack ....$7 – 8

Articulated Truck with Removable Trailer, 3¹⁄₁₆", #50, 1973
1. red cab with purple windows, blue trailer, red trailer base ......$40 – 50
2. red cab with purple windows, metallic gray trailer, red trailer base with tow hook, 2-pack ....$9 – 12
3. red cab with red windows, metallic gray trailer, red trailer base with tow hook, 2-pack ....$9 – 12
4. red cab with red windows, blue trailer, red trailer base ....$40 – 50
5. orange-yellow cab with red windows, light blue trailer, orange yellow trailer base ....$4 – 5
6. orange-yellow cab with purple windows, light blue trailer, orange yellow trailer base, with labels ....$7 – 8
7. orange-yellow cab with purple windows, light blue trailer, orange trailer base, no labels ....$4 – 5
8. orange-yellow cab with purple windows, light blue trailer, yellow trailer base with tow hook, no labels, 2-pack ....$5 – 6
9. yellow cab with red windows, light blue trailer, orange trailer base, no labels ....$4 – 5
10. yellow cab with red windows, light blue trailer, yellow trailer base, no labels ....$4 – 5
11. yellow cab with red windows, dark blue trailer, yellow trailer base with tow hook, no labels, UK issue ....$90 – 120
12. yellow cab with purple windows, light blue trailer, yellow trailer base, no labels ....$4 – 5
13. yellow cab with purple windows, light blue trailer, yellow trailer base, with labels ....$7 – 8
14. yellow cab with purple windows, light blue trailer, yellow trailer base with tow hook, no labels, 2-pack ....$5 – 6

Aston Martin DB-2 Saloon, 2¹⁵⁄₁₆", #53, 1958
1. metallic light green with metal wheels ....$65 – 90
2. metallic light green with gray plastic wheels ....$75 – 100
3. metallic red with gray plastic wheels ....$325 – 375

4. metallic red with black plastic wheels ....$275 – 325

Aston Martin DB-7, #59, 1994; #63, 1994, international
1. metallic red, detailed trim, rubber tires on chrome rims, JC Penney Premiere Collection ....$4 – 5

2. metallic green, "DB-7" and stripe on sides ....$1 – 2
3. metallic green, no markings ......$1 – 2
4. blue, no markings, 6-spoke spiral wheels ....$4 – 5
5. blue, no markings, 5-spoke concave wheels ....$3 – 4

6. silver-blue, detailed trim, rubber tires on chrome rims, Ultra Class ....$9 – 12
7. dark gray, detailed trim, rubber tires on chrome rims, World Class ....$3 – 4
8. metallic gray, detailed trim, rubber tires on chrome rims, international Premiere Collection #1 ....$8 – 10

9. pearl white, detailed trim, rubber tires on chrome rims, Premiere Collection #10 ....$4 – 5

Aston Martin Racing Car, metallic green, 2½", #19, 1961
1. gray driver, "52" decal ....$40 – 50
2. gray driver, "41" decal ....$40 – 50
3. gray driver, "5" decal ....$40 – 50
4. gray driver, "19" decal ....$25 – 35
5. white driver, "19" decal ....$25 – 35
6. white driver, "3" decal ....$40 – 50
7. white driver, "53" decal ....$40 – 50

Atkinson Grit Spreader (see Ford Atkinson Grit Spreader)

Atlantic Prime Mover (see Prime Mover, Rotinoff Super Atlantic Prime Mover)

Atlantic Tractor (see Prime Mover, Rotinoff Super Atlantic Prime Mover)

Atlantic Trailer, 3⅛", #16, 1956
1. tan with metal wheels ......$175 – 200

Atlantic Trailer (Super Atlantic Trailer), 3¼", #16, 1957

1. tan with tan tow bar, gray plastic wheels ....$35 – 45
2. orange with black tow bar, gray plastic wheels ....$100 – 125

3. orange with black tow bar, black plastic wheels .... $30 – 40

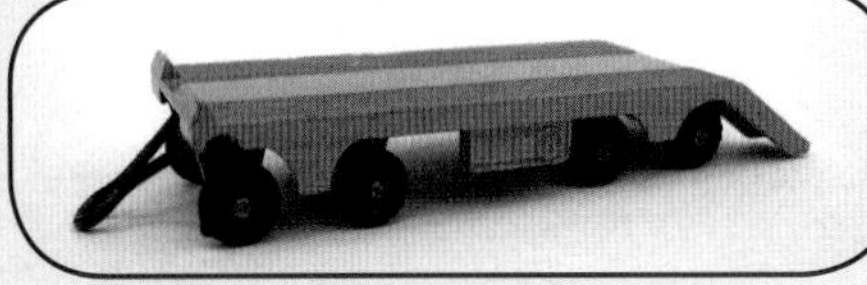

4. orange with unpainted tow bar, black plastic wheels ....$30 - 40

5. orange with orange tow bar, black plastic wheels .... $40 – 50

Atlas Dump Truck, 3", #23, 1975

1. blue with orange dumper ..... $10 – 15

2. blue with yellow dumper .....$9 - 12

3. red with metallic silver dumper ..$9 – 12

Atlas Excavator, #32, 1981; #6, 1990 – 1998; #30, 1999; #10, 1999, Germany; #92, 2000; #72, 2000, international

1. red with black deck, red boom, red scoop, black and white stripes, Thailand cast .... $1 – 2
2. red with black deck, black boom, red scoop, white stripes, Thailand cast .... $1 – 2

3. orange with black deck, black boom, black scoop, England cast ....$7 - 9

4. orange with black deck, black boom, orange scoop ....$1 - 2

5. orange with black deck, orange boom, orange scoop, black and white stripes, Thailand cast .... $1 – 2
6. orange with black deck, orange boom, orange scoop, China cast, Germany issue .... $4 – 5
7. orange with gray deck, gray boom, gray scoop, England cast .... $7 – 9
8. orange with orange deck, black boom, orange scoop, white stripes, 1997 .... $1 – 2
9. fluorescent orange with black deck, black boom, black scoop .... $1 – 2
10. pumpkin orange with black deck, black boom, black scoop, "Blue Ridge Construction," ASAP promotional .... $80 – 120
11. pumpkin orange with black deck, black boom, black scoop, "CAT Service Co.," ASAP promotional .... $80 – 120
12. pumpkin orange with black deck, black boom, black scoop, "Hemler Bros.," ASAP promotional .... $80 – 120
13. pumpkin orange with black deck, black boom, black scoop, "Redi-Way, Inc.," ASAP promotional .... $80 – 120
14. yellow with black deck, metallic gray boom, metallic gray scoop, "X-4970" and dust, 2000 Build It! .... $1 – 2
15. yellow with black deck, metallic gray boom, metallic gray scoop, "X-4970" and dust, "Matchbox 2000," 2000 Build It! .... $3 – 4
16. yellow with black deck, black boom, black scoop, England cast......... $3 – 4
17. yellow with black deck, black boom, black scoop, Macau cast.......... $1 – 2
18. yellow with black deck, black boom, black scoop, Thailand cast........ $1 – 2

19. yellow with black deck, black boom, red scoop, red stripes, Thailand cast .... $1 - 2

20. yellow with black deck, yellow boom, yellow scoop, "JCB" label........... $9 – 10
21. yellow with yellow deck, black boom, black scoop, Macau cast........ $8 – 10

22. yellow with yellow deck, black boom, black scoop, China cast, 5-pack..$1 - 2

23. bright green with black deck, black boom, bright green scoop, black and white stripes, 1998 Stars & Stripes ....$1 - 2

24. blue with blue deck, bright yellow boom, bright yellow scoop, "MC21," "Matchbox," 2003 Hero City 5-pack #4 ....$1 - 2

25. white with black deck, metallic gray boom, black scoop, "X4970" and dust, 1999 Road Work.................... $1 – 2
26. metallic gray with gray deck, orange boom, gray scoop, "MC21," "Matchbox," China cast, 5-pack........... $1 – 2
27. metallic gold with black deck, black boom, black scoop, 1997 75 Challenge............................ $6 – 12

Atlas Skip Truck, 2¹¹⁄₁₆", #37, 1976

1. red with yellow skip, chrome interior, black base, amber windows ...... $6 – 7
2. red with yellow skip, gray interior, black base, amber windows .... $5 – 6

3. red with yellow skip, gray interior, black base, clear windows .....$5 - 6

4. red with yellow skip, gray interior, black base, tinted windows .... $5 – 6
5. red with yellow skip, gray interior, black base, blue windows .... $5 – 6
6. red with yellow skip, gray interior, brown base, clear windows .... $9 – 12
7. red with yellow skip, gray interior, brown base, tinted windows .... $9 – 12
8. red with yellow skip, gray interior, dark gray base, clear windows .... $5 – 6
9. red with yellow skip, gray interior, unpainted base, clear windows.. $5 – 6

10. red with yellow skip, orange interior, black base, clear windows .... $5 – 6
11. red with yellow skip, orange interior, dark gray base, clear windows .. $5 – 6
12. red with blue skip, gray interior, black base, clear windows .... $100 – 150
13. orange with red skip, gray interior, black base, clear windows, Germany issue .... $90 – 120
14. orange with yellow skip, gray interior, black base, clear windows, Germany issue .... $90 – 120
15. blue with yellow skip, black interior, black base, clear windows .... $7 – 8
16. blue with yellow skip, gray interior, black base, clear windows .... $4 – 5
17. blue with yellow skip, gray interior, dark gray base, clear windows .... $4 – 5
18. blue with yellow skip, gray interior, metallic gray base, clear windows .... $4 – 5
19. dark blue with yellow skip, gray interior, dark gray base, clear windows, UK issue .... $200 – 300

Audi Avus Quattro, #12, 1995; #31, 1995, international; #19, 1999; #18, 1999, international

1. chrome burgundy with black interior, tinted windows, "OOOO Avus".. $1 – 2

2. chrome gold with black interior, tinted windows, "OOOO Avus," 5-pack .... $1 – 2
3. chrome green with black interior, tinted windows, "OOOO Avus," 1999 international issue .... $1 – 2
4. chrome orange with red and black interior, clear windows, rubber tires on chrome rims, International Premiere Collection .... $4 – 5
5. chrome red with black interior, tinted windows, "OOOO Avus" .... $1 – 2

6. chrome silver with red interior, clear windows, no markings .... $1 – 2

7. chrome silver with red and black interior, clear windows, "Avus Quattro," rubber tires on chrome rims, Premiere Collection .... $4 – 5
8. iridescent white with red interior, tinted windows, "Avus Quattro," 5-pack .. $1 – 2

9. iridescent white with red and black interior, clear windows, "Avus Quattro," rubber tires on chrome rims, Premiere Collection .... $4 – 5
10. metallic gold with black interior, clear windows, 1997 75 Challenge... $6 – 12
11. metallic green with black interior, tinted windows, "OOOO Avus" .... $1 – 2
12. metallic gray with black interior, clear windows, no markings, ASAP promotional blank........................ $30 – 40
13. metallic gray with black interior, clear windows, "Iscar," ASAP promotional.......................... $75 – 125

14. red with red and black interior, clear windows, rubber tires on chrome rims, Select Class .... $4 – 5
15. white with gray interior, green windows, "Quattro" .... $1 – 2

Audi Quattro, 3", #23, 1982; #25, 1982, international

1. white, "Audi 20," brown and orange accents, England cast .... $3 – 4
2. white, "Audi 20," brown and orange accents, Macau cast .... $3 – 4
3. white, "Audi 20," brown and orange accents, Manaus cast, Brazil issue .... $40 – 60

4. white, "Duckhams," brown and red accents, "Pirelli" .... $4 – 5
5. purple, "Quattro OOOO" .... $4 – 6
6. blue, "Quattro OOOO" .... $8 – 10
7. metallic dark gray with pictogram and "Audi 2584584," China issue .... $40 – 60

8. metallic gray with Audi logo, "Quattro" .... $2 – 4

Audi R8, #14, 2007
metallic charcoal gray .... $1 – 2

Audi RS6 Avant, #5, 2006

1. blue, 2006 #5 .... $1 – 2

Audi TT Hardtop, #44, 2000, US; #37, 1999, Germany; #74, 2000, Germany; #67, 2000, international; #14, 2006
1. red, US issue .... $3 – 4
2. metallic light green, 1999 Germany issue .... $4 – 5

3. metallic dark green, 2001 Eurosports 5-pack .... $1 – 2

4. metallic blue, 2000 International issue ....$3 – 4

5. metallic blue, "TT Coupe," 2000 US issue ....$1 – 2
6. metallic blue, Target Eggmobiles 3-pack .... $9 – 12
7. black, Launcher 5-pack .... $1 – 2
8. metallic gray, 2000 Germany issue .... $4 – 5

9. metallic dark gray, 2006 #15...$1 – 2

Audi TT Convertible Roadster, #37, 1999, Germany; #4, 2001; #22, 2005
1. metallic light green with light tan interior, 1999, Germany issue .... $4 – 6
2. metallic blue with dark gray interior, 10-spoke wheels, 2001 Daddy's Dreams, US issue .... $1 – 2
3. metallic blue with dark gray interior, 5-spoke wheels, 2001 Daddy's Dreams, US issue .... $1 – 2

4. red with white, black and silver Hero City Sports graphics, 2003 Hero City 5-pack #6 ....$1 – 2
5. metallic gray, 2005 #22.......... $1 – 2

6. orange with black interior, detailed lights and grille, 2006 5-pack J4681..............................$1 – 2

Austin 200-Gallon Water Truck, 2³/₈", #71, 1959

1. olive green with black plastic wheels...........................$30 – 40

Austin A50, blue-green, 2⁵/₈", #36, 1957

1. metal wheels...................$35 – 45
2. gray plastic wheels .... $35 – 45

Austin A55 Cambridge, two-tone green, 2³/₄", #29, 1961
1. gray wheels........................ $35 – 45
2. silver wheels....................... $20 – 30
3. black wheels....................... $20 – 30

Austin FX4R London Taxi, 2⁵/₈", #4, 1987; #36, 2005; #35, 2006; #33, 2007#
1. yellow, "ABC Taxi," Preschool/Live & Learn .... $5 – 7

2. black, no markings ....$3 – 5
3. black, "Great Taxi Ride London to Sidney" .... $6 – 8
4. black, "London Taxi" and British flag on left side only .... $3 – 5
5. black, "Old Eight" and British flag .... $80 – 100

6. black, "Taxi"........................$1 – 2

7. red and black, 2005 Superfast #69 ....$1 – 2
8. metallic gray, 2005 #36.......... $1 – 2

9. metal flake silver, 2006 #35...$1 – 2

10. metallic pale blue, 2007 #33....$1 – 2

11. metallic maroon, 2007 5-pack K9612 ....$1 – 2

Austin London Taxi, 2¹/₄", #17, 1960

1. maroon with gray plastic wheels...........................$40 – 50
2. maroon with silver plastic wheels.............................. $65 – 75

Austin Mk 2 Radio Truck, 2³/₈", #68, 1959

1. **olive green with black plastic wheels .... $40 - 50**

Austin Mini Van, #31, 2007
1. light green .... $1 – 2

Auto Medic Tow Truck, #2, 2005; #42, 2007

1. **black and chrome, 2005 #2... $1 - 2**
2. metallic green, 2007 #42........ $1 – 2

Auxiliary Power Truck (see Mack Floodlight Heavy Rescue Auxiliary Power Truck)

Aveling Barford Diesel Road Roller, 1⅞", #1, 1953 (See Road Roller, Diesel)

Aveling Barford Tractor Shovel, 2⅝", #43, 1962
1. yellow with yellow shovel, base and driver .... $40 – 50

2. **yellow with yellow shovel, red base and driver .... $25 - 35**

3. **yellow with red shovel, yellow base and driver .... $25 - 35**
4. yellow with red shovel, base and driver .... $40 – 50

B

Badge Blaster, #2, 2004, vehicle shaped like a policeman's badge (MB618)

1. **silver chrome and red .... $1 - 2**

Badger Cement Truck, Rolamatic, 3", #19, 1976

1. **red with orange-yellow barrel, green windows .... $6 - 9**
2. red with orange-yellow barrel, no windows .... $6 – 9
3. red with orange barrel, purple windows .... $6 – 9
4. red with orange barrel, green windows .... $6 – 9
5. red with gray barrel, no windows.. $6 – 9
6. red with gray barrel, green windows .... $6 – 9
7. red with gray barrel, purple windows .... $6 – 9
8. red with light yellow barrel, green windows .... $6 – 9
9. red with light yellow barrel, purple windows .... $6 – 9

Badger Exploration Truck, with Rolamatic radar antenna, 2⅞", #16, 1974

1. **metallic orange-red with metallic gray base, green windows, ivory radar .... $9 - 12**
2. metallic orange-red with light gray base, green windows, ivory radar .... $5 – 7
3. metallic orange-red with dark gray base, green windows, ivory radar .... $5 – 7
4. metallic orange-red with dark gray base, green windows, black radar .... $5 – 7
5. metallic orange-red with dark gray base, blue-green windows, ivory radar .... $5 – 7
6. metallic orange-red with dark gray base, blue-green windows, black radar .... $5 – 7
7. metallic orange-red with black base, green windows, ivory radar....... $5 – 7
8. metallic orange-red with black base, green windows, black radar...... $5 – 7
9. metallic orange-red with black base, purple windows, ivory radar...... $5 – 7
10. metallic orange-red with black base, blue-green windows, ivory radar.. $5 – 7
11. army green with light gray base, green windows, ivory radar, Two-Pack .... $65 – 85

12. **olive green with light gray base, green windows, ivory radar, Two-Pack .... $6 - 8**

Baja Bandit, #59, 2007
1. 2007 #59 .... $1 – 2

Baja Buggy, 2⅝", #13, 1971
1. metallic light green with orange interior, red flower label, black exhausts .... $12 – 16
2. metallic light green with orange interior, red flower label, red exhausts .... $12 – 16
3. metallic light green with orange interior, orange flower label, black exhausts .... $12 – 16
4. metallic light green with orange interior, orange flower label, red exhausts .... $12 – 16
5. metallic light green with orange interior, Police shield label, red exhausts .... $30 – 45
6. metallic light green with red interior, Police shield label, red exhausts .... $30 – 45
7. metallic light green with red interior, orange flower label, red exhausts .... $12 – 16
8. metallic light green with orange interior from #47 Beach Hopper, orange flower label, red exhausts .... $30 – 45
9. metallic light green with orange interior, no label, red exhausts.......... $12 – 16
10. metallic dark green with orange interior, orange flower label, red exhausts .... $12 – 16
11. metallic green with orange interior, sunburst label, red exhausts...... $24 – 36
12. bright lime green with orange interior, orange flower label, red exhausts, Brazil issue .... $400 – 600

Baja Dune Buggy (see Baja Buggy)

Bass Bus, fish-shaped school bus, #9, 2004 (MB649)

1. yellow, 2004 Ultra Heroes........ $1 – 2

Battering Ram, #90, 2000

1. blue, "Police," white and silver stripes, 2000 Police Patrol ... $1 – 2

2. blue, "Police," white and silver stripes, "Matchbox 2000," 2000 Police Patrol.................................. $3 – 4

3. white, "Metro Patrol," "Police 3," blue, yellow and red design, 2001 On Patrol 5-pack .... $1 – 2

4. pale green with gray and orange graphics .... $1 – 2

5. gray with darker gray and orange graphics, 2007 5-pack K9407 .... $1 – 2

BEA (British European Airways) Coach, 2$^1/_2$", #58, 1958

1. "British European Airways" decals, gray plastic wheels .... $30 – 40

2. "BEA" decals, gray plastic wheels.............................. $40 – 50
3. "BEA" decals, silver plastic wheels........................... $80 – 100
4. "BEA" decals, black plastic wheels........................... $80 – 100

Beach 4x4, #46, 2003; #55, 2004

1. metallic green with yellow interior, black plastic base, 2003 Forest Rescue .... $1 – 2

2. fluorescent lime green with black interior, dark gray plastic base, orange hubs, 2006 10-pack B5609 .... $1 – 2

3. avocado green with black interior, dark gray base, "Diego," 2006 Nickelodeon 5-pack H4108 .... $1 – 2

Beach Buggy, 2$^5/_8$", #30, 1971

1. metallic pink with white interior....$20 – 25
2. metallic pink with yellow interior.....$12 – 16
3. metallic lavender with yellow interior .... $16 – 24

Beach Hopper (Rolamatic), 2$^5/_8$", #47, 1974

1. dark blue, orange interior, metallic gray base.................................. $25 – 30
2. dark blue, orange interior, pink base................................. $12 – 16
3. dark blue, yellow interior, pink base................................. $16 – 24
4. dark blue, orange interior, lavender base................................. $12 – 16
5. dark blue, orange interior, unpainted base................................. $12 – 16

Beach Patrol, #37, 2004 (see All-Terrain Fire Tanker)

Bedford Car Transporter, 3", #11, 1976

Cars are listed in order: top front, top rear, bottom.

1. orange with beige carrier, blue windows; red, yellow, blue cars... $5 – 7

2. orange with beige carrier; blue windows, red, yellow, dark blue cars......... $5 – 7
3. orange with beige carrier; blue windows; yellow, red, blue cars...... $5 – 7
4. orange with beige carrier; blue windows; red, yellow, blue cars...... $5 – 7
5. orange with beige carrier; blue windows; red, blue, blue cars...... $8 – 10
6. orange with beige carrier; blue windows; blue, blue, blue cars... $12 – 16
7. orange with beige carrier; blue windows; yellow, yellow, yellow cars....... $12 – 16
8. orange with beige carrier; blue windows; red, red, red cars...... $12 – 16
9. orange with beige carrier; green windows; red, yellow, blue cars...... $5 – 7
10. orange with beige carrier; purple windows; red, yellow, blue cars...... $5 – 7
11. orange with off-white carrier; blue windows; red, blue, blue cars...... $8 – 10
12. orange with off-white carrier; blue windows; red, yellow, blue cars...... $5 – 7
13. orange with off-white carrier; blue windows; yellow, yellow, blue cars. $8 – 10
14. orange with off-white carrier; blue windows; yellow, yellow, blue cars. $8 – 10
15. orange with gray carrier; blue windows; blue, red, yellow cars............ $8 – 10
16 red with beige carrier; blue windows; red, yellow, blue cars............... $5 – 7
17. red with beige carrier; blue windows; red, orange, blue cars............. $5 – 7
18. red with beige carrier; blue windows; red, orange, red cars........... $8 – 10
19. red with beige carrier; purple windows; red, yellow, blue cars............... $5 – 7
20. red with beige carrier; purple windows; red, orange, blue cars............. $5 – 7
21. red with gray carrier; blue windows; yellow, red, blue cars.................. $5 – 7
22. red with gray carrier; blue windows; red, red, red cars.............. $12 – 16

Bedford Compressor Truck, 2$^1/_4$", #28, 1956

1. orange-yellow, metal wheels .... $35 - 55

Bedford "Dunlop" 12 CWT Van, 2 1/8", #25, 1956
1. blue .... $40 – 55

Bedford Duplé Long Distance Coach, 2 1/4", #21, 1956
1. green .... $45 – 55

Bedford Duplé Long Distance Coach, 2 5/8", #21, 1958
1. light green .... $45 – 60
2. dark green .... $80 – 100

Bedford "Evening News" Van, yellow-orange, 2 1/4", #42, 1957
1. metal wheels .... $40 – 50
2. gray plastic wheels .... $40 – 50
3. black plastic wheels .... $40 – 50

Bedford Horse Box with Two Horses, 2 13/16", #40, 1977; #87, 1999, US; #49, 2000; #2, 1999, international; #29, 2000, international
1. red with beige box, light brown door, green windows, black base, England cast .... $50 – 60
2. red with dark tan box, brown door, green windows, black base, "Manaus" cast, Brazil issue .... $40 – 50
3. red with light brown box, white door, green windows, black base, England cast .... $12 – 16
4. red with light brown box, white door, green windows, metallic gray base, England cast .... $12 – 16
5. orange with beige box, dark brown door, clear windows, black base, England cast .... $9 – 12
6. orange with beige box, dark brown door, clear windows, dark gray base, England cast .... $9 – 12
7. orange with beige box, dark brown door, green windows, dark gray base, England cast .... $5 – 6
8. orange with beige box, dark brown door, green windows, metallic gray base, England cast .... $5 – 6
9. orange with beige box, dark brown door, green windows, unpainted base, England cast .... $5 – 6

10. orange with beige box, light brown door, green windows, black base, England cast .... $5 - 6
11. orange with beige box, light brown door, green windows, black base, England cast .... $5 – 6
12. orange with beige box, dark brown door, purple windows, dark gray base, England cast .... $6 – 8
13. orange with ivory box, light brown door, green windows, black base, England cast .... $5 – 6
14. orange with ivory box, lime green door, green windows, black base, England cast .... $12 – 16
15. orange with light brown box, lime green door, green windows, black base, England cast .... $6 – 8
16. orange with light brown box, white door, green windows, black base, England cast .... $6 – 8
17. orange with light brown box, white door, green windows, black base, Macau cast .... $5 – 6
18. orange with light brown box, white door, green windows, metallic gray base, England cast .... $6 – 8
19. orange with light brown box, white door, green windows, unpainted base, England cast .... $6 – 8
20. orange with clear windows .... $8 – 10
21. orange with purple windows .... $5 – 8
22. dark orange with beige box, brown door, green windows, dark gray base, England cast .... $6 – 8
23. dark orange with light brown box, lime green door, green windows, black base, England cast .... $5 – 6
24. dark orange with light brown box, lime green door, green windows, black base, England cast, black wheel hubs .... $6 – 8
25. dark orange with light brown box, lime green door, green windows, unpainted base, England cast .... $5 – 6
26. dark orange with light brown box, lime green door, green windows, unpainted base, England cast, black wheel hubs .... $6 – 8
27. dark orange with light brown box, white door, green windows, black base, England cast .... $5 – 6
28. yellow with light brown box, lime green door, green windows, black base, England cast .... $6 – 8
29. yellow with light brown box, white door, amber windows, black base, Thailand cast, Farming series gift set .... $4 – 5
30. yellow with light brown box, white door, green windows, black base, England cast .... $6 – 8
31. dark green with beige box, dark brown door, green windows, dark gray base, England cast .... $6 – 8
32. dark green with beige box, dark brown door, green windows, metallic gray base, England cast .... $6 – 8
33. dark green with beige box, dark brown door, green windows, unpainted base, England cast .... $6 – 8
34. dark green with beige box, lime green door, green windows, black base, England cast .... $8 – 10
35. dark green with beige box, lime green door, green windows, metallic gray base, England cast .... $8 – 10
36. dark green with light brown box, white door, green windows, unpainted base, England cast .... $12 – 16
37. dark green with translucent ivory box, dark brown door, green windows, unpainted base, England cast.. $8 – 10
38. light green with beige box, dark brown door, green windows, black base, England cast .... $6 – 8
39. light green with beige box, dark brown door, green windows, unpainted base, England cast .... $6 – 8
40. light green with beige box, white door, green windows, unpainted base, England cast .... $6 – 8
41. blue with yellow box, lime green door, green windows, red base, lime green wheels with blue hubs, Live 'N Learn/Matchbox Preschool series, Thailand cast .... $16 – 24
42. blue with yellow box, lime green door, green windows, red base, lime green wheels with lime green hubs, Live 'N Learn/Matchbox Preschool series, Thailand cast .... $16 – 24
43. blue with yellow box, lime green door, green windows, red base, lime green wheels with red hubs, Live 'N Learn/Matchbox Preschool series, Macau cast .... $6 – 8

44. metallic turquoise with translucent pale gray box, black door, tinted windows, "Kentucky Stables," 1999 Farming series, international window box .... $3 - 4
45. metallic turquoise with translucent pale gray box, black door, tinted windows, "Express," 1999 On the Farm series, China cast, US issue .... $1 – 2
46. white with white box, white door, blue windows, red base, "Circus Circus," Thailand cast, Motor City .... $5 – 6
47. dark gray with mustard yellow box, light brown door, tinted windows, "Express," 2000 Farming .... $1 – 2
48. dark gray with mustard yellow box, light brown door, tinted windows, "Express," "Matchbox 2000," 2000 Farming .... $3 – 4

Bedford Lomas Ambulance, 2 5/8", #14, 1962
1. gray plastic wheels .... $100 – 125
2. silver plastic wheels .... $50 – 60

3. black plastic wheels.......... $15 - 20

Bedford Low Loader, $1\frac{3}{8}$", #27, 1956
1. light blue cab, dark blue trailer............................ $625 - 800

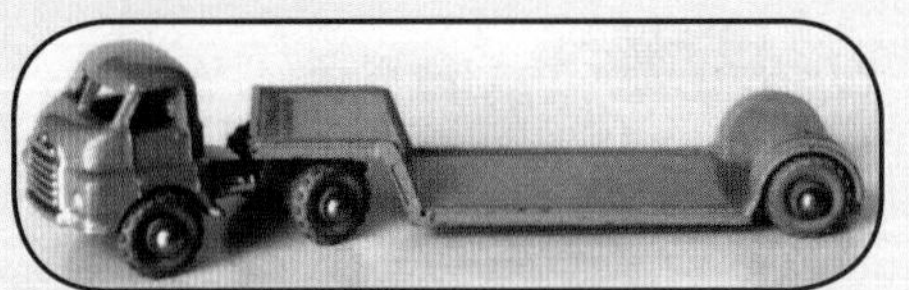

2. dark green cab, tan trailer .. $35 - 60

Bedford Low Loader, $3\frac{3}{4}$", #27, 1959
1. light green cab with metal wheels.............................. $40 - 50
2. light green cab with gray plastic wheels.............................. $65 - 75
3. dark green cab with gray plastic wheels.............................. $75 - 95

Bedford "Matchbox Removal" Van, $2\frac{1}{8}$", #17, 1956
1. maroon or blue body........ $150 - 180
2. green .... $30 - 50
3. light green .... $60 - 75

Bedford Milk Delivery Van, $2\frac{1}{4}$", #29, 1956
1. tan, metal wheels................ $60 - 80
2. tan, gray plastic wheels........ $65 - 85

Bedford Petrol Tanker, with tilt cab, 3", #25, 1964
1. yellow cab, "BP," gray plastic wheels.......................... $140 - 160

2. yellow cab, "BP," black plastic wheels............................ $25 - 40
3. dark blue cab, "ARAL," black plastic wheels............................ $80 - 100

Bedford Tipper Truck, red with tan dumper, $2\frac{1}{8}$", #40, 1957
1. metal wheels...................... $40 - 50
2. gray plastic wheels.............. $50 - 60
3. black plastic wheels............. $25 - 30

Bedford Ton Tipper, gray cab, $2\frac{1}{2}$", #3, 1961
1. maroon dumper, gray wheels .. $90 - 100
2. red dumper, gray wheels ...... $30 - 40

3. maroon dumper, black wheels .... $15 - 20
4. red dumper, black wheels ..... $15 - 20

Bedford Wreck Truck, no number cast in base, 2", #13, 1955
1. tan, metal wheels................ $60 - 80

Bedford Wreck Truck, number 13 cast in base, $2\frac{1}{8}$", #13, 1958
1. tan, metal wheels................ $60 - 80
2. tan, gray plastic wheels...... $80 - 100

Bedford Wreck Truck, 2", 1993, Matchbox Originals replica of #13
1. red with yellow boom, Made in China .... $4 - 5

Beef Hauler (see Dodge Stake Truck)

Beetle 4x4 (see Volkswagen Beetle 4x4)

Beetle Streaker (see Hot Chocolate)

Bentley Continental GT, #1, 2007
1. metallic gray .... $1 - 2

Berkeley Cavalier Travel Trailer, $2\frac{1}{2}$", #23, 1956
1. pale blue, metal wheels, no number on base, faint door outline .... $60 - 80
2. pale blue, metal wheels, number 23 on base, prominent door outline .... $60 - 80
3. lime green, metal wheels, number 23 on base, prominent door outline .... $100 - 120
4. lime green, gray plastic wheels, number 23 on base, prominent door outline.......................... $100 - 120
5. metallic green, gray plastic wheels, number 23 on base, prominent door outline....................... $750 - 1,000

Big Banger, 3", #26, 1972 (similar castings: Cosmic Blues, Flame Out, Pi-Eyed Piper, Red Rider)
1. red, "Big Banger" labels, unpainted metal base, blue windows..... $15 - 20
2. red, "Big Banger" labels, unpainted metal base, amber windows........... $15 - 20
3. red, "Big Banger" labels, chrome plastic base, blue windows, Premiere Collection #13 .... $4 - 5
4. red, "Big Banger" labels, chrome plastic base, blue windows, "Pi-Eyed Piper" on base.............................. $90 - 120

Big Blue (see Hot Chocolate)

Big Bull Bulldozer, $2\frac{3}{8}$", #12, 1975
1. orange with green blade, orange rollers .... $5 - 7
2. orange with green blade, yellow rollers .... $15 - 20
3. orange with green blade, black rollers .... $55 - 65

Billboard Truck, #56, 2003
1. blue, 2003 Kid's Shoppes #56 .... $1 - 2
2. lime green, 2006 5-pack J4682.... $1 - 2

Black Widow, Roman Numeral VIII, 1978 (variation of #41 Siva Spider, 1972)
1. powder blue with clear windows, Roman Numeral Limited Edition .... $12 - 15
2. powder blue with black windows, Roman Numeral Limited Edition .... $9 - 12

Blaze Buster Fire Engine, "Fire" labels, 3", #22, 1975
1. red with white ladder, chrome interior, unpainted base, "Fire" labels .... $275 - 425
2. red with black ladder, chrome interior, unpainted base, "Fire" labels... $25 - 40
3. red with yellow ladder, chrome interior, unpainted base, "Fire" labels ... $6 - 10
4. red with yellow ladder, chrome interior, unpainted base (Manaus, Brazil, cast) .... $40 - 55
5. red with yellow ladder, chrome interior, gray base (Manaus, Brazil, cast) .... $70 - 90
6. red with yellow ladder, chrome interior, black base........................... $6 - 10
7. red with yellow ladder, white interior, black base........................... $6 - 10
8. red with yellow ladder, white interior, charcoal base...................... $6 - 10
9. dark red with yellow ladder, white interior, black base .... $6 - 10
10. dark red with yellow ladder, white interior, charcoal base .... $6 - 10
11. dark red with yellow ladder, white interior, gray-brown base .... $6 - 10
12. dull red with orange-yellow ladder, white interior, gray-brown base .... $6 - 10
13. dull red with orange-yellow ladder, white interior, gray-brown base, "No.32" labels .... $9 - 12

Blimp, #455, 1999
1. red, "Coca-Cola," Premiere Collection .... $7 - 9
2. red, "Coca-Cola," "www.cocacola store.com," Color Comp promotional .... $80 - 120

Bloodmobile, #15, 2003 (see Police Mobile Command Center)

Bluebird Dauphine Travel Trailer, $2\frac{1}{2}$", #23, 1960
1. metallic green with gray plastic wheels.......................... $300 - 350
2. metallic tan with gray plastic wheels.............................. $50 - 60

3. metallic tan with silver wheels....$50 – 60
4. metallic tan with black plastic wheels.......... $80 – 100

Blue Shark, 3", #61, 1971
1. dark blue, "69" label, amber windshield .... $16 – 24
2. dark blue, "69" label, clear windshield .... $16 – 24
3. dark blue, "86" label, amber windshield .... $16 – 24
4. dark blue, "86" label, clear windshield .... $16 – 24
5. dark blue, "scorpion" label, amber windshield .... $30 – 40
6. dark blue, "scorpion" label, clear windshield .... $30 – 40

BMC 1800 Pininfarina, 2¾", #56, 1970

1. metallic gold .... $16 – 24

2. pink .... $20 – 25

3. orange.......... $16 – 24

BMW 3.0 CSL, 2⅞", #45, 1976
1. red .... $70 – 80
2. orange with clear windows...... $8 – 10
3. orange with dark green windows .... $8 – 10

4. orange with green windows ... $7 – 9
5. white, "BMW," "Manhalter" labels, Action System .... $60 – 70
6. white "Polizei" label, amber dome light, Germany/Japan issue .... $40 – 50
7. white, "Polizei" label, blue dome light, Germany/Japan issue .... $40 – 50
8. white, "Polizei" label, green hood and trunk, Germany/Japan issue .... $60 – 70
9. white, no "Polizei" label, green hood and trunk, Germany issue.......... $90 – 120

BMW 323i Cabriolet, 2¾", #39, 1985
1. red, "323i," no tow hook .... $1 – 2
2. red, "323i," tow hook .... $1 – 2
3. red, "Gliding Club," tow hook, Two-Pack (with glider trailer) .... $4 – 5
4. metallic light blue, "323i," no tow hook.......... $3 – 4
5. metallic light blue, "323i," tow hook.......... $1 – 2
6. metallic light blue, dark blue stripe, tow hook, Two-Pack .... $3 – 4
7. dark blue, "323i," "BP," Dutch issue .... $10 – 12
8. white, "323i," "BMW," no tow hook.......... $10 – 12
9. white, "323i," "BMW," tow hook.......... $10 – 12
10. white, "323i," blue and red design, tow hook, Two-Pack .... $3 – 4
11. white, "Alpina," Laser wheels, tow hook.......... $5 – 6
12. white, "Alpina," new Superfast wheels, no tow hook .... $5 – 6
13. white, "Alpina," new Superfast wheels, tow hook.......... $5 – 6
14. white with purple, orange, and blue design, tow hook, Two-Pack ...... $1 – 2

BMW 328i, #69, 1999, Germany
1. metallic dark green, light tan interior, clear windows, 1999.......... $4 – 5
2. metallic blue, light gray interior, tinted windows, 5-pack .... $1 – 2
3. dark metallic blue, black interior, tinted windows, Launcher 5-pack........ $1 – 2

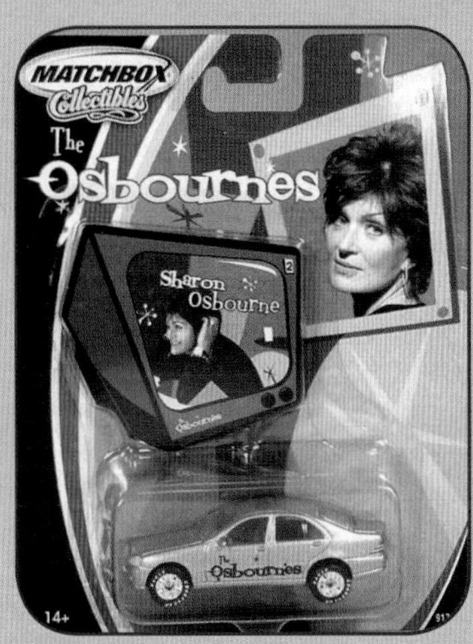

4. metallic silver-blue, rubber tires on chrome rims, Sharon Osbourne, Matchbox Collectibles "The Osbournes" .... $5 – 6
5. dark gray, "BMW328i," light gray interior, clear windows .... $3 – 4

BMW 328i Police Car, #11, 2000; #31, 2001; #29, 2003
1. white and green, "Polizei," blue and green light bar, 2000 .... $3 – 5
2. white with red band, blue stripes, crest, "35 – 1," 2000 .... $3 – 5
3. metallic silver, "Police" with orange band and checks, blue light bar, 2001 ...$1 – 2

4. blue with red and white design, tinted windows, black interior, red light bar, 2001 On Patrol 5-pack... $1 – 2

5. metallic blue with red and yellow design, amber windows, white interior, red light bar, 2003 Police Squad .... $1 – 2

BMW 3-Series Coupe, #83, 2000; #63, 2000, international; #63, 2005

1. metallic blue, "3 Series," gradient black to gray stripe, 5-pack... $1 – 2

2. metallic gray with white and yellow headlights, 2000 Worldwide Wheels.......... $1 – 2
3. metallic gray with white and yellow headlights, "Matchbox 2000," 2000 Worldwide Wheels.......... $3 – 4
4. white with silver headlights, black Matchbox logo, 2003 Auto Carrier Launcher 5-pack .... $1 – 2

5. metallic light blue .... $1 – 2

6. red, 2005 Superfast #71 .....$3 - 4

BMW 5-Series 535i, 3", #26, 1989; #31, 1990, international

1. red, no markings, Show Stoppers, Thailand cast............................... $4 - 5
2. metallic dark gray, no markings, Macau cast..................................... $3 - 4
3. metallic dark gray, no markings, Thailand cast............................... $3 - 4
4. white, "BMW Team," Thailand cast..................................... $3 - 4

BMW 850i, 3", #49, 1993; #2, 1993, international; #2, 2001; #73, 1998, international; #54, 1998, Germany

1. red, "Ripper" on sides, skull and crossbones on hood, 1995 ....$1 - 2

2. red, "Ripper" on sides, no markings on hood, 1996 .... $1 - 2
3. red, detailed trim, black and red interior, rubber tires on chrome rims, Premiere Collection #15....................... $4 - 5
4. red, detailed trim, black and tan interior, rubber tires on chrome rims, JC Penney Premiere Collection............ $4 - 5
5. red, no markings, Kentucky Fried Chicken Kids Meal premium......... $40 - 60
6. metallic red, no markings, 1998 Street Cruisers series, international issue..................................... $1 - 2
7. metallic red, no markings, Germany issue..................................... $4 - 5
8. metallic red, "BMW 850I" on doors, 10-spoke wheels, 2000 Daddy's Dreams .... $1 - 2

9. metallic red, "BMW 850I" on doors, 5-spoke wheels, 2000 Daddy's Dreams ....$4 - 5

10. yellow, "Coca-Cola" and polar bears, 5-pack................................. $1 - 2
11. dark blue, no markings............ $1 - 2
12. maroon with pink and yellow streaks, 1994 .... $1 - 2

13. maroon, detailed trim, rubber tires on chrome rims, Premiere Collection ....$4 - 5

14. purple, detailed trim, rubber tires on chrome rims, Ultra Class .... $9 - 12

15. black, "850i," yellow flash, gold wheel hubs..........................$1 - 2

16. black, "850i," yellow flash, silver wheel hubs .... $3 - 4
17. black, "Go Tigers! 1997," Australia issue.................................... $5 - 6
18. white, Show Stoppers .... $4 - 5

19. metallic silver, clear windows, bright blue interior, 1994 ....$3 - 4

20. metallic gray, detailed trim, chrome windows, rubber tires on chrome rims, World Class .... $4 - 5

21. metallic gray, 2005 Superfast #15 ....$3 - 4

BMW Cabriolet (see 323i Cabriolet)

BMW M1, 3", #52, 1981

1. red, "1," stripes, hood doesn't open..$1 - 2

2. yellow, "11" and stripes, hood doesn't open ....$1 - 2

3. dark yellow, detailed trim, chrome windows, rubber tires on chrome rims, hood doesn't open, World Class.................................... $6 - 8
4. metallic blue, detailed trim, rubber tires on chrome rims, hood doesn't open, Gold Coin Collection .... $16 - 24

5. black, "Pirelli 59," hood doesn't open, Macau cast................$4 - 5

6. black, "Pirelli 59," hood doesn't open, Manaus cast, Brazil issue..... $40 - 50
7. metallic gray, "52," hood opens, clear windows .... $3 - 4
8. metallic gray, "52," hood opens, tinted windows .... $3 - 4
9. metallic gray, "52," hood opens, amber windows .... $12 - 16
10. metallic gray, "52," hood opens, green windows .... $70 - 80

11. white, "BMW M1," hood doesn't open..................................$3 - 4

12. chrome, hood doesn't open, custom...................... $16 - 24

BMW Mini Cooper S (see Mini Cooper S)

BMW X5, #31, 2001, Germany; #31, 2002, USA

1. blue with gray interior, #31, 2002 Cool Rides ....$1 - 2

2. metallic gold, 2003 Hero City 5-pack #11 .... $1 – 2

3. metallic dark olive green, 2005 Superfast #14 .... $3 – 4

BMW Z3, #25, 1997; #61, 1997, international; #5, 1998; #72, 1998, international; #50, 1999; #45, 1999, international; #3, 2000, international; #74, 2002

1. unpainted with tan and black interior, rubber tires on chrome rims, detailed trim, 1997 Inaugural Edition ..... $5 – 6
2. black with dark red interior .... $1 – 2
3. black with dark red interior, plastic base, Target Eggmobile .... $3 – 4
4. black with dark red interior, metal base, Target Eggmobile................ $10 – 12
5. black with dark red interior, "Millions of Reasons To Celebrate! Compaq," ASAP promotional....................... $60 – 90

6. blue with gray interior, "Z3," white splash design bordered in red, 1998 Stars & Stripes................... $1 – 2

7. metallic blue with tan and black interior, rubber tires on chrome rims, detailed trim, 1997 Inaugural Edition ..... $5 – 6
8. metallic red with black interior, silver "Z3," 1999 Drop Tops .... $1 – 2

9. metallic red with black interior, #74, 2002 Kids' Cars of the Year .. $1 – 2

10. metallic red with black interior, silver "Z3" and "007," ASAP promotional..................... $80 – 120
11. metallic gold with black interior, 1997 75 Challenge....................... $6 – 12

12. metallic green with black interior, 2003 5-pack....................... $1 – 2

13. metallic green with tan interior .. $3 – 4
14. metallic gray with gray interior .. $4 – 5

15. metallic gray with maroon and black interior, rubber tires on chrome rims, Premiere Collection #12 .... $4 – 5

16. red with black interior, "3Com," ASAP promotional..................... $80 – 120
17. red with black interior, "Compaq," ASAP promotional....................... $60 – 90
18. red with black interior, "Macola Software," ASAP promotional ... $80 – 120
19. red with black interior, "Millions of Reasons To Celebrate! Compaq," ASAP promotional .... $60 – 90
20. red with black interior, "Retek Broadvision," ASAP promotional..... $80 – 120
21. red with black interior, "Rigid Keenserts," ASAP promotional... $80 – 120

22. red with black interior, "Z3," white splash design bordered in blue, 1998 Stars & Stripes................... $1 – 2

23. red with black interior, "Z3," white splash design bordered in blue, "Espe," ASAP promotional .... $120 – 160
24. red with black interior, "Z3," white splash design bordered in blue, "Fiery Driven," ASAP promotional... $120 – 160

25. red with gray and black interior, rubber tires on chrome rims, Premiere Collection #16 .... $4 – 5

26. white with dark red interior, rubber tires on chrome rims, "Coca-Cola," Premiere Collection .... $7 – 8

27. yellow with dark gray interior, 2006 Superfast #25 .... $3 – 4

BMW Z4, #61, 2004; #26, 2005

1. maroon with tan interior, 2004 #61 .... $1 – 2
2. metallic red with tan interior, 2005 #26 .... $1 – 2

BMW Z8, #9, 2002; #10, 2003; #34, 2005; Superfast #59, 2005

1. metallic blue with tan interior, 2002 Style Champs series .... $1 – 2

2. metallic blue with cream interior, 2003 Family Wheels .... $1 – 2
3. metallic gold with silver-gray interior, 2003 Auto Carrier Launcher 5-pack.................................... $1 – 2
4. metal flake burgundy, 2005 #34.. $1 – 2
5. dark blue with white interior, 2005 Superfast #59....................... $4 – 5

Boat and Trailer, plastic boat, 3¹/₄", #9, 1966

1. white hull, dull blue deck, blue trailer, black plastic wheels ..... $12 – 16

2. white hull, bright blue deck, blue trailer, black plastic wheels .... $5 – 8
3. white hull, blue deck, no label, blue trailer, Superfast wheels, 1969 ... $20 – 25
4. white hull, blue deck, no label, blue trailer, Two-Pack.......................... $4 – 5
5. white hull, blue deck, "8" label, blue trailer, Two-Pack................. $12 – 16
6. white hull, blue deck, no label, orange trailer, Two-Pack..................... $6 – 8

7. white hull, black deck, no label, blue trailer, Two-Pack.................. $65 – 85
8. white hull, white deck, "8" label, orange trailer, Two-Pack.................... $8 – 10

9. white hull, white deck, "Seaspray," black trailer, Two-Pack.......... $4 – 5
10. white hull, white deck, "yellow dash," Two-Pack.............................. $4 – 5
11. blue hull, white deck, "8" label, blue trailer, Two-Pack.................. $12 – 16
12. blue hull, white deck, "8" label, orange trailer, Two-Pack...................... $6 – 8

13. blue hull, blue deck, orange spatter, black trailer, Two-Pack.......... $4 – 5

Bomag Road Roller, #72, 1979; #40, 1991; #68, 1992; #29, 1999; #68, 1991, international; #9, 1998, Germany
1. orange with blue stripes, gray interior, Thailand cast, 1991................ $1 – 2
2. orange with red stripes and design, gray interior, Thailand cast........ $1 – 2
3. orange with black stripes and design, gray interior, Thailand cast........ $1 – 2
4. orange with white roof, black dashes, "R75," China cast, Germany issue . $4 – 5
5. yellow with red interior, yellow hubs, England cast, 1979................ $5 – 6

6. yellow with red interior, chrome hubs, England cast, 1979..... $4 – 5
7. yellow with red stripes, bridge and road graphics, 1992...................... $1 – 2

8. blue with white stripes and "PR-510" and dots, China cast, 1999 Road Work................................. $1 – 2

Boom Fire Truck/Fire Quencher, #33, 2004 (MB613)
1. black, red snorkel, H2O graphics... $1 – 2
2. red with yellow snorkel............. $1 – 2
3. fluorescent lime green with white snorkel.................................. $1 – 2

4. metallic purple, green snorkel, 2006 Nickelodeon 5-pack, H5774... $1 – 2

Boss Mustang (see Ford Mustang 1970 Boss Mustang)

Boulevard Blaster (see Mazda RX7 Savannah)

Bradley M2 Fighting Vehicle, #47, 1998; #83, 1999

1. army green, "Mountain Tiger," "J020764," "476," black base and barrel, 1999 Military Patrol.. $4 – 5
2. army green, black and tan camouflage, army green base, black barrel, Premiere Collection...................... $4 – 5

3. khaki, "T-0927," black star on front and sides, black base and barrel, 1998 Rough 'N Tough........... $1 – 2

4. black with green turret, green tanks, white and red globe graphics, yellow Matchbox logo, gray base and barrel, 2003 Hero City 5-pack #3........ $1 – 2

5. khaki with green and tan camouflage, 2006 Battle Kings Sahara Strike set K5529................ $2 – 3

Bradley M2 Fighting Vehicle, 2001 Feature Cars, with opening features, designed to replace Premiere Collection
1. dark tan with green, black and white camouflage.......................... $9 – 12
2. khaki camouflage with black base and gun, Battle Kings Sahara Strike set, 2006, K5529........................ $1 – 2

Breakdown Van (see Chevrolet Breakdown Van)

BRM Racing Car, black tires on plastic hubs, 2⁵/₈", #52, 1965
1. blue with "5" decal or label...... $8 – 12
2. blue with "3" decal............... $40 – 50
3. red with "5" decal or label..... $20 – 25

Brown Sugar, Roman, numeral VII, 1978 (similar castings: #26 Big Banger, 1972; #26 Cosmic Blues, 1980)

1. brown, Roman Numeral Limited Edition.................................. $9 – 12

Bucket Fire Truck, #2, 2003; #35 Sky Fire, 2004

1. metallic red with metallic gray interior and bumpers, black extending boom, 2003 Sky Fire............ $1 – 2

2. metallic blue with red interior, white bumpers, black non-extending boom, 2004 Sky Fire...................... $1 – 2

Buick LeSabre Stock Car, 3", #10, 1987

1. black with white base, "4" and "355 CID" .... $2 – 4
2. pale purple and white, "Ken Wells," "Quicksilver," Laser wheels .... $6 – 8
3. light green with white base, "4" and "355 CID" .... $3 – 5
4. light brown with white base, "4" and "355 CID" .... $3 – 5
5. orange with white base, "4" and "355 CID" .... $6 – 8

6. **red with white base, "4" and "355 CID" .... 6 – 8**
7. yellow with red base, "10," "Shell," "Marshall" .... $2 – 4
8. white with red base, "10," "Shell," "Marshall" .... $2 – 4
9. red with white base, "07," "Total Racing" .... $2 – 4

Bulldozer (also see Caterpillar Bulldozer, Caterpillar Crawler Bulldozer, Caterpillar D8, Caterpillar Tractor, Case Bulldozer, Ground Breaker)

Bulldozer, #37, 2001; #19, 2002; #67 2003; #32, 2006 (see Super Dozer)

Bulldozer '04, MB624, #17, 2004 (see Rumble Dozer)

Bus (see BEA Coach, Chevrolet Transport Bus, City Bus, Daimler London Bus, Freeman Intercity Commuter, Ikarus Coach, Leyland Royal Tiger Coach, Leyland Titan London Bus, London Bus, London Trolley Bus, School Bus, The Londoner, Volkswagen Transporter Microbus)

Buster, The, stylized pickup truck, #13, 1996; #20, 1998

1. metallic blue with yellow, 1996 ... $1 – 2
2. metallic blue upper, bright yellow lower, hot pink, 1996 .... $4 – 6
3. metallic gold, 1997 75 Challenge ....$12 – 16
4. purple with yellow and white, 1997 .... $1 – 2
5. metallic red with yellow and white, 1998 .... $1 – 2
6. metallic green with yellow and white, 1998 .... $1 – 2
7. metallic light green with yellow and white, 1998 .... $1 – 2
8. metallic blue with yellow, "American Iron Cruise 97" .... $16 – 24

Buzz Copter, dragonfly helicopter, #11, 2004

1. **bright green upper, teal lower, blue tail, silver propellers, blue windows, 2004 Ultra Heroes ....$1 – 2**

C

Cadillac Allante, 3", #65, 1988, international; #72, 1988, USA

1. metallic red, "Official Pace Car 76th Indy," gray interior, clear windshield, Thailand cast .... $8 – 10
2. metallic red with dark gray interior, chrome windshield, rubber tires on gray rims, Thailand cast, World Class ... $4 – 5
3. pink with gray interior, "Cadillac," clear windshield, China cast............. $1 – 2
4. pink with gray interior, "Cadillac," clear windshield, Macau cast............ $1 – 2
5. pink with gray interior, "Cadillac," clear windshield, Thailand cast .... $1 – 2

6. **pink with white interior, green zigzag and blue stripe design, "Cadillac," clear windshield, Thailand cast ...$1 – 2**
7. pink with white interior, green zigzag and blue stripe design, clear windshield, China cast............................ $1 – 2
8. black with red interior, red and silver stripes, clear windshield, Macau cast, Laser wheels .... $4 – 5
9. metallic dark gray with red interior, chrome windshield, rubber tires on gray rims, Macau cast, World Class .. $6 – 8
10. metallic gray with red interior, clear windshield, China cast............. $1 – 2

11. **metallic gray with red interior, clear windshield, Macau cast ....$1 – 2**
12. cream with black and tan interior, clear windshield, rubber tires on gray rims, Thailand cast, JC Penney Premiere Collection 8-car display set........... $4 – 5

13. **white with red and black interior, clear windshield, rubber tires on chrome rims, Thailand cast, Ultra Class...............................$9 – 12**
14. white with red interior, clear windshield, rubber tires on gray rims, China cast, US issue .... $120 – 160

Cadillac Ambulance (see Cadillac S&S Ambulance)

Cadillac Eldorado 1956 Convertible, #501, 2001, Matchbox Collectibles Elvis Presley Collection with Graceland diorama; Superfast #3, 2004; Superfast #18, 2005; Superfast #3, 2007

1. metallic purple, detailed trim, rubber white wall tires on chrome rims, #501, 2001 .... $12 – 16

2. **pale yellow, 2004 Superfast #3..$4 – 5**

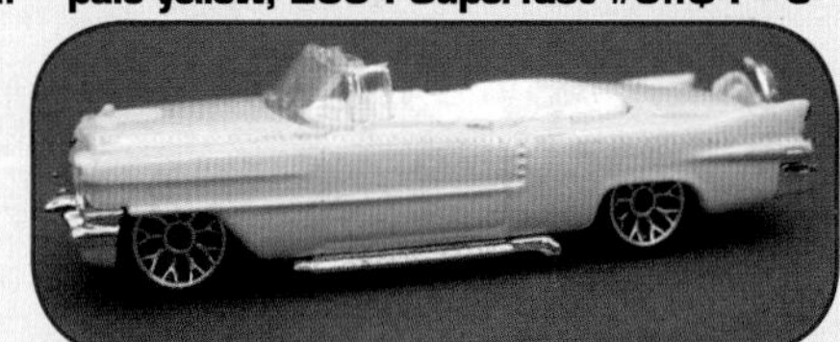

3. **pale green, 2005 Superfast #18...$4 – 5**
4. pale blue, 2006 Superfast #18 .. $4 – 5

5. **black and silver, 2007 Superfast #3 ....$4 – 5**

Cadillac Escalade, #21, 2003; #32, 2005; Superfast #11, 2005

1. **black with yellow and white on sides, "Matchbox Hero City," "Escalade," "21," 2003 Bridge Crew.......$1 - 2**

2. **white with Nickelodeon graphics, 2003 Nickelodeon 5-pack......$1 - 2**

3. **metallic blue, 2005 #32 ....$1 - 2**

4. **black with no graphics, 2005 Superfast #11..............................$4 - 5**

Cadillac Fleetwood 1955, Matchbox Collectibles #500, 2001

1. **pink with white roof, detailed trim, rubber white wall tires on chrome rims, Matchbox Collectibles Elvis Presley Collection with Graceland diorama..........................$12 - 16**
2. bright coral pink with white roof, 2006 5-pack J4677 .... $1 - 2

3. **black with silver trim, 2005 Superfast #25............................$3 - 4**

Cadillac Hearse 1963, #57, 2006; #30, 2007

1. **black, 2006 #57.................$2 - 3**

2. **metallic burgundy green with "Scooby-Doo!" graphics, Scooby-Doo! 5-pack L1574, 2007 ....$5 - 6**
3. white, 2007 #30................... $3 - 4

Cadillac S&S Ambulance, white, $2^{5}/_{8}$", #54, 1965

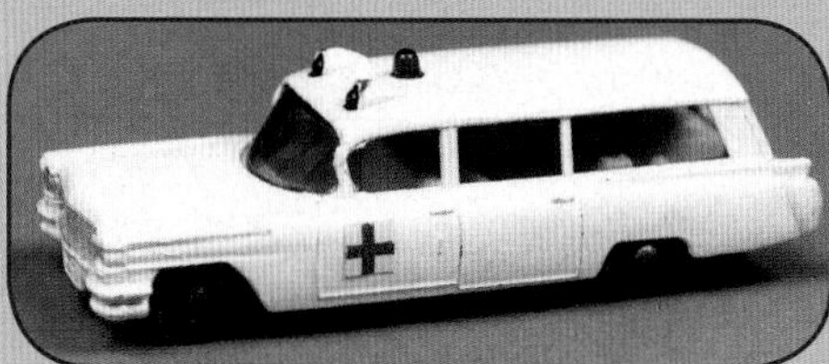

1. **white with black base, black plastic wheels, 1965..................$30 - 40**
2. white with black base, Superfast wheels, 1970............................... $45 - 55

Cadillac Sixty Special, $2^{3}/_{4}$", #27, 1960
1. metallic light green with white roof, silver plastic wheels............ $600 - 800
2. metallic gray with white roof, silver plastic wheels .... $80 - 100
3. metallic gray with pink roof, silver plastic wheels.............................. $70 - 90

4. **lavender with pink roof, red chassis, silver plastic wheels..........$75 - 90**
5. lavender with pink roof, black chassis, silver plastic wheels........... $90 - 110
6. lavender with pink roof, black chassis, gray plastic wheels.............. $75 - 90
7. lavender with pink roof, black chassis, black plastic wheels........... $80 - 100

Camper Motor Home, #65, 2006 (see Truck Camper)

Camaro (see Chevrolet Camaro)

Cap'n Cop, motorcycle with patrolman's helmet, #30, 2004 (MB648)
1. dark blue helmet on blue and yellow motorcycle, silver gray engine, 2004 Ultra Heroes .... $3 - 4

Car Carrier, #16, 2003; #60, 2004; #43, 2007
1. orange with dark gray ramp, blue windows, 2003 Public Works........ $1 - 2

2. **metallic blue with black ramp, black windows, 2006 5-Pack J4674................................$1 - 2**
3. metallic gray with blue ramp, 2007 #43.................................... $1 - 2

Car Transporter (see Bedford Car Transporter)

Caravan Travel Trailer (see Eccles Caravan Travel Trailer)

Caravan Travel Trailer, $2^{11}/_{16}$", #31, 1977; #52, 1999; #47, 1999, international
1. beige, "Mobile 500," Two-Pack .... $3 - 4
2. gray with blue and red stripes, black base, gray door, amber windows.................................... $3 - 4
3. white with unpainted base, door and interior various colors, England casting....................................... $5 - 6
4. white with black base, "Mobile 500," Two-Pack .... $4 - 5
5. white with red door, yellow, orange and red stripes .... $3 - 4
6. white with "Caravan 2000," 5-pack.................................... $1 - 2
7. white with turquoise and blue design, 1999 Beach .... $3 - 4

Carmichael Commando, (European model), 3", #57, 1982
1. red, "Fire" .... $16 - 24
2. white, "Police Rescue".......... $20 - 30

Case Bulldozer, $2^{1}/_{2}$", #16, 1969

1. **green treads.....................$9 - 12**

2. black treads .... $12 – 15

Caterpillar Articulated Dump Truck, #403, 1999, Caterpillar series

1. orange-yellow, "CAT" .... $4 – 5

Caterpillar Backhoe/Loader, #353, 1998 Dirt Machines 2-pack with accessories, retooled Hot Wheels casting

1. orange-yellow, "CAT" on backhoe, tinted windows .... $4 – 6

2. orange-yellow, "CATERPILLAR" at top of windshield, clear windows .... $4 – 6

Caterpillar Bulldozer (also see Caterpillar Crawler, Caterpillar D8, Caterpillar Tractor)

Caterpillar Bulldozer, yellow, no blade braces, 2", #18, 1958

1. yellow with yellow blade .... $55 – 70

Caterpillar Bulldozer, yellow with blade braces, 2¼", #18, 1961

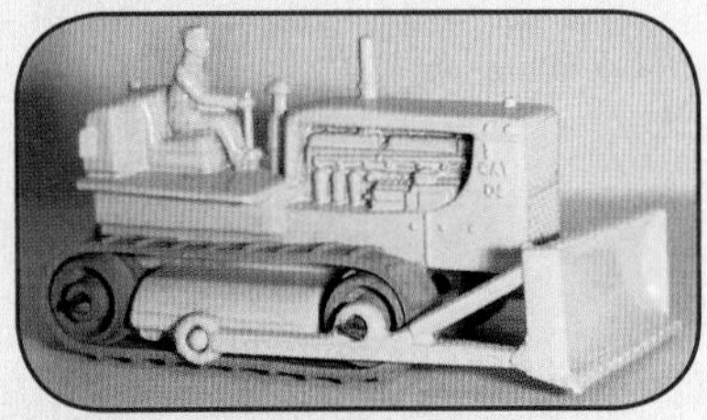

1. metal rollers .... $30 – 40

2. silver plastic rollers .... $85 – 95

3. black plastic rollers............. $20 – 30

Caterpillar Bulldozer, with plastic roof, 2⅝", #64, 1979; #9, 1983, #14, 1998

1. red with lime green blade, blue canopy, gravel design, Thailand cast, Live 'N Learn/Matchbox Preschool ...... $7 – 9

2. red with metallic gray blade, black canopy, no markings, China cast, 1996 .... $1 – 2

3. red with yellow blade, blue canopy, yellow stripes, Macau cast, Live 'N Learn/Matchbox Preschool .... $7 – 9
4. orange with metallic gray blade, black canopy, detailed trim, Thailand cast, Collector's Choice, White Rose Collectibles .... $3 – 4
5. orange with orange blade, black canopy, "Losinger," Macau cast, Swiss issue .... $9 – 12
6. orange with orange blade, black canopy, "Metro DPW" on blade, China cast, 1998 Big Movers .... $1 – 2
7. orange with orange blade, black canopy, black stripes on blade, Thailand cast, 5-pack .... $1 – 2
8. pumpkin orange with gray blade, black canopy, no markings, China cast, 5-pack .... $1 – 2
9. pumpkin orange with metallic gray blade, black canopy, "Amavia," China cast, ASAP promotional ..... $80 – 120
10. pumpkin orange with metallic gray blade, black canopy, "Blue Ridge Construction Co.," China cast, ASAP promotional .... $80 – 120
11. pumpkin orange with metallic gray blade, black canopy, "Cat Service Co.," China cast, ASAP promotional............................ $80 – 120
12. pumpkin orange with metallic gray blade, black canopy, "CT Tank Removal," China cast, ASAP promotional............................ $80 – 120
13. pumpkin orange with metallic gray blade, black canopy, "General Fill," China cast, ASAP promotional ..... $80 – 120
14. pumpkin orange with metallic gray blade, black canopy, "Hemler Bros.," China cast, ASAP promotional .... $80 – 120
15. pumpkin orange with metallic gray blade, black canopy, "LCT," China cast, ASAP promotional .... $80 – 120
16. fluorescent orange with black blade, black canopy, no markings, Thailand cast, 5-pack .... $1 – 2
17. fluorescent orange with gray blade, black canopy, no markings, China cast, 5-pack .... $1 – 2
18. orange-yellow with black blade, yellow canopy, "Matchbox," detailed trim, China cast, Premiere Collection/Convoy................................. $3 – 4
19. orange-yellow with orange-yellow blade, orange-yellow canopy, detailed trim, China cast, Premiere Collection .. $4 – 5
20. orange-yellow with yellow blade, black canopy, no markings, Thailand cast .... $1 – 2
21. orange-yellow with yellow blade, red canopy, red stripes on blade, Thailand cast .... $1 – 2
22. orange-yellow with yellow blade, red canopy, no markings on blade, Thailand cast .... $1 – 2
23. yellow with black blade, black canopy, Caterpillar "C" logo, England cast .... $5 – 6
24. yellow with black blade, tan canopy, Caterpillar "C" logo, England cast.... $5 – 6
25. yellow with black blade, yellow canopy, small Caterpillar "C" logo, detailed trim, China cast, Premiere Collection/Convoy................................. $3 – 4
26. yellow with gray blade, black canopy, no markings, Macau cast, 5-pack .. $3 – 4
27. yellow with gray blade, black canopy, no markings, Thailand cast .... $1 – 2

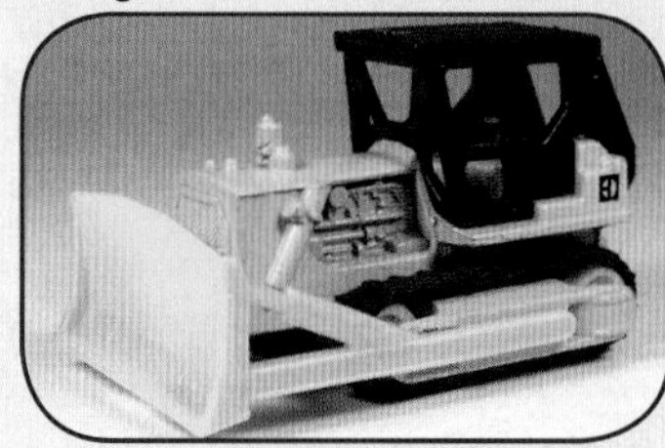

28. yellow with yellow blade, black canopy, Caterpillar "C" logo, England cast .... $5 – 6

29. yellow with yellow blade, black canopy, backwards Caterpillar "C" logo... $6 – 8
30. yellow with yellow blade, black canopy, Caterpillar "C" logo and "Cat," China cast .... $1 – 2
31. yellow with yellow blade, black canopy, Caterpillar "C" logo and "Cat," Macau cast .... $1 – 2
32. yellow with yellow blade, black canopy, no markings, Macau cast .... $1 – 2
33. yellow with yellow blade, black canopy, no markings, Thailand cast .... $1 – 2

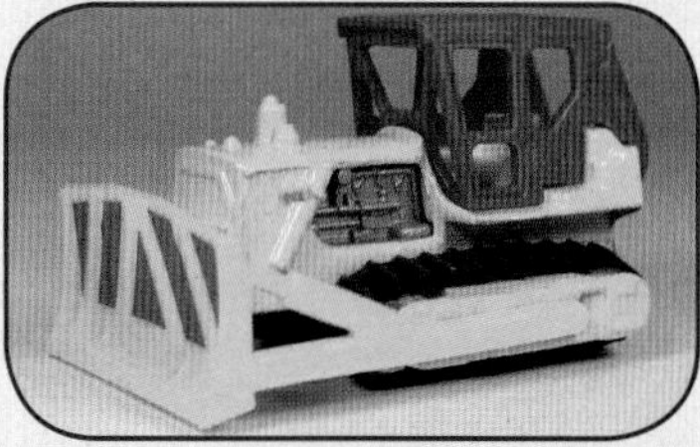

34. yellow with yellow blade, red canopy, red stripes on blade............. $1 – 2

35. yellow with yellow blade, tan canopy, Caterpillar "C" logo, England cast.. $5 – 6

36. yellow with yellow blade, tan canopy, no markings, England cast .... $5 – 6
37. yellow with no blade, black canopy, Caterpillar "C" logo and "Cat," England cast .... $12 – 16
38. fluorescent yellow with gray blade, black canopy, no markings, China cast .... $1 – 2

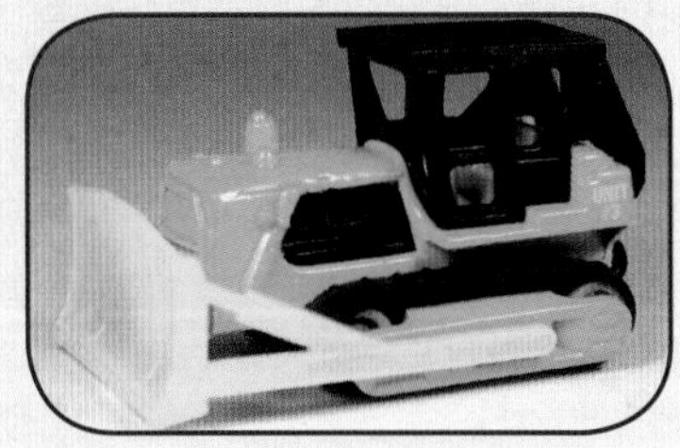

39. fluorescent green with yellow blade, black canopy, "Unit #3," China cast, 1999 Highway Crew 5-pack...$1 – 2

40. fluorescent green with black blade, black canopy, 1998 Big Movers...............................$1 – 2

41. metallic gold with black blade, black canopy, no markings, China cast, 1997 75 Challenge .... $6 – 12

Caterpillar Bulldozer, #345, 1998 Dirt Machines 2-pack with accessories, retooled Hot Wheels casting

1. orange-yellow, "CAT" ....$4 – 5

Caterpillar Challenger AG Tractor, #351, 1998 Dirt Machines 2-pack with accessories, retooled Hot Wheels casting

1. orange-yellow with tinted windows, 1998 Dirt Machines............... $4 – 5
2. orange-yellow with clear windows, Premiere Collection .... $6 – 9

Caterpillar Crawler Bulldozer, $2^{3}/_{8}$", #18, 1964

1. silver plastic rollers........... $90 – 100
2. black plastic rollers............. $15 – 20

Caterpillar D8 Bulldozer with Blade, $1^{7}/_{8}$", #18, 1956

1. yellow with red blade........... $40 – 60

Caterpillar Dump Truck, #344, 1998 Dirt Machines 2-pack with accessories, retooled Hot Wheels casting

1. orange-yellow, "Caterpillar"........ $4 – 5

Caterpillar Excavator, #343, 1998 Dirt Machines 2-pack with accessories, retooled Hot Wheels casting

1. orange-yellow, "CAT" .... $4 – 5

Caterpillar Material Handler, #381, 1999

1. orange-yellow with tinted windows, "CAT," Caterpillar.................... $4 – 5
2. orange-yellow with clear windows, "CAT," Premiere Collection .... $9 – 12

Caterpillar Motor Grader, #350, 1998 Dirt Machines 2-pack with accessories, retooled Hot Wheels casting

1. orange-yellow, "Caterpillar"........ $4 – 5
2. olive green, "Caterpillar" .... $4 – 5

Caterpillar Quarry Dump Truck, #462, 2000

1. orange-yellow with black cab, "CAT," "Caterpillar" .... $6 – 8

Caterpillar Road Roller, #347, 1998 Dirt Machines 2-pack with accessories, retooled Hot Wheels casting

1. orange-yellow, "Caterpillar"........ $4 – 5
2. chrome plated, "Caterpillar" ...... $4 – 5

Caterpillar Scraper, #348, 1998 Dirt Machines 2-pack with accessories, retooled Hot Wheels casting

1. orange-yellow, "CAT" .... $4 – 5
2. chrome plated with black cab and back section, "CAT"........................ $4 – 3

Caterpillar Skidder, #404, 1999

1. orange-yellow, "CAT"

Caterpillar Soil Compactor, #354, 1998 Dirt Machines 2-pack with accessories, retooled Hot Wheels casting

1. orange-yellow, tinted windows, 1998 Dirt Machines ....$4 – 5

2. orange-yellow, clear windows, Premiere Collection...................$6 – 9

Caterpillar Tool Carrier, #382, 1999 Caterpillar series

1. orange-yellow, black forks .... $4 – 5

Caterpillar Tractor, driver, no blade, $1^{1}/_{2}$", #8, 1955

1. orange with orange driver... $80 – 100
2. light yellow with red driver .. $80 – 100
3. dark yellow with dark yellow driver .... $30 – 40

Caterpillar Tractor, driver, no blade, $1^{5}/_{8}$", #8, 1959

1. yellow with metal rollers .... $50 – 60

Caterpillar Tractor, driver, no blade, $1^{7}/_{8}$", #8, 1961

1. metal rollers...................... $45 – 60
2. silver plastic rollers............. $65 – 80
3. black plastic rollers............. $40 – 60

Caterpillar Tractor, no driver, no blade, 2", #8, 1964

1. yellow with black plastic rollers...$15 – 20

Caterpillar Tractor Shovel, #383, 1999

1. orange-yellow with tinted windows, Caterpillar................................. $4 – 5
2. orange-yellow with clear windows, Premiere .... $16 – 24

Caterpillar Trailer, #352, 1998 Dirt Machines 2-pack with accessories, retooled Hot Wheels casting

1. orange-yellow with black treads... $4 – 5

Caterpillar Trailer, #443, 1999

1. orange-yellow, "CAT," "Caterpillar" .. $3 – 4

Caterpillar Wheel Loader, #346, 1998 Dirt Machines 2-pack with accessories, retooled Hot Wheels casting

1. orange-yellow, "CAT" ....$4 – 5

Cattle Trailer, #792, 1979, Two-Pack

1. red with beige stakes, black cattle, England cast.............................. $3 – 4
2. red with beige stakes, brown cattle, England cast.......................... $3 – 4
3. red with orange-yellow stakes, black cattle, England cast .... $3 – 4
4. red with yellow stakes, no cattle, blue wheels with yellow hubs, no origin cast, Live 'N Learn/Matchbox Preschool .... $7 – 9
5. yellow with light brown stakes, brown cattle, England cast................. $3 – 4

6. yellow with light brown stakes, brown cattle, Macau cast .... $3 – 4
7. yellow with light brown stakes, brown cattle, no origin cast................ $3 – 4
8. green with yellow stakes, black cattle, no origin cast .... $3 – 4
9. pale blue with light brown stakes, black cattle, no origin cast................ $3 – 4

Cattle Truck (see Dodge Cattle Truck, Dodge Stake Truck)

Cavalier (see Opel Vectra/Chevrolet Cavalier)

Cement Mixer, 1⅝," #3, 1953

1. **blue with orange metal wheels ....$60 - 85**
2. blue with gray plastic wheels............................ $80 – 100

Cement Mixer 2006, #52, 2006; #47, 2007

1. yellow with metallic gray base and back, red barrel, 2006 #52 .... $1 – 2
2. light green with white barrel, 2007 #47 .... $1 – 2

Cement Mixer Truck, 3", #40, 2001; #22, 2003

1. **white with red drum, 2001 Earth Crunchers...........................$1 - 2**

2. **metallic blue with white drum, 2003 5-pack #9...........................$1 - 2**

3. **white with yellow drum, 2003 Bridge Crew.................................$1 - 2**

4. **orange with yellow drum, 2001 #40 ....$1 - 2**

Cement Truck, Peterbilt (see Peterbilt Cement Truck)

Cement Truck, Badger (see Badger Cement Truck)

Center-Console Boat, #44, 2003 (see Sea Speeder)

Checker Cab/Taxi, #41, 2004; #4, 2005; #42, 2006; Superfast #33, 2006

1. **yellow, 2004 #41, 2005 #4..$1 - 2**

2. **metallic green, 2006 #42 .....$1 - 2**

3. **white with green sides, 2005 Superfast #33.............................$4 - 5**

4. **metallic light blue, "Nami the Navigator," 2006 Shonen Jump's One Piece 5-pack J7421 ....$1 - 2**

5. **beige with checkerboard stripe, "Checker Cab," 2006 Superfast #33 ....$4 - 5**

Chevrolet 1939 Sedan Delivery, #58, 1997, Australia; #245, 1992, White Rose Collectibles (larger than #215, no rear bumper)

1. "1995 Temecula Rod Run," red with white chassis, White Rose Collectibles............................... $12 – 16
2. "49ers 1992," gold with red chassis, White Rose Collectibles............ $4 – 5
3. "Angels 1993," white with dark blue chassis, White Rose Collectibles .... $6 – 8
4. "Astros 1993," dark blue with orange chassis, White Rose Collectibles .... $6 – 8
5. "Bears 1992," orange with dark blue chassis, White Rose Collectibles .... $4 – 5
6. "Bengals 1992," orange with black chassis, White Rose Collectibles .... $4 – 5
7. "Bills 1992," white with dark blue chassis, White Rose Collectibles ...... $4 – 5
8. "Blue Ridge Brewing Co.," "Hawksbill Lager," silver-blue and black with cream chassis, rubber tires on chrome rims, Matchbox Collectibles Microbreweries Collection .... $9 – 12
9. "Boston Celtics 1995," green with white chassis, Australia issue.......... $9 – 12
10. "Braves 1993," white with metallic blue chassis, White Rose Collectibles .. $6 – 8
11. "Brewers 1993," blue with yellow chassis, White Rose Collectibles ...... $6 – 8
12. "Broncos 1992," orange with blue chassis, White Rose Collectibles ...... $4 – 5
13. "Browns 1992," white with brown chassis, White Rose Collectibles ...... $4 – 5
14. "Buccaneers 1992," white with orange chassis, White Rose Collectibles .. $4 – 5
15. "Cardinals 1992," yellow with rust chassis, White Rose Collectibles ...... $4 – 5
16. "Cardinals 1993," red with dark blue chassis, White Rose Collectibles .. $6 – 8

17. "Chargers 1992," yellow with dark blue chassis, White Rose Collectibles .... $4 – 5
18. "Charlotte Hornets 1995," turquoise with blue chassis, Australia issue .... $9 – 12
19. "Chicago Bulls 1995," dark blue with red chassis, Australia issue .... $9 – 12
20. "Chicago Cubs 1993," gray with red chassis, White Rose Collectibles .... $6 – 8
21. "Chiefs 1992," yellow with red chassis, White Rose Collectibles .... $4 – 5
22. "Colts 1992," white with dark blue chassis, White Rose Collectibles .... $4 – 5
23. "Cowboys 1992," metallic gray with dark blue chassis, White Rose Collectibles .... $4 – 5
24. "Dallas Mavericks 1995," green with blue chassis, Australia issue .... $9 – 12

25. "Dallas Stars 1993," black with gold chassis, White Rose Collectibles .... $6 – 8
26. "Denver Nuggets 1995," dark red with dark blue chassis, Australia issue .... $9 – 12
27. "Detroit Pistons 1995," red with blue chassis, Australia issue .... $9 – 12
28. "Dodgers 1993," blue with white chassis, White Rose Collectibles .... $6 – 8
29. "Dolphins 1992," white with turquoise chassis, White Rose Collectibles .... $4 – 5
30. "Dubuque Red," red and black with black chassis, rubber tires on chrome rims, Matchbox Collectibles Microbreweries Collection .... $9 – 12
31. "Eagles 1992," white with green chassis, White Rose Collectibles .... $4 – 5
32. "Expos 1993," blue with red chassis, White Rose Collectibles .... $6 – 8
33. "Falcons 1992," white with red chassis, White Rose Collectibles .... $4 – 5
34. "Florida Panthers 1993," white with dark blue chassis, White Rose Collectibles .... $6 – 8
35. "Gator Lager Beer," yellow and black with green chassis, rubber tires on chrome rims, Matchbox Collectibles Microbreweries Collection .... $9 – 12
36. "Giants 1992," red with dark blue chassis, White Rose Collectibles .... $4 – 5
37. "Giants 1993," gray with black chassis, White Rose Collectibles .... $6 – 8
38. "Golden State Warriors 1995," dark blue with orange-yellow chassis, Australia issue .... $9 – 12
39. "Houston Rockets 1995," dark blue with red chassis, Australia issue .... $9 – 12
40. "Indians 1993," gray with dark blue chassis, White Rose Collectibles .... $6 – 8
41. "Jets 1992," white with green chassis, White Rose Collectibles .... $4 – 5
42. "Knicks 1995," blue-green with orange chassis, Australia issue .... $9 – 12
43. "LA Rams 1992," yellow with blue chassis, White Rose Collectibles .... $4 – 5
44. "Lions 1992," metallic gray with blue chassis, White Rose Collectibles .... $4 – 5
45. "Los Angeles Lakers 1995," lavender with orange-yellow chassis, Australia issue .... $9 – 12
46. "Mariners 1993," metallic gray with blue-green chassis, White Rose Collectibles .... $6 – 8
47. "Marlins 1993," white with light blue chassis, White Rose Collectibles .... $6 – 8
48. "Matchbox Get in the Fast Lane — Hershey 1995," fluorescent orange, US issue .... $9 – 12
49. "Mighty Ducks 1993," white with purple chassis, White Rose Collectibles .... $6 – 8
50. "NY Mets 1993," blue with orange chassis, White Rose Collect ibles .... $6 – 8
51. "Oakland A's 1993," orange-yellow with green chassis, White Rose Collectibles .... $6 – 8
52. "Oilers 1992," white with dark blue chassis, White Rose Collectibles .... $4 – 5
53. "Orioles 1993," orange with black chassis, White Rose Collectibles .... $6 – 8
54. "Orlando Magic 1995," blue with white chassis, Australia issue .... $9 – 12
55. "Pacers 1995," orange-yellow with dark blue chassis, Australia issue .... $9 – 12
56. "Packers 1992," yellow with green chassis, White Rose Collectibles .... $4 – 5
57. "Padres 1993," white with orange chassis, White Rose Collectibles .... $6 – 8
58. "Patroits 1992," white with bright blue chassis, White Rose Collectibles .... $4 – 5
59. "Penn State 1993," white and blue with blue chassis, White Rose Collectibles .... $6 – 8
60. "Phillies 1993," red with white chassis, White Rose Collectibles .... $6 – 8
61. "Phoenix Suns 1995," orange with purple chassis, Australia issue .... $9 – 12
62. "Pioneer Distributors — Gowings," yellow with black chassis, Australia issue .... $12 – 16
63. "Pirates 1993," black with yellow chassis, White Rose Collectibles .... $6 – 8
64. "Raiders 1992," metallic gray with black chassis, White Rose Collectibles .... $4 – 5
65. "Rangers 1993," white with red chassis, White Rose Collectibles .... $6 – 8
66. "Raptors 1995," red with purple chassis, Australia issue .... $9 – 12
67. "Red Ale," yellow and black with red chassis, rubber tires on chrome rims, Matchbox Collectibles Microbreweries Collection .... $9 – 12
68. "Red Sox 1993," dark blue with red chassis, White Rose Collectibles .. $6 – 8
69. "Reds 1993," red with black chassis, White Rose Collectibles .... $6 – 8
70. "Redskins 1992," white with rust chassis, White Rose Collectibles .... $4 – 5
71. "Redskins 1993," rust with yellow chassis, White Rose Collectibles .... $6 – 8
72. "Reithoffer's — Tickets for All Attractions," white with orange chassis, White Rose Collectibles gift set .... $5 – 6
73. "Rockies 1993," black with purple chassis, White Rose Collectibles .... $6 – 8
74. "Royals 1993," pale blue with dark blue chassis, White Rose Collectibles .... $6 – 8
75. "Saints 1992," green-gold with black chassis, White Rose Collectibles .... $4 – 5
76. "Sam Adams," white and black with lavender chassis, rubber tires on chrome rims, Matchbox Collectibles Microbreweries Collection .... $9 – 12
77. "San Andreas Brewing Co.," dark purple and black with blue-green chassis, rubber tires on chrome rims, Matchbox Collectibles Microbreweries Collection .... $9 – 12
78. "San Antonio Spurs 1995," dark blue with orange chassis, Australia issue .... $9 – 12
79. "Seahawks 1992," metallic gray with blue chassis, White Rose Collectibles .... $4 – 5
80. "Seattle Sonics 1995," dark green with orange-yellow chassis, Australia issue .... $9 – 12
81. "Steelers 1992," yellow with black chassis, White Rose Collectibles .... $4 – 5
82. "Tigers 1993," white with blue chassis, White Rose Collectibles .... $6 – 8
83. "Toronto Blue Jays 1993," blue with bright blue chassis, White Rose Collectibles .... $6 – 8
84. "Twins 1993," dark blue with red chassis, White Rose Collectibles .... $6 – 8
85. "Utah Jazz 1995," green with orange-yellow chassis, Australia issue .... $9 – 12
86. "Vancouver Grizzlies 1995," black with turquoise chassis, Australia issue .... $9 – 12
87. "Vikings 1992," yellow with purple chassis, White Rose Collectibles .... $4 – 5
88. "Washington Capitals 20th Anniversary 1974 – 1994," white with blue chassis, White Rose Collectibles .... $6 – 8
89. "White Sox 1993," metallic gray with black chassis, White Rose Collectibles .... $6 – 8
90. "Yankees 1993," white with blue chassis, White Rose Collectibles .... $6 – 8
91. "York Fair 1992," fluorescent orange with lavender chassis, White Rose Collectibles .... $7 – 9

92. "York Fair 1994," light blue with lavender chassis, White Rose Collectibles .... $6 – 8
93. black with money bags and bullet marks, Australia issue .... $5 – 6

Chevrolet 1939 Sedan Delivery, #215 (smaller than #58/#245)

Chevrolet 4x4 Van (see Chevrolet Van 4x4)

Chevrolet Ambulance, 2$^{15}/_{16}$", #41, 1978; #25, 1983; #34, 1999

1. red, "Notarzt," German issue, England cast .... $30 – 40
2. red, "Fire Rescue," gold and white trim, 1996 5-pack, China cast .... $1 – 2
3. red with white, gold and black accents, blue windows, 1996 5-pack .... $2 – 4
4. fluorescent orange, "Ambulance 7," "Intercom City," bar code on base, China cast .... $12 – 16
5. fluorescent orange, "Ambulance 7," "Intercom City," no bar code on base, China cast .... $10 – 12
6. yellow, "Paramedics E11," orange band, China cast .... $10 – 12
7. fluorescent yellow, "Emergency Unit 3," "3 EMT," Collector's Choice, White Rose Collectibles, China cast .... $3 – 4
8. black, "SWAT," "MB County Sheriff," 1999 Law & Order series, China cast .... $1 – 2
9. metallic gray, "Paris Dakar 81," England cast .... $25 – 35

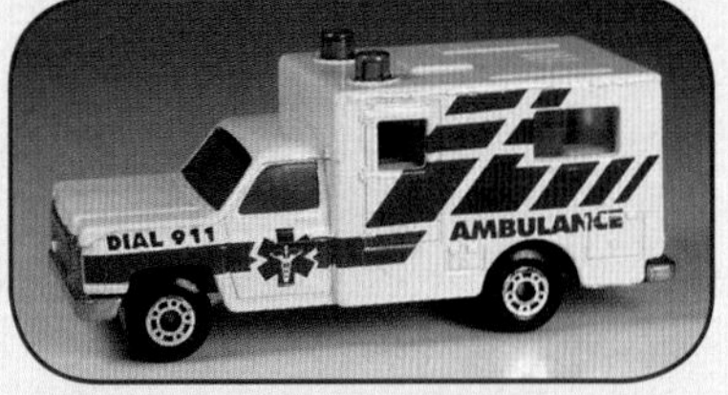

10. white, "Action System," on-package premium, China cast .... $9 – 10

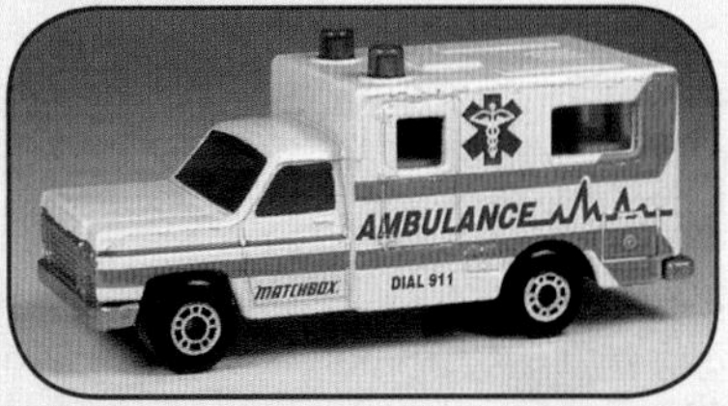

11. white, "Ambulance," "Dial 911," red and blue design, China cast ... $1 – 2

12. white, "Ambulance," "Dial 911," orange and blue design, 1996 .... $1 – 2
13. white, "Ambulance," "EMS" labels, England cast .... $7 – 9
14. white, "Ambulance," cross labels, gray interior, England cast .... $7 – 9
15. white, "Ambulance," cross labels, gray interior, England cast, towing tab on front of base, UK issue .... $40 – 60
16. white, "Ambulance," cross labels, light yellow interior, England cast .... $7 – 9
17. white, "Ambulance," cross labels, orange interior, England cast ... $9 – 12
18. white, "Emergency Medical Services," dark tan interior, England cast ... $7 – 9
19. white, "Emergency Medical Services," gray interior, England cast .... $7 – 9
20. white, "Emergency Medical Services," light yellow interior, England cast ... $7 – 9
21. white, "Emergency Medical Services," orange interior, England cast ... $9 – 12
22. white, "EMT Ambulance," Action Pack, China cast .... $4 – 5
23. white, "LeBonheur Children's Medical Center," orange band on sides, ASAP promotional, China cast .... $30 – 45
24. white, "Manhattan National Life," orange band on sides, ASAP promotional, China cast .... $120 – 160
25. white, "Matchbox Ambulance Dial 911," orange and blue design, 1997 City Streets 5-pack, China cast .... $1 – 2
26. white, "Methodist Healthcare," orange band on sides, ASAP promotional, China cast .... $30 – 45
27. white, "Methodist LeBonheur Healthcare," orange band on sides, ASAP promotional, China cast .... $30 – 45
28. white, "Pacific Ambulance," England cast, Code Red .... $7 – 9
29. white, "Pacific Ambulance," China cast .... $6 – 7
30. white, "Pacific Ambulance," Macau cast .... $6 – 7

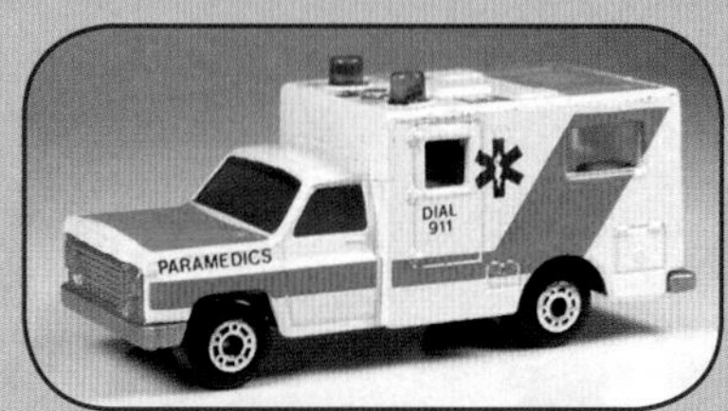

31. white, "Paramedics E11," orange band, China cast .... $1 – 2

32. white, "Paramedics E11," orange band, Macau cast .... $1 – 2
33. white, "Paramedics," "Dial 911," orange band, China cast .... $3 – 4
34. white, no markings, Graffic Traffic, China cast .... $12 – 16
35. white, orange band on sides, ASAP promotional blank, China cast .... $30 – 45

Chevrolet Avalanche, #58, 2002; #49, 2003; #46, 2005; #74, 2006; #4, 2004 Superfast

1. metallic green with dark gray base, 2002 Rescue Rookies #58 .... $1 – 2

2. bright green with dark gray base, 2003 Forest Rescue #49 .... $1 – 2
3. bright green with dark gray base, 2003 Hero City 10-pack #1 .... $1 – 2

4. metallic blue, 2004 Superfast #4 .... $4 – 5

5. dark green with brown base, 2005 #46 .... #2 – 3
6. metallic silver and gray, 2006 #74 .... $1 – 2

7. flat olive green with "Chevy Avalanche Racing Five 46" pale green and yellow graphics, 2007 5-pack K9616 .... $1 – 2

8. yelllow and blue, 2003 5-pack C1817 .... $1 – 2

Chevrolet Bel Air 1955 Convertible, #46, 1999

1. red and ivory two-tone, detailed trim, rubber tires on chrome rims, Premiere Collection .... $9 – 12

2. pale blue, "1999 Matchbox Official Parade Car," gray interior, 1999 Classic Decades .... $1 – 2

3. black, "The Brady Bunch," white stripe, white and black interior, Avon Star Cars .... $12 – 16
4. white, "Coca-Cola," red interior, 5-pack .... $1 – 2

5. bright purple, "Patrick," light blue interior, bright coral pink base, 2003 Nickelodeon Spongebob Squarepants 5-pack .... $1 – 2

6. lime green, Hero City Sports graphics, 2003 Hero City 5-pack #6.. $1 – 2

Chevrolet Bel Air 1955 Hard Top, #73, 1999

1. red, "Midwest Collector's Dinner Model," white roof, white interior, ASAP promotional .... $25 – 35
2. red, "RCA," white roof, white interior, ASAP promotional .... $25 – 35
3. red with white roof, white interior, ASAP promotional blank .... $30 – 40
4. yellow, "Coca-Cola," white roof, black interior, rubber tires on chrome wire rims, Premiere Collection .... $5 – 6
5. yellow, "Coca-Cola," white roof, red interior, Avon Two-Pack .... $4 – 5
6. dark green and cream with silver stripes, cream roof, rubber tires on chrome rims, 1999 First Editions................................. $6 – 8

7. blue, "Bel Air," white stripes, white roof, 1999 Classics .... $1 – 2

8. blue, "Cruisin' New England Magazine," white roof, black interior, Color Comp promotional....................... $45 – 55

9. blue, "D.A.R.E.," white roof, red light bar on roof, 2001 DARE 5-pack.................................. $1 – 2

10. blue, "Matchbox USA Road Race Participant," white roof, white interior, Color Comp promotional .... $80 – 120
11. blue, "Westfield NJ Reunion 2000," "W.H.S.," Color Comp promotional .... $16 – 24
12. bright purple, "Patrick," light blue interior, bright coral pink base, 2003 Nickelodeon Spongebob Squarepants 5-pack.................................... $1 – 2
13. unpainted, rubber tires on chrome rims, 1999 First Editions .... $6 – 8

Chevrolet Bel Air 1955 Police, #507, 2001

1. "D.A.R.E.," metallic blue with white sides, red roof light, 5-pack... $1 – 2

Chevrolet Bel Air 1957, hood opens $2^{15}/_{16}$", #4, 1979; #43, 1990

1. metallic magenta.................... $6 – 8

2. red, "Cherry Bomb," unpainted or metallic gray base, chrome interior .... $3 – 5

3. red, "Cherry Bomb," black base, chrome interior .... $60 – 80
4. black with red hood, flames, chrome interior .... $1 – 2
5. pink with red hood, flames, chrome interior, chrome hubs, rubber tires, Select Class.................................. $4 – 5
6. pale green with red hood, flames, chrome interior, chrome hubs, rubber tires, Select Class .... $4 – 5
7. peach with red hood, flames, chrome interior, chrome hubs, rubber tires, Select Class .... $5 – 8
8. metallic rose red with red hood, flames, chrome interior, chrome hubs, rubber tires, Select Class .... $4 – 5
9. metallic purple with red hood, flames, chrome interior, chrome hubs, rubber tires, Select Class .... $4 – 5
10. red with red hood, chrome interior, "Heinz 57 Chevy"................ $16 – 24
11. metallic purple with "Milky Way," chrome interior, Mail-Away Premium.. $16 – 24
12. black with dark red hood, flames, chrome interior...................... $1 – 2
13. metallic red with red hood, chrome windows, silver stripes, chrome interior, chrome hubs, rubber tires, World Class.................................. $4 – 6
14. yellow with blue and red stripes, "57," black windows, Triple Heat........ $4 – 6

15. red with yellow flame outlines, silver trim, chrome interior .... $1 – 2

16. white with pink and blue accents, chrome interior....................... $1 – 2
17. black with black hood, yellow accents, chrome interior, 5-pack .... $1 – 2
18. metallic blue, chrome interior, Collector's Choice........................... $3 – 4
19. red, "Chubby's Diner," chrome interior .... $8 – 12

20. black with yellow hood, yellow flames, chrome interior, 5-pack................................... $1 – 2

21. pearl white, chrome interior...... $1 – 2
22. metallic gray with red and white interior, white roof, chrome hubs, rubber tires, Premiere Collection .... $4 – 5
23. black with red and white interior, chrome hubs, rubber tires, Premiere Collection .... $4 – 5
24. red with red hood, red and white interior, white roof..................... $12 – 16

25. bright blue with yellow hood, chrome interior, yellow flames, 5-pack.. $1 – 2

26. maroon with maroon hood, red and white interior, white roof, Select Class................................ $4 – 5

27. red with yellow hood, black and chrome interior, orange flames, Premiere Collection, chrome hubs, rubber tires .... $4 – 5
28. black with chrome interior, "Night Stalker," flames........................... $3 – 4
29. black with red hood, yellow flames, chrome interior, chrome hubs, rubber tires, Premiere Collection......... $4 – 5
30. red with yellow flames, black and chrome interior, chrome hubs, rubber tires, U.S. Hot August Nights .. $12 – 16
31. metallic gold with black and chrome interior, chrome hubs, rubber tires, 75 Challenge Winner's Car ... $175 – 250
32. orange with orange hood, chrome interior, "Enjoy Fanta" .... $150 – 200

Chevrolet Bel Air 1957 Hardtop, 1999, Taco Bell; Matchbox mold retooled by Strottman International Inc. through a licensing agreement with Mattel. Strottman manufactures toy premiums for Taco Bell. Base is marked "Made in China by S.I.I."

1. white with green and blue bands, black windows, Taco Bell premium ....$3 – 4

Chevrolet Bel Air 1957 Convertible, #36, 1998; #47, 1999

1. black, "Toy Fair 98 — Matchbox," rubber tires on chrome rims, white interior .... $90 – 120
2. red, silver flash, detailed trim, rubber tires on chrome rims, red and white interior, 1998 First Editions ...... $5 – 6
3. unpainted, rubber tires on chrome rims, red and white interior, 1998 First Editions .... $5 – 6
4. turquoise, silver flash with purple and white accents, white interior, rubber tires on chrome rims, 1998 First Editions (likely a manufacturer packaging error) .... $120 – 160

5. turquoise, silver flash with purple and white accents, white interior, 1998 Classic Decades ....$1 – 2

6. turquoise, silver flash with purple and white accents, white and turquoise interior, rubber tires on chrome rims, Premiere Collection ....$5 – 6

7. turquoise, "Matchbox 2000 Convention — Hershey, PA — Color Comp Inc. Demo Model," white interior, Color Comp promotional .... $20 – 25
8. turquoise, "Cruisin New England Magazine Elite Dream Machines," "Mohegan Sun," white interior, Color Comp promotional .... $40 – 50
9. silver blue, "Coke Brightens Every Bite," red interior, Avon 2-pack .... $6 – 7
10. pale yellow, red and black accents, red interior, 1999 Drop Tops.......... $1 – 2
11. pale yellow, "American Wheels Show," red and black accents, red interior, Color Comp promotional....... $20 – 30
12. pale yellow, "Parsippany Demo Model," "Matchbox USA Toy Show & Convention," Color Comp promotional ..$20 – 25
13. black, "Hero City Sports" graphics, 2003 Hero City 5-pack #6 .... $1 – 2
14. metallic purple with white trim, white interior, chrome hubs, 2006 10-pack B5610................................ $3 – 4

Chevrolet Bel Air 1957 Convertible, 2000 Feature Cars, with opening features, designed to replace Premiere Collection

1. light yellow with cream and black interior .... $9 – 12

Chevrolet Bel Air 1957 Hardtop, #31, 1998

1. blue with blue and white interior, rubber tires on chrome rims, 1998 First Editions .... $5 – 6
2. unpainted metal with gray plastic roof, white interior, rubber tires on chrome rims, 1998 First Editions .... $5 – 6

3. black with white interior, green and white design on sides, 1998 Classic Decades ....$1 – 2

4. black with white interior, green and white design on sides, larger tires, 1998 Classic Decades......... $12 – 16
5. purple with beige roof, "Matchbox Premiere Collectors Club," rubber tires on chrome rims .... $12 – 16
6. red with white interior, 5-pack ... $1 – 2

7. black with white roof, red interior, 2005 Superfast #37 ....$3 – 4

Chevrolet Bel Air 1957 Hardtop, 2000 Feature Cars, with opening features, designed to replace Premiere Collection

1. red with white roof, red and white interior .... $9 – 12
2. baby blue with white roof, blue and white interior .... $12 – 16

Chevrolet Blazer 4x4 (see Chevrolet Blazer 4x4 Police)

Chevrolet Blazer 4x4 Police, 3", #50, 1984 – 1997; #22, 1998; #32, 1999; #71, 2000; #6, 2002; #50, 2004; #24, 2007

1. metallic red, black base, no markings, Thailand cast, 5-pack.............. $1 – 2

2. olive green, "Chief," yellow and brown, 2003 Hero City 5-pack #7 .... #2 – 3

3. blue, "682," green stripes, chrome base, China cast, 5-pack.......... $4 – 5
4. blue, "Police 50," "Police Dial 911," star, chrome base, blue windows, Thailand cast.............................. $1 – 2
5. blue, "Police 50," "Police Dial 911," star, chrome base, red windows, Thailand cast.............................. $1 – 2
6. blue, "Rocky Mountain Rescue MB County 682," China cast, 5-pack..$1 – 2
7. blue and white, "Police 50," "Police Dial 911," China cast, 5-pack .... $1 – 2

8. blue and white, "Police Dial 911," China cast, 1996 ....$1 – 2

9. blue and white, "Police Unit 14," chrome base, Thailand cast, 5-pack.............................$1 – 2
10. blue with black and white accents, orange "50" on roof, blue windows... $1 – 2
11. blue with black and white accents, orange "50" on roof, red windows... $1 – 2
12. purple with orange, red, and black accents, armaments, Roadblasters.. $6 – 8
13. black, "Action Radar," "Xtreme Mission," 5-pack................................. $1 – 2
14. black, "Off Road Patrol Matchbox Police," white canopy, white accents, 1997.. $1 – 2
15. black, "Police Unit 3," gold star, Thailand cast, 5-pack .... $1 – 2
16. black with pink and yellow design, chrome base and windows, Super Trucks................................. $3 – 4
17. brown, "Action Tours," 2000 On Tour..$1 – 2
18. brown, "Action Tours," "Matchbox 2000," 2000 On Tour .... $3 – 4

19. beige and green, "Park Police," China cast, 5-pack .... $1 – 2
20. white, "7 Eleven," black base, Thailand cast .... $5 – 6
21. white, "MB Metro Police," yellow and blue accents, red star, black base, 2001 On Patrol 5-pack .... $1 – 2

22. white, "Emergency Unit 50," "Off Road Patrol," black canopy, chrome base, 1998 To the Rescue series ...... $1 – 2

23. white, "Metro EMS," black base, Thailand cast.............................. $1 – 2

24. white, "Police MB To Protect and Serve," chrome base, China cast, 1999 Law & Order .... $1 – 2
25. white, "Police Unit 3," blue hood and doors, chrome base, Thailand cast, 5-pack .... $1 – 2
26. white, "Sheriff 7," chrome base, Macau cast .... $1 – 2
27. white, "Sheriff 7," black base, Macau cast .... $1 – 2
28. white, "Sheriff 7," black base, Manaus cast, Brazil issue................ $50 – 60
29. white, "Sheriff 7," black base, Thailand cast .... $1 – 2

30. white and black, "Emergency Unit 50," "Off Road Patrol," chrome base, China cast, 1998 To the Rescue .... $1 – 2

31. white and black, "Emergency Unit 50," "Off Road Patrol," chrome base, Thailand cast, 1998 To the Rescue ... $1 – 2
32. white with blue, peach, and magenta design, chrome base and windows, Super Trucks .... $3 – 4

33. white, "Smokey Says...Prevent Forest Fires," green canopy, teal base, red windows, Smokey the Bear, 2002 Safety Stars .... $2 – 4

34. metallic gold, chrome base, 1997 75 Challenge .... $6 – 12
35. khaki camouflage with graphics, 2005 #45 .... $1 – 2

36. white with green stripes on sides, "Park Ranger," gold emblem bordered in green on doors, 2007 #74 .... $1 – 2

37. brown, yellow, and orange camouflage, "Thunder," "Team Matchbox," 2005 #45 .... $1 – 2

Chevrolet Breakdown Van, #21, 1985; #53, 1990

1. army green with metallic gray boom, "Gen IV," "The Lost World," Jurassic Park.................................... $7 – 9
2. black with gray boom, yellow stripes, black hubs, multipack China issue .... $20 – 25
3. black with gray boom, yellow stripes, silver hubs, Commando.............. $5 – 7
4. black with red boom, "24," hand and car logo, multipack .... $1 – 2

5. blue with gray boom, "MB" logo and dirt, 5-pack......................... $1 – 2

6. fluorescent orange with black boom, "Intercom City Auto Services," Intercom City .... $12 – 16
7. lemon yellow with black boom, "Rob's Towing 24 Hours," Action System .... $1 – 2
8. metallic gray with black boom, "Rob's Towing 24 Hours," Action Pack... $1 – 2
9. orange with black boom, "Auto Relay 24 Hr. Tow"................................ $1 – 2
10. orange with orange boom, "Auto Relay 24 Hr. Tow," Action Pack.......... $4 – 5
11. red with green boom, blue wheels, Live 'N Learn/Matchbox Preschool .... $6 – 8
12. red with white boom, "24 Hour Service" .... $1 – 2
13. white and purple with purple boom, "Metro Alarm MA-BU1," 5-pack .... $1 – 2
14. white with black boom, "Auto Rescue," Emergency Pack .... $3 – 4
15. white with white boom, no markings, Graffic Traffic..................... $12 – 16
16. yellow with black boom, "Auto Relay 24 Hr. Tow"................................ $1 – 2

Chevrolet Camaro 1969 RS SS hardtop, Superfast #55, 2004

1. orange with white stripe, 2004 Superfast #55 .... $4 – 5

Chevrolet Camaro 1969 SS 396 convertible, #40, 1997; #33, 1998; #21, 2005

1. red with white racing stripes, black interior, Action Pack .... $1 – 2
2. orange with black stripes, black interior, 5-pack .... $1 – 2
3. orange with white and black stripes, black and white interior, Premiere Collection #20 .... $4 – 5
4. dark green with white side stripes, black and white interior, rubber tires on chrome rims, Premiere Collection #17 .... $4 – 5

5. metallic blue with white racing stripes, black interior, 1998 Classic Decades .... $1 – 2

6. metallic blue with white racing stripes, black interior, "Great Camaro Gathering 1997," promotional............ $40 – 50

7. white with black racing stripes, red interior, 1998 Classic Decades......................... $1 – 2
8. white with "Coca-Cola" and red bands, red and black interior, rubber tires on chrome rims, Premiere Collection .... $5 – 6
9. white with "Coca-Cola" and red bands, red and black interior, rubber tires on chrome rims, "www.cocacolastore.com," Color Comp promotional............................$60 – 80
10. white with "East Coast Camaro Gathering IV," red interior, Color Comp promotional............................... $24 – 36
11. metallic gold with black interior, 1997 75 Challenge....................... $6 – 12

12. orange-red, Rugrats character graphics, 2003 Nickelodeon 5-pack..................................$1 – 2
13. blue with white flames, 2005 #21 .... $1 – 2

14. metallic rose with white trim, gray interior, 2007 Streakers #40.. $4 – 5

15. black with red interior, "One Piece" graphics, 2006 Shonen Jump's One Piece 5-pack J7421.............$2 – 3

Chevrolet Camaro 1969 Z/28, Superfast #7, 2004; Superfast #7, 2007
1. blue, 2004 Superfast #7 .... $4 – 5
2. metallic blue with black roof, 2007 Superfast #7......................... $3 – 4

Chevrolet Camaro 1971 Z/28, #39, 1998; #18, 2000
1. red, "Coca-Cola Play Refreshed," tire marks, Premiere Collection....... $4 – 5
2. metallic green with white stripes, 1998 Classic Decades..................... $1 – 2
3. dark green with white stripes, "Great Camaro Gathering 1999," Color Comp promotional....................... $40 – 50
4. metallic light blue with black stripes, rubber tires on black rims, Premiere Collection.......................... $30 – 40
5. metallic gold with black stripes, 2000 Great Drivers......................... $1 – 2
6. metallic gold with black stripes, "Matchbox 2000," 2000 Great Drivers..$3 – 4

7. olive green, 2005 Superfast #19 ....$1 – 2

Chevrolet Camaro 1993 Z/28 Police, #59, 1995 – 1997; #27, 1998; #98, 1999; #89, 2000; #7, 2002; #30, 2003; #457, 2000; #458, 2000
1. "5," red with crest and white band, 5-pack................................. $1 – 2
2. "5," blue with crest and white band, lace wheels, Launcher 5-pack ... $1 – 2
3. "5," blue with crest and white band, 5-spoke concave wheels, Launcher 5-pack ....$9 – 12
4. "City of Miami 7630," white, rubber tires on chrome rims, Premiere Collection #22...................... $150 – 200
5. "D.A.R.E.," black with yellow and red stripes, 2000 D.A.R.E. .... $4 – 5

6. "D.A.R.E.," orange with dark blue, white and gray accents, 2001 D.A.R.E. ....$1 – 2

7. "D.A.R.E.," white with lion and US flag graphics, 2000 Police Patrol ....$1 – 2
8. "D.A.R.E.," white with lion and US flag graphics, "Matchbox 2000," 2000 Police Patrol.......................... $3 – 4
9. "D.A.R.E.," "Crimestopper," black with stripes and stars, D.A.R.E....... $4 – 5
10. "D.A.R.E. America," "Matchbox," white and black, rubber tires on chrome rims, D.A.R.E. .... $9 – 12
11. "Dial 1-888-Road Rescue," white with dashed road, "Dial" slants left, 1999 At Your Service.......................... $1 – 2
12. "Dial 1-888-Road Rescue," white with dashed road, "Dial" slants right, 1999 At Your Service.................. $40 – 50

13. "Emergency Dial 911," white with black, blue, and silver accents, silver "Police" shield, 2003 Police Squad ....$1 – 2
14. "Highway Patrol," "DWI Enforcement," white, 5-pack........................ $1 – 2
15. "Highway Patrol," black and white, rubber tires on chrome rims, Premiere Collection #8......................... $4 – 5

16. "Highway Patrol," black with white doors, 2006 5-pack J4676 ...$1 – 2

17. "Kansas State Trooper," black with shield on doors, rubber tires on chrome rims, World Class #18 State Police II ....$4 – 5
18. "Matchbox Police," white .... $1 – 2
19. "Matchbox Police," white with blue doors and hood, silver star on door, 1996 Police 5-pack......................... $1 – 2

20. "Matchbox Police 911," black, 1998 To the Rescue ....$1 – 2

21. "Matchbox Police Unit 04," blue with white shield and accents, 1997 Police 5-pack .... $1 – 2
22. "Medford Police," "D.A.R.E. — No Drugs," stripes, white, D.A.R.E... $4 – 5

23. "Nevada Highway Patrol," metallic blue and silver, rubber tires on chrome rims, World Class #18 State Police II .... $4 – 5
24. "NY State Police," bright blue, rubber tires on chrome rims, Premiere Collection #8 .... $4 – 5
25. "Police," gold on white star on doors.. $1 – 2
26. "Police," black on white star on doors.. $1 – 2
27. "Police Unit 4," blue, 5-pack...... $1 – 2

28. "Police," "Unit 6," white with star on blue doors, blue hood, 1996 Police 5-pack .... $1 – 2

29. "Police," "Unit 21," black with shield design on hood, white accents, 1998 To the Rescue .... $3 – 5

30. "Police," "Unit 21," white with blue shield design on hood, blue accents, 1997 .... $1 – 2

31. "Police," "Matchbox Police," black with star on white doors, white hood, 1996 .... $1 – 2

32. "Police D.A.R.E.," "New Rochelle," white and pale blue, D.A.R.E. .... $4 – 5
33. "State Patrol Nebraska," white, rubber tires on chrome rims, Premiere Collection .... $5 – 6

34. "Take a Bite out of Crime," metallic gray with crime dog graphics, 2002 Safety Stars .... $1 – 2
35. "Texas Dept. Public Safety Trooper," white and black, rubber tires on chrome rims, Premiere Collection #8 .... $4 – 5

36. "Utah Highway Patrol," white, rubber tires on chrome rims, World Class #18 State Police II....... $4 – 5
37. "Wyoming Highway Patrol," black and white, rubber tires on chrome rims, Premiere Collection .... $5 – 6

38. metallic gold, 1997 75 Challenge................................ $6 – 12
39. red with silver and blue stripes and crest, 5-pack......................... $1 – 2

40. black with white doors, "Police" and star on doors, 2005 Superfast #30 .... $3 – 4

Chevrolet Camaro 1994 Z/28, #43, 1994 – 1997; #75, 1998
1. red, black roof, detailed trim, rubber tires on chrome rims, Premiere Collection #5 .... $5 – 6
2. metallic red, black roof, detailed trim, rubber tires on chrome rims, Gold Coin Collection .... $16 – 24
3. orange with white stripes, rubber tires on chrome rims, Premiere Collection #14 .... $5 – 6
4. fluorescent orange, "Matchbox Get in the Fast Lane — 95 Premium Show"............................ $40 – 50
5. fluorescent orange, "Matchbox Get in the Fast Lane — Melbourne Motor Show 96".......................... $40 – 50
6. fluorescent orange, "Matchbox Get in the Fast Lane — Sydney Motor Show"........................... $20 – 30
7. yellow, black roof, rubber tires on chrome rims, Special Class #4... $5 – 6
8. dark green, black roof, detailed trim, rubber tires on chrome rims, Premiere Collection #2......................... $5 – 6
9. metallic turquoise, black roof, rubber tires on chrome rims, Special Class #5 .... $5 – 6
10. blue with orange flame and checkered flag design on sides, 1998 Street Cruisers .... $1 – 2

11. blue with black roof, detailed trim, rubber tires on chrome rims, Premiere Collection 8-car display set.................................... $5 – 6

12. metallic purple with orange flame and checkered flag design on sides, 1998 Street Cruisers.......... $1 – 2

13. purple chrome with orange and yellow design on sides, 1997 Sleek Riders 5-pack .... $1 – 2
14. dark purple with black roof, detailed trim, rubber tires on chrome rims, Special Class #2 .... $5 – 6
15. black, "DDCM DuPage Diecast Collectors Meet," ASAP promotional..$20 – 30
16. black, "Novell 6," ASAP promotional................................ $20 – 30

17. black, "RCA," ASAP promotional .... $20 – 30
18. black, "Real Cars Wear Bow Ties," ASAP promotional .... $80 – 120
19. black, "Speed Equipment World," ASAP promotional .... $80 – 120
20. black, no markings, ASAP promotional blank .... $30 – 40

21. black with white, magenta, and cyan stripes on sides and hood, gold chrome wheel hubs, 1994..... $1 – 2

22. black with white, magenta, and cyan stripes on sides only, silver chrome wheel hubs, 1995................ $1 – 2

23. metallic gray with white, magenta, and cyan stripes on sides and hood, 1996 .... $1 – 2
24. metallic gray with white, magenta, and cyan stripes on sides only, 1996 .. $1 – 2
25. dark gray with stripes on sides, 1997 .... $1 – 2
26. white with black roof, chrome windows, rubber tires on chrome rims, World Class.................................... $4 – 5
27. silver with lavender, purple and blue stripes on hood and sides, 1997 Matchcaps........................... $5 – 6
28. gold chrome, blue and yellow design, yellow windows, 1996 5-pack ... $1 – 2
29. metallic gold, "Great Camaro Gathering II 1998," rubber tires on chrome rims, promotional model.............. $40 – 50
30. metallic gold, "Matchbox Collectors Club," rubber tires on chrome rims................................ $12 – 16
31. metallic gold, 1997 75 Challenge .... $6 – 12

Chevrolet Camaro 1998 SS Convertible, #2, 2000

1. dark red, with "Matchbox 2000" logo, black interior, 2000 Open Road series 1................................ $3 – 5

2. dark red, without "Matchbox 2000" logo, black interior, 2000 Open Road series 1.............................. $1 – 2

3. salmon, "Sydney 2000," orange-yellow interior, 5-pack....................... $1 – 2
4. red, Coca-Cola, white interior, Avon 2-pack .... $5 – 6
5. black, Coca-Cola with polar bear, chrome wheels, rubber tires, Premiere Collection .... $5 – 6
6. black, trim detailing, chrome wheels, rubber tires, First Editions .... $5 – 6
7. unpainted, chrome wheels, rubber tires, First Editions .... $5 – 6
8. dark red, with "Matchbox 2000" logo, "South Jersey Camaro Group Productions," "East Coast Camaro Gathering IV," Color Comp promotional ... $30 – 40

9. bright yellow, "The Carrot Show," Looney Tunes Back in Action 5-pack.................................. $1 – 2

10. turquoise, Rugrats characters, "Rocket Power," 2003 Nickelodeon 5-pack................................ $1 – 2

11. metallic light blue with white trim and interior, 2005 Superfast #30 .... $3 – 4

Chevrolet Camaro IROC Z, 3", #51, 1985; #68, 1987

1. red, "Carter," "Goodyear".......... $4 – 5
2. red with white stripes, Show Stoppers................................... $3 – 4
3. metallic red, "Carter," "Goodyear" .... $4 – 5
4. metallic orange, "Carter," "Goodyear" .... $5 – 6
5. yellow, "IROC Z"...................... $1 – 2
6. green, "BP Stunt Team" and stripes, Dutch issue....................... $10 – 12
7. green, "IROC Z"....................... $5 – 6
8. blue, "IROC Z" on sides only ...... $3 – 4
9. blue, "IROC Z" on sides and hood .... $3 – 4

10. metallic blue, "350Z"; pink, purple, and lime green stripes; Triple Heat .. $4 – 5
11. dark purple, "Z28" and silver stripe, Collector's Choice, White Rose Collectibles .... $3 – 4
12. black, "Z28," red accents......... $2 – 4

13. black, "Z28," orange and white accents .... $1 – 2

Chevrolet Camaro IROC Z-28 Police (see Chevrolet Camaro 1994 Z-28 Police)

Chevrolet Camaro Police (see Chevrolet Camaro 1994 Z-28 Police)

Chevrolet Camaro SS (see Chevrolet Camaro 1969 SS 396 Convertible)

Chevrolet Camaro Z-28 (see Chevrolet Camaro 1994 Z-28)

Chevrolet Camaro Z-28 Police (see Chevrolet Camaro 1994 Z-28 Police)

Chevrolet Cavalier (see Opel Vectra/Chevrolet Cavalier GSi 2000)

Chevrolet Corvette 1957 Convertible, #362, 1999

1. red, "Coca-Cola," Santa illustration, white flash, rubber tires on chrome wire rims, Premiere Collection .... $7 – 9
2. red, "Coca-Cola," Santa illustration, white flash, rubber tires on chrome mag rims, Premiere Collection .. $7 – 9
3. red with "FTD" license plate, sold with 1950s diner ceramic planter, sold exclusively through FTD florists ..... $20 – 30
4. red with detailed trim, rubber tires on chrome rims, 1999 First Editions .. $6 – 8
5. yellow, "Coke," white flash, 5-pack.. $4 – 5
6. unpainted, rubber tires on chrome rims, 1999 First Editions .... $6 – 8

7. metallic light blue with white trim and interior, 2005 Superfast #38.. $3 – 4

8. **white with red trim and interior, 2006 5-pack J4677 ....$1 – 2**

Chevrolet Corvette 1957 Hardtop, 2⅞", #75, 1999

1. red with white roof, "Cruisin' New England Magazine All Wheels Festival 2001," white interior and side flash, Color Comp promotional....... $60 – 80
2. red with white roof, "Vettes in Glasstown XXI," "Corvettes Unlimited," white interior and side flash, Color Comp promotional .... $16 – 24

3. **red with white roof, white interior and side flash, chrome base, 1999 Classics.............................$1 – 2**
4. black with black roof, white interior and side flash, black base, rubber tires on chrome rims, Premiere Collection..$6 – 8

Chevrolet Corvette 1961 (see Chevrolet Corvette 1962)

Chevrolet Corvette 1962, 2 15/16", #71, 1982; #32, 1993 reissue; #72, 1994 international reissue (also see Chevrolet Corvette 1962, #374)

1. red, "454 Rat," gold wheels, Macau cast .... $3 – 4
2. red, "454 Rat," silver wheels, China cast .... $1 – 2
3. red, "454 Rat," silver wheels, Macau cast .... $3 – 4
4. red, "62" and white stripes on roof, China cast, Australia issue .... $5 – 6
5. red, "Animal House," white roof and side flash, China cast, Star Cars .... $5 – 6
6. red, "Chubby's," "Pepsi-Cola," China cast, US issue .... $6 – 12
7. red, "Heinz 57," Macau cast, US issue............................. $30 – 40
8. red with white roof and side flash, rubber tires on chrome rims, China cast, 1997 Corvette Premiere Collection....... $5 – 6
9. red with white roof and side flash, Thailand cast, gift set .... $3 – 4
10. red with white stripes, China cast, Australia issue .... $5 – 6
11. pale red, "62" and white stripes on roof, gold 6-spoke spiral wheels, China cast, China issue .... $80 – 120

12. **metallic red, "Corvette 62," China cast, 1996 Racing 5-pack .....$1 – 2**
13. metallic red with white roof, "Matchbox," "DMB & B," rubber tires on chrome rims, Thailand cast, US issue .... $300 – 400
14. metallic red with white roof, rubber tires on chrome rims, Premiere Collection #3 .... $5 – 6
15. orange, "11" and white stripe, Macau cast, New Superfast Wheels .... $4 – 5
16. metallic orange, "4," black roof, rubber tires on black rims, China cast, Whales Project .... $6 – 8
17. metallic orange, "11," white stripes, Macau cast, Laser Wheels....... $4 – 5

18. **yellow with white roof, silver detailed trim, rubber tires on chrome rims, Premiere Collection Select Class #3 ....$5 – 6**
19. yellow with white roof and side flash, gold 6-spoke spiral wheels, China cast, 1997 75 Challenge........... $80 – 120
20. metallic green, "11" and white stripes, Macau cast, Laser Wheels....... $4 – 5
21. turquoise with white roof, chrome windows, rubber tires on gray rims, China cast, World Class................... $4 – 5

22. **blue with white and magenta accents on sides and hood, 1994......$1 – 2**
23. blue with white and magenta accents on sides only, 1996 .... $1 – 2
24. blue with white and red design on sides only, China cast...................... $1 – 2
25. blue with white accents, blue interior, England cast.......................... $4 – 5
26. blue with white accents, chrome interior, England cast .... $4 – 5
27. blue with white roof and side flash, gold 6-spoke spiral wheels, China cast, China issue .... $80 – 120

28. **blue with white roof and side flash, silver detailed trim, rubber tires on chrome rims, 1961 Corvette, 1997 Corvette Premiere Collection... $5 – 6**
29. bright blue, "Firestone," Macau cast, Japan issue......................... $8 – 10
30. metallic blue with blue and red design, Thailand cast......................... $1 – 2
31. metallic blue with magenta and white accents, chrome interior, 1994.. $1 – 2
32. metallic blue with white and red design, China cast............................ $1 – 2
33. metallic blue with white and red design, Thailand cast......................... $1 – 2
34. metallic blue with white roof and side flash, silver 5-spoke spiral wheels, China cast, China issue............... $80 – 120
35. metallic blue with white roof and side flash, rubber tires on chrome rims, 1997 Corvette Premiere Collection .... $5 – 6

36. **purple with fluorescent green-yellow and white tiger stripes, 1997 American Street Machines 5-pack ....$1 – 2**
37. purple with orange and yellow flames, 5-spoke concave wheels, engine cast on hood, China cast, China issue............................. $80 – 120
38. purple with orange and yellow flames, rubber tires on chrome rims, Premiere Collection #11 .... $4 – 5
39. black, "Bloomberg Fair Association," "Millennium 2000," ASAP promotional................................ $60 – 80
40. black, "BS Auto Seaside Oregon," ASAP promotional....................... $16 – 24
41. black, "DDCM DuPage Diecast Collectors Meet," ASAP promotional ...... $16 – 24
42. black, "Matchbox," "Hot August Nights 1998," pink roof, rubber tires on chrome rims, US issue .... $16 – 20
43. black, "Matchbox USA 18th Convention & Toy Show," ASAP promotional................................ $16 – 24
44. black, "X Xedia," ASAP promotional............................... $80 – 120
45. black, no markings, ASAP promotional blank................................ $35 – 45
46. black with silver, blue, and purple accents, engine cast on hood, rubber tires on chrome rims, Premiere Collection #9 .... $4 – 5
47. black with white roof and side flash, Collector's Choice, White Rose Collectibles, China cast............................ $3 – 4
48. black with white roof and side flash, rubber tires on chrome rims, 1997 Corvette Premiere Collection.......... $5 – 6

49. white with blue base, red accents, silver interior .... $8 – 10
50. white with fluorescent orange flames, 5-spoke concave wheels, China cast .... $1 – 2

51. white with fluorescent orange flames, 6-spoke spiral wheels, China cast .... $3 – 4
52. white with fluorescent orange flames, Hong Kong cast .... $3 – 4
53. white with fluorescent orange flames, Macau cast .... $3 – 4
54. white with no markings, China cast, Graffic Traffic .... $7 – 9
55. white with red accents, blue interior, England cast .... $8 – 10
56. white with red accents, chrome interior, England cast .... $8 – 10
57. white with red flames, Hong Kong cast .... $3 – 4
58. white with red flames, Macau cast .... $3 – 4
59. white with white roof and side flash, rubber tires on chrome rims, 1997 Corvette Premiere Collection ..... $5 – 6
60. metallic silver with white roof and side flash, gold 6-spoke spiral wheels, China cast, China issue .... $80 – 120

61. metallic silver with white roof and side flash, detailed trim, rubber tires on chrome rims, 1961 Corvette, 1997 Corvette Premiere Collection .... $5 – 6

62. metallic gold with white roof, silver detailed trim, rubber tires on chrome rims, Premiere Collection World Class #6 .... $5 – 6
63. metallic gold, 5-spoke concave wheels, China cast, 1997 75 Challenge .. $6 – 12

Chevrolet Corvette 1962, #374, 1998, Taco Bell; Matchbox mold retooled by Strottman International Inc. through a licensing agreement with Mattel. Strottman manufactures toy premiums for Taco Bell. Base is marked "Made in China by S.I.I."

1. black with Taco Bell logo and red bands on sides .... $4 – 5

Chevrolet Corvette 1983/1984 Convertible, with roll bar, 3", #14, 1983; #69, 1983; #28, 1990

1. red upper, light gray lower, black interior, "Vette," silver and black stripes .... $3 – 5
2. red upper, metallic silver lower, black interior, blue and silver, Dinky, 1983 .... $9 – 12
3. red and white upper and lower, black interior, "350 CID" .... $4 – 6
4. red and white upper, red lower, black interior, "Chef Boyardee," on-package promotional .... $15 – 20
5. red and white upper, red lower, black interior, "Chef Boyardee," Laser Wheels, on-package promotional ..... $80 – 100
6. red and white upper, red lower, "350 CID" .... $3 – 5
7. gray upper, lavender lower, interior replaced by gold chrome armament, Roadblasters .... $6 – 9
8. gray upper, bluish purple lower, interior replaced by gold chrome armament, Roadblasters .... $6 – 9
9. metallic silver with red interior, "83 Vette" .... $4 – 6

Chevrolet Corvette 1987/1988 Convertible, with no roll bar, 3", #14, 1987; #28, 1990, international

1. red upper and lower, flame, black interior, clear windshield .... $9 – 12

2. red upper and lower, "Corvette" and logo, black interior, clear windshield .... $1 – 2
3. red upper and lower, "Corvette" and "Matchbox Line Preview 1994," black interior, clear windshield ... $300 – 400

4. red upper and lower, detailed trim, black and red interior, clear windshield, rubber tires on chrome rims, Ultra Class .... $9 – 12
5. red to orange upper, metallic gray lower, "Corvette" and logo, black interior, clear windshield, Super Color Changers .. $3 – 5
6. metallic red upper and lower, rubber tires on chrome rims, detailed trim, gray and black interior, clear windshield, Corvette Premiere Collection .... $4 – 6
7. orange-yellow upper and lower, "Corvette" and logo, black interior, clear windshield .... $1 – 2

8. yellow upper and lower, detailed trim, black and gray interior, clear windshield, rubber tires on chrome rims, Corvette Premiere Collection .... $4 – 6

9. lemon yellow upper and lower, black interior, clear windshield, "Corvette" and logo .... $1 – 2
10. yellow upper and lower with black interior, clear windshield, "Corvette" and logo .... $2 – 4
11. lime green upper and lower, "Rally Official," "Joe Bulgin," black interior, clear windshield, rubber tires on gray rims, Whales Project .... $7 – 9
12. metallic yellow-green upper and lower, detailed trim, gray and black interior, clear windshield, rubber tires on chrome rims, Corvette Premiere Collection .... $4 – 6

13. bright green upper and lower, pink side molding, "White's Guide Car of the Month — December 1998," white interior, clear windshield, Color Comp promotional .... $12 – 16
14. bright green upper and lower, "70th Shenandoah Apple Blossom Festival 1997," white interior, clear windshield .... $12 – 16
15. dark green upper and lower, detailed trim, black and gray interior, clear windshield, rubber tires on chrome rims, Corvette Premiere Collection ..... $4 – 6
16. blue-green upper and lower, "Corvette," black interior, clear windshield, Show Stoppers .... $3 – 4

17. bright blue upper and lower, white stripes, black and red interior, clear windshield, rubber tires on chrome rims, Premiere Collection .... $4 – 6
18. metallic blue upper and lower, black and gray interior, chrome windshield, rubber tires on chrome rims, World Class .. $6 – 8

19. metallic lavender upper and lower, white graphics, orange interior, clear windshield .... $1 – 2
20. purple upper and lower, "Corvette," black interior, clear windshield ... $3 – 5
21. purple upper and lower, detailed trim, gray and black interior, clear windshield, rubber tires on chrome rims, Corvette Premiere Collection .... $4 – 6
22. black upper, green-gold lower, gray and black interior, clear windshield, gold hubs, China issue .... $100 – 150

23. black upper and lower, pink and yellow graphics, fluorescent yellow interior, clear windshield .... $1 – 2

24. black upper and lower, detailed trim, red interior, clear windshield, White Rose Collector's Choice .... $3 – 5
25. black upper and lower, "Corvette Cologne," red and black interior, clear windshield, rubber tires on chrome rims .... $12 – 16
26. black upper and lower, detailed trim, red and black interior, clear windshield, rubber tires on chrome rims, Corvette Premiere Collection .... $4 – 6
27. white and red upper, red lower, black interior, clear windshield, "350 CID," Laser wheels .... $4 – 6
28. white and red upper, red lower, "350 CID," black interior, clear windshield, new Superfast wheels .... $4 – 6

29. white upper and lower, stripes and zigzag, pink interior, clear windshield, Dream Machines 3-pack .... $2 – 4
30. white upper and lower, maroon interior, chrome windshield, rubber tires on gray rims, World Class .... $3 – 5

31. white upper and lower, orange and blue, blue interior, clear windshield .... $1 – 2
32. metallic gold upper and lower, black interior, clear windshield, 1997 75 Challenge .... $6 – 12
33. metallic light bronze upper and lower, detailed trim, gray and black interior, clear windshield, rubber tires on chrome rims, Corvette Premiere Collection .... $4 – 6
34. metallic light bronze upper and lower, fluorescent yellow interior, clear windshield, gold hubs, China issue .... $100 – 150

35. metallic burgundy with gray Chevrolet bowtie on front of hood, "Corvette" on doors and windshield .... $2 – 3

Chevrolet Corvette 1997, #4, 1997; #58, 1998

1. red, "8th Toy Show Demo Model — Hershey," Color Comp promotional .... $25 – 35
2. red, "Corvette" on windshield, black interior .... $1 – 2
3. red, "Corvette Cologne," chrome hubs, rubber tires, black interior .... $30 – 45
4. red, "Corvette Expo," ASAP promotional .... $50 – 100
5. red, "Fiery Driven," black interior, ASAP promotional .... $100 – 125
6. red, "Launch Commemorative Jan. 6th, 1997," black interior .... $175 – 225
7. red, "Matchbox USA Hershey 2001," Color Comp promotional .... $25 – 35
8. red, "Mid Town Bank," ASAP promotional .... $100 – 150

9. red, chrome hubs, rubber tires, gray and black interior, Corvette Premiere Edition .... $4 – 6
10. maroon, "Frohe Weihnachten" .... $20 – 30
11. metallic red, chrome hubs, rubber tires, gray and black interior, Corvette Premiere Edition .... $4 – 6
12. yellow, "Corvette" with white and black checks, play set .... $6 – 8
13. green, chrome hubs, rubber tires, gray and black interior, Corvette Premiere Edition .... $4 – 6

14. blue, "Corvette" on windshield, #58, 1998 .... $1 – 2
15. metallic blue, chrome hubs, rubber tires, 1997 Inaugural Edition .... $5 – 7
16. lavender, lime interior, "Scooby Do," "Like Who," "Daphne," Warner Bros.................................... $6 – 8
17. black, "Coca-Cola," Premiere Collection................................... $5 – 7
18. black, chrome hubs, rubber tires, red and black interior, Corvette Premiere Edition .... $4 – 6
19. dark gray, chrome hubs, rubber tires, Toys "R" Us gift set................. $4 – 6
20. metallic gray, chrome hubs, rubber tires, gray and black interior, Corvette Premiere Edition .... $4 – 6

21. white, chrome hubs, rubber tires, red and black interior, Corvette Premiere Edition....................... $4 – 6
22. white, no markings, ASAP blank .... $25 – 50
23. white, "Lucent Technologies," red "Gigaspeed" graphics, ASAP promotional .... $100 – 150
24. white, "Lucent Technologies," black "Gigaspeed/Optispeed" graphics, ASAP promotional .... $25 – 50
25. white, "Route 66 Promotions," ASAP promotional .... $25 – 50
26. white, "Progress Pit Crew," ASAP promotional .... $100 – 150
27. white, "Sandvik Coromant," ASAP promotional .... $100 – 150
28. white, "Cisco Systems," ASAP promotional............................ $100 – 150
29. white, "Colorado Auto Auctions," ASAP promotional .... $25 – 50

30. white, "White's Guide Car of the Month #7," ASAP promotional ....$9 - 12
31. white, "Datamax," ASAP promotional .... $75 – 125
32. white, "RCA," ASAP promotional ..$25 – 50
33. white, "Progressive AE," ASAP promotional .... $75 – 125
34. white, "Kitchen Aid," ASAP promotional .... $100 – 150
35. white, "IBM" on left side, ASAP promotional .... $100 – 150
36. white, "Pras," ASAP promotional .$15 – 25
37. white, "ND Go Irish," ASAP promotional .... $15 – 25
38. white, "Consumer Finance Services," ASAP promotional .... $100 – 150
39. white, "Serena," ASAP promotional .... $100 – 150
40. white, "Alabama Crimson Tide," ASAP promotional .... $75 – 125
41. white, "Huskers," ASAP promotional .... $12 – 16
42. white, "Novell," ASAP promotional .... $20 – 25
43. white, "Eds," "eds.com," ASAP promotional .... $40 – 50
44. white, "Bud's Cruise-In," ASAP promotional .... $50 – 100
45. white, "Phillips," "Sy's Samson," ASAP promotional .... $50 – 100
46. unpainted, chrome hubs, rubber tires, 1997 Inaugural Edition............ $5 – 7
47. metallic gold, 1997 75 Challenge .... $6 – 12

Chevrolet Corvette 1997, 1999, Taco Bell; Matchbox mold retooled by Strottman International Inc. through a licensing agreement with Mattel. Strottman manufactures toy premiums for Taco Bell. Base is marked "Made in China by S.I.I."
1. green with blue and white design, black windows, Taco Bell .... $3 – 4

Chevrolet Corvette 1998, 2000 Feature Cars, with opening features, designed to replace Premiere Collection
1. dark blue with gray interior ..... $9 – 12

Chevrolet Corvette 1998 Convertible, 2000 Feature Cars, with opening features, designed to replace Premiere Collection
1. red with tan and black interior .. $9 – 12

Chevrolet Corvette 2000, #57, 2001; #11, 2002; #8, 2003
1. metallic burgundy with black interior, no markings, 2001 Wheeled Envy .. $1 – 2

2. metallic silver with black interior, "Corvette" in white on sides, 2002 Style Champs...................... $1 - 2

3. metallic green with butterscotch interior, yellow and white on sides, 2003 Family Wheels .... $1 - 2

4. metallic red with green, black, and white graphics, tan interior ... $1 - 2

Chevrolet Corvette C6 2005, #63, 2004; #5, 2005; #20, 2006; #22, 2007 (MB630)
1. metallic gray, 2004 #63 .... $1 – 2
2. metallic copper, 2005 #5......... $1 – 2
3. metallic silver, 2006 #20......... $1 – 2

4. dark blue, 2007 #22 .... $1 - 2

5. black, 2005 Superfast #24... $3 - 4

Chevrolet Corvette Grand Sport, 3", #2, 1990; #15, 1990; #3, 1998
1. metallic blue with "15" on doors, black base.................................... $3 – 5
2. metallic blue with "Corvette" on doors, black base............................ $3 – 5
3. metallic red with "63," black base................................ $15 – 20
4. metallic red with "63," chrome base.................................. $5 – 10
5. metallic blue with "15" on doors, black base................................... $4 – 5
6. metallic blue with "Heinz 57".. $20 – 25
7. white with red stripes, "Corvette," black base.................................... $1 – 2
8. bright yellow with purple and black, dark gray base.............................. $1 – 2
9. metallic blue with "2" on doors, from 40th Anniversary Corvette Collection, 1993 .... $5 – 7
10. chrome plated, white base........ $3 – 5
11. dark orange, black tire tread .... $1 – 2
10. metallic red, chrome windows, black base, World Class .... $12 – 16
11. metallic red, chrome windows, chrome base, World Class .... $4 – 6
12. white and blue with "9" and red stripes, Goodyear tires .... $6 – 8

13. white with red accent stripe, "Corvette," 1993...................... $2 - 4
14. orange with black tire tread pattern, 1994 .... $1 – 2

15. white with black widow graphics, 1995 .... $1 - 2

16. black with black widow graphics, 1996 .... $3 - 5

17. dark purple with orange flames .... $1 – 2
18. light metallic blue, chrome wheels, rubber tires, Premiere Collection.... $4 – 6
19. 1998 Stars & Stripes series 1 .. $3 – 5
20. metallic gray with "50" and white stripes, chrome wheels, rubber tires, Premiere Collection .... $4 – 6
21. metallic gold, Challenge.......... $5 – 10

22. white with "4" and black stripes, chrome wheels, rubber tires, Select Class................................ $4 – 6
23. dark gray, chrome wheels, rubber tires, Corvette Premiere.................. $4 – 6

24. blue, chrome wheels, rubber tires, Corvette Premiere............... $4 – 6
25. white with orange flames, chrome wheels, rubber tires, Premiere Collection .... $4 – 6
26. lemon yellow, chrome wheels, rubber tires, Corvette Premiere........... $4 – 6
27. metallic gold, chrome wheels, rubber tires, Corvette Premiere........... $4 – 6
28. metallic green, chrome wheels, rubber tires, Corvette Premiere........... $4 – 6

29. black, chrome wheels, rubber tires, Corvette Premiere............... $4 – 6
30. red with white stripe................ $3 – 5
31. black, gold 6-spoke pinwheel wheels, Challenge series prize.......... $60 – 80
32. gold, gold 6-spoke pinwheel wheels, Challenge series prize.......... $60 – 80
33. blue with white stripe............... $1 – 2

34. metallic blue with yellow flames .... $2 – 3

Chevrolet Corvette Hardtop, 3 1/16", #62, 1979; #21, 1983
1. "Angels 1992," yellow, rubber tires on gray rims, White Rose Collectibles.................................. $4 – 5
2. "Astros 1992," white, rubber tires on gray rims, White Rose Collectibles.................................. $4 – 5
3. "Athletics 1992," green, rubber tires on gray rims, White Rose Collectibles.................................. $4 – 5
4. "Brut," "Faberge," green, gray interior, clear windows, Macau cast, Team Matchbox............................. $3 – 4
5. "Blue Jays 1992," blue, rubber tires on gray rims, White Rose Collectibles.................................. $4 – 5
6. "Braves 1992," metallic blue, rubber tires on gray rims, White Rose Collectibles.................................... $4 – 5
7. "Brewers 1992," blue, rubber tires on gray rims, White Rose Collectibles.................................. $4 – 5
8. "Cardinals 1992," red, rubber tires on gray rims, White Rose Collectibles.................................. $4 – 5
9. "Coca-Cola Play Refreshed," red band, black interior, tinted windows, Premiere Collection .... $4 – 5
10. "Cooperstown 1993," white, rubber tires on gray rims, White Rose Collectibles.................................... $4 – 5
11. "Cubs 1992," red, rubber tires on gray rims, White Rose Collectibles.... $4 – 5
12. "Dodgers 1992," blue, rubber tires on gray rims, White Rose Collectibles.................................. $4 – 5
13. "Expos 1992," blue, rubber tires on gray rims, White Rose Collectibles.................................. $4 – 5
14. "Giants 1992," gray, rubber tires on gray rims, White Rose Collectibles.................................. $4 – 5
15. "Indians 1992," blue, rubber tires on gray rims, White Rose Collectibles............................... $4 – 5
16. "Mariners 1992," blue, rubber tires on gray rims, White Rose Collectibles............................... $4 – 5
17. "Marlins 1992," white, rubber tires on gray rims, White Rose Collectibles.................................. $4 – 5
18. "Mets 1992," blue, rubber tires on gray rims, White Rose Collectibles.... $4 – 5
19. "Orioles 1992," black, rubber tires on gray rims, White Rose Collectibles.................................. $4 – 5

20. "Pace Car" on sides and trunk, metallic gray with blue accents .... $6 – 8
21. "Pace Car" on sides only, metallic gray with blue accents .... $6 – 8
22. "Padres 1992," white, rubber tires on gray rims, White Rose Collectibles.................................. $4 – 5
23. "Phillies 1992," red, rubber tires on gray rims, White Rose Collectibles.................................. $4 – 5
24. "Pirates 1992," black, rubber tires on gray rims, White Rose Collectibles.................................. $4 – 5
25. "Rangers 1992," red, rubber tires on gray rims, White Rose Collectibles.................................. $4 – 5
26. "Reds 1992," red, rubber tires on gray rims, White Rose Collectibles.... $4 – 5
27. "Red Sox 1992," blue, rubber tires on gray rims, White Rose Collectibles.................................. $4 – 5
28. "Rockies 1992," blue, rubber tires on gray rims, White Rose Collectibles.................................. $4 – 5
29. "Royals 1992," blue, rubber tires on gray rims, White Rose Collectibles.................................. $4 – 5
30. "The Force," black, gray interior, clear windows, Macau cast .... $3 – 4
31. "The Force," black, gray interior, opaque windows, Macau cast .... $9 – 12
32. "The Force," black, red plastic base, gray interior, clear windows, Manaus cast, Brazil issue................ $40 – 50
33. "Tigers 1992," orange, rubber tires on gray rims, White Rose Collectibles.................................. $4 – 5
34. "Turbo Vette," black, red interior, clear windows, Macau cast, New Superfast Wheels................................ $4 – 5
35. "Turbo Vette," black, red interior, clear windows, Macau cast, Laser Wheels................................ $4 – 5
36. "Turbo Vette," metallic red, red interior, clear windows, Macau cast, Laser Wheels............................ $12 – 16
37. "Twins 1992," blue, rubber tires on gray rims, White Rose Collectibles.................................. $4 – 5
38. "White Sox 1992," black, rubber tires on gray rims, White Rose Collectibles.................................. $4 – 5
39. "Yankees 1992," white, rubber tires on gray rims, White Rose Collectibles.................................. $4 – 5
40. red with white hood and sides, black interior, clear windows, England cast .... $5 – 6
41. red with white hood and sides, gray interior, clear windows, no "Corvette" cast at rear or front, England cast .... $40 – 50
42. red with white hood and sides, gray interior, clear windows, England cast .... $5 – 6
43. red with white hood and sides, black interior, clear windows, England cast .... $5 – 6

44. red with white hood only, black interior, clear windows, England cast ..... $5 – 6
45. black with green and orange stripes on hood, gray interior, clear windows, England cast............................... $4 – 5
46. black with green and orange stripes on hood, gray interior, opaque windows, England cast...................... $12 – 16
47. black with yellow and orange stripes on hood, gray interior, clear windows, Macau cast.......................... $3 – 4
48. metallic gray with white and purple design, purple interior, clear windows, China cast.......................... $9 – 12
49. white with red stripes, maroon interior, Thailand cast......................... $3 – 4

Chevrolet Corvette Pace Car, #21, 1983 (see Chevrolet Corvette Hardtop)

Chevrolet Corvette Police, #464, 2000
1. "D.A.R.E. America," "Moorehead Police," white, triangular roof lights, D.A.R.E. .... $4 – 5
2. "D.A.R.E. Suffern Police," yellow with purple flames, D.A.R.E............ $4 – 5

Chevrolet Corvette Stingray III Convertible, #38, 1994; #2, 1998

1. red, "7-Eleven" .... $5 – 6
2. red, "Matchbox USA 97," black interior, chrome windshield, rubber tires on chrome rims, promotional.. $120 – 160

3. red with white and blue accents, light gray interior, tinted windshield, 1998 Stars & Stripes.......... $1 – 2
4. red with detailed trim, black interior, chrome windshield, rubber tires on chrome rims, US on-package premium .... $30 – 40
5. red, detailed trim, brown and black interior, clear windshield, rubber tires on chrome rims, Premiere Collection #12 .... $4 – 5
6. metallic dark red, detailed trim, two-tone gray interior, clear windshield, rubber tires on chrome rims, Premiere Collection #16 .... $4 – 5
7. fluorescent orange, "Ice Breaker," gray interior .... $8 – 10
8. fluorescent orange and yellow, "Matchbox Get in the Fast Lane," "Toy Fair 1995," US issue .... $20 – 25
9. fluorescent orange and yellow, "Matchbox Get in the Fast Lane," "Toy Fair 1995," UK/German issue.... $20 – 25
10. lemon yellow with detailed trim, two-tone gray interior, rubber tires on chrome rims, clear windshield, Premiere Collection #5 .... $4 – 5
11. fluorescent yellow, "Ice Breaker," gray interior .... $8 – 10
12. blue with orange and white accents, "Corvette," 1998 Stars & Stripes .... $1 – 2

13. blue chrome with pink and orange design, light gray interior, clear windshield, 1997 Sleek Riders 5-pack................................ $1 – 2
14. metallic blue with detailed trim, two-tone gray interior, rubber tires on chrome rims, clear windshield, Premiere Collection #2 .... $4 – 5
15. purple, white interior, tinted windshield, 5-pack.................................. $1 – 2
16. purple with pink and white accents, dark gray interior, clear windshield, 1994 .... $1 – 2

17. purple with pink and white accents, gray interior, tinted windshield .. $1 – 2
18. purple with pink and white accents, light gray interior, tinted windshield ... $1 – 2
19. purple, detailed trim, dark gray interior, chrome windshield, rubber tires on chrome rims, World Class........ $4 – 5
20. black, detailed trim, red and gray interior, clear windshield, rubber tires on chrome rims, Gold Coin Collection.................................$16 – 24
21. black and fluorescent orange, white interior, tinted windshield, 5-pack.. $3 – 4

22. white with red and yellow design, red interior, tinted windshield, 1996.. $3 – 4
23. white with blue and black spray design, blue interior, tinted windshield, 5-pack.................................... $1 – 2
24. white, detailed trim, brown and black interior, clear windshield, rubber tires on chrome rims, Select Class #4 .... $4 – 5
25. metallic silver with white and peach accents, white interior, amber windshield .... $4 – 5
26. metallic silver, detailed trim, dark gray interior, clear windshield, rubber tires on chrome rims, Select Class #2 .. $4 – 5
27. metallic gold with black interior, clear windshield, 1997 75 Challenge .... $12 – 16

Chevrolet Corvette T-Roof, 3¹/₁₆", #40, 1982; #58, 1992 – 1997; #74, 1998; #62, 1982, international
1. red, "Vette," "Chevy" logo, white interior, China cast............................. $1 – 2
2. red, "Vette," white stripe, white interior, 1993, Thailand cast................ $1 – 2
3. red with white accents, no "Corvette" cast on front or rear .... $35 – 45
4. red with white accents, "Corvette" cast on front and rear .... $4 – 6
5. red with white and purple design, black interior, 1998 Street Cruisers... $1 – 2

6. red with detailed trim, black and red interior, rubber tires on chrome rims, Corvette Premiere Collection.................................... $4 – 5
7. candy apple red with black and white design, black and white interior, rubber tires on chrome rims, Premiere Collection #9................................ $4 – 5
8. candy apple red with black and white design, purple interior, Canadian issue .... $60 – 80
9. metallic red, "Turbo Vette," Laser Wheels............................... $8 – 10
10. salmon pink, detailed trim, white and black interior, rubber tires on chrome rims, Gold Coin Collection ..... $16 – 24
11. orange with chrome windshield, rubber tires on gray rims, World Class .. $6 – 8
12. yellow, "Corvette," metallic gray interior, Macau cast.......................... $1 – 2
13. yellow, "Corvette," metallic gray interior, China cast............................. $1 – 2
14. yellow with purple and blue accents.. $2 – 4

15. yellow with detailed trim, black and white interior, rubber tires on chrome rims, Corvette Premiere Collection .... $4 – 5
16. green, "Brut," "Faberge" .... $8 – 10
17. green with white and purple design, black interior, China cast .... $1 – 2
18. dark green, detailed trim, orange interior, Thailand cast, Collector's Choice, White Rose Collectibles .... $3 – 4
19. dark green, detailed trim, white and black interior, rubber tires on chrome rims, Corvette Premiere Collection .... $4 – 5
20. metallic green, white accents with lavender border .... $1 – 2
21. blue with flames, red interior, silver wheel hubs, Macau cast .... $3 – 4
22. blue with flames, red interior, gold wheel hubs, Macau cast .... $5 – 6
23. blue with flames, red interior, New Superfast wheels, Macau cast .... $80 – 100
24. blue with yellow and red stripes, red interior, Manaus cast, Brazil issue .... $40 – 50
25. teal blue with pink interior, white and pink grid design, Thailand cast .. $1 – 2
26. metallic blue with chrome windshield, dark gray interior, World Class .. $6 – 8
27. metallic blue with white and red accents, 1994 .... $2 – 4
28. bright blue, detailed trim, white and black interior, rubber tires on chrome rims, Corvette Premiere Collection .... $4 – 5
29. black with chrome windshield, World Class .... $6 – 8
30. black "22," green and orange stripes, clear windows, rubber tires on black rims, Whales Project .... $6 – 8
31. black, detailed trim, red and black interior, rubber tires on chrome rims, Corvette Premiere Collection .... $4 – 5
32. black with opaque windows, green and orange stripes .... $8 – 10
33. black with clear windows, yellow and orange stripes .... $2 – 4
34. black with gray interior, "The Force" .... $2 – 4
35. black with red interior, "The Force" graphics, Manaus cast, Brazil issue .... $20 – 30

36. metallic gray with white and purple design, purple interior, China cast .... $1 – 2
37. metallic dark gray, "Corvette," white stripes, white interior, Corvette 40th Anniversary set .... $3 – 4
38. dark cream with red and gray stripes, red interior, Manaus cast, Brazil issue .... $40 – 50

39. white front, black rear, pink blotch design, pink interior, China cast .... $1 – 2
40. white front, black rear, pink blotch design, pink interior, Thailand cast .... $1 – 2
41. white with pink design, black interior, China cast .... $1 – 2
42. white with stripes, gray interior, England cast .... $5 – 6
43. white with stripes, red interior, Macau cast .... $3 – 4
44. white, detailed trim, red and black interior, rubber tires on chrome rims, Corvette Premiere Collection .... $4 – 5
45. black with "Turbo Vette" .... $4 – 6
46. metallic silver, purple interior, gray base .... $1 – 2
47. metallic gold, black interior, 1997 75 Challenge .... $6 – 12
48. various baseball team logos (29 variations) .... $4 – 6

Chevrolet Corvette T-Top (see Chevrolet Corvette T-Roof)

Chevrolet El Camino 1970, #32, 1998; #74, 1999; #60, 2000

1. red, "Coca-Cola It's the Real Thing," metallic gray metal base, Avon .. $4 – 5
2. red and white, "Coca-Cola," rubber tires on chrome rims, Premiere Collection .... $5 – 6
3. red with white stripes on hood, rubber tires on chrome rims, 1998 First Editions .... $5 – 6
4. maroon, chrome plastic base, "Canyon Base," 5-pack .... $1 – 2
5. maroon, metallic gray metal base, "Canyon Base," Target Eggmobiles 5-pack .... $9 – 12
6. metallic blue, "Freestyle," skateboarder, 2000 Speedy Delivery .... $1 – 2
7. metallic blue, "Freestyle," skateboarder, "Matchbox 2000," 2000 Speedy Delivery .... $3 – 4

8. metallic gold with black stripes on hood, chrome base, 1998 Classic Decades .... $1 – 2

9. metallic gold with black stripes on hood, translucent white base, 1998 Classic Decades .... $60 – 80
10. unpainted with no markings, rubber tires on chrome rims, 1998 First Editions .... $5 – 6

11. yellow with dark brown and blue design, 1999 Classics .... $1 – 2
12. metallic greenish-gold, "Back in Action," Daffy Duck graphics, Looney Tunes 5-pack .... $2 – 3
13. metallic gold with black stripes on hood, "El Camino SS 454," 2005 Superfast #29 .... $3 – 4

Chevrolet Highway Maintenance Truck, 3$^{1}/_{16}$", #45, 1990 – 1997; #11, 1998; #79, 2000; #20, 2003; #69, 1990, international; #44, 2007

1. "Airways Plowing," white, blue dumper and plow, 1999 Airport 5-pack .... $1 – 2
2. "Aspen Snow Removal," red, gray dumper and plow, Action Pack .... $4 – 5
3. "Blue Ridge Construction," pumpkin orange, gray dumper and plow, ASAP promotional .... $80 – 120
4. "CAT Service Co.," pumpkin, gray dumper and plow, ASAP promotional .. $80 – 120
5. "DOT 13," fluorescent yellow, gray dumper and plow, 2000 Snow Explorer .... $1 – 2
6. "DOT 13," "Matchbox 2000," fluorescent yellow, gray dumper and plow, 2000 Snow Explorer .... $3 – 4
7. "DOT 103," orange, black dumper and plow, 1999 Highway Haulers .... $1 – 2
8. "Hemler Bros.," pumpkin orange, gray dumper and plow, ASAP promotional .... $80 – 120

9. "Highway Crew," fluorescent green, black dumper, yellow plow, 1999 Highway Crew 5-pack .... $1 – 2

10. "Highway Dept.," white, blue dumper and plow, 1995 .... $1 – 2

11. "Highway Maintenance 45," orange, gray dumper and plow, Collector's Choice, White Rose Collectibles .. $4 – 5
12. "Intercom City," green, yellow dumper and plow .... $8 – 10
13. "International Airport Authority 45," dark orange, red dumper and plow .. $9 – 12
14. "International Airport Authority 45," yellow, red dumper and plow .... $1 – 2
15. "International Airport Authority 45," yellow, yellow dumper and plow ..... $1 – 2
16. "Matchbox," pumpkin orange, gray dumper and plow, 5-pack .... $1 – 2
17. "Matchbox Road Crew," red, black dumper and plow, 1998 Big Movers ... $1 – 2
18. "Minnesota Guidestar," pumpkin orange, gray dumper and plow, ASAP promotional .... $80 – 120
19. "Redi-Way Inc.," pumpkin orange, gray dumper and plow, ASAP promotional .... $80 – 120

20. "Road Crew," red, black dumper and plow, 1997 .... $1 – 2

21. "Road Crew," orange, black dumper and plow, 1997 .... $1 – 2

22. "Test Centre," orange, gray dumper and plow, polar bear design, Launcher 5-pack .... $1 – 2

23. metallic green, orange dumper and plow, charging ram design, 2003 Public Works .... $1 – 2

24. metallic gold, black dumper and plow, 1997 75 Challenge .... $6 – 12
25. black with orange dumper and plow, 2002 Matchbox Across America 50th Birthday Series #39 North Dakota — Central Collection .... $4 – 5

26. orange with yellow plow and dumper .... $1 – 2

27. orange with black plow and dumper, silver trim, "Engineering," "222," seal on door, 2006 5-pack J4680 .... $1 – 2

28. yellow with yellow plow, black dumper, 2007 #44 .... $1 – 2

Chevrolet Impala, metallic blue with light blue roof, 2¾", #57, 1961

1. gray plastic wheels, black base .... $150 – 175

2. silver plastic wheels, black base .... $70 – 90

3. silver plastic wheels, dark blue base .... $70 – 90
4. silver plastic wheels, light blue base .... $70 – 90
5. silver plastic wheels, pale light blue base .... $80 – 100
6. black plastic wheels, black base..$70 – 90

Chevrolet Impala Police, #34, 2000; #53, 2001; #5, 2002; #53, 2003; #3, 2005

1. black, "Test Mission," yellow and red with white space shuttle design, 2000 Space Mission 5-pack .. $1 – 2

2. blue with white and yellow accents, "53 Crossing Guard," 2003 School Time .... $1 – 2

3. blue with light blue, white and yellow design, 2003 Hero City 5-pack #2 .... $1 – 2

4. white, "D.A.R.E.," 2002 Safety Stars .... $1 – 2

5. white with blue design, "Cleveland, Ohio, Police," 2000 Matchbox USA .... $1 – 2

6. white with blue design, "Cleveland, Ohio, Police," "Matchbox 2000," 2000 Matchbox USA .... $3 – 4
7. white and blue, "Metro Alarm," "Police," 5-pack .... $1 – 2
8. yellow-orange and blue, "Sydney 2000," 5-pack .... $1 – 2
9. blue with white, yellow and black graphics, 2001 #53 .... $1 – 2
10. 2002 Matchbox Across America 50th Birthday Series #9 New Hampshire — Northeastern Collection .... $4 – 6
11. 2002 Matchbox Across America 50th Birthday Series #10 Virginia — Southern Collection .... $4 – 6
12. black with white door panels and graphics, 2005 #3 .... $1 – 2

Chevrolet Impala Police, 2000 Feature Cars, with opening features, designed to replace Premiere Collection

1. "Chevrolet Police Vehicle," white ....$9 – 12
2. "FDMB R32," white, K.B. Toys exclusive .... $9 – 12
3. "NYPD 2419," white............. $9 – 12
4. "State Highway Patrol Ohio," dark gray .... $9 – 12
5. "Twp of Franklin," "43-5," white with red band .... $9 – 12

Chevrolet Impala Taxi Cab, 3", #20, 1965

1. orange with gray wheels, ivory interior .... $250 – 350
2. orange with black wheels, ivory or red interior .... $20 – 25

3. yellow with black wheels, ivory or red interior .... $12 – 16

Chevrolet K-1500 4x4 Pick-Up, #72, 1996; #54, 1998; #100, 1999

1. red with yellow lightning bolt, black and white specks on sides, 1998 Rugged Riders 5-pack .... $1 – 2

2. fluorescent orange with blue snow-capped mountain design, 1996 Off-Road 5-pack .... $1 – 2

3. yellow with red and white design on sides, 1998 Rough 'N Tough.. $1 – 2

4. fluorescent green with orange lightning bolt, black and white specks on sides, 1997 Rugged Riders 5-pack .... $1 – 2

5. blue, "Evergreen Landscaping," "Keeping Lawns Beautiful," 1999 At Your Service........................ $1 – 2

6. metallic blue with green and white design on sides, 1998 Rough & Tough .... $1 – 2

7. metallic blue with red and white accents .... $1 – 2
8. black, "Farm Credit Services," yellow and pink accents, ASAP promotional.......................... $120 – 160

9. black with yellow and pink accents .... $1 – 2

10. white, "World Cup Field Maintenance," "France 98," 1998 World Cup 5-pack.................................... $1 – 2
11. metallic gold, no markings, 1997 75 Challenge.......................... $12 – 16

12. dark green camouflage, black base and roll bar, Battle Kings Jungle Recon set, 2006, K5530 ...... $1 – 2

13. flat green with beige mud spatter design, "F9N4," 2006 5-pack J4671................................ $1 – 2

Chevrolet K-1500 Pickup 1980, 1999, Taco Bell; Matchbox mold retooled by Strottman International Inc. through a licensing agreement with Mattel. Strottman manufactures toy premiums for Taco Bell. Base is marked "Made in China by S.I.I."

1. blue with white wave design, black windows, Taco Bell premium.......... $3 – 4

Chevrolet Lumina Stock Car, 3", #54, 1990; #267, 1994, White Rose Collectibles

1. "3," "GM Parts," black, Goodyear rubber tires on gray rims, Winross promotional, White Rose Collectibles ... $20 – 30
2. "7 Time Champion 3," gold plated, Goodyear rubber tires on black rims, White Rose Collectibles........... $4 – 5
3. "98 Cutler-Hammer," white, ASAP promotional .... $60 – 80
4. "AC Delco 52," Goodyear rubber tires on black rims, White Rose Collectibles.................................. $4 – 5
5. "Active 32," red, Goodyear slicks, White Rose Collectibles.................... $4 – 5
6. "American Zoom 93," white and blue, white, Goodyear slicks, White Rose Collectibles........................... $12 – 16
7. "Avis," white, Goodyear slicks, ASAP promotional...................... $60 – 80
8. "Baltimore Colts 29," white, Hoosier rubber tires on black rims, White Rose Collectibles....................... $20 – 30
9. "Caterpillar," black and orange-yellow, Goodyear rubber tires on black rims, White Rose Collectibles........... $4 – 5
10. "Champion 4," black, Hot Stocks................................ $3 – 4
11. "Cintas 87," white, Goodyear slicks, White Rose Collectibles.......... $8 – 10
12. "City Chevrolet 46," green and lime, China cast............................ $4 – 5
13. "City Chevrolet 46," green and lime, Macau cast, Days of Thunder ... $7 – 9
14. "Dentyne 87," red and white, Goodyear slicks, White Rose Collectibles .. $4 – 5
15. "Detroit Gasket," "MGM Brake 70," red, Goodyear rubber tires on black rims, White Rose Collectibles........... $4 – 5
16. "Dewalt 08," yellow, Goodyear slicks, White Rose Collectibles........... $4 – 5
17. "Dewalt 08," yellow, Goodyear rubber tires on black rims, White Rose Collectibles.................................. $5 – 6
18. "Drive," "A-Pix Entertainment," white, Goodyear slicks, ASAP promotional........................... $120 – 160
19. "Dupont 24," metallic blue and fluorescent orange, Goodyear slicks, White Rose Collectibles.................... $4 – 5
20. "Dupont 24," metallic blue and fluorescent orange, Goodyear rubber tires on black rims, Team Convoy, White Rose Collectibles............................ $5 – 6

21. "Dupont 24," "1993 Rookie of the Year," metallic blue and fluorescent orange, Goodyear rubber tires on black rims, Team Convoy, White Rose Collectibles .... $4 – 5
22. "Dupont 99," metallic blue, Goodyear slicks, White Rose Collectibles .. $4 – 5
23. "Dupont Automotive Finishes 2," metallic blue, Goodyear rubber tires on black rims, White Rose Collectibles .... $4 – 5
24. "Enck's Custom Catering 71," blue, Goodyear slicks, White Rose Collectibles .... $4 – 5
25. "Exxon 51" with signature, black, China cast, Days of Thunder ... $4 – 5
26. "Exxon 51" with signature, black, Macau cast, Days of Thunder .. $7 – 9
27. "Exxon 51," no signature, black, Macau cast, Days of Thunder .... $30 – 40
28. "FDP Brakes 9," metallic turquoise and pink, Goodyear slicks, White Rose Collectibles .... $4 – 5
29. "Fiddle Faddle 34," red, Goodyear rubber tires on black rims, White Rose Collectibles .... $4 – 5
30. "Ferree Chevrolet 49," white and orange, White Rose Collectibles .... $4 – 5
31. "Freedom Village," "Jasper 55," white, Goodyear slicks, White Rose Collectibles .... $4 – 5
32. "Goodwrench," "GM," "Mom N Pops," "Western Steer," black, Goodyear slicks, on-package premium, White Rose Collectibles .... $7 – 9
33. "GM," "Goodwrench," black, Goodyear slicks, Team Convoy, White Rose Collectibles .... $5 – 7
34. "Goodwrench 3," "GM," "Western Steer," black, 9-spoke Goodyear slicks, White Rose Collectibles .... $4 – 5
35. "Goodwrench 3," "GM," "Western Steer," black, Goodyear slicks, White Rose Collectibles .... $6 – 8
36. "Goodwrench 3," "GM," "Western Steer," black, Goodyear rubber tires on black rims, Team Convoy, White Rose Collectibles .... $6 – 8
37. "Goodwrench 3," "GM," "Western Steer," black, Goodyear rubber tires on gray rims, Team Convoy, White Rose Collectibles .... $7 – 9
38. "Goodwrench 3," "GM," black, Goodyear rubber tires on gray rims, White Rose Collectibles Winross promotional .... $20 – 30
39. "Goodwrench 3," "GM," large "Goodwrench" on sides, revised small logos, black, Goodyear rubber tires on gray rims, Team Convoy, White Rose Collectibles .... $5 – 6
40. "Goodwrench 3," "Melbourne Motor Show," black, Goodyear rubber tires on black rims, promotional ... $20 – 30
41. "Goodwrench 3," "Sydney Motorshow 1997," black, Goodyear rubber tires on black rims, promotional ... $20 – 30
42. "Hardees 18," bright orange and blue, Macau cast, Days of Thunder .. $7 – 9
43. "Hardees 18," bright orange and blue, China cast, Days of Thunder ... $4 – 5
44. "Hendricks 25," white and green, Goodyear rubber tires on gold rims, Team Convoy, White Rose Collectibles .... $7 – 9
45. "Ica Citrix," "CDN," Goodyear slicks, ASAP promotional .... $80 – 120
46. "Ideal," white, Goodyear slicks, ASAP promotional .... $80 – 120
47. "Interstate Batteries 18," lime green and black, White Rose Collectibles .... $4 – 5
48. "Ireland 31," black, Goodyear slicks, White Rose Collectibles .... $4 – 5
49. "Ithaca Finish First," "607-257-8901," white, Goodyear slicks, ASAP promotional .... $60 – 80
50. "Kandi & Steve," "October 1, 1994," purple, Goodyear rubber tires on black rims, White Rose Collectibles .... $400 – 500
51. "Kellogg's 5," gray, Goodyear rubber tires on black rims, White Rose Collectibles .... $5 – 6
52. "Kellogg's Corn Flakes," red and yellow, Goodyear rubber tires on black rims, White Rose Collectibles .... $4 – 5
53. "Kellogg's Corn Flakes," red and yellow, yellow disc wheels, Team Convoy, White Rose Collectibles .... $5 – 6
54. "Kodak 4," orange-yellow, Goodyear rubber tires on black rims, White Rose Collectibles .... $4 – 5
55. "Kodak Film 4 Racing," orange-yellow, Goodyear rubber tires on black rims, Team Convoy, White Rose Collectibles .... $6 – 8
56. "Kodak Film 4 Racing," orange-yellow, Goodyear slicks, White Rose Collectibles .... $4 – 5
57. "Kodak Funsaver 4," orange and white, Goodyear rubber tires on black rims, White Rose Collectibles .... $4 – 5
58. "Lifetime Achievement Award-Harry Gant," gold plated, Team Convoy, White Rose Collectibles .... $20 – 30
59. "Lipton Tea 74," pink-red and yellow, Goodyear rubber tires on black rims, White Rose Collectibles .... $4 – 5
60. "Luxaire 99," white, Goodyear rubber tires on black rims, White Rose Collectibles .... $4 – 5
61. "Mac Tool Distributors 10," yellow, White Rose Collectibles .... $16 – 24
62. "Mac Tool Distributors 10," "Champion 3," yellow, Goodyear slicks, Hot Stocks .... $3 – 4
63. "Mac Tools 7," yellow, White Rose Collectibles .... $8 – 10
64. "Mac Tools 10," yellow, White Rose Collectibles .... $8 – 10
65. "Manheim 41," fluorescent yellow and lime green, Goodyear slicks, White Rose Collectibles .... $4 – 5
66. "Manheim Auctions 7" in black letters, fluorescent lime green, Hoosier rubber tires on black rims, White Rose Collectibles .... $4 – 5
67. "Manheim Auctions 7" in white letters, fluorescent lime green, Goodyear rubber tires on lime green rims, White Rose Collectibles .... $4 – 5
68. "Matchbox," "White Rose 29," white, Goodyear slicks, White Rose Collectibles .... $4 – 5
69. "Matchbox," "White Rose 29," "Brad's Toys," white, Goodyear slicks, White Rose Collectibles .... $7 – 9
70. "Matchbox," "White Rose 29," "Cars Plus," white, Goodyear slicks, White Rose Collectibles .... $7 – 9
71. "Matchbox," "White Rose 29," "Craig Hill," white, Goodyear slicks, White Rose Collectibles .... $7 – 9
72. "Matchbox," "White Rose 29," "Diecast Toy Exchange," white, Goodyear slicks, White Rose Collectibles .... $7 – 9
73. "Matchbox," "White Rose 29," "Kiddie Kar Kollectibles," white, Goodyear slicks, White Rose Collectibles .... $7 – 9
74. "Matchbox," "White Rose 29," "Matchbox Road Museum," white, Goodyear slicks, White Rose Collectibles .... $7 – 9
75. "Matchbox-White Rose Collectibles 29," dark blue and yellow, Hoosier rubber tires on black rims, White Rose Collectibles .. $4 – 5
76. "Matchbox Motorsports 35," fluorescent green, black grille, Goodyear slicks .... $3 – 4
77. "Matchbox Motorsports 35," fluorescent green, without black grille, Goodyear slicks .... $1 – 2
78. "Matchbox Motorsports 35," dark blue .... $3 – 4
79. "Matchbox Racing 1," white and metallic blue, Hot Stocks .... $3 – 4
80. "Matchbox Racing 7," red and yellow, Goodyear slicks, Hot Stocks .... $3 – 4
81. "Matchbox USA 12," yellow and red, Goodyear slicks .... $7 – 9
82. "Matchbox USA 13," yellow and red, Goodyear slicks .... $7 – 9
83. "Matchbox USA 14," metallic gray, Goodyear slicks, Parlor City Collectibles .... $8 – 10
84. "Meineke 41," black and yellow, Goodyear rubber tires on black rims, White Rose Collectibles .... $5 – 6
85. "Mello Yello 51," black, Macau cast .... $6 – 8
86. "Mello Yello 51," black, China cast, Days of Thunder .... $4 – 5
87. "Molly Black Gold 98," black, Goodyear slicks, White Rose Collectibles .. $4 – 5
88. "MW Windows," "Freedom 14," white, Goodyear slicks, White Rose Collectibles .... $4 – 5
89. "Nationwide Auto Parts," yellow, Goodyear slicks .... $30 – 40
90. "Penrose 44," "Firecracker Sausage," "Big Mama," maroon, White Rose Collectibles .... $7 – 9

91. "Performance Parts 12," red with white-lettered Goodyear slicks .... $1 – 2
92. "Performance Parts 12," red with yellow-lettered Goodyear slicks, Aquafresh on-package premium .... $5 – 6

93. "Performance Parts 12," purple with yellow-lettered Goodyear slicks, White Rose Collector's Choice...$5 – 6

94. "Performance Parts 12," baby blue with Goodyear slicks, Collectors Choice, White Rose Collectibles .... $4 – 5
95. "PG Tags," white, UK on-package premium .... $90 – 120
96. "Phil Parsons Racing 29," "Matchbox," dark purple and white, White Rose Collectibles .... $16 – 24
97. "Pic N Pay," "Shoe World 32," yellow, Goodyear rubber tires on black rims, White Rose Collectibles.......... $9 – 12
98. "Pic N Pay Shoes," "Shoe City 32," yellow, Goodyear slicks, White Rose Collectibles .... $4 – 5
99. "Polaroid 46," orange, Goodyear rubber tires on black rims, White Rose Collectibles .... $20 – 30
100. "Purolator 10," fluorescent orange and white, Goodyear slicks, White Rose Collectibles .... $4 – 5
101. "Purolator 10," fluorescent orange and white, Goodyear rubber tires on gray rims, Team Convoy, White Rose Collectibles .... $5 – 6
102. "Raybestos 12" without "Tic Tac," metallic blue and white, White Rose Collectibles .... $80 – 100
103. "Raybestos 12," "Tic Tac," metallic blue and white, White Rose Collectibles .... $4 – 5
104. "Rookie of the Year 1993," gold plated, Goodyear rubber tires on black rims, Team Convoy, White Rose Collectibles .... $8 – 10
105. "Six Time Champion 3 Dale Earnhardt," gold plated, White Rose Collectibles .... $20 – 30
106. "Slim Jim 44," maroon, White Rose Collectibles .... $7 – 9
107. "Stanley 92," black, Goodyear rubber tires on black rims, White Rose Collectibles .... $5 – 6
108. "Stanley Tools 92," black, Goodyear slicks, White Rose Collectibles .. $4 – 5
109. "Steph & Mike," "The Desenbergs," "December 10, 1994," Goodyear rubber tires on black rims, White Rose Collectibles .... $400 – 500
110. "Sunoco Ultra 94," dark blue, Goodyear slicks, White Rose Collectibles .... $4 – 5
111. "Superflo 46," pink and white, Macau cast, Days of Thunder............. $7 – 9
112. "Superflo 46," pink and white, China cast, Days of Thunder............. $4 – 5
113. "Team Goodyear 11," white, Hot Stocks .... $3 – 4
114. "Team Goodyear 22," orange, Hot Stocks .... $3 – 4
115. "Texas Pete," "Lozito's 87," yellow and white, White Rose Collectibles .. $5 – 6
116. "Tracey Lawrence," "Yamaha 1," orange-red and white, Goodyear rubber tires on black rims, White Rose Collectibles .... $9 – 12
117. "US Transplant Olympics — Tyler Elliott," white, Goodyear slicks, Color Comp promotional.............. $30 – 40
118. "Vermont Teddy Bear," blue-green and purple, Goodyear rubber tires on black rims, White Rose Collectibles .... $4 – 5
119. "Virginia Is for Lovers 25," black, white, Goodyear slicks, White Rose Collectibles .... $4 – 5
120. "Western Auto 17"; white, gray, and black; Goodyear rubber tires on black rims; White Rose Collectibles.... $4 – 5
121. "WFE 69," black, Goodyear slicks, White Rose Collectibles........ $16 – 24
122. "White Rose Collectibles 29," "Matchbox," dark purple and white, White Rose Collectibles .... $4 – 5
123. "White Rose Collectibles 94," white, light blue and dark blue, White Rose Collectibles .... $30 – 40
124. "White Rose Series II in '94," white and dark blue, White Rose Collectibles .... $5 – 6
125. Lightning Wheels, yellow and orange with purple spatter and lightning bolts, chrome and black windows .....$3 – 5
126. Lightning Wheels, yellow and orange, red spatter and lightning bolts, chrome and black windows ....$4 – 5
127. Lightning Wheels, green and white with purple spatter and lightning bolts, chrome and black windows .....$4 – 5
128. Lightning Wheels, white and yellow with pink spatter and lightning bolts, blue chrome and black windows .... $8 – 10
128. Lightning Wheels, white and black .... $8 – 10
130. yellow, Goodyear slicks, White Rose Collectibles........................ $16 – 24
131. white with no markings, Thailand cast, Graffic Traffic................. $6 – 8
132. white with no markings, China cast, ASAP promotional blank .... $20 – 30
133. chrome plated, no markings, Goodyear slicks, customized model ..$15 – 20

Chevrolet Monte Carlo, #283, 1995, White Rose Collectibles

1. "1995 Champion-Lipton Tea 74," gold plated, Goodyear rubber tires on black rims, White Rose Collectibles..$20 – 30
2. "1995 Rookie of the Year — Ricky Craven 41," gold plated, Goodyear rubber tires on black rims, White Rose Collectibles .... $20 – 30
3. "Bell South Mobility 87," blue and white, Goodyear rubber tires on black rims, White Rose Collectibles........ $12 – 16
4. "Budweiser 25," red, Goodyear rubber tires on black rims, White Rose Collectibles, sealed in plexiglas box.. $20 – 25
5. "Budweiser 25," red, Goodyear rubber tires on black rims, White Rose Collectibles, sealed in glass bottle ... $30 – 40
6. "Burger King 87," black and orange-yellow, Goodyear rubber tires on black rims, White Rose Collectibles.. $8 – 10
7. "Burger King 87," purple and yellow, Goodyear rubber tires on black rims, White Rose Collectibles............ $4 – 5
8. "Caterpillar," "Cat 95," black, Goodyear rubber tires on black rims, Team Convoy, White Rose Collectibles...... $7 – 9
9. "Caterpillar," "Cat 96," orange-yellow, Goodyear rubber tires on black rims, White Rose Collectibles........... $4 – 5
10. "Caterpillar 96," black and orange-yellow, Goodyear rubber tires on black rims, White Rose Collectibles.... $4 – 5
11. "Channellock 10," blue, Goodyear rubber tires on black rims, White Rose Collectibles .... $4 – 5
12. "Coor's Light 40," dark blue, metallic gray and pale yellow, Goodyear rubber tires on black rims, White Rose Collectibles, sealed in glass bottle ... $30 – 40
13. "Dewalt 1," orange-yellow, Goodyear rubber tires on black rims, White Rose Collectibles .... $4 – 5
14. "Dupont 24," metallic blue and fluorescent orange, Goodyear rubber tires on black rims, White Rose Collectibles .... $4 – 5
15. "Dupont 95 Points Champion," gold plated, Goodyear rubber tires on black rims, White Rose Collectibles........ $20 – 30
16. "Fina 74," blue, Goodyear rubber tires on black rims, White Rose Collectibles .... $4 – 5
17. "Fina 74 – 1996 Champion," gold plated, Goodyear rubber tires on black rims, White Rose Collectibles........ $20 – 30
18. "Goodwrench 3," black, Goodyear rubber tires on black rims, White Rose Collectibles .... $4 – 5
19. "Hyde Tools 08," blue and white, Goodyear rubber tires on black rims, White Rose Collectibles.................... $4 – 5
20. "Hype 88," black, Goodyear rubber tires on black rims, White Rose Collectibles .... $4 – 5

21. "Interstate Batteries," green and black, Goodyear rubber tires on black rims, White Rose Collectibles............ $4 – 5
22. "Kellogg's 5," yellow and red, Goodyear rubber tires on black rims, White Rose Collectibles............................ $4 – 5
23. "Kellogg's Corn Flakes 5," "1996 Champion," gold plated, Goodyear rubber tires on black rims, White Rose Collectibles................................ $20 – 30
24. "Kellogg's Corn Flakes 5," lemon and red, Goodyear rubber tires on black rims, White Rose Collectibles.... $4 – 5
25. "Kodak Film 4," orange-yellow, Goodyear rubber tires on black rims, White Rose Collectibles............................ $4 – 5
26. "Kodiac 41," white and green, Goodyear rubber tires on black rims, White Rose Collectibles, sealed in plexiglas box .... $20 – 30
27. "Lance Snacks 43," blue, Goodyear rubber tires on black rims, White Rose Collectibles................................ $4 – 5
28. "Lance Snacks 43"; blue, white, and red; Goodyear rubber tires on black rims; White Rose Collectibles.... $4 – 5
29. "Lipton Tea 74," red, Goodyear rubber tires on black rims, White Rose Collectibles.................................... $4 – 5
30. "Matchbox 1995," "1," fluorescent pink, Goodyear rubber tires on black rims, White Rose Collectibles, 1995 Hershey, PA, convention raffle prize..$100 – 150
31. "Matchbox 1995," "1," fluorescent yellow, Goodyear rubber tires on black rims, White Rose Collectibles, 1995 Hershey, PA, convention raffle prize .... $100 – 150
32. "Rookie of the Year — Ricky Craven 41," gold plated .... $20 – 25
33. "Royal Oak Charcoal," red and yellow, Goodyear rubber tires on black rims, White Rose Collectibles............ $4 – 5
34. "Skoal 33," green and white, Goodyear rubber tires on black rims, White Rose Collectibles, sealed in plexiglas box .... $30 – 40
35. "The Budget Gourmet," white, Goodyear rubber tires on black rims, White Rose Collectibles............................ $4 – 5
36. "White Rose Collectibles 96"; blue, white, and dark rose; Goodyear rubber tires on black rims; White Rose Collectibles.................................. $9 – 12

Chevrolet Panel Van, #215, 1995, rear bumper, smaller than #245 (also see Chevrolet Panel Van #245)

1. red, "Texaco," rubber tires on chrome rims, Premiere Collection .... $4 – 5
2. metallic red, "American Iron Cruise 95"................................ $15 – 20
3. fluorescent orange, "Matchbox — Get in the Fast Lane — Hershey Convention 1996"............................ $10 – 12
4. metallic green, "25th Anniversary S.J.S.R.A. South Jersey Shore Rod Run," Color Comp promotional..$16 – 24
5. metallic green, "American Iron Cruise 1998," custom promotional.. $16 – 24
6. metallic green, "Season's Greetings — Matchbox Collectors Club 1995"...$10 – 12
7. purple, "Continental Aero"..... $12 – 16
8. metallic gray, "Andale — www.andale.com," ASAP promotional ...... $60 – 80
9. metallic gray, "Hot August Nights," Color Comp promotional.............. $16 – 24
10. metallic gray, "Penn State," ASAP promotional .... $16 – 24
11. metallic gray, no markings, ASAP promotional blank .... $35 – 45
12. white, "1st Annual Salmon River Festival," rubber tires on chrome rims, Color Comp promotional.............. $15 – 20
13. white, "Alpenglow," "Apple House," rubber tires on chrome rims, Color Comp promotional....................... $20 – 30
14. white, "FAO Schwarz World of Wheels," rubber tires on chrome rims, Color Comp promotional.............. $60 – 80
15. white, "Mac's Roller Rink, Inc.," rubber tires on chrome rims, Color Comp promotional .... $20 – 30
16. white, "Omps Funeral Home," rubber tires on chrome rims, Color Comp promotional .... $15 – 20
17. white, no markings, rubber tires on chrome rims, Color Comp promotional blank................................ $35 – 45

Chevrolet Panel Van, #245, 1993 White Rose Collectibles, no rear bumper, larger than #215 (also see Chevrolet Panel Van #215)

1. black with gold fenders, "Dallas Stars 1993"............................ $12 – 16

Chevrolet Pro Stocker, 3", #34, 1981

1. white with no markings .... $16 – 24
2. white, "Lightning," "34," metallic gray base.................................... $6 – 8
3. white, "Lightning," "34," red base................................ $16 – 24

4. white, "Lightning," "34," unpainted base.................................. $6 – 8

5. light orange, "4" and stripe....... $3 – 4

6. white, "Pepsi Challenger," "14," red interior.............................. $3 – 4

7. white, "Pepsi Challenger," "14," black interior, Team Matchbox....... $70 – 90
8. white, "Superstar 217," Team Matchbox .... $4 – 5
9. black, "Halley's Comet"........... $9 – 12

10. white and orange, "21," "355 CID".................................. $5 – 6

11. white, "7-Up," red interior......... $4 – 5
12. white, "7-Up," black interior .. $80 – 120
13. blue and white, "70 Bailey Excavating," White Rose Collectibles........... $5 – 6

Chevrolet Sedan Delivery (see Chevrolet 1939 Sedan Delivery)

Chevrolet Silverado 1999, #86, 1999; #49, 2002; 54, 2005

1. red, "Classic Home Builders," chrome plastic grille and base, 5-pack ... $1 – 2
2. red with tool designs, chrome plastic grille and base, 5-pack............ $1 – 2

3. yellow, "Aqua Centre" on sides, multicolor on hood, chrome plastic grille and base, 2000 Ocean Dock 5-pack................................. $1 – 2

4. yellow, "Hammer & Nails Quality Carpentry," black plastic grille and base, 2002 Hammer and Nails....... $1 – 2

5. white, "5 Alarm," "Hangar 34," "67," chrome plastic grille and base, Launcher 5-pack.............................. $1 – 2
6. white, "Action Radar," "Xtreme Mission," red plastic grille and base, 5-pack..$1 – 2

7. white, "Fresh Eggs," "Farm Fresh Dairy," brown mud, chrome plastic grille and base, 1999 On the Farm.................................$1 – 2

8. white; "HQ Chief"; aqua, green, and black design; green plastic grille and base; 2003 Hero City 5-pack #7 .... $2 – 3

9. black, "24/7 M," orange and white graphics, 2005 5-pack H4108 ....$1 – 2

Chevrolet Silverado 1999 4x4, #70, 1999; #11, 2000; #7, 2001; #22, 2002; #65, 1999, international

1. yellow, "Zero," mountain design, 5-pack..................................... $1 – 2

2. purple, "Surfshop — The Hottest Boards on the Beach!" 2000 To the Beach.................................$1 – 2
3. purple, "Surfshop — The Hottest Boards on the Beach!" "Matchbox 2000," 2000 To the Beach .... $3 – 4
4. purple, 2002 Great Outdoors ... $1 – 2

5. black, "Canyon Mission," 1999 Ranger Patrol international ....$3 – 4
6. black, "Game Warden," "Protect Wild Life," 1999 Ranger Patrol US ... $1 – 2

7. white, "Fast Ride Snowboards 22," 2001 Team Tundra .... $1 – 2

Chevrolet Silverado SS, #54, 2005; Superfast #13, 2005; #10, 2006

1. blue, 2005 #54 .... $1 – 2

2. metallic green, 2005 Superfast #13 ....$1 – 2

3. metallic gold, 2006 #10 ....$1 – 2

Chevrolet SSR, #70, 2002; #57, 2003; #18, 2007

1. metallic blue, 2002 Kids' Cars of the Year..................................... $1 – 2

2. yellow, "Tony's Pizza," 2003 #57 Kid's Shoppes.......................$1 – 2

3. yellow, 2006 Shonen Jump's One Piece 5-pack J7421.............$2 – 3

4. yellow, no markings, 2005 Superfast #21 ....$3 – 4

5. metallic bright lime green, 2007 #18, K9480 .... $1 – 2

6. lime green, 2007 #18, K9480 ....$1 – 2

7. metallic purple, 2006 Superfast #21 ....$3 – 4

8. metallic maroon, "Construction," "Building Cities for Tomorrow," white and orange graphics with circular seal...................................$1 – 2

Chevrolet Suburban 2000, #80, 2000; #477, 2000; #60, 2000, international; #40, 2005

1. white, "zero test base," "Matchbox 2000," red and black design, 2000 Snow Explorer......................... $3 – 4

2. white, "zero test base," red and black design, 2000 Snow Explorer ....$1 – 2
3. white with blue logo, ASAP promotional................................ $60 – 80

4. blue with red roof lights, white and yellow, 2003 Hero City 5-pack #2 .... $1 – 2
5. black, "D.A.R.E. America," "Pima County Sheriff," D.A.R.E. .... $4 – 5
6. yellow with red stripes and graphics, Fire Chief, 2005 #40 .... $1 – 2

7. pearl white with white interior, amber windows, "M Construction," "Surveyor," 2005 5-pack H4108 .... $1 – 2

Chevrolet Suburban, 2000 Feature Cars, with opening features, designed to replace Premiere Collection
1. "Chevrolet Police Vehicle," white .... $9 – 12
2. "DC1," "City of Miami," "Fire Rescue," red .... 9 – 12
3. "FDMB," "TR3," white, K.B. Toys exclusive .... $9 – 12
4. "Fire MBFD 45," red and white .... $9 – 12
5. "NYPD," white .... $9 – 12

Chevrolet Suburban Fire Chief (see Chevrolet Suburban 2000)

Chevrolet Super Truck, 1995, #284, White Rose Collectibles
1. "3 — 1995 Super Truck Champion," gold plated, Goodyear rubber tires on black rims .... $20 – 25
2. "Dupont 24," metallic blue and orange, Goodyear rubber tires on black rims .... $4 – 5
3. "Goodwrench 3," black, Goodyear rubber tires on black rims .... $4 – 5
4. "Lance Snacks 43"; blue, white, and red; Goodyear rubber tires on black rims .... $4 – 5
5. "Manheim Auctions 33," purple, Goodyear rubber tires on black rims .... $4 – 5
6. "Quaker State 24," white and green, Goodyear rubber tires on black rims .... $4 – 5
7. "Sears Diehard 1," black, Goodyear rubber tires on black rims .... $4 – 5
8. "The Magic Mile 96," black, Goodyear rubber tires on black rims ...... $8 – 10
9. "Total 6"; white, blue, and red; Goodyear rubber tires on black rims . $4 – 5
10. "Westview Capital 33," purple, Goodyear rubber tires on black rims .. $4 – 5

Chevrolet Tahoe 1997, #46, 1998; #99, 1999; #28, 2000; #33, 2001; #51, 2002

1. bright yellow with "Coca-Cola" and logo on side, Matchbox Collectibles .... $12 – 16
2. yellow with red windows, 2004 Coca-Cola 5-pack .... $6 – 8
3. red with black flare and mud spatter, gray interior, play set .... $12 – 16

4. metallic red, "454," white and yellow design, tan interior, 1998 To the Rescue .... $1 – 2
5. metallic red, "454," "Matchbox Madness," white and yellow design, tan interior, Color Comp promotional ..$80 – 120

6. metallic burgundy, 2005 Superfast #74 .... $3 – 4
7. dark green, silver band, detailed trim, rubber tires on chrome rims, tan and black interior, 1998 First Editions 2-car set .... $5 – 6

8. pale green, "National Parks Forest Ranger" graphics, #72, 2007..$1 – 2
9. bright blue, "Sydney 2000," red interior, 5-pack .... $1 – 2
10. black, "Hammer Demolition," 2002 Hammer and Nails .... $1 – 2
11. black, "Chicago Bulls 23," "Michael Jordan," white interior, NBA 2-pack... $6 – 8

12. black with white doors, "City Airport Police," "K-9 Terminal Patrol," "Airport Security Services," 2006 5-pack J4676 .... $1 – 2
13. metallic gray, "Clogs," blue interior, 1999 At Your Service series, Canada/Mexico issue, not released in US .... $12 – 16
14. metallic gray, "Coca-Cola" and logo, red interior, 5-pack .... $1 – 2
15. white, "Chicago Bulls 23," "Michael Jordan," black interior, NBA 2-pack.. $6 – 8
16. white, "Rough Riders," red interior, ASAP promotional .... $80 – 120
17. white, "Ford Tough Mud Run," red interior, ASAP promotional....... $80 – 120
18. unpainted, rubber tires on chrome rims, tan interior, 1998 First Editions 2-car set .... $5 – 6
19. yellow, "Public Works," 2006 J4674 5-pack .... $3 – 4

Chevrolet Tahoe 1997 Police/Fire Chief, #30, 1998; #78, 1999; #33, 2000; #28, 2001
1. red, "City of Seattle," rubber tires on chrome rims, Premiere Collection .... $6 – 8

2. red, "Fire 3 Dept.," "Dial 911," "Fire Chief," 2000 Fire Fighters..... $1 – 2
3. red, "Fire 3 Dept.," "Dial 911," "Fire Chief," "Matchbox 2000," 2000 Fire Fighters .... $10 – 12
4. red, "5 Alarm," "67," "Hangar 34," Action Launcher Airplane set .... $1 – 2
5. metallic red, "Fire Chief," 2000 Fire Fighters .... $1 – 2
6. blue, "City of Cleveland Ohio," red interior, 2000 Matchbox USA .... $1 – 2
7. blue, "City of Cleveland Ohio," "Matchbox 2000," red interior, 2000 Matchbox USA .... $3 – 4
8. green and yellow, "York Fair Police 1998," US issue .... $8 – 10
9. army green, "Military Police," rubber tires on green rims, Premiere Collection .... $12 – 16
10. blue, "Wisconsin State Police," rubber tires on chrome rims, Premiere Collection .... $12 – 16
11. black, "Matchbox Official Collectors Club" .... $7 – 9

12. **black, "NJ Diecast Collectors Club," 1998, ASAP promotional .. $20 – 25**
13. black, "Official Matchbox Collectors Club," "Matchbox USA Membership Drive 2001," Color Comp promotional.................................. $20 – 25
14. black, "Official Matchbox Collectors Club," "Penn Matchbox Collectors Club 2001," Color Comp promo -tional................................. $20 – 25

15. **metallic gray with red interior, "Matchbox FDMB" on shield with flame graphics, "14," 2001 Action Launcher Fire Truck set .... $3 – 4**
16. white, "Fire Chief," red and black design, 1999 Fire Rescue.................. $1 – 2
17. white, "H2O Force"; red, orange, and black design; 2001 Flame Eaters .. $1 – 2
18. white, "Nassau County Police," stripes, Color Comp promotional....... $20 – 25
19. white, "Open Space Officer," ASAP promotional .... $80 – 120

20. **white, "Police," "Dial 911," blue accents, red trim, 1998 To the Rescue .... $1 – 2**
21. white, "Police," "Matchbox," two-tone blue stripes, Pleasant Books..... $4 – 5
22. white, "Salt Lake City Police," rubber tires on chrome rims, Premiere Collection #23........................... $20 – 25
23. white, "Thomas Hines Retired Finally," ASAP promotional............ $80 – 120
24. white, no markings, ASAP promotional blank............................... $30 – 40

Chevrolet Tahoe 1997, 1999, Taco Bell; Matchbox mold retooled by Strottman International Inc. through a licensing agreement with Mattel. Strottman manufactures toy premiums for Taco Bell. Base is marked "Made in China by S.I.I."

1. white with green, blue, and black design, black windows, Taco Bell premium................................ $3 – 4

Chevrolet Transport Bus, #24, 1999; #73, 2000

1. **blue with red and yellow, 2000 Wilderness Road Trip 5-pack ...... $1 – 2**

2. **green, "National," 1999 Speedy Delivery .... $1 – 2**
3. dark green, "National," 1999 Canadian issue................................ $15 – 20

4. **ivory, "Metro Motel Shuttle" and globe design, 2000 On Tour... $1 – 2**
5. ivory, "Metro Motel Shuttle" and globe design, "Matchbox 2000," 2000 On Tour.................................... $3 – 4
6. red, "Coca-Cola" and polar bears, Premiere Collection...................... $5 – 6
7. white, black interior, clear windows, ASAP promotional blank....... $30 – 45
8. white, "Serving Meridian Since 1927," ASAP promotional............ $80 – 120
9. white, "Happy Birthday Michelle," ASAP promotional..................... $80 – 120

10. **red with white trim, "Transport Services," "Fire Rescue Team," 2006 5-pack J4678 .... $1 – 2**

11. **pearl white with "Airport Shuttle" graphics, 2007 5-pack K9613 .... $1 – 2**

Chevrolet Van, 2 15/16", #68, 1979; #44, 1982; #26, 1991 (similar casting: Chevrolet Van 4x4)

1. red-orange, "Claws," black and white accents, 1997 .... $1 – 2
2. orange, "Matchbox Collectors Club," blue windows, England cast .. $20 – 30
3. orange with blue and red stripes, blue windows, Macau cast, Premiere Collection #13............................... $4 – 5
4. orange with no markings, blue windows, England cast........................ $9 – 12
5. orange with wide blue and narrow red stripes, clear windows, England cast................................ $35 – 45
6. orange with wide blue and narrow red stripes, blue windows, England cast.................................... $4 – 5
7. orange with wide blue and narrow white stripes, blue windows, England cast.................................... $5 – 6
8. orange with wide red and narrow black stripes, blue windows, England cast.................................... $5 – 6
9. orange with wide red and narrow black stripes, green windows, England cast.................................... $7 – 9
10. orange with wide red and narrow black stripes, orange windows, England cast.................................... $5 – 6
11. orange with wide red and narrow black stripes, red windows, England cast.................................... $5 – 6
12. dark orange with wide blue and narrow red stripes, blue windows, England cast................................ $16 – 24
13. fluorescent orange and white, "Purolator 10," blue windows, Thailand cast, Team Convoy, White Rose Collect -ibles.................................... $5 – 6
14. orange-yellow, "DeWalt 08," clear windows, Thailand cast, Team Convoy, White Rose Collectibles........... $5 – 6
15. orange-yellow, "Kodak Film 4 Racing," blue windows, Thailand cast, Team Convoy, White Rose Collectibles...... $5 – 6
16. yellow, "Matchbox Collecting," kangaroo illustration, blue windows, Australia issue................................ $12 – 16
17. yellow, "Pennzoil 30," blue windows, Thailand cast, Team Convoy, White Rose Collectibles........................... $5 – 6
18. yellow, "Pepsi Challenge," blue windows, Macau cast, Team Matchbox.... $5 – 6

19. yellow, "STP Son of a Gun," blue windows, Macau cast, Team Matchbox.......................... $60 – 80
20. green, "Chevy," brown stripes, blue windows, England cast............... $9 – 12
21. green, "Chevy," yellow stripes, blue windows, England cast............... $9 – 12
22. pale blue, "Boston Gas," blue windows, Thailand cast, US issue...... $80 – 120
23. blue and fluorescent orange, "43 STP Oil Treatment," blue windows, Thailand cast, Team Convoy, White Rose Collectibles.................................... $5 – 6
24. blue and dark orange, "21st National Truckin' VAM," Thailand cast, US issue.................................. $9 – 12
25. black, "Automodels 98912244," "Melbourne Motorshow," blue windows, Thailand cast, Australian custom promotional issue............... $16 – 24
26. black, "Automodels 98912244," "Sydney Motorshow," blue windows, Thailand cast, Australian custom promotional issue................................ $16 – 24
27. black, "Goodwrench 5 Time National Champion Dale Earnhardt," blue windows, Thailand cast, Team Convoy, White Rose Collectibles........... $5 – 6
28. black, "Goodwrench Racing Team Pit Crew," blue windows, Macau cast, Team Convoy, White Rose Collectibles............................ $5 – 6
29. black, "Goodwrench Racing Team Pit Crew," blue windows, Thailand cast, Team Convoy, White Rose Collectibles.................................... $5 – 6
30. black, "Pontiac Excitement 2," blue windows, Thailand cast, Team Convoy, White Rose Collectibles........... $5 – 6
31. black and green, "Mello Yello 42," blue windows, Thailand cast, Team Convoy, White Rose Collectibles........... $5 – 6
32. metallic gray, "Vanpire," blue windows, England cast.......................... $4 – 5
33. pearl silver, "Vanpire," blue windows, Macau cast.......................... $4 – 5
34. white, "25" and green accents, blue windows, Thailand cast, Team Convoy, White Rose Collectibles........... $5 – 6
35. white, "Adidas," blue windows, England cast, German issue .... $40 – 50
36. white, "American International Recovery" in black lettering, blue windows, Thailand cast, ASAP promotional issue........................... $120 – 160
37. white, "American International Recovery" in blue lettering, blue windows, Thailand cast, ASAP promotional issue........................... $120 – 160
38. white, "Bulldog Castor Co.," blue windows, China cast, ASAP promotional issue............................... $20 – 30
39. white, "Consolidated Engineering," blue windows, Thailand cast, ASAP promotional issue.................... $120 – 160
40. white, "MCI Scholar Award," blue windows, Thailand cast, ASAP promotional issue........................... $120 – 160
41. white, "Huffman," blue windows, China cast, ASAP promotional issue..$30 – 40
42. white, "RCA," blue windows, China cast, ASAP promotional issue....... $25 – 35
43. white, "Sears Home Central," blue windows, Thailand cast, ASAP promotional issue.............................. $30 – 40
44. white, "Sears May I Reward," blue windows, Thailand cast, ASAP promotional issue.............................. $30 – 40
45. white, "USA 1," blue windows, England cast... $9 – 12
46. white, no markings, blue windows, Thailand cast, ASAP promotional blank............................... $30 – 40
47. white and maroon, "Dr. Pepper," blue windows, Macau cast, Team Matchbox.................................. $8 – 10
48. white and yellow, "Renault Canon Williams," Thailand cast, Nigel Mansell .... $5 – 6
49. white with purple and lime green graphics, 1996 .... $1 – 2

Chevrolet Van, #40, 2007

1. orange with black red and white trim..$1 – 2

Chevrolet Van 4x4, 2 7/8", #68, 1979; #44, 1982; #26, 1991; #96, 1998; #10, 1993, international; #39, 2006 (similar casting: Chevrolet Van)

1. **red, "Claws," black and white rip graphics, 1997 ....$1 – 2**
2. red, "Coca-Cola," polar bears at pool table, 5-pack .... $1 – 2

3. **fluorescent yellow with blue and pink graphics, 1994 ....$1 – 2**
4. green and purple, "23rd National Truck-In"..................................... $9 – 12
5. metallic green, "Ridin' High," no graphics on hood .... $4 – 5
6. metallic green, "Ridin' High," black horseshoes, white "4x4" on hood..$4 – 5
7. metallic green, "Ridin' High," white horseshoes, black "4x4" on hood...... $8 – 10
8. metallic emerald green, black horseshoes, white "4x4" on hood .. $16 – 24

9. **metallic blue with white snowflake and cross on sides, 2003 Hero City 5-pack #8...........................$2 – 4**
10. black, "S.W.A.T. Unit 5," gold star, 5-pack................................... $1 – 2
11. black, "Stegosaurus," skeleton graphics, 5-pack

12. **black with pink and light green graphics, 1993 Off Road 5-pack..................................$1 – 2**

13. **white; "100 Amazing Flavors"; "Ice Cream"; purple, orange, and lime green graphics; 1999 At Your Service..................................$1 – 2**
14. white, "Castrol Racing Team," Australia issue.................................. $8 – 10
15. white, "Matchbox Collectors Club 20th Anniversary, ASAP promotional................................ $12 – 16

16. **white, "Matchbox Motorsports," with yellow, orange, and red design, 1993 ....$1 – 2**

17. white, "Matchbox Racing" .... $3 – 4
18. white, "Surf's Up," wave design, 5-pack .... $1 – 2
19. white, "Tokyo Giants," "Egawa 30," Japanese issue .... $10 – 12
20. white, "Tokyo Giants," "Hara 8," Japanese issue .... $10 – 12
21. white, "Tokyo Giants," "Matsumoto 2," Japanese issue .... $10 – 12
22. white, "Tokyo Giants," "Nakahata 24," Japanese issue .... $10 – 12
23. white, "Tokyo Giants," "Nishimoto 26," Japanese issue .... $10 – 12
24. white, "Tokyo Giants," "Shinozuka 6," Japanese issue .... $10 – 12
25. white, "Tokyo Giants," "Yamakura 15," Japanese issue .... $10 – 12
26. white, no markings, Graffic Traffic, labels included with set .... $12 – 16

27. white with purple and green graphics, 1996 .... $1 – 2

28. metallic gold, 1997 75 Challenge .... $6 – 12
29. white with "Lesney Trucking Rentals" graphics, 2006 #39 .... $1 – 2

30. pearl white with "Matchbox" logo, thick blue and thin red stripes, 2007 #39 (K2616 on 2006 package) .... $1 – 2

31. aqua with "The Mystery Machine" graphics, Scooby-Doo! 5-pack L1574, 2007 .... $5 – 6
32. turquoise with "Manny" graphics, "Ice Age 2: The Meltdown" 5-pack J4720 .... $2 – 3

33. metallic gold with white, orange, and black graphics, "370 Racing Parts," 2006 5-pack J4675 .... $1 – 2

Chevy (see Chevrolet)

Chevy Pro Stocker (see Chevrolet Pro Stocker)

Chevy SSR (see Chevrolet SSR)

Chevy Van (see Chevrolet Van)

Chevy Van 4x4 (see Chevrolet Van 4x4)

Chop Suey Motorcycle, 2¾", #49, 1973

1. magenta with chrome handlebars .... $400 – 450
2. magenta with orange handlebars .... $16 – 24
3. magenta with red handlebars .... $12 – 16
4. magenta with black handlebars .... $20 – 25
5. magenta with dark red handlebars .... $12 – 16

Chrysler Atlantic, #11, 1997; #19, 1998, #39, 1999; #34, 2000

1. metallic gold with tan interior, 1997 .... $3 – 4
2. metallic gold with black interior, chrome wheel hubs, 1997 75 Challenge .... $6 – 12
3. metallic gold with black interior, black wheel hubs, 1997 75 Challenge .... $30 – 40

4. metallic gold with brown interior, 1998 Cool Concepts .... $1 – 2

5. metallic gold with light tan interior, 1999 Car Shows .... $1 – 2
6. metallic gold with brown interior, rubber tires on chrome rims, "Matchbox," "www.Matchboxtoys.com" .... $9 – 12
7. metallic gold with brown and tan interior, rubber tires on chrome rims, Chrysler gift set .... $4 – 6
8. metallic gold with tan interior, "Merry Christmas 1997 Seasons Greetings from Color Comp," Color Comp promotional .... $100 – 150

Chrysler Panel Cruiser, #30, 2002

1. metallic gold with wood panel graphics, 2002 Cool Rides .... $1 – 2

2. white, "Richie's Burgerama," 2003 Mom and Pop Shops .... $1 – 2

Chrysler PT Cruiser Convertible, #72, 2003

1. metallic red with "72," 2003 Car Shop .... $1 – 2

2. yellow, 2005 Superfast #10 .... $3 – 4

3. metallic red, 2006 Superfast #10 .... $3 – 4

4. yellow with "Diego" illustration, 2007 Nick Jr. Go Diego Go 5-pack L1575 .... $2 – 3

Chrysler Voyager, #262, 1994, Belgium, modified casting of #64/#68 Dodge Caravan

1. blue with detailed trim .... $16 – 24
2. blue with detailed trim, "Kipling" label on roof .... $16 – 20

Citroen 15CV (European model), 3", #44, 1983

1. dark green with chrome base, China cast, 1983 Dinky Collection from Matchbox .... $9 – 12
2. dark blue with chrome base, Macau cast .... $3 – 4

3. black with chrome base, England cast .... $3 – 4

4. black with chrome base, Macau cast .... $3 – 4
5. black with gray base, China cast .. $5 – 7

Citroen CX Ambulance (European model), 3", #12, 1980 (similar casting: Citroen CX Station Wagon)

1. white with red interior, metallic gray base, blue windows, "Ambulance," England cast .... $3 – 5
2. white with red interior, black base, blue windows, "Ambulance," England cast .... $3 – 5
3. white with red interior, unpainted base, blue windows, "Ambulance," England cast .... $3 – 5
4. white with red interior, metallic gray base, blue windows, "Marine Division Police," Two Pack, England cast .. $3 – 5
5. white with red interior, unpainted base, blue windows, "Marine Division Police," Two Pack, England cast .... $3 – 5
6. white with red interior, pearly silver base, blue windows, "Marine Division Police," Two Pack, Macau cast .. $5 – 7

Citroen CX Station Wagon, 3", #12, 1979 (similar casting: Citroen CX Ambulance)

1. metallic light blue with ivory interior, metallic gray base, blue windows .... $12 – 16

2. metallic light blue with ivory interior, metallic gray base, clear windows .... $6 – 9

3. metallic light blue with yellow interior, metallic gray base, clear windows .... $6 – 9
4. metallic light blue with tan interior, unpainted base, clear windows .. $6 – 9
5. metallic light blue with tan interior, black base, clear windows .... $6 – 9
6. metallic light blue with tan interior, dark gray base, clear windows .... $6 – 9
7. metallic light blue with tan interior, metallic gray base, clear windows .... $6 – 9
8. metallic dark blue with ivory interior, metallic gray base, clear windows .... $6 – 9
9. metallic dark blue with yellow interior, metallic gray base, clear windows .... $6 – 9
10. metallic dark blue with yellow interior, metallic gray base, blue windows .. $6 – 9
11. metallic dark blue with red interior, metallic gray base, clear windows .... $200 – 275
12. yellow with red interior, black base, clear windows .... $6 – 9
13. yellow with red interior, dark gray base, clear windows .... $6 – 9
14. yellow with red interior, black base, clear windows, "Team" in blue, Two Pack .... $5 – 7
15. yellow with red interior, black base, clear windows, "Team" in black, Two Pack .... $5 – 7
16. yellow with red interior, dark gray base, clear windows, "Team" in blue ... $5 – 7
17. yellow with red interior, black base, blue windows, "Team" in black, Two Pack .... $5 – 7
18. yellow with red interior, black base, blue windows, no markings, Two Pack .... $6 – 9
19. yellow with red interior, metallic gray base, clear windows, no markings, Two Pack .... $6 – 9

Citroen DS19, yellow, 2½", #66, 1959

1. gray plastic wheels .... $50 – 60
2. silver plastic wheels .... $120 – 130

Citroen SM, 3", #51, 1972

1. metallic orange with orange interior .... $25 – 35
2. metallic orange with ivory interior .... $10 – 12

3. metallic orange with yellow interior .... $10 – 12

4. metallic orange with tan interior .... $10 – 12
5. metallic blue, no markings .... $16 – 24
6. metallic blue, "8" .... $10 – 12
7. metallic blue with roof rack ... $60 – 80

City Bus, #19, 2005; Superfast #60, 2005; #33, 2006; #35, 2007

1. white, "Metro Shuttle," "MBTA," 2005 .... $1 – 2
2. white with silver red and orange, black trim, "METRO CITY BUS," 2005 Superfast #60 .... $3 – 4

3. silver with orange trim, "Native American Iconography & Symbolism," 2006 #33 .... $1 – 2

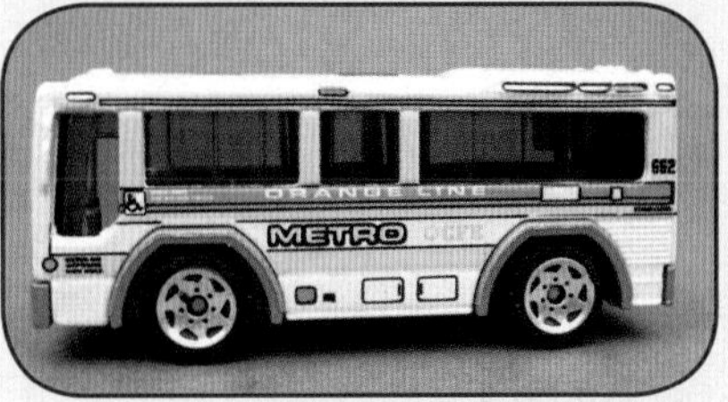

4. white with orange, yellow, silver, and black trim, "Metro Orange Line," 2006 5-pack J4674 .... $1 – 2

5. yellow with "Airport Express" graphics, 2007 5-pack K9613 .... $1 – 2

6. metallic rose and silver, "Los Angeles Metro Rapid" graphics, 2007 #35, L4817 .... $1 – 2

7. white with "Go Diego Go" graphics, 2007 Nick Jr. Go Diego Go 5-pack L1575 .... $2 – 3

City Police, #66, 2004

1. white with blue and red-orange cityscape graphics, "Matchbox Police Hero City," 2004 #66 .... $1 – 2

2. metal flake green, Danny Phantom illustration, 2006 Nickelodeon 5-pack H5774....................$1 – 2

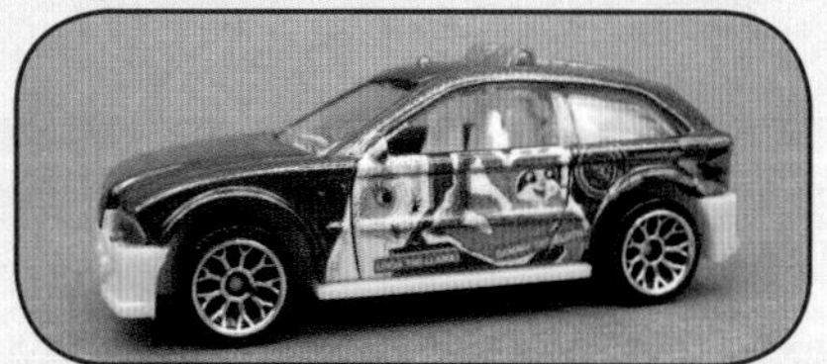

3. metallic purple with yellow base, white interior, 2006 Nickelodeon 5-pack H4108.....................$1 – 2

Claas Combine Harvester, 3", #65, 1967

1. red with black plastic wheels .... $15 – 20

Clipper, fantasy car with opening cockpit, 3", #39, 1973

1. hot pink, yellow interior, amber windows, unpainted base, chrome tailpipes............................ $200 – 300
2. metallic magenta, yellow interior, amber windows, green base, chrome tailpipes................................ $12 – 16
3. metallic magenta, yellow interior, amber windows, green base, white tailpipes................................ $12 – 16
4. metallic magenta, yellow interior, amber windows, unpainted base, chrome tailpipes................................ $12 – 16
5. metallic magenta, yellow interior, amber windows, unpainted base, white tailpipes................................ $12 – 16
6. metallic magenta, yellow interior, clear windows, green base, chrome tailpipes................................ $12 – 16
7. metallic magenta, yellow interior, clear windows, green base, white tailpipes................................ $12 – 16

Combine Harvester (see Claas Combine Harvester)

Combine Harvester, 2¾", #51, 1978; #89, 1999; #47, 2000; #3, 2000, Germany

1. red with yellow rotor and chute .. $5 – 6
2. orange with yellow rotor and chute, no origin cast, Brazil issue .... $400 – 600
3. orange-yellow with red rotor and chute, "2" and stripes, Motor City..................................... $1 – 2
4. orange-yellow with maroon rotor and chute, "2" and stripes, Motor City..................................... $1 – 2

5. yellow with red rotor and chute, "2" with stripes, Motor City/1978 Farm Set ....$2 – 3

6. lime green and blue with yellow rotor, lime green chute, Matchbox Preschool/Live 'N Learn .... $7 – 10
7. green with yellow rotor and chute, German issue .... $4 – 5
8. dark green with yellow rotor and chute, no origin cast, Brazil issue ..$400 – 600

9. dark green with yellow rotor and chute, China cast, 2000 Farming ....$1 – 2

10. dark green with yellow rotor and chute, "Matchbox 2000," China cast, 2000 Farming................................ $3 – 4

11. dark blue with yellow rotor and chute, 1999 On the Farm .....$1 – 2

Command Vehicle, 3¼", #54, 1984, radar, beacons and lights on forward part of roof (similar castings: Airport Foam Pumper, Mobile Home, NASA Tracking Vehicle)

1. army green, "9," red and white diagonal stripes, black wheels, Commando Strike Team.....................$4 – 5

2. army green, "9," red and white diagonal stripes, chrome wheels, Commando Strike Team........................ $20 – 25

3. blue with white graphics, "Police Command Center," 1997 Police 5-pack.................................$2 – 3

4. black, "LS150," yellow design, black wheels, Commando Dagger Force ....$4 – 5

5. black with green and tan camouflage, 5-pack ....$2 – 3

6. white, "NASA Space Shuttle Command Center," Macau cast................ $3 – 4
7. white, "NASA Space Shuttle Command Center," Thailand cast.............. $1 – 2

Commer 30 CWT "Nestle's" Van, gray plastic wheels, 2⅜", #69, 1959

1. maroon...........................$30 – 40

2. dark red .... $30 – 40
3. red .... $60 – 70

Commer Ice Cream Canteen, 2 7/16", #47, 1963
1. blue with gray plastic wheels .... $150 – 175

2. blue with black plastic wheels.......................... $30 – 35
3. metallic blue with black plastic wheels...................... $100 – 120
4. ivory with square roof decal, striped side decals, black wheels...... $60 – 70
5. ivory with oval roof decal, plain side decals, black plastic wheels .. $40 – 50

Commer Milk Delivery Truck, 2 1/4", #21, 1961
1. silver wheels...................... $25 – 35
2. gray wheels....................... $65 – 75

3. black wheels .... $15 – 25

Commer Pickup, 2 1/2", #50, 1958
1. dark tan with metal wheels ... $75 – 90
2. light tan with metal wheels ... $75 – 90
3. light tan with gray plastic wheels............................ $80 – 100
4. dark tan with gray plastic wheels........................... $80 – 100
5. dark tan with silver plastic wheels.......................... $130 – 160
6. red and white with silver plastic wheels........................ $750 – 1000
7. red and gray with silver plastic wheels.......................... $175 – 225
8. red and gray with gray plastic wheels.......................... $135 – 165
9. red and gray with black plastic wheels.......................... $130 – 160

Compressor Truck (see Bedford Compressor Truck, Thames Trader Compressor Truck)

Corvette (see Chevrolet Corvette)

Cosmic Blues, 3", #26, 1980; #41, 1993 (similar castings: Big Banger, Flame Out, Pi -Eyed Piper, Red Rider)
1. white with blue "Cosmic Blues," clear windows, Hong Kong cast .... $40 – 50
2. white with chrome exhausts, blue "Cosmic Blues," blue windows, Hong Kong cast .... $4 – 5
3. white with chrome exhausts, blue "Cosmic Blues," blue windows, Macau cast .... $1 – 2
4. white with chrome exhausts, blue "Cosmic Blues," blue windows, China cast .... $1 – 2
5. blue with chrome exhausts, white "Cosmic Blues," blue windows, China cast .... $1 – 2
6. blue with black exhausts, white "Cosmic Blues," blue windows, China cast..$1 – 2

7. bright orange-yellow with black exhausts, "Hemi," magenta and black design, 1993..............$1 – 2

8. black with gray exhausts, fluorescent orange and white flames, 1996 .... $1 – 2

9. metallic green with orange and white flames, 1997 ....$1 – 2
10. orange-red with gray exhausts, "Dandelion," "Dyslexicon" .... $9 – 12
11. metallic gold with black exhausts, 1997 75 Challenge....................... $6 – 12

Cosmobile, 2 7/8", #68, 1975
1. metallic red upper, beige lower, chrome interior, amber windows .... $16 – 24
2. metallic red upper, beige lower, white interior, amber windows .... $16 – 24
3. metallic avocado upper, black lower, chrome interior, purple windows, Adventure 2000 .... $30 – 40
4. metallic avocado upper, black lower, white interior, purple windows, Adventure 2000 .... $30 – 40
5. metallic avocado upper, black lower, chrome interior, amber windows, Adventure 2000 .... $30 – 40
6. metallic blue upper, black lower, chrome interior, purple windows, Adventure 2000.............................. $50 – 60
7. metallic blue upper, yellow lower, chrome interior, amber windows............................... $12 – 16
8. metallic blue upper, yellow lower, white interior, amber windows .... $12 – 16

Cougar (see Mercury Cougar 1968)

Crane, #72, 2001; #24, 2003 (see Rescue Crane)

Crane Truck, 2 15/16", #49, 1976
1. red with yellow boom, green windows, German issue .... $70 – 80
2. yellow with yellow boom, green windows.................................. $5 – 6
3. yellow with black boom, blue windows................................. $9 – 12
4. yellow with black boom, green windows.................................. $5 – 6
5. yellow with black boom, purple windows.................................. $5 – 6
6. yellow with black boom, red windows.................................. $5 – 6

Crash Hopper, grasshopper wrecker, #12, 2004 (MB622)

bright green, 2004 Ultra Heroes ... $1 – 2

Crime Capper (see Police Hat)

Critter Cruncher Exterminator Truck (see All-Terrain Fire Tanker)

Crown Victoria (see Ford Crown Victoria)

Cycle with Sidecar (see Police Motorcycle)

D

D.I.R.T. Modified Racer, #217, 1992, White Rose Collectibles
1. "35," blue .... $7 – 9
2. "Alfair Studio 21"; red, white, and black .... $7 – 9
3. "Auto Palace 72," red .... $6 – 8
4. "BR Dewitt 12," orange and yellow.. $7 – 9
5. "Doherty Bros. 115," white and black .... $7 – 9
6. "Freightliner 6," white .... $6 – 8
7. "Kinney 9," orange and white .... $6 – 8
8. "Philis Chevrolet 1," brown........ $6 – 8
9. "Pontiac — Kneisel Race Cars 44," white and orange .... $7 – 9
10. "R.P. LeFrois 14," white........... $7 – 9
11. "Smith Brothers 74," dark blue and white.................................. $7 – 9
12. "Steak Out Restaurants 1," white...$7 – 9
13. "Turbo Blue 7X," light orange .... $6 – 8
14. "Wheels 91," light orange .... $6 – 8

15. "White Rose Collectibles 1," light blue .... $70 - 90

D-Type Jaguar (see Jaguar D-Type)

DAF 3300 Space Cab, #15, 1999
1. orange, "DAF 3300 SC56"....... $3 - 4

DAF Girder Truck, $2\frac{5}{8}$", #58, 1968
1. **cream with 8 red girders in back, black plastic wheels, 1968.. $12 - 16**
2. cream with 8 red girders in back, Superfast wheels, 1970 ...... $70 - 90
3. metallic gold with 8 red girders in back, Superfast wheels, 1970 ...... $24 - 32

DAF Tipper Container Truck, 3", #47, 1968
1. blue with yellow container, gray container cover, black plastic wheels.. $25 - 30
2. metallic silver with yellow container, gray container cover, black plastic wheels.................................. $6 - 9
3. metallic silver with yelow container, gray container cover, Superfast wheels, 1970 .... $30 - 40

Daimler Ambulance, $1\frac{7}{8}$", #14, 1956
1. .... $50 - 65

Daimler Ambulance, $2\frac{1}{8}$", #14, 1958
1. metal wheels .... $35 - 45

2. **gray plastic wheels .... $30 - 40**
3. silver plastic wheels......... $100 - 125

Daimler London Bus, 3", #74, 1966
1. "Baron of Beef," red, Superfast wheels.......................... $200 - 250
2. "Beefeater Gin," red, Superfast wheels.......................... $400 - 500
3. "Esso Extra Petrol," red, black plastic wheels.............................. $15 - 20
4. "Esso Extra Petrol," red, Superfast wheels, ... $20 - 30
5. "Esso Extra Petrol," green, black plastic wheels.............................. $15 - 20

6. **"Esso Extra Petrol" decals, cream, black plastic wheels......... $20 - 30**

7. **"Esso Extra Petrol" labels, cream, black plastic wheels......... $16 - 24**
8. "Fly Cyprus Airways," "London Frankfurt Athens Nicosia," red, Superfast wheels.......................... $350 - 450
9. "Inn on the Park," red, Superfast wheels .... $250 - 300
10. "The Miniature Vehicle," "N.A.M.C.," red, Superfast wheels...... $250 - 300

Datsun 126X, 3", #33, 1973; BR5-6, 1985
1. yellow with orange base, no markings .... $12 - 16
2. yellow with unpainted base, no markings .... $30 - 45
3. yellow with orange base, orange and red flames .... $16 - 24

4. **yellow with orange base, black and red flames .... $16 - 24**
5. dark blue with black windows, England cast, Super GT BR5-6, 1985 .... $4 - 6
6. silver with black windows, England cast, Super GT BR5-6, 1985 .... $4 - 6
7. silver with black windows, China cast, Super GT BR5-6, 1985 .... $8 - 10
8. powder blue with black windows, China cast, Super GT BR5-6, 1985 .... $3 - 5
9. beige with black windows, China cast, Super GT BR5-6, 1985 .... $3 - 5

Datsun 260Z 2+2, #67, 1978
1. metallic burgundy, doors open, Lesney England cast.......................... $4 - 5
2. metallic purple, doors open, Lesney England cast............................. $9 - 12
3. metallic magenta, doors open, Lesney England cast.......................... $6 - 8
4. metallic blue, doors open, Lesney England cast............................. $7 - 9
5. black, doors cast shut, black interior, clear windows, Matchbox International England cast.......................... $5 - 6
6. black, doors cast shut, black interior, opaque windows, Matchbox International England cast .... $9 - 12
7. black, doors cast shut, white interior, clear windows, Matchbox International England cast.......................... $3 - 4
8. black, doors cast shut, white interior, opaque windows, Matchbox International England cast .... $9 - 12
9. metallic gray, doors open, red interior, Lesney England cast .... $3 - 4
10. metallic gray, doors open, light yellow interior, Lesney England cast..... $7 - 9
11. metallic gray, doors cast shut, red interior, black base, clear windows, China cast .... $9 - 12
12. metallic gray, doors cast shut, black interior, black base, clear windows, China cast......................... $12 - 16
13. metallic gray, doors cast shut, black interior, black base, clear windows, Matchbox International England cast .... $6 - 8
14. metallic gray, doors cast shut, black interior, metallic gray base, clear windows, Matchbox International England cast .... $4 - 5
15. metallic gray, doors cast shut, black interior, opaque windows, Matchbox International England cast....... $9 - 12
16. metallic gray with green and blue accents, doors cast shut, black interior, China cast, Chinese issue.. $150 - 200
17. metallic gray with red and black accents, doors open, white interior, Lesney England cast .... $3 - 4
18. metallic gray with two-tone blue accents, doors cast shut, black interior, black base, Matchbox International England cast .... $3 - 4
19. metallic gray with two-tone blue accents, doors cast shut, black interior, metallic gray base, Matchbox International England cast.............................. $5 - 6

Datsun 280ZX, hood doesn't open, 3", #24, 1981
1. black with white interior........... $3 - 4
2. black with red interior .... $4 - 5

Datsun 280ZX 2+2, hood opens, 3", #24, 1983

1. **black with gold pin stripes..... $3 - 4**

2. **black, "Turbo ZX," silver wheels............................... $3 - 4**
3. black, "Turbo ZX," gold wheels .. $9 - 12
4. white, "Turbo 33," Japan issue... $9 - 12

5. **black with orange, yellow, and white, "Turbo" ....$4 – 5**
6. gray with orange, yellow, and white accents, Laser Wheels .... $7 – 8
7. red with black and orange with armaments, Roadblasters .... $7 – 9
8. metallic red, China issue ...... $60 – 80

Datsun 280ZX Police Car, #44, 1987, Japan
1. white and black, Japanese pictograms, red dome lights, tan interior, Macau cast .... $9 – 12

Datsun Fairlady Z, #78, 1981; #5, 1981, Japan
1. red, Japan cast, Japan issue .... $16 – 24
2. black, "Z," Hong Kong cast, issued in US as Phantom Z .... $6 – 8
3. black, no markings, Australia issue and US Speedsticks issue.............. $3 – 4
4. pearl white, no markings, Australia issue .... $16 – 24
5. pearl silver, Japan cast, Japanese issue .... $16 – 24

Deep Diver (see Submersible)

Delivery Truck, #48, 2000; #28, 2000, international; #41, 2006 (similar casting: Flatbed Truck)
1. red with white container, barn and rooster labels .... $1 – 2
2. red with white container, barn and rooster, "Matchbox 2000"........ $3 – 4
3. metallic dark orange with gray container, "Test Mission," 2000 Space Mission 5-pack .... $1 – 2
4. dark orange with bright blue container, "MC – 09" and rhinoceros head, Matchbox City 5-pack .... $1 – 2
5. fluorescent yellow with black box, rhino graphics, 2003 Hero City 5-pack #4 .... $1 – 2
6. white with brown box "Zolo" illustration, 2006 Shonen Jump's One Piece 5-pack J7421 .... $1 – 2
7. blue with white box, 2006 Superman 5-pack J4725 .... $1 – 2
8. yellow, "DHL," #41 Fast Freight Truck, 2006 .... $1 – 2

Demolition Machine/Wall Eater, #38, 2001; #25, 2003

1. **white with blue boom, dark blue base, "Matchbox 43," 2001 #38 ....$1 – 2**

2. **metallic blue with orange boom, 2003 Bridge Crew #25.........$1 – 2**

3. **orange with blue boom, 2003 Hero City 5-pack #9 ....$1 – 2**

Dennis Fire Escape, #9, 1955
1. no front bumper, no number cast 2¹/₄"................................ $45 – 60

Dennis Fire Escape, with front bumper, number 9 cast, 2³/₈", #9, 1957
1. metal wheels...................... $50 – 60
2. gray plastic wheels.......... $125 – 150

Dennis Fire Escape, 1988, commemorative replica of #9, 2¹/₄"
1. made in China, red reels (1988), from 40th Anniversary Gift Set .... $8 – 10
2. yellow reels, 1991 Matchbox Originals .... $2 – 4

Dennis Refuse Truck, dark blue with gray container, 2¹/₂", #15, 1963
1. no porthole in rear hatch...... $45 – 50
2. porthole in rear hatch.......... $15 – 20

Dennis Sabre Fire Engine, open back with raising ladder; #44, 2002; #61, 2003; #34, 2004; #46, 2006
1. red, "44," white and silver accents, 2002 Airport Alarm .... $1 – 2

2. **red, "Matchbox," with white, blue, and yellow graphics, metallic gray ladder, white boom, blue windows, 2003 Pumper Squad series #61 ......$1 – 2**

3. yellow with red, maroon, silver, and white graphics, red windows, metallic gray plastic base, 2003 Hero City 5-pack #1 .... $1 – 2

4. **metallic gray with red ladder and boom, "Metro Alarm," 2004 #34 ....$1 – 2**

5. **metallic red with metallic gray ladder and boom, amber windows, 2006 #46 ....$1 – 2**

6. **red with white front and trim, 2005 Superfast #11 ....$3 – 4**

Dennis Sabre Ladder Fire Truck (see Dennis Sabre Fire Engine)

Dennis Sabre Fire Truck, closed back, ladder on roof, #68, 1999, international; #30, 2001; #13, 2005; #46, 2006
1. red, "35 – 3," white dashes, silver panels, blue windows, white ladder .. $3 – 4

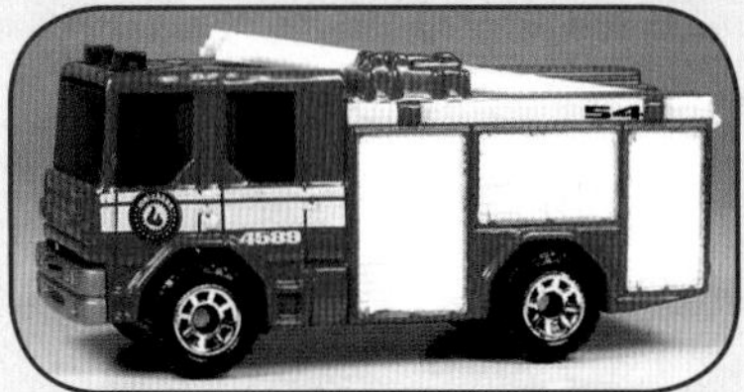

2. **red with white stripes and panels, "4589," "54," "Matchbox" in circle, blue windows, white ladder, 2000 5 Alarm 5-pack ....$1 – 2**

3. **red with silver panels, "9-1-1 Emergency," yellow and white stripes, shield .... $4 – 5**
4. red, "London Fire Brigade," silver panels, yellow windows, metallic gray ladder .... $3 – 4

5. **red, "Metro Alarm," "WR-1168," yellow bands, 5-pack................ $1 – 2**
6. red with yellow and silver panels, 1999 Fire Rescue international......... $3 – 4

7. **black, "Oregon 33," "Mount Hood Fire Rescue," volcano and mountain graphics, red windows, Matchbox Across America 50th Birthday Series #33 — Western Collection .... $4 – 5**
8. red with wide white and gray bands on sides, blue windows, metallic gray ladder, 2005 #13...................... $1 – 2

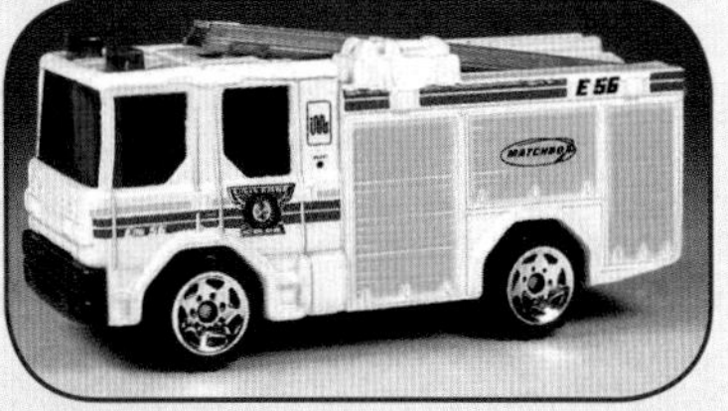

9. **white with yellow panels, "Universe Action Base," red stripes, shield, metallic gray ladder, blue windows, 2001 Flame Eaters .... $1 – 2**
10. white with red stripe on sides, "Alarm," yellow ladder, red windows........ $3 – 4
11. white with multicolored graphics, blue ladder, red windows................ $1 – 2

12. **yellow with red graphics trimmed in white, white ladder, red windows, 2003 Hero City 5-pack #7 .... $1 – 2**
13. yellow with red graphics trimmed in white, red ladder, red windows, 2003 Hero City 5-pack #2 .... $1 – 2
14. red with white and gray trim, 2005 #13.................................... $1 – 2

Desert Dawg 4x4 Jeep, $2\frac{5}{8}$", #20, 1982; #14, 1987

1. white with red roof, "Desert Dawg" graphics, England cast............ $2 – 4

Desert Thunder V16, #63, 2007 .... $1 – 2

DeTomaso Pantera, 3", #8, 1975; BR 39 – 40, 1986 (similar castings: Greased Lightning)

1. white with blue base, "8" label on hood .... $8 – 12
2. white with umpainted base, "8" label on hood .... $8 – 12
3. white with blue base, "9" label on hood .... $15 – 20
4. white with blue base, sunburst label on hood .... $20 – 25
5. white with lavender base, "8" label on hood, Brazil issue............... $60 – 80
6. blue with black base .... $4 – 6
7. maroon, China cast, Super GT BR 39 – 40, 1986............................ $3 – 5
8. orange, China cast, Super GT BR 39 – 40, 1986............................ $3 – 5
9. fluorescent yellow, China cast, Neon Racers BR 39 – 40, 1986....... $4 – 6

DeTomaso Pantera Greased Lightning, 3", #8, 1983

1. red with white base, black interior, Macau cast.......................... $6 – 9
2. red with white base, black interior, Hong Kong cast .... $6 – 9

Diesel Road Roller (see Road Roller, Diesel)

Diesel Shunter Locomotive, 3", #24, 1978

1. dark green with red metal undercarriage, red base, "Rail Freight".. $9 – 12
2. dark green with red metal undercarriage, red base, "D1496-RF"..... $9 – 12
3. yellow with red metal undercarriage, red base, "D1496-RF," England cast .... $5 – 6
4. yellow with red metal undercarriage, red base, "D1496-RF," no origin cast .... $80 – 120
5. yellow with yellow plastic undercarriage, black base, "D1496-RF," England cast .... $80 – 120
6. yellow with red plastic undercarriage, black base, "D1496-RF," Macau cast, Motor City............................ $3 – 4

Dirt Bike, #93, 1999; #13, 2000; #33, 2001; #73, 1999, international

1. red with black seat, blue-gray rider with brown jacket, 1999 Mountain Cruisers .... $1 – 2

2. **red with black seat, yellow rider with red jacket, 2000 To the Beach.................................. $1 – 2**
3. red with black seat, red rider with black jacket, "Matchbox 2000," 2000 To the Beach .... $3 – 4
4. red with black seat, red rider with black jacket, 2000 To the Beach....... $1 – 2
5. orange with purple seat, white rider with red jacket, 2001 Sand Blasters............................... $1 – 2

6. **yellow with blue seat, red rider with black jacket, Wilderness Tour 5-pack.................................. $1 – 2**
7. yellow, blue rider with orange jacket, 5-pack................................. $1 – 2

Dirt Hauler Quarry Truck (see Faun Earth Mover Dump Truck)

Dirt Machine, #37, 2001; #19, 2002; #67 2003 (see Super Dozer)

Dirt Modified Racer (see D.I.R.T. Modified Racer)

Dodge Airflow Van 1938, #338, 1998, Matchbox Collectibles

1. "Catamount Porter," mustard yellow with black roof........................... $9 – 12
2. "Continental Aero," "Purple Plastic Inserts...," purple................. $9 – 12
3. "Penn Brewery St. Nikolaus Bock Bier," red .... $9 – 12
4. "Zephyr Golden Ale," yellow..... $9 – 12

Dodge Caravan, $2\frac{7}{8}$", #68, 1984; #64, 1985, international

1. red, "Red Arrows," "Royal Air Force," red door, Thailand cast, Motor City .... $4 – 5

2. burgundy, "Expressly for Dodge Las Vegas," England cast .... $90 – 120
3. burgundy with black stripe, England cast, US issue .... $18 – 24
4. black, "Adidas" on hood, silver stripe, black door, England cast, US issue .... $275 – 325
5. black with green and yellow stripes, black door, Macau cast, Dutch issue .... $9 – 12
6. black with no stripe, England cast .... $4 – 6
7. black with silver side stripe, black door, England cast.......................... $4 – 5
8. black with silver side stripe, black door, Macau cast.......................... $3 – 4
9. black with silver and gold stripes, black door, Macau cast .... $3 – 4
10. black with silver and gold stripes, black door, China cast...................... $4 – 5
11. black with silver and gold stripes, black door, Manaus cast, Brazil issue .... $40 – 50
12. gray and blue, "British Airways," gray door, barcode base, Thailand cast, Intercom City..................... $40 – 50
13. gray and blue, "British Airways," gray door, Thailand cast, Motor City.. $4 – 5
14. metallic gray with black stripe, gray door, England cast.................. $7 – 9
15. metallic gray with no stripe, black door, England cast.......................... $6 – 8
16. white, "Caravan" and stripe, white door, Macau cast........................... $3 – 4
17. white, "Fly Virgin Atlantic," white door, Macau cast, gift set .... $4 – 5
18. white, "NASA Shuttle Personnel," white door, Macau cast................... $4 – 5
19. white, "Pan Am," white door, Macau cast, gift set.......................... $4 – 5

Dodge Cattle Truck (also see Dodge Stake Truck)

Dodge Cattle Truck, with cattle and ramp tailgate, $2^{1}/_{2}$", #37, 1966

1. **yellow with gray cattle compartment, metal base, black plastic wheels............................$12 – 16**
2. yellow with gray cattle compartment, plastic base, black plastic wheels .... $20 – 25
3. yellow with brown cattle compartment, metal base .... $120 – 160
4. yellow with gray cattle compartment, Superfast wheels, 1970 ..... $30 – 40
5. yellow with metallic gray cattle compartment, Superfast wheels, 1970..$30 – 40

Dodge Challenger, with hood grilles, no scoop, $2^{15}/_{16}$", #1, 1976 (similar casting: Revin' Rebel, Dodge Challenger Hot Rod)

1. **red with chrome interior, dot-dash wheels..............................$8 – 10**
2. red with white interior, 5-arc wheels.................................. $4 – 6
3. red with red interior .... $9 – 12

4. **blue with red interior ....$5 – 8**

Dodge Challenger, Revin' Rebel, cast hood scoop, $2^{7}/_{8}$", #1, US, 1982; #34, international, 1991

1. **orange with blue roof, "Revin' Rebel" ....$5 – 8**
2. orange with blue roof, no markings .... $10 – 15

3. **orange with white roof, "Revin' Rebel" ....$8 – 12**

Dodge Challenger Hot Rod, plastic hood scoop, $2^{7}/_{8}$", #1, 1983

1. **yellow with black roof, "Toyman," England cast.......................$3 – 5**
2. yellow with black roof, "Toyman," Macao cast .... $2 – 4
3. yellow with black roof, "Toyman," China cast .... $2 – 4
4. yellow with black roof, no markings, China cast............................. $3 – 5

5. **white with white roof, no markings, (Graffic Traffic) ....$5 – 7**

6. **light blue with black roof, "Challenger," (Action Pack with accessories) ....$4 – 6**
7. white with black roof, "Toyman," China cast .... $4 – 6

8. **metallic blue with white roof, "Hemi," "Challenger," 1993..............$2 – 4**

9. **fluorescent yellow with black spatter accents, black roof, hot pink interior, 1994 ....$1 – 2**

10. **white with purple spatter accents, black roof, fuchsia interior, 1996 .... $1 – 2**

11. dark purple with black roof, fluorescent yellow hood scoop and interior, gray plastic base, Thailand cast........ $2 – 4

12. dark purple with black roof, fluorescent yellow hood scoop and interior, chrome plastic base, China cast.................................. $4 – 6
13. dark purple with black roof, fluorescent yellow hood scoop and interior, gray plastic base, China cast .... $45 – 60
14. red with black roof, chrome wheels, rubber tires (Premiere Collection #11)................................... $5 – 8

15. bright green with black hood scoop, roof, and zebra-stripe graphics .... $2 – 3

Dodge Challenger/Mitsubishi Galant Eterna, 2⅞", #63, 1980; #79, 1981; #J-22, 1979, Japan

1. bright red with cream interior, black base, J-22, 1979, Made in Japan, Japan issue..................... $20 – 25
2. yellow with cream interior, black base, J-22, 1979, Made in Japan, Japan issue................................ $20 – 25
3. two-tone green with white "2," white interior, Japan cast .... $16 – 24
4. green with black "2," green interior, Japan cast........................ $16 – 24
5. light green, "Hot Points," Hong Kong cast, issued in US as Hot Points Challenger .... $6 – 8
6. light green, Hong Kong cast, Australia issue and US Speedsticks issue.. $3 – 4
7. dark green, Hong Kong cast, Australia issue and US Speedsticks issue.. $3 – 4

Dodge Charger (see Orange Peel Dodge Charger)

Dodge Charger Concept, #61, 2005; Superfast #75, 2005; #12, 2006; #50, 2007
1. metallic red, 2005 #61 .... $1 – 2
2. metallic gray, 2005 Superfast #75.................................... $4 – 5

3. dark teal blue, 2006 #12...... $1 – 2

4. yellow, 2007 Superfast #75.. $3 – 4
5. black with white sides, "Police," 2007 #50.................................... $1 – 2

Dodge Charger Mk III concept car, 2⅞", #52, 1970
1. metallic red with metallic green base................................ $12 – 16
2. metallic magenta with metallic green base................................ $12 – 16
3. metallic light green with red base, "5" on roof, side labels............. $16 – 24
4. metallic light green with red base, "Castrol" label .... $600 – 800
5. metallic light green with red base, no label................................ $12 – 16
6. metallic light green with unpainted base, no label .... $12 – 16
7. purple with green base......... $16 – 24

Dodge "Copperhead" Concept, #40, 1999
1. unpainted, rubber tires on chrome rims, 1999 First Editions .... $5 – 6
2. metallic copper, rubber tires on chrome rims, 1999 First Editions .... $5 – 6

3. metallic copper, 1999 Car Shows............................... $1 – 2

Dodge Crane Truck, 2¾", #63, 1968
1. yellow with green windows, red hook, black plastic wheels, 1968... $12 – 16
2. yellow with green windows, yellow hook, black plastic wheels, 1968... $12 – 16
3. yellow with green windows, Superfast wheels, 1970.................... $30 – 40

Dodge Dakota Pickup, 3", #50, 1989; #17, 1990
1. red with black and white stripes, chrome roll bar...................... $4 – 6

2. red, "Dakota ST," black and white stripes, chrome roll bar .... $1 – 2

3. bright red, "Sandy," cartoon map of Texas, 2003 Nickelodeon Spongebob Squarepants 5-pack............. $2 – 3
4. dark red, "Dakota ST," black and white stripes, black roll bar.............. $1 – 2
5. metallic green with "MB Construction," black roll bar, Action Pack......... $4 – 6
6. white with no markings, white roll bar, Graffic Traffic..................... $12 – 16
7. blue with "Dakota ST" and stripes, black roll bar, gift set .... $9 – 12
8. fluorescent orange, "Fire Chief 1," "Intercom City," white roll bar .... $12 – 16

9. purple with yellow and pink on sides, chrome roll bar, 1997 Rugged Riders 5-pack............................... $1 – 2
10. olive with white bands, black roll bar, China multipack.................. $24 – 36

11. yellow, "Highway Crew," "Crew Chief," black roll bar, 1999 Highway Crew 5-pack........................ $1 – 2

12. black and gray with logo on door and gray and beige spots, Salvage Yard 5-pack .... $1 - 2

13. black and gray, "Hershey 99" in silver print, black roll bar, 1999 Color Comp promotional .... $9 – 12
14. black and gray, "Hershey 99" in gold print, black roll bar, 1999 Color Comp promotional .... $9 – 12

15. metallic blue with gray plastic base, red interior and roll bar, monkey and wrench, 2003 Hero City 5-pack #11 .... $1 - 2

Dodge Dart Phoenix 1961, 1:72, Superfast #27, 2005

1. white with black interior .... $4 - 5

2. red with beige interior .... $4 - 5

3. silver with white interior .... $4 - 5

Dodge Daytona 1984 Turbo Z, 2⁷/₈", #28, 1984

1. red with yellow and blue "Turbo Z," silver wheels .... $1 - 2

2. red with yellow and blue "Turbo Z," "new Superfast" wheels .... $6 – 7
3. metallic burgundy with metallic gray lower body, "Expressly for Dodge Las Vegas," England cast .... $90 – 120

4. metallic burgundy with metallic gray lower body, England cast .... $4 - 5

5. metallic burgundy with metallic gray lower body, Macau cast .... $60 – 80
6. metallic burgundy with gold lower body, plastic armament, Roadblasters ... $7 – 8
7. dark blue with black lower body, "5 Goat Racing Team," Hong Kong issue .... $10 – 12
8. white with blue lower body, red and blue stripes, new Superfast wheels ... $4 – 5
9. white with blue lower body, red and blue stripes, Laser Wheels .... $4 – 5

10. metallic silver with black lower body, red and black stripes, Macau cast .... $3 - 4

Dodge Delivery Truck, 2³/₄", #72, 1982

1. "Big Top Circus," red with white container, Thailand cast .... $4 – 5
2. "British Airways Cargo," light gray and dark blue, Thailand cast, Motor City .... $4 – 5
3. "C Plus Orange," dark green with orange container, Macau cast, Canadian issue .... $12 – 16
4. "H & B," "Harris & Bailey Ltd.," red with red container, Thailand cast, UK issue .... $12 – 16
5. "Hertz," orange-yellow with orange-yellow container, Macau cast .... $3 – 4
6. "Hertz," yellow with yellow container, Macau cast .... $3 – 4
7. "Jetspress Road Express," white with white container, Macau cast, Australia issue .... $7 – 9
8. "Kellogg's" labels, red with white container, gold wheels, England cast .. $5 – 6
9. "Kellogg's" labels, red with white container, silver wheels, England cast .... $5 – 6
10. "Kellogg's" labels, red with white container, silver wheels, Macau cast .. $5 – 6
11. "Kellogg's," "Milch-Laite-Latte," red with white container, Macau cast, German/Swiss issue .... $40 – 50
12. "Kit Kat," red with red container, red with red container, Macau cast, UK on-package premium .... $8 – 10
13. "Matchbox USA Sheraton Inn 1989," red with white container, Macau cast, US issue .... $9 – 12
14. "MD," white with white container, Thailand cast, UK issue .... $12 – 16
15. "Minties," green with white container, Macau cast, Australia issue ...... $7 – 9
16. "Mitre 10," blue with blue container, Macau cast, Australia issue ...... $7 – 9
17. "Nestles Chokito," red with red container, Macau cast, Australia issue .... $7 – 9
18. "Pepsi" labels, red with white container, gold wheels, England cast .... $5 – 6
19. "Pepsi" labels, red with white container, silver wheels, England cast .... $5 – 6
20. "Pirelli Gripping Stuff," white with white container, Macau cast, Team Convoy .... $4 – 5
21. "Risi," orange yellow with yellow container, Macau cast, Spanish issue ... $20 – 30
22. "Royal Mail Parcels," red with red container, Macau cast, UK issue .... $6 – 8
23. "Smith's" labels, red with white container, gold wheels, England cast, UK on-package premium .... $5 – 6
24. "Smith's" labels, red with white container, silver wheels, England cast, UK on-package premium .... $5 – 6
25. "St. Ivel Gold," blue with blue container, Thailand cast, UK on-package premium .... $12 – 16
26. "Stena Line Freight," blue with blue container, Thailand cast, UK issue ... $12 – 16
27. "Street's Ice Cream," white with white container, Macau cast, Australia issue .... $7 – 9
28. "Wigwam," white with white container, Thailand cast, Convoy series, Dutch issue .... $8 – 10
29. "XP Express Parcels Systems," white with white container, Macau cast, Team Convoy .... $4 – 5
30. "XP Express Parcels Systems," white with white container, Thailand cast, Team Convoy .... $4 – 5
31. "Yorkie," blue with blue container, Macau cast, UK on-package premium .... $8 – 10

Dodge Dragster, 3", #70, 1971 (similar casting: Orange Peel Dodge Charger)

1. pink, "Castrol" label, black base .... $800 – 1000
2. pink, "Rat Rod" label, black base .... $30 – 40
3. pink, "Wildcat" label, black base .... $30 – 40
4. pink, snake label, black base .... $16 – 24
5. pink, snake label, unpainted base .... $16 – 24
6. pink, snake label, dark gray base .... $16 – 24

7. pink, snake label, green base.. $16 – 24
8. pink, snake label, lavender base.............................. $16 – 24
9. pink, snake label, tan base.... $16 – 24
10. pink, snake label, yellow base.. $16 – 24
11. pink, star flame label, black base.............................. $250 – 300

Dodge Dump Truck, 3", #48, 1966
1. red, black plastic wheels, 1966 ... $7 – 9
2. blue cab, yellow dumper, Superfast wheels, 1970.................... $30 – 40
3. metallic blue cab, yellow dumper, Superfast wheels, 1970.............. $30 – 40

Dodge Magnum Police, #30, 2005; #38, 2006

1. black and white, 2005 #30 ... $1 – 2

2. metallic gray with white panel, Police graphics on sides, red roof light, 2006 #38 .... $1 – 2

Dodge Magnum R/T, #8, 2007

1. metallic dark blue, 2007 #8 .. $1 – 2

Dodge Ram SRT-10 4x4, #66, 2003; #74, 2004; #59, 2005

1. black with red windows, red "Dodge" and Dodge Ram logo, 2003 Heavy Movers.............................. $1 – 2

2. metallic blue, 2005 10-pack #2 .... $1 – 2

3. olive green, 2006 5-pack J4675................................ $1 – 2
4. blue, 2005 #59 .... $1 – 2

5. gold with black graphics, 2007 5-pack K9407 .... $1 – 2

6. flat brown, black windows, "07," beige and red mud splatter graphics, 2006 5-pack J4679 .... $1 – 2

Dodge Stake Truck, 2⅞", #4, 1967; reissued as Cattle Truck #71, 1976 – 1991; #12, 1992 – 1997; reissued as Beef Hauler #88, 1999, #50, 2000; #30, 2000, international, England cast except where noted
1. red with cream stake bed, two black steers, blue windows, #71 Cattle Truck.................................. $4 – 5
2. red with cream stake bed, two brown steers, blue windows, #71 Cattle Truck.................................. $4 – 5
3. red with beige stake bed, two black steers, purple windows, #71 Cattle Truck.................................. $4 – 5
4. red with beige stake bed, two black steers, red windows, #71 Cattle Truck.................................. $4 – 5
5. red with yellow stake bed, no steers, red windows, blue wheels with yellow hubs, Matchbox Preschool/Live 'N Learn .... $7 – 9
6. metallic orange with orange-yellow stake bed, two black steers, blue windows, #71 Cattle Truck.................... $4 – 5
7. metallic orange with orange-yellow stake bed, two black steers, light green windows, #71 Cattle Truck............ $4 – 5
8. metallic orange with orange-yellow stake bed, two black steers, orange windows, #71 Cattle Truck.................... $4 – 5
9. metallic orange with orange-yellow stake bed, two black steers, purple windows, #71 Cattle Truck.................... $4 – 5
10. orange-yellow with green stake bed, Superfast wheels, no livestock, #4, 1970.............................. $20 – 30
11. yellow with blue-green stake bed, regular wheels, no livestock, #4, 1967.......................... $160 – 240
12. yellow with brown stake bed, amber windows, black tow hook, #71....... $4 – 5
13. yellow with brown stake bed, amber windows, no tow hook, #71 .... $8 – 10
14. yellow with brown stake bed, clear windows, #71 .... $4 – 5
15. yellow with brown stake bed, red windows, black tow hook, #71....... $4 – 5
16. yellow with brown stake bed, red windows, black tow hook, #71, Macau cast .... $1 – 2
17. yellow with brown stake bed, red windows, no tow hook, #71 .... $8 – 10

18. yellow with green stake bed, regular wheels, no livestock, #4, 1967 .... $12 – 16
19. yellow with green stake bed, Superfast wheels, no livestock, #4, 1970............................ $90 – 120
20. yellow with red stake bed, two black steers, #1, 1999 Beef Hauler, China cast.................................... $1 – 2

21. yellow with red stake bed, "Target Beef," two black steers, #1, 1999 Beef Hauler, China cast......... $1 – 2
22. yellow with tan stake bed, amber windows, no tow hook #71 .... $5 – 6
23. yellow with tan stake bed, red windows, no tow hook #71 .... $5 – 6

24. green with yellow stake bed, two black steers, #12, 1992 Cattle Truck .... $4 – 6

25. green with yellow stake bed, two black steers, #71, Macau cast, Two-Pack .... $1 – 2
26. green with yellow stake bed, two black steers, #71, Thailand cast, Two-Pack .... $1 – 2
27. dark green with beige stake bed, two steers, orange windows, #71 ... $7 – 9
28. dark green with light brown stake bed, two steers, amber windows, #71 .... $7 – 9
29. dark green with light brown stake bed, two steers, clear windows, #71 ... $7 – 9
30. dark green with light brown stake bed, two steers, orange windows, #71 .... $7 – 9
31. dark green with light brown stake bed, two steers, red windows, #71 .. $7 – 9
32. dark green with orange-yellow stake bed, two steers, orange windows, #71 .... $4 – 5
33. dark green with orange-yellow stake bed, two steers, red windows, #71 .... $4 – 5
34. metallic green with brown stake bed, two steers, amber windows, #71 .... $7 – 9
35. metallic green with brown stake bed, two steers, clear windows, #71 ... $7 – 9
36. metallic green with brown stake bed, two steers, red windows, #71 .. $7 – 9
37. light green with beige stake bed, two steers, orange windows, #71 ... $7 – 9
38. light green with orange-yellow stake bed, two steers, orange windows, #71 .... $4 – 5
39. light green with orange-yellow stake bed, two steers, red windows, #71 .... $4 – 5
40. blue with brown stake bed, amber windows, two dark brown steers, #50/30, 2000 Farm .... $1 – 2
41. blue with brown stake bed, amber windows, two dark brown steers, "Matchbox 2000," #50/30, 2000 Farm .... $3 – 4
42. pale blue with brown stake bed, two black steers, red windows, #71, Macau cast .... $3 – 4

Dodge Viper GTS Coupe, #1, US, 1997; #35, international, 1997; #1, 1998; #19, 1999; #5, 2001

1. metallic blue with white stripes, chrome wheels, rubber tires, 1997 Inaugural Edition .... $6 – 8
2. unpainted, chrome wheels, rubber tires, 1997 Inaugural Edition............ $6 – 8

3. metallic blue with white stripes, 5-spoke wheels.................... $2 – 4

4. black with orange interior, chrome wheels, rubber tires, Matchbox Convention .... $12 – 16
5. red with black interior, chrome wheels, rubber tires, Premiere Collection #14 .... $6 – 8
6. red with black interior, 5-spoke wheels, Premiere Collection #14 .... $45 – 60

7. white with blue stripes, 1998 Stars & Stripes series 1 .... $2 – 4

8. metallic gold with black interior, 75 Challenge series, 1997.......... $8 – 12
9. bright blue with white stripes, Chrysler Gift Set.................................... $4-6
10. blue with black interior, New York Knicks, NBA.......................... $5 – 7
11. light blue with white interior, Utah Jazz, NBA.................................... $5 – 7
12. teal blue with black interior, Detroit Pistons, NBA............................. $5 – 7
13. lavender and white with white interior, Los Angeles Lakers, NBA......... $5 – 7
14. black with gray interior, Orlando Magic, NBA.................................... $5 – 7
15. black and white with red interior, Chicago Bulls, NBA........................ $5 – 7
16. orange and black with red-orange interior, Atlanta Hawks, NBA........... $5 – 7
17. red with white interior, Houston Rockets, NBA .... $5 – 7
18. dark purple and black with orange interior, Phoenix Suns, NBA .... $5 – 7
19. orange-yellow with green interior, Seattle Supersonics, NBA.............. $5 – 7
20. white with purple interior, Charlotte Hornets, NBA............................. $5 – 7
21. yellow and red with black interior, Miami Heat, NBA .... $5 – 7
22. green and white with black interior, Boston Celtics, NBA .... $5 – 7
23. red and black with white interior, Portland Trailblazers, NBA............. $5 – 7
24. white with dark blue interior, Warriors, NBA.................................... $5 – 7
25. yellow and white with dark blue interior, Indiana Pacers, NBA.............. $5 – 7
26. lavender and blue with orange interior, Cleveland Cavaliers, NBA......... $5 – 7
27. black and green with blue interior, Timberwolves, NBA .... $5 – 7
28. metallic gray with red interior, New York Nets, NBA .... $5 – 7
29. metallic brown with red interior, Denver Nuggets, NBA .... $5 – 7
30. bright yellow with black interior, 5-pack.................................... $2 – 4
31. metallic gray with black interior, chrome wheels, rubber tires, Premiere Collection .... $5 – 7
32. 1998 Stars & Stripes series 1 ... $3 – 5

33. metallic gray with tan interior, Mattel Wheels #19, 1999 .... $2 – 4

34. metallic gray with tan interior, Matchbox 2000 on window.................... $3 – 5
35. white with black interior, blue "Midwest Regional Matchbox Convention" on hood, Color Comp .... $30 – 35
36. white with black interior, red "Midwest Regional Matchbox Convention" on hood, Color Comp .... $30 – 35
37. white with black interior, no graphics, concave star wheels, Color Comp blank .... $30 – 40
38. metallic dark gray with metallic gray interior, 5-pack....................... $1 – 2

39. bright blue with metallic gray interior, yellow stripes and "Viper," 2001 #5 Daddy's Dreams .... $1 – 2

40. metallic gray with tan interior, "Celebrating Dr. Roy R. Gal Ph. D. Astrophysics," "California Institute of Technology," Color Comp .... $45 – 55
41. metallic dark gray with metallic gray interior, 5-pack....................... $1 – 2
42. white with black interior, "Hope Spring 2000," Color Comp............ $12 – 16
43. white with black interior, "Hope Spring 2001," Color Comp............ $12 – 16
44. white with black interior, "Savannah 2001," Color Comp............ $25 – 30

45. metallic light blue, "Alicia" graphics, 2006 Nickelodeon 5-pack H4108 .... $1 – 2

Dodge Viper GTS-R, #56, 2001; #10, 2002; #54, 2005; #68, 2006; #17, 2007

1. **red with silver stripes, 2001 Wheeled Envy....................$2 – 4**

2. **metallic blue with white "Viper GTSR" on sides, black plastic base, 2002 Style Champs series ... $3 – 4**

3. **black with gold "Dodge" graphics, Dodge Ram logo, snake's head, gold wheel hubs, 2003 Hero City 5-pack #12 ....$4 – 6**
4. red with no stripes, 2005 Road Rush #64 .... $1 – 2

5. **yellow with black stripes, 2005 Superfast series................. $4 – 5**
6. black with no markings, light gray interior, 2006 #68........................ $1 – 2
7. light blue, 2007 #17.............. $1 – 2

Dodge Viper RT/10, #10, 1994; #12, 1994, international; #56, 1998; #67, 1998, international; #37, 1999; #32, 1999, international; #43, 2000; #66, 2000, international

1. red with black interior, clear windshield, gold wheel hubs .... $1 – 2

2. **red with black interior, clear windshield, silver wheel hubs........$1 – 2**
3. red with black interior, tinted windshield, silver wheel hubs.................... $1 – 2
4. red with black interior, chrome windshield, rubber tires on gray rims, World Class.................................. $3 – 5
5. red with black and brown interior, clear windshield, rubber tires on chrome rims, Premiere Collection......... $4 – 6
6. red with twin yellow stripes, black and gray interior, clear windshield, rubber tires on chrome rims, Gold Collection.......................... $35 – 55

7. **red with black interior, tinted windshield, yellow wheel hubs, 5-pack...................................$1 – 2**
8. red with black interior, tinted windshield, #43, 2000.......................... $1 – 2
9. red with black interior, tinted windshield, "Matchbox 2000," #43, 2000................................. $3 – 5
10. red with black interior, clear windshield, #66, 2000.......................... $1 – 2
11. red with black interior, clear windshield, "16th Annual Matchbox USA Convention 1997" decals, silver wheel hubs.................................. $12 – 16
12. red with black interior, clear windshield, "Compaq," ASAP promotional.............................. $50 – 75
13. red with black interior, clear windshield, "NCR," ASAP promotional.............................. $50 – 75
14. red with black interior, clear windshield, small "R," ASAP promotional.............................. $30 – 40
15. red with black interior, clear windshield, "G" in circle, ASAP promotional.............................. $16 – 24
16. red with black interior, clear windshield, "Mahle," ASAP promotional.............................. $30 – 40
17. red with black interior, clear windshield, "Rensselaer Polytechnic," ASAP promotional...................... $16 – 24
18. red with black interior, clear windshield, "Microsoft," ASAP promotional............................ $75 – 125
19. red with black interior, clear windshield, "Citrix Silver," ASAP promotional .... $75 – 125
20. red with black interior, clear windshield, "Intel Pill Pushing the Limits," ASAP promotional .... $75 – 125
21. red with black interior, clear windshield, "Skip Barber Driving School," ASAP promotional .... $50 – 75
22. red with black interior, clear windshield, "Huskers" on left side, ASAP promotional .... $12 – 16
23. red with black interior, clear windshield, "Novell 6," ASAP promotional..$20 – 25
24. red with black interior, clear windshield, "A-Pix Entertainment," "Drive," ASAP promotional................... $120 – 160
25. red with black interior, clear windshield, "Lucent Technologies," ASAP promotional............................... $25 – 45
26. red with black interior, tinted windshield, "Fiery Driven," ASAP promo tional..........................$100 – 150
27. red with black interior, clear windshield, "Fiery Driven," ASAP promo tional..........................$100 – 150
28. red with black interior, clear windshield, "1998 Sales Meeting," ASAP promotional................... $100 – 150
29. red with black interior, clear windshield, "Concept 4," "Interact," ASAP promotional............................... $16 – 24
30. red with black interior, clear windshield, "Yasnac PCNC," "Yaskawa Can Fly!" ASAP promotional .... $50 – 75
31. red with black interior, clear windshield, "Moore," ASAP promotional.......................... $100 – 150
32. red with black interior, clear windshield, "Nebraska," ASAP promotional..$12 – 16
33. red with black interior, clear windshield, "Huffhines Dodge," ASAP promotional........................... $100 – 150
34. red with black interior, clear windshield, "Oberon Software," ASAP promotional............................. $75 – 125
35. red with black interior, clear windshield, "X," ASAP promotional .... $75 – 125
36. red with black interior, clear windshield, "RCA," ASAP promotional ..... $20 – 25
37. red with black interior, clear windshield, "Season's Greetings Color Comp Inc.," "Christmas 1998," Color Comp promotional........................... $250 – 300
38. red with black interior, clear windshield, "Marathon Ashland," ASAP promotional .... $75 – 125
39. red with black interior, clear windshield, "Faith," "Sunday School Evangelism Strategy," ASAP promotional........................... $100 – 150
40. red with black interior, tinted windshield, "Matchbox Collectors," "Color Comp Inc. Conference," Color Comp promotional............................... $30 – 45
41. red with black interior, clear windshield, "Project Vertigo," "Citrix Developer Network," ASAP promotional.... $75 – 125
42. red with black interior, clear windshield, "Citrix Vertigo," ASAP promotional............................. $75 – 125
43. red with black interior, clear windshield, "Me, Mom & Matchbox," Color Comp promotional....................... $16 – 24
44. green with tan interior, clear windshield, "Me, Mom & Matchbox," Color Comp promotional..................... $80 – 100

45. yellow with black interior, clear windshield, "Me, Mom & Matchbox," Color Comp promotional .... $16 – 24

46. white with black interior, clear windshield, "98 White's Guide," ASAP promotional .... $30 – 35

47. red with black interior, clear windshield, yellow lettered "White's Guide Car of the Month #8 July 1999," ASAP promotional .... $9 – 12

48. red with black interior, clear windshield, white lettered "White's Guide Car of the Month #8 July 1999," ASAP promotional .... $9 – 12

49. red with black interior, tinted windshield, "Hope Spring Cancer Support Center 1997" .... $16 – 24

50. green with tan interior, tinted windshield, "Hope Spring Cancer Support Center 1997" .... $90 – 120

51. green with tan interior, tinted windshield, no markings.............. $3 – 4

52. green with twin white stripes, gray and black interior, clear windshield, rubber tires on chrome rims, Premiere Collection .... $4 – 6

53. metallic green with black and gray interior, clear windshield, rubber tires on chrome rims, Select Class.... $12 – 15

54. dark gray with black and gray interior, clear windshield, rubber tires on chrome rims, Australia issue Premiere Collection .... $9 – 12

55. yellow with black interior, clear windshield, #56, 1998 .... $1 – 2

56. yellow, black interior, tinted windshield, #56, 1998 .... $1 – 2

57. yellow with black and gray interior, clear windshield, rubber tires on chrome rims, Premiere Collection .... $8 – 10

58. yellow with black interior, chrome windshield, "California Viper's Club," rubber tires on gray rims................ $15 – 20

59. yellow with black interior, tinted windshield, "Matchbox Forum 1998," "First Shot" .... $20 – 25

60. yellow with black interior, tinted windshield, "Matchbox Convoys Collectors Club," "M3CG," Color Comp promotional .... $30 – 45

61. yellow with black interior, clear windshield, "Pratiker" .... $45 – 65

62. yellow with black interior, tinted windshield, "PMCC Happy Holidays," Color Comp promotional .... $30 – 45

63. yellow with black interior, tinted windshield, "Color Comp Demo Model 2000," Color Comp promotional .... $20 – 25

64. yellow with black interior, tinted windshield, "NJ Diecast Collectors Club" .... $30 – 45

65. yellow with black interior, tinted windshield, "Matchbox Forum International Matchbox Collectors Club Deutschland" .... $30 – 45

66. yellow with black interior, tinted windshield, "Keystone Kollectible Kars," Color Comp promotional .... $16 – 24

67. blue with metallic gray interior, clear windshield, "Keystone Kollectible Kars," Color Comp promotional .... $16 – 24

68. red with black interior, clear windshield, "Keystone Kollectible Kars," Color Comp promotional .... $16 – 24

69. black with gray interior, chrome windshield, rubber tires on gray rims, "Matchbox 1995 Line Preview" .... $275 – 350

70. black with tan interior, clear windshield, 5-pack .... $1 – 2

71. black with twin silver stripes, gray and black interior, clear windshield, rubber tires on chrome rims, Select Class................................ $4 – 6

72. white with black interior, clear windshield, "69th Shenandoah Apple Blossom Festival 1996" .... $12 – 15

73. white with black interior, clear windshield, "Merry Christmas Ad-Ventures" .... $20 – 25

74. white with twin red stripes, black and gray interior, clear windshield, rubber tires on chrome rims, Select Class.................................... $4 – 6

75. white with brown interior, clear windshield, "Viper," 5-pack .... $1 – 2

76. white with black interior, clear windshield, "1st Annual Golf Outing — Mattel," Color Comp.............. $300 – 375

77. white with twin white stripes; black, blue and gray interior; clear windshield; rubber tires on chrome rims; Premiere Collection .... $5 – 7

78. white with blue stripes, tan interior, clear windshield, "District 16B Lion's Club New Jersey," Color Comp promotional .... $25 – 40

79. metallic blue with twin white stripes, gray and black interior, clear windshield, rubber tires on chrome rims, Premiere Collection .... $4 – 6

80. blue with twin yellow stripes, gray interior, clear windshield, "Praktiker" .... $16 – 24

81. gold with black interior, clear windshield, no markings, 1997 75 Challenge .... $12 – 16

82. dark blue, 2005 Superfast #65 .... $3 – 4

Dodge Wreck Truck, "BP," 3", #13, 1965

1. green cab, yellow body, black plastic wheels, prototype.......... $900 – 1000

2. yellow cab, green body, black plastic wheels............................$10 – 15
3. yellow cab, green body, Superfast wheels, 1970.................... $60 – 80

Dodge Zoo Truck, #72, 1992, international
1. white with red, orange, and yellow stripes, blue windows, metallic gray cage, brown lions, Thailand cast, Motor City...................................... $4 – 5

Double Decker (see Routemaster Double Decker Bus)

Dragon Wheels (see Hot Chocolate)

Draguar (see Hot Rod Draguar)

Drott Excavator, $2^5/_8$", #58, 1962
1. red with silver motor and base, metal rollers .... $25 – 35
2. red with silver motor and base, silver rollers .... $80 – 100
3. red with silver motor and base, black rollers .... $25 – 35
4. orange with silver motor and base, black rollers .... $35 – 45
5. orange with orange motor and base, black rollers .... $35 – 45

DUKW Army Amphibian, $2^3/_4$", #55, 1958
1. metal wheels..................... $30 – 45
2. gray plastic wheels............. $30 – 45

3. black plastic wheels..........$30 – 45

Dumper, $1^5/_8$", #2, 1953
1. green metal wheels .... $120 – 150
2. unpainted metal wheels........ $45 – 60

Dumper, $1^7/_8$", #2, 1957

1. with driver.......................$45 – 60

Dumper, Muir Hill, red with green dumper, black plastic wheels, $2^3/_{16}$", #2, 1961
1. "Laing" decals..................... $20 – 25
2. "Muir Hill" decals................. $65 – 80

Dump Truck (also see Articulated Dump Truck, Atlas Earth Mover Dump Truck, Caterpillar Dump Truck, DAF Tipper Truck, Dodge Dump Truck, 8-Wheel Tipper, Euclid Quarry Truck, GMC Highway Maintenance Truck, GMC Tipper Truck, Leyland Articulated Truck, Mack Dump Truck, Peterbilt Quarry Truck, Quarry Truck)

Dump Truck/Earth Hauler Quarry Truck, #55, 2002; #69, 2003; #75, 2004; #56, 2005

1. metallic red with metallic gray plastic dumper with "Matchbox Demolition Force" and wrecking ball on sides, 2002 Rescue Rookies..$1 – 2

2. metallic red with metallic gray plastic dumper with "Matchbox Demolition Force" and wrecking ball on sides, Christmas 2002 3-pack with gift box..............................$4 – 5

3. red with black dumper, 2003 Heavy Movers................................ $1 – 2

4. gray -green with yellow dumper, Hero City graphics, Earth Hauler #75, 2004 ....$1 – 2

5. metallic greenish yellow with black dumper, "Matchbox Mover 536," 2005 10-pack #2................$1 – 2
6. orange with black dumper, "MHC," 2005 #56............................ $1 – 2

7. orange with white dumper, "M Construction," with black, orange, and yellow graphics, 2005 5-pack H4108...............................$1 – 2

Dune Buggy (also see Dune Buggy 2006)

Dune Buggy/Sand Speeder, #92, 1999; #15, 2000; #35, 2001; #46, 2002; #72, 1999, international
1. red, "Beach Patrol," black interior, black roll cage, "Matchbox 2000," 2000 To the Beach............................. $3 – 4
2. red, "Beach Patrol," black interior, black roll cage, 2000 To the Beach ... $1 – 2
3. red, "Beach Patrol," blue interior, yellow base, red roll cage, 2002 Sand Castle Rescue Team 5-pack .... $4 – 5
4. red with orange interior, blue engine 2003 Hero City 5-pack #5 .... $1 – 2
5. orange with phosphorescent yellow roll cage, blue interior, 2003 Camp Fun 3-pack with flashlight .... $4 – 5

6. yellow with red interior, blue roll cage, yellow base, 2002 Weekend Cruisers .... $1 – 2

7. light blue with white band, metallic gray interior, black roll cage, #92, 1999 Mountain Cruisers....... $1 – 2
8. pale blue with dark blue band, mountain scene, light blue base, metallic gray interior, 1999 Mountain Cruisers series
9. turquoise, "Rt450," mountain scene, black interior, metallic gray roll cage, yellow base, 1999 Mountain Cruisers international .... $3 – 4

10. blue with black interior, gray engine, "H4M," 2006 5-pack J4671.. $1 – 2
11. purple, "Sand Blaster," black interior, black roll cage, yellow base, 2001 Sand Blasters................................ $1 – 2
12. black, "Rugged Adventures," "88," orange interior, yellow roll cage, orange base.................................... $3 – 4
13. black with purple and blue stingrays design, black roll cage, metallic red base, 5-pack .... $1 – 2

14. light gray with dark gray interior, blue engine .... $1 – 2
15. red with black roll cage, red engine, "Beach Patrol," #15, 2000 To the Beach .... $1 – 2

16. black with black interior, red engine, #15, 2000 To the Beach....... $1 – 2

Dune Buggy 2006, MB685, #51, 2006

1. khaki and black, #51, 2006 .. $1 – 2

2. fluorescent red-orange with blue, black, and white graphics, white roll bar, blue interior, gloss black base, 2007 5-pack K9616 .... $1 – 2

3. metallic blue with black, white, and red graphics, red roll bar, black interior, 2007 #64, K9503 .... $1 – 2
4. white with metallic silver base, blue and metallic gray interior, "Sand Speeder," "429," 2007 5-pack K9617..... $1 – 2
5. metallic blue with black, white, and red graphics, white roll bar, black interior, 2007 10-pack B5610............ $1 – 2

Dune Man Volkswagen Beetle, 2 13/16", #49, 1984 (similar castings: Hi Ho Silver, Hot Chocolate, Sand Digger, Volks Dragon, Big Blue)
1. red .... $3 – 4

Dunes Racer 4x4 Pickup, 3", #13, 1982; #63, 1984, #76 error package (similar castings: Mini Pickup 4x4, Mountain Man)
1. white, #63 on package .... $4 – 6

2. white, #76 on package.......... $3 – 5

3. white, #13 on package.......... $2 – 4

Duracell Delivery Truck, #9, 2005
1. orange cab, 2005 #9.............. $1 – 2

E

E-Type Jaguar (see Jaguar E-Type)

Earth Hauler Quarry Truck, #56, 2005 (see Dump Truck)

Earth Mover (see Faun Earth Mover Dump Truck)

Eccles Caravan Travel Trailer, 3", #57, 1970
1. light yellow with orange roof, brown stripe and flower label, green interior, black axle cover .... $12 – 16

2. dark yellow with dark orange roof, black stripe and flower label, white interior, black axle cover .... $6 – 8
3. dark yellow with dark orange roof, dots label, white interior, black axle cover................................. $9 – 12

4. beige with orange roof, stripe label, green interior, black axle cover............................ $12 – 16
5. beige with orange roof, brown stripe and flower label, green interior, black axle cover .... $12 – 16
6. beige with orange roof, brown stripe and flower label, green interior, red axle cover................................ $12 – 16
7. beige with dark orange roof, black stripe and flower label, white interior, black axle cover .... $6 – 8
8. beige with dark orange roof, stripe and seagull label, white interior, black axle cover.................................... $9 – 12
9. white with dark orange roof, "Sun Set" design, white interior, black axle cover................................ $10 – 14

Eight-Wheel Crane Truck, 3", #30, 1965
1. mint green, black plastic wheels, preproduction................... $900 – 1000

2. green, black plastic wheels, 1965 .... $5 – 10
3. red with orange boom, Superfast wheels, 1970................ $400 – 500
4. red with gold boom, Superfast wheels, 1970.............................. $40 – 50

Eight-Wheel Tipper (see AEC Ergomatic Eight-Wheel Tipper)

Emergency Power Truck, #60, 2002; #68, 2003

1. red with white light tower, 2002 Rescue Rookies .... $1 – 2

2. orange with white light tower, 2003 Heavy Movers .... $1 – 2

Emergency Rescue, #11, 2003

1. yellow with brown base, grille, and back; amber windows; orange, brown, and green graphics; 2006 Creepy Cars J1818 (2-pack of plastic skulls with toy inside)....... $1 – 2

2. metal flake silver with red base, grille, and back; blue windows; red, yellow, and blue graphics; 2003 Hospital #11 .... $1 – 2

Emergency Response 4x4, #11, 2003
1. metallic silver with red gear and base, 2003 Hospital .... $1 – 2

ERF 68G Truck "Ever Ready For Life," blue, $2^{5}/_{8}$", #20, 1959

1. gray plastic wheels .... $40 – 50
2. silver plastic wheels .... $85 – 95
3. black plastic wheels .... $45 – 55

Euclid Quarry Truck, $2^{5}/_{8}$", #6, 1964
1. yellow with black plastic wheels .... $10 – 15

Excavator (see Atlas Excavator, Caterpillar Excavator)

Extending Ladder Fire Engine (also see Extending Ladder Fire Truck)

Extending Ladder Fire Engine, 3", #18, 1984; #23, 1998; #79, 1999; #32, 2000; #29, 2001; #4, 2003
1. fluorescent orange with "4" and checkered bar accents, 1994 .... $1 – 2
2. fluorescent orange, "5," "Intercom City" graphics, black base with bar code .... $12 – 16
3. fluorescent orange, "5," "Intercom City," chrome base .... $9 – 12
4. fluorescent orange with white accents .... $1 – 2
5. metallic gold with white ladder, 1997 75 Challenge .... $6 – 12
6. metallic maroon with gray ladder, gold design, "14" and "Matchbox," Pleasant Books.................................. $5 – 7

7. red with gray ladder, gold stripe, 5-pack.................................. $1 – 2

8. red with gray ladder, "54" and "Matchbox" in circle, 5-pack . $2 – 3
9. red with gray ladder, "FDMB-E64" and "Ladder 3 Fire Rescue," rubber tires on chrome rims, K-B Toys Feature Car .... $6 – 9
10. red with white ladder, no markings .... $1 – 2
11. red with white ladder, yellow accents, "Metro Alarm" flame logo, 2003 Hero City 5-pack #7 .... $1 – 2
12. red with white ladder, "Fire Dept." "7," shield .... $1 – 2
13. red with white ladder, Japanese lettering .... $10 – 15
14. red with white ladder, "3" and crest................................... $3 – 5
15. red with white ladder, "Fire Dept.," no origin cast......................... $10 – 15
16. red with white ladder, "4" and checkered bar accents......................... $8 – 10
17. red with white ladder, "FD No. 1," 5-pack .... $1 – 2

18. red with white "12th," gold "Rescue Squad," gold trim graphics, 1995..$1 – 2
19. red with white upper, gold and black accents, "FD No.1" on gold shield (1996 5-Pack)........................ $2 – 4
20. red with white "12th Rescue Squad," white trim, 1996 .... $1 – 2
21. red with white stripes on sides, "Matchbox Fire Dept." in black .... $1 – 2

22. red with white ladder, "Metro Fire Department," Collector's Choice, White Rose Collectibles.........$3 – 5
23. red with white ladder, white accents, "Laurel Springs Fire Rescue," rubber tires on chrome rims, Premiere Collection 21 .... $4 – 6
24. red with white ladder, white accents, "City of Miami," rubber tires on chrome rims, Premiere Collection .... $4 – 6
25. red with white ladder, white accents, "Cleveland Fire Div.," 2000 Matchbox USA .... $1 – 2
26. red with white ladder, white accents, "Cleveland Fire Div.," "Matchbox 2000," 2000 Matchbox USA.............. $3 – 5
27. red with white ladder, white accents, "Westworth Fire Dept. 8," 2001 Flame Eaters .... $1 – 2
28. red with yellow ladder, blue tires, Live 'N Learn/Matchbox Preschool .... $7 – 9

29. red with yellow ladder; black plastic base; gold, white, and yellow accents; 2003 Sky Fire.........$1 – 2

30. red and white with gray ladder, 2007 Superfast #10 ....$1 – 2
31. white with gray ladder, "Metro Alarm," orange and red stripes, 5-pack... $1 – 2

32. white with metallic gray ladder, blue, metallic gray metal base, 2001 Flame Eaters ....$3 – 4
33. white with orange ladder, 1996.. $1 – 2
34. white with red ladder, red bands and yellow hash marks on ladder, 5-pack.................................... $1 – 2

35. white with translucent red ladder, red band, 1998 To the Rescue ...... $1 – 2
36. white with white ladder, Graffic Traffic.............................. $12 – 16
37. white with white ladder, red accents, "Springfield Fire Dept.," rubber tires on chrome rims, Premiere Collection 7 .... $4 – 6
38. yellow with white ladder, no markings .... $4 – 6

39. yellow with gray ladder, "Matchbox Fire Dept." and red stripe, 5-pack..................................$1 – 2
40. yellow with gray ladder, "Ladder 3 Bay District," rubber tires on chrome rims, Premiere Collection 7 .... $4 – 6
41. yellow with gray ladder, "Park Ridge Fire Dept.," rubber tires on chrome rims, Premiere Collection 21 .... $4 – 6
42. yellow with gray ladder, "21" and crest, 1999 Fire Rescue.................. $1 – 2
43. yellow with gray ladder, "21 Laurel Ladder" and crest, 1999 Fire Rescue.. $1 – 2
44. 2002 Matchbox Across America 50th Birthday series #20, Mississippi — Southern Collection .... $4 – 6

Extending Ladder Fire Truck, #1, 2005 (see Ladder King)

Extending Ladder Fire Truck, #27 Flame Thrower, 2006
1. red with metallic silver trim, 2006 #27 .... $1 – 2

F

F1 Racer, 2⅞", #16, 1984, USA; #6, 1985, Europe; Indy Racer, #65, 1985
1. "123456" and flames, white with red airfoil, blue wheels, red driver, Matchbox Preschool/Live 'N Learn series, Macau cast .... $7 – 9
2. "123456" and flames, white with red airfoil, blue wheels, red driver, Matchbox Preschool/Live 'N Learn series, Thailand cast.............................. $7 – 9
3. "Agfa Film 29," white and dark orange with orange driver, "Agfa" on orange airfoil, Thailand cast, US issue .... $8 – 10
4. "Agfa Film 29," white and red with red driver, "Agfa" on red airfoil, Thailand cast, US issue .... $8 – 10
5. "Amway," "Speedway 22," white with pink driver, bright pink and blue accents, "Rain-X" on pink airfoil, China cast, Indy 500 .... $4 – 5
6. "Amway," "Speedway 22," white, bright pink and blue with pink driver, bright pink and blue accents, "Rain-X" on pink airfoil, Thailand cast, Indy 500...... $4 – 5
7. "Bosch STP 20," dark blue with red driver, "Goodyear" on red airfoil, chrome lettering on wheels, Macau cast ... $5 – 6
8. "Bosch STP 20," dark blue with red driver, "Goodyear" on red airfoil, unchromed lettering on wheels, Macau cast... $5 – 6
9. "Fiat 3," red with black driver, "Pirelli" on black airfoil............................ $3 – 5
10. "Havoline 86," black with black driver, "Havoline" on black airfoil, China cast, Indy 500.............................. $4 – 5

11. "Hyflo Exhausts 5," white with purple driver, "Hyflo Exhausts" on fuchsia airfoil, Thailand cast ....$1 – 2
12. "Indy 11," lemon yellow and black with lemon yellow driver, "Goodyear" on lemon yellow airfoil, China cast, Indy 500 .... $4 – 5
13. "Indy 11," lemon yellow and black with lemon yellow driver, "Indy" on lemon yellow airfoil, China cast, Indy 500.. $5 – 6
14. "Kraco 18," orange-yellow and blue with orange-yellow driver, "Kraco" on orange-yellow airfoil, Thailand cast, Indy 500 .... $4 – 5
15. "Kraco," "Otter Pops 18," orange-yellow and blue with yellow driver, "Kraco" on yellow airfoil, China cast, Indy 500 .... $4 – 5
16. "Matchbox," "Goodyear," white with blue driver, "Shell" on blue airfoil....... $3 – 5
17. "Matchbox Racing Team," red with red driver, "Goodyear" on red airfoil, Macau cast, Super Color Changers...... $4 – 5

18. "Matchbox Racing Team," pink with red driver, "Goodyear" on red airfoil, Macau cast, Super Color Changers...... $4 – 5
19. "Matchbox Racing Team," light peach with with red driver, "Goodyear" on red airfoil, Macau cast, Super Color Changers...................................... $4 – 5
20. "Matchbox Racing Team," orange with with red driver, "Goodyear" on red airfoil, Macau cast, Super Color Changers.............................. $4 – 5
21. "Matchbox Racing Team," yellow with dark red driver, "Goodyear" on dark red airfoil, Macau cast .... $3 – 4
22. "Matchbox Racing Team," yellow with red driver, "Goodyear" on red airfoil, black exhausts, China cast........ $1 – 2
23. "Matchbox Racing Team," yellow with red driver, "Goodyear" on red airfoil, black exhausts, Macau cast...... $1 – 2
24. "Matchbox Racing Team," yellow with red driver, "Goodyear" on red airfoil, black exhausts, Thailand cast.... $1 – 2
25. "Matchbox Racing Team," yellow with red driver, "Goodyear" on red airfoil, chrome exhausts, Macau cast .. $3 – 4
26. "Matchbox Racing Team," yellow with maroon driver, "Goodyear" on red airfoil, black exhausts, Thailand cast.... $1 – 2
27. "Matchbox Racing Team," light green with with red driver, "Goodyear" on red airfoil, Macau cast, Super Color Changers.............................. $4 – 5
28. "Mitre 10," "M10," blue with blue driver, "Mitre 10" on blue airfoil, Thailand cast, Convoy Australia issue .... $6 – 8
29. "Mitre 10," "Larkham," "Taubmans 3," blue and white with blue driver, "Mitre 10" on blue airfoil, Thailand cast, Team Convoy Australia issue .... $7 – 9
30. "Mr. Juicy," "Sunkist," with white, orange, and green with yellow driver, "Watson's" on yellow airfoil, Hong Kong issue...$24 – 30
31. "Rad 5," black with green and white stripes, black driver, "Rad" on black airfoil, Thailand cast.................... $1 – 2
32. "Rad 5," black with white stripes, black driver, "Rad" on black airfoil, Thailand cast, Aquafresh on-package premium.............................. $5 – 6
33. "Tech Racing 3," red with black driver, black airfoil, Thailand cast......... $1 – 2
34. "Valvoline 5," blue and white with dark blue driver, "Valvoline" on blue airfoil, China cast, Indy 500 .... $4 – 5
35. chrome with red driver, "Goodyear" on red airfoil, Thailand cast, custom promotional .... $16 – 24

FAB 1 (see Lady Penelope's FAB 1)

Fairlady Z (see Datsun Fairlady Z)

Fandango, 3", #35, 1975; BR 31-32, 1985
1. red, "35" label, red base, red interior, silver propeller.................... $60 – 80
2. red, "35" label, red base, ivory interior, silver propeller.................... $12 – 16
3. red, "35" label, unpainted base, ivory interior, silver propeller........... $9 – 12
4. red, "35" label, unpainted base, ivory interior, blue propeller............ $9 – 12
5. red, "35" label, unpainted base, white interior, blue propeller............ $9 – 12
6. red, "35" label, white base, ivory interior, silver propeller .... $9 – 12
7. red, "35" label, white base, ivory interior, red propeller.................... $9 – 12
8. red, "35" label, white base, ivory interior, blue propeller................... $9 – 12
9. red, "35" label, black base, white interior, blue propeller, UK issue ... $75 – 90
10. red, sunburst label, unpainted base, white interior, blue propeller.. $16 – 24
11. yellow, England cast, Super GT BR 31-32, 1985 .... $4 – 6
12. yellow, China cast, Super GT BR 31-32, 1985 .... $3 – 45
13. lemon yellow, China cast, Super GT BR 31-32, 1985 .... $8 – 10
14. maroon, England cast, Super GT BR 31-32, 1985 .... $4 – 6
15. maroon, China cast, Super GT BR 31 -32, 1985 .... $8 – 10
16. purple, "35" label, gray base, white interior, light blue propeller, UK issue .... $600 – 800
17. white, "6" label, red base, red interior, silver propeller.................... $16 – 24
18. white, "35" label, red base, red interior, red propeller .... $9 – 12
19. white, "35" label, red base, red interior, silver propeller...................... $9 – 12
20. white, "35" label, unpainted base, red interior, silver propeller........... $9 – 12
21. gray, China cast, Super GT BR 31-32, 1985 .... $3 – 45

Farm Trailer, #711, 1993 Farming series
1. yellow, black tires on gray rims.. $3 – 4

Fast Freight Truck, #41, 2006 (see Delivery Truck)

Faun Crane Truck (see Faun Mobile Crane)

Faun Dump Truck (see Faun Earth Mover Dump Truck)

Faun Earth Mover Dump Truck, $2\frac{3}{4}$", #58, 1976; #9, 1989; #53, 1989; #9, 1997; #27, 1999; #95, 2000; #18, 2002; #47, 2006
1. red with metallic gray dumper, no markings, 1997 .... $1 – 2
2. red with black dumper, no markings .. $1 – 2

3. primer pale red with light gray dumper, black and brown rust and primer colors, no markings, 5-pack... $1 – 2
4. bright orange with metallic gray dumper, no markings .... $1 – 2

5. bright orange with gray dumper, "MC18," "Matchbox" and rhinoceros graphics, 2003 Hero City 5-pack #4.............................. $1 – 2

6. bright orange with gray dumper, 2007 .... $1 – 2
7. bright orange with bright orange dumper .... $1 – 2
8. bright orange with black dumper, no markings, 1996 .... $1 – 2

9. fluorescent light orange, black dumper, no markings .... $3 – 4
10. light orange with red dumper, no markings, Action Systems Pack........ $1 – 2
11. orange-yellow with red dumper, no markings, China cast...................... $1 – 2
12. orange-yellow with orange-yellow dumper, orange stripes, China cast, Action Pack .... $3 – 4
13. orange-yellow with orange-yellow dumper, no markings, England cast ... $4 – 6
14. orange-yellow with plastic dumper, black stripes, "Dirt Hauler," 2007 Superfast #15.................................... $4 – 5
15. yellow with yellow dumper, no markings, England cast.......................... $4 – 6

16. yellow with red dumper, no markings, England cast .... $30 – 40

17. yellow with yellow dumper, "CAT" logo, England cast.......................... $5 – 7
18. yellow with metallic silver dumper, orange stripes, Macau cast...... $3 – 4
19. yellow, metallic silver dumper, orange stripes, China cast................. $3 – 4

20. metallic green with yellow Matchbox logo, yellow dumper with black vertical stripes, 2002 Build It Right .... $1 – 2
21. blue, yellow dump, orange stripes and tools, China cast, Live 'N Learn/Preschool .... $4 – 5

22. dusty blue with pale gray dumper, 2000 Build It! .... $1 – 2
23. dusty blue with pale gray dumper, "Matchbox 2000," 2000 Build It! .... $3 – 4
24. dusty white with green dumper, 1999 Road Work........................... $1 – 2
25. white with yellow dumper, "MC18," "Matchbox," rhinoceros head, 5-pack.................................... $1 – 2
26. metallic gold with metallic gold dumper, no markings, 1997 75 Challenge .... $12 – 16

Faun Mobile Crane, 3", #42, 1985 – 1997; #15, 1998

1. red, black crane cab, metallic gray crane, 1998 Big Movers.......... $1 – 2
2. yellow, "Reynolds Crane Hire," England cast.................................... $3 – 4
3. yellow, "Reynolds Crane Hire," Macau cast.................................... $1 – 2
4. yellow, "Reynolds Crane Hire," China cast.................................... $1 – 2
5. yellow, "Reynolds Crane Hire," Thailand cast.................................... $1 – 2
6. yellow, no markings, yellow plastic crane cab, black crane, Motor City..... $3 – 4

7. yellow, road and bridge graphic, red plastic crane cab, black crane.. $1 – 2
8. yellow, fluorescent orange crane cab, "IC" and checkerboard pattern, Intercom City .... $12 – 16
9. orange, road and bridge graphic, gray crane cab, black crane, light gray boom, 1996 .... $1 – 2

10. orange, black crane cab, metallic gray crane, 1997 .... $1 – 2
11. orange, gray crane cab, black crane.. $1 – 2
12. blue-green, black crane cab, metallic gray crane, dolphin and waves design, Action Pack............................. $4 – 5

13. blue, purple crane cab, gray and brown crane, dirt pattern, 5-pack.................................. $1 – 2
14. blue, purple crane cab, gray and brown crane, dirt pattern, "Hershey 99," Color Comp promotional.............. $12 – 16

15. pale blue, black crane cab, metallic gray crane .... $1 – 2
16. metallic gold, black crane cab, black crane, 1997 75 Challenge ..... $6 – 12
17. orange with gray dumper, 2006 #47.................................... $1 – 2

FedEx Delivery Truck (see Ford Box Van)

Ferrari 308 GTB, 2 15/16", #70, 1981

1. red, "Data East," "Secret Service," red base, Macau cast, Canadian issue................................ $70 – 90
2. red, "Ferrari" logo on hood, red base, Macau cast............................ $3 – 4
3. red, "Ferrari" logo on hood, red base, Thailand cast, Motor City.......... $3 – 4
4. red, "Ferrari" on sides, gray plastic base, Manaus cast, Brazil issue.............................. $20 – 30
5. red, "Magnum P. I.," red plastic base, black roof, China cast, Star Cars.. $5 – 6
6. red, "Pioneer 39," blue base, Macau cast .... $3 – 4
7. red with chrome windows, red base, rubber tires on chrome rims, World Class, Macau cast.................. $6 – 8
8. red with no markings, red base, clear windows, England cast............ $3 – 4
9. red with no markings, orange-red base, clear windows, England cast ..... $3 – 4
10. dark red, "Ferrari" and logo, pearl silver base, clear windows, Macau cast.. $3 – 4
11. orange-red, "Ferrari" and logo, pearl silver base, clear windows, Macau cast.................................... $3 – 4
12. orange-red, "Ferrari" logo, orange-red base, amber windows, England cast .... $3 – 4
13. orange-red, "Ferrari" logo, orange-red base, clear windows, England cast.................................... $3 – 4
14. orange-red, "Ferrari" logo, metallic gray base, clear windows, England cast.................................. $9 – 12
15. orange-red, no markings, orange-red base, clear windows, England cast.................................... $3 – 4
16. orange, "12 Rat Racing Team," blue base, Macau cast, Hong Kong issue................................ $9 – 12
17. yellow, "Ferrari 308 GTB," red base, Macau cast, Laser Wheels....... $4 – 5
18. yellow, "Ferrari 308 GTB," red base, Macau cast, New Superfast Wheels................................ $4 – 5
19. yellow with geometric design, yellow base, 1993 Dream Machines 3-pack, Thailand cast......................... $3 – 4
20. white with no markings, white base, green windows, Graffic Traffic, Macau cast .... $12 – 16

Ferrari 360 Spider, #7, 2003; #16, 2005

1. metallic gray with black interior, 2003 Family Wheels............ $1 – 2
2. yellow with tan interior, 2005 #16.................................... $1 – 2

Ferrari 456 GT, #17, 1994, US; #41, 1994, international; #29, 1997; #82, 2000

1. black, rubber tires on chrome rims, Premiere Collection #15 .... $4 – 5
2. metallic blue, "456 GT" in yellow on sides, gold 6-spoke spiral wheels, 1994 .... $1 – 2
3. metallic gold, 75 Challenge series, 1997 .... $12 – 16

4. metallic pale gold, #82, 2000 Worldwide Wheels.......................... $1 – 2
5. metallic pale gold, #82, "Matchbox 2000," 2000 Worldwide Wheels ....$3 – 4

6. metallic purple with white abstract design on sides, no markings on hood or roof, fluorescent yellow interior, 1996 ....$1 – 2

7. metallic purple with white design on sides, roof, and hood, "Matchbox Rush Racing," pale gray interior, 1997 ....$1 – 2

8. red, 2005 Superfast #17 .....$3 – 4

9. metallic red with no markings, butterscotch interior, 5-spoke wheels, 1996 ....$1 – 2

10. metallic red with no markings, butterscotch interior, 6-spoke pinwheel wheels, 1997......................$1 – 2

11. metallic red, Ferrari logo, rubber tires on chrome rims, J C Penney's Premiere Collection .... $4 – 5
12. metallic red, small logo on hood, 1998 ....$2 – 3
13. metallic dark red, Ferrari logo, 5-spoke wheels................................ $1 – 2
14. pale yellow, small Matchbox logo, 1997 .... $3 – 4

Ferrari Berlinetta, 3", #75, 1965
1. red, black tires on chrome wheels, prototype.................... $1,200 – 1,600
2. red, plain grille, Superfast wheels, 1970.............................. $30 – 40
3. red, silver grille, Superfast wheels, 1970.............................. $30 – 40

4. metallic green, unpainted base, black tires on spoked wheels, 1965 ....$16 – 24
5. metallic green, metallic gray base, black tires on spoked wheels, 1965...$65 – 85
6. metallic green, unpainted base, black tires on chrome wheels, 1966.............................. $16 – 24
7. metallic green, plain grille, Superfast wheels, 1970.................. $80 – 100
8. metallic light blue-green, black tires on spoked wheels, 1965...... $160 – 240

Ferrari F1 Racing Car, red, 2⅝", #73, 1962
1. white driver....................... $20 – 30
2. gray driver .... $20 – 30

Ferrari F40, 3", #24, 1989; #70, 1989; #57, 1998; #19, 1999; #23, 2000
1. black with black and chrome windows, Lightning.............................. $4 – 5
2. black with clear windows, "It's Matchbox '93 Tyco" .... $40 – 50
3. black with clear windows, tan and black interior, rubber wheels on chrome rims, International Premiere Collection #2.................................... $4 – 5
4. red chrome with clear windows, white interior, light blue and yellow design, 5-pack................................ $1 – 2
5. silver chrome with clear windows, custom model .... $15 – 20
6. silver chrome with pink windows...$3 – 4

7. light blue chrome with red windows, 1997 Sleek Riders 5-pack .....$1 – 2
8. metallic burgundy with clear windows, white interior, light blue and yellow design, 5-pack....................... $1 – 2
9. metallic gold with clear windows, black interior, 6-spoke wheels, 1997 75 Challenge................................. $6 – 12
10. metallic gold with clear windows, black interior, 5-spoke concave wheels, 1997 75 Challenge..................... $30 – 50
11. metallic gray with clear windows, red and black interior, rubber tires on chrome rims, Premiere Collection #19.................................... $4 – 5
12. gradient metallic purple to metallic pink, 1996.................................. $1 – 2
13. gradient metallic red to black, clear windows, black interior, 5-pack....... $1 – 2
14. gradient metallic red to purple, clear windows, black interior............ $1 – 2

15. gradient white to orange, clear windows, black interior, 1996 Super Cars 5-pack ....$1 – 2

16. orange with opaque yellow windows, black spots ....$1 – 2

17. purple with orange windows, orange and white design, 1997 Super Cars 5-pack ....$1 – 2
18. red with opaque yellow windows, black spots, 1994......................... $3 – 4
19. red with black windows, Triple Heat .... $4 – 5
20. red with clear windows, black interior, Ferrari logo .... $1 – 2
21. red with clear windows, black interior, Ferrari logo, painted tail lights, Show Stoppers.............................. $3 – 4
22. red with clear windows, black interior, Ferrari logo, Intercom City base................................ $40 – 60

23. red with clear windows, black interior, "Ferrari," "Pininfarina" on doors, 1999 Top Class .... $1 – 2
24. red with clear windows, black interior, "Ferrari," no "Pininfarina" on doors, 1999 Top Class .... $1 – 2
25. red with clear windows, black interior, "Old Eight," UK issue .... $80 – 120
26. red with clear windows, black and red interior, detailed trim, Gold Coin Collection .... $16 – 24
27. red with chrome windows, rubber tires on chrome rims, Ferrari logo, World Class.................................. $6 – 8
28. red with chrome and black windows, Lightning............................... $3 – 4

29. red with tinted windows, brown interior, 2000 Italian Stars......... $1 – 2
30. red with tinted windows, brown interior, "Matchbox 2000," 2000 Italian Stars.................................. $3 – 4
31. silver with pink windows, yellow and pink stripes................................. $4 – 5
32. white with blue chrome and black windows, Lightning...................... $4 – 5
33. white with clear windows, Collector's Choice, White Rose Collectibles .. $3 – 4

34. white with clear windows, black horse, red stripe, 1998 Super Car................................. $1 – 2
35. yellow and white with chrome windows, rubber tires on gray rims, World Class .... $6 – 8
36. yellow with clear windows, black and red interior, rubber tires on gray rims, Premiere Collection #10 .... $4 – 5
37. yellow with clear windows, black interior, red stripe, black horse on hood.. $1 – 2
38. yellow with blue chrome and black windows, Lightning...................... $3 – 4
39. yellow with red racing stripe, black horse on hood, 1997 .... $1 – 2

Ferrari F50 Coupe, #75, 1996 – 1997; #59, 1998; #21, 2000; #35, 1999, international; #16, 2000, international

1. red, "Citrix," "SD2000," black interior, ASAP promotional .... $80 – 120

2. red, "Ferrari," "50," gradient white to yellow stripes, black interior, 1997 Racing 5-pack .... $1 – 2

3. red, "Go Swans! 1997," gray interior, 5-spoke concave wheels, Australia issue .... $4 – 5
4. red, "Novell 6," black interior, clear windows, ASAP promotional ...... $20 – 30
5. red, "Novell 6," black interior, tinted windows, ASAP promotional ...... $20 – 30
6. red with Ferrari logo, black interior, 5-spoke concave wheels............. $1 – 2

7. red with Ferrari logo, black interior, 6-spoke spiral wheels........... $1 – 2

8. red with detailed trim, black interior, rubber tires on chrome rims, Ultra Class............................... $9 – 12
9. red with no markings, black interior, ASAP promotional blank .... $30 – 40
10. yellow, "Ferrari" and logo, black interior, 5-spoke concave wheels, 5-pack... $1 – 2
11. yellow, "Ferrari" and logo, black interior, 5-spoke wheels, 5-pack .... $1 – 2
12. yellow, "Ferrari" and logo, black interior, 10-spoke wheels, 5-pack .... $7 – 9
13. yellow with detailed trim, black and red interior, rubber tires on chrome rims, Toys "R" Us gift set................. $4 – 5
14. yellow with Ferrari logo, black interior, 5 -spoke concave wheels.......... $1 – 2
15. black with Ferrari logo, brown interior .... $1 – 2

16. black with Ferrari logo, red interior, 1998 Super Cars .... $1 – 2
17. metallic gray, "Ferrari" and logo, red interior, 5-pack....................... $1 – 2
18. metallic gray with detailed trim, black and red interior, rubber tires on chrome rims, Premiere Collection #15 .. $4 – 5
19. metallic gray with Ferrari logo, "Matchbox 2000," black interior, 5-spoke concave wheels, 2000 Italian Stars.. $7 – 9
20. metallic gray with Ferrari logo, "Matchbox 2000," black interior, 5-spoke wheels, 2000 Italian Stars .... $3 – 4
21. metallic gray with Ferrari logo, black interior, 5-spoke wheels, 2000 Italian Stars................................... $1 – 2
22. metallic gray with Ferrari logo, black interior, 5-spoke concave wheels, 2000 Italian Stars........................... $1 – 2
23. metallic gold, black interior, 1997 75 Challenge .... 12 – 16

Ferrari F50 Spyder, #75, 1996 (planned but never issued)

Ferrari Testarossa, 3", #75, 1987; #78 error package, 1996; #25, 2000; #20, 2000, international

1. red, "1," face and checkered flag, yellow wheels with blue hubs, Macau cast, Live 'N Learn/Matchbox Preschool................................$7 – 9
2. red, "Lloyds," "Ferrari," China cast, UK issue...........................$8 – 10
3. red, "Redoxon," Macau cast, Hong Kong issue......................$30 – 40
4. red with clear windows, detailed trim, rubber tires on chrome rims, Thailand cast, Premiere Collection #19 ..$4 – 5
5. red with chrome windows, detailed trim, rubber tires on gray rims, Macau cast, World Class ....$6 – 8
6. red with chrome windows, detailed trim, rubber tires on gray rims, Thailand cast, World Class...........$6 – 8
7. red with Ferrari logo, China cast..................................$1 – 2
8. red with Ferrari logo, 8-dot wheels, Thailand cast.......................$1 – 2
9. red with Ferrari logo, 6-spoke spiral wheels, Thailand cast............$4 – 5
10. red with small Ferrari logo, painted tail lights, Thailand cast, Show Stoppers ....$3 – 4
11. red with silver accents and logos, Macau cast, New Superfast Wheels ....$9 – 12
12. metallic red with silver accents, Macau cast, Laser Wheels .....$4 – 5
13. metallic red 6-spoke spiral wheels, Thailand cast.......................$1 – 2
14. dark red to orange with Ferrari logos, Macau cast, Super Color Changers............................$4 – 5
15. yellow with detailed trim, rubber tires on chrome rims, Thailand cast, international Premiere Collection #2 .. $4 – 5
16. yellow with small logo, 5-spoke concave wheels, China cast, German issue.................................$5 – 6
17. yellow with red, blue and yellow accents, armaments, Roadblasters .... $4 – 5
18. yellow, "9 Rabbit Racing Team," Macau cast, Hong Kong issue.............................$10 – 12

19. fluorescent yellow with black accent stripes, pink flash, Thailand cast................................ $1 - 2
20. metallic blue with small Ferrari logo, Collector's Choice, White Rose Collectibles.................................... $3 - 4
21. black with detailed trim, rubber tires on chrome rims, Thailand cast, Premiere Collection #10....................... $4 - 5
22. black with Ferrari logo, silver accents, New Superfast Wheels .... $4 - 5
23. black with small logo, 5-spoke concave wheels, China cast, 2000 Italian Stars.................................. $1 - 2

24. black with small logo, "Matchbox 2000," 5-spoke concave wheels, China cast, 2000 Italian Stars ....$3 - 4
25. metallic gray with detailed trim, rubber tires on chrome rims, Thailand cast, Gold Coin Collection .... $20 - 30
26. metallic pearl gray with gold accents, Laser Wheels....................... $4 - 5
27. white, "Miami Vice," China cast, Star Cars.................................. $5 - 6
28. white with chrome windows, detailed trim, rubber tires on gray rims, Thailand cast, World Class.................. $6 - 8
29. white with no markings, China cast, Graffic Traffic..................... $12 - 16

Ferret Scout Car, 2¼", #61, 1959

1. olive green with black plastic wheels .... $15 - 25

Fiat 1500, with luggage on roof, 2½", #56, 1965

1. turquoise..........................$8 - 12
2. red .... $80 - 90

Fiat Abarth, 2 15/16", #9, 1982; #74, 1984
1. white, "Matchbox," red interior.. $3 - 4
2. white, "Matchbox," black interior .... $160 - 200

3. white, "Alitalia"...................$4 - 5

4. white with red, orange and yellow stripe, Macau cast ....$9 - 12
5. white, "Matchbox 11," Manaus cast, Brazil issue .... $45 - 55

Field Car 2⅝", #18, 1969 — based on an International Scout
1. yellow with black plastic tires on green plastic wheel hubs........... $250 - 300
2. yellow with black plastic tires on red wheel hubs, unpainted base...... $6 - 9
3. black plastic tires on red wheel hubs, black painted base................ $9 - 12
4. yellow with Superfast wheels, unpainted base................................ $24 - 32
5. yellow with Superfast wheels, metallic gray base.......................... $32 - 36
6. light olive green with Superfast wheels................................. $6 - 8
7. dark olive green with Superfast wheels............................ $70 - 90
8. white with checked design label, Superfast wheels.................... $400 - 500
9. orange with Superfast wheels, black interior .... $5 - 7
10. orange with Superfast wheels, "179," black interior .... $6 - 8
11. orange with Superfast wheels, white interior .... $6 - 9
12. orange with Superfast wheels, "179," white interior....................... $9 - 12
13. metallic red with Superfast wheels................................. $5 - 7
14. dark yellow with checked design label, Superfast wheels .... $5 - 7

Field Gun, 3", #32, 1978
1. army green, army green guard, no base.................................... $6 - 7

2. army green, army green guard, tan plastic base, black wheel hubs ..$6 - 7
3. army green, army green guard, tan plastic base, chrome wheel hubs .... $30 - 40
4. army green, black guard, tan plastic base, black wheel hubs, UK issue............................... $80 - 90
5. green, green guard, tan plastic base, black wheel hubs, UK issue.. $80 - 120

Fire Chief Car (resembles a Ford Torino), 3", #64, 1976; BR 17-18, 1985
1. red, 1976 .... $10 - 12
2. red, "Rescue," England cast, Super GT BR 17-18, 1985 .... $4 - 6
3. red, "Rescue," China cast, Super GT BR 17-18, 1985 .... $8 - 10
4. orange, "Rescue," China cast, Super GT BR 17-18, 1985 .... $3 - 5
5. blue, "Police," China cast, Super GT BR 17-18, 1985 .... $3 - 5
6. white, "Police," England cast, Super GT BR 17-18, 1985 .... $4 - 6
7. white, "Police," China cast, Super GT BR 17-18, 1985 .... $8 - 10

Fire Crusher 4x4, #32, 2004 (see Fire Truck 4x4)

Fire Crusher/Ladder Truck, #27, 2001; #25, 2002; #3, 2003
1. metallic red with white ladder, "5 Alarm Force," "Base 525," 2001 Flame Eaters .... $1 - 2
2. metallic orange, 2002 Red Hot Heroes .... $1 - 2

3. white with red ladder, 2003 Sky Fire .... $1 – 2

Fire Engine (also see Snorkel Fire Engine, Extending Ladder Fire Engine)

Fire Engine 2006 (Flame Tamer), #27, 2006

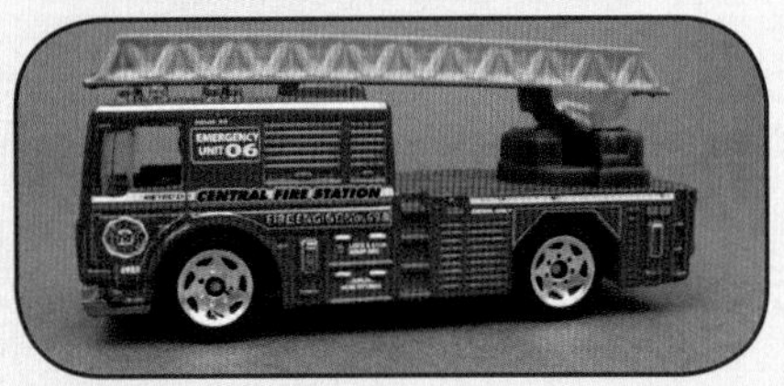

1. red with thin white stripes, silver-gray ladder on dark gray base, silver-gray chassis, "Central Fire Station," 2006 #27 .... $1 – 2

Fire Flooder, #31, 2004 (see Airport Fire Tanker)

Fire Freezer, #4, 2004, fire extinguisher vehicle (MB619)

1. 2004 Ultra Heroes .... $1 – 2

Fire Hovercraft, 2⅞", #62, 2001; #35, 2002; #64, 2003

1. black hull, red deck, yellow water gun and engines, 2001 Scuba Dudes .. $1 – 2

2. red hull, white deck, sky blue water gun and engines, 2002 Ultimate Rescue .... $1 – 2

3. red hull, white deck, sky blue water gun and engines, in Christmas box, 2002 .... $3 – 4

4. dark red hull, white deck, yellow water gun and engines, 2003 Pumper Squad .... $1 – 2

5. black hull. dark gray deck, black water gun and engines, Battle Kings Night Landing set, 2006, K5532...... $1 – 2

6. red hull, gray base, white deck, dark gray gun and engines, 2006 5-pack J4673............................... $1 – 2

Fire Pumper (also see Highway Fire Pumper)

Fire Pumper, 3", #29, 1966

1. red, "Denver" decals, regular wheels .... $9 – 12

2. red, shield labels, regular wheels .. $9 – 12
3. red, no labels, regular wheels ... $8 – 10
4. red, no water gun cast, Superfast wheels, 1970..................... $60 – 80
5. red, water gun cast, Superfast wheels, Code Red............................ $9 – 12

Fire Quencher (see Boom Fire Truck)

Fire Truck (see Airport Fire Truck, All-Terrain Fire Tanker, Bucket Fire Truck, Extending Ladder Fire Engine, Extending Ladder Fire Truck, Fire Crusher, Fire Ladder Truck, Fire Pumper, Fire Truck 4x4, Snorkel Fire Engine, etc.)

Fire Rescue, Real Talkin', electronic sounds and lights

1. fluorescent neon yellow......... $5 – 6

Fire Truck 4x4/4x4 Fire Crusher, #32, 2004

1. metallic red with black base, pearl white back, "Alarm Unit," 2004 .... $1 – 2

2. red with metallic gray base and back, 2006 5-pack J4678 .... $1 – 2

3. black with red base, blue back, Spongebob Squarepants graphics, 2006 Nickelodeon 5-pack H5774 .... $1 – 2

4. red with "Scooby-Doo!" graphics, Scooby-Doo! 5-pack L1574, 2007 .... $3 – 4

Fire Water Pumper, #75, 2002; #62, 2003

1. **dark red with metallic gray base, "Eng. 922," 2002 Rescue Rookies .... $1 – 2**

2. **red, "Hero City," burning cityscape and fireman graphics, 2003 Pumper Squad .... $1 – 2**

3. **red, "Rescue Heroes" and fireman illustration, 2003 Rescue Heroes 5-pack.................................. $1 – 2**

4. **red with red wheel hubs, metallic silver chassis, "Water Pumper," 2006 5-pack J4678 .... $1 – 2**

FJ Holden Van (see Holden FJ Van)

Flame Chopper, fireman's axe, #5, 2004
1. 2004 #5 .... $3 – 4

Flame Out, #67, 1983 (similar castings: Big Banger, Cosmic Blues, Pi-Eyed Piper, Red Rider)
1. white with red and orange flames, red windows, Macau cast .... $5 – 6

Flame Tamer, #27, 2006; #51, 2007
1. red with metallic silver trim, 2006 #27 .... $1 – 2

Flamin' Manta, Roman Numeral IX, 1978 (variation of #7 Hairy Hustler, 1971)
1. yellow, Roman Numeral Limited Edition .... $9 – 12

Flareside Pickup (see Ford Flareside Pickup)

Flat Car with container, 3", #25, 1978
1. beige container, "NYK" .... $12 – 16
2. beige container, "Sea/Land" ... $8 – 12
3. blue container, "United States Line" .... $45 – 60
4. blue container, "Sea/Land" labels .... $45 – 60
5. dark brown container, "NYK" ..... $7 – 9
6. light brown container, "NYK" ... $16 – 24
7. orange container, "NYK" .... $45 – 60
8. orange container "OCL" .... $45 – 60
9. red container, "NYK" .... $45 – 60
10. tan container, "NYK" .... $7 – 9
11. tan container, "United States Line" .... $10 – 12
12. tan container, "Sea/Land" .... $7 – 9
13. tan container, "OCL" .... $12 – 16
14. white container, no labels (labels included with play set) .... $12 – 16
15. yellow container, no labels (labels included with play set)................ $12 – 16

Flatbed Truck, #41, 2000 (similar casting: Delivery Truck)
1. lemon yellow with gray flat bed, metallic gray base, "HB Show Cars"....... $1 – 2
2. lemon yellow with gray flat bed, metallic gray base, "HB Show Cars," "Matchbox 2000"................................. $3 – 4
3. orange with black flatbed, metallic gray base, "Auto Club" .... $3 – 5

4. **metallic blue with black flatbed, metallic gray base, monkey and wrench design, 2003 Hero City 5-pack #11........................... $1 – 2**

Floodlight Heavy Rescue Auxiliary Power Truck (see Mack Floodlight Heavy Rescue Auxiliary Power Truck)

Flying Beetle, Roman Numeral IV, 1978 (variation of #11 Flying Bug, 1972)

1. **orange, Roman Numeral Limited Edition.............................. $9 – 12**

Flying Bug Volkswagen Beetle, $2\frac{7}{8}$", #11, 1972 (similar casting: Flying Beetle)

1. **metallic red, yellow jets, driver with chrome helmet .... $15 – 20**

Foam Fire Truck (see All-Terrain Fire Tanker)

Foden 15-Ton Sugar Container Truck, "Tate & Lyle," $2\frac{5}{8}$", #10, 1961
1. crown decal on back, gray wheels .... $65 – 80

2. **no crown decal on back, gray wheels .... $30 – 40**
3. silver wheels .... $65 – 80
4. black wheels .... $30 – 40

Foden Cement Truck (see Foden Concrete Truck, Foden "Ready-Mix" Concrete Truck)

Foden Concrete Truck, 3", #21, 1968
1. yellow with red base, black plastic wheels .... $6 – 9
2. yellow with green base, Superfast wheels .... $24 – 36

Foden "Ready-Mix" Concrete Truck, $1\frac{3}{4}$", #26, 1956

1. **orange with orange mixer, metal wheels, gold grille........... $65 – 85**
2. orange with orange mixer, metal wheels, silver grille......................... $35 – 50
3. orange with orange mixer, silver plastic wheels.......................... $135 – 160
5. orange with orange mixer, silver metal wheels, China casting, 1993 Matchbox Originals .... $3 – 5

Foden "Ready-Mix" Concrete Truck, $2\frac{1}{2}$", #26, 1961
1. orange with gray mixer, gray metal wheels.......................... $400 – 450
2. orange with orange mixer, gray plastic wheels.............................. $35 – 45
3. orange with orange mixer, silver plastic wheels.......................... $130 – 150

4. orange with orange mixer, black plastic wheels .... $15 – 20

Ford '33 Coupe (see Ford 1933 Coupe)

Ford '33 Hot Rod (see Ford 1933 Coupe)

Ford '33 Street Rod (see Ford 1933 Coupe)

Ford 1921 Model T (see Ford Model T 1921 Van)

Ford 1933 Coupe, #34, 1998; #13, 1999, Australia; #20, 2000

1. black, "IMCC Est. 1998," "Join Today," custom .... $30 – 40
2. black with red stripes, rubber tires on chrome rims, First Editions .... $5 – 6

3. gray with purple door, dirt and "MB" door logo, 5-pack .... $1 – 2

4. gray with purple door, dirt and "American Iron Cruise Night," Color Comp promotional .... $12 – 16
5. metallic hot pink with accents ... $1 – 2
6. maroon, "IMCC Est. 1998," "Join Today," Goodyear slicks, custom .... $20 – 30
7. maroon with black and yellow design, Goodyear slicks, 1998 Classic Decades .... $1 – 2
8. metallic purple, no markings, Goodyear slicks, 2000 Great Drivers .... $1 – 2
9. metallic purple, "Matchbox 2000," Goodyear slicks, 2000 Great Drivers .... $3 – 4
10. metallic purple, "Midwest Regional Convention," "MRMC 2000," custom .... $20 – 25
11. metallic purple, "Midwest Regional Convention," "MRMC 2000 Vendor," custom .... $30 – 40
12. purple, "Hot August Nights 2000" .... $16 – 24
13. purple with amber roof lights, "D.A.R.E." and graphics, 2001 D.A.R.E. 5-pack .... $1 – 2
14. red and white, "Coca-Cola," rubber tires, Premiere Collection .... $5 – 6
15. unpainted, "IMCC Est. 1998," "Join Today," custom .... $30 – 40
16. unpainted with no markings, rubber tires on chrome rims, First Editions .... $5 – 6
17. yellow, "American Graffiti," rubber tires on gray rims, Star Cars .... $12 – 16
18. yellow, "2001 Ballarat 12th Super Southern Swapmeet," custom .. $12 – 16
19. yellow, "Cruise Down Memory Lane," "Corvettes Unlimited," Color Comp promotional .... $16 – 24
20. yellow, "Cruisin New England Magazine All Wheels Festival 2001," Color Comp promotional .... $50 – 60
21. yellow with black roof, "Glenside Motor Vehicle Show 2000," Color Comp promotional .... $20 – 25
22. yellow with black roof, "Matchbox 2000 Demo Model — Color Comp Inc.," Color Comp promotional .... $24 – 32
23. yellow with black roof, "Midwest Regional Convention," custom .... $20 – 25
24. yellow with black roof, Goodyear slicks, Australia issue .... $3 – 4

25. bright orange-red with flame graphics, 2005 Superfast #13 ...... $3 – 4

Ford 1933 Police Coupe, #508, 2001

1. metallic purple, "D.A.R.E.," black and orange design, amber roof light, 5-pack .... $1 – 2

2. black with white door, 2006 10-pack B5609 .... $2 – 3

3. metallic blue with white door, 2006 10-pack 1 B5609 .... $2 – 3

Ford 3-Ton 4x4 Army Ambulance, 2½", #63, 1959

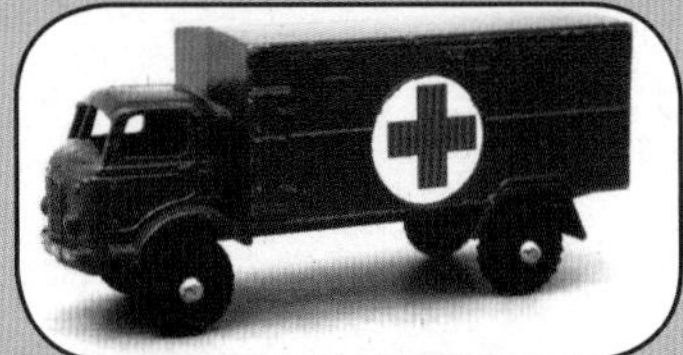

1. olive green with black plastic wheels .... $40 – 50

Ford Ambulance, #51, 1997; #25, 1998; #5, 1999; #87, 2000; #17, 1997, international

1. "27 Matchbox Ambulance," "48-91," "Newfield Ambulance Corps," white with chrome base, Color Comp promotional .... $20 – 30

2. "27 Matchbox Ambulance," "Dial 911 Ambulance," white with chrome base, blue and silver design ... $1 – 2

3. "27 Matchbox Ambulance," yellow with chrome base, red and white design, 1998 To the Rescue .. $1 – 2

4. "27 Matchbox Ambulance," yellow with translucent white base, red and white design, 1998 To the Rescue ... $60 – 80
5. "5 Alarm Ambulance," white with chrome base, 5-pack .... $1 – 2
6. "Alice 106 FM," white with chrome base, ASAP promotional issue .... $120 – 160
7. "Ambulance," "EMS" logo, metallic silver with chrome base, dark blue bands, 5-pack .... $4 – 5
8. "Ambulance-Ridge, New York," bright blue with chrome base, 1999 Matchbox USA .... $1 – 2
9. "Ambulance 3-1926," white with chrome base, olive and blue stripes, 5-pack .... $1 – 2
10. "Ambulance Dial 911," white with chrome base, rubber tires on chrome rims, 1997 Inaugural issue ...... $5 – 6
11. "American International Recovery," white with chrome base, ASAP promotional issue .... $120 – 160
12. "Bill Cairns Realtor," white with chrome base, ASAP promotional issue ... $12 – 16
13. "County EMS," burgundy cab, white box, burgundy accents, 1998 Around Town 5-pack .... $1 – 2

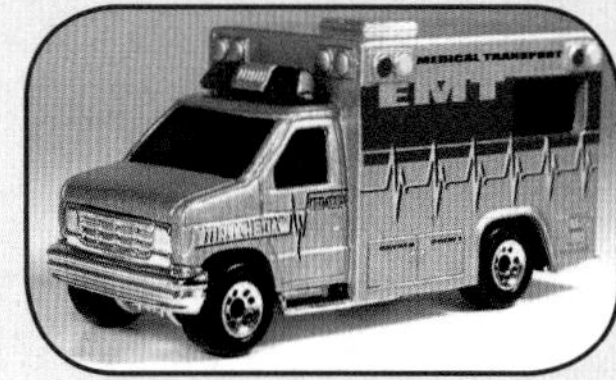

14. "EMT," "Matchbox Medical Transport," metallic silver with chrome base, red band, yellow design, 2000 Police Patrol .... $1 – 2
15. "EMT," "Matchbox Medical Transport," "Matchbox 2000," metallic silver with chrome base, red band, yellow design, 2000 Police Patrol .... $3 – 4
16. "Fire Rescue," red with chrome base, white band, rubber tires on chrome rims, Premiere Collection #21 .. $4 – 5
17. "FSU," white with chrome base, ASAP promotional issue .... $12 – 16
18. "Flight Crew Transport," dark blue with chrome base, rubber tires on chrome rims, Premiere Collection ..... $30 – 40
19. "Kimball Day Hospital," white with chrome base, ASAP promotional issue .... $12 – 16
20. "Las Vegas Fire Department," white with chrome base, rubber tires on chrome rims, Premiere Collection ..... $12 – 16
21. "Matchbox Dial 911 Ambulance," white with blue and silver accents ...... $1 – 2
22. "Metro Alarm," "Ambulance," orange and white with chrome base, 5-pack... $1 – 2
23. "Midwest Regional Matchbox Convention" in gold lettering, white with chrome base, ASAP promotional issue......... $12 – 16
24. "Midwest Regional Matchbox Convention" in green lettering, white with chrome base, ASAP promotional issue .... $60 – 70
25. "Midwest Regional Matchbox Convention" in red lettering, white with chrome base, ASAP promotional issue......... $30 – 40
26. "NAEMT/MAEMT 25 Years of Service," white with chrome base, ASAP promotional issue .... $12 – 16
27. "Police"; "Metropolitan Police"; white with chrome base; red, yellow, and blue stripes; 2000 Police Patrol ...... $3 – 4
28. "Squantz Engine Co.," white with chrome base, ASAP promotional issue... $12 – 16
29. "Sugar Grove Fire Department 2000," white with chrome base, ASAP promotional issue .... $16 – 24
30. "Windham Hospital EMS" (left side only), white with chrome base, ASAP promotional issue .... $12 – 16
31. "Windham Hospital EMS," "2000," white with chrome base, ASAP promotional issue .... $12 – 16
32. "York Fair Emergency 1997," yellow with chrome base, White Rose Collectibles .... $7 – 9
33. metallic gold with chrome base, 1997 75 Challenge .... $6 – 12
34. red with chrome base, yellow and red snake and rod design, 5-pack.... $1 – 2
35. unpainted with chrome base, rubber tires on chrome rims, 1997 Inaugural issue .... $5 – 6
36. white with chrome base, no markings, ASAP promotional blank .... $30 – 40

Ford Anglia, light blue, 2⅝", #7, 1961
1. gray plastic wheels .... $20 – 25
2. silver plastic wheels .... $20 – 25
3. black plastic wheels .... $15 – 20

Ford Atkinson Grit Spreader, 2⅝", #70, 1966

1. red cab, light yellow hopper, black plastic wheels, 1966 .... $12 – 16
2. red cab, dark yellow hopper, black plastic wheels, 1966 .... $30 – 40
3. red cab, yellow hopper, Superfast wheels, 1970..................... $35 – 45

Ford Boss Mustang, 2⅞", #44, 1972, #11, 1982 (see Ford Mustang Boss 302 1970)

Ford Boss Mustang 1970, #37, 1998 (see Ford Mustang Boss 302 1970)

Ford Box Truck (see Ford Box Van)

Ford Box Van, #23, 1999, #59, 2000
1. blue-green with white interior, blue windows, fish logo, 5-pack............. $1 – 2

2. green with yellow interior, "Hey Arnold" and cartoon head, 2003 Nickelodeon 5-pack .... $3 – 4
3. red with red interior, "Coca-Cola," black and white design .... $3 – 4

4. white with white interior, clear windows, "FedEx," 1999 Speedy Delivery .... $1 – 2
5. white with white interior, clear windows, no markings, ASAP promotional blank .... $30 – 45
6. white with white interior, clear windows, "County Line," ASAP promotional .... $80 – 120
7. white with white interior, clear windows, "Flowers Make It Special," "Roques," ASAP promotional .... $80 – 120
8. white with white interior, blue windows, "FedEx," 2000 Speedy Delivery.. $1 – 2
9. white with white interior, blue windows, "FedEx," "Matchbox 2000," 2000 Speedy Delivery .... $3 – 4
10. white with black interior, clear windows, "FedEx," 2000 Speedy Delivery.. $1 – 2

11. white with black interior, amber windows, red and black design, "Matchbox," "8945," "54," circle logo, 2000, 5 Alarm 5-pack............. $1 – 2
12. white with black interior, "Merry Christmas 1999," "Last Delivery — Matchbox Forum," custom model......... $24 – 32
13. white with black interior, clear windows, no markings, ASAP promotional blank .... $30 – 45
14. yellow with red interior, clear windows, "Coca-Cola," rubber tires on chrome rims, Premiere Collection .... $5 – 6

15. black, Texaco graphics, 2002 Matchbox Collectibles .... $12 – 16

16. yellow with "The Backyardigans" graphics, 2006 Nickelodeon 5-pack H4108 .... $1 – 2

17. flat black, "Emergency Response Police SWAT," 2006 5-pack J4676................................ $1 – 2

18. red with Coca-Cola graphics... $4 - 6 F0497

Ford Bronco 1972 4x4, #58, 2007
1. blue .... $1 – 2

Ford Bronco II 4x4, 3", #35, 1989; #39, 1990; #51, 1998; #25, 1999

1. red with yellow "4x4 Bronco," white splash design, 1993 Off Road 5-pack................................. $1 - 2

2. red, "Luigi's Pizza," 1998 Rough 'N Tough................................ $1 - 2
3. red, "Vinnie's Pizza," 1999 Speedy Delivery .... $1 – 2
4. red, map and compass design, yellow tires, Live 'N Learn/Matchbox Preschool .... $7 – 9
5. orange to dark brown, "Bronco" and stripes, Super Color Changer.... $4 – 5
6. fluorescent orange with black zebra stripes, 5-pack....................... $1 – 2
7. yellow, "4x4," red flames, red interior, on-package premium, US issue... $7 – 9
8. yellow, "World 4 Kids," blue interior, Australia issue.................... $20 – 25
9. metallic green with beige trim, Collector's Choice, White Rose Collectibles ... $4 – 5

10. purple with white stripes, modified base and interior, play set ..... $4 - 5
11. metallic blue, "4x4 Bronco," white splash design .... $1 – 2
12. metallic purple with white zebra stripes, 1998 Rugged Riders 5-pack..... $1 – 2
13. black, "Kidz 1.75 FM," pink and yellow stripes, Australia issue............ $5 – 6
14. black, "Piranha" on hood, orange piranha design, orange interior....... $1 – 2
15. black, "Piranha" on hood, orange piranha design, red interior........... $1 – 2
16. black, without "Piranha" on hood, orange piranha design, red interior....... $1 – 2
17. white, "Rescue Unit," "Police," shield on door, black hood, black side design, Emergency EM-71 .... $1 – 2

18. white, "Police," orange "PD-22" on roof, 1995 Emergency 5-Pack .. $2 - 4

19. white with black zebra stripes, black interior, 1996 Off Road 5-pack.................................. $1 - 2
20. white, "Bronco" and stripes, red interior .... $2 – 4
21. white, "Coast Guard Beach Patrol," red interior .... $1 – 2
22. white, "Luigiís Pizza," red interior, 1997 .... $1 – 2
23. dark brown to orange, "Bronco" and stripes, red interior, Super Color Changer .... $4 – 5
24. metallic silver with orange piranha design, blue interior................. $3 – 4
25. metallic gold, black interior, 1997 75 Challenge........................... $6 – 12
26. 2002 Matchbox Across America 50th Birthday series #41 Montana-Western Collection .... $4 – 5

Ford Camper Pickup Truck (see Ford Pickup Camper)

Ford Capri, 3", #54, 1971; BR 37-38, 1986 (similar casting: Hot Rocker, Maxi Taxi)

1. metallic bright pink.......... $12 - 16

2. orange............................. $9 - 12
3. purple.............................. $12 – 15
4. cream, China cast, Super GT BR 37-38, 1986 .... $3 – 5
5. blue, China cast, Super GT BR 37-38, 1986 .... $3 – 5

Ford Cargo Skip Truck, $2^{13}/_{16}$", #70, 1988; #45, 1987, international; #317, 1999, Action Packs
1. red with metallic gray cage, metallic gray arms with lever, "Big Top Circus," Action Pack.......................... $4 – 5
2. orange-yellow with no stripe, red plastic skip, China cast .... $1 – 2
3. yellow with orange stripe, gray metal skip, Macau cast.................... $1 – 2
4. yellow with orange stripe, gray metal skip, Thailand cast.................. $1 – 2
5. yellow with orange stripe, gray plastic skip, Macau cast.................... $1 – 2
6. yellow with orange stripe, gray plastic skip, Thailand cast.................. $1 – 2
7. yellow with orange stripe, red plastic skip, Thailand cast.................. $1 – 2
8. bright green with orange cage, black arms with lever, dark green camouflage, "The Lost World," Jurassic Park... $4 – 5
9. blue with red metal skip, yellow wheels with orange hubs, Macau cast, Matchbox Preschool/Live 'N Learn..... $7 – 9
10. khaki with black cage, black arms with lever, green stripes, Action Pack .. $3 – 4

Ford Corsair with boat and rack on roof, $2^{5}/_{8}$", #45, 1965
1. gray wheels....................... $30 – 40
2. black wheels...................... $12 – 16

Ford Cortina 1600 GL, $3^{1}/_{16}$", #55, 1979
1. red, clear windows, doors cast shut .... $4 – 5
2. red, clear windows, white and orange flames, China issue .... $160 – 240
3. metallic red, clear windows, doors open .... $5 – 6
4. metallic red, opaque white windows, doors cast shut .... $12 – 16
5. orange-red, "Nigel Cooper for Matchbox Toys," "Christmas 96," clear windows, Bulgarian cast, UK issue .... $9 – 12
6. green, clear windows, doors open .... $5 – 6

7. metallic green, clear windows, doors open.................................. $5 - 6

8. metallic tan, black stripe, clear windows, doors open .... $4 – 5

Ford Cortina GT, 2⅞", #25, 1968

1. metallic light brown, no roof rack, regular wheels .... $6 – 9
2. metallic light brown with roof rack, regular wheels .... $9 – 12
3. metallic light brown, Superfast wheels, 1970 .... $60 – 80
4. metallic blue, Superfast wheels, 1970 .... $20 – 25

Ford Coupe (see Ford 1933 Coupe)

Ford Courier Delivery Van, 3", #38, 1992, European model
1. red, "Australian Matchbox News," no side cast windows, Australian issue .... $16 – 24
2. red, "Australian Matchbox News," "Club Member" on roof, no side cast windows, Australia issue .... $80 – 120
3. red, "Axa Insurance?" no side cast windows, UK issue .... $80 – 120
4. red, "Ford County Emergency Services," no side cast windows, US issue .... $16 – 24
5. red, no markings, side cast windows .... $12 – 16
6. dark blue, "Australian Matchbox News," no side cast windows, Australian issue .... $80 – 120
7. dark blue, "Axa," no side cast windows, UK issue .... $20 – 25
8. dark blue, "Benedick's Coffee Service," no side cast windows, US issue .... $16 – 24
9. dark blue, "Matchbox — The Ideal Premium," no side cast windows, Germany issue .... $20 – 25
10. dark purple, "Milka," no side cast windows .... $1 – 2
11. light purple, "Milka," no side cast windows .... $3 – 4
12. white, "Courier," no side cast windows, UK issue .... $12 – 16
13. white, "Dent Magician," no side cast windows, UK issue .... $50 – 60

Ford Crown Victoria Police, #54, 1997; #28, 1998; #33, 1999; #86, 2000; #49, 2001 (also see Ford Crown Victoria Police 2006)
1. "Aegis NT New World Systems," white with red roof lights, ASAP promotional .... $60 – 80
2. "Atlanta Police," white with blue roof lights, rubber tires on chrome rims, Premiere Collection #22 .. $200 – 250
3. "C.E.R.T.," "Toy Show Police," "Color Comp Emergency Response Team," "Emergency Demo Model," white with red triangular roof lights, Color Comp promotional .... $30 – 40
4. "D.A.R.E.," white with blue flames, red triangular roof lights, D.A.R.E. .. $4 – 5
5. "Dallas Police," white with red and blue roof lights, rubber tires on chrome rims, Premiere Collection #22 .... $300 – 350
6. "Drive," "A-Pix Entertainment," white with red roof lights, ASAP promotional .... $120 – 160
7. "Freeport Police," white with red roof lights, ASAP promotional ...... $30 – 40
8. "IACP," white with red dome light, ASAP promotional .... $60 – 80
9. "If You Don't Collect Matchbox...Get Out of the Way," white with red triangular roof lights, Color Comp promotional .... $30 – 40
10. "Justice for Police Officer Daniel Faulkner," "4699," "Philadelphia Police," white with red triangular roof lights, Color Comp promotional .... $30 – 50
11. "Matchbox FDMB" on shield with flame graphics, "14," white with red roof lights, 2001 Action Launcher Fire Truck .... $3 – 4
12. "MBI Special Agents" on hood, black with blue roof lights, blue, white and red accents, 2001 Pull Over .... $1 –
13. "Metropolis Museum," black, 2007 Superman 5-pack .... $2 – 3
14. "Minnesota State Patrol," metallic burgundy with red roof lights, rubber tires on chrome rims, World Class series 18 State Patrol II .... $4 – 5
15. "Missouri State Police," white with red and blue roof lights, rubber tires on chrome rims, World Class State Patrol .... $4 – 5
16. "Montana Highway Patrol," black with blue roof lights, white roof, rubber tires on chrome rims, World Class series 18 State Patrol II .... $4 – 5
17. "Nassau County Police," white with red roof lights, ASAP promotional ..$30 – 40
18. "National Law Enforcement Officers Memorial 2001," white with red bar roof lights, ASAP promotional .. $60 – 80
19. "North Dakota State Patrol," white with red roof lights, rubber tires on chrome rims, World Class State Patrol .. $4 – 5
20. "Ocean City New Jersey Police" on shield, white with red triangular roof lights, blue and orange stripes, 2000 Police Patrol .... $1 – 2
21. "Police," "D.A.R.E.," white with red and blue roof lights, D.A.R.E. .... $4 – 5
22. "Police," "To Serve and Protect — Scotchguard," white with red triangular roof lights, Color Comp promotional ..$30 – 50
23. "Police D-19," black and white with red roof lights .... $5 – 6
24. "Police K-9 Canine Unit," blue with red roof lights .... $1 – 2
25. "Police Landover Hills," "D.A.R.E.," white with red and blue roof lights, D.A.R.E. .... $4 – 5

26. "Police Sheriff Warrant Division," white with black and gold stripes, 2006 5-pack J4676 .... $1 – 2

27. "Police Unit 22," "D22" on roof, blue with red roof lights, white and pale orange design, 1997 .... $3 – 4
28. "Police Unit 22," "D22" on roof, black with red roof lights, 1998 To the Rescue .... $1 – 2
29. "Police" with red and white design, blue with red roof lights, 1999 Law & Order .... $1 – 2
30. "Police" with red and blue stripes, white with red triangular roof lights, 1999 Law & Order .... $1 – 2
31. "Police" with blue checkerboard pattern, white with red and blue roof lights, Australia issue .... $16 – 24
32. "Rhode Island State Police," gray with red roof lights, rubber tires on chrome rims, Premiere Collection .... $6 – 8
33. "Route 66 Promotions," white with red roof lights, ASAP promotional .... $20 – 30

34. "South Dakota Highway Patrol," white with red and blue roof lights, rubber tires on chrome rims, World Class series 18 State Patrol II .... $4 – 5

35. "Station 02"; red with red roof lights; white, silver, and yellow graphics; 2003 Hero City 5-pack #1............................ $1 – 2

36. "Verona Police," white with red triangular roof lights, black interior, Color Comp promotional........................ $20 – 30
37. "Verona Police," white with red triangular roof lights, gray interior, Color Comp promotional........................ $60 – 80
38. "Verona Police," "Verona PBA," white with red triangular roof lights, black interior, Color Comp promotional................................ $20 – 30
39. "Wanaque Police," "D.A.R.E.," black with red triangular roof lights, D.A.R.E. .... $4 – 5
40. blue with red and yellow stripes and crest, red roof lights, 5-pack..... $1 – 2
41. blue with red and yellow stripes and crest, red roof lights, Target Eggmobile 3-pack.............................. $12 – 16

42. white with yellow roof lights, 2002 McDonald's Happy Meal premium with set of labels to apply ..... $3 - 4
43. white with red roof lights, ASAP promotional blank........................ $30 – 40
44. white with red triangular roof lights, Color Comp promotional blank............................... $30 – 40
45. metallic gold with red roof lights, 1997 75 Challenge...................... $6 – 12

Ford Crown Victoria Police 2006, #26, 2006

1. "Highway Patrol," black with white doors, 2006 #26 ....$1 - 2

2. white with red and orange trim, chrome 5-spoke wheels, 2007 Superfast #48 ....$3 - 4

3. white with blue and black trim, black wheels, 2007 #49, K9493....$1 - 2

Ford Customline Station Wagon, $2^3/_4$", #31, 1957
1. yellow with metal wheels ...... $35 – 45
2. yellow with gray plastic wheels .... $40 – 50

Ford Dump/Utility Truck, #91, 2000; #71, 2000, international (see Ford F-150 Pickup)

Ford Dump Truck, #91, 2000; #71, 2000, international (see Ford F-150 Pickup)

Ford Escort, BR 25-26, 1985
1. red, England cast, Super GT BR 25-26, 1985 .... $4 – 6
2. blue, England cast, Super GT BR 25-26, 1985 .... $6 – 8
3. beige, England cast, Super GT BR 25-26, 1985 .... $4 – 6
4. yellow, England cast, Super GT BR 25-26, 1985 .... $12 – 15
5. purple, China cast, Super GT BR 25-26, 1985 .... $3 – 5

Ford Escort Cabriolet (see Ford Escort XR3/XR3i Cabriolet)

Ford Escort Cosworth (see Ford Escort RS Cosworth)

Ford Escort RS200 (see Ford RS200)

Ford Escort RS Cosworth, #52, 1994 – 1997; #15, 2001, UK
1. red, "5," yellow splash design, black spoiler, 5-spoke wheels .... $1 – 2
2. red, "5," yellow splash design, black spoiler, 6-spoke wheels .... $4 – 5

3. metallic red with lime and white design, red spoiler $1-2
4. metallic red with lime and white design, black spoiler .... $3 – 4

5. black, "1," yellow and white accents, yellow spoiler, 1997 .... $1 - 2
6. black, "1," yellow and white accents, black spoiler .... $1 – 2

7. white, "Ford" logo on hood, "23," "Goodyear," black and orange graphics, white spoiler, 1996 Racing 5-pack ....$1 - 2

8. white, "Matchbox 3," yellow and dark blue design, dark blue spoiler, 1997 Racing 5-pack ....$1 - 2

9. white, "Mobil 1," "5," "Michelin," blue design, white spoiler, white base ....$1 - 2
10. white, "Mobil 1," "5," "Michelin," blue design, white spoiler, blue base... $4 – 5
11. white, "MOL," orange and two-tone green stripes, white spoiler, Hungarian issue .... $30 – 40
12. white with British flag, red spoiler, 2001 Union Jack series, UK issue...... $4 – 5
13. metallic gold, black spoiler, 1997 75 Challenge .... $6 – 12

Ford Escort RS2000, 3", #9, 1978

1. white with tan interior, "Dunlop," "Ford," "Shell" labels ....$4 - 5
2. white with red interior, "Dunlop," "Ford," "Shell" labels .... $150 – 180
3. white with tan interior, "Phantom" labels .... $4 – 6
4. blue with tan interior, "Phantom" labels .... $4 – 6

5. green with tan interior, white with red interior, "Dunlop," "Ford," "Shell" labels .... $4 – 6
6. green with tan interior, seagull labels .... $4 – 6
7. green with white interior, seagull labels .... $4 – 6
8. green with red interior, seagull labels .... $150 – 180

Ford Escort XR3/XR3i Cabriolet, $2^3/_4$", #17, 1985, US; #37, 1985, international

1. white with "XR3i," silver wheel hubs, Macau cast .... $2 – 4
2. white with "XR3i," gold wheel hubs, Macau cast .... $4 – 6
3. white with "XR3i," Thailand cast .. $2 – 4

4. white with "3" and orange stripes, new Superfast wheels .... $4 – 6

5. white with black trim, red interior, "Ocean Explorer" graphics, 1999 Beach Fun 5-pack .... $1 – 2
6. red with "XR3i" and "FORD" ... $9 – 12
7. metallic blue with "3" and stripes, Laser wheels .... $4 – 6

8. metallic blue with white and orange spatter .... $2 – 4
9. dark blue with "XR3i," Macau cast ... $2 – 4
10. dark blue with "XR3i," Thailand cast .... $2 – 4

Ford Expedition, #67, 1999; #54, 2000; #28, 2002; #62, 1999, international; #73, 2006

1. yellow, "Base 2000," "3456/54," red bands, Launcher 5-pack .... $1 – 2
2. yellow, "Coca-Cola," red band and polar bears, rubber tires on chrome rims, Premiere Collection .... $6 – 8
3. yellow, "Rescue," "Mountain Patrol," red stripes, 1999 Ranger Patrol US issue .... $1 – 2
4. yellow with red stripes and medical cross, 1999 Ranger Patrol international issue .... $3 – 4
5. dusty army green, "Military Police," "Matchbox 2000," 2000 Military .... $3 – 4

6. dusty army green, "Military Police," 2000 Military .... $1 – 2
7. bright blue, detailed trim, rubber tires on chrome rims, 1999 First Editions .... $5 – 6
8. unpainted, rubber tires on chrome rims, 1999 First Editions .... $5 – 6
9. black, "09-99," red and black design, 5-pack .... $1 – 2
10. black, "09-99," red and white design, Target Eggmobile 3-pack .... $3 – 4
11. black, "Scooby-Doo," "Iriuih-Irioih," "Scooby Dooby Doo!" Warner Brothers .... $6 – 8
12. white, "100 Ford Motor Company 100 Years," 2003 Avon 2-pack .... $5 – 6

13. metal flake silver, "RR Road Rescue Fire Patrol," purple base, 2002 Red Hot Heroes .... $1 – 2

14. khaki with black and brown camouflage, 2006 #73 .... $1 – 2

Ford Expedition Fire Chief (see Ford Expedition Police)

Ford Expedition Police, #50, 2001; #5, 2003; #27, 2005

1. blue, "State Patrol," yellow roof light, chrome base, 2001 Pull Over .... $1 – 2
2. metallic blue, "042076," storm graphics, amber roof light, Launcher 5-pack .... $1 – 2

3. white, round "Matchbox" fire logo, red stripes, "54," "3460," red roof light, 2000 5 Alarm 5-pack .. $1 – 2
4. white and metallic red, "Fire Chief PTF01," "Matchbox PTF 2001," red roof light, rubber tires on chrome rims .... $50 – 60
5. white with orange accents, amber roof light, 2002 Matchbox Across America 50th Birthday series #47 New Mexico — Western Collection .... $5 – 6

6. white with black, red, yellow, and bronze design, blue roof light, "Metro Alarm," 2003 Sky Fire .... $1 – 2
7. black and white, 2005 #27 ..... $1 – 2

Ford Explorer Sport Trac, #23, 2001; #24, 2002; #40, 2003; #47, 2004

1. black with purple base, "Tune-Up Auto Parts" and graphics, 2003 Mom and Pop Shops .... $1 – 2
2. black with white splashes, "Coca-Cola," white interior .... $5 – 6

3. metallic blue with black base, 2003 Hero City 5-pack #12 ....$1 - 2
4. orange-red with chrome base, "2001 Matchbox Toy Show," "Hershey Matchbox Pennsylvania," rubber tires on chrome rims .... $20 – 25

5. red with gray base, gray interior, 2001 Sun Chasers ....$1 - 2
6. red with silver-gray base, black interior, white accents, shield graphics ... $3 – 4
7. white with orange-yellow base, blue interior, 2002 Matchbox Across America 50th Birthday #45 Utah — Western Collection .... $4 – 6

8. white with gray base, red and black "Huskies Dog Sled Team," 2002 Great Outdoors ....$1 - 2

9. yellow with lime green base, 2003 Rescue Heroes 5-pack ....$1 - 2
10. red, "Alamo" graphics .... $3 – 4
11. metallic light blue with red base, white interior, red windows, graphics .. $1 – 2
12. modified, 2004 #47 .... $1 – 2

13. yellow with white, red and black diagonal stripes, dark gray base, "Beach Patrol Lifeguard," 2007 5-pack K9617 ....$1 - 2
14. metallic blue, 2007 Superfast #61

Ford F-100 1956 Pickup, #48, 1997; #35, 1998; #21, 1999; #56, 2000; #15, 2001; #66, 2006; #56, 2007

1. red, "2nd Annual Mattel Open," Color Comp promotional issue .. $120 – 160
2. red, "Bendigo 1999 National Swap Meet," Australia issue .... $16 – 24
3. red, "Coca-Cola in Bottles," rubber tires on chrome rims, Premiere Collection .... $5 – 6
4. red, "Matchbox Madness," Color Comp promotional issue .... $80 – 120
5. red, "Matchbox USA," "www.matchboxusa.com," white roof, promotional .... $12 – 16

6. red, "Mr. Timmerman's," 2001 Highway Heroes ....$1 - 2

7. red, "Texaco" logo, "Jimmy's Auto Service" on doors, 2000 Speedy Delivery ....$1 - 2
8. red, "Texaco" logo, "Jimmy's Auto Service" on doors, "Matchbox 2000," 2000 Speedy Delivery .... $3 – 4
9. red, detailed trim, rubber tires on chrome rims, Premiere Collection #17 .... $4 – 5

10. red with chrome base and grille, white interior, no markings, 1998 Classic Decades ....$1 - 2
11. metallic red, "Happy Days," Star Cars .... $5 – 6

12. metallic red with chrome base and grille, butterscotch interior, 2006 Superfast #26 ....$4 - 5
13. red and white, "Coca-Cola," Avon 2-pack .... $4 – 5
14. orange, "MBRR Service," rubber tires on chrome rims, Color Comp promotional .... $30 – 40
15. orange with chrome trim .... $1 – 2
16. yellow with mud spray, 5-pack ... $1 – 2

17. bright green, "Fresh Produce Delivery," 1999 Speedy Delivery ..$1 - 2

18. flat green with white splatter accents, "Farm Fresh Produce" in yellow oval, 2007 #56 ....$1 - 2
19. turquoise, with pink and purple pinstripes, rubber tires on chrome rims, Premiere Collection #20 .... $4 – 5

20. blue with chrome base and grille, cream interior, 2005 Superfast #26 ....$4 - 5
21. dark blue with white flames ...... $1 – 2
22. metallic blue, "Matchbox Toy Show Hershey 98," rubber tires on chrome rims .... $12 – 16

23. dark purple with white and pink flames ....$3 - 4
24. black, "Great Connecticut Toy Show 2000," Color Comp promotional issue .... $12 – 16

25. black, "Great White Adventures," Australia issue .... $3 – 4
26. black with white roof, rubber tires on chrome rims, 1997 Inaugural Edition .... $5 – 6

27. white with yellow plastic base, monkey and wrench design, 2003 Hero City 5-pack #11 .... $1 – 2
28. metallic gold, 1997 75 Challenge .... $6 – 12
29. unpainted, rubber tires on chrome rims, 1997 Inaugural Edition .... $5 – 6
30. metallic light blue with chrome hubs, 2006 #66 .... $1 – 2

Ford F-150 1997 Pickup, #65, 1997; #50, 1998; #69, 1999; #21, 2002

1. red, "4X4 Off Road," black interior, chrome base, 1998 Rough 'N Tough .... $1 – 2

2. blue with orange and white "State Park Fish Farm Catch & Release Patrol Vehicle," 1999 Ranger Patrol .... $1 – 2
3. black with black and tan interior, Goodyear rubber tires, 1997 First Editions .... $5 – 6
4. black with black and tan interior, Goodyear rubber tires, "Matchbox," "MDM," "630-681-2101" .... $40 – 50
5. white, "Action Radar," "Xtreme Mission," 5-pack .... $1 – 2
6. white, "Texaco — A World of Energy," black bedliner, Premiere Collection .. $5 – 6

7. white with red, yellow, and gray electrician graphics, 2003 Hero City 5-pack #8 .... $1 – 2
8. metallic olive gold, blue accents, 2002 Great Outdoors .... $1 – 2
9. unpainted, tan interior, Goodyear rubber tires, 1997 First Editions .... $5 – 6
10. unpainted, tan interior, Goodyear rubber tires, "Matchbox," "MDM," "630-681-2101" .... $40 – 50

Ford F-150 4x4 Pickup, #65, 1995; #53, 1998; #14, 2000

1. red, "Beach Patrol Unit 44," black roll bar, China cast, 2000 To the Beach .... $1 – 2
2. red, "Beach Patrol Unit 44," "Matchbox 2000," black roll bar, China cast, 2000 To the Beach .... $3 – 4
3. red, "Ford," white and blue accents, chrome roll bar, China cast, 5-pack .... $1 – 2
4. red with white accents on sides, black roll bar, China cast, 1995 .... $1 – 2
5. red with white accents on sides, black roll bar, Thailand cast, 1995 .... $1 – 2
6. red with white accents on sides, chrome roll bar, Thailand cast, 1995 .... $1 – 2
7. red with white and blue splash, blue Ford logo on doors, chrome roll bar, 1997 Rugged Riders 5-pack .... $1 – 2
8. fluorescent yellow with orange and blue rhinoceros head on doors, 2003 Hero City 5-pack #4 .... $1 – 2
9. metallic blue with silver accents on sides, black roll bar, China cast, 1996 .... $1 – 2
10. metallic blue, "Whirlpool," black roll bar, China cast, ASAP promotional .... $120 – 160
11. purple with light green accents on sides, chrome roll bar, China cast, 1998 5-pack .... $1 – 2
12. purple with light green accents on sides, metallic gray roll bar, 1996 Off Road 5-pack .... $1 – 2
13. black, "Black Star Ranch," mud spatter, green roll bar, China cast, 5-pack .. $1 – 2
14. black, "Don't Mess With Texas," mud spatter, green roll bar, China cast, 5-pack .... $1 – 2
15. black, "MC15" and rhinoceros head, dark green roll bar, China cast, 5-pack .... $1 – 2
16. black with red accents on sides, chrome roll bar, China cast, 1997 .... $1 – 2
17. white with orange and blue accents, blue Ford logo, blue roll bar, China cast, 1998 Rough 'N Tough .... $1 – 2
18. metallic gold with white and blue splash design, blue Ford logo on sides, chrome roll bar, China cast, 1998 Rugged Riders 5-pack .... $1 – 2
19. metallic gold with chrome roll bar, 1997 75 Challenge .... $6 – 12

Ford F-150 Dump/Utility Truck, #91, 2000; #13, 2001; #71, 2000, international; #39, 2005 (similar casting: Ford F-150 Rescue Pickup)

1. red, "Matchbox Bilt," "CM-3527," white stripes, 8-spoke wheels, 2000 Build It! .... $3 – 4
2. red, "Matchbox Bilt," "CM-3527," white stripes, 8-spoke wheels, 2000 Build It! series, "Matchbox 2000" .... $4 – 5
3. red, "Matchbox Bilt," "CM-3527," white stripes, 7-spoke sawblade wheels, 2000 5-pack .... $12 – 16

4. orange-red with yellow dumper, "Rescue Heroes," graphics, yellow dumper, 7-spoke sawblade wheels, 2003 Rescue Heroes 5-pack .... $1 – 2
5. black with checkerboard design and winged logo, 7-spoke sawblade wheels, 2001 Highway Heroes .... $3 – 4
6. black with checkerboard design and winged logo, 8-spoke wheels, 2001 Highway Heroes .... $5 – 6
7. red with gray dumper, "Haulin' Shaun," #39, 2005 .... $1 – 2

Ford F-150 Lightning (see Ford SVT F-150 Lightning)

Ford F-150 Rescue Pickup, with boat ramp and inflatable raft, #43, 2001; #42, 2003 (similar casting: Ford F-150 Dump/Utility Truck)

1. red, "Matchbox FDMB" on shield, flame graphics, metallic gray ramp, yellow raft, 2001 Action Launcher Fire Truck set .... $3 – 4

2. red, "MBFD," white ramp, yellow raft, 2001 Rescue Squad ..... $1 – 2

3. yellow, 2002 Matchbox Across America 50th Birthday series #32 Minnesota-Central Collection .... $4 – 6

4. white, "MHC Beach Patrol," yellow ramp, yellow raft, 2003 Beach Patrol .... $1 – 2

Ford F-250 Dump Truck, #39, 2005 (see Ford F-150 Dump/Utility Truck, Ford F-150 Rescue Pickup)

Ford F-350 (see Ford F-150 Dump Truck, Ford F-150 Rescue Pickup)

Ford F-350 KME Pumper, 2000 Feature Cars, with opening features, designed to replace Premiere Collection

1. fluorescent yellow, "Base 24" ... $9 – 12
2. white and red, "Elizaville" ...... $12 – 16
3. white and red, "Trucksville" .. $12 – 16

Ford F-350 Pickup, 2000 Feature Cars, with opening features, designed to replace Premiere Collection

1. metallic gray .... $9 – 12
2. metallic pale brown .... $9 – 12

Ford F-800 Delivery Truck, FS001/WR002, container doesn't extend over cab, White Rose Collectibles

1. "ABC Sports," white with white container .... $12 – 16
2. "All Star Game 1996," red with white container .... $9 – 12
3. "All Star Game 1997 — Indians," white with white container .... $7 – 9
4. "American Lung Association," white with white container .... $8 – 10
5. "Atlanta Braves 1996," red with blue container .... $7 – 9
6. "Baltimore Orioles 1996," orange with black container .... $7 – 9
7. "Bill Elliot," "M," "10," red with white container, Team Convoy .... $7 – 9
8. "Boston Red Sox 1996," dark blue with red container .... $7 – 9
9. "California Angels 1996," metallic gray with dark blue container .... $7 – 9
10. "Cat Racing," white with white container, Team Convoy .... $7 – 9
11. "Chicago Cubs 1996," blue with white container .... $7 – 9
12. "Chicago White Sox 1996," black with white container .... $7 – 9
13. "Cincinnati Reds 1996," white with red container .... $7 – 9
14. "Cleveland Indians 1996," red with dark blue container .... $7 – 9
15. "Colorado Rockies 1996," purple with metallic gray container .... $7 – 9
16. "Detroit Tigers 1996," dark blue with orange container .... $7 – 9
17. "Dutch Valley," blue with white container .... $7 – 9
18. "Florida Marlins 1996," black with turquoise container .... $7 – 9
19. "Houston Astros 1996," gold with dark blue container .... $7 – 9
20. "Hulkster," "Hogan 43," red with orange-yellow container, Team Convoy ... $8 – 10
21. "KC Royals 1996," blue with white container .... $7 – 9
22. "Los Angeles Dodgers 1996," white with blue container .... $7 – 9
23. "Milwaukee Brewers 1996," dark blue with gold container .... $7 – 9
24. "Minnesota Twins 1996," red with dark blue container .... $7 – 9
25. "Montreal Expos 1996," red with blue container .... $7 – 9
26. "New York Mets 1996," orange with blue container .... $7 – 9
27. "New York Yankees 1996," white with blue container .... $7 – 9
28. "NY Yankees World Series 1996," white with white container .... $8 – 10
29. "Oakland Athletics 1996," yellow with green container .... $7 – 9
30. "Philadelphia Phillies 1996," blue with red container .... $7 – 9
31. "Pittsburgh Pirates 1996," yellow with black container .... $7 – 9
32. "Preston — The 151 Line," orange with white container .... $16 – 24
33. "Quality You Can See — Maple Donuts," white with white container ..... $8 – 10
34. "Rutters Dairy Celebrates 75 Years," green with white container ... $16 – 24
35. "San Diego Padres 1996," dark blue with orange container .... $7 – 9
36. "San Francisco Giants 1996," black with orange container .... $7 – 9
37. "Seattle Mariners 1996," blue-green with dark blue container .... $7 – 9
38. "St. Louis Cardinals 1996," dark blue with red container .... $7 – 9
39. "Texas Rangers 1996," light gray with red container .... $7 – 9
40. "Toronto Blue Jays 1996," blue with dark blue container .... $7 – 9
41. "UGI Gas Service," white with white container .... $9 – 12
42. "We Are Penn State 95," dark blue, white container with blue roof .. $8 – 10
43. "World Series 1995 — Atlanta Braves Champs," blue with white container .... $9 – 12
44. "World Series 1995 — Atlanta Braves Champs," red with white container .... $9 – 12
45. "York Daily Record," white with white container .... $7 – 9
46. "York Fair 1995," green with orange-yellow container .... $8 – 10

Ford F-800 Delivery Van, FS002, 1995, container extends over cab, White Rose Collectibles

1. "All Star Game 1997," blue with white container .... $7 – 9
2. "Nittany Lions — PSU 1996," metallic silver with metallic silver container .... $8 – 10
3. "Penn State 1996," white with white container .... $8 – 10
4. "York Fair 1996," beige with beige container .... $8 – 10

Ford F-Series (see Ford F-150 Dump Truck, Ford F-150 Rescue Pickup)

Ford Fairlane Fire Chief Car, $2^7/_8$", #59, 1963

1. red with gray plastic wheels ..$80 – 100
2. red with silver plastic wheels . $125 – 150
3. red with black plastic wheels ...$20 – 25

Ford Fairlane Police Car, $2^5/_8$", #55, 1963

1. dark blue with black plastic wheels .... $180 – 200
2. light blue with gray plastic wheels .... $80 – 100
3. light blue with silver plastic wheels .... $80 – 100

4. light blue with black plastic wheels .... $65 – 90

Ford Fairlane Station Wagon, $2^3/_4$", #31, 1960

1. yellow, silver plastic wheels .. $100 – 120
2. green with pink roof, silver plastic wheels .... $40 – 50
3. green with pink roof, gray plastic wheels .... $40 – 50
4. green with pink roof, black plastic wheels .... $100 – 120

Ford Fairlane Sunliner, 1956

1. yellow and white, Matchbox Collectibles Barrett-Jackson .... $4 – 5

Ford Falcon, #61, 2001, international

1. metallic blue .... $1 – 2

2. green, "Coca-Cola," US issue .. $4 – 5

Ford Falcon Forte, #63, 1997, Australia; #68, 1998, international; #12, 2000, international; #4, 2002, US; #49, 2004

1. "Australia's First," gold, rubber tires on chrome rims, Australian inaugural issue .... $12 – 16
2. "Australia's First," unpainted, rubber tires on chrome rims, Australian inaugural issue .... $12 – 16
3. "Australian Open 1997," white, rubber tires on chrome rims, Australia issue .... $8 – 10
4. "Blues 1998," white and dark blue, Australia issue .... $4 – 5
5. "Brisbane 1998," yellow and purple, Australia issue .... $4 – 5
6. "Castrol 25," white, rubber tires on chrome rims, Australia issue ....$16 – 24
7. "Cats 1998," white and black, Australia issue .... $4 – 5

8. **"Coca-Cola," white, US issue ... $4 – 5**
9. "Crows 1998," red and dark blue, Australia issue .... $4 – 5
10. "Eagles 1998," yellow and dark blue, Australia issue .... $4 – 5
11. "Ford," maroon with white stripes, 2000 Australian Adventure international .... $3 – 4
12. "Ford 75," white and dark blue, Australia issue .... $3 – 4
13. "Ford Falcon 4," metallic purple, 1998 Street Cruisers international .... $1 – 2
14. "Go Cats! 1997," white, Australia issue ....$4 – 5
15. "Great Strides," "Cystic Fibrosis Foundation," "Ford," maroon with white stripes, Color Comp promotional ....$20 – 30
16. "Kangaroos 1998," white and blue, Australia issue ....$4 – 5
17. "Midwest Regional Matchbox Convention 2000," "Toy Show Demo Model," "Ford," maroon with white stripes, Color Comp promotional .....$12 – 16
18. "Mitre 10 Accent Paint Racing," blue, rubber tires on yellow rims, Australia issue ....$8 – 10
19. "Official Matchbox Collectors Club," "Australian Matchbox News," white, rubber tires on chrome rims ..$16 – 24
20. "Official Matchbox Collectors Club," "Australian Matchbox News," gold, rubber tires on chrome rims ....$16 – 24
21. "Official Matchbox Collectors Club," "Australian Matchbox News," unpainted, rubber tires on chrome rims ....$16 – 24

22. **"Roy Roo's Taxi," picture of Sydney Opera House on doors, yellow with black plastic base, 2002 Hometown Heroes ....$1 – 2**
23. "Special Edition Puerto Rico," Puerto Rican flag, maroon, "Ford" and white stripes, Color Comp promotional .... $9 – 12
24. "Swans 1998," white and red, Australia issue .... $4 – 5
25. "Tigers 1998," yellow and black, Australia issue .... $4 – 5
26. yellow taxi, 2004 #49 .... $1 – 2

Ford Falcon Taxi (see Ford Falcon Forte)

Ford Flareside Pickup, $2^7/_8$", #53, 1982; #55, 1994 – 1998 (compare to Ford Flareside Pickup with Load)

1. red, "326 Baja Bouncer," 8-spoke wheels, Macau cast .... $25 – 30
2. red, "326 Baja Bouncer," 8-spoke wheels, Manaus cast, Brazil issue .....$80 – 120
3. red, "Bill Elliott 11," racing slicks, Team Convoy, White Rose Collectibles ..$6 – 8

4. **red with orange and yellow flames, racing slicks, chrome windows, 1994 ....$1 – 2**

5. **orange, "326 Baja Bouncer," clear windows ....$3 – 4**
6. fluorescent orange with black front end .... $2 – 4
7. yellow, "Ford 460," black interior, racing slicks with chromed lettering, Macau casting .... $3 – 4

8. **yellow, "Ford 460," black interior, racing slicks with unchromed lettering, Macau casting ....$1 – 2**
9. yellow, "Ford 460," black interior, racing slicks with unchromed lettering, Thailand casting .... $3 – 4
10. yellow, "Ford 460," black interior, 8-spoke wheels, Macau casting ...$40 – 50
11. yellow, "Ford 460," white interior, 8-spoke wheels, Macau casting ....$200 – 250
12. yellow with black interior, 8-spoke wheels .... $35 – 40
13. yellow with black interior, racing slicks .... $2 – 4
14. fluorescent yellow with no interior, chrome windows, Super Trucks ... $3 – 4
15. orange, "326 Baja Bouncer," white interior, black base .... $1 – 2

16. **fluorescent orange with black design on front, chrome base, white interior ....$1 – 2**
18. lime green, yellow base, red interior, red racing slicks, Matchbox Preschool/Live 'N Learn .... $7 – 8
19. khaki green with purple and blue design, racing slicks, plastic armament, Roadblasters .... $7 – 8
20. blue, "326 Baja Bouncer," blue windows ....$50 – 60
21. blue, "326 Baja Bouncer," clear windows .... $3 – 4

22. **light blue, "F-150" with white accents, yellow interior, chrome base ... $1 – 2**
23. metallic blue, "326 Baja Bouncer," white interior .... $3 – 4
24. dark blue, "QC Quality Care 15," chrome interior, racing slicks with unchromed lettering, Team Convoy, White Rose Collectibles .... $4 – 5
25. metallic blue with no interior, chrome windows, Super Trucks .... $3 – 4

26. dark purple with white accents, gray interior, chrome base, 1998 Rough 'N Tough .... $1 - 2

27. black with flames on front, yellow tailpipes, roll bar, grille, and interior, chrome base, 1998 Rugged Riders 5-pack .... $1 - 2

28. gray with purple and magenta flames on front, purple tailpipes, roll bar, grille and interior, 1996 Off Road 5-pack .... $1 - 2

29. metallic gray, "Jay's Flight Team," racing slicks, Avon Light & Sound .... $1 – 2
30. metallic gray, "Jay's Flight Team," racing slicks, includes black launcher and white glider, Action System .... $3 – 4
31. white, "Deb," racing slicks, UK on-package premium .... $40 – 50

32. white with silver band, red stripe, chrome interior, clear windows, Collector's Choice, White Rose Collectibles .... $3 - 4

33. metallic gold, chrome base, black interior, 1997 75 Challenge .... $6 – 12

Ford Flareside Pickup with Load, 1994, White Rose Collectibles

1. "Angels 94," dark blue .... $4 – 5
2. "Astros 94," gold .... $4 – 5
3. "Athletics 94," dark green .... $4 – 5
4. "Baltimore Football 94," white .. $4 – 5
5. "Blue Jays 94," light blue .... $4 – 5
6. "Braves 94," metallic blue .... $4 – 5
7. "Brewers 94 — 25th Anniversary," dark green .... $4 – 5
8. "Cubs 94," red .... $4 – 5
9. "Dodgers 94," blue .... $4 – 5
10. "Expos 94," blue .... $4 – 5
11. "Giants 94," orange .... $4 – 5
12. "Indians 94," red .... $4 – 5
13. "Mariners 94," dark blue-green $4 – 5
14. "Marlins 94," blue-green .... $4 – 5
15. "Mets 94," blue .... $4 – 5
16. "Orioles 94," black .... $4 – 5
17. "Padres 94," orange .... $4 – 5
18. "Penn State Nittany Lions 94," dark blue .... $4 – 5
19. "Phillies 94," red .... $4 – 5
20. "Pirates 94," black .... $4 – 5
21. "Rangers 94," khaki gray .... $4 – 5
22. "Red Sox 94," dark gray .... $4 – 5
23. "Reds 94," black .... $4 – 5
24. "Rockies 94," purple .... $4 – 5
25. "Royals 94," gold .... $4 – 5
26. "St. Louis Cardinals 94," blue ... $4 – 5
27. "Tigers 94," orange .... $4 – 5
28. "Twins 94," blue .... $4 – 5
29. "White Sox 94," metallic gray ... $4 – 5
30. "Yankees 94," red .... $4 – 5

Ford Focus, #84, 2000; #55, 2003; #64, 2000, international; #68, 2005; Superfast #63, 2006

1. metallic red-orange, "Matchbox 2000," 2000 Worldwide Wheels .... $3 – 4

2. metallic red-orange, 2000 Worldwide Wheels .... $1 - 2

3. yellow with black side stripe, 2003 Hero City 5-pack #12 .... $1 - 2

4. metallic yellow with black hood, 2005, #68 .... $1 - 2

5. orange, 2005 Superfast #63 .. $3 - 4

6. blue, Ford 100th Anniversary, 2003 .... $3 - 4

7. metallic blue, 2001 Eurosports 5-pack .... $1 - 2

8. purple, "Focus," 5-pack .... $1 – 2

9. white with black and green Bears soccer graphics, 2003 School Time series #55 .... $1 - 2

10. metallic silver, 2006 Superfast #63 .... $4 - 5

Ford Galaxie Fire Chief Car, 2⁷/₈", #59, 1966

1. red, black plastic wheels, blue roof light, 1966 .... $30 - 40

2. red, black plastic wheels, red roof light, 1966 .... $350 – 500

3. red, Superfast wheels, 1970 ..$40 – 50

Ford Galaxie Police Car, 2⅞", #55, 1966
1. white with blue dome light ..$200 – 300
2. white with red dome light .... $50 – 60

Ford Grit Spreader (see Ford Atkinson Grit Spreader)

Ford Group 6, 3", #45, 1970; BR 19-20, 1985
1. red, England cast, Super GT BR 19-20, 1985 .... $4 – 6
2. red, China cast, Super GT BR 19-20, 1985 .... $8 – 10

3. dark red, China cast, Super GT BR 19-20, 1985 ....$3 - 5
4. yellow, England cast, Super GT BR 19-20, 1985 .... $8 – 10
5. dark enamel green, unpainted base, clear windows, round "7" label ....$1,200 – 1,600
6. metallic green, black base, amber windows, "45" label .... $12 – 16
7. metallic green, black base, clear windows, "45" label .... $12 – 16
8. metallic green, black base, clear windows, round "7" label .... $12 – 16
9. metallic green, black base, clear windows, square "7" label .... $12 – 16
10. metallic green, gray base, amber windows, "45" label .... $12 – 16
11. metallic green, gray base, clear windows, "45" label .... $12 – 16
12. metallic green, black base, clear windows, "45" label .... $12 – 16
13. metallic green, pink base, amber windows, "45" label .... $12 – 16
14. metallic green, pink base, clear windows, "45" label .... $12 – 16
15. metallic green, unpainted base, clear windows, round "7" label ..... $12 – 16
16. metallic green, unpainted base, clear windows, square "7" label .... $12 – 16
17. metallic green, yellow base, amber windows, "45" label .... $12 – 16
18. metallic green, yellow base, clear windows, "45" label .... $12 – 16
19. fluorescent lime green, China cast, Neon Racers BR 19-20, 1985 .... $4 – 6
20. purple, amber windows, "45" label .... $12 – 16
21. purple, amber windows, eyes label .... $12 – 16
22. gray, China cast, Super GT BR 19- 20, 1985 .... $3 – 5
23. white, England cast, Super GT BR 19-20, 1985 .... $4 – 6
24. white, China cast, Super GT BR 19-20, 1985 .... $8 – 10

Ford GT, 2⅝", #41, 1965 (also see Ford GT 2005 Concept)
1. yellow with black plastic tires, yellow wheel hubs, "6" decals .... $60 – 80
2. white with black plastic tires, red wheel hubs, "6" decal .... $100 – 120

3. white with black plastic tires, yellow wheel hubs, "6" decal ....$8 - 12
4. white with black plastic tires, yellow wheel hubs, "9" decals .... $12 – 16
5. white with black plastic tires, yellow wheel hubs, "6" label .... $7 – 12
6. white with black plastic tires, yellow wheel hubs, "9" label .... $7 – 12
7. white with Superfast wheels, "6" label ....$12 – 16
8. white with Superfast wheels, cat head label .... $16 – 24
9. yellow with Superfast wheels, Italian issue .... $700 – 900
10. metallic orange with Superfast wheels ....$12 – 16

Ford GT 2005 Concept, #49, 2005; #9, 2006; #13, 2007
1. red with white stripes, 2005 #49 ..$1 – 2
2. black with silver stripes .... $1 – 2

3. yellow with black stripes, 2006 5-pack J4672 ....$1 - 2

4. light blue with orange stripes, 2006 #9 ....$1 - 2

5. metallic gold with black stripes, 2007 #13, K9474 ....$1 - 2

6. orange with black stripes, 2007 #13, L5029 ....$1 - 2

Ford Heavy Wreck Truck, "Esso," 3", #71, 1968
1. red cab, "Esso," white bed, amber windows, black plastic wheels, prototype .... $300 – 400

2. red cab, "Esso," white bed, green windows, black plastic wheels, 1968 .... $25 - 35
3. red cab, "Esso," white bed, Superfast wheels, 1970 .... $35 – 45
4. olive green, "3LGS64," Superfast wheels, Two-Pack .... $12 – 15
5. blue, Superfast wheels, multi-pack .... $200 – 250

Ford Hot Rod (see Ford '33 Street Rod)

Ford IMSA Mustang (see Ford Mustang IMSA)

Ford Kennel Truck, with four dogs, 2¾", #50, 1969
1. metallic green, tinted canopy, white grille, black plastic wheels, 1969 ...$16 – 24
2. metallic green, tinted canopy, chrome grille, black plastic wheels, 1969 ....$20 – 25
3. metallic green, clear canopy, white grille, black plastic wheels, 1969 .... $16 – 24
4. metallic green, clear canopy, chrome grille, black plastic wheels 1969 .... $20 – 25
5. metallic green, chrome grille, Superfast wheels, 1970 .... $30 – 40
6. apple green, chrome grille, Superfast wheels, 1970 .... $30 – 40

Ford Lotus Europa (see Lotus Europa)

Ford LTD Police, 3", #51, 1988; #16, 1990; #24, 1998; #2, 1999 (similar casting: Ford LTD Taxi)
1. black, "Police Unit 3," gold star, 5-pack .... $1 – 2
2. black and tan, "Florida State Trooper," Premiere Collection #8 .... $4 – 6

3. black and white, "42" in shield .. $6 – 9

4. blue with white trim, black shield, "Police," "16," White Rose Collector's Choice ....$4 – 5

5. blue with white band, "Unit 22" on hood, "Matchbox Police" shield, 1997 Police 5-pack ....$1 – 2

6. bright blue with yellow accent stripe on sides, "State Police," 1996 ...... $1 – 2
7. dark blue, "Police," "R-25," Triple Heat ....$3 – 5
8. dark blue and gray, "Virginia State Police," Premiere Collection #8 ....$4 – 6

9. metallic blue with yellow accent stripe on sides, "State Police," 1996 ....$1 – 2

10. metallic copper, "Sheriff" and "S-27," 1997 ....$1 – 2

11. metallic gold, no markings, 1997 75 Challenge .... $12 – 16
12. metallic gray, "Police," shield and red design, 5-pack .... $1 – 2
13. purple to red, "Police," with "PD-21" on roof, Color Changers .... $3 – 5

14. red, "Dan's Pocket Cruisers," "Police," "1994," customized .... $5 – 10

15. red, "Fire Chief," "FD No. 1" in gold crest, multipack .... $1 – 2
16. red, "Fire Dept. Fire Chief," Motor City .... $2 – 4
17. red, "Police," with "PD-21" on roof .... $3 – 5
18. white, "17 Police," multipack ....$1 – 2
19. white, "Corvette Unlimited Salutes Vineland Police NJ," Color Comp promo .... $80 – 120
20. white, "New Jersey Police," Premiere Collection #8 .... $4 – 6
21. white, policeman caricature, Live 'N Learn/Preschool .... $6 – 9
22. white, "Police," with "PD-21" on roof, "Intercom City" .... $12 – 16

23. white with blue doors and hood, "Police" on hood, "Police Dept No. 1" on doors, 1996 Police 5-pack ..$1 – 2

24. white, "Ridge, New York, Police," 1999 Matchbox USA ....$1 – 2

25. white, "Sheriff," "S-27," 1998 ..$1 – 2

26. white with black accents, shield on door, "Police," with "PD-21" on roof, 1995 ....$1 – 2

27. white with blue accents, shield on door, "Police," with "PD-21" on roof, 1995 ....$5 – 7

28. white with bright orange and yellow accents, "Dial 911 Metro," 1993 Emergency 5-pack .... $3 – 5
29. white with no markings, Graffic Traffic .... $12 – 16

Ford LTD US Taxi, 3", #53, 1992; #56, 1992; #9, 1999 (similar casting: Ford LTD Police)

1. yellow, "Radio XYZ Cab" and checkerboard pattern ....$4 – 5

2. yellow, "Taxi," black checks, Star Cars ....$5 – 6

3. yellow with black checks and airplane silhouette on doors, 1999 Air Traffic .... $1 – 2
4. pumpkin orange, "Taxi," 5-pack .. $1 – 2
5. pumpkin orange, "Cabbies for Life," ASAP promotional issue .... $80 – 120
6. pumpkin orange, "Ronnie & Rene August 19, 2000," ASAP promotional issue .... $80 – 120

Ford Model A Coupe, 2 13/16", #73, 1979; #55, 1991

1. red with blue and yellow design, red fenders, clear windows, racing slicks on back axle, Thailand cast, 1995 Hot Rods 5-pack ....$1 – 2

2. red with black fenders, clear windows, Macau cast .... $3 – 4
3. red with dark green fenders, clear windows, China cast, UK on-package premium .... $16 – 24
4. red with dark green fenders, clear windows, Macau cast, UK on-package premium .... $16 – 24
5. red with dark green fenders, clear windows, Thailand cast, UK on-package premium .... $16 – 24

6. metallic red with detailed trim, racing slicks on back axle, Thailand cast, Collector's Choice, White Rose Collectibles .... $4 – 5
7. orange-yellow, "GT" and yellow jacket, white fenders, Thailand cast, White Rose Collectibles .... $7 – 9
8. yellow, "PAVA," red fenders, clear windows, racing slicks on back axle, Macau cast, Danish issue .... $9 – 12
9. metallic green with dark green fenders, green windows, England cast ... $5 – 6

10. metallic green with dark green fenders, no windows, England cast ....$5 - 6

11. light blue with clown illustration, clear windows, racing slicks on back axle, Thailand cast, Motor City .... $8 – 10
12. dark blue with green and pink grid design, clear windows, racing slicks on back axle, Thailand cast, multi-pack .... $1 – 2
13. purple with stripes, yellow fenders, clear windows, racing slicks on back axle, Macau cast .... $4 – 5
14. purple with stripes, yellow fenders, clear windows, racing slicks on back axle, Thailand cast .... $3 – 4

15. black with flames, black fenders, clear windows, racing slicks on back axle, Macau cast ....$3 - 4

16. dark gray, "The Untouchables," bullet holes, clear windows, China cast, Star Cars .... $5 – 6
17. cream, "Hershey 2000," "Matchbox USA," England cast, Color Comp promotional .... $80 – 120

18. cream with dark green fenders, green windows, spare tire cast into fender, England cast ....$7 - 9

19. cream with dark green fenders, green windows, England cast .... $5 – 6
20. cream with dark green fenders, no windows, England cast .... $5 – 6
21. beige with brown fenders, amber windows, England cast .... $5 – 6

22. beige with brown fenders, clear windows, England cast ....$5 - 6

23. beige with brown fenders, clear windows, Macau cast .... $3 – 4
24. white with zigzag design, clear windows, racing slick on back axle, Thailand cast .... $3 – 4
25. metallic gold, "Matchbox Collectors Club," clear windows, Thailand cast .... $12 – 16
26. metallic gold, "American Iron Cruise 96," "Memory Lane," Thailand cast, custom promotional .... $20 – 30

Ford Model A Van, 3", #38, 1982 – 1997

1. "1st M.I.C.A. Australia Convention," yellow with green fenders, green roof, Australia issue .... $9 – 12
2. "1st M.I.C.A. European Convention," red with yellow fenders, black roof, Germany issue .... $15 – 20
3. "2nd M.I.C.A. Convention," black, black roof .... $400 – 500
4. "2nd M.I.C.A. NA Convention 1989," black, orange roof .... $7 – 9
5. "3rd M.I.C.A. Australia Convention," yellow-orange with green fenders and roof, Australia issue .... $9 – 12
6. "3rd M.I.C.A. Australia Convention," fluorescent orange with blue fenders and roof, screw-mounted base, promotional .... $90 – 120
7. "3rd M.I.C.A. Convention," yellow, red roof, UK issue .... $9 – 12
8. "8th M.I.C.A. Event," red with yellow fenders, dark blue roof, UK issue .... $12 – 16
9. "10th M.I.C.A. Convention," silver black fenders, black roof, UK issue ... $9 – 12
10. "15th Anniversary Matchbox USA 1991," chrome plated with red fenders, red roof, promotional .... $40 – 50
11. "72nd Shenandoah Apple Blossom Festival," white with black fenders and roof, US issue .... $9 – 12
12. "75th Anniversary Borough of Newfield," blue with black fenders and roof, Color Comp promotional .... $12 – 16
13. "2000 Southern California Rod Run Sept. 4th 2000," white with black fenders and roof, ASAP promotional ....$80 – 120
14. "Acco Chain & Lifting Products," white with black fenders and roof, ASAP promotional .... $40 – 60
15. "Adelaide Crows," dark blue with red fenders, yellow roof, Australia issue .... $8 – 10
16. "Adelaide Super Sixers," dark blue with red fenders and roof, Australia issue ....$8 – 10
17. "Aldershot — 4th M.I.C.A. Convention," green, rust roof, UK issue ..... $9 – 12
18. "Alex Munro Master Butcher," red, black roof, UK issue .... $9 – 12
19. "Alka-Seltzer," dark blue .... $5 – 6
20. "Arnott's Biscuits," red with black fenders and roof, Australia issue ... $8 – 10
21. "Asda Baked Beans," red, red roof, on-package premium, UK issue .. $8 – 10
22. "Atlanta Braves 1990," white with blue fenders, white roof, White Rose Collectibles .... $4 – 5
23. "Atlanta Braves 1991," blue with red fenders, white roof, White Rose Collectibles .... $4 – 5
24. "Atlanta Falcons 1990," red with black fenders, light gray roof, White Rose Collectibles .... $4 – 5
25. "Atlanta Falcons 1991," red with black fenders and roof, White Rose Collectibles .... $4 – 5
26. "Aukland Warriors," green with blue fenders and roof, Australia issue .... $8 – 10
27. "Australia Post," orange-red with black fenders and roof .... $6 – 8
28. "Auto 1," white with blue fenders, red roof, Australia issue .... $6 – 8
29. "Automodel Exchange," maroon with beige fenders and roof, Australia issue .... $8 – 10
30. "Avant Garde Drum & Bugle Corps," white with black fenders and roof, ASAP promotional .... $12 – 16
31. "Bakker Bros. Seeds," white with black fenders and roof, ASAP promotional .... $40 – 50
32. "Balmain Tigers," orange with white fenders, black roof, Australia issue .... $8 – 10
33. "Baltimore Colts 1990," white with blue fenders and roof, White Rose Collectibles .... $4 – 5
34. "Baltimore Colts 1991," dark blue with white fenders and roof, White Rose Collectibles .... $4 – 5
35. "Baltimore Orioles 1989," black with orange fenders and roof, White Rose Collectibles .... $7 – 9
36. "Baltimore Orioles 1990," black with orange fenders, black roof, White Rose Collectibles .... $4 – 5
37. "Baltimore Orioles 1991," orange with black fenders, white roof, White Rose Collectibles .... $4 – 5

38. "Barratt's Sherbet," yellow, black chassis, red roof, on-package premium, UK issue .... $12 – 16
39. "Barratt's Sherbet," yellow, black chassis and roof, UK issue .... $9 – 12
40. "Barratt's Sherbet," yellow, red chassis and roof, UK issue .... $9 – 12
41. "Bass Museum," blue with black fenders, red roof .... $6 – 8
42. "Bayer Aspirin," tan with brown fenders, tan roof .... $5 – 6
43. "BBC 1925," green, black roof, UK issue .... $7 – 9
44. "Beechworth Bakery," brown with black fenders, brown roof, Australia issue .... $6 – 8
45. "Beechworth Bakery," brown with black fenders, yellow roof, Australia issue .... $20 – 25
46. "Beechworth Bakery," red with black fenders and roof, Australia issue .... $4 – 5
47. "Ben Franklin," white with blue fenders, red roof .... $600 – 800
48. "Bendigo National Swapmeet," white with blue fenders, red roof, Australian promotional issue................ $12 – 16
49. "Big Apple Circus," blue with blue fenders and roof .... $6 – 8
50. "Big Apple Circus," red with blue fenders, white roof, US issue ..... $60 – 80
51. "Big Ben," white with black fenders, red roof, Australia issue .... $7 – 9
52. "Big Sister," red, black roof, on-package premium, Australia issue .... $7 – 9
53. "Boston Bruins 1917," tan with brown fenders, white roof; "Boston Bruins 1992," black with yellow fenders, white roof. White Rose Collectibles 2-pack ....$12 – 16 for set of two
54. "Boston Red Sox 1990," white with red fenders, white roof, White Rose Collectibles .... $4 – 5
55. "Boston Red Sox 1991," dark blue with red fenders, white roof, White Rose Collectibles .... $4 – 5
56. "Brew Works," white with black fenders and roof, ASAP promotional .... $120 – 160
57. "Brisbane Bears," red with yellow fenders, red roof, Australia issue ... $8 – 10
58. "Brisbane Broncos," light purple with white fenders, yellow roof, Australia issue .... $8 – 10
59. "Brisbane Bullets," yellow with blue fenders, yellow roof, Australia issue .... $8 – 10
60. "Buffalo Bills 1990," blue with red fenders, white roof, White Rose Collectibles .... $4 – 5
61. "Buffalo Bills 1991," white with dark blue fenders, red roof, White Rose Collectibles .... $4 – 5
62. "C-B Bulldogs," white with blue fenders, white roof, Australia issue ..... $8 – 10
63. "Cadbury's Chocolate," purple with gold fenders, purple roof, Australia issue .... $16 – 24
64. "California Angels 1990," white with red fenders, yellow roof, White Rose Collectibles .... $4 – 5
65. "California Angels 1991," yellow with red fenders, dark blue roof, White Rose Collectibles .... $4 – 5
66. "Camperdown Cumberland," white with blue fenders, blue roof, Australia issue ....$12 – 16
67. "Canada Dry," metallic green, Canada issue .... $9 – 12
68. "Canadian Tire," red with black fenders and roof, rubber tires, Canada issue ....$5 – 6
69. "Canada Tire Associate Store," red with black fenders and roof, rubber tires, Canada issue .... $5 – 6
70. "Canadian Tire Corp'n," red with black fenders and roof, rubber tires, Canada issue .... $5 – 6
71. "Canberra Cannons," red with blue fenders, red roof, Australia issue ... $8 – 10
72. "Canberra Raiders," bright lime green with white fenders, blue roof, Australia issue .... $8 – 10
73. "Carlton Blues," dark blue, Australia issue .... $8 – 10
74. "Carmelle," green, green roof, Saudi Arabia issue .... $16 – 24
75. "Carroll County Fair," white with black fenders and roof, ASAP promotional .... $60 – 80
76. "Cave Creek Chili Beer," fluorescent orange with black fenders and roof, Matchbox Collectibles .... $9 – 12
77. "Champion," blue with black fenders, white roof, England cast .... $6 – 8
78. "Champion," blue with black fenders, white roof, Macau cast .... $5 – 6
79. "Celebrate Michigan's Greatness," "Governor John Engler 1999 Inauguration," white with black fenders and roof, ASAP promotional .... $80 – 120
80. "Celebrating a Decade of Matchbox Conventions 1991," yellow with black fenders and roof .... $9 – 12
81. "Cheeses of England & Wales," blue, black roof, on-package premium, UK issue .... $12 – 16
82. "Chester Heraldry Centre," pale blue, dark gray roof, UK issue .... $7 – 9
83. "Chester Toy Museum," pale blue, dark gray roof, UK issue .... $7 – 9
84. "Chesty Bonds," white, black roof, Australia issue .... $6 – 8
85. "Chicago Bears 1990," white with dark blue fenders, orange roof, White Rose Collectibles .... $4 – 5

86. "Chicago Bears 1991," white with orange fenders, dark blue roof, White Rose Collectibles .... $4 – 5
87. "Chicago Black Hawks 1917," black with red fenders, white roof; "Chicago Black Hawks 1992," white with black fenders, white roof. White Rose Collectibles 2-pack ....$12 – 16 for set of two
88. "Chicago Cubs 1990," white with blue fenders, red roof, White Rose Collectibles .... $4 – 5
89. "Chicago Cubs 1991," red with white fenders and roof, White Rose Collectibles .... $4 – 5
90. "Chicago White Sox 1990," white with blue fenders, white roof, White Rose Collectibles .... $4 – 5
91. "Chicago White Sox 1991," white with black fenders, dark gray roof, White Rose Collectibles .... $4 – 5
92. "Cincinnati Bengals 1990," black with orange fenders, white roof, White Rose Collectibles .... $4 – 5
93. "Cincinnati Bengals 1991," orange with black fenders and roof, White Rose Collectibles .... $4 – 5
94. "Cincinnati Reds 1990," white with red fenders, white roof, White Rose Collectibles .... $4 – 5
95. "Cincinnati Reds 1991," red with white fenders and roof, White Rose Collectibles .... $4 – 5
96. "City Ford," black, Australia issue .... $8 – 10
97. "Clemson University 1992," orange with blue fenders, white roof, White Rose Collectibles .... $5 – 7
98. "Cleveland Browns 1990," orange with brown fenders, white roof, White Rose Collectibles .... $4 – 5
99. "Cleveland Browns 1991," brown with brown fenders, orange roof, White Rose Collectibles .... $4 – 5
100. "Cleveland Indians 1990," white with blue fenders, white roof, White Rose Collectibles .... $4 – 5
101. "Cobb of Knightsbridge," brown with black fenders and roof, UK issue, Macau cast .... $8 – 10
102. "Cobb of Knightsbridge," brown with black fenders and roof, UK issue, Thailand cast .... $9 – 12
103. "Coca-Cola," cream with red roof, Australia issue .... $16 – 24
104. "Coca-Cola Quality Assurance," red with black fenders and roof, Premiere Collection .... $5 – 6
105. "Collingwood Magpies," black with white fenders, black roof, Australia issue .... $8 – 10
106. "Continental Aero," purple with black fenders and roof, US issue .... $9 – 12
107. "Cooter's Garage," "Christmas 2000," white with black fenders and roof, Color Comp promotional .... $30 – 40
108. "Corning Building Co.," white with black fenders and roof, ASAP promotional .... $80 – 120

109. "Cronulla Sharks," light blue with black fenders, bright blue roof, Australia issue .... $8 – 10
110. "Dairylea," light yellow, light blue and light blue roof, on-package premium, UK issues .... $16 – 24
111. "Dale Farms," dark blue with white fenders, red roof, UK issue ...... $7 – 9
112. "Dallas Cowboys 1990," silver with dark blue fenders, dark blue roof, White Rose Collectibles .... $4 – 5
113. "Dallas Cowboys 1991," dark blue with silver fenders, dark blue roof, White Rose Collectibles .... $4 – 5
114. "De Post," red with black fenders, black roof .... $6 – 8
115. "Delacre World's Finest Belgian Chocolate Biscuits," white with black fenders and roof, Color Comp promotional .... $160 – 240
116. "Denver Broncos 1990," orange with blue fenders, orange roof, White Rose Collectibles .... $4 – 5
117. "Denver Broncos 1991," orange with dark blue fenders, dark blue roof, White Rose Collectibles .... $4 – 5
118. "Detroit Lions 1990," silver with light fenders, white roof, White Rose Collectibles .... $4 – 5
119. "Detroit Lions 1991," blue with silver fenders, white roof, White Rose Collectibles .... $4 – 5
120. "Detroit Redwings 1917," red with white fenders, white roof; "Detroit Redwings 1992," white with red fenders, white roof. White Rose Collectibles 2-pack ....$12 – 16 for set of two
121. "Detroit Tigers 1990," white with blue fenders, orange roof, White Rose Collectibles .... $4 – 5
122. "Detroit Tigers 1991," silver with dark blue fenders, orange roof, White Rose Collectibles .... $4 – 5
123. "Dewhurst Master Butcher," red, black roof, UK issue .... $9 – 12

124. "Dixie Lexington Brewery," "Kentucky Pride," cream with green fenders, dark green roof, rubber tires, Matchbox Collectibles ....$9 – 12

125. "Drink Coca-Cola," yellow, red bottles graphics, red roof, Swiss issue ...$9 – 12
126. "Drink Coca-Cola," yellow, green roof, Canadian issue .... $8 – 10
127. "Drink Coca-Cola," yellow, brown bottles graphics, red roof, Canadian issue .... $8 – 10
128. "Dusseldorf Deutschland 94," white with red fenders, lime green roof, Germany issue .... $12 – 16
129. "Dutchway Farm Market," white with black fenders and roof, ASAP promotional .... $12 – 16
130. "Eastern Suburbs," blue with red fenders, red roof, Australia issue ....$8 – 10
131. "Essendon Bombers," black with red fenders, black roof, Australia issue .... $8 – 10
132. "Farmers Insurance Group," white with black fenders and roof, ASAP promotional .... $120 – 160
133. "Fish Tales Ales," green with gold fenders and roof, rubber tires, Matchbox Collectibles .... $9 – 12
134. "Fitzroy Lions," blue with red fenders, blue roof, Australia issue .... $8 – 10
135. "Ford Motor Company 100 Years," blue with white roof, 2003 Avon 2-pack .... $5 – 6
136. "Fred Meyer 75th Anniversary," green with black fenders and roof, US issue .... $10 – 15
137. "Fremantle Dockers," purple with red fenders, purple roof, Australia issue .... $8 – 10
138. "Fresh Dairy Cream," blue, white roof, on-package premium, UK issue ..$9 – 12
139. "Geelong Cats," dark blue with white fenders, dark blue roof, Australia issue .... $8 – 10
140. "Geelong Supercats," dark blue and white with red fenders, red roof, Australia issue .... $8 – 10
141. "Georgia," white with red fenders, black roof, White Rose Collectibles ......$5 – 6
142. "Gold Coast Rollers," white with green fenders, turquoise roof, Australia issue .... $8 – 10
143. "Gold Coast Seagulls," white with black fenders, white roof, Australia issue .... $8 – 10
144. "Gowings," black, Australian issue .... $9 – 12
145. "Greater Pennsylvania Toy Show," brown with light brown fenders, white roof, promotional .... $9 – 12
146. "Green Bay Packers 1990," olive green with light yellow fenders, white roof, White Rose Collectibles ... $4 – 5
147. "Green Bay Packers 1991," olive green with yellow fenders, yellow roof, White Rose Collectibles .... $4 – 5
148. "Green's Sponge Mixture," green, green roof, on-package premium, UK issue .... $9 – 12
149. "Guernsey Post," blue, blue roof, UK issue .... $6 – 8
150. "Guernsey Post Office," blue with white roof .... $6 – 8
151. "H. H. Brain," cream with green roof, on-package premium, UK issue .... $20 – 25
152. "Hansell's," white with red fenders, white roof, on-package premium, Australia issue .... $8 – 10
153. "Hawthorn Hawks," brown with yellow fenders, brown roof, Australia issue .... $8 – 10
154. "Hershey, Penn. — MICA 7," black with maroon fenders, maroon roof, promotional .... $12 – 16
155. "Historical Collection," "Powerhouse," green, black roof, Australia issue .... $7 – 9
156. "Houston Astros 1990," white with blue fenders, white roof, White Rose Collectibles .... $4 – 5
157. "Houston Astros 1991," orange with dark blue fenders, yellow roof, White Rose Collectibles .... $4 – 5
158. "Houston Oilers 1990," bright blue with red fenders, bright blue roof, White Rose Collectibles .... $4 – 5
159. "Houston Oilers 1991," bright blue with red fenders, white roof, White Rose Collectibles .... $4 – 5
160. "Hudson Lager," bright blue with yellow fenders and roof, rubber tires, Matchbox Collectibles .... $9 – 12
161. "I.O.M. Post Office," red, black roof, UK issue .... $7 – 9
162. "Illawarra Hawks," red and white with red fenders, red roof, Australia issue .... $8 – 10
163. "Illawarra Steelers," red with white fenders, red roof, Australia issue .... $8 – 10
164. "Indiana 1991," white with red fenders, dark blue roof, White Rose Collectibles .... $4 – 5
165. "Indiana Hoosiers 1993," cream with red fenders, red roof, White Rose Collectibles .... $5 – 6
166. "Ironbridge Telford — MICA 9," white with red fenders, pale powder roof, UK issue .... $12 – 16
167. "Isle of Man TT86," pale blue with dark blue fenders, red roof, UK issue .... $6 – 8
168. "Isle of Man TT87," black with red fenders, red roof, UK issue ...... $6 – 8
169. "Isle of Man TT88," yellow with black fenders, red roof, UK issue ...... $6 – 7
170. "Isle of Man TT89," cream with red fenders, red roof, UK issue ...... $6 – 8
171. "Isle of Man TT90," blue with red fenders, yellow roof, UK issue .. $6 – 8
172. "Isle of Man TT91," pale blue with blue fenders, red roof, UK issue .... $6 – 8
173. "Jacky Maeder," white, black roof, Swiss issue .... $9 – 12
174. "James Neale & Sons," yellow, white roof, UK issue .... $9 – 12
175. "John West Salmon," green, red roof, on-package premium, Australia issue .... $9 – 12
176. "Johnnie Walker," dark purple with black fenders, black roof, UK issue .... $20 – 25
177. "Johnnie Walker," dark purple with black fenders, black roof, on-package premium, UK issue............. $20 – 25
178. "Johnson's Seeds," cream, brown roof, on-package premium, UK issue .... $9 – 12

179. "Jordan's," cream, black roof, on-package premium, UK issue .. $12 – 16
180. "Junior Matchbox Club," yellow, blue roof, Canadian issue .... $7 – 9
181. "Junior Matchbox Club — The Gang," light blue, blue roof, Canadian issue .... $7 – 9
182. "Kansas City Chiefs 1990," white with red fenders, yellow roof, White Rose Collectibles.......................... $4 – 5
183. "Kansas City Chiefs 1991," yellow with red fenders, white roof, White Rose Collectibles..................... $4 – 5
184. "Kansas City Royals 1990," pale blue with blue fenders, white roof, White Rose Collectibles..................... $4 – 5
185. "Kansas City Royals 1991," blue with baby blue fenders, white roof, White Rose Collectibles..................... $4 – 5
186. "Kathy's Tortuga," white with black fenders and roof, Color Comp promotional................................ $16 – 24
187. "Kellogg's," blue with black fenders, white roof, on-package premium, Macau cast, UK issue..................... $8 – 10
188. "Kellogg's," blue with black fenders, white roof, on-package premium, Thailand cast, Swedish issue ...... $40 – 60
189. "Kellogg's Eggo," yellow with black fenders, red roof, on-package premium, US issue........................... $12 – 16
190. "Kellogg's Frosted Mini Wheats," orange with black fenders, black roof, on-package premium, US issue ...$9 – 12
191. "Kellogg's Raisin Bran," red-pink with black fenders, black roof, on-package premium, US issue .... $9 – 12
192. "Kellogg's Rice Krispies," blue, black roof, on-package premium, US issue .....$5 – 6
193. "Kellogg's Rice Krispies," blue, white roof, on-package premium, UK issue .... $9 – 12
194. "Krispy Kreme Doughnuts," white with black fenders and roof, ASAP promotional............................ $120 – 160
195. "Larklane Motor Museum," beige with brown fenders, brown roof, UK issue .... $6 – 8
196. "LaRue Bros. Auto Inc.," brown with light brown fenders, white roof, promotional................................. $9 – 12
197. "Left Hand Brewing Co.," blue with black fenders and roof, rubber tires, Matchbox Collectibles .... $9 – 12
198. "Lightwater Theme Park Valley," blue, cream roof, UK issue .... $7 – 9
199. "Lion's Club Fund Raising Activity," white with black fenders and roof, Color Comp promotional .... $30 – 40
200. "Los Angeles Dodgers 1991," silver with blue fenders, orange roof, White Rose Collectibles .... $4 – 5
201. "Los Angeles Dodgers 1990," white with blue fenders, white roof, White Rose Collectibles .... $4 – 5
202. "Los Angeles Kings 1993," black with silver fenders, silver roof, White Rose Collectibles .... $7 – 9
203. "Los Angeles Rams 1990," yellow with blue fenders, yellow roof, White Rose Collectibles .... $4 – 5
204. "Los Angeles Rams 1991," yellow with dark blue fenders, dark blue roof, White Rose Collectibles .... $4 – 5
205. "Lyceum Theatre," blue, black roof, UK issue .... $7 – 9
206. "Lyon's Tea," dark blue with black fenders, white roof, UK issue ... $7 – 9
207. "Magic," black with red fenders, blue roof, Australia issue .... $8 – 10
208. "Manx Cattery," red, black roof, UK issue .... $12 – 16
209. "Matchbox," white with black fenders, red roof, Australia issue ...... $24 – 32
210. "Matchbox Collectors Club 1989," silver with silver fenders, black roof, promotional .... $120 – 160
211. "Matchbox Collectors Club 1990," fluorescent green with fluorescent orange fenders, black roof, promotional .... $90 – 120
212. "Matchbox Collectors Club 1991," white with dark pink fenders, black roof, promotional .... $60 – 80
213. "Matchbox Collectors Club 1992," brass plated with black fenders, black roof, promotional .... $50 – 70
214. "Matchbox Collectors Club 1993," black with green fenders, green roof, promotional....................... $20 – 25
215. "Matchbox Collectors Club Christmas 1994".................................. $6 – 8
216. "Matchbox Convention 2000 — Hershey Demo Model," brown with brown fenders, white roof, Color Comp promotional................................ $40 – 50
217. "Matchbox Convention 2001 — Hershey Demo Model," white with black fenders and roof, Color Comp promotional....................................$16 – 24
218. "Matchbox Dinky Toy Convention 1991," yellow with black fenders, black roof, UK issue......................................$9 – 12
219. "Matchbox for Serious Collectors," yellow with black roof, Germany issue . $9 – 12
220. "Matchbox on the Move in '84," blue with black fenders, white roof....$30 – 50
221. "Matchbox on the Move in '84," "Toy Fair 84," blue with black fenders, white roof......................................$30 – 50
222. "Matchbox Series Model A Ford Van," yellow, black roof.........................$3 – 4
223. "Matchbox Speedshop," blue, orange pinstripes, nonchrome-lettered wheels ....$1 – 2
224. "Matchbox Speedshop," blue, yellow pinstripes, nonchrome-lettered wheels ....$1 – 2
225. "Matchbox Speedshop," blue, yellow pinstripes, chrome-lettered wheels ....$80 – 120
226. "Matchbox USA," white with blue fenders, red roof .... $24 – 36
227. "Matchbox USA 9th Annual Convention 1990," white with maroon fenders, white roof .... $8 – 10
228. "Matchbox & Lesney Toy Museum," brown with white roof .... $6 – 12
229. "Matchbox — Get in the Fast Lane," fluorescent orange with yellow fenders, orange roof......................... $8 – 10
230. "Matchbox — This Van Delivers" with phone number on doors, blue, red roof, UK issue.......................... $16 – 24
231. "Matchbox — This Van Delivers" without phone number on doors, blue, red roof, Hong Kong issue .... $60 – 80
232. "Matchbox 1991," blue with red fenders, white roof, China issue .. $60 – 80
233. "Matchbox 1991," green with yellow fenders, white roof, China issue .... $60 – 80
234. "Matchbox 1991," maroon with maroon fenders, white roof, China issue .... $60 – 80
235. "Matchbox 1991," orange with black fenders, white roof, China issue .... $60 – 80
236. "Matchbox 1991," silver with black fenders, orange roof, China issue .... $60 – 80
237. "Matchbox 1991," white with red fenders, blue roof, China issue ..$60 – 80
238. "Matchbox 33000," white with black fenders and roof, ASAP promotional .... $80 – 120
239. "Matchbox 40th Anniversary 1990," blue, blue roof .... $8 – 10
240. "Matthew Walker," white with white fenders, white roof, UK issue.. $9 – 12
241. "McVities Digestive," red with black fenders, black roof, on-package premium, UK issue..................... $12 – 16
242. "Melbourne Demons," dark blue with red fenders, blue roof, Australia issue .... $8 – 10
243. "Melbourne Tigers," red with yellow fenders, red roof, Australia issue ......$8 – 10
244. "Melcer Tile 30 Years," white with black fenders and roof, ASAP promotional........................... $120 – 160
245. "Memories 1993," gold with black fenders, black roof, promotional .... $400 – 600
246. "Merry Christmas 1993," green with red fenders, red roof, promotional .... $30 – 50
247. "Mervyn Wynne," red with black fenders, black roof, UK issue...... $12 – 16
248. "Mervyn Wynne," black island design on doors, red with black fenders, black roof, UK issue .... $20 – 25
249. "Miami Dolphins 1990," blue-green with orange fenders, white roof, White Rose Collectibles.................... $4 – 5
250. "Miami Dolphins 1991," orange with blue-green fenders, blue-green roof, White Rose Collectibles........... $4 – 5
251. "MICA" and kangaroo, tan with blue fenders, blue roof, Australia issue .... $8 – 10
252. "MICA" and kangaroo, beige with blue fenders, blue roof, base secured by screws, Australia issue .... $100 – 150

253. "Milk of Magnesia," blue with dark blue fenders, blue roof......... $5 – 6
254. "Milwaukee Brewers 1991," white with yellow fenders, white roof, White Rose Collectibles .... $4 – 5
255. "Milwaukee Brewers 1990," white with blue fenders, white roof, White Rose Collectibles .... $4 – 5
256. "Minnesota Twins 1990," white with blue fenders, white roof, White Rose Collectibles .... $4 – 5
257. "Minnesota Twins 1991," dark blue with red fenders, white roof, White Rose Collectibles .... $4 – 5
258. "Minnesota Vikings 1990," purple with purple fenders, yellow roof, White Rose Collectibles .... $4 – 5
259. "Minnesota Vikings 1991," yellow with purple fenders, purple roof, White Rose Collectibles .... $4 – 5
260. "Mitre 10," blue with black fenders, blue roof, Australia issue.........................$8 – 10
261. "Moorland Centre," light gray, dark gray roof, UK issue............ $7 – 9
262. "Montreal Expos 1990," white with red fenders, white roof, White Rose Collectibles....................... $4 – 5
263. "Montreal Canadiennes 1917," red with blue fenders, white roof; "Montreal Canadiennes 1992," white with red fenders, white roof. White Rose Collectibles 2-pack.....$12 – 16 for set of two
264. "Montreal Expos 1991," baby blue with red fenders, white roof, White Rose Collectibles .... $4 – 5
265. "Moto Master," black with red fenders and roof, rubber tires, Canada issue............................... $5 – 6
266. "Nat West Action Bank," blue, gray roof, UK issue................... $7 – 9
267. "New England Ice Cream 508-580-6100," white with black fenders and roof, ASAP promotional ......$120 – 160
268. "New England Patriots 1990," red with white fenders, blue roof, White Rose Collectibles .... $4 – 5
269. "New England Patriots 1991," dark blue with red fenders, red roof, White Rose Collectibles .... $4 – 5
270. "New Orleans Saints 1990," gold with black fenders, white roof, White Rose Collectibles .... $4 – 5
271. "New Orleans Saints 1991," white with gold fenders, black roof, White Rose Collectibles .... $4 – 5
272. "New York Jets 1990," white with green fenders, green roof, White Rose Collectibles .... $4 – 5
273. "New York Jets 1991," white with green fenders, green roof, White Rose Collectibles .... $4 – 5
274. "New York Mets 1990," white with blue fenders, white roof, White Rose Collectibles .... $4 – 5
275. "New York Mets 1991," orange with blue fenders, white roof, White Rose Collectibles .... $4 – 5
276. "New York Rangers 1917," red with red fenders, white roof; "New York Rangers 1992," white with blue fenders, white roof. White Rose Collectibles 2-pack .... $12 – 16 for set of two
277. "New York Rangers 1990," white with blue fenders, white roof, White Rose Collectibles .... $4 – 5
278. "New York Rangers 1991," red with blue fenders, white roof, White Rose Collectibles .... $4 – 5
279. "New York Yankees 1991," white with red fenders, dark blue roof, White Rose Collectibles .... $4 – 5
280. "New York Yankees 1990," white with blue fenders, white roof, White Rose Collectibles .... $4 – 5
281. "Newcastle Falcons," dark blue with red fenders, red roof, Australia issue ....$8 – 10
282. "Newcastle Knights," blue with red fenders, red roof, Australia issue ....$8 – 10
283. "No. Melbourne Kangaroos," white with blue fenders, white roof, Australia issue..........................$8 – 10
284. "No. Melbourne Giants," turquoise with purple fenders, white roof, Australia issue......................$8 – 10
285. "No. Queensland Cowboys," dark blue with gray fenders, gray roof, Australia issue.................$8 – 10
286. "No. Sydney Bears," black with white fenders, black roof, Australia issue ....$8 – 10
287. "North America M.I.C.A. Convention 1988," orange, black roof .... $7 – 9
288. "North Carolina 1992," pale blue with pale blue fenders, white roof, White Rose Collectibles .... $5 – 7
289. "Notre Dame 1991," yellow with green fenders, white roof, White Rose Collectibles .... $4 – 5
290. "Oakland Athletics 1990," yellow with green fenders, white roof, White Rose Collectibles .... $4 – 5
291. "Oakland Athletics 1991," green with yellow fenders, white roof, White Rose Collectibles .... $4 – 5
292. "Oakland Raiders 1990," silver with black fenders, black roof, White Rose Collectibles .... $4 – 5
293. "Oakland Raiders 1991," black with silver fenders, white roof, White Rose Collectibles .... $4 – 5
294. "Old Tymers Model A Club Rod Run," white with black fenders and roof, ASAP promotional ..$80 – 120
295. "Open Every Day," pale blue with dark gray fenders, dark gray roof ....$12 – 16
296. "P.M.G.," orange with black fenders, black roof, Australia issue .... $9 – 12
297. "Parramatta Eels," blue with yellow fenders, blue roof, Australia issue .... $8 – 10
298. "Pava," yellow, red roof, Denmark issue..............................$9 – 12
299. "Penn State 1990," blue with white fenders, white roof, White Rose Collectibles.......................... $7 – 9
300. "Penn State 1990," white with blue fenders, white roof, White Rose Collectibles.......................... $7 – 9
301. "Penn State 1991," white with dark blue fenders, dark blue roof, White Rose Collectibles .... $7 – 9
302. "Penrith Panthers," black with red fenders, black roof, Australia issue ....$8 – 10
303. "Pepsi," white with blue fenders, red roof.......................... $5 – 6
304. "Pepsi-Cola," white with black fenders and roof, ASAP promotional ..$60 – 80
305. "Pepsi," "Come Alive," white with blue fenders, red roof.........$8 – 10
306. "Perth Wildcats," white with yellow fenders, white roof, Australia issue ....$8 – 10
307. "PG Tips," cream with green fenders, red roof, on-package premium, UK issue ....$12 – 16
308. "Philadelphia Eagles 1990," silver with green fenders, white roof, White Rose Collectibles .... $4 – 5
309. "Philadelphia Eagles 1991," silver with green fenders, green roof, White Rose Collectibles .... $4 – 5
310. "Philadelphia Flyers 1993," orange with black fenders, black roof, White Rose Collectibles .... $7 – 9
311. "Philadelphia Phillies 1990," white with maroon fenders, white roof, White Rose Collectibles .... $4 – 5
312. "Philadelphia Phillies 1991," maroon with maroon fenders, white roof, White Rose Collectibles .... $4 – 5
313. "Pittsburgh Pirates 1991," black with yellow fenders, white roof, White Rose Collectibles .... $4 – 5
314. "Pittsburgh Pirates 1990," white with black fenders, black roof, White Rose Collectibles .... $4 – 5
315. "Pittsburgh Steelers 1990," yellow with black fenders, yellow roof, White Rose Collectibles .... $4 – 5
316. "Pittsburgh Steelers 1991," yellow with black fenders, black roof, White Rose Collectibles .... $4 – 5
317. "Postes Canada Post," red with black fenders, black roof ..... $6 – 8
318. "Pritt Stick," red with black fenders, black roof, on-package premium, UK issue ....$8 – 10
319. "Pure Cod Liver Oil," dark cream with blue fenders, cream roof .... $5 – 6
320. "RACQ," yellow with bright blue fenders, blue roof, Australia issue ....$12 – 16
321. "Rayner's Crusha," red, on-package premium, UK issue ....$9 – 12
322. "RCA, white with black fenders and roof, ASAP promotional ...$30 – 40

323. "Reichspost," yellow with black fenders, white roof .... $6 – 8
324. "Ribena," blue, black roof, UK issue ....$9 – 12
325. "Richmond Tigers," black with yellow fenders, black roof, Australia issue ....$8 – 10
326. "Ritz Carlton Hotel & Casino," white with black fenders and roof, ASAP promotional ....$320 – 480
327. "Ritz Carlton Hotel, Spa & Casino" graphics, white with black fenders and roof, ASAP promotional .... $240 – 320
328. "River Horse Lager," green with yellow fenders and roof, Matchbox Collectibles ....$9 – 12

329. "Roosevelt for President 1932," "White's Guide Car #1 Presidential Campaign Series," white with black fenders and roof, Color Comp promotional ....$16 – 24
330. "Route 11 Potato Chips," white with black fenders and roof, Color Comp promotional ....$16 – 24
331. "Rowntree's Table Jelly," green, yellow roof, on-package premium, UK issue ....$9 – 12
332. "Royal Mail," red, black roof, gold grille, UK issue .... $7 – 9
333. "Rugby Child Development Centre," white with blue fenders, blue roof, UK issue ....$8 – 10
334. "Rutter Bros. Dairy," white with black fenders, black roof, White Rose Collectibles .... $7 – 9
335. "Sammler Treffen 1988," dark blue with black fenders, yellow roof, 1997 German promotional ....$180 – 240
336. "San Diego Chargers 1990," dark blue with yellow fenders, white roof, White Rose Collectibles ...... $4 – 5
337. "San Diego Chargers 1991," yellow with dark blue fenders, dark blue roof, White Rose Collectibles ...$4 – 5
338. "San Diego Padres 1990," white with brown fenders, orange roof, White Rose Collectibles ...... $4 – 5
339. "San Diego Padres 1991," silver with dark blue fenders, orange roof, White Rose Collectibles ...... $4 – 5
340. "San Francisco 49ers 1990," gold with red fenders, white roof, White Rose Collectibles .... $4 – 5
341. "San Francisco 49ers 1991," red with gold fenders, gold roof, White Rose Collectibles .... $4 – 5
342. "San Francisco Giants 1990," blue with white fenders, white roof, White Rose Collectibles .... $4 – 5
343. "San Francisco Giants 1990," white with black fenders, white roof, White Rose Collectibles ...... $4 – 5
344. "San Francisco Giants 1991," lavender gray with black fenders, orange roof, White Rose Collectibles ... $4 – 5
345. "San Francisco Giants 1991," white with dark blue fenders, dark blue roof, White Rose Collectibles .... $4 – 5
346. "San Jose Sharks 1993," white with metallic turquoise fenders, black roof, White Rose Collectibles ...$7 – 9
347. "Sea Eagles," dark red with white fenders, dark red roof, Australia issue ....$8 – 10
348. "Season's Greetings From Color Comp Inc.," white with red fenders, green roof, Color Comp promotional ....$120 – 160
349. "Seattle Mariners 1990," white with blue fenders, yellow roof, White Rose Collectibles .... $4 – 5
350. "Seattle Mariners 1991," yellow with blue fenders, blue roof, White Rose Collectibles .... $4 – 5
351. "Seattle Seahawks 1990," silver with blue fenders, white roof, White Rose Collectibles .... $4 – 5
352. "Seattle Seahawks 1991," dark blue with green fenders, white roof, White Rose Collectibles ...... $4 – 5
353. "Selfridge & Co.," dark green with black roof, UK issue .... $6 – 8
354. "Shell Motor Oil," yellow with red fenders, yellow roof, Australia issue ....$16 – 24
355. "Ship McQuaid," white with black fenders and roof, ASAP promotional ....$30 – 40
356. "Shipyard Brewing," white with blue fenders and roof, rubber tires, Matchbox Collectibles ....$9 – 12
357. "Silvo," blue with black fenders, black roof, UK issue ....$8 – 10
358. "Smith Kline Beecham," white with black fenders and roof, ASAP promotional ....$120 – 160
359. "Smith's Crisps," dark blue with red fenders, yellow roof, Australia issue ....$16 – 24
360. "Smith's Potato Crisps," blue, white roof, on-package premium, Australia issue ....$8 – 10
361. "So. Queensland Crushers," dark blue with red fenders and roof, Australia issue ....$8 – 10
362. "So. Sydney Rabbitohs," bright green with red fenders, bright green roof, Australia issue ....$8 – 10
363. "South Jersey Ghost Research," white with black fenders and roof, Color Comp promotional ...$20 – 25
364. "Special Edition 76," white with blue fenders and roof .... $2 – 3

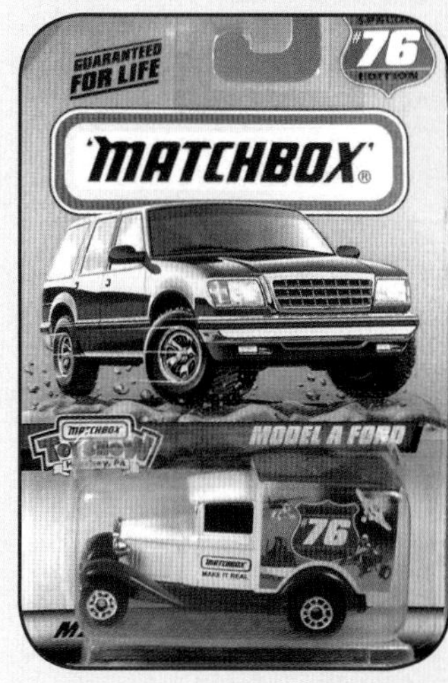

365. "Special Edition 76," white with blue fenders and roof, "Matchbox Make It Real" on doors, in "Matchbox Toy Show, Hershey, PA" pkg. ....$9 – 12
366. "St. George," white with red fenders, white roof, Australia issue ..... $8 – 10
367. "St. Kilda Saints," white with red roof, Australia issue ....$8 – 10
368. "St. Louis Cardinals 1990," white with rust fenders, maroon roof, White Rose Collectibles ...... $4 – 5
369. "St. Louis Cardinals 1990," white with red fenders, white roof, White Rose Collectibles .... $4 – 5
370. "St. Louis Cardinals 1991," white with red fenders, white roof, White Rose Collectibles .... $4 – 5
371. "St. Louis Cardinals 1991," maroon with white fenders, white roof, White Rose Collectibles ...$4 – 5
372. "Street's Ice Cream," light brown with red fenders and roof, Australia issue ....$16 – 24
373. "Swarfega," blue, black roof, on-package premium, UK issue .. $20 – 25
374. "Sydney Kings," purple with yellow fenders, white roof, Australia issue ....$8 – 10
375. "Sydney Swans," white with red fenders, red roof, Australia issue ....$8 – 10
376. "Syracuse University 1992," orange with blue fenders, white roof, White Rose Collectibles ...... $5 – 7
377. "Tampa Bay Buccaneers 1990," orange with black fenders, black roof, White Rose Collectibles .... $4 – 5
378. "Tampa Bay Buccaneers 1991," orange with red fenders, white roof, White Rose Collectibles ...... $4 – 5
379. "Tandy Electronics," red, blue roof, Australia issue ....$12 – 16
380. "Tassie Devils," yellow with red fenders, red roof, Australia issue ..$8 – 10

381. "Temecula Rod Run 1996," white, clear windows, racing slicks on back axle, Thailand cast, White Rose Collectibles .... $9 – 12
382. "Ten Years Lion," white, blue roof, UK issue .... $8 – 10
383. "Tennessee Vol. 1992," white with orange fenders, white roof, White Rose Collectibles .... $5 – 7
384. "Texaco Petroleum Products," black with green fenders and roof, Premiere Collection .... $5 – 6
385. "The Australian," white with black fenders, black roof, Australia issue .... $7 – 9
386. "The New Crawford," white with black fenders and roof, ASAP promotional .... $80 – 120
387. "Tiger Balm," red with dark blue fenders, red roof .... $5 – 6
388. "Tittensor First School," gray with red fenders, red roof, UK issue ... $6 – 8
389. "TMLP," white with black fenders and roof, ASAP promotional ...... $30 – 40
390. "Tom's Antiques Art & Collectibles," white with black fenders and roof, ASAP promotional .... $40 – 50
391. "Toronto Blue Jays 1990," white with blue fenders, white roof, White Rose Collectibles .... $4 – 5
392. "Toronto Blue Jays 1991," blue with blue fenders, white roof, White Rose Collectibles .... $4 – 5
393. "Toronto Maple Leafs 1917," dark blue with white fenders, white roof; "Toronto Maple Leafs 1992," white with blue fenders, white roof. White Rose Collectibles 2-pack .... $12 – 16 for set of two
394. "Townsville Suns," yellow with salmon pink fenders, red roof, Australia issue .... $8 – 10
395. "Toy Collectors Pocket Guide," yellow with green fenders, green roof, UK issue .... $7 – 9
396. "Transply," white with black fenders and roof .... $60 – 80
397. "True Value Hardware," lime green with orange fenders, orange roof, Australia issue .... $8 – 10
398. "Two Men and a Truck," white with black fenders and roof, ASAP promotional .... $12 – 16
399. "Tyco — Portland, Oregon," white with black fenders and roof, ASAP promotional .... $120 – 160
400. "Tyne Brand," dark blue with black fenders and roof, on-package premium, UK issue .... $12 – 16
401. "Tyne Brand," orange-red with black fenders and roof, on-package premium, UK issue .... $12 – 16
402. "U.S. Mail," white .... $6 – 8
403. "Unionville Community Fair 2000," white with black fenders and roof, ASAP promotional .... $30 – 40
404. "Uniroyal Royal Care," black, Canada issue .... $20 – 25
405. "University of Colorado 1992," yellow with black fenders, white roof, White Rose Collectibles .... $5 – 7
406. "University of Michigan 1992," yellow with dark blue fenders, yellow roof, White Rose Collectibles .... $5 – 7
407. "University of Washington 1992," yellow with purple fenders, white roof, White Rose Collectibles .... $5 – 7
408. "UNLV 1991," silver with red fenders, white roof, White Rose Collectibles .... $4 – 5
409. "Vegemite," yellow with red fenders, yellow roof, Australia issue .... $8 – 10
410. "Vick's," green with blue fenders, green roof .... $5 – 6
411. "Vileda," red with white fenders, white roof, on-package premium, UK issue .... $9 – 12
412. "W.H. Smith & Sons," red, black roof, on-package premium, UK issue .... $20 – 25
413. "W.H. Smith & Sons," yellow, black roof, UK issue .... $12 – 16
414. "Washington Capitals 1993," white with red fenders, blue roof, White Rose Collectibles .... $7 – 9
415. "Washington Redskins 1990," rust with yellow fenders, white roof, White Rose Collectibles .... $4 – 5
416. "Washington Redskins 1991," yellow with maroon fenders, maroon roof, White Rose Collectibles .... $4 – 5
417. "Weetabix," "Sanitarium Food," green, on-package premium, Australia issue .... $8 – 10
418. "Welcome Ye to Chester," yellow, blue roof, promotional UK issue .... $16 – 24
419. "West Coast Eagles," blue and yellow fenders, blue roof, Australia issue .... $8 – 10
420. "Western Reds," red with white fenders and roof, Australia issue .. $8 – 10
421. "Western Suburbs," black with white fenders, black roof, Australia issue .... $8 – 10

422. "White's Guide Car of the Month #6 May, 1999," white with black fenders and roof, Color Comp promotional .... $16 – 24
423. "William Lusty," cream with green fenders, green roof, UK issue .. $7 – 9
424. "William Lusty," green with green fenders, green roof, UK issue .. $7 – 9
425. "XIth MICA Convention," rust with cream fenders, cream roof, UK issue ... $12 – 16
426. "Yardley," light gray with brown fenders, brown roof, UK issue ..... $9 – 12
427. "York Fair 1989," yellow, green roof, White Rose Collectibles .... $7 – 9
428. "York Fair 1990 — 225 Years," cream with red fenders, red roof, White Rose Collectibles .... $6 – 8
429. "York Fair 1991," silver with turquoise fenders, turquoise roof, White Rose Collectibles .... $6 – 8
430. "York Fair 1993," cream with blue fenders, green roof, White Rose Collectibles .... $5 – 6
431. "Young's Sheep Dips," green, Australia issue .... $8 – 10
432. Australian six-piece set: "Aeroplane Jelly," "Billy Tea," "IXL," "Milo," "Uncle Toby's," "Violet Crumble" ..... $12 – 16 for set of six in original box
433. Australian six-piece set: "Hardy's Black Bottle," "Houghton White Burgundy," "McWilliams Cream Sherry," "Penfold's," "Tyrell's Dry Red," "Yalumba Port" .... $40 – 50 for set of six in original box
434. Australian six-piece set: "Big Apple Circus," "Chipperfield's Circus," "Circus Barum," "Circus Krone," "Circus Oz," "Gerry Cottle's Circus" .. $30 – 40 for set of six in original box
435. white, white fenders, white roof, no markings, Graffic Traffic ...... $12 – 16
436. white with black fenders and roof, no markings, ASAP promotional blank .... $30 – 40

Ford Model T 1921 Van, $2\frac{7}{8}$", #44, 1990

1. "15 Jaar Model Auto 97," yellow with black fenders, Dutch issue .. $12 – 16
2. "1896 1996," red with black fenders, UK issue .... $16 – 24
3. "1939 – 1945," "War & Occupation Museum," white with black fenders, Dutch issue .... $20 – 30
4. "3rd MICA NA Convention 1990," ivory with dark blue roof and fenders, US issue .... $10 – 12
5. "4th MICA NA Convention," "Detroit Motor City," black, US issue .. $10 – 12
6. "5th Anniversary Australian Matchbox News," white with black fenders .... $16 – 24
7. "5th MICA Convention 1990," ivory with dark blue roof and fenders, UK issue .... $10 – 12
8. "8th Super Southern Swapmeet," red with black fenders, Australia issue .... $9 – 12
9. "8th Super Southern Swapmeet," yellow with black fenders, Australia issue .... $9 – 12
10. "16th Matchbox USA Toy Show," white with black fenders, US issue .. $12 – 16
11. "16th Matchbox USA Toy Show," yellow with black fenders, US issue .. $12 – 16
12. "40th Anniversary Spar," white with black fenders, UK issue .. $120 – 160

13. "50 Years Liberation," "War & Occupation Museum," white with black fenders, Dutch issue .... $20 – 30
14. "Adtrucks," yellow with black fenders, UK issue .... $12 – 16
15. "Adtrucks 2001," UK issue .. $12 – 16
16. "Anderson Valley," gold with green roof and fenders, Matchbox Collectibles #5 .... $9 – 12
17. "Bala Lake Railway," yellow with black fenders, UK issue .... $12 – 16
18. "Barrettine — The Independent Choice," ivory with blue fenders, UK issue .... $12 – 16
19. "BASC," "Beccles Amateur Sailing Club," dark blue with black fenders, UK issue .... $40 – 50
20. "Bendigo National Swapmeet 1996," red with black fenders, Australia issue .... $20 – 30
21. "Bendigo National Swapmeet 1996," white with black fenders, Australia issue .... $20 – 30
22. "Biddestone Village," white with black fenders, UK issue .... $12 – 16

23. "Bird's Custard Powder," yellow with red roof, blue fenders, China cast .... $3 – 4
24. "Bird's Custard Powder," yellow with red roof, blue fenders, Macau cast .... $1 – 2
25. "Bishop's Move," yellow with black fenders, UK issue .... $12 – 16
26. "Bostik," ivory with black fenders, UK issue .... $12 – 16
27. "Bradford AFC," red with black fenders, UK issue .... $20 – 30
28. "Catalogue of Matchbox Toys," ivory with black fenders, US issue .. $16 – 24
29. "Catalogue of Matchbox Toys," yellow with black fenders, US issue .. $60 – 80
30. "CE Engineering Europe Ltd.," white with black fenders, UK issue ... $12 – 16
31. "Chesdale," yellow with blue roof and fenders, Australian on-package premium .... $8 – 12
32. "Chester Doll Hospital," "World's Largest Matchbox Display," white with light blue roof and fenders, UK issue .... $9 – 12
33. "Coca-Cola," red with white fenders, Premiere Collection .... $5 – 6
34. "Continental Aero," purple with black fenders, US issue .... $12 – 16
35. "Craig's," blue with red roof and fenders, Australian on-package premium .... $8 – 12
36. "Crazy Clown," red with dark blue roof and base, Australia issue .... $9 – 12
37. "Cromer Carnival 1996," white with black fenders, UK issue ..... $20 – 30
38. "Cromer Carnival 1997," red with black fenders, UK issue ..... $12 – 16
39. "Dale Farm," white with red roof, dark blue fenders, UK issue .... $8 – 11
40. "Daybreak at Lowestoft," "The Sunrise Coast," "The Dawn of a New Millenium," UK issue .... $12 – 16
41. "DM David Meek," dark blue with black fenders, UK issue .... $60 – 80
42. "Dunaskin," white with black fenders, UK issue .... $12 – 16
43. "Dyspraxia Foundation," white with black fenders, UK issue ..... $12 – 16
44. "Encyclopedia of Matchbox Toys," ivory with black fenders, US issue .... $40 – 50
45. "Encyclopedia of Matchbox Toys," red with black fenders, UK issue .... $12 – 16
46. "Encyclopedia of Matchbox Toys" in black lettering, yellow with black fenders, US issue .... $20 – 30
47. "Encyclopedia of Matchbox Toys" in blue lettering, yellow with black fenders, US issue .... $20 – 30
48. "Evening Gazette Car Awards 1997," yellow with black fenders, UK issue .... $12 – 16
49. "Farnham Maltings 1 – 7th January 1996," white with black fenders, UK issue .... $20 – 30
50. "Farnham Maltings 2 – 10th March 1996," white with black fenders, UK issue .... $20 – 30
51. "Farnham Maltings 3 – 26th May 1996," ivory with white roof, blue fenders, UK issue .... $20 – 30
52. "Farnham Maltings 3 – 26th May 1996," white with blue fenders, UK issue .... $20 – 30
53. "Farnham Maltings 4 – 8th September 1996," white with black fenders, UK issue .... $20 – 30
54. "Farnham 6 – 16th March 1997," white with black fenders, UK issue .... $12 – 16
55. "Farnham 7 – May 1997," white with black fenders, UK issue ...... $12 – 16
56. "Farnham 8 – 11th September 1997," white with black fenders, UK issue .... $12 – 16
57. "Ferne Animal Sanctuary," white with black fenders, UK issue ...... $12 – 16
58. "Financial Times," white with black roof and fenders, UK issue .... $9 – 12
59. "Finlaystone," white with black fenders, UK issue .... $12 – 16
60. "Finlaystone," yellow with black fenders, UK issue .... $12 – 16
61. "Firehouse Brewing Co.," black with red roof and fenders, Matchbox Collectibles #2 .... $9 – 12
62. "Ford Motor Company," yellow with black fenders, UK issue ...... $20 – 30

63. "Ford Motor Company 100 Years," blue with white roof, black fenders, 2003 Matchbox Collectibles .... $9 – 12
64. "Ford on Show," dark blue with black fenders, UK issue .... $80 – 120
65. "Freihofer's," white with black fenders, US issue .... $12 – 16
66. "Garde D'Or," white with black fenders, UK issue .... $12 – 16
67. "Glenturret," white with black fenders, UK issue .... $12 – 16
68. "Goodyear Tire & Rubber Co," light blue with black roof, dark blue fenders .... $2 – 4
69. "Goodyear Tyres," powder blue with black roof, dark blue fenders ... $1 – 2
70. "Great Yarmouth," "The Bloaters," yellow with black fenders, UK issue .... $12 – 16
71. "Great Yarmouth," "Wellesley Main Grandstand," yellow with black fenders, UK issue .... $12 – 16
72. "Greetings from Philadelphia 1992," "MICA NA," ivory, dark blue roof and fenders .... $12 – 16
73. "Haig's Chocolates," beige with red fenders, spoked wheels, Australia issue .... $12 – 16
74. "Holy Cow," "Ambler Gambler," green with black roof, red fenders, Matchbox Collectibles #3 .... $9 – 12
75. "Jacob's," orange with black fenders, Irish on-package premium ... $20 – 30
76. "Kellogg's Apple Jacks," fluorescent green with black roof and fenders, US on-package premium .... $9 – 12
77. "Kellogg's Corn Flakes," dark blue with black roof and fenders, Australia on-package premium .... $16 – 24
78. "Kellogg's Corn Pops," yellow with red roof, blue fenders, US on-package premium .... $9 – 12
79. "Kellogg's Eggo," yellow with red roof, black fenders, US on-package premium .... $20 – 30
80. "Kla-Ora," yellow with black fenders, UK issue .... $12 – 16
81. "Klaus Toys," red with green roof, red fenders, Holiday Express Train, Color Comp promotional .... $40 – 50

82. "Kraft," blue with yellow roof and fenders, Australian on-package premium ..$9 – 12
83. "Lloyds," white with red roof, dark blue fenders, UK issue .... $12 – 16
84. "Lowestoft Town Football Club," "Blues of Crown Meadow," white with blue roof, black fenders, UK issue .... $30 – 40
85. "Lowestoft Town Football Club," "Blues of Crown Meadow" with "John Grose Ford" on roof, white with black fenders, UK issue .... $200 – 250
86. "Lowestoft Town Football Club," "John Grose Ford," white with blue roof, black fenders, UK issue .... $30 – 40
88. "Matchbox Collectibles," green with red roof, green fenders, Holiday Express Train, Color Comp promotional ...$40 – 50
89. "Matchbox Drive Your Name Home," dark blue with black fenders, UK issue .... $20 – 30
90. "Matchbox Drive Your Name Home," red with black fenders, UK issue .. $20 – 30
91. "Matchbox Official Visitor," red with black fenders, UK issue .... $60 – 80
92. "Matchbox Drive Your Name Home," white with black fenders, UK issue .... $20 – 30
93. "Matchbox Toy Delivery," red with black roof, Collector's Choice, White Rose Collectibles .... $4 – 5
94. "Matchbox USA 15th Annual Toy Show," dark blue with black fenders, US issue .... $20 – 30
95. "Matchbox USA 15th Annual Toy Show," red with black fenders, US issue .... $20 – 30
96. "Matchbox USA 15th Annual Toy Show," yellow with black fenders, US issue .... $100 – 150
97. "Matchbox USA 95," dark blue with black fenders .... $20 – 30
98. "Matchbox USA 96," red with black fenders .... $20 – 30
99. "Matchbox USA 96," white with black fenders .... $20 – 30
100. "Mars," black, UK issue ... $12 – 16
101. "Mars," red, UK issue ...... $16 – 24
102. "MCCD 1998," ivory with black fenders, Germany issue .... $40 – 60
103. "MCCD 1998," red with black fenders, Germany issue .... $16 – 24
104. "MCCD 1998," white with black fenders, Germany issue .... $16 – 24
105. "MCCD 1998," yellow with black fenders, Germany issue .... $60 – 80
106. "MD," white with black fenders, UK issue .... $12 – 16
107. "Merry Christmas Australian Matchbox," red with black fenders .... $16 – 24
108. "Merry Christmas," "Best Wishes from Carr Collectibles," red with black fenders, UK issue .... $40 – 50
109. "MICA 7," "I Could Have Danced All Night," white with light blue roof and fenders, UK issue .... $12 – 16
110. "MICA NA Convention," "Detroit Motor City," black .... $10 – 12
111. "Mt. Wilson Wheat Beer," pink with dark green roof and fenders, Matchbox Collectibles .... $9 – 12
112. "Mundesley Inshore Lifeboat," white with black fenders, UK issue .. $12 – 16
113. "NGK — The Heartbeat of the Engine," white with black fenders, UK issue .... $60 – 80
114. "NGK — The UK's No. 1 Professional Plug," white with black fenders, UK issue .... $70 – 90
115. "North Coast Brewing Company-Scrimshaw," blue with red roof and fenders, Matchbox Collectibles #1 .... $9 – 12
116. "North Walsham Carnival 1996," white with black fenders, UK issue .... $20 – 30
117. "Norwich Citadel-Salvation Army," ivory with black fenders, UK issue .... $12 – 16
118. "Norwich Citadel-Salvation Army," yellow with black fenders, UK issue .... $12 – 16
119. "Open Business Solutions," white with black fenders, UK issue .... $16 – 24
120. "P.M.G.," orange-red with black roof and fenders, Australia issue .... $8 – 12
121. "PARA 90," white with light blue roof and fenders, UK issue .... $10 – 12
122. "PG Tips," ivory with red roof, green fenders, UK on-package premium .... $16 – 24
123. "Philadelphia MICA NA," black .... $12 – 16
124. "Pool's Plus, Inc.," dark blue with red roof and fenders, ASAP promotional .... $16 – 24
125. "QATC & EMC Projects," "QA Testing Centre," yellow with black fenders, UK issue .... $20 – 30
126. "Red Tail Ale," red with blue roof, gold fenders, Matchbox Collectibles #6 .... $9 – 12
127. "Ritz Carlton Hotel, Spa & Casino," dark blue with red roof and fenders, ASAP promotional .... $200 – 300
128. "Royal Mail GR," red with black hood, roof and fenders, UK issue .... $9 – 12
129. "Runnymeade Meccano Guild," red with green roof, black fenders, UK issue .... $12 – 16
130. "Runnymeade Meccano Guild," white with black fenders, UK issue .. $12 – 16
131. "SAE International," black, US issue .... $45 – 55
132. "Seadog Brewing Co.," blue with red roof and fenders, Matchbox Collectibles .... $9 – 12
133. "Springfest Extravaganza 1996," red with black fenders, Australia issue .... $20 – 30
134. "Squidward" illustration, white with metallic light blue roof, blue fenders, 2003 Nickelodeon Spongebob Squarepants 5-pack .... $2 – 3
135. "St. Marien Sandersleben," red with black fenders, Germany issue .$30 – 40
136. "St. Marien Sandersleben," white with black fenders, Germany issue ..$40 – 50
137. "St. Marien Sandersleben," yellow with black fenders, Germany issue .... $16 – 24
138. "Starlec," white with black fenders, UK issue .... $12 – 16
139. "Stirling Old Town Jail," dark blue with black fenders, UK issue .... $60 – 80
140. "Swarfega," dark green with black roof, dark gray base, UK on-package premium .... $45 – 55
141. "The Royal Tournament," white with black fenders, UK issue .... $20 – 30
142. "The Royal Tournament" with "Earl's Court," white with black fenders, UK issue .... $150 – 200
143. "The Story of Mann," ivory with black fenders, UK issue .... $12 – 16
144. "The Sunrise Coast," UK issue .....$12 – 16
145. "TTK," dark blue with black fenders, UK issue .... $40 – 50
146. "Vegemite," yellow with red roof and fenders, Australian on-package premium .... $8 – 12
147. "Weidman's Brewery," yellow with blue fenders, Matchbox Collectibles #4 .... $9 – 12
148. "Welcoming the New Millennium," beige with black roof and fenders, UK issue .... $20 – 30
149. "Welcoming the New Millennium," red with black fenders, UK issue ...$20 – 30
150. "Williams Lusty," black, UK issue . $7 – 9
151. "Your Own Promotional Vehicle," "Matchbox — Put Your Logo Here," Australian Special Edition in gift box .... $100 – 150
152. "Zonker Stout," pale orange with orange red roof and fenders, Matchbox Collectibles .... $9 – 12
bright blue with red roof and fenders, no markings, ASAP promotional blank .... $30 – 40

Australian 2-packs with pewter medallion:

1. "St. Kilda Saints 1897"; "St. Kilda Saints 1996" .... $45 – 65 pair
2. "Essendon Bombers 1897," "Essendon Bombers 1996" .... $45 – 65 pair
3. "Fitzroy Lions 1897," "Fitzroy Lions 1996" .... $45 – 65 pair
4. "Carlton Blues 1897," "Carlton Blues 1996 .... $45 – 65 pair
5. "Melbourne Demons 1897," "Melbourne Demons 1996" .... $45 – 65 pair
6. "Collingwood Magpies 1897," "Collingwood Magpies 1996" ... $45 – 65 pair
7. "South Melbourne 1897," "1996" .... $45 – 65 pair
8. "Geelong Cats 1897," "Geelong Cats 1996" .... $45 – 65 pair

Ford Mondeo, #40, 1995; #33, 1995, international

1. blue, "151CS" on hood, blue "Mondeo" on white field, tan interior, Thailand cast .... $1 – 2

2. blue, "151CS" on hood, red "Mondeo" on white field, tan interior, Thailand cast .... $1 – 2
3. blue, "Ford" logo, tan interior, Thailand cast .... $1 – 2
4. white, "Airport Security," dark blue interior, China cast .... $12 – 16

Ford Mustang (also see Ford SVT Mustang)

Ford Mustang, 2⅞", #8, 1966
1. white with red interior, black plastic tires and chrome hubs .... $30 – 40
2. orange with black plastic tires with chrome hubs .... $400 – 500
3. white with red interior, Superfast wheels ....$60 – 80
4. red with red interior, Superfast wheels .... $300 – 400
5. red-orange with red interior, Superfast wheels .... $300 – 400
6. red with ivory interior, Superfast wheels ....$45 – 60
7. red-orange with ivory interior, Superfast wheels .... $45 – 60

Ford Mustang 1964 — ½ Convertible, 2000 Feature Cars, with opening features, designed to replace Premiere Collection
1. black with red interior .... $9 – 12

Ford Mustang 1964 — ½ Soft Top, 2000 Feature Cars, with opening features, designed to replace Premiere Collection
1. dark green with white roof, tan interior .... $12 – 16

Ford Mustang 1965 Fastback, #72, 1999 (see Ford Mustang GT 1965 Fastback)

Ford Mustang 1968 Cobra Jet (see Ford Mustang Cobra Jet 1968)

Ford Mustang 1999 Convertible, #36, 1999; #3, 2000; #12, 2002
1. black, "Toy Fair 2000 Matchbox," gray interior, rubber tires on chrome rims ....$60 – 80
2. black with tan interior, detailed trim, rubber tires on chrome rims, Premiere Collection .... $7 – 8
3. blue with white interior, white stripes, 5-pack .... $1 – 2
4. bronze with black interior, silver stripes and horse logo, "Mustang," 5-pack ....$1 – 2
5. light red, "Subway," tan interior, "Subway Mfg. By b. little" cast into base .. $4 – 5
6. red with black interior, white band and stripes, 5-pack .... $1 – 2

7. metallic red with purple interior, "Mustang" and graphics, 2002 Style Champs ....$1 – 2

8. white with red interior, "Coca-Cola," Coke bottles and water droplets graphics on hood, 5-pack ......$1 – 2
9. white with tan interior, black stripes, "Mustang," 1999 Car Shows ... $1 – 2
10. yellow, "Mustang," black interior, 2000 Open Road .... $1 – 2
11. yellow, "Mustang," "Matchbox 2000," black stripes, black interior, 2000 Open Road .... $3 – 4
12. metallic green with dark gray interior, 2007 10-pack B5609 .... $1 – 2

Ford Mustang 1999 Hardtop Coupe, #17, 2000, US; #8, 2000, Mexico; #68, 2000, international; #3, 2001; #12, 2002
1. red with rubber tires on chrome rims, 1999 First Edition .... $6 – 9
2. unpainted with rubber tires on chrome rims, 1999 First Edition .... $6 – 9
3. orange and white, "Matchbox 2," "Mattel Wheels" .... $15 – 20
4. metallic green with white headlights, ivory interior, 2000 Great Drivers ....$1 – 2

5. metallic green with white headlights, ivory interior, "Matchbox 2000," 2000 Great Drivers ....$3 – 4
6. white with red stripes, "Mustang," 5-spoke wheels, 2000 international issue .... $3 – 4
7. white with red stripes, "Mustang," 10-spoke wheels, 2000 international issue .... $9 – 12

8. white with silver and black horse, red accent and "Mustang" on sides, red and blue stripes, "Thirty Fifth Anniversary" on hood, 2001 Daddy's Dreams ....$1 – 2
9. metallic red with purple and white design, "Mustang," 2002 Style Champs ....$1 – 2
10. black with dual white stripes, 5-pack .... $1 – 2
11. red with rubber tires on chrome rims, "MDM," "Matchbox," custom ..$20 – 25
12. unpainted with rubber tires on chrome rims, "MDM," "Matchbox," custom .... $20 – 25
13. red with "Coca-Cola" and polar bears design, Avon 2-pack, chrome hubs .... $5 – 7
14. red with "Coca-Cola" and polar bears design, Avon 2-pack, black hubs ....$9 – 12
15. cream, "Scooby Doo!" "Like Wow!" "Fred," Warner Bros. promotional ....$6 – 8
16. red with "Coca-Cola" and polar bears design, rubber tires on chrome rims, Premiere Collection .... $7 – 9
17. black with dual white stripes, 5-pack ....$1 – 2

Ford Mustang 1999 Police, #460/509, 2000

1. "D.A.R.E.," metallic red with amber roof lights, D.A.R.E. 5-pack ..$1 – 2
2. "D.A.R.E. Police," black with blue and red roof lights, D.A.R.E. .... $4 – 5

Ford Mustang 2000 Convertible, #3, 2000; #12, 2002

1. yellow with black interior, "Mustang," black, 2000 Open Road series 1 .... $1 – 2
2. metallic red with purple interior, "Mustang," purple, black and white, 2002 Style Champs series 3 .... $1 – 2

Ford Mustang Boss 302 1970, 2⅞", #44, 1972; #11, 1982; #37, 1998
1. orange, "Boss" outlined on sides, 1982 ....$7 – 9

2. orange, "Boss" in black on sides, 1982 .... $7 – 9
3. orange, "Boss" in white on sides, 1982 .... $7 – 9
4. orange with no markings, 1982 .. $7 – 9
5. yellow with black hood, no markings, 1972 .... $7 – 9
6. dark green, "Cobra Mustang," limited edition, 1972 .... $9 – 12
7. lemon yellow with black stripe, lemon yellow plastic base, white and black interior, rubber tires on chrome rims, 1998 First Editions .... $5 – 6
8. lemon yellow, "Coca-Cola," black interior, metallic gray metal base, Avon .. $6 – 7
9. pale blue, no markings, white and black interior, rubber tires on chrome rims, pale blue plastic base .... $5 – 6

10. metallic purple, "Boss 302" and stripes, yellow interior, chrome plastic base, 1998 Classic Decades .... $1 – 2

11. metallic purple, "Boss 302" and stripes, yellow interior, translucent white base, 1998 Classic Decades .... $60 – 80
12. metallic purple, "Boss 302," "South Jersey Mustang" and stripes, yellow interior, chrome plastic base, Color Comp promotional .... $30 – 40
13. unpainted, no markings, white interior, chrome plastic base, rubber tires on chrome rims, 1998 First Editions .... $5 – 6
14. black with silver design, light gray interior, chrome plastic base, Real Talkin' .... $4 – 5
15. black with silver design, light gray interior, translucent white plastic base .... $60 – 80

16. white with black stripes, 2005 Superfast #28 .... $4 – 5

Ford Mustang Cobra, #44, 1972 (see Ford Mustang Boss 302 1970)

Ford Mustang Cobra SVT Convertible, #71, 1995; #73, 1998

1. red with no markings, butterscotch interior, 1999 Beach Fun 5-pack .... $1 – 2

2. red with no markings, tan interior, 5-pack .... $1 – 2
3. red with detailed trim, rubber tires on chrome rims, Premiere Collection #2 .... $5 – 6
4. metallic red with cobra on black hood, Thailand cast, 1995 .... $1 – 2

5. metallic red with lime green horse head on sides, chrome wheel hubs, 1998 Street Cruisers .... $1 – 2

6. metallic red with lime green horse head on sides, black wheel hubs, 1998 Street Cruisers .... $16 – 24
7. pink, "71st Shenandoah Apple Blossom Festival 1998," Thailand cast, US issue .... $9 – 12

8. pink, "White's Guide Car of the Month #2," "January 1999" .... $12 – 16

9. pumpkin orange with detailed trim, white and gray interior, rubber tires on chrome rims, Gold Coin Collection .... $16 – 24
10. metallic orange with detailed trim, tan and brown interior, rubber tires on chrome rims, gift set .... $5 – 6
11. green with white and gray interior, detailed trim, rubber tires on chrome rims, Select Class .... $5 – 6
12. bright blue, "District 16 Convention Lion's Club," gray interior, Color Comp promotional .... $16 – 24
13. bright blue with no markings, gray interior, China cast, 5-pack .... $1 – 2

14. metallic blue with brown and tan interior, rubber tires on chrome rims, Premiere Collection #16 ...... $4 – 5

15. metallic blue with lime green horse logo on sides, translucent yellow interior, Thailand cast .... $1 – 2
16. metallic blue with white and gray interior, detailed trim, rubber tires on chrome rims, Select Class #4 .... $5 – 6

17. purple with white and black interior, rubber tires on chrome rims, JC Penney Premiere Collection 8-car display set .... $4 – 5

18. black with cobra on gray hood, Thailand cast, 1996 .... $4 – 5

19. black with detailed trim, rubber tires on chrome rims, Select Class #2 .. $5 – 6

20. white, "Pace Car," Ford logo, black speckle pattern, blue interior, 1997 Convertibles 5-pack .. $1 – 2

21. white with cobra on black hood, green interior, Thailand cast, 1998 5-pack .... $1 – 2
22. white with detailed trim, rubber tires on chrome rims, Premiere Collection #5 .... $5 – 6
23. metallic gold with no markings, Thailand cast, 1997 75 Challenge .... $6 – 12
24. gold with white and gray interior, detailed trim, rubber tires on chrome rims, Premiere Collection #14 .... $4 – 5

Ford Mustang Cobra Jet 1968, #69, 1997; #40, 1998

1. red with white and black stripes, rubber tires on chrome rims, Premiere Collection #20 .... $4 – 5
2. maroon with black and white stripes, rubber tires on chrome rims, Toys "R" Us gift set .... $4 – 5
3. yellow, "Coca-Cola," rubber tires on chrome rims, Premiere Collection .... $6 – 8

4. yellow with white and purple accents, 1998 Classic Decades .... $1 – 2
5. green with gold side stripes and black hood band, rubber tires on chrome rims, Premiere Collection .... $6 – 8
6. dark green, "Ice Cold Coca-Cola," Avon 2-pack .... $4 – 5

7. blue with white and orange accents, chrome interior, 1998 Classic Decades .... $1 – 2
8. blue with white and orange accents, translucent white interior, 1998 Classic Decades .... $60 – 80
9. dark blue with black and gold stripes, rubber tires on chrome rims, Premiere Collection ... $7 – 9
10. silver-blue with black band and stripes, 5-spoke wheels, 5-pack .... $1 – 2
11. silver-blue with black band and stripes, 10-spoke wheels, 5-pack .... $1 – 2
12. silver-blue with black stripes, rubber tires on chrome rims, Matchbox Collectibles .... $16 – 24
13. black with red pinstripes, rubber tires on chrome rims, 1997 Inaugural Edition .... $5 – 6
14. unpainted, rubber tires on chrome rims, 1997 Inaugural Edition .... $5 – 6
15. white, "Coca-Cola Play Refreshed," Premiere Collection .... $4 – 5
16. white with black on hood and red pinstripes, rubber tires on chrome rims, Premiere Collection #17 .... $4 – 5
17. metallic gold with black stripes, 5-pack .... $1 – 2

Ford Mustang Fastback 1965, #72, 1999 (see Ford Mustang GT 1965 Fastback)

Ford Mustang GT, #74, 1984, oversized chrome engine (see Ford Mustang GT350)

Ford Mustang GT 1965 Fastback, #72, 1999 (similar casting: Ford Mustang Fastback)
1. red, "Matchbox Toy Show," "Toy Show 98," black interior, rubber tires on chrome rims .... $9 – 12
2. red with white stripes, black and white interior, rubber tires on chrome rims, gift set .... $5 – 6

3. orange, 2005 Superfast #8 .. $3 – 4
4. white, "Cruisin New England Magazine All Wheels Festival 2001," Color Comp promotional .... $60 – 80

5. white, "Mustang," blue stripes, large 5-spoke concave wheels, 1999 Classics .... $1 – 2
6. white, "Mustang," blue stripes, small 5-spoke concave wheels, 1999 Classics .... $6 – 8

7. dark green with mag wheels, 2003 My Classic Car with Dennis Gage .... $4 – 5

Ford Mustang GT 1968, 2003
1. blue with white C-stripe, "Ford Motor Company 100 Years," 2003 Avon 2-pack .... $5 – 6

Ford Mustang GT 1998, 2003
1. red, "Ford Motor Company 100 Years," 2003 Avon 2-pack .... $5 – 6

Ford Mustang GT Concept, #6, 2005; #19, 2006; #6, 2004 Superfast; #6, 2005 Superfast
1. metallic green, 2004 Superfast #6 .... $4 – 5
2. red, 2005 #6 .... $1 – 2
3. metallic gray, 2005 Superfast #6 .... $4 – 5

4. yellow, 2006 #19 .... $1 – 2

5. copper, 2007 5-pack K9615 .. $1 – 2
6. black and gold with white trim, 2007 Streakers #6, J6555 .... $4 – 5

7. antifreeze green with black racing stripes, 2007 #16, K9479 .. $1 – 2

8. metallic gray, 2005 Superfast #6 .... $3 – 4

Ford Mustang GT350, with chrome oversized engine, 2⁷/₈", #23, 1979
1. white with blue accents .... $10 – 15

2. white with red graphics, racing slicks on back axle, Thailand cast ... $1 – 2

3. red with black stripes, racing slicks on back axle, China cast .... $1 – 2
4. light orange with yellow and blue stripes, racing slicks on back axle, China cast .... $3 – 4
5. light orange with yellow and blue stripes, racing slicks on back axle, Macau cast .... $3 – 4
6. dark orange with yellow and blue stripes, racing slicks on back axle, Macau cast .... $3 – 4
7. dark orange with orange and blue stripes, racing slicks on back axle, Macau cast .... $3 – 4

8. pearl silver with purple and yellow stripes, racing slicks on back axle, China cast ....$3 – 4

Ford Mustang IMSA, 3", #11, 1983; #67, 1983

1. black with red and white stripes, "Ford Mustang" ....$1 – 2
2. black with yellow and green flames ....$1 – 2
3. black with yellow and green stripes ....$1 – 2
4. yellow with black and red stripes, "47" ....$4 – 5
5. red with no markings ....$10 – 12
6. orange with yellow flames, 1993 ....$1 – 2
7. orange with yellow and blue flames ....$1 – 2

8. **fluorescent orange with black wavy lines, black plastic base .... $1 – 2**
9. fluorescent orange with black wavy lines, black metal base, Hungary issue ....$16 – 24
10. bright red with spatter accents, 1994 ....$1 – 2

Ford Mustang Mach III Convertible, #15, 1994, US; #28, 1994, international; #4, 1998

1. red; hood has black lines through blue field bordered in white, 1994 ... $1 – 2
2. red; hood has white stars on blue field; red stripes on trunk and sides, 1995 ....$1 – 2
3. red with rubber tires on gray rims, World Class Super Series 1994 – 1995 ....$3 – 5
4. metallic red, "Mach III" ....$1 – 2
5. yellow, "Nationwise Auto Parts" ....$16 – 24
6. yellow with rubber tires on chrome rims, Gold Coin Collection ..$16 – 24
7. metallic gold, 1997 75 Challenge ....$6 – 12
8. metallic green with rubber tires on chrome rims, Matchbox European Premiere Series 2, 1997 ......$4 – 6

9. **light blue with orange stripe down middle and on front, 1997 Cars of the Future 5-pack .... $1 – 2**
10. metallic blue, "Mach III," trim detail, rubber tires on chrome rims, Premiere Collection World Class Series 12 — Convertibles ....$4 – 6
11. purple with neon yellow tiger stripes on doors, 1999 ....$1 – 2
12. dark purple with green stripes, 5-pack ....$1 – 2

13. **black; hood has black lines through dark blue field bordered in white, 1994 .... $1 – 2**
14. black; hood has white stars on blue field; red stripes on trunk and sides, 1996 ....$1 – 2
15. white; hood has white stars on blue field; red stripes on trunk and sides, 1997 ....$1 – 2

16. **white, white stars on red field on hood, blue stripes on trunk and sides, 1998 Stars & Stripes.. $1 – 2**
17. pearly white, "Ice Crusher" ...$9 – 12

Ford Mustang Piston Popper (Rolamatic), 2$^{13}/_{16}$", #10, 1973; #60, 1982 reissue

1. orange, "Sunkist," red interior, black base, Macau cast ....$5 – 6
2. orange, "Sunkist," red interior, unpainted base, Hong Kong cast ....$5 – 6
3. yellow, "Hot Popper," flames ...$6 – 8
4. yellow, "60," red interior, England cast ....$6 – 8
5. yellow, "60," white interior, England cast ....$12 – 16
6. yellow, design on trunk, England cast ....$8 – 10
7. yellow, no markings, red interior, England cast ....$8 – 10
8. metallic blue, "Superfast" cast ....$80 – 100
9. metallic blue, "Rolamatic" cast ....$9 – 12
10. white, no markings ....$250 – 350

Ford Mustang Wildcat Dragster, 2$^{7}/_{8}$", #8, 1970

1. "Wildcat" labels ....$20 – 30
2. "Rat Rod" labels ....$30 – 45
3. no labels ....$20 – 30
4. sailboat labels ....$30 – 45

Ford Panel Van, #38, 2000; #474, 2000; #52, 2002; #23, 2000, international

1. **red with "Paramedic" graphics, blue light bar on roof, 2006 5-pack J4678 .... $1 – 2**

2. **metallic red, "Elemental Hero Burstinatrix," 2006 Yu-Gi-Oh GX 5-pack H5775 .... $1 – 2**

3. **olive green with "USOPP" graphics, 2006 Shonen Jump's One Piece 5-pack J7421 .... $1 – 2**

4. **turquoise with "24/7," "Matchbox Hero City 555-2134," running plumber cartoon illustration, 2003 Hero City 5-pack #8 .... $2 – 3**
5. white, "Camp Sunshine," Color Comp promotional ....$20 – 30
6. white, "M.J. Engineering & Land Surveying, P.C.," Color Comp promotional ....$20 – 30
7. white, "MICA Hershey 2000," Color Comp promotional ....$16 – 24

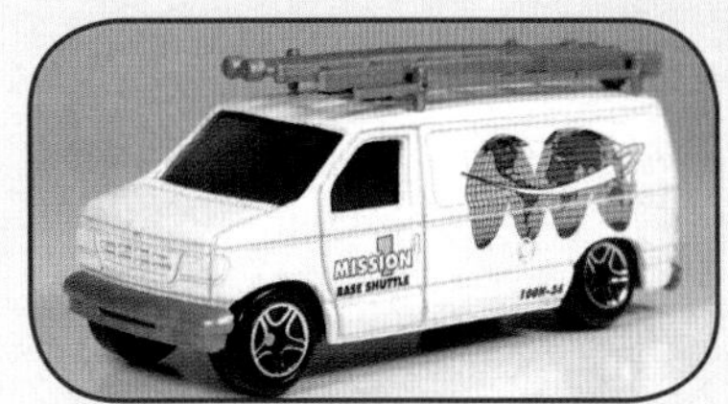

8. white with metallic gray ladders on roof, "Mission 1 Base Shuttle" on doors, world atlas and space shuttle design, Mission Ford Van from 2000 Space Explorer set ... $1 – 2
9. white with metallic gray ladders on roof, "Mission 1 Base Shuttle" on doors, "Matchbox 2000," world atlas and space shuttle design Mission Ford Van from 2000 Space Explorer .... $3 – 4
10. white, "Virtek," Color Comp promotional .... $20 – 30
11. white, no markings, Color Comp promotional blank .... $30 – 40

12. gray with bullet holes, 2006 Superman 5-pack J4725 .... $1 – 2

13. metallic gray with blue ladders on roof, "H + N 24 Hour Emergency Service," "For All Your Plumbing Needs," 2002 Hammer and Nails series, 2003 Hero City ..... $1 – 2
14. black, "D.A.R.E. Dover Police," D.A.R.E. series .... $4 – 5

Ford Pickup 1956 (see Ford F-100 1956 Pickup)

Ford Pickup, red with white topper, 2³/₄", #6, 1968
1. white grille, black plastic wheels .. $9 – 12
2. chrome grille, black plastic wheels .... $12 – 15
3. chrome grille, unpainted base, Superfast wheels .... $45 – 60
4. chrome grille, black base, Superfast wheels .... $45 – 60
5. chrome grille, green base, Superfast wheels .... $45 – 60
6. chrome grille, metallic green base, Superfast wheels .... $45 – 60
7. chrome grille, gray base, Superfast wheels .... $45 – 60
8. white grille, green base, Superfast wheels .... $45 – 60
9. white grille, gray base, Superfast wheels .... $45 – 60
10. white grille, black base, Superfast wheels .... $45 – 60
11. white grille, unpainted base, Superfast wheels .... $45 – 60

Ford Pickup Camper, 3", #38, 1980
1. red with beige camper .... $5 – 6
2. orange-red with beige camper .. $5 – 6
3. orange-red with beige camper, "35" on base .... $60 – 80

Ford Prefect, 2¹/₄", #30, 1956
1. light blue .... $100 – 125
2. gray -brown or olive brown ... $35 – 50

Ford Probe GT, #44, 1994
1. metallic red, "Princeton Nassau-Conover," orange and yellow design .... $16 – 24

2. metallic red with orange and yellow design, 1994 .... $1 – 2
3. metallic blue with gray flames, oversized engine, rubber tires on chrome rims, Premiere Collection #9 .... $4 – 5
4. purple with green and white design, 1996 .... $1 – 2

5. black with blue and pink design, 1995 .... $1 – 2
6. black with peach and white design .. $1 – 2

7. metallic bronze with blue and white design .... $1 – 2
8. metallic gold, 1997 75 Challenge .... $12 – 16

Ford Racing Van, #6, 1988 (see Ford Supervan II)

Ford Refuse Truck, 3", #7, 1966
1. orange cab, gray container, black plastic wheels .... $12 – 16
2. orange cab, gray container, Superfast wheels, 1970 .... $30 – 40

Ford RS200, 2⁷/₈", #34, 1987

1. white with blue graphics, "7" .. $1 – 2

2. white with red graphics, "7" ... $1 – 2

3. blue with white graphics, "2" .. $1 – 2
4. white with no markings, Graffic Traffic .... $12 – 16
5. dark blue with no markings, Germany issue .... $10 – 12
6. orange, "Enjoy Fanta," China issue .... $160 – 200

Ford RS2000 (see Ford Escort RS2000)

Ford Scissors Truck, #7, 1999; #37, 2000, US; #22, 2000, international

1. white with white container, "World Jets," 1999 Air Traffic .... $1 – 2
2. white with white container, "World Airways," 5-pack .... $1 – 2
3. white with white container, "LSG Sky Chefs" .... $1 – 2

4. light gray with white container, "VentureStar," 2000 Space Explorer .... $1 – 2
5. light gray with white container, "VentureStar," "Matchbox 2000," 2000 Space Explorer .... $3 – 4
6. white with white container, blue and green labels, 5-pack .... $1 – 2

7. red with white container, shipping docks and ship labels, 2000 Ocean Dock 5-pack .... $1 – 2

8. red with gray container, jet and globe labels, Action System .... $4 – 5

Ford Shelby Cobra Concept, #42, 2005; #8, 2006; #11, 2007

1. metallic red, 2006 #8 .... $1 – 2

2. metallic blue with silver racing stripes, 2005 #42 .... $1 – 2

3. black with silver racing stripes, 2006 5-pack J4672 .... $1 – 2

4. white with blue racing stripes, 2007 411 .... $1 – 2

Ford Sierra (see Ford Sierra XR4Ti)

Ford Sierra XR4Ti, 3", #15, 1983; #55, 1983; #40, 1990

1. black upper, dark gray lower, white and green stripes, "85" .... $3 – 5

2. black upper, black lower, "Texaco 6," "Pirelli" .... $2 – 4

3. dark blue upper, black lower, "Duckhams Race Team," Team Convoy .... $4 – 6
4. ivory upper, dark gray lower, black roof, wide stripe, "55" .... $9 – 12
5. metallic green upper, dark gray lower, black roof, Laser Wheels .... $4 – 6
6. metallic green upper, dark gray lower, black roof, Superfast wheels .. $9 – 12

7. metallic gray upper, dark gray lower body, "Ford XR4i Sport" on hood, red interior, clear windows .... $4 – 6

8. red upper, black lower, "Tizer The Appetizer," Team Convoy .... $4 – 6
9. red upper, black lower, "Fire Dept." Siren Force .... $9 – 12
10. red upper, yellow lower, blue roof graphics, Live 'N Learn/Preschool ... $12 – 16
11. white upper, red lower, black interior, "Virgin Atlantic" .... $4 – 6
12. white upper, red lower, red interior, "Virgin Atlantic" .... $12 – 16
13. white upper, gray lower, white interior, clear windows, gray metal base .... $90 – 120

14. white upper, gray lower, red spoiler, red interior, clear windows, gray metal base .... $4 – 6

15. white upper, gray lower, white spoiler, red interior, clear windows, gray metal base .... $4 – 6

16. white upper, white lower, "Sheriff," Siren Force/Rescue 911 .... $9 – 12
17. white upper, black lower, "Police," Light & Sound .... $2 – 4
18. white upper, black lower, "Gemini," "N Cooper," "1" .... $2 – 4

19. yellow upper, black lower, black roof panel, "XR 4x4" .... $6 – 9

20. yellow upper, black lower, black roof panel, "Matchbox Taxi Co. 555-7800," Light & Sound .... $4 – 6
21. yellow upper, dark gray lower, gray roof panel, "XR 4x4" .... $40 – 60
22. yellow-orange upper, black lower, "Airport Security," red roof lights, Siren Force/Rescue 911 .... $9 – 12
23. yellow-orange, "Airport Security," green roof lights, Siren Force/Rescue 911 .... $20 – 25

Ford Skip Truck (see Ford Cargo Skip Truck)

Ford Street Rod 1933

Ford Sunliner 1956, Superfast #45, 2006

1. black and pearl with red interior, 2006 Superfast #45 .... $4 – 5

Ford Super Truck, FST, 1996, White Rose Collectibles

1. "Exide 7," black .... $4 – 5
2. "Larry's Heavenly," "Petron Plus 78," white .... $6 – 8
3. "Ortho 21," yellow .... $4 – 5
4. "Quaker State 24," white and green $4 – 5
5. "Remax 6," white and red .... $6 – 8
6. "Team ASE 2," blue and white .. $4 – 5

Ford Supervan II, 2$^{15}/_{16}$", #6, 1985, international; #72, 1987, US

1. white with "Ford Supervan" ...... $3 – 5

2. white with red and blue "Starfire" graphics .... $4 – 6

3. white with "Fuji Racing Team" ... $4 – 6
4. white with roof lights, "Ambulance," Siren Force .... $12 – 16
5. white with roof lights, "Ambulance," "Rescue 911" .... $12 – 16
6. white with no markings, Graffic Traffic .... $4 – 6
7. red with roof lights, "Fire Observer," Siren Force .... $12 – 16
8. red with roof lights, "Fire Observer," "Rescue 911" .... $12 – 16
9. red with "Tizer Flavoured Soft Drink" .... $4 – 6

10. dark blue with "Duckhams QXR Engine Oils" .... $4 – 6
11. dark blue with lights, "Police Control Unit," Siren Force .... $12 – 16
12. dark blue with lights, "Police Control Unit," "Rescue 911" .... $12 – 16
13. dark gray, "Danger High Explosive," "Heavy Load," weapons, Roadblasters .... $3 – 5
14. light gray, "Danger High Explosive," "Heavy Load," weapons ...... $15 – 20
15. yellow with "Service Car BP Oil" .... $12 – 15
16. yellow with "Goodyear Pit Stop" .. $4 – 6

Ford SVT F – 150 Lightning, #18, 2005; #6, 2006; Superfast #2, 2005

1. metallic silver, 2005 Superfast #2 .... $4 – 5

2. metallic gray, 2005 #18 ...... $1 – 2

3. pearl white, 2006 #6 .... $1 – 2

Ford SVT Lightning (see Ford SVT F-150 Lightning)

Ford SVT Mustang Cobra, Superfast #22, 2005; Superfast #66, 2006 (see Ford Mustang SVT Convertible)

Ford Thames Estate Car, yellow and turquoise, 2⅛", #70, 1959

1. no windows, gray plastic wheels .... $30 – 40
2. clear windows, gray plastic wheels .... $30 – 40
3. green windows, gray plastic wheels .... $30 – 40
4. clear windows, silver plastic wheels .... $30 – 40
5. green windows, silver plastic wheels .... $30 – 40
6. green windows, black plastic wheels .... $25 – 35

Ford Thames "Singer" Van, 2⅛", #59, 1958

1. light green with gray plastic wheels .... $30 – 40
2. light green with silver plastic wheels .... $80 – 100
3. dark green with gray plastic wheels .... $100 – 120

4. dark green with silver plastic wheels .... $110 – 135

Ford Thames Trader (see Thames Trader)

Ford Thames Trader Compressor Truck (see Thames Trader Compressor Truck)

Ford Thames Trader Wreck Truck (see Thames Trader Wreck Truck)

Ford Thunderbird, 2⅝", #75, 1960

1. ivory and pink, gray plastic wheels .... $50 – 60
2. ivory and pink, silver plastic wheels .... $50 – 60
3. ivory and pink, black plastic wheels .... $80 – 100

Ford Thunderbird 1957, #42, 1982; #16, 2000; #27, 2007

1. red with white interior .... $4 – 5

2. red with white interior, "White's Guide Car of the Month #3," "February 1999" .... $6 – 8
3. red, "Celebrating Patsy," white interior .... $12 – 16
4. red, detailed trim, white and red interior, rubber tires on chrome rims, Special Class .... $4 – 5

5. metallic red, detailed trim, white and red interior, whitewall rubber tires on chrome rims, Premiere Collection #6 .... $4 – 5
6. pink, "Pinky," "Happy Days," white and pink interior, Avon Star Cars .. $9 – 12

7. pink with pink interior, 2005 Superfast #1 .... $3 – 4
8. yellow, detailed trim, black and white interior, rubber tires on chrome rims, Premiere Collection #17 .... $4 – 5

9. pale yellow with light gray interior, 2000 Great Drivers .... $1 – 2
10. pale yellow with light gray interior, "Matchbox 2000," 2000 Great Drivers .... $3 – 4
11. pale yellow with black and white interior, rubber tires on chrome rims, Matchbox Collectibles Elvis Presley series, includes Graceland diorama and Plexiglas cover .... $12 – 16
12. pale yellow with white interior, 2007 #27, K9483 .... $1 – 2
13. light green, 2007 #27 .... $1 – 2
14. blue with yellow and orange flames, detailed trim, white and red interior, rubber tires on chrome rims, Premiere Collection #11 .... $4 – 5
15. blue with yellow and orange flames, white interior, China issue .... $60 – 80
16. turquoise, "Chubby's," white interior .... $9 – 12

17. turquoise with red and white "Hero City Sports" graphics, 2003 Hero City 5-pack #6 .... $1 – 2
18. turquoise, detailed trim, white and turquoise interior, rubber tires on chrome rims, Matchbox Collectibles Train Set .... $12 – 16
19. black with red interior .... $4 – 5
20. black, detailed trim, red and white interior, rubber tires on chrome rims, Premiere Collection #3 .... $4 – 5

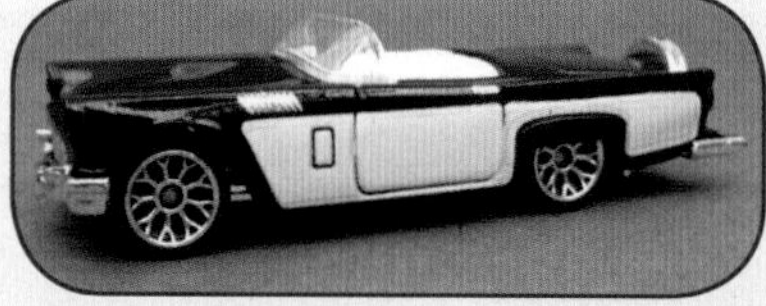

21. black with beige side panels, white interior, 2006 5-pack #4677 .. $1 – 2
22. ivory and red two-tone .... $4 – 5

23. white with red interior .... $1 – 2

24. white with black interior, Superfast #1, 2006 .... $3 – 4
25. white with red and pink interior, detailed trim, white and red interior, rubber tires on chrome rims, Gold Coin Collection .... $16 – 24
26. metallic silver, T-Bird design, detailed trim, blue and white interior, rubber tires on chrome rims, Premiere Collection #20 .... $4 – 5

Ford Thunderbird 1996, WRP02, 1996, White Rose Collectibles, Goodyear rubber tires on chrome rims
1. "Badcock 12," orange and blue ..$9 – 12
2. "Caterpillar 97," orange-yellow .. $4 – 5
3. "Circuit City 8," dark red .... $4 – 5
4. "Family Channel 16," metallic blue and white .... $4 – 5
5. "Hayes Modems 15," purple and turquoise .... $9 – 12
6. "Jasper," "Federal Mogul 77," white .... $4 – 5
7. "Mac Tonight," blue .... $20 – 30
8. "McDonald's," "Monopoly 94," red .... $9 – 12
9. "McDonald's 94," red .... $4 – 5
10. "McDonald's 94," red and white .. $4 – 5
11. "McDonald's 94," red and white with red wheels, Team Convoy .... $7 – 9
12. "Miller Lite," dark blue and white, sealed in plexiglas box .... $25 – 35
13. "Miller Racing 2," black, sealed in glass bottle on wooden stand .... $60 – 80
14. "New Holland 94," blue .... $4 – 5
15. "QC Quality Care," "Red Carpet Lease 88," blue .... $4 – 5
16. "QVC 7," brown-gold .... $4 – 5
17. "Remington 75," metallic green, sealed in glass bottle .... $30 – 40
18. "Remington 75," olive green, tan and black camouflage, sealed in glass bottle ....$30 – 40
19. "Remington Stren 75," purple, sealed in glass bottle .... $30 – 40
20. "Spam 9," blue .... $4 – 5
21. "Valvoline 6," white and blue ..... $4 – 5

Ford Thunderbird Concept, 2000 Feature Cars, with opening features, designed to replace Premiere Collection
1. red .... $9 – 12
2. pale yellow .... $9 – 12

Ford Thunderbird Stock Car, 3", #7, 1993, US; #39, 1995, international; #64, 1998, US; #268, 1994, White Rose
1. "1994 Most Popular Driver — Bill Elliott," gold plated, Goodyear rubber tires on black rims, White Rose .....$20 – 30
2. "1994 Rookie of the Year — 8 Jeff Burton," gold plated, Goodyear rubber tires on black rims, White Rose .. $20 – 30
3. "Baby Ruth 1," white, white-lettered Goodyear slicks, White Rose .... $4 – 5
4. "Baby Ruth," white, yellow-lettered Goodyear slicks, White Rose .... $4 – 5
5. "Bill Elliot 11," red, white-lettered Goodyear slicks, White Rose .... $4 – 5
6. "Bill Elliot 11," red, white-lettered Goodyear slicks, White Rose Team Convoy .... $4 – 5
7. "Bojangles," "Easter Seals 7," white, yellow-lettered Goodyear slicks, White Rose .... $20 – 25
8. "Bojangles 98," black, Goodyear rubber tires on black rims, White Rose Team Convoy .... $5 – 6
9. "Bojangles 98," yellow, Goodyear rubber tires on black rims, White Rose Team Convoy .... $5 – 6
10. "Bojangles 98," yellow, yellow-lettered Goodyear slicks, White Rose .... $4 – 5
11. "BP Car Care 25," green, Australia issue .... $20 – 25
12. "Bud 11," flat black, Goodyear rubber tires on black rims, White Rose Ertl set ....$24 – 36
13. "Budweiser 11," red, Goodyear rubber tires on black rims, White Rose Ertl set ....$24 – 36
14. "Burn Foundation," "Motorsports 96," black, Goodyear rubber tires on black rims, White Rose .... $8 – 10
15. "Cappio 48," black, yellow-lettered Goodyear slicks, White Rose .... $4 – 5
16. "Carr Auto Care 4," black .... $1 – 2
17. "Carr Auto Care 4," blue .... $4 – 5
18. "Cellular One 7," black and red, yellow-lettered Goodyear slicks, White Rose ....$6 – 9
19. "Citgo 21," white and red, yellow-lettered Goodyear slicks, White Rose ..... $4 – 5
20. "Citgo 21," red and orange, Goodyear rubber tires on black rims, White Rose .... $4 – 5
21. "Country Time 68," fluorescent pink, yellow-lettered Goodyear slicks, White Rose .... $4 – 5
22. "Country Time 68," fluorescent yellow, yellow-lettered Goodyear slicks, White Rose Team Convoy .... $4 – 5
23. "Evan Carr," black, racing accents, white-lettered Goodyear slicks .. $1 – 3
24. "Exide 99," black, Goodyear rubber tires on black rims, White Rose ...... $4 – 5
25. "Exide Batteries," black, Goodyear rubber tires on black rims, White Rose .... $4 – 5
26. "Factory Stores of America," blue, Goodyear rubber tires on black rims, White Rose .... $4 – 5
27. "Family Channel 7," white, yellow-lettered Goodyear slicks, White Rose .... $12 – 16
28. "Family Channel 16," metallic blue and white, Goodyear rubber tires on black rims, White Rose .... $4 – 5
29. "Fingerhut 98," black, Goodyear rubber tires on black rims, White Rose .. $4 – 5
30. "Fingerhut 98," black and pink, Goodyear rubber tires on black rims, White Rose .... $4 – 5
31. "Ford 1" and checkered flag, white, Goodyear tires on chrome rims, Show Stoppers .... $3 – 4
32. "Ford Motorsports 2," black, Goodyear rubber tires on black rims, White Rose .... $4 – 5
33. "Hanes 7," white, yellow lettered Goodyear slicks, White Rose .... $20 – 25
34. "Havoline," "Texaco 28," black, white-lettered Goodyear slicks, White Rose .... $4 – 5
35. "Havoline 28," black, Goodyear rubber tires on black rims, White Rose .. $4 – 5
36. "Heilig-Meyers 90," turquoise and black, Goodyear rubber tires on black rims, White Rose .... $4 – 5
37. "Hooters 7," gray, white lettered Goodyear slicks, White Rose .... $9 – 12
38. "Hooters 7," white and orange, Goodyear slicks, White Rose Team Convoy .... $12 – 16
39. "Hooters 7," "Classic," "Naturally Fresh," white and orange, white-lettered Goodyear slicks, White Rose .... $6 – 9
40. "Hooters 7," without "Classic," "Naturally Fresh," white, white-lettered Goodyear slicks, White Rose .... $9 – 12
41. "Hooters 19," white, Hoosier rubber tires on black rims, White Rose .. $4 – 5
42. "K-Mart," "Little Caesar's 37," purple, Goodyear rubber tires on black rims, White Rose .... $4 – 5
43. "Kleenex 40," blue, Goodyear rubber tires on black rims, White Rose .. $4 – 5
44. "Kleenex 40," blue, Goodyear slicks, White Rose .... $12 – 16
45. "Kyle Wieder 11," blue, racing accents, white lettered Goodyear slicks .. $1 – 2
46. "Joltage Batteries 12," black, yellow-lettered Goodyear slicks, 5-pack .. $1 – 2

47. "Joltage Batteries 12," black, six-hole spiral wheels, 1996 Racing 5-pack .... $1 – 2
48. "Lowe's 11," bright blue and yellow, Goodyear rubber tires on black rims, White Rose .... $4 – 5
49. "Luxaire 1," white, black-lettered Goodyear slicks, White Rose .... $12 – 16
50. "Mane N Tail," "Straight Arrow 12," multicolor, Goodyear rubber tires on black rims, White Rose .... $4 – 5
51. "Matchbox," "USA Bobsled 7," white, yellow-lettered Goodyear slicks, White Rose .... $12 – 16

52. "Matchbox," "White Rose 1," white, yellow-lettered Goodyear slicks, White Rose .... $4 – 5
53. "Matchbox," "White Rose 7," white, yellow-lettered Goodyear slicks, White Rose .... $12 – 16
54. "Matchbox 92," yellow, white-lettered Goodyear slicks, White Rose ... $21 – 27
55. "Maui 17," white, white-lettered Goodyear slicks, White Rose .... $4 – 5
56. "Maxwell House 22," blue, white-lettered Goodyear slicks, White Rose ..... $4 – 5
57. "Maxwell House 22," blue, yellow-lettered Goodyear slicks, White Rose ..... $4 – 5
58. "McDonald's," "Batman Forever 94," black, Goodyear rubber tires on black rims, White Rose .... $12 – 16
59. "McDonald's 94," red, Goodyear rubber tires on black rims, White Rose .. $4 – 5
60. "Meineke," black, yellow-lettered Goodyear slicks, White Rose .... $4 – 5
61. "Melling 9," red, white-lettered Goodyear slicks, White Rose .... $4 – 5
62. "Mitre 10," Stanley," blue, yellow-lettered Goodyear slicks, Australia issue .... $6 – 8
63. "Motorcraft Quality Parts 15," red, white-lettered Goodyear slicks, White Rose .... $4 – 5
64. "Nationwise Auto Parts," yellow, yellow-lettered Goodyear slicks ...... $24 – 36
65. "Naturally Fresh," bright blue, yellow-lettered Goodyear slicks, White Rose .... $6 – 8
66. "New Holland 94," blue, Goodyear rubber tires on black rims, White Rose .... $4 – 5

67. "Peterson Pistons 17," blue, 5-spoke concave wheels, 1998 Motor Sports #64 .... $1 – 2

68. "Peterson Pistons 17," red, 1997 Racing 5-pack .... $1 – 2
69. "Petron," black, Goodyear rubber tires on black rims, White Rose .. $16 – 24
70. "Phillips 66," "Trop Artic," black, white-lettered Goodyear slicks, White Rose .... $4 – 5
71. "Phillips 66," "Trop Artic," bright red, white-lettered Goodyear slicks, White Rose .... $4 – 5
72. "Phillips 66," "Trop Artic," dark red, white-lettered Goodyear slicks, White Rose .... $4 – 5
73. "Purex 83," bright blue, yellow-lettered Goodyear slicks, White Rose .... $4 – 5
74. "Purex Dial 40," blue and orange, Goodyear rubber tires on black rims, White Rose .... $4 – 5
75. "Quaker State 26," green, Goodyear rubber tires on black rims, White Rose .... $4 – 5
76. "Quaker State 26," green, white-lettered Goodyear slicks, White Rose .... $4 – 5
77. "Quality Care 15," metallic blue and pale blue, Goodyear rubber tires on black rims, White Rose .... $4 – 5

78. "Racetech," blue, white-lettered Goodyear slicks, 1994 .... $1 – 2
79. "Racetech Radios 16," blue, gold chrome spokes, yellow-lettered Goodyear slicks .... $1 – 2
80. "Racetech Radios 16," blue, gold chrome spokes, white-lettered Goodyear slicks, Aquafresh promo .... $5 – 6
81. "Racetech Radios," dark blue, white-lettered Goodyear slicks, 5-pack .. $1 – 2
82. "Radical Cams 10," checkered flag, bright pink, yellow-lettered Goodyear slicks .... $1 – 2
83. "Radical Cams 10," checkered flag, bright pink, white-lettered Goodyear slicks .... $1 – 2

84. "Radical Cams 10," checkered flag, bright pink, six whole spiral wheels .... $1 – 2
85. "Raybestos 8," blue and white, Goodyear rubber tires on black rims, White Rose .... $4 – 5
86. "Raybestos 8," metallic blue, Hoosier rubber tires on black rims, White Rose .... $4 – 5
87. "Raybestos 8," metallic blue, yellow-lettered Goodyear slicks, White Rose .... $4 – 5
88. "Smokin' Joe 23," yellow and purple, Goodyear rubber tires on black rims, White Rose, sealed in plexiglas box with yellow platform base .... $20 – 30
89. "Smokin' Joe 23," yellow and purple, Goodyear rubber tires on black rims, White Rose, sealed in plexiglas box with purple platform base .... $20 – 30
90. "Snickers 8," brown and red, white-lettered Goodyear slicks, White Rose .... $4 – 5
91. "Texaco," "Havoline 28" in bright orange, black, white-lettered Goodyear slicks, White Rose .... $9 – 12
92. "Texaco," "Havoline 28" in bright orange, black, Goodyear rubber tires on black rims, White Rose .... $9 – 12
93. "Texaco 28," flat black, white-lettered Goodyear slicks, White Rose team Convoy .... $9 – 12
94. "TIC Financial 0," black, yellow-lettered Goodyear slicks, White Rose .... $6 – 9
95. "USA Bobsled Project 7," white, yellow-lettered Goodyear slicks, White Rose .... $12 – 16
96. "Valvoline," "Cummins 6," white and dark blue, Goodyear rubber tires on black rims, White Rose .... $4 – 5
97. "Valvoline 6," white, yellow-lettered Goodyear slicks, White Rose .... $4 – 5
98. "Valvoline 6," "Reese's," with white, red, and dark blue, Goodyear rubber tires on black rims, White Rose .... $4 – 5
99. "White Rose Collectibles 00," orange, Goodyear rubber tires on black rims, White Rose .... $12 – 16
100. "Wieder Racing 7," dark blue, yellow-lettered Goodyear slicks .... $1 – 2
101. "Wieder Racing 7," dark blue, concave 5-spoke wheels .... $3 – 4

102. "Weider Racing 7," dark blue, 6-spoke spiral wheels $1-2
103. "Wynn Dixie 60," black, Goodyear rubber tires on black rims, White Rose .... $4 – 5
104. white, no markings, gold chromed spokes, yellow-lettered Goodyear slicks .... $4 – 5
105. metallic gold, 1997 75 Challenge .... $6 – 12

Ford Thunderbird Turbo Coupe, 3", #59, 1988; #61, 1988, international; #28, 1992, international reissue

1. red, "Turbo Coupe" .... $1 – 2
2. red, detailed trim, rubber tires on chrome rims, Premiere Collection Special Class #2 .... $4 – 5
3. metallic red, Thailand cast, Show Stoppers .... $4 – 5
4. dark green, detailed trim, rubber tires on chrome rims, Premiere Collection #4 .... $4 – 5

5. metallic blue with purple and pink stripes .... $1 – 2
6. purple, "Turbo Coupe," Macau cast . $1 – 2
7. purple, "Turbo Coupe," Thailand cast $1 – 2
8. dark purple to pink, "Turbo Coupe," Super Color Changers .... $4 – 5
9. black, detailed trim, rubber tires on chrome rims, Premiere Collection Special Class #5 .... $4 – 5

10. metallic gray, detailed trim, red interior, chrome windows, rubber tires on gray rims, World Class .... $6 – 8
11. metallic gray, detailed trim, black interior, chrome windows, rubber tires on gray rims, World Class ...... $60 – 70
12. dark gray, detailed trim, rubber tires on chrome rims, JC Penney Premiere Collection .... $4 – 5
13. white, detailed trim, rubber tires on chrome rims, Gold Coin Collection .... $16 – 24
14. dark brown to pale green, "Turbo Coupe," Super Color Changers ... $4 – 5
15. metallic gold, "56 Motorcraft," Laser Wheels .... $4 – 5

16. metallic gold, detailed trim, rubber tires on chrome rims, Premiere Collection #1 .... $4 – 5

Ford Tractor, 2 1/8", #39, 1967

1. dark blue with yellow engine cowl .... $15 – 20
2. dark blue with blue engine cowl .. $20 – 30
3. light blue with yellow engine cowl ... $20 – 30
4. orange with orange engine cowl .... $90 – 120

Ford Tractor, 2 3/16", #46, 1978
1. yellow with orange stripe, black interior, no harrow, metallic silver base, orange hubs, Macau cast, 2-pack .... $1 – 2
2. yellow with orange stripe, black interior, red harrow, metallic silver base, orange hubs, Macau cast, gift set .... $1 – 2

3. green, black interior, no harrow, metallic silver base, orange hubs, Macau cast .... $1 – 2
4. green, black interior, no harrow, metallic silver base, orange hubs, Thailand cast, 2-pack .... $1 – 2
5. green, black interior, yellow harrow, metallic silver base, orange hubs, Thailand cast, Motor City .... $1 – 2
6. green, white interior, red harrow, metallic silver base, orange hubs, Macau cast, Motor City .... $1 – 2
7. green, yellow interior, yellow harrow, unpainted base, yellow wheel hubs, England cast .... $6 – 8
8. lime green, yellow interior, yellow harrow, unpainted base, yellow wheel hubs, England cast .... $6 – 8
9. blue, yellow interior, no harrow, unpainted base, black wheel hubs, England cast, 2-pack .... $4 – 5
10. blue, yellow interior, orange harrow, black wheel hubs, unpainted base, England cast .... $4 – 5
11. blue, yellow interior, yellow harrow, unpainted base, black wheel hubs, England cast .... $4 – 5
12. blue, yellow interior, yellow harrow, unpainted base, yellow wheel hubs, England cast .... $4 – 5
13. blue, yellow interior, yellow harrow, unpainted base with towing tab, yellow wheel hubs, no origin cast, Brazil issue .... $70 – 90
14. blue, white interior, yellow harrow, unpainted base, black front hubs, yellow rear hubs, England cast .... $4 – 5
15. blue, white interior, yellow harrow, unpainted base, yellow front and rear hubs, England cast .... $4 – 5

16. blue, yellow interior, no harrow, metallic silver base, gold hubs, Macau cast, 2-pack .... $3 – 4

Ford Tractor, #236, 1993, Farming Series set

1. blue with red scoop, Farming .. $6 – 8
2. dark blue with yellow harrow, Action Pack .... $4 – 5

Ford Transit (see Ford Transit Pickup, Ford Transit Van, Ford Transit Ambulance)

Ford Transit Ambulance, with roof light, #21, 1999, Germany; #14, 2003 (similar casting: Ford Transit Van)
1. red, "112 Feuerwehr," 1999, Germany issue .... $5 – 6
2. red with yellow stripes, "London Fire Brigade" .... $4 – 5
3. yellow with blue stripes, "Medic" .. $3 – 4
4. white with yellow and orange stripes, blue tinted windows and roof light, 2003 Hospital .... $1 – 2

Ford Transit Pickup, light to dark orange with cargo load of varying shades of brown or tan, 2 3/4", #66, 1977
1. amber windows, light yellow interior, unpainted base .... $7 – 9
2. amber windows, olive green interior, unpainted base .... $7 – 9
3. amber windows, tan interior, unpainted base .... $7 – 9
4. amber windows, white interior, unpainted base .... $7 – 9
5. blue-green windows, cream interior, black base .... $7 – 9
6. blue-green windows, cream interior, unpainted base .... $7 – 9
7. blue-green windows, cream interior, unpainted base with towing tab, Brazil issue .... $40 – 60
8. blue-green windows, light yellow interior, unpainted base .... $7 – 9
9. blue-green windows, olive green interior, unpainted base .... $7 – 9
10. blue-green windows, tan interior, unpainted base .... $7 – 9
11. dark green windows, olive green interior, unpainted base .... $7 – 9
12. green windows, cream interior, dark gray base .... $7 – 9
13. green windows, light yellow interior, dark gray base .... $7 – 9

Ford Transit Van, 2⅞", #60, 1987 – 1989; #57, 1990 – 1997; #49, 2002; #50, 2003; #5, 1998, international; #25, 1999, international; #13, 2001, UK; #11, 2005 (left-hand drive unless noted; similar casting: Ford Transit Ambulance; also see Ford Transit Van 2006)

1. "14th Annual Toy Show — Ft. Washington, PA," red, US issue ... $20 – 30
2. "24 Hour Roofing," metallic blue, 2002 Hammer and Nails ..... $1 – 2
3. "24th Annual Truck-In 1996," red, US issue .... $20 – 30
4. "24th Annual Truck-In 1996," white, US issue .... $12 – 16
5. "97.5 PST," dark blue, US issue .... $20 – 30
6. "97.5 PST," white, US issue .... $16 – 24
7. "Abbey Stainless," white, UK issue .... $12 – 16
8. "AC Auto Clenz," white, UK issue .... $60 – 100
9. "American International Recovery," white, ASAP promotional ....$100 – 150
10. "Anglian Self Drive," "Norflex," white, UK issue ....$120 – 180
11. "Auckland Warriors," green with blue roof, Australia issue .... $12 – 16
12. "Australia Post," red, Australia issue .... $7 – 9
13. "Australia Post-We Deliver," orange-red with white roof, left-hand drive, Australia issue .... $4 – 5
14. "Australia Post-We Deliver," red, right-hand drive, Australia issue .... $7 – 9
15. "Australia Telecom," white, Australia issue .... $7 – 9
16. "Balmain Tigers," black with red roof, Australia issue .... $12 – 16
17. "Belfast Evening Telegraph," red, Ireland issue ....$120 – 160
18. "Bell South Americast," white, ASAP promo ....$120 – 160
19. "Blick," red, Switzerland issue .. $9 – 12
20. "Brantho-Korrux," red, Germany issue .... $30 – 40
21. "Brisbane Broncos," light yellow with purple roof, Australia issue .... $12 – 16
22. "British Telecom," yellow ...... $5 – 6
23. "Cadbury Flakes," yellow .... $1 – 2
24. "Canberra Raiders," lime green with yellow roof, Australia issue .... $12 – 16
25. "Canterbury-Bankstown Bulldogs," black with dark blue roof, Australia issue .... $12 – 16
26. "Citizens Communications," white, ASAP promo .... $30 – 40
27. "Coca Cola," yellow, rubber tires on chrome rims, Premiere Collection .... $5 – 7
28. "Coca Cola" with hockey player bear, red and white, FAO Schwarz multi-pack .... $4 – 6

29. **"Coca-Cola" with line of bottles and couple, metallic silver, 2003 .... $4 – 6**
30. "Coca-Cola" with two polar bears, red and white .... $16 – 24
31. "Coldseal," white, UK issue .. $12 – 16
32. "Council of Councils," "C of C The Old Ship," metallic gray, UK issue .... $60 – 120
33. "Council of Councils," "C of C The Old Ship," white, UK issue ..... $16 – 24
34. "Council of Councils," "France — Windsor-London-Stonehenge," metallic gray, UK issue .... $16 – 24
35. "Council of Councils," "France — Windsor-London-Stonehenge," white, UK issue .... $16 – 24
36. "Council of Councils," "I Did the Pub Crawl," metallic gray, UK issue .... $60 – 120
37. "Council of Councils," "I Did the Pub Crawl," white, UK issue ... $16 – 24
38. "Cronulla Sharks," black with light blue roof, Australia issue ....$12 – 16
39. "Day Break at Lowestoft," "The Sunrise Coast," metallic gray, UK issue .... $16 – 24
40. "Day Break at Lowestoft," "The Sunrise Coast," white, UK issue .... $16 – 24
41. "DCS," white .... $90 – 120
42. "Delta Precision Ltd.," white, UK issue .... $12 – 16
43. "Disaster Care," white, UK issue .... $12 – 16
44. "Eastern Suburbs Roosters," bright blue with red roof, Australia issue .... $12 – 16
45. "EFI Disc Brakes," white, UK issue .... $12 – 16
46. "Envelopes UK," white, UK issue .... $12 – 16
47. "Euro Dollar," white, UK issue .... $12 – 16
48. "Eurolines," white, UK issue .... $12 – 16
49. "Evening Gazette," white, UK issue .... $15 – 20
50. "Express Post," yellow, right hand drive, Australia issue .... $4 – 5
51. "Fastway Couriers," white, Australia issue .... $6 – 8
52. "Federal Express," white, left-hand drive, China cast .... $1 – 2
53. "Federal Express," white, left-hand drive, Macau cast .... $3 – 4
54. "Federal Express," white, right-hand drive, China cast .... $4 – 5
55. "Garden Festival Wales," white, Wales issue .... $7 – 9
56. "GCS Service Inc. Communications Food Service Equipment," white .... $60 – 120
57. "Gold Coast Seagulls," black with red, Australia issue .... $12 – 16
58. "Grafi Press," white and orange, Netherlands issue .... $15 – 20
59. "Grime Busters," white, UK issue .... $12 – 16
60. "Hankook Tyres," red, Malta issue .... $12 – 16
61. "Hankook Tyres," white with black roof logo, Malta issue ..... $16 – 24
62. "Hankook Tyres," white with blue roof logo, Malta issue .... $16 – 24
63. "Hankook Tyres," white with orange roof logo, Malta issue ..$120 – 160
64. "Hankook Tyres," white with red roof logo, Malta issue ....$120 – 160
65. "Hankook Tyres," white with white roof, US issue .... $30 – 40
66. "Hannant's," white, UK issue ...$12 – 16
67. "Hilton" in black letters, white and teal, US issue .... $16 – 24
68. "Hilton" in red letters, white and teal, US issue .... $20 – 30
69. "Illawarra Steelers," white with orange roof, Australia issue ....$12 – 16
70. "Isotar," "Perform," "Powerplay," metallic gray, Swiss issue ... $9 – 12
71. "JCB Job Site," white, right hand drive .... $7 – 9
72. "Kellogg's," white, Action System on-package premium, Swiss issue .... $70 – 80
73. "Kellogg's," white, right hand drive, Action System on-package premium, Swiss issue .... $70 – 80
74. "Kingston Communications," white, UK issue .... $12 – 16
75. "Kiosk," white, Swiss issue .. $9 – 12
76. "Kit Kat," red, UK issue ... $30 – 40
77. "Lincare," white, ASAP promotional ....$100 – 150
78. "Long Time Vanners 1983 – 1999," white, UK issue .... $16 – 24
79. "Long Time Vanners 1999 Club Member," dark blue, UK issue .. $12 – 16
80. "Long Time Vanners Club Member," metallic gray, UK issue .... $30 – 40
81. "Long Time Vanners Yet Another Millennium," white, UK issue .. $16 – 24
82. "Lufthansa 88 – 786," white .. $3 – 5
83. "Magna," red, UK issue ..$120 – 160
84. "Matchbox," white .... $3 – 4
85. "Manly Sea Eagles," dark lavender with white roof, Australia issue ... $12 – 16
86. "McKesson," white, US issue .... 70 – 80
87. "Menrose Extractor Fans," red, UK issue .... $12 – 16
88. "Midwest Diecast Miniatures," dark blue, US issue .... $12 – 16
89. "Morgan Lovell," white, UK issue .... $12 – 16
90. "Motorsport," red .... $3 – 4
91. "National Windscreens," white, UK issue .... $12 – 16

92. "Newcastle Knights," white with bright blue roof, Australia issue .... $12 – 16
93. "NGK — The World's Only," white, UK issue .... $60 – 80

94. "Nickelodeon," metallic purple with Rugrats graphics, 2003 Nickelodeon 5-pack .... $2 – 3
95. "North Queensland Cowboys," dark gray with white roof, Australia issue .... $12 – 16
96. "North Sydney Bears," black with red roof, Australia issue .... $12 – 16
97. "NSVA — 25 years of Vanning," white, UK issue .... $16 – 24
98. "NSVA 25th Anniversary Committee Van," dark blue, UK issue .. $120 – 160
99. "NSVA 25th Anniversary Committee Van," white, UK issue ...... $120 – 160
100. "NSVA 25th Anniversary Members Van," dark blue, UK issue .... $30 – 40
101. "NSVA Van 23 Years on the Road Committee Van," white, UK issue .... $120 – 160
102. "NSVA Van 23 Years on the Road Members Van," white, UK issue .... $30 – 40
103. "NSVA Van Nationals Billing Northampton," white, UK issue .... $12 – 16
104. "OCS," pale blue and white, Australia issue .... $16 – 24
105. "Ormond St. Appeal," white, right hand drive .... $6 – 8
106. "Ovomaltine," orange, Switzerland issue .... $9 – 12
107. "Panasonic Colin Smith," white, UK issue .... $12 – 16
108. "Parcel Post," white, Australia issue .... $5 – 7
109. "Parramatta Eels," bright blue with yellow roof, Australia issue .... $12 – 16
110. "Penrith Panthers," lemon yellow with red roof, Australia issue ...... $12 – 16
111. "Peter Cox Preservation," white, right hand drive, UK issue .... $8 – 10
112. "Phoenix Natural Gas," white, UK issue .... $12 – 16
113. "Pickfords Record Management," white, UK issue .... $40 – 60

114. "Police 3," "S.W.A.T.," blue, red star over white circle design, 2001 On Patrol 5-pack .... $2 – 4
115. "Poltransplant Navartis," white, Poland issue .... $90 – 120
116. "Rentokil Initial," white, UK issue .... $12 – 16
117. "Rotamole," "Pitmole," white, UK issue .... $120 – 180
118. "Royal Mail," red, right hand drive, UK issue .... $6 – 8

119. "Ryder Truck Rental," yellow .. $3 – 4

120. "S.W.A.T. 64437-998-01," "MB Police 3," blue with red, white, and silver design, 2001 On Patrol 5-pack .... $1 – 2
121. "Scooter's Snowboard Shoppe," dark blue, US issue .... $20 – 30
122. "Scooter's Snowboard Shoppe," white, US issue .... $16 – 24
123. "Siemen's," white, UK issue .. $12 – 16
124. "SLP Engineering Ltd.," white, UK issue .... $15 – 20
125. "SLP Engineering Ltd.," "Lowestoft," white, UK issue .... $15 – 20
126. "Smith Kline Beecham," white, ASAP promotional .... $60 – 100
127. "Smoke Detectors Save Lives," red, US issue .... $16 – 24
128. "South Queensland Crushers," red with gold roof, Australia issue .... $12 – 16
129. "South Sydney Rabbitohs," green with red roof, Australia issue ...... $12 – 16
130. "St. George Dragons," white with red roof, Australia issue .... $12 – 16
131. "Standish Van Hire," white, UK issue .... $12 – 16
132. "Starlec," white, UK issue .. $12 – 16
133. "Stegosaurus" and skeleton design, black .... $1 – 2
134. "Supertoys," white, Ireland issue .. $20 – 30
135. "Taronga Zoomobile," metallic green, Australia issue .... $7 – 9
136. "The Sunrise Coast," metallic gray, UK issue .... $16 – 24
137. "The Sunrise Coast," white, UK issue .... $12 – 16
138. "Transit," yellow, 2005 #11 .. $1 – 2
139. "Transit" in red and black, metallic gray, UK issue .... $80 – 120
140. "Transit" in red and black, white, UK issue .... $40 – 50
141. "Transit" in red and blue, metallic gray, UK issue .... $80 – 120
142. "Transit" in red and blue, white, UK issue .... $40 – 50
143. "Transit Ford," "C of C Ford," "Transit Plant Trip 2000," metallic gray, UK issue .... $16 – 24
144. "Transit Ford," "C of C Ford," "Transit Plant Trip 2000," white, UK issue .... $16 – 24
145. "Transit Ford," "NSVA," "Show & Shine," metallic gray, UK issue .... $16 – 24
146. "Transit Ford," "NSVA," "Show & Shine," white, UK issue ...... $16 – 24
147. "Trophy Gold Pet Foods," white, UK issue .... $12 – 16
148. "Ultra Link," white, UK issue .... $140 – 180
149. "Unichem," white, right hand drive, UK issue .... $8 – 10
150. "Upright," metallic gray, UK issue .... $30 – 40
151. "Van Club — 25th Van Nationals — England," white, UK issue .... $12 – 16
152. "Van Club – 26 Years of Vanning," white, UK issue .... $12 – 16
153. "Viewmaster," red, US issue with wooden box, viewer and special reel .... $90 – 100
154. "Viewmaster," white, US issue .... $20 – 30
155. "Vinnie's," red .... $3 – 4

156. "Water & Power," yellow lower, white upper, 2006 5-pack J4682 ...... $1 – 2
157. "Waterway Recovery Group," red, UK issue .... $12 – 16
158. "Web Force," white, UK issue .... $12 – 16
159. "Welcoming the New Millennium" in red, white, UK issue .... $12 – 16
160. "Welcoming the New Millennium" in black, white, UK issue .... $12 – 16
161. "Wella," white, Germany issue . $7 – 9
162. "Western Reds," red with yellow roof, Australia issue .... $12 – 16
163. "Western Suburbs Magpies," white, Australia issue .... $12 – 16
164. "Windscreen Auto," white, UK issue .... $120 – 160
165. "Wigwam," white, Dutch issue .... $8 – 10
166. "Wishing Well Appeal," white, UK issue .... $7 – 9

167. "www rent-a-van," white, UK issue .... $12 – 16
168. "XP Express Parcels," white, UK issue .... $5 – 6
169. "XP Express Parcels," white, right-hand drive, UK issue .... $7 – 9
170. red, no markings, left-hand drive .... $3 – 4
171. red, no markings, right-hand drive, UK issue .... $40 – 50
172. yellow, 2001 Union Jack series, UK issue .... $4 – 6
173. yellow with British flag, blue and red stripes .... $3 – 4
174. lime green with no markings, Dutch issue .... $12 – 16
175. light blue, surfing design ...... $2 – 4
176. white, no markings, Graffic Traffic .... $12 – 16
177. white, no markings, ASAP promotional blank .... $20 – 25
178. white with red cross and stripes, gray rectangle, Macau cast .... $3 – 4
179. white with red cross and stripes, gray rectangle, China cast .... $3 – 4
180. white with surfboard design, 1998 .... $1 – 2
181. white with surfing scene, 1998 Around the Town international .. $1 – 2

Ford Transit Van 2006, #28, 2006; #37, 2007

1. metallic blue-gray, 2006 #28 ..... $1 – 2

2. metallic light blue, "Bilstein Shock Absorbers," 2007 #37 .... $1 – 2

3. metallic gray, "Genuine Ford Parts," 2007 #37 .... $1 – 2

Ford Utility Truck, 3", #74, 1987, international; #33, 1989 – 1997; #9, 1998; #15, 1999

1. red with white boom, "Matchbox Fire Dept.," 2000 Fire 5-pack ..... $1 – 2

2. red with yellow boom, "53," yellow wheels, Matchbox Preschool/Live 'N Learn .... $6 – 8
3. orange with white boom, "P & L Response Unit 20," 1998 Big Movers .... $1 – 2

4. yellow with red front end, "Energy Inc.," Action Pack .... $4 – 5

5. yellow, "Telephone Co.," "Unit 4" .. $1 – 2

6. green, "Intercom City," "Service" ... $8 – 10

7. metallic green with metallic gray base, white boom, "Tree Care" and tree, 1996 .... $1 – 2

8. blue with yellow boom, white lettering, yellow accents, White Rose Collectibles .... $6 – 8

9. blue with yellow boom, "P & L Co," "Response Unit," "20," 1997 .. $1 – 2

10. metallic gold with black boom, 1997 75 Challenge .... $12 – 16

11. metallic silver with red boom, "Global Electric," 1997 City Streets 5-pack .... $1 – 2

12. metallic silver with yellow boom, "Ideal Power," "Clean Safe Power," 1999 Highway Haulers .... $1 – 2

13. metallic silver with black boom, "55," black, white and yellow graphics, yellow wheel hubs, 2006 5-pack J4682 .... $1 – 2

14. black with green boom, "Highway Crew," "Caution High Voltage," "Unit 45," 1999 Highway Crew 5-pack .... $1 – 2

15. gray with orange front end, "Energy Inc." .... $1 – 2

16. beige with bright green base and boom, green "Tree Care" and tree design, 1995 .... $1 – 2

17. white with white boom, ASAP promotional blank .... $30 – 40
18. white with white boom, "American International Recovery," ASAP promotional .... $60 – 80
19. white with white boom, "Bell Atlantic," ASAP promotional .... $60 – 80
20. white with white boom, "Georgia Power Co.," ASAP promotional .... $80 – 120
21. white with white boom, "GI," ASAP promotional .... $120 – 160
22. white with white boom, "Gulf Power," ASAP promotional .... $60 – 80
23. white with white boom, "LCEC," ASAP promotional .... $40 – 60
24. white with white boom, "MTI" on left side, ASAP promotional .... $60 – 80
25. white with white boom, "Pac Tel," ASAP promotional .... $80 – 120
26. white with white boom, "RMLD," ASAP promotional .... $30 – 40
27. white with white boom, "Verizon," ASAP promotional .... $80 – 120
28. white with white boom, "Western States Co-Op," ASAP promotional .. $80 – 120
29. white with white boom, "Xcel Energy," ASAP promotional .... $80 – 120
30. white with white boom, yellow sun and green line logo, ASAP promotional .... $60 – 80

Ford Wildlife Truck (Rolamatic) with lion under transparent canopy, $2^3/_4$", #57, 1973 (similar casting: Ford Kennel Truck)

1. yellow with red windows, amber canopy .... $6 – 8
2. yellow with red windows, blue canopy .... $6 – 8
3. yellow with red windows, clear canopy .... $6 – 8
4. yellow with red windows, tinted canopy .... $6 – 8
5. yellow with orange windows, tinted canopy .... $6 – 8
6. yellow with no windows, clear canopy .... $6 – 8
7. white with red windows, blue canopy .... $6 – 8
8. white with red windows, clear canopy, stripes .... $6 – 8
9. white with red windows, tinted canopy, stripes .... $6 – 8
10. white with orange windows, blue canopy, stripes .... $6 – 8
11. white with orange windows, clear canopy, stripes .... $6 – 8
12. white with orange windows, tinted canopy, stripes .... $6 – 8
13. white with purple windows, blue canopy, stripes .... $6 – 8
14. white with purple windows, clear canopy, stripes .... $6 – 8
15. white with purple windows, tinted canopy, stripes .... $6 – 8

Ford Wreck Truck, 3", #61, 1978

1. red with amber windows, green booms, black hooks .... $200 – 300
2. red with amber windows, red booms, black hooks .... $7 – 9
3. red with amber windows, red booms, red hooks .... $7 – 9
4. red with amber windows, white booms, black hooks .... $5 – 6
5. red with amber windows, white booms, red hooks .... $5 – 6
6. red with amber windows, white booms, red hooks, "24 Hour" .... $6 – 8
7. red with blue windows, white booms, red hooks .... $5 – 6
8. red with blue windows, white booms, white hooks .... $9 – 12
9. orange-red with amber windows, white booms, red hooks, Manaus cast, Brazil issue .... $250 – 350
10. yellow with amber windows, green booms, black hooks .... $6 – 8
11. yellow with amber windows, green booms, red hooks .... $6 – 8
12. yellow with amber windows, red booms, black hooks .... $5 – 6
13. yellow with amber windows, red booms, red hooks .... $5 – 6
14. yellow with amber windows, white booms, red hooks .... $5 – 6
15. white with amber windows, white booms, red hooks, red stripe label, Manaus cast, Brazil issue ...$500 – 600

Ford Zephyr 6 Mk III, $2^5/_8$", #33, 1963

1. turquoise with gray plastic wheels .... $50 – 60
2. turquoise with silver plastic wheels .... $50 – 60

3. turquoise with black plastic wheels ....$20 - 30

Ford Zodiac Convertible, pink, $2^5/_8$", #39, 1957

1. pink with tan interior and base, metal wheels .... $450 – 600
2. pink with turquoise interior and base, metal wheels .... $80 – 100
3. pink with turquoise interior and base, gray plastic wheels .... $100 – 125
4. pink with turquoise interior and base, silver plastic wheels .... $175 – 225

Ford Zodiac Mk II, $2^5/_8$", #33, 1957

1. light blue or light blue-green, no windows, metal wheels .... $30 – 40
2. dark green. no windows, metal wheels .... $30 – 40
3. dark green, no windows, gray plastic wheels .... $40 – 50
4. metallic gray and orange, no windows, gray plastic wheels .... $40 – 50
5. tan and orange to light orange, no windows, gray plastic wheels ... $40 – 50
6. tan and orange with green windows, gray plastic wheels .... $40 – 50
7. tan and orange with green windows, silver plastic wheels .... $40 – 50

Ford Zodiac Mk IV, $2^3/_4$", #53, 1968

1. metallic silver blue, unpainted base, black plastic wheels .... $7 – 9
2. light metallic green, unpainted base, black plastic wheels .... $500 – 600
3. metallic light blue, unpainted base, Superfast wheels .... $400 – 450
4. metallic green, unpainted base, Superfast wheels .... $18 – 24
5. apple green, unpainted base, Superfast wheels .... $24 – 32

Fordson Power Major Farm Tractor, blue, 2", #72, 1959

1. gray front wheels, gray rear tires on orange wheels .... $40 – 50
2. black front wheels, black rear tires on orange wheels .... $35 – 45
3. gray front and rear tires on orange wheels .... $40 – 50
4. gray front and rear tires on yellow wheels ....$90 – 100
5. black front and rear tires on yellow wheels ....$90 – 100
6. black front and rear tires on orange wheels .... $40 – 50

Fork Lift (also see Power Lift)

Fork Lift, #63, 2002; #70, 2003; #28, 2005

1. orange with black fork lift boom, yellow and blue graphics, 2002 Rescue Rookies ....$1 - 2

2. lime green with gray fork lift boom, 2005 #28 .... $1 – 2

3. white with black fork lift boom, "562 Lift Truck Mechanical," seal design, 2006 5-pack J4680 ....$1 - 2

4. **white with bright red fork lift boom, "MCH" and graphics .... $1 – 2**
5. white with red fork lift boom, 2003 Heavy Movers .... $1 – 2

Fork Lift Truck, 2½", #15, 1972

1. **plastic steering wheel, "Lansing Bagnall" labels, gray forks .... $12 – 16**
2. plastic steering wheel, "T6AD" labels, gray forks, Brazil issue ... $250 – 400
3. no steering wheel, "Lansing Bagnall" labels, gray forks .... $12 – 16
4. no steering wheel, "Lansing Bagnall" labels, long red forks, part of King Size model .... $20 – 25
5. no steering wheel, "Lansing Bagnall" labels, black forks .... $12 – 16
6. no steering wheel, "Lansing Bagnall" labels, yellow forks .... $12 – 16
7. cast steering wheel, "Lansing Bagnall" labels, yellow forks .... $9 – 12
8. cast steering wheel, "HI LIFT" labels, black roof, long black forks, part of King Size model .... $20 – 25
9. cast steering wheel, "HI LIFT" labels, no roof, black forks .... $12 – 16

Fork Lift Truck, 3⅛", #28, 1991; #61, 1992 (see Sambron Jack Lift)

Formula 1 (see Formula One Racing Car, Formula Racer)

Formula 5000, 3", #36, 1975
1. orange, "5000" labels .... $9 – 12
2. red, "5000" labels .... $8 – 10
3. red, "Texaco" on hood .... $8 – 10
4. red, "Texaco" on hood, towing tab on base, UK issue .... $50 – 60
5. white, "Texaco" on hood, towing tab on base, UK issue .... $350 – 450

Formula One Racing Car, 2⅞", #34, 1971
1. metallic pink, "16" and "Wynn's" labels, UK issue .... $100 – 150
2. metallic pink, "16" label only .. $16 – 24
3. orange, "16" label .... $12 – 16
4. yellow, "15" label .... $12 – 16
5. yellow, "16" label .... $12 – 16
6. metallic blue, "15" label .... $12 – 16
7. blue, "15" label .... $12 – 16
8. blue, "16" label .... $12 – 16

Formula Racer, #28, 1982; #16, 1984; #74, 1996; #61, 1998 (see Williams Renault Formula Racer)

Four-Wheeler, #91, 1999; #63, 2000; #34, 2001; #71, 1999, international; #43, 2000, international

1. **red with black chassis, white cross, yellow driver, 2002 Sand Castle Rescue Team 5-pack .... $1 – 2**
2. red with metallic gray chassis, "5," mud spray, black driver, 2001 Sand Blasters .... $1 – 2
3. red with metallic gray chassis, "400," blue stripes, yellow driver with black pants, 5-pack .... $1 – 2

4. **red with blue chassis, orange driver, 2003 Hero City 5-pack #5 ... $1 – 2**
5. light red with metallic gray chassis, "Matchbox 2000," white and black design, gray driver with dark gray pants, 2000 Great Outdoors ... $1 – 2
6. light red with metallic gray chassis, white and black design, gray driver with dark gray pants, 2000 Great Outdoors .... $1 – 2
7. green with metallic gray chassis, brown mud, brown driver with black pants, 5-pack .... $1 – 2

8. **olive green with metallic gray chassis, beige driver with blue pants, 1999 #71 Mountain Cruisers .. $1 – 2**

9. **blue with pale gray rider, 2007 5-pack K9616 .... $1 – 2**

Freeman Inter-City Commuter Coach, 3", #22, 1970

1. **metallic red-orange .... $20 – 25**

2. **metallic magenta .... $20 – 25**
3. metallic purple .... $20 – 25
4. metallic gold .... $20 – 25

Freeway Gas Tanker, 3", #63, 1973 (goes with #63 Freeway Gas Tanker Trailer, 1978)
1. "Aral," blue cab, purple windows, blue and white tank .... $30 – 40
2. "BP," white cab, purple windows, white and yellow tank .... $60 – 80
3. "BP," white cab, purple windows, white and green tank .... $9 – 12
4. "Burmah," red cab, purple windows, red and white tank .... $7 – 9
5. "Burmah," red cab, purple windows, red and white tank with tow hook, Two-Pack .... $7 – 9
6. "Castrol," red cab, purple windows, red and white tank .... $100 – 125
7. "Chevron," red cab, purple windows, red and white tank .... $7 – 9
8. "Chevron," red cab, purple windows, red and white tank with tow hook, Two-Pack .... $7 – 9
9. "Exxon," white cab, purple windows, white tank .... $8 – 10

10. "Exxon," white cab, purple windows, white tank with tow hook, Two-Pack .... $7 – 9
11. "Exxon," white cab, purple windows, yellow and white tank .... $20 – 30
12. "Exxon," red cab, purple windows, white tank with tow hook, Two-Pack ..$60 – 80

13. "K 95 High Octane," olive green cab, purple windows, olive green tank, Two-Pack ....$8 – 10
14. "K 95 High Octane," dark army green cab, purple windows, dark army green tank .... $70 – 90
15. "Shell," white cab, amber windows, white and yellow tank .... $7 – 9
16. "Shell," white cab, red windows, white and yellow tank .... $7 – 9
17. "Shell," white cab, purple windows, white and yellow tank .... $7 – 9
18. "Shell," white cab, purple windows, white and yellow tank with tow hook, Two-Pack .... $7 – 9
19. "Shell," yellow cab, purple windows, white and yellow tank .... $9 – 12
20. Canadian flag labels, army green cab, purple windows, army green tank, Two-Pack .... $300 – 400
21. French flag labels, army green cab, purple windows, army green tank, Two-Pack .... $70 – 90

Freeway Gas Tanker Trailer 3", #63, 1978 (issued as part of Two-Pack with #63 Freeway Gas Tanker, 1973)
1. "BP" labels, yellow coupling, yellow base ....$40 – 50
2. "BP" labels, white coupling, yellow base .... $7 – 9
3. "Burmah" labels, red coupling, red base .... $7 – 9
4. "Chevron" labels, red coupling, red base .... $7 – 9
5. "Exxon" labels, red coupling, white base .... $60 – 80
6. "Exxon" labels, yellow coupling, white base .... $8 – 1
7. "Shell" labels, yellow coupling, yellow base .... $7 – 9

Front End Loader Tractor, #40, 2006 (see Tractor Shovel)

G

Galant Eterna (see Dodge Challenger/Mitsubishi Galant Eterna)

General Service Lorry, 2⅝", #62, 1959
1. olive green with black plastic wheels .... $40 – 50

Glider Trailer, #794, 1976, with white glider and wings
1. red with amber canopy, "Gliding Club," England cast .... $400 – 450
2. red with clear canopy, "Auto Glide," no origin cast .... $3 – 4
3. yellow with amber canopy, "Gliding Club," England cast .... $3 – 4
4. lemon yellow with clear canopy, purple and pink spatters, no origin cast ...$3 – 4
5. green with clear canopy, "Seagull Gliding Club," England cast .... $3 – 4
6. green with clear canopy, England cast .... $3 – 4
7. dark green with amber canopy, "Seagull Gliding Club," England cast .... $3 – 4
8. dark blue with clear canopy, yellow stripes, no origin cast .... $3 – 4

GMC Bucket Truck, #99, 2000
1. dark blue, "Power Inc.," white boom and bucket, 2000 On the Road Again .... $1 – 2
2. dark blue, "Power Inc.," white boom and bucket, "Matchbox 2000," 2000 On the Road Again .... $3 – 4

3. metallic gray with black boom and bucket, black and yellow graphics, "55" ....$1 – 2

GMC Dump Truck (see GMC Tipper Truck)

GMC Refrigerator Truck, 3", #44, 1967

1. red with turquoise container, black plastic wheels ....$6 – 9
2. red with turquoise container, Superfast wheels, 1970 .... $50 – 60
3. yellow with red container, Superfast wheels .... $20 – 30
4. yellow with turquoise container, Superfast wheels .... $2,000 – 2,500

GMC Terradyne, #62, 2002; #58, 2003

1. metallic gray, no markings, 2002 Rescue Rookies ....$1 – 2
2. metallic green, "Extreme," 2003 Kid's Shoppes .... $1 – 2

3. burgundy with Dora graphics, 2006 Nickelodeon 5-pack H4108 ...$1 – 2

GMC Tipper Truck, 2⅝", #26 ,1968

1. red with metallic gray dumper, regular wheels, 1968 ....$6 – 9
2. red with metallic gray dumper, Superfast wheels, 1970 .... $30 – 40

GMC Utility Truck, #99, 2000 (similar casting: GMC Bucket Truck, Guzzler)

1. metallic chartreuse (greenish gold) with gray boom and auger, "470," 2005 5-pack H4108 ....$1 – 2

2. **metallic purple with white boom and auger, orange and white graphics, 2000 On the Road Again #99 ...$1 - 2**

3. **white with dark gray boom and auger, black and orange graphics, 2006 5-pack J4680 ....$1 - 2**

GMC Wrecker, 2⅞", #21, 1987; #71, 1987; #72, 1989; #63, 1998; #14, 1999; #48, 2006

1. red with chrome plastic base, white accents, "Ron's Towing," Collector's Choice, White Rose Collectibles ..$4 – 5
2. red with chrome plastic base, "Parkhill Towing," fluorescent yellow boom, no printing on hood .... $1 – 2

3. **red with chrome plastic base, "Matchbox 24 Hour Towing," yellow and white accents ....$1 - 2**
4. red with chrome plastic base, "Ron's," yellow and white accents, black boom, 1999 Highway Haulers .... $1 – 2

5. **orange, "Zentner 24 Hour Towing" graphics, 2006 #48 ....$1 - 2**
6. metallic gold with chrome plastic base, black boom, 1997 75 Challenge ....$6 – 12
7. metallic green with chrome plastic base, "Ron's," yellow and white design, 2000 Police Patrol .... $1 – 2
8. metallic green with chrome plastic base, "Ron's," "Matchbox 2000," yellow and white design, 2000 Police Patrol .... $3 – 4
9. metallic purple with chrome plastic base, white boom, yellow and white design .... $1 – 2

10. **metallic purple with chrome plastic base, "Parkhill Towing," "24 Hour Towing" on hood, fluorescent yellow boom, 1996 ....$1 - 2**
11. metallic purple with chrome plastic base, "Parkhill Towing," black boom, no printing on hood, international issue .... $7 – 9
12. metallic purple with chrome plastic base, "Parkhill Towing," fluorescent yellow boom, no printing on hood ... $1 – 2
13. black with chrome plastic base, "Official Wrecker Indy 500" .... $8 – 10
14. black with chrome plastic base, "Matchbox," yellow and white design, 1998 Motor Sports .... $1 – 2
15. black with chrome plastic base, "Police Emergency Unit 4" and gold star, 5-pack ....$1 – 2
16. black with chrome plastic base, "Service GMC," yellow and white design, 1998 Motor Sports .... $1 – 2
17. black with chrome plastic base, "Service GMC," "Matchbox," yellow and white design, Pleasant Books issue ... $4 – 5
18. white with unpainted metal base, "Accessory Wholesalers Inc." ..$20 – 25
19. white with unpainted metal base, "Frank's Getty," "557-1117," Macau cast .... $3 – 4
20. white with chrome plastic base, "3 Rescue" .... $1 – 2
21. white with chrome plastic base, "CAA Member Service," red windows, blue boom, Canadian issue ..... $120 – 160
22. white with chrome plastic base, "CAA Member Service," amber windows, blue boom, Canadian issue .... $12 – 16

23. **white with chrome plastic base, "Frank's Getty," "557-1117," China cast ....$1 - 2**
24. white with chrome plastic base, "Frank's Getty," "557-1117," Macau cast ....$1 – 2
25. white with chrome plastic base, "Frank's Getty," "557-1117," no origin cast ....$4 – 5
26. white with chrome plastic base, "Frank's Getty," "557-1117," Thailand cast ....$1 – 2
27. white with chrome plastic base, "Frank's Getty," no phone number, China cast ....$1 – 2
28. white with chrome plastic base, "Frank's Getty," no phone number, Thailand cast ....$1 – 2
29. white with chrome plastic base, "Matchbox 24 Hr. Towing," 5-pack ...... $3 – 4

30. **white with chrome plastic base, "Police," "Metro Emergency," 1993 Emergency 5-pack ....$1 - 2**
31. white with chrome plastic base, "Helmrich Towing & Recovery," Color Comp promotional .... $80 – 120
32. white with chrome plastic base, "Riehl's Towing," Color Comp promotional ....$80 – 120
33. white with chrome plastic base, white boom, "Alenco Service," ASAP promotional .... $80 – 120
34. white with chrome plastic base, white boom, "American International Recovery," ASAP promotional ... $120 – 160
35. white with chrome plastic base, white boom, "Matchbox 33000," ASAP promotional .... $60 – 80
36. white with chrome plastic base, white boom, "Phil's Body Works," ASAP promotional .... $120 – 160
37. white with chrome plastic base, white boom, "PTROI," ASAP promotional .... $30 – 40
38. white with chrome plastic base, white boom, no markings, ASAP promotional blank .... $25 – 30
39. white with chrome plastic base, "3 Rescue" .... $3 – 4

40. **pearl white, "24 Hr. Tow Service," 2005 Superfast #39 ....$3 - 4**

Go Rolla, #19, 2004

1. 2004 Ultra Heroes .... $3 – 4

Golden X, Roman Numeral X, 1978 (variation of #33 Datsun 126X, 1973)

1. yellow, Roman Numeral Limited Edition ....$15 – 20
2. gold plated, Roman Numeral Limited Edition .... $9 – 12

Golf Cart, #75, 2000; #55, 2000, international
1. gray, "Canyon Golf 232," 2000 On Tour .... $3 – 4
2. gray, "Canyon Golf 232," "Matchbox 2000," 2000 On Tour .... $4 – 5
3. gray, "Canyon Golf 232," "PMCC Christmas Dinner," Color Comp promotional .... $20 – 30
4. white, "3rd Annual Mattel Open," Color Comp promotional .... $20 – 30
5. white, "EMC2 Where Information Lives," "Global Financial Services," ASAP promotional .... $35 – 45
6. white, "RCA," ASAP promotional .... $25 – 35
7. white, "Together for Tyler," "Memorial Golf Tournament," Color Comp promotional .... $20 – 30
8. white, no markings, ASAP/Color Comp promotional blank .... $30 – 40

Golf V GTI (see Volkswagen Golf V GTI)

Grain Grabber (see Combine Harvester)

Gran Fury Police (see Plymouth Gran Fury Police)

Grand Prix Racer, 3", #74, 1988; #14, 1989
1. red, "Fiat 27," black metal base ..$3 – 4
2. red, "Fiat 27," black plastic base .... $16 – 24
3. red, "Kids World," "Fiat," Australia issue .... $45 – 55
4. red, "Scotch," "Target," Indy 500 ..$4 – 5
5. red, "Scotch 9," Indy 500 .... $4 – 5
6. orange, lavender, and white, "Indy 1," Indy 500 .... $4 – 5
7. orange and white, "Indy 4," Indy 500 .... $4 – 5
8. fluorescent orange and yellow, "Matchbox Get in the Fast Lane 7," Collector's Choice, White Rose Collectibles ..$4 – 5
9. yellow, "Pennzoil 2," Indy 500 ... $4 – 5
10. yellow, "Pennzoil 4," Indy 500 ... $4 – 5
11. yellow, "Pennzoil 8," Indy 500 ... $4 – 5
12. yellow, "Squirt," on-package premium .... $20 – 30
13. green and white, "4," black lines ..$1 – 2
14. blue, "Mackenzie," Indy 500 ..... $4 – 5
15. blue, "Panasonic," Indy 500 ..... $4 – 5
16. blue and white, "Valvoline," "Kraco 3," Indy 500 .... $4 – 5
17. blue and yellow, "Panasonic 11," Indy 500 .... $4 – 5

18. purple, "Matchbox 20," fluorescent yellow airfoil and base, 1997 Racing 5-pack .... $1 – 2
19. black, "Indy 5," green and pink spatter, Indy 500 .... $4 – 5
20. white, "7," blue dots .... $1 – 2
21. white, "Indy 500," "77," Indy 500 ...$4 – 5
22. white, "XP 6," Dutch issue ..... $9 – 12
23. white and black, "Havoline," "K-Mart," Indy 500 .... $4 – 5
24. white and black, "Texaco," "K-Mart," Indy 500 .... $4 – 5
25. white and blue, "Indy 76," Indy 500 .... $4 – 5

26. white and orange, "4," black lines, 1996 Racing 5-pack .... $1 – 2
27. white and pale blue, "15," "Goodyear," "Shell" .... $4 – 5
28. metallic tan, "Peugeot," "Special 11," international issue .... $3 – 4
29. chrome plated, custom promotional .... $16 – 24

Greased Lightning (see DeTomaso Pantera Greased Lightning)

Greyhound Bus, 3", #66, 1967
1. metallic gray, clear windows, black plastic wheels, 1967 .... $175 – 225

2. metallic gray, amber windows, black plastic wheels, 1967 .... $20 – 30

3. metallic gray, amber windows, black base, 1970, Superfast wheels .... $30 – 40
4. metallic gray, amber windows, pink base, 1970, Superfast wheels ....$30 – 40
5. metallic gray, amber windows, yellow base, 1970, Superfast wheels ....$30 – 40

Ground Breaker (Bulldozer), #48, 2007
1. yellow with black base and interior .... $1 – 2

Gruesome Twosome, 2 7/8", #4, 1971; BR 3-4, 1985
1. metallic gold with amber windows .... $125 – 150
2. metallic gold with purple windows .... $12 – 16
2. metallic orange-gold with purple widows .... $12 – 16
3. red with purple windows ...... $16 – 24
4. yellow, England cast, Super GT BR 3-4, 1985 .... $4 – 6
5. powder blue, England cast, Super GT BR 3-4, 1985 .... $4 – 6
6. dark blue, England cast, Super GT BR 3-4, 1985 .... $6 – 8
7. yellow, China cast, Super GT BR 3-4, 1985 .... $8 – 10
8. white with black windows, China cast, Super GT BR 3-4, 1985 .... $3 – 5
9. white with translucent white windows, China cast, Super GT BR 3-4, 1985 .... $20 – 25
10. gray, China cast, Super GT BR 3-4, 1985 .... $3 – 5
11. fluorescent orange, China cast, Neon Racers BR 3-4, 1985 .... $4 – 6

Guzzler/Mini Tanker (Utility Truck on base), #53, 2006; #39, 2007

1. gold cab, chrome tank with "Phillips 66" emblem, 2006 #53 .... $1 – 2

2. dark green cab, chrome tank, "Aviation Fuel," 2007 5-pack K9613; 2007 #39 .... $1 – 2
3. green with white tank, "Air Products," 2007 #39 .... $1 – 2

H

Hairy Hustler, 2 7/8", #7, 1971 (similar casting: Flamin' Manta)
1. metallic orange-red with purple windows, "5" labels .... $120 – 160
2. metallic orange-red with amber windows, "5" labels .... $16 – 24
3. metallic orange-red with amber windows, scorpion label .... $30 – 40
4. white with amber windows, no labels ....$60 – 80

5. white with amber windows, checkers and stripes .... $16 – 24
6. yellow, England cast, Super GT BR 13-14, 1985 .... $5 – 10
7. green, England cast, Super GT BR 13-14, 1985 .... $4 – 6
8. dark green, England cast, Super GT BR 13-14, 1985 .... $8 – 10
9. gray, China cast, Super GT BR 13-14, 1985 .... $3 – 5
10. yellow, China cast, Super GT BR 13-14, 1985 .... $8 – 10
11. red, China cast, Super GT BR 13-14, 1985 .... $3 – 5

Halftrack (see Army M3 Halftrack Personnel Carrier)

Harley-Davidson Chopper, #50, 1993, Harley-Davidson series
1. red, chrome handlebars .... $3 – 4
2. metallic maroon, chrome handlebars .... $3 – 4
3. fluorescent orange, black flames, chrome handlebars .... $3 – 4
4. yellow, chrome handlebars .... $3 – 4
5. yellow chrome, chrome handlebars .... $3 – 4
6. turquoise, chrome handlebars ....$12 – 16
7. blue, chrome handlebars .... $3 – 4
8. metallic blue, chrome handlebars .... $3 – 4
9. dark purple, chrome handlebars ....$9 – 12
10. black, chrome handlebars .... $3 – 4
11. metallic gray, chrome handlebars .... $3 – 4

Harley-Davidson Electraglide, #50, 1993 Harley-Davidson series
1. red, "Harley-Davidson," chrome handlebars, black saddlebags .... $3 – 4
2. metallic red, "Harley-Davidson," chrome handlebars, black saddlebags .. $9 – 12
3. orange-red, "PMG," orange handlebars, orange saddlebags, Australia issue .... $12 – 16
4. gold chrome, "Harley-Davidson," chrome handlebars, black saddlebags ... $3 – 4
5. metallic blue, "MBPD," chrome handlebars, black saddlebags .... $3 – 4
6. dark blue, "Harley-Davidson," chrome handlebars, black saddlebags ... $3 – 4
7. black, "Harley-Davidson," chrome handlebars, black saddlebags .... $3 – 4
8. black, "MBPD," chrome handlebars, black saddlebags .... $3 – 4
9. pale gray, "MBPD," chrome handlebars, black saddlebags .... $3 – 4
10. white, "Police," chrome handlebars, blue saddlebags .... $3 – 4
11. white, "MBPD," chrome handlebars, white saddlebags .... $3 – 4

Harley-Davidson H-D FXSTS Springer Softail, #393, 1995
1. metallic blue .... $4 – 5
2. metallic turquoise .... $4 – 5
3. metallic purple .... $4 – 5
4. metallic red .... $4 – 5

Harley-Davidson H-D Knucklehead, #394, 1995
1. pale blue .... $4 – 5
2. black .... $4 – 5

Harley-Davidson Motorcycle, 2 11/16", #50, 1980
1. red, chrome handlebars, no driver, China cast, Harley-Davidson ..... $3 – 4
2. metallic red, chrome handlebars, no driver, Thailand cast, Harley-Davidson .... $3 – 4
3. orange-red, "PMG," orange-red handlebars, no driver, China cast, Australia issue .... $5 – 6
4. orange-red, "PMG," orange-red handlebars, no driver, Thailand cast, Australia issue .... $5 – 6
5. metallic orange, black handlebars, tan driver, England cast .... $4 – 5
6. metallic orange, chrome handlebars, no driver, Thailand cast, Harley-Davidson ....$3 – 4
7. metallic dark orange, chrome handlebars, no driver, Thailand cast, Harley-Davidson gift set .... $3 – 4
8. metallic dark orange, chrome handlebars, no driver, China cast, Harley-Davidson .... $3 – 4
9. fluorescent orange, chrome handlebars, no driver, Thailand cast, Harley-Davidson .... $3 – 4
10. metallic yellow, chrome handlebars, no driver, Thailand cast, Harley-Davidson .... $3 – 4
11. fluorescent yellow, chrome handlebars, no driver, Thailand cast, Harley-Davidson gift set .... $3 – 4
12. gold plated, chrome handlebars, no driver, Thailand cast, Harley-Davidson .... $3 – 4
13. metallic turquoise, chrome handlebars, no driver, Thailand cast, Harley-Davidson gift set .... $3 – 4
14. metallic turquoise, chrome handlebars, no driver, Thailand cast, Harley-Davidson .... $3 – 4
15. metallic blue, chrome handlebars, no driver, Thailand cast, Harley-Davidson .... $3 – 4
16. dark purple, chrome handlebars, no driver, Thailand cast, Harley-Davidson .... $4 – 3
17. metallic brown, black handlebars, brown driver, Macau cast .... $3 – 4
18. metallic tan, black handlebars, no driver, England cast .... $4 – 5
19. metallic dark gray, chrome handlebars, no driver, Thailand cast, Harley-Davidson .... $3 – 4
20. metallic gray, chrome handlebars, no driver, Thailand cast, Harley-Davidson .... $3 – 4
21. white, chrome handlebars, no driver, Thailand cast, Harley-Davidson play set .. $3 – 4

Harley-Davidson Motorcycle and Sidecar, 2 5/8", #66, 1962

1. metallic bronze with black tires ....$85 – 95

Hatra Tractor Shovel, 3", #69, 1965
1. orange with orange shovel, orange wheels, gray tires .... $60 – 80
2. orange with orange shovel, red wheels, black tires .... $90 – 120
3. orange with orange shovel, yellow wheels, black tires .... $30 – 40
4. orange with yellow shovel, orange wheels, black tires .... $600 – 800
5. yellow with yellow shovel, red wheels, black tires .... $275 – 350

6. yellow with yellow shovel, yellow wheels, black tires ....$20 – 30

Hay Trailer, 3 1/4", #40, 1967
1. blue with yellow plastic fences, yellow hubs, black plastic tires .... $6 – 9

Hay Trailer, 1993 Farming Series set

1. yellow ....$3 – 5

Hearse, 1959 Cadillac, #57, 2006 (see Cadillac Hearse 1959, #57, 2006)

Heavy Rescue Auxiliary Power Truck (see Mack Floodlight Heavy Rescue Auxiliary Power Truck)

Helicopter (also see Air-Lift Helicopter, Hospital Helicopter, Mission Chopper, Rescue Chopper, Sea Rescue Helicopter, Seasprite Helicopter)

Helicopter, with pilot, large windows, 3", #75, 1982; #29, 1998; #6, 1999

1. red with red base, "Fire Dept." China cast .... $1 – 2

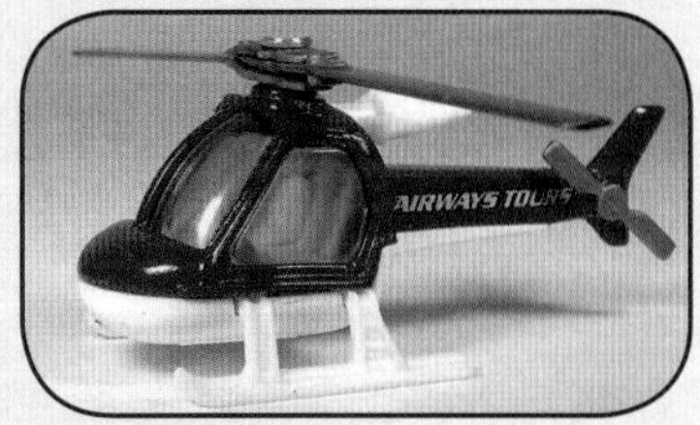

2. red with white base, "Airways Tours," China cast .... $1 – 2

3. red with white base, "Fire Dept." Macau cast .... $3 – 4

4. red with white base, "Fire Dept." Thailand cast .... $1 – 2
5. red with white base, "Red Rebels," Macau cast, Motor City .... $3 – 4
6. red with white base, "Red Rebels," Thailand cast, Motor City .... $1 – 2
7. red with white base, "Royal Air Force," Thailand cast, Motor City .... $3 – 4
8. orange with brown base, "Magnum P.I.," brown stripes, China cast, Avon Star Cars .... $9 – 12
9. yellow with black base, "702," black stripes, China cast, Germany issue .... $4 – 5
10. black with black base, "Air Car," Macau cast, Convoy .... $3 – 4
11. black with black base, "Air Car," Thailand cast, Convoy .... $3 – 4
12. metallic gray with orange base, "600," England cast, Convoy .... $3 – 4
13. metallic gray with orange base, "600," Macau cast, Convoy .... $3 – 4
14. metallic gray with black base, "600," England cast, Convoy .... $3 – 4
15. white with red base, "35-2," medic logo and red stripes, China cast ...... $3 – 4

16. white with red base, "87," yellow design, China cast, 1999 Air Traffic .... $1 – 2

17. white with red base, "Aerobatic Team," Thailand cast .... $3 – 4

18. white with red base, "Fire Dept." black interior, China cast, 1998 To the Rescue .... $1 – 2

19. white with red base, "Fire Dept." white interior, China cast .... $1 – 2
20. white with red base, "Fire Rescue," China cast, Avon Action Pack ... $1 – 2
21. white with red base, "NASA," Macau cast .... $3 – 4
22. white with red base, "Virgin Atlantic," Macau cast, gift set .... $3 – 4
23. white with orange base, "MBTV News," England cast .... $4 – 5
24. white with orange base, "Police," China cast, Action Pack .... $3 – 4
25. white with orange base, "Police 36," England cast .... $16 – 24
26. white with orange base, "Rescue," Macau cast .... $3 – 4
27. white with fluorescent orange base, "Air Rescue 10," "IC" logo, Thailand cast, Intercom City .... $12 – 16
28. white with fluorescent orange base, blue checkerboard design, Thailand cast, Emergency Pack .... $1 – 2
29. white with yellow base, "123456," Macau cast, Live 'N Learn/Matchbox Preschool .... $7 – 9
30. white with yellow base, "123456," Thailand cast, Live 'N Learn/Matchbox Preschool .... $7 – 9
31. white with yellow base, "JCB," Macau cast, gift set .... $5 – 6
32. white with yellow base, "Fire Dept." Macau cast .... $3 – 4
33. white with yellow base, "Fire Dept." Thailand cast .... $3 – 4
34. white with black base, "MBTV News," England cast .... $9 – 12
35. white with black base, "Newscam," "News 8," China cast, Real Talkin' .... $3 – 4
36. white with black base, "Police 36," England cast .... $5 – 6
37. white with black base, "Rescue," England cast .... $3 – 4
38. white with black base, "Rescue," Macau cast .... $3 – 4
39. white with black base, "Rescue," Thailand cast, Motor City .... $3 – 4
40. white with black base, Japanese lettering, Japanese gift set .... $10 – 12
41. metallic gold with white base, China cast, 1997 75 Challenge ...... $6 – 12

Hellraiser, 3", #55, 1975

1. white with red stripes, white stars on blue field .... $16 – 24
2. blue with red stripes, white stars on blue field .... $12 – 16
3. blue with no labels .... $12 – 16
4. blue with "3" label .... $12 – 16

Hero City Taxi, #43, 2004 (see Taxi)

Hi Ho Silver! Volkswagen Beetle (similar castings: Hot Chocolate, Volks Dragon, Sand Digger, Dune Man, Big Blue)

1. metallic silver with red interior, "Hi Ho Silver!" .... $9 – 12

Hi-Tailer Team Matchbox Racer, 3", #56, 1974; BR 33-34, 1986

1. white, unpainted base .... $8 – 10
2. white, red base .... $9 – 12
3. lemon, China cast, Super GT BR 33-34, 1986 .... $4 – 5
4. yellow, China cast, Super GT BR 33- 34, 1986 .... $4 – 5
5. white, China cast, Super GT BR 33- 34, 1986 .... $4 – 5

Highway Fire Pumper, #1, 2003

1. metallic red with white plastic parts, 2003 Sky Fire #1 .... $1 – 2

Highway Maintenance Truck (see Chevrolet Highway Maintenance Truck)

Hillman Minx, $2^5/_8$", #43, 1958

1. green with metal wheels .. $200 – 225
2. blue-gray with gray roof, metal wheels .... $40 – 50
3. blue-gray with gray roof, gray plastic wheels .... $40 – 50
4. turquoise with ivory roof, gray plastic wheels .... $30 – 40

Holden Commodore, #54, 1997, Australia; #64, 1998, international; #11, 2000, international

1. "50," unpainted, rubber tires on chrome rims, promotional .... $16 – 24
2. "50th Anniversary," metallic silver, rubber tires on chrome rims, promotional .... $16 – 24
3. "99 Holden Commodore," pumpkin orange, 1998 Motor Sports series, international issue .... $4 – 5
4. "Australia's First," metallic silver, rubber tires on chrome rims, Australian Inaugural issue .... $12 – 16
5. "Bombers," red and dark blue, Australia issue .... $4 – 5
6. "Bulldogs 1998," red and black, Australia issue .... $4 – 5
7. "Castrol 11," white, rubber tires on chrome rims, Australia issue ....$16 – 24
8. "Commodore Race Team 25," white, Australia issue .... $4 – 5
9. "Demons 1998," red and dark blue, Australia issue .... $4 – 5
10. "Fremantle 1998," red and green, Australia issue .... $4 – 5
11. "Hawks 1998," yellow and brown, Australia issue .... $4 – 5
12. "Holden," white, 2000 Australian Adventure series, international issue ... $4 – 5

13. "Magpies 1998," white and black, Australia issue .... $4 – 5
14. "Olympic Torch Relay," metallic gray, Australia issue .... $9 – 12
15. "Power 1998," turquoise and black, Australia issue .... $4 – 5
16. "Saints 1998," white and red, Australia issue .... $4 – 5
17. unpainted, rubber tires on chrome rims, Australian Inaugural issue .... $12 – 16

Holden Commodore Police Car, #35, 2001, international

1. blue, "Police," crest and blue designs .... $1 – 2

Holden Pickup, 2⅞", #60, 1977 (similar casting: Holden Ruff Trek)

1. red with "500" labels, yellow motorcycles, red interior .... $9 – 12

2. **red with "500" labels, yellow motorcycles, yellow interior ....$8 – 10**
3. red with "500" labels, olive green motorcycles, red interior .... $12 – 16
4. red with star label, yellow motorcycles, yellow interior .... $20 – 30
5. red with sunburst label, olive motorcycles, red interior .... $12 – 16
6. maroon with "500" labels, yellow motorcycles, orange interior .... $12 – 16
7. metallic blue with "Paris Dakar" labels, yellow motorcycles, yellow interior, French issue .... $40 – 50
8. cream with "Honda" labels, red motorcycles, red interior .... $16 – 24

9. **cream with "Superbike" label, red motorcycles, red interior ......$7 – 9**
10. cream with "Superbike" label, yellow motorcycles, red interior .... $9 – 12
11. cream with "Superbike" label, yellow motorcycles, tan interior .... $7 – 9
12. white with "Superbike" label, red motorcycles, red interior .... $12 – 16

Holden Ruff Trek Pickup, with tires in back, 2⅞", #58, 1983 (similar casting: Holden Pickup)

1. yellow, "Matchbox Rescue Team Support," black cargo, clear windows, red interior, Macau cast, Motor City ..$4 – 5
2. yellow, "Matchbox Rescue Team Support," black cargo, clear windows, red interior, Thailand cast, Motor City ..$4 – 5
3. dark blue, "STP," "Goodyear," black cargo, clear windows, red interior, Macau cast, Team Matchbox ..$50 – 60
4. white, "217," black cargo, amber windows, red interior, Macau cast, Team Matchbox .... $4 – 5

5. **white, "217," black cargo, clear windows, red interior, Macau cast, Team Matchbox ....$4 – 5**
6. white, "7-Up," black cargo, clear windows, red interior, Macau cast, Team Matchbox .... $4 – 5
7. white, "Brut," "Faberge," black cargo, clear windows, black interior, Macau cast, Team Matchbox .... $4 – 5
8. white, "Brut," "Faberge," black cargo, clear windows, red interior, Macau cast, Team Matchbox .... $50 – 60
9. white, "Ruff Trek," black cargo, amber windows, red interior, Macau cast, Japanese issue .... $8 – 10
10. white with flames, black cargo, clear windows, black interior, Macau cast, James Bond gift set .... $9 – 12

11. **metallic tan, "Ruff Trek," black cargo, amber windows, Macau cast ....$3 – 4**
12. brown with red, yellow and blue accents, green cargo, armaments, Macau cast, Roadblasters .... $7 – 9
13. brown with red, yellow and blue accents, green cargo, armaments, Thailand cast, Japanese issue, Tomy box ... $12 – 16

Holden FJ Van, #282, 1995, Australia; #40, 1998, international; #21,1999, international; #14, 2000, international

1. "Auto One," white, Australia issue .... $5 – 6
2. "Automodels for Model Cars 1995," black, Australia issue .... $30 – 40
3. "Automodels for Model Cars 1996," black, Australia issue .... $30 – 40
4. "Bears," burgundy and yellow, Australia issue .... $4 – 5
5. "Bevic," baby blue, Australia issue ....$20 – 30
6. "Blues," white and dark blue, Australia issue .... $4 – 5
7. "Bombers," red and black, Australia issue .... $4 – 5
8. "Bulldogs, red and blue, Australia issue ....$4 – 5
9. "Cats," white and dark blue, Australia issue .... $4 – 5
10. "Coca-Cola Good with Food," green, Avon 2-pack .... $6 – 8
11. "Crows," yellow and dark blue, Australia issue .... $4 – 5
12. "Demons," red and dark blue, Australia issue .... $4 – 5
13. "Dockers," red and green, Australia issue .... $4 – 5
14. "Hawks," brown and yellow, Australia issue .... $4 – 5
15. "Kangaroos," white and dark blue, Australia issue .... $4 – 5
16. "Kids World," white, 1995 Australia issue .... $5 – 6

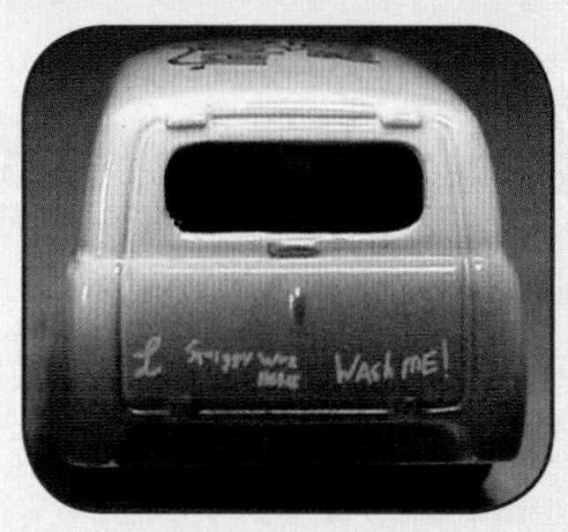

17. **"Laverne & Shirley," "Shotz," Star Cars series, US issue ....$5 – 6**
18. "Lions," red and blue, Australia issue $4 – 5
19. "Magpies," white and black, Australia issue .... $4 – 5
20. "Matchbox," red, 1998 international issue .... $1 – 2
21. "Premiers 1995," white and dark blue, Australia issue .... $4 – 5
22. "Royal Mail," orange-red, Australia issue .... $5 – 6
23. "Saints," light red and black, Australia issue .... $4 – 5
24. "Sunday Age/View," black, Australia issue .... $30 – 40
25. "Sydney," red and white, Australia issue .... $4 – 5

26. "Tigers," yellow and black, Australia issue .... $4 – 5
27. "True Blue," blue, Australia issue ....$4 – 5
28. "West Coast," yellow and blue, Australia issue .... $4 – 5
29. "Your Own Promotional Van," "Matchbox — Your Logo Here," blue, Australia issue .... $20 – 30
30. green with fruit design, 1999 Special Delivery international .... $3 – 4
31. black, no markings, Australia issue .....$5 – 6
32. beige with surfer design, 2000 Australia issue .... $3 – 4

Honda CB750 (see Police Motorcyclist)

Honda ATC, #23, 1985
1. red .... $9 – 12
2. fluorescent green .... $5 – 8

Honda Element, #36, 2004; #47, 2005
1. metallic green, 2004 #36 .... $2 – 3

2. black, 2005 #47 ....$1 – 2
3. metallic orange, 2006 #36 ..... $1 – 2

Honda Ridgeline, #57, 2007

1. metallic light blue, 2007 #57 ..$1 – 2

Honda Motorcycle and Trailer, 2⅞", #38, 1967
1. orange trailer with no decals, blue-green motorcycle, black plastic wheels ....$30 – 40
2. orange trailer with "Honda" decals, blue-green motorcycle, black plastic wheels ....$45 – 60

3. yellow with "Honda" decals, blue-green motorcycle, black plastic wheels ....$30 – 40
4. yellow with "Honda" labels, blue-green motorcycle, black plastic wheels ....$30 – 40
5. orange trailer with blue-green motorcycle, Superfast wheels .... $7 – 9
6. yellow trailer with blue motorcycle, Superfast wheels, 1970 ..... $16 – 24
7. yellow with purple motorcycle, Superfast wheels .... $25 – 35
8. yellow trailer with pink motorcycle, Superfast wheels .... $25 – 35
9. yellow trailer with blue-green motorcycle, Superfast wheels .... $7 – 9

Honda Passport (see Isuzu Rodeo)

Hondarora Motorcycle, 2⅜", #18, 1975
1. red with chrome handlebars, black seat, chrome engine, wire wheels, no rider, England cast .... $12 – 16

2. red with black handlebars and seat, chrome engine, wire wheels, no rider, England cast ....$6 – 8
3. red with black handlebars and seat, chrome engine, mag wheels, no rider, England cast .... $6 – 8
4. red with black handlebars and seat, black engine, mag wheels, no rider, England cast .... $6 – 8
5. red with black handlebars, white seat, chrome engine, wire wheels, no rider, England cast .... $100 – 150
6. orange with black handlebars and seat, chrome engine, wire wheels, no rider, England cast .... $8 – 12
7. dark olive green with black handlebars and seat, black engine, wire wheels, no rider, England cast .... $60 – 80
8. light olive green with black handlebars and seat, black engine, wire wheels, no rider, England cast .... $4 – 6
9. metallic red with black handlebars and seat, black engine, wire wheels, no rider, England cast .... $40 – 50
10. metallic red with black handlebars and seat, chrome engine, wire wheels, no rider, England cast .... $80 – 120
11. metallic green with black handlebars and seat, chrome engine, mag wheels, no rider, England cast .... $6 – 8

12. metallic green with black handlebars and seat, black engine, mag wheels, no rider, England cast ....$6 – 8
13. yellow with black handlebars and seat, chrome engine, mag wheels, no driver, England cast .... $5 – 7
14. yellow with black handlebars and seat, chrome engine, mag wheels, tan driver, England cast .... $5 – 7
15. yellow with black handlebars and seat, chrome engine, mag wheels, brown driver, England cast .... $5 – 7
16. yellow with black handlebars and seat, chrome engine, mag wheels, green driver, England cast .... $60 – 80
17. yellow with black handlebars and seat, chrome engine, mag wheels, tan driver, Macau cast .... $4 – 6
18. metallic silver with black handlebars and seat, black engine, mag wheels, red rider, Macau cast .... $9 – 12
19. metallic silver with black handlebars, dark gray seat, black engine, mag wheels, red rider, Macau cast ...$9 – 12
20. orange with black handlebars and seat, chrome engine, mag wheels, tan rider, Macau cast .... $4 – 6

Horse Box (see AEC Ergomatic Horse Box, Bedford Horse Box)

Horse Drawn Milk Float, 2¼", #7, 1955
1. orange with silver bottles, metal wheels, made in England .... $300 – 400

2. orange with white bottles, metal wheels, made in England $90 – 120
2. orange with orange bottles, metal wheels, made in England ... $90 – 120
3. orange with gray plastic wheels, made in England .... $150 – 175

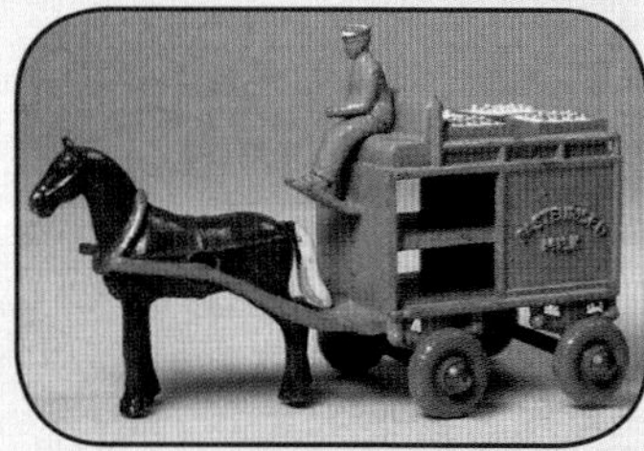

4. orange, 1988 40th Anniversary Gift Set, made in China ....$9 – 12
5. light blue, 1991 Matchbox Originals, made in China .... $4 – 6

Hospital Helicopter/Rescue Helicopter, #63, 2002; #13, 2003; #48, 2004

1. white metal upper, blue plastic lower and tail, red and blue "Med Alarm," #63 Rescue Helicopter, 2002 ..$1 - 2

2. black metal upper, red plastic lower and tail, red and yellow, #13 Hospital Helicopter, 2003 Hospital ...$1 - 2

3. metallic blue upper, white lower, orange "Shuttle" and graphics, 2007 5-pack K9613 ....$1 - 2

4. olive green with dark gray tail and runners, red windows and prop, 2007 5-pack K9407 ....$1 - 2

Hot Chocolate Volkswagen Beetle, $2^{13}/_{16}$", #46, 1982; Dragon Wheels, #43, 1972 (similar castings: Beetle Streaker, Big Blue, Dragon Wheels, Dune Man, Hi Ho Silver, Sand Digger, Volks Dragon)

1. black with metallic brown sides, no roof stripes, "Hot Chocolate" on base, Hong Kong cast .... $9 – 12

2. black with metallic brown sides, white roof stripes, "Hot Chocolate" on base, Hong Kong cast ......$5 - 6
3. metallic blue, "Big Blue," "Beetle Streaker" on base, Macau cast .... $4 – 5
4. metallic blue, "Big Blue," "Beetle Streaker" on base, Hong Kong cast ... $4 – 5
5. blue, "Big Blue," "Beetle Streaker" on base, Hong Kong cast .... $4 – 5
6. green, "Dragon Wheels" tampo, "Beetle Streaker" on base, China cast, Premiere Collection #13 .... $5 – 6
7. green, "Dragon Wheels" label, England cast .... $16 – 24

Hot Head, fire truck with fireman's hat, #28, 2004 (MBG39)

1. red truck with chrome hat, 2004 Ultra Heroes .... $3 – 4

Hot Points Challenger (see Dodge Challenger/Mitsubishi Galant Eterna)

Hot Rocker, 3", #67, 1973 (similar casting: Ford Capri, Maxi Taxi)

1. metallic lime green .... $12 – 16
2. metallic green .... $12 – 16

3. orange-red ....$12 - 16

Hot Rod Draguar, $2^{13}/_{16}$", #36, 1970

1. metallic red .... $16 – 24
2. metallic pink .... $16 – 24

Hot Smoker, Roman Numeral V, 1978 (variation of #70 Dodge Dragster, 1971 and #74 Orange Peel Dodge Charger, 1981)

1. yellow, Roman Numeral Limited Edition ....$9 – 12

Hovercraft, $3^{1}/_{8}$", #2, 1976

1. metallic light green ....$5 - 10
2. avocado green, Adventure 2000.. 8 – 12

Hovercraft, $2^{7}/_{8}$", #62, 2001; #35, 2002 (see Fire Hovercraft)

Hovercraft SRN6, 3", #72, 1972

1. white .... $6 – 8

Hoveringham Tipper, $2^{7}/_{8}$", #17, 1963

1. red cab, orange tipper .....$15 - 20

Hummer/Humvee, small opening rear hatch, #3, 1994; #48, 1998; #53, 2000; #32, 2002

1. army green with white star on doors and hood, "A-4873-2," with roof-mounted gun, 1996 ....$1 - 2
2. army green with brown and black camouflage, with roof-mounted gun, 1996 5-pack .... $2 – 4

3. army green with yellow lettering, roof-mounted gun, #81, 1999 Military Patrol series 17 ....$1 - 2
4. army green, "Unit 5 Communications," with roof-mounted gun, Real Talkin' ....$1 – 2
5. army green, green hubs with rubber tires, with roof-mounted gun, Premiere Collection .... $5 – 6

6. **metallic green, no gun, with roof-mounted gun, 2002 Cool Rides ..$2 – 4**
7. dark green with roof-mounted gun, "Gen IV," "The Lost World," Jurassic Park play set .... $4 – 5

8. **khaki with dark brown star on doors and hood, "A-4873-2," with roof-mounted gun, 1998 ....$1 – 2**

9. **khaki with light green and tan camouflage, no gun, Battle Kings Sahara Strike set, 2006, K5529 .....$1 – 2**

10. **khaki with green and brown camouflage, with roof-mounted gun, 5-pack .... $1 – 2**

11. **khaki with mud splash, "Alpha Co.," with roof-mounted gun, 2000 Military ....$1 – 2**
12. khaki with mud splash, "Alpha Co.," with roof-mounted gun, "Matchbox 2000," 2000 Military .... $3 – 4

13. **khaki with brown camouflage, roof-mounted gun, 1995 ....$1 – 2**

14. **khaki with brown and white camouflage, bright orange vertical bar on rear hatch, with roof-mounted gun .... $2 – 4**

15. **khaki with brown and white camouflage, bright orange cross on rear hatch, with roof-mounted gun, 1994 ....$2 – 4**

16. **black with green and brown camouflage, with roof-mounted gun, 5-pack ....$1 – 2**
17. gray with brown and white camouflage, pink cross, with roof-mounted gun .... $1 – 2

18. **white with blue hood, "Police," "Police Unit 7," with roof-mounted gun, 1996 Police 5-pack ....$1 – 2**

19. **white with gray and army green camouflage, with roof-mounted gun, 1997 Tundra Defense Force 5-pack ....$1 – 2**

Hummer H1 Rescue Vehicle, with large opening compartment, ATV molded into interior, #33, 2002; #65, 2003

1. metallic red with opening metallic gray hatch, "Matchbox FDMB" on shield with flame graphics, "14," 2001 Action Launcher Fire Truck set .... $3 – 4
2. yellow with opening white hatch, burning cityscape and fireman graphics, 2003 Pumper Squad .... $1 – 2
3. fluorescent yellow #65, 2003 .. $1 – 2

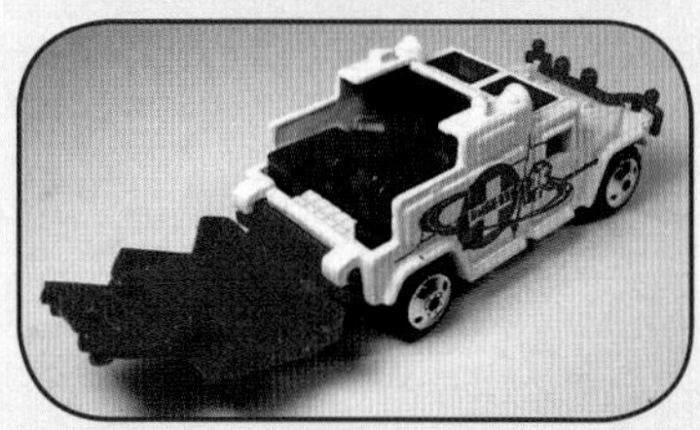

4. **white with opening red hatch, black interior, red and blue "BASE 33," 2002 Ultimate Rescue ....$1 – 2**

5. **white with gray camouflage graphics, black hatch, Battle Kings Polar Rescue set, 2006, K5537 ....$1 – 2**

Hummer H2 SUV Concept, #73, 2003; #35, 2005; #75, 2006

1. **yellow, 2003 Car Shop ....$1 – 2**

2. **gray, no graphics 2005 #35 ....$1 – 2**

3. gray with Spongebob Squarepants graphics, 2006 Nickelodeon 5-pack H5774 .... $2 – 3

4. white with gray and black camouflage, 2006 #75 .... $1 – 2

Hummer H3, #25, 2005; #59, 2006; #73, 2007

1. yellow, 2005 #25 .... $1 – 2

2. black, 2005 10-pack #2 (also sold as #25 in 2006 blister pack) .. $1 – 2

3. metallic gray, 2006 #59 ...... $1 – 2

4. flat dark gray, "03," pale gray interior, 2006 5-pack J4679 .... $1 – 2

5. metallic dark blue, dark gray interior, 2006 #59 .... $1 – 2

6. white, "National Park Forest Ranger" graphics, 2007 #73 .... $1 – 2

Hummer Rescue Vehicle (see Hummer H1 Rescue Vehicle)

Hummer School Bus, #16, 2001; #69, 2002; #52, 2003; #42, 2004; #44, 2005 (MB614)

1. yellow, "Burton Hill Elementary Buffalos," 2001 City Dudes .... $1 – 2

2. yellow, "Bulldogs Football," "State Champions 2002," 2002 Kids' Cars of the Year .... $1 – 2

3. yellow, "Hero City Elementary Bears," 2003 School Time .... $1 – 2

4. yellow, "Hero City Elementary Bears" on white banner, 2004 #42 .... $1 – 2

5. white, "Blue's Clues" graphics ... $2 – 3

Humvee (also see Hummer)

Humvee, #375, 1998, Taco Bell; Matchbox mold retooled by Strottman International Inc. through a licensing agreement with Mattel. Strottman manufactures toy premiums for Taco Bell. Base is marked "Made in China by S.I.I."

1. black with white and red swirls, metallic silver windows, Taco Bell premium .... $4 – 5

Huski-Patrol, snowmobile, #24, 2004

1. chrome cowl, red seat, yellow base, 2004 Ultra Heroes .... $3 – 4

Hydroplane, #44, 1999: #10, 2000; #39, 1999, international

1. red, "Coca-Cola" and polar bears design, Premiere Collection .... $5 – 6
2. red, "Coca-Cola," "www.cocacolastore.com," polar bears design, Color Comp promotional .... $60 – 80

3. red with white base, black wing, with purple, blue, and white graphics, 1999 Ocean .... $1 – 2

4. dark blue, "492," red and white design, red base, metallic gray wing, black wheels, 5-pack .... $1 – 2
5. dark blue, "492," red and white design, red base, metallic gray wing, white wheels, 5-pack .... $4 – 5

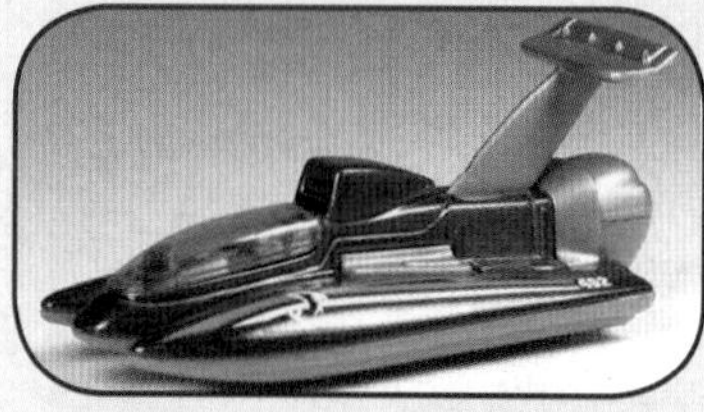

6. bright blue, "492," orange and white design, orange base, metallic gray wing, 2000 Ocean Explorer .. $1 – 2

7. bright blue, "492," "Matchbox 2000," orange and white design, orange base, metallic gray wing, 2000 Ocean Explorer .... $3 – 4

I

Ice Breaker, #61, 2002; #38, 2004

1. metallic red hull, white cabin, blue deck and stacks, white cross, illustration on sides, 2002 Rescue Rookies, 2003 Hero City .... $1 – 2

2. blue hull, white cabin, aqua deck and stacks, Spongebob Squarepants graphics, 2003 Nickelodeon 5-pack .... $1 – 2

3. yellow hull, blue deck, red cabin, green rhinoceros and other graphics on side .... $1 – 2
4. sky blue hull, red hull, white cabin, Clifford the Big Red Dog graphics ... $1 – 2
5. blue hull; red deck; silver cabin; "Hero City Guard Unit"; red, white, and light blue graphics .... $1 – 2

Ice Cream Canteen (Commer Ice Cream Canteen)

Ice Cream Truck, #65, 2002; #60, 2003; #59, 2004

1. white with yellow plastic base, red door, "Jimmie's Ice Cream," 2002 Kids' Cars of the Year .... $1 – 2

2. white with blue trim, ice cream cone graphics, 2003 Kid's Shoppes ... $1 – 2

Ice Maker (see Zamboni)

Ikarus Coach, #67, 1987; #2, 1998, international

1. "2384584," "FT," Chinese pictograms, white with green roof, tinted windows, China cast, Chinese issue .... $40 – 50
2. "Airport Limousine 237," white and orange with white roof, tinted windows, China cast, Japanese gift set .. $9 – 12
3. "Canary Island," white with white roof, tinted windows, China cast, UK issue .... $8 – 10

4. "City Line Tourist," white with green roof, tinted windows, China cast .... $3 – 4

5. "Down The Shore Tours of New Jersey," light blue .... $1 – 2

6. "España," white with white roof, tinted windows, China cast .... $1 – 2

7. "Gibraltar," white with red roof, clear windows, Macau cast, Spain issue .... $6 – 8
8. "Gibraltar," white with red roof, tinted windows, China cast, Spain issue .... $6 – 8
9. "Ikarus," cream with cream roof, tinted windows .... $3 – 4
10. "Marti," beige with brown roof, tinted windows, China cast, Switzerland issue .... $9 – 12

11. "Shuttle," purple with purple roof, tinted windows, China cast, 5-pack .... $1 – 2

12. "Voyager," white with orange roof, amber windows, Macau cast ... $3 – 4

13. "Voyager," white with orange roof, clear windows, Macau cast .. $3 – 4

14. "Voyager," white with orange roof, tinted windows, China cast .... $3 – 4
15. "Voyager," white with orange roof, tinted windows, Macau cast .... $3 – 4
16. "World Cup Tour Bus," white with red roof, blue windows, China cast, 5-pack .... $1 – 2
17. yellow with white roof, sunset scene, tinted windows, China cast, 1998 Around the Town international .. $1 – 2
18. light blue, Matchbox Across America 50th Birthday Series #3 New Jersey — Northeastern Collection .... $4 – 5
19. white with red roof, smiling face design, tinted windows, China cast, 5-pack .. $4 – 5
20. white with white roof, no markings, Graffic Traffic .... $9 – 12
21. white with white roof, tinted windows, China cast, ASAP promotional blank .... $30 – 40

IMSA Mazda (see Mazda IMSA)

IMSA Mustang (see Ford Mustang IMSA)

Indy Racer, #65, 1985 (see F1 Racer, #16, 1984)

Inflatable Raft and Trailer, #793, 1984, part of Two-Pack except where noted

1. red deck, white hull, black motor, blue "SR," England cast, black trailer, England cast .... $6 – 8

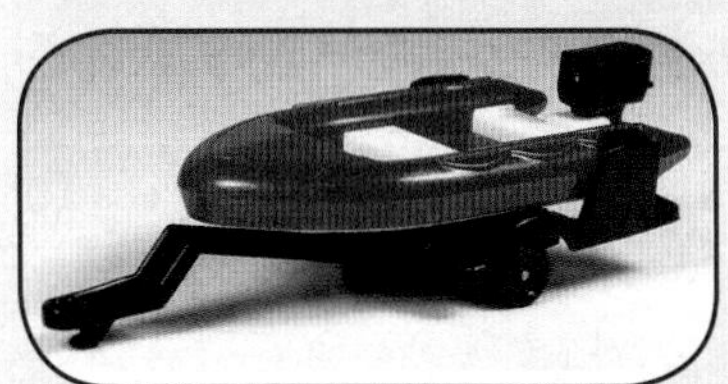

2. red deck, white hull, black motor, 1999 Beach Fun 5-pack .... $2 – 3

3. red deck, yellow hull, black motor, "Red Valley Camp," no origin cast, black trailer, no origin cast, 1997 Land Sea & Air 5-pack .... $1 – 2

4. red deck, yellow hull, black motor, "Red Valley Camp," no origin cast, black trailer, China cast, 1997 Land Sea & Air 5-pack .... $1 – 2

5. orange deck, black hull, black motor, "R1," no origin cast, white trailer, "Rescue" and stripes, no origin cast ... $3 – 4
6. orange deck, black hull, black motor, blue "SR," no origin cast, black trailer, no origin cast .... $3 – 4
7. orange deck, black hull, white motor, anchor emblem, no origin cast, white trailer with black and orange stripes, no origin cast .... $3 – 4
8. orange deck, black hull, white motor, no origin cast, white trailer with dark blue and red stripes, no origin cast ... $3 – 4
9. orange deck, metallic gray hull, white motor, "Rescue," no origin cast, white trailer with anchor design, no origin cast .... $3 – 4
10. orange deck, white hull, black motor, blue "SR," England cast, black trailer, England cast .... $3 – 4
11. orange deck, white hull, black motor, blue "SR," Macau cast, black trailer, Macau cast .... $3 – 4
12. orange deck, white hull, black motor, red "SR," England cast, black trailer, England cast .... $3 – 4

13. orange deck, white hull, black motor, England cast, black trailer, England cast ....$3 - 4
14. lemon yellow deck, white hull, black motor, blue "SR," England cast, black trailer, England cast .... $6 – 8
15. dark blue deck, gray hull, white motor, no origin cast, white trailer with blue and red stripes, no origin cast ... $3 – 4
16. black deck, orange hull, white motor, no origin cast, black trailer, "2," no origin cast .... $3 – 4

International 4700 Armored Car, #58, 2000; #17, 2001; #38, 2003; #53, 2001, international; #75, 2005

1. lime green with piggy bank illustration, "MHC Bank," 2003 Mom and Pop Shops .... $1 – 2
2. lime green with piggy bank illustration, "MHC Bank," 2003 Hero City 10-pack #2 .... $1 – 2

3. metallic blue-gray, "Mr. Krabs" and cartoon illustration, 2003 Nickelodeon Spongebob Squarepants 5-pack ..$1 - 2

4. light gray, "Matchbox Armored Car Service," blue windows, #58, 2000 Speedy Delivery ....$1 - 2
5. light gray, "Matchbox Armored Car Service," "Matchbox 2000," blue windows, #58, 2000 Speedy Delivery .... $3 – 4
6. pearl gray, red and yellow crest, tinted windows, 5-pack .... $1 – 2
7. blue, "Money Mobile," 2001 City Dudes #17 .... $1 – 2
8. 2002 Matchbox Across America 50th Birthday series #36 Nevada — Western Collection .... $5 – 6
9. beige and brown, "AMSA," blue windows, Color Comp promotional, repainted, rivets glued .... $40 – 50
10. white, "Selmac Savings," blue windows, ASAP promotional .... $80 – 120
11. white, no markings, blue windows, ASAP promotional blank .... $30 – 40
12. metallic dark gray, 2005 #75 .. $1 – 2

13. black with red graphics, orange lettering "iNAT International Armored Transport," 2007 #38 ....$1 - 2

International CXT, #29, 2006; #60, 2007

1. yellow, 2006 #29 ....$1 - 2

2. blue with red and white graphics, 2007 #60 ....$1 - 2
3. red, 2007 Superfast #73 .... $3 – 4

International Fire Pumper, #76, 1999; #30, 2000; #27, 2002; #66, 1999, international; #58, 2005

1. red, "73rd Apple Blossom Festival" .... $9 – 12
2. red, "Fort Wayne Fire Dept.," rubber tires on chrome rims, Premiere Collection .... $16 – 24
3. red, "Hot Springs Vol. Fire Dept.," Color Comp promotional .... $20 – 30

4. red, "Matchbox" logo, "Station 5," yellow and white trim, 2003 Hero City 5-pack #1 ....$1 - 2
5. red, "MB Fire Dept No. 7," stripes, door crest, 1999 Fire Rescue .... $1 – 2
6. red, "Metro Alarm," black stripe, 5-pack ....$1 – 2
7. red with white roof and back section, stripes, door crest, 1999 Fire Rescue international .... $3 – 4

8. red with yellow flame and hood trim, Kidde First Alert Carbon Monoxide Detector on-package premium ..$4 - 5 (+ cost of various detectors/alarms if still in package)

9. metallic red, "Fire Hunter AMR 977," yellow, red and black design, 2002 Red Hot Heroes ....$1 - 2
10. metallic red with white plastic parts, 2003 Sky Fire #1 .... $1 – 2

11. orange-red with self-stick set of labels, McDonald's Happy Meal premium .... $1 – 2

12. orange-yellow, "6532," "54," black bands, "Matchbox" in circular logo, 2000 5 Alarm 5-pack .... $1 – 2

13. yellow, "Metro Alarm" graphics, "WR-1168," 2003 Hero City 5-pack #7 .... $1 – 2

14. white, "Engine Co. 34," 5-pack ... $3 – 4

15. white, "Engine Co. 77," pale green trim, black detail, 1998 Emergency Rescue 5-pack .... $1 – 2

16. white and red, "Radio E-75" ... $9 – 12

17. white, "99 Pumper," 2005 10-pack #2 .... $1 – 2

18. metallic gold, "MB Fire Dept. No. 7," "Matchbox 2000," 2000 Fire Fighters .... $3 – 4
19. metallic gold, "MB Fire Dept. No. 7," 2000 Fire Fighters .... $1 – 2
20. olive green with white roof, 2005 #58 .... $1 – 2

International Fire Truck (see International Fire Pumper)

International Pumper (see International Fire Pumper)

Iron Fairy Crane, 3", #42, 1969

1. red with yellow crane, black plastic wheels .... $12 – 16

2. red with yellow crane, Superfast wheels, 1970 .... $70 – 90
3. red with lime green crane, Superfast wheels .... $300 – 400
4. orange-red with yellow boom, Superfast wheels .... $50 – 60
5. orange-red with lime green, Superfast wheels .... $50 – 60

Iso Grifo, 3", #14, 1968; BR 3-4, 1985

1. metallic blue with light blue interior, black plastic wheels on chrome hubs, 1968 .... $6 – 9
2. enamel dark blue with light blue interior, Superfast wheels, 1969 ..... $20 – 25
3. enamel dark blue with dark blue interior, Superfast wheels, 1969 ..... $20 – 25
4. enamel dark blue with white interior, Superfast wheels, 1969 ..... $20 – 25
5. metallic dark blue with white interior, Superfast wheels .... $20 – 25

6. enamel light blue with white interior, Superfast wheels .... $20 – 25

7. enamel blue with white interior, Superfast wheels .... $20 – 25
8. enamel pale blue with white interior, Superfast wheels, Japan issue ...$20 – 25
9. cream with black windows, England cast, Super GT BR 3-4, 1985 .. $3 – 5
10. cream with translucent white windows, England cast, Super GT BR 3-4, 1985 .... $12 – 15
11. yellow with black windows, England cast, Super GT BR 3-4, 1985 .... $8 – 10
12. light blue with black windows, England cast, Super GT BR 3-4, 1985 .. $4 – 6
13. metallic blue with black windows, England cast, Super GT BR 3-4, 1985 .... $3 – 8
14. metallic blue with translucent white windows, England cast, Super GT BR 3-4, 1985 .... $12 – 15
15. bright green with black windows, China cast, Neon Racers BR 3-4, 1985 .....$3 – 5
16. metallic blue with black windows, China cast, Super GT BR 3-4, 1985 .... $8 – 10
17. cream with black windows, China cast, Super GT BR 3-4, 1985 .... $6 – 8
18. yellow with black windows, China cast, Super GT BR 3-4, 1985 .... $3 – 5

Isuzu Amigo, 2⁷⁄₈", #52, 1991

1. red, "Amigo," silver and orange stripes .... $3 – 4
2. light yellow, pink stripes and patterns, gray interior, Dream Machines 3-pack .... $3 – 4
3. metallic blue, "Isuzu Amigo," gray interior .... $6 – 8

4. dark blue with green design, gray interior, 1999 Beach Fun 5-pack .... $1 – 2

5. purple, "Hadrosaur," skeleton design, black interior .... $1 – 2

6. white, "Surf Shop," "Surf's Up," orange and blue design, black interior, 1999 Beach .... $1 – 2

7. white with blue design, fluorescent orange interior, 1997 Land Sea & Air 5-pack .... $1 – 2

8. mustard yellow with "Go Diego Go" and graphics, 2006 Nickelodeon 5-pack H4108 .... $1 – 2

Isuzu Rodeo/Vauxhall Opel Frontera/ Honda Passport, #56, 1995; #100, 2000; #59, 1995, international

1. red, "Power Parts 21," blue and white accents, "Rodeo" on gray base .... $3 – 4
2. metallic red, no markings, "Frontera" on black base .... $3 – 4

3. yellow, "555 — RES — Q Roadside Rescue," "Rodeo" on black base, 2000 On the Road Again ...... $1 – 2
4. yellow, "555 — RES — Q Roadside Rescue," "Matchbox 2000," "Rodeo" on black base, 2000 On the Road Again .... $3 – 4
5. green, "Brontosaurus" and skeleton, no name on gray base, 5-pack ...... $1 – 2
6. blue, red tail lights, "Opel Frontera" on black base, 1995 Germany issue .$4 – 5

7. black with bright pink mud splash pattern on sides only, "Rodeo" on gray base .... $1 – 2

8. black with bright pink mud splash pattern on sides and hood, "Rodeo" on gray base .... $1 – 2
9. black with red and white design, "Rodeo" on gray base, 5-pack .... $1 – 2
10. black with red and white design, "Frontera" on gray base, 5-pack .... $1 – 2
11. metallic gray, no markings, "Frontera" on black base .... $1 – 2
12. pink-beige, "Operations Safari 1999," "Matchbox," green camouflage, "Rodeo" on black base .... $20 – 25

13. white, "Wilderness Tours," "Rodeo" on turquoise base, Wilderness Tours 5-pack .... $1 – 2

14. white with bright pink mud splash pattern on sides only, "Rodeo" on gray base .... $3 – 4
15. white with brown mud splash pattern on sides only, "Frontera" on black base .... $4 – 5
16. white with orange and blue design, "Frontera" on black base, international issue .... $3 – 4
17. white with no markings, "Frontera" on black base .... $12 – 16
18. white with no markings, "Frontera" on turquoise base, Wilderness Tours 5-pack .... $1 – 2
19. metallic gold, no markings, "Rodeo" on gray base, 1997 75 Challenge ...$6 – 12

J

J. R. Bumper, #10, 2004

1. brown, orange and blue, 2004 Ultra Heroes .... $3 – 4

Jaguar 3.4 Litre Sedan, 2½", #65, 1959
1. metallic blue, gray plastic wheels .... $30 – 40
2. blue, gray plastic wheels ...... $30 – 40

Jaguar 3.8 Litre Saloon, 2⅝", #65, 1962
1. red with gray wheels .... $25 – 35
2. red with silver wheels .... $35 – 45
3. metallic red with silver wheels ...$35 – 45

4. red with black wheels ...... $20 – 30

Jaguar D-Type, green, 2³⁄₁₆", #41, 1957
1. metal wheels, "41" decal ..... $30 – 40
2. gray plastic wheels, "41" decal ...$40 – 50

Jaguar D-Type, green, 2⁷⁄₁₆", #41, 1960
1. gray plastic wheels, "41" decal .... $40 – 50
2. silver plastic wheels, "19" decal .... $125 – 150
3. black plastic tires on spoked hubs .... $40 – 50
4. black plastic tires on red hubs .... $175 – 200

Jaguar E-Type, 2⅝", #32, 1962
1. metallic red, clear windows, gray plastic tires on wire wheels .... $110 – 140
2. metallic red, green windows, gray plastic tires on wire wheels ..... $80 – 110

3. metallic red, clear windows, black plastic tires on wire wheels (with or without Union Jack on roof) .$60 – 80
4. metallic bronze, clear windows, black tires on wire wheels .... $75 – 100

Jaguar E-Type Coupe 1961, #4, 2006; #28, 2007

1. red with silver interior, red plastic chassis, 2006 #4 .... $1 – 2

2. pea green with chrome interior, pea green chassis, 2007 #28 ..... $1 – 2

3. black, 2007 Superfast #58, J6620 .... $4 – 5

4. white, 2007 5-pack K9612 .. $1 – 2

Jaguar Mark 10, metallic tan, 2¾", #28, 1964

1. gray plastic wheels .... $140 – 160

2. black plastic wheels .... $15 – 20

Jaguar SS-100, 3", #47, 1982

1. red with partially painted hood, England cast .... $9 – 12
2. red with red hood, England cast .. $4 – 5

3. red with red hood, Macau cast .... $4 – 5

4. blue with gray hood, Macau cast .... $5 – 6
5. dark green, Thailand cast, UK on-package premium, US gift set .. $12 – 16
6. metallic gray with dark gray hood, Thailand cast, gift set .... $4 – 5

Jaguar XJ-6, 3", #1, 1987; #41, 1987; #14, 2001, UK (similar casting: Jaguar XJ6 Police)

1. metallic red, tan interior, doors open .... $1 – 2

2. green, "Redoxon," "Jaguar," maroon interior, doors open, Hong Kong issue .... $20 – 25
3. dark green, black and tan interior, detailed trim, doors don't open, chrome windows, rubber tires on gray rims, Ultra Class .... $9 – 12
4. blue, tan interior, doors don't open, Show Stoppers .... $3 – 4
5. blue, gray interior, British flag, 2001 Union Jack series, UK issue ..... $4 – 5
6. metallic blue, tan interior, detailed trim, doors don't open, chrome windows, rubber tires on gray rims, World Class .... $3 – 4
7. black, "W&M" and crest, maroon interior, doors open, on-package premium, UK issue .... $30 – 40
8. metallic dark gray, black and red interior, detailed trim, doors don't open, chrome windows, rubber tires on gray rims, JC Penney Premiere Collection .... $4 – 5
9. metallic silver with white interior .. $3 – 4
10. white, black interior, doors open, part of King Size set .... $9 – 12
11. white with no markings, Graffic Traffic .... $6 – 8

Jaguar XJ-6 Police, 3", #1, 1991; #27, 1998, international (similar casting: Jaguar XJ6)

1. white, "Police," blue and yellow stripes .... $4 – 5

2. white, "Police," orange and blue shield, blue checkerboard design, blue interior, doors don't open .. $1 – 2

Jaguar XJ-220, 3⅛", #31, 1993; #75, 1998, international; #12, 2001, international

1. blue with white interior, "Old Eight," UK issue .... $80 – 120
2. blue with yellow and green accents, 1997 .... $1 – 2

3. metallic blue with white interior, clear windows, 1993 .... $1 – 2

4. blue with ivory interior, clear windows, Jaguar logo .... $4 – 5
5. blue with white interior, tinted windows, "50," "XJ220," gift set .... $4 – 5
6. chrome plated with white interior, amber windows, Graffic Traffic .... $3 – 4
7. fluorescent orange with black accents, 1996 .... $1 – 2
8. fluorescent yellow and orange with blue interior, bright blue design, 1994 .... $1 – 2

9. gradient metallic red to black with yellow interior, 2001 Union Jack series, international issue .... $1 – 2

10. green with gray and black interior, rubber tires on chrome rims, Premiere Collection #19 .... $4 – 5

11. green with ivory interior, tinted windows, white and lime green flames .... $1 – 2

12. green with tan interior, "Jaguar," 1998 Street Cruisers series, international issue .... $1 – 2
13. metallic blue with gray and black interior, rubber tires on chrome rims, international Premiere Collection #2 .. $4 – 5
14. metallic gold with black interior, clear windows, 1997 75 Challenge .. $6 – 12
15. metallic gray with blue interior, tinted windows, blue and yellow design .. $1 – 2
16. metallic gray with red interior, clear windows, 1993 Show Stoppers .... $3 – 4
17. metallic maroon with gray and black interior, rubber tires on chrome rims, Premiere Collection #10 .... $4 – 5
18. metallic purple with chrome windows, rubber tires on chrome rims, 1995 World Class .... $3 – 5
19. metallic silver-blue with chrome interior, 1998 Street Cruisers, international issue .... $3 – 4

20. metallic turquoise with yellow interior, tinted windows, yellow and white flames .... $1 – 2

21. red with silver-gray interior, British flag and white band, 1997 .... $3 – 4

Jaguar XK6 2006, #3, 2006; #21, 2007

1. **green, 2005 Superfast #57 ... $3 - 4**
2. metallic silver, 2006 #3 .... $1 - 2
3. white, 2007 5-pack K9615 ..... $1 - 2
4. black, 2007 #21 .... $1 - 2

Jaguar XK8 Convertible 1997, #71, 1998; #48, 1999; #43, 1999, international; #2, 2000, international; #2, 2001, UK; #43, 2002, international; #24, 2006

1. **metallic red with gray interior, silver headlights, 1999 Roadsters international .... $4 - 5**
2. metallic red with metallic gray interior, silver headlights, 10-spoke wheels, 2002 Roadsters international .. $3 - 4
3. metallic red with tan and black interior, detailed trim, rubber tires on chrome rims, 1998 First Editions .... $5 - 6
4. green with gray interior, no markings, 5-spoke wheels .... $3 - 4
5. green with gray interior, no markings, 10-spoke wheels, Target Eggmobile 3-pack .... $9 - 12
6. green with metallic gray interior, white Jaguar design, 1999 Drop Tops ... $1 - 2
7. green with tan interior, no markings, Germany issue .... $4 - 5
8. green with cream interior, 2005 Superfast #69 .... $3 - 4

9. **green with butterscotch interior, no markings, #24, 2007, K2614 .... $1 - 2**

10. **metallic blue, silver "Jaguar XK8" and design and interior, 1998 Street Cruisers .... $1 - 2**
11. metallic blue with black interior, red tail lights, white Matchbox logo, 2003 Auto Carrier Launcher 5-pack .... $1 - 2
12. **metallic light blue with silver headlights, black interior, 2001 Eurosports 5-pack .... $1 - 2**
13. unpainted with pale tan interior, rubber tires on chrome rims, 1998 First Editions .... $5 - 6

Jaguar XK-120, 3", #22, 1984

1. **black with orange interior, Collectors Choice, White Rose Collectibles .... $3 - 5**

2. **black with light brown interior, Select Class #3 .... $4 - 5**
3. dark green with red interior, no markings .... $4 - 5

4. **dark green with tan and brown interior, rubber tires on chrome rims, Premiere Collection #3 .... $4 - 5**
5. dark green with tan interior, no markings, China issue .... $80 - 120
6. pale olive with maroon interior .. $3 - 4
7. ivory with red interior, "414" .... $1 - 2
8. red with white interior, Show Stoppers .... $3 - 4
9. red with white interior, "Coca-Cola," rubber tires on chrome rims, Premiere Collection .... $4 - 5

10. **red with light brown interior, rubber tires on chrome rims, Premiere Collection #6 .... $4 - 5**
11. red with tan interior, no markings, China issue .... $80 - 120
12. white with chrome windshield, rubber tires on chrome rims, World Class .... $6 - 8

13. **white with blue and fluorescent orange flames, Dream Machines .... $4 - 5**

Jaguar XK-140 Coupe, 2 3/8", #32, 1957
1. ivory .... $40 - 50
2. red .... $75 - 100
3. Matchbox Originals replica, 1993, black with silver metal wheels .... $3 - 5

Jaguar XK Coupe, #3, 2006; #21, 2007

1. **silver, 2006 #3 .... $1 - 2**

2. **black, 2007 #21 .... $1 - 2**

3. **white, 2007 5-pack K9615 .. $1 - 2**

Jaguar XKE (see Jaguar E-Type)

Javelin AMX (see AMC Javelin AMX)

Javelin AMX Pro Stocker (see AMC Javelin AMX Pro Stocker)

Jeep, #38, 1976, with or without gun, no roof (similar casting: U.S. Mail Jeep, Sleet 'N Snow, Jeep 4x4)
1. light army green, no gun, star in circle label on hood, black hubs .... $20 - 25
2. light army green, no gun, "21*11" label, black hubs .... $9 - 12
3. light army green, with gun, star in circle label on hood, black hubs ...... $9 - 12
4. light army green, with gun, "21*11" label, silver hubs .... $9 - 12
5. light army green, with gun, "21*11" label, black hubs .... $6 - 8
6. green, with gun, "21*11" label, silver hubs, UK issue .... $160 - 240

7. green, with gun, no label, silver hubs, UK issue .... $160 – 240
8. dark army green, no gun, "21*11" label, black hubs .... $70 – 90
9. red, no gun, "Gliding Club," silver hubs, Two-Pack .... $360 – 480
10. yellow, no gun, "Gliding Club," silver hubs, Two-Pack .... $9 – 12
11. yellow, no gun, "Gliding Club," black hubs, Two-Pack .... $9 – 12

Jeep, Army, #38, 1976 (see Jeep, #38)

Jeep 1960, #505, 2001
1. pink with white roof, pink stripes, rubber white wall tires on chrome rims, Matchbox Collectibles Elvis Presley Collection with Graceland diorama ...... $12 – 16

2. olive drab, "Matchbox Collectibles," "The Osbournes with Jack Osbourne" on package .... $4 – 5

Jeep 4x4, with or without roof, 2 7/16", #5, 1982, US; #20, 1982, US; #14, 1984, international; #56, 1990, international (similar castings: US Mail Jeep, 4x4 Jeep Eagle, 4x4 Golden Eagle Off-Road Jeep, Jeep Laredo, Jeep Wrangler)

1. beige with beige roof, camouflage .... $1 – 2
2. beige with black roof, camouflage ... $1 – 2
3. black with red roof, "Laredo," Macau cast .... $14 – 21
4. black with white roof, "Laredo," red and white trim, red interior, Macau cast .... $1 – 2
5. black with white roof, "Laredo," red and white trim, red interior, Hong Kong cast .... $25 – 30
6. black with white roof, "Laredo," red and white trim, red interior, Thailand cast .... $1 – 2
7. blue, "Mork & Mindy," Star Cars ... $6 – 9

8. metallic blue with pink, white, and yellow accents, no roof, 1993 5-pack .... $3 – 4
9. brown, "Golden Eagle," no roof ... $3 – 4
10. pale brown with pale brown roof, "V-9873-3," 5-pack .... $1 – 2
11. metallic copper with red roof, England cast .... $3 – 5
12. army green with black roof, "RB104," play set .... $1 – 2
13. army green with black roof, "V-9872-3" .... $1 – 2

14. army green with army green roof, white star, "V-9872-3," 1996 .... $1 – 2
15. army green with tan roof, camouflage, Macau cast, black metal base, Commando .... $5 – 7
16. army green with tan roof, camouflage, Macau cast, black plastic base, Commando .... $5 – 7
17. army green with plastic armaments, Roadblasters .... $7 – 8
18. light army green with army green roof, red cross, "M*A*S*H," Star Cars .... $5 – 7
19. pale army green with pale olive roof, white cross, "RB104," play set . $1 – 2

20. metallic gray, "Bad to the Bone" on hood, black interior, no roof, 1996 .... $3 – 4

21. fluorescent pink with white interior, no roof, 1993 Dream Machines 3-pack .... $3 – 4
22. metallic purple, "Bad to the Bone" on hood, teal blue interior, no roof, 1995 .... $1 – 2
23. red, "Golden Eagle," metal base, no roof .... $3 – 4
24. red, "Golden Eagle," plastic base, no roof .... $1 – 2
25. red, "Wolff Systems" .... $20 – 25
26. red with white roof, "Golden Eagle," Macau cast .... $9 – 12

27. tan with tan roof, brown camouflage .... $1 – 2
28. dark tan, "Golden Eagle," red roof, England cast .... $21 – 28
29. metallic dark tan, "Golden Eagle," no roof .... $4 – 5
30. metallic light tan, "Golden Eagle," no roof .... $4 – 5
31. metallic turquoise, "Jeep," no roof, White Rose Collector's Choice .. $3 – 4
32. white, "Desert Dawg," red roof, England cast .... $4 – 6
33. white with black cow spots, 5-pack .... $1 – 2
34. yellow "50th Anniversary Jeep" graphics, no roof .... $16 – 24

35. yellow with lime green roof, Macau cast, Matchbox Preschool/Live 'N Learn .... $7 – 9

36. yellow with black roof, pink and blue design on hood, 5-pack .... $1 – 2

37. metallic gold, 75 Challenge .. $12 – 16

38. khaki with brown stripes, black spots on white .... $1 – 2

Jeep Cherokee, 2⅞", #27, 1987; #73, 1994; #1, 1996, international; #36, 1998; #97, 1999

1. red with black lower, gold trim and shield, 5-pack .... $1 – 2
2. red with black lower, "Fire Chief," "FD No. 1," 5-pack .... $1 – 2

3. red with black lower, "Matchbox Fire Chief," 1999 Fire 5-pack ...... $1 – 2

4. red with black lower, "Fire Chief," rubber tires on chrome rims, Premiere Collection #7 .... $4 – 5
5. red with blue lower; blue, white, and gold winged design; 5-pack ...... $1 – 2
6. orange-red with black lower, "Hilti expertise in every case" .... $12 – 16
7. yellow, "Forest Ranger County Park" .... $8 – 10
8. yellow, "BP Chief," green and red stripes, Netherlands issue ... $10 – 12
9. yellow, "Mr. Fixer" .... $1 – 2
10. green, no markings, Thailand cast, Belgium issue .... $20 – 25
11. metallic green with light tan interior and trim, black base, 1997 Rugged Riders 5-pack .... $1 – 2
12. light green to dark brown, "Mr. Fixer," Super Color Changers .... $4 – 5

13. dark green with tan lower, no markings, 1997 Rugged Riders 5-pack, China cast .... $1 – 2

14. blue, "Hellman's," "Best Foods" .... $80 – 120
15. blue with black lower, "Camp Jeep 2000," 5-pack .... $1 – 2
16. turquoise with black lower, "Animal Rescue," 2000 international Rescue .. $1 – 2

17. purple with orange and ivory flames, 1994 .... $1 – 2

18. black with pink-red and white flames .... $1 – 2
19. black, no markings, ASAP promotional blank .... $30 – 40
20. black, "American International Recovery," ASAP promotional ... $120 – 160
21. black, "Linux Solutions," ASAP promotional .... $80 – 120
22. black, "Microsoft," ASAP promotional .... $80 – 120
23. white, "AT&T Network Management Services," ASAP promotional .... $80 – 120
24. white, "Giant," ASAP promotional .... $80 – 120
25. white, "Linux Solutions," ASAP promotional .... $80 – 120
26. white, "Microsoft," ASAP promotional .... $80 – 120
27. white, "National Ski Patrol" .... $9 – 12
28. white, "Quadtrak" .... $4 – 5

29. white, "Rescue EMT," 2000 City Streets 5-pack .... $1 – 2

30. white, "Unix User Conference San Jose, ASAP promotional .... $80 – 120
31. white, "V8 Splash," ASAP promotional .... $120 – 160
32. white with black lower, no markings, ASAP promotional blank ...... $30 – 40

33. white with black lower, "MBX Coast Guard," 2006 5-pack J4673 .. $1 – 2

34. white with blue lower, "Water Works City Division" logo, teal blue wave design, 1999 At Your Service .. $1 – 2

35. white with blue lower, black and orange design, polar bear logo, Launcher 5-pack .... $1 – 2
36. white with dark blue lower, "Rescue EMT," "Dial 911," orange and blue stripes, 2000 City Streets 5-pack .... $1 – 2
37. white with orange lower, blue and red design, Launcher 5-pack .... $1 – 2

38. white with red lower, red flame, gold and black star, "Chief" on sides, 2003 Hero City 5-pack #7 ... $1 – 2

39. beige, "Holiday Club," Two-Pack .. $3 – 4
40. brown, "Mr. Fixer" .... $3 – 5

41. metallic silver with black lower, "Sport," red stripe, 1987 #27 .. $3 – 4

Jeep CJ-5, Standard, 2⅜", #72, 1966

1. yellow with red interior, black plastic tires on plastic wheel hubs, 1966 .... $16 – 20

2. yellow with white interior, black plastic tires on plastic wheel hubs, prototype .... $1,200 – 1,600
3. yellow, Superfast wheels, 1970 .... $35 – 45

Jeep CJ – 6, $2\frac{15}{16}$", #53, 1977
1. red with tan canopy, orange-yellow interior, metallic gray base .... $5 – 6

2. red with tan canopy, orange-yellow interior, unpainted base .... $5 – 6
3. red with tan canopy, orange-yellow interior, unpainted base, black hubs .. $6 – 7
4. red with tan canopy, black interior, unpainted base .... $7 – 8
5. yellow with brown canopy, black interior, black base .... $6 – 7
6. green with tan canopy, orange-yellow interior, unpainted base .... $7 – 8
7. green with tan canopy, orange-yellow interior, metallic gray base .... $7 – 8
8. green with tan canopy, black interior, metallic gray base .... $5 – 6

Jeep Compass, #51, 2004; #23, 2005; #72, 2006 (MB627)
1. metallic green, 2004 #51 .... $3 – 4
2. red, "N Canyon," 2005 #23 .... $1 – 2

3. metallic blue with pale brown mud splash graphics, rally markings, 2005 #72 .... $1 – 2

Jeep Eagle 4x4 (see Jeep 4x4)

Jeep Gladiator Pickup Truck, $2\frac{5}{8}$", #71, 1964
1. red with green interior .... $40 – 50

2. red with white interior ..... $20 – 25

Jeep Golden Eagle Off-Road Jeep (see Jeep 4x4)

Jeep Grand Cherokee, Superfast #64, 2005
1. red, "Camp Jeep 2000," black stripes and design, 5-pack .... $1 – 2
2. red, "Metro Alarm," yellow band, 5-pack .... $1 – 2

3. gradient red, "Hospitality," "Coca-Cola," yellow interior, rubber tires on chrome rims, Matchbox Collectibles Coca-Cola Collection .... $5 – 6

4. black with yellow, red, and white "Metro Alarm" graphics, 2003 Hero City 5-pack #7 .... $1 – 2

5. metallic dark gray, 2005 Superfast #64 .... $4 – 5

Jeep Grand Cherokee with raft on roof, 3", #65, 2000; #22, 2001; #48, 2002; #45, 2000, international

1. yellow with black doors, "H4M," 2006 5-pack J4671 .... $1 – 2

2. pale green with wood grain side panels, gray raft, gray base, 2007 5-pack K9617 .... $1 – 2

3. dark blue with yellow raft, "Action Canyon," 2001 Sun Chasers .. $1 – 2

4. purple with river rafting graphics, yellow raft, 2003 Hero City .. $1 – 2

5. metallic silver with red raft, "Grand Cherokee," 2000 Great Outdoors series, 5-spoke wheels .... $1 – 2
6. metallic silver with red raft, "Grand Cherokee," "Matchbox 2000," 2000 Great Outdoors series, 5-spoke wheels .... $3 – 4
7. metallic silver with red raft, "Grand Cherokee," 2000 Great Outdoors series, 10-spoke wheels ...... $12 – 16

Jeep Grand Cherokee, 2000 Feature Cars, with opening features, designed to replace Premiere Collection
1. red, "FDMB," "EMT," red, KB Toys exclusive .... $9 – 12
2. maroon .... $9 – 12
3. metallic gray, "FDMB," "EMT," KB Toys exclusive .... $9 – 12

Jeep Hot Rod, $2^{5}/_{16}$", #2, 1971

1. pink with green base .... $15 – 20

2. fuchsia with green base ... $20 – 25
3. red with green base .... $20 – 25
4. red with white base .... $15 – 25
5. light olive .... $10 – 15
6. dark olive .... $70 – 80

Jeep Hurricane, 1:58, #43, 2005; #58, 2006 (MB670)

1. bright orange with tan interior, dark gray base and grille, 2007 5-pack K9616 .... $1 – 2

2. olive green with black interior, silver gray base and grille, 2005 #43, 2006 #58 .... $1 – 2

3. metallic dark gray with red interior, silver gray base and grille, 2005 10-pack #2 .... $1 – 2
4. black with metallic gray base, red interior, 2007 Superfast #68 .... $4 – 5

Jeep Laredo (see Jeep 4x4)

Jeep Liberty, 2002; 3", #71, 2001; #69, 2006

1. "Police," red with blue and yellow trim, 2001 .... $4 – 5

2. yellow with Looney Tunes "Back in Action" illustration, Looney Tunes Back in Action 5-pack .... $2 – 3

3. metallic gold with black plastic base, monkey and wrench graphics, 2003 Hero City 5-pack #11 .... $1 – 2

4. dark olive green with pale green mud splash graphics, 2006 #69 .. $1 – 2

5. blue with Superman logo and graphics, 2007 Superman 5-pack .. $2 – 3

Jeep Off-Road 4x4, with black roll cage and winch, white antenna, $2^{7}/_{8}$", #37, 1984 – 1997; #52, 1998; #25, 1994, international; #57, 1998, Germany

1. metallic red, black base, Germany issue .... $5 – 6

2. metallic red, gray base, 1996 Off-Road 5-pack .... $1 – 2
3. pink, "Cool Mud" .... $4 – 5

4. fluorescent orange with black graphics, "Cool Mud," 1997 .... $1 – 2

5. yellow with red flames, 1998 Rugged Riders 5-pack .... $1 – 2
6. yellow with blue roll cage, "Wilderness Tours," Wilderness Tours 5-pack ..$1 – 2

7. yellow with blue roll cage, blue and red circle design, Wilderness Tours 5-pack .... $1 – 2
8. lime green with green roll cage, black antenna, "Jeep" and mud design, 5-pack .... $1 – 2

9. blue with white splash design, 1998 Rough 'N Tough .... $1 – 2

10. pale blue with blue and black graphics, "Cool Mud" .... $4 – 5

11. metallic blue with orange flames, 1997 Rugged Riders 5-pack .. $1 – 2
12. black with red, orange and yellow design .... $3 – 4
13. metallic gray with purple and pink flames, Action System .... $1 – 2
14. beige with green stripes, Action System/Action Pack .... $1 – 2

15. white with blue, red and orange design ....$1 – 2
16. metallic gold, 1997 75 Challenge .... $12 – 16

Jeep Rescue Concept, #67, 2005; #62, 2006 (MB677)

1. metallic lime green, black tires, 2005 #67 ....$1 – 2

2. orange with light brown mud graphics, "25," light brown tires and base, 2006 #62 ....$1 – 2

3. metallic red with wreath, "2006 Happy Holidays," Christmas 2006 Coal Cars J1821, packaged in plastic "lump of coal" ....$1 – 2

4. bronze with "Rescue 677" graphics, 2007 5-pack K9616 ....$1 – 2

Jeep, U.S. Mail (see U.S. Mail Jeep)

Jeep Willys II, #71, 2003; #53, 2004

1. metallic light blue with dark gray roll cage, black base, 2003 Car Shop #71 ....$1 – 2
2. white with blue roll cage and base, "Sid" illustration, 2006 "Ice Age 2, The Meltdown" 5-pack J4720 .... $2 – 3

Jeep Wrangler 1998, #68, 1999; #9, 2000; #25, 2001; #63, 1999, international

1. red with orange stripes, "City Zoo Keeper Services," 2007 #71 .. $1 – 2

2. metallic orange, "Tours," butterscotch roll cage, base, and roof rack with gear, green interior, 2001 Sun Chasers ....$1 – 2
3. metallic orange, "Matchbox New York Toy Fair 2000," "Matchbox 2000" ....$50 – 75
4. yellow, "Coca-Cola," red interior and roll cage, black base, Premiere Collection .... $5 – 6
5. yellow, "Coca-Cola," "www.cocalastores.com," red interior and roll cage, black base, Premiere Collection .... $60 – 80

6. yellow with brown interior, black base, 2006 5-pack J4679 ....$1 – 2
7. green, "Forest Ranger," black roll cage and base, 1999 Ranger Patrol international .... $3 – 4
8. green with yellow and white accents, black roll cage and base, 1999 Ranger Patrol US .... $1 – 2
9. green, "Jeep," "Matchbox," mud spatter, gray interior, black roll cage and base, Pleasant Books issue .... $4 – 5

10. metallic dark green with butterscotch roll cage, gray interior, 2006 Superfast #29 ....$3 – 4
11. blue, "10-17MB," octopus graphics, metallic gray roll cage and base, no roof rack or gear, 2000 Ocean Explorers .... $1 – 2
12. blue, "10-17MB," "Matchbox 2000," octopus graphics, metallic gray roll cage and base, no roof rack or gear, 2000 Ocean Explorers .... $3 – 4

13. metallic blue, metallic gray roll cage, interior and base, no roof rack or gear, 2000 Ocean Explorers ... $1 – 2

14. metallic blue with fishing pole graphics, bright red interior, phosphorescent (glow-in-the-dark) roll cage, roof rack, and gear, 2003 Camp Fun 3-pack .... $1 – 2
15. beige, "Black Star Ranch" and mud spatter, black roll cage and base, 5-pack .... $1 – 2
16. metallic gray, "Jeep" and mud spatter, gray interior, black roll cage and base, 5-pack .... $1 – 2
17. white, "Base 2000," red roll cage and interior, black base, Launcher 5-pack .... $1 – 2

18. white with butterscotch interior, 2005 Superfast #3 .... $3 – 4

19. white with butterscotch interior, black base, "Beach Rescue 06," 2007 5-pack K9617 .... $1 – 2

Jiminy Cricketís Old Timer, WD-8, 1979
1. Hong Kong casting .... $35 – 45
2. Macau casting .... $60 – 80

John Deere Tractor, 2¹/₈", #50, 1964
1. gray plastic tires .... $25 – 30
2. black plastic tires .... $20 – 25

John Deere Trailer with three barrels, 2⁵/₈", #51, 1964
1. gray plastic tires .... $25 – 30
2. black plastic tires .... $20 – 25

Jumbo Crane (see Taylor Jumbo Crane)

Jumbo Jet Motorcycle, 2³/₄", #71, 1973
1. dark blue, red elephant's head .... $16 – 24

Jumbo Sweeper, #20, 2004
1. 2004 Ultra Heroes .... $3 – 4

K

Karrier Bantam 2-Ton Coca-Cola Lorry, 2¹/₄", #37, 1957
1. no base, uneven caseload .. $75 – 100
2. no base, even caseload .... $60 – 75

3. black base, even caseload, gray plastic wheels, 1960 .... $50 – 60
4. black base, even caseload, silver plastic wheels .... $125 – 150
5. black base, even caseload, black plastic wheels .... $50 – 60

Karrier Refuse Truck, 2³/₈", #38, 1957
1. grayish brown with metal wheels .... $100 – 125
2. dark gray with metal wheels . $30 – 40
3. dark gray with gray plastic wheels .... $30 – 40

4. silver with gray plastic wheels .... $40 – 50

Kennel Truck (see Ford Kennel Truck)

Kenworth COE Aerodyne, 2³/₄", #45, 1982 (other variations exist as part of Convoy series)
1. white with brown and blue stripes, England cast .... $4 – 5
2. white with brown and blue stripes, Macau cast .... $3 – 4
3. metallic silver with purple and orange .... $3 – 4
4. white with "Chef Boyardee" labels, US on-package premium .... $40 – 50
5. red with yellow, orange, and white stripes .... $1 – 2

Kenworth Conventional Aerodyne, 2³/₄", #41, 1982 (other versions exist as part of Convoy and White Rose Race Transporter series)
1. red with black and white flared stripes, Lesney England cast .... $4 – 5
2. red with black and white straight stripes, Lesney England cast .... $4 – 5
3. red with black and white straight stripes, Matchbox International England cast .... $4 – 5
4. red with black and white curved stripes, Matchbox International England cast .... $4 – 5
5. blue, Macau cast .... $5 – 6
6. black with orange, yellow and white stripes, Macau cast .... $5 – 6
7. metallic gray with red and blue stripes, Macau cast .... $4 – 5

Kenworth T-2000, #13, 1998 – 1999
1. metallic red, chrome interior and base, rubber tires on chrome rims, 1998 First Editions .... $6 – 9
2. unpainted, chrome interior and base, rubber tires on chrome rims, 1998 First Editions .... $6 – 9

3. bright blue, metallic gray interior and base, "Eagle Express," stripes, 1999 Highway Haulers .... $1 – 2
4. bright blue, metallic gray interior and base, "Express," stripes, 1999 Highway Haulers .... $1 – 2
5. dark gray, chrome interior and base, rubber tires on chrome rims, "Matchbox Toy Show 2000" .... $7 – 9

Kilo King, #28, 2005 (see Fork Lift)

King Tow, #11, 2001; #1, 2002; #17 Tow Truck, 2003
1. black with gray boom, chrome plastic base, "Auto Max Crash 00-207-600," 2001 Highway Heroes .... $1 – 2
2. black with black boom, chrome plastic base, "Matchbox Mattel Toy Fair 2001" .... $30 – 40

3. metallic blue with red boom, chrome plastic base, "All-Star Towing," 2002 Hometown Heroes .... $1 – 2

4. red with bright blue boom, yellow plastic base, monkey and wrench design, 2003 Hero City 5-pack #11 .... $1 – 2

5. metallic gray with red boom, red plastic base, snarling dog design, 2003 Public Works .... $1 – 2

6. white, "Police 3" graphics, 2001 On Patrol 5-pack .... $1 – 2

L

Ladder Fire Truck (see Extending Ladder Fire Engine)

Ladder King ("MB660 Fire Ladder Truck" on base), #1, 2005; #52, 2007

1. red with chrome trim, white ladder, 2005 #1 .... $1 – 2

2. red with metallic gray trim, white graphics, base and ladder, 2007 #52, K9491 .... $1 – 2

Lady Bug, Roman Numeral VI, 1978 (variation of #31 Volks Dragon, 1971, and #15 Hi Ho Silver! 1971)

1. red, Roman Numeral Limited Edtion .... $15 – 20

2. black, Roman Numeral Limited Edition .... $9 – 12

Lady Penelope's FAB 1, "Thunderbirds" TB 005, 1992

1. pink with cream interior, clear windows, chrome base .... $9 – 12

Laing Dumper (see Dumper, Muir Hill)

Lamborghini Countach, with opening rear cowl, $2\frac{7}{8}$", #27, 1973

1. yellow with chrome interior, purple windows, "3" .... $12 – 16

2. yellow with chrome interior, red windows, "3" .... $12 – 16

3. yellow with chrome interior, amber windows, "3" .... $12 – 16
4. dark green with light gray interior, blue-green windows, "Shell" labels, UK issue .... $600 – 800
5. red with chrome interior, amber windows, "3" .... $12 – 16
6. red with chrome interior, red windows, "3" .... $12 – 16
7. red with chrome interior, amber windows, "8," yellow and blue design .... $9 – 12
8. red with chrome interior, blue-green windows, "8," yellow and blue design .... $9 – 12
9. red with chrome interior, red windows, "8," yellow and blue design ..... $9 – 12
10. red with gray interior, blue-green windows, "8," yellow and blue design .... $9 – 12
11. red with gray interior, blue-green windows, "8," green and blue design .... $9 – 12
12. red with gray interior, green windows, "8," green and blue design ..... $9 – 12
13. red with gray interior, green windows, "8," yellow and blue design ..... $9 – 12
14. red with gray interior, tinted windows, "8," yellow and blue design ..... $9 – 12
15. red with gray interior, tinted windows, no design, UK issue .... $160 – 240
16. red with tan interior, blue-green windows, "8," yellow and blue design .... $9 – 12
17. red with tan interior, clear windows, "8," yellow and blue design .... $9 – 12
18. red with tan interior, green windows, "8," yellow and blue design ..... $9 – 12
19. red with tan interior, purple windows, "8," yellow and blue design ..... $9 – 12
20. red with white interior, blue-green windows, "8," yellow and blue design .... $9 – 12
21. red with white interior, clear windows, "8," yellow and blue design ..... $9 – 12
22. red with yellow interior, blue-green windows, "8," yellow and blue design .... $9 – 12
23. red with yellow interior, tinted windows, "8," yellow and blue design ..... $9 – 12

Lamborghini Countach LP500S, no opening features, 3", #67, 1985 – 1997; #60, 1998; #16, 1999; #24, 2000; #11, 1985 – 1997, international; #19, 2000, international

1. red, "Countach," "Lamborghini," clear windows, gold wheels, Thailand cast .... $3 – 4
2. red, "Countach," clear windows, red metal base, Thailand cast .... $1 – 2
3. red, "Countach," clear windows, red plastic base, 5-spoke concave wheels, Thailand cast .... $1 – 2
4. red, "Countach," clear windows, red plastic base, 6-spoke wheels, Thailand cast .... $4 – 5
5. red, "Countach," clear windows, barcode base, Thailand cast, Intercom City .... $40 – 50

6. red, "Countach," clear windows, China cast .... $1 – 2

7. red, "Countach," detailed trim, chrome windows, rubber tires on gray rims, China cast, World Class .... $6 – 8

8. red with white "lamborghini" and bull logo, black interior, 1996 Super Cars 5-pack .... $1 – 2

9. red, detailed trim, rubber tires on chrome rims, Premiere Collection .... $5 – 6

10. red, detailed trim, rubber tires on chrome rims, Thailand cast, Ultra Class .... $9 – 12

11. red, Lamborghini logo on hood, silver wheels, Macau cast .... $3 – 4
12. red, Lamborghini logo on hood, gold wheels, Macau cast .... $9 – 12
13. red with green "15" and "BP," Macau cast, Dutch issue .... $9 – 12

14. red chrome with purple, white, and yellow design, Thailand cast, 1997 Sleek Riders 5-pack ....$1 – 2

15. metallic red with white "lamborghini" and bull logo on sides, 1995, Thailand cast ....$1 – 2
16. metallic light red, "Lamborghini," "Bloomberg," Thailand cast, ASAP promotional .... $120 – 160
17. orange, detailed trim, rubber tires on chrome rims, Thailand cast, Gold Coin Collection .... $16 – 24
18. yellow, "10 Tiger Racing Team," Macau cast, Hong Kong issue .... $9 – 12
19. yellow, "Lamborghini" in script, 2000 Italian Stars .... $1 – 2

20. yellow, "Lamborghini" in script, "Matchbox 2000," 2000 Italian Stars ....$3 – 4
21. yellow, "Lamborghini" and "Countach," Macau cast .... $3 – 4
22. yellow, "LP500," chrome windows, rubber tires on gray rims, Macau cast, World Class .... $6 – 8
23. fluorescent yellow and metallic blue with blue design on sides and hood, pink interior, Thailand cast, 1994 .... $1 – 2
24. fluorescent yellow and metallic blue with blue design on sides only, pink interior, Thailand cast, Aquafresh on-package premium .... $5 – 6
25. fluorescent green, Thailand cast, Show Stoppers .... $3 – 4
26. dark green, "Lamborghini," Thailand cast, 1998 Super Cars .... $1 – 2

27. metallic light blue, "Lamborghini" in script, China cast, 1999 Top Class ....$1 – 2
28. metallic blue with pink windows, Thailand cast, 5-pack .... $5 – 6
29. metallic purple, detailed trim, rubber tires on chrome rims, Thailand cast, Premiere Collection #10 .... $4 – 5
30. black, "5" and stripes, silver wheels, Macau cast .... $3 – 4
31. black, "5" and stripes, gold wheels, Macau cast .... $4 – 5
32. black, "LP500" and stripes, New Superfast Wheels, Macau cast .... $12 – 16
33. black with white "Lamborghini" and bull on sides, Thailand cast, 1997 .. $1 – 2
34. pearl ivory, "Countach" and logo, Thailand cast, Triple Heat .... $4 – 5
35. pearl silver, "LP500S" and stripes, Macau cast, Laser wheels .... $4 – 5
36. metallic silver with lavender, blue, and white design, Thailand cast, Matchcaps .... $4 – 5
37. metallic gray, "Countach," detailed trim, Thailand cast, Collector's Choice, White Rose Collectibles .... $3 – 4

38. white, "lamborghini" and bull logo, red windows, 1997 Super Cars 5-pack ....$1 – 2
39. white, "LP500S" and stripes, New Superfast Wheels, Macau cast .. $4 – 5
40. white, detailed trim, rubber tires on chrome rims, international Premiere Collection #2 .... $4 – 5
41. white with no markings, China cast, clear windows, silver wheels, Graffic Traffic .... $12 – 16
42. white with no markings, Thailand cast, pink windows, gold wheels, Graffic Traffic .... $3 – 4
43. chrome with no markings, Macau cast, custom promotional .... $16 – 24
44. metallic gold, Thailand cast, 1997 75 Challenge .... $12 – 16

Lamborghini Diablo, 3", #22, 1992; #49, 1992, international; #17, 2000, international

1. red with black interior, chrome windows, rubber tires on gray rims, World Class ....$6 – 8
2. red with black interior, clear windows, "Diablo," Thailand cast, UK issue ....$60 – 80
3. red with black and red interior, rubber tires on chrome rims, Premiere Collection Select Class series 4 .... $4 – 5
4. red with fluorescent yellow interior, black spots, 1996 .... $4 – 5
5. fluorescent pink with black interior, clear windows, black spots, 5-pack ... $1 – 2
6. yellow with black interior, clear windows, "Diablo," silver chrome hubs, 1992 ....$1 – 2
7. yellow with black interior, clear windows, "Diablo," gold chrome hubs, 1992 ....$3 – 4
8. yellow with gray and black interior, clear windows, rubber tires on gray rims, Australia Premiere Collection series 1 .... $4 – 5

9. yellow chrome with black interior, clear windows, orange, white and pink design, 5-pack ....$1 – 2

10. fluorescent yellow with bright pink interior, black spots, clear windows, 1995 ....$1 – 2
11. fluorescent yellow with black interior, clear windows, Show Stoppers .. $4 – 5
12. metallic gold with gray and black interior, clear windows, rubber tires on chrome rims, Premiere Collection series 19 ....$4 – 5
13. metallic gold with black interior, clear windows, 1997 75 Challenge ....$6 – 12
14. blue with brown interior, clear windows, white "Diablo," white and black design, 1997 ....$1 – 2
15. blue with gray and blue interior, rubber tires on chrome rims, Premiere Collection Select Class series #2 ....$4 – 5
16. bright blue with gray interior, 2000 Italian Stars ....$1 – 2
17. bright blue with gray interior, "Matchbox 2000," 2000 Italian Stars .. $3 – 4
18. metallic blue with pink and white accents, 1994 ....$1 – 2

19. metallic blue with white and black accents, "Diablo," 1997 .... $1 - 2

20. metallic blue to black gradient with orange interior, clear windows, orange and white flash design .... $1 – 2

21. metallic blue with orange and white accents, orange interior, gold wheels spiral 5-spoke wheels, 1992 #22 .... $1 - 2

22. metallic turquoise with black and gray interior, clear windows, rubber tires on chrome rims, Japan Premiere Collection .... $4 – 5

23. metallic pinkish purple with blue and black interior, clear windows, rubber tires on chrome rims, Premiere Collection World Class series 3 .... $4 – 5

24. dark purple with orange interior, clear windows, white spots, 5-pack .... $1 - 2

25. dark purple with gray interior, clear windows .... $4 – 5

26. metallic purple with black and gray interior, clear windows, rubber tires on chrome rims, Premiere Collection Select Class series 5 .... $4 – 5

27. metallic purple, 2005 Superfast #72 .... $3 - 4

28. black with black interior, chrome windows, rubber tires on gray rims, World Class .... $3 – 4

29. black with red interior, clear windows, "Lamborghini," international issue .... $1 – 2

30. white with blue and gray interior, clear windows, rubber tires on chrome rims, Gold Coin Collection .... $16 – 24

31. metallic gray with blue and black interior, clear windows, rubber tires on chrome rims, Premiere Collection World Class series 6 .... $4 – 5

32. silver with white interior, amber windows, orange and yellow flames .. $4 – 5

Lamborghini Marzal, with Superfast wheels, 2³/₄", #20, 1969; BR 27-28, 1985

1. metallic red .... $16 – 24

2. metallic red with labels, gift set .... $20 - 25

3. salmon .... $16 – 24
4. salmon with labels, gift set .. $20 – 25
5. yellow .... $40 – 50
6. fluorescent pink .... $12 – 16
7. fluorescent pink .... $16 – 24
8. green, "8" graphics, England cast, Super GT BR 27-28, 1985 .... $4 – 6
9. green, "16" graphics, England cast, Super GT BR 27-28, 1985 .... $12 – 15
10. blue, England cast, Super GT BR 27-28, 1985 .... $8 – 10
11. cream, England cast, Super GT BR 27-28, 1985 .... $4 – 6
12. white, England cast, Super GT BR 27-28, 1985 .... $12 – 15
13. cream, China cast, Super GT BR 27-28, 1985 .... $8 – 10
14. yellow, China cast, Super GT BR 27-28, 1985 .... $3 – 5
15. green, China cast, Super GT BR 27-28, 1985 .... $8 – 10
16. red, China cast, Super GT BR 27-28, 1985 .... $3 – 5

Lamborghini Miura, 2³/₄", #33, 1969

1. yellow with ivory interior, black plastic wheels on chrome hubs ...... $60 – 75

2. yellow with red interior, black plastic wheels on chrome hubs .... $6 - 9

3. metallic gold with ivory interior, black plastic wheels on chrome hubs .... $60 – 75
4. yellow, red interior, Superfast wheels, 1970 .... $80 – 100
5. metallic dark orange, red interior, Superfast wheels, 1970 .... $30 – 45
6. metallic light orange, red interior, Superfast wheels, 1970 .... $20 – 25
7. metallic gold, red interior, Superfast wheels, 1970 .... $20 – 25
8. metallic gold, ivory interior, Superfast wheels, 1970 .... $16 – 24

Lambretta TV175 Scooter and Sidecar, 2", #36, 1961

1. metallic green, black wheels .. $60 – 75

Land Rover, with driver, 1³/₄", #12, 1955

1. olive green, metal wheels .... $40 – 50

Land Rover, without driver, no roof, olive green, 2¹/₄", #12, 1959

1. gray plastic wheels .... $85 – 100
2. black plastic wheels .... $25 – 30

Land Rover 90 (see Land Rover Ninety)

Land Rover Defender 110, 1997, #55, 2006; #65 2007

1. white, 2006 #55 (J2379 on 2006 package) .... $1 - 2

2. metallic green, 2007 #55 .... $1 - 2

3. red with black base and interior, yellow, black and white graphics, 2007 #65 .... $1 - 2

Land Rover Discovery, #67, 2001; #50, 2003

1. metallic red with black trim, cream interior, 2005 Superfast #51 .. $3 - 4

2. **orange with white diagonal door stripes, "MBX Coast Guard," 2006 5-pack J4673 .... $1 – 2**
3. green camouflage, 2002 Matchbox Across America 50th Birthday Series #14 Vermont — Northeastern Collection .... $4 – 6
4. metallic light olive green with red windows, "Bighorn Forest" graphics, 2003 #50 .... $1 – 2

5. **metallic green with maroon, orange and yellow Adventure graphics, 2005 #50 .... $1 – 2**
6. metallic blue-gray, 2001 Storm Watch #67 .... $1 – 2

7. **metallic bronze with red windows, "Bighorn Forest" graphics, 2003 Forest Rescue .... $1 – 2**

Land Rover Fire Truck, $2^{7}/_{8}$", #57, 1966
1. "Kent Fire Brigade," red, gray plastic wheels, 1966 .... $325 – 475
2. "Kent Fire Brigade," red, black plastic wheels, 1966 .... $9 – 12
3. "Kent Fire Brigade," red, Superfast wheels, 1970 .... $50 – 60

Land Rover Freelander, #66, 1999; #64, 2000; #9, 2001; #61, 1999, international; #44, 2000, international

1. **yellow with metallic gray fenders; red, maroon, silver, and white accents, 2003 Hero City 5-pack #1 .... $1 – 2**
2. metallic pale green with green fenders, "Canyon Base," 5-pack .... $1 – 2

3. **metallic blue with blue fenders, "Canyon Park," green band and door crest, 2000 Great Outdoors .. $1 – 2**
4. metallic blue with blue fenders, "Canyon Park," "Matchbox 2000," green band and door crest, 2000 Great Outdoors series, 5-spoke wheels .... $3 – 4
5. metallic blue with blue fenders, "Canyon Park," "Matchbox 2000," green band and door crest, 2000 Great Outdoors series, 5-spoke concave wheels .. $6 – 8

6. **metallic blue with black fenders, light blue, white, and black graphics, "1," "406," "Team Freelander," 2006 5-pack J4675 .... $2 – 3**

7. **bright blue with bright orange fenders, "Powder," "Turbo," unpainted metal base, 2001 Team Tundra .... $1 – 2**
8. metallic gray with dark gray fenders, "Canyon Park," green band and door crest, 1999 Ranger Patrol international .... $1 – 2
9. metallic gray with dark gray fenders, "Canyon Park," "Ranger," green band and door crest, 1999 Ranger Patrol US series, larger 5-spoke concave wheels .... $1 – 2
10. metallic gray with dark gray fenders, "Canyon Park," "Ranger," green band and door crest, 1999 Ranger Patrol US series, smaller 5-spoke concave wheels .... $6 – 8

Land Rover Ninety, $2^{1}/_{2}$", #35, 1990, US; #16, international, 1990; #53, 1998, international; #41, 1998, Germany; #58, 2004
1. red with white roof, "County," blue and gray stripes .... $1 – 2
2. red with white roof, "Red Arrows," "Royal Air Force," Motor City .... $4 – 5

3. **red with white roof, "Red Valley Camp," 1997 Land Sea & Air 5-pack .... $1 – 2**

4. **orange with black roof, "Safari Park," black tiger stripes, 1993 Off-Road 5-pack .... $1 – 2**
5. yellow with black roof, "Canyon," crest and dashes design .... $3 – 4
6. yellow with white roof, "Park Ranger" .... $1 – 2
7. yellow with black roof, "Mountain Trails," 5-pack .... $1 – 2

8. **green with white roof, yellow and orange stripes, Motor City ... $1 – 2**
9. dark green with black roof, "0321" and tree design, Germany issue ..... $4 – 5

10. **dark green with white roof, "55," white and gray stripe graphics, 2006 5-pack J4679 .... $1 – 2**
11. blue with white roof, yellow and orange stripes, Motor City .... $3 – 4

12. **blue with white roof, no graphics .... $3 – 4**
13. dark blue with white roof, "Royal Navy" .... $3 – 4

14. black with gray roof, gray and yellow camouflage, Commando .... $5 – 6

15. black with white roof, gray and white stripes, Superfast #18 2006 ....$3 – 4
16. light gray and navy blue with light gray roof, red stripes .... $4 – 5
17. white with black roof, "Land Rover," 1998 international Rough and Tough .... $1 – 2
18. white with black roof, "Metropolitan Police," stripes, UK issue .... $3 – 4
19. white with blue roof, "Alitalia" ... $4 – 5
20. white with blue roof, "KLM" ...... $4 – 5
21. white with blue roof, "SAS" .... $4 – 5
22. white with green roof, "Garden Festival Wales," Wales issue .... $7 – 8
23. white with white roof, "Bacardi Rum," on-package premium .... $30 – 40
24. white with white roof, "Circus Circus," Motor City .... $3 – 4
25. white with white roof, "County," black and red stripes .... $1 – 2
26. white with white roof, "Rescue Police," checkerboard pattern, Emergency .... $1 – 2
27. white with white roof, "Rijkspolitie," "55," Netherlands issue .... $4 – 5
28. white with white roof, black and red stripes, "Country" .... $2 – 4
29. white with white roof, bright pink, bright yellow and blue splash design ... $4 – 5
30. white with white roof, no markings, Graffic Traffic .... $12 – 16

Land Rover Safari (see Safari Land Rover)

Land Rover SVX, #52, 2004; #12, 2005; #63, 2006 (MB628)

1. olive green with black roll cage, 2006 #63 ....$1 – 2
2. khaki with black roll cage, 2005 #12 J5596 .... $1 – 2

3. blue with black roll cage, 2006 #63 J5596 ....$1 – 2

4. metallic gold, "Elemental Hero Avian," 2006 Yu-Gi-Oh GX 5-pack H5775 ....$1 – 2

5. black with metallic gray roll cage and base, #52, 2004 ....$1 – 2

6. white with red diagonal stripes, anchor logo, black roll cage and base, "MBX Coast Guard," 2006 5-pack J4673 ....$1 – 2

Lexus GS430, #23, 2007
1. black .... $1 – 2

Leyland Articulated Tanker, 3", #14, 1982, international
1. red with white tank, "Elf" labels .. $3 – 5
2. yellow with white tank, "Shell," Japan issue .... $9 – 12
3. red with white tank, "Shell" .. $65 – 90
4. black with black tank, "Gas," Commando .... $5 – 6

Leyland Articulated Truck, 3", #30, 1982
1. blue cab, metallic gray trailer, no markings $3 – 4
2. blue cab, metallic gray trailer, "International" .... $5 – 7

3. red cab, metallic gray trailer, no markings ....$8 – 10
4. red cab, yellow trailer, "International" .... $6 – 8
5. blue cab, yellow trailer, "International" .... $6 – 8
6. bright blue cab, yellow trailer, "International" .... $4 – 5
7. bright blue cab, bright blue trailer, "Paul's," UK issue .... $30 – 40

Leyland Petrol Tanker with 3", #32, 1968

1. green with white tank, "BP" labels, silver grille, black plastic wheels .... $6 – 9
2. green with white tank, "BP" labels, white grille, black plastic wheels ...... $9 – 12
3. dark blue with white tank, "Aral" labels, silver grille, black plastic wheels .... $40 – 50
4. blue with white tank, "Aral," Superfast wheels .... $60 – 80
5. green cab with white tank, chrome base, "BP," Superfast wheels ...$16 – 24
6. green cab with white tank, gray base, "BP," Superfast wheels .... $20 – 25
7. red cab with white tank, "N. A. M. C.," "The Miniature Vehicle," 1972 .... $500 – 750
8. purple cab with metallic gray tank, "National Association of Matchbox Collectors," 1972 .... $200 – 250
9. purple cab, metallic gray tank, chrome base, no labels, 1994 .... $150 – 200

Leyland Pipe Truck, with six pipes, 2⁷/₄", #10, 1966

1. red with chrome grille and base, gray pipes, black plastic wheels ...$40 – 50
2. red with white grille and base, gray pipes, black plastic wheels ... $20 – 30
3. red with chrome grille and base, gray pipes, Superfast wheels ...... $40 – 50
4. orange with chrome grille and base, yellow pipes, Superfast wheels ... 20 – 30
4. orange with gray grille and base, gray pipes, Superfast wheels ...... $20 – 30
5. orange with gray grille and base, yellow pipes, Superfast wheels ...... $20 – 30

Leyland Royal Tiger Coach, metallic blue, 3", #40, 1961
1. gray wheels .... $35 – 45
2. silver wheels .... $25 – 35

3. black wheels ....$20 – 30

Leyland Site Office Truck, 2½", #60, 1966

1. blue, yellow plastic building with green roof, black plastic wheels, 1966 ....$15 – 20

2. blue, yellow plastic building with green roof, Superfast wheels, 1970 ....$30 – 40

Leyland Tanker, #32 (see Leyland Petrol Tanker)

Leyland Tanker, with separate tank trailer (European model), 3⅛", #14, 1982

1. red cab with "ELF" and red stripe ...$4 – 6
2. yellow cab with "Shell," white tank with yellow base .... $6 – 8
3. red cab with "Shell," white tank with red base .... $40 – 50
4. black cab tank, "GAS" .... $4 – 6

Leyland Titan London Bus (see London Bus, Leyland Titan)

Limousine, #66, 2002; #32, 2003

1. metallic red with silver Matchbox logo, 2003 Auto Carrier Launcher 5-pack ....$1 – 2

2. metallic lavender with "Skeletor" and graphics, 2003 He-Man/Masters of the Universe 5-pack ....$1 – 2

3. black, 2002 Kids' Cars of the Year .... $1 – 2

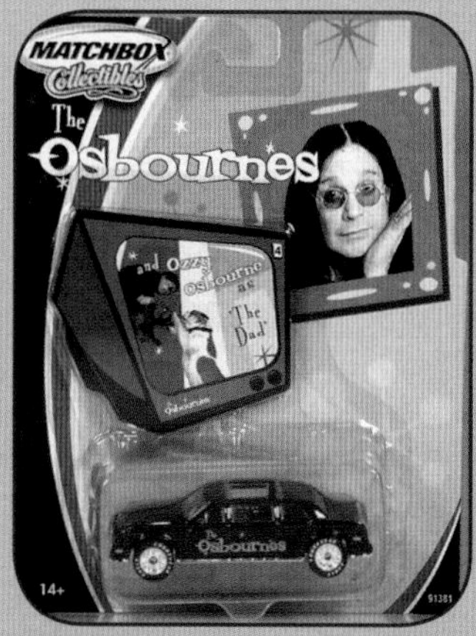

4. black, "The Osbournes," "Ozzie Osbourne 'The Dad'" on package, 2003 Matchbox Collectibles ..$4 – 6

5. metallic gray, "Matchbox VIP Shuttle," 2003 Airport ....$1 – 2

6. metallic gray, "Matchbox VIP Shuttle," 2003 Hero City 10-pack #2 .... $1 – 2

Lincoln Continental, 2¾", #31, 1964

1. metallic blue, black plastic wheels ....$15 – 20
2. mint green, black plastic wheels ....$6 – 10
3. metallic lime green, black plastic wheels .... $500 – 600
4. mint green, Superfast wheels, 1970 .... $2,000 – 2,500
5. green-gold, Superfast wheels, 1970 .... $50 – 60

Lincoln Continental Mark V, 3", #28, 1979

1. red with white roof, tan interior ...$4 – 5
2. red with white roof, gray interior ...$5 – 6
3. red with white roof, brown interior ...$5 – 6

4. red with white roof, light brown interior ....$6 – 7

Lincoln Navigator, #20, 2005; #67, 2006

1. burgundy, 2005 #20 .... $1 – 2

2. white, 2005 Superfast #32 .. $4 – 5

3. black, 2006 #67 ....$1 – 2

Lincoln Premiere 1957, Superfast #50, 2004

1. metallic gold, 2004 Superfast #50 ....$3 – 4

2. pale yellow, 2005 Superfast #50 ....$3 – 4

3. two-tone blue, 2006 5-pack J4677 ....$1 – 2

4. pink, Matchbox Collectibles Barrett-Jackson ....$4 – 5

Lincoln Town Car, 3", #43, 1989; #24, 1990

1. metallic red, brown landau roof .. $4 – 5

2. metallic red ....$1 – 2

3. yellow with blue wheels, Live 'N Learn/ Matchbox Preschool .... $12 – 16

4. black with chrome windows, whitewall rubber tires on gray rims, World Class .... $7 – 9

5. metallic dark gray, purple landau roof, rubber tires on chrome rims, Ultra Class .... $9 - 12

6. white with metal base .... $1 – 2

7. white with plastic base .... $1 - 2

8. metallic silver with pink and yellow design, Dream Machines ...... $3 - 4

Litter Bug, insect garbage truck, #15, 2004

1. 2004 Ultra Heroes $3-4

Lock Boxer, armored car with dog's head, #23, 2004 (MB646)

1. white cab, gold armored car, metallic teal base, 2004 Ultra Heroes $3-4

Lockheed Martin X-33 Reusable Launch Vehicle (RLV), #36, 2000; #21, 2000, international

1. white with black base, "Venture Star," "USA," "X-33 RLV" on base ...... $1 – 2
2. white with black base, "Venture Star," "USA," "X-33 RLV" on base, "Matchbox 2000" .... $3 – 4

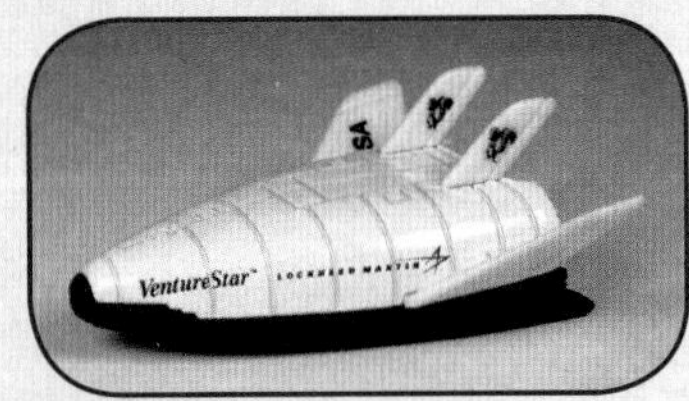

3. white with black base, "Venture Star," "USA," "X-33 Lockheed" on base, 2000 Space Mission 5-pack .... $1 - 2

4. white with black base, "Citrix MetaFrame XP," "X-33 Lockheed" on base, Color Comp promotional ...... $25 – 35

London Bus (also see Daimler London Bus, Double Decker Bus, Routemaster London Bus, The Londoner)

London Bus, red, 2", #5, 1954

1. "Buy Matchbox Series," metal wheels, made in England .... $60 – 70
2. "Buy Matchbox Series," 1988 40th Anniversary Gift Set replica, made in China .... $8 – 10
3. "Matchbox Originals," 1991 Matchbox Originals replica, made in China ... $2 – 4

London Bus, 2¼", #5, 1957

1. metal wheels, "Buy Matchbox Series" .... $45 – 60
2. gray plastic wheels, "Buy Matchbox Series" .... $65 – 80

London Bus, red body, plastic wheels, 2 9/16", #5, 1961

1. "Player's Please," gray wheels .... $100 – 125
2. "Visco Static," gray wheels ... $35 – 45
3. "Drink Peardrax," gray wheels .... $150 – 175
4. "Drink Peardrax," black wheels .... $150 – 175
5. "Baron of Beef," gray wheels .... $175 – 200
6. "Baron of Beef," black wheels .... $175 – 200
7. "Visco Static," black wheels .. $30 – 40

London Bus, Routemaster, #5, 1965 (See London Routemaster Bus)

London Bus, The Londoner, with solid door in left side center, small windows, 3," #17, 1972

1. red, "Swinging London" labels, black base .... $9 - 12

2. red, "Swinging London" labels, gray base .... $9 – 12
3. red, "Swinging London" labels, unpainted base with cast screw mounts ... $15 – 20
4. gold plated, "Swinging London" labels, unpainted base with cast screw mounts .... $800 – 1,200
5. silver plated, "Swinging London" labels, unpainted base with cast screw mounts .... $800 – 1,200
6. red, "Preston Guild Merchant 1972" .... $175 – 225
7. red, "London Kensington Hilton" .... $175 – 225
8. red, "Typhoo Tea" .... $300 – 350
9. red, "Impel 73" .... $60 – 80

10. red, "Berger Paints" .... $9 - 12

11. red, "ICP Interchemicals & Plastics" .... $800 – 1,200
12. red, "Borregard Paper" .. $800 – 1,200
13. red, "Sellotape Selbstklebander" .... $800 – 1,200
14. red, "Sellotape Packaging Systems" .... $175 – 225
15. red, "Sellotape Electrical Tapes" .... $800 – 1,200
16. red, "Sellotape International Operations" .... $800 – 1,200
17. red, "Chambourcy Yogurt" ... $90 – 120
18. red, "Esso Extra Petrol" .... $40 – 50
19. butterscotch and ivory, "Berger Paints" .... $175 – 225
20. butterscotch and ivory, "Impel 76" .... $90 – 120
21. red, "Selfridges" .... $65 – 75
22. red, "Aviemore Centre," "Santa Claus Land" .... $75 – 100
23. red, "Amcel" .... $180 – 240
24. red, "Baron of Beef" .... $180 – 240
25. yellow and red, "Swinging London" .... $400 – 500
26. red, "AIM Building Fund 1976" .... $45 – 60
27. red with no labels .... $6 – 9
28. white and red, "Berger Paints" .... $400 – 500
29. white and blue, "Berger Paints" .... $200 – 250
30. yellow and blue, "Berger Paints" .... $600 – 800
31. metallic red, "Lufthansa" ... $600 – 800
32. red, "Army & Navy" .... $55 – 70
33. red, "Eduscho Kaffee" ..... $600 – 800
34. orange, "Jacob's Biscuit Makers" .... $35 – 50
35. red, "Jacob's Biscuit Makers" .. $70 – 90
36. red, "Ilford Hp5 Film" ...... $400 – 500
37. red, "Museum of London" .... $60 – 90
38. red, "Silver Jubilee" .... $200 – 250

39. metallic gray, "Silver Jubilee" .... $12 - 16

40. metallic gray, "Berger Paints" .... $80 – 120

41. blue, "Deutschlands Autopartner" ....$40 – 60

42. blue, "Matchbox 1953 – 1978" ....$40 – 60

43. orange, "Matchbox 1953 – 1978" .... $80 – 120
44. red, "Matchbox 1953 – 1978" ..$7 – 10
45. red, "Busch Gardens" .... $50 – 70
46. red, "The Bisto Bus" .... $10 – 15
47. red, "3rd A.I.M. Inc. Convention & Toy Show" .... $40 – 50
48. red, "Matchbox Collectors Club 1997," "Hershey 1997" .... $16 – 24

London Bus, Leyland Titan, with double doors on left side, large windows, 3", #17, 1982; #51, 1984; #28 1990; #2, 2002

1. Red, "Berger Paints" labels .. $12 – 15
2. red, "Laker Skytrain" labels .... $9 – 12
3. white upper, light blue lower, "Matchbox No. 1," "Montepna" .... $30 – 40
4. red, "Matchbox No. 1," "Montepna" ....$30 – 40
5. dark green, "Chesterfield Centenary" labels .... $12 – 16

6. red, "Matchbox London Bus," England cast ....$5 – 8

7. red, "Matchbox London Bus," Macau cast .... $2 – 4
8. red, "Nice To Meet You! Japan 1984," Japan issue .... $16 – 24
9. red, Japanese writing on labels, Japan issue .... $16 – 24
10. red, "York Festival & Mystery Plays" .... $12 – 16
11. dark blue, "Nestle Milkybar" ... $12 – 16
12. red, "Nestle Milkybar" .... $12 – 16
13. dark green, "Rowntree Fruit Gums" ....$12 – 16
14. red, "Rowntree Fruit Gums" ... $8 – 10
15. dark blue, "Keddies No. 1 In Essex" .... $50 – 70
16. maroon, "Rapport" .... $9 – 12
17. white upper, black lower, "Torvale Fisher Engineering Co." .... $9 – 12
18. white upper, orange lower, "W H Smith Travel" .... $12 – 16
19. red, "You'll [Love] New York" ..... $2 – 4
20. "Space For Youth 1985," "Staffordshire Police" .... $9 – 12
21. blue, "Cityrama" .... $9 – 12
22. red, no labels, England cast ..... $4 – 6
23. red, no labels, China cast .... $6 – 8
24. red, "Nurenburg 1986," Macau cast .... $120 – 160
25. red, "First M.I.C.A. Convention," Macau cast .... $240 – 300
26. red, "First M.I.C.A. Convention," England cast .... $240 – 300
27. red, "First M.I.C.A. Convention," England cast .... $240 – 300
28. "M.I.C.A. Matchbox Intl. Collectors Association" .... $9 – 12
29. red, "Around London Tour Bus," China cast .... $2 – 4
30. blue, "National Tramway Museum," China cast .... $9 – 12
31. white upper, red lower, "Midland Bus Transport Museum," China cast .... $9 – 12
32. red, "Band-Aid Plasters Playbus," China cast .... $9 – 12
33. blue, "National Girobank," China cast .... $9 – 12
34. red, "Matchbox — Niagara Falls," China cast .... $6 – 8
35. red, "Feria Del Juguete Valencia," "12 Febrero 1987" .... $180 – 240
36. beige upper, blue lower, "West Midlands Travel," China cast .... $9 – 12
37. white, "Denney — Happy 1000th Birthday, Dublin" .... $8 – 10
38. red, "123abc," "My First Matchbox — Nurenburg 1990" .... $12 – 16
39. red, "123abc," Matchbox Preschool/ Live 'N Learn .... $6 – 8
40. yellow, "It's The Real Thing — Coke," China cast .... $15 – 20
41. maroon, "Corning Glass Center," China cast .... $9 – 12
42. chrome, "Celebrating a Decade of Matchbox Conventions" .... $30 – 45
43. red, "Markfield Project Support Appeal 92," China cast .... $16 – 24
44. red, "London Wide Tour Bus," China cast .... $2 – 4
45. white, no labels, China cast, Graffic Traffic .... $12 – 16

46. red, "Union Jack Tours," #2, 2002 Hometown Heroes ....$1 – 2

47. red, "Takashimaya," Japan issue .... $120 – 150
48. white with no markings, ASAP promotional blank .... $20 – 25
49. white, "American International Recovery" on roof, ASAP promotional .... $125 – 175
50. orange, "Fanta" labels on sides, "Enjoy Fanta" on roof, China issue .... $175 – 225

51. red, scenery design, 2000 On Tour ....$1 – 2

52. red, scenery design, "Matchbox 2000," 2000 On Tour .... $3 – 4
53. red, "Scansource & Symbol" on roof, ASAP promotional .... $75 – 125
54. red, "www.citrix.com/cdn" on sides, "Citrix Meta Frame for Unix Operating Systems" on roof, ASAP promotional .... $75 – 125
55. red, "www.mbxroad.com" on sides, "Matchbox Road Museum" on roof, Color Comp promotional ...... $16 – 24

London Routemaster Bus, 2¾", #5, 1965

1. "Longlife" decals .... $9 – 12
2. "Visco Static" decals or stickers ..$9 – 12
3. "Baron of Beef" .... $180 – 200

London Taxi (see Austin FX4R London Taxi, Austin London Taxi)

London Trolley Bus, red, 2⅝", #56, 1958

1. black rods, metal wheels .. $180 – 200
2. red rods, metal wheels .... $35 – 45
3. red rods, gray plastic wheels ..$25 – 40

Lotus Elise, #69, 2000, international; #8, 2005

1. yellow with black interior, tinted windows, 2000 international .... $3 – 4

2. metallic green with black metal base, 2003 Hero City 5-pack #12, US issue ....$1 – 2

3. yellow with green and black graphics, 2005 #8 .... $1 – 2

Lotus Europa, Superfast wheels, 2⅞", #5, 1969; BR 9-10, 1985

1. metallic blue, does not say "Superfast" on base .... $80 – 100
2. metallic blue, says "Superfast" on base .... $12 – 16
3. metallic blue, "20" labels, gift set .... $16 – 24
4. metallic lavender, no labels .. $12 – 16
5. metallic lavender, "20" labels, gift set .... $16 – 24
6. black, "JPS," Japan issue .... $20 – 25
7. black, no labels .... $16 – 24
8. Bulgarian issue, various colors .... $40 – 50

9. white, England cast, Super GT BR 9-10, 1985 .... $4 – 6
10. metallic blue, England cast, Super GT BR 9-10, 1985 .... $4 – 6
11. purple, China cast, Super GT BR 9-10, 1985 .... $3 – 5
12. white, China cast, Super GT BR 9-10, 1985 .... $8 – 10
13. blue, China cast, Super GT BR 9-10, 1985 .... $3 – 5

Lotus Exige, #12, 2007

1. metallic yellow, 2007 #12 ....$1 - 2

2. antifreeze green, 2007 #12, L5031 ....$1 - 2

Lotus Racing Car, $2^3/_4$", #19, 1966
1. orange with black tires on yellow plastic hubs .... $25 – 30
2. green with black tires on yellow plastic hubs .... $15 – 20

3. purple with Superfast wheels, 1970 ....$40 - 50

Lotus Super Seven, 3", #60, 1971
1. orange with flames label ...... $16 – 24
2. yellow with flames label .... $60 – 80

3. yellow with checkerboard pattern and "60" ....$20 - 30

Luna-C (see UFO)

LVTP7 Landing Craft, 2001 Feature Cars, with opening features, designed to replace Premiere Collection
1. beige with black painted treads ...$9 – 12

Lyons Maid Ice Cream Truck (see Commer Ice Cream Canteen)

LZ Chopper (see Sea Rescue Helicopter)

M

M1 A1 Abrams Tank (see Abrams M1 A1 Tank)

M1 Abrams Tank (see Abrams M1 A1 Tank)

M2 Bradley Tank (see Bradley M2 Fighting Vehicle)

M3 Army Halftrack Personnel Carrier (see Army M3 Halftrack Personnel Carrier)

M4 A3 Sherman Tank (see Sherman M4 A3 Tank)

Mack CH600 Aerodyne, 3", #8, 1990, US; #39, 1990, international; other variations in Convoy and White Rose series
1. white with black and red stripes ..$1 – 2
2. red and white, "Coke," chrome hubs, rubber tires .... $5 – 6

Mack Dump Truck, $2^5/_8$", #28, 1968
1. orange with black plastic tires on orange plastic hubs .... $9 – 12
1. metallic dull gold, Superfast wheels, 1970 .... $24 – 36
2. dark olive green, Superfast wheels, Two-Pack .... $70 – 90

3. light olive green, Superfast wheels, Two-Pack ....$6 - 8

Mack Floodlight Heavy Rescue Auxiliary Power Truck, 3", #57, 1991 – 1997; #21, 1998; #77, 1999; #45, 2001; #42, 2002; #50, 1991, international

1. "42 Metro," yellow with red roof, black, red and white design, 2002 Airport Alarm ....$1 - 2
2. "Acorn Hill Fire Dept.," red and white with white roof, rubber tires on chrome rims, Premiere Collection #7 ... $4 – 5

3. "Action Metro Base," "33," safety green with blue roof, white and black design, "Action Metro" shield, 1999 Fire Rescue ....$1 - 2
4. "American International Recovery," red with white roof, ASAP promotional .... $120 – 160

5. "Bridge & Highway Dept." red with white roof, "57," "Give Us a Brake," black roadway design, red lettering, 1998 To the Rescue ....$1 - 2
6. "Bridge & Highway Dept." yellow with white roof, "57" .... $3 – 4

7. "Bridge & Highway Dept," white with white roof, "57," "Give Us a Brake," black roadway design, red lettering, 1996 ....$1 - 2
8. "Clearbrook Fire & Rescue," red with white roof .... $9 – 12
9. "Eagle Point Fire Rescue," metallic red and white with white roof, rubber tires on chrome rims, Premiere Collection #21 .... $4 – 5
10. "Emergency Power" in blue field, red with white roof, "77," white accents, blue shield on doors, 1998 Emergency Rescue 5-pack .... $1 – 2

11. "Emergency Power 34," red with white roof, 5-pack ....$4 - 5

12. "Fire Rescue Unit 2," orange-red with white roof, "Action System," on-package premium .... $8 – 10
13. "Fire Rescue Unit 2," fluorescent orange with white roof, black and white checkerboard design .... $1 – 2
14. "Floodlight Rescue Unit," metallic gold, 1997 75 Challenge .... $12 – 16
15. "Floodlight Heavy Rescue," red with white roof, "Fire Rescue Unit 2," gift set .... $9 – 12
16. "Floodlight Heavy Rescue," fluorescent orange with white roof, "Fire Rescue Unit 2," blue and white checkerboard design .... $5 – 6

17. "Floodlight Heavy Rescue," fluorescent orange with white roof, "Newfield Borough Fire Co.," "Fire Rescue Unit 2," 1995 .... $1 – 2
18. "Floodlight Heavy Rescue," yellow with white roof, "Newfield Borough Fire Co.," shield on doors, 1995 .... $1 – 2
19. "Floodlight Rescue Unit," red with white roof, "Fire Rescue" .... $6 – 8
20. "Garage 33," red with white roof, "5 Alarm," Launcher 5-pack .... $1 – 2
21. "Garage 33," yellow with white roof, "5 Alarm," Launcher 5-pack .... $1 – 2
22. "Houston Fire Dept. 11," white and red with white roof, "Heavy Rescue," Premiere Collection .... $5 – 6
23. "Main Transit Fire Dept. Amherst NY," red with white roof, ASAP promotional .... $16 – 24

24. "Matchbox Fire Rescue," red with white roof, "Fire Dept." white bands, 1997 Fire 5-pack .... $1 – 2

25. "Matchbox Fire Rescue," white with white roof, "Fire Dept.," red bands, 2000 Fire 5-pack .... $1 – 2
26. "Metro Alarm," white and green with black roof, "MA-RC1," 5-pack ... $1 – 2
27. "Reithoffer's," orange with white roof, White Rose Collectibles gift set .. $5 – 6
28. "Shrewsbury Fire Co.," red with white roof, White Rose Collectibles ..$12 – 16
29. "Sugar Grove Fire Department" on left side only, red with white roof, ASAP promotional .... $16 – 24
30. "Sugar Grove Fire Department 2000," red with white roof, ASAP promotional .... $20 – 25

31. "Universe Alarm Centre," white with white roof, red and black design, 2001 Rescue Squad .... $1 – 2
32. red with white roof, no markings, ASAP promotional blank .... $30 – 40
33. white with white roof, no markings, Graffic Traffic .... $12 – 16

Mack Junior Van 1937, #339, 1998, Matchbox Collectibles
1. "Arapahoe Amber Ale," dark green .... $9 – 12
2. "Continental Aero," "Purple Plastic Inserts...," purple .... $9 – 12
3. "Dixie Jazz Beer," black .... $9 – 12
4. "Pony Express," yellow .... $9 – 12

Magirus-Deutz Six-Wheel Crane Truck, 2⅝", #30, 1961
1. tan with red boom, gray plastic wheels .... $2000 – 3000
2. tan with orange boom, gray plastic wheels .... $2000 – 3000
3. metallic silver with orange boom, orange metal hook, gray plastic wheels ..$70 – 90
4. metallic silver with orange boom, silver metal hook, gray plastic wheels ..$70 – 90
5. metallic silver with orange boom, silver metal hook, silver plastic wheels ..$70 – 90
6. metallic silver with orange boom, silver metal hook, black plastic wheels ..$60 – 80
7. metallic silver with orange boom, gray plastic hook, gray plastic wheels ......$70 – 90

8. metallic silver with orange boom, gray plastic hook, black plastic wheels .... $60 – 80

Maintenance Truck (see Chevrolet Highway Maintenance Truck)

Mark 10 Jaguar (see Jaguar Mark 10)

Marshall Horse Box Mk 7, red cab, brown horse box, 2", #35, 1957
1. metal wheels .... $35 – 45
2. gray plastic wheels .... $40 – 50
3. silver plastic wheels .... $80 – 100
4. black plastic wheels .... $125 – 150

Maserati 4CL T/1948 Racer, 2½", #52, 1958

1. red with black plastic wheels .... $50 – 70
2. red with black plastic tires on spoked wheels .... $100 – 125

3. yellow with black tires on spoked wheels .... $60 – 80

Maserati Bora, 3", #32, 1972; BR 29-30, 1985 (similar casting: Sunburner)
1. metallic burgundy with unpainted metal base, "8" label .... $60 – 80

2. metallic burgundy with green base, "8" label .... $9 – 12
3. metallic gold with metallic gray base .... $16 – 24
4. beige, China cast, Super GT BR 29-30, 1985 .... $3 – 5
5. fluorescent lime, China cast, Neon Racer BR 29-30, 1985 .... $4 – 6

6. yellow, England cast, Super GT BR 29-30, 1985 .... $5 – 10
7. yellow, China cast, Super GT BR 29-30, 1985 .... $8 – 10
8. powder blue, China cast, Super GT BR 29-30, 1985 .... $3 – 5
9. light blue, England cast, Super GT BR 29-30, 1985 .... $5 – 10
10. light blue, China cast, Super GT BR 29-30, 1985 .... $8 – 10

11. dark blue, England cast, Super GT BR 29-30, 1985 .... $6 – 10

Massey Harris Tractor, with fenders, 1⁵/₈", #4, 1954

1. red, made in England .... $60 – 75
2. red, from 40th Anniversary Gift Set, made in China, 1988 .... $8 – 10
3. green, Matchbox Originals, made in China, 1991 .... $3 – 4

Massey Harris Tractor, no fenders, 1⁵/₈", #4, 1957

1. red .... $50 – 70

Matra Rancho, 2⁷/₈", #37, 1982, international

1. turquoise, no markings, blue tailgate, turquoise base .... $9 – 12
2. light blue, no markings, blue tailgate, light blue base .... $9 – 12
3. blue, "Marine Rescue," blue tailgate, yellow base .... $4 – 5

4. **dark blue, "Surf Rescue," black tailgate, white base ....$5 – 6**
5. dark blue, "Surf Rescue," black tailgate, yellow base .... $5 – 6
6. dark blue, "Surf Rescue," blue tailgate, white base .... $5 – 6
7. dark blue, no markings, blue tailgate, black base, silver wheel hubs ... $8 – 10
8. dark blue, no markings, blue tailgate, black base, gold wheel hubs .. $16 – 24
9. dark blue, no markings, blue tailgate, dark blue base, silver wheel hubs .... $16 – 24
10. dark blue, no markings, blue tailgate, yellow base, silver wheel hubs ...$16 – 24
11. dark blue, no markings, yellow tailgate, yellow base, gold wheel hubs ...$20 – 25
12. orange, "Surf 2," orange tailgate, black base .... $3 – 4
13. yellow, no markings, yellow tailgate, yellow base .... $7 – 9

14. **yellow, red stripes, yellow tailgate, yellow base, silver wheel hubs ....$8 – 10**
15. yellow, red stripes, yellow tailgate, yellow base, gold wheel hubs .... $16 – 24

16. **fluorescent yellow, "Marine Rescue," fluorescent yellow tailgate, yellow base ....$1 – 2**
17. black, "Surf 2," orange tailgate, black base .... $3 – 4
18. white, no markings, white tailgate, white base, Graffic Traffic (stickers and markers included with set) .... $12 – 16

Maxi Taxi, 3", #72, 1973 (similar castings: Ford Capri, Hot Rocker)

1. yellow, "M" on roof, Hong Kong cast .... $8 – 10
2. yellow, "M" on roof, Macau cast ..$4 – 5
3. yellow, "I" on roof, Hong Kong cast .... $3 – 4
4. yellow, no markings, Hong Kong cast .... $4 – 5

Mazda IMSA, 3", #6, 1983, US; #7, 1983, Europe

1. dark blue, red interior, white and orange, Macau cast .... $3 – 4
2. dark blue, red interior, white and stripes, Manaus (Brazil) cast .... $40 – 50

Mazda RX-7, with no spoiler, #31, 1982

1. white with wide stripe on sides, ivory interior .... $4 – 5
2. white with thin stripe on sides, ivory interior .... $4 – 5
3. white with wide stripe on sides, tan interior .... $4 – 5
4. white with thin stripe on sides, tan interior .... $4 – 5
5. black with gold stripe on sides, tan interior .... $4 – 5

Mazda RX-7, with spoiler, #31, 1983

1. **black with gold stripe on sides, Macau cast ....$3 – 4**

2. **white with "7" and stripe accents, Macau cast ....$3 – 4**
3. black with "RX7" and "MAZDA," Manaus cast, Brazil issue .... $40 – 50

Mazda RX-7, #8, 1994; #54, 1994, international; #67, 1998; #41, 1998, international; #20, 1999

1. fluorescent orange, "Matchbox Get In The Fast Lane," "Toy Fair 1994" ...$40 – 50
2. black, no graphics, chrome windows, gray wheel hubs, rubber tires, World Class .... $3 – 4

3. **black with silver stripes, "Mazda," 1999 ....$1 – 2**
4. blue, rubber tires on chrome rims, Gold Collection .... $16 – 24
5. red with black and yellow on roof and hood .... $1 – 2
6. red with black and yellow on hood .... $3 – 4

7. **red with trim detail, rubber tires on chrome rims, Premiere Collection ....$4 – 5**
8. red, "Go Bombers! 1997," Australia issue .... $4 – 5
9. red, rubber tires on chrome rims, Premiere Collection .... $5 – 6

10. **metallic bronze to black gradient, no graphics, 1998 ....$1 – 2**
11. metallic gold, no graphics, 1997 75 Challenge .... 12 – 16

12. **metallic green to black gradient, no ....$1 – 2**

13. **metallic green, rubber tires on chrome rims, JC Penney Premiere Collection ....$4 – 5**

14. metallic orange to black gradient, no graphics, 1998 .... $1 - 2
15. metallic silver with red blotch ... $4 - 5
16. metallic yellow to red gradient, no gradients .... $1 - 2
17. lavender chrome with yellow and blue, 5-pack .... $1 - 2

18. purple chrome with yellow and orange, 5-pack .... $1 - 2
19. yellow-orange with black and pink on hood and sides .... $1 - 2
20. yellow-orange with black and pink on sides only, Aquafresh promotional .... $5 - 6
21. yellow-orange with black and pink on hood and sides, "Nationwise Auto Parts" on roof .... $25 - 35
22. yellow, rubber tires on chrome rims, Premiere Collection .... $4 - 5

Mazda RX-7 Savannah, no spoiler, #76, 1981; #2, 1981, Japan
1. yellow with stripe and "RX7," Japan cast, Japan issue .... $16 - 24
2. green with stripe and "RX7," Japan cast, Japanese issue .... $16 - 24
3. light green, no markings, Hong Kong cast, Australia issue .... $16 - 24
4. blue, no markings, Hong Kong cast, Speedsticks, US issue .... $4 - 5
5. blue with black stripe, "RX7," Hong Kong cast, US issue .... $25 - 35
6. blue with red and white stripes, issued in US as Boulevard Blaster, Hong Kong cast .... $6 - 8

Mazda RX500, 3", #66, 1971
1. red with amber windows, chrome interior, unpainted base, "77," England cast .... $9 - 12
2. red with amber windows, chrome interior, white base, "77," England cast .... $9 - 12
3. red with amber windows, tan interior, white base, "77," England cast .. $9 - 12
4. red with purple windows, chrome interior, white base, "77," England cast .... $12 - 16
5. red with purple windows, chrome interior, white base, "Castrol" labels, England cast .... $700 - 900
6. red with purple windows, chrome interior, white base, England cast .. $20 - 30
7. red with purple windows, tan interior, white base, England cast ..... $20 - 30
8. orange with amber windows, chrome interior, unpainted base, England cast .... $60 - 80
9. orange with purple windows, chrome interior, unpainted base, England cast .... $12 - 16
10. orange with purple windows, chrome interior, white base, England cast .... $12 - 16

11. green with amber windows, chrome interior, pearl silver base, "66," Hong Kong cast .... $12 - 16

Mazda Savanna RX-7 (see Mazda RX-7 Savannah)

Mechanical Horse and Trailer, #10, 1955
1. red cab, gray trailer, metal wheels $2^3/_8$" .... $60 - 75

Mechanical Horse and Trailer, red cab, tan trailer, $2^{15}/_{16}$", 10-B, 1958
1. metal wheels .... $45 - 60
2. gray plastic wheels .... $50 - 60

Mercedes **(see Mercedes-Benz)**

Mercedes-Benz 220 SE, $2^3/_4$", #53, 1963
1. maroon with gray plastic wheels .... $25 - 30
2. red with gray plastic wheels .... $25 - 30
3. maroon with silver plastic wheels .... $30 - 35

4. maroon with black plastic wheels .... $25 - 30
5. red with black plastic wheels .... $100 - 120

Mercedes-Benz 230 SL Convertible, 3", #27, 1966

1. ivory, regular wheels .... $6 - 8
2. white, regular wheels .... $8 - 10

3. ivory with red interior, Superfast wheels .... $30 - 40
4. off-white with red interior, Superfast wheels .... $30 - 40
5. yellow with red interior, Superfast wheels .... $20 - 25
6. yellow with black interior, Superfast wheels .... $16 - 24

Mercedes-Benz 280 GE Ambulance, #10, 2005
1. white with black roof, graphics, 2005 #10 .... $1 - 2

Mercedes-Benz 280 GE G-Wagon, 3", #30, 1984; #40, 2000 (also see Mercedes-Benz 280 GE Ambulance)
1. red with black roof, "Mission Satellite Top Secret," 2000 Space Explorer ... $1 - 2
2. red with black roof, "Mission Satellite Top Secret," "Matchbox 2000," 2000 Space Explorer .... $3 - 4
3. red with gray roof, "Matchbox Rescue Unit," Light & Sound .... $4 - 5
4. red with red roof, "Fire Metro Airport," Siren Force/Rescue 911 .... $10 - 12
5. red with white roof, "Matchbox Fires Rescue Dept.," Avon Light & Sound .... $5 - 6
6. red with white roof, "Matchbox Rescue Unit," "Fire Dept.," Light & Sound .. $4 - 5
7. red with white roof, "Rescue Unit" and checkerboard pattern, Motor City .. $1 - 2
8. orange with white roof, "Lufthansa" .... $4 - 5
9. fluorescent orange with white roof, "Auto Rescue 24 Hr. Towing," Thailand cast .... $1 - 2
10. fluorescent orange with white roof, "Police 8," "Intercom City" .... $12 - 16
11. fluorescent orange with white roof, "Rescue" and checkerboard pattern, Emergency Pack .... $1 - 2
12. yellow with black roof, "Tough Construction — Construction Foreman," Light & Sound .... $4 - 5

13. yellow with blue roof, red and white on doors with "S.C.U.B.A." and "Beach Patrol," 2002 Sand Castle Rescue Team 5-pack with plastic bucket .... $3 - 4

14. yellow with white roof, "Beach Patrol Unit 2," Light & Sound .... $4 – 5
15. army green with tan roof, "LS 2014," Commando .... $5 – 6
16. blue with blue roof, "SWAT Unit Team Support," Siren Force/Rescue 911 .... $10 – 12
17. white with orange roof, "Ambulance" and checkerboard pattern, Motor City .... $4 – 5
18. white with fluorescent orange roof, "Marine Rescue" and checkerboard pattern, Emergency Pack .... $1 – 2
19. white with green roof, Polizei, Germany issue .... $4 – 5
20. white with green roof and doors, "Polizei" .... $6 – 7

21. white with turquoise roof, "Beach Patrol," "S.C.U.B.A." and graphics, 2003 Hero City 5-pack #5 ...$2 – 3
22. white with blue roof, "Test Centre," Launcher 5-pack .... $1 – 2
23. white with white roof, "Auto Rescue 24 Hr. Towing," Siren Force/Rescue 911 .... $10 – 12
24. white with white roof, "Polizei," checkerboard pattern, Two-Pack .... $3 – 4
25. white with white roof, "Polizei," green doors .... $3 – 4
26. white with white roof, "Polizei," green doors and hood .... $1 – 2
27. white with white roof, "Lufthansa," Macau cast .... $5 – 6
28. white with white roof, "Lufthansa," Thailand cast .... $1 – 2
29. beige with dark green roof, green stripes, Avon Light & Sound ..... $5 – 6
30. butterscotch with black roof, graphics, 2006 5-pack .... $2 – 3
31. metallic gray with black roof, red stripe and fish design, 5-pack .... $3 – 4
32. metallic gray with black roof, "Marine Research," 5-pack .... $1 – 2

Mercedes-Benz 300 E, 3", #58, 1987
1. metallic light blue, dark blue interior, Macau cast .... $1 – 2
2. metallic light blue, dark blue interior, Thailand cast .... $1 – 2
3. blue-gray, "Go Blues! 1997," gray interior, China cast, Australia issue .. $4 – 5
4. white, "Polizei 5075," green stripe, silver star, tan interior, Thailand cast .... $1 – 2
5. white, "Polizei 5075," green stripe, tan interior, China cast .... $3 – 4
6. white, "Polizei 5075," green stripe, tan interior, Thailand cast .... $1 – 2
7. white, "Rijkspolitie," dark blue interior, Thailand cast, Dutch Convoy issue .... $5 – 6

Mercedes-Benz 300 SE, with 2⁷/₈", #46, 1968
1. green, black plastic wheels .. $16 – 24

2. metallic blue, black plastic wheels, 1968 ....$30 – 36
3. metallic blue, Superfast wheels, 1970 .... $80 – 100
4. metallic orange, Superfast wheels .... $20 – 25
5. metallic gold, Superfast wheels .... $20 – 25
6. army green with "Staff" labels, Superfast wheels .... $9 – 12
7. metallic gray, Superfast wheels .... $90 – 120

Mercedes-Benz 350 SL Convertible (also Mercedes Tourer), 3", #6, 1973
1. orange with black roof .... $9 – 12
2. yellow with black roof .... $6 – 9
3. metallic gray with black roof, no markings $30 – 45
4. metallic gray with black roof, "Rennservice" labels, Germany issue .. $40 – 50
5. metallic orange with black roof ..$9 – 12
6. metallic orange with white roof .. $6 – 9
7. maroon with white roof .... $9 – 12
8. red with white roof .... $6 – 9
9. blue with no roof .... $6 – 9
10. purple with no roof .... $9 – 12
11. white with no roof, translucent red interior .... $9 – 12
12. pale gray with no roof, translucent white interior, UK issue .... $40 – 50
13. beige with no roof, translucent white interior, UK issue .... $40 – 50
14. red with no roof, translucent white interior .... $40 – 50
15. black with no roof, white interior .... $40 – 50

Mercedes-Benz 430 Wagon, #68, 1999, Germany
1. metallic dark blue .... $4 – 5
2. white, "Euro Taxi" and green band .... $4 – 5

Mercedes-Benz 450 SEL/Taxi/Polizei, 3", #56, 1979
1. metallic blue with tan interior ... $3 – 4
2. metallic blue with red interior ... $6 – 8

3. beige with ivory "Taxi" sign on roof, tan interior ....$3 – 4
4. beige with ivory "Taxi" sign on roof, brown interior .... $4 – 5
5. white with blue roof light .... $8 – 10
6. white and green, "Polizei," blue roof light ....$3 – 4
7. white and green, no markings, blue roof light .... $3 – 4

Mercedes-Benz 500 AMG (see Mercedes-Benz AMG 500 SEC)

Mercedes-Benz 500 SEC (see Mercedes-Benz AMG 500 SEC)
1. black, 2006 #2 .... $1 – 2
2. metallic blue, 2007 #20 .... $1 – 2

Mercedes-Benz 500 SL Convertible, 3", #12, 1990; #33, 1990, international
1. red with white interior, clear windshield, Show Stoppers .... $3 – 4
2. red with gray and black interior, clear windshield, rubber tires on chrome rims, Premiere Collection .... $4 – 6
3. bright green with reddish brown interior, Mattel Wheels 5-pack .... $1 – 2
4. bright green with reddish brown interior, "Merry Christmas," "Ad-Ventures 1999," Color Comp promotional .... $20 – 25
5. dark blue with two-tone gray interior, clear windshield, rubber tires on chrome rims, Premiere Collection .... $4 – 6
6. black with dark gray interior, chrome windshield, rubber tires on gray rims, World Class .... $6 – 9

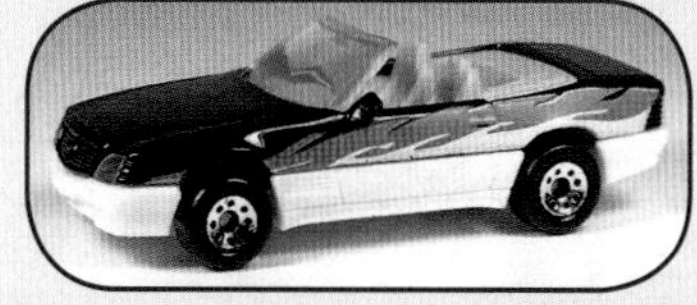

7. black upper with white lower, light gray interior, pink and white, clear windshield ....$1 – 2
8. black with black interior, clear windshield, rubber tires on chrome rims, Premiere Collection .... $4 – 6
9. metallic gray with dark blue interior, clear windshield .... $1 – 2
10. metallic gray with maroon interior, chrome windshield, rubber tires on gray rims, World Class .... $6 – 9

11. white upper with gray lower, brown interior, "500SL," clear windshield .... $1 – 2
12. white with maroon and black interior, rubber tires on chrome rims, Gold Collection .... $15 – 20

13. metallic silver with black interior, no markings, ASAP promotional blank ..$35 – 45
14. metallic silver with black interior, "Personal Lines 25 Years," ASAP promotional .... $50 – 100
15. metallic silver with black interior, "Citrix Technology Directions 2000," ASAP promotional .... $75 – 125
16. metallic silver with black interior, "Classic Collision," ASAP promotional ....$75 – 125
17. metallic silver with black interior, "Thunder Machines AMG Line," ASAP promotional .... $75 – 125

Mercedes-Benz 600 SL/SEL, 3", #38, 1992; #39, 1991, international
1. metallic red, detailed trim, two-tone gray interior, clear windows, rubber tires on chrome rims, Ultra Class .... $9 – 12
2. dark green, detailed trim, two-tone gray interior, clear windows, rubber tires on chrome rims, Australian Premiere Collection #1 .... $4 – 5
3. blue, detailed trim, two-tone gray interior, clear windows, rubber tires on chrome rims, Premiere Collection #2 .... $4 – 5
4. silver blue, detailed trim, two-tone gray interior, clear windows, rubber tires on chrome rims, JC Penney Premiere Collection .... $4 – 5

5. metallic silver, light gray interior, clear windows ....$1 – 2
6. black, detailed trim, two-tone gray interior, clear windows, rubber tires on chrome rims, Premiere Collection #5 .... $4 – 5
7. white, detailed trim, two-tone gray interior, clear windows, rubber tires on chrome rims, Special Class #2 .. $4 – 5
8. metallic brown, light gray interior, clear windows, Show Stoppers .... $3 – 4

Mercedes-Benz A-Class, #56, 1999; #51, 1999, international
1. red, "New Hope Auto Show 2000" with kayak and splash design, purple interior, Color Comp promotional ...... $16 – 24

2. red with kayak and splash design, purple interior, 1999 Wilderness Adventure ....$1 – 2
3. red with no design, black interior, 1999 Forest Run international .... $3 – 4

4. yellow with "Scrat" illustration, 2006 Ice Age 2 5-pack J4720 .... $2 – 3

5. black with silver trim, 2005 Superfast #32 ....$3 – 4
6. metallic gray, "New Hope Auto Show 2000," Color Comp promotional .... $16 – 24
7. metallic gray, no design, black interior, 2000 German Classics international ....$3 – 4

8. white with snowflake design on sides, "Alarm," 2003 Hero City 5-pack #8 ....$4 – 6

Mercedes-Benz AAV, #319, 1997, Jurassic Park; #337, 1997, Jurassic Park
1. light green, "The Lost World," green camouflage, roof turret with arms .....$6 – 8
2. light green, "The Lost World," green camouflage, roof luggage rack ... $6 – 8

Mercedes-Benz Actros 1857 Semi-Tractor, #64, 1999, Germany; #71, 2005
1. yellow with black base, no markings, China cast .... $6 – 8
2. metallic burgundy, 2005 #71 .. $1 – 2

3. metallic green with beige graphics, 2006 J4674 5-pack ....$4 – 5

Mercedes-Benz AMG 500 SEC, #43, 1984
1. red, "AMG," black interior, clear windows, Macau cast .... $3 – 4
2. red, "AMG" and stripes, black interior, clear windows, new Superfast wheels .... $5 – 6
3. red with green and yellow stripes, brown interior, clear windows, Dutch issue ....$10 – 12
4. metallic red, "AMG" and stripes, black interior, clear windows, Laser wheels .... $5 – 6
5. army green, "Matchbox Military Police MP-090196," Light & Sound ... $5 – 6
6. black, "500SEC," brown interior .. $3 – 4
7. black, "500SEC" and stripes, brown interior, black base .... $3 – 4
8. black, "500SEC" and stripes, brown interior, silver base .... $5 – 6
9. black, "Redoxon," "500SEC," brown interior, Hong Kong issue .... $20 – 25
10. black, "Pace Car Heuer," "Rescue 911," black metal base, Siren Force .. $8 – 10
11. black, "Pace Car Heuer," "Rescue 911," black plastic base, Siren Force .. $8 – 10

12. black, "Pace Car Heuer," Siren Force .... $6 – 8
13. metallic gray, "Police 17," blue stripes, Light & Sound .... $5 – 6
14. ivory, "Emergency Doctor," "Rescue 911," black metal base, Siren Force .... $8 – 10

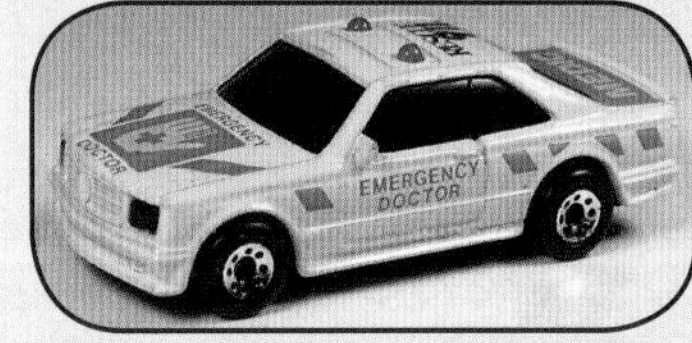

15. ivory, "Emergency Doctor," black metal base, Siren Force .... $6 – 8
16. ivory, "Emergency Doctor," black plastic base, Siren Force .... $6 – 8
17. white, "500SEC" and silver stripes, brown interior, Saudi Arabian issue .... $20 – 25
18. white, "AMG," blue interior, Macau cast .... $4 – 5
19. white, "AMG," black interior ..... $7 – 9
20. white, "1 Pig Racing Team," brown interior, Hong Kong issue .... $10 – 12
21. white, "7," red and blue design, black interior, gold chrome 8-dot wheels, Macau cast .... $4 – 5
22. white, "7," red and blue design, black interior, silver chrome 8-dot wheels, Macau cast .... $4 – 5
23. white, "7," red and blue design, black interior, new Superfast wheels, Macau cast .... $80 – 120
24. white with detailed trim, chrome windows, rubber tires on gray rims, World Class .... $7 – 9

25. white, "Police," "Rescue 911," red and blue stripes, Siren Force ....$8 – 10

26. white, "Police," red and blue stripes, black metal base, Siren Force .. $8 – 10
27. white, "Police," red and blue stripes, black plastic base, Siren Force .. $8 – 10
28. white, "Police 17," blue stripes, Light & Sound .... $5 – 6

Mercedes-Benz AMG C-Class, #35, 1996; #75, 1996, international

1. metallic blue, "25 Camsport," 1996 ....$1 – 2

2. metallic gold, 1997 75 Challenge ....$6 – 12
3. yellow, "25 Camsport," black and red accents, 1997 .... $1 – 2
4. metallic gray, "Team Matchbox 1," rubber tires on chrome rims, Premiere Collection #15 .... $4 – 5

5. silver with blue and white graphics, "Camsport," "25 Rally Systems," 1997 Racing 5-pack ....$2 – 3

Mercedes-Benz "Binz" Ambulance, 2⁷/₈", #3, 1968

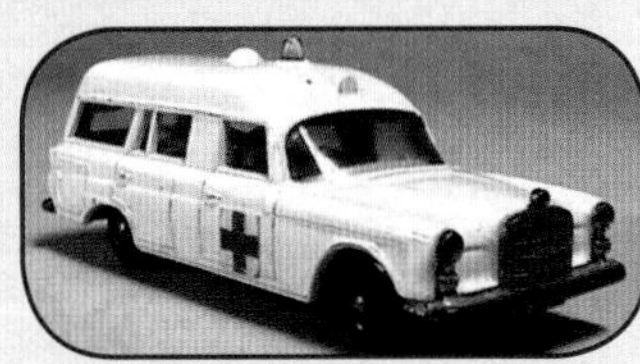

1. ivory, black plastic wheels, with patient on stretcher, rear hatch opens ....$20 – 25

2. ivory, Superfast wheels, with patient on stretcher, rear hatch opens, 1970 ....$25 – 30
3. ivory, Superfast wheels, rear hatch doesn't open .... $12 – 16
4. olive, Superfast wheels, rear hatch doesn't open, Two-Pack .... $12 – 16

Mercedes-Benz C-Class Taxi, Superfast #11, 2006

1. burgundy, 2006 Superfast #11 ..$4 – 5

Mercedes-Benz CLK Convertible, #71, 1999, Germany; #1, 2000, USA; #62, 2005

1. metallic burgundy with black interior, 2005 Superfast #67 ....$3 – 4

2. maroon with butterscotch interior, 2005 10-pack #2 .... $1 – 2

3. brown, 2005 #62 ....$1 – 2

4. metallic green with black interior, 1999 Germany issue .... $4 – 6

5. metallic green with tan interior, 2000 Open Road series 1 .....$1 – 2

6. metallic green with tan interior, "Matchbox 2000" on windshield, 2000 Open Road series 1 .... $3 – 4

7. white, "Hero City Sports" graphics, 2003 Hero City 5-pack #6 ...$1 – 2

Mercedes-Benz CLS-500, 1:65, #2, 2006; #20, 2007

1. metallic burgundy, 2006 #2 .. $1 – 2

2. metallic dark green, 2007 5-pack K9615 .... $1 – 2

3. metallic dark blue, 2007 #20 ..$1 – 2

Mercedes-Benz Coach, 2⁷/₈", #68, 1965

1. turquoise .... $150 – 175
2. orange .... $12 – 15

Mercedes-Benz Container Truck, 3", #42, 1977

1. red with beige container, "Sea/Land" labels .... $6 – 8
2. red with beige container, "N.Y.K." labels .... $6 – 8
3. red with beige container, "O.C.L." labels .... $12 – 16
4. red with beige container, "Confern" labels, Germany issue .... $40 – 50
5. red with white container, "Matchbox" labels .... $9 – 12
6. red with white container, "Mayflower" labels .... $9 – 12
7. red with white container, "Confern" applied over "Mayflower" ...... $50 – 60
8. yellow with yellow container, "Deutsche Bundespost," Germany issue . $30 – 40
9. green with green container, "Confern" applied over "Mayflower" .. $120 – 160
10. green with green container, "Mayflower" labels .... $7 – 9
11. blue with blue container, "Karstadt," Germany issue .... $40 – 50

Mercedes-Benz E-430 Wagon, #34, 2001; #22, 2006

1. metallic green, "Polizei," "K-9," 2001 .... $3 – 4

2. turquoise with red metal base, amber windows, mountain graphics, light blue interior, 2003 5-pack #10 ....$1 – 2

3. **black, 2006 #22 ....$1 - 2**

Mercedes-Benz E-Class 1997, #70, 1998; #65, 1999; #65, 1999, international

1. metallic pink, "Matchbox USA 20th Anniversary Convention," "Color Comp Inc. Conference," Color Comp promotional ....$30 – 40

2. **metallic dark gray, "E Class," red pinstripe, red interior, 1998 Street Cruisers ....$1 - 2**
3. metallic gray, "Intergalactic Research," 1999 Science Fiction .... $1 – 2
4. cream, "Taxi 23000," Germany issue ....$4 – 5

Mercedes-Benz G-Wagon (see Mercedes-Benz 280 GE G-Wagon)

Mercedes-Benz GTC, #35, 1996

1. metallic cornflower blue with white and coral pink rally accents .... $1 – 2

Mercedes-Benz Lorry, 3", #1, 1968

1. **black plastic wheels, mint green with orange canopy ....$10 - 15**
2. black plastic wheels, mint green with yellow canopy .... $15 – 20
3. Superfast wheels, metallic gold with orange canopy .... $20 – 30
4. Superfast wheels, metallic gold with yellow canopy .... $15 – 20
5. Superfast wheels, red with yellow canopy, "Transcontinental Haulage" (Two-Pack) .... $5 – 10
6. Superfast wheels, light olive with tan canopy, "USA48350" (Two-Pack) .... $10 – 15
7. Superfast wheels, dark olive with tan canopy, "USA48350" (Two-Pack) ....$75 – 90
8. Superfast wheels, light olive with tan canopy, "4TS 702K" (Two-Pack) ....$5 – 10
9. Superfast wheels, blue with orange-yellow canopy, blue windows, "IMS" (Two-Pack) .... $15 – 25
10. Superfast wheels, blue with orange-yellow canopy, purple windows, "IMS" (Two-Pack) .... $45 – 60

Mercedes-Benz ML-430, #63, 1999, Germany; #57, 2000, international; #77, 2000 US

1. metallic maroon, "Matchbox," "Midwest Diecast Miniatures Customer Appreciation," custom promotional .... $16 – 24
2. metallic maroon, 5-spoke concave wheels, 1999 Germany issue .. $5 – 6
3. metallic maroon, 10-spoke wheels, Target Eggmobiles 3-pack .... $16 – 20
4. dark green, no markings, 5-pack ..$1 – 2

5. **bright green, "Rugrats" and cartoon character illustrations, 2003 Nickelodeon 5-pack ....$1 - 2**

6. **blue with "Superman" logo and graphics, 2006 Superman 5-pack J4725 ....$2 - 3**

7. **metallic blue with "The Osbournes" on sides, Matchbox Collectibles, Kelly Osbourne's car ....$3 - 4**
8. dark blue, "If You Don't Collect Matchbox...Get Out of the Way," custom promotional .... $16 – 24
9. dark blue, "Matchbox 2000," 2000 Snow Explorer #77 .... $3 – 4

10. **dark blue, 2000 Snow Explorer #77 ....$1 - 2**

11. **white and pale yellow, "Coca-Cola," "The Pause That Refreshes," illustration in circle, pale yellow lower half, rubber tires on chrome rims, Matchbox Collectibles Coca-Cola Collection .... $5 - 6**

Mercedes-Benz S - 500, #66, 1999, Germany; #32, 2000, international; Superfast #5, 2005

1. yellow with blue stripe, 5-spoke concave wheels, 5-pack .... $3 – 4
2. yellow with blue stripe, 10-spoke wheels, 5-pack .... $1 – 2
3. black, 2000 German Classics series, international issue .... $3 – 4
4. metallic gray, 1999 German issue .... $4 – 5

5. **dark blue, 2005 Superfast #5 ....$4 - 5**

6. **pearl white, 2004 Superfast #60 ....$3 - 4**

Mercedes-Benz Sauber Group C Racer, 3", #46, 1985; #66, 1985

1. red, "BASF Cassettes," black airfoil, gold wheels, Macau cast .... $4 – 5
2. red, "BASF Cassettes," black airfoil, silver wheels, Macau cast .... $4 – 5
3. red, "Royal Mail Swiftair," red foil, Macau cast, UK issue .... $6 – 8
4. red and white, "Champion 51," maroon airfoil, China cast .... $1 – 2
5. red and white, "Champion 51," maroon airfoil, Thailand cast .... $1 – 2

6. **red and white, "Champion 51," red airfoil, China cast .... $1 - 2**
7. pale red with black, white and yellow accents, armaments, no airfoil, Roadblasters .... $6 – 8
8. fluorescent pink and blue, "Matchbox" and flames, blue airfoil, chrome and black windows, China cast, Lightning Wheels .... $4 – 5
9. fluorescent orange and yellow with lightning bolts, fluorescent yellow airfoil, blue chrome and black windows, China cast, Lightning Wheels .... $4 – 5
10. fluorescent yellow and orange, "Lightning," fluorescent yellow airfoil, blue chrome and black windows, China cast, Lightning Wheels .... $4 – 5
11. yellow and red, "Matchbox USA 11th Annual Convention & Toy Show 1992," red airfoil, China cast .... $12 – 15
12. yellow with orange and blue accents, blue airfoil, Macau cast, New Superfast Wheels .... $4 – 5
13. yellow with orange and blue accents, blue airfoil, Macau cast, Laser Wheels .... $4 – 5
14. pale blue, "Grand Prix 46," black foil, Macau cast .... $5 – 6
15. blue and fluorescent pink, "Lightning" and flames, blue foil, China cast, Lightning Wheels .... $4 – 5
16. black, "Cargantua," black airfoil, Macau cast, New Superfast Wheels ..$16 – 24

17. **white, "50," red stripes, blue graphics, blue airfoil, silver wheels, China cast .... $1 - 2**

18. **white, "50," blue and pink accents, pink airfoil, gold wheels, Thailand cast .... $1 - 2**
19. white, "50," blue on sides only, pink on hood only, pink airfoil, silver wheels, China cast .... $1 – 2
20. white, "50," blue on sides only, pink on hood only, pink airfoil, silver wheels, Thailand cast .... $1 – 2
21. white, "50," blue and pink accents, pink airfoil, silver wheels, Thailand cast .... $1 – 2
22. white, "Castrol Sauber 61," black airfoil, gold wheels, Macau cast .... $3 – 4
23. white, "Castrol Sauber 61," black airfoil, silver wheels, Macau cast .... $1 – 2
24. white, "Grand Prix 46," black airfoil, gold wheels, Thailand cast .... $1 – 2
25. white, "Grand Prix 46," black airfoil, silver wheels, China cast .... $1 – 2
26. white, "Grand Prix 46," black airfoil, 6-spoke spiral wheels, China cast ... $1 – 2
27. white, "Grand Prix 46," black airfoil, 6-spoke spiral wheels, Thailand cast .... $4 – 5
28. white, "Grand Prix 46," black airfoil, 8-dot silver wheels, Macau cast .. $1 – 2
29. white, "Grand Prix 46," black airfoil, 8-dot silver wheels, Thailand cast .... $1 – 2
30. white, "Jr. Matchbox Collector's Club," black airfoil, Macau cast, Australia issue .... $9 – 12
31. white and orange, "Bisotherm," "Baustein," orange airfoil, Macau cast, Swiss issue .... $10 – 12
32. white with blue and pink accents, pink airfoil .... $1 – 2
33. white with white airfoil, gold wheels, no markings, Thailand cast, Graffic Traffic .... $8 – 10
34. chrome plated with black airfoil, no markings, Macau cast, custom promotional .... $16 – 24

Mercedes-Benz Scaffold Truck, $2^1/_2$", #11, 1969

1. **metallic gray with yellow scaffolding, black plastic wheels .... $15 - 20**
2. metallic gray with yellow scaffolding, Superfast wheels .... $30 – 40

Mercedes-Benz SL-55 AMG Convertible, #48, 2005; #11, 2006; #19, 2007

1. **metallic silver, 2005 #48 (H1850 on 2006 package) .... $1 - 2**

2. **metallic burgundy, 2006 5-pack J4672 .... $1 - 2**
3. **metallic red, 2006 #11 .... $1 - 2**

4. **black, 2007 5-pack K9615 .. $1 - 2**
5. red with black interior, 2007 #19 .. $1 – 2

Mercedes-Benz Tourer (see Mercedes-Benz 350SL Convertible)

Mercedes-Benz Trac 1600 Turbo Farm Tractor, $2^3/_4$", #73, 1990; #90, 1999; #46, 2000; #27, 1991, international; #5, 1999, international; #26, international

1. mustard yellow and brown, "Power," China cast, 2000 Farming ...... $1 – 2
2. mustard yellow and brown, "Power," "Matchbox 2000," China cast, 2000 Farming .... $3 – 4
3. green, "FA2318," black interior, China cast, Germany issue .... $5 – 6
4. green, no markings, yellow interior, Thailand cast, Team Convoy Two-Pack .... $3 – 4
5. dark green, no markings, green interior, Thailand cast, 1999 Farming ... $3 – 4
6. light green, no markings, green interior, Macau cast .... $1 – 2
7. light green, no markings, green interior, Thailand cast .... $1 – 2
8. light green, "MB Trac," green interior, Thailand cast .... $1 – 2

9. **blue and orange-red, "Chiefton Power," China cast, 1999 Farming .... $1 - 2**
10. "Iowa," Matchbox Across America 50th Birthday Series #29 — Central Collection .... $4 – 5

Mercedes-Benz Trailer, $3^1/_2$", #2, 1968

1. **black plastic wheels, mint green with orange canopy .... $10 - 12**

2. black plastic wheels, mint green with yellow canopy .... $16 – 18
3. Superfast wheels, metallic gold with orange canopy .... $20 – 25
4. Superfast wheels, metallic gold with yellow canopy .... $15 – 20
5. Superfast wheels, red with yellow canopy, "Transcontinental Haulage" .... $5 – 7
6. Superfast wheels, light olive with tan canopy, "USA48350" .... $10 – 12
7. Superfast wheels, dark olive with tan canopy, "USA48350" .... $70 – 85
8. Superfast wheels, light olive with tan canopy, "4TS 702K" .... $10 – 12
9. Superfast wheels, dark olive with tan canopy, "4TS 702K" .... $70 – 85
10. Superfast wheels, blue with orange-yellow canopy, "IMS" .... $15 – 20
11. Superfast wheels, yellow with white canopy, "Alpine Rescue," Two-Pack .... $4 – 6
12. Superfast wheels, yellow with no canopy, no markings .... $3 – 5
13. Superfast wheels, red with white canopy, "Unfall Rettung," Two-Pack .... $4 – 6
12. Superfast wheels, white with orange canopy, "C & S" .... $4 – 6
13. Superfast wheels, red with white canopy, "Big Top Circus" .... $5 – 7

Mercedes-Benz TV News Truck, 3", #68, 1989 – 1997; #62, 1999; #98, 2000; #73, 1989 – 1997, international; #3, 1998, international

1. "Action News 6," white with yellow roof with lime green TV camera and antenna, China cast, ASAP promotional .... $16 – 24
2. "Action Radar," "Xtreme Mission," lime green with metallic gray roof with metallic gray TV camera and antenna, China cast, 5-pack .... $1 – 2
3. "Action TV," black with football graphics, yellow roof with yellow TV camera and antenna, China cast, 5-pack .... $1 – 2
4. "Action TV," black with soccer ball graphics, yellow roof with yellow TV camera and antenna, China cast, 5-pack .... $3 – 4
5. "American International Recovery," white with yellow roof with lime green TV camera and antenna, China cast, ASAP promotional .... $120 – 160
6. "Fox 8 WJW Cleveland," white with black roof with white TV camera and antenna, China cast, ASAP promotional .... $16 – 24
7. "Fox 8 WJW Cleveland," white with yellow roof with lime green TV camera and antenna, China cast, ASAP promotional .... $16 – 24
8. "Intercom City TV," white with blue roof with white TV camera and antenna, Thailand cast, Intercom City .... $8 – 10

9. "Intergalactic Research," red with black roof with metallic gray TV camera and antenna, 1999 Science Fiction ....$1 – 2

10. "Live Action News 99," white with blue roof, fuchsia rocker panels, 2006 5-pack J4679 ....$1 – 2

11. "Matchbox Cable TV," yellow with black roof with red TV camera and antenna, 1997 City Streets 5-pack ....$1 – 2

12. "Matchbox Channel 4," black with red roof, yellow TV camera and antenna, China cast, 1998 Around Town 5-pack .... $1 – 2

13. "MBTV Mobile One," "75 News," blue with metallic gray roof with light orange TV camera and antenna, Thailand cast ....$1 – 2

14. "MBTV Mobile One," "75 News," blue with metallic gray roof with orange TV camera and antenna, Macau cast .... $1 – 2
15. "MBTV Mobile One," "75 News," blue and metallic gray roof with orange TV camera and antenna, Thailand cast .... $1 – 2
16. "Mission Impossible," black with dark gray roof with dark gray TV camera and antenna, China cast, Star Cars .... $5 – 6
17. "RCA," white with yellow roof, lime green TV camera and antenna, China cast, ASAP promotional .... $25 – 35
18. "Rock TV," blue and white with metallic gray roof .... $2 – 4

19. "Rock TV," white with multicolor diagonal lines, blue roof with white TV camera and antenna, Thailand cast ....$1 – 2

20. "Sky Satellite Television," white with dark blue roof with white TV camera and antenna, Thailand cast .... $1 – 2

21. "Sky Satellite TV," white with blue roof with white TV camera and antenna, China cast .... $3 – 4
22. "Super RTL Live!" blue with red roof with light gray TV camera and antenna, China cast, Germany issue .. $4 – 5
23. "TV 6," blue with yellow roof, lime green TV camera and antenna, China cast, 1998 Around the Town international .... $1 – 2
24. "Weather, News at Noon, Sports," TV camera graphics, metallic gray with black roof with metallic gray TV camera and antenna, tinted windows, China cast, 2000 On the Road Again .. $1 – 2
25. "Weather, News at Noon, Sports," TV camera graphics, "Matchbox 2000," metallic gray with black roof with metallic gray TV camera and antenna, tinted windows, China cast, 2000 On the Road Again .... $3 – 4
26. "Weather, News at Noon, Sports," TV camera graphics, metallic gray with black roof with metallic gray TV camera and antenna, blue windows, China cast, 2000 On the Road Again .... $20 – 30
27. "World Cup Mobile Unit Television," white with blue roof with red TV camera and antenna, China cast, 5-pack ... $3 – 4
28. "World Cup Mobile Unit Television," white with blue roof with white TV camera and antenna, China cast, Action Pack .... $1 – 2

29. white with black roof, red TV camera and antenna, globe and satellite design, China casting ....$3 – 4
30. white with white roof, brown TV camera and antenna, no markings, Graffic Traffic ....$12 – 16
31. white with white roof, orange TV camera and antenna, no markings, Graffic Traffic ....$12 – 16
32. white with yellow roof, lime green TV camera and antenna, China cast, ASAP promotional blank ....$30 – 40
33. white with purple roof, metallic gray TV camera and antenna, Thailand cast, 2006 5-pack J4679 ....$1 – 2

Mercedes-Benz Unimog, $2^1/_2$", #49, 1967
1. tan with turquoise chassis, black tires on plastic hubs ....$9 – 12
2. blue with red chassis, black tires on plastic hubs ....$7 – 10
3. blue with red chassis, Superfast wheels, 1970 ....$20 – 30
4. metallic light blue with red chassis, Superfast wheels ....$20 – 30
5. army green with star label, Superfast wheels ....$80 – 120
6. army green with "A" label, Superfast wheels ....$9 – 12

Mercedes-Benz Unimog, #46, 2007
1. orange with black base ....$1 – 2

Mercedes-Benz Unimog with snowplow, 3", #48, 1984
1. red, "UR83," white canopy, white stripes on red plow, Macau cast ....$3 – 4
2. yellow, "Rescue," white canopy, black stripes on white plow, England cast ....$9 – 12
3. yellow, "Rescue," white canopy, black stripes on yellow-orange plow, England cast ....$4 – 5
4. yellow, "Rescue," white canopy, black plow, England cast ....$4 – 5
5. yellow, "Rescue," no canopy, black stripes on yellow-orange plow, England cast ....$4 – 5
6. yellow, "Rescue," white canopy, black stripes on yellow plow, Macau cast ....$3 – 4
7. bright green, "The Lost World," metallic gray plow, includes metal dinosaur, Jurassic Park ....$7 – 8
8. white, "C&S," black stripes on orange plow, Macau cast ....$3 – 4
9. white, "C&S," black stripes on orange plow, Thailand cast ....$3 – 4
10. white with gray and army green camouflage, army green plow and canopy, China cast ....$3 – 4
11. white with gray and army green camouflage, army green plow and canopy, Thailand cast ....$3 – 4
12. white with red and blue stripes, no canopy, plastic armament, Roadblasters, Macau cast ....$7 – 8
13. white with red and dark blue stripes, no canopy, plastic armament, packaged in Tomy box, Japanese issue ..... $9 – 12

Mercury Capri (see Ford Capri, Hot Rocker, Maxi Taxi)

Mercury Commuter Police Station Wagon, 3", #55, 1971 (similar casting: Mercury Commuter Station Wagon)
1. white with red roof lights ..... $16 – 24
2. white with amber roof lights ..$90 – 120

Mercury Commuter Station Wagon, $3^1/_8$", #73, 1968 (similar casting: Mercury Commuter Police Station Wagon)
1. metallic lime green, black plastic tires on chrome hubs, 1968 .... $16 – 20
2. metallic lime green, Superfast wheels, 1970 .... $20 – 30
3. red, Superfast wheels, cow head label .... $80 – 120
4. red, Superfast wheels, cat head label ....$20 – 30

Mercury Cougar (also see Mercury Cougar 1968, Mercury Cougar Rat Rod, Mercury Cougar Villager)

Mercury Cougar 1968, doors open, 3", #62, 1968 (similar casting: Mercury Cougar Rat Rod)
1. pale yellow, black plastic wheels on chrome hubs, 1968 .... $750 – 800

2. metallic pale green, black plastic wheels on chrome hubs, 1968 ....$6 – 9
3. metallic pale green, Superfast wheels, 1970 .... $30 – 40
4. metallic green, Superfast wheels, 1970 ....$30 – 40

Mercury Cougar 1968, doors don't open, Superfast #62, 2005

1. metallic pale green, 2005 Superfast #62 ....$4 – 5

Mercury Cougar Rat Rod, doors don't open, 3", #62, 1970
1. fluorescent lime green "Rat Rod" .... $16 – 24
2. fluorescent lime green "Wildcat" ....$25 – 30

Mercury Cougar Villager Station Wagon, 3", #74, 1978
1. metallic light green with green tailgate .... $3 – 4
2. metallic dark green with green tailgate .... $3 – 4
3. olive green with green tailgate, Brazil issue .... $400 – 500
4. metallic dark blue with blue tailgate .... $3 – 4

Mercury Park Lane Fire Chief, #59, 1971 (see Mercury Park Lane Police/Fire Chief)

Mercury Park Lane Police, 3", #55, 1968; Mercury Park Lane Fire Chief, #59, 1971, Superfast wheels unless noted)
1. red, "Fire" in shield label on doors, no hood label .... $40 – 50
2. red, "Fire Chief" hood label, "Fire" in shield label on doors, #59 .... $6 – 8
3. red, "Fire Chief" in square hood label, shield label on doors, clear windows, #59 .... $12 – 16
4. red, "Fire Chief" in square hood label, helmet and axes label on doors, clear windows, #59 .... $12 – 16
5. red, "Fire Chief" red and yellow hood label, helmet and axes label on doors, clear windows, #59 .... $12 – 16
6. red, "Los Angeles Fire Dept.," Code Red .... $7 – 9
7. red, helmet and axes label on hood, shield label on doors, clear windows, #59 .... $12 – 16
8. red, helmet and axes label on hood and doors, clear windows, #59 .... $9 – 12
9. red, helmet and axes on hood, no label on doors, clear windows, #59 ..$9 – 12
10. red, no hood label, "Fire" in shield label on doors, #59 .... $6 – 8
11. red, purple windows, #59 ... $30 – 40
12. metallic blue, bar lights, yellow, blue and red trim, plastic armaments, Roadblasters .... $6 – 8
13. black, Halley's Comet Commemorative Car, New Superfast wheels, 1986 .... $8 – 10
14. white, "201" on hood, "Metro" on sides .... $9 – 12
15. white, "Los Angeles Police," blue windows, Code Red .... $7 – 9
16. white, "Los Angeles Police," clear windows, Code Red .... $7 – 9
17. white, "Los Angeles Police" on hood, "Metro Police" on doors, blue windows .... $30 – 40
18. white, "Metro" on hood, shield on doors, blue windows .... $9 – 12
19. white, "Metro" on hood, shield on doors, clear windows .... $9 – 12
20. white, "Metro" on hood, shield on doors, tinted windows .... $9 – 12
21. white, "Metro Police," blue windows .... $9 – 12
22. white, "Metro Police," clear windows .... $9 – 12

23. white, "Metro Police," tinted windows .... $9 – 12

24. white, "Police" with shield, clear windows, black tires on chrome hubs .... $9 – 12

25. white, "Police" labels, purple windows ....$35 – 45
26. white, "State Police," gray base, bar lights, blue windows, Laser Wheels ....$4 – 5
27. white, "State Police," gray base, bar lights, blue windows, New Superfast ....$4 – 5
28. white, "State Police," black base, bar lights, blue windows, New Superfast ....$9 – 12
29. white, "State Police" in orange and blue, black base, bar lights, blue windows, 8-dot wheels ....$80 – 120
30. white, no hood label, "Police" in shield label on doors, purple windows ....$40 – 50
31. white, no labels, blue windows ...$9 – 12
32. white, no labels, clear windows ...$9 – 12
33. white, Superfast wheels, 1970 ..$16 – 24
34. white with black fenders, "Metro," clear windows ....$9 – 12
35. white with black fenders, "Police" in shield, blue windows .... $9 – 12
36. white with black fenders, "Police" in shield, clear windows .... $9 – 12
37. white with black fenders, "Police" in shield, purple windows .... $40 – 50
38. white with shield and "Police" labels, blue dome light, black plastic wheels, #55, 1968 ....$40 – 50
39. white with red dome light, black plastic wheels, #55, 1968 .... $250 – 350

Mercury Sable Wagon, 3", #33, 1988; #55, 1988
1. white with gray side stripe, metallic gray base, white hatch, China cast ....$3 – 4
2. white with gray side stripe, metallic gray base, white hatch, Macau cast ..$3 – 4
3. white with gray side stripe, metallic gray base, clear hatch, China cast, Chinese issue ....$30 – 50
4. metallic pale green with woodgrain side panels, "The Brady Bunch," Star Cars ....$5 – 6

Merryweather Marquis Fire Engine, red, 2¼", #9, 1959
1. tan ladder, gray plastic wheels ..$60 – 80

2. gold ladder, gray plastic wheels .... $60 – 80
3. gold ladder, black plastic wheels ....$40 – 60
4. silver ladder, black plastic wheels ....$60 – 80
5. tan ladder, black plastic wheels ....$60 – 80

Merryweather Fire Engine, Superfast only, 3", #35, 1969
1. metallic red with light gray base held on by two clips ....$16 – 24
2. bright red with black base held on by four rivets ....$20 – 25
3. bright red with light gray base held on by two clips ....$12 – 16
4. bright red with light gray base held on by four rivets ....$6 – 12
5. bright red with tan base held on by two clips ....$20 – 25

Meteor Sports Boat and Trailer, tan deck, blue hull, 2⅜", #48, 1958
1. metal wheels ....$40 – 50
2. gray plastic wheels ....$60 – 80
3. silver plastic wheels ....$80 – 100

Mexican Volkswagen Taxi, #44, 2004 (see Volkswagen Taxi)

MG 1100, with driver and dog, 2⅝", #64, 1966

1. green with black plastic wheels .... $20 – 30
2. green with Superfast wheels ....$200 – 300
3. light blue with Superfast wheels ....$40 – 50
4. dark blue with Superfast wheels ....$40 – 50

MG Midget Sports Car, 2", #19, 1956
1. with driver, made in England ..$50 – 75
2. Matchbox Originals commemorative replica, green, 1993, made in China ..$3 – 5

MGA 1960, #502, 2001, Matchbox Collectibles Elvis Presley Collection with Graceland diorama
1. maroon, detailed trim, rubber whitewall tires on chrome rims ....$12 – 16

MGA Sports Car, white, 2¼", #19, 1958
1. metal wheels, gold grille ....$80 – 100
2. metal wheels, silver grille .....$60 – 80
3. gray plastic wheels ....$80 – 100
4. silver plastic wheels ....$125 – 150

MGF 1.8L 1997, #66, 1998; #41, 1999, international; #4, 2000, international; #2, 2001?
1. red, 2000 Open Road international ....$3 – 4
2. red, Target Eggmobiles 3-pack ....$4 – 5
3. bright red, #2 ....$3 – 4

4. bright red, "Coca-Cola," 5-pack .... $1 – 2

5. yellow with orange band and "MG" logo, 1998 Street Cruiser ....$1 – 2
6. lime green, 5-pack ....$1 – 2
7. white, 1998 Street Cruiser international ....$3 – 4
8. 1999 Roadsters international .. $1 – 2

Midnight Magic, 3", #51, 1982 (similar casting: Tanzara)
1. black with silver sides, pearly silver base, Macau cast ....$3 – 4
2. black with silver sides, pearly silver base, Hong Kong cast ....$4 – 5
3. black with silver sides, pearly white base, Macau cast ....$3 – 4
4. black with silver sides, unpainted base, Hong Kong cast ....$3 – 4
5. white with red and blue graphics, unpainted base, China cast, Premiere Collection #13 ....$5 – 6

Military Jeep (see Jeep 4x4 Laredo)

Military Tank, 2⅞", #70, 1993 (see Weasel)
1. tan (khaki) camouflage ....$1 – 2
2. army green (olive), 1996 ....$1 – 2

Mini Cooper S, #75, 2003; #65, 2004; #7, 2005; #6, 2007

1. red with white roof, 2003 Car Shop #75 .... $1 – 2

2. red with Union Jack on roof, 2003 Car Shop #75 .... $1 - 2

3. red with red roof, 2007 #6 .. $1 - 2
4. yellow with black roof and rally stripes, 2004 #65 .... $1 – 2

5. green with white roof, 2006 Superfast #12 .... $4 - 5
6. blue with white roof, 2005 #7 ... $1 – 2

Mini Ha Ha Mini Cooper, 2³/₈", #14, 1975
1. red with blue windows .... $16 – 24

Mini Pickup 4x4 (see Toyota Mini-Pickup 4x4)

Mini Tanker (see Guzzler/Mini Tanker)

Missile Launcher, #82, 1999; #52, 2000
1. green with brown launcher, metallic light blue-gray base, "Man-At-Arms" and graphics, 2003 Masters of the Universe series .... $2 – 3

2. light green, "476 — Unit 61," 1999 Military Patrol .... $1 - 2

3. tan with brown dirt, "United States," "MLS 62," "314 6985," "10," 2000 Military .... $1 - 2
4. tan with brown dirt, "United States," "MLS 62," "314 6985," "10," "Matchbox 2000," 2000 Military .... $3 – 4

5. khaki camouflage, black base, Battle Kings Sahara Strike set, 2006, K5529 .... $1 - 2

Mission Chopper with retractable tail, 3", #46, 1985 – 1997; #49, 1998; #31, 1999; #66, 2000; #55, 2001; #57, 1985 – 1997, international; #44, 2006
1. red with white base and skids, tail, and blades, "Rebels," "Rescue," "Air 1," Motor City .... $1 – 2
2. red with white base and skids, tail, and blades, "Sheriff Air 1" .... $1 – 2
3. yellow with blue base and skids, white tail and blades, "Canon," Nutmeg promotional issue .... $3 – 4
4. green with white base and skids, tail, and blades, "Polizei," Convoy .... $3 – 4
5. green with green base and skids, tail, and blades, brown and black camouflage, 1996 5-pack .... $1 – 2
6. army green with tan base and skids, tan tail, and blades, star and emblem, Sky Busters SB-12 1992 .... $1 – 2
7. army green with black base and skids, black tail, and blades, "AC15," Commando .... $5 – 6

8. army green with black base, skids, and blades, army green tail, white star, "AT-7521," 1996 .... $1 - 2
9. fluorescent green with black base, blades, and skids, fluorescent blue tail, "12 Air Patrol," 5-pack .... $1 – 2

10. fluorescent green with blue base, skids, and tail, black blade, "12 Air Patrol," 1997 Land Sea & Air 5-pack .... $1 - 2

11. blue with white base and skids, blue tail, metallic gray blade, "Air Rescue," "Police," 1997 Police 5-pack .... $1 - 2
12. dark blue with metallic gray base and skids, white tail and blades, orange design .... $1 – 2
13. dark blue with metallic gray base and skids, metallic gray tail and blades, bull's-eye design, Macau cast ... $3 – 4
14. dark blue with metallic gray base and skids, white tail and blades, bull's-eye design, Thailand cast .... $3 – 4

15. light purple with blue base and skids, yellow tail and blades, "Hanger 12," 2000 Air Travel .... $1 - 2
16. light purple with blue base and skids, yellow tail and blades, "Hanger 12," "Matchbox 2000," 2000 Air Travel .... $3 – 4
17. black with black base and skids, tail, and blades, "INGEN," "Lost World," gray armament attached, Jurassic Park .... $7 – 9
18. black with blue base and skids, tail, and blades, "SWAT Stand Clear 00256," 5-pack .... $1 – 2

19. black with brown base and skids, tail, and blades, green and brown camouflage, 5-pack ....$1 - 2

20. black with gray base and skids, tail, and blades, "AC99" Commando ...... $5 – 6
21. black with tan base, skids, and blades, black tail, tan and green camouflage, 5-pack .... $1 – 2
22. black with white base and skids, tail, and blades, "Police," Convoy cast ..... $3 – 4
23. black with white base and skids, tail, and blades, "Police Unit 2," gold star, 5-pack ....$1 – 2
24. light gray with black base and skids, tail, and blades, black camouflage, 5-pack .... $1 – 2

25. khaki with black base and skids, tail, and blades, "AT-7521," black star, 1998 Rough 'N Tough ....$1 - 2

26. khaki with black base, blades, and skids, khaki tail, brown camouflage, 1997 Desert Assault Force 5-pack ....$1 - 2

27. khaki with khaki base and skids, khaki tail and blades, green and brown camouflage, 1995 Military 5-pack ....$1 - 2

28. white with black base and skids, black tail and blades, "Unit 2," "Police," star crest, 1996 Police 5-pack ....$1 - 2

29. white with black base and skids, black tail and blades, "Unit 3," "Police," 5-pack ....$1 – 2
30. white with black base and skids, black tail and blades, black camouflage ......$1 – 2
31. white with black base and skids, white tail and blades, "Police" .... $1 – 2
32. white with blue base and skids, tail, and blades, "Police Air Search" .... $1 – 2
33. white with blue base and skids, white tail and blades, "Rescue" and green crest, 5-pack .... $4 – 5
34. white with blue base and skids, white tail and blades, "Intercom City," "Police," Intercom City .... $9 – 12
35. white with fluorescent orange base and skids, white tail and blades, "Politie 06-11," Dutch Convoy issue ..... $4 – 5

36. white with fluorescent orange base and skids, white tail and blades, "Metro SWAT 7," 1993 Emergency 5-pack ....$1 - 2

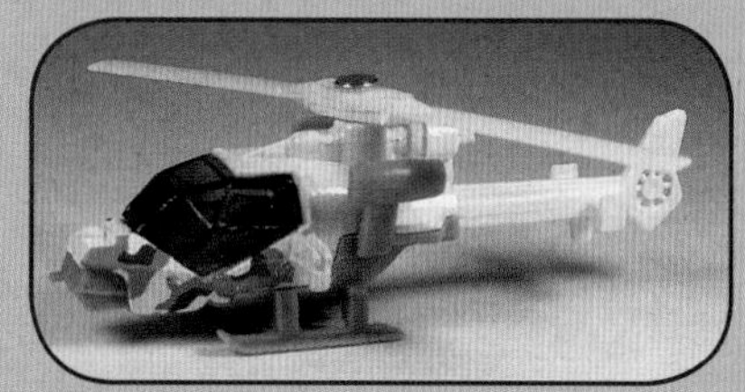

37. white with gray base and skids, white tail and blades, gray and army green camouflage, 5-pack .....$1 - 2

38. white with gray base and skids, white tail and blades, gray camouflage, 1997 Tundra Defense Force 5-pack ... $1 – 2
39. white with red base and skids, tail, and blades, "Sky," Nutmeg promotional issue .... $3 – 4
40. white with red base and skids, red tail, white blades, "Aces," Convoy issue ....$3 – 4
41. white with tan base and skids, tail, and blades, "Rescue" and green logo, 5-pack .... $4 – 5
42. white with white base and skids, tail, and blades, "Storm Troopers Reunion at the Mark 2000," ASAP promotional .... $80 – 120
43. white with white base and skids, tail, and blades, ASAP promotional blank .... $30 – 40
44. metallic gold with black base and skids, tail, and blades, 1997 75 Challenge .... $6 – 12
45. dark olive green, "Police," 2006 #44 .... $1 – 2

Mission Helicopter (see Mission Chopper)

Mission Ford Van (see Ford Panel Van)

Mitsubishi Eclipse, #37, 2005; #13, 2006; #2, 2007

1. metallic yellow, 2005 #37 (H1839 on 2006 package) ....$1 - 2

2. metallic gray, 2006 #13 (J5593 on 2006 package) ....$1 - 2

3. pearl white, 2006 5-pack J4672 ....$1 - 2

4. metallic blue, 2007 #2 ....$1 - 2

Mitsubishi Spyder, 1994, #28, 1995; #22, 1995, international; #69, 1998; #49, 1999

1. black with dark gray and black interior, detailed trim, rubber tires on chrome rims, Premiere Collection #1 ... $4 – 5

2. black with red interior, "Spyder" on sides, 1997 Convertibles 5-pack .... $1 - 2

3. black with red interior, "The Red Back" with spider and web design, Australia issue .... $4 – 5
4. blue with gray interior, "Spyder" on sides, 1998 Street Cruisers .... $1 – 2

5. dark green with tan interior, "Spyder," 1998 Street Cruisers .... $1 – 2
6. dark green with tan interior, "Fujihara Tuning Pros," ASAP promotional ....$80 – 120
7. dark green with tan interior, "Yamaha Mufflers," ASAP promotional .... $80 – 120
8. metallic blue with gray and black interior, detailed trim, rubber tires on chrome rims, Gold Coin Collection .... $16 – 24
9. metallic blue with pale green interior, light green splash design on sides and hood .... $1 – 2

10. metallic blue with pale green interior, no markings ....$3 – 4

11. metallic blue with white interior, no markings ....$1 – 2
12. metallic gold with black interior, 1997 75 Challenge .... $6 – 12

13. metallic silver with red and black interior, detailed trim, rubber tires on chrome rims, JC Penney Premiere Collection ....$4 – 5
14. red with dark gray interior, no markings .... $1 – 2
15. red with dark gray interior, skeleton and "Raptor," 5-pack .... $1 – 2
16. red with dark gray and black interior, detailed trim, rubber tires on chrome rims, Premiere Collection #1 ... $4 – 5

17. yellow with dark gray interior, "Spyder" on sides, 1997 ......$1 – 2
18. yellow with gray and black interior, detailed trim, rubber tires on chrome rims, Premiere Collection #12 ... $4 – 5
19. white with maroon and black interior, detailed trim, rubber tires on chrome rims, Premiere Collection #16 ... $4 – 5

Mitsubishi Galant Eterna (see Dodge Challenger/Mitsubishi Galant Eterna)

Mixopotamus, hippo-shaped cement truck, #18, 2004
1. 2004 Ultra Heroes .... $1 – 2

Mobile Canteen Refreshment Bar, 2⁵⁄₈", #74, 1959
1. white with blue base and interior, gray wheels .... $300 – 350
2. pink with light blue base and interior, gray wheels .... $400 – 500
3. coral ivory with blue base and interior, gray wheels .... $300 – 350
4. ivory with blue base and interior, gray wheels .... $300 – 350
5. silver with gray wheels .... $30 – 40
6. silver with silver plastic wheels .... $30 – 40
7. silver with black plastic wheels .... $30 – 40

Mobile Crane (see Faun Mobile Crane)

Mobile Home, 3¹⁄₄", #54, 1980 (see Motor Home; similar castings: Airport Foam Pumper, Command Vehicle, NASA Tracking Vehicle)

Moby Quick (see Power Boat)

Mod Rod, 2⁷⁄₈", #1, 1971
1. yellow with red wheels, wildcat label .... $25 – 45
2. yellow with black wheels, wildcat label .... $15 – 20
3. yellow with black wheels, flower label .... $15 – 20
4. yellow with black wheels, spotted cat label .... $20 – 25
5. yellow with black wheels, scorpion label .... $30 – 45
6. silver plated with black wheels, stripes .... $60 – 80

Mod Tractor, 2⁵⁄₈", #25, 1972
1. metallic bright lavender, black base, red seat .... $40 – 50
2. metallic bright lavender, black base, yellow seat, headlights cast on fenders .... $14 – 16
3. metallic bright lavender, black base, yellow seat, no headlights cast on fenders .... $12 – 14
4. metallic bright lavender, unpainted base, yellow seat .... $12 – 14
5. red with black base, yellow seat, Two-Pack .... $9 – 12

Model A Ford (see Ford Model A)

Model T Ford (see Ford Model T)

Modified Racer, 2¹⁵⁄₁₆", #12, 1989; #32, 1990
1. red, "2X," Nutmeg Collectibles ... $5 – 6
2. red, "37," Nutmeg Collectibles ... $5 – 6
3. red, "CraZ 8," Nutmeg Collectibles .. $5 – 6
4. red, "Jamie Tomaino," "42," Nutmeg Collectibles .... $5 – 6
5. red, "Jan Leaty," Nutmeg Collectibles .... $5 – 6
6. red, "Jerry Cook," "38," Nutmeg Collectibles .... $5 – 6
7. red, "Mike," "15," Nutmeg Collectibles .... $5 – 6
8. red, "Parts Peddler," "69," Nutmeg Collectibles .... $5 – 6
9. red, "Sherri Cup," "12," Nutmeg Collectibles .... $5 – 6
10. red, "Spearpoint Auto," 21," Nutmeg Collectibles .... $5 – 6
11. red, "Wayne Anderson," "15," Nutmeg Collectibles .... $5 – 6
12. red with black interior, chrome exhaust pipes, "12" and stripes .... $4 – 5
13. red with orange-yellow interior, black exhaust pipes, "12" and stripes, Nutmeg Collectibles .... $5 – 6
14. red with red interior, black exhaust pipes, "36," Nutmeg Collectibles ...$5 – 6
15. orange, "73," Nutmeg Collectibles ....$5 – 6
16. orange, "BR DeWitt," "61," Nutmeg Collectibles .... $5 – 6
17. orange to red with black interior, black exhaust pipes, "12," Super Color Changers .... $4 – 5
18. orange to red with black interior, chrome exhaust pipes, "12," Super Color Changers .... $4 – 5
19. orange with black interior, chrome exhaust pipes, "12," Macau cast ..$1 – 2
20. orange with black exhaust pipes, "12," China cast .... $1 – 2
21. orange-yellow, "4 Bugs," Nutmeg Collectibles .... $5 – 6
22. orange-yellow, "Satch Wirley," "4," Nutmeg Collectibles .... $5 – 6
23. yellow, "Miller Brick Co.," "56," Nutmeg Collectibles .... $5 – 6
24. yellow, "Reggie 44," "Magnum Oils," Nutmeg Collectibles .... $5 – 6
25. powder blue, "5," Nutmeg Collectibles .... $5 – 6
26. blue, "Jimmy Spencer," "24," Nutmeg Collectibles .... $5 – 6
27. blue, "Mike McLaughlin," "3," Nutmeg Collectibles .... $5 – 6
28. blue and metallic gray, "Collector's Toys 95," "Gary's," metallic gray interior, chrome exhaust pipes, Parlor City Collectibles .... $7 – 8
29. dark blue, "Doug Heveron," "3," Nutmeg Collectibles .... $5 – 6
30. dark blue, "Hummels," "11," Nutmeg Collectibles .... $5 – 6

31. dark blue, "Ron Bouchard," "3," Nutmeg Collectibles .... $5 – 6
32. dark blue with black interior, chrome exhaust pipes, "12" .... $9 – 12
33. metallic blue, "JVB27-Jan Leaty," Nutmeg Collectibles .... $5 – 6
34. dark purple with black interior, black exhaust pipes, "12," Action Pack ..$4 – 5
35. black, "Fyne Lyne," "39," Nutmeg Collectibles .... $5 – 6
36. black, "George Kent," "21," Nutmeg Collectibles .... $5 – 6
37. black, "NY," "7," Nutmeg Collectibles .... $5 – 6
38. black, "Rick Fuller," "44," Nutmeg Collectibles .... $5 – 6
39. black and gold, "O," Nutmeg Collectibles ....$5 – 6
40. black with white interior, chrome exhausts, "1," pink and white stripes, 5-pack .... $1 – 2
41. white, "1," Nutmeg Collectibles .. $5 – 6
42. white, "Maynard Troyer," Nutmeg Collectibles .... $5 – 6
43. white, "Phil's Chevrolet," "99," Nutmeg Collectibles .... $5 – 6
44. white, "Polar," "77," Nutmeg Collectibles .... $5 – 6
45. white, "Tony 1," "Universal Joint Sales," Nutmeg Collectibles .... $5 – 6
46. white, "U2 Jamie," Nutmeg Collectibles .... $5 – 6
47. white and blue, "ADAP 15," Nutmeg Collectibles .... $5 – 6
48. white and orange, "Perth Amboy Spring," "17," Nutmeg Collectibles .... $5 – 6
49. white and powder blue, "Tony Ferrante," "31," Nutmeg Collectibles .... $5 – 6
50. white with no markings, lavender interior, black exhaust pipes, Graffic Traffic .... $12 – 16
51. white with translucent blue interior, black exhaust pipes, "41" and stripes, Nutmeg Collectibles .... $5 – 6
52. chrome plated, with black interior, black exhaust pipes, custom .... $16 – 24

Monteverdi Hai, 2⅞", #3, 1973; BR 15-16, 1985 (similar casting: Rallye Royale)

1. orange with metallic gray base, ivory interior .... $16 – 24
2. orange with unpainted base, yellow interior, "3" labels .... $12 – 16
3. orange with unpainted base, yellow interior, no labels .... $12 – 16
4. orange with unpainted base, ivory interior .... $12 – 16
5. orange with unpainted base, ivory interior, "3" label .... $12 – 16
6. orange with unpainted base, ivory interior, "16" label .... $16 – 24
7. orange with black base, ivory interior, "3" label .... $12 – 16
8. orange with black base, ivory interior, "6" label .... $16 – 24
9. green with black windows, no graphics, England cast, Super GT BR 15-16, 1985 .... $12 – 15
10. green with black windows, white and gold, England cast, Super GT BR 15-16, 1985 .... $5 – 8
11. black with translucent white windows, England cast, Super GT BR 15-16, 1985 .... $15 – 20
12. yellow, England cast, Super GT BR 15-16, 1985 .... $45 – 60
13. light tan, England cast, Super GT BR 15-16, 1985 .... $4 – 6
14. tan, England cast, Super GT BR 15-16, 1985 .... $6 – 8
15. gold, England cast, Super GT BR 15-16, 1985 .... $8 – 10
16. white, China cast, Super GT BR 15-16, 1985 .... $30 – 40
17. orange, China cast, Super GT BR 15-16, 1985 .... $3 – 5
18. green, China cast, Super GT BR 15-16, 1985 .... $8 – 10
19. blue, China cast, Super GT BR 15-16, 1985 .... $3 – 5
20. fluorescent pink, China cast, Neon Racer BR 15-16, 1985 .... $4 – 6

Morris J2 "Builders Supply" Pickup, light blue, 2¼", #60, 1958

1. **open rear window, gray plastic wheels, red and black decals .... $80 – 100**
2. open rear window, gray plastic wheels, red and white decals .... $60 – 80
3. open rear window, silver plastic wheels, red and black decals .... $100 – 120
4. open rear window, silver plastic wheels, red and white decals .... $80 – 100
5. open rear window, black plastic wheels, red and white decals .... $60 – 80
6. no rear window, black plastic wheels, red and white decals .... $60 – 80
7. no rear window, black plastic wheels, red and black decals .... $80 – 100

Morris Mini (see Racing Mini)

Morris Minor 1000, 2", #46, 1958

1. light tan with metal wheels .. $700 – 900
2. dark green with metal wheels ...$50 – 60
3. dark green with gray plastic wheels .... $60 – 80
4. dark blue with gray plastic wheels .... $80 – 100

Motor Home (see Police Mobile Command Center, Truck Camper)

Motor Home, 3¼", #54, 1980 (similar castings: Airport Foam Pumper, Command Vehicle, NASA Tracking Vehicle)

1. **beige ....$4 – 5**
2. white .... $4 – 5
3. white with stripes .... $5 – 6

Motorcycle Trailer, #791, 1979

1. red with yellow motorcycles, England cast, Two-Pack .... $3 – 4
2. yellow with black motorcycles, England cast, Two-Pack .... $3 – 4
3. yellow with dark green motorcycles, England cast, Two-Pack .... $16 – 24
4. yellow with red motorcycles, England cast, Two-Pack .... $3 – 4
5. yellow with red motorcycles, Macau cast, Two-Pack .... $3 – 4
6. yellow with red motorcycles, no origin cast, Two-Pack .... $3 – 4
7. yellow with yellow motorcycles, England cast .... $8 – 10
8. blue with yellow motorcycles, England cast, Two-Pack .... $3 – 4
9. black with dark red motorcycles, China cast, 5-pack .... $1 – 2
10. black with dark red motorcycles, no origin cast, 5-pack .... $1 – 2
11. pearl gray with black motorcycles, no origin cast, Two-Pack .... $3 – 4
12. beige with black motorcycles, no origin cast, Two-Pack .... $3 – 4

Mountain Man (see Toyota Mini Pickup 4x4)

Muir Hill Dumper (see Dumper, Muir Hill)

Mush Puppy, dog-shaped snow vehicle, #21, 2004 (MB642)

1. 2004 Ultra Heroes .... $3 – 4

Mustang (see Ford Mustang)

Mustang, 1970 Boss (see Ford Mustang Boss 302 1970)

Mustang Cobra (see Ford Mustang Cobra)

Mustang GT350 (see Ford Mustang GT350)

Mustang Mach III (see Ford Mustang Mach III)

N

NASA Rocket Transporter (see Rocket Transporter; similar casting: Airplane Transporter)

NASA Tracking Vehicle, 3$\frac{1}{4}$", #54, 1982, radar toward rear of roof (similar castings: Airport Foam Pumper, Command Vehicle, Mobile Home)

1. white, no side accents, clear windows, England cast .... $5 – 6
2. white with side accents, clear windows, England cast .... $4 – 5
3. white with side accents, clear windows, Macau cast .... $3 – 4
4. white with side accents, blue windows, Macau cast .... $4 – 5

New Ford Transit (see Ford Transit Van)

Nissan 300ZX, no opening parts, 3", #61, 1990 – 1997; #37, 1991, international; #43, 1998

1. metallic red with chrome windows, dark gray interior, rubber tires on gray rims, World Class .... $6 – 8
2. metallic red, "Turbo Z," black and chrome windows, no interior, pink and red Lightning Wheels, on-package premium .... $6 – 8
3. metallic red, "Turbo Z," black and chrome windows, no interior, silver and yellow Lightning Wheels, on-package premium .... $6 – 8
4. pearl pink, "Turbo Z," blue chrome and black windows, peach and silver Lightning Wheels .... $3 – 4
5. orange-yellow, "D.A.R.E.," "Sanibel Police," D.A.R.E. .... $4 – 5
6. yellow, "300ZX" on doors, clear windows, white interior .... $1 – 2
7. yellow, "300ZX" on doors, tinted windows, white interior .... $1 – 2
8. yellow, "Turbo Z," black and chrome windows, Lightning Wheels .... $3 – 4
9. yellow, "Nationwide Auto Parts," "300ZX," clear windows, gray interior ....$30 – 40

10. **yellow, "North American Diecast Toy Collectors Association 1st Anniversary November 1994," custom ...$12 – 16**
11. yellow, detailed trim, black and gray interior, rubber tires on chrome rims, Premiere Collection #15 .... $4 – 5
12. bright orange, "300ZX," blue chrome and black windows, Lightning Wheels .... $3 – 4
13. teal blue with yellow and pink streaks, clear windows, pink interior ..... $1 – 2

14. **metallic teal blue with yellow accents, hot pink interior, 1994 .... $2 – 4**
15. metallic teal blue with hot pink, yellow, and green accents, chrome and black windows .... $3 – 5
16. metallic blue, "300ZX," chrome and black windows, Lightning Wheels ....$3 – 4
17. metallic blue with silver and black riveted-steel plate design on hood, pink interior, 1995 .... $1 – 2
18. black with orange and white lines on hood, white lines on sides, clear windows, fluorescent orange interior ....$4 – 5
19. black with orange-red and white graffiti, orange-red interior .... $1 – 2

20. **black with white swirls, clear windows, pink interior ....$1 – 2**
21. pearl white, detailed trim, chrome windows, dark gray interior, rubber tires on gray rims, World Class .... $6 – 8
22. pearl white, detailed trim, chrome windows, pink interior, rubber tires on gray rims, World Class .... $6 – 8
23. pearl white, detailed trim, chrome windows, white interior, rubber tires on gray rims, World Class .... $6 – 8
24. white, "ZX," orange and yellow design, 1998 Asian Cars series, international issue .... $1 – 2
25. white with hot pink accents, blue chrome and black windows ...... $3 – 5
26. white, lime, and pink, "Z," "Turbo," black and chrome windows, Lightning Wheels ....$3 – 4
27. white, orange, and black, "Z," "Turbo," black and chrome windows, Lightning Wheels .... $3 – 4
28. metallic gray and metallic blue, clear windows, fluorescent orange interior .... $1 – 2
29. metallic silver with yellow and orange accents, "ZX" on doors, 1997 ... $1 – 2

30. **metallic gold, 1997 75 Challenge .... $12 – 16**
31. chrome plated, Macau cast, custom .... $16 – 24
32. chrome plated, Thailand cast, custom ....$16 – 24

Nissan 300ZX Turbo, hood opens, 2$\frac{7}{8}$", #24, 1987

1. pearl gray with gold stripes, "Turbo" .... $3 – 4
2. white, "Fujicolor" .... $3 – 4
3. red with red and orange stripes ..$4 – 5
4. metallic red with red and orange stripes, Laser Wheels .... $4 – 5
5. white, "96," "BP Racing Team," Netherlands issue .... $10 – 12
6. yellow, "4 Monkey Racing Team," Hong Kong issue .... $10 – 12

Nissan 350Z, #62, 2004; #29, 2005 (MB611)

1. **metallic blue, 2004 #62 ......$1 – 2**
2. black with white graphics, 2005 #29 .... $1 – 2

3. **white with "Avatar: The Last Airbender" graphics, 2006 Nickelodeon 5 pack H5774 ....$2 – 3**

4. **metallic orange, 2005 Superfast #34 ....$3 – 4**

Nissan Prairie, 2$\frac{7}{8}$", #31, US, 1991; #21, international, 1991; #45, 1998, international

1. dark green, gold "Nissan," 1998 Asian Cars .... $1 – 2
2. metallic blue, silver sides .... $6 – 7
3. metallic silver, "Nissan" .... $3 – 4
4. red, "Nissan" .... $9 – 12
5. white, no markings, Graffic Traffic .... $12 – 16
6. white, "Aqua" and diver design, 5-pack .... $1 – 2
7. white, "Paramedic PS" .... $3 – 4

8. yellow "City Wide Taxi Service," 1998 Around Town 5-pack .... $1 – 2

Nissan Xterra, #32, 2001; #65, 2001, international; #47, 2002; #39, 2003

1. metallic silver, "Matchbox" logo, "Xterra," gradient yellow to red kayaks, 2001 Sand Blasters .....$1 – 2

2. blue, "Kayaking Adventures" and wave design, yellow kayaks, 2001 international issue .... $3 – 4
3. white with red, yellow and black graphics, 2002 Weekend Cruisers ... $1 – 2

4. metallic dark gold, no kayaks, 2002 Matchbox Across America 50th Birthday series #16 Tennessee — Southern Collection ....$4 – 6

5. dark blue with red plastic base, "MHC Outfitters," 2003 Mom and Pop Shops/ 2003 Hero City 10-pack #2 .... $1 – 2

6. yellow, no kayaks, 2004 #40 ...$1 – 2

7. red with white kayaks, "MBX Coast Guard," 2006 5-pack J4673 ......$1 – 2

Nissan Z (see Nissan 350Z)

O

Off-Road Rider 4x4 all-terrain vehicle, #54, 2006; #70, 2007

1. yellow with red, black and white graphics, 2006 #54; 2007 #70 .....$1 – 2

Oldsmobile Aerotech, 3", #62, 1989; #64, 1989

1. fluorescent orange, "Aerotech," Thailand cast .... $1 – 2

2. metallic purple and white, "Aerotech," purple flash, gold wheels, Thailand cast ....$1 – 2

3. metallic purple and white, "Aerotech," purple flash, silver wheels, China cast .... $1 – 2
4. metallic purple and white, "Aerotech," purple flash, silver wheels, Thailand cast ....$1 – 2
5. metallic purple and white, purple flash without "Aerotech," silver wheels, China cast .... $1 – 2

6. metallic silver, "Quad 4," "Aerotech," "Oldsmobile," Macau cast .....$1 – 2

7. metallic silver, "Quad 4," "Aerotech," "Oldsmobile," Thailand cast ...... $1 – 2

Opel Calibra DTM, #66, 1997; #65, 1998

1. orange with purple and white "33 Opel Racing," "Calibra" accents ...... $3 – 4

2. orange-yellow, "Sydney 2000," orange – yellow interior, 5-pack .... $1 – 2
3. orange-yellow, "Sydney 2000," orange-yellow interior, small wheels, Five-pack ....$4 – 5
4. white, "Coca-Cola" and polar bear graphics, red interior, 5-pack .... $1 – 2

5. white with blue and red "World Cup," "France 98" accents, red interior, yellow spoiler, 1998 World Cup 5-pack ....$1 – 2

6. white with blue and red "World Cup," "France 98" accents, yellow interior, yellow spoiler, 1998 Motor Sports ....$1 – 2

7. white with blue and red "World Cup," "France 98" accents, blue interior, yellow spoiler, Action Pack .... $1 – 2
8. metallic gold, no markings, 1997 75 Challenge .... $6 – 12

Opel Diplomat, $2\frac{7}{8}$", #36, 1966

1. metallic gold with gray motor, black plastic wheels .... $15 – 20

2. metallic gold with chrome motor, black plastic wheels ....$15 – 20

3. sea green with gray motor, black plastic wheels .... $2,000 – 2,500
4. metallic gold, Superfast wheels, 1970 ....$40 – 50

Opel Frogster, #74, 2003; #17, 2005

1. metallic green with red graphics on sides, red interior, dark tinted windshield, 2003 #74 Car Shop ..... $1 – 2

2. metallic green with no graphics, red interior, black hood with silver emblem, light tinted windshield, 2005 10-pack #2 ....$1 – 2

Opel Frontera (see Isuzu Rodeo)

Opel Kadett (see Vauxhall Astra/Opel Kadett)

Opel Kadett Police (see Vauxhall Astra/ Opel Kadett Police)

Opel Speedster, #6, 2003; #16, 2006

1. **metallic silver with red interior, 2003 Family Wheels .... $1 – 2**
2. yellow with black interior, #2006 #16 .... $1 – 2

Opel Vectra/Chevrolet Cavalier GSi 2000, 3", #22, 1990; #41, 1991

1. **metallic red .... $3 – 5**
2. green, Germany gift set ...... $10 – 12

Open Back Truck (see Toyota Mini Pickup 4x4)

Orange Peel Dodge Charger, 3", #74, 1981 (similar casting: Dodge Dragster)
1. pink with snake illustration, China cast, Premiere Collection #13 .... $4 – 5
2. purple with white, yellow and green flames, China cast, Adventure 2000 .... $1 – 2
3. white, "Orange Peel," Hong Kong cast .... $4 – 5
4. white, "Orange Peel," Macau cast .. $4 – 5

Over-Under Rescue Boats, #61, 2001; #38, 2002; #43, 2003

1. **white deck, metallic purple hull, yellow-orange "Rescue" on sides, bright orange interior, 2001 Scuba Dudes .... $1 – 2**

2. **light blue deck, dark blue hull, yellow, white, and blue lighthouse on sides, fluorescent interior, 2002 Nite Glow .... $1 – 2**
3. red deck, metallic blue hull, amber windows, metallic gray interior, 2003 Beach Patrol .... $1 – 2
4. red deck, metallic blue hull, amber windows, metallic gray interior, 2003 Hero City 10-pack #1 .... $1 – 2

P

Pannier Tank Locomotive, 3", #47, 1979
1. dark green with black base ...... $5 – 6
2. light green with black base ...... $5 – 6
3. light green with brown base ... $8 – 10
4. light green with dark gray base .. $5 – 6
5. light green with unpainted base .. $5 – 6
6. light green with blue-gray base ... $5 – 6

Pantera (see DeTomaso Pantera)

Passenger Coach (see Railway Passenger Coach)

Personnel Carrier (see M3 Army Halftrack Personnel Carrier, Army Saracen Personnel Carrier)

Personnel Carrier, 3", #54, 1976

1. **army green with beige plastic figures seated in back .... $5 – 6**
2. army green, no rear seats .... $5 – 6

Peterbilt Cement Truck, 3", #19, 1982; #8, 1998; #26, 1999; #93, 2000; #73, 2000, international
1. red, face and stripes, yellow wheels, lime green barrel, Live 'N Learn/Matchbox Preschool .... $5 – 7
2. red, black barrel, white barrel base, 1996 .... $1 – 2
3. red, black barrel, chrome barrel base, 1997 .... $1 – 2
4. red, orange barrel, Manaus cast, Brazil issue .... $35 – 40
5. red, white barrel, white stripes, packaged as #10 Peterbilt Quarry Truck, 1998 .... $24 – 32

6. **metallic red with white stripes, black barrel, metallic gray barrel base, 1998 Big Movers .... $1 – 2**
7. dusty red, white barrel, 1999 Road Work .... $1 – 2
8. light pink, "Readymix," white barrel, Australia issue .... $9 – 12
9. dirty pink, cream barrel with red stripes .... $1 – 2
10. orange-yellow, "Pace Construction," orange barrel .... $5 – 6
11. orange-yellow, "Pace Construction," red barrel .... $1 – 2
12. orange, black barrel .... $1 – 2
13. orange, cream barrel, translucent gray base, China cast .... $4 – 6
14. fluorescent orange, no markings, black barrel, 5-pack .... $1 – 2
15. fluorescent orange, no markings, gray barrel, 5-pack .... $1 – 2
16. pumpkin orange, "Matchbox," gray barrel, 5-pack .... $1 – 2
17. yellow, "Dirty Dumper," orange barrel .... $45 – 60
18. yellow, "Pace Construction," gray barrel .... $1 – 2
19. yellow, "Pace Construction," dark gray barrel, Motor City .... $3 – 4

20. **yellow, "Pace Construction," red barrel .... $2 – 4**

21. **lemon yellow, "Highway Crew," green barrel, 1999 Highway Crew 5-pack .... $1 – 2**
22. metallic green, "Big Pete," orange barrel .... $3 – 5
23. bright green, "Matchbox," "MC05," white barrel, 5-pack .... $1 – 2

24. **powder blue, black barrel, metallic gray barrel base, white stripes .... $3 – 4**
25. blue, "Kwik Set Cement," yellow barrel .... $1 – 2
26. blue, "Kwik Set Cement," orange barrel .... $9 – 12

27. dark blue with silver drum, orange barrel base, 2003 Hero City 5-pack #4 ....$1 - 2
28. metallic gold, white barrel, 1997 75 Challenge .... $6 - 12
29. white, "Cement Company," orange barrel, Manaus cast, Brazil issue ..$35 - 40
30. white, no markings, gray barrel, ASAP promotional blank .... $30 - 40
31. white, "Hemler Bros.," gray barrel, ASAP promotional .... $80 - 120
32. white, "CAT Service Co.," gray barrel, ASAP promotional .... $80 - 120
33. white, "Redi-Way, Inc.," gray barrel, ASAP promotional .... $80 - 120
34. white, "Blue Ridge Construction," gray barrel, ASAP promotional .. $80 - 120

35. dirty white, "Bilt," red barrel with white markings, pale gray base and grille, gray barrel base, 2000 Build It ....$1 - 2
36. dirty white, "Bilt," "Matchbox 2000," red barrel with white markings, pale gray base and grille, gray barrel base, 2000 Build It .... $4 - 5

Peterbilt Conventional, $2^3/_4$", #43, 1982 (other variations exist as part of Convoy and White Rose Race Transporter series)
1. black with white and red design, amber windows, England (L) cast .... $5 - 6
2. black with white and red design, clear windows, England (L) cast .... $5 - 6
3. black with white and red "Ace" graphics, amber windows, England (L) cast ..$5 - 6
4. black with white and red "Ace" graphics, amber windows, England (M) cast ..$3 - 4
5. black with white and red "Ace" graphics, clear windows, England (L) cast ...$5 - 6
6. black with white and red "Ace" graphics, clear windows, England (M) cast ...$5 - 6
7. black with white and red "Z" graphics, amber windows, England (M) cast ..$4 - 5
8. black with white and red "Z" graphics, clear windows, Macau cast ...... $3 - 4
9. black with white and red "Z" graphics, clear windows, England (M) cast ...$4 - 5
10. black with white and brown "Ace" graphics, clear windows, England (L) cast ....$5 - 6
11. black with white and black "Ace" graphics, clear windows, England (L) cast ...$5 - 6
12. white with "NASA" and rocket graphics, clear windows, Macau cast ...... $4 - 5

Peterbilt Dump Truck, 3", #30, 1982, US; #23, 1982, international; #19, 1997; #10, 1998

1. red with gray dumper, white stripes, 1998 Big Movers ....$1 - 2
2. red with red dumper, "530SP," Manaus cast, Brazil issue .... $40 - 50
3. red with gray dumper, "530SP" and stripes, Manaus cast, Brazil issue ....$40 - 50
4. red with yellow dumper, "Joe Diesel," face and yellow design, play set ...$5 - 6
5. orange with gray dumper, "Losinger," Macau cast, Swiss issue ..... $10 - 12
6. fluorescent orange with black dumper, 5-pack .... $1 - 2
7. pumpkin orange with gray dumper, "Matchbox," 5-pack .... $1 - 2
8. pumpkin orange with gray dumper, no markings, ASAP promotional blank .....$20 - 30
9. orange-yellow with plow, "CAT," play set .... $5 - 7
10. orange-yellow with red dumper, "Pace Construction" .... $3 - 4
11. orange-yellow with red dumper, no markings .... $1 - 2

12. yellow with red dumper, "Pace Construction" ....$1 - 2
13. yellow with red dumper, "Pace," "Intercom City" .... $12 - 16
14. yellow with gray dumper, "Dirty Dumper," England cast .... $3 - 4
15. yellow with gray dumper, "Dirty Dumper," Macau cast .... $1 - 2
16. yellow with gray dumper, "Pace," Macau cast .... $1 - 2
17. yellow with gray dumper, "Pace," Thailand cast .... $1 - 2

18. yellow with yellow dumper, "CAT," Dirt Machines Dirt Movers set ...... $1 - 2
19. white with gray dumper, "Cement Company," Manaus cast, Brazil issue .... $40 - 50
20. white with gray dumper, "Construction," Manaus cast, Brazil issue .... $40 - 50
21. white with gray dumper, no markings, ASAP promotional blank ...... $30 - 40
22. white with gray dumper, "Coast to Coast Hydraulics," ASAP promotional ..$20 - 30
23. white with gray dumper, "CAT Service Co.," ASAP promotional .... $80 - 120
24. white with gray dumper, "Redi-Way Inc.," ASAP promotional .... $80 - 120
25. white with gray dumper, "Blue Ridge Construction," ASAP promotional .... $80 - 120
26. white with gray dumper, "Hemler Bros.," ASAP promotional .... $80 - 120
27. white with turquoise dumper, "Sagamore Insurance" .... $90 - 120
28. metallic gold with gray dumper, 1997 75 Challenge .... $80 - 120

Peterbilt Petrol Tanker (see Peterbilt Tanker)

Peterbilt Quarry Truck (see Peterbilt Dump Truck)

Peterbilt Tanker, 3", #56, 1982; #12, 1999; #5, 1982, international; #7, 1998, international; #12, 1999, international
1. red, "Amoco" on tank, "Getty" on door, chrome tank .... $50 - 70
2. red, "Getty," chrome tank .... $3 - 4

3. fluorescent yellow, "Airways Caution Jet Fuel," chrome tank, 1999 Airport 5-pack ....$1 - 2
4. army green, "Gas," army green tank, Commando .... $5 - 6
5. lime green, yellow tank, red wheels, Matchbox Preschool/Live 'N Learn ....$7 - 9

6. blue, "Fresh Milk," white tank, Farm gift set ....$20 - 30
7. blue, "Milk" with red "Milk" on door, white tank .... $5 - 6
8. blue, "Milk" with white "Milk" on door, white tank .... $4 - 5

9. blue, "Milk" with no markings on door, white tank .... $4 – 5

10. blue, "QTD-94712," maroon and white stripes, chrome tank with printed gauges, flammable symbol and pipes, 5-pack ....$1 – 2

11. blue, "Test Mission, gray tank, 2000 Space Mission 5-pack ....$1 – 2

12. blue, white tank, no markings ... $6 – 8
13. black, "Amoco," black tank .... $4 – 5
14. black, "Amoco," chrome tank ..$60 – 80
15. black, "Amoco," white tank .. $40 – 60
16. black, "Indy Racing Fuel," black tank, Indy 500 .... $12 – 16
17. black, "Matchbox," "Getty," black tank, Manaus cast, Brazil issue .... $40 – 50
18. black, "Supergas," yellow tank .. $3 – 4
19. black, "Supergas," orange-yellow tank .... $3 – 4
20. black, "Supergas," chrome tank ..$60 – 70
21. black, "Texaco," chrome tank, rubber tires on chrome rims, Premiere Collection .... $4 – 5

22. black and white, "Official Indy Fuel Truck," black tank ....$8 – 10

23. white, "100% Divine," chrome tank, ASAP promotional .... $80 – 120
24. white, "American International Recovery," ASAP promotional ... $120 – 160
25. white, "Amoco," white tank ...... $3 – 4
26. white, "Ampol," gray tank, Australia issue .... $8 – 10
27. white, "Arco Lar 75," chrome tank, ASAP promotional .... $80 – 120
28. white, "Blue Ridge Construction," chrome tank, ASAP promotional .... $80 – 120
29. white, "BP," green tank, Australia issue .... $9 – 12
30. white, "BP Super," chrome tank, ASAP promotional .... $80 – 120
31. white, "CT Tank Removal," chrome tank, ASAP promotional .... $80 – 120
32. white, "Darry Brothers," chrome tank, ASAP promotional .... $80 – 120
33. white, "Dairy Line," cream tank, black cow spots, 1999 Highway Haulers ....$1 – 2
34. white, "Dairy Line" on cab only, cream tank, black cow spots, 1999 Highway Haulers international .... $9 – 12
35. white, "Esso," cream tank, Manaus cast, Brazil issue .... $40 – 50
36. white, "Fullbright Oil Co.," chrome tank, ASAP promotional .... $80 – 120
37. white, "Giant Industries," chrome tank, ASAP promotional .... $80 – 120
38. white, "Hemler Bros.," chrome tank, ASAP promotional .... $80 – 120
39. white, "Maalcovich Pumping," chrome tank, ASAP promotional .... $80 – 120
40. white, "Shell," gray tank .... $3 – 4

41. white, "Shell," chrome tank ..$1 – 2

42. white, "Shell" with "IC" on doors, chrome tank, Intercom City .... $12 – 16
43. white, "Supergas," yellow tank ..$30 – 40
44. white, "Systend Dairies," chrome tank, ASAP promotional .... $80 – 120

45. white, "White's Guide Car of the Month #10 September 1999," chrome tank, ASAP promotional ....$10 – 15

46. white, "Wisconsin," Matchbox Across America 50th Birthday series #30, Central Collection .... $5 – 6
47. white, cream tank, black cow spots, international issue
48. white, chrome tank, no markings, ASAP promotional blank .... $30 – 40
49. white, white tank, chrome pipes, no markings .... $40 – 60
50. white, white tank, gray pipes, no markings, Graffic Traffic .... $12 – 16
51. white and red, "Avia," white tank, Belgian issue .... $16 – 24

Peterbilt Wreck Truck, 3", #61, 1982

1. red, "Police," black booms, Manaus cast, Brazil issue .... $40 – 50
2. orange, "Eddie's Wrecker," black booms, amber windows .... $5 – 6
3. orange, "Eddie's Wrecker," black booms, clear windows .... $5 – 6
4. orange with black stripes, dark green booms, plastic armament, Roadblasters, Macau cast .... $7 – 9
5. orange with black stripes, dark green booms, Tomy box, Japan issue, Thailand cast .... $9 – 12
6. yellow, "Metro Recovery," blue booms, amber windows, 5-pack .... $1 – 2
7. yellow with car design, blue booms, amber windows, 5-pack .... $3 – 4
8. army green, "8," red and white stripes, black booms, Commando .... $5 – 6
9. blue, "C.P. City Police," black booms, Manaus cast, Brazil issue .... $40 – 50
10. blue with no markings, black booms, amber windows .... $160 – 240
11. white, "911," blue booms .... $3 – 4
12. white, "Police PD-22" and checkerboard pattern, orange booms, clear windows ....$3 – 4
13. white, "Police M9," "Intercom City," orange booms, clear windows, Intercom City .... $8 – 10
14. white, "SFPD" and star, orange booms, clear windows .... $1 – 2
15. white with black "9," black booms, Manaus cast, Brazil issue .... $40 – 50
16. white with black "9," black booms, amber windows .... $3 – 4
17. white with black "9," black booms, clear windows .... $1 – 2
18. white with blue "9," black booms, amber windows .... $3 – 4
19. white with blue "9," blue booms, amber windows .... $1 – 2
20. white with blue "9," blue booms, clear windows .... $1 – 2
21. white with no markings, black booms, Macau cast .... $3 – 4

Petrol Tanker (see Bedford Petrol Tanker)

Peugeot 205 Turbo 16, $2\frac{11}{16}$", #15 1985; #25, 1991

1. white with red "205" and stripes Macau cast .... $3 – 5
2. white with black "205" and stripes Macau cast .... $3 – 5
3. white with purple "205" and stripes Macau cast .... $3 – 5
4. white with purple "205" and stripes China cast .... $3 – 5
5. white with black "205," Manaus cast Brazil issue .... $35 – 45
6. white with black "205," "Matchbox 11, Manaus cast, Brazil issue .... $35 – 45
7. orange-red with "Michelin," "Bilstein, "48" .... $3 – 5
8. green with no markings, Germany gi set .... $9 – 12
9. yellow with "Peugeot 205," "Bilstein, "48" .... $3 – 5
10. dark gray with "Shell 37" and pink and yellow, Manaus cast, Brazil issue ......$40 – 50

Peugeot Quasar, 2¾", #25, 1985, US; #49, 1987, international
1. maroon with yellow accents ..... $1 – 2
2. orange, "Fanta," China issue .. $160 – 180
3. yellow, "3," stripes and flames, Matchbox Preschool/Live 'N Learn .... $7 – 9
4. dark blue, "9" and pink stripes, new Superfast wheels .... $4 – 5
5. metallic blue, "9" and pink stripes, Laser wheels .... $4 – 5
6. purple, "Quasar" .... $1 – 2
7. black with bright green and orange stripes, armaments, Roadblasters ....$6 – 8
8. white, "Quasar" .... $3 – 4

Phantom Z (see Nissan Fairlady Z)

Pi-Eyed Piper, 2⅞", #48, 1972 (similar castings: Big Banger, Cosmic Blues, Flame Out, Red Rider)
1. blue, "8" label on roof, amber windows ....$16 – 24
2. blue, "8" label on roof, blue windows .... $16 – 24
3. blue, "8" label on roof, "Red Rider" on base, Premiere Collection #13 ..$4 – 5

Pickfords Removals Van, 2⅝", #46, 1960
1. dark blue, "Pickfords Removers & Storers," gray wheels .... $60 – 75
2. dark blue, "Pickfords Removers & Storers," silver wheels .... $100 – 120
3. green, "Pickfords Removers & Storers," gray wheels .... $40 – 50
4. green, "Pickfords Removers & Storers," silver wheels .... $75 – 90

5. **green, "Pickfords Removers & Storers," black wheels ....$20 – 25**
6. tan, "Beales Bealson," sunburst, black wheels .... $300 – 325

Pickup Camper 4x4, 3", #57, 1982; #35, 1986

Pickup (see Mini Pickup 4x4, Jeep Gladiator, etc.)

Pipe Truck (see Leyland Pipe Truck)

Piston Popper (see Ford Mustang Piston Popper)

Plane Transporter (see Airplane Transporter)

Planet Scout, 2¾", #59, 1971
1. red upper, beige lower, amber windows .... $12 – 16
2. metallic green upper, lime lower, amber windows .... $12 – 16
3. metallic green upper, apple green lower, amber windows .... $12 – 16
4. avocado upper, black lower, amber windows, Adventure 2000 .... $30 – 40
5. avocado upper, black lower, purple windows, Adventure 2000 .... $30 – 40
6. metallic blue upper, black lower, purple windows, Adventure 2000 ... $50 – 60

Plymouth Barracuda 1970, #4, 2004 Superfast
1. silver, 2004 Superfast #4 .... $4 – 5

Plymouth Gran Fury Police, 3", #10, 1979
1. white with "Police" and shield, England cast .... $3 – 5
2. white with "Metro," blue windows, England cast .... $3 – 5
3. white with "Metro," dark gray windows, England cast .... $4 – 6
4. white with "Metro," blue windows, Macau cast .... $4 – 6
5. white with blue "Police," blue windows, Macau cast .... $3 – 5
6. white with "Police SFPD," dark blue windows .... $3 – 5
7. white with "Police SFPD," green windows .... $80 – 100
8. white with "Sheriff SP-5," dark blue windows .... $3 – 5
9. black and white, "Adam 12," "Police," Star Cars .... $5 – 7

Plymouth Prowler, with metal base, MLB97, 1997, White Rose Collectibles (compare to Plymouth Prowler with plastic base)
1. "Anaheim Angels 1997," pearl white ....$5 – 6
2. "Arizona Diamondbacks Inaugural Season 1998," metallic purple ...... $5 – 6
3. "Atlanta Braves 1997," metallic tan ....$5 – 6
4. "Baltimore Orioles 1997," black ..$5 – 6
5. "Boston Red Sox 1997," metallic red ....$5 – 6
6. "Chicago Cubs 1997," metallic blue ....$5 – 6
7. "Chicago White Sox 1997," black ..$5 – 6
8. "Cincinnati Reds 1997," metallic red ....$5 – 6
9. "Cleveland Indians 1997," metallic gray .... $5 – 6
10. "Colorado Rockies 1997," metallic purple .... $5 – 6
11. "Detroit Tigers 1997," metallic orange ....$5 – 6
12. "Florida Marlins 1997," metallic gray .... $5 – 6
13. "Houston Astros 1997," pearl white ....$5 – 6
14. "Kansas City Royals 1997," metallic tan ....$5 – 6
15. "Milwaukee Brewers 1997," metallic green .... $5 – 6
16. "Los Angeles Dodgers 1997," metallic blue .... $5 – 6
17. "Minnesota Twins 1997," metallic blue ....$5 – 6
18. "Montreal Expos 1997," pearl white ....$5 – 6
19. "New York Mets 1997," metallic orange ....$5 – 6
20. "New York Yankees 1997," metallic gray ....$5 – 6
21. "Oakland A's 1997," metallic green ....$5 – 6
22. "Philadelphia Phillies 1997," metallic red ....$5 – 6
23. "Pittsburgh Pirates 1997," black ..$5 – 6
24. "San Diego Padres 1997," metallic gray ....$5 – 6
25. "San Francisco Giants 1997," black ....$5 – 6
26. "Seattle Mariners 1997," metallic tan .... $5 – 6
27. "St. Louis Cardinals 1997," metallic gray .... $5 – 6
28. "Tampa Bay Devil Rays Inaugural Season 1998," metallic purple .... $5 – 6
29. "Texas Rangers 1997," metallic red ....$5 – 6
30. "Toronto Blue Jays 1997," metallic blue ....$5 – 6
31. "World Series 1997 Champions Marlins," turquoise .... $5 – 6
32. "World Series 1997 Champions Marlins," turquoise, sealed in bat-shaped glass bottle .... $40 – 50

Plymouth Prowler, with plastic base, #34, 1995 – 1997; #18, 1998; #4, 2000; #58, 2001; #6, 1995, international; #17, 2006 (compare to Plymouth Prowler, with metal base)
1. red with black interior, "Prowler" ..$1 – 2

2. **metallic red with black interior, gray grille, no markings ....$3 – 4**
3. red with black interior, detailed trim, rubber tires on chrome rims, Select Class #4 .... $4 – 5

4. **red with gray and red interior, detailed trim, rubber tires on chrome rims, JC Penney Premiere Collection .... $4 – 5**
5. orange with gray interior, detailed trim, rubber tires on chrome rims, Premiere Collection #16 .... $4 – 5
6. metallic orange with gray interior, detailed trim, rubber tires on chrome rims, Premiere Collection .... $5 – 6

7. yellow, "Matchbox 1996 Line Preview," gray interior, rubber tires on chrome rims .... $300 – 400
8. yellow with black interior, blue and red stripes, 5-pack .... $1 – 2
9. yellow with gray and black interior, detailed trim, rubber tires on chrome rims, Select Class #5 .... $4 – 5
10. yellow with black interior, no markings, Color Comp promotional blank ..$30 – 40
11. yellow with black interior, "Convention 2000 Lion's Club — Honolulu Hawaii," Color Comp promotional ...... $30 – 40
12. yellow with black interior, "Tyler Elliot Memorial Model," "10," Color Comp promotional .... $20 – 30

13. blue with green interior, green and white design, 5-pack .... $1 – 2
14. metallic dark blue with black interior, detailed trim, rubber tires on chrome rims, International Premiere Collection #1 .... $9 – 12

15. metallic blue with orange base and interior, Jimmy Neutron illustration, 2003 Nickelodeon 5-pack ..... $1 – 2
16. purple, "16th Annual Matchbox USA Convention 1997," custom .. $12 – 16
17. purple, "Great Strides," "Cystic Fibrosis Foundation," Color Comp promotional .... $20 – 25
18. purple, "Mattel Wheels — Driving to Win," custom .... $300 – 500
19. purple, "Thank You for Buying from the Chris Getz Collection," Color Comp promotional .... $20 – 25
20. purple with black interior, no markings, Color Comp promotional blank ..$30 – 40

21. purple with gray interior, silver grille, 1995 .... $1 – 2
22. purple with gray interior, plain grille, 1997 .... $1 – 2
23. purple with gray interior, detailed trim, rubber tires on chrome rims, Premiere Collection #14 .... $4 – 5
24. purple with plain gray base, gray and purple interior, detailed trim, rubber tires on chrome rims, Premiere Collection World Class #1 .... $9 – 12
25. purple with detailed base, gray and purple interior, detailed trim, rubber tires on chrome rims, Premiere Collection World Class #1 .... $125 – 175
26. purple with white interior, detailed trim, rubber tires on chrome rims, Chrysler gift set .... $4 – 5
27. metallic gold with black interior, 6-spoke spiral wheels, 1997 75 Challenge .... $6 – 12
28. metallic gold with black interior, 5-spoke concave star wheels, 1997 75 Challenge .... $20 – 30
29. metallic tan with black interior, 1998 Cool Concepts .... $1 – 2
30. metallic tan with black interior, "White's Guide Movie #1," ASAP promotional .... $60 – 80
31. black with plain grille, "Prowler" on sides, purple interior, 1998 5-pack ..... $1 – 2
32. black with gray grille, "Prowler" on sides, purple interior, 1998 Cool Concepts ..... $1 – 2
33. black with orange interior, "Toy Fair 97," "Matchbox," US issue .... $80 – 120
34. black with yellow interior, "Toy Fair 97," "Matchbox," UK issue .... $20 – 25
35. black with red interior, detailed trim, rubber tires on chrome rims, Gold Coin Collection .... $16 – 24

36. black with red interior, no markings, 2000 Open Road .... $1 – 2
37. black with red interior, "Matchbox 2000," 2000 Open Road .... $3 – 4
38. gray with gray and purple interior, detailed trim, rubber tires on chrome rims, Select Class #1 .... $9 – 12
39. metallic gray with gray and purple interior, detailed trim, rubber tires on chrome rims, Premiere Collection #4 ... $4 – 5
40. white with blue interior, "Beep Beep the Clown," Color Comp promotional .... $40 – 50
41. white with purple interior, "Prowler" on sides, plain grille, 5-pack .... $1 – 2

42. white with purple interior, "Prowler" on sides, gray grille, 1998 Cool Concepts .... $1 – 2
43. white with blue interior, "Tyco Playtime Toy Fair 96" .... $40 – 50
44. white with blue interior, "Tyco Playtime Dallas 96" .... $40 – 50
45. white with blue interior, "Tyco Playtime Hong Kong 96" .... $40 – 50
46. metallic bronze with yellow "Prowler" on sides, 2001 Wheeled Envy ...... $1 – 2
47. metallic orange, 2006 #17 ..... $1 – 2
48. gray, 2006 #17 .... $1 – 2

Police Bus (see School Bus)

Police Car, #53, 2002; #27, 2003; #68, 2004; #71, 2006

1. pearl white with blue, yellow and gray design, 2002 Rescue Rookies .... $1 – 2
2. black with yellow door, "Highway Patrol," blue plastic base, red windows, 2003 Police Squad .... $1 – 2

3. blue with white, gold and black graphics, white plastic base, amber windows, 2003 Hero City 5-pack #7 .... $1 – 2

4. metallic silver with brown base, red interior, He-Man graphics, 2003 Masters of the Universe .... $1 – 2

5. black with white doors, blue windows, "Police" in black with blue outline, 2006 #71 .... $1 – 2
6. black with white hood and doors, blue windows, "Police Rescue" and "Sheriff 102" on shield .... $1 – 2

Police Hat (on base; Crime Capper on pkg.), #26, 2004

1. white with dark blue base and cap, "Metro Police," 2004 Ultra Heroes ....$1 – 2

Police Helicopter, #70, 2004 (see Sea Rescue Helicopter)

Police Launch, 3", #52, 1976; #80, 1999

1. red deck, white hull, "2416-134," blue sash design, yellow figures, 1998 Emergency Rescue 5-pack .... $2 – 3

2. orange deck white hull with black and red graphics, blue figures, "Mission H2O," 2006 Christmas Coal Cars 2-pack J1821 (each packaged in black plastic "lump of coal") .. $3 – 4

3. yellow deck, black hull, "Rescue B-1," red and white stripes, cast horns, red figures, Real Talkin' .... $4 – 5
4. yellow and black deck, white hull, "Base 2000," blue and black stripes, blue figures, Launcher 5-pack .... $1 – 2

5. blue deck, white hull, "OD-593," light blue band, compass design, yellow figures, 2000 Ocean Dock 5-pack ....$1 – 2

6. metallic blue deck, dark blue hull, storm design, blue figures, Launcher 5-pack ....$1 – 2
7. white deck, blue hull, "Amity Police," "Jaws" labels, cast horns, light blue figures, Star Cars .... $6 – 8
8. white deck, blue hull, "Police" labels, light blue figures, England cast ... $5 – 6
9. white deck, blue hull, "Police" labels, cast horns, light blue figures, England cast .... $6 – 8
10. white deck, blue hull, "Police" labels, cast horns, light blue figures, no origin cast, Brazil issue .... $60 – 80
11. white deck, blue hull, "123," rope pattern, red figures, Matchbox Preschool/ Live 'N Learn .... $7 – 9
12. white deck, dark blue hull, "Police," orange stripes, cast horns, China cast, Action Pack .... $3 – 4
13. white deck, red hull, "LA Fire," orange-yellow figures, England cast, Code Red ....$7 – 9
14. white deck, red hull, "LA Fire," light blue figures, England cast, Code Red .... $12 – 16

15. white deck, red hull, white "UT-35-091M" and graphics, cast horns, China cast, 1999 Fire Rescue ..$1 – 2

16. white deck, red hull, white "UT-35-091M" and graphics, no horns, China cast, Target Eggmobile .... $6 – 8
17. white deck, white hull, white figures, Graffic Traffic, China cast .... $6 – 8
18. black deck, dark gray hull, tan and gray camouflage, dark gray figures, Macau cast, Commando .... $5 – 6

Police Mobile Command Center, #44, 2001; #15 Bloodmobile, 2003 (similar casting: Truck Camper)

1. pearl white with blue door, blue and red, "Police," red roof lights, #44, 2001 Rescue Squad ....$1 – 2

2. white with red door and red, black, and gray, "Metro Base 15," blue roof lights, #15 Bloodmobile, 2003 Hospital ....$1 – 2

Police Moto (see Police Motorcycle)

Police Motorcycle, #35, 1999; 46, 2001

1. black with gray handlebars and saddlebags, "Police," 1999 Law & Order ....$1 – 2

2. blue with black handlebars and saddlebags, "Radio," 5-pack .... $1 – 2
3. black with gray handlebars, black saddlebags, "MB1," 2001 Pull Over ....$1 – 2

Police Motorcycle with Sidecar/Police Moto ("Cycle with Sidecar" on base), #59, 2002; #28, 2003; #40, 2004

1. yellow with yellow plastic fairing, blue seat, yellow base, 2003 Hero City 10-pack #1 .... $1 – 2

2. metallic blue with white plastic fairing, seat, and base, "No. 420 Police," 2002 Rescue Rookies $1 – 2

3. metallic blue with yellow plastic fairing, blue seat, and base, 2003 Police Squad ....$1 – 2

4. metallic blue with white plastic fairing, yellow seat, and base, 2003 Rescue Heroes 5-pack ....$1 – 2

5. metallic red with white fairing, seat, and base, 2004 #40 Police Moto .. $1 – 2

Police Motorcyclist, Honda CB750 with rider, 2½", #33, 1977

1. black with "L.A.P.D." label ...... $8 – 10
2. black with "Police" .... $3 – 4
3. ivory with "Polizei" label, wire wheels, Germany issue .... $25 – 40
4. white with "Polizei" label, wire wheels, Germany issue .... $25 – 40
5. white with "Polizei" label, mag wheels, Germany issue .... $25 – 40
6. white with "Police" label, wire wheels, white seat .... $6 – 8
7. white with "Police" label, mag wheels, white seat .... $6 – 8
8. white with "Police" label, mag wheels, green seat .... $16 – 24
9. white with "Police" label, mag wheels, black seat, black engine .... $3 – 4
10. white with "Police" label, mag wheels, black seat, chrome engine .... $6 – 8
11. white with "4" label, mag wheels, red seat, no rider .... $12 – 16
12. white with "Honda" and "Police" labels .... $3 – 4

13. white with Japanese lettering ....$9 – 12

Police Patrol (see Range Rover Police Patrol)

Police SUV, #26, 2003

1. **blue with yellow base, red windows, "Marvin the Martian" logo, Looney Tunes Back in Action 5-pack ......$2 – 3**

2. **pearl white with painter illustration, "365-555-3214," 2003 Hero City 5-pack #8 ....$1 – 2**

3. **metal flake gray with dark blue plastic base; blue windows; red, white, and two-tone blue; 2003 Police Squad ....$1 – 2**

Police Trouble Tracker, 3", #52, 2001 (similar casting: Troop Carrier)

1. blue with khaki canopy, red tinted windows, "Police," 2001 Police ..... $1 – 2

Pontiac Convertible, 2¾", #39, 1962

1. metallic lavender .... $80 – 100
2. yellow .... $30 – 40

Pontiac Fiero, 2$^{13}/_{16}$", #2, 1985

1. white upper, blue lower, "Goodyear," silver wheels .... $3 – 5
2. white upper, blue lower, "Goodyear," gold wheels .... $5 – 10
3. white upper, red lower, "GT Fiero" ....$3 – 5
4. yellow upper, orange lower, "Protech," new Superfast wheels .... $5 – 7
5. yellow upper, orange lower, "Protech," 8-dot silver wheels .... $60 – 80
6. yellow upper, gold lower, "Protech," Laser wheels .... $4 – 6
7. black upper, red lower, "2 Dog Racing Team" .... $10 – 15
8. fluorescent orange upper, black lower, black flames, "Turbo" .... $5 – 7

Pontiac Firebird, 2⅞", #4, 1975

1. **metallic blue with dual chrome hood scoops ....$6 – 8**

Pontiac Firebird Formula, #20, 1997; #72, 1998 (see Pontiac Firebird Ram Air 1997)

Pontiac Firebird Formula, #377, 1998, Taco Bell; Matchbox mold retooled by Strottman International Inc. through a licensing agreement with Mattel. Strottman manufactures toy premiums for Taco Bell. Base is marked "Made in China by S.I.I."

1. black with metallic silver windows, "Taco Bell," red and white flames, Taco Bell ....$4 – 5

Pontiac Firebird Racer S/E, #12, 1982; #51, 1984; #60, 1984; #12, 1986; #48, 1993 (see Pontiac Firebird S/E)

Pontiac Firebird Ram Air 1997, #20, 1997; #72, 1998

1. **yellow, 1997 ....$1 – 2**
2. metallic gold, 1997 75 Challenge series, Thailand cast .... $10 – 12
3. metallic gold, 1997 75 Challenge series, China cast .... $8 – 10

4. **black, 1998 Street Cruisers series, China cast ....$1 – 2**
5. black, 1998 Street Cruisers series, Thailand cast .... $1 – 2
6. metallic gray, rubber tires on chrome hubs, Premiere Collection #14 ..$4 – 6
7. red, rubber tires on chrome hubs, Premiere Collection .... $6 – 9
8. yellow, "Coca-Cola Play Refreshed," Premiere Collection .... $4 – 6

Pontiac Firebird S/E, 3", #12, 1982; #51, 1984; #60, 1984; #12, 1986; #48, 1993

1. red, "Firebird," tan interior, clear windows .... $5 – 7
2. red, "Maaco" labels, red interior, clear windows .... $9 – 12
3. dark red, no markings, tan interior, clear windows .... $4 – 6
4. dark red, no markings, tan interior, amber windows .... $5 – 7
5. dark red, no markings, yellow interior, clear windows .... $4 – 6
6. dark red, no markings, yellow interior, amber windows .... $4 – 6

7. **fluorescent pink with fluorescent yellow and white accents on sides and hood, 1994 ....$1 – 2**
8. fluorescent pink with fluorescent yellow and white accents on sides, not on hood, 1996 .... $1 – 2
9. fluorescent pink with yellow and white design, bright yellow plastic base, Thailand cast .... $1 – 2
10. yellow, "10," red and white, plastic base, New Superfast Wheels ....$16 – 24
11. yellow, "Pirelli 56" .... $5 – 6
12. yellow, "Son of a Gun 55" ...... $5 – 6
13. pale green to dark brown, "Fast Eddie's 15," Super Color Changers .... $8 – 10
14. metallic turquoise with yellow and white hood and sides design, bright yellow plastic base, China cast ... $3 – 4
15. blue with white interior; blue windows; red, orange, and yellow stripes; black metal base....................... $9 – 12
16. blue with white interior; blue windows; red, orange, and yellow stripes; white metal base .... $4 – 6
17. blue with white interior; blue windows; red, orange, and yellow stripes; white plastic base .... $5 – 7
18. light blue, "10," blue and yellow, metal base, New Superfast Wheels .. $4 – 5
19. light blue, "10," blue and yellow, plastic base, New Superfast Wheels .. $8 – 10
20. light blue with red interior; clear windows; green, yellow, and white stripes; Dinky .... $12 – 16
21. metallic blue, "10," blue and yellow, blue metal base, Laser Wheels.. $4 – 5
22. metallic blue, "10," blue and yellow, blue plastic base, Laser Wheels .... $8 – 10
23. metallic blue with white interior; blue windows; red, orange, and yellow stripes; Laser Wheels .... $4 – 6
24. purple, "Firebird," red interior, clear windows, Super Color Changers ..$4 – 5
25. purple with yellow and white design, bright yellow plastic base, Thailand cast .... $7 – 9

26. black, "Firebird," red interior, opaque windows .... $12 – 16
27. black, "Firebird," red interior, clear windows .... $3 – 5
28. black, "Firebird," tan interior, clear windows .... $4 – 6
29. black, "Go Pies! 1997," Australia issue .... $1 – 2
30. black, "Halley's Comet," gray interior, clear windows, 1986 .... $9 – 12
31. black, "Knight Rider," tan interior, Star Cars .... $9 – 12
32. black with red interior, clear windows, hot pink and bright blue accents .. $4 – 5
33. metallic gray with two-tone blue design, rubber tires on chrome rims, Premiere Collection #9 .... $4 – 5
34. white, "6 Horse Racing Team," Hong Kong issue .... $9 – 12
35. white, "Fast Eddie's 15," blue metal base .... $3 – 4
36. white, "Fast Eddie's 15," blue plastic base, China cast .... $7 – 9
37. white, "Fast Eddie's 15," blue plastic base, Macau cast .... $4 – 5
38. white, "Fast Eddie's 15," blue plastic base, Thailand cast .... $3 – 4
39. dark brown to pale green, "Fast Eddie's 15," blue metal base, Super Color Changers .... $8 – 10

Pontiac Firebird S/E Police, #456, 2000

1. red, "D.A.R.E.," "Police," D.A.R.E. .... $4 – 5
2. black and white, "D.A.R.E. to Resist Drugs & Violence," D.A.R.E. .... $4 – 5

Pontiac Firebird Trans Am, #16, 1979

1. metallic tan .... $6 – 9
2. metallic gold .... $6 – 9
3. white .... $5 – 7
4. dark blue, Manaus casting, Brazil issue .... $60 – 80

Pontiac Firebird Trans Am T-Roof, #35, 1982; #16, 1983, international

1. black, firebird design on hood, "Turbo," England cast .... $3 – 4

2. black, firebird design on hood, "Trans Am," Macau cast .... $3 – 4

3. black, orange tiger stripes, Macau cast, UK on-package premium ..... $12 – 16

4. metallic silver, firebird design on hood, Macau cast .... $3 – 4

5. red, "3 Rooster Racing Team," Macau cast, Hong Kong issue .... $9 – 12
6. black, "Smokey & the Bandit," Star Cars $6 – 7

Pontiac Grand Prix, 3", #22, 1964

1. red with black plastic wheels ....$16 – 24

2. red with Superfast wheels, 1970 .... $2,000 – 2,500

3. purple with Superfast wheels .... $55 – 65

Pontiac Grand Prix, 1994, approximately 1:43 scale, from White Rose Collectibles

1. yellow and black, red, and blue, "Black Flag 43," "French's 43" .... $35 – 40
2. dark blue and white, "Cobra 24" ..$12 – 16
3. light blue, "USA Bobsled Team 43" .... $12 – 16
4. silver gray, metallic blue and pink, "Coors Light 42" .... $20 – 25

Pontiac Grand Prix 1996, WRP01, 1996, White Rose Collectibles

1. "MBNA America 72," black ...... $5 – 6
2. "Skittles 36," "Starburst," red and blue ....$5 – 6
3. "White Rose Collectibles," "December 25," dark green .... $60 – 80
4. "White Rose Collectibles," "Merry Christmas 1997," red .... $50 – 60

Pontiac Grand Prix Stock Car, #35, 1992; #22, 1993, international; #269, 1994, White Rose

1. "Black Flag 43"; "French's 43"; yellow, black, red, and blue; Goodyear rubber tires on black rims; White Rose Collectibles .... $40 – 50
2. "Black Flag 43," Goodyear rubber tires on black rims, White Rose Collectibles ....$4 – 5
3. "Cobra 24," dark blue and white, Goodyear rubber tires on black rims, White Rose Collectibles .... $12 – 16
4. "Coors Light 42," metallic blue and pink, Goodyear rubber tires on black rims, White Rose Collectibles, sealed in plexiglas box with metallic gray stand .....$20 – 30
5. "Coors Light 42," metallic blue and pink, Goodyear rubber tires on black rims, White Rose Collectibles, sealed in plexiglas box with white stand ..... $20 – 30
6. "Country Time 68," yellow, Goodyear slicks, White Rose Collectibles ... $4 – 5
7. "Evinrude 80," blue and white, Goodyear slicks, White Rose Collectibles ... $4 – 5
8. "French's 43," yellow, Goodyear rubber tires on black rims, White Rose Collectibles .... $4 – 5
9. "Hulkster 43," red, Goodyear rubber tires on black rims, Team Convoy, White Rose Collectibles .... $7 – 9
10. "Kendall 40," black, Goodyear rubber tires on black rims, White Rose Collectibles .... $4 – 5
11. "Medford Speed Shop," "Valtrol 48," white and yellow, Goodyear slicks, White Rose Collectibles .... $5 – 6
12. "Mello Yello 42," black and green, Goodyear slicks, White Rose Collectibles ....$4 – 5
13. "Mello Yello 42," black and green, Goodyear rubber tires on black rims, White Rose Collectibles .... $5 – 6
14. "Nastrak 1," white and red, Goodyear slicks, White Rose Collectibles ... $4 – 5
15. "Nastrak 2," red, Goodyear slicks, White Rose Collectibles .... $4 – 5
16. "Nastrak 3," red and yellow, Goodyear slicks, White Rose Collectibles ... $4 – 5
17. "Nastrak 4," red and brown, Goodyear slicks, White Rose Collectibles ... $4 – 5
18. "Nastrak 5," red and yellow, Goodyear slicks, White Rose Collectibles ... $4 – 5
19. "Nastrak 6," blue and white, Goodyear slicks, White Rose Collectibles ... $4 – 5

20. "Outlaw Auto 7," black ....$3 – 4

21. "Pennzoil 30," yellow, Goodyear slicks, White Rose Collectibles .... $4 – 5
22. "Pennzoil 30," yellow, Goodyear rubber tires on black rims, White Rose Collectibles .... $4 – 5
23. "Pennzoil 30," yellow, Goodyear rubber tires on gray rims, White Rose Collectibles .... $5 – 6
24. "Pontiac Excitement 2," black, Goodyear slicks, White Rose Collectibles ... $4 – 5
25. "Pontiac Excitement 2," black, Goodyear rubber tires on black rims, White Rose Collectibles .... $5 – 6
26. "Pro Auto 10," yellow .... $1 – 2
27. "Richard Petty Pit Tour 43," blue, Goodyear rubber tires on black rims, White Rose Collectibles .... $12 – 16
28. "Rumple 70," "Son's," blue, Goodyear rubber tires on black rims, White Rose Collectibles .... $5 – 6
29. "STP 43," blue, Goodyear slicks, White Rose Collectibles .... $4 – 5
30. "STP 43," blue, Goodyear rubber tires on blue rims, White Rose Collectibles .... $5 – 6

31. "USA Bobsled Team 43," light blue, Goodyear rubber tires on black rims, White Rose Collectibles .... $12 – 16
32. "White House Apple Juice 4," yellow, Goodyear slicks, White Rose Collectibles, on-package premium ...... $5 – 6
33. "White Rose Collectibles 93," white and black, Goodyear slicks, White Rose Collectibles .... $30 – 35

Pontiac GTO (see Pontiac GTO 1970 "The Judge")

Pontiac GTO 1970 "The Judge," #70, 1996 – 1997; #38, 1998; #71, 1999; #65, 2005

1. red with yellow and blue trim, 5-spoke concave wheels .... $3 – 4
2. red with yellow and blue trim, 6-spoke spiral wheels .... $120 – 160

3. **red with yellow and blue trim, 5-spoke wheels, 2005 Superfast #18 ....$3 – 4**
4. orange with blue and red trim, rubber tires on chrome rims, Premiere Collection .... $6 – 8
5. orange with yellow and blue trim, 5-spoke concave wheels .. $120 – 160
6. orange with yellow and blue trim, 6-spoke spiral wheels, 1996 .... $1 – 2
7. yellow with green and blue flames, rubber tires on chrome rims, Premiere Collection #11 .... $4 – 5

8. **yellow with red and blue trim, 1998 Classic Decades ....$1 – 2**
9. dark green with orange and yellow trim, 6-spoke spiral wheels, Chinese issue .... $80 – 120
10. dark green with orange and yellow trim, rubber tires on chrome rims, Select Class #3 .... $4 – 5
11. metallic blue with red and white trim, rubber tires on chrome rims, Gold Coin Collection .... $16 – 24
12. dark blue with white, yellow, orange, and red trim, rubber tires on chrome rims, Premiere Collection #20 .... $4 – 5
13. dark purple with detailed trim, rubber tires on chrome rims, Matchbox Collectibles .... $16 – 24

14. **black with orange and white band, "GTO," 1999 Classics series .. $2 – 3**
15. black with yellow and red trim .. $1 – 2

16. **black with orange and yellow pinstriping, "The Judge," 1997 American Street Machines 5-pack .. $2 – 3**
17. dark gray with red and white trim, rubber tires on chrome rims, Premiere Collection #17 .... $4 – 5
18. white, "Coca-Cola Play Refreshed," rubber tires on chrome rims, Premiere Collection .... $4 – 5
19. white with blue and yellow trim, rubber tires on chrome rims, Premiere Collection #6 .... $6 – 8
20. metallic silver with blue and yellow trim, 6-spoke spiral wheels, Chinese issue .... $80 – 120

21. **metallic silver with blue and yellow trim, rubber tires on chrome rims, Premiere Collection #3 .... $6 – 8**
22. metallic gold with no trim, 1997 75 Challenge .... $6 – 12

23. **metallic light bronze, 2005 #65 .... $1 – 2**

Pontiac Piranha, #73, 2002; #59, 2003

1. **purple with silver doors, "Piranha" and illustration on sides, 2002 Kids' Cars of the Year ....$1 – 2**

2. **yellow with fishbowl, cat, bird, and dog design, 2003 Kid's Shoppes .....$1 – 2**

3. **metallic gray with "Elemental Hero Sparkman" graphics, 2006 Yu-Gi-Oh GX 5-pack H5775 ....$2 – 3**

4. **flat black with maroon argyle pattern, 2007 5-pack K9407 ....$1 – 2**

Pontiac Solstice, (MB612) #64, 2004; #14, 2006; #14, 2007

1. bright sky blue, 2004 #64 ...... $1 – 2

2. **teal blue, 2006 #14 ....$1 – 2**
3. periwinkle blue, #2007 #14 (K2619 on 2006 package) .... $1 – 2

4. **metallic purple with green stripe graphics, 2007 Streakers #42 ....$4 – 5**

Pontiac Stock Car, 3", #35, 1993

1. yellow, "Seaside 15," Goodyear slicks 1993 .... $4 – 5

2. **yellow, "Pro Auto 10," Goodyear slicks, 1994 .... $1 – 2**
3. black, "Dirt Devil," Goodyear slicks, White Rose Collectibles .... $4 – 5
4. black, "Dirt Devil," rubber tires on black rims, White Rose Collectibles ... $4 – 5
5. black, "Duron 66," Goodyear slicks, White Rose Collectibles .... $9 – 12
6. orange, "Burn Foundation," "Motorsports 94," Goodyear slicks .. $16 – 24
7. purple, "JP Graphics," Goodyear slicks .... $1 – 2

Pontiac T-Roof (see Pontiac Firebird Trans Am T-Roof)

Pontiac Trans Am (see Pontiac Firebird Trans Am)

Pontiac Vibe, #51, 2003; Superfast #23, 2005

1. **metallic silver, 2003 School Time .... $1 – 2**

2. **black, 2005 Superfast #23 .. $4 – 5**

Pony Trailer, with two horses, 2⁵⁄₈", #43, 1968

1. orange, Superfast wheels .... $5 – 6

2. **yellow, black plastic wheels .. $7 – 9**
3. yellow, Superfast wheels ...... $20 – 25
4. green, white roof, "Polizei," Superfast wheels .... $4 – 5
5. beige, brown tailgate, Superfast wheels .... $5 – 6
6. beige, lime green tailgate, Superfast wheels .... $9 – 12
7. beige, white tailgate, Superfast wheels .... $3 – 4
8. white, blue-gray tailgate, "Polizei," Superfast wheels .... $1 – 2
9. **white, lime green tailgate, Superfast wheels .... $1 – 2**
10. white, red roof, white tailgate, Superfast wheels .... $1 – 2

Pop-Up Camper, #62, 2000; #42, 2000, international

1. **red with white and black road design, white roof, tan interior, 2000 Great Outdoors .... $1 – 2**
2. red with white and black road design, "Matchbox 2000," white roof, tan interior, 2000 Great Outdoors .... $3 – 4

3. **red-orange with forest, camper, and moon illustration, phosphorescent green roof, 2003 Camp Fun 3-pack with flashlight .... $1 – 2**
4. metallic pale green with green and blue graphics, blue roof, 5-pack ...... $1 – 2

5. **white with red roof, footprints and turquoise graphics, aqua interior, teal base, 2003 5-pack #10 ... $1 – 2**

Porsche 910, 2⁷⁄₈", #68, 1970

1. red, "45" label on hood, amber windows .... $16 – 24
2. red, "45" label on hood, clear windows .... $16 – 24
3. red, "68" label on hood, amber windows .... $12 – 16
4. red, "68" label on hood, clear windows .... $12 – 16
5. red, "68" label on hood and sides, amber windows, gift set ...... $12 – 16
6. red, scorpion label on hood, amber windows .... $180 – 240
7. metallic red .... $12 – 15
8. white, amber windows .... $40 – 50
9. fluorescent orange, China cast, Neon Racer BR 35-36, 1985 .... $4 – 6
10. lime green, China cast, Super GT BR 35-36, 1985 .... $3 – 5
11. light blue, England cast, Super GT BR 35-36, 1985 .... $4 – 6
12. light blue, "Drive" graphics, England cast, Super GT BR 35-36, 1985 .... $8 – 10
13. light blue, China cast, Super GT BR 35-36, 1985 .... $8 – 10
14. dark blue, England cast, Super GT BR 35-36, 1985 .... $4 – 6
15. white, China cast, Super GT BR 35-36, 1985 .... $8 – 10
16. silver, "49" graphics, England cast, Super GT BR 35-36, 1985 .... $8 – 10
17. silver, "Drive" graphics, England cast, Super GT BR 35-36, 1985 .... $4 – 6
18. silver, China cast, Super GT BR 35-36, 1985 .... $8 – 10

Porsche 911 Carrera Cabriolet, #17, 1999, US; #72, 1999, Germany; #50, 2003, international; #14, 2005; #10, 2007

1. red with black interior, 5-spoke wheels, 1999 Germany issue .... $5 – 6
2. red with black interior, 10-spoke wheels, Target Eggmobile 3-pack .... $5 – 6

3. **metallic burgundy with gray interior, 2005 Superfast #36 .... $3 – 4**
4. yellow with black interior, 1999 Germany issue .... $5 – 6
5. lime green with dark gray interior, 2007 #10 .... $1 – 2
6. blue with black interior, 2005 #14 .... $1 – 2

7. **dark blue with tan interior, 2003 international issue .... $1 – 2**

8. **black with gray interior, 2001 Eurosports 5-pack .... $1 – 2**
9. metallic graphite gray with light gray interior, black plastic base, 2001 Eurosports 5-pack .... $1 – 2

10. metallic silver with red interior, 2003 Auto Carrier Launcher 5-pack .. $1 – 2

Porsche 911 GT1, #68, 1998; #45, 2000; #58, 1998, international; #31, 1999, international; #35, 2000, international

1. metallic red, 2001 Eurosports 5-pack ....$1 - 2
2. yellow, "911GT1," 2000 Show Cars ...$1 – 2
3. yellow, "911GT1," "Matchbox 2000," 2000 Show Cars .... $3 – 4
4. metallic blue, "911GT1," Germany issue .... $4 – 5
5. metallic blue, "Matchbox," "GT1" ..$3 – 4
6. metallic gray, "Porsche" .... $3 – 4

7. white, "911 GT1," 1998 Street Cruisers ....$1 - 2

8. white with no markings 2005 Superfast #70 ....$3 - 4
9. white, "Citrix Vertigo," "CDN," ASAP promotional .... $80 – 120
10. white, "Citrix Vertigo," "Citrix.com," "CDN," ASAP promotional .. $80 – 120
11. white with upside-down "V" and radiating lines, ASAP promotional ...... $60 – 80

Porsche 911 GT3, #3, 2007
1. metallic gray .... $1 – 2

Porsche 911 Turbo, #3, 1978 (also see Porsche 911 Turbo, #69, 2005)
1. red, black base, tan interior, "Porsche 90 Turbo," clear windows, England cast ....$4 – 6
2. red, blue-gray base, tan interior, "Porsche 90 Turbo," clear windows, England cast .... $4 – 6
3. red, dark gray base, tan interior, "Porsche 90 Turbo," clear windows ....$4 – 6
4. red, dark gray base, white interior, "Porsche 90 Turbo," clear windows ....$4 – 6
5. red, black base, white interior, "Porsche 90 Turbo," clear windows .... $4 – 6
6. red, black base, tan interior, "Porsche 90 Turbo," opaque windows ..$12 – 16
7. red, black base, tan interior, no markings, clear windows, Macau cast ..$4 – 6
8. red, black base, tan interior, clear windows, "Porsche" and "Porsche 911," Macau cast .... $1 – 2
9. red, black base, brown interior, clear windows, "Porsche 90 Turbo," Macau cast .... $3 – 5
10. red, black base, blue interior, clear windows, "8 Dragon Racing Team," Macau cast, Hong Kong issue .... $9 – 12
11. red, black base, tan interior clear windows, "Porsche" and "Porsche 911," Thailand cast .... $1 – 2
12. red, black base, tan interior, clear windows, "Porsche 90 Turbo," Manaus cast, Brazil issue .... $30 – 40
13. orange-red, black base, white interior, "Porsche 90 Turbo," clear windows, England cast .... $6 – 9
14. metallic green, dark gray base, red interior, England cast .... $8 – 12
15. metallic green, black base, red interior, England cast .... $8 – 12
16. metallic green, dark gray base, light orange interior, England cast .... $4 – 6
17. metallic green, black base, light orange interior, England cast .... $4 – 6
18. metallic green, blue-gray base, light orange interior, England cast .... $6 – 9
19. metallic green, unpainted base, light orange interior, England cast .... $6 – 9
20. metallic green, dark gray base, ivory interior, England cast .... $8 – 12
21. blue, black base, blue interior, clear windows, "Porsche," Thailand cast, 5-pack ....$1 – 2
22. metallic dark blue, black base, white interior, clear windows, "Wrangler 47," Macau cast, UK issue .... $9 – 12
23. dark blue, black base, tan interior, clear windows, "Porsche" and yellow stripes, Macau cast .... $3 – 4
24. dark blue, black base, tan interior, clear windows, "Porsche" and yellow stripes, Thailand cast .... $1 – 2

25. blue with orange and white streaks, clear windows, cream interior, 1997 Super Cars 5-pack ....$2 - 3
26. pale blue, black base, blue interior, clear windows, "Boss 14," multipack, Macau cast .... $4 – 6
27. yellow, black base, tan interior, clear windows, Porsche logo, Thailand cast, gift set .... $4 – 5
28. pale yellow, black base, black interior, clear windows, "Porsche" and spatter, Two-Pack, Thailand cast .... $3 – 4
29. metallic brown, unpainted base, ivory interior, England cast ....$40 – 55
30. metallic brown, black base, ivory interior, England cast ....$8 – 12
31. black, black base, tan interior, amber windows, "Porsche 90 Turbo," Macau cast ....$3 – 5
32. black, black base, tan interior, clear windows, "Porsche," Macau cast .... $9 – 12
33. black, black base, black interior, clear windows, "90 Porsche Turbo," "BP," Macau cast, Netherlands issue .... $9 – 12
34. black, black base, tan interior, clear windows, "Porsche" and "Porsche 911," multipack, Macau cast ..$3 – 4
35. black, black base, tan interior, clear windows, "Porsche 90 Turbo," Manaus cast, Brazil issue ....$30 – 40
36. black, black base, peach interior, clear windows, gold "Porsche," Thailand cast, Sports Pack ....$3 – 4
37. gray, brown base, red interior, England cast ....$8 – 12
38. gray, dark gray base, red interior, England cast ....$8 – 12
39. metallic gray, black base, ivory interior, England cast ....$7 – 9
40. metallic gray, dark gray base, ivory interior, England cast ....$7 – 9
41. metallic gray, black base, red interior, England cast ....$4 – 6
42. metallic gray, brown base, red interior, England cast ....$8 – 12
43. metallic gray, dark gray base, red interior, England cast ....$4 – 6
44. metallic gray, brown base, tan interior, England cast ....$8 – 12
45. metallic gray, black base, tan interior, England cast ....$5 – 7
46. metallic gray, dark gray base, tan interior, England cast ....$6 – 9
47. white, black base, tan interior, clear windows, "Boss 14," Macau cast, Japan issue ....$9 – 12
48. white, black base, tan interior, clear windows, "Boss 14," Macau cast ....$4 – 6
49. white, black base, blue interior, clear windows, "Boss 14," "14," Thailand cast, Sports Pack ....$3 – 4
50. white, black base, blue interior, clear windows, "Boss 14," Macau cast ....$4 – 6
51. white, black base, tan interior, clear windows, "Porsche," "3," Macau cast .... $9 – 12
52. white, black base, red interior, clear windows, small Porsche logo, Thailand cast, Show Stoppers ....$3 – 4
53. white, black base, tan interior, clear windows, "Matchbox Fun Club," Thailand cast, UK issue ....$9 – 12

Porsche 911 Turbo, #9, 2003; #69, 2005; #25, 2006 (also see Porsche 911 Turbo, #3, 1978)

1. **red with yellow and black on sides, 2003 Family Wheels #9 ....$1 - 2**

2. **metallic red, 2005 #69 ....$1 - 2**

3. **metallic pale blue, 2006 #25 ...$1 - 2**

4. **metallic gray, 2005 Superfast #20 .... $3 - 4**

Porsche 928, doors open except where noted, 3", #59, 1980

1. orange, "Lufthansa," red interior, clear windows, pearl silver base .... $5 – 6
2. yellow, "Porsche 928" and logo, red interior, clear windows, pearl silver base ....$12 – 16
3. metallic blue with brown interior, clear windows, black base .... $5 – 6
4. metallic blue with brown interior, clear windows, dark gray base .... $5 – 6
5. metallic blue with brown interior, clear windows, metallic gray base ..... $5 – 6
6. metallic blue with tan interior, clear windows, black base .... $5 – 6
7. black, "Porsche" and stripe, brown interior, clear windows, metallic gray base .... $9 – 12
8. black, "Porsche" and stripe, red interior, clear windows, metallic gray base ..$4 – 5
9. black, "Porsche" and stripe, red interior, clear windows, unpainted base .. $4 – 5
10. black, "Porsche" and stripe, red interior, clear windows, pearly silver base ..$3 – 4
11. black, "Porsche" and stripe, red interior, light amber windows, pearly silver base ....$3 – 4
12. dark gray, chrome windows, detailed trim, rubber tires on gray rims, doors don't open, Macau cast, World Class .... $6 – 8
13. dark gray, chrome windows, detailed trim, rubber tires on gray rims, doors don't open, Thailand cast, World Class ....$6 – 8
14. metallic light gray with purple and blue design, red interior, clear windows ... $4 – 5
15. metallic gray "928S," detailed trim, purple and gray interior, clear windows, rubber tires on chrome rims, JC Penney Premiere Collection .... $4 – 5
16. pearl silver, "Martini Racing Porsche," red interior, clear windows, Japan issue .... $8 – 10
17. white, "56 Porsche" with red stripes, red interior, clear windows, white base, doors don't open .... $12 – 16
18. white and metallic blue, "28" with "Cale Jenkins," red interior, clear windows, Laser Wheels .... $4 – 5
19. white and metallic blue, "28" with "Cale Jenkins," red interior, clear windows, New Superfast wheels .... $4 – 5
20. white and metallic blue, "28" without "Cale Jenkins," red interior, clear windows, Laser Wheels .... $4 – 5
21. white and metallic blue, "28" without "Cale Jenkins," red interior, clear windows, New Superfast wheels ... $4 – 5
22. metallic tan with ivory interior, clear windows, black base .... $5 – 6
23. metallic tan with brown interior, amber windows, black base .... $5 – 6
24. metallic tan with brown interior, amber windows, brown base .... $8 – 10
25. metallic tan with brown interior, clear windows, black base .... $5 – 6
26. metallic tan with brown interior, orange windows, black base .... $5 – 6
27. metallic tan with light tan interior, clear windows, black base .... $5 – 6
28. metallic tan with tan interior, amber windows, black base .... $5 – 6
29. metallic tan with tan interior, amber windows, brown base .... $8 – 10

Porsche 935, 3", #55, 1983; #41, 1983

1. red, "41 Porsche," Macau cast ... $1 – 2
2. red, "Autotech 35," New Superfast wheels .... $4 – 5
3. red, "Porsche" logo, Thailand cast .. $3 – 4
4. metallic red, "Autotech 35," Laser Wheels .... $4 – 5
5. light yellow with chrome windows, detailed trim, rubber tires on gray rims, World Class .... $6 – 8
6. yellow, "Porsche 10," Macau cast .. $3 – 4
7. yellow, "Porsche 10," Thailand cast ....$3 – 4
8. light blue, "Elf 71 Sachs," silver wheels ....$3 – 4
9. light blue, "Elf 71 Sachs," gold wheels ....$50 – 70
10. light blue, "Far Porsche 71 Sachs," Manaus cast, Brazil issue .... $40 – 60
11. black, "11 Ox Racing Team," Hong Kong issue .... $9 – 12
12. black, "935," chrome and black windows, Lightning Wheels .... $3 – 4
13. pearl ivory, detailed trim, chrome windows, rubber tires on gray rims, World Class .... $6 – 8
14. white, "935," fluorescent orange accents, blue chrome and black windows, Lightning Wheels .... $3 – 4
15. white, "Cadbury Buttons," UK issue ....$9 – 12
16. white, "Elf," "Porsche," "Sachs," green wavy line and lavender stripes, Manaus cast, Brazil issue .... $40 – 60
17. white, "Porsche 10," gold wheels .. $5 – 6
18. white, "Porsche 10," silver wheels .. $3 – 4

Porsche 944, 3", #71, 1988; #59, 1991

1. red, "944 Turbo," "Credit Charge," doors open, Macau cast, UK issue ... $9 – 12
2. red, "944 Turbo," detailed trim, doors open, Thailand cast, International Premiere Collection #2 .... $4 – 5

3. **red, "944 Turbo" on sides, large logo on hood, doors open, Macau cast .... $1 – 2**
4. metallic red, detailed trim, doors open, Thailand cast, Gold Coin Collection .... $16 – 24
5. yellow, doors open, Collector's Choice, White Rose Collectibles .... $4 – 5
6. metallic green, "944 Turbo," "American International Recovery," doors open, Thailand cast, ASAP promotional .... $120 – 160
7. metallic green, "944 Turbo" and logo, doors open, Thailand cast .... $1 – 2
8. black, "944 Turbo" and logo, doors open, Macau cast .... $3 – 4
9. black, "944 Turbo" on sides, doors don't open, detailed trim, chrome windows, rubber tires on gray rims, Macau cast, World Class .... $7 – 9
10. black, "944 Turbo" on sides, doors don't open, detailed trim, chrome windows, rubber tires on gray rims, Thailand cast, World Class .... $7 – 9
11. white, "Duckhams," doors open, Macau cast, UK on-package premium .. $16 – 24
12. white, "Duckhams," doors open, Thailand cast, UK on-package premium .... $16 – 24
13. pearl white, "944 Turbo," detailed trim, doors open, Thailand cast, Premiere Collection #19 .... $4 – 5

Porsche 959, $2^{7}/_{8}$", #7, 1987; #51, 1994; #17, 1999

1. **metallic dark orange with black and white stripes, "959," "Porsche," #17, 1999 Top Class ....$2 – 3**

2. **lime green with black and yellow graphics, #51, 1996 ....$1 – 2**
3. purple with "Porsche 959" .... $4 – 5
4. magenta with "Rage" graphics, black and yellow accents .... $1 – 2
5. hot pink with "Rage" on doors, accent on hood and roof .... $1 – 2
6. pink with "Porsche 959" .... $3 – 5
7. black with "Porsche" logo .... $5 – 6
8. gray with "Porsche 959" .... $2 – 4
9. metallic pearl gray with "Porsche" on doors .... $2 – 4
10. metallic pearl gray with "Porsche," chrome wheels, rubber tires, World Class .... $6 – 9
11. white with "Lloyds" .... $10 – 12
12. white with "Porsche" on doors, white wheels .... $4 – 6
13. white with "Porsche" on doors, silver wheels .... $2 – 4
14. white with "Pace Car," "Shell" .... $4 – 5
15. white with "Pirelli Gripping Stuff 313" .... $4 – 6
16. white with "Porsche 959," with red, yellow, and black stripes .... $8 – 10
17. white with "Redoxon" .... $25 – 35
18. chrome with no markings .... $16 – 24

Porsche Boxster, #55, 1999; #5, 2000; #50, 1999, international

1. metallic red with gray and black interior, rubber tires on chrome rims, First Editions .... $6 – 8
2. light green, "Porsche Boxster," gold stripe, 5-pack .... $1 – 2
3. blue with rust interior, "Millennium Convention," Color Comp promotional ..$30 – 40
4. purple, "Millennium Toy Show," Color Comp promotional .... $12 – 16
5. metallic gray with rust interior, 1999 Beach .... $1 – 2
6. metallic gray with black interior, 2000 Open Road .... $1 – 2
7. metallic gray with black interior, "CFS Bowl 2000," ASAP promotional ......$60 – 80
8. metallic gray with rust interior, "Grand Opening Mattel — Die Cast Factory," "Matchbox," Color Comp promotional ....$250 – 300

9. **metallic gray with rust interior, silver trim on windshield, 1999 Beach ..$4 – 5**

10. **metallic gray with black interior, "Matchbox 2000," 2000 Open Road ....$3 – 4**

11. **metallic silver with red interior, 2003 Hero City 5-pack ....$1 – 2**

12. **white with black interior, 2003 Hero City 5-pack #12 ....$1 – 2**
13. white with black interior, detailed headlights and taillights, 2006 5-pack J4681 .... $1 – 2
14. unpainted with gray interior, rubber tires on chrome rims, First Editions ... $6 – 8

Porsche Cayenne Turbo, #60, 2005; #61, 2006; #25, 2007

1. black, 2005 #60 .... $1 – 2
2. metallic gray, 2006 #61 .... $1 – 2

3. **metallic light blue, 2006 #61, K2617 ....$1 – 2**

4. **metallic blue, 2006 5-pack J4672 ....$1 – 2**

5. **dark blue, 2007 #25, K9512 ..$1 – 2**

Porsche Turbo (see Porsche 911 Turbo)

Postal Service Delivery Truck, #97, 2000

1. **white, "United States Postal Service," 2000 On the Road Again ....$4 – 5**
2. white, "United States Postal Service," "Matchbox 2000," 2000 On the Road Again .... $5 – 6
3. white, "United States Postal Service," "Skillman, NJ 08558" decals, Color Comp promotional .... $20 – 30
4. black with haunted house graphics, 2006 play set .... $4 – 5

Pound Hound, bulldog with wrecking ball, #22, 2004

1. gold with brown base, yellow wrecking ball and boom, 2004 Ultra Heroes ...$1 – 2

Power Boat (Moby Quick), #21, 2001

1. **red deck, white hull, white "Unit 26," yellow "1462-PP12," 2001 Sun Chasers ....$1 – 2**

2. **orange deck with orange and black accents, white hull, black foil, 2007 5-pack K9617 ....$1 – 2**

3. blue deck, white hull, "Police," 2006 Superman 5-pack J4725 ......$2 - 3

4. white deck, black hull, yellow, white and blue "05 Police," 2003 Hero City 5-pack #2 ....$1 - 2

Power Lift, #45, 2007

1. yellow with gray fork lift, metallic gun metal gray base, 2007 #45, K7471 ....$1 - 2

Pressure Refueler (see RAF 10-Ton Pressure Refueling Tanker)

Prime Mover Truck Tractor (also see Rotinoff Super Atlantic Prime Mover), 2¹/₈", #15, 1956

1. yellow with metal wheels .. $500 – 700
2. orange with metal wheels .... $25 – 50
3. orange with plastic wheels ..$175 – 200

Prime Mover (see Rotinoff Super Atlantic Prime Mover)

Q

Q-B Roller, football-shaped vehicle, #8, 2004

1. football with wheels, 2004 Ultra Heroes ....$3 – 4

Quarry Truck (also see Articulated Dump Truck, Atlas Dump Truck, DAF Tipper Truck, Dodge Dump Truck, 8-Wheel Tipper, Euclid Quarry Truck, GMC Highway Maintenance Truck, GMC Tipper Truck, Leyland Articulated Truck, Mack Dump Truck, Peterbilt Quarry Truck, Quarry Truck)

Quarry Truck, Euclid (see Euclid Quarry Truck)

Quarry Truck, 2¹/₈", #6, 1955

1. metal wheels .... $40 – 55
2. gray plastic wheels .... $150 – 200
3. Matchbox Originals, 1993, blue with gray dumper, silver metal wheels, made in China .... $4 – 6

Quarry Truck, 2¹/₂", #6, 1957 (see Euclid Quarry Truck)

R

Racing Mini, #29, 1971

1. metallic orange ....$20 - 25

2. orange ....$12 - 16

3. red .... $15 – 20

Racing Porsche (see Porsche 935)

Radar Plane, #41, 2001; #40, 2002; #34, 2003

1. orange-yellow with white base, orange wings and radar, 2003 Airport .. $1 – 2
2. yellow with white base, orange-yellow wings and radar, 2003 Hero City 10-pack #2 .... $1 – 2
3. blue with gray base, yellow wings and radar, 2001 Rescue Squad ..... $1 – 2

4. black with red base, blue wings and radar, 2003 Hero City 5-pack #3 ....$1 - 2

5. black with black base, phosphorescent wings and radar, 2002 Nite Glow ....$1 - 2

Radar Truck (see Weather Radar Truck)

RAF 10-Ton Pressure Refueling Tanker, 2⁵/₈", #73, 1959

1. blue-gray with gray plastic wheels ....$5 - 10

Railway Passenger Coach, 3¹/₁₆", #44, 1978

1. red, "431 432" labels, beige roof, England cast .... $5 – 6
2. red, "431 432" labels, beige roof, Macau cast .... $3 – 4
3. red, "431 432" labels, beige roof, China cast .... $1 – 2
4. red, "431 432," "Kellogg's" labels, beige roof, Kellogg's on-package premium, China cast, Netherlands issue .... $20 – 30
5. red, "5810 – 6102" labels, beige roof, England cast .... $9 – 12
6. red, "GWR" labels, beige roof, England cast .... $9 – 12
7. red, "NYK" labels, beige roof, no origin cast, Brazil issue .... $120 – 160
8. green, "431 432" labels, beige roof, England cast .... $9 – 12
9. green, "5810-6102" labels, England cast .... $7 – 8
10. green, "British Railways," China cast ....$3 – 4
11. lime green, yellow, and red, Live 'N Learn/Matchbox Preschool series, Macau cast .... $7 – 8
12. lime green, yellow, and red, Live 'N Learn/Matchbox Preschool series, China cast .... $7 – 8
13. white, no markings, Graffic Traffic, China cast .... $12 – 16

Rallye Royale, 2⁷/₈", #14, 1981 (similar casting: Monteverdi Hai, 1973)

1. metallic silver upper, black lower body, "14" .... $9 – 12
2. metallic silver upper, black lower body, "8" .... $9 – 12

3. white upper, red-orange lower body, "8" ....$9 - 12

Range Rover Police Patrol (Rolamatic), 2⁷/₈", #20, 1975

1. white, "Police" labels, frosted windows, orange dome, orange spinner .. $9 – 12
2. white, "Police" labels, frosted windows, blue dome, orange spinner ...... $7 – 9
3. white, "Police" labels, frosted windows, yellow dome, blue spinner, large "Police" labels .... $7 – 9
4. white, "Police" labels, frosted windows, yellow dome, blue spinner, small "Police" labels .... $20 – 25
5. white, "Police" labels, frosted windows, yellow dome, orange spinner, large "Police" labels .... $7 – 9
6. white, "Police" labels, frosted windows, yellow dome, orange spinner, small "Police" labels .... $20 – 25
7. white, "Police" labels, frosted windows, blue dome, blue spinner, unpainted base .... $7 – 9
8. white, "Police" labels, frosted windows, blue dome, blue spinner, black base .... $9 – 12
9. white, "Police" labels, frosted windows, blue dome, orange spinner, unpainted base .... $20 – 25
10. white, "Police" labels, frosted windows, blue dome, orange spinner, black base .... $9 – 12
11. white, "Police" labels, amber frosted windows .... $9 – 12
12. white, "Police" labels, blue frosted windows .... $9 – 12
13. white, "Police" labels, yellow frosted windows .... $9 – 12
14. white, checkered "Police" labels .. $9 – 12
15. white, "Ambulance" labels .... $20 – 25
16. white, "County Sheriff" .... $9 – 12
17. white, "Site Engineer" labels ... $20 – 25
18. white and black with Japanese letters .... $9 – 12
19. beige, "Paris Dakar 83," "Lesney England" cast .... $7 – 9
20. beige, "Paris Dakar 83," "Matchbox International England" cast .... $7 – 9
21. blue, "Paris Dakar 81" .... $40 – 60
22. dark army green, "Ambulance" labels .... $70 – 90
23. dark army green, "Police" labels .. $70 – 90
24. light army green, "Ambulance" labels .... $7 – 9
25. light army green, red and yellow "Police" labels, black hubs .... $7 – 9
26. light army green, "Police" labels, chrome hubs .... $8 – 10
27. metallic tan, "Paris Dakar 83" .. $7 – 9
28. orange, "Site Engineer" labels .. $16 – 24
29. orange, "Police" labels .... $20 – 25
30. orange, "Ambulance" labels ... $20 – 25

Range Rover Sport, #50, 2006

1. **black with gray interior, 2006 #50 .... $1 – 2**
2. metallic orange, 2006 #50 ..... $1 – 2

3. **metallic orange, 2007 Superfast #54 .... $3 – 4**

Rapid Rescue Helicopter, #73, 2005 (see Rescue Chopper)

1. green and black, 2005 #73 .... $1 – 2

Real Talkin' Beach Patrol .... $5 – 6

Real Talkin' Ice Cream Truck .... $5 – 6

Real Talkin' UFO Landing Set #35240 ... $7 – 8

Real Talkin' UFO Landing Helicopter ... $5 – 6

Real Talkin' UFO Landing UFO ...... $5 – 6

Real Talkin' Waste Hauler .... $5 – 6

Real Talkin' Wrecker .... $5 – 6

Red Rider, 2⅞", #48, 1982 (similar castings: Big Banger, Cosmic Blues, Flame Out, Pi-Eyed Piper)

1. red, England cast .... $5 – 6
2. red, Hong Kong cast .... $5 – 6
3. red, Macau cast .... $1 – 2
4. red, China cast .... $1 – 2

Refueler (see RAF 10-Ton Pressure Refueling Tanker)

Refuse Truck, 3", #36, 1980; #7, 1998; #3, 1999; #35, 2000; #19, 2001

1. red with yellow container and hatch, "Colectomatic" embossed on front of container, England cast .... $3 – 4
2. red with yellow container and hatch, no "Colectomatic" on container, England cast .... $20 – 25
3. red with yellow container and hatch, "Refuse Disposal," China cast .. $9 – 12

4. **red with metallic gray container and hatch, black recycling illustration, China cast .... $1 – 2**
5. orange with dark blue container and hatch, "Metro DPW Unit 17" ... $1 – 2

6. orange with gray container and hatch, "Refuse Disposal," China cast ... $1 – 2
7. orange-red with light gray container, black recycle logos, 1996 .... $1 – 2
8. orange with orange container and hatch, "Metro DPW Unit 17," recycle symbol, 1998 Big Movers .... $1 – 2
9. orange with white container and hatch, "Refuse Disposal," China cast ... $1 – 2

10. bright orange with white container and hatch, "Disposal Unit 24," red recycling symbol, 1994 ....$3 – 4

11. light orange with dark blue container and hatch, "Metro DPW" on doors, "Unit 17," white recycle symbol, 1998 Big Movers ....$1 – 2

12. light orange with metallic gray container, "Ridge, NY Recycles," 1999 Matchbox USA .... $1 – 2
13. fluorescent pale orange with white container, no markings .... $1 – 2
14. yellow with white container, "Disposal Unit" .... $1 – 2
15. green with metallic gray container, "Recycle," 1998 Around Town 5-pack .. $1 – 2
16. green with yellow container and hatch, "State City," China cast .... $1 – 2
17. green with yellow container and hatch, "Refuse Disposal," China cast ... $1 – 2
18. dark green with metallic gray container and hatch, "Recycle," China cast, 5-pack .... $1 – 2
19. blue with orange container and hatch, "Metro" labels, England cast .... $3 – 4
20. blue with orange container, yellow hatch, "Metro" labels, England cast .... $6 – 7

21. blue with orange container and hatch, "Metro D.P.W. 66" labels, Macau cast ....$3 – 4

22. blue with yellow container and hatch, "Metro D.P.W. 66" labels, England cast .... $4 – 5
23. blue with white container and hatch, "City of Cleveland Ohio," 2000 Matchbox USA .... $1 – 2
24. blue with white container and hatch, "City of Cleveland Ohio," "Matchbox 2000," 2000 Matchbox USA ... $3 – 4
25. bright blue with white container and hatch, "Fort Worth," metallic gray metal base, 2001 City Dudes .... $1 – 2
26. magenta with yellow container and hatch, England cast .... $3 – 4
27. metallic gold with white container and hatch, 1997 75 Challenge .... $6 – 12

28. white with green container and hatch, "Waste Management," 2006 Superfast #22 ....$3 – 4

29. white with blue container and hatch, "Metro D.P.W. 66" labels, Macau cast ....$3 – 4

30. white with blue container and hatch, "Metro D.P.W. 66" labels, China cast .... $3 – 4
31. white with blue container and hatch, "Mill Run" and flag, China cast, 5-pack .... $1 – 2
32. white with blue container and hatch, globe, China cast, 5-pack .... $3 – 4
33. white with blue container and hatch, cartoon character, China cast, 5-pack .... $4 – 5
34. white with blue container and hatch, Japanese lettering, Macau cast, Japan issue .... $10 – 12
35. white with white container and hatch, "Bulldog Castor Co.," ASAP promotional .... $80 – 120
36. white with white container and hatch, "Renfro Cartage," ASAP promotional .... $80 – 120
37. white with white container and hatch, "Waste Industries," ASAP promotional .... $80 – 120
38. white with white container and hatch, "Vince Coleen," heart design, ASAP promotional .... $120 – 150
39. white with white container and hatch, maroon design, ASAP promotional .... $80 – 120
40. white with white container and hatch, ASAP promotional blank ...... $30 – 40

Renault 5TL LeCar, 2 11/16", #21, 1978

1. blue with red interior, black base, clear windows, no markings .... $10 – 12
2. blue with red interior, dark gray base, clear windows, no markings .. $10 – 12
3. blue with tan interior, black base, amber windows, no markings .... $5 – 6
4. blue with tan interior, black base, clear windows, no markings .... $5 – 6
5. blue with tan interior, dark gray base, amber windows, no markings ... $5 – 6
6. blue with tan interior, dark gray base, clear windows, no markings ..... $5 – 6
7. blue with tan interior, metallic gray base, amber windows, no markings ... $5 – 6
8. blue with tan interior, metallic gray base, clear windows, no markings ..... $5 – 6
9. pale blue with tan interior, black base, clear windows, Manaus cast, Brazil issue .... $80 – 120
10. metallic gray with black interior, black base, clear windows, "Scrambler" ....$5 – 6
11. metallic gray with red interior, black base, amber windows, "LeCar" .. $5 – 6
12. metallic gray with red interior, black base, clear windows, "A5" ... $16 – 24
13. metallic gray with red interior, black base, clear windows, "LeCar" ... $5 – 6
14. metallic gray with red interior, black base, clear windows, no markings .... $20 – 25
15. metallic gray with red interior, blue-gray base, orange windows, "LeCar" .... $5 – 6
16. metallic gray with red interior, dark gray base, amber windows, "LeCar" .. $5 – 6
17. metallic gray with red interior, dark gray base, clear windows, "LeCar" ... $5 – 6
18. metallic gray with red interior, gray-brown base, clear windows, "LeCar" .... $5 – 6
19. metallic gray with tan interior, metallic gray base, clear windows, "A5" ....$16 – 24
20. metallic gray with red interior, metallic gray base, clear windows, no markings .... $16 – 24
21. metallic gray with tan interior, metallic gray base, clear windows, no markings .... $20 – 25
22. red with orange interior, orange base, clear windows, "Turbo," Japan issue ....$16 – 24
23. red with tan interior, black base, clear windows, "Turbo" .... $20 – 25
24. white with dark yellow interior, black base, clear windows, "Renault" .. $4 – 5
25. white with light yellow interior, dark gray base, clear windows, "Renault" .. $4 – 5

26. white with tan interior, black base, clear windows, "Renault" ......$4 – 5

27. white with tan interior, black base, clear windows, "Roloil" .... $4 – 5
28. white with tan interior, black base, clear windows, "Roloil," Manaus cast, Brazil issue .... $40 – 60
29. white with tan interior, cream base, clear windows, "Roloil," Manaus cast, Brazil issue .... $40 – 60
30. white with tan interior, dark gray base, clear windows, "Renault" .... $4 – 5
31. white with tan interior, orange base, clear windows, "Roloil" .... $16 – 24
32. white with white interior, black base, clear windows, "Renault" .... $5 – 6
33. white with white interior, black base, clear windows, "Roloil" .... $4 – 5
34. yellow with gray -yellow interior, dark gray base, clear windows, "LeCar" .... $5 – 6
35. yellow with red interior, black base, clear windows, "LeCar" .... $10 – 12
36. yellow with red interior, black base, clear windows, "Le Toy Show," "Matchbox Road Museum," Color Comp promotional .... $30 – 40
37. yellow with red interior, metallic gray base, clear windows, "LeCar" ..$10 – 12
38. yellow with tan interior, black base, amber windows, "LeCar" .... $5 – 6
39. yellow with tan interior, black base, clear windows, "LeCar" .... $5 – 6
40. yellow with tan interior, black base, amber windows, "Le Toy Show," "Matchbox Road Museum," Color Comp promotional .... $30 – 40
41. yellow with tan interior, black base, clear windows, "Le Toy Show," "Matchbox Road Museum," Color Comp promotional .... $30 – 40
42. yellow with tan interior, dark gray base, amber windows, "LeCar" .... $5 – 6
43. yellow with tan interior, dark gray base, clear windows, "LeCar" .... $5 – 6
44. yellow with tan interior, metallic gray base, amber windows, "LeCar" .. $5 – 6
45. yellow with tan interior, metallic gray base, clear windows, "LeCar" ... $5 – 6
46. yellow with tan interior, metallic gray base, clear windows, "Le Toy Show," "Matchbox Road Museum," Color Comp promotional .... $30 – 40

Renault 11 Turbo Alliance, $2^{15}/_{16}$", #33, 1987; #43, 1987

1. black .... $3 – 4
2. metallic blue, "Taxi Parisien" roof sign, James Bond .... $12 – 16

Renault 17TL, 3", #62, 1974

1. dark red, "9" label on hood .... $8 – 10
2. orange-red, "6" label on hood .. $8 – 10
3. orange-red, "9" label on hood .. $8 – 10
4. orange-red, "Fire" label on hood ...$12 – 16

Renault Alliance (see Renault 11 Turbo Alliance)

Renault LeCar (see Renault 5TL LeCar)

Rescue Boat (see Over-Under Rescue Boats)

Rescue Chopper, #60, 1999; #55, 1999, international; #7, 2000; #73, 2005

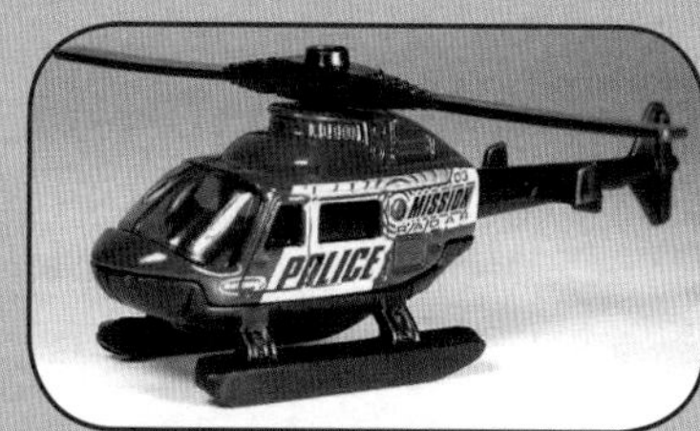

1. **blue; "Police"; white, silver, and red design; black base and tail; 2003 Hero City 5-pack #2 .... $1 – 2**
2. light blue, "Res-026," "067/299," dark blue base, tail, and blades .... $1 – 2
3. bright blue, "Sydney 2000," orange-yellow base, tail, and blades, 5-pack .... $1 – 2

4. **olive green with black base and tail, red windows, 2005 #73 .... $1 – 2**
5. white, "Alpine Rescue," blue base and tail, metallic gray blades, 1999 Wilderness Adventure .... $1 – 2
6. white, "Alpine Rescue," "Matchbox," dark blue base and tail, metallic gray blades, Pleasant Books issue ... $4 – 5
7. white, "Med Air," yellow and dark blue stripes, red base and tail, black blades, 5-pack .... $1 – 2

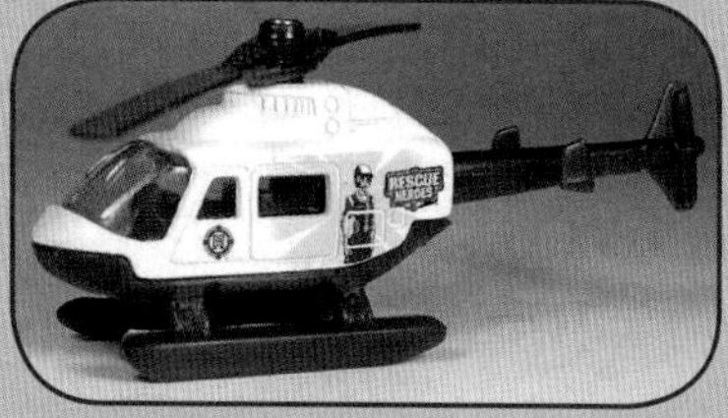

8. **white, "Rescue Heroes," purple base, tail and blades, 2003 Rescue Heroes 5-pack .... $1 – 2**
9. white with bright orange and lime green design, blue base and tail, metallic gray blades, 2000 Ocean Explorer ... $1 – 2

10. **white with bright orange and lime green design, "Matchbox 2000," blue base and tail, metallic gray blades, 2000 Ocean Explorer ... $3 – 4**
11. white with red and yellow design, blue base and tail, metallic gray blades, 1999 Forest Run international .. $1 – 2

Rescue Crane, #72, 2001; #24, 2003; #53, 2005

1. **red with orange crane, metallic gray boom, black plastic base, 2001 X-Treme Rescue .... $1 – 2**

2. **red with orange crane, yellow boom, gray plastic base, 2003 5-pack C1817 .... $1 – 2**

3. **yellow with green crane, red boom, metallic gray plastic base, 2003 Bridge Crew .... $1 – 2**

4. **white with red crane, yellow boom, black plastic base, 2003 Hero City 5-pack #9 .... $1 – 2**
5. dark gray with silver turret, white boom, brown base, 2005 #53 .... $1 – 2

Rescue Helicopter (see Hospital Helicopter)

Rescue Radar Plane (see Radar Plane)

Rhino Rod, #53, 1994 – 1997; #43, 1998; #24, 1994, international

1. **black with white eyes, 5-spoke concave wheels ....$4 – 5**

2. **dark gray with red eyes, 6-spoke gold wheels ....$1 – 2**

3. **dark gray with orange eyes, 6-spoke silver wheels ....$1 – 2**
4. dark gray with black eyes, 6-spoke silver wheels .... $1 – 2
5. dark gray with white eyes, 6-spoke silver wheels .... $1 – 2
6. metallic dark gray with yellow eyes, 5-spoke concave wheels, 1998 Animals ....$1 – 2
7. light gray with red eyes, 5-spoke concave wheels .... $1 – 2
8. metallic gold with black eyes, 5-spoke concave wheels, 1997 75 Challenge .... $6 – 12

Ridge Raider, #62, 2007
1. 2007 #62 .... $1 – 2

Rig Digger, bulldozer with hardhat, #29, 2004
1. red and yellow with silver tracks and base, 2004 Ultra Heroes .... $3 – 4

Road Dragster, 2⁷⁄₈", #19, 1970
1. red, "8" labels .... $16 – 24
2. red-orange, "8" labels .... $16 – 24
3. red-orange, no labels .... $16 – 24
4. red-orange, scorpion labels .. $40 – 60
5. light red, "Wynn's" labels ... $100 – 150
6. purple, "8" labels .... $20 – 30
7. purple, scorpion labels .... $40 – 60
8. metallic red, "8" labels .... $300 – 450

Road Roller (also see Bomag Road Roller, Road Roller Paver)

Road Roller, Diesel, 1⁷⁄₈", #1, 1953
1. dark green with red metal wheels ....$100 – 150
2. light green with red metal wheels ....$150 – 200
3. commemorative replica, green, 1988, made in China, 40th Anniversary Gift Set .... $8 – 12
4. dark blue, 1991 Matchbox Originals, made in China .... $4 – 6
5. orange, 1992 Matchbox Originals, made in China .... $4 – 6

Road Roller, 2¹⁄₄", #1, 1955
1. green with red metal wheels, dark tan driver .... $80 – 100
2. green with red metal wheels, light tan driver .... $80 – 100

Road Roller, 2³⁄₈", #1, 1958
1. light green with red metal wheels ....$115 – 140
2. dark green with red metal wheels ....$90 – 110

Road Roller, Aveling Barford, 2⁵⁄₈", #1, 1962
1. green with red plastic rollers ...$25 – 40

Road Roller, Bomag, #72, 1979; #40, 1991; #68, 1992; #68, 1991, international (see Bomag Road Roller)

Road Roller Paver, #36, 2001; #20, 2002; #23, 2003; #71, 2004; #70, 2005

1. **red with metallic gray interior, black cage, 2002 Build It Right! ....$1 – 2**

2. **red with yellow interior, metallic gray cage, 2003 Bridge Crew ......$1 – 2**

3. **orange with dark gray interior, black cage ....$1 – 2**

4. **light orange with metallic gray interior, blue cage, 2001 Earth Crunchers ....$1 – 2**
5. yellow with black and white graphics, "492," "Road Roller," dark gray rollers, metallic gray interior, black roll cage, 2007 5-pack K9618 .... $1 – 2

6. **lime green with gray interior, yellow cage, 2003 Hero City 5-pack #9 ....$1 – 2**

Road Tanker, 1³⁄₄", #11, 1955
1. green with metal wheels .. $400 – 500
2. dark yellow with metal wheels .... $75 – 100
3. yellow with metal wheels ...... $50 – 60
4. red with metal wheels, "Esso" decal on rear .... $50 – 60
5. red with metal wheels, "Esso" decal on sides .... $125 – 150

Road Tanker "Esso," red, 2¹⁄₂", #11, 1958
1. gold trim, metal wheels .... $40 – 50
2. silver trim, metal wheels ..... $30 – 40
3. gray plastic wheels .... $30 – 40
4. silver plastic wheels .... $150 – 175
5. black plastic wheels .... $80 – 100

Robot Truck, #37, 2002

1. **black with white, yellow, and blue city scene, phosphorescent chassis and dish, 2002 #37 Nite Glow .... $1 – 2**

2. black, "Jimmy Neutron," 2003 Nickelodeon 5-pack .... $1 – 2

Rocket Transporter, 3", #60, 1990; #63, 1999; #39, 2000; #40, 1985, international; #58, 1999, international; #24, 2000 – 2001, international (similar castings: Airplane Transporter)

1. red with yellow stripes, "Test Mission," yellow rockets, chrome hubs, 2000 Space Mission 5-pack .. $1 – 2

2. lemon yellow with "Mission 1 Missiles," metallic gray rockets, 2000 Space Explorer .... $1 – 2
3. lemon yellow with "Mission 1 Missiles," metallic gray rockets, "Matchbox 2000," 2000 Space Explorer .... $3 – 4
4. lime green with "Intergalactic Defence," black rockets, 1999 international Science Fiction .... $1 – 2
5. lime green with "Intergalactic Defense," black rockets, 1999 Science Fiction .... $1 – 2
6. green with black and brown camouflage, green rockets, black hubs, Thailand cast, 5-pack .... $1 – 2

7. army green with "T7871-6" and star, army green rockets, black hubs, Thailand cast, 1996 .... $1 – 2

8. black with yellow and gray camouflage, dark gray rockets, black hubs, China cast, Commando .... $30 – 40

9. black with green and brown camouflage, black rockets, black hubs, China cast, 5-pack .... $1 – 2

10. black with green and brown camouflage, black rockets, black hubs, Thailand cast, 5-pack .... $1 – 2
11. black with skull and crossbones, red rockets, black hubs, Thailand cast, Australia issue .... $4 – 5

12. white with "NASA" logo, U.S. flag, white rockets, chrome hubs, Macau cast .... $1 – 2

13. white with "NASA" logo, U.S. flag, white rockets, chrome hubs, China cast .... $1 – 2
14. white with "NASA" logo and checkerboard design, white rockets, chrome hubs, China cast .... $1 – 2
15. white with "NASA" logo and checkerboard design, white rockets, chrome hubs, Thailand cast .... $1 – 2
16. white with gray and army green camouflage, army green rockets, black hubs, Thailand cast .... $1 – 2
17. white with gray and army green camouflage, army green rockets, chrome hubs .... $9 – 12

18. white with gray and army green camouflage, gray rockets, black hubs, Thailand cast, 1997 Tundra Defense Force 5-pack .... $1 – 2

19. khaki with "T7871-6" and star, light brown rockets, Thailand cast, 5-pack .... $1 – 2

20. khaki with brown and olive green camouflage, khaki rockets, black hubs, 1995 Military 5-pack .. $1 – 2

21. beige with brown camouflage, beige rockets, black hubs, Thailand cast .... $1 – 2

22. beige with brown camouflage, black rockets, black hubs, Thailand cast, 1997 Desert Assault 5-pack .. $1 – 2

Rod Roller, 2⁵⁄₈," #21, 1973

1. yellow with green base, metallic red rear wheels .... $20 – 25

2. yellow with green base, red rear wheels .... $16 – 24
3. yellow with green base, black rear wheels .... $12 – 16

4. yellow with black base, black rear wheels .... $16 – 24

Rolls-Royce Phantom V, 2⁷⁄₈", #44, 1964

1. metallic tan, gray plastic wheels .... $80 – 100

2. metallic tan, black plastic wheels .... $15 – 20

3. metallic gray, black plastic wheels .... $30 – 40

Rolls-Royce Silver Cloud, metallic blue, 2⁵⁄₈", #44, 1958

1. metal wheels .... $30 – 40
2. gray plastic wheels .... $40 – 50
3. silver plastic wheels .... $40 – 50

Rolls-Royce Silver Cloud, 3", #62, 1985, US; #31, 1987, international

1. purple, rubber tires on chrome rims, Gold Coin Collection .... $20 – 30
2. metallic gray, England cast, James Bond set .... $9 – 12

3. **cream, England cast .... $1 – 2**
4. cream, Macau cast .... $1 – 2
5. cream, Thailand cast .... $1 – 2
6. metallic gold, chrome windows, rubber tires on gray rims, Macau cast, World Class .... $6 – 8
7. metallic gold, chrome windows, rubber tires on gray rims, Thailand cast, World Class .... $6 – 8

Rolls-Royce Silver Shadow, 3", #24, 1967

1. **metallic red, with black plastic tires on chrome hubs, 1967 .... $6 – 9**

2. **metallic red with black base, Superfast wheels .... $12 – 16**
3. metallic red with gray base, Superfast wheels .... $12 – 16
4. metallic red with metallic green base, Superfast wheels .... $16 – 24
5. metallic red with pink base, Superfast wheels .... $16 – 24
6. metallic gold with black base, Superfast wheels, Japan issue .... $16 – 24
7. metallic gold with unpainted base, Superfast wheels, Japan issue .... $16 – 24

Rolls-Royce Silver Shadow II, 3 1/16", #39, 1979

1. metallic red, brown interior, clear windows, unpainted base, England cast .... $5 – 6
2. metallic red, ivory interior, clear windows, unpainted base, England cast .... $5 – 6
3. metallic red, light yellow interior, clear windows, unpainted base, England cast .... $4 – 5
4. metallic maroon, white interior, clear windows, metallic silver base, Macau cast .... $5 – 6
5. metallic purple, white interior, clear windows, black base, England cast .. $5 – 6
6. metallic purple, white interior, clear windows, metallic gray base, England cast .... $5 – 6
7. metallic purple, white interior, clear windows, unpainted base, England cast .... $5 – 6
8. metallic tan, white interior, amber windows, unpainted base, England cast .... $4 – 5
9. metallic tan, white interior, amber windows, metallic gray base, England cast .... $4 – 5
10. metallic tan, white interior, clear windows, unpainted base, England cast .... $3 – 4
11. metallic tan, white interior, clear windows, metallic gray base, England cast .... $3 – 4
12. metallic tan, white interior, tinted windows, unpainted base, England cast .... $3 – 4

13. **metallic gray, red interior, clear windows, unpainted base, England cast .... $5 – 6**
14. gray, red interior, clear windows, unpainted base, England cast ... $5 – 6
15. black, gray interior, clear windows, black base, China cast, China issue ... $60 – 80

Rolls-Royce Silver Shadow Convertible Coupe, Superfast wheels only, 3", #69, 1969

1. **metallic blue, orange-brown interior, tan tonneau, black base .... $20 – 30**
2. metallic blue, orange-brown interior, tan tonneau, dark yellow base ... $20 – 30
3. metallic blue, orange-brown interior, tan tonneau, light yellow base .... $20 – 30
4. metallic gold, ivory interior, black tonneau, black base .... $20 – 30
5. metallic gold, ivory interior, black tonneau, silver base .... $20 – 30
6. metallic gold, orange-brown interior, black tonneau, black base .... $20 – 30
7. metallic gold, orange-brown interior, black tonneau, dark gray base .... $20 – 30
8. metallic gold, orange-brown interior, black tonneau, light yellow base .... $20 – 30
9. metallic gold, orange-brown interior, black tonneau, silver base .... $20 – 30
10. metallic gold, orange-brown interior, tan tonneau, black base .... $20 – 30
11. metallic gold, orange-brown interior, tan tonneau, dark yellow base ... $20 – 30
12. metallic gold, orange-brown interior, tan tonneau, light yellow base .... $20 – 30
13. metallic gold, orange-brown interior, tan tonneau, silver base .... $20 – 30
14. metallic gold, orange-brown interior, tan tonneau, tan base .... $20 – 30

Rolls-Royce Silver Spirit, 3", #66, 1988; #55, 1990

1. **metallic red, tan interior, China cast .... $1 – 2**
2. metallic red, tan interior, Macau cast .... $1 – 2
3. metallic red, tan interior, Thailand cast .... $1 – 2
4. metallic red with crest, cream interior, Thailand cast .... $1 – 2
5. metallic green-gold, tan interior, Macau cast .... $4 – 5
6. metallic tan, tan interior, Macau cast .... $3 – 4

Rompin' Rabbit 4x4 (see Volkswagen Rompin' Rabbit 4x4)

Rotinoff Super Atlantic Prime Mover, orange, 2 5/8", #15, 1959

1. gray plastic wheels .... $350 – 425

2. **black plastic wheels .... $30 – 45**

Rotovator, 1993 Farming Series (MB713)

1. **blue with gray rotors .... $3 – 4**

Rotwheeler, lower jaw moves when rolled, #73, 1995; #42, 1998; #47, 1995, international

1. **red with black collar, China cast, 1998 Animals ....$1 - 2**
2. red with black collar, Thailand cast, 1998 Animals .... $1 – 2

3. **black with red collar, Thailand cast .... $1 - 2**

4. **brown with black collar, Thailand cast ....$1 - 2**
5. metallic gold, Thailand cast, 1997 75 Challenge .... $6 – 12

Routemaster Bus, #5, 1965 (see London Bus)

Routemaster Double Decker Bus, #56, 2006; #34, 2007

1. **red, "The British Invasion Continues," 2006 #56 ....$1 - 2**
2. blue, "Matchbox Toys," 2007 #34 ..$1 – 2

Rover 3500, 3", #8, 1982, international
1. metallic bronze, tan interior ..... $3 – 5
2. metallic bronze, white interior .. $4 – 6

Rover 3500 Police, 3", #8, 1982, international

1. **white with "Police" graphics, England cast ....$3 - 4**
2. white with "Police" graphics, Macau cast .... $3 – 4
3. white with "Police" graphics, China cast .... $4 – 5
4. white with "Police" graphics, Manaus (Brazil) cast .... $30 – 45
5. white with no markings, England cast, Graffic Traffic .... $4 – 5

Rover Sterling, $2^{15}/_{16}$", #2, 1988; #31, 1988
1. metallic red with no markings ... $3 – 4
2. metallic pearl gray with red, white, and blue stripes, Laser wheels .... $5 – 6
3. blue with yellow base, blue wheels, no hood, Matchbox Preschool/Live 'N Learn .... $7 – 9
4. yellow with no markings .... $9 – 12
5. metallic gray, "Rover Sterling" ... $3 – 4
6. white with no markings, Graffic Traffic ....$12 – 16

Ruff Trek Holden Pickup (see Holden Ruff Trek Pickup)

Ruff Rabbit (see Volkswagen Ruff Rabbit)

Rumble Dozer, #17, 2004
1. 2004 Ultra Heroes .... $1 – 2
2. 2004 5-pack C1817 .... $1 – 2

Runway Hero (see Airport Fire Pumper)

Runway Patrol, #45, 2006 (see Airport Fire Tanker)

S

S.2 Jet, $2^{7}/_{8}$", #2, 1981
1. black with yellow base, yellow wings, England cast .... $4 – 6
2. light blue with white base, white wings, England cast .... $3 – 5
3. light blue with white base, gray wings, England cast .... $3 – 5

4. **dark blue with white base, white wings, Macau cast ....$3 - 5**
5. dark blue with white base, white wings, China cast .... $3 – 5
6. dark blue with white base, white wings, Hong Kong cast .... $20 – 25
7. dark olive green, black base, dark olive green wings, Commando .... $5 – 7

S & S Ambulance (see Cadillac S & S Ambulance)

S-Cargo, snail-shaped delivery truck, #13, 2004
1. pearl white, 2004 Ultra Heroes ..$1 – 2

S. P. Gun (see Self Propelled Gun)

Saab 9000, $2^{15}/_{16}$", #15, 1988; #22, 1989

1. **metallic red with brown interior ..$1 - 2**
2. metallic blue with gray interior, "Saab Turbo" and stripes, Laser Wheels .... $8 – 10
3. white with brown interior, "Saab 22" and stripes .... $3 – 4
4. metallic gray with brown interior, "Saab 22" and stripes .... $9 – 12
5. dark blue with brown interior, Germany gift set .... $9 – 12

6. **dark ivory with yellow and brown interior, rubber tires on chrome rims, Ultra Class ....$9 - 12**

Saab Sonnet, $2^{3}/_{4}$", #65, 1973; BR 11-12, 1985
1. blue with yellow interior, unpainted base ....$12 – 16
2. white with yellow interior, unpainted base ....$300 – 400
3. orange with no interior, England cast, Super GT BR 11-12, 1985 .... $5 – 6
4. orange with no interior, China cast, Super GT BR 11-12, 1985 ....$8 – 10
5. green with no interior, China cast, Super GT BR 11-12, 1985 .... $4 – 5
6. blue with no interior, England cast, Super GT BR 11-12, 1985 ....$8 – 10

7. pale blue with no interior, China cast, Super GT BR 11-12, 1985 ..... $4 – 5
8. tan with no interior, England cast, Super GT BR 11-12, 1985 .... $6 – 8
9. tan with no interior, China cast, Super GT BR 11-12, 1985 .... $8 – 10

Safari Land Rover, $2^{3}/_{8}$", #12, 1965
1. green with brown luggage on roof, black plastic wheels .... $9 – 12

2. blue with brown luggage on roof, black plastic wheels .... $9 – 12
3. blue with tan luggage, black plastic wheels .... $9 – 12
4. gold with tan luggage, black plastic wheels .... $80 – 100
5. bright blue, Superfast wheels, 1970 .... $1,250 – 1,750
6. metallic gold, Superfast wheels, 1970 .... $24 – 36

Saladin Armoured Car, $2^{1}/_{2}$", #67, 1959

1. olive green with black plastic wheels .... $30 – 40

Sambron Jack Lift/Fork Lift Truck, $3^{1}/_{16}$," #48, 1977; #28, 1991; #61, 1991, international
1. orange-yellow with red stripes, 1994 gift set .... $3 – 4
2. yellow, no markings, black base, silver hubs, 1977 .... $6 – 7
3. yellow, no markings, brown base, silver hubs, 1977 .... $9 – 12
4. yellow, no markings, dark gray base, silver hubs, 1977 .... $6 – 7
5. yellow, no markings, dark gray base, yellow hubs, 1977 .... $6 – 7
6. yellow, "Sambron," black base, silver hubs, 1977 .... $400 – 500
7. lime green with red and white stripes, 1991 .... $1 – 2
8. bright green with red and white stripes, 1994 .... $1 – 2

9. white with red stripes, 1993 Team Convoy .... $4 – 5

Sand Digger Volkswagen Beetle, $2^{13}/_{17}$", #49, 1983 (similar castings: Hi Ho Silver, Hot Chocolate, Volks Dragon, Dune Man, Big Blue)

1. metallic green .... $3 – 4

Sand Racer, $2^{11}/_{16}$", #72, 1984

1. white, "Goodyear," "Union 211," Macau cast .... $20 – 30

Sand Speeder (see Dune Buggy)

Saracen Personnel Carrier, Army green, $2^{1}/_{4}$", #54, 1958
1. black plastic wheels .... $20 – 35

Sauber Group C Racer (see Mercedes-Benz Sauber Group C Racer)

Savannah RX7 (see Mazda RX7 Savannah)

Scaffold Truck (see Mercedes-Benz Scaffold Truck)

Scammell Breakdown Truck, olive green, black plastic wheels, $2^{1}/_{2}$", #64, 1959

1. green metal hook .... $30 – 40
2. silver metal hook .... $30 – 40
3. gray plastic hook .... $25 – 35

Scammell Mountaineer Snowplow, 3", #16, 1964
1. gray plastic wheels .... $80 – 90
2. black plastic wheels .... $15 – 20

Scania T142, 3", #8, 1986; #71, 1986; #72, 1986; other variations exist in Convoy series
1. white with red, orange, and yellow stripes .... $3 – 4
2. blue with red, orange, and yellow stripes .... $3 – 4
3. white with red and black stripe .. $3 – 4

School Bus, 3", #47, 1985; #12, 1998; #1, 1999; #31, 2000; #15, 2002
1. "1+2=3 abc," orange-yellow, green wheels with blue hubs, Matchbox Preschool/Live 'N Learn .... $7 – 9
2. "1+2=3 abc," orange-yellow, green wheels with green hubs, Matchbox Preschool/Live 'N Learn .... $5 – 7
3. "1+2=3 abc," orange-yellow, green wheels with red hubs, Matchbox Preschool/Live 'N Learn .... $7 – 9
4. "Atlantic Coast Surety," orange-yellow, ASAP promotional .... $80 – 120
5. "Cap'n Crunch," "Quaker Oats," orange-yellow, ASAP promotional .. $120 – 160

6. "Carpenter High School," orange-yellow, China cast .... $1 – 2
7. "Downington Area School District," orange-yellow, ASAP promotional .... $30 – 40
8. "Durham," orange-yellow, ASAP promotional .... $60 – 80
9. "George Dapper, Inc. Iselin, NJ," orange-yellow, ASAP promotional .. $80 – 120
10. "Govt. Property," army green .. $10 – 12
11. "Govt. Property," "Commando" hood logo, army green, China issue .. $30 – 40
12. "Harvey World Travel," yellow, Australia issue .... $9 – 12
13. "Hofstra University," blue .... $9 – 12
14. "Horlicks School Bus," yellow, Hong Kong issue .... $20 – 30
15. "JMOA Engineering PC – K – 12 Specialists," orange-yellow, ASAP promotional .... $80 – 120
16. "Martin Luther King Drug Free," orange-yellow, ASAP promotional .. $80 – 120
17. "Matchbox Elementary," "Matchbox," orange-yellow, Pleasant Books .. $4 – 5

18. "Matchbox Elementary School," orange-yellow ....$1 - 2

19. "Matchbox Elementary School," "Enjoy Fanta," orange-yellow ...... $160 – 200

20. "Montgomery High School," orange-yellow, promotional .... $16 – 24

21. "Mt. Laurel Preschool," bright pink, 1994 Collectors Choice from White Rose Collectibles ....$4 - 5

22. "ND Irish Mobile," orange-yellow, ASAP promotional .... $20 – 30

23. "Oaklyn Middle School PS33," "Go Team Go," orange-yellow, 1997 ..$1 - 2

24. "Oaklyn Middle School PS33," "Go Team Go," yellow, 1998 Big Movers .. $1 – 2

25. "Off to Northwestern," orange-yellow, ASAP promotional .... $30 – 40

26. "On My Way to Bowdoin," orange-yellow, ASAP promotional .... $16 – 24

27. "On My Way to Cal Poly," orange-yellow, ASAP promotional .... $16 – 24

28. "On My Way to Maryland," orange-yellow, ASAP promotional .... $30 – 40

29. "On My Way to RPI," orange-yellow, ASAP promotional .... $16 – 24

30. "On My Way to UCLA," orange-yellow, ASAP promotional .... $60 – 80

31. "On My Way to UGI," orange-yellow, ASAP promotional .... $30 – 40

32. "Penn State," "The Loop," white and dark blue, White Rose Collectibles ..... $7 – 9

33. "Police 88," blue, Action Pack .. $4 – 5

34. "Police Transport" with coiled barbed wire graphics, red with silver painted metal base, 2002 To the Rescue .... $1 - 2

35. "RCA," orange-yellow, ASAP promotional ....$20 – 30

36. "Ridge, NY Elementary," "Go Ridge Go," orange-yellow, 1999 Matchbox USA .... $1 – 2

37. "Rutgers," orange-yellow, ASAP promotional .... $25 – 35

38. "Sage," orange-yellow, ASAP promotional .... $80 – 120

39. "School District 2," dark orange, China cast, gift set .... $9 – 12

40. "School District 2," orange-yellow, China cast ....$1 - 2

41. "School District 2," orange-yellow, Thailand cast .... $12 – 16

42. "School District 2," yellow, China cast ....$1 - 2

43. "School District 2," yellow, Macau cast ....$1 – 2

44. "School District 2," "Chef Boyardee," orange-yellow, on-package premium .... $10 – 12

45. "School District 2," "Chef Boyardee," yellow, on-package premium .... $10 – 12

46. "St. Paul Public Schools," orange-yellow, China cast .... $40 – 50

47. "St. Thomas Elementary School, Rocky River, Ohio," 2000 Matchbox USA ....$1 - 2

48. "St. Thomas Elementary School, Rocky River, Ohio," "Matchbox 2000," 2000 Matchbox USA .... $3 – 4

49. "Storm Troopers Reunion at the Mark 2000," orange-yellow, ASAP promotional .... $80 – 120

50. "Van Lear," orange-yellow, ASAP promotional .... $80 – 120

51. "Vancom," orange-yellow .... $80 – 120

52. "White's Guide Car of the Month" in black lettering, orange-yellow, ASAP promotional ....$6 - 8

53. "White's Guide Car of the Month" in red lettering, orange-yellow, ASAP promotional ....$6 - 8

54. "Wolfington," orange-yellow, ASAP promotional .... $60 – 80

55. orange-yellow, no markings, ASAP promotional blank .... $30 – 40

56. metallic gold, 1997 75 Challenge .... $12 – 16

57. white with "Blue's Clues" graphics, 2006 Nickelodeon 5-pack H4108 .... $1 – 2

58. yellow with "Turck senso plex" on roof, "senso plex Der Vor-Ort-Bus" on sides ....$20 – 25

School Bus, #16, 2001; #69, 2002; #52, 2003; #42, 2004; #44, 2005 (see Hummer School Bus)

Scion xB (see Toyota Scion xB)

Scissors Truck (see Ford Scissors Truck)

Sea Plane (see Seaplane)

Sea Rescue Boat, #43, 1999; #26, 2000; #38, 1999, international

1. red deck, white hull, dark blue railings, "489-4" and blue stripes, black wheels, 5-pack ....$1 - 2

2. red deck, white hull, dark blue railings, "489-4" and blue stripes, white wheels, 5-pack .... $4 – 5
3. blue deck, white hull, white railings, "Base 2000," 2000 Launcher 5-pack .... $1 – 2
4. dark blue deck, orange hull, red railings, lifesaver and storm logo, Launcher 5-pack .... $1 – 2
5. white deck, black hull, metallic gray railings, red and silver stripes, 1999 Ocean series, international ...... $1 – 2
6. white deck, black hull, metallic gray railings, red and silver stripes, "World Ocean Explorer," 1999 Ocean series, US issue .... $1 – 2
7. white deck, metallic gold hull, black railings, red and black stripes, 2000 Fire Fighters .... $1 – 2
8. white deck, metallic gold hull, black railings, red and black stripes, "Matchbox 2000," 2000 Fire Fighters ...... $4 – 5
9. white deck, white hull, white railings, "The Perfect Storm," ASAP promotional ....$80 – 120
10. white deck, white hull, white railings, ASAP promotional blank ...... $30 – 40

Sea Rescue Helicopter, #41, 2003; Police Helicopter #70, 2004; LZ Chopper, #70, 2006

1. white with red base, propeller, and tail, red and blue swirl, 2003 Beach Patrol ....$1 – 2

2. dark blue with blue base and tail, metallic gray rotors, 2004 Police Helicopter #70....................$1 – 2

3. orange with white base, gray tail and rotors, LZ Chopper, #70, 2006 ....$1 – 2

4. black with dark gray, Battle Kings Night Landing set, 2006, K5532 ....$1 – 2

Sea Speeder, #68, 2001; #44, 2003

1. white deck, yellow hull, red canopy, blue radar, "NJBP" and graphics on sides, 2001 Storm Watch .... $1 – 2
2. red deck, white hull, metallic gray canopy and radar, "MHC Beach Patrol," 2003 Beach Patrol .... $1 – 2
3. red deck, white hull, metallic gray canopy and radar, "MHC Beach Patrol," 2003 Hero City 10-pack #2 .... $1 – 2
4. metallic gray deck, metallic blue hull, red canopy, black radar, 2002 Christmas 3-pack .... $3 – 4

Seafire Boat, $2^{15}/_{16}$", #5, 1975

1. red deck, white hull, no graphics, with trailer .... $9 – 12
2. red deck, blue hull, no graphics, with trailer .... $30 – 40
3. red deck, yellow hull, no graphics, with trailer .... $40 – 50
4. red deck, white hull, "Surf Rider," silver stripes, white plastic trailer ...... $3 – 4
5. yellow deck, blue hull, "460," black plastic trailer .... $4 – 5

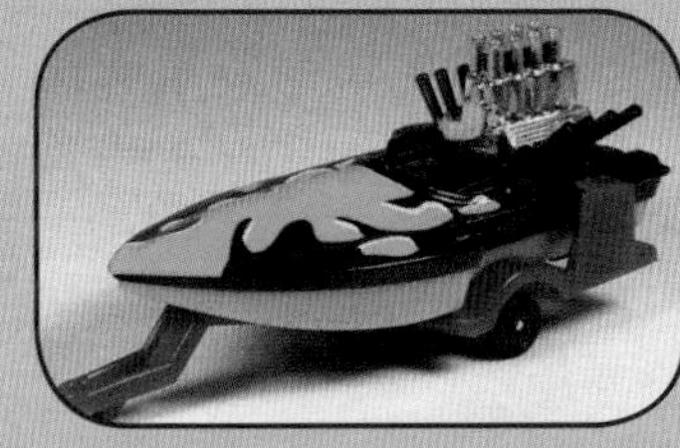

6. navy blue deck, green hull, black plastic trailer ....$1 – 2
7. black deck, yellow hull, no graphics ..$9 – 12
8. white deck, blue hull, no graphics, with or without trailer .... $12 – 16
9. white deck, brown hull, no graphics, with or without trailer .... $90 – 120
10. white deck, red hull, red and black, black plastic trailer .... $4 – 5

11. white deck, fluorescent orange hull, no graphics, black plastic trailer ...$1 – 2
12. white deck, white hull, "Bacardi," white metal trailer .... $12 – 16

Seaplane, #42, 1999; #67, 2000; #37, 1999, international; #47, 2000, international

1. red, red wings, white base, "EB32," red and black stripes, 2000 Air Traffic ....$1 – 2
2. red, red wings, white base, "EB32," red and black stripes, "Matchbox 2000," 2000 Air Traffic .... $3 – 4

3. yellow, yellow wings, metallic gray base, blue stripes, Water Wings, 1999 Ocean ....$1 – 2
4. dark blue, dark blue wings, white base, 5-pack .... $1 – 2

5. cream, blue wings, blue base, blue stripes, 2000 Ocean Dock 5-pack ....$1 – 2

6. white with teal wings and base, "Beach Patrol," 2003 Hero City 5-pack #5 ....$1 – 2
7. white, gray wings, red base, "Coca-Cola" and reclining woman, Premiere Collection ....$5 – 6
8. white, gray wings, red base, "Coca-Cola" and reclining woman, "www.cocacolastores.com," Color Comp promotional ....$60 – 80

9. white, white wings, white base, no markings, ASAP promotional blank .... $30 – 40
10. white, white wings, white base, "The Perfect Storm," ASAP promotional .... $80 – 120

11. white, red wings, red base, "Beach Patrol," 2002 Sand Castle Rescue Team 5-pack with sand bucket ...$1 – 2

Seasprite Helicopter, small windows, 2¾", #75, 1977

1. white, "Rescue" labels, blue windows .... $5 – 6
2. white, "Rescue" labels, green windows .... $5 – 6
3. white, "Rescue" labels, purple windows .... $5 – 6
4. white, "Rescue" labels, red windows .... $5 – 6
5. cream, "Rescue" labels, blue windows, Brazil issue .... $300 – 400
6. dark green, "Rescue" labels, blue windows, Brazil issue .... $300 – 400

Security Truck (see Armored Truck)

Seeder, #712, 1993 Farming Series

1. green .... $3 – 4

Self-Propelled Gun, Rolamatic, 2⅝", #70, 1976

1. olive green, black treads .... $3 – 4

2. olive green, tan treads .... $3 – 4

3. olive green with tan and black camouflage, tan treads, China cast, Commando .... $7 – 9
4. olive green with tan and black camouflage, tan treads, Macau cast, Commando .... $5 – 6
5. black with gray and yellow camouflage, tan treads, Commando .... $5 – 6

Setra Coach, 3", #12, 1970

1. metallic gold with tan roof, clear windows .... $20 – 25
2. metallic gold with white roof, clear windows .... $15 – 20
3. yellow with white roof, clear windows .... $12 – 16
4. yellow with white roof, green windows .... $60 – 80
5. burgundy with white roof, clear windows .... $12 – 16
6. burgundy with white roof, green windows .... $12 – 16
7. purple with white roof, green windows .... $12 – 16

Shelby Cobra 427 S/C 1965, Superfast #1, 2004

1. red, 2004 Superfast #1 ...... $5 – 6

2. red, My Classic Car with Dennis Gage .... $5 – 6

3. metallic blue, 2006 5-pack J4677 .... $2 – 3

Sherman M4 A3 Tank, #85, 1999; #51, 2000

1. light green with white "Power Striker," "476," "No. 33857," 1999 Military Patrol .... $1 – 2
2. light olive green with white "Power Striker," "476," "No. 33857," Premiere Collection .... $4 – 5
3. olive green with tan camouflage, white star, 1999 Military Patrol .... $1 – 2
4. olive green with mud spatter, "Matchbox 2000," 2000 Military .... $3 – 4
5. olive green with mud spatter, 2000 Military .... $1 – 2

Sherman M4 Tank, 2001 Feature Cars, with opening features, designed to replace Premiere Collection

1. olive green with light blue camouflage, star .... $9 – 12

Shovel Nose Tractor Shovel (see Tractor Shovel)

Shunter (see Diesel Shunter Locomotive)

Side Tipper, #720, 1977, Two-Pack

1. yellow with red tipper, England cast .. $3 – 4
2. yellow with red tipper, China cast .. $3 – 4
3. yellow with black tipper, England cast $4 – 5
4. yellow with red tipper, Macau cast .. $3 – 4
5. blue, "ABCD," yellow tipper, Macau cast, Live 'N' Learn/Matchbox Preschool .... $7 – 9

Silver Streak, Roman Numeral I, 1978 (variation of #1 Mod Rod, 1971)

1. yellow with silver motor, Roman Numeral Limited Edition .... $15 – 20
2. yellow with black motor, Roman Numeral Limited Edition .... $20 – 25
3. silver plated with black motor, Roman Numeral Limited Edition .... $9 – 12

Site Dumper, 2⅝", #26, 1976

1. yellow with yellow dumper, black interior .... $5 – 6

2. **yellow with red dumper, black interior .... $5 - 6**
3. orange-red with orange-red dumper, white interior .... $200 – 300
4. orange-red with metallic gray dumper, white interior .... $5 – 6
5. orange-red with metallic gray dumper, white interior, yellow hubs .... $7 – 8
6. red with metallic gray dumper, white interior, yellow hubs .... $12 – 16

Site Hut Truck (see Leyland Site Office Truck)

Site Office Truck (see Leyland Site Office Truck)

Siva Spider, 3", #41, 1972; BR 7-8, 1985

1. **red with black trim ....$12 - 16**
2. red with silver trim .... $16 – 24
3. orange-yellow, England cast, Super GT BR 7-8, 1985 .... $8 – 10
4. yellow, England cast, Super GT BR 7-8, 1985 .... $8 – 10
5. dark blue with black trim ..... $16 – 24
6. light blue with black trim ...... $16 – 24

Six-Wheel Quarry Truck (see Quarry Truck)

Six-Wheel Crane Truck (see Magirus-Deutz Six-Wheel Crane Truck)

Ski Boat (see Wave King)

Skip Truck (see Atlas Skip Truck, Ford Cargo Skip Truck)

Skoda 130LR Rally (European model), 2⁷⁄₈", #44, 1988

1. **white, "Skoda 44" ....$4 - 5**

Sky Fire (see Bucket Fire Truck)

Sleet-N-Snow, Roman Numeral II, 1978 (variation of U.S. Mail Jeep, #5, 1978)
1. blue, Roman Numeral Limited Edition .... $9 – 12
2. olive, Roman Numeral Limited Edition .... $15 – 20
3. yellow, Roman Numeral Limited Edition .... $15 – 20

Slingshot Dragster, 3", #64, 1971
1. pink, "9" with flames label .... $16 – 24
2. orange, "9" with flames label .. $120 – 160
3. metallic blue, "3" with stripe lable .... $20 – 30

4. **metallic blue, "9" with flames label ....$16 - 24**
5. metallic blue, star with flames label .... $60 – 80

Snack Truck, #96, 1998 (see Chevrolet Van 4x4)

Snorkel Fire Engine, with closed cab, 3", #13, 1977

1. **red with blue windows, yellow boom and bucket, unpainted base ..$6 - 9**
2. red with blue windows, yellow boom and bucket, metallic gray base .... $6 – 9
3. red with amber windows, yellow boom and bucket, unpainted base ... $12 – 16
4. dark red with blue windows, yellow boom and bucket, unpainted base ..... $6 – 9
5. dark red with blue windows, yellow boom and bucket, metallic gray base . $6 – 9
6. dark red with blue windows, white boom and bucket, unpainted base ..... $6 – 9
7. dark red with blue windows, yellow boom, white bucket, gray base, UK issue .... $60 – 80

Snorkel Fire Engine, with open cab, 2¹³⁄₁₆", #63, 1982; #26, 1998; #4, 1999; #27, 2000

1. **"12th Rescue Squad," red with gold outline, metallic gray boom, China cast, 1995 .... $1 - 2**
2. "12th Rescue Squad," red with white outline, metallic gray boom, China cast, 1995 .... $1 – 2
3. "FD No. 1 Fire Dept.," gold and black trim, red lower, white upper, metallic gray boom, China cast, 1996 5-Pack .... $1 – 2
4. "Fire Dept." and shield, red with white boom, China cast ...... $1 – 2
5. "Fire Dept." and shield, fluorescent lime yellow with white boom, China cast, Action Pack .... $4 – 5
6. "J.D.F.D. Fire Rescue 25," red with black boom, China cast, 2000 Fire Fighters .... $1 – 2
7. "J.D.F.D. Fire Rescue 25," red with black boom, "Matchbox 2000," China cast, 2000 Fire Fighters .... $3 – 4
8. "Los Angeles," red with white boom, England cast, Code Red ...... $7 – 9
9. "Matchbox Fire Dept.," red with white bands, metallic gray boom, China cast, 2000 Fire 5-pack .... $1 – 2

10. **"Matchbox Fire Dept.," red with metallic gray boom, China cast, 1998 To the Rescue ....$1 - 2**

11. **"Matchbox Fire Dept.," maroon with white bands, 1997 ....$1 - 2**
12. "Matchbox Fire Dept.," dark purple with metallic gray boom, China cast .. $1 – 2
13. **"Matchbox Fire Dept.," white with red bands, metallic gray boom, China cast, 1997 Fire 5-pack ....$1 - 2**

14. "Metro Alarm," "MA-ST1," red with gray boom, China cast, 5-pack .... $1 – 2
15. "Metro Fire," red with white boom, Macau cast .... $1 – 2
16. "Metro Fire," red with white boom, China cast .... $1 – 2
17. "Rescue Unit Fire 1," red with checkerboard design, white boom, China cast .... $9 – 12
18. "Rescue Unit Fire 1," fluorescent orange with blue and white checkerboard design, white boom, "IC" logo, China cast, Intercom City .... $12 – 16

19. "Rescue Unit Fire 1," fluorescent orange with blue and white checkerboard design, white boom, China cast ....$1 – 2
20. "Ridge, NY Fire & Rescue," red with white boom, 1999 Matchbox USA ....$1 – 2
21. "Richfield Co.," red with black boom, rubber tires on chrome rims, China cast, Premiere Collection #7 ... $4 – 5
22. "Screamin' Red Fire Engines" in red print, white with white boom, China cast, ASAP promotional ...... $12 – 16
23. "Screamin' Red Fire Engines" in purple print, white with white boom, China cast, ASAP promotional ...... $12 – 16
24. "Seaside Fire Co.," "Snorkel Unit 2," metallic red with white boom, rubber tires on chrome rims, Premiere Collection #21 .... $4 – 5
25. red with Japanese lettering, white boom, China cast, Japan issue .... $10 – 12

26. turquoise with blue boom, separate labels included, McDonald's Happy Meal premium ....$4 – 5

27. white with gray boom, no markings, China cast, ASAP promotional blank .... $30 – 40
28. white with white boom, no markings, China cast, Graffic Traffic (labels included in set) .... $12 – 16

29. white with cityscape graphics, yellow boom, 2003 Hero City Fire Station .... $4 – 5
30. metallic gold with black boom, no markings, China cast, 1997 75 Challenge .... $6 – 12

Snow Doctor, halftrack vehicle, #6, 2001; #68, 2002

1. metallic blue with pearl white back section, 2001 Team Tundra ..$1 – 2

2. metallic rust with blue back section, 2002 Kids' Cars of the Year ... $1 – 2

3. yellow with white back section, 2003 Hero City 5-pack #8 ....$1 – 2

Snow Groomer, #57, 1999; #78, 2000; #52, 1999, international

1. orange, "FF-525," mountain scene, black plow and hatch, 1999 Forest Run international .... $3 – 4

2. orange, "Hill Top Unit 3 Resort," white snow spatter, black plow and hatch, 1999 Wilderness Adventure ....$1 – 2
3. blue, "42-06," metallic gray plow and hatch, cross and white design, 5-pack .... $1 – 2

4. metallic silver with blue plow and hatch, white and blue graphics, 2000 Snow Explorer ....$1 – 2
5. metallic silver with blue plow and hatch, white and blue graphics, "Matchbox 2000," 2000 Snow Explorer .... $3 – 4

6. gray with green plow and hatch, with purple, white, and green graphics, 2003 Hero City 5-pack #8 ...$1 – 2
7. white, "Test Centre," blue plow and hatch, polar bear graphics and hash marks, Launcher 5-pack .... $1 – 2

8. white with red band, yellow hash marks, black plow and hatch, 1998 Emergency Rescue 5-pack... $1 – 2

Snowmobile/Turbo Ski, #94, 1999; #76, 2000; #8, 2001; #74, 1999, international; #56, 2000, international

1. **red with white design, black seat, yellow rider with black jacket, 1999 Mountain Cruisers series #19 ...$2 - 3**
2. yellow with "8" and blue hash marks, black seat, dark gray rider, 5-pack ....$1 – 2
3. black with fluorescent yellow flash, red seat, dark blue rider with fluorescent green jacket, 2000 Snow Explorer ....$1 – 2
4. black with fluorescent yellow flash, red seat, dark blue rider with fluorescent green jacket, "Matchbox 2000," 2000 Snow Explorer .... $3 – 4
5. white upper with blue snowflake design, red lower with "+ Alarm" and graphics, black seat, red rider, 2003 Hero City 5-pack #8 .... $2 – 4

6. **white upper, orange lower, "TC-3," "Test Centre," hash marks, black seat, orange rider with blue jacket, Launcher 5-pack ....$1 - 2**
7. white upper, burgundy lower, light blue snowflake design, 2003 Hero City 5-pack #8 .... $1 – 2
8. "Colorado," Matchbox Across America 50th Birthday Series #38 — Western Collection .... $5 – 6

Snow Trac Tractor, $2^{3}/_{8}$", #35, 1964
1. white treads, "Snow Trac" decals .... $20 – 25
2. white treads, plain sides ...... $20 – 25
3. white treads, "Snow Trac" cast into sides .... $20 – 25
4. gray treads, "Snow Trac" cast into sides ....$30 – 40

Soopa Coopa, $2^{7}/_{8}$", #37, 1972
1. blue .... $16 – 24
2. pink with unpainted base, flower label ....$20 – 25
3. pink with red base, flower label ..$60 – 80
4. orange with "Jaffa Mobile" label, on-package premium .... $120 – 160

Space Buggy, #25, 2004
1. white cab, blue body, yellow components, amber windows, 2004 Ultra Heroes .... $3 – 4

Speedboat (see Sea Speeder)

Sports Boat and Trailer (see Meteor Sports Boat and Trailer)

Sports Boat and Trailer, with outboard motor, $2^{5}/_{8}$", #48, 1961
1. gray wheels .... $60 – 75
2. black wheels .... $30 – 40

Sprint Racer, $2^{15}/_{16}$", #34, 1990
1. red, "Allweld 14," Nutmeg Collectibles .... $5 – 6
2. red, "Gambler 4," Nutmeg Collectibles .... $5 – 6
3. red, "IW Lew," Nutmeg Collectibles ... $5 – 6
4. red, "Joe Gaerte 7," Nutmeg Collectibles .... $5 – 6
5. red, "Lucky 7" .... $1 – 2

6. **red, "Rollin Thunder 2" ....$1 - 2**
7. red, "Schoff 23S," Nutmeg Collectibles ....$5 – 6
8. red, "Williams 5M" in blue letters, Nutmeg Collectibles .... $5 – 6
9. red, "Williams 5M" in white letters, Nutmeg Collectibles .... $80 – 120
10. orange, "Williams Payless 5M," Nutmeg Collectibles .... $5 – 6
11. yellow, "Ben Cook & Sons 33X," Nutmeg Collectibles .... $5 – 6
12. yellow, "D. Blaney," "Vivarin 7C," Nutmeg Collectibles .... $5 – 6
13. yellow, "F&G Classics East 17," Nutmeg Collectibles .... $5 – 6
14. yellow, "Vivarin," "7c," "D. Blaney," purple background, Nutmeg Collectibles ....$5 – 6
15. yellow, "Vivarin," blue background, Nutmeg Collectibles .... $8 – 10
16. light blue, "Schnee-D. Krietz 69," Nutmeg Collectibles .... $5 – 6
17. blue, "Ben Allen 1A," Nutmeg Collectibles .... $5 – 6
18. metallic blue, "Rollin Thunder," "2" ....$9 – 12
19. metallic blue, "Lucky 7," Action Pack ....$4 – 5
20. purple, "Hot Shot 34," 5-pack .. $1 – 2
21. black, "Doug Wolfgang 49," Nutmeg Collectibles .... $5 – 6
22. black, "Gebhart's 4J," Nutmeg Collectibles .... $5 – 6
23. black, "JW Hunt 69," Nutmeg Collectibles .... $5 – 6
24. black, "TMC 1," Nutmeg Collectibles .... $5 – 6
25. white, "Alvis O Rock 69," Nutmeg Collectibles .... $5 – 6
26. white, "Maxim 11," Nutmeg Collectibles ....$5 – 6
27. white, "Schnee 8D," Nutmeg Collectibles .... $5 – 6
28. white, "Valvoline 11," Nutmeg Collectibles .... $5 – 6
29. white, "Vanermark & Wahlie Im," Nutmeg Collectibles .... $5 – 6
30. white, "Weitkerk's Livestock 29," Nutmeg Collectibles .... $5 – 6
31. white, red and dark blue, "Casey Luna 10," Nutmeg Collectibles .... $5 – 6

Squad Runner, SUV with helmet and goggles, #27, 2004 (MB626)
1. khaki camouflage with brown helmet, black base, 2004 Ultra Heroes ... $1 – 2

Squawkie-Talkie, #3, 2004 (MB641)
1. 2004 Ultra Heroes .... $3 – 4

SRN6 Hovercraft (see Hovercraft SRN6)

Stake Truck, maroon, $2^{3}/_{8}$", #20, 1956
1. gold grille and fuel tanks, metal wheels .... $80 – 100
2. silver grille and fuel tanks, metal wheels ....$30 – 50
3. maroon grille and fuel tanks, metal wheels .... $30 – 50
4. silver grille and fuel tanks, gray plastic wheels .... $100 – 125
5. dark red grille and fuel tanks, gray plastic wheels .... $90 – 120

Standard Jeep CJ5 (see Jeep CJ5 Standard)

Sterling (see Rover Sterling)

Stinger, helicopter-style fantasy vehicle, #68, 1995 – 1997; #41, 1998

1. **orange and black, 1995, Thailand cast ....$1 - 2**

2. **yellow and black, 1996, Thailand cast ....$1 - 2**

3. **green and black, 1998 Animals series, China cast ....$1 - 2**
4. green and black, 1998 Animals series, Thailand cast .... $1 – 2
5. metallic gold and black, 1997 75 Challenge series, Thailand cast .... $6 – 12

Stingeroo, 3-wheel motorcycle, 3", #38, 1973
1. purple with chrome handlebars .... $350 – 450
2. purple with purple handlebars ... $16 – 24
3. purple with blue-gray handlebars .... $20 – 25

Stoat Armored Truck, 2⁵⁄₈", #28, 1974
1. metallic gold with chrome hubs .... $10 – 12
2. army green with black hubs ..... $7 – 9
3. army green with chrome hubs .. $8 – 10
4. dark olive green with black hubs .... $70 – 90

Street Cleaner/Street Sweeper, #96, 2000; #20, 2001; #3, 2002; #18, 2003; #33, 2005
1. orange-yellow, "City Streets Department," dark blue bucket and brushes, black base, Pleasant Books issue .... $5 – 6
2. dark green, "City Service DOT 042076," fluorescent yellow bucket and brushes, black base, 7-spoke sawblade front wheels, 2001 City Dudes .... $1 – 2
3. dark green, "City Service DOT 042076," fluorescent yellow bucket and brushes, black base, 8-spoke front wheels, 2001 City Dudes .... $5 – 6

4. purple with bright green bucket and brushes, black base, 2002 Hometown Heroes .... $1 – 2
5. dark cream, "Metro Disposal," red bucket and brushes, metallic gray base, 2000 On the Road Again .... $1 – 2
6. dark cream, "Metro Disposal," red bucket and brushes, metallic gray base, "Matchbox 2000," 2000 On the Road Again .... $3 – 4

7. white with red dust bucket and brushes, orange base, 2003 Public Works .... $1 – 2
8. metallic gold, 2005 #33 .... $1 – 2

9. white with gray base, black brushes, "City Works," 2007 5-pack K9618 .... $1 – 2

Street Streak concept car, #62, 1996 – 1997; #16, 1998

1. red upper, black lower, chrome windows, 1997 Cars of the Future 5-pack .... $1 – 2

2. metallic red upper, metallic gray lower, chrome windows, 1997 .... $1 – 2
3. bright orange upper, black lower, black windows .... $1 – 2

4. blue upper, metallic gray lower, chrome windows, 1998 Cool Concepts series, China cast .... $1 – 2
5. blue upper, metallic gray lower, chrome windows, 1998 Cool Concepts series, Thailand cast .... $1 – 2
6. purple upper, white lower, tinted windows .... $4 – 5
7. metallic gold, tinted windows, 1997 75 Challenge .... $6 – 12

Street Sweeper (see Street Cleaner)

Stretcha Fetcha Ambulance, 2³⁄₄", #46, 1972
1. red, "Unfall Rettung" label, yellow interior, blue windows, red base, Germany issue .... $40 – 50
2. bright green, "Viper Van," ivory interior, amber windows, white base .. $12 – 16
3. bright green, "Viper Van," yellow interior, amber windows, black base ... $12 – 16
4. bright green, "Viper Van," yellow interior, amber windows, unpainted base .... $12 – 16
5. bright green, "Viper Van," yellow interior, amber windows, white base .. $12 – 16
6. white, "Ambulance" labels, ivory interior, blue windows, red base .... $12 – 16
7. white, "Ambulance" labels, yellow interior, amber windows, red base .. $16 – 24
8. white, "Ambulance" labels, yellow interior, blue windows, red base .. $12 – 16
9. white, "Ambulance" labels, yellow interior, blue windows, unpainted base .... $12 – 16
10. white, no labels, yellow interior, blue windows, red base .... $12 – 16
11. white, red cross labels, yellow interior, amber windows, red base ... $16 – 24
12. white, red cross labels, yellow interior, blue windows, red base .... $12 – 16

Studebaker Lark Wagonaire, with hunter and 1 or 2 dogs, 3", #42, 1965
1. blue with white sliding roof ... $12 – 16

Submersible, #45, 1999; #6, 2000; #64, 2001; #40 Deep Diver, 1999, international
1. orange-yellow and blue, purple window, globe design, white and blue wave graphics, 1999 Oceanics series, international issue .... $1 – 2
2. orange-yellow and blue, purple window, globe design, "World Ocean Exploration," 1999 Ocean series, US issue .... $1 – 2

3. lime green and blue, amber window, globe design, white and blue wave graphics, 2000 Ocean Explorer .. $1 – 2
4. lime green and blue, amber window, globe design, white and blue wave graphics, "Matchbox 2000," 2000 Ocean Explorer .... $3 – 4
5. 2001 Scuba Dudes .... $1 – 2

6. yellow and blue, amber window, "Base 2000," "BX-22775," Launcher 5-pack .... $1 – 2

7. metallic blue and yellow, blue window, globe design, yellow and red wave graphics, Pleasant Books issue .... $5 – 6

8. red and blue, amber window, "#042076" and storm graphics, Launcher 5-pack .... $1 – 2

Sugar Container Truck (see Foden 15-Ton Sugar Container Truck)

Sunburner (loosely based on Dodge Viper), 3", #15, 1992, USA; #41, 1992, international

1. fluorescent yellow with sun and flames on hood .... $2 – 4

2. white with sun and flames on hood .. $4 – 6

3. metallic blue with white racing stripes, 1993 .... $2 – 4

Sunburner Celica (see Toyota Celica XX)

Sunburner Maserati Bora, 3", #37, 1982

1. black with yellow and red flames, England cast .... $4 – 5
2. black with green and red flames, England cast .... $4 – 5
3. black with yellow and red flames, Macau cast .... $4 – 5
4. black with yellow and red flames, Hong Kong cast .... $4 – 5

Sunkist Mustang Piston Popper (see Ford Mustang Piston Popper)

Super Atlantic (see Atlantic Trailer, Prime Mover, Rotinoff Super Atlantic Prime Mover)

Super Dozer, #37, 2001; #19, 2002; #67 2003; #72, 2004; #32, 2006

1. red, "Matchbox 48," yellow plow, 2001 Earth Crunchers .... $1 – 2

2. orange with metallic gray plow, 2006 10-pack B5610 .... $1 – 2

3. yellow with black plow, 2003 Heavy Movers .... $1 – 2
4. yellow with red plow, 2003 Hero City 5-pack #9 .... $1 – 2
5. yellow with black plow, brown base, 2005 5-pack H4108 .... $1 – 2
6. blue with yellow plow, 2002 Build It Right .... $1 – 2

7. white with red-orange plow, 2004 #72, 2006 #32 .... $1 – 2

Super Porsche (see Porsche 935)

Swamp Rat airboat, 3", #30, 1976

1. army green with tan hull, "Swamp Rat" labels .... $6 – 8
2. army green with tan hull, no labels .... $5 – 7
3. army green with tan hull, camouflage, tan driver, Commando .... $5 – 6
4. army green with tan hull, camouflage, black driver, Commando ...... $12 – 16

Swing Wing Jet, 3", #27, 1981

1. red with white base, white wings .... $3 – 4
2. red with white base, gray wings .. $5 – 6
3. black with gray base, gray wings, Commando .... $5 – 6
4. gray with gray base, gray wings, "Top Gun," Star Car .... $7 – 8

T

T-Bird Concept (see Ford Thunderbird Concept)

T-Bird Stock Car (see Ford Thunderbird Stock Car)

T-Bird Turbo Coupe (see Ford Thunderbird Turbo Coupe)

Tailgator, #27, 1994; #45, 1998

1. bright green with gold-trimmed wheels, 1994 .... $1 – 2

2. bright green with silver-trimmed wheels, 1994 .... $1 – 2

3. dark green, 1996 .... $1 – 2

4. metallic gold, silver-trimmed wheels, 1997 75 Challenge .... $12 – 16
5. metallic gold with yellow base, gold-trimmed wheels, China issue .... $120 – 160

6. purple, 1997 .... $1 – 2

7. black, 1998 Animals .... $1 – 2

Tanker Truck (also see Guzzler, #53, 2006)

Tanker Truck, #54, 2002; #48, 2003

1. metallic red with translucent blue tank, 2002 Rescue Rookies .. $1 – 2

2. **red with white tank, with red, maroon, and silver, metallic gray plastic base, 2003 Hero City 5-pack #1 ..... $1 – 2**
3. white with translucent blue tank, 2003 Forest Rescue .... $1 – 2
4. white with translucent blue tank, 2003 Hero City 10-pack #1 .... $1 – 2

5. **white with translucent blue tank, "Tuga the Sea Turtle" graphics, 2006 Nickelodeon 5-pack H4108 .... $1 – 2**

Tanzara, 3", #53, 1972 (similar casting: Midnight Magic)
1. orange with chrome interior, amber windows .... $12 – 16
2. orange with chrome interior, blue-green windows .... $12 – 16
3. white with chrome interior, amber windows .... $20 – 25
4. white with orange stripes, chrome interior, amber windows .... $12 – 16
5. white with red stripes, chrome interior, amber windows .... $12 – 16
6. white with red stripes, chrome interior, blue-green windows .... $16 – 24
7. white with red stripes, red interior, amber windows .... $30 – 40

Taxi (also see Austin FX4R London Taxi, Chevrolet Impala Taxi, Taxi Cab)

Taxi Cab/Hero City Taxi, #36, 2003; #43, 2004; #49, 2006

1. **yellow, "Taxi," "36," wavy checked stripe design, 2003 Mom and Pop Shops .... $1 – 2**

2. **white with diagonal white and green stripes, 2006 #49 .... $1 – 2**
3. yellow with green, white, and black graphics, 2007 10-pack B5609 .. $1 – 2

Taxi FX4R (see Austin FX4R London Taxi)

Taylor Jumbo Crane, 3", #11, 1965
1. yellow weight box .... $15 – 20
2. red weight box .... $12 – 15

Team Matchbox Racer (see Hi-Tailer Team Matchbox Racer)

Team Matchbox Formula 1 Racer, 2 7/8", #24, 1973
1. yellow with white driver, "8" label .... $250 – 300
2. yellow with white driver, "4" label .... $350 – 400
3. metallic blue with white driver, "1" label .... $350 – 400
4. metallic blue with white driver, "5" label .... $350 – 400
5. metallic green with white driver, "5" label .... $50 – 60
6. red with white driver, "8" label .. $7 – 9
7. red with white driver, "8" label, label on base, UK issue .... $60 – 70
8. red with white driver, "44" label .. $6 – 8
9. red with yellow driver, "44" label .... $20 – 25
10. orange with tan driver, "44" label .... $60 – 80
11. orange with yellow driver, "44" label .... $60 – 80

Thames (also see Ford Thames)

Thames Trader Compressor Truck, yellow, 2 3/4", #28, 1959
1. gray plastic wheels .... $160 – 180
2. black plastic wheels .... $30 – 40

Thames Trader Wreck Truck, 2 1/2", #13, 1961
1. gray wheels .... $40 – 50
2. black wheels .... $30 – 40

The Buster (see Buster, The)

The Londoner (see London Bus, The Londoner)

The Wall Eater (see Demolition Machine)

Thunderbird (see Ford Thunderbird)

Tipper Truck (see Articulated Dump Truck, Atlas Dump Truck, DAF Tipper Truck, Dodge Dump Truck, 8-Wheel Tipper, Euclid Quarry Truck, GMC Highway Maintenance Truck, GMC Tipper Truck, Leyland Articulated Truck, Mack Dump Truck, Peterbilt Quarry Truck, Quarry Truck)

Tipping Trailer, 1993 Farming Series set

1. **red with black tailgate, black tires on gray rims .... $3 – 4**

Toe Joe Wreck Truck, 2 3/4", #74, 1972
1. red with green booms, black hooks, black base .... $175 – 225
2. red with red booms, black hooks, black base .... $175 – 225
3. red with red boom, red hooks, black base .... $175 – 225
4. yellow-orange with red booms, black hooks, unpainted base .... $4 – 5
5. yellow-orange with "Hitchhiker" label, unpainted base .... $150 – 200
6. yellow with green booms, black hooks, unpainted base .... $16 – 24
7. yellow with red booms, black hooks, black base .... $4 – 5
8. yellow with red booms, black hooks, unpainted base .... $4 – 5
9. lime green with green booms, red hooks, black base .... $5 – 6
10. lime green with green booms, red hooks, metallic gray base .... $5 – 6
11. lime green with green booms, red hooks, unpainted base .... $5 – 6
12. lime green with green booms, black hooks, unpainted base .... $5 – 6
13. dark lime green with white booms, black hooks, black base .... $150 – 200
14. dark lime green with green booms, red hooks, black base .... $5 – 6
15. dark lime green with red booms, black hooks, black base .... $16 – 24
16. dark lime green with red booms, black hooks, unpainted base .... $16 – 24

Tow Truck, #17, 2003 (see King Tow)

Tow Truck, #2, 2005 (see Auto Medic)

Tow Truck, #1, 2005 (see Auto Medic)

Tow Truck, #11, 2001; #16, 2003 (see King Tow)

Tow Truck, #13, 1955 (see Bedford Wreck Truck)

Tow Truck, #13, 1958 (see Bedford Wreck Truck)

Tow Truck, #13, 1961 (see Ford Thames Trader Wreck Truck)

Tow Truck, #13, 1965 (see Dodge Wreck Truck)

Tow Truck, #21, 1987; #71, 1987; #72, 1989; #63, 1998; #14, 1999 (see GMC Wrecker)

Tow Truck, #42, 2007 (see Auto Medic)

Tow Truck, #61, 1978 (see Ford Wreck Truck)

Tow Truck, #61, 1982 (see Peterbilt Wreck Truck)

Tow Truck, #71, 1968 (see Ford Heavy Wreck Truck)

Tow Truck, #74, 1972 (see Toe Joe Wreck Truck)

Toyman Dodge Challenger (see Dodge Challenger Hot Rod)

Toyota Celica GT, 2¹⁵/₁₆", #25, 1978

1. blue, "78," flat base, small rear wheels .... $5 – 6
2. yellow, "Yellow Fever," raised base, small rear wheels .... $40 – 50
3. yellow, "Yellow Fever," raised base, large rear wheels .... $5 – 6

Toyota Celica Supra, #30, 1995 (see Toyota Supra)

Toyota Celica XX, #77, 1981; #J-21, 1979, Japan

1. red, "Sunburner," US issued Sunburner Celica .... $6 – 8
2. red, no markings, Hong Kong cast, Australia issue and US Speedsticks issue .... $4 – 5
3. red, Japan cast, Japan issue ....$16 – 24
4. ivory, Japan cast, Japan issue ....$16 – 24

Toyota Mini Pickup 4x4, issued with or without roof foil, roll bar or tires in back, 2³/₄", #57, 1982; #13, 1983; #76, 1996 (also issued as Dunes Racer, Mini Pickup 4x4, Mountain Man, 4x4 Open Back Truck; similar casting: Toyota Mini Pickup Camper)

1. red with chrome windows, white and black splash design, yellow zigzag design, chrome plastic base, black roll bar, Super Trucks .... $3 – 5
2. dark red with white, silver and black stripes, no roof foil or roll bar .. $5 – 6
3. orange-red with white, silver, and black stripes, no roof foil or roll bar .. $5 – 6
4. orange with purple windows, "FWD," unpainted metal base, England cast .... $5 – 6
5. orange with orange windows, "FWD," unpainted metal base, England cast .... $5 – 6
6. orange with red windows, "FWD," unpainted metal base, England cast .... $5 – 6
7. yellow with red windows, "4X4," unpainted metal base, England cast .... $5 – 6
8. yellow with red windows, "4X4," metallic gray metal base, England cast .. $5 – 6
9. yellow with red windows, "4X4 Goodyear," pearly silver metal base, Macau cast .... $4 – 5
10. yellow with red windows, "4X4 Goodrich," pearly silver metal base, Macau cast .... $4 – 5
11. light blue, "Mountain Man" on roof, no roof foil or roll bar, black metal base .... $3 – 4
12. light blue, "Mountain Man" on roof, no roof foil or roll bar, black plastic base .... $1 – 2
13. metallic blue with red windows, pink, pink roll bar, black plastic base, Thailand cast .... $1 – 2
14. metallic purple with red windows, skeleton and triceratops, orange roll bar, 5-pack .... $1 – 2
15. white with red windows, "Bob Jane T-Mart," pearly silver metal base, Macau cast, Australia issue .... $12 – 16

16. **white with red windows, "63" and stripes, black metal base, Macau cast ....$1 – 2**
17. white with red windows, "63" and stripes, black plastic base, Macau cast .... $1 – 2
18. white with red windows, "63" and stripes, black plastic base, Thailand cast .... $1 – 2
19. white with chrome windows, blue and pink, pink roll bar, chrome plastic base, Thailand cast, Super Trucks ..... $4 – 5

20. **white with red windows, black bats and dripping blood, red roll bar, black tires in back, red plastic base, Thailand cast ....$1 – 2**

Toyota Mini Pickup Camper, 2³/₄", #22, 1982 (similar casting: Toyota Mini Pickup 4x4)

1. metallic silver with white stepped roof, yellow and black design, "Big Foot" ....$5 – 6
2. metallic silver with white stepped roof, yellow and black design, no side design, "Big Foot" .... $7 – 8
3. metallic silver with white flat roof, yellow and black design, "Big Foot," England cast .... $5 – 6
4. metallic silver with white flat roof, yellow and black design, "Big Foot," Hong Kong cast .... $7 – 8
5. metallic silver with white flat roof, yellow and black design, "Big Foot," Macau cast .... $5 – 6
6. metallic silver with black roll bar, yellow and black design, "Big Foot" .. $40 – 50
7. red with white flat roof, "Aspen Ski Holidays," metal base .... $4 – 5
8. red with white flat roof, "Aspen Ski Holidays," plastic base .... $3 – 4
9. white with white flat roof, "SLD Pump Service" .... $12 – 16

Toyota MR2, 2⁷/₈", #9, 1987; #74, 1987

1. white with "MR2 Pace Car" ...... $3 – 4
2. blue with "MR2" and pink stripes, new Superfast wheels .... $4 – 5
3. metallic blue with "MR2" and pink stripes, Laser Wheels .... $5 – 6
4. green with "7 Snake Racing Team" ...$9 – 12

Toyota Scion xB, #24, 2005; Superfast #64, 2005; #5, 2006; #7, 2007

1. **metallic gray, 2005 #24 ......$1 – 2**

2. **metallic burgundy, 2005 Superfast #64 ....$1 – 2**
3. pearl white, 2006 #5 .... $1 – 2

4. **light orange, #7, 2007 ....$1 – 2**

Toyota Supra, 3", #39, 1982; #60, 1984, international

1. red, "Twin Cam 24," amber windows, black base, Japanese issue ... $8 – 10
2. red, "Twin Cam 24," clear windows, black base, Japan issue .... $8 – 10
3. white, "41," red and black rally accents, amber windows, black base, 1982 .. $3 – 4
4. white, "41," red and black rally accents, amber windows, dark gray base, 1982 .... $3 – 4

5. **white, "41," red and black rally accents, clear windows, black base, 1982 .... $3 – 4**
6. white, "Supra," pinstripes, amber windows, black base .... $3 – 4
7. white, "Supra," pinstripes, clear windows, black base .... $3 – 4
8. white with red, blue, and yellow design, clear windows, black base, issued as a Dinky Toy, 1983 .... $9 – 12

Toyota Supra, #30, 1995; #44, 1998, international; #70, 2000, international

1. dark gray with red and black interior, clear windows, rubber tires on chrome rims, Premiere Collection #4 .... $4 – 5
2. black with black interior, tinted windows, red stripe, "Matchbox," 2000 Power international .... $1 – 2
3. black with tan interior, clear windows, "Supra," 1998 Asian Cars international .... $1 – 2
4. black with tan and black interior, clear windows, rubber tires on chrome rims, Gold Coin Collection .... $16 – 24
5. blue with black interior, green windows, ASAP promotional blank ...... $30 – 40
6. blue with black interior, green windows, "HEDIS Group," ASAP promotional .... $80 – 120
7. blue with black interior, green windows, "Mas 90 User Conference Lexington," ASAP promotional .... $80 – 120
8. blue with black interior, green windows, "Lucent Technologies," ASAP promotional .... $80 – 120
9. blue with black interior, green windows, "Wenchey's Antiques...," ASAP promotional .... $15 – 20
10. blue with white interior, clear windows, pink, orange and white design, 5-pack .... $1 – 2
11. chrome blue with white interior; clear windows; pink, orange, and white design; 5-pack .... $1 – 2

12. **chrome silver with purple interior, clear windows, lavender and pink design on sides and hood, 1997 .... $1 – 2**
13. fluorescent orange with red interior, clear windows, "Matchbox Get in the Fast Lane," "Toy Fair 1996," rubber tires on chrome rims .... $20 – 30
14. metallic gold with black interior, clear windows, 1997 75 Challenge .. $6 – 12
15. red with yellow interior, tinted windows, white and orange design on sides .... $3 – 4

16. **red with metallic gray interior, tinted windows, black and white design on sides, 1997 Super Cars 5-pack .... $1 – 2**
17. white with gray interior, red and yellow flames on sides and hood .... $1 – 2
18. white with red interior, red and yellow flames on sides and hood, 1996 .... $1 – 2

19. **white with red interior, red and yellow flames on sides only .... $1 – 2**
20. white with red and black interior, detailed trim, rubber tires on chrome rims, Premiere Collection #1 ... $4 – 5

21. **yellow with gray interior, rubber tires on chrome rims, Premiere Collection 8-car display set .... $4 – 5**

Tractor (also see Ford Tractor)

Tractor, #54, 2007

1. **red with black interior, white graphics, metallic gray chassis, 2007 #54 .... $1 – 2**
2. blue with black interior, white wheel hubs, 2007 #54 .... $1 – 2

Tractor Cab, #31, 2005; #34, 2006

1. gray, 2005 #31 .... $1 – 2

2. **yellow, 2006 #34 .... $1 – 2**

3. **metallic blue, 2007 Superfast #49 .... $4 – 5**

Tractor Plow, #30, 2006

1. **yellow and black with silver metal plow and base, 2006 #30 .... $1 – 2**

2. **red with gray lower body, silver metal plow and base, 2007 5-pack K9618 .... $1 – 2**

Tractor Shovel, 2⅞", #29, 1976; #13, 1998; #237, 1993; #29, 1997; #13, 1998; #28, 1999; #94, 2000; #39, 2001; #52, 2005; #40, 2006

1. red with black shovel, chrome hubs, black motor .... $1 – 2
2. red with metallic gray shovel, gray motor, 1997 .... $1 – 2

3. **red with metallic gray shovel, black motor, 1998 Big Movers ...... $1 – 2**
4. red with metallic gray shovel, chrome hubs, black motor, "Thomae Mucusolvan," Germany issue .... $30 – 40

5. red with red fork on metallic gray arms, black motor, 1993 Farming Series set .... $4 – 6
6. orange with black shovel, chrome hubs, black motor, white roof, Germany issue .... $4 – 5
7. orange with black shovel, silver motor, 2006 #40 .... $1 – 2

8. orange with metallic gray shovel, chrome hubs, black motor, no markings .... $1 – 2
9. orange with metallic gray shovel, chrome hubs, black motor, black stripes .... $1 – 2

10. orange with metallic gray shovel, orange hubs, chrome motor, 2006 #40 .... $1 – 2
11. light orange with black shovel, gray motor .... $9 – 10
12. light orange with black shovel, chrome hubs, black motor, "Thomae Mucosolvan," Macau cast, Germany issue .... $25 – 35
13. light orange with red shovel, chrome hubs, black motor, red stripes, Action System/Action Pack .... $1 – 2
14. dark orange with black shovel, chrome hubs, gray motor .... $9 – 10
15. dark orange with red shovel, chrome hubs, gray motor .... $60 – 80
16. fluorescent orange with black shovel, chrome hubs, black motor, 5-pack .. $1 – 2
17. fluorescent orange with metallic gray shovel, chrome hubs, black motor, 5-pack .... $1 – 2
18. pumpkin orange with gray shovel, chrome hubs, black motor, 5-pack .... $1 – 2
19. pumpkin orange with gray shovel, chrome hubs, gray motor, "Hemler Bros.," ASAP promotional .. $80 – 120
20. pumpkin orange with gray shovel, chrome hubs, gray motor, "Redi-Way," ASAP promotional .... $80 – 120
21. pumpkin orange with gray shovel, chrome hubs, gray motor, "Blue Ridge Construction," ASAP promotional .... $80 – 120
22. pumpkin orange with gray shovel, chrome hubs, gray motor, "CAT Service Co.," ASAP promotional .... $80 – 120
23. yellow with black shovel, chrome hubs, black motor, "Thomae Mucosolvan," Germany issue .... $30 – 40
24. light yellow with red shovel, chrome hubs, chrome motor .... $9 – 12
25. light yellow with red shovel, black hubs, chrome motor .... $12 – 18
26. light yellow with black shovel, chrome hubs, black motor, "Thomae Mucosolvan," Germany issue .... $20 – 30
27. light yellow with black shovel, chrome hubs, black motor, "Thomae Mucosolvan," Germany issue .... $20 – 30
28. dark yellow with black shovel, chrome hubs, black motor, "Thomae Mucosolvan," Thailand cast, Germany issue .... $30 – 40
29. dark yellow with black shovel, chrome hubs, black motor, "Thomae Mucosolvan," Macau cast, Germany issue .... $20 – 30
30. dark yellow with black shovel, chrome hubs, black motor, no markings ... $5 – 6
31. dark yellow with black shovel, chrome hubs, black motor, black stripes, "C" .... $3 – 4
32. dark yellow with black shovel, chrome hubs, black motor, black stripes, England cast .... $3 – 4
33. dark yellow with black shovel, chrome hubs, black motor, black stripes, Thailand cast .... $1 – 2
34. dark yellow with black shovel, chrome hubs, gray motor, black stripes .. $3 – 4
35. dark yellow with black shovel, chrome hubs, gray motor, no markings .. $3 – 4
36. dark yellow with maroon shovel, chrome hubs, black motor .... $5 – 6
37. dark yellow with maroon shovel, yellow hubs, black motor .... $7 – 8
38. dark yellow with red shovel, chrome hubs, chrome motor .... $7 – 8
39. dark yellow with red shovel, chrome hubs, black motor, no markings ... $5 – 6
40. dark yellow with red shovel, chrome hubs, black motor, red stripes .. $1 – 2
41. dark yellow with black shovel, chrome hubs, black motor, black stripes, Team Convoy .... $1 – 2
42. green with black shovel, chrome hubs, black motor, "Thomae Mucosolvan," Germany issue .... $40 – 50
43. green with dirt, gray shovel, chrome hubs, gray motor, metallic gray roof, 2000 Build It! .... $1 – 2
44. green with dirt, gray shovel, chrome hubs, gray motor, metallic gray roof, "Matchbox 2000," 2000 Build It! .... $3 – 4
45. lime green with yellow shovel, chrome hubs, chrome motor, Germany issue .... $150 – 175
46. bright green with metallic gray shovel and engine, yellow wheel hubs, 2007 10-pack B5610 .... $1 – 2
47. blue with red shovel, yellow wheels with orange hubs, red motor, Matchbox Preschool/Live 'N Learn .... $7 – 8
48. blue with black shovel, chrome hubs, black motor, "Thomae Mucosolvan," Germany issue .... $30 – 40
49. blue with black shovel, chrome hubs, black motor, "Spasmo Mucosolvan," Germany issue .... $12 – 16

50. blue with white shovel, chrome hubs, gray motor, 2001 Earth Crunchers .... $1 – 2
51. purple with black shovel, black motor, green and orange design, plastic armaments, Roadblasters .... $7 – 8

52. white with metallic gray shovel, chrome hubs, metallic gray motor, 1998 Big Movers .... $1 – 2
53. beige with dirt, metallic gray shovel, chrome hubs, metallic gray motor, "3-MB34," 1999 Road Work .... $1 – 2
54. metallic gold with black shovel, chrome hubs, black motor, 1997 75 Challenge .... $12 – 16
55. dull gold with black shovel, chrome hubs, black motor, Germany issue .... $80 – 120

Tractor Shovel, 2000, Subway, "Mfd. by b. little" on base
1. pumpkin orange with black scoop and engine, black hubs .... $1 – 2

Trailer Caravan, 2$^7/_8$", #23, 1965

1. yellow .... $12 – 16

2. pink .... $12 – 16

Trailer Caravan (see Eccles Caravan)

Trans Am (see Pontiac Firebird Trans Am)

Trans Am T-Roof (see Pontiac Firebird Trans Am T-Roof)

Trash Titan, #72, 2005; #36, 2006

1. metallic green, 2005 #72 .... $1 – 2

2. yellow with metallic gray base, "Industrial Waste," 2006 #36 .... $1 – 2

3. blue with gray base, "New Castle Waste Contractors Organic Recyclables," 2007 5-pack K9618 ... $1 – 2

4. white, "Dump or Recycle" graphics, 2006 5-pack J4682 .... $1 – 2

Trash Truck, #57, 2002; #19, 2003; #56, 2004

1. black with black dumper, metallic gray container and base, orange forks, 2002 Rescue Rookies ... $1 – 2

2. black with black dumper, metallic gray container and base, orange forks, Christmas 2002, boxed 3-pack .... $2 – 3

3. yellow with dark green dumper, black container and base, metallic gray forks, 2003 Public Works .... $1 – 2

Travel Trailer (see Eccles Caravan Travel Trailer, Caravan Travel Trailer)

Travel Trailer (see Caravan Travel Trailer)

Travel Trailer (see Trailer Caravan)

Triumph Motorcycle and Sidecar, #4, 2⅛", 1960

1. metallic silver blue with black plastic tires .... $90 – 120

Trojan 1-Ton "Brooke Bond Tea" Van, red, 2¼", #47, 1958

1. metal wheels .... $30 – 40

2. gray plastic wheels .... $40 – 50

Trolley Bus (see London Trolley Bus)

Troop Carrier, #36, 2002 (similar casting: Police Trouble Tracker)

1. white with black canopy, with blue, turquoise, and yellow, "Metro Police," 2003 Hero City 5-pack #2 .... $1 – 2

2. flat primer brown with white interior and bed, with orange, tan, and black graphics, 2007 10-pack B5610 ...... $1 – 2

3. olive green, 2003 Hero City 5-pack #8 .... $1 – 2

Truck Camper, #58, 1999; #61, 2000; #53, 1999, international; #41, 2000, international; #65 2006 (similar casting: Police Mobile Command Center)

1. bright orange, 2002 Matchbox Across America 50th Birthday Series #44 Wyoming — Western Collection .... $4 – 5
2. cream with blue and lavender design, blue windows, 5-pack .... $1 – 2
3. light gray, "Candy Hill Campgrounds," red and yellow stripes, blue windows, Color Comp promotional ...... $20 – 30
4. light gray, "Matchbox 2000," red and yellow stripes, blue windows, 2000 Great Outdoors .... $3 – 4

5. light gray with red and yellow stripes, blue windows, 2000 Great Outdoors .... $1 – 2

6. white, "34 States and Still Going," black and yellow US map design, yellow windows, 1999 Wilderness Adventure .... $1 – 2

7. white with blue and yellow design, yellow windows, 1999 Forest Run international .... $1 – 2

8. white with red and black stripes, blue windows, 5-pack .... $1 – 2

9. white with "Free Spirit" graphics, 2006 #65 .... $1 – 2

Truck Camper Police (see Police Mobile Command Center)

Turbo Fury, 3", #69, 1973

1. red, "69" label, amber windshield .... $16 – 24
2. red, "69" label, clear windshield .... $16 – 24

3. red, "86" label, clear windshield ....$16 – 24
4. red, scorpion label, clear windshield ....$35 – 45

Turbo Ski (see Snowmobile)

TV News Truck (see Mercedes-Benz TV News Truck)

TV Service Van, with ladder, antenna, and three TV sets, $2\frac{1}{2}$", #62, 1963
1. gray plastic wheels, "Rentaset" decals ....$125 – 150
2. gray plastic wheels, "Radio Rentals" decals ....$180 – 200
3. black plastic wheels, "Rentaset" decals ....$30 – 35
4. black plastic wheels, "Radio Rentals" decals ....$40 – 50

TVR Tuscan S, #23, 2006

1. metallic blue, 2006 #23 ......$1 – 2

2. metallic green, 2005 Superfast #35 ....$3 – 4

3. white with "Jaden Yuki" graphics, 2006 Yu-Gi-Oh GX 5-pack H5775 ....$1 – 2

Tyre Fryer, 3", #42, 1972
1. blue ....$12 – 16
2. orange "Jaffa Mobile," on-package premium, UK issue ....$90 – 120

Tyrone Malone Bandag Bandit, 3", #65, 1982 (similar casting: Tyrone Malone Super Boss)
1. black with green and white stripes, "Tyrone" and four stripes on airfoil, England cast ....$4 – 5
2. black with green and white stripes, "Tyrone" and two stripes on airfoil, England cast ....$4 – 5

3. black with green and white stripes, no markings on airfoil, England cast ....$4 – 5
4. black with yellow and white stripes, "Tyrone" on airfoil, Macau cast ..$1 – 2
5. black with yellow and white stripes, "Tyrone" and four stripes on airfoil, Macau cast ....$1 – 2
6. black with yellow and white stripes, no markings on airfoil, China cast ...$5 – 6

Tyrone Malone Super Boss, 3", #66, 1982 (similar casting: Tyrone Malone Bandag Bandit)

1. white, "Super Boss," "Detroit Diesel" on roof, decal, no stripes on spoiler, Macau cast ....$1 – 2
2. white, "Super Boss," "Detroit Diesel" on roof, tampo, no stripes on spoiler, Macau cast ....$1 – 2
3. white, "Super Boss," "Detroit Diesel" on roof, four stripes on spoiler, Macau cast ....$1 – 2
4. white, "Super Boss," "Detroit Diesel" on roof, no markings on spoiler, Macau cast ....$1 – 2
5. white, "Super Boss," "Detroit Diesel" on roof, no markings on spoiler, green windows, England cast ....$3 – 4
6. white, "Super Boss," "Detroit Diesel" on roof, no markings on spoiler, red windows, England cast, Convoy ... $8 – 10
7. white, "Super Boss," four stripes on spoiler, green windows, England cast ....$3 – 4
8. white, "Super Boss," four stripes on spoiler, Macau cast ....$1 – 2
9. white, "Super Boss," two stripes on spoiler, green windows, England cast ....$3 – 4
10. white, "Super Boss," no markings on spoiler, green windows, England cast ....$3 – 4
11. white, "Super Boss," no markings on spoiler, China cast ....$3 – 4
12. white, no markings, China cast, Graffic Traffic ....$12 – 16

13. tan with orange, yellow, and black stripes, metallic gray armament replaces spoiler, Macau cast, Roadblasters ....$6 – 8

U

UFO, #61, 1999; #56, 1999, international

1. lavender with blue-green windows, 1999 Science Fiction ....$1 – 2

2. pale bronze, Real Talkin' ....$5 – 6

Ultralight (see Aero Junior)

Unimog (see Mercedes-Benz Unimog)

US Mail Jeep, "No. 5 U.S. Mail Truck" on base, no gun, $2\frac{3}{8}$", #5, 1978 (similar casting: Army Jeep, with or without gun, #38, Sleet 'N' Snow)
1. blue, white roof, "U. S. Mail" .... $6 – 8
2. pale blue, white roof, "U. S. Mail" ..$9 – 12

US Mail Truck (see US Mail Jeep, Postal Service Delivery Truck)

US Taxi (see Ford LTD US Taxi)

Utility Truck, #74, 1987; #33, 1989; #9, 1998; #15, 1999 (see Ford Utility Truck)

Utility Truck, #39, 2007 (see Guzzler/Mini Tanker)

V

Vantastic, $2\frac{7}{8}$", #34, 1975; BR 23-24, 1986
1. orange with exposed engine, unpainted base, blue-green windows, fish design label ....$80 – 120
2. orange with exposed engine, white base, blue-green windows, fish design labels ....$12 – 16
3. orange with exposed engine, white base, blue-green windows, stripes labels ....$12 – 16
4. orange, no exposed engine, white base, blue-green windows, "34" hood label ....$9 – 12

5. orange, no exposed engine, white base, sunburst hood label .... $16 – 24
6. orange, no exposed engine, white base, "Jaffamobile" label .... $400 – 450
7. orange, no exposed engine, white tab base, "34" label, UK issue ... $70 – 90
8. orange, no exposed engine, white tab base, "3" label, UK issue ... $80 – 120
9. beige, China cast, Super GT BR 23- 24, 1986 .... $4 – 5
10. blue, China cast, Super GT BR 23-24, 1986 .... $4 – 5

Vauxhall Astra GTE/Opel Kadett, 2¾", #48, 1987, Europe

1. **red, "GTE" and stripes ....$3 – 4**
2. yellow, "Mobile Phone," "Telecom" .... $4 – 5
3. yellow, no markings, Germany issue ....$10 – 12
4. black, "BP 52," "7," yellow stripe, Dutch issue ....$9 – 12
5. white, "AC Delco 48," silver wheels .... $1 – 2
6. white, "AC Delco 48," white wheels .... $3 – 4
7. white, "STP," "Sphere Drake" ....$1 – 2

Vauxhall Astra Police/Opel Kadett Police, 2⅞", #8, 1987; #24, 1999, international

1. white, "Police," red and blue stripes, white wheel hubs .... $5 – 6
2. white, "Police," red and blue stripes, silver wheel hubs .... $3 – 4
3. white and dark green, "Polizei" ... $5 – 6
4. white, "Police," orange and blue stripes and face on hood, yellow hubs, Live 'N Learn/Preschool .... $4 – 5
5. white, "Police," yellow stripes, orange dot on roof .... $1 – 2
6. white, "Police," yellow stripes, no orange dot on roof .... $1 – 2
7. white, "Police," peach and yellow stripes .... $1 – 2
8. white, "59" in shield, yellow and black checks .... $1 – 2
9. white, "Police," "Hertfordshire" .... $1 – 2
10. black, "Police," commando emblem ....$16 – 24
11. white, "World Cup Security," "France 98" .... $1 – 2
12. metallic gray, "Police," red and blue stripes .... $1 – 2

Vauxhall Cresta sedan, 2½", #22, 1956

1. **red with white or ivory roof, no windows ....$30 – 50**

Vauxhall Cresta sedan, 2⅝", #22, 1958

1. ivory, no windows, metal wheels ....$40 – 50
2. ivory, no windows, gray plastic wheels .... $40 – 50
3. ivory, green windows, gray plastic wheels .... $45 – 55
4. ivory and turquoise, green windows, gray plastic wheels .... $350 – 400
5. gray and turquoise, green windows, gray plastic wheels .... $65 – 75
6. bronze and turquoise, green windows, gray plastic wheels .... $65 – 75
7. gray and pink, green windows, gray plastic wheels .... $50 – 60
8. gray and pink, green windows, silver plastic wheels .... $50 – 60
9. gold, green windows, gray plastic wheels .... $50 – 60
10. gold, green windows, silver plastic wheels .... $50 – 60
11. copper, green windows, gray plastic wheels .... $50 – 60
12. copper, green windows, silver plastic wheels .... $50 – 60
13. copper, green windows, black plastic wheels .... $35 – 45

Vauxhall Frontera (see Isuzu Rodeo)

Vauxhall Guildsman, Superfast wheels, 3", #40, 1971

1. pink, "40," green windows, unpainted base .... $16 – 24
2. pink with flames label, green windows, metallic gray base .... $12 – 16
3. pink with flames label, green windows, unpainted base .... $12 – 16
4. red, "40," amber windows, metallic gray base .... $12 – 16
5. red, "40," amber windows, unpainted base .... $12 – 16

6. **red, "40," green windows, unpainted base ....$12 – 16**
7. red with flames label, amber windows, unpainted base .... $12 – 16
8. red with flames label, green windows, unpainted base .... $12 – 16

Vauxhall Victor Estate Car, yellow, 2⅝", #38, 1963

1. green interior, gray plastic wheels ....$30 – 35
2. green interior, silver plastic wheels ....$35 – 40
3. green interior, black plastic wheels ....$25 – 30
4. red interior, silver plastic wheels .... $25 – 30
5. red interior, black plastic wheels .... $25 – 30

Vauxhall Victor Sedan, 2⅜", #45, 1958

1. red with no windows, metal wheels ....$900 – 1000
2. yellow with no windows, metal wheels ....$30 – 40
3. yellow with no windows, gray plastic wheels .... $30 – 40
4. yellow with green windows, gray plastic wheels .... $30 – 40
5. yellow with clear windows, gray plastic wheels .... $30 – 40
6. yellow with green windows, silver plastic wheels .... $40 – 50
7. yellow with green windows, black plastic wheels .... $20 – 30

Vectra Cavalier (see Opel Vectra/Chevrolet Cavalier)

Volks Dragon Volkswagen Beetle, red, 2½", #31, 1971 (similar castings: Hi Ho Silver, Hot Chocolate, Sand Digger, Dune Man, Big Blue)

1. red with unpainted base, purple windows, ivory interior, eyes sticker ....$12 – 16
2. red with unpainted base, purple windows, yellow interior, eyes sticker ......$12 – 16
3. red with unpainted base, clear windows, yellow interior, eyes sticker .. $12 – 16
4. red with metallic gray base, clear windows, yellow interior, eyes sticker ....$12 – 16
5. red with metallic gray base, purple windows, yellow interior, eyes sticker ..$12 – 16
6. red with unpainted base, purple windows, yellow interior, flower sticker .... $16 – 24
7. red with metallic gray base, purple windows, yellow interior, flower sticker ....$16 – 24
8. red with unpainted base, purple windows, yellow interior, no sticker ....$12 – 16
9. red with metallic gray base, purple windows, white interior, eyes sticker ....$12 – 16

Volkswagen 1200 Sedan, metallic light blue, 2½", #25, 1960

1. gray plastic wheels, clear windows .... $40 – 50
2. gray plastic wheels, green windows .... $40 – 50
3. silver plastic wheels, green windows .... $50 – 60
4. black plastic wheels, green widows .... $100 – 120

Volkswagen 1500 Saloon, 2⅞", #15, 1968

1. ivory with "137" on doors, black plastic wheels, 1969 ....$9 – 12

2. ivory with "137" on doors, Superfast wheels, 1970 ....$20 – 25

3. metallic red with "137" on doors, Superfast wheels ....$24 – 36

Volkswagen 1600TL, 2³/₄", #67, 1967

1. red with no roof rack, black plastic tires on chrome hubs ....$16 – 24
2. red with maroon roof rack, black plastic tires on chrome hubs .... $40 – 50
3. metallic purple, no roof rack, black plastic tires on chrome hubs ... $300 – 400
4. red, Superfast wheels, 1970 ....$90 – 120
5. metallic purple, Superfast wheels, 1970 .... $25 – 35
6. pink, Superfast wheels .... $20 – 30

Volkswagen Beetle 1962, #53, 1999; #12, 2000; #48, 1999, international; #21, 2006; #29, 2007
1. red, no markings, 2006 #21 ... $1 – 2
2. red with black roof, "Coca-Cola," Avon 2-pack .... $6 – 8
3. red with black roof, silver pinstripes, 5-pack .... $1 – 2

4. red with fishing graphics, 2003 5-pack #10 ....$1 – 2
5. red and white with black roof, "Things Go Better with Coke," rubber tires on chrome rims, Target multipack .... $5 – 6

6. orange, no markings, 2007 #29 ....$1 – 2
7. orange with black roof, "Xtreme Mission 33," 5-pack .... $1 – 2
8. pumpkin orange, "Scooby-Doo!" "Jinkies," "Velma," Warner Brothers .... $6 – 8
9. yellow with black roof, rubber tires on chrome rims, FAO Schwarz multipack .... $7 – 9

10. lime green, "Nickelodeon," Spongebob Squarepants illustration, 2003 Nickelodeon 5-pack ....$2 – 3

11. sea green, 2007 5-pack K9612 ....$1 – 2
12. light blue with black roof, "Beetle," 5-pack .... $1 – 2

13. metallic silver-blue, "Massachusetts," 2002 Matchbox Across America 50th Birthday Series — Northeastern Collection ....$4 – 5
14. metallic purple with black roof, with black, blue, and lavender fish design, 5-pack .... $1 – 2

15. black with turquoise sides, black roof, "Matchbox," 1999 Beach ..... $1 – 2
16. white with black roof, turquoise sides, "Northern New Jersey Toy Show," Color Comp promotional .... $16 – 24

17. white with turquoise sides, black roof, 2000 To the Beach ......$1 – 2
18. white with turquoise sides, black roof, "Matchbox 2000," 2000 To the Beach .... $3 – 4
19. white and red, "Coca-Cola," rubber tires on chrome rims, Premiere Collection .... $5 – 6

20. metallic gold with "Scooby-Doo!" graphics, Scooby-Doo! 5-pack L1574, 2007 ....$4 – 5

Volkswagen Beetle 4x4, front opens, #31, 2001; #45, 2002; #74, 2005; #64, 2006
1. yellow with black base, "Desert Rescue," 2001 Sand Blasters .... $1 – 2
2. yellow with red plastic base, 2002 Weekend Cruisers .... $1 – 2
3. yellow with black plastic base, 2003 Beach Patrol .... $1 – 2
4. yellow with black plastic base, 2003 Hero City 10-pack #1 .... $1 – 2
5. yellow with blue plastic base, 2003 Hero City 5-pack #7 .... $1 – 2
6. yellow with black plastic base, "MHC Beach Patrol," 2004 #54 .... $1 – 2
7. tan camouflage, 2005 #74 ..... $1 – 2
8. dark green, 2006 #64 .... $1 – 2

Volkswagen Beetle Big Blue (see Big Blue Volkswagen Beetle)

Volkswagen Beetle Dragon Wheels (see Dragon Wheels Volkswagen Beetle)

Volkswagen Beetle Dune Man (see Dune Man Volkswagen Beetle)

Volkswagen Beetle Flying Bug (see Flying Bug Volkswagen Beetle)

Volkswagen Beetle Hi Ho Silver! (see Hi Ho Silver! Volkswagen Beetle)

Volkswagen Beetle Hot Chocolate (see Hot Chocolate Volkswagen Beetle)

Volkswagen Beetle Sand Digger (see Sand Digger Volkswagen Beetle)

Volkswagen Beetle Taxi, #31, 2003, #41, 2005

1. **green with white roof, 2003 Airport .... $3 – 4**
2. green with white roof, 2003 Hero City 10-pack #2 .... #3 – 4

3. **yellow with checkerboard graphics, 2005 #41 .... $1 – 2**
4. pearl with yellow accents, checkerboard graphics, "Yellow Stripe Taxi," 2005 J4674 5-pack .... $1 – 2

Volkswagen Beetle Volks Dragon (see Volks Dragon)

Volkswagen Camper, raised 6-windowed roof, 2⁵⁄₈", #34, 1967
1. metallic silver .... $35 – 50

Volkswagen Camper, low windowless roof graphics, 2⁵⁄₈", #34, 1968
1. metallic silver .... $25 – 40

Volkswagen Camper/Dormobile, with opening roof, 2¹⁄₈", #23, 1970
1. blue with orange interior and roof .... $16 – 24
2. orange with orange interior and roof ....$150 – 200
3. orange with white interior, orange roof .... $12 – 16
4. olive with no interior, blue windows .... $7 – 9
5. white with no interior, "Pizza Van" ....$10 – 15

Volkswagen Caravette Camper, light green, 2³⁄₄", #34, 1962
1. gray plastic wheels .... $40 – 50
2. black plastic wheels .... $40 – 50

Volkswagen Concept 1, #49, 1996 – 1997; #17, 1998; #18, 1999; #42, 2000; #60, 2001 (also see Volkswagen Concept 1 Convertible, Volkswagen Concept 1 Police)
1. red, "17th Annual Matchbox USA Convention 1998," black roof, promotional .... $15 – 20
2. red, "Coca-Cola," white wave, rubber tires on chrome rims, Premiere Collection .... $5 – 6
3. red, "Coca-Cola," "Always Coca-Cola," white roof, rubber tires on chrome rims, Premiere Collection .... $5 – 6
4. red, "Mark 1 V.W.S.," rubber tires on chrome rims .... $9 – 12
5. red, "Matchbox Collectors Club Deutschland," promotional ... $16 – 24
6. red, 2002 Matchbox Across America 50th Birthday Series #1 Delaware — Northeastern Collection .... $4 – 5
7. red with black fenders, opaque metallic silver windows, 1999 Taco Bell Matchbox Madness .... $3 – 4
8. red with black roof, 1997 .... $4 – 5
9. red, "MICA Hershey 1999," Color Comp promotional .... $20 – 30
10. dark red, "8th Toy Show Demo Model Hershey," Color Comp promotional ....$16 – 24
11. dark red, "20th Annual MBUSA Demo Model," Color Comp promotional ....$16 – 24
12. dark red, "Matchbox," gold glitter, short card, "A Target Exclusive" on package .... $3 – 4
13. maroon, "Hope Spring Cancer Support Centre 1998," black roof, promotional .... $120 – 160
14. orange, "Bill Cairns Realtor," ASAP promotional .... $30 – 40
15. orange, "Hope Spring Cancer Support Centre 1998," black roof, promotional .... $20 – 30
16. orange, "Matchbox Convention Hershey PA 1999 Demo Model," Color Comp promotional .... $30 – 40
17. orange, "MICA Hershey 1999," Color Comp promotional .... $20 – 30
18. orange, "Matchbox World of Wheels," black roof, Color Comp promotional ....$120 – 160
19. orange, "RLI," black roof, ASAP promotional .... $80 – 120
20. orange, "www.sachs.com," ASAP promotional .... $120 – 160

21. **orange with black roof, 1998 Cool Concepts ....$1 – 2**
22. pumpkin orange, "Hope Spring Cancer Support Centre 1998," black roof, promotional .... $120 – 160
23. yellow, "10 Jahre Mauerfall," "Berlin 1989 1999," promotional ... $30 – 40
24. yellow, "Happy New Millennium," "Y2K Bug," promotional .... $20 – 30
25. yellow with yellow roof, Germany issue .... $4 – 5
26. green, "17th Annual Matchbox USA Convention 1998," black roof, promotional .... $15 – 20

27. **green with black roof, green base, 1997 ....$1 – 2**
28. green with black roof, red base, 1997 .... $120 – 160

29. **light green ....$1 – 2**
30. light lime green, white flowers and globe design, rubber tires on chrome rims ....$12 – 16
31. metallic lime green, white headlights .... $4 – 5
32. metallic lime green, white headlights, "Matchbox," Pleasant Books issue ..$4 – 5

33. **light blue, "Looney Tunes Paris," Pepe Le Pew, Looney Tunes Back in Action 5-pack ....$2 – 3**

34. **metallic purple with black roof, 1997 Cars of the Future 5-pack ....$1 – 2**
35. black with yellow stripes, 2000 Show Cars .... $1 – 2

36. black with yellow stripes, "Matchbox 2000," 2000 Show Cars .... $3 – 4
37. brown, "Hope Spring Cancer Support Centre 1998," black roof, promotional .... $120 – 160
38. white, "Blue Angels," ASAP promotional .... $16 – 24
39. white, "Happy New Millennium," "Y2K Bug," promotional .... $20 – 30
40. white, "New Way Lunch," ASAP promotional .... $60 – 80
41. white, "RCA," ASAP promotional .... $20 – 30

42. white with light blue stripes, VW logo and interior, 1999 Top Class .... $1 – 2
43. metallic gold, 1997 75 Challenge .... $6 – 12
44. metallic silver, rubber tires on chrome rims, FAO Schwarz multipack ... $7 – 9

Volkswagen Concept 1, 1998, Taco Bell; Matchbox mold retooled by Strottman International, Inc., through a licensing agreement with Mattel. Strottman manufactures toy premiums for Taco Bell. Base is marked "Made in China by S.I.I."
1. red with black fenders, metallic silver windows, swirl design and lines, Taco Bell premium .... $4 – 5
2. green with metallic silver windows, play set .... $9 – 12
3. metallic gold, 1997 Challenge 75 series #49 .... $4 – 6

Volkswagen Concept 1 Cabriolet (see Volkswagen Concept 1 Convertible)

Volkswagen Concept 1 Convertible, #81, 2000; #1, 2001; #61, 2000, international; #73, 1999, Germany; #38, 2005
1. red with red trim on windshield, black interior, rubber tires on chrome rims, FAO Schwarz gift set .... $7 – 9
2. blue with no trim on windshield, light tan interior, 1999 Germany issue $9 – 12
3. blue with blue trim on windshield, light tan interior, 1999 Germany issue ......$5 – 6

4. metallic blue with cream interior .... $3 – 4

5. orange with black interior, 2004 Superfast #22 ....$3 – 4
6. white, "Coca-Cola," 5-pack .... $1 – 2
7. white with white trim on windshield, tan interior, 2000 Worldwide Wheels ..$1 – 2
8. white with white trim on windshield, tan interior, "Matchbox 2000," 2000 Worldwide Wheels .... $3 – 4
9. metallic silver with silver trim on windshield, "Beetle," 2001 Daddy's Dreams .... $1 – 2

10. metallic silver, "Coca-Cola" with bottle in red circle, red interior, Matchbox Collectibles Coca-Cola Collection ....$3 – 4

Volkswagen Concept 1 Police, #465, 2000

1. "D.A.R.E.," yellow with black hood and doors, 5-pack ....$1 – 2
2. "D.A.R.E. Bellevue Police," white and black, D.A.R.E. .... $4 – 5

3. "Police Parking Enforcement," white with black doors, seal, 2006 5-pack J4676 ....$1 – 2

Volkswagen Delivery Van, #72, 2000; #52, 2000, international; #31, 2006 (similar casting: Volkswagen Transporter)
1. yellow, "Custom Signs & Painting" graphics, 2007 #36 .... $1 – 2

2. yellow, "Matchbox Delivery Service," 2007 5-pack K9612 ....$1 – 2

3. green, "Georgia," Matchbox Across America 50th Birthday Series #4 Southern Collection ....$4 – 5

4. blue, "Spongebob," cartoon illustrations, yellow base, 2003 Nickelodeon Spongebob Squarepants 5-pack ....$1 – 2
5. metallic light blue, "TNT Tours," motorcycle design, 2000 On Tour .... $1 – 2
6. metallic light blue, "TNT Tours," motorcycle design, "Matchbox 2000," 2000 On Tour ....$3 – 4
7. metallic blue with blue, yellow and black fish design, 5-pack ....$1 – 2
8. white, "All You Need To Know About Matchbox...," "Shabbir's Matchbox Website 5th Anniversary," Color Comp promotional ....$25 – 35
9. white, "Coca-Cola Sign Of Good Taste," red roof, Avon Two-Pack ....$6 – 8
10. white, "Farewell Vaarwell Wiedersehen 2000," "Welcom Welkom Willkommen 2001," "Matchbox Forum 2000 – 2001," Color Comp promotional ....$20 – 30
11. white, "Flashback Toys & Collectibles," Color Comp promotional ... $35 – 45
12. white, "Iron City Beer," Color Comp promotional ....$35 – 45
13. white, "Manawatu Model Diecast Collectors New Zealand 2001," Color Comp promotional ....$20 – 30
14. white, "MICA Goes To Hershey 2001," "Friday June 22 2001," Color Comp promotional ....$20 – 30
15. white, "MICA Goes To Hershey 2001," "Saturday June 23 2001," Color Comp promotional ....$20 – 30
16. white, "MICA Goes To Hershey 2001," "Sunday June 24 2001," Color Comp promotional ....$20 – 30
17. white, "RCA," ASAP promotional ....$25 – 35
18. white, "Scooby-Doo Christmas," Color Comp promotional .... $80 – 120

19. white, "Tyler James Elliot Memoriam Model 1," Monarch butterfly and sky design, Color Comp promotional ....$35 – 45
20. white, "We've Scored 20th Anniversary Matchbox USA Convention," Color Comp promotional .... $16 – 24
21. white with chrome base, ASAP/Color Comp promotional blank ...... $35 – 45

22. beige with "Automotive Parts & Service" graphics, 2006 #31 .....$1 – 2

Volkswagen Golf with rack and surfboards, 2⁷/₈", #7, 1976
1. red with yellow interior .... $6 – 8
2. yellow with "ADAC" labels, roof light and antenna, no rack, Germany and Japan issue .... $40 – 50
3. yellow with red interior .... $6 – 8

4. metallic green with yellow interior ....$6 – 8
5. metallic green with red interior ..$9 – 12
6. black with red stripe graphics, no rack ....$6 – 8
7. black with red and orange stripe, "9" graphics, no rack, Dinky issue ...$9 – 12
8. metallic silver with red interior .. $4 – 6
9. metallic silver with tan interior ....$30 – 40
10. metallic silver with blue interior ....$300 – 400

Volkswagen Golf GTi, 2⁷/₈", #33, 1986; #56, 1986; #63, 1991
1. red, "Golf GTi" .... $3 – 4
2. white, "Federal Express" .... $4 – 5
3. white, "Quantum," UK issue ..... $6 – 8
4. dark gray, Two-Pack .... $3 – 4
5. yellow, "PTT," Swiss issue .... $9 – 12
6. white, "Abstract" and graphics, UK issue .... $4 – 5
7. white, "Lippische Landes-Zeitung," Germany issue .... $16 – 24

Volkswagen Golf GTI, 2006, Superfast #35, 2007
1. white, 2007 Superfast #35 ..... $3 – 4

Volkswagen Golf V GTI, #1, 2006; #5, 2007

1. red, 2006 #1 ....$1 – 2

2. black, 2007 #5, K9465 ....$1 – 2
3. metallic gold .... $1 – 2

Volkswagen Rabbit (see Volkswagen Golf)

Volkswagen Lady Bug

Volkswagen Microbus, #72, 2002; #54, 2003; Superfast #31, 2004; #51, 2005

1. metallic two-tone light blue, no markings, 2002 Kids' Cars of the Year .... $1 – 2

2. metallic blue, "Hero City Elementary," 2003 School Time #54 ..$1 – 2

3. metallic red and silver, 2004 Superfast ....$4 – 5

4. metallic light blue with gray, silver and light blue trim, 2005 #51 ....$1 – 2

5. pearl white with light blue panels, dark blue accents, 2003 Hero City 5-pack #11 ....$1 – 2

Volkswagen Panel Transporter (see Volkswagen Delivery Van)

Volkswagen Rompin' Rabbit 4x4, 2⁷/₈", #7, 1982
1. white with "Rompin' Rabbit" ...... $6 – 8
2. yellow with "Ruff Rabbit" .... $4 – 5

Volkswagen Ruff Rabbit 4x4, 2⁷/₈", #7, 1983 (also Rompin' Rabbit)

1. yellow with black rabbits, "Ruff Rabbit" on sides ....$3 – 5

Volkswagen Taxi/Mexican Volkswagen Taxi, #44, 2004 (see Volkswagon Beetle Taxi)
1. green lower, white upper body, 2004 #44 .... $3 – 4
2. yellow, checkerboard pattern, 2005 10-pack #2 .... $2 – 3

Volkswagen Transporter/Ambulance Vanagon, 2⁷/₈", #20, 1986, international
1. white with ambulance markings and roof lights .... $3 – 5
2. black with green cross, "LS2081," Commando .... $4 – 6
3. white with no markings, Graffic Traffic ....$12 – 16

Volkswagen Transporter Microbus, 1967, #64, 1999; #57, 2000; #12, 2001; #59, 1999, international; #52, 2000, international (similar casting: Volkswagen Delivery Van)

1. **red and white, "We Have Visitors," "They Are Here," 1999 Science Fiction US .... $1 – 2**
2. red and white with black and white illustrations, 1999 Science Fiction international .... $3 – 4

3. **green, blue windows with curtains, 2002 Wilderness Tours 5-pack .... $1 – 2**
4. lime green, "Scooby-Doo," "Zoinks," "Shaggy," orange-yellow interior, clear windows, Warner Bros. .... $6 – 8
5. light sea green and white with gray interior, clear windows, "Coca-Cola," rubber tires on chrome rims, Premiere Collection .... $5 – 6
6. light sea green and white with gray interior, clear windows, "Coca-Cola" and "www.cocacolastore.com," rubber tires on chrome rims, Color Comp promotional .... $60 – 80
7. metallic blue, "TNT," 2001 World Tour international .... $3 – 4
8. turquoise and white, detailed trim, rubber tires on chrome rims, FAO Schwarz multipack .... $5 – 6

9. **turquoise, dark blue and white with red, blue, and white stripes, orange interior, "VW Transporter," 2001 Highway Heroes .... $1 – 2**

10. **blue lower with white upper, Superfast #17, 2006 .... $3 – 4**

11. **black, "Richie's Pizzeria," red interior, 2000 Speedy Delivery ..... $1 – 2**
12. black, "Richie's Pizzeria," "Matchbox 2000," red interior, 2000 Speedy Delivery .... $3 – 4
13. black, "Action Radar," "Xtreme Mission," gray interior, tinted windows, 5-pack .... $1 – 2

14. **white with red, yellow and teal bicycle and sun design, aqua interior, teal base, yellow windows, 2003 5-pack #10 .... $1 – 2**

Volkswagen Van, blue "Matchbox Express," 2¼", #34, 1957
1. metal wheels .... $45 – 55
2. gray plastic wheels .... $55 – 65
3. silver plastic wheels .... $80 – 100
4. black plastic wheels .... $125 – 150

Volkswagen W12 Concept, #57, 2005
1. metallic light bronze, 2005 #57 ... $1 – 2

2. **metallic red with butterscotch interior, "Baby Jaguar," 2006 Nickelodeon 5-pack H4108 .... $1 – 2**

3. **dark purple with black interior, 2007 5-pack K9615 .... $1 – 2**

Volvo 480ES, European model, 2⅞", #69, 1989
1. metallic pearl gray, "Volvo 480," green stripes, Laser Wheels .... $4 – 5
2. white, "480ES," gray metal base, Macau cast .... $3 – 4
3. white, "480ES," "Volvo," gray metal base, Macau cast .... $3 – 4
4. white, "480ES," "Volvo," gray plastic base, China cast .... $6 – 8
5. white, "480ES," "Volvo," gray plastic base, Macau cast .... $3 – 4
6. white, "Toys City" label on roof, gray metal base, Macau cast, Malaysian issue .... $80 – 120

Volvo 760 (European model), 3", #62, 1987
1. burgundy .... $8 – 10
2. purple, China cast .... $3 – 4
3. dark purple, China cast .... $3 – 4
4. metallic gray with detailed trim, rubber tires on chrome rims, Ultra Class .. $9 – 12
5. metallic dark gray, China cast ... $3 – 4
6. metallic pearl gray, Macau cast ... $3 – 4
7. white, China cast, Graffic Traffic .. $12 – 16

Volvo Aquarium Truck, with accessories, #389, 1998
1. blue-green with dolphin and waves design .... $4 – 5

Volvo C30, #4, 2007
1. metallic light blue .... $1 – 2

Volvo Cable Truck, with two metallic gray cable spools on back, 3", #26, 1984
1. orange with black base, blue windows .... $20 – 25
2. orange with dark gray base, blue windows .... $20 – 25
3. orange with red base, blue windows .... $20 – 25
4. orange with red base, green windows .... $20 – 25
5. red with black base, blue windows .... $30 – 40
6. yellow with black base, blue windows .... $25 – 30

Volvo Container Truck, 3$^{1}/_{16}$", #20, 1986; #23, 1985; #62, 1990; #44, 1998; #1, 1998, international
1. red with blue container, "Matchbox" with red arrow, international issue ... $1 – 2
2. red with brown container, "Merkur Kaffee" labels, Swiss issue .... $10 – 12
3. red with red container, "Coca-Cola" with polar bears, tinted windows ... $12 – 16
4. red with red container, "Coca-Cola" with polar bears, blue windows ... $30 – 45
5. red with red container, "Coca-Cola" with polar bears, amber windows ... $30 – 45
6. red with orange container, "Coca-Cola" with polar bears, tinted windows .... $80 – 120

7. **red with white container, "Big Top Circus" .... $1 – 2**
8. red with white container, "Denner," Swiss issue .... $10 – 12

9. red with yellow container, "Matchbox Animals" with dinosaur illustration, 1998 Animals .... $1 - 2

10. orange with orange container, "Allied Van Lines," 1999 Speedy Delivery .... $1 - 2
11. orange with orange container, "Allied," "Pickfords" .... $1 - 2
12. orange with orange container, "Enjoy Fanta," China issue .... $160 - 240
13. orange with orange container, "Polar Power," White Rose gift set ..... $4 - 5

14. orange with yellow container, black design and "Matchbox" logo on doors, "Get in the Fast Lane" ... $1 - 2

15. orange with yellow container, no design or logo on doors, "Get In The Fast Lane" .... $1 - 2

16. orange with yellow container, "N.A.D.T.C.A." label on doors, "North American Diecast Toy Collectors Association Second Anniversary November 1995" label on container, custom issue .... $9 - 10

17. orange with yellow container, "Matchbox Collector Edgar M. Strauss" label on container, custom issue .... $12 - 16

18. yellow with yellow container, Action System," on-package offer .... $10 - 12
19. green with gray container, "Hikkoshi Semmon Center," Japan issue .... $12 - 16
20. green with white container, "M" and green stripes, Swiss issue ... $10 - 12
21. blue with blue container, "Allders," UK issue .... $7 - 9
22. blue with blue container, "Comma Performance Motor Oils," UK on-package offer .... $8 - 10
23. blue with blue container, "Crooke's Healthcare" .... $7 - 9
24. blue with red container, "Christiansen," Belgium issue .... $10 - 12
25. blue with white container, "Big Top Circus," gift set .... $10 - 12
26. blue with white container, "Coldfresh" labels .... $4 - 5
27. blue with white container, "MB1-75 #1 in Volume Sales," UK issue .. $40 - 50
28. blue with white container, "Unic" .. $10 - 12
29. blue with white container, "Kellogg's," "Milch-Lait-Latte," Switzerland-Germany issue .... $40 - 50

30. blue with yellow container, "Airways Air Cargo," 5-pack .... $1 - 2

31. turquoise with black container, "Matchbox Auto Products," 5-pack .... $1 - 2

32. turquoise with black container, "Matchbox Auto Products," Corvette illustration, 5-pack .... $1 - 2
33. purple with purple container, "Continental Aero" .... $10 - 12

34. black with black container, "Cool Paint Co.," 1993 .... $1 - 2

35. black with yellow container, "Matchbox Auto Products," 1997 ... $1 - 2

36. gray with gray container, "Supersaver Drugstores" .... $9 - 12
37. white and red with white container, "Auto Palace" .... $6 - 8
38. white with blue container, "The Matchbox Times," 1998 Around Town 5-Pack .... $1 - 2
39. white with light blue container, "Co-Op People Who Care," UK issue .... $7 - 9
40. white with light blue container, "99 Tea," UK on-package offer .... $8 - 10

41. white with ivory container, "Federal Express" on container .... $3 - 4

42. white with white container, "Automotive Distributing Company," ASAP promotional .... $60 - 80
43. white with white container, "Bill Cairns — Let Bill Move You," ASAP promotional .... $25 - 50
44. white with white container, "Bulldog Castor Co.," ASAP promotional .... $30 - 40
45. white with white container, "Cendant Mobility," "We treat each move like it's our own," ASAP promotional ... $60 - 80
46. white with white container, "Certainteed," "Synergy," ASAP promotional .... $50 - 75
47. white with white container, "Certainteed HVAC Insulation Products," ASAP promotional .... $80 - 120
48. white with white container, "CFU" in red on right side only, ASAP promotional .... $30 - 45
49. white with white container, "CFU" in blue on right side only, ASAP promotional .... $60 - 80
50. white with white container, "Cookman Accounting Services," ASAP promotional .... $24 - 32
51. white with white container, "Dupont Answers," ASAP promotional .. $60 - 80
52. white with white container, "Dupont Floor Covering," ASAP promotional .... $60 - 80
53. with white container, "Dupont Floor Finishes," ASAP promotional .... $50 - 75
54. white with white container, "e-cycled.com," ASAP promotional ..... $60 - 80
55. white with white container, "Family Trust," Canadian issue .... $10 - 12
56. white with white container, "Federal Express" on container .... $4 - 5
57. white with white container, "Federal 57" on container, "XP Parcels" on doors .... $16 - 24
58. white with white container, "Federated Realty Group Inc.," ASAP promotional .... $45 - 65
59. white with white container, "Harty Press," ASAP promotional .. $125 - 175
60. white with white container, "Hi-Speed," "Garvens," ASAP promotional .. $40 - 50

61. white with white container, "Kellogg's," "Milch-Lait-Latte," Switzerland-Germany issue .... $40 – 50
62. white with white container, "Kit Kat," UK issue .... $30 – 40
63. white with white container, "Kuthasta Investment Supplies Group," ASAP promotional .... $30 – 40
64. white with white container, "Matchbox asi 33000," ASAP promotional .... $80 – 120
65. white with white container, "Nestle," ASAP promotional .... $30 – 40
66. white with white container, "Office Depot," ASAP promotional ... $30 – 45
67. white with white container, "PC Van Go" on left side only, ASAP promotional .... $60 – 90
68. white with white container, "RCA," ASAP promotional .... $21 – 28
69. white with white container, "Scotch Corner" labels .... $9 – 12
70. white with white container, "TNT Ipec," Team Convoy .... $4 – 6
71. white with white container, "Transply, Inc.," ASAP promotional ...... $60 – 80
72. white with white container, "Two Men and a Truck," ASAP promotional .... $12 – 16
73. white with white container, "UNIC" .$8 – 10
74. white with white container, "XP Parcels" ....$5 – 7
75. white with white container, "Yorkie" .... $30 – 40
76. white with white container, no markings, ASAP promotional blank ...... $16 – 24

77. metallic gold with black container, no labels, 1997 75 Challenge .. $6 – 12

Volvo Covered Tilt Truck, 3", #26, 1984, international; #49, 1990, US; #4, 1999, international
1. army green with tan canopy, "LS2020," Commando .... $16 – 24
2. black with dark gray canopy, "LS1506," Commando .... $16 – 24
3. blue with blue canopy, "Henniez," Swiss issue .... $10 – 12
4. dark blue with yellow canopy, "Michelin" .... $1 – 2
5. metallic blue with yellow canopy, no markings, England cast .... $24 – 36
6. metallic blue with yellow canopy, "Fresh Fruit Co.," England cast .... $4 – 5
7. metallic blue with yellow canopy, "Fresh Fruit Co.," Macau cast .... $3 – 4
8. pumpkin orange with turquoise canopy, apple design, 1998 Farming international .... $1 – 2
9. pumpkin orange with no canopy, "www.matchboxclub.de," Germany promotional .... $30 – 40
10. red with green canopy, yellow wheels, Live 'N Learn/Matchbox Preschool ....$7 – 8
11. red with no canopy, "123" on doors, Live 'N Learn/Matchbox Preschool ... $7 – 8
12. red with white canopy, "Big Top Circus," Adventure 2000 .... $3 – 4
13. white with white canopy, "Federal Express" .... $3 – 4
14. white with white canopy, "Pirelli Gripping Stuff" .... $1 – 2
15. yellow with yellow canopy, "Ferrymasters Groupage" .... $3 – 4

Volvo Stake Truck, #315, 1997
1. blue, "MB Builders," wall frame payload, Action Pack .... $4 – 5
2. blue, no markings, straw bale payload, Action Pack .... $4 – 5

Volvo Tilt Truck (see Volvo Covered Tilt Truck)

Volvo XC90, #55, 2005; #60, 2006

1. metallic silver, 2005 #55..... $1 – 2

2. metallic red, 2006 #60 .... $1 – 2
3. gray, 2007 #24 .... $1 – 2

Volvo Zoo Truck, 3", #35, 1982, international
1. red with blue cage, yellow lions ..$20 – 25
2. red with gray cage, tan or brown lions ....$20 – 25
3. red with gray cage, white lions.. $30 – 40
4. orange with gray cage, tan or yellow lions .... $20 – 25

VW (see Volkswagen)

W

Wall Eater (see Demolition Machine)

Watercraft with Trailer, #51, 1999; #46, 1999, international; #8, 2000

1. teal blue hull, white deck, red seat and handlebars, yellow trailer, 2003 Hero City 5-pack #10 ....$1 – 2
2. white hull with turquoise and purple design, turquoise deck, purple seat and handlebars, purple trailer, 1999 Beach series (US), 1999 Seaside series (international) .... $1 – 2

3. white hull with orange and blue design, orange deck, blue seat and handlebars, blue trailer, 2000 Ocean Explorer ....$1 – 2
4. white hull with orange and blue design. orange deck, blue seat and handlebars, blue trailer, "Matchbox 2000," 2000 Ocean Explorer .... $3 – 4
5. white hull with yellow stripe, red deck, black seat and handlebars, black trailer, 2000 Ocean Dock 5-pack ....$1 – 2
6. white hull with purple and blue octopus design, yellow deck, black seat and handlebars, gray trailer, 5-pack ..... $1 – 2

Water Cannon Fire Truck, #45, 2006 (see Airport Fire Tanker)

Water Pumper (see Fire Water Pumper)

Wave King Speedboat and Skier, #41, 1999; #24, 2001; #36, 1999, international
1. yellow deck, white hull, two-tone blue design, blue driver and skier, 1999 Ocean .... $1 – 2
2. blue-gray deck, black hull, maroon and white design, yellow driver, no skier, 5-pack .... $1 – 2

3. turquoise deck; white hull; blue, purple, and orange design; purple interior; 2001 Sun Chasers ....$1 – 2

Weasel Armored Vehicle, 2⅞", #73, 1974; Military Tank, #70, 1993; #77, 1996 error package
1. green with black and brown camouflage, Thailand cast, 5-pack .... $1 – 2
2. olive green, "M-3173," star, black hubs, Thailand cast, packaged as #73 ..$3 – 4
3. olive green, "M-3173," star, black hubs, Thailand cast, packaged as #77 ..$3 – 4
4. olive green, black hubs, England cast, Two-Pack .... $7 – 9

5. olive green with tan and black camouflage, black hubs, Macau cast, Commando .... $5 – 6
6. olive green, silver hubs, England cast, Two-Pack .... $7 – 9
7. dark army green, black hubs, Two-Pack .... $70 – 90
8. metallic green, England cast, silver hubs .... $5 – 6
9. black with yellow and gray camouflage, Macau cast, Commando .... $5 – 6
10. beige with brown, black and white camouflage, black hubs, China cast .. $1 – 2
11. beige with brown, black and white camouflage, black hubs, Thailand cast .... $1 – 2

12. khaki with brown and green camouflage, 1995 Military 5-pack .. $1 – 2
13. army green, 1996 .... $1 – 2

Weather Radar Truck, 3", #66, 2001; #43, 2002; #35, 2003; #67, 2004; #15, 2005
1. metallic dark red with blue tinted windows, metallic gray radar, 2001 Storm Watch .... $1 – 2

2. metallic gray with smoke tinted windows, red radar, 2002 Airport Alarm .... $1 – 2

3. black with blue tinted windows, blue radar, 2003 Airport .... $1 – 2
4. black with blue tinted windows, blue radar, 2003 Hero City 10-pack #2 .... $1 – 2
5. pale gray-green, "Satellite Radar," detailed graphics, 2003 Matchbox Heroes .... $3 – 4
6. dark olive green, 2005 #15 .... $1 – 2

7. white with gray camouflage, Battle Kings Polar Rescue set, 2006, K5537 .... $1 – 2

Weatherhill (see Weatherill)

Weatherill Hydraulic Excavator, yellow, 2³/₈", #24, 1956
1. orange with metal wheels .... $60 – 80
2. yellow with metal wheels .... $80 – 100

Weatherill Hydraulic Excavator, 2⁵/₈", #24, 1959
1. yellow with gray plastic wheels .... $30 – 40
2. yellow with black plastic wheels .... $20 – 30

Web Wheeler, spider motorcycle, #14, 2004 (MB650)
1. 2004 Ultra Heroes .... $3 – 4

Whistle Car, #1, 2004 (MB617)

1. silver chrome with blue fenders, red windows .... $1 – 2

Whistle Wagon (see Whistle Car)

Whitewater Raft Boat, #59, 1999; #65, 2001; #54, 1999, international; #37, 2000, international; #14, 2001, international

1. red deck, white hull, "Beach Patrol S.C.U.B.A." graphics on yellow trailer, graphics, 2002 Sand Castle Rescue Team 5-pk .... $3 – 4
2. red deck, yellow hull, "Base 1," "A1697-935L," black trailer with "Base 1," 2001 Rescue series, UK issue .... $4 – 5

3. red deck, orange hull, turquoise engine, "Beach Patrol S.C.U.B.A." graphics on white trailer, 2003 Hero City 5-pack #5
4. orange deck, orange hull, "RNLI Lifeboats," blue trailer with "Lifeboats," "RNLI," UK issue .... $4 – 5
5. yellow deck, turquoise hull, "Water Rescue," black trailer, 2000 Rescue series, international issue .... $4 – 5
6. yellow deck, metallic blue hull, "River Research," lime trailer, Pleasant Books issue .... $6 – 8

7. blue deck, white hull, "Action Canyon," blue trailer, 1999 Wilderness Adventure .... $1 – 2
8. white deck, yellow hull, "Louisiana," Matchbox Across America 50th Birthday Collection #18 — Southern Collection .... $5 – 6

White Lightning, Roman Numeral III, 1978 (variation of #48 Pi-Eyed Piper, 1972 and #48 Red Rider 1982)
1. cream, Roman Numeral Limited Edition .... $9 – 12
2. white, Roman Numeral Limited Edition .... $9 – 12

Wildcat Dragster (see Ford Mustang Wildcat Dragster)

Wildlife Truck (see Ford Wildlife Truck)

Williams Honda F1 Grand Prix Racer, 3", #74, 1988; #14, 1989
1. white and light blue, "Goodyear," "Shell," "15" .... $3 – 5
2. red, "Fiat," "27," metal base .... $2 – 4
3. red, "Fiat," "27," plastic base ... $8 – 10
4. red, "Scotch," "Target" .... $3 – 5
5. yellow, "Pennzoil," "2" .... $3 – 5
6. yellow, "Pennzoil," "4" .... $3 – 5
7. dark orange and white, "Indy," "4" ... $3 – 5
8. chrome with no markings .... $16 – 24
9. blue, "Panasonic," "7" .... $3 – 5
10. white and blue, "Indy," "76" ...... $3 – 5
11. white and black, "Havoline," "Kmart," "6" .... $3 – 5
12. orange, lavender, and white, "Indy" .... $4 – 6

13. white and pink with blue spots, "7," 1994 .... $1 – 3

Williams Renault Formula Racer, 3⅛", #28, 1982; #16, 1984; #74, 1996; #61, 1998; #246, 1994, Nigel Mansell issue

1. red, "Ferrari 27 Pioneer," black airfoil, F1 issue .... $4 – 5
2. red, "Fiat 3," black "Pirelli" on airfoil .. $2 – 4
3. red, "Fiat 27," red airfoil, F1 issue .... $4 – 5
4. metallic red, Manaus cast, Brazil issue .... $40 – 50
5. orange, "MB Racing 1," dark blue airfoil .... $1 – 2

6. **yellow, "MB Racing 1," red airfoil, 1998 Motor Sports .... $1 – 2**
7. yellow, "Matchbox Racing Team," dark red "Goodyear" on airfoil .... $2 – 4
8. dark green, Manaus cast, Brazil issue .... $40 – 50
9. blue, "Renault Elf O" with red, white, and gold trim, F1 issue .... $4 – 5
10. blue, "Sasol 14," black airfoil, F1 issue .... $4 – 5
11. blue, "Sasol 14," blue airfoil, F1 issue .... $4 – 5
12. blue and white, "Cannon Williams O," white airfoil, F1 issue .... $4 – 5
13. blue and white, "Cannon Williams 5," white airfoil, Nigel Mansell issue .. $5 – 6
14. blue and white, "Renault Elf O," white airfoil, F1 issue .... $4 – 5
15. pale blue, Manaus cast, Brazil issue .... $40 – 50
16. black, "Liqui Moly 30," black airfoil, F1 issue .... $4 – 5
17. white, "Belterra," ASAP promotional issue .... $60 – 80
18. white, "Citrix CDN," ASAP promotional issue .... $60 – 80
19. white, "Comp USA," "SAP, $," ASAP promotional issue .... $30 – 40
20. white, "Footwork 9," white airfoil, F1 issue .... $4 – 5
21. white, "Hewlett Packard," "HP2000C," "From Fast to 4X Faster," ASAP promotional issue .... $80 – 120
22. white, "IBM Infinity," ASAP promotional issue .... $80 – 120
23. white, "IFS," ASAP promotional issue .... $60 – 80
24. white, "Indy 98 Rotary," ASAP promotional issue .... $60 – 80
25. white, "Loctite," "Hitachi 72," white airfoil, F1 issue .... $4 – 5
26. white, "MB Racing 1," dark blue airfoil .... $1 – 2

27. **white, "MB Racing 1," orange airfoil .... $1 – 2**
28. white, "Matchbox," "Goodyear," blue "Shell" on airfoil .... $3 – 5
29. white, "Mr. Juicy," "Sunkist," orange and green, yellow "Watson's" on airfoil .... $20 – 25
30. white, "Network Associates," ASAP promotional issue .... $60 – 80
31. white, "Protective," ASAP promotional issue .... $60 – 80
32. white, "RCA," ASAP promotional issue .... $25 – 35
33. white, "Site Smith," ASAP promotional issue .... $25 – 35
34. white, "STB," ASAP promotional issue .... $60 – 80
35. white, "Sun Microsystems," "Java," ASAP promotional issue .... $80 – 120
36. white, "Uliveto," "Lee Cooper," "Ford 9, white airfoil, F1 issue .... $4 – 5
37. white, "UR #1," "Sealed Air," ASAP promotional issue .... $60 – 80

38. **white, "White's Guide August 1999 Car of the Month #9" in black lettering, ASAP promotional issue .... $12 – 16**

39. **white, "White's Guide August 1999 Car of the Month #9" in red lettering, ASAP promotional issue .... $12 – 16**
40. white, four grasped hands logo, ASAP promotional issue .... $60 – 80
41. white, no markings, ASAP promotional blank .... $35 – 45
42. metallic tan, England cast .... $4 – 5
43. metallic tan, Macau cast .... $4 – 5
44. metallic tan, Manaus cast, Brazil issue .... $40 – 50
45. metallic gold with black airfoil, 1997 75 Challenge .... $6 – 12

Willys '33 Street Rod, 2$^{15}/_{16}$", #69, 1982

1. blue with orange and white flames, "313" on roof, pearl silver metal base, Macau cast .... $1 – 2
2. blue with red and white flames, "313" on roof, light gray metal base, Hong Kong cast .... $1 – 2

3. **blue with red and white flames, "313" on roof, black plastic base, China cast .... $1 – 2**
4. blue with red and white flames, "313" on roof, black plastic base, Macau cast .... $1 – 2
5. blue with red and white flames, "313" on roof, pearl silver metal base, Macau cast .... $1 – 2

6. **metallic blue with pink and white design, 1996 Hot Rods 5-pack .... $1 – 2**
7. turquoise with pink, purple, and white design, China cast .... $1 – 2

8. **turquoise with pink brush stroke on white band, 1997 American Street Machines 5-pack .... $1 – 2**
9. metallic turquoise with pink and white design, black plastic base, China cast .... $1 – 2
10. purple, "Bad to the Bone" and crossbones, black plastic base, China cast, Australia issue .... $4 – 5
11. black with pink and white design, black plastic base, China cast .... $6 – 8
12. black with red flames, "313" on roof, black plastic base, China cast, US on-package premium .... $8 – 10
13. white with orange flames, "313" on roof, metallic gray metal base, England cast .... $4 – 5
14. white with orange flames, "313" on roof, unpainted metal base, England cast .... $4 – 5
15. white with red flames, "313" on roof, unpainted metal base, England cast .... $4 – 5
16. white with red flames, "313" on roof, metallic gray metal base, England cast .... $4 – 5

17. pearl, "Grease" and silver flash, China cast, Star Cars .... $5 – 6
18. pearl with pink and yellow flames, "Pro Street," black plastic base, China cast, 1993 .... $1 – 2
19. pearl with pink and yellow flames, without "Pro Street," black plastic base, China cast .... $3 – 4

Wolseley 1500 sedan, 2 1/8", #57, 1958
1. pale yellow-green with gold grille ..$60 – 80
2. pale yellow-green with silver grille ..$40 – 50
3. pale green with silver grille ... $40 – 50
4. pale gray with silver grille ..$110 – 120

Woosh-N-Push, 2 7/8", #58, 1972
1. metallic red with light yellow interior, "2" label .... $16 – 24
2. magenta with light yellow interior, "2" label .... $16 – 24
3. magenta with light yellow interior, "8" label .... $16 – 24
4. yellow with red interior, flower label .... $16 – 24
5. yellow with red interior, "2" label .... $16 – 24

Wreck Truck, #1, 2005 (see Auto Medic)

Wreck Truck, #11, 2001; #16, 2003 (see King Tow)

Wreck Truck, #13, 1955 (see Bedford Wreck Truck)

Wreck Truck, #13, 1958 (see Bedford Wreck Truck)

Wreck Truck, #13, 1961 (see Ford Thames Trader Wreck Truck)

Wreck Truck, #13, 1965 (see Dodge Wreck Truck)

Wreck Truck, #21, 1987; #71, 1987; #72, 1989; #63, 1998; #14, 1999 (see GMC Wrecker)

Wreck Truck, #61, 1978 (see Ford Wreck Truck)

Wreck Truck, #61, 1982 (see Peterbilt Wreck Truck)

Wreck Truck, #71, 1968 (see Ford Heavy Wreck Truck)

Wreck Truck, #74, 1972 (see Toe Joe Wreck Truck)

Wrecker (see Auto Transport, Car Carrier, King Tow, Tow Truck, Wreck Truck, etc.)

X

X-33 RLV Reusable Launch Vehicle (see Lockheed Martin X-33 Reusable Launch Vehicle)

Y-Nossarus, dump truck with rhinoceros head, #16, 2004 (MB624)

1. **yellow with blue and red graphics, blue dumper, black base .... $1 – 2**

2. **yellow with orange to black graphics, black dumper, metallic gray base, 2004 Ultra Heroes .... $1 – 2**

Z

Z28 (see Chevrolet Camaro 1969 Z28)

Zamboni Ice Maker, #285, 1995, White Rose Collectibles
1. red lower, white upper, "White Rose Collectibles — No. 1 in Sports 1995" ..$90 – 120

Zoo Truck (see Volvo Zoo Truck)

NUMBERS

0-4-0 Steam Locomotive, England cast unless noted, 3", #43, 1978; #63, 1992
1. red, "4345" labels, England cast ..$5 – 6
2. red, "4345" labels, Macau cast, Motor City .... $4 – 5
3. red, "4345" labels, China cast ... $3 – 4
4. red, "NP" labels, England cast ...$9 – 12
5. red, white "North Yorkshire Moors Railway," Macau cast, UK issue ..... $7 – 9
6. red, white and black "North Yorkshire Moors Railway," Macau cast, Swiss issue .... $16 – 24
7. metallic red, "4345" labels, no origin cast, Brazil issue .... $160 – 240
8. yellow, "123," "456," China cast, Live 'N Learn/Matchbox Preschool ..... $7 – 9
9. yellow, "123," "efg," China cast, Live 'N Learn/Matchbox Preschool ..... $7 – 9
10. green, "4345" labels, England cast .... $9 – 12
11. green, "4345" labels, Macau cast, Motor City .... $4 – 5
12. green, "NP" labels, England cast ..$6 – 8
13. green, "British Railways," China cast, UK issue .... $3 – 4
14. green with red, black, and white "British Railways" printing, China cast, US issue ....$1 – 2
15. green with red and white "British Railways" printing, China cast, US issue ....$1 – 2
16. green, "British Railways," Macau cast, UK issue .... $8 – 10
17. green, "Kellogg's" rooster head, China cast, on-package premium, French, Dutch, UK issue .... $80 – 120
18. green, "West Somerset Railway," UK issue .... $6 – 8
19. green, white emblem, Macau cast .... $16 – 420
20. dark green, "GWR," Macau cast, UK issue .... $6 – 8
21. blue, "Hutchinson," Macau cast, UK issue .... $7 – 9
22. blue, red accents, Macau cast, UK issue .... $7 – 9
23. black, "British Railways," Macau cast, UK issue .... $7 – 9
24. white with no markings, China cast, Graffic Traffic .... $12 – 16
25. rust, "Gold Rush Australia," China cast, Australia issue .... $5 – 6

'33 Ford Coupe (see Ford 1933 Coupe)

'33 Ford Hot Rod (see Ford 1933 Coupe)

'33 Ford Street Rod (see Ford 1933 Coupe)

'33 Willys Street Rod (see Willys 1933 Coupe)

'56 Ford Pick-Up (see Ford Pick-Up 1956)

'57 Chevy Bel Air (see Chevrolet Bel Air 1957)

'57 Chevy Bel Air Convertible (see Chevrolet Bel Air Convertible 1957)

'57 Chevy Bel Air Hardtop (see Chevrolet Bel Air Hardtop 1957)

'57 Corvette Hardtop (see Chevrolet Corvette 1957 Hardtop)

'57 T-Bird (see Ford Thunderbird 1957)

'62 Corvette (see Chevrolet Corvette 1962)

'62 VW Beetle (see Volkswagen Beetle 1962)

'68 Cougar (see Mercury Cougar 1968)

'68 Mercury Cougar (see Mercury Cougar 1968)

'68 Mustang Cobra Jet (see Ford Mustang 1968 Cobra Jet)

'69 Camaro SS 396 (see Chevrolet Camaro 1969 SS 396)

'70 Boss Mustang (see Ford Mustang 1970 Boss Mustang)

'70 El Camino (see Chevrolet El Camino 1970)

'70 Pontiac GTO (see Pontiac 1970 GTO "The Judge")

'71 Camaro (see Chevrolet Camaro 1971)

'94 Camaro-28 (see Chevrolet Camaro 1994 Z-28)

'97 Chevy Tahoe (see Chevrolet Tahoe 1997)

'97 Corvette (see Chevrolet Corvette 1997)

'97 Firebird Formula (see Pontiac Firebird 1997 Formula)

'97 Firebird Ram Air (see Pontiac Firebird 1997 Ram Air)

'97 Ford F-150 (see Ford F-150 1997)

'97 Mercedes E Class (see Mercedes-Benz 1997 E Class)

'97 MGF (see MGF 1997)

'97 Land Rover Defender 110 (see Land Rover Defender 110, 1997)

'98 Jeep Wrangler (see Jeep Wrangler 1998)

'99 Camaro Convertible (see Chevrolet Camaro 1999 Convertible)

10-Ton Pressure Refueler (see RAF 10-Ton Pressure Refueling Tanker)

1921 Ford Model T Van (see Ford Model T 1921 Van)

1933 Ford Coupe (see Ford 1933 Coupe)

1933 Ford Hot Rod (see Ford 1933 Coupe)

1933 Ford Street Rod (see Ford 1933 Coupe)

1933 Willys Street Rod (see Willys Street Rod 1933)

1939 Chevrolet Sedan Delivery (see Chevrolet 1939 Sedan Delivery)

1956 Ford Pick-Up (see Ford F-100 1956)

1956 Ford Sunliner (see Ford Sunliner 1956)

1957 Ford Thunderbird (see Ford Thunderbird, 1957)

1957 Thunderbird (see Ford Thunderbird, 1957)

1961 Dodge Dart Phoenix (see Dodge Dart Phoenix 1961)

1963 Cadillac Hearse, #57, 2006 (see Cadillac Hearse 1963, #57, 2006)

1965 Shelby Cobra 427 S/C (see Shelby Cobra 427 S/C 1965)

1967 Volkswagen Transporter (see Volkswagen Transporter Microbus, 1967)

1968 Cougar (see Mercury Cougar 1968)

1968 Mercury Cougar (see Mercury Cougar 1968)

1969 Chevrolet Camaro SS 396 (see Chevrolet Camaro 1969 SS 396)

1969 Camaro Z28 (see Chevrolet Camaro 1969 Z28)

1970 Boss Mustang (see Ford Mustang 1970 Boss Mustang)

1970 Pontiac GTO (see Pontiac GTO 1970 "The Judge")

1984 Dodge Daytona Turbo Z (see Dodge Daytona 1984 Turbo Z)

1997 Land Rover Defender 110 (see Land Rover Defender 110, 1997)

1998 Jeep Wrangler (see Jeep Wrangler 1998)

1999 Ford Mustang Coupe (see Ford Mustang 1999 Coupe)

2000 Chevrolet Corvette (see Chevrolet Corvette 2000)

2000 Chevrolet Suburban (see Chevrolet Suburban 2000)

2005 Ford GT Concept (see Ford GT 2005 Concept)

2006 Cement Mixer (see Cement Mixer 2006)

2006 Dune Buggy (see Dune Buggy 2006)

2006 Ford Crown Victoria Police (see Ford Crown Victoria Police 2006)

2006 Ford Transit Van (see Ford Transit Van 2006)

2006 Mixer (see Cement Mixer 2006)

2½ Ton Truck, 2001 Feature Cars, with opening features, designed to replace Premiere Collection

1. dark tan with green, black, and white camouflage, dark olive green canopy ...$9 – 12

4x4 Buggy (see Beach 4x4)

4x4 Chevy Blazer Police (see Chevy Blazer Police 4x4)

4x4 Chevy Van (see Chevrolet Van 4x4)

4x4 Fire Crusher, #32, 2004 (see Fire Truck, 4x4)

4x4 Fire Truck (see Fire Truck, 4x4)

4x4 Golden Eagle Off-Road Jeep (see Jeep Eagle)

4x4 Desert Dawg Jeep (see Desert Dawg 4x4 Jeep)

4x4 Dunes Racer (see 4x4 Mini-Pickup)

4x4 Jeep (see Jeep 4x4, Jeep Off-Road 4x4)

4x4 Fire Truck (see Fire Truck 4x4)

4x4 Mini Pickup (see Mini-Pickup 4x4)

4x4 Off-Road Jeep (see Jeep Off-Road 4x4)

4x4 Open Back Truck (see Mini-Pickup 4x4)

4x4 Pickup Camper (see Pickup Camper 4x4)

4-Wheeler (see Four-Wheeler)

6-Wheel Quarry Truck (see Quarry Truck)

6-Wheel Crane Truck (see Magirus-Deutz Six-Wheel Crane Truck)

8-Wheel Crane Truck (see Eight-Wheel Crane Truck)

8-Wheel Tipper (see AEC Ergomatic Eight-Wheel Tipper)

2008 MATCHBOX 1 - 100 SERIES

Manufacturer numbers and serial number on package.

1. 68 Citroen DS, black, MB 735, M4380 ....$1 – 2
2. 69 Cadillac Sedan DeVille (NEW), MB 739 .... $1 – 2
3. '68 Mercury Cougar, red, MB 637, M5289 .... $1 – 2
4. '65 Alfa Romeo Giulia Sprint, MB 715 .... $1 – 2
5. '71 Chevelle SS Convertible, MB 610 .... $1 – 2
6. '61 Jaguar E-Type Coupe, MB 688 .... $1 – 2
7. '65 Austin Mini Van, MB 713B... $1 – 2
8. '70 Chevy El Camino, MB 328... $1 – 2
9. 2008 Chevy Corvette (NEW), MB 74 .... $1 – 2
10. 2008 Lotus (NEW), MB 750... $1 – 2
11. Shelby Cobra GT 500 Convertible (NEW), MB 744 .... $1 – 2
12. Morgan Aeromax (NEW), MB xxx .. $1 – 2
13. '65 Ford Mustang, MB 342 .... $1 – 2
14. Dodge Charger, metallic lime with black hood, MB 676, M5288........... $1 – 2
15. Lotus Exige, light blue, MB 706, M5290 .... $1 – 2
16. Ford F-150 Lightning, MB 663.. $1 – 2
17. Porsche 911 GT3, MB 729 ..... $1 – 2
18. Audi R 8, MB 726 .... $1 – 2
19. Porsche 911 Carrera Cabrio, MB 423 .... $1 – 2
20. Audi TT Roadster, MB 441 .... $1 – 2
21. Ford Mustang GT, MB 609...... $1 – 2
22. TVR Tuscan S, MB 595 .... $1 – 2
23. Nissan 350 Z, MB 611 .... $1 – 2
24. Dodge Viper GTS-R, MB 517 .... $1 – 2

25. Chevrolet Corvette Convertible, metallic gold with black interior, MB 515... $1 – 2
26. Future Honda (NEW), MB xxx.... $1 – 2
27. Mazda 2 (NEW), MB xxx .... $1 – 2
28. VW Golf GTi, MB 684............ $1 – 2
29. Smart Cabrio, MB 561 .... $1 – 2
30. Mitsubishi Eclipse, metallic purple, MB 668, M5303 .... $1 – 2
31. Scion xB, charcoal with orange and white design, MB 665, M5310.. $1 – 2
32. VW Beetle Convertible, MB 438 .. $1 – 2
33. Jaguar XK, metallic maroon, MB 692, M5286 .... $1 – 2
34. Mercedes-Benz CLS 500, MB 683 .... $1 – 2
35. Mercedes-Benz SL 55 AMG, MB 673 .... $1 – 2
36. Audi RS6 Avant, MB 696 .... $1 – 2
37. Lexus GS 430, MB 714.......... $1 – 2
38 Volvo C 30, MB 711B .... $1 – 2
39. Bentley Continental GT, MB 727... $1 – 2
40. Range Rover Sport, MB 691 ... $1 – 2
41. Lincoln Navigator, MB 645 ...... $1 – 2
42. Porsche Cayenne Turbo, MB 675 .... $1 – 2
43. Volvo XC 90, metallic blue, MB 674, M5312 .... $1 – 2
44. Cadillac Escalade, MB 567 ...... $1 – 2
45. Subaru Impreza Police (NEW), MB 751 .... $1 – 2
46. VW Caddy (NEW), MB 741 ..... $1 – 2
47. Garbage Truck (NEW), MB 742.. $1 – 2
48. Car Carrier, MB 708 .... $1 – 2
49. Chevy Van, white, "Water & Power," MB 709B .... $1 – 2
50. City Bus, MB 662 .... $1 – 2
51. GMC Wrecker, MB 188.......... $1 – 2
52. Austin FX4 Taxi, MB 667 .... $1 – 2
53. London Double Decker Bus, gold, MB 694, M5338 .... $1 – 2
54. DAF XF 95 Space Cab, MB 702B ... $1 – 2
55. Cadillac Hearse, MB 700 .... $1 – 2
56. VW Beetle Taxi, MB 578 .... $1 – 2
57. Quarry King (NEW), MB 737 ... $1 – 2
58. Scraper (NEW), MB 745 .... $1 – 2
59. Ground Breaker, MB 707 .... $1 – 2
60. Power Lift, dark green and black, MB 704, M5325 .... $1 – 2
61. Mercedes-Benz Unimog U300, MB 728 .... $1 – 2
62. 2006 Cement Mixer, MB 690 ... $1 – 2
63. Dirt Hauler, MB 710B .... $1 – 2
64. Ford F-100 Panel Van, orange (NEW), MB 733, M2634 .... $1 – 2
65. Tractor, MB 703 .... $1 – 2
66. Tractor Plow, MB 686 .... $1 – 2
67. Gas Tanker, MB 695 .... $1 – 2
68. International CXT, white with "Farm" graphics, MB 687, M5341 ..... $1 – 2
69. Highway Maintenance Truck, MB 652 .... $1 – 2
70. 2006 Ford Crown Victoria, MB 689 .... $1 – 2
71. Dodge Magnum Police, MB 680 .. $1 – 2
72. 2006 Ford Transit, MB 693 .... $1 – 2
73. Ladder Truck, MB 660 .... $1 – 2
74. Dennis Sabre, red with white and yellow stripes, MB 402, M5345 .... $1 – 2
75. Pierce Fire Engine (NEW) .... $1 – 2
76. '75 VW 181 (NEW), MB 738 .. $1 – 2
77. Motor Home Toy Box (NEW) .... $1 – 2
78. '75 Chevrolet Stepside (NEW), MB 736 .... $1 – 2
79. VW T2 Bus, orange (NEW), MB 734, M2633 .... $1 – 2
80. 2007 Honda Ridgeline, MB 705B .. $1 – 2
81. 2006 Dune Buggy, dark brown MB 685, M5352 .... $1 – 2
82. Jeep 4x4, light blue with black interior, MB 131, M5356 .... $1 – 2
83. Hummer H3, MB 666 .... $1 – 2
84. Jeep Rescue, MB 677 .... $1 – 2
85. Land Rover Discovery, MB 524 .. $1 – 2
86. Chevrolet Avalanche, MB 546 ... $1 – 2
87. Chevrolet Silverado SS, MB 672 .. $1 – 2
88. Rock Crawler II (NEW), MB 748 ... $1 – 2
89 '72 Ford Bronco 4x4, MB 720B .... $1 – 2
90. Baja Bandit, MB 731 .... $1 – 2
91. VW 4x4, MB 723 .... $1 – 2
92. Ridge Raider, MB 716 .... $1 – 2
93. Land Rover Defender 110, brown, "D.E.R. 22," MB 697, M5351 .. $1 – 2
94. Off-Road Rider, MB 699 .... $1 – 2
95. Jeep Hurricane, green-gold, MB 670 .... $1 – 2
96. GMC Terradyne, MB 555 .... $1 – 2
97. Chevrolet K-1500 Pickup, MB 249 .. $1 – 2
98. Desert Thunder V16, MB 712B .. $1 – 2
99. Jeep Wrangler, MB 369B .... $1 – 2
100. Hummer H2 SUV Concept, MB 526 .... $1 – 2

MATCHBOX CHARACTER TOYS

In 1979, Lesney established an agreement with Universal of Hong Kong to produce a series of toys based on Disney characters. It is interesting to note that Universal later purchased Matchbox from Lesney in 1982 and Dinky Toys shortly thereafter.

Disney Series 1979 – 1980

Donald Duck's Beach Buggy, WD-2, 1979
1. Hong Kong casting .... $25 – 30
2. Macau casting .... $65 – 80

Donald Duck's Ice Cream Truck, WD-11, 1980
1. Hong Kong casting .... $35 – 45
2. Macau casting .... $60 – 80

Donald Duck's Jeep, WD-6, 1979
1. white with white base, Hong Kong casting .... $25 – 35
2. white with black base, Macau casting .... $60 – 80

Goofy's Beetle, WD-3, 1979
1. Hong Kong casting with ears not connected at shoulders .... $80 – 100
2. Hong Kong casting with ears connected at shoulders .... $25 – 30
3. Macau casting with ears connected at shoulders .... $65 – 80

Goofy's Train, blue, WD-9, 1980
1. Hong Kong casting .... $35 – 45
2. Macau casting .... $60 – 80

Goofy's Train, red, WD-10, 1980
1. Hong Kong casting .... $60 – 80
2. Macau casting .... $70 – 90

Jiminy Cricket's Old Timer, WD-8, 1979
1. Hong Kong casting .... $35 – 45
2. Macau casting .... $60 – 80

Mickey Mouse Corvette, WD-12, 1980
1. Hong Kong casting .... $30 – 40
2. Macau casting .... $60 – 80

Mickey Mouse's Fire Engine, WD-21, 1979
1. Hong Kong casting, no casting to hold ladder .... $65 – 80
2. Hong Kong casting, with casting to hold ladder .... $25 – 30
3. Macau casting, with casting to hold ladder .... $65 – 80

Mickey Mouse's Jeep, WD-5, 1979
1. "MM" on hood, Hong Kong casting ... $30 – 40

2. **"Mickey's Mail Jeep" on hood, Hong Kong casting .... $25 – 35**
3. "Mickey's Mail Jeep" on hood, Macau casting .... $60 – 80

Minnie Mouse's Lincoln, WD-4, 1979

1. **Hong Kong casting .... $25 – 30**
2. Macau casting .... $65 – 80

Pinnochio's Traveling Theater, WD-7, 1979

Pinocchio's Traveling Theater, WD-7

1. **Hong Kong casting .... $35 – 45**

2. Macau casting .... $60 – 80

Popeye Series, King Features 1981

With the modest success of the Disney series, a follow-up offering featuring Popeye the Sailor Man characters was produced in 1982. Issues were designated CS, presumably for Cartoon Series, implying that later additions were being considered.

Bluto's Road Roller, CS-14, 1981 ...$35 – 45

Olive Oyl's Sports Car, CS-15, 1981 .. $35 – 45

Popeye's Spinach Wagon, CS-13, 1981 .... $35 – 45

Looney Tunes Series, Warner Brothers 1994

Most familiar of the character toy series from Matchbox is this offering from 1994, thanks to a limited licensing agreement obtained from Warner Brothers.

Bugs Bunny Mercedes Sauber Group C Racer, 1994 ....$4 – 5

Bugs Bunny Chevrolet Lumina Stock Car, 1994 ....$4 – 5

Daffy Duck 4x4 Pickup, 1994 .....$4 – 5

Road Runner Dodge Dragster, 1994 ..$4 – 5

Tasmanian Devil Sprint Racer, 1994 ..$4 – 5

Wile E. Coyote Chevrolet Lumina Stock Car, 1994 .... $4 – 5

Sesame Street 1998

Previously, Hasbro had the license to produce Sesame Street preschool toys. For 1998, Mattel issued 12 diecast-and-plastic models under the Tyco Preschool/Matchbox brand. Models are made in China, distributed by Mattel Australia Proprietary, Ltd., and sold (in the US) in sets of three for $5.99 or individually for $1.97 each. The 1999 models are packaged under the Fisher-Price brand, but on the base is printed either "Matchbox" or "Tyco." Some 1998 models are no more than repackaged models from the previous year. Altogether, 19 different models result from several vehicles with different drivers and color schemes.

Baby Bear's Buggy, lime green with orange roll bar and base, blue wheels ....$4 – 5

Bert's Tow Truck, lime green with blue boom, orange base, yellow wheels ....$4 – 5

Big Bird's Buggy, lime green with blue roll bar, orange base, yellow wheels ..$4 – 5

Big Bird's Fire Engine, red and white with yellow wheels ....$4 – 5

Big Bird's Mail Truck, red cab, white container, blue base and wheels ... $4 – 5

Cookie Monster's Airplane, white with yellow trim and propeller, red base, blue wheels .... $4 – 5

Cookie Monster's School Bus, yellow with blue base, red wheels .... $4 – 5

Elmo's Cement Mixer, blue and red with yellow base, silver barrel, red wheels .... $4 – 5

Elmo's Dump Truck .... $4 – 5

Elmo's Locomotive, blue with red smokestack and wheels, yellow trim ..$4 – 5

Elmo's Taxi, yellow with red base, blue wheels .... $4 – 5

Ernie's Cement Mixer, yellow with red barrel and wheels .... $4 – 5

Ernie's Dump Truck .... $4 – 5

Ernie's Police Car .... $4 – 5

Fozzie Bear's Dump Truck, blue with red dumper, yellow base, red wheels ...$4 – 5

Fozzie Bear's Police Car, white with black doors, orange base, blue wheels ..$4 – 5

Grover's Helicopter, red and yellow with blue skids, silver propeller and tailfin ....$4 – 5

Oscar the Grouch's Garbage Truck, silver with orange container, yellow base, lime green wheels .... $4 – 5

Telly's Front Loader, yellow with lime green scoop and wheels ....$4 – 5

Zoe's Convertible, red with yellow base, blue wheels .... $4 – 5

Star Cars Collection

Star Cars Series I, 1998:
1. #1 "Grease" '33 Willys .... $4 – 6
2. #2 "Taxi" Sunshine Cab Ford LTD ..$4 – 6
3. #3 "Brady Bunch" Mercury Sable Station Wagon .... $4 – 6
4. #4 "Happy Days" '56 Ford Pick-Up ....$4 – 6
5. #5 "MASH" 4077 Jeep CJ ...... $4 – 6
6. #6 "Mission: Impossible" Surveillance Van .... $4 – 6

Star Cars Series 2, 1998:
1. #7 "Magnum P.I." Ferrari 308 GTS ....$4 – 6
2. #8 "Miami Vice" Ferrari Testarossa Convertible .... $4 – 6
3. #9 "Jaws" Amity Police Launch with Shark .... $4 – 6
4. #10 "Animal House" '62 Corvette ....$4 – 6
5. #11 "Adam-12" Police Car ...... $4 – 6
6. #12 "Smokey & The Bandit" Pontiac Trans Am T-Roof .... $4 – 6

Star Cars Series 3, 1999:
1. #13 "Mork & Mindy" Jeep CJ .. $4 – 6
2. #14 "Laverne & Shirley" Shotz Brewery FJ Holden Panel Van .... $4 – 6
3. #15 "Knight Rider" Trans Am ... $4 – 6
4. #16 "The Untouchables" Ford Model T ....$4 – 6
5. #17 "American Graffiti" Hot Rod ...$4 – 6
6. #18 "Top Gun" Fighter Jet .... $4 – 6

Star Cars Character Cars:
1. Ace Ventura, Ford LTD Police Car, #96114 .... $10 – 14
2. Animal House, 1962 Chevrolet Corvette, #96112, 2000 .... $9 – 12
3. Fonzie, Harley-Davidson Motorcycle, #98111, 2000 .... $8 – 10
4. Frankenstein, Ford Model T Van, #96107, 2000 .... $9 – 12
5. Freddy Krueger, Chevrolet Van, #38247, 2000 .... $8 – 10
6. Gilligan, "S. S. Minnow" Police Launch, #96110, 2000 .... $8 – 10
7. I Dream of Jeannie, '69 Camaro, #96106, 2000 .... $8 – 10
8. Jason, Jeep Cherokee, #38248, 1999 ....$8 – 10
9. Leatherface, '56 Ford Pick-up, #92082, 2001 .... $10 – 14
10. Rocky, Pontiac Trans Am T-Roof, #96113, 2000 .... $9 – 12
11. The Mask, Ford LTD Police Car, #96109, 2000 .... $8 – 10
12. Wolfman, Ford Model A Van, #96108, 2000 .... $9 – 12

Thunderbirds

The *Thunderbirds* live-action movie released in theaters in 2004 recalled the animated adventures of the Tracy family and its secret high-tech "International Rescue" organization. The original 1960s children's television series was produced by Gerry Anderson, applying his trademark "Supermarionation" — animation using marionette puppets — and the show had high drama and spectacular special effects. Matchbox produced a series of Thunderbirds vehicles in 1992 to celebrate the TV show's re-release in Great Britain.

Thunderbird Vehicles and Sets:
1. International Rescue Set ..... $40 – 60
2. Lady Penelope's Fab 1, TB-005, 1992 .... $12 – 16
3. The Mole, #41785 .... $12 – 16

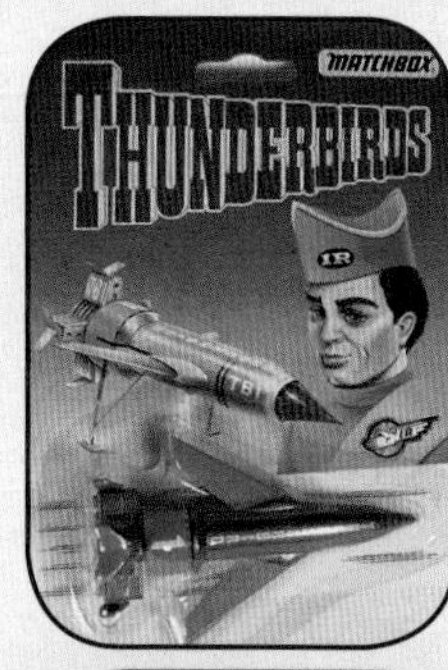

4. **Thunderbird 1, TB-001, 1992 ..$9 – 12**
5. Thunderbird 2 and 4, TB-002, 1992 .... $18 – 24
6. Thunderbird 3, TB-003, 1992 ..$9 – 12
7. Thunderbirds Gift Set by Vivid Imaginations of Canada, 1991 ...... $75 – 100
8. Thunderbirds Anniversary Set, 1996, gold plated .... $120 – 160
9. Tracy Island play set, #41720 ....$9 – 120

Thunderbirds Action Figures, 1994:
1. Alan Tracy .... $35 – 45
2. Gordon Tracy .... $35 – 45
3. Scott Tracy .... $35 – 40
4. Virgil Tracy .... $35 – 45

Stingray

After the success of the Thunderbirds vehicles and sets, Matchbox issued a series of Stingray vehicles and action figures from another of Gerry Anderson's '60s television action-adventure shows.

Stingray Vehicles and Play Sets:
1. Marineville Playset .... $60 – 80
2. Stingray Action Playset .... $40 – 50

3. Stingray and Terrorfish, #43200 .. $12 – 16

Stingray Action Figures:
1. Commander Shore .... $8 – 10
2. Marina .... $8 – 10
3. Phones .... $8 – 10
4. Titan .... $8 – 10
5. Troy Tempest .... $8 – 10

ACCESSORY PACKS

Occasionally, Matchbox offered items designated Accessory Packs, which included, at different times, service station accessories, road signs, buildings, a strange noisemaker, and one car transporter.

Brrroomstick (noisemaker), A3, 1971, packaged with 2 cars .... $8 – 12 (not including value of cars in package)

Car Transporter, A2, 1957
1. blue cab and trailer, black lettered decals, metal wheels .... $150 – 175
2. blue cab and trailer, orange-lettered decals, gray plastic wheels .. $150 – 175
3. blue cab and trailer, orange-lettered decals, black plastic wheels ....$200 – 250
4. red cab, gray trailer, orange-lettered decals, black plastic wheels ....$250 – 300

Garage, A3, 1957 .... $65 – 90

Home Store, A5, 1961 .... $70 – 90

Pumps and Sign, Esso, A1, 1957 ...$80 – 100

Pumps and Sign, BP, A1, 1963 .. $60 – 80

Roadsigns, A4, 1960 .... $60 – 80

Service Ramp, A1, 1970, ... $30 – 45

LARGER MATCHBOX MODELS

These include Kingsize, Speed Kings, Super Kings, Models of Yesteryear, Matchbox Collectibles, and the Dinky Collection from Matchbox.

AC Mack (see Mack Model AC Truck)

A.E.C. S-Type Omnibus, 1922, Models of Yesteryear Y-23, introduced in 1982; Matchbox Collectibles European Transports YET-05, introduced in 1996
1. "Haig," brown, Y-23 .... $18 – 24
2. "Kennedy's," green, YET-05 .. $24 – 32
3. "Lifebuoy Soap," blue, Y-23 .. $14 – 18
4. "Maples Furniture," red, Y-23 ...$18 – 24
5. "Rice Krispies," brown, Y-23 .. $18 – 24
6. "Schweppes Tonic Water," red with dark brown interior, red wheels, Y-23 ..$20 – 30
7. "Schweppes Tonic Water," red with light tan interior, red wheels, Y-23 ..$18 – 24
8. "The RAC," red, Y-23 .... $18 – 24

A.E.C. Y-Type Lorry, 1916, Models of Yesteryear Y-6, introduced in 1958
1. dark gray with black plastic wheels .... $1,250 – 1,400
2. dark gray with metal wheels ..$90 – 100
3. light gray with metal wheels ... $80 – 90

Ahrens-Fox N-S-4 Fire Engine, 1927, 7", Matchbox Collectibles Fire Engine Collection .... $30 – 40

Ahrens-Fox Quad Fire Engine, 1930, YSFE-01, Matchbox Collectibles Fire Engine Collection, introduced in 1994
1. red with wooden stand ...... $90 – 120

Aircraft Transporter (also see Scammell Aircraft Transporter, Army Aircraft Transporter)

Aircraft Transporter, 8", Kingsize K-13, 1976
1. metallic gray, white airplane with no labels .... $18 – 24
2. metallic gray, white airplane with stripes ....$18 – 24
3. red, white airplane with "X4" label .... $18 – 24
4. red, brown airplane with "12" label, white wings .... $20 – 30

Airport Fire Tender (see Airport Rescue Fire Tender)

Airport Rescue Fire Tender, $5^{5}/_{16}$", Kingsize K-75, 1980
1. yellow, "Airport Fire Tender" ... $14 – 18
2. yellow, "Securite Aeroport," France issue .... $60 – 80
3. yellow, "Flughafan-Feurwehr," Germany issue .... $40 – 60

Albion 6-Wheeler, 1938, Models of Yesteryear Y-42, introduced in 1991 .... $18 – 24

Allchin Traction Machine, 1926, Models of Yesteryear Y-1, introduced in 1956
1. diagonal red painted treads, copper boiler door .... $75 – 90
2. diagonal red painted treads, gold boiler door .... $75 – 90

3. diagonal unpainted treads, copper boiler door ....$90 – 100

4. diagonal unpainted treads, gold boiler door .... $85 – 100
5. diagonal unpainted treads, silver boiler door .... $125 – 150
6. straight unpainted treads, copper boiler door .... $125 – 150
7. smooth unpainted treads, gold boiler door .... $500 – 600

Allis-Chalmers Earth Scraper, $5^{7}/_{8}$", Kingsize K-6, 1961 .... $100 – 125

Ambulance, (also see DAF Ambulance) $4^{3}/_{8}$", Kingsize K-49, 1973
1. red with ivory roof, white interior, "Malteser," Germany issue .... $35 – 50
2. white with red roof, red interior, "Ambulance" .... $14 – 18
3. white with red roof, white interior, "Ambulance" .... $20 – 30

AMC Javelin (see Javelin AMX)

American General Locomotive, 1862, Models of Yesteryear Y-13, introduced in 1959

1. dark green ....$70 – 85
2. light green .... $300 – 350

AMX Javelin (see Javelin AMX)

Animal Transporter, $12^{5}/_{16}$", Kingsize K-8, 1980 .... $25 – 40

Armored Car Transporter, $7^{1}/_{2}$", Matchbox Military MM-2 (South Africa and Germany only), 1973 .... $16 – 20

Army Aircraft Transporter, 8", Battle Kings BK-114, 1977 .... $45 – 60

Army Ambulance (see DAF Ambulance)

Army Helicopter (see Kaman Seasprite Army Helicopter)

Army Petrol Tanker, 9", Battle Kings BK-115, 1977 .... $60 – 85

Army Tank (see M48A2 Tank, Chieftain Tank, King Tiger Tank)

Articulated Container Truck (see Scammell Articulated Container Truck

Articulated Horse Box (see Dodge Articulated Horse Box)

Articulated Petrol Tanker, 8", Matchbox Military MM-1 (South Africa and Germany only), 1973 ....$16

Articulated Tipper Truck, 8", Kingsize K-18, 1974
1. dark blue cab, "Hoch & Tief," Germany issue .... $50 – 70
2. metallic red cab .... $20 – 30
3. metallic silver cab .... $20 – 30
4. red cab .... $20 – 30
5. white cab, "Condor" .... $50 – 70
6. yellow cab .... $20 – 30

Aston-Martin DB4, 1960, DYB-06, introduced in 1998
1. metallic gray .... $24 – 32

Atkinson Logger, Matchbox Collectibles Steam-Powered Vehicles Collection .... $24 – 32

Atkinson Steam Wagon, 1918, Matchbox Collectibles Age of Steam YAS-10, introduced in 1997
1. "City of Westminster Works, Sewers & Highways" .... $30 – 45

Atkinson Steam Wagon, 1920, Models of Yesteryear Y-18, introduced in 1986; Matchbox Collectibles "Great Beers of the World" Collection YGB-03, YGB-22, introduced in 1996
1. "Beamish Special Stout Cork," YGB-22 .... $18 – 24
2. "Blue Circle Portland Cement," yellow, Y-18 .... $18 – 24
3. "Burghfield Mills Reading," red, Y-18 .... $18 – 24
4. "Sand & Gravel," green, Y-18 ..$20 – 30

5. "Swan Brewery Co. Ltd.," green, YGB-03 ....$18 – 24

Auburn 851 Boattail Speedster, 1933, Models of Yesteryear Y-19, introduced in 1980
1. khaki and beige with silver disc wheels, whitewall tires .... $20 – 30

2. khaki and beige with red disc wheels, whitewall tires ....$18 – 24
3. cream with red disc wheels ... $18 – 24
4. white with blue side accents, blue spoked wheels .... $20 – 30
5. beige and cream with chrome spoked wheels .... $20 – 30

Audi Quattro, Kingsize K-95, 1982

1. metallic blue .... $10 – 14
2. metallic gray .... $10 – 14
3. white, "Audi Sport" .... $12 – 16
4. white, "Pirelli," "Duckhams" .... $9 – 12

Austin/BMW/Rosengart Special Limited Edition Set: 1928 Austin, 1928 BMW Dixi, 1928 Rosengart, Models of Yesteryear Y-65, introduced in 1992 .... $50 – 60

Austin 7, 1959, introduced in 1997

1. red .... $24 – 32

Austin A40, 1953, The Dinky Collection DY-15, introduced in 1990
1. "Brooke Bond Tea," red .... $12 – 16
2. "Dinky Toys," yellow .... $12 – 16
3. "Matchbox at Rugby," yellow, approximately 50 produced .... $600 – 800

Austin Mini Cooper S, The Dinky Collection DY-21, introduced in 1991
1. cream with black roof .... $12 – 16

Austin Healy 100, 1956, The Dinky Collection DY-30, introduced in 1992; DYG-04, introduced in 1998
1. cream .... $24 – 32
2. dark green .... $18 – 24

Austin Van 4-Vehicle Christmas Treasures Set
1. YCC-01, introduced in 1994 ...$60 – 80 boxed set
2. YCC-02, introduced in 1995 ...$30 – 40 boxed set
3. YCC-03, introduced in 1996 ...$24 – 32 boxed set

Auto Tanker (see BP Auto Tanker)

Aveling Barford Tractor Shovel, $4^1/_8$", Kingsize K-10, 1963
1. blue-green, black plastic tires on silver metal hubs .... $90 – 120
2. blue-green, black plastic tires on red plastic hubs .... $90 – 120

Aveling Porter Steam Roller, 1920, approx. 3", Models of Yesteryear Y-11, introduced in 1958 .... $65 – 80

Aveling Porter Steam Roller, 1920, approx. 4", Models of Yesteryear Y-21, introduced in 1987
1. green with gray roof, inscription underneath roof .... $20 – 30
2. green with gray roof, no inscription underneath roof .... $275 – 325

B Type London Bus (see London Bus, 1911 B Type)

Bandalero, $4^1/_2$", Kingsize K-36, 1972 ...$14 – 18

Barracuda, $4^1/_4$", Kingsize K-51, 1973
1. blue .... $14 – 18
2. white .... $16 – 20

Bazooka, $4^3/_8$", Kingsize K-44, 1973
1. "Bazooka" labels .... $14 – 18
3. "Firestone" labels .... $16 – 20

Bedford Articulated Truck (see Bedford Ice Cream Truck)

Bedford Courier Car Transporter, $10^5/_{16}$", Kingsize K-10, 1981 .... $20 – 30

Bedford Emergency Van, Kingsize K-143, 1987 .... $9 – 12

Bedford Fire Tanker, YFE-04, Matchbox Collectibles Fire Engine Collection, introduced in 1995
1. red, "Belrose Volunteer Bush Fire Brigade," Australia issue .... $90 – 120
2. red, no markings .... $35 – 50

Bedford Fire Truck, 1939, Matchbox Collectibles Fire Engine Collection YFE-17, introduced in 1997
1. "City of Manchester," "Fire Brigade" .... $35 – 50

Bedford Ice Cream Truck, $4^5/_{16}$", Major Pack M-2, 1957
1. "Wall's Ice Cream," metal wheels .... $150 – 200

2. "Wall's Ice Cream," gray plastic wheels ....$150 – 200

Bedford KD Truck, 1939, Models of Yesteryear Y-63, introduced in 1992 .... $25 – 40

Bedford Pickup, Matchbox Collectibles "Great Beers of the World" Collection YGB-24, introduced in 1996
1. "Toohey's" .... $18 – 24

Bedford Tractor and York Trailer, $4^5/_8$", Major Pack M-2, 1961

1. "Davies Tyres," orange cab, orange trailer base and doors, gray plastic tires .... $475 – 525
2. "Davies Tyres," orange cab, orange trailer base and doors, black plastic tires .... $150 – 200
3. "LEP," silver cab, maroon trailer base and doors, black plastic tires .... $475 – 525
4. "LEP," silver cab, black trailer base and doors, black plastic tires ... $150 – 200
5. "LEP," silver cab, black trailer base, orange doors, black plastic tires .... $150 – 200

Bentley 4.5 Litre Supercharged, 1929, Models of Yesteryear Y-5, introduced in 1962
1. metallic green .... $40 – 60
2. metallic apple green .... $375 – 400
3. silver plated .... $60 – 70

Bentley 4.5 Litre Supercharged, 1930, Models of Yesteryear Y-2, introduced in 1984
1. dark blue .... $14 – 18

2. dark green .... $14 – 18
3. purple .... $18 – 24

Bentley LeMans, 1929, Models of Yesteryear Y-5, introduced in 1958
1. gray tonneau .... $150 – 175
2. green tonneau .... $65 – 80

Bentley R-Type Continental, 1955, the Dinky Collection DY-13, introduced in 1990

1. metallic dark blue .... $18 – 24
2. metallic light blue .... $12 – 16

Benz Fire Engine, 1912, Matchbox Collectibles Fire Engine Collection YFE-20, introduced in 1998 .... $35 – 50

Benz Limousine, 1910, Models of Yesteryear Y-3, introduced in 1966; Medallion Series YMS-02, introduced in 1996
1. cream with green roof, green seats and grille, high-cast headlights ... $40 – 60
2. cream with green roof, green seats and grille, low-cast headlights ..... $30 – 40
3. cream with green roof, red seats and grille, high-cast headlights ... $40 – 60
4. cream with pale lime green roof, green seats and grille .... $125 – 150
5. cream with pale lime green roof, red seats and grille .... $125 – 150
6. black with blue sides, black roof, brown grille .... $20 – 30
7. dark blue with gold pinstripe trim, YMS-02 .... $20 – 30

8. dark green with black roof, red grille .... $18 – 24
9. dark green with black roof, green grille .... $20 – 30
10. dark green with lime green roof ..$50 – 60
11. light green with black roof .... $20 – 30
12. light green with green roof ... $60 – 75
13. light green with pale lime green roof .... $30 – 45

Berlin Bus (see The Londoner)

Bertone Runabout, 4", Kingsize K-31, 1972
1. orange with green windows ...$14 – 18
2. orange with clear windows ... $16 – 20

Big Tipper, $4^{11}/_{16}$", Kingsize K-4, 1974 $15 – 20

Blaze Trailer Fire Chief's Car, 4," K-40, 1973 .... $14 – 18

BMW 507, 1957, Models of Yesteryear Y-21, introduced in 1988; Matchbox Collectibles Y-33, introduced in 1998
1. blue, Y-21 .... $20 – 30

2. beige, Y-33 .... $35 – 50

BMW 7-Series, Kingsize K-147, 1988
1. black .... $8 – 10
2. metallic gray, white and black interior, Ultra Class, China cast .... $16 – 20
3. metallic gray, black interior, China cast .... $8 – 10

4. metallic light blue, Macau cast ...$8 – 10
5. metallic light blue, China cast .. $8 – 10
6. red, China cast, Australia issue ..$20 – 30

BMW 7-Series Police Car, Kingsize K-154, 1988; Emergency EM-4, 1991 .... $9 – 12

BMW Motorcycle and Rider, $4^{5}/_{16}$", Kingsize K-82, 1981
1. metallic gray .... $14 – 18
2. black, "Polizei," Germany issue ...$20 – 30

BMW Police Car, Kingsize K-142, 1987 .... $9 – 12

Boat Transporter (see Power Boat and Transporter)

BP Auto Tanker, 4", Major Pack M-1, 1961

1. yellow and green with "BP" decals, black plastic tires .... $50 – 75

Brabham BT 44B, $4^{1}/_{4}$", Kingsize K-41, 1977; K-72 1980
1. red, "Martini-Brabham 7," K-41 ..$14 – 18
2. red, "Martini-Brabham 7," K-72 ..$14 – 18
3. blue-green, K-72 .... $15 – 20

Breakdown Tow Truck, 5", Kingsize K-11, 1976
1. red, "Falck Zonen," Switzerland issue ....$80 – 110
2. yellow, "AA" .... $14 – 18
3. yellow, "Shell Recovery" .... $14 – 18

Bridge Transporter, $13^{1}/_{8}$", Kingsize K-44, 1981 .... $120 – 150

Bugatti Type 35, 1923, Models of Yesteryear Y-6, introduced in 1961
1. blue with red dash and floor, black tires, gold grille .... $30 – 40
2. blue with red dash and floor, black tires, blue grille .... $75 – 85
3. blue with red dash and floor, gray tires .... $100 – 120
4. blue with white dash and floor .... $135 – 155

5. red with black dash and floor ..$135 – 150
6. red with white dash and floor ..$30 – 50

Bugatti Type 44, 1927, Models of Yesteryear Y-24, introduced in 1983
1. black with black interior, yellow accents .... $20 – 30

2. black with tan interior, red accents .... $18 – 24
3. black with tan interior, yellow accents .... $14 – 18
4. gray with tan interior, plum accents .... $20 – 30

Bugatti Type 51, 1932, Models of Yesteryear Y-11, introduced in 1987
1. blue .... $14 – 18

Bugatti Royale, 1930, Models of Yesteryear Y-45, introduced in 1991 ..... $18 – 24

Buick Skylark Convertible, 1953
1. light blue, the Dinky Collection DY-29, introduced in 1992 .... $18 – 24
2. light green, DYM-37798 ..... $40 – 50

3. pale yellow, DYG-04, introduced in 1996 .... $18 – 24

4. pale yellow, Matchbox Collectibles Oldies but Goodies I, issued 2004 ... $9 – 12

Buick Special, 1958; DYG-11, introduced in 1998; Matchbox Collectibles Oldies but Goodies II
1. metallic teal, DYG-11 .... $20 – 30
2. metallic teal, Oldies but Goodies II .... $9 – 12

Building Transporter, $5^3/_4$", Kingsize K-13, 1971 .... $20 – 30

Burrel Traction Engine, 1912, Matchbox Collectibles Age of Steam YAS-08, introduced in 1997 .... $25 – 40

Busch Steam Fire Engine, 1905, Models of Yesteryear Y-43, introduced in 1991; YSFE-03, Matchbox Collectibles Fire Engine Collection, introduced in 1996
1. Y-43 .... $50 – 60
2. YSFE-03 .... $60 – 70

Cadillac, 1913, Models of Yesteryear Y-6, introduced in 1967
1. gold plated .... $150 – 175
2. green .... $24 – 32

3. metallic gold, "1913" on base ...$20 – 30

4. metallic gold, "913" on base .. $50 – 60

5. silver plated .... $125 – 150

Cadillac 452 V-16, 1933, Models of Yesteryear Y-34, introduced in 1990; Matchbox Collectibles Cars of the Rich & Infamous DYM35181, introduced in 1999
1. dark blue .... $18 – 24
2. dark green .... $30 – 40
3. white .... $18 – 24

Cadillac Convertible, 1959, DYG-05, introduced in 1996
1. black .... $18 – 24

Cadillac Coupe DeVille, 1959, The Dinky Collection DY-7, introduced in 1989; Matchbox Collectibles Budweiser Sports Cars DYM-37597, introduced in 1999
1. "Coca-Cola," Matchbox Collectibles Coca-Cola Collection, 1:43 .... $12 – 18
2. black, Matchbox Collectibles Oldies but Goodies I .... $9 – 12
3. Golf, DYM-37597 .... $30 – 40
4. pale blue, DY-7 .... $20 – 30
5. pink, DY-7 .... $18 – 24

Cadillac Eldorado, 1953, DYG-13, introduced in 1998; Matchbox Collectibles Oldies but Goodies II, issued 2004
1. black with white roof, DYG-13 ..$20 – 30
2. black with white roof, Oldies but Goodies II .... $9 – 12

Cadillac Fire Engine, 1933, Models of Yesteryear
1. Y-61, introduced in 1992 .... $20 – 30

2. YFE-03, Matchbox Collectibles Fire Engine Collection, introduced in 1994 .... $25 – 30

Cadillac V-16 (see Cadillac 452 V-16)

Camaro (see Chevrolet Camaro)

Cambuster, $4^3/_8$", Kingsize K-43, 1973
1. yellow with black base, amber windows .... $14 – 18
2. yellow with black base, clear windows .... $14 – 18
3. yellow with black base, green windows .... $14 – 18
4. yellow with yellow base, amber windows .... $14 – 18
5. yellow with yellow base, green windows .... $14 – 18

Camping Cruiser Motor Coach, $4^3/_8$", Kingsize K-27, 1971
1. yellow with orange roof .... $14 – 18

Car Recovery Vehicle, Kingsize K-2, 1977
1. green, "Car Recovery" labels, with K-37 Sand Cat .... $20 – 30
2. green, "24 Hour" labels, with K-37 Sand Cat .... $20 – 30
3. metallic blue, "24 Hour" labels, with K-59 Ford Capri II .... $20 – 30
4. tan and white, "Race Haulage" labels, with K-60 Cobra Mustang .... $35 – 50
5. yellow, "im Auftrag des ADAC" labels, with K-48 Mercedes Benz 350 SLC, Germany issue .... $45 – 60

Car Transporter, $10^1/_2$", Kingsize K-10, 1976
1. "4" .... $25 – 40
2. "Auto Transport" .... $25 – 40
3. wild horse design .... $30 – 45

Cargo Hauler, $8^3/_4$", Kingsize K-33, 1978
1. blue, "Gauntlet" .... $20 – 30
2. blue, "US Steel" .... $20 – 30
3. yellow, "Gauntlet" .... $30 – 50
4. yellow, "K" .... $20 – 30
5. yellow, "MW" .... $20 – 30

Cargo Hauler and Pallet Loader, with K-15 Fork Lift, $7^1/_2$", Kingsize K-20, 1973 .... $20 – 30

Caterpillar Bulldozer, $3^5/_{16}$", Kingsize K-3, 1960 .... $65 – 90

Caterpillar Earth Scraper, $4^1/_2$", Major Pack M-1, 1957 .... $125 – 175

Caterpillar Traxcavator, $4^1/_8$", Kingsize K-8, 1970
1. yellow .... $25 – 40
2. silver-gray, Mexico issue ...... $65 – 90

Caterpillar Traxcavator Road Ripper, $5^1/_2$", Kingsize K-42, 1979; Construction CS-1, 1991
1. yellow with yellow metal shovel, black roof, England cast, K-42 ..... $18 – 24
2. yellow with yellow plastic shovel, black roof, England cast, K-42 ..... $14 – 18
3. yellow with red plastic shovel, red roof, China cast, CS-1 .... $14 – 18

Cement Mixer (see GMC Cement Mixer, Cement Truck)

Cement Truck, 4", Kingsize K-26, 1980
1. blue with red base, "Hoch & Tief," Germany issue .... $30 – 50

2. red with red base, "McAlpine" .. $20 – 30
3. yellow with black base, "McAlpine" .. $14 – 18
4. yellow with red base, "McAlpine" .. $18 – 24

Chevelle (see Chevrolet Chevelle)

Chevrolet 3100 Pickup, 1955, 4³/₈", Matchbox Collectibles Fabulous Fifties Road Service YRS-04, introduced in 1996; YIS-01, introduced in 1998

1. "Harley-Davidson Motorcycles," black, porcelain crates in back, Matchbox Collectibles YIS-01 .... $30 – 40
2. "Ray's Dixie Gasoline AAA Service," YRS-04 .... $30 – 40

Chevrolet 3100 Pickup, 1956, 4¹/₂", Matchbox Collectibles Fabulous Fifties Road Service YRS-03, introduced in 1996; YIS-03, introduced in 1998
1. "Chevrolet Motors," "Chevrolet Genuine Parts," blue with two porcelain engine blocks in back, YIS-03 .... $30 – 40
2. "Harris Bros. Mobilgas," dark blue with accessories in back, YRS-03 .. $30 – 40

Chevrolet 3100 Pickup, 1957, 4³/₈", YRS-05, YIS-04
1. turquoise with white top, Matchbox Collectibles '57 Chevys Collection, YRS-05 .... $25 – 35

2. "AA American Ground Service," white, porcelain luggage in back, YIS-04, introduced in 1998 .... $30 – 40

Chevrolet Bel Air, 1955, DYG-16, introduced in 1998; Matchbox Collectibles Oldies but Goodies II, issued 2004
1. red and cream, DYG-16 ...... $20 – 30
2. red and cream, Oldies but Goodies II .... $9 – 12

Chevrolet Bel Air, 1957, The Dinky Collection DY-2, introduced in 1989; DYG-02, introduced in 1996; Matchbox Collectibles '57 Chevys Collection; Budweiser Sports Cars DYM-37600, introduced in 1999; Oldies but Goodies I, issued 2004
1. black with flames, Matchbox Collectibles .... $12 – 16
2. Boxing, DYM-37600 .... $30 – 40
3. metallic lavender with white roof, '57 Chevys Collection .... $24 – 36
4. red with white roof, DY-2 ..... $18 – 24
5. red with white roof, DYG-02 .. $18 – 24
6. red with white roof, Oldies but Goodies I .... $9 – 12

Chevrolet Bel Air Convertible, 1957, the Dinky Collection DY-27, introduced in 1991
1. red, Matchbox Collectibles '57 Chevys .... $25 – 40
2. red and yellow, Matchbox Collectibles Coca-Cola Collection .... $12 – 18
3. sky blue with brown and blue interior, DY-27 .... $100 – 150
4. sky blue with cream and blue interior, DY-27 .... $20 – 30

Chevrolet Bel Air Nomad, 1957, Matchbox Collectibles '57 Chevys VCV-01, introduced in 1998
1. black with white roof .... $20 – 30

Chevrolet Camaro SS396, 1968, Matchbox Collectibles Muscle Cars YMC-06, 1997
1. black with red pinstripes, YMC-06 .... $30 – 40
2. black, "Coca-Cola — It's Twice Time" .... $30 – 40

Chevrolet Camaro Turbo, 4⁵/₈", Specials SP11/12, 1984; Kingsize K-10, 1989, Turbo Specials TS1, Muscle Cars, LA Wheels
1. black with orange and black stripes, chromed rims, Muscle Cars .. $8 – 10
2. red, "56," chromed rims, Specials SP12 .... $8 – 10
3. white, "7 Total," chromed rims, Specials SP12 .... $8 – 10
4. white, "7 Total," unchromed rims, Turbo Specials TS1 .... $8 – 10
5. white, "Firestone 4," unchromed rims, Turbo Specials TS1 .... $8 – 10

6. white, "Goodyear 18," chromed rims, Specials SP11 .... $8 – 10
7. white, "Michelin 3," chromed rims, Specials SP11 .... $8 – 10
8. white, "Michelin 3," unchromed rims, LA Wheels, Kingsize K-10 ..... $8 – 10
9. white with orange and black stripes, chromed rims, Muscle Cars .. $8 – 10
10. yellow, "7 Total," unchromed rims, LA Wheels, Kingsize K-10........... $8 – 10

Chevrolet Chevelle SS396, 1966, Matchbox Collectibles Muscle Cars YMC-08, introduced in 1998
1. metallic red .... $30 – 40

Chevrolet Chevelle SS454, 1970, Matchbox Collectibles Muscle Cars YMC-01, introduced in 1996
1. red, no markings .... $30 – 40
2. red, "Mattel Annual Operations Meeting 1998" .... $800 – 1000

Chevrolet Corvette, pewter, the Dinky Collection DY-923, introduced in 1992 .... $40 – 50

Chevrolet Corvette, 1956, the Dinky Collection DY-23, introduced in 1991; DYG-06, introduced in 1996; Matchbox Collectibles Oldies but Goodies I, issued 2004
1. black, DYG-06 .... $18 – 24
2. black, Oldies but Goodies I ..... $9 – 12
3. metallic copper, DY-23 .... $18 – 24
4. red, DY-23 .... $12 – 16

Chevrolet Corvette, 1957
1. white, Matchbox Collectibles '57 Chevys .... $25 – 40
2. baby blue with removable hardtop, Matchbox Collectibles Corvette Collection .... $20 – 30

Chevrolet Corvette, 1993 40th Anniversary Edition, burgundy, Matchbox Collectibles Corvette Collection . $20 – 30

Chevrolet Corvette, 1997, red, Matchbox Collectibles Corvette Collection .... $20 – 30

Chevrolet Corvette Convertible, 1953, white, Matchbox Collectibles Corvette Collection .... $20 – 30

Chevrolet Corvette Split Window Stingray, 1963, silver, Matchbox Collectibles Corvette Collection .... $20 – 30

Chevrolet Corvette Stingray Convertible, 1969, yellow, Matchbox Collectibles Corvette Collection .... $20 – 30

Chevrolet Corvette Caper Cart (see Corvette Caper Cart)

Chevrolet Impala, 1959, DYG-09, introduced in 1998; Matchbox Collectibles Oldies but Goodies II, issued 2004
1. white, DYG -09 .... $20 – 30

2. white, Oldies but Goodies II .... $9 – 12

Chevrolet Nomad (see Chevrolet Bel Air Nomad)

Chevrolet Model AK Half-Ton Pickup, 1941, YTC-01, introduced in 1999

1. **blue, no markings .... $30 – 40**

Chevrolet Pickup, 1955, 1:43 scale, 4¼"
1. "Budweiser," red and white, Matchbox Collectibles YVT-04, introduced in 1999 .... $30 – 40
2. "Chevrolet General Parts & Service," Matchbox Collectibles American Giants Collection .... $30 – 40
3. "Fred's Service," "Emergency AAA," red with accessories in back, Matchbox Collectibles Road Service YRS-01, introduced in 1996 .... $30 – 40
4. "Harley-Davidson," Matchbox Collectibles American Giants Collection .... $30 – 40
5. red with porcelain Christmas tree, Matchbox Collectibles Santa Claus Collection YSC-02, introduced in 1996 .... $50 – 70

Chevrolet Pickup, 1957, 1:43 scale, 4¼"
1. "American Airlines," Matchbox Collectibles American Giants Collection .... $30 – 40
2. "The Coca-Cola Bottling Company... It's The Real Thing," "Atlanta Bottling Co.," red, YPC-02, introduced in 1998 .... $30 – 40

Chieftain Tank, 4¾", Battle Kings BK-103, 1974 .... $35 – 50

Chrysler Town and Country, 1947, DYG-10, introduced in 1998; Matchbox Collectibles Oldies but Goodies II, issued 2004
1. tan with woodtone sides, DYG-10 .... $20 – 30
2. tan with woodtone sides, Oldies but Goodies II .... $9 – 12

Churchill Mk. IV, Matchbox Collectibles Great Tanks of World War II DYM-37584, issued 2000 .. $30 – 40

Citroen 15CV, 1952, The Dinky Collection DY-22, introduced in 1991
1. 1.black .... $12 – 16
2. 1.cream .... $12 – 16

Citroen 2CV, 1949, VEM-03, introduced in 1997

1. **metallic light gray .... $24 – 32**

Citroen 2CV, 1957, The Dinky Collection DY-32, introduced in 1992; Exclusive Editions DYM-36840, introduced in 1999
1. gray, DY-32 .... $18 – 24
2. yellow and black, DYM-36840 ..$40 – 50

Citroen H-Type Van, 1947, Matchbox Collectibles "Taste of France" Collection, introduced in 1993
1. "Brie Marcillat," cream, YTF-04 .... $18 – 24
2. "Brisbane International Motor Show," metallic gray with maroon roof .... $60 – 80
3. "Champagne Taittinger," metallic gray with maroon roof, YTF-05 .... $18 – 24
4. "Evian," pink, YTF-01 ...... $18 – 24
5. "Martell Cordon Bleu," cream and dark blue, YTF-02 .... $18 – 24
6. "Moutarde de Meaux Pommery," cream with red roof, YTF-06 .... $18 – 24
7. "Yoplait," white and lime green, YTF-03 .... $18 – 24

Citroen SM, 4½", Kingsize K-33, 1972 .... $14 – 18

Citroen SM Doctor's Emergency Car, 4½", Kingsize K-62, 1977 .. $14 – 18

Claas Matador Combine Harvester, 5½", Kingsize K-9, 1967

1. **green with no driver, green and white "Claas" label .... $40 – 60**
2. green with white driver, green and white "Claas" decal .... $40 – 60
3. green with white driver, green and white "Claas" label .... $40 – 60
4. red with tan driver, green and white "Claas" label .... $60 – 80
5. red with tan driver, red and white "Claas" decal .... $40 – 60
6. red with no driver, red and white "Claas" decal .... $40 – 60

Cobra Mustang (see Ford Cobra Mustang)

Command Force, set of four vehicles, Adventure 2000 K-2005, 1977 .... $65 – 90
Includes:
- #68 Cosmobile, 3"
- #59 Planet Scout, 3"
- #2 Hovercraft, 3"
- K-2004 Rocket Striker, 4⅜"

Commer 8-CWT Van, 1948, the Dinky Collection DY-8, introduced in 1989
1. "His Master's Voice," dark blue .... $12 – 16
2. "Sharp's Toffee," red .... $12 – 16

Construction Transporter, 6⅜", Kingsize K-36, 1978
1. with #26 Site Dumper and #29 Tractor Shovel .... $20 – 30
2. with #26 Site Dumper and #48 Sambron Jacklift .... $20 – 30
3. with Superkings Mercury, lime green......................... $25 – 40

Container Truck (see Scammell Container Truck)

Cooper-Jarrett Interstate Double Freighter with Hendrickson Relay Tractor, 11⅛", Major Pack M9, 1962
1. gray trailers .... $175 – 225

2. **silver trailers .... $175 – 225**

Cord 812, 1937, Models of Yesteryear Y-18, introduced in 1979; Matchbox Collectibles Cars of the Rich & Infamous DYM-35178, introduced in 1999
1. dark blue, DYM35178........ $30 – 40
2. metallic red with white roof, silver disc wheels, Y-18 .... $18 – 24
3. metallic red with white roof, silver spoked wheels, Y-18........... $20 – 30
4. plum with white roof, chrome spoked wheels, Y-18 .... $30 – 40
5. yellow with tan roof, chrome spoked wheels, Y-18 .... $20 – 30

Corvette Caper Cart, 4¼", Kingsize K-55, 1975
1. dark blue .... $14 – 18
2. light blue.......................... $18 – 24
3. metallic orange................. $14 – 18

Corvette Power Boat Set, 10⅛", Kingsize K-58, 1975 (K-55 Corvette Caper Cart with K-25 Seaburst Power Boat and Trailer)............................ $30 – 40

Crane Truck (see Mobile Crane, Military Crane Truck)

Crescent Limited Locomotive and Coal Tender on wooden stand with two track sections, YSL-001, introduced in 1994 (made by Mantua) .... $200 – 250

Crossley, 1918, Models of Yesteryear Y-13, introduced in 1973

1. **blue-gray with tan roof and canopy, "RAF" .... $60 – 75**
2. blue-gray with olive roof and canopy, "RAF" .... $70 – 85
3. blue-gray with black roof and canopy, "RAF" .... $275 – 325
4. cream with green roof and canopy, "Carlsberg" .... $18 – 24

5. **dark green with cream roof and canopy, "Waring's" .... $20 – 30**
6. gold plated with black roof and canopy, cross labels .... $50 – 60
7. gold plated with black roof and coal load, "Coal and Coke" .... $50 – 60
8. red with black roof and coal load, "Coal and Coke" .... $18 – 24
9. yellow with black roof and coal load, "Kohle & Koks" .... $18 – 24

Crossley Beer Lorry, 1918, Models of Yesteryear Y-26, introduced in 1984

1. "Gonzales Byass," white with maroon canopy .... $18 – 24

2. **"Lowenbrau," light blue with tan canopy, brown barrels .... $18 – 24**
3. "Romford Brewery," black with black canopy, dark brown barrels... $18 – 24

Crusader Tank, 4³/₈", Adventure 2000 K-2003, 1977 .... $40 – 65

Cuda 440 6-Pack, 1971 (see Plymouth 'Cuda 440 6-Pack)

Curtiss-Wright Rear Dumper, 5³/₄", King Size K-7, 1961 .... $100 – 125

DAF 3300 Space Cab, 7³/₄", tractor tanker trailer, Matchbox Collectibles Official Gas Tankers Collection

1. "British Petroleum" .... $18 – 24

DAF Aircraft Transporter, Kingsize K-128, 1986

1. red, light brown jet plane, Macau cast .... $16 – 20
2. red, metallic gray airplane with red pontoons, China cast, Great Britain issue .... $40 – 60

DAF Ambulance, 3³/₄", Battle Kings BK-112, 1977 .... $40 – 65

DAF Car Transporter, 9", Kingsize K-11, 1969

1. metallic blue with gold trailer, black plastic tires...... $90 – 120
2. yellow with yellow and orange trailer, black plastic tires .... $55 – 75
3. yellow with yellow and red trailer, Superfast wheels .... $30 – 50
4. yellow with yellow and orange trailer, Superfast wheels............ $30 – 50

DAF Helicopter Transporter, Kingsize K-126, 1986; Emergency EM-9, 1991

1. "Coast Guard," white, EM-9 .. $18 – 24
2. "Royal Navy," blue, K-126 .. $18 – 24

Daimler, 1911, Models of Yesteryear Y-13, introduced in 1966; Medallion Series YMS-05, introduced in 1996

1. blue .... $20 – 30
2. gold plated .... $50 – 60

3. **maroon with gold pinstripe trim, YMS-05 .... $20 – 30**
4. silver plated .... $50 – 60

5. **yellow .... $30 – 40**

Datsun 260Z Rally Car, 4¹/₈", Kingsize K-52, 1974

1. yellow .... $14 – 18
2. metallic gray .... $14 – 18
3. green (from K-76 Volvo Rally Set) .... $14 – 18

Delahaye 145, 1946, the Dinky Collection DY-14, introduced in 1990

1. metallic dark blue .... $12 – 16
2. metallic red .... $12 – 16

DeSoto, 1948, DYG-14, introduced in 1998

1. burgundy, DYG-14 .... $20 – 30
2. burgundy, Matchbox Collectibles Oldies but Goodies II .... $9 – 12

Diamond T, 1933, YVT-01, introduced in 1999

1. "Budweiser — King of Bottled Beers," red and white, YVT-01, introduced in 1999 .... $30 – 40
2. Diamond T, 1948, Matchbox Collectibles Big Rig Cabs DYM35216, introduced in 1999 .... $40 – 50

Diddler Trolley Bus, 1931, Models of Yesteryear Y-10, introduced in 1988; Matchbox Collectibles European Transports YET-03, introduced in 1996

1. "Ronuk," "Jeyes' Kills," red, Y-10 .... $30 – 40

2. **"Lion Black Lead," red, YET-03 ... $24 – 32**

Diesel Road Roller, 3¹/₄", Kingsize K-9, 1962

1. green with gray driver .... $90 – 120
2. green with red driver .... $60 – 80

Digger and Plow, 5¹/₈", Kingsize K-25, 1977, Construction CS-7, 1991

1. red .... $25 – 40
2. orange .... $20 – 30
3. yellow .... $18 – 24
4. green, CS-7 .... $18 – 24

Digger and Plough Transporter (see Peterbilt Digger and Plough Transporter)

Dinkum Dumper, 4¹/₄", Major Pack M-10-A, 1962
1. black plastic tires on silver metal rims .... $85 – 100
2. black plastic tires on red plastic rims .... $85 – 100

Doctor's Emergency Car (see Citroen SM Doctor's Emergency Car)

Dodge Airflow Van, 1937
1. red and white, "Anheuser-Busch Budweiser Everywhere". YVT-02, introduced in 1999 .... $30 – 40
2. yellow and red, "Coca-Cola," Matchbox Collectibles Coca-Cola Collection .... $12 – 18

3. **yellow and green, "Zephyr," Great Beers of the World .... $12 – 18**

Dodge Ambulance, 5⁵/₁₆", K-38, 1980
1. "Ambulance" .... $18 – 24
2. "Notarzt," Germany issue ..... $30 – 50

Dodge Articulated Horse Box, 6¹/₂", Kingsize K-18, 1966

1. **red cab, unpainted base, tan horse box, black plastic tires .... $60 – 80**
2. red cab, gray base, tan horse box, black plastic tires .... $30 – 50

Dodge Challenger R/T, 1971, Matchbox Collectibles Muscle Cars YMC-02, introduced in 1998
1. purple .... $30 – 40

Dodge Charger, 4¹/₂", Kingsize K-22, 1969
1. dark blue .... $60 – 80

Dodge Charger, 1969, Matchbox Collectibles Muscle Cars YMC-10, introduced in 1998; Budweiser Sports Cars DYM-37598, introduced in 1999; VCV01-M, introduced in 2000

1. **orange-red, VCV01-M .... $30 – 40**
2. orange-red, YMC-10 .... $30 – 40
3. Racing, DYM-37598 .... $30 – 40

Dodge Custom Van, 5⁵/₁₆", Kingsize K-80, 1980 .... $14 – 18

Dodge Delivery Van, 5⁵/₁₆", Kingsize K-11, 1981
1. blue, "Frankfurter Allgemeine," Germany issue .... $40 – 60
2. blue, "Suchard Express," France issue .... $40 – 60
3. yellow, "Michelin" .... $15 – 20
4. yellow, "Suchard Express," France issue .... $60 – 80

Dodge Dragster, 4¹/₂", Kingsize K-22, 1971
1. orange, "Bender" .... $18 – 24
2. orange, "Dinamite" .... $20 – 30
3. pink .... $12 – 18 (see Drag Pack)
4. purple .... $12 – 18 (see Drag Pack)

Dodge Monaco and Travel Trailer, 8¹/₄", Kingsize K-68, 1979 .... $16 – 20

Dodge Monaco Fire Chief, 4¹/₂", Kingsize K-67, 1978

1. **yellow, "Hackensack" .... $18 – 24**
2. red, "Fire Chief" .... $18 – 24

Dodge Power Wagon, 1946, YTC-02, introduced in 1999
1. dark green, no markings ...... $30 – 40

2. **red, no markings .... $30 – 40**

Dodge Route Van Canteen, Matchbox Collectibles Fire Engine Collection YFE-16
1. red, "Springfield Fire Brigade Auxiliary" .... $35 – 50

Dodge Routemaster, Matchbox Collectibles "Power of the Press" YPP-04, introduced in 1995

1. **"New York Times" .... $20 – 30**
2. "Express Delivery" .... $50 – 70

Dodge Tractor with Twin Tippers, 11⁷/₈", Kingsize K-16, 1966
1. green with yellow dump trailers, black tires on red hubs .... $150 – 200
2. yellow with pale blue dump trailers, Superfast wheels .... $90 – 120

Drag Pack, 11", Kingsize K-28, 1971
1. lime green Mercury Commuter, pink K-22 Dodge Dragster .... $25 – 40
2. lime green Mercury Commuter, purple K-22 Dodge Dragster .. $25 – 40
3. metallic green Mercury Commuter, pink K-22 Dodge Dragster .. $25 – 40
4. metallic green Mercury Commuter, purple K-22 Dodge Dragster .... $25 – 40

Duesenberg Model J Town Car, 1930, Models of Yesteryear Y-4, introduced in 1976; Matchbox Collectibles Cars of the Rich & Infamous DYM35182, introduced in 1999
1. red, DYM35182 .... $30 – 40

2. **brown and beige .... $18 – 24**
3. light blue .... $18 – 24

4. **metallic red with black roof .... $20 – 30**
5. silver and blue, China cast .... $30 – 30
6. silver and blue, Macau cast .. $18 – 24
7. two-tone green with green roof .. $20 – 30
8. white with yellow roof .. $1,800 – 2,400

Duke of Connaught Locomotive, 1903, Models of Yesteryear Y-14, introduced in 1959 .... $70 – 85

Dump Truck (also see Tipper Truck)

Dyson Low Loader with Bulldozer (see Ford Tractor with Dyson Low Loader and Case Tractor Bulldozer)

Easy Rider motorcycle, 4³/₄", Kingsize K-47, 1973
1. light brown driver .... $14 – 18
2. orange driver .... $14 – 18
3. white driver .... $60 – 80

Emergency Van (see Bedford Emergency Van)

Emergency Set, Emergency EM-50, 1991 .... $45 – 50
Includes:
Snorkel Fire Engine
Fire Spotter Plane
BMW 730 Police
Helicopter
Ford Transit Ambulance
plus accessories

E.R.A. Remus, 1936, Models of Yesteryear Y-14, introduced in 1986
1. black with chrome plated wheels .... $18 – 24
2. blue with yellow wheels, England cast .... $14 – 18
3. blue with yellow wheels, China cast .... $30 – 40

ERF Simon Snorkel Fire Engine, 8$^1/_4$", K-39, 1980; Emergency EM-10, 1991

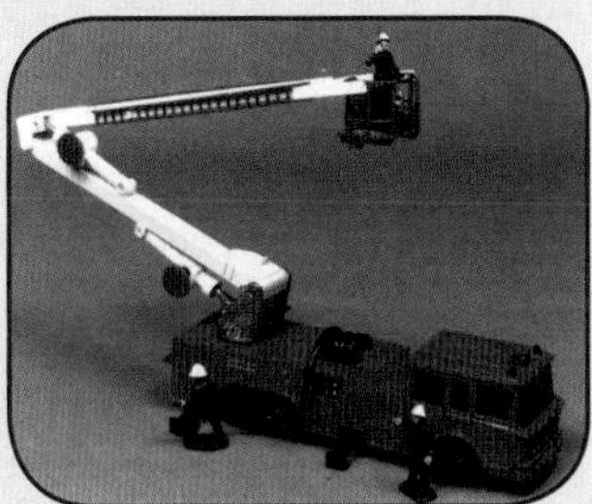

1. K-39 .... $20 – 30
2. EM-10 .... $14 – 18

Europa Caravelle Caravan (see Jaguar and Europa Caravelle Caravan, Volvo and Europa Caravelle Caravan)

Farm Unimog and Livestock Trailer (see Mercedes Benz Farm Unimog and Livestock Trailer)

Ferrari 512 BB (Berlinetta Boxer), 4$^{11}/_{16}$", Specials SP3/4, 1984; Superkings K-3/K-4, 1989; also issued as Super GT Sports, Turbo Specials, Muscle Cars, Alarm Cars, Graffic Traffic, LA Wheels
1. black, "Michelin 88," Specials SP4..$8 – 10
2. blue, "Pioneer 11," Specials SP3....$8 – 10
3. lime green, "Michelin 88," LA Wheels.......................... $8 – 10
4. orange, "147," Specials SP3 .. $8 – 10
5. red, "European University 11," Specials SP4 .... $8 – 10
6. white, "147," LA Wheels........ $8 – 10
7. white, "Pioneer 11," Turbo Specials TS6 .... $10 – 12
8. white, no markings, Graffic Traffic .... $14 – 18
9. white and black, pink flames, "512" .... $7 – 9
10. Ferrari Dino 246/V12, 1957, Models of Yesteryear Y-16, introduced in 1986 .... $18 – 24

Ferrari Dino 246 GTS, 1973, The Dinky Collection DY-24, introduced in 1991; DY-922, introduced in 1992
1. red, DY-24 .... $18 – 24
2. pewter, DY-922 .... $40 – 50

Ferrari F40, 4$^5/_{16}$", Kingsize K-8/K-9, 1989
1. lime green with clear windows, Matchbox Preschool/Live 'N Learn... $8 – 10
2. red with black windows, Alarm Car .... $8 – 10
3. red with clear windows, Kingsize K-8, 1989 .... $14 – 18
4. white with amber windows, Graffic Traffic .... $14 – 18
5. white with black windows, Alarm Car .... $8 – 10
6. Racer, Kingsize K-9 .... $14 – 18

Ferrari Testarossa, Kingsize K-149, 1988
1. red, China cast .... $8 – 10
2. red, Macau cast .... $8 – 10
3. red with detail trim, Ultra Class, China cast .... $16 – 20

Ferrari Testarossa Rally, Kingsize K-155, 1988
1. yellow .... $8 – 10

Fiat 500, 1966, VEM-06, introduced in 1997
2. light green .... $24 – 32

Fire Chief's Car (see Blaze Trailer Fire Chief's Car)

Fire Control Range Rover, 4$^1/_8$", Kingsize K-64, 1978
1. "Fire Control" .... $14 – 18
1. "Falck Zonen," Switzerland issue .... $50 – 70

Fire Engine (see Magirus Deutz Fire Engine, Iveco Fire Engine)

Fire Rescue Set-Unimog and Magirus Deutz Fire Engine, Kingsize K-119, 1985; Kingsize K-138 with roof lights on fire engine that steer front wheels, 1986 .... $30 – 40

Fire Spotter Airplane Transporter, Kingsize K-112, 1985; K-134, 1986; Emergency EM-11, 1991
1. K-112 .... $20 – 30

2. K-134 with roof lights that steer front wheels .... $18 – 24
3. EM-11 .... $14 – 18

Fire Tender, 6$^1/_8$", Kingsize K-9, 1973
1. red with amber windows, "7" in circle labels .... $90 – 120

2. red with amber windows, "Denver," "Fire Dept." labels .... $20 – 25
3. red with amber windows, "Fire" labels .... $18 – 24
4. red with clear windows, "Fire" labels .... $18 – 24

Flight Hunter, 4$^{13}/_{16}$", Adventure 2000 K-2002, 1977 .... $40 – 65

Foden Breakdown Truck, 4$^3/_4$", Kingsize K-12, 1963
1. green with silver metal hubs, no cast roof lights .... $70 – 90

2. green with red plastic hubs, no cast roof lights .... $70 – 90
3. green with red plastic hubs, cast roof lights .... $70 – 90

Foden Coal Truck, Matchbox Collectibles Steam-Powered Vehicles Collection .... $24 – 32

Foden Ready-Mix Concrete Truck, 4$^1/_2$", Kingsize K-13, 1963
1. orange, "Ready-Mix," black plastic tires on silver metal hubs .... $70 – 90

2. orange, "Ready-Mix," black plastic tires on red plastic hubs .... $70 – 90
3. orange, "RMC," black plastic tires on red plastic hubs .... $70 – 90

Foden Steam Wagon, 1922, Models of Yesteryear Y-27, introduced in 1985; Matchbox Collectibles Age of Steam YAS-12, introduced in 1997

1. "F. Parker & Co.," rust brown, Matchbox Collectibles .... $90 – 120
2. "Frasers," dark green with trailer ..$30 – 40
3. "Guiness," dark blue .... $18 – 24
4. "Hovis," brown .... $18 – 24
5. "Joseph Rank," dark green .. $18 – 24
6. "McMullen," black .... $18 – 24
7. "Pickfords," blue, no tow hook ...$18 – 24
8. "Pickfords," blue, with tow hook ....$30 – 40
9. "R. Brett & Sons," gray, YAS-12 .... $30 – 40
10. "Spillers," cream .... $18 – 24
11. "Tate & Lyle," light brown ..... $18 – 24

Foden Steam Wagon, 1927, Matchbox Collectibles "Great Beers of the World" Collection YGB-11, introduced in 1994

1. "Whitbrea's Ale & Stout" ..... $18 – 24

Foden Tipper Truck, 4$\frac{1}{4}$", King Size K-5, 1961

1. black plastic tires on silver metal wheels .... $70 – 95

2. **black plastic tires on red plastic wheels ....$65 – 90**

Fokker DR-1 Bi-Plane, Matchbox Collectibles, 2004 .... $16 – 24

Ford AA (see Ford Model AA)

Ford Aeromax, 7", tractor-trailer, Matchbox Collectibles North American Brewmasters Collection

1. "Red Dog" .... $16 – 20

Ford Aeromax, 7$\frac{3}{4}$", tractor-tanker-trailer, Matchbox Collectibles Official Gas Tankers Collection

1. "Sunoco" $25

Ford Aeromax Box Truck, Matchbox Collectibles Exlusive Editions DYM-36097, introduced in 1999

1. "Jack Daniel's," DYM-36097 ...$40 – 50

Ford Bronco, 1969, Ford 100th Anniversary Series, 1:43, introduced in 2003

1. **orange red with white roof .... $16 – 20**

Ford Capri Mk 2, 4$\frac{1}{8}$", Kingsize K-59, 1976

1. beige with black roof, red interior ..$14 – 18
2. beige with brown roof, red interior .... $14 – 18
3. metallic silver with metallic silver roof, white interior .... $18 – 24
4. white with black roof, red interior ....$14 – 18
5. white with white roof, red interior .... $16 – 20

Ford Cobra Mustang (see Ford Mustang Cobra)

Ford Delivery Van, 4$\frac{5}{16}$", Kingsize K-29, 1978

1. blue cab, "Elefanten Junge Mode," Germany issue .... $35 – 50
2. blue cab, "Jelly Babies" .... $35 – 50
3. blue cab, "TAA," UK issue .... $35 – 50
4. orange and white cab, "U-Haul" ....$18 – 24

5. **orange cab, "U-Haul" .... $20 – 30**
6. red cab, "Avis" .... $18 – 24
7. red cab, "TAA," UK issue ..... $40 – 60
8. turquoise cab, "75 Express" .. $35 – 50
9. white cab, "Avis" .... $40 – 60
10. white cab, dark green chassis, "Mr. Softy," Germany issue .... $35 – 50
11. white cab, white chassis, "Mr. Softy" .... $25 – 40

Ford E83W 10CWT Van, 1950, the Dinky Collection DY-4, introduced in 1989

1. "Heinz 57 Varieties," yellow-orange .... $12 – 16
2. "Radio Times," olive green ... $12 – 16

Ford E83W 10CWT Van and Support Trailer, 1950, Matchbox Collectibles Fire Engine Collection YFE-18, introduced in 1997

1. "Emergency Fire Services," YFE-18 .... $35 – 50

Ford F-100 1953, 4$\frac{1}{2}$", Matchbox Collectibles Fabulous Fifties Road Service Collection YRS-02, introduced in 1996

1. "Flying A Tire Service," black with accessories in back .... $30 – 40

Ford F-100 1954, 5$\frac{1}{8}$", Matchbox Collectibles Fabulous Fifties Road Service Collection YRS-04, introduced in 1996; YIS-05, introduced in 1998

1. "Sinclair Snow Plow," YRS-04 .... $30 – 40
2. "PRR," porcelain rail and accessories in back, YIS-05 .... $30 – 40

Ford F-100 1955, 4$\frac{1}{2}$", Matchbox Collectibles Fabulous Fifties Road Service Collection YRS-06, introduced in 1996

1. "Santa Fe Red Crown Gasoline," white, "Route US 66" on canopy, YRS-06 .... $45 – 60
2. "Santa Fe Red Crown Gasoline," white, "Route US 84" on canopy, YRS-06 .... $30 – 40
3. "County Fire Marshall," red, fire equipment and dalmatians in back .... $40 – 55
4. "Peoria Tractor & Equipment Co.," "Caterpillar," porcelain tool box and tires in back, Matchbox Collectibles YIS-02 .... $30 – 40

Ford F-150, 1953, Matchbox Collectibles YIS-06, introduced in 1998

1. **"Genuine Ford Parts," "Factory Service," red .... $30 – 40**

Ford Fairlane, 1956, DYG-12, introduced in 1998; Matchbox Collectibles Oldies but Goodies II, issued 2004

1. white and blue, DYG-12 .... $20 – 30
2. white and blue, Oldies but Goodies II ..$9 – 12

Ford Fairlane 500XL, 1966, Matchbox Collectibles Muscle Cars YMC-09, introduced in 1998

1. dark blue .... $30 – 40

Ford Fire Truck, 1953, introduced in 1997

1. "Garden City F. D. No. 1," Matchbox Collectibles Fire Engine Collection YFE-14 ....$35 – 50

Ford Galaxie XL 1966, Matchbox Collectibles YMS09

1. **dark blue .... $20 – 25**

Ford LTS Series Tractor and Articulated Tanker, 11$\frac{1}{2}$", Kingsize K-16, 1974

1. "Aral," blue cab .... $50 – 70
2. "BP," white cab .... $500 – 650
3. "Chemco," black cab .... $20 – 30
4. "Exxon," white cab .... $20 – 30
5. "LEP International Transport," metallic red .... $500 – 650
6. "Quaker State," green cab, Canada issue .... $90 – 120
7. "Shell," white cab .... $20 – 30
8. "Texaco," green cab, US issue ....$90 – 120

9. "Texaco," metallic red .... $20 – 30
10. "Texaco," red cab .... $20 – 30
11. "Total," white cab .... $50 – 70

Ford Model A Breakdown Truck, 1930, Models of Yesteryear Y-7, introduced in 1984

1. "Barlow Motor Sales," orange, England cast .... $14 – 18
2. "Barlow Motor Sales," orange, Macau cast .... $20 – 30
3. "Shell," yellow .... $14 – 18

Ford Model A Fire Chief's Car, YFE-12, Matchbox Collectibles Fire Engine Collection, introduced in 1996 ..... $25 – 30

Ford Model A Pickup, 1930, Models of Yesteryear Y-35, introduced in 1990; YPC-05, introduced in 1998

1. "Coca-Cola," "Atlanta Bottling Company — Atlanta, Georgia," ice chest in back ....$30 – 40
2. "From Our Devon Creamery — Ambrosia" .... $18 – 24
3. "W. Clifford & Sons," "Fresh Farm Milk" .... $18 – 24

Ford Model A Van, 1930, Models of Yesteryear Y-22, introduced in 1982; Matchbox Collectibles "Great Beers of the World" Collection YGB-01, introduced in 1993; "Power of the Press" YPP-08, introduced in 1995; YWG-01, introduced in 1997; Charity series YCH-07, introduced in 1998

1. "Ballantine's," dark blue, YWG-01 ....$20 – 30
2. "Canada Poste," red with black roof, Y-22 .... $18 – 24
3. "Castlemaine XXXX," YGB-01 ..$18 – 24
4. "Cherry Blossom," white with black roof, Macau cast, Y-22 .... $18 – 24
5. "Cherry Blossom," white with black roof, China cast, Y-22 .... $30 – 40
6. "Coca-Cola," yellow and red, Matchbox Collectibles Coca-Cola Collection .... $12 – 18
7. "Lyon's Tea," blue with white roof, Macau cast, Y-22 .... $18 – 24
8. "Lyon's Tea," blue with white roof, China cast, Y-22 .... $30 – 40
9. "Maggi's," yellow with red roof, Y-22 .... $18 – 24
10. "OXO," red with black roof, Y-22 .... $14 – 18
11. "Pratt's," white with black roof, Y-22 .... $18 – 24
12. "Ronald McDonald House," white with red roof, YCH-07, Australia issue .... $30 – 40
13. "Spratt's," reddish brown with white roof, Y-22 .... $18 – 24
14. "The Washington Post," YPP-08 ..$18 – 24

15. "Toblerone," beige with red roof, Y-22 ....$18 – 24
16. "Walter's Palm Toffee," cream with red roof, Y-22 .... $18 – 24

Ford Model A Woody Wagon, 1929, Models of Yesteryear Y-21, introduced in 1981

1. "A&J Box," metallic bronze and brown ....$18 – 24
2. "A&J Box," rust and brown .. $18 – 24
3. "Carter's Seeds," blue and cream .... $18 – 24

4. yellow and brown .... $20 – 30

Ford Model A Wreck Truck, Models of Yesteryear Y-7

1. orange, "Barlow Motor Sales" ..$20 – 30

Ford Model AA 1½ Ton Pickup Truck, 1932, Models of Yesteryear Y-62, introduced in 1992; Matchbox Collectibles "Great Beers of the World" Collection YGB-05, introduced in 1993; YGB-16, introduced in 1995; YGB-20, introduced in 1996; Matchbox Collectibles "Power of the Press" YPP-05, introduced in 1995; Matchbox Collectibles Santa Claus Collection YSC-03, introduced in 1996; YPC-06, introduced in 1998

1. "Carlsberg Pilsner," YGB-05 ... $18 – 24
2. "Corona Extra," YGB-16 .... $18 – 24
3. "Delicious, Refreshing Coca-Cola," yellow and red, cases in back .... $30 – 40
4. "G. W. Peacock," Y-62 .... $25 – 40
5. "Happy Holidays from Clayton Feed & Grain," Matchbox Collectibles ..$30 – 50

6. "Los Angeles Times," YPP-05 $20 – 30
7. "Stroh's Beer," YGB-20 .... $18 – 24
8. "Teacher's," brown, YWG-06 ..$20 – 30

Ford Model AA Fire Engine, 1932, YFE-06, Matchbox Collectibles Fire Engine Collection, introduced in 1995; YFE-28, introduced in 1999; Matchbox Collectibles Santa Claus Collection YSC-04, introduced in 1997

1. red, no markings, YFE-06 .... $25 – 30
2. red, "Clayton Fire Brigade," Santa and Mrs. Claus in back with presents, YSC-04 .... $50 – 65
3. green, "White Mountain National Forest," "Prevent Forest Fires," YFE-29 ....$40 – 55

Ford Model AA Open Fire Engine, YFE-09, Matchbox Collectibles Fire Engine Collection, introduced in 1996; Matchbox Collectibles Santa Claus Collection YSC-03, introduced in 1997

1. red, no markings, YFE-09 .... $25 – 30
2. red with porcelain Santa in back, YSC-03 .... $60 – 80

Ford Model T, 1911, Models of Yesteryear Y-1, introduced in 1965; Matchbox Collectibles Medallion Series YMS-01, introduced in 1996

1. black with black seats, black roof, Y-1 .... $375 – 450
2. black with tan seats, black roof, Y-1 .... $20 – 30
3. black with gold pinstripes, brown seats, black roof, YMS-01 .... $20 – 30

4. cream, Y-1 .... $20 – 30

5. red, Y-1 .... $20 – 30
6. silver plated, Y-1 .... $50 – 60
7. white, Y-1 .... $30 – 40

Ford Model T Fire Engine, 1916, $4^3/_4$", Matchbox Collectibles Fire Engine Collection YFE-22 .... $35 – 50

Ford Model T Tanker, 1912, Models of Yesteryear Y-3, introduced in 1982
1. "BP," dark green with red tank, white roof, gold spoked wheels ..... $40 – 60
2. "BP," dark green with red tank, white roof, red spoked wheels ...... $12 – 18
3. "Carnation Farm Products," cream with maroon tank, white roof ...... $18 – 24
3. "Castrol," dark green with dark green tank, white roof, gold spoked wheels .... $18 – 24
4. "Castrol," dark green with dark green tank, white roof, red spoked wheels .... $30 – 35
5. "Express Dairy," blue with blue tank, white roof, gold spoked wheels ....$18 – 24

6. "Express Dairy," blue with blue tank, white roof, red spoked wheels .... $30 – 35
7. "Mobiloil," blue and red with blue tank and roof, red 12-spoke wheels .... $18 – 24
8. "Mobiloil," blue and red with blue tank and roof, red 24-spoke wheels .... $30 – 40
9. "Red Crown Gasoline," red with red tank and roof ....$20 – 30
10. "Shell," yellow with yellow tank, white roof ....$18 – 24
11. "Zerolene," green with white tank, white roof, gold spoked wheels ... $90 – 120

Ford Model T Truck, 1912 (see Ford Model T Van, 1912)

Ford Model T Van, 1912, Models of Yesteryear Y-12, introduced in 1979; Matchbox Collectibles "Great Beers of the World" Collection YGB-14, introduced in 1995; Matchbox Collectibles "Great Beers of the World" Collection YGB-19, introduced in 1996; Matchbox Collectibles Charity Series YCH-01, introduced in 1995; YWG-05, introduced in 1997; YPC-04, introduced in 1998
1. "25th Anniversary," green with gray roof, yellow wheels ...$18 – 24
2. "Arnott's Biscuits," red with black roof, gold wheels .... $175 – 225
3. "Bang & Olufsen," white and maroon with black roof, red wheels .... $275 – 325
4. "Bird's Custard," blue with yellow roof, red wheels .... $18 – 24
5. "Cada Toys," yellow with black roof, red wheels .... $275 – 325
6. "Camberley News," yellow with black roof, red wheels .... $275 – 325

7. "Coca-Cola," cream with black roof, red wheels .... $40 – 60
8. "Coca-Cola," cream with black roof, silver wheels .... $60 – 75
9. "Coleman's Mustard," yellow with black roof, red wheels .... $18 – 24
10. "Coleman's Mustard," yellow with black roof, silver wheels .... $30 – 40
11. "Deans for Toys," yellow with black roof, red wheels .... $275 – 325
12. "Harrods," dark green with beige roof, gold wheels .... $18 – 24
13. "Ice Cold Coca-Cola Sold Here," red and yellow .... $30 – 40
14. "Kirin Lager," YGB-14 .... $18 – 24
15. "Model Collectors Extravaganza," yellow with black roof, red wheels .. $275 – 325

16. "Pepsi-Cola," white with red roof, blue fenders .... $18 – 24
17. "Ronald McDonald House," YCH-01, Australia issue .... $150 – 200
18. "Sheep Dip, The Original Oldbury," olive green, YWG-05 .... $20 – 30
19. "Smith's Crisps," blue with white roof, red wheels .... $18 – 24
20. "Suze," yellow with black roof, red wheels .... $18 – 24
21. "Suze," yellow with black roof, silver wheels .... $30 – 40
22. "Yuengling's, YGB-19 .... $18 – 24

Ford Model TT Van, 1926, Models of Yesteryear Y-21, introduced in 1989; Matchbox Collectibles Y-39, introduced in 1996; Matchbox Collectibles "Great Beers of the World" Collection YGB-02, introduced in 1993; YGB-13, introduced in 1995; YWG -02, introduced in 1997; YVT-03, introduced in 1999
1. "3rd MICA Convention Sydney" .... $90 – 120
2. "Anchor Steam Beer," YGB-13 .... $18 – 24
3. "Anheuser-Busch Bottled Beer," black and red, YVT-03 .... $30 – 40
4. "Antiques Road Show-Next Generation 1992," black .... $1,750 – 2,000

5. "Beck & Co.," YGB-02 .... $18 – 24
6. "Coca-Cola," yellow and red, Matchbox Collectibles Coca-Cola Collection .... $12 – 18
7. "Drambuie," black, Y-21 ...... $18 – 24
8. "Jack Daniel's Old No. 7 Brand," Y-39 .... $40 – 55
9. "Long John," black, YWG-02 ...$20 – 30
10. "My Bread," beige, Y-21 ...... $18 – 24
11. "O for an Osram," green with red roof, Y-21 .... $18 – 24

Ford Model TT Van YCH-02/1 & Ford Model A Van YCH-02/2, Matchbox Collectibles Charity Series YCH-02
1. YCH-02/1: "Ronald McDonald Charities of Australia," red and yellow; YCH-02/2: "Camp Quality," light blue, Australia issue, 1996 .... $150 – 200
2. YCH-02/1: "Ronald McDonald Charities of Australia," red; YCH-02/2: "Camp Quality," two-tone blue, Australia issue, 1996 .... $400 – 600
3. YCH-02/1: "Tyco," red and yellow; YCH-02/2: "Matchbox," two-tone blue, Hong Kong issue, 1997 .... $1,600 – 2,000

Ford Model TT Van 2-Vehicle Set, issued in Australia, 1989
1. "Pro Hart" and "Lunchtime," dark green; "Jenny Kee" and "Waratah," dark blue .... $800 – 1,000

Ford Mustang, 1964½, Matchbox Collectibles Budweiser Sports Cars DYM-37619, introduced in 1999
1. Rodeo .... $30 – 40

Ford Mustang II, 4¼", Kingsize K-60, 1976
1. metallic blue .... $14 – 18

Ford Mustang Boss 429, 1970, Matchbox Collectibles Muscle Cars YMC-05, introduced in 1997
1. orange, YMC-05 .... $30 – 40
2. yellow, "It's the Real Thing," "Coca-Cola" .... $30 – 40

Ford Mustang Cobra, 4¼", Kingsize K-60, 1978
1. enamel red, part of K-2 Car Recovery Vehicle .... $24 – 32
2. metallic red, part of K-2 Car Recovery Vehicle .... $24 – 32
3. white .... $14 – 18

Ford Mustang Fastback, 1967 (see Ford Mustang GT 2+2 Fastback Coupe, 1967)

Ford Mustang GT 2+2 Fastback Coupe, 1967, the Dinky Collection DY-16, introduced in 1990; DYG-01, introduced in 1996; Matchbox Collectibles Oldies but Goodies I, issued 2004
1. dark blue, DYG-01 .... $18 – 24
2. dark blue, Matchbox Collectibles Oldies but Goodies I .... $9 – 12
3. dark green, DY-16 .... $12 – 16
4. metallic light green, DY-16 .. $18 – 24
5. red, Matchbox Collectibles ... $20 – 30
6. white, DY-16 .... $18 – 24

Ford Pickup, 1940, YTC-03, introduced in 1999

1. **dark red, YTC-03 .... $30 – 40**
2. red and black, "Budweiser," YVT-05 .... $30 – 40

Ford Pickup, 1953, 1:43 scale, 4½"
1. "Ford Genuine Parts," Matchbox Collectibles American Giants Collection .... $30 – 40

Ford Pickup, 1954 (see Ford F-100, 1954)

Ford Pickup, 1955, 1:43 scale, 4½"
1. "Caterpillar," Matchbox Collectibles American Giants Collection .. $30 – 40

2. Matchbox Collectibles Coca-Cola Collection, yellow and red .... $12 – 18

Ford Sierra RS500 Cosworth, Kingsize K-162, 1989
1. black upper, gray lower .... $8 – 10
2. white upper, gray lower .... $8 – 10
3. white upper and lower .... $8 – 10
4. white upper and lower, "Caltex Bond," Australia issue .... $30 – 40

Ford Sierra XR4, Kingsize K-100, 1983 .... $12 – 16

Ford Sierra XR4i Rally, Kingsize K-158, 1988
1. white, "Total" .... $20 – 30

Ford Thunderbird Convertible, 1955, the Dinky Collection DY-31, introduced in 1992; DYG-08, introduced in 1996; Matchbox Collectibles Oldies but Goodies I, issued 2004
1. black, "Americans Prefer Taste," "Coca-Cola" .... $30 – 40
2. red, DY-31 .... $18 – 24
3. turquoise, DYG-08 .... $18 – 24
4. turquoise, Oldies but Goodies I ..$9 – 12

Ford Tractor Transporter with Three Tractors, 9", Kingsize K-20, 1968
1. blue cab, metallic silver trailer, Superfast wheels, three orange tractors, Mexico issue .... $250 – 300
2. blue cab, metallic gold trailer, Superfast wheels, three orange tractors, Mexico issue .... $250 – 300
3. blue cab, yellow trailer, Superfast wheels, three orange tractors, Mexico issue .... $250 – 300
4. fluorescent red cab, Superfast wheels, three blue tractors .... $150 – 200
5. red cab, metallic silver trailer, Superfast wheels, three orange tractors, Mexico issue .... $250 – 300

6. **red cab, red trailer, black plastic tires, three blue tractors .... $150 – 200**

Ford Tractor with Dyson Low Loader and Case Tractor Bulldozer, 11", Kingsize K-17, 1966
1. fluorescent red cab, lime green trailer, "Taylor Woodrow," Superfast wheels, orange and yellow bulldozer ... $60 – 80
2. green cab and trailer, "Laing," black plastic tires, red and dark yellow bulldozer .... $110 – 130
3. green cab and trailer, "Taylor Woodrow," black plastic tires, red and dark yellow bulldozer .... $110 – 130
4. lime green cab and trailer, "Taylor Woodrow," Superfast wheels, orange and yellow bulldozer .... $90 – 110

Ford Transcontinental Double Freighter, 11", Kingsize K-21, 1979
1. blue, "Santa Fe" .... $25 – 40
2. blue, "Sunkist" .... $40 – 60
3. green, "Nichts geht uber Barenmarke," Germany issue .... $50 – 70
4. green, "Polara," Germany issue ..$50 – 70
5. yellow, "Continental" .... $25 – 40
6. yellow, "Danzas" .... $50 – 70
7. yellow, "Weetabix," UK issue .. $50 – 70

Ford Transit Ambulance, Kingsize K-169; Emergency EM-7, 1991 .... $9 – 12

Ford Transit Van, Kingsize K-167, 1989; Construction CS-2, 1991
1. lavender, "Milka" .... $14 – 18
2. light blue, "Surf N Sun" .... $9 – 12
3. light orange, "Miller Construction," CS-2 .... $9 – 12

Ford U-Haul Truck (see Ford Delivery Van)

Ford V-8 Pilot, 1949, the Dinky Collection DY-5, introduced in 1989
1. black .... $12 – 16
2. metallic gray with black roof .. $12 – 16
3. tan with black roof .... $12 – 16

Fordson Tractor and Farm Trailer, 6¼", Kingsize K-11, 1963
1. blue with blue steering wheel, plastic tires on orange plastic hubs .... $65 – 85
2. blue with blue steering wheel, plastic tires on red plastic hubs ... $65 – 85
3. blue with silver steering wheel, plastic tires on orange metal hubs .. $65 – 85
4. blue with silver steering wheel, plastic tires on orange plastic hubs .... $65 – 85

Forestry Range Rover and Trailer, Kingsize K-89, 1982 .... $18 – 24

Forestry Unimog and Trailer, Kingsize K-98, 1979 .... $40 – 60

Fowler B6 Showman's Engine, Models of Yesteryear Y-19, introduced in 1986; Matchbox Collectibles Age of Steam YAS05, introduced in 1996
1. maroon, "John Hoadley's Mammoth Fair" .... $20 – 30

Fowler B6 Showman's Engine with Crane, Matchbox Collectibles Age of Steam YAS-07, introduced in 1997
1. black, "John Hoadley's Mammoth Fair," "Marstons Road Services Ltd."

Fowler Big Lion Showman's Engine, 1924, Models of Yesteryear Y-9, introduced in 1958 .... $80 – 110

Freightliner Cabover Semi Tractor-Trailer, 11", 1:58, "Beefeater," The Spirit of London $75

Freightliner COE, 4½", Matchbox Collectibles Highway Commanders, 1:58 ....$35 – 50

Freightliner COE, 12", 1:58, the Spirit of Budweiser .... $75 – 90

Freightliner Container Truck, Kingsize K-187, 1997; K-190, 1996

1. "Beefeater — The Spirit of London," Matchbox Collectibles K-187 ...$60 – 80
2. "ingle ells ingle ells — Don't forget the J & B," Matchbox Collectibles K-190 ....$120 – 150

Fruehauf Hopper Train (see GMC Tractor and Fruehauf Hopper Train)

Fuzz Buggy, 4½", K-41, 1973

1. white with black base .... $14 – 18
2. white with red base .... $18 – 24

Garage Transporter, Kingsize K-113, 1985 .... $20 – 30

Garrett Steam Wagon, 1929, Matchbox Collectibles Age of Steam YAS-09, introduced in 1997

1. "Rainford Potteries Ltd.," dark blue .... $30 – 45

Garrett Steam Wagon, 1931, Models of Yesteryear Y-37, introduced in 1990; Y-48, introduced in 1996; Matchbox Collectibles "Great Beers of the World" Collection YGB-03, introduced in 1993; YGB-15, introduced in 1995

1. "Chester Mystery Players," Y-48 ....$50 – 65
2. "Chubb's Safe Deposits," Y-37 ....$18 – 24
3. "Flower's Fine Ale," YGB-15 .. $18 – 24
4. "Milkmaid Brand Milk," Y-37 ....$18 – 24
5. "Pickfords Removals & Warehousing," Y-48 ....$50 – 65
6. "The Swan Brewery Ltd.," YGB-03 ....$18 – 24

GMC Ambulance, 1937, Matchbox Collectibles Fire Engine Collection YFE-30, introduced in 1999

1. white .... $40 – 55

GMC Cement Mixer, 5¾", King Size K-6, 1971 .... $20 – 30

GMC Rescue Vehicle, YFE-10, Matchbox Collectibles Fire Engine Collection, introduced in 1996 .... $25 – 30

GMC Tractor and Fruehauf Hopper Train, Major Pack M-4, 1964; Kingsize K-4, 1967, 11¼"

1. gray plastic tires on red rims, Major Pack M-4 .... $175 – 225

2. **black plastic tires on red rims, Major Pack M-4 ....$125 – 175**
3. gray plastic tires on red rims, Kingsize K-4 .... $200 – 250

4. **black plastic tires on red rims, Kingsize K-4 ....$125 – 175**

GMC Van, 1937, Models of Yesteryear Y-12, introduced in 1988; Matchbox Collectibles "Great Beers of the World" Collection YGB-08, introduced in 1994; Matchbox Collectibles "Power of the Press" YPP-07, introduced in 1996; YWG-04, introduced in 1997; YPC-02, introduced in 1998

1. "Baxter's," cream .... $18 – 24
2. "Drink Coca-Cola Special Delivery," "Nine Million Drinks A Day," YPC-02 ...$30 – 40
3. "Goanna," dark blue .... $18 – 24

4. **"Goblin," black with black roof ...$18 – 24**
5. "Goblin," black with gray roof ...$50 – 60
6. "Laphroaig Islay Malt Whisky," white, YWG-04 .... $20 – 30
7. "Steinlager," YGB-08 .... $18 – 24
8. "The Australian," YPP-07 ..... $18 – 24

GMC Van, 1948, YVT-06, introduced in 1999

1. "Budweiser Lager Beer," with red, white, and metallic silver .... $30 – 40

Gold State Coach (see Her Majesty Queen Elizabeth II's Gold State Coach)

Grain Transporter, 11⅞", King Size K-3, 1980

1. red cab, "Kellogg's" .... $30 – 40
2. green, "Heidelberger Zement," Germany issue .... $50 – 75

Gran Fury (see Plymouth Gran Fury)

Grand Prix Mercedes, 1908 (see Mercedes, 1908 Grand Prix)

Gus's Gulper, 4¼", K-38, 1973

1. pink .... $14 – 18
2. white .... $175 – 225

Guy Warrior Car Transporter, 8¼", Major Pack M-8, 1964; King Size K-8, 1967

1. blue-green with orange trailer, gray plastic tires on orange rims, Major Pack M-8 .... $100 – 125
2. blue-green with orange trailer, gray plastic tires on orange rims, King Size K-8 ....$65 – 90
3. blue-green with orange trailer, black plastic tires on orange rims, King Size K-8 .... $65 – 90
4. blue-green with orange trailer, black plastic tires on red rims, King Size K-8 ....$65 – 90
5. blue-green with yellow trailer, black plastic tires on red rims, King Size K-8 ....$500 – 600
6. yellow with yellow trailer, black plastic tires on red rims, King Size K-8 ....$50 – 75

Gypsy Caravan, Matchbox Collectibles "Historical Series" Collection YHS-01, introduced in 1993 .... $60 – 75

Half Track APC (see M3A1 Half Track APC)

Harley-Davidson Cafe Racer, #76320, 1993 .... $20 – 30

Harley-Davidson Chopper, Kingsize K-83, 1994

1. black, Harley-Davidson series ... $8 – 10
2. blue, Harley-Davidson series .. $8 – 10
3. gold plated, Harley-Davidson series ...$8 – 10
4. metallic red, Harley-Davidson series ....$8 – 10
5. purple, Harley-Davidson series ..$8 – 10
6. red, Harley-Davidson series ... $8 – 10

Harley-Davidson Electraglide Motorcycle, 3", Harley-Davidson Series #76246 .... $12 – 16

Harley-Davidson Electraglide Motorcycle, Harley-Davidson Series #76300, 1993 .... $20 – 30

Harley-Davidson Electraglide Motorcycle and Rider, 4⁵⁄₁₆", Kingsize K-83, 1981

1. black, "Harley-Davidson," no rider, Harley-Davidson series .... $8 – 10
2. black and white, "California Highway Patrol," Harley-Davidson series ....$8 – 10 (0098)
3. black and white, "Kansas Highway Patrol," Harley-Davidson series ....$8 – 10
4. cream, "Florida State Trooper," Harley-Davidson series .... $8 – 10
5. dark blue, "Harley-Davidson," no rider, Harley-Davidson series .... $8 – 10
6. dark blue, "Virginia State Police," no rider, Harley-Davidson series .. $8 – 10
7. gold plated, "Harley-Davidson," no rider, Harley-Davidson series .. $8 – 10

8. purple, "Harley-Davidson," no rider, Harley-Davidson series .... $8 – 10
9. red, "Harley-Davidson," no rider, Harley-Davidson series .... $8 – 10
10. white, "MBPD 17," no rider, Harley-Davidson series .... $8 – 10
11. white, "Police," England cast .. $14 – 18
12. white, "Police," Macau cast ... $9 – 12

Harley-Davidson Electraglide Motorcycle and Sidecar, 1:10, Harley-Davidson Series #76310, 1993 .... $55 – 65

Harley-Davidson Fat Boy, 1:9, 1995 .... $45 – 55

Harley-Davidson Sportster, 3", Harley-Davidson Series #76246

Harley-Davidson Sportster, #76330, 1993 .... $20 – 30

Harley-Davidson Sportster, Kingsize K-83, Harley-Davidson series, 1994
1. black .... $8 – 10
2. blue .... $8 – 10
3. fluorescent yellow .... $8 – 10
4. gold plated .... $8 – 10
5. purple .... $8 – 10
6. red .... $8 – 10
7. turquoise .... $8 – 10
8. yellow .... $8 – 10

Hatra Tractor Shovel, 5 7/8", King Size K-3, 1965 .... $60 – 85

Heavy Breakdown Truck, 5 1/8", Kingsize K-14, 1977 .... $16 – 20

Heavy Breakdown Wreck Truck (see Foden Breakdown Truck)

Helicopter (also see Kaman Seasprite Army Helicopter)

Helicopter, Emergency EM-13, 1991 .. $9 – 12

Helicopter Transporter, Kingsize K-92, 1982 .... $20 – 30

Hendrickson Relay Double Freighter (see Cooper-Jarrett Interstate Double Freighter with Hendrickson Relay Tractor)

Her Majesty Queen Elizabeth II's Gold State Coach, Models of Yesteryear Y-66 Special Limited Edition introduced in 1992 .... $40 – 60

Hercules Mobile Crane, 6 1/8", Kingsize K-12, 1975

1. **yellow, "Laing" .... $20 – 30**
2. two-tone blue, "Hoch & Tief," Germany issue .... $50 – 70

Highway Rescue Vehicle, 5 5/16", Kingsize K-77, 1980
1. white, "Highway Rescue System" .... $14 – 18
2. white, "Secours Routier," France issue .... $60 – 80
3. white, "Strassen Service," Germany issue .... $50 – 60

Hispano Suiza, 1938, Models of Yesteryear Y-17, introduced in 1973
1. green .... $20 – 30; with diorama .... $24 – 32

2. **metallic red .... $18 – 24**
3. two-tone light blue .... $18 – 24

4. **pea green and tan .... $20 – 30**

Holden 50/2106 Utility, 1951, Australia issue, Holden series YHN-03, introduced in 1997; Charity series YCH-11, introduced in 1998
1. "12th Super Southern Swapmeet Ballarat 2001," lime green with purple canopy, YCH-11 .... $30 – 40
2. "The HouseThat Love Built... Melbourne Australia," lime green with white canopy, YCH-11 .... $30 – 40
3. khaki tan with removable brown canopy, YHN-03 .... $45 – 60

Holden FJ/2104 Panel Van, 1955, Australia issue, Holden series YHN-01, introduced in 1997; Charity series YCH-10, introduced in 1998
1. "Ronald McDonald House-Sydney Newcastle," pale blue .... $30 – 40
2. beige, "Temora District Ambulance," YHN-01 .... $45 – 60
3. gray, YHN-01 .... $45 – 60
4. yellow, "Automodels Sydney," "Autuomodels Solingen," YHN -01 .. $45 – 60

Holden FJ/2106 Utility, 1954, Australia issue, Holden series YHN-02, introduced in 1997
1. midnight blue with removable black canopy .... $45 – 60

Hot Fire Engine, 3 3/8", Kingsize K-53, 1975 .... $14 – 18

Hover Raider, 4 7/8," Battle Kings BK-105, 1974 .... $35 – 50

Hovercraft (see SRN6 Hovercraft)

Hoveringham Tipper Truck, 4 1/4", King Size K-1, 1964
1. red cab, orange dumper, "Hoveringham" decals .... $60 – 80
2. red cab, orange dumper, "Hoveringham" labels .... $60 – 80

Howitzer (see Self Propelled 155mm Howitzer, Troop Carrier with 226mm Howitzer)

International C Series Pickup, 1934, YTC-06, introduced in 1999
1. dark purple .... $30 – 40

International Tractor (see McCormick International Tractor)

Interstate Double Freighter (see Cooper – Jarrett Interstate Double Freighter with Henderson Relay Tractor)

Iveco Double Tipper, Kingsize K-145, 1988 .... $20 – 30

Iveco Fire Engine, Emergency EM-5, 1991 .... $9 – 12

Iveco Racing Car Transporter "Ferrari," Kingsize K-136, 1986 .... $20 – 30

Iveco Refuse Truck, Kingsize K-133, 1986
1. blue cab, blue container ...... $60 – 80
2. blue cab, white container ... $90 – 120
3. maroon cab, maroon container .. $12 – 16

4. white cab, white container ..... $12 - 16

Iveco Petrol Tanker, Kingsize K-109, 1984; K-131 with roof lights that steer front wheels, 1986
1. red, "Texaco," K -131 .... $18 – 24
2. white, "Texaco," K-131 .... $18 – 24
3. yellow, "Shell," K-109 .... $9 – 12
4. yellow, "Shell," K-131 .... $9 – 12

Iveco Semi Tanker; Kingsize K-127, 1989
1. blue cab, "British Farm Produce-Milk" .... $30 – 50

Iveco Skip Truck, Kingsize K-141, 1987 .... $9 – 12

Iveco Tanker (see Iveco Semi Tanker, Iveco Petrol Tanker)

Iveco Tipper Truck, Kingsize K-139, 1987; Construction CS-6, 1991

1. Macau cast, K-139 .... $12 - 16
2. China cast, CS-6 .... $9 – 12

Jaguar and Europa Caravelle Caravan, $10^5/_8$", Kingsize K-69, 1980 (also see Volvo and Europa Caravan)
1. blue Jaguar, white caravan .. $30 – 40
2. blue Jaguar, beige caravan .. $30 – 40
3. light brown Jaguar, white caravan .... $30 – 40
4. red Jaguar, white caravan ... $30 – 40

Jaguar E-Type, pewter, The Dinky Collection DY-921, introduced in 1992 ..$40 – 50

Jaguar E-Type Series 1.5 Convertible, top up, 1967, The Dinky Collection DY-1, introduced in 1989
1. black, black roof .... $18 – 21
2. dark green, black roof .... $12 – 16
3. yellow, black roof .... $18 – 21

Jaguar E-Type Series 1.5 Convertible, top down, 1967, The Dinky Collection DY-18, introduced in 1990; Matchbox Collectibles DYB-02, introduced in 1998
1. black, DY-18 .... $18 – 24
2. red, DY-18 .... $12 – 16
3. red, DYB-02 .... $24 – 36

Jaguar SS100, 1936, Models of Yesteryear Y-1, introduced in 1977
1. cream, England cast .... $14 – 18

2. dark green, England cast ...... $14 - 18
3. dark yellow with whitewall tires, Macau cast .... $18 – 24; with diorama .... $20 – 30
4. light yellow with whitewall tires, England cast .... $80 – 100
5. metallic red, China cast .... $18 – 24
6. silver and blue, England cast ...$14 – 18

Jaguar SS100, Models of Yesteryear Y-901, introduced in 1991
1. pewter cast .... $80 – 100

Jaguar XJ6, Kingsize K-146, 1988
1. dark green .... $14 – 18

2. metallic red ....$9 - 12
3. white, China cast .... $8 – 10
4. white, Macau cast .... $14 – 18

Jaguar XJ6 Police Car, Kingsize K-153, 1988; Emergency EM-3, 1991 ..$9 – 12

Jaguar XJ12 Police, $4^3/_4$", Kingsize K-66, 1978 .... $18 – 24

Jaguar XK150, 1960, DY-36, introduced in 1995
1. cream .... $18 – 24

Javelin AMX, $4^1/_4$", Kingsize K-54, 1975
1. burgundy .... $14 – 18
2. red .... $14 – 18
3. black .... $18 – 24

Javelin Drag Racing Set, $9^3/_4$", Kingsize K-57, 1975
1. K-54 Javelin with K-39 Milligan's Mill .... $30 – 40
2. K-54 Javelin with K-38 Gus's Gulper .... $30 – 40

JCB Excavator, $9^7/_8$", Kingsize K-41, 1981; K-170, 1989, Construction CS-9, 1991
1. K-41 .... $30 – 50
2. K-170 .... $20 – 30
3. CS-9 .... $20 – 30

Jennings Cattle Truck, $4^3/_4$", Major Pack M-7, 1960
1. gray plastic wheels .... $150 – 200
2. black plastic wheels .... $150 – 200

Kaman Seasprite Army Helicopter, $5^7/_8$", Battle Kings BK-118, 1978 .. $60 – 85

Karmann Ghia (see Volkswagen Karmann Ghia)

Kenworth, 7", tractor-trailer, Matchbox Collectibles North American Brewmasters Collection
1. "Corona" .... $16 – 20

Kenworth Aerodyne, $7^3/_4$" tractor-tanker-trailer, Matchbox Collectibles Official Gas Tankers Collection
1. "Mobil" .... $20 – 30

Kenworth COE, 7" tractor-trailer, Matchbox Collectibles North American Brewmasters Collection
1. "Moosehead" .... $16 – 20

Kenworth Semi Tractor-Trailer, The Power of Harley, 1:58 scale, 12" $75

Kenworth Tanker, $12^1/_2$", 1:58, Matchbox Collectibles "The Spirit of Shell"; Exclusive Editions DYM-36838, introduced in 1999
1. "Gulf," DYM -36838 .... $40 – 50
2. The Spirit of Shell .... $75 – 90

Kenworth W900, $5^1/_2$", Matchbox Collectibles Highway Commanders, 1:58 ....$35 – 50

King Tiger Tank, $4^1/_2$", Battle Kings BK-104, 1974 .... $35 – 50

Kremer Porsche CK.5 Racer, $4^1/_{16}$", Specials SP-1/2, 1984; Superkings K-1/K-2, 1989; also issued as Super GT Sports, Turbo Specials, Muscle Cars, Alarm Cars, Graffic Traffic, LA Wheels
1. black, "35 Porsche," LA Wheels ..$14 – 18
2. maroon, "Michelin 15," Turbo Specials TS3 .... $8 – 10
3. pearl silver, "19" and stripes, Specials SP2 .... $8 – 10
4. white, "22 Grand Prix," Specials SP1 .... $8 – 10
5. white, "35 Porsche," Specials SP1 ...$8 – 10
6. white, "35 Porsche," Turbo Specials TS3 .... $8 – 10
7. white, "Lloyd's 1," British issue ......$25 – 40
8. white, green and yellow, "2," Specials SP2 .... $8 – 10
9. white, no markings, Graffic Traffic .... $14 – 18

KW Dart Dump Truck, $5^5/_8$", King Size K-2-B, 1964 .... $75 – 100

Lagonda Drophead Coupe, 1938, Models of Yesteryear Y-11, introduced in 1973
1. beige with black chassis ...... $18 – 24
2. copper with gold chassis ..... $18 – 24
3. gold with purple chassis .. $900 – 1000

4. gold with red chassis .... $400 - 500
5. gold with maroon chassis .... $50 – 60
6. plum with black interior .... $20 – 30

7. plum with maroon interior ... $35 – 40

Lamborghini Diablo, Kingsize K-173, 1992
1. black .... $9 – 12
2. yellow .... $9 – 12

Lamborghini Miura, 4", Kingsize K-24, 1969
1. blue .... $15 – 20
2. burgundy .... $15 – 20
3. metallic bronze .... $15 – 20
4. red .... $40 – 60

Lamp Maintenance Set, Kingsize K-93, 1982 .... $16 – 20

Lancia Rallye, $4\frac{7}{16}$", Specials SP5/6, 1984; Superkings K-5, 1989; also issued as Super GT Sports, Turbo Specials, Muscle Cars, Alarm Cars, Graffic Traffic, LA Wheels
1. dark blue, "Pirelli 16," LA Wheels ..$8 – 10
2. green, "Pirelli 116," Specials SP5 ..$8 – 10
4. white, "102," Turbo Specials TS5 ..$8 – 10
5. white, "Martini Racing 1," Specials SP6 .... $8 – 10
6. white, no markings, Graffic Traffic .... $14 – 18
7. yellow, "102," Specials SP5 ... $8 – 10

Land Rover Fire Engine, 1952, Matchbox Collectibles Fire Engine Collection YFE-02, introduced in 1994; YFE-25, introduced in 1999

1. red, with trailer, YFE-02 .... $25 – 30
2. yellow, YFE-02 .... $90 – 110
3. dark blue, "Royal Navy Rescue," YFE-25 ....$40 – 55

Land Rover Fire Truck (see Land Rover Fire Engine)

Land Rover Pilot Car, Kingsize K-144, 1987
1. green, "Veterinary Surgeon," Great Britain issue .... $18 – 24
2. orange, "Heathrow Airport," Great Britain issue .... $9 – 12
3. orange, "Road Maintenance," US issue ....$9 – 12
4. yellow, "Frankfurt Flughafen," Germany issue .... $9 – 12

Land Rover Series 1, 1949, the Dinky Collection DY-9, introduced in 1989

1. green .... $12 – 16
2. yellow, "AA Road Service" .... $18 – 24

Leyland 3-Ton Lorry, 1920, Models of Yesteryear Y-9, introduced in 1985

Leyland 4-Ton Van, 1914, Models of Yesteryear Y-7, introduced in 1957
1. three lines of text, cream roof, black plastic wheels .... $1,250 – 1,500
2. three lines of text, cream roof, metal wheels .... $80 – 100
3. three lines of text, white roof, metal wheels .... $80 – 100
4. two lines of text, cream roof, metal wheels .... $900 – 1000

Leyland Car Recovery Vehicle, Kingsize K-140, 1987 .... $9 – 12

Leyland Car Transporter, Kingsize K-120, 1986 .... $18 – 24

Leyland Cement Truck, Kingsize K-123, 1986; Construction CS-3, 1991 ....$9 – 12

Leyland Cub Fire Engine
1. YFE-08, Matchbox Collectibles Fire Engine Collection, introduced in 1995 ....$25 – 30
2. YSFE-02, Matchbox Collectibles Fire Engine Collection, introduced in 1996 ....$50 – 60

Leyland Cub Hook and Ladder Truck, 1936, Models of Yesteryear Y-9, introduced in 1989 .... $125 – 150

Leyland Skip Truck, Kingsize K-151, 1988; Construction CS-4, 1991 ...... $9 – 12

Leyland Tipper, $4\frac{1}{2}$", King Size K-4, 1970; K-37, 1979
1. dark red cab, metallic silver dumper, "LE Transport" labels, black plastic tires, K-4 .... $15 – 20
2. dark red cab, metallic silver dumper, "W. Wates" labels, black plastic tires, K-4 .... $40 – 55
3. orange-red cab, metallic lime green dumper, "W. Wates" labels, black plastic tires, K-4 .... $55 – 70
4. orange-red cab, metallic lime green dumper, "W. Wates" labels, Superfast wheels, K-4 .... $25 – 40
5. orange-red cab, metallic lime green dumper, no labels, Superfast wheels, K-4 .... $25 – 40
6. orange-red cab, pea green dumper, "W. Wates" labels, black plastic tires, K-4 .... $40 – 55
7. pale blue cab, metallic silver dumper, miner and cave graphics, Superfast wheels, Mexico issue, K-4 .... $60 – 85
8. pale green cab and dumper, "W. Wates" labels, black plastic tires, K-4 ....$500 – 750

9. yellow with red dumper, "Laing," K-37 ....$14 – 18

Leyland Titan TD1 London Bus, 1929, Models of Yesteryear Y-5, introduced in 1989; Matchbox Collectibles European Transports YET-02, introduced in 1996
1. "MICA for collectors of Matchbox," maroon .... $30 – 40
2. "Newcastle Brown Ale," maroon ...$18 – 24
3. "Robin, the New Starch," lime green.......................... $18 – 24
4. "Swan Fountpens," blue, issued in frame with one assembled and one disassembled .... $80 – 100
5. "Van Houten's Cocoa," YET-02 ..$24 – 32

Leyland Truck with three interchangeable backs, Kingsize K-150, 1988
1. blue cab .... $18 – 24
2. yellow cab .... $12 – 16

Lightning, $4\frac{1}{4}$", Kingsize K-35, 1972
1. red, "35 Team Matchbox" .... $15 – 20
2. red, "Flame Out," UK issue .. $180 – 240
3. white, "35 Team Matchbox" .. $15 – 20
4. white, "35 STP Champion" ... $15 – 20

Lincoln Zephyr, 1938, Models of Yesteryear Y-64, introduced in 1992; Matchbox Collectibles Cars of the Rich & Infamous DYM-35180, introduced in 1999
1. cream, Y-64 .... $40 – 55

2. light rose, DYM-35180 .... $30 – 40
3. purple, Y-64 .... $20 – 30

Log Transporter (see Mercedes Benz Log Transporter)

London Bus (also see Leyland Titan TD1 London Bus)

London Bus, 1911 B Type, Models of Yesteryear Y-2, introduced in 1956
1. eight over four windows ...... $65 – 80

2. four over four side windows ... $250 - 300

London E Class Tram Car, 1907, Models of Yesteryear Y-3, introduced in 1956
1. "Dewars" .... $475 - 500

2. "News of the World" .... $60 - 80

London Horse Drawn Bus, 1899, Models of Yesteryear Y-12, introduced in 1959

1. beige driver and seats .... $65 - 75
2. light pink driver and seats .... $80 - 90

London Omnibus, Matchbox Collectibles "Historical Series" Collection YHS-02, introduced in 1993 .... $60 - 75

Londoner Bus (see The Londoner)

Lotus Super Seven, 1961, DYB-07, introduced in 1998
1. red with black doors .... $24 - 32

Low Loader with Bulldozer (see Ford Tractor with Dyson Low Loader and Case Tractor Bulldozer, Scammell Crusader Low Loader with Bulldozer)

M3A1 Half Track APC, 3⅞", Battle Kings BK-108, 1974 .... $35 - 50

M48A2 Tank, 4⅝", Battle Kings BK-102, 1974 .... $35 - 50

M551 Sheridan Tank, 4⅛", Battle Kings BK-109, 1975 .... $35 - 50

Mack 7" Tractor-Trailer, Matchbox Collectibles North American Brewmasters Collection
1. "Honey Brown Lager" .... $16 - 20

Mack AC Tanker, 1930, Models of Yesteryear Y-23, introduced in 1989; YFE-11, Matchbox Collectibles Fire Engine Collection, introduced in 1996

1. "Conoco" .... $16 - 24
2. "Texaco" .... $16 - 24
3. Fire Tanker .... $20 - 30

Mack AC Truck, 1920, Models of Yesteryear Y-30, introduced in 1985; Y-33, introduced in 1990; Matchbox Collectibles "Great Beers of the World" Collection YGB-09, introduced in 1994; YGB-23, introduced in 1996; "Power of the Press" YPP-06, introduced in 1995; Charity series YCH-06, introduced in 1998; YPC-03, introduced in 1998

1. "Acorn Storage," light blue, Y-30 ..$18 - 24
2. "Artic Ice Cream," cream, Y-30 ...$18 - 24
3. "Coca-Cola," "Stoneleigh Pharmacy Drink Coca-Cola," black, YPC-03 ... $30 - 40
4. "Goodyear," blue, Y-33 .... $18 - 24
5. "Kiwi Boot Polish," red, Y-30 .. $18 - 24
6. "Moosehead Beer," YGB-09 ... $18 - 24

7. "Pravda," YPP-06 .... $20 - 30
8. "Ronald McDonald House," white and red, YCH-06, Australia issue ...$30 - 40
9. "Tsingtau Beer," YGB-23 ...... $18 - 24

Mack B, 1956, Matchbox Collectibles Big Rig Cabs DYM35214, introduced in 1999; Classic 1950's Automobilia DYM-35265, DYM-35266, DYM-35268, introduced in 1999
1. "Champion," DYM-35268 .... $30 - 40
2. "Pennzoil," DYM-35265 ...... $30 - 40
3. "Texaco," DYM-35266 .... $30 - 40
4. yellow with black fenders, DYM-35214 .... $40 - 50

Mack B Tractor-Trailer, 1956; Matchbox Collectibles Tractor Trailers DYM-34557, issued 2000
1. "McDonald's" .... $80 - 100

Mack Canvasback Truck, 1920, Models of Yesteryear Y-30, introduced in 1985
1. "Consolidated Transport," yellow ..$18 - 24

Mack CH600, 5¾", Matchbox Collectibles Highway Commanders; Budweiser Rigs DYM-36672, introduced in 1998
1. "Bud Lite," DYM-36672 ...... $48 - 54
2. Highway Commanders .... $35 - 50
3. "Safeway," Highway Cruisers Safeway Exclusive .... $12 - 16

Mack CH600, 7¾" tractor-tanker-trailer, Matchbox Collectibles Official Gas Tankers Collection
1. "Citgo" .... $20 - 30
2. "Shell" .... $20 - 30

Mack Fire Engine, 1911, 5⅞", YFE-01, Matchbox Collectibles Fire Engine Collection, introduced in 1994 ..... $30 - 40

Mack Junior, Matchbox Collectibles MB339

1. "Pony Express Beer," yellow with red fenders .... $12 - 16

Mack Model AC (see Mack AC Truck, Mack AC Tanker)

Mack Petrol Tanker (see Mack AC Tanker)

Mack Pumper, 1911, Matchbox Collectibles Fire Engine Collection YFE-24, introduced in 1998 .... $35 - 50

Mack Pumper, 1935, Matchbox Collectibles Fire Engine Collection YFE-15, introduced in 1997 .... $35 - 50

Magirus Deutz Fire Engine, Kingsize K-110, 1985; K-132 with roof lights that steer front wheels, 1986 ..$9 - 12

Marauder, 4⅛", Kingsize K-45, 1973 .... $14 - 18

Maserati 250F, 1957, Models of Yesteryear Y-10, introduced in 1986 ..$18 - 24

Maserati Bora, 4", Kingsize K-56, 1975
1. metallic gray .... $14 - 18
2. metallic gold .... $70 - 90
3. red .... $18 - 24

Massey Ferguson Combine Harvester, 4⅝", Major Pack M-5, 1959
1. orange plastic front wheels, black plastic rear wheels .... $100 - 125
2. orange plastic front and rear wheels ....$100 - 125
3. silver metal front wheels, black plastic rear wheels .... $100 - 125
4. yellow plastic front wheels, black plastic rear wheels .... $700 - 900
5. yellow plastic front and rear wheels .... $100 - 125

Massey Ferguson Farm Set, tractor with accessories, Action Farming FM-8, 1991 .... $18 – 24

Massey Ferguson Tractor (see Massey Ferguson Tractor and Hay Trailer, Massey Ferguson Tractor and Rotary Rake, Massey Ferguson Tractor and Trailer, Massey Ferguson Farm Set)

Massey Ferguson Tractor and Hay Trailer, $8^7/_8$", Kingsize K-35, 1979; Action Farming FM-6, 1991
1. red, England cast .... $18 – 24
2. red, Early Learning Centre, Macau cast .... $14 – 18
3. red, FM-6, China cast .... $14 – 18

Massey Ferguson Tractor and Rotary Rake, Kingsize K-87, 1981; Action Farming FM-7, 1991
1. red with orange frame, K-87 ..$18 – 24
2. green with green frame, FM-7 ...$14 – 18

Massey Ferguson Tractor and Trailer, 8", King Size K-3, 1970 .... $35 – 60

Matchbox Racing Car Transporter (see Racing Car Transporter, Matchbox)

Matra Rancho, Kingsize K-90, 1982; Emergency EM-2, 1991
1. red, "Fire Control Unit," EM-2 .. $9 – 12
2. red, China cast, K-90 .... $9 – 12
3. red, England cast, K-90 ...... $14 – 18
4. red, Macau cast, K-90 .... $12 – 15
5. white, England cast, part of K-104 .... $9 – 12
6. yellow, England cast, K-90 ... $14 – 18

Matra Rancho Rescue Set, Kingsize K-104, 1983; K-109, 1984
1. packaged as K-104, 1983 .. $20 – 30
2. packaged as K-109, 1984 .. $30 – 40

Maxwell Roadster, 1911, Models of Yesteryear Y-14, introduced in 1965; Medallion Series YMS-06, introduced in 1996
1. beige .... $18 – 24
2. gold plated .... $50 – 60
3. red with gold pinstripe trim, YMS-06 .... $20 – 30
4. silver plated .... $50 – 60
5. turquoise with gold gas tank .. $40 – 60

6. **turquoise with copper gas tank ..$20 – 30**

McCormick International Tractor, $2^{13}/_{16}$", King Size K-4, 1960
1. red with black plastic tires on green metal hubs .... $65 – 90
2. red with black plastic tires on orange plastic hubs .... $65 – 90
3. red with black plastic tires on red metal hubs .... $65 – 90

4. **red with black plastic tires on red plastic hubs .... $65 – 90**

Mercedes, 1908 Grand Prix, Models of Yesteryear Y-10, introduced in 1958
1. cream .... $70 – 85
2. white .... $125 – 150

Mercedes Benz 190E 2.3 16V, Kingsize K-115, 1985
1. black .... $8 – 10
2. metallic gray .... $8 – 10

3. **metallic light blue ....$8 – 10**

4. **metallic light green ....$8 – 10**
5. white, England cast .... $9 – 12
6. white, "Fuji," Macau cast .... $8 – 10
7. white, "Fuji," China cast .... $8 – 10

Mercedes Benz 190E Police, Emergency EM-15, 1993 .... $9 – 12

Mercedes Benz 190E Taxi, Kingsize K-166, 1989 .... $8 – 10

Mercedes Benz 300SL "Gullwing," 1955, the Dinky Collection DY-12, introduced in 1990; DY-924, introduced in 1992
1. black, DY-12 .... $12 – 16
2. pewter, DY-924 .... $40 – 50
3. white, DY-12 .... $20 – 30

Mercedes Benz 300SL Convertible, 1962, the Dinky Collection DY-33, introduced in 1995
1. dark blue .... $18 – 24

Mercedes Benz 350SLC, $4^1/_8$", Kingsize K-48, 1973
1. metallic copper .... $14 – 18
2. metallic gray with black roof (part of K-2 Car Recovery Vehicle) .... $14 – 18

Mercedes Benz 36/220, 1928, Models of Yesteryear Y-10, introduced in 1963
1. cream .... $75 – 80
2. gold plated .... $50 – 60
3. silver plated .... $50 – 60

4. **white ....$120 – 140**

Mercedes Benz 500SL, Kingsize K-172, 1991; Ultra Class, 1991
1. metallic gray .... $8 – 10
2. metallic red .... $8 – 10
3. red, Ultra Class .... $14 – 18

Mercedes Benz 540K, 1937, Models of Yesteryear Y-20, introduced in 1981

1. **black with chrome spoked wheels ...$20 – 30**
2. metallic gray with red disk wheels ....$30 – 40
3. metallic gray with red spoked wheels ....$30 – 40
4. metallic gray with silver disk wheels .... $25 – 30

5. **metallic gray with silver spoked wheels ....$14 – 18**
6. red with red spoked wheels .. $18 – 24; with diorama, ... $20 – 30
7. white with red spoked wheels ..$18 – 24

Mercedes Benz 770, Matchbox Models of Yesteryear Y-40, introduced in 1991; Matchbox Collectibles Y-53, introduced in 1998; Matchbox Collectibles Cars of the Rich & Infamous DYM-35185, introduced in 1999

1. black with white roof, DYM-35185 ....$30 - 40

2. red with black roof, Y-40 .... $35 - 45
3. dark gray, Y-40 .... $18 - 24
4. reddish brown, Y-53 .... $35 - 50

Mercedes Benz Ambulance (see Mercedes Benz "Binz" Ambulance)

Mercedes Benz "Binz" Ambulance, King Size K-6, 1967; K-26, 1971; K-63, 1977
1. black plastic tires on silver hubs, K-6 .... $30 - 50
2. Superfast wheels, K-26 or K-63 ....$14 - 18

Mercedes Benz Bus, 1950, The Dinky Collection DY-10, introduced in 1989 ....$60 - 80

Mercedes Benz Container Truck, Kingsize K-124, 1986
1. white cab, "7-Up" .... $18 - 24
2. metallic gray, "Taglich Frisch," Germany issue .... $40 - 50

Mercedes Benz Crane Truck, Kingsize K-148, 1988 .... $16 - 20

Mercedes Benz Farm Unimog and Livestock Trailer, 8⁷/₈", Kingsize K-32, 1978 .... $15 - 20

Mercedes Benz Garage Transporter, Kingsize K-135, 1986 .... $20 - 30

Mercedes Benz KS15 Fire Engine, YFE-07, Matchbox Collectibles Fire Engine Collection, introduced in 1995 .... $25 - 30

Mercedes Benz L5 Truck, 1932, Models of Yesteryear Y-6, introduced in 1988; Y-41, introduced in 1991; Matchbox Collectibles "Great Beers of the World" Collection YGB-06, introduced in 1993; YGB-17, introduced in 1995; YGB-21, introduced in 1996; Matchbox Collectibles "Power of the Press" YPP-03, introduced in 1996; Matchbox Collectibles Charity series YCH-08, introduced in 1998

1. "Berliner Morgenpost," YPP-03 ....$20 - 30
2. "DAB Pils-Das Bier Von Weltreut," YGB-21 .... $18 - 24
3. "Henniger-Brau," YGB-17 ..... $18 - 24
4. "Holsten Brauerei," YGB-06 ... $18 - 24
5. "Howaldtswerks AG Kiel," Y-41 ...$18 - 24
6. "Ronald McDonald House," yellow and red, YCH-08, Australia issue ...$30 - 40
7. "Stuttgarter Hofbrau," Y-6 ... $18 - 24

Mercedes Benz Ladder Truck, YFE-05, Matchbox Collectibles Fire Engine Collection, introduced in 1995 ..... $25 - 30

Mercedes Benz Log Transporter, 12⁵/₈", Kingsize K-43, 1981
1. yellow with orange boom, brown logs, England cast .... $20 - 30

Mercedes Benz Lorry (see Mercedes Benz Truck)

Mercedes Benz Pipe Transporter, 12⁵/₈", Construction CS-11, 1991
1. yellow with red boom, gray pipes, China cast .... $16 - 20

Mercedes Benz Police Car, 4¹/₄", Kingsize K-61, 1976
1. white with green hood and doors, "Polizei," Germany issue ...... $30 - 40
2. white with white hood and doors, "Police" .... $14 - 18

Mercedes Benz Power Launch Transporter, Kingsize K-129, 1986; Emergency EM-12, 1991
1. K-129 .... $18 - 24
2. EM-12 .... $14 - 18

Mercedes Benz SS Coupe, 1928, Models of Yesteryear Y-16, introduced in 1972
1. blue and gray with blue chassis, black roof .... $20 - 30
2. blue and light blue with blue chassis, black roof .... $20 - 30
3. blue and beige with blue chassis, black roof .... $20 - 30
4. dark green with dark green chassis, black roof .... $18 - 24
5. light green with emerald green chassis, black roof .... $175 - 225
6. light green with light green chassis, black roof .... $18 - 24
7. light green with light green chassis, green roof .... $125 - 150

8. metallic gray with red chassis, black roof .... $60 - 75
9. white with white chassis, black roof .... $18 - 24

Mercedes Benz Truck, 1920, Matchbox Collectibles Y-32, introduced in 1998
1. "O'Neill Family Products" ...... $35 - 50

Mercedes Benz Truck, 1932 (see Mercedes Benz L5 Truck, 1932)

Mercedes Benz Type 770, 1931 (see Mercedes Benz 770)

Mercedes Benz Unimog and Compressor, 7¹/₄", Kingsize K-30, 1978
1. beige .... $16 - 20
2. gray .... $30 - 50

Mercedes Benz Unimog Snow Plow, Kingsize K-163, 1989
1. orange, China cast .... $10 - 13
2. orange, Macau cast .... $12 - 16

Mercedes Benz Unimog Tar Sprayer, Construction CS-5, 1991 .... $9 - 12

Mercer Raceabout, 1913, Models of Yesteryear Y-7, introduced in 1961
1. gold plated with gold grille ...$225 - 250
2. lilac with gray tires .... $100 - 125

3. lilac with black tires .... $40 - 60
4. silver plated with silver grille .... $180 - 200
5. yellow with yellow grille .... $24 - 32
6. yellow with gold grille .... $24 - 32

Mercury Capri (see Ford Capri Mk 2)

Mercury Commuter and Dodge Dragster (see Drag Pack)

Mercury Commuter and Lightning Racer (see Race Pack)

Mercury Commuter and Thunderclap Racer (see Race Pack)

Mercury Commuter Police Station Wagon, 4³/₈", Kingsize K-23, 1969
1. white with black plastic tires .. $50 - 70
2. white with Superfast wheels .. $25 - 40

Mercury Commuter Station Wagon (see Drag Pack, Race Pack)

Mercury Cougar, 4$^{1}/_{8}$", Kingsize K-21, 1968
1. metallic gold with red interior ..$60 – 85
2. metallic gold with white interior .... $80 – 110

Mercury Cougar Dragster, 4$^{1}/_{8}$", K-21, 1971
1. burgundy, "Dinamite" .... $18 – 24
2. pink, "Dinamite" .... $18 – 24
3. purple, "Bender" .... $20 – 30
4. purple, "Dinamite" .... $18 – 24

Merryweather Fire Engine, 6", Kingsize K-15, 1964

1. red with black plastic tires on red plastic hubs .... $70 – 90
2. red with Superfast wheels ... $40 – 60
3. metallic red with Superfast wheels .... $40 – 60

Merryweather Fire Engine, 1868, Models of Yesteryear Y-46, introduced in 1991; Matchbox Collectibles Special Fire Engine Collection YSFE-05
1. red, "Tehidy House," with firemen, Y-46 .... $50 – 60
2. red, no markings, no firemen, YSFE-05 .... $60 – 80

Merryweather Fire Engine, 1904, Matchbox Collectibles Fire Engine Collection YFE-19, introduced in 1998 .. $30 – 40

Messerschmitt KR200, 1955, VEM-04, introduced in 1997

1. yellow with black fenders .... $24 – 32

MGB, DYB-05, introduced in 1998
1. pale yellow with black roof .... $24 – 32

MGB GT, 1965, the Dinky Collection DY-3, introduced in 1989
1. blue with black roof .... $12 – 16
2. orange .... $12 – 16

MGB GT V-8, 1973, the Dinky Collection DY-19, introduced in 1990
1. red .... $18 – 24

2. reddish brown .... $12 – 16

MG TD, 1945, Models of Yesteryear Y-8, introduced in 1978
1. green with tan roof, red 12-spoked wheels .... $30 – 40
2. green with tan roof, silver 12-spoked wheels .... $18 – 24
3. green with tan roof, tan interior, silver 24-spoked wheels .... $75 – 90
4. green with tan roof, black interior, silver 24-spoked wheels .... $60 – 75
5. red with tan roof, red interior, silver 24-spoked wheels .... $60 – 75
6. red with tan roof, black interior, silver 24-spoke wheels .... $14 – 18
7. red with brown roof, black interior, silver 24-spoke wheels .... $14 – 18
8. blue with tan roof .... $14 – 18

9. cream with tan roof .... $14 – 18

Military Ambulance (see DAF Ambulance)

Military Crane Truck, 6$^{1}/_{8}$", Battle Kings BK-113, 1977 .... $55 – 80

Military Tank (see M48A2 Tank, Chieftain Tank, King Tiger Tank)

Milligan's Mill, 4$^{1}/_{2}$", K-39, 1973
1. dark green, flames label on roof, orange interior and roll bar, blue windows ......$14 – 18
2. dark green, flames label on roof, orange interior and roll bar, clear windows .....$14 – 18
3. dark green, flames label on roof, yellow interior and roll bar, clear windows ....$14 – 18
4. dark green, stars and stripes label on roof, orange interior and roll bar, clear windows .... $16 – 20
5. light green, flames label on roof, orange interior and roll bar, clear windows ....$14 – 18

Mini Cooper S, 1964 (see Austin Mini Cooper S, 1964)

Missile Launcher, 4$^{3}/_{8}$", Battle Kings BK-111, 1975 .... $40 – 65

Mobile Crane, Kingsize K-114, 1985; Construction CS-8, 1991 .... $18 – 24

Mobilgas Petrol Tanker, 3$^{7}/_{8}$", Major Pack M-8, 1960
1. gray plastic tires .... $175 – 225
2. black plastic tires .... $475 – 525

Mod Tractor and Trailer, 7$^{3}/_{4}$", King Size K-3, 1974

1. blue-green, no labels .... $65 – 90
2. metallic blue, star inside circle label .... $65 – 90
3. metallic blue, stars and stripes labels .... $20 – 30

Morgan, 1955, DYB-03, introduced in 1998
1. black .... $24 – 32

Morris 10 CWT Van, 1929, Models of Yesteryear Y-19, introduced in 1987; Y-47, introduced in 1991
1. "Antiques Road Show 1991," black with yellow roof .... $1,750 – 2,000
2. "Brasso," blue, China cast ... $30 – 40
3. "Brasso," blue, Macau cast ... $18 24
4. "Chocolat Lindt," black with yellow roof .... $18 – 24
4. "Michelin," blue .... $18 – 24
5. "Sainsbury," brown .... $18 – 24

Morris Cowley Bullnose, 1926, Models of Yesteryear Y-8, introduced in 1958 ... $60 – 80

Morris Light Van, 1929, Matchbox Collectibles "Great Beers of the World" Collection YGB-04, introduced in 1993; YWG-03, introduced in 1997
1. "Cutty Sark Scots Whisky," yellow, YWG-03 .... $20 – 30
2. "Fuller's," green, YGB-04 ..... $18 – 24

Morris Pantechnicon, 1933, Models of Yesteryear Y-31, introduced in 1990; Matchbox Collectibles "Great Beers of the World" Collection YGB-18, introduced in 1995; "Power of the Press" YPP-02, introduced in 1995; Charity series YCH-09, introduced in 1998
1. "Cascade," YGB-18 .... $18 – 24
2. "Classic Toys for a Jolly Colorful Read" .... $60 – 80
3. "Kemp's Biscuits," Y-31 .... $16 – 20
4. "Ronald McDonald House," blue with dark blue roof and fenders, YCH-09, Australia issue .... $30 – 40

5. "The Times," YPP-02 .... $20 – 30
6. "Weetabix," Y-31 .... $16 – 20

Morris Van (see Morris 10 CWT Van, Morris Light Van)

Motor Coach (see Camping Cruiser Motor Coach)

Motorcycle Racing Set, Kingsize K-91, 1982
1. metallic gray Plymouth Gran Fury with two #33 Honda CB750 motorcycles .... $40 – 60

Motorcycle Transporter, $4^3/_4$", King Size K-6, 1975 .... $12 – 16

Muir Hill Dumper, 3", King Size K-2, 1960
1. gray plastic tires on green metal hubs .... $75 – 90
2. black plastic tires on green metal hubs .... $75 – 90

Muir Hill Tractor and Trailer, $9^1/_2$", King Size K-5-C, 1972
1. two-tone blue, Germany issue ...$50 – 75
2. yellow .... $25 – 40

Muir Tractor and Back Shovel, Action Farming FM-2, 1991 .... $9 – 12

Muir Tractor and Back Shovel with trailer, Action Farming FM-5, 1991 ...$14 – 18

Mustang (see Ford Mustang II, Ford Cobra Mustang, Ford Mustang Boss 429)

Mustang Cobra (see Ford Cobra Mustang)

Nash Metropolitan, 1958, DYG-15, introduced in 1998; Matchbox Collectibles Oldies but Goodies II, issued 2004
1. white and turquoise, DYG-15 ..$20 – 30
2. white and turquoise, Oldies but Goodies II .... $9 – 12

Nissan 270ZX, 4", Kingsize K-42, 1973 .... $14 – 18

O & K Excavator, $4^7/_8$", King Size K-1, 1970
1. black plastic tires on red rims, amber windows .... $45 – 65
2. Superfast wheels, amber windows .... $20 – 25
3. Superfast wheels, clear windows .... $20 – 25

Oldsmobile 442, 1970, Matchbox Collectibles Muscle Cars YMC-11, introduced in 1998
1. white .... $30 – 40

Opel Coupe, 1909, Models of Yesteryear Y-4, introduced in 1966; Medallion Series YMS-03, introduced in 1996
1. gold plated with red roof ...... $50 – 60
2. orange with black roof .... $20 – 30
3. red with tan roof .... $20 – 30
4. silver plated with red roof .... $50 – 60
5. white with smooth tan roof, maroon seats .... $25 – 30

6. white with smooth tan roof, red seats .... $20 – 30

7. white with textured tan roof, red seats .... $40 – 60
8. yellow with black pinstripe trim, black roof, YMS-03 .... $20 – 30

Packard Landaulet, 1912, Models of Yesteryear Y-11, introduced in 1964; Medallion Series YMS-04, introduced in 1996
1. beige and brown .... $20 – 30

2. red .... $24 – 32

3. pearl white, YMS-04 .... $20 – 30

Packard Victoria, 1930, Models of Yesteryear Y-15, introduced in 1969
1. beige with white roof .... $40 – 60
2. beige with tan roof .... $20 – 30
3. beige with rust roof .... $30 – 35

4. black and red with black roof .. $18 – 24

5. black and red with white roof ..$14 – 18
6. gold plated with maroon roof ..$50 – 60

7. metallic tan with brown fenders, maroon roof .... $20 – 30

8. metallic lime green with dark green fenders, maroon roof .... $18 – 24

Pallet Loader and Forklift, $5^5/_8$," Kingsize K-34, 1979 .... $40 – 60

Panther Type A, Matchbox Collectibles Great Tanks of World War II DYM-37581, issued 2000 .. $30 – 40

Panzer IV Type F1 Tank, Matchbox Collectibles Great Tanks of World War II DYM-37580, issued 2000 .. $30 – 40

Panzer IV Type H/J Tank, Matchbox Collectibles Great Tanks of World War II DYM-37586, issued 2000 .. $30 – 40

Pepsi Delivery Truck, $5^5/_{16}$," K – 40, 1980
1. white with red roof, "Pepsi Cola" .... $18 – 24
2. white with blue roof, "Pepsi Cola" .... $18 – 24
3. white, "Froliches Durstloschen," Germany issue .... $40 – 60

Peterbilt, 1939, Matchbox Collectibles Big Rig Cabs DYM-35217, introduced in 1999; Classic 1950's Automobilia DYM-35267, DYM-35269, DYM-35270, introduced in 1999
1. "Michelin," DYM-35269 ...... $30 – 40
2. "Pep Boys," DYM-35267 ..... $30 – 40
3. "Sinclair," DYM-35270 .... $30 – 40
4. red with black engine cowl, DYM-35217 .... $40 – 50

Peterbilt, 7", tractor-trailer, Matchbox Collectibles North American Brewmasters Collection
1. "Miller Genuine Draft" .... $16 – 20
2. "Pabst Blue Ribbon" .... $16 – 20

Peterbilt, $7^3/_4$", tractor-tanker-trailer, Matchbox Collectibles Official Gas Tankers Collection
1. "Texaco" .... $20 – 30

Peterbilt 359, $5^1/_2$", 1:58, Matchbox Collectibles Highway Commanders .....$35 – 50

Peterbilt 359 Transporter, 12," 1:58, flatbed with two cab assemblies .. $75 – 90

Peterbilt Container Truck, Kingsize K-186, 1995
1. "Jim Beam 200 Years," black cab, Matchbox Collectibles .... $55 – 75
2. "Matchbox," blue, Matchbox Collectibles .... $150 – 200
3. "Tyco International," white cab .... $800 – 1,000

Peterbilt Digger and Plough Transporter, Kingsize K-108, 1984 .... $20 – 30

Peterbilt Refrigerator Truck, $11^7/_8$," Kingsize K-31, 1978
1. "Acorn Duro-Penta," white, South America .... $600 – 800
2. "Burger King," white .... $60 – 80
3. "Christian Salvesen," white... $60 – 80
4. "Coca Cola," red.......... $50 – 70
5. "Euro-Express," light blue ..... $40 – 60
6. "Glaces Gervais," white, France issue .... $90 – 120
7. "Iglo Langnese," white .... $60 – 80
8. "Pepsi Cola," white .... $50 – 70

9. "Trink 10," white, Germany issue ....$60 – 80

Peterbilt Refuse Truck, Kingsize K-111, 1985 .... $14 – 18

Peterbilt Tanker, Kingsize K-103, 1983; K-127, 1986
1. metallic gray cab, K-103 ..... $30 – 40

2. white cab, K-103 .... $18 – 24

Peterbilt Tipper, Kingsize K-105, 1985 .... $10 – 12

Peterbilt Tractor-Trailer, 11", 1:58, The Jack Daniel's Edition .... $75 – 90

Peterbilt Tractor-Trailer, 12", 1:58, "Tis the Season for Coca-Cola" ... $75 – 90

Peterbilt Wrecker (see Peterbilt Wreck Truck)

Peterbilt Wreck Truck, 6⁵/₁₆", Kingsize K-20, 1979; K-121, 1986

1. black and white, "Police," K-121 ...$18 – 24
2. dark blue, K -121 .... $16 – 20
3. dark green, K-20 .... $18 – 24
4. lime green, K -20 .... $20 – 30
5. white, K -20 .... $60 – 80

Peterbilt Wreck Truck and Porsche 959, Emergency EM-8, 1991 ...... $14 – 18

Petrol Tanker (also see Army Petrol Tanker)

Petrol Tanker (see Ford LTS Series Tractor and Articulated Tanker)

Peugeot, 1907, Models of Yesteryear Y-5, introduced in 1969
1. bronze with black roof ..... $125 – 150

2. bronze with bronze roof .... $20 – 30
3. metallic orange with metallic orange roof .... $20 – 30
4. metallic orange with black roof ....$125 – 150

5. yellow with amber windows, black roof .... $20 – 30
6. yellow with clear windows, black roof .... $60 – 75

Peugeot 305, 4¹/₂", Kingsize K-84, 1981
1. blue .... $14 – 18
2. metallic blue .... $12 – 16
3. white .... $12 – 16

Pickford 200-Ton Transporter, 11", Major Pack M-6, 1960 .... $175 – 225

Pipe Truck (also see Log Transporter)

Pipe Truck, 8", Kingsize K-10, 1967
1. lavender with labels, gray pipes, Superfast wheels .... $25 – 40
2. lavender with labels, yellow pipes, Superfast wheels .... $25 – 40
3. metallic purple with labels, yellow pipes, Superfast wheels .... $25 – 40
4. metallic purple with labels, orange pipes, Superfast wheels ...... $25 – 40
5. yellow with decals, gray pipes, black plastic tires on red hubs ...... $60 – 80
6. yellow with labels, gray pipes, black plastic tires on red hubs .... $60 – 80

Plymouth 'Cuda 440 6-Pack, Matchbox Collectibles Muscle Cars YMC-02, introduced in 1997
1. yellow .... $30 – 40

Plymouth Barracuda, 1971, Matchbox Collectibles Budweiser Sports Cars DYM-37599, introduced in 1999
1. Fly Fishing .... $30 – 40

Plymouth Gran Fury (also see Motorcycle Racing Set)

Plymouth Gran Fury Fire Chief Car, 5³/₈", Kingsize K-78, 1990

1. maroon ....$9 – 12
2. orange .... $9 – 12
3. red, "IAAFC," White Rose Collectibles promotional .... $14 – 18
4. white .... $9 – 12

Plymouth Gran Fury Police Car, 5³/₈", Kingsize K-78, 1979; Emergency EM-1, 1991

1. black and white, "City Police" ....$9 – 12
2. black, blue interior, "Police" .. $24 – 36
3. black, white interior, "Police" $18 – 24
4. blue .... $14 – 18
5. blue and white, "Police" .... $14 – 18
6. blue and white, "Polizei" .... $14 – 18
7. white .... $9 – 12
8. yellow, EM-1 .... $8 – 10

Plymouth Gran Fury Taxi, 4³/₈", Kingsize K-79, 1979
1. yellow .... $14 – 18

Plymouth GTX, 1970, Matchbox Collectibles Muscle Cars YMC-07, introduced in 1998
1. bright green with white stripes .... $30 – 40

Plymouth Road Runner Hemi, 1970, Matchbox Collectibles Muscle Cars YMC-04, introduced in 1997
1. metallic lime green .... $30 – 40

Plymouth Trail Duster Rescue Vehicle, 4¹/₂", Kingsize K-65, 1978
1. red, "Emergency Rescue" .... $14 – 18
2. green, "Bergrettungswacht," Germany issue .... $40 – 60

Pontiac GTO, 1967, Matchbox Collectibles Muscle Cars YMC-03, introduced in 1997

1. metallic light blue with dark blue roof .... $30 – 40

Porsche 356A Coupe, 1958, the Dinky Collection DY-25, introduced in 1991
1. metallic gray .... $12 – 16

Porsche 911 Carrera, Kingsize K-168, 1989; Ultra Class, 1991

1. red .... $8 – 10
2. metallic white, Ultra Class ... $14 – 18

Porsche 944, Kingsize K-98, 1983 .... $40 – 60

Porsche 959, 4³/₈", Specials SP13/14, 1986; Kingsize K-11, 1989; Turbo Specials TS8; LA Wheels

1. black, "Michelin 44," unchromed rims, LA Wheels .... $8 – 10
2. black, "Turbo," chromed rims, Alarm Cars .... $16 – 20
3. dark blue, "Turbo," chromed rims, Alarm Cars .... $16 – 20
4. metallic silver, "3," stripes, unchromed rims, gray interior, Kingsize K-12 .... $14 – 18
5. metallic silver, "3," stripes, unchromed rims, tan interior, Turbo Specials TS8 .... $14 – 18
6. red, "Michelin 44," chromed rims, SP13 .... $8 – 10
7. red, cartoon design, white rims, Live 'N Learn/Matchbox Preschool ... $8 – 10
8. white, "53," stripes, chromed rims, SP14 .... $8 – 10
9. white, "959," with red, green, and black lines .... $8 – 10
10. white, "Porsche 959," chromed rims, Kingsize K-11 .... $14 – 18
11. white, no markings, unchromed rims, Graffic Traffic .... $14 – 18
12. yellow, "53," stripes, unchromed rims, LA Wheels .... $8 – 10

Porsche 959 Racer, 4³/₈", Kingsize K-12, 1989 (see Porsche 959)

Porsche Polizei, 4⁷/₈", Kingsize K-71, 1979

1. white and green with two #33 Honda CB750 motorcycles, Germany issue .... $60 – 80

Porsche Racing Car Transporter (see Racing Car Transporter, Porsche)

Porsche Turbo 911, 4⁵/₈", Kingsize K-70, 1979

1. black .... $9 – 12
2. green .... $14 – 18
3. lime green .... $14 – 18
4. metallic red .... $9 – 12
5. red, Hong Kong issue .... $16 – 20

Porsche Turbo 944, Kingsize K-156, 1988

1. red, "Pioneer," "Elf," "18" .... $8 – 10

Porsche Turbo 944 Rally, Kingsize K-157, 1988

1. light orange, "Turbo Porsche 944" .... $8 – 10

Power Boat and Trailer (see Seaburst Power Boat and Trailer)

Power Boat and Transporter, 10¹/₈", Kingsize K-27, 1978

1. orange, "Benihana" .... $18 – 24
2. orange, "Matchbox" .... $18 – 24
3. red, "Benihana" .... $18 – 24
4. red, "Miss Embassy" .... $18 – 24
5. red, "Matchbox" .... $18 – 24
6. white, "Benihana" .... $18 – 24
7. white, "Miss Embassy" .... $18 – 24
8. white, "Miss Solo" .... $18 – 24

Power Boat Transporter (see Mercedes Benz Power Launch Transporter, Power Boat and Transporter, Power Launch Transporter)

Power Launch Transporter, Kingsize K-107, 1984 .... $18 – 24

Preston London Tram, 1920, Models of Yesteryear Y-15, introduced in 1987; Matchbox Collectibles European Transports YET-01, introduced in 1996

1. "Golden Shred," orange, Y-15 ...$18 – 24
2. "Swan Soap," blue, Y-15 ...... $18 – 24
3. "Swan Vestas," red, Y-15 ... $18 – 24; disassembled in framed display .... $80 – 100
4. "Yorkshire Relish," blue, YET-01 .... $24 – 32
5. "Zebra Grate," brown, Y-15 ... $18 – 24

Prime Mover with Caterpillar Crawler, 12¹/₂", Kingsize K-8, 1962 .... $200 – 250

Prince Henry Vauxhall, 1914, Models of Yesteryear Y-2, introduced in 1970; Medallion Series YMS-07, introduced in 1996

1. blue with red seats ...... $900 – 1,200

2. **metallic blue with white seats ...$20 – 30**
3. gold plated .... $50 – 60

4. **green with gold pinstripe trim, YMS-07 .... $20 – 30**

5. **metallic red with white seats .. $20 – 30**
6. silver plated .... $50 – 60

Queen Elizabeth II's Gold State Coach (see Her Majesty Queen Elizabeth II's Gold State Coach)

Race Pack, 11", Kingsize K-46, 1973

1. Mercury Commuter and K-34 Thunderclap Racer .... $30 – 50
2. Mercury Commuter and K-35 Lightning Racer .... $30 – 50

Race Car Transporter (also see Racing Car Transporter)

Race Car Transporter, 5¹/₈", Major Pack M-6, 1965, Kingsize K-5, 1967

1. **green with black plastic tires on red rims, Major Pack M-6 .... $50 – 75**
2. green with black plastic tires on red rims, Kingsize K-5 .... $45 – 60

Race Car Transporter, 6¹/₈", Kingsize K-7, 1973

1. white, "Martini Racing," with #56 Hi-Tailer Team Matchbox Racer in red .... $45 – 60
2. white, "Martini Racing," with #56 Hi-Tailer Team Matchbox Racer in white .... $35 – 50
3. yellow, "Team Matchbox," with #34 Formula One Racing Car in pink .... $30 – 45
4. yellow, "Team Matchbox," with #24 Team Matchbox Formula 1 Racer in green .... $65 – 90
5. yellow, "Team Matchbox," with #24 Team Matchbox Formula 1 Racer in red .... $25 – 40
6. yellow, "Team Matchbox," with #34 Formula One Racing Car in yellow .... $30 – 45

Race Rally Support Set, Kingsize K-102, 1983 .... $18 – 24

Racing Car Transporter, Porsche, Kingsize K-159, 1988 .... $20 – 30

Racing Car Transporter, Matchbox, Kingsize K-160, 1989 .... $20 – 30

Racing Porsche, Kingsize K-101, 1983
1. metallic beige .... $20 – 30
2. red .... $9 – 12
3. white .... $9 – 12

Raider Commander, 6⁵/₁₆", Adventure 2000 K-2001, 1977 .... $40 – 65

Rancho (see Matra Rancho)

Range Rover, Kingsize K-164, 1989, Action Farming FM-1, 1991
1. beige, Great Britain issue .... $12 – 16
2. dark blue .... $8 – 10
3. dark green with sheep, shepherd, and dog, FM-1 .... $8 – 10
4. white .... $8 – 10

Range Rover and Trailer (see Forestry Range Rover and Trailer)

Range Rover Fire Engine (see Fire Control Range Rover)

Range Rover Police, Kingsize K-165, 1989; Emergency EM-6, 1991 .... $9 – 12

Range Rover Police Set, Kingsize K-97, 1983 .... $14 – 18

Range Rover Polizei Set, Kingsize K-99, 1979 .... $90 – 120

ReadY-Mix Concrete Truck (see Foden Ready-Mix Concrete Truck)

Recovery Vehicle, 5¹/₈", Battle Kings BK-110, 1975 .... $40 – 65

Refrigerator Truck (see Peterbilt Refrigerator Truck)

Refuse Truck (see SD Refuse Truck)

Renault AG (see Renault Type AG)

Renault Bus, 1910, Models of Yesteryear Y-44, introduced in 1991
1. orange-yellow with red roof, "Wesserling-Bassang" .... $80 – 100
2. orange yellow with black roof, "Wesserling-Bassang" .... $18 – 24

Renault Two-Seater, 1911, Models of Yesteryear Y-2, introduced in 1963

1. **green .... $24 – 32**
2. silver plated .... $50 – 60

Renault Type AG, 1910, Models of Yesteryear Y-25, introduced in 1983; Matchbox Collectibles "Great Beers of the World" Collection YGB-07, introduced in 1994; Matchbox Collectibles "Power of the Press" YPP-01, introduced in 1995; Matchbox Collectibles "European Transports" YET-06, introduced in 1996
1. "British Red Cross Society–St. John Ambulance Association," olive.. $20 – 30
2. "Delhaize," green, Y-25 .... $18 – 24
3. "Duckham's Oils," metallic gray, Y-25 .... $18 – 24
4. "Eagle Pencils," light blue, Y-25 .... $18 – 24
5. "James Neale & Sons," yellow, Y-25 .... $18 – 24
6. "Kronenburg," YGB-07 .... $18 – 24

7. **"Le Figaro," YPP-01 .... $20 – 30**
8. "Perrier," green with gold spoked wheels, Y-25 .... $18 – 24
9. "Perrier," green with red spoked wheels, Y-25 .... $30 – 40

10. **"St. Symphorien Coise Paris," pale green, YET-06 .... $24 – 32**
11. "Suchard Chocolat," lavender, Y-25 .... $18 – 24
12. "Tunnock," red, Y-25 .... $18 – 24

REO Pickup, 1939, YTC-04, introduced in 1999
1. cream .... $30 – 40

Riley MPH, 1934, Models of Yesteryear Y-3, introduced in 1974
1. blue with 12-spoke silver wheels ..$18 – 24

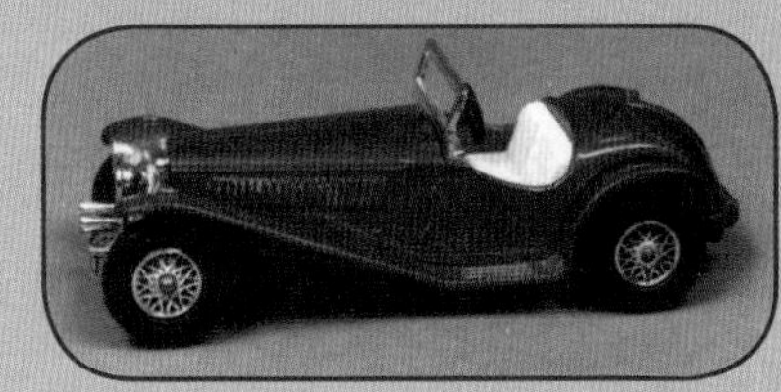

2. **metallic dark red with 24-spoke silver wheels .... $20 – 30**
3. metallic light red with 24-spoke silver wheels .... $20 – 30
4. metallic light red with 12-spoke red wheels .... $30 – 40
5. metallic purple with 24-spoke silver wheels .... $30 – 40
6. metallic purple-red with 24-spoke silver wheels .... $20 – 30
7. metallic red with 12-spoke silver wheels ....$50 – 60

RJ Racing Ferrari 512 BB (see Ferrari 512 BB)

Road Construction Set-Ford Truck, Compressor Trailer and Unimog, Kingsize K-118, 1985 .... $40 – 50

Road Construction Set-DAF Truck, Compressor Trailer and Unimog, Kingsize K-137, 1986 .... $40 – 50

Road Ripper (see Caterpillar Traxcavator Road Ripper)

Road Runner Hemi (see Plymouth Road Runner Hemi)

Rocket Launcher (see Self Propelled Rocket Launcher)

Rocket Striker, 4³/₈", Adventure 2000 K-2004, 1977 .... $40 – 65

Rolls-Royce, 1912, Models of Yesteryear Y-7, introduced in 1968
1. gold plated .... $50 – 60
2. metallic gold with red seats and grille ....$25 – 30
3. metallic gold with black seats and grille ....$18 – 24
4. metallic silver with ribbed gray roof .... $180 – 200
5. metallic silver with ribbed red roof ....$30 – 40

6. **metallic silver with smooth gray roof .... $24 – 32**
7. metallic silver with smooth red roof .... $30 – 40
8. silver plated .... $50 – 60
9. yellow .... $14 – 18

Rolls-Royce Armored Car, 1920, Models of Yesteryear Y-38, introduced in 1990 .... $25 – 30

Rolls-Royce Fire Engine, 1920, Models of Yesteryear Y-6, introduced in 1977
1. red with 12-spoke gold wheels, black seat .... $14 – 18
2. red with 12-spoke gold wheels, red seat ....$140 – 160

3. **red with 12-spoke silver wheels, black seat .... $20 – 30**
4. red with 24-spoke gold wheels, black seat .... $20 – 30

Rolls-Royce Phantom I, 1926, Models of Yesteryear Y-36, introduced in 1990 ....$18 – 24

Rolls-Royce Silver Ghost, 1906, Models of Yesteryear Y-10, introduced in 1969
1. gold plated .... $50 – 60
2. lime green .... $20 – 30
3. silver plated .... $50 – 60
4. silver with red wheels, maroon seats ....$20 – 30
5. silver with red wheels, yellow seats ....$25 – 30

6. **white with silver wheels .... $18 – 24**
7. white with red wheels .... $25 – 30

Rolls-Royce Silver Ghost, 1907, Models of Yesteryear Y-15, introduced in 1960
1. gold plated with black tires .. $50 – 65

2. **metallic pale green with black tires ....$20 – 30**
3. metallic pale green with gray tires .... $50 – 65
4. silver plated with black tires ... $50 – 65

Rolls-Royce Silver Spirit, Kingsize K-161, 1989

1. **metallic gray ....$8 – 10**
2. metallic red .... $12 – 15

Royal Mail Horse Drawn Coach, 1820, Models of Yesteryear Y-39, introduced in 1990 .... $50 – 60

Ruston Bucyrus Power Shovel, 3⅞", Major Pack M-4, 1959
1. gray or green treads, yellow or red decals .... $150 – 200

S. P. Howitzer (see Self Propelled 155mm Howitzer)

Sand Cat, 3⅜", Kingsize K-37, 1973
1. orange .... $14 – 18
2. red (from Car Recovery Vehicle, Kingsize K-2) .... $14 – 18
3. gold plated, mounted on ashtray, Gift Ware .... $60 – 80

Santa Fe Locomotive (see American General Locomotive)

Scammell 100-Ton Truck-Trailer with GER Class E 2-4-0 Steam Locomotive, 1929, Models of Yesteryear YS16, introduced in 1989 .... $80 – 100

Scammell Aircraft Transporter, Kingsize K-106, 1984 .... $18 – 24

Scammell Articulated Container Truck, 9⅞", Kingsize K-17, 1974
1. blue cab, "Gentransco" .... $20 – 30
2. blue cab, "Pppick-up a Penguin," UK issue .... $20 – 30
3. metallic red cab, "Gentransco" ...$20 – 30
4. metallic red, "Ginny Vogue Dolls," US issue .... $300 – 450
5. white cab, "7-Up" .... $20 – 30
6. yellow cab, "DBP," Germany issue ....$40 – 60
7. yellow cab, "Deutsche Bundespost," Germany issue .... $40 – 60
8. yellow cab, "Gentransco" ..... $20 – 30

Scammell Container Truck, 5½", Kingsize K-14, 1971; K-24, 1977
1. "LEP," K-14 .... $18 – 24

2. **"Crowe," K-24 .... $14 – 18**
3. "Gentransco," K-24 .... $16 – 20
4. "Michelin," K-24 .... $16 – 20
5. "Bauknecht Kemplettkuchen," Germany issue, K-24 .... $30 – 50

Scammell Crane Truck, 6", Kingsize K-12, 1970
1. orange with Superfast wheels ..$20 – 30
2. silver-gray with Superfast wheels, Mexico issue .... $60 – 80
3. yellow with black plastic tires on red plastic rims .... $45 – 60

Scammell Crusader Low Loader with Bulldozer, 11", Kingsize K-23, 1974
1. dark blue cab, "Hoch & Tief," Germany issue .... $50 – 70
2. metallic blue cab .... $20 – 30
3. orange cab .... $20 – 30
4. red cab .... $20 – 30
5. yellow cab .... $20 – 30

Scammell Heavy Wreck Truck, 4¾", Kingsize K-2, 1969
1. gold with amber windows .... $25 – 40
2. white with amber windows ... $25 – 40
3. white with green windows .. $90 – 120

Scammell Tipper Truck, 4¾", Kingsize K-19, 1967
1. red cab, black plastic tires ... $50 – 70
2. metallic red, Superfast wheels .... $30 – 50

Scania Digger Transporter, Kingsize K-130, 1986; Construction CS-10, 1991
1. K-130 .... $20 – 30
2. CS-10 .... $14 – 18

Scania Transporter with Traxcavator Bulldozer, Kingsize K-117, 1985 ...$24 – 32

Scania Vabis Bus/Postbus, 1922, Models of Yesteryear Y-16, introduced in 1988; Matchbox Collectibles Y-35, introduced in 1997; Matchbox Collectibles European Transports YET-04, introduced in 1996; Matchbox Collectibles Santa Claus Collection YSC-01, introduced in 1995

1. **"Kaffe DG Rich," dark blue, YET-04 ....$24 – 32**
2. dark green, Y-35 .... $24 – 32
3. red, Y-35 .... $24 – 32
4. white with porcelain Christmas tree on roof, YSC-01 .... $120 – 160
5. yellow, Y-16 .... $24 – 32

SD Refuse Truck, 4⅝", Kingsize K-7, 1967

1. red cab, metallic gray container, "Cleansing Service," black plastic tires ....$40 – 55
2. red cab, metallic gray container, "Cleansing Service," Superfast wheels ....$20 – 30
3. dark blue, orange container, yellow, black and white labels, Superfast wheels, Mexico issue .... $60 – 85

Seaburst Power Boat and Trailer, 6", Kingsize K-25, 1971 .... $14 – 18

Seagrave AC53 Fire Engine, 1907, 4 1/2", Matchbox Collectibles Fire Engine Collection YFE-21, introduced in 1998
1. white, "V.F.D." .... $35 – 50

Seasprite Army Helicopter (see Kaman Seasprite Army Helicopter)

Security Truck, 12 7/8", Kingsize K-19, 1979
1. white with yellow roof, "Group 4" labels .... $16 – 20
2. white with orange roof, "Group 4" labels ....$16 – 20
3. white with orange roof, "Fort Knox" labels .... $16 – 20

Sedan and Europa Caravan (see Jaguar and Europa Caravan, Volvo and Europa Caravan)

Self Propelled 155mm Howitzer, 4 1/4", Battle Kings BK-107, 1974 .. $35 – 50

Self Propelled Rocket Launcher, 4 1/8", Battle Kings BK-117, 1977 .. $50 – 75

Sentinel Steam Wagon, Models of Yesteryear Y-4, introduced in 1956
1. black plastic wheels .... $200 – 250
2. unpainted metal wheels .... $50 – 60

Shand-Mason Horse Drawn Fire Engine with Driver and Two Firemen, Models of Yesteryear Y-4, introduced in 1960
1. black horses, "London" .... $140 – 165
2. gray horses, "Kent" .... $275 – 300
3. white horses, "Kent" .... $150 – 175
4. white horses, "London" ... $140 – 165

Sheridan Tank (see M551 Sheridan Tank)

Sherman Tank, 3 5/8", Battle Kings BK-101, 1974 .... $35 – 50

Sherman M4A3 105mm Tank, Matchbox Collectibles Great Tanks of World War II DYM-37579, DYM-37585, issued 2000 .... $30 – 40

Shovel Nose, 4", Kingsize K-32, 1972
1. yellow with black interior, clear windows ....$14 – 18
2. yellow with black interior, amber windows .... $14 – 18
3. yellow with yellow interior, clear windows ....$20 – 30

Shovel Tractor with Ducks, Chicken, and Rooster, Action Farming FM-3, 1991 ....$9 – 12

Showman's Engine, Matchbox Collectibles Steam-Powered Vehicles Collection ....$24 – 32

Shuttle Launcher, 4 3/8", Adventure 2000 K-2006, 1982 .... $90 – 120

Simplex, 1912, Models of Yesteryear Y-9, introduced in 1968; Medallion Series YMS-08, introduced in 1998

1. lime green with smooth tan roof ....$30 – 40
2. dark green with smooth tan roof ....$30 – 40
3. dark green with textured tan roof ....$40 – 60

4. dark red with gold pinstripe trim, YMS-08 .... $20 – 30
5. metallic gold with textured black roof .... $50 – 60
6. pale gold with black roof ...... $50 – 60
7. orange-red with black roof ... $18 – 24

8. dark red with black roof .... $18 – 24
9. dark red with yellow roof ..... $18 – 24
10. yellow with black roof .... $14 – 18; with diorama, ... $18 – 24
11. yellow with yellow roof .... $20 – 30; with diorama .... $30 – 35

Skip Truck (see Leyland Skip Truck)

Snorkel Fire Engine (see ERF Simon Snorkel Fire Engine)

Spyker, 1904, Models of Yesteryear Y-16, introduced in 1961
1. light green with black tires .... $1,600 – 2,000
2. maroon with black tires .. $1,000 – 1,200
3. yellow with gray tires ...... $100 – 110
4. yellow with black tires .... $24 – 32
5. silver plated .... $50 – 60

SRN6 Hovercraft, 5", Kingsize K-22, 1974
1. blue deck, white hull, "SRN6," "Seaspeed" .... $14 – 18
2. white deck, black hull, "Calais-Ramsgate," "Hoverlloyd" ..... $14 – 18
3. white deck, black hull, "SRN6," "Seaspeed" .... $14 – 18
4. white deck, white hull, "SRN6," "Seaspeed" .... $60 – 80

Stephenson's Rocket Steam Tractor and Wagon, YAS-01, Matchbox Collectibles Steam-Powered Vehicles Collection .... $24 – 32

Street Rod, 4", Kingsize K-50, 1973
1. green .... $14 – 18
2. orange with gold plated fenders, mounted on pen stand, Gift Ware .. $60 – 80

Studebaker Golden Hawk, 1958, The Dinky Collection DY-26, introduced in 1991; DYG-03, introduced in 1996; Matchbox Collectibles Oldies but Goodies I, issued 2004
1. blue-green, DYG-03 .... $18 – 24
2. blue, Oldies but Goodies I .... $9 – 12

3. metallic gold, DY-26 .... $18 – 24

Studebaker Coupe Express K-Model Pick-up, 1938, YTC-05, introduced in 1999

1. yellow .... $30 – 40

Stutz, 1914, Models of Yesteryear Y-8, introduced in 1969
1. blue with black roof .... $12 – 18

2. metallic red with copper gas tank .... $20 - 30
3. metallic red with gold gas tank ....$60 – 75

Stutz Bearcat, 1931, Models of Yesteryear Y-14, introduced in 1974; Matchbox Collectibles Cars of the Rich & Infamous DYM-35179, introduced in 1999
1. blue with chrome wheels, Y-14 .... $20 – 30
2. cream and red with red wheels, Y-14 .... $30 – 40
3. cream with silver wheels, Y-14 ....$18 – 24

4. metallic lime with silver wheels, Y-14 .... $18 - 24
5. yellow and black, DYM-35179 ..$30 – 40

Sunbeam Motorcycle and Milford Sidecar, Models of Yesteryear Y-8, introduced in 1962
1. black sidecar seat .... $1,250 – 1,500
2. bright green sidecar seat ..$400 – 500-

3. dark green sidecar seat .... $40 - 60

Surtees F1 Racer, $4^{1}/_{4}$", Kingsize K-44, 1977; K-73, 1980
1. white, "Chesterfield 18," K-44 on base ....$14 – 18
2. white, "Chesterfield 18," K-73 on base .... $35 – 45
3. light tan, K-73 on base ...... $18 – 24

Suzuki Motorcycle and Rider, $4^{5}/_{16}$", Kingsize K-81, 1981
1. white .... $14 – 18
2. dark blue .... $14 – 18

Suzuki Santana/Samurai, Kingsize K-179, 1992, Emergency EM-14, 1993 ..$9 – 12

Suzuki Santana/Samurai Police, Emergency EM-14, 1991 .... $9 – 12

T -34/76 Tank, Matchbox Collectibles Great Tanks of World War II DYM-37583, issued 2000 .... $30 – 40

Talbot Van, 1927, Models of Yesteryear Y-5, introduced in 1978; Matchbox Collectibles "Great Beers of the World" Collection YGB-10, introduced in 1994
1. "1st Dutch Swapmeet," blue and gray with black roof .... $275 – 325
2. "2nd AIM Convention," green with black roof .... $150 – 175
3. "AIM 25th Anniversary 1970 – 1995," black with yellow roof .... $50 – 60
4. "Bees Art," yellow with black roof .... $275 – 325
5. "Chivers," cream with green roof, red spoked wheels .... $14 – 18
6. "Chocolat Menier," blue with black roof, red spoked wheels .... $30 – 40
7. "Chocolat Menier," blue with black roof, silver spoked wheels .... $20 – 30
8. "Crawley Swapmeet," blue with black roof .... $275 – 325
9. "Dunlop," black with yellow roof ..$18 – 24
10. "EverReady," blue with white roof ..$18 – 24
11. "Frasers," blue with black roof ....$325 – 375
12. "Greenwich Appeal," yellow with black roof .... $275 – 325
13. "Ironbridge Museum," yellow with black roof .... $275 – 325
14. "Langendorf," yellow with black roof ....$40 – 60
15. "Lipton's," green with black roof, green spoked wheels .... $20 – 30
16. "Lipton's," green with black roof, silver spoked wheels .... $30 – 40
17. "Lyle's Golden," green with white roof .... $18 – 24
18. "Merita," yellow with black roof ...$40 – 60
19. "Nestle's," light blue with gray roof, red spoked wheels .... $20 – 30
20. "Nestle's Milk," blue with black roof .... $90 – 120
21. "Rose's Lime Juice," cream with black roof .... $18 – 24
22. "South Pacific Export Lager," YGB-10 .... $18 – 24
23. "Taystee," yellow with black roof, red disc wheels .... $30 – 40

24. "Taystee," yellow with black roof, red spoked wheels .... $14 - 18

25. "Wright's Coal Tar," brown with beige roof, silver or gold spoked wheels .... $14 – 18

Tank (see Chieftain Tank, King Tiger Tank, M48A2 Tank, M551 Sheridan Tank, Crusader Tank, etc.)

Tank Transporter (also see Thornycroft Antar Tractor, Sanky 50-Ton Tank Transporter, Centurion Mk III Tank)

Tank Transporter with M48A2 Tank, $10^{1}/_{2}$", Battle Kings BK-106, 1974 .... $50 – 75

Tanker Truck (see Peterbilt Tanker)

Taylor Jumbo Crane, 5", Kingsize K-14, 1964 .... $50 – 70

The Londoner, $4^{3}/_{4}$", Kingsize K-15, 1973, doors on left side except where noted

1. beige, doors on right side, "Berlin ist eine Reise Wert!" .... $14 - 18
2. blue, "Alton Towers," UK issue ..$20 – 30
3. cream upper, blue lower, "Telegraph & Argus," UK issue .... $20 – 30
4. metallic silver, "Cada Toys," promotional .... $225 – 275
5. metallic silver, "London Dungeon" ..$20 – 30
6. metallic silver, "Silver Jubilee 1952 – 1977," UK issue .... $20 – 30

7. metallic silver, "The Royal Wedding" ....$30 - 50
8. pale blue upper, white and dark blue lower, "123 – 1984 Parish Church 750th Anniversary," UK issue ..$20 – 30
9. pale blue upper, white lower, "Macleans Toothpaste," UK issue .... $20 – 30

10. red, "Around London Tour Bus" ..$10 – 12
11. red, "Besuchen Sie Berlin Haupstadt Der DDR," Germany issue ... $30 – 50
12. red, "Enter a Different World — Harrod's" .... $20 – 30
13. red, "Firestone" .... $20 – 30
14. red, "Hamley's" .... $20 – 30
15. red, "Harrods for more than money can buy" .... $20 – 30
16. red, "London Dungeon" .... $16 – 20
17. red, "London Wide Tour Bus" ..$14 – 18
18. red, "Matchbox" on roof, Chinese pictograms on sides, China issue ....$300 – 500
19. red, "Nestle Milkybar" .... $16 – 20
20. red, "Petticoat Lane" ..... $14 – 18
21. red, "Swinging London Carnaby Street," bell cast .... $30 – 50
22. red, "Swinging London Carnaby Street," no bell cast ...... $14 – 18
23. red, "The Planetarium" ... $14 – 18
24. red, "Tourist London — By Bus" .... $20 – 30
25. white upper, red lower, "Nestle Milkybar" .... $16 – 20
26. yellow, "1234" with blue and red stripes on sides, "Save the Children" on roof, Live 'N Learn/Matchbox Preschool .... $8 – 10
27. yellow upper, brown lower, "London Wide Tour Bus" .... $14 – 18

Thomas Flyabout, 1909, Models of Yesteryear Y-12, introduced in 1967
1. gold plated .... $50 – 60
2. metallic bright blue with yellow seats and grille .... $900 – 1,000

3. metallic bright blue with dark red seats and grille .... $20 – 30
4. metallic fuscia .... $20 – 30
5. metallic red .... $60 – 75
6. silver plated .... $50 – 60

Thornycroft Antar Tractor, Sanky 50-Ton Tank Transporter, Centurion Mk III Tank, $4^{1}/_{2}$", Major Pack M-3, 1959 ....$150 – 200

Thunderclap, 4", Kingsize K-34, 1972
1. black, "Matchbox 1" .... $14 – 18
2. yellow, "Matchbox 34" .... $14 – 18

Tipper Truck (see Scammell Tipper Truck, also see Dump Truck)

Toyota 4x4 Hi-Lux, Kingsize K-171, 1989, Action Farming FM-4, 1991
1. white .... $18 – 24
2. red with milk cans and cow, FM-4 .... $9 – 12

Tractor Transporter (see Ford Tractor Transporter with three tractors)

Tractor Transporter with two MB25 Mod Tractors, $6^{3}/_{8}$", Kingsize K-21, 1974
1. blue with yellow ramp .... $20 – 30

Transcontinental Double Freighter (see Ford Transcontinental Double Freighter)

Traxcavator Road Ripper (see Caterpillar Traxcavator Road Ripper)

Triumph Dolomite, 1939, the Dinky Collection DY-17, introduced in 1990
1. red .... $20 – 30

Triumph Stag, 1969, the Dinky Collection DY-28, introduced in 1992
1. dark green .... $18 – 24
2. white .... $12 – 16

Triumph TR4A – IRS, 1965, the Dinky Collection DY-20, introduced in 1991
1. white .... $12 – 16

Triumph TR8, DYB-01, introduced in 1998
1. dark green with brown roof .. $20 – 30

Troop Carrier with 226mm Howitzer, $8^{7}/_{8}$", Battle Kings BK-116, 1977 .... $60 – 85

Tucker Torpedo, 1948, the Dinky Collection DY-11, introduced in 1990; DYG-06, introduced in 1996
1. dark green, DYG-06 .... $18 – 24
2. dark green, Matchbox Collectibles Oldies but Goodies I, issued 2004 ... $9 – 12
3. metallic blue, DY-11 .... $18 – 24
4. metallic red, DY-11 .... $18 – 24

5. yellow, Matchbox Collectibles .. $35 – 45

6. bronze, Barrett-Jackson Collection, 2003 .... $10 – 14

U-Haul Truck (see Ford Delivery Van)

Unic Taxi, 1907, Models of Yesteryear Y-28, introduced in 1984
1. blue .... $14 – 18

2. maroon .... $14 – 18
3. white .... $14 – 18

Unimog (see Mercedes Benz Unimog)

Volkswagen Beetle, 1968, Matchbox Collectibles Budweiser Sports Cars DYM-37622, introduced in 1999
1. Bowling .... $30 – 40

Volkswagen Cabrio, 1949, VEM-01, introduced in 1997
1. black .... $24 – 32

Volkswagen Deluxe Sedan, 1951, the Dinky Collection DY-6, introduced in 1989
1. black .... $18 – 24
2. pale blue .... $20 – 30
3. red .... $18 – 24

Volkswagen Golf, Kingsize K-86, 1981
1. black .... $9 – 12
2. white .... $9 – 12
3. yellow, "ADAC Straflenwacht," Germany issue .... $30 – 40

Volkswagen Karmann Ghia, 1968, DY-35, introduced in 1995
1. red .... $18 – 24

Volvo Ambulance, Kingsize K-96, 1984 .... $14 – 18

Volvo and Europa Caravelle Caravan, $10^{5}/_{8}$", Kingsize K-69, 1980
1. light brown Volvo, light yellow caravan ....$30 – 40
2. red Volvo, white caravan ...... $30 – 40

Volvo Estate Car, $5^{3}/_{8}$", Kingsize K-74, 1980
1. blue .... $14 – 18
2. dark red .... $14 – 18
3. light brown, part of K-69 ..... $18 – 24
4. red, part of K-69 .... $18 – 24

Volvo Rally Set, $10^{5}/_{8}$", Kingsize K-76, 1981

1. white Volvo, green Datsun ... $30 – 40

Wirlbelwind Flak PZ IV Tank, Matchbox Collectibles Great Tanks of World War II DYM-37582, issued 2000 .. $30 – 40

Walker Electric Van, 1919, Models of Yesteryear Y-29, introduced in 1985
1. "Harrods Ltd.," olive .... $18 – 24
2. "Harrod's Special Bread," olive ..$14 – 18
3. "His Master's Voice," dark blue ..$14 – 18
4. "Joseph Lucas," green .... $14 – 18

Wall's Ice Cream Truck (see Bedford Ice Cream Truck)

Waterous Fire Engine, 1906, 5", Matchbox Collectibles Fire Engine Collection YFE-23, introduced in 1998 .. $35 – 50

Weatherill Hydraulic Excavator, 3 1/16", Kingsize K-1, 1960 .... $100 – 125

Wells Fargo Stage Coach, Matchbox Collectibles "Historical Series" Collection YHS-03, introduced in 1993 ..$60 – 75

Wolesley Hornet, 1962, VEM-05, introduced in 1997

1. burgundy .... $24 – 32

Wreck Truck (see Peterbilt Wreck Truck)

Yorkshire Steam Wagon, 1917 Type WA, Models of Yesteryear Y-8, introduced in 1987; Y-32, introduced in 1990; Matchbox Collectibles "Great Beers of the World" Collection YGB-12, introduced in 1994; Matchbox Collectibles Age of Steam YAS-11, introduced in 1997
1. "Fyffes," yellow, Y-8 .... $18 – 24
2. "Great Western Railway Co. 1087," YAS-11 .... $25 – 40
3. "Johnny Walker Whisky," purple, Y-8 .... $18 – 24
4. "Lowenbrau," YGB-12 .... $18 – 24
5. "Samuel Smith," green, disassembled in framed display, Y-8 .... $125 – 150
6. "Samuel Smith," purple, Y-32 ..$18 – 24
7. "William Prichard Millenium Flour," dark blue, Y-8 .... $18 – 24

ZakSpeed Ford Mustang, 5 1/16", Specials SP7/8, 1984; Superkings K-6, 1989; also issued as Super GT Sports, Turbo Specials, Muscle Cars, Alarm Cars, Graffic Traffic, LA Wheels
1. black, "83," Specials SP8 ...... $8 – 10
2. black, "83," Turbo Specials TS2 ....$8 – 10
3. blue, "QXR Duckhams," Specials SP7 .... $8 – 10
4. blue, "QXR Duckhams" Superkings K-6 .... $8 – 10
5. orange, blue and red, "20," Superkings K-1 .... $8 – 10
6. orange with black stripes, Muscle Cars .... $8 – 10

7. pearl white, "Motul 28," Specials SP8 .... $8 – 10
8. white, "Ford 16," Specials SP7 ..$8 – 10
9. white with blue stripes, Muscle Cars .... $8 – 10
10. yellow, blue and red, "20," Turbo Specials TS2 .... $8 – 10

155mm Self Propelled Howitzer (see Self Propelled 155mm Howitzer)

Two Packs (TP), Twin Packs (TP), Trailers, Matchmates, 900 Series Long Haul (TP), Convoy (CY), Super Rigs (CY), Highway Express (HE)

Variously sold as Two Packs, Twin Packs, or Trailers, the series is defined by its packaging of a vehicle usually accompanied by a trailer. Some of these trailers were never sold separately. One such trailer available only as part of a set is the Glider Trailer, included with TP-7 in 1977, TP-102 in 1984, TP-118 in 1987, and TP-122 in 1989. These sets first appeared in the 1976 catalog, although packages of two complementary models were available as early as 1968, with models such as #1 Mercedes Benz Lorry and matching #2 Mercedes Benz Trailer. The pair was reintroduced as TP-1 in 1976, with Superfast wheels. Since most models in this series are available separately, values listed below are for sets in their original containers. The information in parentheses ( ) indicates the model number and year each vehicle was introduced separately.

1982 saw the introduction of the new Convoy series, derived from the semi tractor-trailers from the Twin Pack/900 Long Haul Series of the previous year (see Twin Pack listing). The Convoy series designation was changed to HE, for Highway Express, in 1983 and changed back to Convoy the following year. When Tyco purchased Matchbox in 1992, it changed the name again, this time to Super Rigs.

All models are approximately 7 1/2" long. When White Rose Collectibles started a cooperative marketing effort with Matchbox, it produced a series of racing transporters based on Convoy models and called Superstar Transporters.

Note: The abbreviation "C.O.E." stands for "Cab Over Engine."

Aircraft Transporter, DAF, Convoy CY-21, 1987; CY-108, 1992
1. black, "AC102," CY-21 .... $30 – 35
2. red cab, carriage, and trailer base with "SB-37 Hawk," CY-108 .... $9 – 12
3. white, "Airtrainer," CY-21 ..... $10 – 12
4. white, "Red Rebels," CY-21 ...... $7 – 9
5. white, no markings, Graffic Traffic .... $12 – 15
6. white, "Aerobatic Team," "Flying Aces," CY-21 .... $12 – 15

Aircraft Transporter, Kenworth C.O.E., Convoy CY-12, 1984
1. white cab with blue and dark green tampos, blue plane, "DARTS," England cast ....$12 – 15
2. white cab with blue and brown tampos, blue plane, "DARTS," England cast .... $12 – 15
3. white cab with two-tone blue tampos, blue plane, "DARTS," Macau cast .....$10 – 12

Aircraft Transporter, Mack, Convoy CY-29, 1991
1. red with red plane, "RED REBELS" tampo .... $4 – 5

Alvis Stalwart and Dodge Wrecker (see Military Alvis Stalwart and Dodge Wrecker)

Ambulance and Fire Chief, TP-10, 1978 (see Fire Chief and Ambulance)

Articulated Dump Truck (also see Articulated Tipper)

Articulated Dump Truck, Kenworth C.O.E. Aerodyne, Convoy CY-20, 1987
1. yellow, "TAYLOR WOODROW" ... $7 – 9
2. red with yellow trailer, red design .... $4 – 6
3. yellow, "EUROBRAN" .... $7 – 9
4. yellow with black and white road design .... $7 – 9

Articulated Dump Truck, Scania T142, Convoy CY-20, 1987

1. pink, "READYMIX" .... $16 – 20

Articulated Petrol Tanker and Trailer, TP-2, 1976

1. green windows, red cab and trailer, white tank, "Exxon" labels ..... $14 – 18
2. amber windows, red cab and trailer, white tank, "Exxon" labels ..... $14 – 18

Articulated Truck (#50, 1973) **and Trailer** (#50, 1980), TP-16, 1980

1. yellow cab, blue dumper, trailer with blue dumper .... $14 – 18
2. red cab, metallic gray dumper, trailer with metallic gray dumper .... $24 – 32

Articulated Tipper, Peterbilt, Convoy CY-106, 1990, Australia

1. pink cab, gray dumper with black base, "Readymix" .... $14 – 16

BMW 323i Cabriolet (#39, 1985) **and Caravan** (#31, 1977), TP-123, 1989

1. metallic silver blue with dark blue stripe, gray caravan with orange stripe .... $9 – 12
2. white with geometric design, white caravan with matching design ...... $9 – 12

BMW 323i Cabriolet (#39, 1985) **and Glider Trailer,** TP-118, 1987

1. red with "Gliding Club," red glider trailer with "Auto Glide" .... $14 – 18

BMW 323i Cabriolet (#39, 1985) **and Inflatable Raft,** TP-127, 1991

1. white with red and blue design, dark blue raft with gray hull, white trailer with red and blue design .... $9 – 12

Boat Transporter, TP-26, 1979 (see Long Haul Boat Transporter)

Boat Transporter, Kenworth Conventional Sleeper Cab, Convoy CY-4, 1982; HE-2, 1983

1. orange cab, boat with orange hull, green windows .... $10 – 12
2. orange cab, boat with orange hull, red windows .... $10 – 12
3. orange cab, boat with orange hull, clear windows .... $10 – 12

Bomag Road Roller (#72, 1979; #40, 1991; #68, 1992) **and Faun Mobile Crane** (#42, 1985-1997), CS-83, 1992

1. yellow road roller, yellow crane with red cab, plastic accessories .... $7 – 9

Box Car, Kenworth Conventional, Convoy CY-36, 1992

1. white, "Charitoys" labels ...... $30 – 35
2. orange cab, black container, "TRICK TRUCKIN'" .... $4 – 5
3. fluorescent orange, yellow container, "MATCHBOX — GET IN THE FAST LANE" .... $4 – 5

Box Car, Peterbilt, Convoy CY-19, 1987

1. white, "ANSETT WRIDGWAYS" ..$16 – 20

Box Container Truck, TP-24, 1979 (see Long Haul Box Container Truck)

Box Truck, DAF, Convoy CY-9, 1982; HE-9, 1982; TP-24, 1982; CY-24, 1988

1. yellow cab and container, Macau cast, "IPEC" .... $12 – 15
2. red, "FERRARI" .... $7 – 9
3. blue, "PICKFORDS" .... $12 – 15
4. white, "PORSCHE" .... $7 – 9
5. white, "CIRCUS CIRCUS" .... $7 – 9
6. white, "SAUDIA" .... $60 – 75
7. blue, "MITRE 10 RACING" .... $10 – 12
8. white, black container, "BASSETT'S LIQUORICE ALLSORTS" .... $10 – 12
9. white, yellow container, "BASSETT'S JELLY BABIES" .... $10 – 12
10. dark green, "JAGUAR" .... $7 – 9
11. orange and red, "PARCEL POST" ..$10 – 12
12. white, "RENAULT ELF," "CANON WILLIAMS" .... $10 – 12

Box Truck, Ford Aeromax, CY-39 Convoy, 1994; CY-39 Super Rigs, 1995

1. blue, "Hawaiian Punch" .... $7 – 9
2. light orange, "Honey Nut Cheerios" .. $7 – 9
3. red, "Heinz Tomato Ketchup Squeezable!" .... $7 – 9
4. white, "Pepsi," "Diet Pepsi" ...... $4 – 5
5. yellow, "Cheerios" .... $4 – 5

Box Truck, Kenworth Conventional Aerodyne, Convoy CY-8, 1982; HE-8, 1983; Convoy CY-9, 1982; HE-9, 1982; TP-24, 1982; Super Rigs, 1995

1. red, red container with white roof, black doors, England cast, "REDCAP" .... $40 – 50
2. red, red container with black roof and doors, England cast, "REDCAP" .... $80 – 100
3. red, red container with black roof, white doors, England cast, "REDCAP" ....$80 – 100
4. red, "Skittles" .... $9 – 12
5. black cab, black container, England cast, "MIDNIGHT X-PRESS" .... $10 – 12
6. black cab, black container, Macau cast, "MIDNIGHT X-PRESS" .... $7 – 9
7. black cab, black container, Macau, "MOVING IN NEW DIRECTIONS" .... $150 – 175
8. black cab, black container, Macau, "MOVING IN NEW DIRECTIONS," "Personal Contact is Barry Oxford" on roof ....$275 – 300
9. black cab, black container, Macau, "MOVING IN NEW DIRECTIONS," "Personal Contact is Anita Jones" on roof ....$275 – 300
10. black cab, black container, Macau, "MOVING IN NEW DIRECTIONS," "Personal Contact is Keith Mottram" on roof ....$275 – 300
11. black cab, black container, Macau, "MOVING IN NEW DIRECTIONS," "Personal Contact is Terry Blyton" on roof ....$275 – 300
12. black cab, black container, Macau, "MOVING IN NEW DIRECTIONS," "Personal Contact is Jenny Brindley" on roof ....$275 – 300
13. black cab and container, Macau cast, "STANLEY" .... $12 – 15
14. orange, "Reese's" .... $9 – 12
15. white cab and container, Macau cast, "PAUL ARPIN VAN LINES" .... $12 – 15
16. white cab, container, "Matchbox Compliments Macau Diecast Co. Ltd." ....$800 – 1,000
17. white cab and container, "PAUL ARPIN VAN LINES" with "NFL" logo ... $12 – 18
18. white, "Matchbox — In Celebration of Universal Group's 20th Anniversary" ....$1,250 – 1,500
19. white cab and container, Macau cast, "Canadian Tire" .... $12 – 15
20. white cab and container, Macau, "Merry Christmas 1988 MICA Members" ....$20 – 25
21. blue cab and container, Macau cast, "Mitre 10" .... $12 – 15
22. blue cab and container, Macau cast, "Spaulding" .... $30 – 40
23. white cab and container, Macau, "Merry Christmas MICA Members 1990" .... $20 – 25
24. black cab and container, Thailand cast, "MIDNIGHT X-PRESS" .... $4 – 5
25. black cab and container, Thailand cast, "COOL PAINT CO." .... $4 – 5
26. white cab and container, "HERSHEY'S" .... $4 – 5
27. white cab and container, "TRUCKIN' USA" .... $4 – 5

Box Truck, Kenworth C.O.E. Aerodyne, Convoy CY-8, 1982; HE-8, 1983; Convoy CY-9, 1982; HE-9, 1982; TP-24, 1982

1. black with "Harley-Davidson" tampos, Macau cast .... $7 – 9
2. black cab, black container, England cast, "MIDNIGHT X-PRESS" .... $40 – 50
3. red cab, white container, "Pizza Hut" .... $9 – 12
4. red cab and container, "NINTENDO," Thailand cast .... $4 – 5
5. silver-gray, blue roof and doors, Macau, "MATCHBOX SHOWLINER" ....$325 – 375
6. white, "KFC" .... $7 – 9
7. white, England cast, "MATCHBOX" .... $60 – 75
8. white, England cast, "REDCAP" ..$40 – 50
9. white, red container, white roof and doors, "SKI FRUIT YOGURT" ..$80 – 100
10. white, red container, white roof, red doors, England cast, "REDCAP" .... $40 – 50
11. white, white container, roof and doors, Macau, "K-Line" .... $300 – 400

12. white cab, container, roof and doors, Macau cast, "MATCHBOX" ... $12 – 15
13. white, Macau cast, "Matchbox," "This Truck Delivers 1988" .... $40 – 50
14. white, Macau cast, "Matchbox," "This Truck Delivers 1989" ...... $200 – 250
15. white with red container, roof and doors, Macau cast, "K-Line" .... $175 – 225

Box Truck, Mack Convoy CY-27, 1989

1. white, "A GREAT NAME IN TRUCKS — MACK" .... $12 – 15
2. chrome, black container, "Celebrating a Decade of Matchbox Conventions 1991" .... $30 – 40

Box Truck, Scania, Convoy CY-4, 1985, Australia; Convoy CY-16, 1985

1. white cab, and container, black trailer, "Ansett" labels, Australia ..... $12 – 15
2. white with "7-Up" labels .... $12 – 15
3. white with upside down "7-Up" labels .... $30 – 35
4. white with dark blue container, "DUCK-HAM'S" .... $12 – 15
5. purple with purple trailer, "EDWIN SHIRLEY" .... $12 – 15
6. white with "WIMPEY" tampo .. $12 – 15
7. white with "SIGNAL TOOTH-PASTE" .... $12 – 15
8. white with red container, "HEINZ TOMATO KETCHUP SQUEEZABLE" .. $12 – 15
9. yellow with white container, "WEET-ABIX" ....$12 – 15
10. blue, "MATEY BUBBLE BATH" ..$12 – 15
11. white, "GOLDEN WONDER POTATO CRISPS" .... $12 – 15
12. white, "MERCHANT TIRE & AUTO CENTERS" .... $12 – 15
13. white, "Merry Christmas 1988 MICA Members" .... $25 – 30
14. yellow, "WEETABIX" .... $12 – 15
15. purple, "RIBENA" .... $12 – 15
16. white, "Merry Christmas 1989 MICA Members" .... $30 – 35
17. white, "GOODYEAR VECTOR" .... $7 – 9
18. white, "SAUDIA" .... $60 – 75
19. red with white trailer, "KENTUCKY FRIED CHICKEN" .... $12 – 15

Breakdown Set, TP-6, 1976. Variations:
Toe Joe (#74, 1972) **and Racing Mini** (#29, 1970)

1. red Toe Joe with green booms, orange Racing Mini with "29" labels .... $250 – 300
2. red Toe Joe with red booms, orange Racing Mini with "29" labels .... $250 – 300
3. yellow Toe Joe with red booms, orange Racing Mini with "29" labels .. $14 – 18
4. yellow Toe Joe with green booms, orange Racing Mini with "29" labels .... $14 – 18
5. green Toe Joe with green booms, orange Racing Mini with "29" labels .... $14 – 18
6. green Toe Joe with green booms, orange Racing Mini with "3" labels .... $16 – 20

Toe Joe (#74, 1972) **and Range Rover Police Patrol** (#20, 1975)

7. yellow Toe Joe with red booms, orange Police Patrol with "Site Engineer" labels .... $30 – 40
8. green Toe Joe with green booms, orange Police Patrol with "Site Engineer" labels .... $30 – 40
9. green Toe Joe with white booms, orange Police Patrol with "Site Engineer" labels .... $250 – 300

Toe Joe (#74, 1972) **and Volkswagen 1500** (#15, 1968)

10. red Toe Joe with red booms, white Volkswagen with "137" labels .... $250 – 300
11. yellow Toe Joe with red booms, white Volkswagen with "137" labels .... $36 – 48

Toe Joe (#74, 1972) **and Saab Sonnet** (#65, 1973)

12. yellow Toe Joe with red booms, metallic blue Saab .... $36 – 54

Ford Wrecker (#61, 1978) **and Racing Mini** (#29, 1970)

13. red wrecker with white booms, orange Racing Mini with "29" labels .. $14 – 18
14. red wrecker with white booms and "24 Hour," orange Racing Mini with no labels .... $14 – 18
15. red wrecker with red booms, orange Racing Mini with "3" labels ... $16 – 20
16. red wrecker with green booms, orange Racing Mini with "29" labels ... $250 – 300
17. yellow wrecker with red booms, orange Racing Mini with "29" labels .. $14 – 18

Car Transporter, Kenworth C.O.E., Convoy CY-1, 1982; HE-1, 1983

1. red cab, red trailer with beige ramp and white stripes .... $10 – 12
2. red cab with "4" label on roof, red trailer with beige ramp and no stripes ....$175 – 200
3. red cab with no label on roof, red trailer with beige ramp and no stripes ....$10 – 12
4. yellow cab, dark blue trailer, yellow ramp .... $6 – 9
5. blue cab, blue trailer, yellow ramp ....$4 – 6

Caterpillar Bulldozer (#64, 1979) **and Tractor Shovel** (#29, 1976 – 1997), CS-81, 1992

1. yellow bulldozer with red roof, yellow tractor shovel with red shovel, plastic accessories .... $7 – 9

Cattle Truck and Trailer, TP-19, 1979; TP-103, 1984 (see Dodge Stake Truck and Trailer)

Circus Set, TP-128, 1992, Variations:
Volvo Covered Truck (#23, 1985; #20, 1986; #62, 1990) **and Trailer** (#2, 1968)

1. red with white canopies, "Big Top Circus" .... $16 – 20

Dodge Truck (Zoo Truck #72, 1992 with container replacing cage) **and Trailer** (#2, 1968)

1. red truck with white container, red trailer with white canopy, "Big Top Circus" ....$14 – 18

Citroen CX Station Wagon (#12, 1979) **and Boat** (#9, 1966), TP-109, 1984

1. white Citroen with "Marine," boat has blue deck, white hull, no label, blue trailer .... $16 – 20
2. white Citroen with "Marine," boat has blue deck, white hull, "8" label, blue trailer .... $16 – 20
3. white Citroen with "Marine," boat has white deck, blue hull, "8" label, blue trailer .... $16 – 20
4. white Citroen with "Marine," boat has white deck, blue hull, "8" label, orange trailer .... $16 – 20
5. white Citroen with "Marine," boat has white deck, blue hull, no label, orange trailer .... $30 – 40
6. white Citroen with "Ambulance," boat has white deck, blue hull, "8" label, orange trailer .... $16 – 20
7. white Citroen with "Ambulance," boat has white deck, white hull, "8" label, orange trailer .... $16 – 20

Citroen and Motorcycle Trailer with three plastic motorcycles, TP-21, 1979 (see Motorcycle Set)

Citroen Matchmates, M-01, 1984

1. white Citroen CX Station Wagon (#12, 1979) with "Marine," black Citroen 15CV (#44, 1983) .... $14 – 18

Construction Low Loader, Convoy CY-203, 1989

1. yellow, with Atlas Excavator .. $10 – 12

Container Truck, DAF, Convoy CY-25, 1989

1. yellow, "IPEC" .... $12 – 15
2. blue, "CROOKES HEALTHCARE" .... $12 – 15
3. white and orange, "UNIGATE" ..$12 – 15
4. red, "ROYAL MAIL PARCELS" ..$12 – 15
5 blue, "COMMA PERFORMANCE OIL" .... $12 – 15
6. white, "LEISURE WORLD" .... $12 – 15
7. white, "PEPSI TEAM SUZUKI" ..$12 – 15
8. white and orange, "TNT IPEC" ...$10 – 12
9. white, "PIONEER" .... $12 – 15
10. metallic gold cab, black container, "DURACELL" .... $12 – 15
11. yellow, "ZWEIFEL POMY CHIPS" .... $12 – 15
12. green, "M" and orange stripe ..$12 – 15
13. white, "TOBLERONE" .... $10 – 12
14. white, "PIRELLI GRIPPING STUFF" .... $10 – 12

15. white, "XP" .... $10 – 12
16. white, "HB RACING" .... $10 – 12
17. white, "GARDEN FESTIVAL WALES" .... $12 – 15
18. brown, light gray container, "UNITED PARCEL SERVICE" .... $20 – 25

Container Truck, Ford Aeromax, Convoy CY-37, 1993
1. yellow, "Radical Cams" .... $4 – 5

Container Truck, Kenworth, Convoy CY-38, 1993
1. black, "Matchbox Racing 5" ..... $4 – 5

Container Truck, Mack, Convoy CY-28, 1989
1. white with white containers, "BIG TOP CIRCUS" .... $12 – 15
2. white, "DHL Worldwide Express" ...$7 – 9
3. red with white containers, "BIG TOP CIRCUS" .... $4 – 6

Container Truck, Scania, Convoy CY-18, 1986
1. blue cab with black interior, "VARTA BATTERIES" .... $35 – 40
2. blue cab with gray interior, "VARTA BATTERIES" .... $12 – 15
3. white, "WALL'S ICE CREAM" .. $12 – 15
4. red, "KIT KAT" .... $12 – 15
5. orange, "BREAKAWAY" .... $12 – 15
6. white, "7-Up" .... $12 – 15

Cougar (see Mercury Cougar)

Cougar Dragster (see Mercury Cougar Dragster)

Corvette Matchmates, M-03, 1984
1. red 1984 Corvette Convertible (#14, 1983; #69, 1983; #28, 1990) and metallic silver pearl Corvette (#62, 1979; #21, 1983) .... $14 – 18

Covered Container Truck, TP-23, 1979 (see Long Haul Covered Container Truck)

Covered Truck, Kenworth Conventional Aerodyne, Convoy CY-5, 1982; HE-5, 1982; TP-23, 1982
1. white cab, white trailer with green cover, "INTERSTATE TRUCKING" .... $8 – 12
2. green cab, white trailer, England cast, "INTERSTATE TRUCKING" ..... $15 – 20

Covered Truck, Peterbilt Conventional Aerodyne, Convoy CY-5, 1982; HE-5, 1982; TP-23, 1982
1. green cab, white trailer, Macau cast, "INTERSTATE TRUCKING" labels .... $12 – 15
2. yellow cab, silver trailer with yellow cover graphics, "MICHELIN" tampo .... $10 – 12
3. orange, Macau cast, "WALT'S FARM FRESH PRODUCE" .... $7 – 9
4. orange, Thailand cast, "WALT'S FARM FRESH PRODUCE" .... $4 – 6

Covered Truck, Scania, Convoy CY-23, 1988
1. yellow, "MICHELIN" .... $10 – 12

DAF Road Train, Kingsize K-122, 1986
1. white, "Eurotrans" .... $20 – 30
2. white, "Toblerone"............... $20 – 30

Datsun 260Z 2+2 (# 67, 1978) **and Caravan** (#31, 1977), TP-107, 1984
1. metallic gray Datsun with two-tone stripes, white Caravan with "Mobile 500" .... $14 – 18

Diesel Shunter (#24, 1978) **and Side Tipper,** TP-20, 1979; TP-125, 1991
1. yellow Shunter, yellow Side Tipper with red dumper, England cast, TP-20, 1979 .... $14 – 18
2. yellow Shunter, yellow Side Tipper with black dumper, England cast, TP-20, 1979 .... $16 – 20
3. yellow Shunter, yellow Side Tipper with red dumper, China cast, TP-125 .... $9 – 12

Dodge Stake Truck (#4, 1967 – 1970; issued as Dodge Cattle Truck #71, 1976 – 1991) **and Trailer,** TP-19, 1979; TP-103, 1984
1. red with beige stakes, black cows, TP-19 .... $14 – 18
2. red with beige stakes, brown cows, TP-19 .... $14 – 18
3. red with beige stakes, brown cows, TP-103 .... $9 – 12
4. red with orange stakes, dark brown cows, TP-19 .... $16 – 20
5. yellow with light brown stakes, reddish brown cows, TP-103 .... $9 – 12
6. pale blue with light brown stakes, black cows, TP-103 .... $9 – 12
7. green with yellow stakes, black cows, TP-103 .... $8 – 10

Double Container Truck, TP-22, 1979 (see Long Haul Double Container Truck)

Double Container Truck, DAF, Convoy CY-26, 1989
1. light blue with dark blue containers, "P & O" .... $12 – 15

Double Container Truck, Ford Aeromax, Convoy CY-111, 1993 from White Rose Collectibles
1. black, "Charitoys 1993" ...... $35 – 40

Double Container Truck, Kenworth Conventional Aerodyne, Convoy CY-3, 1982; HE-3, 1982; TP-22
1. red cab, black trailer, "UNIROYAL" labels ....$10 – 12
2. white cab, black trailer, "FEDERAL EXPRESS" .... $10 – 12

Double Container Truck, Peterbilt Conventional Aerodyne, Convoy CY-3, 1982; HE-3, 1982; TP-22, 1982
1. red cab, black trailer, "UNIROYAL" labels ....$10 – 12
2. red cab, white trailer, "UNIROYAL" labels .... $16 – 20
3. red cab, yellow trailer, "LINFOX" tampo .... $12 – 15

Double Tanker Set (Freeway Gas Tanker #63, 1973, and Freeway Gas Tanker Trailer, #63, 1978), TP-17, 1979
1. red cab/white trailer with "Burmah" labels, red and white tanker trailer with "Burmah" labels ..... $14 – 18
2. red cab/white trailer with "Chevron" labels, red and white tanker trailer with "Burmah" labels .... $14 – 18
3. red cab/red trailer with "Chevron" labels, red and white tanker trailer with "Chevron" labels ..... $14 – 18
4. red cab/white trailer with "Exxon" labels, white tanker trailer with "Exxon" labels ....$120 – 160
5. white cab/yellow trailer with "Shell" labels, yellow and white tanker trailer with "Shell" labels ..... $14 – 18
6. white cab/white trailer with "Exxon" labels, white tanker trailer with "Exxon" labels .... $14 – 18
7. white cab/yellow trailer with "Exxon" labels, yellow and white tanker trailer with "Exxon" labels .... $30 – 40
8. white cab/green trailer with "BP" labels, white and green tanker trailer with "BP" labels .... $24 – 36

Emergency Center, Peterbilt, Convoy CY-34, 1992
1. fluorescent orange .... $6 – 9

Emergency Set, TP-7, 1976. Variations:

Stretcha Fetcha (#46, 1972) **and Mercury Fire Chief** (#59, 1971)
1. white Stretcha Fetcha, white Mercury Fire Chief .... $14 – 18

Stretcha Fetcha (#46, 1972) **and Fire Chief** (#64, 1976)
1. white Stretcha Fetcha, red Fire Chief .... $14 – 18

Farming Twin Pack, FM-100, 1993
1. Mercedes Benz Trac 1600 Turbo Farm Tractor (#73, 1990) and Seeder (#712, 1993) .... $5 – 7
2. Mercedes Benz Trac 1600 Turbo Farm Tractor (#73, 1990) and Farm Trailer (#711, 1993) .... $5 – 7
3. Tractor Shovel (#29, 1976 – 1997; #237, 1993; #13) and Tipping Trailer (#710, 1993) .... $5 – 7
4. Ford Tractor (#236, 1993) and Farm Trailer (#711, 1993) .... $5 – 7
5. Ford Tractor (#236, 1993) and Rotovator (#713, 1993) .... $5 – 7

Field Car (#18, 1969) and Honda Motorcycle Trailer (#38, 1967), TP-8, 1977
1. dark orange Field Car with no labels, orange trailer with "Honda" labels .... $16 – 20
2. dark orange Field Car with "179," orange trailer with no labels .. $20 – 25
3. orange Field Car with checkerboard label, orange trailer with "Honda" labels .... $14 – 18
4. orange Field Car with checkerboard label, orange trailer with no labels .... $14 – 18
5. yellow Field Car with checkerboard label, orange trailer with no labels .... $14 – 18
6. yellow Field Car with checkerboard label, yellow trailer with "Honda" labels .... $14 – 18
7. yellow Field Car with checkerboard label, yellow trailer with no labels .. $14 – 18
8. white Field Car with checkerboard label, orange trailer with "Honda" labels .... $500 – 700

Field Car (#18, 1969) **and Team Matchbox Racer** (#24, 1973), TP-9, 1978
1. red Field Car with "44" label, red Team Racer with "44" label .... $14 – 18
2. orange Field Car with "44" label, orange Team Racer with "44" label ... $80 – 120
3. orange Field Car with checkerboard label, orange Team Racer with "44" label .... $80 – 120

Field Car and Volkswagen Van (see Military Field Car and Volkswagen Van)

Fire Chief and Ambulance, TP-10, 1978. Variations:

Fire Chief (#64, 1976) **and Mercedes Benz Ambulance** (#3, 1968)
1. red Fire Chief, white ambulance .... $14 – 18

Mercury Park Lane Fire Chief (#59, 1971) and Mercedes Benz Ambulance (#3, 1968)
1. red Mercury Fire Chief, white ambulance .... $14 – 18

Fire Engine, Kenworth C.O.E. Aerodyne, Convoy CY-13, 1984
1. red with "DENVER" label, white "8," "FIRE DEPT.," England ...... $600 – 750

Fire Engine, Peterbilt Conventional, Convoy CY-13, 1984
1. red with white "8" and "FIRE DEPT.," white ladder, England cast ... $15 – 20

Fire Engine, Peterbilt custom cab with roof lights, Convoy CY-13, 1984
1. red with "8" and "FIRE DEPT.," Macau cast .... $10 – 12
2. red with "8" and "FIRE DEPT.," Thailand cast .... $4 – 5

3. fluorescent orange, "CITY FIRE DEPT. 15," Thailand .... $4 – 6

Flareside Pickup and Seafire Boat (see Ford Flareside Pickup and Seafire Boat)

Ford Aeromax Box Truck, 1995 Super Rigs

1. "Hawaiian Punch," blue ....$7 – 8

2. "Honey Nut Cheerios," butterscotch .... $7 – 8

3. "Oreo," blue ....$7 – 8

4. "Pepsi," white ....$7 – 8

Ford Cortina 1600 GL (#55, 1979) **and Pony Trailer** (#43, 1968), TP-111, 1984
1. metallic red Ford Cortina with black stripe, beige Pony Trailer with silver horseshoes design .... $9 – 12
2. metallic tan Ford Cortina with black stripe, beige Pony Trailer with horsehead label .... $9 – 12

Ford Escort RS2000 (#9, 1978) **and Boat** (#9, 1966), TP-109, 1984
1. dark green Escort with seagull labels, boat has white deck, blue hull, "8," orange trailer .... $60 – 80

Ford Escort XR3i (#17, 1985) **and Boat** (#9, 1966), TP-115, 1987
1. white Ford Escort with "XR3i," white boat with "Seaspray," black trailer .... $9 – 12
2. metallic blue Ford Escort with spatter design, blue boat with spatter design, black trailer .... $9 – 12

Ford Escort XR3i (#17, 1985) **and Glider Trailer,** TP-102, 1984
1. light green Ford Escort, dark green trailer with seagull labels ..... $16 – 20
2. dark green Ford Escort, dark green trailer with seagull labels .... $9 – 12

Ford Flareside Pickup (#53, 1982) **and Seafire Boat** (#5, 1975), TP-119, 1987
1. yellow pickup with "Ford," yellow Seafire with blue hull, "460" .... $9 – 12

Ford Matchmates, M-02, 1984
1. white, red, and blue Ford Model A Van (#38, 1982 – 1997) with "Pepsi," tan and brown Ford Model A (#73, 1979; #55, 1991) .... $14 – 18

Ford Tractor (#46, 1978) **and Hay Trailer** (#40, 1967), TP-11, 1979
1. blue tractor, yellow hay trailer with no stakes .... $16 – 20
2. blue tractor, blue hay trailer with black stakes .... $16 – 20
3. blue tractor, beige hay trailer with black stakes .... $180 – 220
4. lime green tractor, beige hay trailer with black stakes .... $180 – 220
5. lime green tractor, red hay trailer with black stakes .... $16 – 20

Ford Tractor (#46, 1978) **and Hay Trailer** (#40, 1967), TP-108, 1984
1. blue tractor, red hay trailer .... $9 – 12
2. yellow tractor, yellow hay trailer ... $9 – 12
3. green tractor, yellow hay trailer ... $9 – 12

Freeway Gas Tanker and Tanker Trailer (see Double Tanker Set)

Gas Tanker (also see Double Tanker Set, Petrol Tanker, Tanker)

Gas Tanker, Ford Aeromax, Convoy CY-7, 1999
1. bright blue cab, chrome tank, "Exxon," Premiere Collection

Gas Tanker, Kenworth, Convoy CY-105, 1989
1. white with gold and black stripes .... $12 – 15
2. white with "Shell" tampo ...... $12 – 15

Glider Set, TP-7, 1977. Variations:

Field Car (#18, 1969) **with Glider and Trailer**
1. yellow Field Car with checkerboard label, yellow trailer with "Gliding Club" labels .... $40 – 50

Ford Escort (#9, 1978) **with Glider and Trailer**
1. green Ford with seagull labels, green trailer with seagull labels .... $9 – 12

Jeep (#38, 1976) **with Glider and Trailer**
1. red Jeep with black base, red trailer with "Gliding Club" labels .. $900 – 1,200
2. yellow Jeep with black base, yellow trailer with "Gliding Club" labels .. $14 – 18

3. yellow Jeep with white base, yellow trailer with "Gliding Club" labels .. $14 – 18
4. yellow Jeep with white base, yellow trailer with no labels .... $14 – 18

Graffic Traffic Metal Flakes, 1994
1. Ford Thunderbird (#7, 1993) and Lamborghini Countach (#67, 1985 – 1997) ....$6 – 8
2. Chevrolet Lumina (#54, 1990; #267, 1994) and Sauber Group C Racer (#46/#66, 1985) .... $6 – 8

Grove Crane, Convoy CY-30, 1992
1. orange-yellow, red crane cab, yellow boom, "AT1100 Grove" .... $6 – 9

Helicopter Transporter, Kenworth C.O.E., HE-11, 1983; Convoy CY-11, 1984. Includes 75-F Helicopter with pilot and large windows
1. silver-gray cab, "ACE HIRE," 75-F in silver-gray with "600," England cast ..$10 – 12
2. silver-gray cab, "ACE HIRE," 75-F in pearl silver with "600," Macau cast ......$7 – 9
3. black cab, "AIR CAR," 75-F in black with "AIR CAR," Macau cast .... $7 – 9
4. dark blue cab, 75-F in white with "RESCUE," Macau cast .... $10 – 12
5. black cab, "AIR CAR," 75-F in black with "AIR CAR," Thailand cast .... $4 – 5

Helicopter Transporter, Mack, Convoy CY-33, 1992
1. white with Mission Chopper ..... $6 – 9
2. white with Mission Chopper, "Rijkspolitie" ....$20 – 25

Highway Tanker and Trailer (see Double Tanker Set)

Holiday Set, TP-4, 1976. Variations: **AMX Javelin** (#9, 1972) **and Eccles Caravan** (#57, 1970)
1. lime green Javelin (doors open), yellow caravan with flower and stripe label ....$14 – 18
2. dark green Javelin (doors cast shut), yellow caravan with flower and stripe label .... $14 – 18
3. metallic blue Javelin (doors cast shut), yellow caravan with flower and stripe label .... $14 – 18

Datsun 260Z (#67, 1978) **and Eccles Caravan** (#57, 1970)
1. blue Datsun, yellow caravan with flower and stripe label .... $40 – 50

Ford Capri (#54, 1971) **and Eccles Caravan** (#57, 1970), 1976
1. orange Ford, cream caravan with flower and stripe label .... $20 – 30

Maserati Bora (#32, 1972) **and Eccles Caravan** (#57, 1970)
1. metallic gold Maserati, beige caravan with flower and stripe label .... $30 – 40
2. metallic gold Maserati, beige caravan with dots label .... $30 – 40
3. metallic gold Maserati, beige caravan with seagull label ..... $30 – 40

Renault 5TL (#21, 1978) **and Eccles Caravan** (#57, 1970)
1. blue Renault, yellow caravan with flower and stripe label .... $40 – 50

Vauxhall Guildsman (#40, 1971) **and Eccles Caravan** (#57, 1970)
1. red Guildsman with label, yellow caravan with flower and stripe label ....$20 – 30
2. red Guildsman with label, yellow caravan with dots label ....$20 – 30
3. red Guildsman with label, yellow caravan with no label ....$20 – 30
4. red Guildsman with printed design, yellow caravan with flower and stripe label ....$20 – 30
5. red Guildsman with no label, white caravan with seagull label ..$30 – 40
6. pink Guildsman with label, yellow caravan with flower and stripe label ....$30 – 40

Volkswagen Golf (#7, 1976) **and Eccles Caravan** (#57, 1970)
1. red Golf, yellow caravan with flower and stripe label .... $20 – 25
2. yellow Golf, yellow caravan with flower and stripe label .... $20 – 25
3. green Golf, yellow caravan with flower and stripe label .... $16 – 20
4. green Golf, beige caravan with flower and stripe label .... $16 – 20
5. green Golf, beige caravan with seagull label .... $20 – 25

Horse Box Transporter, Kenworth Conventional Sleeper Cab, Convoy CY-6, 1982; HE-6, 1983
1. green cab, "BLUE GRASS FARMS" .... $10 – 12
2. green cab, tan trailer, no tampo ....$10 – 12
3. green cab, silver trailer, "BLUE GRASS FARMS" ....$10 – 12
4. green cab, beige trailer, green and orange stripes with horse silhouette ....$7 – 9

Indy 500 Closest Finish Ever, #32660, 1993
1. Two Formula Racers (#28, 1982; #16, 1984; #74, 1996; #61, 1998; #246, 1994), Valvoline, Mackenzie ....$8 – 10

Isuzu Amigo (#52, 1991) and Seafire (#5, 1975), TP-129, 1992
1. red Isuzu, red Seafire with white hull and "Surf Rider," white plastic trailer .... $9 – 12

Jaguar Matchmates, M-03, 1984
1. green Jaguar XK-120 (#22, 1984) and red Jaguar SS-100 (#47, 1982) ......$14 – 18

Javelin and Pony Trailer, TP-3, 1976 (see Pony Trailer Set)

Jeep and Glider Trailer, TP-7, 1977 (see Glider Set)

Jeep Cherokee (#27, 1987) **and Caravan** (#31, 1977), TP-116, 1987
1. beige Jeep Cherokee with "Holiday Club," beige Caravan with "500" ...... $9 – 12

Jeep Matchmates, M-03, 1984
1. brown Jeep (#5, 1982) and black Jeep (#20, 1982) .... $14 – 18

Kenworth Aerodyne Box Truck, 1995 Super Rigs

1. **"Reese's," orange ....$7 – 8**

2. **"Skittles," red ....$7 – 8**

3. **"Trick Truckin'," fluorescent orange with black trailer ....$7 – 8**

Kenworth C.O.E. Box Truck, 1995 Super Rigs

1. **"KFC," white ....$7 – 8**

2. **"Pizza Hut," red with white trailer .... $7 – 8**

Kenworth Matchmates, M-06, 1984
1. black Kenworth Conventional Aerodyne (#41, 1982) and metallic silver pearl Kenworth COE Aerodyne (#45, 1982) .... $14 – 18

Lamborghini Miura, Kingsize K-24, 1969
1. metallic red .... $40 – 60
2. metallic bronze .... $14 – 18
3. metallic burgundy .... $14 – 18
4. metallic blue .... $14 – 18

Land Rover Ninety (#35, 1990) **and Pony Trailer** (#43, 1968), TP-130, 1992
1. white Land Rover, white Pony Trailer with red roof, red and black stripes .... $9 – 12

Land Rover Ninety (#35, 1990) **and Seafire Boat** (#5, 1975), TP-121, 1989
1. white Land Rover with "County," white Seafire with red hull, red design, white plastic trailer with blue and red design .... $9 – 12
2. white Land Rover with "Bacardi," white Seafire with white hull, "Bacardi," white metal trailer (from #9 Boat and Trailer, 1966), UK promotional .... $60 – 80

Locomotive (0-4-0 Steam Locomotive #43, 1978) **and Passenger Coach** (#44, 1978), TP-124, 1991
1. green Locomotive with "British Railways," green Coach with "British Railways" .... $9 – 12

Long Haul Boat Transporter, TP-26, 1979
1. blue tractor with green windows, metallic gray trailer with beige and red boat .... $40 – 50
2. blue tractor with amber windows, metallic gray trailer with beige and red boat .... $14 – 18

Long Haul Box Container Truck, TP-24, 1979
1. red tractor, solid-lettered "Firestone" labels .... $30 – 40
2. red tractor, outline-lettered "Firestone" labels .... $40 – 50
3. red tractor, "Matchbox" labels .. $14 – 18
4. yellow tractor, "Matchbox" labels .... $40 – 50

Long Haul Covered Container Truck, TP-23, 1979
1. red tractor with amber windows, solid lettered "Firestone" labels .... $14 – 18
2. red tractor with amber windows, outline-lettered "Firestone" labels .... $14 – 18
3. red tractor with no windows, outlined lettered "Firestone" labels.... $14 – 18

Long Haul Double Container Truck, TP-1
1. red tractor with amber windows, beige containers with "OCL" labels $14 – 18
2. red tractor with amber windows, light blue containers with "Sealand" labels .... $120 – 160
3. red tractor with amber windows, off-white containers with "OCL" labels .... $14 – 18
4. red tractor with amber windows, red containers with "NYK" labels .... $120 – 160
5. red tractor with amber windows, yellow containers with "OCL" labels .. $14 – 18
6. bronze tractor with amber windows, beige containers with "OCL" labels .... $14 – 18
7. bronze tractor with amber windows, cream containers with "OCL" labels .... $14 – 18
8. bronze tractor with amber windows, off-white containers with "OCL" labels............................ $14 – 18
9. bronze tractor with no windows, beige containers with "OCL" labels .. $14 – 18
10. dark green tractor with amber windows, beige containers with "OCL" labels .... $120 – 160
11. dark green tractor with amber windows, orange containers with "OCL" labels .... $160 – 200

Long Haul Pipe Truck, TP-25, 1979
1. yellow tractor with amber windows, metallic gray flatbed with orange pipes............................ $40 – 50
2. yellow tractor with amber windows, black flatbed with orange pipes........................... $40 – 50
3. dark green tractor with amber windows, metallic gray flatbed with orange pipes .... $14 – 18
4. dark green tractor with amber windows, black flatbed with orange pipes .... $14 – 18
5. bronze tractor with amber windows, black flatbed with orange pipes .... $80 – 100

Low Loader with Dodge Delivery Truck, Scania, Convoy CY-803, 1992, Europe
1. red .... $20 – 25

Mack Auxiliary Power Truck (#57, 1991 – 1997) and Chevrolet Ambulance (#41, 1978; #25, 1983), EM-83, 1992
1. fluorescent orange power truck, white ambulance, plastic accessories ... $7 – 9

Mack CH600, Highway Cruisers Twin Pack

1. **"Safeway," white, with assorted Matchbox car in package .... $8 – 12**

Matra Rancho (#37, 1982), Inflatable Raft and Trailer, TP-110, 1984
1. navy blue Matra with design and white base, orange raft with white hull, no markings, black trailer, England cast .... $14 – 18
2. navy blue Matra with design and white base, orange raft with white hull, "SR," black trailer, England cast............................ $14 – 18
3. navy blue Matra with design and white base, yellow raft with white hull, "SR," black trailer, England cast.. $16 – 20
4. black Matra with design and white base, orange raft with white hull, "SR," black trailer, England cast .... $14 – 18
5. orange Matra with design and black base, orange raft with white hull, "2," white trailer, England cast ... $14 – 18

Mercedes (see Mercedes Benz)

Mercedes Benz 280 GE G-Wagon (#30, 1984) and Dinghy, TP-131, 1992
1. white Mercedes Benz with orange roof and "Marine Rescue," fluorescent orange dinghy with gray hull and "Rescue," white trailer................ $9 – 12

Mercedes Benz 280 GE G-Wagon (#30, 1984) **and Pony Trailer** (#43, 1968), TP-117, 1987
1. white Mercedes Benz with "Polizei" and checkerboard design, white Pony Trailer with "Polizei" and checkerboard design .... $9 – 12
2. white Mercedes Benz with green "Polizei," green Pony Trailer with "Polizei"............................ $9 – 12

Mercedes Benz 300 SE Staff Car (#46, 1968) and Mercedes Benz Ambulance (#3, 1968), TP-14, 1979
1. olive green Staff Car, olive green Ambulance.............................. $16 – 20

Mercedes Benz Ambulance and Mercury Fire Chief, TP-10, 1978 (see Fire Chief and Ambulance)

Mercedes Benz Ambulance and Staff Car, TP-14, 1979 (see Mercedes Benz 300 SE Staff Car and Mercedes Benz Ambulance)

Mercedes Benz C.111, Kingsize K-30, 1972
1. metallic gold, with battery compartment, Germany issue ...... $135 – 160
2. metallic gold .... $15 – 20
3. lime green .... $14 – 18
4. blue .... $14 – 18

Bulgaria casting, various colors.. $35 – 60

Mercedes Benz Covered Truck (#1, 1968) and Trailer (#2, 1968), TP-1, 1976

1. **red with yellow canopies, "Transcontinental" labels .... $14 – 18**
2. powder blue with yellow canopies, "I.M.S." labels .... $24 – 32

Mercedes Benz G-Wagon and Dinghy, TP-131, 1992 (see Mercedes Benz 280 GE G-Wagon and Dinghy)

Mercedes Benz G-Wagon and Horse Box, TP-117, 1987 (see Mercedes Benz 280 GE G-Wagon and Pony Trailer)

Mercedes Benz G-Wagon and Inflatable Raft, TP-131, 1992 (see Mercedes Benz 280 GE G-Wagon and Dinghy)

Mercedes Benz Military Covered Truck (#1, 1968) **and Trailer** (#2, 1968), TP-15, 1977
1. army green truck, army green trailer with "48350USA" labels .... $150 – 180
2. army green truck with "48350USA" labels, army green trailer with "4TS702K" labels .... $150 – 180
3. olive green truck, olive green trailer with "48350USA" labels .....$16 – 20
4. olive green truck, olive green trailer with "4TS702K" labels .... $16 – 20

Mercedes Benz Staff Car and Ambulance, TP-14, 1979 (see Mercedes Benz 300 SE Staff Car and Mercedes Benz Ambulance)

Mercedes Benz Trac 1600 Turbo Farm Tractor (#73, 1990) **and Hay Trailer** (#40, 1967), TP-126, 1991
1. yellow and green tractor, yellow hay trailer............................... $9 – 12

Mercedes Benz Unimog (#49, 1967) **and Trailer** (#2, 1968), TP-112, 1984
1. yellow with white canopies, "Alpine Rescue"............................... $14 – 18
2. red with white canopies, "Unfall Rettung"............................... $14 – 18
3. white with orange canopies, "GES"............................ $14 – 18

Mercedes Benz Unimog (#49, 1967) **and Weasel** (#73, 1974),TP-13, 1979
1. olive green Unimog with "A" label, olive green Weasel................... $14 – 18

Mercury Fire Chief and Mercedes Benz Ambulance, TP-10, 1978 (see Fire Chief and Ambulance)

Mercury Police and Merryweather Fire Engine, TP-2, 1979 (see Police Car and Fire Engine)

Mercury Police and Blaze Buster Fire Engine, TP-2, 1980 (see Police Car and Fire Engine)

Military Alvis Stalwart (#61, 1966) **and Ford Heavy Wreck Truck** (#71, 1968), TP-16, 1979
1. olive green Alvis Stalwart with "3LGS64" labels, olive green wreck truck .... $16 – 20

Military Ambulance and Staff Car (see Mercedes Benz Staff Car and Ambulance)

Military Dump Truck (Mack Dump Truck #28, 1968) **and Case Bulldozer** (#16, 1969), TP-16, 1977
1. army green dump truck, army green bulldozer...................... $150 – 175
2. olive green dump truck, olive green bulldozer .... $16 – 20

Military Field Car (#18, 1969) **and Motorcycle** (Hondarora #18, 1975), TP-11, 1977
1. olive green Field Car with star label, olive green Hondarora......... $30 – 50

Military Field Car (#18, 1969) **and Volkswagen Van** (#23, 1970), TP-12, 1977
1, olive green Field Car with "3RA391" label, olive green Volkswagen Van with "Ambulance" labels .... $16 – 20

Military Jeep (Jeep #38, 1976, or Jeep Hot Rod #2, 1971) **and Motorcycle** (Hondarora #18, 1975), TP-11, 1977
1. army green Jeep with star label, no gun, army green Hondarora .... $150 – 180
2. olive green Jeep with star label, no gun, olive green Hondarora......... $16 – 20
3. olive green Jeep with "21*11" label, no gun, olive green Hondarora.. $16 – 20
4. olive green Jeep with "21*11" label, gun, olive green Hondarora.. $16 – 20

Military Mercedes Benz Covered Truck and Trailer, TP-15, 1977 (see Mercedes Benz Military Covered Truck (#1, 1968) and Trailer (#2, 1968)

Military Scout (Stoat Armored Truck #28, 1974) and Armored Car (Weasel #73, 1974), TP-13, 1977
1. army green Stoat, army green Weasel..................... $150 – 175
2. olive green Stoat, oliver green Weasel....................... $14 – 18

Military Tanker (Freeway Gas Tanker #63, 1973) **and Radar Truck** (Badger Exploration Truck #16, 1974), TP-14, 1977
1. army green tanker with Canadian flag label, army green radar truck...................... $160 – 180
2. army green tanker with French flag label, army green radar truck.................. $150 – 175
3. olive green tanker with "High Octane" labels, olive green radar truck .. $16 – 20

Military Unimog and Weasel (see Mercedes Benz Unimog and Weasel)

Mission Launch Adventure Pack

1. **Kenworth C.O.E. Rocket Transporter and figures .... $15 – 20**

Miura (see Lamborghini Miura)

Kenworth C.O.E. Rocket Transporter and figures .... $15 – 20

Miura Seaburst Set, 10", Kingsize K-29, 1971 (K-24 Lamborghini Miura and K-25 Seaburst Power Boat) ....$25 – 40

Mod Tractor (#25, 1972) and Hay Trailer (#40, 1967) TP-2, 1976
1. red tractor, yellow hay trailer ...$16 – 20

Money Box Armored Car, Kingsize K-88, 1981
1. white, "Fort Knox" .... $12 – 16
2. white, "Matchbox" .... $12 – 16
3. white, "Volksbank Raiffeisenbank," Germany issue .... $40 – 50
4. red, "Caisse D'Epargne" ...... $30 – 40

Motorcycle Set with three plastic motorcycles, TP-21, 1979. Variations:

Renault 5TL (#21, 1978) and Motorcycle Trailer
1. blue Renault, blue trailer with yellow motorcycles .... $16 – 20

Datsun 260Z (#67, 1978) and Motorcycle Trailer
1. blue Datsun, blue trailer with yellow motorcycles .... $16 – 20
2. blue Datsun, blue trailer with lemon yellow motorcycles................ $16 – 20

Citroen SM (#51, 1972) and Motorcycle Trailer

1. blue Citroen, blue trailer, yellow motorcycles .... $9 – 12
2. blue Citroen, blue trailer, red motorcycles .... $30 – 40

NASA Tracking Vehicle, Peterbilt, Convoy CY-15, 1985
1. white with white trailer, "NASA" tampos .... $7 – 9

Nigel Mansell Twinpacks, NM-810, 1994
1. Formula 1 (#246, 1994) and Grand Prix Racer (#74, 1988; #14, 1989) .... $5 – 7
2. Formula 1 (#246, 1994) and Mission Chopper (#46, 1985 – 1997)... $5 – 7
3. Formula 1 (#246, 1994) and Chevy Van (#68, 1979; #44, 1982; #26, 1991) .... $5 – 7

Peterbilt Quarry Truck (#30, 1982) and Atlas Excavator (#32, 1981), CS-82, 1992
1. yellow quarry truck with red dumper, yellow excavator with red bucket, plastic accessories .... $7 – 9

Petrol Tanker (also see Gas Tanker, graphics, Mack AC Tanker, Tanker)

Petrol Tanker, Kenworth C.O.E., Convoy CY-7, 1982; HE-7, 1983
1. white, "SUPERGAS" .... $10 – 12

Petrol Tanker, Peterbilt Conventional Aerodyne, Convoy CY-7, 1982; HE-7, 1983
1. black, "SUPERGAS" .... $10 – 12

Petrol Tanker, Scania, Convoy CY-17, 1985
1. white with white tank, "AMOCO" ..$7 – 9
2. red with red tank, "TIZER".... $12 – 15
3. white with white tank, "Diet 7 – Up" .... $12 – 15
4. orange with red tank, "CADBURY'S FUDGE" .... $12 – 15
5. white with chrome tank, "SHELL" .. $7 – 9
6. white with white tank, "FEOSO" .... $40 – 45

Pipe Truck, TP-25, 1979 (see Long Haul Pipe Truck)

Pipe Truck, Mack, Convoy CY-31, 1992
1. red with yellow plastic pipes ..... $6 – 9

Police Car and Fire Engine, TP-2, 1979. Variations:

Mercury Police (#55, 1971) and Merryweather Fire Engine (#35, 1969), 1979
1. white police car, red fire engine .... $14 – 18

Mercury Police (#55, 1971) and Blaze Buster Fire Engine (#22, 1975), 1980
1. white police car, red fire engine .... $16 – 20

Pony Trailer Set, TP-3. Variations:

AMX Javelin (#9, 1972) and Pony Trailer (#43, 1968)
1. red Javelin (doors cast shut(, beige Pony Trailer .... $75 – 100
2. green Javelin (doors cast shut), beige Pony Trailer .... $14 – 18
3. green Javelin (doors cast shut), orange Pony Trailer .... $14 – 18
4. lime green Javelin (doors open), orange Pony Trailer .... $14 – 18
5. metallic blue Javelin (doors open), orange Pony Trailer .... $14 – 18
6. blue Javelin (doors cast shut), beige Pony Trailer .... $14 – 18
7. blue Javelin (doors cast shut) with white design, beige Pony Trailer.... $16 – 20

Jeep CJ6 (#53, 1977) **and Pony Trailer** (#43, 1968)
1. red Jeep, orange Pony Trailer .. $20 – 30
2. red Jeep, beige Pony Trailer .. $20 – 30

Field Car (#18, 1969) **and Pony Trailer** (#43, 1968)
1. red Field Car with "44" label, beige Pony Trailer .... $30 – 40

Porsche 911 Turbo (#3, 1978) **and Caravan** (#31, 1977), TP-113, 1985
1. black Porsche with gold design, white Caravan with "Mobile 500" .. $16 – 20

Porsche 911 Turbo (#3, 1978) **and Glider Trailer,** TP-122, 1989
1. dark blue Porsche with yellow design, dark blue trailer with white glider and yellow design .... $9 – 12
2. yellow Porsche with spatter design, yellow trailer with spatter design and bright pink glider .... $9 – 12

Power Launch Transporter, DAF, Convoy CY-22, 1987
1. white, "LAKESIDE" with "SHARK" on boat .... $10 – 12
2. white, "P&G," "CG22" .... $10 – 12
3. white, "COAST GUARD" .... $7 – 9
4. white, "RESCUE 3" .... $4 – 5

Power Launch Transporter, Kenworth C.O.E., Convoy CY-14, 1985
1. white with white boat .... $10 – 12

Quarry Truck and Excavator, CS-82, 1992 (see Peterbilt Quarry Truck and Atlas Excavator)

Racing Car Transporter, Kenworth C.O.E., HE-10, 1983; Convoy CY-10, 1984
1. white with "TYRONE MALONE" and MB-66 Super Boss with green windows .... $15 – 20
2. white with "TYRONE MALONE" and MB-66 Super Boss with red windows .... $20 – 25

Renault 5TL (#21, 1978) and Motorcycle Trailer, TP-106, 1984
1. white Renault with green design, yellow trailer with red motorcycles... $14 – 18
2. white Renault with pink and yellow design, yellow trailer with red motorcycles .... $14 – 18
3. white Renault with pink and yellow design, yellow trailer with olive green motorcycles .... $16 – 20
4. white Renault with pink and yellow design, yellow trailer with black motorcycles .... $16 – 20
5. white Renault with pink and yellow design, silver pearl trailer with black motorcycles .... $16 – 20

Road Roller and Crane, CS-83, 1992 (see Bomag Road Roller and Faun Mobile Crane)

Rocket Transporter, Kenworth C.O.E., Convoy CY-2, 1982; HE-2, 1983
1. silver-gray cab, trailer with Sky Busters SB-3 Space Shuttle .... $15 – 18
2. silver-gray cab, trailer with white plastic rocket .... $10 – 12
3. pearl silver cab, white rocket ... $7 – 9
4. white cab, white rocket .... $6 – 9
5. white cab, chrome rocket........ $4 – 5

Rocket Transporter, Kenworth T2000, Convoy CY-2, 1982; HE-2, 1999
1. black cab, black trailer, chrome trim, Germany .... $10 – 12

Shovel Transporter, Mack, Convoy CY-32, 1992
1. orange-yellow with MB-29 Shovel Nose Tractor .... $6 – 9

Shunter and Tipper, TP-20, 1979; TP-125, 1991 (see Diesel Shunter and Side Tipper)

Skip Truck, 4⁵⁄₁₆", Kingsize K-28, 1978
1. orange, "Hales" .... $14 – 18
2. red, "Hales" .... $14 – 18
3. blue and red, "Hoch & Tief," Germany issue .... $30 – 50

Snorkel (#63, 1982) **and Foam Pumper** (#54, 1984), EM-81, 1992
1. fluorescent orange snorkel, fluorescent orange pumper, plastic accessories .... $7 – 9

Stretcha Fetcha and Fire Chief, TP-7, 1976 (see Emergency Set)

Superstar Transporter, Ford Aeromax, Convoy CY-109, 1991. Two versions were issued as "Convoy/Super Rigs" models. The rest are White Rose Collectibles variations.
1. red, "Melling Performance" .. $12 – 15
2. red, "Motorcraft" .... $21 – 15

White Rose Collectibles variations:

3. white, "Hooters Racing" ...... $12 – 15
4. black, "Texaco Havoline," "Davey Allison" .... $12 – 15
5. white with dark blue container, "Goodyear Racing" .... $12 – 15
6. white with dark blue container, "Penn State Nittany Lions" .... $12 – 15

7. rust, "Washington Redskins Super Bowl Champions" .... $12 – 15
8. white, "Snickers Racing Team" .. $12 – 15
9. black, "Stanley Mechanic Tools 92" .... $12 – 15
10. green with red container, "Merry Christmas White Rose Collectibles 1992" .... $200 – 250
11. gold, "Folger's" .... $20 – 25
12. blue with white container, "Bill Elliot 9" .... $20 – $25

Superstar Transporter, Ford Aeromax, Convoy CY-113, 1994, from White Rose Collectibles

1. metallic blue, "Family Channel" .. $12 – 15
2. blue, "Quality Care Racing" .... $12 – 15
3. white, "7 Exide Batteries" .... $12 – 15
4. white, "Hooters Racing" ...... $12 – 15
5. black, "Fingerhut Racing" ..... $12 – 15
6. white with blue container, "Colts 94" .... $10 – 12
7. white with light blue container, "Oilers 94" .... $10 – 12
8. white with dark blue container, "Chargers 94" .... $10 – 12
9. white with black container, "Raiders 94" .... $10 – 12
10. white with red container, "Bills 94" .... $10 – 12
11. yellow with red container, "Cardinals 94" .... $10 – 12
12. yellow with red container, "KC Chiefs 94" .... $10 – 12
13. yellow with green container, "Packers 94" .... $10 – 12
14. yellow with black container, "Steelers 94" .... $10 – 12
15. orange with red container, "Buccaneers 94" .... $10 – 12
16. orange with white container, "Browns 94" .... $10 – 12
17. orange with white container, "Bengals 94" .... $10 – 12
18. orange with turquoise container, "Dolphins 94" .... $10 – 12
19. red-brown with yellow container, "Redskins 94" .... $10 – 12
20. red with dark blue container, "Patriots 94" .... $10 – 12
21. red with black container, "Falcons 94" .... $10 – 12
22. silver and gray with dark blue container, "Cowboys 94" .... $10 – 12
23. gold with red container, "SF 49ers" .... $10 – 12
24. green and gold with black container, "Saints 94" .... $10 – 12
25. purple with yellow container, "Vikings" .... $10 – 12
26. dark blue with white container, "Giants 94" .... $10 – 12
27. dark blue with orange container, "Broncos 94" .... $10 – 12
28. bright blue with yellow container, "Broncos 94" .... $10 – 12
29. blue with yellow container, "Rams 94" .... $10 – 12
30. blue with gray container, "Lions 94" .... $10 – 12
31. green with gray container, "Eagles 94" .... $10 – 12
32. green with white container, "Jets 94" .... $10 – 12
33. bright green with gray container, "Seahawks 94" .... $10 – 12

Superstar Transporter, Kenworth, Convoy CY-104, 1989. Matchbox issued this truck in three series, Superstar Transporters from White Rose Collectibles, "Days of Thunder" models based on the movie of the same name, and Indy 500 series models, resulting in over 50 total variations of this model.

Superstar Transporters from White Rose Collectibles:

1. white cab with "STP" logo, white container, "Richard Petty," "STP" .... $325 – 400
2. white, "Neil Bonnett," "CITGO" .... $100 – 125
3. white, "Hardee's Racing" .. $100 – 125
4. black, silver-gray base, Macau cast, "Goodwrench Racing Team" .. $200 – 275
5. white with blue container, "Goodyear Racing" .... $75 – 100
6. white cab with red and blue tampos, white container, "Richard Petty," "STP" .... $100 – 125
7. black, black base, Thailand cast, "Goodwrench Racing Team" ...... $100 – 125
8. gold cab, no "6" on doors, gold container, "Folger's" .... $60 – 75
9. gold cab with "6" on doors, gold container, "Folger's" .... $30 – 40
10. white, "Trop Artic," "Dick Trickle" .... $40 – 50
11. black, "Goodwrench Racing Team" and car pictured .... $25 – 30
12. dark blue, "94 Sunoco," no "Sterling Marlin" .... $400 – 425
13. dark blue, "94 Sunoco," "Sterling Marlin" .... $375 – 400
14. white, "Crown Moroso" .... $60 – 75
15. black, "Texaco Havoline," " Davey Allison" .... $24 – 32
16. white, "Richard Petty" with portrait .... $40 – 50
17. dark blue with white container, "Penn State 1855 – 1991" .... $12 – 15
18. white, "Trop Artic," "Lake Speed" .... $25 – 30
19. blue, "Maxwell House Racing" .. $12 – 15
20. white, "Ken Schraeder 25" ... $12 – 15
21. orange-yellow, "Kodak Racing" .. $12 – 15
22. white, "Purolator" .... $20 – 25
23. white, "Western Auto 17" .... $16 – 20
24. white, "Country Time" .... $16 – 20
25. black, "MAC Tools" .... $30 – 35
26. black, "Mello Yello 42" .... $16 – 20
27. black, "Alliance" .... $20 – 25
28. yellow, "Pennzoil," "Waltrip" ... $12 – 15
29. white, "STP-Richard Petty Fan Appreciation Tour 1992" .... $20 – 25
30. white, "Baby Ruth Racing" .... $12 – 15
31. black, "Goodwrench Racing Team" with checkered flags .... $15 – 20
32. metallic blue, "Raybestos" ..... $12 – 15
33. black, "Slim Jim Racing Team" .. $12 – 15
34. white and green, "Quaker State" .... $12 – 15
35. blue and white, "Evinrude 98" ... $12 – 15
36. white, "Jasper Engines 55" ... $12 – 15
37. black, "MAC Tools Racing," "Harry Gant" .... $15 – 20
38. black, "Martin Birrane — Team Ireland" .... $12 – 15
39. white, "Penn State Nittany Lions — Happy Valley Express" .... $12 – 15

"Days of Thunder" Versions:

40. black, "Exxon 51" .... $30 – 40
41. black and green, "Mello Yello 51" .... $30 – 40
42. orange, "Hardees 18" .... $30 – 40
43. pink with white container, "Superflo" .... $30 – 40
44. white, "City Chevrolet" .... $30 – 40

Indy 500 Versions:

45. white and blue, "Valvoline" ..... $10 – 12
46. yellow, "Pennzoil 4" .... $10 – 12
47. yellow, Pennzoil 2" .... $10 – 12
48. white, "Panasonic" .... $10 – 12
49. white, "K-Mart," "Havoline" .... $12 – 15

Superstar Transporter, Kenworth, Convoy CY-110, 1992 from White Rose Collectibles

1. black, "Rusty Wallace — Pontiac" . $12 – 15
2. black, "TIC Racing 8" .... $12 – 15
3. orange, "Pic-N-Pay Shoes" .... $12 – 15

Superstar Transporter, Kenworth T600, Convoy CY-112, 1994 from White Rose Collectibles

1. red with green container, "Merry Christmas 1993" .... $175 – 225
2. black with yellow container, "White Rose Series II in '94" .... $12 – 15
3. yellow, "White House Apple Juice Racing" in pink lettering .... $12 – 15
4. yellow, "White House Apple Juice Racing" in red lettering .... $20 – 25
5. dark blue with yellow container, "Matchbox," "White Rose 29" .... $12 – 15
6. black with red container, "Phillies — National League Champions 1993" .... $12 – 15
7. white, "Factory Stores of America" .... $12 – 15
8. yellow with red container, "Kellogg's Racing 5" .... $12 – 15
9. white, "Manheim Auctions 7" .. $12 – 15
10. black, "Shoe World 32" .... $12 – 15
11. black, "Baltimore Orioles 94" .. $12 – 15
12. black with red container, "65th All Star Game — Pittsburgh Pirates 1994" .... $12 – 15
13. purple with black container, "Colorado Rockies" .... $12 – 15
14. black, "Carolina Panthers — Inaugural Season 1995" .... $12 – 15

Toe Joe (#74, 1972) **and Racing Mini** (#29, 1970; see Breakdown Set, TP-6, 1976)

Tractor and Trailer, TP-2, 1976 (See Mod Tractor and Hay Trailer)

Tractor and Hay Trailer, TP-11, 1979, TP-108, 1984 (see Ford Tractor and Hay Trailer)

Tractor and Hay Trailer, TP-126, 1991 (see Mercedes Benz Trac 1600 Turbo Farm Tractor and Hay Trailer)

Transport Set, The Londoner Bus (#17, 1972) **and SRN6 Hovercraft** (#72, 1972), TP-8, 1976
1. red bus with "Swinging London" labels, white hovercraft................. $16 – 20

Unimog (see Mercedes Benz Unimog)

Volkswagen Golf (#7, 1976) **and Pony Trailer** (#43, 1968), TP-114, 1985
1. black Golf with red design, beige Pony Trailer with silver shoes design..$16 – 20

Volkswagen Golf GTi (#33, 1986; #56, 1986; #63, 1991) **and Inflatable Raft**, TP-120, 1989
1. dark gray Volkswagen, orange raft with black hull, white trailer with red and blue design .... $9 – 12

Volkswagen Van and Field Car (see Military Field Car and Volkswagen Van)

Volvo Covered Truck and Trailer, TP-128, 1992 (see Circus Set)

Water Sporter, TP-18, 1979. Variations:

AMX Javelin (#9, 1972) **and Seafire** (#5, 1975)
1. red Javelin, dark red Seafire with white hull .... $60 – 80

Volkswagen Golf (#7, 1976) **and Seafire** (#5, 1975)
2. red Golf, red Seafire with white hull ....$14 – 18
3. red Golf, white Seafire with brown hull ....$120 – 160
4. red Golf, white Seafire with blue hull ....$16 – 20

Weekender Set, TP-5, 1976. Variations:
Ford Capri (#54, 1971) **and Boat and Trailer** (#9, 1966), 1980
1. orange Capri, blue and white Boat and Trailer..............................$16 – 20

Hot Rocker (#67, 1973) **and Boat and Trailer** (#9, 1966)
2. red-orange Hot Rocker, blue and white Boat and Trailer ....$16 – 20

Ford Escort RS2000 (#9, 1978) **and Boat and Trailer** (#9, 1966)
3. white Escort with "Dunlop" labels, blue and white Boat and Trailer ...$40 – 60
4. white Escort with "Phantom" labels, blue and white Boat and Trailer .... $40 – 60
5. blue Escort with "Phantom" labels, blue and white Boat and Trailer ...$40 – 60

Lotus Europa (#5, 1969) **and Boat and Trailer** (#9, 1966)
6. black Europa with "JPS," blue and white Boat and Trailer ....$40 – 60

Porsche 911 Turbo (#3, 1978) **and Boat and Trailer** (#9, 1966)
7. brown Porsche, blue and white Boat and Trailer........................$40 – 60

Volkswagen Golf (#7, 1976) **and Boat and Trailer** (#9, 1966)
8. red Golf, blue and white Boat and Trailer..............................$14 – 18

Wrecker and Car (see Breakdown Set)

Zoo Truck and Eccles Caravan, TP-124, 1989 .... $18 – 24

MATCHBOX BUILDINGS

Auto Park, AP-1, 1971 .... $140 – 180

Compact Garage, MG-7, 1984 ... $24 – 32

Deluxe Garage, MG-6, 1984 .... $24 – 32

Emergency Station, 580101, 1974 .... $60 – 80

Gearshift Garage, MG-9, 1987 .. $24 – 32

Matchbox Fire Station, MF-1, 1963
1. ivory with green roof, brick front .... $180 – 220
2. white with red roof, brick front ....$80 – 110
3. white with red roof, smooth front .... $120 – 160

Matchbox One Story Garage, MG-1, 1959
1. yellow .... $180 – 240
2. red .... $180 – 240

Matchbox Service Station, MG-1, 1968 ....$80 – 110

Matchbox Two Story Garage, MG-1, 1961
1. "Esso," yellow with red base .... $180 – 240
2. "BP," white with green base .... $120 – 160

Service Station, MG-2, 1979 ... $60 – 80

Super Garage, MG-4, 1981 ..... $50 – 70

Texaco Garage, MG-3, 1979 .... $60 – 80

SEA KINGS

In 1976, a line of military ship models was introduced and named Sea Kings. The series, however, was short lived and only produced 10 models.

Aircraft Carrier, $8^3/_4$", SK-304, 1976 ... $12

Anti-Aircraft Cruiser, $8^1/_8$", SK-310, 1977 ....$12
Battleship, $8^1/_2$", SK-303, 1976 ....$12
Convoy Escort, $7^7/_8$", SK-306, 1976 ....$12
Corvette, $7^7/_8$", SK-302, 1976 ....$12
Frigate, $8^5/_8$", SK-301, 1976 ....$12
Guided Missile Destroyer, $8^{15}/_{16}$", SK-308, 1976 ....$12
Helicopter Carrier, $8^1/_4$", SK-307, 1976 .... $12
Submarine, $8^1/_8$", SK-309, 1977 ....$12
Submarine Chaser, $7^7/_8$", SK-305, 1976 .... $12

SKY BUSTERS, AIRPORT/ AIRFORCE

These small scale aircraft, typically about $3^1/_2$" long, were introduced in 1973. Around 1995, Sky Busters were issued as Airport or Airforce models, depending on whether the model represented a commercial or military aircraft. Current models are available in blister packs for around $4.00 each and are divided into two groups for marketing purposes, as either commercial or military models.

A300 Airbus, SB-28, 1981
1. white and silver-gray, "Lufthansa" ....$6 – 8
2. white, "Alitalia" .... $6 – 8
3. white, "Air France" .... $6 – 8
4. light blue and silver-gray, "Korean Air" .... $6 – 8

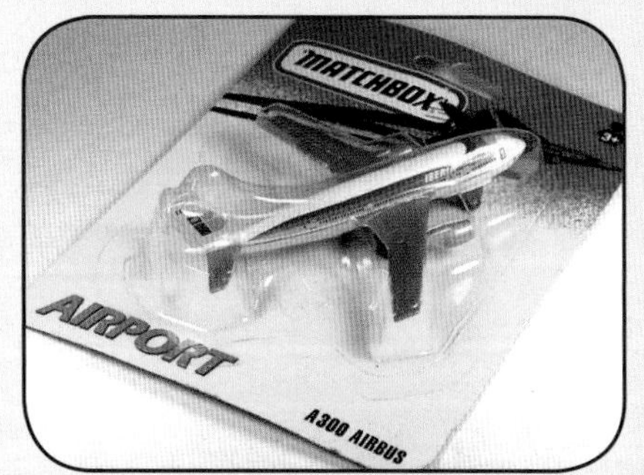

5. **white, "Iberia" ....$6 – 8**
6. white, "Air Inter" .... $60 – 75
7. white and silver-gray, "Swissair" .. $6 – 8
8. white, "Air Malta" .... $15 – 18

A300B Airbus, SB-3, 1973
1. white and gray, "Air France" ... $8 – 10
2. white and gray, "Lufthansa" ...... $6 – 8

Alpha Jet, SB-11, 1973
1. metallic red and white .... $8 – 10
2. blue and red .... $10 – 12
3. blue .... $8 – 10
4. white and red .... $8 – 10

Bell Jet Ranger Helicopter, SB-33, 1990
1. white and blue, "Sky Ranger" .... $4 – 5

B.AE 146, SB-38, 1992
1. white, "Dan-Air" .... $4 – 5

2. white, "Thai" ....$6 – 8

Boeing 737-300, SB-40, 1992
1. white and dark blue, "Brittania" .. $4 – 5

2. light blue and silver-gray, "KLM" ...$4 – 5

Boeing 747, SB-10, 1973
1. white and dark blue, "BOAC" .. $8 – 10

2. white and dark blue, "British Airways" .... $8 – 10
3. white and dark blue, "Qantas" .. $8 – 10
4. white and silver-gray, "United States of America" .... $12 – 15
5. white and silver-gray, "MEA" ....$12 – 15
6. white and silver plated, "BOAC," on ashtray/stand .... $40 – 50
7. white and gold plated, "British Airways," on ashtray/stand .... $40 – 50
8. white with silver wings, "El Al" .. $8 – 10
9. white and dark blue, "British" .. $12 – 15
10. white and silver-gray, "Cathay Pacific" .... $6 – 8
11. white and silver-gray, "British Caledonia" ....$8 – 10
12. white and silver-gray, "Lufthansa" ..$6 – 8
13. white and silver-gray, "Pan Am" .... $12 – 15
14. white, "Virgin" .... $6 – 8
15. light blue and silver-gray, "KLM" ...$6 – 8
16. white and silver-gray, Air Nippon" .... $12 – 15
17. lime and white, "Aer Lingus" ..... $6 – 8
18. white, "South African Airways" .... $12 – 415
19. white and silver-gray, "Saudi" .... $4 – 5
20. white and silver-gray, "Olympic" ....$4 – 5

Boeing 747-400, SB-31, 1990
1. light gray and dark blue, "British Airways" .... $5 – 6
2. white and silver-gray, "Cathay Pacific" .... $4 – 5
3. white and silver-gray, "Lufthansa" ....$4 – 5
4. white and silver-gray, "Signapore Airlines" .... $4 – 5

Boeing Stearman Biplane, SB-39, 1992
1. orange-yellow, "Crunchie," printing on underside of wings .... $25 – 30
2. orange-yellow, "Crunchie," no printing on underside of wings .... $4 – 5
3. white, "Circus Circus" .... $4 – 5

Cessna 210, SB-14, 1973
1. orange-yellow and white .... $8 – 10

Cessna 210 Float Plane, SB-26, 1981
1. red and white .... $6 – 8
2. black and white .... $6 – 8
3. red, "Fire" .... $4 – 5
4. white, "007 James Bond" ...... $8 – 10

Cessna 402, SB-9, 1973
1. light green and white .... $8 – 10
2. dark green and white .... $5 – 7
3. brown and beige .... $6 – 8
4. white and red, "DHL World-Wide Express" .... $5 – 6
5. blue and yellow .... $4 – 6

Corsair A7D, SB-2, 1973
1. dark green and white .... $8 – 10
2. khaki and white with brown and green camouflage .... $6 – 8
3. orange and white .... $5 – 6

Corsair F4U, SB-16, 1975
1. metallic blue .... $6 – 8
2. orange .... $6 – 8

Douglas DC-10, SB-13, 1973
1. white and red, "Swissair" .... $8 – 10
2. white and silver-gray, "Swissair" .... $8 – 10
3. whiteand silver-gray, "United" ... $8 – 10
4. white and silver-gray, "Lufthansa" ...$6 – 8
5. white and silver-gray, "Alitalia" .... $6 – 8
6. white, "Thai," Macau cast .... $6 – 8
7. white, "Thai," Thailand cast ...... $4 – 5
8. silver and red, "Aeromexico" .... $6 – 8
9. silver-gray, "American" .... $6 – 8
10. white, "UTA" .... $60 – 75
11. white, "Scandinavian" .... $4 – 5
12. white and silver-gray, "Sabena" .... $4 – 5

Douglas Skyhawk, SB-12, 1973
1. dark blue and white, "Navy" .... $8 – 10
2. dark blue and white, "Marines" ..$8 – 10

F-16, SB-24, 1979
1. white and red, "USAF," no side labels .... $6 – 8
2. white and red, "USAF," "United States Air Force" on sides .... $5 – 6
3. white with no markings, Graffic Traffic .... $6 – 8

Fairchild A10 Thunderbolt (dubbed "Warthog" during Desert Storm, Persian Gulf War), SB-32, 1990
1. dark gray with green camouflage ..$4 – 5

Grumman F-14 Tomcat, SB-30, 1989

1. gray and white, "Navy" ....$4 – 5

Harrier Jet, SB-27, 1981
1. white and red .... $6 – 8
2. light gray and white .... $5 – 6
3. dark blue and white, "Royal Navy" ..$5 – 6
4. light green and white, "Marines" ..$5 – 6

Hawk, SB-37, 1992
1. red, "Royal Air Force" .... $5 – 7

Helicopter, SB-20, 1977

1. olive, "Army" ....$8 – 10
2. white and light blue, "Coast Guard" ..$6 – 8
3. white and red, "Police" .... $6 – 8
4. dark blue and white, "Air-Aid" ... $6 – 8
5. dark blue, "Gendarmerie JAB" .... $60 – 75

Helicopter (also see Rescue Helicopter)

Junkers 87B, SB-7, 1973
1. green with swastikas .... $8 – 10
2. black with swastikas .... $80 – 90
3. black with beige and brown .... $8 – 10

Learjet, SB-1, 1973
1. yellow and white, "D-IDLE" ...... $8 – 10
2. red, "Datapost" .... $6 – 8
3. purple and white, "Federal Express" .... $5 – 7

4. white, "G-JCB" .... $6 – 8
5. white, "U. S. Air Force" .... $4 – 5
6. purple, "U. S. Air Force" .... $5 – 6
7. white and orange, "Q-Xpress Freight Delivery Service" .... $4 – 6
8. white, "DHL" .... $4 – 5

Lightning SB-21 1977
1. olive .... $8 – 10
2. silver-gray .... $8 – 10

Lockheed A130 (see Lockheed C-130 Hercules)

Lockheed C-130 Hercules, SB-34, 1990

1. white, "USCG" ....$4 – 5

Lockheed F-117A Stealth, SB-26, 1990; SB-36, 1991

1. dark gray, "USAF" ....$4 – 5
2. white, no markings, Graffic Traffic ..$5 – 6

Lockheed SR-71 Blackbird, SB-29, 1989
1. black, "U. S. Air Force" .... $4 – 5

MIG 21, SB-6, 1973
1. blue and white .... $8 – 10
2. silver-gray .... $5 – 6
3. black .... $5 – 6
4. light purple .... $5 – 6
5. silver .... $4 – 5

MiL M24 Hind-D Chopper, SB-35, 1990
1. brown and gray .... $4 – 5

2. camouflage khaki and army green .. $4 – 5

Military Helicopter, Sky Busters 2003

1. avocado green and bright purple ..$4 – 5

Mirage F1, SB-4, 1973
1. red with bull's-eye on wings .... $8 – 10
2. orange and brown, "122-18" ... $5 – 6
3. yellow .... $4 – 5
4. white, "ZE-164" .... $4 – 5
5. pink .... $5 – 6
6. blue .... $4 – 5

Mission Chopper, SB – 12, 1992 variation of #46, 1985 – 1997
1. army green with tan base and skids, tan tail and blades, star and emblem .... $1 – 2

NASA Space Shuttle, SB-3, 1980
1. white and gray .... $5 – 6

Phantom F4E SB-15 1975
1. metallic red and white .... $6 – 8
2. cherry red and white .... $6 – 8
3. gray, "Marines," Macau cast .... $5 – 6
4. gray, "Marines," Thailand cast .. $3 – 4
5. pink, "Marines" .... $5 – 6

Piper Comanche, SB-19, 1977
1. red and yellow .... $6 – 8
2. white, "XP" .... $6 – 8
3. beige and dark blue, "Comanche," Macau cast .... $5 – 6
4. beige and dark blue, "Comanche," Thailand cast .... $4 – 5

Pitts Special Biplane, SB-12, 1980
1. metallic red and white .... $6 – 8
2. dark green and white .... $8 – 10
3. blue and white .... $8 – 10
4. red, "Fly Virgin Atlantic" .... $4 – 5
5. white, no markings, Graffic Traffic ....$6 – 8
6 white, "Circus Circus" .... $6 – 8

Ram Rod, SB-17, 1976
1. red .... $8 – 10

Rescue Helicopter, SB-25, 1979
1. yellow .... $6 – 8
2. white .... $8 – 10
3. dark blue, "Royal Air Force Rescue" ....$6 – 8
4. white, "Shell" .... $6 – 8
5. white and red, "007" .... $8 – 10

Rescue Plane, 2002

1. yellow, green and blue-gray ....$4 – 5

Search Plane, 2002
1. red, "Mission Base" ....$4 – 5

Space Shuttle (see NASA Space Shuttle)

Spitfire, SB-8, 1973
1. dark brown and gold .... $12 – 15
2. metallic green and gold .... $8 – 10
3. gold plated on pen stand ..... $40 – 50
4. light brown and khaki .... $8 – 10
5. khaki with green camouflage .. $20 – 25

SST Super Sonic Transport, SB-23, 1979
1. white, "Air France" .... $5 – 7
2. white, "Singapore" .... $15 – 20
3. white, "Supersonic Airlines" ...... $4 – 5
4. white, "Singapore Airlines" ... $75 – 100

5. white, "British Airways" ....$4 – 5
6. white, "Heinz 57" .... $20 – 25
7. white with no markings, Graffic Traffic .... $5 – 6

Starfighter F104, SB-5, 1973
1. white with maple leaf labels .... $8 – 10
2. red with maple leaf labels ...... $8 – 10

Tornado, SB-22, 1978

1. **light gray and white .... $6 – 8**
2. dark gray and white .... $6 – 8
3. red and white .... $6 – 8
4. light purple and white .... $4 – 5

Transport Helicopter, Sky Busters, 2003

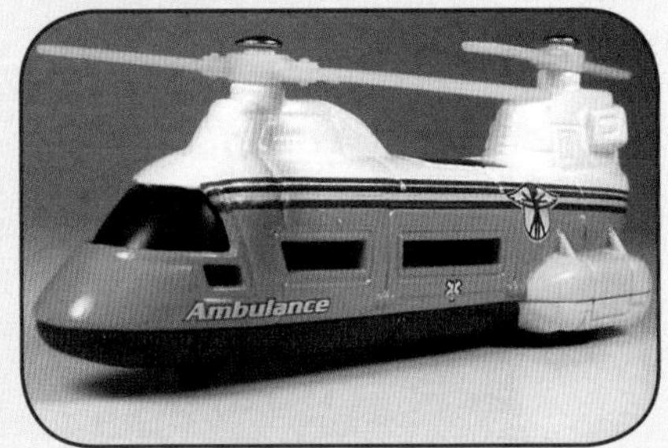

1. **turquoise and white .... $4 – 5**

2. **orange, white and red .... $4 – 5**

Wild Wind, SB-18, 1976
1. lime green and white .... $8 – 10

MATCHBOX DOLLS, ACTION FIGURES, AND MISCELLANEOUS TOYS

ABBA — introduced in 1978
Anna, AB-101 .... $90 – 120
Bennie, AB-103 .... $90 – 120
Bjorn, AB-104 .... $90 – 120
Frida, AB-102 .... $90 – 120

Disco Girls — Vogue dolls, introduced in 1974
Britt, DG-101 .... $40 – 50
Dee, DG-100 .... $40 – 50
Disco Bride, DG-150 .... $40 – 50
Disco Darling, DG-153 .... $40 – 50
Disco Date, DG-151 .... $40 – 50
Disco Deb, DG-152 .... $40 – 50
Domino graphics, DG-102 .... $40 – 50
Tia, DG-103 .... $40 – 50
Tony, DG -104 .... $40 – 50

Fighting Furies — action figures, introduced in 1974
Black McCoy, FF-103 .... $50 – 60
Captain Peg Leg, FF-100 .... $50 – 60
Crazy Horse, FF-104, FF-106 ..... $50 – 60
Ghost of Captain Kidd, FF-102 .... $50 – 60
Hook, FF-101 .... $50 – 60
Kid Cortez, FF-105 .... $50 – 60

Miss Matchbox — character dolls, introduced in 1974
Alice in Wonderland, M01 .... $16 – 20
Blue Belle, M11 .... $16 – 20
Calamity Jane, M04 .... $16 – 20
Cookie Kate, M09 .... $16 – 20
Cosy Cathy, M07 .... $16 – 20
Jilly Jodhpur, M08 .... $16 – 20
Mod Millie, M14 .... $16 – 20
Party Patti, M13 .... $16 – 20
Penny Playmate, M16 .... $16 – 20
Polly Painter, M05 .... $16 – 20
Sailor Sue, M02 .... $16 – 20
Sally Stewardess, M15 .... $16 – 20

PEE-WEE'S PLAYHOUSE

Of special note is a popular line of toys spawned from the TV series *Pee-Wee's Playhouse*, a popular but controversial cutting-edge show for kids hosted by Paul Ruben as Pee-Wee Herman. The show only lasted for two years, from 1989 to 1990, but generated a lot of fans as well as detractors. Values on the various characters from the show have risen steadily since the show's demise and Ruben's notorious incident in an adult movie theater.

Pee-Wee's Playhouse Characters
Billy Baloney, 1989 .... $40 – 55
Chairry, small, 1989 .... $12 – 16
Chairry, large, 1989 .... $40 – 55
Conkey, 1989 .... $16 – 20
Cowboy Curtis, 1989 .... $12 – 16
Globey & Randi, 1989 .... $16 – 20
Jambi & The Puppet Band, 1989 .. $16 – 20
King of Cartoons, 1989 .... $16 – 20
Magic Screen, 1989 .... $12 – 16
Miss Yvonne, 1989 .... $12 – 16
Pee Wee Herman, articulated arms and legs, 5 3/4" tall, 1989 .... $12 – 16
Pee Wee Herman and Scooter, 1989 .... $30 – 40
Pee Wee Herman doll, Non-Talking, 1989 .... $40 – 55
Pee Wee Herman doll, Talking, 1989 .... $40 – 55
Pee Wee Herman Ventriloquist's Dummy, 1990 .... $90 – 120
Pee Wee's Playhouse Playset, #3550, 1989 .... $90 – 120
Pee Wee's Scooter riding toy, 1989 .... $275 – 325
Pterri, small, 1989 .... $16 – 20
Pterri, large, 1989 .... $40 – 55
Reba, 1990 .... $18 – 24
Ricardo, 1990 .... $16 – 20
Vance the Talking Pig, 1990 .... $40 – 55

Pooch Troup — plush toys, introduced in 1989
Colonel Ollie Collie .... $24 – 32
Doc Bernard .... $24 – 32
Sergeant Barker .... $24 – 32
Top Dog .... $24 – 32

Popsicle Kids — introduced in 1990
Berry Blue $12-16
Grape Cakes $12-16
La De Lime $12-16
Lotta Lime $12-16
Merry Cherry $12-16
Ooh La Orange $12-16

Real Models — introduced in 1990
Beverly Johnson .... $20 – 30
Cheryl Tiegs .... $20 – 30
Christie Brinkley .... $20 – 30

RUBIK'S
Rubik's Clock, 1989 .... $18 – 22
Rubik's Cube, 1989 .... $9 – 12
Rubik's Dice, 1990 .... $18 – 22
Rubik's Fifteen, 1990 .... $18 – 22
Rubik's Illusion Game, 1989 .... $18 – 22
Rubik's Link The Rings, 1987 .... 12 – 16
Rubik's Magic Picture Games, 1988
Crazy Orchestra .... $7 – 9
Dinosaur Days .... $7 – 9
Monster Sports .... $7 – 9
Octopus's Garden .... $7 – 9
Rubik's Magic Puzzle, 1987 .... $12 – 16
Rubik's Magic Strategy Game, 1987 .... $20 – 30
Rubik's Tangle, 1990 .... $18 – 22
Rubik's Triamid, 1990 .... $18 – 22

Suky, Susy, Patty Dolls — introduced in 1976
Ballerina, S01 .... $12 – 16
Bedtime, S07 .... $12 – 16
Horse Rider, S04 .... $12 – 16
Nurse, S02 .... $12 – 16
Shopper, S06 .... $12 – 16
Skater, S05 .... $12 – 16
Swimmer, S08 .... $12 – 16
Tennis Pro, S03 .... $12 – 16

Resources

Force, Edward. *Matchbox and Lledo Toys.* Atglen, PA: Schiffer Publishing, 1988.

———. *Miniature Emergency Vehicles.* Atglen, PA: Schiffer Publishing, 1985.

Kelly, Douglas R. *Die Cast Price Guide, Post-War: 1946 – Present.* Dubuque, IA: Antique Trader Books, 1997.

Mack, Charlie. *The Encyclopedia of Matchbox Toys,* revised and expanded 3rd ed. Atglen, PA: Schiffer Publishing, 2002.

Ragan, Mac. *Diecast Cars of the 1960s.* St. Paul, MN: MBI Publishing Company, 2000.

———. *Matchbox Cars.* St. Paul, MN: MBI Publishing Company, 2002.

Rettig, Jerry. *American Wheels.* ELC, 2000.

Schiffer Nancy. *Matchbox Toys,* revised 5th ed. Atglen, PA: Schiffer Publishing, 2000.

Scholl, Richard. *Matchbox — The Official 50th Anniversary Commemorative Edition.* New York, NY: Universe Publishing, 2002.

Stearns, Dan, ed. *Standard Encyclopedia of Diecast Vehicles, Identification and Values.* Iola, WI: Krause Publications, 2002.

Stephan, Elizabeth A, ed. *O'Brien's Collecting Toy Cars & Trucks, Identification & Value Guide,* 3rd ed. Iola, WI: Krause Publications, Inc., 2000.

———. *Today's Hottest Diecast Vehicles.* Iola, WI: Krause Publications, Inc., 2000.